The Princeton Encyclopedia of American Political History

The Princeton Encyclopedia

ADVISORS

Richard R. John

Ira I. Katznelson

Jack N. Rakove

Julian E. Zelizer

# of American Political History

Volume II

EDITOR

Michael Kazin

Georgetown University

ASSOCIATE EDITORS

Rebecca Edwards

Vassar College

Adam Rothman

Georgetown University

PRINCETON UNIVERSITY PRESS

PRINCETON AND OXFORD

Published by Princeton University Press, 41 William Street, Princeton, New Jersey 08540

In the United Kingdom: Princeton University Press, 6 Oxford Street, Woodstock, Oxfordshire OX20 1TW

Library of Congress Cataloging-in-Publication Data

The Princeton encyclopedia of American political history / Michael Kazin, editor . . . [et al.].

v. cm.

Includes bibliographical references and index.

ISBN 978-0-691-12971-6 (hardcover : alk. paper) 1. United States—Politics and government—Encyclopedias. 2. Political science—United States—History—Encyclopedias. I. Kazin, Michael, 1948– II. Title: Encyclopedia of American political history.

E183.P85 2010

973.03—dc22 2009032311

This book has been composed in Adobe Garamond and Myriad Pro

Printed on acid-free paper.

press.princeton.edu

Printed in the United States of America

10 9 8 7 6 5 4 3 2 1

Contents

Alphabetical List of Entries

Topical List of Entries

federalism
feminism
labor movement and politics
nativism
New Left
pacifism
populism
progressivism (*see* progressivism and the Progressive Era, 1890s–1920; Progressive parties)
Prohibition and temperance
radicalism
socialism
woman suffrage

Political Parties

American (Know-Nothing) Party
Anti–Masonic Party
conservative third parties since the New Deal
Democratic Party
Federalist Party
Free Soil Party
Greenback-Labor Party
labor parties
Libertarian Party
Liberty Party
National Republican Party
Progressive parties
Republican Party
Whig Party

Ideas, Philosophies, and Religions
(*see also* **Movements**)

Americanism
anarchism
antiparty sentiment
Catholics and politics
communism
conservatism
democracy
federalism
feminism
Jews and politics
liberal consensus and American exceptionalism
liberalism
Muslims and politics
political culture
Protestants and politics
radicalism
religion and politics
republicanism
socialism

War and Foreign Policy

armed forces, politics in the
Caribbean, Central America, and Mexico, interventions in, 1903–34
Civil War and Reconstruction
foreign observers of U.S. politics
foreign policy and domestic politics
Iraq wars of 1991 and 2003
Korean War and cold war
Mexican-American War
Spanish-American War and Filipino Insurrection
transnational influences on American politics
veterans
Vietnam and Indochina wars
war and politics
war for independence
War of 1812
World War I
World War II

Founding Documents

Articles of Confederation
Bill of Rights
Constitution, federal
Declaration of Independence

Regions

Alaska and Hawai'i
Great Plains, the
Middle Atlantic, the
Midwest, the
New England
Pacific Coast, the
Rocky Mountain region
South since 1877, the

Ethnic and Racial Groups

African Americans and politics
Asian immigrants and politics
Caribbean immigrants and politics
European immigrants and politics
Latinos and politics
Native Americans and politics
race and politics

Contributors

Sean Adams
History Department, University of Florida
energy and politics

Patrick Allitt
Department of History, Emory University
religion and politics since 1945

John Ashworth
School of American and Canadian Studies, University of Nottingham
Democratic Party, 1828–60

Dean Baker
Center for Economic Policy and Research, Washington, D.C.
economy and politics since 1970

Paula Baker
Department of History, Ohio State University
campaign law and finance to 1900; campaign law and finance since 1900

James M. Banner Jr.
National History Center
Federalist Party

Lois Banner
Department of History, University of Southern California
feminism

Kyle Barbieri
Hillsborough Community College and Polk Community College, Florida
Republican Party, 1968–2008 *(coauthor)*

Stephen Bates
Hank Greenspun School of Journalism and Media Studies, University of Nevada–Las Vegas
political advertising

David H. Bennett
Department of History, Maxwell School, Syracuse University
nativism

Edward D. Berkowitz
Elliott School of International Affairs, George Washington University
Social Security

Frederick J. Blue
Department of History (emeritus), Youngstown State University
Free Soil Party

Stuart M. Blumin
Department of History, Cornell University
antiparty sentiment

Matthew Bowman
Department of History, Georgetown University
conservative third parties since the New Deal; Electoral College; inaugural addresses of U.S. presidents; Libertarian Party; party nominating conventions

Amy Bridges
Department of Political Science, University of California–San Diego
cities and politics

Contributors

Stephen Brooks
Department of Political Science, University of Windsor
foreign observers of U.S. politics

Joshua Brown
American Social History Project/Center for Media and Learning, Graduate Center, City University of New York
cartooning

W. Elliot Brownlee
Department of History, University of California–Santa Barbara
taxation since 1913

Frank M. Bryan
Department of Political Science, University of Vermont
New England

Richard Buel Jr.
Department of History (emeritus), Wesleyan University
War of 1812

Paul Buhle
Departments of History and American Civilization, Brown University
anarchism

Charles W. Calhoun
Department of History, East Carolina University
Republican Party to 1896

Christopher Capozzola
Department of History, Massachusetts Institute of Technology
World War I

Daniel Carpenter
Department of Government, Harvard University
regulation

Robert W. Cherny
Department of History, San Francisco State University
the Great Plains; the Pacific Coast

Elisabeth S. Clemens
Department of Sociology, University of Chicago
interest groups

Dorothy Sue Cobble
Department of Labor and Employment Relations, Rutgers University
women and politics, 1920–70

Michael Cornfield
Graduate School of Political Management, George Washington University
Internet and politics

Edward Countryman
Department of History, Southern Methodist University
colonial legacy

Matthew J. Countryman
Department of History, University of Michigan
race and politics since 1933

Douglas Craig
School of Social Sciences, Australian National University
radio and politics

Joe Creech
Lilly Fellows Program and Christ College, Honors College of Valparaiso University
religion and politics, 1865–1945

Joseph Crespino
Department of History, Emory University
South since 1877, the

Donald T. Critchlow
Department of History, Saint Louis University
conservatism *(coauthor)*

Elliott Currie
Department of Criminology, Law, and Society, University of California–Irvine
crime

John Patrick Diggins, deceased
Graduate Center, City University of New York
liberal consensus and American exceptionalism

John Dinan
Department of Political Science, Wake Forest University
state constitutions

Ellen Carol DuBois
Department of History, University of California–Los Angeles
woman suffrage

Gerald Early
American Culture Studies, Washington University in St. Louis
popular music and politics

Max M. Edling
Department of History, Uppsala University
Constitution, federal

Rebecca Edwards
Department of History, Vassar College
gender and sexuality

Robin L. Einhorn
Department of History, University of California–Berkeley
taxation to 1913

Richard E. Ellis
Department of History, University at Buffalo, State University of New York
Democratic Party, 1800–28

Nicole Etcheson
Department of History, Ball State University
Midwest, the

Michael W. Flamm
Department of History, Ohio Wesleyan University
conservative ascendancy, 1980–2008

Maureen A. Flanagan
Department of History, Michigan State University
progressivism and the Progressive Era, 1890s–1920

Anne L. Foster
Department of History, Indiana State University
Spanish-American War and Filipino Insurrection

Steve Fraser
New York University
business and politics

Kevin Gaines
Department of History, University of Michigan
African Americans and politics

Michael A. Genovese
Department of Political Science, Loyola Marymount University
presidency to 1860

Michael Gerhardt
School of Law, University of North Carolina–Chapel Hill
impeachment

Steven M. Gillon
Department of History, University of Oklahoma
Democratic Party, 1932–68

Marcia Tremmel Goldstein
Department of History, University of Colorado
Rocky Mountain region *(coauthor)*

Lewis L. Gould
Department of History (emeritus), University of Texas–Austin
Gilded Age, 1870s–90s; Republican Party; Republican Party, 1896–1932

Amy S. Greenberg
Department of History, Pennsylvania State University
Mexican-American War

Eric Allen Hall
Department of History, Purdue University
sports and politics *(coauthor)*

Richard F. Hamm
Department of History, University at Albany, State University of New York
Prohibition and temperance

Stanley Harrold
Department of Social Sciences, South Carolina State University
abolitionism

D. G. Hart
Intercollegiate Studies Institute
religion and politics to 1865

David C. Hendrickson
Department of Political Science, Colorado College
Articles of Confederation

Williamjames Hull Hoffer
Department of History, Seton Hall University
Supreme Court

Susan Hoffmann
Department of Political Science, University of Western Michigan
banking policy

David A. Horowitz
Department of History, Portland State University
anti-statism

Jane Armstrong Hudiburg
Annapolis, Maryland
Senate

Andrew Hunt
Department of History, University of Waterloo
pacifism

Sarah E. Igo
Department of History, University of Pennsylvania
public opinion polls

Maurice Isserman
Department of History, Hamilton College
communism; era of confrontation and decline, 1964–80; New Deal Era, 1932–52

Meg Jacobs
Department of History, Massachusetts Institute of Technology
consumers and politics

Dennis W. Johnson
Graduate School of Political Management, George Washington University
campaign consultants

Robert D. Johnston
Department of History, University of Illinois–Chicago
class and politics since 1877

Jeffrey P. Jones
Department of Communication and Theatre Arts, Old Dominion University
television and politics

Stephen Kantrowitz
Department of History, University of Wisconsin–Madison
Reconstruction Era, 1865–77

Michael B. Katz
Department of History, University of Pennsylvania
welfare

Michael Kazin
Department of History, Georgetown University
Americanism; Democratic Party, 1800–2008; populism

Alexander Keyssar
John F. Kennedy School of Government, Harvard University
voting

Michael Kimmage
History Department, Catholic University of America
politics in the American novel

Michael J. Klarman
Harvard Law School
segregation and Jim Crow

Jennifer Klein
Department of History, Yale University
economy and politics, 1945–70

James T. Kloppenberg
Department of History, Harvard University
liberalism

Gary J. Kornblith
Department of History, Oberlin College
class and politics to 1877

J. Morgan Kousser
Division of the Humanities and Social Sciences, California Institute of Technology
race and politics, 1860–1933

Alan M. Kraut
Department of History, American University
European immigrants and politics; health and illness

Kathleen Smith Kutolowski
Department of History, College at Brockport, State University of New York
Anti-Masonic Party

David E. Kyvig
Department of History, Northern Illinois University
amendment process

Matthew D. Lassiter
Department of History, University of Michigan
suburbs and politics

Mark Lause
Department of History, University of Cincinnati
Greenback-Labor Party

Steven F. Lawson
Department of History, Rutgers University
civil rights

Allan J. Lichtman
Department of History, American University
elections and electoral eras; presidency, 1860–1932; presidency, 1932–2008

Patricia Nelson Limerick
Center of the American West, University of Colorado
Rocky Mountain region *(coauthor)*

James Livingston
Department of History, Rutgers University
economy and politics, 1860–1920

John Majewski
Department of History, University of California–Santa Barbara
economy and politics to 1860

Chandra Manning
Department of History, Georgetown University
Civil War and Reconstruction; sectional conflict and secession, 1845–65

Glenna Matthews
Independent Scholar, Laguna Beach, California
women and politics since 1970

Joseph A. McCartin
Department of History, Georgetown University
labor movement and politics

Stuart McConnell
History, Pitzer College
veterans

Lisa McGirr
Department of History, Harvard University
conservative interregnum, 1920–32

Alan McPherson
School of International and Area Studies, University of Oklahoma
foreign policy and domestic politics, 1865–1933

Yanek Mieczkowski
Division of Social Sciences, Dowling College
Republican Party, 1932–68

David Montejano
Department of Comparative Ethnic Studies, University of California–Berkeley
Latinos and politics

Kathleen M. Moore
Religious Studies Department, University of California–Santa Barbara
Muslims and politics

James A. Morone
Department of Political Science, Brown University
political culture

Kevin P. Murphy
Department of History, University of Minnesota
homosexuality

Teresa Murphy
Department of American Studies, George Washington University
women and politics, 1828–65

Mark A. Noll
Department of History, University of Notre Dame
Protestants and politics

James Oakes
Graduate Center, City University of New York
race and politics to 1860

David O'Brien
History Department, College of the Holy Cross
Catholics and politics

Peter S. Onuf
Department of History, University of Virginia
federalism

Jeffrey Ostler
Department of History, University of Oregon
Native Americans and politics

Meredith Oyen
Department of History, Georgetown University
Asian immigrants and politics

Jeffrey L. Pasley
Department of History, University of Missouri
era of new republic, 1789–1827

William Pencak
Department of History and Religious Studies, Pennsylvania State University
Middle Atlantic, the

Michael Perman
Department of History, University of Illinois–Chicago
Democratic Party, 1860–96

Elisabeth Israels Perry
Department of History, Saint Louis University
women and politics, 1865–1920

Christopher Phelps
School of American and Canadian Studies, University of Nottingham
radicalism

Sarah T. Phillips
Department of History, Columbia University
economy and politics, 1920–45

Kim Phillips-Fein
Gallatin School, New York University
era of consensus, 1952–64

Dan Plesch
Center for International Studies and Diplomacy, University of London
United Nations

Charles L. Ponce de Leon
Department of History, California State University–Long Beach
press and politics

Kevin Powers
Department of History, Georgetown University
cabinet departments; labor parties; Progressive parties

Richard Gid Powers
College of Staten Island, and Graduate Center, City University of New York
anticommunism

Jack N. Rakove
Department of History, Stanford University
Bill of Rights

Donald J. Ratcliffe
Faculty of History, University of Oxford
National Republican Party

Eric Rauchway
Department of History, University of California–Davis
assassination, presidential; globalization

William J. Reese
Departments of Educational Policy Studies and History, University of Wisconsin–Madison
education and politics

Brian Holden Reid
Department of War Studies, King's College London
armed forces, politics in the

Joanne Reitano
Social Science Department, La Guardia Community College, City University of New York
tariffs and politics

Leo P. Ribuffo
Elliott School of International Affairs, George Washington University
Democratic Party, 1968–2008

Andrew Rich
Franklin and Eleanor Roosevelt Institute
think tanks

Randy Roberts
Department of History, Purdue University
sports and politics *(coauthor)*

Adam Rome
Department of History, Pennsylvania State University
environmental issues and politics

Steven J. Ross
Department of History, University of Southern California
politics in American film

Doug Rossinow
History Department, Metropolitan State University
New Left

Adam Rothman
Department of History, Georgetown University
Liberty Party; slavery

Andrew J. Rotter
Department of History, Colgate University
Vietnam and Indochina wars

Mark Rozell
School of Public Policy, George Mason University
Republican Party, 1968–2008 *(coauthor)*

Anne Sarah Rubin
History Department, University of Maryland–Baltimore County
Confederacy

Leonard J. Sadosky
Department of History, Iowa State University
Declaration of Independence; foreign policy and domestic politics to 1865

Nick Salvatore
Industrial and Labor Relations School and Program in American Studies, Cornell University
socialism

Elizabeth Sanders
Department of Government, Cornell University
agrarian politics

David Sarasohn
The Oregonian
Democratic Party, 1896–1932

Gregory Schneider
Department of Social Sciences, Emporia State University
conservatism *(coauthor)*

Robert Schulzinger
Department of History, University of Colorado–Boulder
Korean War and cold war

Carlos A. Schwantes
Department of History, University of Missouri–St. Louis
transportation and politics

William G. Shade
Department of History (emeritus), Lehigh University
Whig Party

Robert E. Shalhope
Department of History, University of Oklahoma
republicanism

Michael Sherry
Department of History, Northwestern University
war and politics

John Shy
Department of History, University of Michigan
war for independence

David J. Siemers
Political Science, University of Wisconsin–Oshkosh
anti-Federalists

Stephen Skowronek
Department of Political Science, Yale University
presidency, the

Jason Scott Smith
Department of History, University of New Mexico
patronage

Bartholomew H. Sparrow
Department of Government, University of Texas–Austin
territorial government

Jeremi Suri
Department of History, University of Wisconsin–Madison
transnational influences on American politics

Jon C. Teaford
Department of History, Purdue University
local government; state government

Daniel J. Tichenor
Department of Political Science, University of Oregon
immigration policy

Anand Toprani
Department of History, Georgetown University
Iraq wars of 1991 and 2003

Frank Towers
History Department, University of Calgary
American (Know-Nothing) Party

Contributors

Gil Troy
Department of History, McGill University
campaigning

Cyrus Veeser
Department of History, Bentley College
Caribbean, Central America, and Mexico, interventions in, 1903–34

Penny M. Von Eschen
Department of History, University of Michigan
foreign policy and domestic politics since 1933

Samuel Walker
School of Criminology and Criminal Justice, University of Nebraska–Omaha
civil liberties

Irma Watkins-Owens
Department of History, Fordham University
Caribbean immigrants and politics

Harry L. Watson
Department of History and Center for the Study of the American South, University of North Carolina–Chapel Hill
Jacksonian era, 1828–45

Robert Westbrook
Department of History, University of Rochester
democracy

Richard D. White Jr.
Public Administration Institute, Louisiana State University
civil service

John S. Whitehead
Department of History, University of Alaska Fairbanks
Alaska and Hawai'i

Stephen J. Whitfield
Department of American Studies, Brandeis University
Jews and politics

Allan M. Winkler
Department of History, Miami University
World War II

Rosemarie Zagarri
Department of History, George Mason University
women and politics to 1828

Julian E. Zelizer
Department of History, Princeton University
House of Representatives

Aristide R. Zolberg
Department of Political Science, New School for Social Research
citizenship

The Princeton Encyclopedia of American Political History

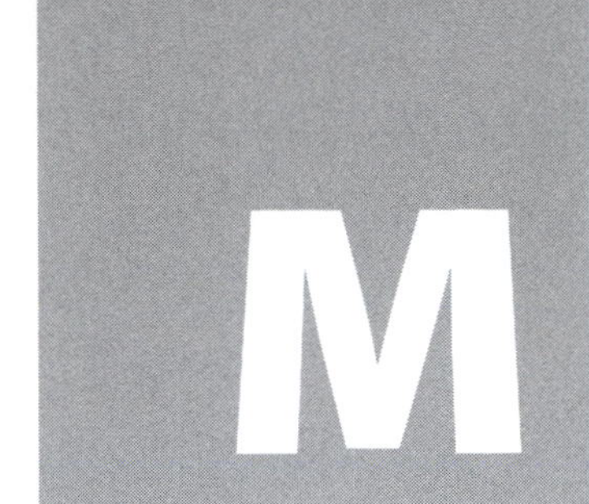

Mexican-American War

Often called America's "forgotten" war, the 1846–48 conflict with Mexico was brief, bloody, and a great short-term success for the United States. After a string of impressive military victories under General Zachary Taylor in Texas and Mexico's northeast between May 1846 and February 1847, General Winfield Scott's troops completed an amphibious assault on the port of Vera Cruz in Mexico's south and marched west to the capital, ultimately occupying Mexico City in September 1847. In early 1848, Mexico ratified the Treaty of Guadalupe Hidalgo, transferring 500,000 square miles, almost half of its territory, to the United States in exchange for $15 million. The U.S. states of California, New Mexico, Nevada, and Utah, as well as parts of Arizona, Colorado, and Wyoming are all products of the Mexican cession. The ratified treaty arrived in the United States on the Fourth of July in 1848 to ecstatic celebration. That the nation had "won an empire" in this war seemed providential to many Americans, proof of the country's Manifest Destiny to expand across the continent.

The long-term implications of the war were less than positive, however. The question of the status of slavery in the newly acquired territories greatly exacerbated sectional tensions and eventually contributed to both the collapse of the Second Party System and southern secession. The war with Mexico was the first war fought by America for reasons other than self-defense; it set a precedent for military action in Latin America in the name of American interests, and permanently damaged relations with Mexico. This little-remembered war had far-reaching effects, ultimately transforming America's foreign relations and internal politics almost as dramatically as it altered the nation physically.

The Road to War

Hostilities between the United States and Mexico officially erupted when President James K. Polk ordered General Taylor to move his army in Texas into a disputed area between the Nueces River and the Río Grande. After the Texas rebellion of 1836, both Mexico and the newly independent Republic of Texas claimed this area, although Texas's claims were somewhat speculative (the republic also claimed Santa Fe, the capital city of Mexico's province of New Mexico). In fact, Mexico refused to recognize the independence of Texas, considering it a rebel province. Although most Texans favored joining the United States, attempts to annex Texas in the late 1830s and early 1840s failed because both Democrats and Whigs recognized that annexation would inflame sectional tensions and likely result in a war with Mexico. President John Tyler, a Whig in name but Democrat in policy, fastened on the idea of annexing Texas in the hope that this stance would win him the presidency in 1844. It did not, but his proposal was met with an outpouring of popular and congressional support. Tyler invited Texas to join the union at the close of his presidential term in 1845.

Democrat James K. Polk entered office immediately after on an explicitly expansionist platform and pledged himself to gaining Mexico's Alta California. During his first year as president, he unsuccessfully attempted to buy California and New Mexico for more than twice the amount the United States eventually paid in 1848. After Mexican cavalry crossed the Río Grande and attacked a U.S. patrol, Polk addressed Congress on May 11, 1846, and reported that "Mexico has passed the boundary of the United States, has invaded our territory and shed American blood upon the American soil." Although many representatives had serious doubts about Polk's claims and suspected that the president had provoked war by moving U.S. troops into an area rightfully

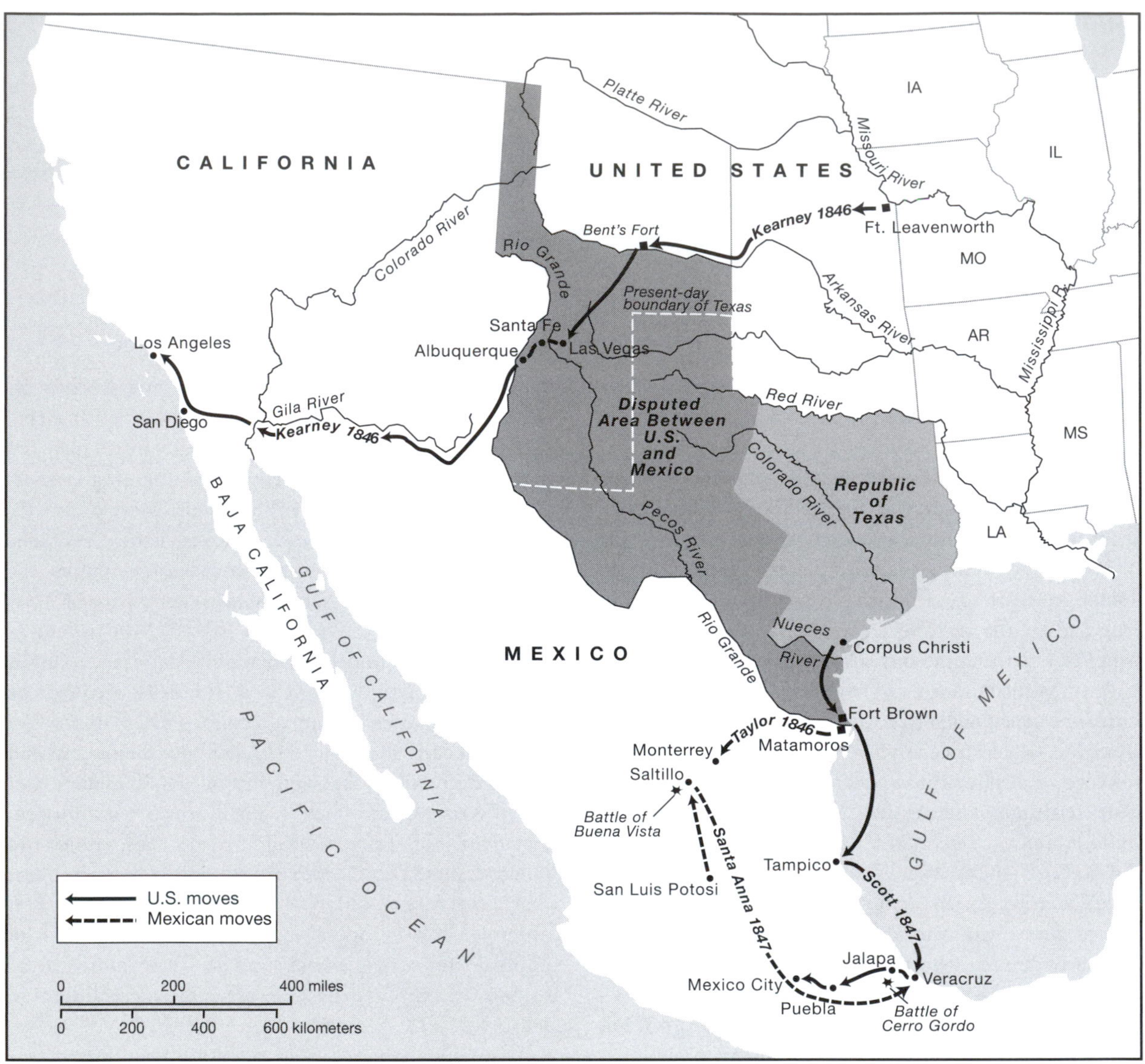

Major Campaigns of the Mexican-American War

claimed by Mexico, Congress overwhelmingly supported the declaration of war.

Dissent

The Whig minority in Congress opposed territorial expansion generally and expansion into potential new slave territories in particular. But with memories of the disastrous collapse of the Federalist Party over the War of 1812 firmly in mind, the vast majority of congressional Whigs supported Polk's call for volunteers and voted for funds to fight Mexico. Only 14 members of the House, all of whom represented heavily antislavery constituencies in the Northeast and upper Midwest, voted against the declaration of war.

The American public, schooled in the ideology of Manifest Destiny and firmly convinced of the racial and cultural inferiority of Mexicans, largely embraced this war. But a vigorous antiwar movement, centered in New England and led by abolitionists, offered sharp critiques of its morality. Antiwar activists argued that the war was unjust, that might did not make right, and that the conflict was evidence of a "slave power" manipulating the government in order to expand slavery. These positions would ultimately emerge as the consensus view by the late nineteenth century.

During the first year of the war, the antiwar movement had a limited impact. But as war dragged on, dissent became widespread. By late 1847, mainstream congressional Whigs, including some from southern and western districts, openly protested the war and called for its immediate end. Freshman representative Abraham Lincoln demanded to know the "exact spot" where American blood had supposedly been shed. Presidential hopeful Henry Clay gained national attention when he called for mass protests against the war. The antiwar movement has been discounted by some scholars as ineffective, but it played a clear role in pressuring President Polk to come to terms with Mexico at the close of the war.

Soldiers and the Military Front

Polk's initial call for troops resulted in an outpouring of volunteer enthusiasm, but most soldiers found service in Mexico disillusioning. The Mexican-American War had the highest casualty rate of any American conflict, almost 17 percent of the 79,000 American soldiers who served in it died, mainly from disease. Although the regulars in the army did most of the hard fighting and both Taylor and Scott regularly condemned the volunteers for lack of discipline (they were responsible for most of the atrocities committed against Mexican civilians), it was the volunteers who won most of the acclaim back home. The working men who made up the bulk of both army regulars and volunteers may have believed that service in Mexico would result in an increase in their class status at home, but their harsh treatment by officers tended to reinforce their subservient position in industrializing America. Desertion rates were high, particularly among Catholic immigrants who felt divided loyalties fighting a Catholic country under an army openly hostile to their faith. Some of these men joined the San Patricio Battalion and fought for Mexico. Many more American soldiers embraced the "free soil" political movement upon returning home, convinced that democracy and economic opportunity could flourish only for working men in slavery-free territories.

At the outset of the war, most European observers predicted that Mexico, fighting at home with a large standing army, would easily defeat the invaders from the north. But General Stephen W. Kearny's troops easily conquered New Mexico, Taylor's troops prevailed in a number of bloody clashes in northeastern Mexico, Scott battered his way to the capital, and an initial revolt of Anglo settlers under the command of Captain John C. Frémont in California (known as the Bear Flag Revolt) culminated in the surrender of Mexican *Californios* to American forces in January 1847. Factors internal to Mexico greatly aided the U.S. cause. Chronic political instability, a series of popular uprisings against national and state governments, wars between Mexican settlers and independent Native Americans in the border region, and the inept military leadership of General Antonio López de Santa Anna all hampered Mexico's ability to repulse the invaders.

Polk had secured the northern half of Mexico by the end of February 1847, and dispatched diplomat Nicholas Trist to negotiate a treaty of peace soon after. But the incensed Mexican government refused to come to terms, even after the fall of Mexico City. American forces in the capital were subject to brutal attacks by guerrilla partisans, and General Scott came to believe that the long-term occupation of central Mexico by the United States was untenable. But extreme Democratic expansionists increasingly called for the annexation of all of Mexico as spoils of war, and Polk recalled Trist in the fall of 1847 in hopes of gaining a larger settlement from Mexico than he had originally authorized. With the support of General Scott, and in sympathy with Mexico's plight, Trist disobeyed the president and negotiated a treaty on his own. Polk agreed to the terms of the Treaty of Guadalupe Hidalgo, both because of growing antiwar sentiment at home and because the annexation of the densely populated southern part of Mexico was opposed on racial grounds by many in both the North and South.

War and the Democratic Party

There was initial support for the war among northern Democrats who believed expansion was healthy for democracy, desired California's ports in order to commercially expand into Asia, and saw the annexation of Texas and California as the best means of preventing British encroachment in North America. Yet many came to view Polk's war with Mexico with suspicion, born of the belief that the war was being waged in the interest of southern slaveholders. When Pennsylvania Democratic congressman David Wilmot offered a rider to a war appropriations bill in August of 1846 on the floor of the House that banned slavery from any territory won from Mexico, he revealed the increasing sectional rift and growing power of free soil ideology in the North.

Democrats faced other struggles during "their" war. Polk had pledged to serve only one term in office, and there was no clear front-runner for the Democratic nomination in 1848. The two heroes of the engagement, Zachary Taylor and Winfield Scott, were Whigs. Despite Polk's attempts to brevet Democratic generals, including Franklin Pierce, the president's fears were realized when the Whigs won the presidency in 1848 with Taylor at the head of the ticket. This was the second and last time the Whigs would win the presidency before the party collapsed over the issue of slavery in the 1850s. Winfield Scott, the Whig Party's final presidential candidate, was defeated by Pierce in 1852.

Popular Reception of the War

In the eyes of many U.S. citizens, virtually every battle in the Mexican-American War made manifest the heroism and superior fighting abilities of the North American. In the battle of Buena Vista, less than 5,000 U.S. soldiers defeated a Mexican army of 15,000. At Cerro Gordo, U.S. forces flanked and drove a much larger Mexican army out of a defensive position, clearing the way to march on the capital, where they successfully stormed Chapúltepec Castle, which guarded Mexico City.

The first war covered by newspaper correspondents was closely followed at home, and these victories became cultural events, celebrated not only in the press, but also in fiction, music, and art. This war marked the first encounter of most white Americans with Mexicans and disrupted the reigning division between black and white that structured American racism. Dime-novel accounts of the war celebrated romance between U.S. soldiers and light-skinned Mexican women, while casting dark-skinned Mexican men as villains. The years following the war saw an explosion of filibustering expeditions by American men into Mexico, the Caribbean, and Central America. American filibusters were motivated to invade foreign countries without governmental sanction by a belief that the continued territorial expansion of America was God's will, by greed for land, and by visions of international romance. For these mercenaries, the key lessons taught by the Mexican-American War were that violence was an acceptable means to gain new territory, and that victory was inevitable over the racial inferiors of Latin America.

Sectional Crises

The status of slavery in the Mexican cession led to repeated sectional crises. Despite its support among northern representatives of both parties, the Wilmot Proviso never became law because of southern strength in the Senate. The question of whether to allow slavery in the new territories took on concrete importance when California applied for statehood in 1849. When President Zachary Taylor proposed outlawing slavery from all the new territories, including California, furious Southerners threatened to secede from the Union. Only Henry Clay's Compromise of 1850 calmed the storm by offering Southerners a strict fugitive slave law and the possibility of a new slave state in the unorganized New Mexico territory through the doctrine of "popular sovereignty."

But this compromise was only temporary. The Second Party System was yet another casualty of the war. The platforms of both major parties, which studiously avoided discussing slavery, began to seem increasingly irrelevant to voters in both the North and South, opening up room for the new Republican Party to make a strong showing in the North in 1856 with presidential candidate John C. Frémont, hero of the Bear Flag Revolt.

Lasting Memory and Hemispheric Impact of the War

Both supporters and opponents agreed that the Mexican-American War marked a turning point in the nation's history. In 1848 Captain James Henry Carleton wrote that "the Battle of Buena Vista will probably be regarded as the greatest ever fought on this continent." The Civil War quickly proved him wrong, however, and completely overshadowed the war in Mexico. While in Mexico La Invasíon Norteamericana exerted a powerful force in the political realignment of the late nineteenth century, the creation of a centralized state, and the forging of a common Mexican identity, the half-life of this war north of the border was remarkably short. Representations of even the most dramatic victories of the conflict disappeared after 1860, and veterans of the 1848 conflict struggled to gain public recognition and financial support from a society that had no heart for revisiting the Halls of the Montezumas.

In 1885 former president Ulysses S. Grant, who like most Civil War generals had gained key military experience in the Mexican conflict, described the war with Mexico as "one of the most unjust ever waged by a stronger against a weaker nation." He declared the Civil War "our punishment" for that "transgression." At the time this view was a mainstream one. While Grant had been a member of the pro-war Democratic Party in the 1840s and 1850s, he was a Union general and Republican president and accepted the antiwar Whig Party as his party's forebear. Although the Democrats promoted and won the war with Mexico, it was a pyrrhic victory for the party. Ultimately the views of Whigs, who maintained that the war was unjust, immoral, and part of a land grab on the part of slaveholders, held sway. The 1847 resolution by the Massachusetts House of Representatives that "an offensive and unnecessary war is one of the highest crimes which man can commit against society; but when is superadded a war for the extension of slavery, its criminality stands out in the boldest possible relief" had become the dominant belief among Republicans after the Civil War.

But white Americans of all parties and all sections of the country in the later nineteenth century tried to forget the Mexican conflict and to reimagine the bloody 1840s as a peaceful period, when sectional harmony and common purpose advanced Manifest Destiny. By the fiftieth anniversary of the war in 1898, politicians and historians seemed comfortable writing a history of America's military past in which the war with Mexico and its veterans were absent. Congress debated whether to fight a war for empire in 1898 without acknowledging that it was the fiftieth anniversary of the successful conclusion of the first war for empire. The 1848 war posed some difficulties for those who endorsed a history in which Americans always behaved from selfless motives. In 1898 both supporters and opponents of imperialism maintained that the United States had always firmly and consistently disavowed empire.

Since many scholars now explain the war fought by the United States in 1898 as part of a regional struggle for dominance, a process that started with the Monroe Doctrine, this amnesia was significant. Some historians have suggested that the war with Mexico was unnecessary: Polk could have gained Mexico's northern territories through steady diplomatic negotiations and without either the loss of life or principle that the war entailed. In either case, many would now consider Ralph Waldo Emerson prophetic for predicting in 1846 that "the United States will conquer Mexico," but that "Mexico will poison us."

See also sectional conflict and secession, 1845–65.

FURTHER READING

DeLay, Brian. *War of a Thousand Deserts: Indian Raids and the U.S.-Mexican War*. New Haven, CT: Yale University Press, 2008.

Foos, Paul. *A Short Offhand Killing Affair: Soldiers and Social Conflict during the Mexican-American War*. Chapel Hill: University of North Carolina Press, 2002.

Greenberg, Amy S. *Manifest Manhood and the Antebellum American Empire*. New York: Cambridge University Press, 2005.

Griswold del Castillo, Richard. *The Treaty of Guadalupe Hidalgo*. Norman: University of Oklahoma Press, 1990.

Hietala, Thomas. *Manifest Design: American Exceptionalism and Empire*. Ithaca, NY: Cornell University Press, 2003.

Levinson, Irving W. *Wars within War: Mexican Guerrillas, Domestic Elites, and the United States of America*. Fort Worth: Texas Christian University Press, 2005.

Pletcher, David. *The Diplomacy of Annexation: Texas, Oregon, and the Mexican War*. Columbia: University of Missouri Press, 1973.

Reséndez, Andrés. *Changing National Identities at the Frontier: Texas and New Mexico, 1800–1850*. New York: Cambridge University Press, 2005.

Robinson, Cecil. *The View from Chapultepec: Mexican Writers on the Mexican-American War*. Tucson: University of Arizona Press, 1989.

Schroeder, John H. *Mr. Polk's War: American Opposition and Dissent, 1846–1848*. Madison: University of Wisconsin Press, 1973.

Winders, Richard. *Mr. Polk's Army: The American Military Experience in the Mexican War*. College Station: Texas A&M University Press, 2001.

AMY S. GREENBERG

Middle Atlantic, the

Just three Middle Atlantic states, among the most populous in the nation between 1820 and 1940 and industrial leaders for much of American history, have wielded huge potential influence in American politics, particularly in the election of presidents and the make-up of Congress. Yet they have realized this potential only intermittently, as great wealth and diverse populations have made them notorious for political corruption and the politics of compromise.

Leading banks, industries, and railroads were the glue that held these diverse states together. From the Civil War until the mid-twentieth century, Pennsylvania was dominated politically by the Pennsylvania Railroad, Standard Oil, the great steel and coal companies, the Mellon Bank interests (including the Aluminum Corporation of America), and the Pennsylvania Association of Manufacturers. In New York during the same period, the New York Central and Erie Railroads, along with Wall Street bankers, notably J. P. Morgan, wielded the most influence. In New Jersey, the Camden and Amboy Railroad before the Civil War and the Pennsylvania Railroad afterward came to dominate the state. In each state, the enormous discrepancy between private and public wealth ensured that state legislators were almost invariably willing to do the bidding of the capitalists.

New York

New York was founded as New Netherland in 1624 by the Dutch East India Company for two purposes: sending furs, especially for beaver hats, to Holland, and supplying the newly acquired Dutch colony of Brazil with provisions such as fish and grain. Peter Minuit, the first governor, instituted the patroon system in 1629, which the English continued under the name of proprietary estates, in which wealthy men who brought at least 50 settlers to the colony received large tracts of land that they leased to tenants.

New Netherland was governed autocratically by a series of governors, none of whom could maintain order effectively among the diverse population of Dutch, English (on eastern Long Island), and, after 1654, Swedes in the Delaware Valley, whom Governor Pieter Stuyvesant conquered. Stuyvesant was so unpopular that when an English fleet arrived in 1664, the population refused to fight. The renamed New York was then ruled as a proprietary colony by the Duke of York, the future King James II. Conflict between the influential English and Anglican minority and the Dutch characterized New York politics until the mid-1730s, when the proprietary Livingston family of upstate New York and the French Huguenot merchant Delanceys of New York City became leading rivals until the American Revolution.

New York anticipated the party politics that did not develop elsewhere until the 1790s or later. Each faction ran complete slates of candidates, distributed literature, held rallies, and articulated specific policies.

As with Pennsylvania and New Jersey, New York's assembly never supported the American Revolution, and leadership before 1775 fell to New York City merchants and sea captains, who, in 1766, led the fight against British soldiers at what became known as the Battle of Golden Hill. But New York's revolution did not lead to a major class conflict because members of the elite, such as the intermarried Jay and Livingston families, took a strong stand for resistance and independence. In 1777 John Jay (governor, 1795–1801) drafted most of a constitution that gave equal political rights to all citizens regardless of religion. But until 1795, the anti-Federalist supporters of states' rights dominated New York, with George Clinton holding the governorship for 18 years. Alexander Hamilton and John Jay, along with James Madison, wrote the *Federalist Papers* to convince New Yorkers to support the U.S. Constitution, but only the threat to remove heavily Federalist New York City from the state and join the union convinced the upstate opposition to support ratification. New York was the eleventh state to ratify.

New York continued to lead the nation in political mobilization in the nineteenth century. Aaron Burr (senator, 1791–97) earned his spot as vice president on Thomas Jefferson's 1800 ticket when he was a principal organizer of the nation's first urban political machine, known as Tammany Hall after the meeting place of New York Democrats. On the state level, Martin Van Buren (senator, 1821–28; president, 1837–41) did likewise, earning a similar position from Andrew Jackson in 1833. Van Buren wrote the first theoretical defense of the two-party system as well, arguing that a legitimate opposition encouraged voter participation, especially in an era when nearly every government job was a political appointment.

During the Civil War, New York State, especially the New York City area, was the most pro-southern in the North. The city was the center of the cotton export trade, and by 1860, its population was three-fourths immigrant or first-generation (mostly Irish) American—poor workers who had little sympathy with southern slaves and competed for jobs with local African Americans. Mayor Fernando Wood hoped the city would secede and form the state of Islandia to join the South. In 1863 the city descended into chaos for seven days after the draft was instituted on July 4, and between 100 and 1,000 people died in the ensuing riots. Only the arrival of Union troops from Gettysburg, Pennsylvania, ended the disturbances; had Lee won that pivotal battle, Union control over its largest city might have ended.

With the most patronage positions up for grabs, the New York Republican and Democratic parties led the nation in corruption. William M. "Boss" Tweed, a

Democrat who dominated the city in the 1860s, had a Republican counterpart in Senator Roscoe Conkling (1867–81), who persuaded his party to nominate the former head of the New York customhouse, Chester Arthur, for vice president in 1880. Republican president Rutherford Hayes had dismissed Arthur for his willingness to overlook corruption where more of the nation's imports landed than anywhere else. Earlier, New Yorkers of both parties had joined together and nominated Republican editor of the New York *Tribune* Horace Greeley to run for president in 1872 against the scandal-ridden administration of Ulysses S. Grant. The Democratic Party endorsed him as well. New York Governor Grover Cleveland was the only Democratic president between the Civil War and Woodrow Wilson, who would become president in 1913: in 1884 Cleveland defeated the notoriously corrupt James G. Blaine, a Maine senator, despite having admitted to fathering and supporting an illegitimate child. When a New York Republican minister denounced the Democrats as the party of "Rum, Romanism, and Rebellion," his speech backfired, giving Cleveland a minuscule margin in his home state.

With Theodore and Franklin Roosevelt and Alfred E. Smith (governor, 1923–29), New York became a national leader in progressive reform in both political parties. Laws that protected women and children at work, supported labor unions, provided old-age and disability insurance, and furthered public education were a model for the New Deal; Governor Herbert Lehman (1933–44) was a firm friend of Franklin Roosevelt and his policies. New York public housing and road construction led the nation: by the 1930s, New York City had five times the highway mileage of any other city, as well as the largest city and regional railroad system.

Following World War II, New York continued to lead the nation in expenditures, including a huge highway system, state university, and capitol complex in Albany built under Governor Nelson Rockefeller (1959–73), which greatly expanded the state's debt. In the 1960s, New York and many of the state's older cities were plagued by poverty, riots, and a flight to the suburbs. New York City went bankrupt in 1975 and had to be bailed out by the state government. Under Mayor Ed Koch (1978–89), the city regained much of its prosperity by promoting international tourism and investment, but at the expense of the poor and the middle class, who found it increasingly hard to pay the astronomical city rents. The suburbs continued to grow while urban and rural areas of upstate New York declined in population.

In the twentieth century, New York was the only state to have important liberal and conservative parties that ran candidates of their own as well as endorsing those of the major parties. Liberal Republican John Lindsay won election as mayor of New York City (1966–73) when conservative Republicans ran candidates—including columnist William F. Buckley Jr.—who took votes away from the Democratic machine's choice. Lindsay ran on the Republican-Liberal ticket to win his first term and Democratic-Liberal for his second. When Buckley's brother James (senator, 1981–87) defeated longtime liberal Republican senator Jacob Javits (1957–81) in the 1980 primary, Javits refused to give up his Liberal Party line, taking enough votes away from Democrat Elizabeth Holtzman to cost her the election.

New York also attracted celebrity candidates from other states: the Buckleys from Connecticut, Senator Robert F. Kennedy from Massachusetts, and Senator Hillary Rodham Clinton from Arkansas. In the late twentieth and early twenty-first centuries, New York voters were independent and unpredictable: they elected two Republican mayors, Rudolph Giuliani (1994–2001) and Michael Bloomberg (2001–), in heavily Democratic New York City and a conservative Republican governor, George Pataki (1995–2006), to succeed the liberal Democrat Mario Cuomo (1983–94). Until the Democrats' victory in the election of 2008, the state senate had been in Republican hands, the assembly in Democratic, since the 1960s. Candidates for judges were almost invariably endorsed by the Democratic, Republican, Conservative, and Liberal parties.

Pennsylvania

Pennsylvania began in 1682, when William Penn became the proprietor of the colony. Penn recruited English Quakers as well as German pacifists to receive freeholds in a colony that would grant religious toleration to all peaceful inhabitants (although only Christians could vote and hold office before the constitution of 1790). Penn recruited whole communities, which settled together, thereby preventing serious internal conflict until the Scots-Irish settled the western frontier in the 1750s. He bought the western land fairly from the Indians, although the "treaty" made famous in Benjamin West's 1771 painting was actually 12 treaties with small groups in the Philadelphia area.

Penn's colonists did not appreciate his largesse. They opposed his design for an appointed council and did not want to pay rents or taxes without an assembly's consent;

Penn lost so much money on Pennsylvania that when he tried to sell it in the 1690s to pay off his debts, there were no buyers. After 19 constitutions or instruments of government either proposed or attempted, in 1701 Penn and the colonists finally settled on a system unique among the 13 colonies in having a one-house legislature, the assembly. With representation set by county, the three original counties that favored the Quaker Party dominated the legislature; their opponents, the Proprietary Party, supported the Penn family interests and mostly consisted of Presbyterians and Anglicans.

When warfare broke out in 1754 over whether the French or British should rule what is now western Pennsylvania, the Indians from whom Pennsylvania had purchased land attacked all along the frontier, driving settlement back beyond the Susquehanna River and turning Lancaster, York, and Reading into refugee centers. The assembly insisted the proprietors pay taxes for frontier defense; eight pacifist Quakers resigned in 1756 rather than approve funds for war, but the party kept control. It sent Benjamin Franklin to London to lobby for Pennsylvania's becoming a royal province; during the 1760s and 1770s, when most colonies were resisting British taxes and commercial regulation, leaders of both Pennsylvania factions were trying to impress the home government with their loyalty.

As a result, Philadelphia artisans and politicized Pennsylvania German farmers, led by notable Philadelphians including Franklin, Thomas Paine (author of *Common Sense*), painter Charles Willson Peale, astronomer David Rittenhouse, and Dr. Benjamin Rush, took control of the revolution, ousted the assembly, and drew up a new constitution in 1776. Abolishing the office of governor for a mere "president," who simply presided over the assembly, the document was both the most and least democratic of all the state constitutions: most democratic in that tax-paying men could vote and the assembly was reapportioned to favor the previously underrepresented backcountry, but least democratic in that only those who swore an oath to the government on the Bible could participate in the new order. Pennsylvania also adopted the nation's first system of rotation in office (no one could serve in the assembly more than four out of seven years), authorized the Council of Censors to judge whether laws violated the constitution, and required two consecutive assemblies to pass nonemergency legislation, to give people a chance to look over the new laws. But the new government proved both tyrannical in suppressing opponents and enforcing price fixing and ineffective in collecting taxes and keeping order. Businessmen headed by U.S. superintendent of finance Robert Morris formed the Republican (later Federalist) Party to oppose the Constitutionalists (later anti-Federalists). Bringing fiscal stability to the state with the first bank on the North American continent in 1781, they also supported commercial and industrial development. After they took over the state in 1786, they brought it into line for the U.S. Constitution, and replaced Pennsylvania's own constitution in 1790, restoring a strong senate and governor.

Aside from the struggle over the nature of its government, Pennsylvania endured more unrest than any other state between 1750 and 1800. It had fought with three of its neighbors—Maryland in the south, Virginia in the west, and Connecticut in the north—over its boundaries, and only settled them in 1763, 1781, and 1786, respectively. Two of the three "rebellions" in the early republic (more accurately, cases of tax resistance)—the Whiskey Rebellion of 1794 and Fries's Rebellion in 1799—occurred in Pennsylvania when the federal government appointed unpopular individuals to collect new taxes.

Between 1800 and the Civil War, Pennsylvanians of every political persuasion dedicated themselves to economic growth. They strongly favored government support for internal improvements, differing primarily over whether this should occur through legislative grants, borrowing, or assistance to banks. Pennsylvania staked its industrial growth on high tariffs, but by the 1850s, after most of the schemes for canals and railroads failed, the state was controlled by the pro–southern Democratic machine headed by James Buchanan.

Buchanan's disastrous presidency and the invasion of Pennsylvania twice by Confederate forces (at Gettysburg in 1863 and Chambersburg in 1864) led to a Republican ascendancy that even the Great Depression barely interrupted, and which ultimately survived until the 1950s. The state legislature became notorious as the servant of business interests: Pennsylvania was the only state in the union that allowed corporations to recruit government police forces (the infamous "coal and iron police") and allowed the Pennsylvania Railroad to create corporations, such as John D. Rockefeller's South Improvement Company, which drilled and processed most of western Pennsylvania's oil. Tom Scott, President of the Pennsylvania Railroad, helped negotiate the deal that in 1876 made Republican Rutherford B. Hayes president in a disputed election with Samuel Tilden; the next year, Hayes ordered federal troops to break the national railroad strike.

Even Pennsylvania Democratic reformers such as lawyer J. Mitchell Palmer could not defeat boss Boies Penrose in the first direct election of a senator held in the state in 1914; six years later, Penrose solved an impasse at the Republican National Convention and secured the presidential nomination for Warren Harding, with his chief supporter Andrew Mellon of Pittsburgh becoming secretary of the treasury. Nor could William Wilson, secretary of the United Mine Workers—in whose northeastern Pennsylvania strike of 1903 the federal government intervened on the workers' behalf for the first time —defeat William Vare, the boss of Philadelphia, in the dishonest senate election of 1926. Vare had previously arranged for his wife to be the first woman in the Pennsylvania state legislature as a sop to women's rights. Ultraconservative Pennsylvania supported neither woman suffrage nor Prohibition.

Only in 1922 and again in 1930 was a reformer, Gifford Pinchot, elected governor. Pinchot had won the support of the Mellons and the Pennsylvania Association of Manufacturers, which, represented by its president Joseph Grundy, ran the state most of the time between Penrose's death in 1921 and his own (at the age of 99) in 1961. The first chief of the National Forest Service, Pinchot pushed for conservation of the formerly magnificent woods that had allowed Pennsylvania to lead the nation in lumber production during the 1860s and 1870s. He also favored employment projects, especially roads and public construction, during the New Deal, as did his successor Democrat George Earle (1935–39): both men supported unions and the right of workers to strike. But the Republican legislature refused even to set up a system for distributing much of the New Deal monies to which the state was entitled, just as, in the 1920s, it had refused to enforce Prohibition, leading Pinchot to rely on funds from the Women's Christian Temperance League. The Pennsylvania Turnpike, the nation's first limited access high-speed highway, was built only when President Roosevelt approved $20 million in federal funds to do so.

After World War II, Pennsylvania became a two-party state. Popular governors included Democrats George Leader (1955–59), David Lawrence (1959–63), and Ed Rendell (2003–) as well as Republicans William Scranton (1963–67) and Tom Ridge (1995–2001). Once a leader in American industry, Pennsylvania now confronted deindustrialization: numerous small cities as well as Pittsburgh and Philadelphia lost one-third to one-half of their population between 1960 and 2008.

New Jersey

New Jersey began as two colonies: East Jersey, with its capital at Perth Amboy, opposite New York City, and West Jersey, with its capital at Burlington opposite Philadelphia, in 1676. Although the colony united in 1702, its economy and politics reflected this geographic divide. West Jersey was heavily Quaker, settled with freehold farms, and used Philadelphia as its major port; East Jersey was settled largely by Scots, had large proprietary estates, and fell within New York's orbit. At first New Jersey was considered too insignificant to have its own royal governor, and shared one with New York until 1738. During the 1750s, Scottish proprietors attempted to collect their rents and control the settlement on their estates, which led to land riots. Only the American Revolution and the ousting of the largely loyalist owners settled the problem. New Jersey accepted the U.S. Constitution with alacrity, fearing that otherwise it would be swallowed by its stronger neighbors. But the divisions continued: the state had to pass a law in 1790 preventing people from bringing their guns to polling places.

New Jersey set up one of the weakest state governments in the nation: the executive had no appointive powers, it was the next to last state to have free public education, and, as late as 1960, had neither a sales nor an income tax. In the nineteenth century, it was overwhelmingly Democratic until the Republicans supplanted the Democrats after William McKinley defeated William Jennings Bryan in the presidential election of 1896. Conservative New Jersey gave African American men the vote only when compelled to, along with the South, by the Fifteenth Amendment to the Constitution in 1870. Republican rule was briefly interrupted when a division between Republican reformers and conservatives permitted the election of Woodrow Wilson, a Democratic governor (1911–13) who supported such innovations as the direct primary, laws protecting workers, and regulation of public utilities. Wilson had won election as the choice of Boss James Smith of Newark, and infuriated Democratic regulars when he decided to become a reformer.

In later years, New Jersey, like New York, behaved unpredictably in state elections, although consistently in presidential races, voting Democratic in every national contest between 1992 and 2008. Republican moderates won election as governor, including Tom Kean (1982–90) and Christine Todd Whitman (1994–2001). Democratic governor James Florio (1990–94) generated a backlash against his party when he raised taxes significantly to improve public services. As in Pennsylvania, state taxes were low (New Jersey had some of the lowest gasoline prices in the nation), which put the burden of solving urban problems on cities. Many New Jersey residents lived in suburban areas and were more closely linked, economically and psychologically, with the communities in Pennsylvania and New York, especially Philadelphia and New York City, where they worked.

Compromise and Corruption

New Jersey and Pennsylvania, and frequently New York, have been bastions of corruption and compromise through much of their history, from their refusal to endorse independence in 1776 to the vast influence corporations and railroads exercised over state legislatures. As the nation moved to a service economy, representatives of urban ethnic groups, middle-class suburbs, business interests, farmers, and post-industrial cities all had to cooperate to solve the problems of a region that had lost national importance to the South and the West. Nevertheless, all three states proved capable of electing energetic officials whose civic commitment extended beyond enriching corporations and satisfying the wishes of political machines. Mayors Giuliani (1994–2001) and Bloomberg (2002–) of New York City and Governor Jon Corzine (2006–) of New Jersey won national attention for their efforts to control fiscal expenditures, promote economic growth, and improve some of the nation's most polluted environments. At the same time, perpetual squabbling in the state legislatures continued to stymie meaningful advances in educational reform and improved health care.

See also local government; patronage; state government.

FURTHER READING

Beers, Paul D. *Pennsylvania Politics: Today and Yesterday*. University Park: Pennsylvania State University Press, 1980.

Fleming, Thomas. *New Jersey: A History*. New York: Norton, 1984.

Hofstadter, Richard. *The Rise of a Party System: The Growth of the Idea of Legitimate Opposition in the United States, 1780–1840*. Berkeley: University of California Press, 1969.

Klein, Milton M., ed. *The Empire State: A History*. Ithaca, NY: Cornell Universtiy Press, 2005.

Klein, Philip, and Ari Hoogenboom. *A History of Pennsylvania*. University Park: Pennsylvania State University Press, 1980.

Lehne, Richard, and Lana Rosenthal, eds. *Politics in New Jersey*. New Brunswick, NJ: Rutgers University Press, 1979.

Miller, Randall, and William Pencak, eds. *Pennsylvania: A History of the Commonwealth*. University Park: Pennsylvania State University Press, 2002.

Reynolds, John F. *Testing Democracy: Electoral Behavior and Political Reform in New Jersey, 1880–1920*. Chapel Hill: University of North Carolina Press, 1988.

Riordan, William, ed. *Plunkett of Tammany Hall*. New York: E. P. Dutton, 1963.

Salmore, Barbara G., and Stephen A. Salmore. *New Jersey Politics and Government: The Suburbs Come of Age*. 3rd ed. New Brunswick, NJ: Rutgers University Press, 2008.

Schneier, Edward V., and Brian Murtaugh. *New York Politics: A Tale of Two States*. Armonk, NY: M. E. Sharpe, 2001.

Treadway, Jack M. *Elections in Pennsylvania: A Century of Partisan Conflict*. University Park: Pennsylvania State University Press, 2005.

WILLIAM PENCAK

Midwest, the

In his recent polemic *What's the Matter with Kansas?* Thomas Frank examined that state to discover "how conservatives won the heart of America." For many Americans, Frank's assessment that the Midwest is fundamentally conservative, unprogressive, and even backward politically is self-evident. An earlier generation, however, saw the Midwest as a laboratory for democratic ideas and causes. John Barnhart, author of a 1953 history on the settlement of the Ohio River Valley, applied historian Frederick Jackson Turner's emphasis on the frontier's importance for democracy to that region. Barnhart's thesis was that in Ohio's territorial period, democracy triumphed over the elitism of the Federalist Party. Although it is no longer fashionable among historians to see a causal connection between the settlement of the frontier and the advance of democracy, many of the issues and problems of U.S. politics have been worked out in the Midwest. Even William Allen White, the newspaper editor who first asked the question "What's the matter with Kansas?" in an 1896 editorial, was ridiculing a movement—populism—that many contemporary historians view as a radical solution to the economic ills of the late nineteenth century. And Frank's maligned conservatives were, in the 1980s, part of a revolution to remake American society and politics. Far from being backward, the Midwest has been at the forefront of political debate in the nation.

Native and Euro-Americans

The first political systems of the Midwest were the consensus-based tribal politics of the Native Americans. The collective decision making and noncoercive nature of the Native American political tradition ran contrary to the European colonizers' hierarchical systems. As European alliances became important to the tribes, tribal politics began to revolve much more around diplomacy and trade relations. Historian Richard White has posited a "middle ground" in which Native Americans and Euro-Americans accommodated and adapted to each other. That relationship eroded, however, when Euro-Americans achieved dominance in the early nineteenth century. Rather than accommodate Native Americans, Americans sought to expel them.

The removal period of the early 1800s saw some tribes displaced from certain areas of the Midwest, often to more western parts of the region. In states that had undergone removal, the families and bands that remained often lost their tribal status. Some, such as the Miami, engaged in a long political struggle to regain that status. Even among current Native Americans with tribal status, resentment at government encroachments on tribal sovereignty conflicts with fears that government moves toward "self-determination" will mean the end of the federal aid the tribes receive.

For Euro-Americans in the Midwest, the American Revolution brought new forms of government. The national government, under the Articles of Confederation, possessed a vast colonial territory: the region between the Appalachian Mountains and the Mississippi River. Congress resolved the issue of governance through the Northwest Ordinance, which established the Northwest Territory and provided for stages of government as the territory grew in population. In the earliest stages, government was autocratic under a federally appointed governor and judges. As population increased, the territory acquired an elected legislature, but the governor retained absolute veto power. When the population reached a certain level, voters could elect a constitutional convention and apply for statehood. If admitted, the new state entered on an equal footing with its predecessors. The ordinance acknowledged both the democratic underpinnings of the American system and a good deal of distrust in the pioneers' capabilities to govern properly. It also, however, laid the groundwork for territorial government not only in the Midwest but in all regions of future U.S. expansion. As well, the trend from the earliest settlement of Ohio was for autocratic features to erode in favor of democracy. The population benchmarks required for the government to move to the next stage were often waived, governors of future territories lost their absolute veto, and the presumption became that settlers were fit for statehood as soon as they desired it. In fact, the national government, or political parties that sought to gain electoral votes, would often push for statehood before many settlers felt ready to bear the financial burden of extra taxation that statehood entailed.

Creating the Midwest

The Midwest achieved statehood during the nineteenth century, a period when expanding democracy was the norm. James H. Madison, an expert in Midwestern history, includes the following states in the region: Ohio (which achieved statehood in 1803), Indiana (1816), Illinois (1818), Missouri (1821), Michigan (1837), Iowa (1846), Wisconsin (1848), Minnesota (1858), Kansas (1861), Nebraska (1867), South Dakota (1889), and North Dakota (1889). State constitutions provided for strong legislatures and weak governors. Ohio's 1803 constitution did not even give the governor a veto. Some early state constitutions gave the legislature extensive control over appointments or required frequent elections of both the legislative and executive branches. Frequent elections gave the people more control over their representatives. Nineteenth-century notions of democracy, however, were limited only to white men. When Indiana revised its constitution in 1851, it specifically limited suffrage to white males. Many Midwestern states had black exclusion laws that forbade blacks to settle in them or required the posting of a bond. Although these laws were often flouted, they demonstrated the pervasive hostility to African Americans and became the basis for harassing blacks who incurred community wrath—often for abolitionist activity.

Attitudes toward African Americans depended in part on sectional differences. New England migrants who settled Ohio's Western Reserve formed abolition societies and voted Whig or Republican, while the Kentuckians in the lower North favored the Democrats. In general, regional differences in housing styles, foodways, and political culture would be subordinated to a general sense of American westernness. Stephen A. Douglas and Abraham Lincoln demonstrated the subordination of region of origin to party politics when they clashed in the 1858

A family with their covered wagon during the Great Western Migration, Loup Valley, Nebraska, 1866. (National Archives)

Illinois senatorial race. The Democrat, Douglas, a Vermont native, rejected the East's confining morality and deference to hierarchy. The Republican, Lincoln, a Kentucky native, rejected the South's economic backwardness and embraced the very movements Douglas abhorred—temperance and antislavery. Both men, of course, considered themselves Westerners and believed their positions represented the best interests of the Midwest. The place where this emphasis on westernness failed, perhaps, was the Kansas Territory. Since Kansas was at the center of a sectional storm over slavery, settlers from New England, the Midwest, and Missouri were unable to forget their regions of origin and forge a common western identity. Rather, they adhered to free soil or proslavery political positions, keenly aware of region.

The Midwest was at the forefront of disputes over democracy during the Civil War. The Peace Democrats, or Copperheads, took their nickname from a poisonous snake indigenous to the Midwest. The Copperheads advocated constitutional liberty, which they believed the administration of President Abraham Lincoln threatened. They opposed military arrests and trials of civilians, the suspension of habeas corpus, and the suppression of free speech and the press. Deeply racist, they also opposed emancipation, as well as civil and political rights for African Americans. Many Midwesterners believed that Copperhead objections to Republican wartime policy constituted active support of the Confederacy. In 1863 the military's arrest of the leading Peace Democrat, former congressman Clement Vallandigham of Ohio, became a cause célèbre. Because Vallandigham had spoken against the war, he was arrested and tried by a military tribunal. President Lincoln commuted his sentence to exile to the Confederacy. While never a threat to the war effort, the Copperheads represented deep discontent in the white Midwest with many of the Lincoln administration's policies, particularly on civil liberties and race.

African Americans

Although the Midwest had long been hostile to blacks, African American migration to the Midwestern states increased after the Civil War. The suppression of African American political rights at the end of Reconstruction prompted a migration of so-called Exodusters (so named because of their exodus from the increasingly repressive southern states). Segregation of schools, workplaces, housing, and social venues existed formally and informally in the Midwest, but voting was nonetheless allowed. By the early 1900s, industrialization stimulated black migration. Factory owners sometimes recruited black workers as strikebreakers, but, in general, the availability of jobs just as surely brought African Americans from the South. Race riots occasionally marred the Midwest's reputation as a refuge from the Jim Crow South. In 1908 a race riot erupted in Springfield, Illinois—Abraham Lincoln's hometown—when whites attacked blacks in reaction to their growing presence. During World War II, a terrible race riot occurred in Detroit, where black and white workers clashed. By contrast, race riots during the 1960s were more often associated with black frustration at poor housing and menial jobs, as was the case with a Detroit riot in 1967.

Civil rights leaders worked to improve conditions in the Midwest as well as in the South. The lead case in the U.S. Supreme Court's groundbreaking school desegregation case, *Brown v. Board of Education of Topeka*, was that of an African American family, the Browns, against the school board of Topeka, Kansas. In the all-white Chicago suburb of Cicero, Martin Luther King Jr. drew attention to segregation in the North by means of a peaceful march. By 2008 the rise of Illinois senator Barack Obama to the U.S. presidency indicated the progress that Midwestern African Americans had achieved.

Ethnocultural versus Economic Issues

After the Civil War, the Midwest became a political battleground. Several Midwestern states possessed both divided electorates and considerable electoral votes. Moreover, government's growing involvement in regulating the economy was of special interest to residents of the region. As a heavily agricultural area, but also one of growing industry, the Midwest faced the social and economic changes of the age. The temperance, Greenback (labor), and grange or populist movements all drew great attention in the Midwest.

Quantitative analyses of Midwestern politics in the late nineteenth century argue that voters split along ethnic and religious—rather than along class—lines. In this formulation, pietists (evangelical Protestants) backed the Republican Party, and ritualists (Catholics) backed the Democrats. The 1896 presidential election between William McKinley and William Jennings Bryan, both Midwesterners, shifted the dynamic. Pietists embraced the Presbyterian Bryan, but ritualists were repelled from the Democratic Party. The result was a new ascendancy for the Republican Party in the Midwest as the "party of prosperity."

However, pietism was not dead, and soon saw results in the Prohibition movement. Both major anti-alcohol organizations, the Women's Christian Temperance Union and the Anti-Saloon League, originated in the Midwest. The Eighteenth Amendment to prohibit alcohol was ratified by most Midwestern state legislatures, and the enforcement legislation, the Volstead Act, took the name of Minnesota congressman Andrew Volstead.

The Midwest also became a center of resistance to Prohibition. Al Capone, a Chicago gangster, gained notoriety as a supplier of bootleg liquor. Because the legalization of alcohol not only promised to undermine this flourishing criminal subculture but also to stimulate a flagging economy, the Midwest decisively supported repealing Prohibition in the early years of the Great Depression.

Ethnicity was an important element of the struggle over Prohibition. Among the bootleggers' customers were ethnic, urban voters who supported the repeal of Prohibition, while native-born, rural Protestant Midwesterners opposed it, embracing the crusade against alcohol. These ethnic voters resulted from the waves of migration into the Midwest from the early nineteenth century on. Irish, Germans, and Scandinavians came first, followed by the late-nineteenth- and twentieth-century migration of southern and eastern Europeans. Democrats welcomed the immigrants, but the Whig Party, and later the Republican Party—although attractive to some immigrant groups such as the Germans—were more hesitant to embrace the new constituencies.

Issues such as slavery, alcohol, and economics helped determine the partisan split of immigrant groups. German voters were more receptive to the middle-class aspirations of Republicans than were the Irish. Although German voters might have disliked Republican temperance proclivities, they were more likely to appreciate Republican moral qualms about slavery and invocations of the superiority of a free-labor society. In the post–Civil War period, Democrats continued to appeal to immigrants for their defense of cultural traditions, such as drinking alcohol, and their closer identification with the working class, to which many immigrants belonged.

More recently, many political alliances have been reshaped by Hispanic migration, especially from Mexico, and by migration from Asia, Southeast Asia, Africa, and the Mideast. Federal immigration legislation in 1965, which removed quotas that favored western and northern Europeans, coincided with shifting patterns of migration by bringing more persons from developing nations. As immigrants became more involved in civic life, their presence often provoked a nativist backlash. Political movements to deny immigrants the right to hold office, to enforce the legal prohibition of alcohol, or to deny amnesty for illegal immigrants have all grown from nativist sentiment.

The increasing presence of women on the Midwestern public stage in the late nineteenth and early twentieth centuries dovetailed with the growing movement for their own rights. Although the women's rights movement originated in the northeast, Midwestern women took part in meetings before the Civil War. It was at an Akron, Ohio, women's rights gathering that Sojourner Truth delivered her famous "Aren't I a Woman?" speech, reminding the audience that nineteenth-century gender roles made no allowance for the situation of black women. Clarina Nichols took a notable role at the convention that wrote Kansas's constitution.

Nonetheless, women's activism was still seen as an extension of their role in the home. During the Civil War, women supported the war effort through aid societies, sanitary fairs, and nursing. Although Mary Livermore, a Chicagoan and organizer of sanitary commission fairs, became a suffrage advocate, the movement was not as strong in the Midwest. In the post–Civil War period, many women turned their activism toward temperance. Midwestern women joined the Women's Christian Temperance Union (WCTU) and participated in its crusades against the saloon. Kansan Carrie Nation and her hatchet became national symbols of the WCTU's campaign against alcohol.

Their battle against the liquor interests persuaded many women of the need for the vote. Midwestern states began to permit women to vote, often in local elections, before the passage of the Nineteenth Amendment. The leader of the campaign for the woman suffrage amendment was an Iowan, Carrie Chapman Catt. A generation later, the feminist movement would also have Midwestern roots. Betty Friedan from Peoria, Illinois, was living the life of a suburban housewife and mother when she wrote her protest against women's isolation in the home, *The Feminine Mystique*, in 1963. All the Midwestern states except Illinois ratified the equal rights amendment, although Nebraska and South Dakota later rescinded their ratifications. After the expansion of women's rights to include reproductive rights, the National Abortion Rights Action League was founded in Chicago to protect against attacks—both political and physical—on abortion rights.

Women had, of course, never been entirely isolated in the domestic sphere. Economic necessity as well as the desire for a career often drove women to work outside the home. During the nineteenth century, certain occupations such as teaching and nursing had become feminized. But women also worked in the emerging factories.

The new industrial order, in fact, stimulated some of the most important political developments in Midwestern history. Early factory labor was dangerous, subject to the boom and bust periods of the business cycle, and largely unregulated. Manufacturers' reliance on holding companies and trusts allowed them to build near monopolies in certain industries. Amid a political culture of lax ethics, politicians took money and gifts from industrialists, thereby compromising their ability to speak for the people. Some of the most famous protests against the new industrial order arose out of the Midwest. In 1894 Jacob Coxey, an Ohio manufacturer, led an army of the unemployed in a march on Washington, D.C. Although they drew attention to the hardships created by the Panic of 1893, they gained little from the government except arrest for walking on the grass.

Industrialization stimulated the political movement of progressivism. Progressives sought to ameliorate its worst effects through social reform and government regulation. Jane Addams pioneered the settlement house movement when she and Ellen Gates Starr opened Hull House in an immigrant neighborhood in Chicago in 1889. Settlement houses provided social services for their neighbors, such as day care and vocational training, but they also played an active role in civic life. Settlement house workers helped immigrants prepare for naturalization and campaigned for regulation and services from city government. Midwestern mayors such as Hazen Pingree of Detroit, Samuel Jones of Toledo, and Tom Johnson of Cleveland led early reforms against the boss-dominated politics of their cities. Samuel M. "Golden Rule" Jones, a Christian Socialist, advocated public ownership of utilities. Robert M. "Fighting Bob" La Follette of Wisconsin, the great leader of Midwestern progressivism, began his career by winning election against his state's Republican machine. By 1900 the machine was broken, and La Follette and his followers were implementing the "Wisconsin idea" of expanded democracy, whose major reforms included direct primaries, initiative and referendum, campaign finance, civil service, and antilobbying laws; government regulation of transportation, public utilities, industry, and banking; state income and inheritance

The Haymarket Square Riot took place on the night of May 4, 1886. Published in *Frank Leslie's Illustrated Newspaper*, May 15, 1886. (C. Bunnell and Chas Upham/ Library of Congress)

taxes; child labor, industrial safety, pure food and workmen's compensation laws. Although La Follette lost influence in the national party, the Wisconsin reforms became a model for national progressivism.

Radicalism versus Reaction

While Progressives accepted the capitalist economic order, some Midwesterners rebelled against it. The Midwest was the site of labor unrest that galvanized the nation. Chicago, a major railroad hub, was caught up in the national railroad strike of 1877. In 1886 strikes in Chicago for the eight-hour day panicked middle-class residents, who feared the violent rhetoric of many in the labor movement. When police fired into a crowd of strikers at the McCormick Harvester plant, labor leaders organized a protest meeting at the Haymarket. A bomb was thrown among the police who came to the meeting, and the police opened fire. Eight anarchists were convicted of conspiracy for murder, although little evidence connected them to the bomb.

During the depression of 1893–94, workers in Pullman, Illinois—who built railroad cars—went on strike over wage cuts. The strike became national when the American Railway Union agreed to support the Pullman workers. Eugene V. Debs, the leader of the American Railway Union, converted to socialism while in jail during the Pullman strike. Debs emerged from prison determined to change the economic system. A Hoosier, Debs pioneered an indigenous, American version of socialism, but socialism still was too radical and—despite Debs—too foreign for most Midwesterners.

Industrial workers were not the only people turning to organization to resolve their economic difficulties. Farmers also adopted cooperative arrangements, such as those offered by the Patrons of Husbandry (also known as the Grange) or the Farmers' Alliance. The Granger laws, aimed at regulating the railroads on which farmers relied, were passed in many states. The Farmers' Alliance, which began in Texas, took hold in the Midwest with a program of cooperative marketing and proposals for a government-run subtreasury that was intended to expand the money supply. Unable to achieve these reforms through the two-party system, the Alliance turned to political action with the creation of the Populist Party in 1892. It was the strength of the Populists in Kansas that provoked White to pose the question "What's the Matter with Kansas?" for the first time. However, the Populists' venture as a third party was short-lived: when they decided to fuse with the Democrats in 1896, they lost both the election and their identity as an influential party.

But Midwestern radicalism did not expire with the demise of the Populists. Before World War I, North Dakota farmers responded to the monopoly practices of grain elevators and railroads by forming the Non-Partisan League. Radicalism spread to other parts of the Midwest, where the Farmer-Labor party allied farmers with miners and industrial workers. During the war, the party lost power because adherents were accused of being pro-German.

A reactionary movement saw surprising growth in parts of the Midwest with the rise of the Ku Klux Klan in the 1920s; this second Klan movement was as much anti-immigrant and anti-Catholic as it was antiblack. Klansmen, ostensibly representing moral rectitude and Americanism, enforced the vice laws, such as Prohibition, that immigrants often flouted. The Klan reached its apex of political power in Indiana, where the governor had ties to the group. Ironically, the Indiana Klan collapsed under the weight of a sex scandal when its leader kidnapped and raped a young woman who then committed suicide.

The Klan was one manifestation of another side of Midwestern politics. In contrast to the discontent and push for reform demonstrated by farmers and laborers, there were powerful impulses of conformity. The pioneering sociological study by Robert S. Lynd and Helen Merrell Lynd, *Middletown*, found the Klan to be an offshoot of that impulse. Muncie, Indiana—the site of *Middletown*—possessed a business class that promoted civic boosterism, local and national patriotism, and encouraged voting a straight ticket. In this environment, citizens knew less and less about their candidates and their local government. Peer pressure kept those who might dissent from the local ethic quiet. In Middletown, the emphasis was on "getting a living," not on political activism.

While the Midwest saw much protest against the emerging industrial-capitalist order, it also saw the rise of powerful conservatives who were part of that order. William McKinley, the Ohio Republican who concentrated on tariff reform, was bankrolled by Mark Hanna, the epitome for many in the Progressive Era of the money bag–carrying plutocrat. Herbert Hoover, a self-made man, championed a philosophy of "rugged individualism." Conservative or so-called Bourbon Democrats, such as J. Sterling Morton of Nebraska, were more comfortable with industrialization than their Populist-oriented counterparts. In some parts of the Midwest, a more symbiotic than antagonistic relationship existed between farm and factory. Midwestern industrial centers such as Chicago and Omaha, Nebraska, provided markets for farmers' output.

The Midwestern protest tradition reasserted itself during the Great Depression. The Farm Holiday Association dramatized the plight of farmers through farm strikes and by pouring milk onto roads in an attempt to raise its price. President Franklin D. Roosevelt's New Deal brought Midwestern farmers the Agricultural Adjustment Act, which paid farmers not to plant and formed the basis of much modern farm policy. The American Farm Bureau emerged as spokesman for the farm interest. Although its roots were in the cooperative movements of the nineteenth century, it came to represent the farmer as small businessman. The Farm Bureau became a powerful lobbying force, closely allied to the Farm Bloc—congressmen and senators from farm states who have a major say in agricultural policy. The New Deal thus turned agrarian activism in a more conservative direction.

The Great Depression also renewed labor activism, which had been crushed by government suppression during and after World War I, and had remained dormant during the affluence of the 1920s. Flint, Michigan, home to a General Motors factory, became the site of a major sit-down strike that inspired similar labor actions across the country. Through such strikes, and New Deal legislation, labor won the right to organize.

World War II brought prosperity that continued into the postwar period, and that prosperity brought increased conservatism. As white workers could afford a middle-class income, they became increasingly concerned with rising taxes that redistributed income to the poor and to African Americans. By the 1980s, they became known as Reagan Democrats, traditionally working-class Democratic voters who voted for Republican Ronald Reagan because they liked his antitax stance and anticommunism. Ironically, the emergence of Reagan Democrats coincided with the decline of industry and working-class affluence. Filmmaker Michael Moore caught the emergence of the Rust Belt in *Roger & Me*, a profile of Flint's decline as General Motors closed its plants there. Industry's decline crippled labor's political power.

Liberals and Conservatives

During the post–World War II period, the Midwest was home to both a vibrant liberalism and a rising conservatism. Iowan Henry A. Wallace, who had a long career as secretary of agriculture under President Franklin D. Roosevelt and then as his vice president, would run for president himself in 1948 as the candidate of the left-wing Progressive Party. Conservatism would see its triumph with the election of Illinois-born Ronald Reagan in 1980.

Some of the best-known national spokesmen for postwar liberalism were from the Midwest. Throughout his long career as mayor of Minneapolis, senator from Minnesota, vice president, and presidential candidate, Hubert Humphrey worked for the ideals of the New Deal and the Great Society, a social safety net, and civil rights. Humphrey, along with the 1972 Democratic presidential candidate, South Dakota senator George McGovern, embodied the big-government liberalism that conservatives attacked. In addition, McGovern was identified with a youth movement that wanted to legalize marijuana and end the Vietnam War.

The student movement had its birth in the Midwest with the Port Huron Statement, which was issued by Students for a Democratic Society (SDS) in 1962. With roots in the Old Left, SDS initially focused on civil rights but quickly moved to antiwar protest. Student rallies against the Vietnam War at campuses throughout the country became a hallmark of the era. On May 4, 1970, a protest at Kent State University in Ohio turned deadly when National Guardsmen fired on protesters and bystanders, killing four and wounding several others.

At the same time, the Midwest was home to much dissatisfaction with the direction of liberalism. The cold war's animus toward radicals undermined progressivism in the Midwest. Senator Robert Taft of Ohio, known as "Mr. Republican," viewed government as the source of oppression not social welfare. He not only opposed the New Deal but also voted against U.S. entry into the North American Treaty Organization. Taft's fellow senator, Joseph McCarthy of Wisconsin, gave his name to the era's anti-Communist preoccupations, making exaggerated charges of Communist infiltration into the federal government and the Hollywood entertainment industry. One manifestation of the New Right was the John Birch Society, founded in Indianapolis in 1958, which advanced theories of left-wing subversion and claimed, for a time, that President Dwight Eisenhower was a Communist.

Although the "Birchers" might be dismissed as cranks, the conservative ideals of small government and anticommunism went mainstream with the election of Ronald Reagan in 1980. Although Reagan built his political career in California, he always acknowledged his Midwestern upbringing as key to his individualistic values. As president, he presided over major tax cuts, a military buildup, and cuts in social welfare programs. Many Midwestern politicians carried out Reagan's philosophy at the state level. Governor Tommy Thompson of Wisconsin, for example, became nationally known for innovative conservative stands on welfare reform, for support of school choice and voucher programs, and for using the line-item veto—a power Reagan continually lamented the president lacked—to cut state spending.

As the history of the Midwest in the period after World War II reveals, it is a misconception to see the region as monolithically liberal or conservative. Just as the famous 1896 presidential election pit William McKinley of Ohio against William Jennings Bryan of Nebraska, who were styled as standard-bearers of money power versus the people, respectively, late-twentieth-century elections have featured Midwesterners of very different viewpoints. The witty Adlai Stevenson, governor of Illinois and defender of liberal "eggheads," was twice defeated for the presidency by Dwight D. Eisenhower of Kansas. In 1984 Ronald Reagan defeated a protégé of Hubert Humphrey, Minnesota's Walter Mondale, who crippled his chances by pledging to raise taxes.

In addition, Midwestern politics is still capable of producing its share of candidates who are not easily categorized. Former independent Minnesota governor—and former professional wrestler—Jesse Ventura supported tax rebates when the state was running a surplus, but vetoed a bill to promote recitation of the Pledge of Allegiance in public schools—a key test of patriotism for many conservatives in the 1990s.

Once a stronghold of Republican "red states," electoral maps of the Midwest offer only a superficial understanding of political divisions. Since World War II, Indiana usually voted Republican for president, but Minnesota was a Democratic stronghold. At the turn of the twenty-first century, the region became increasingly competitive. Minnesota, Michigan, and Ohio were battlegrounds during the 2000 and 2004 elections. In the Midwest, Democratic U.S. Senate candidates were successful almost two-thirds of the time in the last third of the twentieth century, while House of Representative seats split fairly evenly between the two parties. In the 2008 presidential primary race, two of the leading Democratic candidates, Barack Obama and Hillary Clinton, had ties to Illinois, while Republican candidate Mitt Romney originally hailed from Michigan. In addition, the Midwest still plays a crucial role in selecting candidates via the primary and caucus system. Iowa, by virtue of its first-in-the-nation place in the presidential selection process, has a disproportionate say in picking the major party nominees.

Indiana, which had not given its electoral vote to a Democrat since 1964, went for Obama in 2008. This deviation from its staunchly Republican record may be temporary. It remains to be seen whether Obama will emphasize pragmatism or progressivism, but the election of the first Midwestern president in a generation reaffirms the centrality of the region in the nation's politics.

See also Great Plains; Rocky Mountain region.

FURTHER READING

Barnhart, John D. *Valley of Democracy: The Frontier versus the Plantation in the Ohio Valley, 1775–1818.* Bloomington: Indiana University Press, 1953.

Berman, William C. *America's Right Turn: From Nixon to Clinton.* Baltimore, MD: Johns Hopkins University Press, 1998.

Davis, Allen F. *Spearheads for Reform: The Social Settlements and the Progressive Movement.* New York: Oxford University Press, 1967.

Frank, Thomas. *What's the Matter with Kansas? How Conservatives Won the Heart of America.* New York: Henry Holt, 2004.

Goodwyn, Lawrence. *The Populist Moment; A Short History of the Agrarian Revolt in America.* New York: Oxford University Press, 1978.

Hurt, R. Douglas. *American Agriculture: A Brief History.* Ames: Iowa State University Press, 1994.

Kleppner, Paul. *The Cross of Culture: A Social Analysis of Midwestern Politics, 1850–1900.* New York: Free Press, 1970.

Lynd, Robert S., and Helen Merrell Lyud. *Middletown: A Study in American Culture.* New York: Harcourt, Brace, and Co., 1929.

Madison, James H., ed. *Heartland: Comparative Histories of the Midwestern States.* Bloomington: Indiana University Press, 1988.

Middleton, Stephen. *Race and the Legal Process in Early Ohio.* Athens: Ohio University Press, 2005.

Onuf, Peter S. *Statehood and Union: A History of the Northwest Ordinance.* Bloomington: Indiana University Press, 1987.

White, Richard. *The Middle Ground: Indians, Empires, and Republics in the Great Lakes Region, 1650–1815.* New York: Cambridge University Press, 1991.

NICOLE ETCHESON

Muslims and politics

Muslims have lived in the United States for many generations, yet they have existed at the margins of the nation's political history. As early as the seventeenth century, a significant portion of black Africans brought to the Americas as slaves were Muslim. The rate of voluntary immigration from the Muslim world, low between the Civil War and World War II, gained momentum after U.S. immigration policies were altered in the mid-1960s to end the use of a national origins system that favored immigration from Europe. Many Muslim arrivals between 1875 and 1945 were from Arabic-speaking countries and were rural, unskilled, or semiskilled laborers. Within a generation, most were absorbed into American society, sometimes even marrying outside the faith and adopting Americanized names (for instance, Mohammed became Mo or Mike). Many intended to stay temporarily to earn and save money. In more recent decades, however, a new wave of immigration—this time of urban elites seeking higher education and economic opportunities—resulted in unprecedented numbers of Muslims settling permanently in the United States. This phenomenon has made a Muslim presence more discernible.

Muslims are one of the fastest growing minority communities in the nation's largest cities. Dispersed throughout the United States, with concentrations on the East and West Coasts and in the upper Midwest, Muslims comprise a mosaic of ethnic, sectarian, and socioeconomic diversity. Muslims trace their origins to more than 80 countries and multiple sectarian orientations. Estimates of the size of the U.S. Muslim population vary widely, from 1.4 million (0.6 percent of the general population) to 6 million (roughly 2 percent of the general population) or more. However, because the U.S. Census Bureau does not collect data on religious affiliation, it is difficult to determine exactly how many Muslims reside in the United States. A 2007 survey by the Pew Research Center estimated that there are at least as many Muslims as Buddhists or Hindus in the United States. Other researchers say that their numbers are greater, perhaps similar to the population numbers for Jews or Mormons.

The American Muslim population defies easy categorization when it comes to political beliefs. Comprised largely of persons of Arab, South Asian, and African American descent, followed by those of several smaller ethnic groups—Turks, Iranians, Bosnians, Indonesians,

Malaysians, and others—the population is vast, and the umbrella term *American Muslim* is almost too broad to describe a coherent group.

It would be difficult to characterize American Muslims as predominately conservative or liberal. While a large percentage expresses a preference for a larger government providing more public services, many are not consistently liberal in their views. A solid majority opposes homosexuality and believes that government should do more to protect "morality" in society. The 9/11 terrorist attacks cast a long shadow over American Muslims, and many worried about government surveillance, job discrimination, and street harassment. In the 2000 presidential election, most voters who identified themselves as Muslims supported George W. Bush by a wide margin, yet in 2004, their preference changed to John Kerry. Anxiety and fear about personal liberty in the "war on terror" after 9/11 was a likely cause of this realignment, since many Muslims felt the brunt of profiling and discrimination at the hand of government surveillance and security agencies as well as extralegal acts by individuals and groups. Muslim Americans have been mobilized by the backlash against terror and a common tendency to conflate terrorists with Muslims writ large.

Still, overall, American Muslims express positive attitudes about living in the United States, and the majority come from the middle class and are highly educated. The Muslim population is youthful, and the young generation participates in several Muslim organizations that have intensified efforts to train the next generation's leaders. The vast majority of Muslims believe they should be engaged in American political life and civic affairs, and do not see a conflict between being devout and living in a modern society. Political and civic engagement includes voting in elections, contributing time and money to voluntary associations, participating in interfaith activities, supporting political candidates, calling or writing the media or an elected official about an issue, attending a rally or convention on behalf of a cause or political candidate, and being active in a political party.

Increasing participation by American Muslims in local school boards, city councils, interfaith alliances, and electoral politics is evident. A nationwide survey of American Muslims in 2004 reported a high rate of political participation when compared to the general population. According to this survey, 61 percent of Muslim Americans voted in the 2000 elections, compared to slightly more than 50 percent of the general voting-age population. For the first time, in 2000, both the Democrat and Republican nominating conventions opened with Muslim prayers included among the rituals of the party gatherings.

How did American Muslims become relevant in American politics? Are they a potential voting bloc? Many are deeply vested in civic engagement as individuals and through Islamic organizations, local and national meetings and conferences, and interfaith dialogue. What follows is an overview of the broad contours of the history of Muslim presence in the United States and its contributions to law and politics.

Diversity among the Muslims of America

A major challenge to understanding the history of American Muslims is appreciating the wide spectrum of the many communities that are considered "Muslim." American Muslims are a diverse population, one that is largely immigrant. Lacking hard numbers, researchers have approximated that the ratio of foreign-born to U.S.-born Muslim Americans is two to one. Of those born in the United States, about half are African American (roughly 20 percent of the total U.S. Muslim population). There are differences in beliefs and practice between Sunnis and Shi'as—two major sectarian groupings—and also a range of variation within both affiliations. Additionally, a growing number of Sufis who teach mysticism includes many Euro-American converts. Large numbers of native-born Americans of African, Hispanic, and European backgrounds have converted to Islam or, as some would have it, "reverted" (returned) to the faith. Thus the population can be generally divided between those who are called "indigenous" Muslims and those who are foreign-born. Finally, there are those born to immigrants and converts. Each of these sources accounts for a considerable share of the total U.S. Muslim population, and each constitutes an important facet of the political history of American Muslims.

Interrupted by slavery, African American Muslim history restarted its thread in the early twentieth century, with the creation of Islamic organizations as alternatives to the racially segregated churches associated with slavery and Jim Crow. Up and down the East Coast and in the Midwest, African American Islamic communities began to appear in the early 1900s. The Moorish Science Temple (1913), the Universal Islamic Society (1926), and the Nation of Islam (NOI; 1930) developed from small communities of black Muslims. Members of these groups created self-help philosophies emphasizing the value of sustaining economic investment. These nascent communities sought to be self-sufficient and avoided contact with non-Muslims. Islamic practices of prayer, modest dress, and fasting, as well as abstinence from "slave behaviors" of eating pork and drinking alcohol, were maintained and used to propagate the idea that Islam was the true religion for black people (who were, it was argued, by nature, Muslims). These communities grew out of the pan-African movements of the turn of the twentieth century; many proclaimed an esoteric and sometimes racist theology (for instance, that white people were devils).

In spite of major doctrinal differences with the orthodox or mainstream beliefs and practices of Islam, by the middle of the twentieth century, these African American Muslim communities had grown rapidly. Their popularity was largely based on their particularistic expression of black nationalism. In 1964 Malcolm X became the first prominent leader of the NOI to repudiate the separatist and racist teachings of the group's leader Elijah Muhammad in favor of a broader vision.

Elijah Muhammad's son, Warith Deen Mohammed, assumed the leadership of the NOI upon his father's death in 1975. With classical training in Arabic and Islamic sciences, Mohammed moved away from the teachings of his father to align the NOI with a mainstream Sunni understanding of Islam. Mohammed's organization is now named the American Society of Muslims and is often referred to simply as the ministry of Warith Deen Mohammed. After stepping down as leader, Mohammed remained active until his death in 2008 in a Chicago-based ministry with an organization dedicated to interfaith relations called The Mosque Cares. While Mohammed forged closer ties with mainstream Muslim organizations and Muslims outside the United States, Minister Louis Farrakhan split from the group in 1977 to revive the doctrines and practices of the former NOI leader Elijah Muhammad. Minister Farrakhan, now leading a small number of members of the NOI, continues to garner media attention.

The pioneering efforts made by African American Muslims to secure political and legal rights have made a significant contribution to the political history of American Muslims. In particular, their struggle in the prisoners' rights movement of the 1960s and 1970s secured for inmates the rights to pray, receive services of imams and Muslim newsletters, eat halal foods, and wear religious insignia and clothing. These courtroom victories opened the way for other Muslims to make broader claims on American society in further arenas, such as employment discrimination, protection from hate crimes, and zoning restrictions on the construction of mosques.

African American Muslims have had other significant firsts in public affairs. In 1991 Imam Siraj Wahaj became the first Muslim invited to give the invocation prayer at the opening of the U.S. Congress. In 2006 U.S. Representative Keith Ellison (Democrat, Minnesota) became the first Muslim elected to Congress, followed shortly thereafter by the election of the second Muslim congressman, U.S. Representative André Carson (Democrat, Indiana). The first American Muslim judges, male and female, were also African American. Judge Adam Shakoor was also Detroit's first Muslim deputy mayor. The first female Muslim judge was Sheila Abdus-Salaam, a justice on the New York State Supreme Court. These achievements have paved the way for Muslims to participate more actively in politics and law.

American Muslim Nongovernmental Organizations

American Muslims were subject to discrimination as early as the late nineteenth century. Candidates for public office in some locations proposed that Muslims should not be allowed to vote. Federal courts in the early 1900s denied citizenship to several Muslim residents because of the practice of polygamy, repudiated under American law, even when those aspiring toward citizenship neither practiced nor supported it. Nativists in the same period targeted Muslims, along with Catholics and Jews, as a threat to jobs and as a source of cultural defilement. Public anxiety over cultural pollution was used to justify the early-twentieth-century legislation of immigration quotas that affirmed many of the societal prejudices about the supposedly innate characteristics of those from the Muslim world (wicked, autocratic, unclean, oversexed), among other ethnic and religious minorities.

Yet for the most part, Muslims residing in the United States remained silent about these violations of their civil rights until late in the twentieth century. With a few notable exceptions, Muslim engagement with the American legal and political systems in any sustained way began only a decade or two before the fateful 9/11 attacks. A collective Muslim voice in the policy arena was not apparent until the 1980s, when a handful of national nongovernmental organizations (NGOs) were formed. The most prominent are the American-Arab Anti-Discrimination Committee (established 1980); the Islamic Society of North America (founded in 1982) and its affiliated organizations—including the Muslim Student Association, the Islamic Medical Association, the American Muslim Engineers and Scientists, and the American Muslims Social Scientists; and Warith Deen Mohammed's national ministry. Two local organizations established in the 1980s became major national NGOs in the 1990s: the Muslim Public Affairs Council (MPAC), founded in southern California in 1988, and the American Muslim Alliance/American Muslim Taskforce, founded in northern California in 1989. Subsequently several national organizations were founded in Washington, D.C. (see table 1). These Muslim NGOs represent a variety of missions, and, in general, aim to produce leaders in media and politics and to articulate policy concerns regarding American domestic and foreign policy.

What explains the organization building by American Muslims at the close of the twentieth century? By then there were sufficient numbers of Muslims in the United States to achieve momentum behind politicization efforts, and that momentum fueled continued institutional growth. Conflicts in the 1980s and 1990s in Afghanistan, Lebanon, Israel/Palestine, Somalia, and the Persian Gulf brought increasing numbers of Muslim refugees to the United States. At the same time, negative media portrayals of Muslims and Islam were omnipresent, and when a variety of terrorist acts were blamed on Muslims, the political goals of the emerging American Muslim community began to shift. To compound this, ethnogenesis—the process by which minority groups foster a sense of common identity by forming panethnic coalitions to address a common political problem—was underway. In other words, while many people had been defined by national origins rather than religion—for instance, as Arab American, African American, Turkish American, and the like—an overarching strategy of constructing a *Muslim* narrative began to emerge. Growth in mosques and Islamic centers, Islamic schools, social service organizations, charities, and finance companies attests to the multiethnic coalition building going on and the increased salience of *Muslim* as a public identity. Newly organized Muslim American political coalitions began to expand their goals and audiences, to engage in political lobbying, and to encourage Muslims to run for electoral office. They mobilized their constituents to work on the future of civil and human rights, participation in the electoral process, media campaigns, and interfaith cooperation with Jewish and Christian leaders regarding U.S. policy in the Middle East.

Table 1
Major American Muslim Nongovernmental Organizations

Name	Date Founded
American Muslim Alliance/American Muslim Taskforce on Civil Rights and Elections	1989
Council on American Islamic Relations (CAIR)	1994
Institute for Social Policy Understanding (ISPU)	2002
Islamic Society of North America (ISNA)	1982
Muslim Alliance in North America (MANA)	2005
Muslim Public Affairs Council (MPAC)	1988
Muslim Student Association (MSA)	1963
Muslim Women Lawyers for Human Rights (KARAMAH)	1993
National Association of Muslim Lawyers (NAML)	2000
South Asian Americans Leading Together (SAALT)	2000

Political Action

In 2000 many of these organizations mobilized the "Muslim vote" to support Republican presidential candidate George W. Bush because he was perceived to be more equitable in the Israeli-Palestinian conflict than Democratic candidate Al Gore and his running mate Joe Lieberman. A significant moment in solidifying American Muslim support occurred during the election campaign when Bush announced his opposition to the secret evidence provision of the 1996 Antiterrorism and Effective Death Penalty Act, a federal law that allowed law enforcement to use evidence in prosecuting terrorism suspects without showing it to the defendant (ironically a precursor of the Bush-supported 2001 USA PATRIOT Act, which once again reinstated strict surveillance and secret evidence measures).

Many of these Muslim NGOs responded to the post-9/11 backlash against American Muslims by drawing media attention to hate crimes, employment discrimination, and school expulsions of young students for wearing clothing that expressed their Islamic faith. Key issues these organizations face include Islamophobia; advocacy for due-process protections in the justice system, in particular for terrorism suspects; cultural awareness training for law enforcement, politicians, and court officers; and U.S. foreign policy regarding Afghanistan, Iraq, Iran, Israel, and Kashmir.

Like other Americans, many Muslims in the United States are divided about the appropriate role for religion in the nation's public life. Approximately half of American Muslims believe that members of religious congregations (including mosques) should stay out of political matters, while roughly the same number believe they should express their views on social and political questions. Nearly two-thirds of American Muslims lean toward or identify with the Democratic Party, compared with just over half the general public. Some American Muslims oppose gay rights and abortion, and have joined Orthodox Jews and evangelical Protestants and Catholics on these issues. Others are more concerned about the environment, poverty, and the rights of minorities and women around the world.

The ability of American Muslims to participate in and affect civic life has been influenced by a variety of factors. Unlike more homogeneous groups, American Muslims do not share a common language or historical experience, which makes the adoption of a collective group consciousness more challenging. Until the end of the twentieth century, ethno-linguistic, class, and sectarian divisions among Muslims hindered the development of shared civic interests. The articulation of what it means to be a Muslim American in a secular and pluralist polity has been highly variegated due to the circumstances of history and the disjuncture between indigenous and immigrant Islam. This articulation also has been challenging because the sense of a collective identity has been imposed from outside by circumstances that thrust American Muslims into the center of the civic arena. When the Murrah Federal Building in Oklahoma City was destroyed in 1995 and suspicion automatically fell on Islamist radicals, American Muslims responded by advocating civil rights and improving the public image of Islam in America. Such organizations as the Council on American-Islamic Relations (CAIR) were formed and, more recently, responded to the negative backlash after the 9/11 attacks by Muslim extremists on American targets.

The role of Muslims in U.S. political history has not been limited to political action groups and civil rights advocacy. Since the 1990s, a renewed sense of voluntarism and increasing congregationalism characterize the development of a Muslim American public identity. A connection between religious duties and civic interests has translated into the establishment of several community-based service providers that identify as Muslim, including domestic violence shelters, family counseling centers, low-income housing projects, foster care placement agencies, and clinics providing physical and mental health care. Muslim philanthropies and financial institutions providing "sharia-compliant" mortgages and insurance also demonstrate the desire to contribute Islamic values and norms to a wider notion of Muslim American citizenship. These institutions represent the integration of individual piety, communal identity, and citizenship in a manner that enables Muslim Americans to participate in the American political system while maintaining a connection to the broader Muslim world.

See also religion and politics since 1945.

FURTHER READING

Abdo, Geneive. *Mecca and Main Street: Muslim Life in America after 9/11*. New York: Oxford University Press, 2006.

Curtis, Edward E., IV, ed. *The Columbia Sourcebook on Muslims in the United States*. New York: Columbia University Press, 2008.

Haddad, Yvonne Yazbeck, Jane I. Smith, and Kathleen M. Moore. *Muslim Women in America: The Challenge of Islamic Identity Today*. New York: Oxford University Press, 2006.

Jackson, Sherman A. *Islam and the Blackamerican: Looking Toward the Third Resurrection*. New York: Oxford University Press, 2005.

Jamal, Amaney. "The Political Participation and Engagement of Muslim Americans: Mosque Involvement and Group Consciousness." *American Politics Research* 33, no. 4 (2005), 521–44.

Leonard, Karen. *Muslims in the United States: The State of Research*. New York: Russell Sage Foundation, 2003.

Moore, Kathleen. "Muslims in the United States: Pluralism under Exceptional Circumstances." *Annals of the American Academy of Political and Social Science* 612 (July 2005), 116–32.

Pew Research Center. *"Muslim Americans: Middle Class and Mostly Mainstream*. Washington, DC: Pew Research Center for the People and the Press, 2007.

Strum, Philippa, ed. *Muslims in the United States: Identity, Influence, Innovation*. Washington, DC: Woodrow Wilson International Center for Scholars, 2006.

KATHLEEN M. MOORE

National Republican Party

The National Republican Party took its name in late 1830 and served until 1834 as the main opposition to the Jacksonian Democrats. It found its electoral base among those who had supported the reelection of John Quincy Adams in 1828, and ran the campaign opposing Andrew Jackson's reelection in 1832. Some modern historians claim that the National Republicans did not constitute a real party, but in many northern and border states they proved effective and popular forerunners of the later Whig Party.

The origins of the party may be found in two tendencies apparent by 1824: the hostile reaction, especially among New Englanders, to the extension of slavery conceded in the Missouri Compromise; and the powerful demand among farming communities in the middle Atlantic, border, and northwestern states to strengthen the home market through the so-called American System—encouraging industry with protective tariffs and improving communications by building roads and canals with federal money. When the confused presidential election of 1824 had to be decided by the House of Representatives, the two tendencies came together in the election of John Quincy Adams, with the support of Henry Clay. President Adams advocated an ambitious program of internal improvements, and Congress voted an unprecedented amount of money for such improvements. Though the administration lost control of the House of Representatives in 1827, a highly protective tariff was passed in 1828, with the assistance of northern Jacksonians. Thus, the campaign to reelect Adams could reasonably claim to have delivered on its policies, in the face of strong opposition from southern Jacksonians.

In the 1828 presidential election, Adams's supporters demonstrated a degree of party organization and a willingness to cultivate popular appeals that historians have sometimes denied. A small central committee in Washington organized the interchange of information, raised money to finance local party newspapers, and established a Washington-based campaign paper titled *We the People*. In 12 states, state management committees organized state delegate conventions to name a pro-Adams "People's Ticket" for the Electoral College, and ensured that a clearly identified Adams man ran in each congressional district. They defended their record as democrats, stressed the importance of the American System to all "laboring men," and condemned Jackson for his record of violence, supposed adultery, and scorn for constitutional restraints. In the election, the Adams-Clay coalition held on to its earlier support, but apparently the preferences of new voters, notably in some critical northern states, gave the election to Jackson.

After 1828 the disillusioned Adams-Clay men transformed themselves into an opposition party, taking the title *National Republican* for the midterm elections. Initially they criticized Jackson's administration as weak and corrupt and then denounced his major policies: the Maysville Road Veto of 1830 destroyed the American System; his Indian Removal Act of 1830 betrayed treaty obligations to native peoples and would expand slavery within the Old South; his veto of the bill rechartering the second Bank of the United States disregarded established constitutional principles and endangered the nation's prosperity. This powerful focus on national politics was weakened in several northern states by the distraction of Anti-Masonry.

Many National Republicans resisted on principle the Anti-Masons' demand that no one who was affiliated with Masonry should be nominated for office, and so the many Anti-Masons in the National Republican ranks could pursue their political objectives only by forming a third party. Inevitably, in many northern states, this new party opposed the National Republicans in state and local elections, associating them with Freemasonry and secret aristocratic advantage. However, this cleavage did not greatly weaken the National Republican campaign in the 1832 presidential election, because most Anti-Masons who had opposed Jackson in 1828 were unwilling to support the Anti-Masonic presidential ticket if it would assist Jackson's reelection. In New York, Pennsylvania, and Ohio, the National Republicans made formal coalitions with the Anti-Masons, conceding the state election to the Anti-Masons in return for their agreement on a joint presidential ticket that would vote in the Electoral College for whoever could defeat Jackson.

In the 1832 campaign, the National Republicans expanded on the measures used in 1828. In December 1831, they held the first national nominating convention, complete with keynote address and floor demonstrations on behalf of their candidate, Henry Clay. In May 1832, they issued the first formal party platform, which laid down what would later be regarded as Whig principles. A vigorous populistic campaign, notable for the innovative use of political cartoons, pulled out a popular vote that correlated closely with that of 1828, but Jackson again won the popular vote and a majority in the Electoral College.

The National Republicans failed in both presidential campaigns partly because of Jackson's charisma but mainly because the anti-southern issues that gave them life restricted their reach. The party ran powerfully in 12 northern and border states, which together elected over half of both the U.S. House of Representatives and the Electoral College. It won its largest majorities in New England, regularly secured about half the vote in the large states of New York and Ohio (though not Pennsylvania), and found substantial support in the border states, in Louisiana and parts of Appalachia. But it never broke significantly into the older seaboard South, the Cotton Kingdom, or the far frontiers of Missouri and Illinois. Exclusion from much of the South meant that, unlike the Jacksonians, National Republicans had to carry almost all the marginal constituencies to win a national election.

In 1833 President Jackson's renewed attack on the national bank brought on a crisis that emphasized the urgency of strengthening the anti-Jacksonian opposition. Leading Anti-Masons, such as William Henry Seward and Thurlow Weed, saw the need to rejoin old allies but recognized that antagonism between Anti-Masons and National Republicans in state contests obstructed the road to reunion. Similarly, the appearance within the South of discontent with Jackson's actions in the nullification and bank crises created the opportunity for a genuinely national opposition party, but only if the National Republicans could shake off their identification with anti-southernism. So, in 1834 the name *National Republican* was quietly dropped and all elements began to adopt the name *Whig*. The Whigs would become the major national party opposing the Democrats over the next 20 years, but the party was not an entirely new creation. In the 12 states where a competitive anti-Jacksonian opposition had existed from 1827 through 1833, the Whigs drew on the National Republicans' organizational experience, adopted their program, and built upon the body of popular support for them.

See also Anti-Masonic Party; Jacksonian era, 1828–45; Whig Party.

FURTHER READING

Chase, James S. *Emergence of the Presidential Nominating Convention*. Chicago: University of Illinois Press, 1973.

Howe, Daniel Walker. *The Political Culture of the American Whigs*. Chicago: Chicago University Press, 1979.

Ratcliffe, Donald J. "The Forgotten Origins of the Northern Whigs, 1827–1833." *Proceedings of the Ohio Academy of History* (2002), 69–78.

———. *The Politics of Long Division: The Birth of the Second Party System in Ohio, 1818–1828*. Columbus: Ohio State University Press, 2000.

Watson, Harry L. *Liberty and Power: The Politics of Jacksonian America*. New York: Hill and Wang, 1990.

DONALD J. RATCLIFFE

Native Americans and politics

An understanding of Native Americans and politics begins with recognition of the sovereignty of tribal nations and the limits of this sovereignty under U.S. colonialism. Sovereignty is grounded in the fact of indigenous self-government and autonomy prior to the European invasion of North America. Although the United States has affirmed tribal sovereignty through treaties, federal legislation, and court decisions, these affirmations, even at their most expansive, have always entailed restrictions on sovereignty, while segments of American society have consistently sought to undermine even the most circumscribed theories and practices of sovereignty. From 1776 to the present, Native American tribes that have become subject to U.S. rule have fought to preserve their communities and reclaim their sovereignty.

Treaties and Removal

After winning independence, the United States regarded tribes that had supported the British as conquered peoples, unilaterally imposing treaties that stipulated land cessions. Realizing that these treaties threatened to provoke costly resistance, U.S. leaders soon modified this approach. By the late 1780s, the federal government adopted a policy of negotiating treaties with tribes in which they would exchange their land for payment, usually in the form of assistance toward becoming "civilized." Government officials asserted federal, over state, authority in tribal relations. To regulate the pace of settlement and trade, Congress passed the Northwest Ordinance in 1787 and the Trade and Intercourse Act in 1790. The ultimate goal, as articulated by Thomas Jefferson and other policymakers, was for Indians to become "assimilated" into American civilization.

Federal policy was ineffective in preventing speculators, slave owners, and settlers from overrunning aboriginal lands. In the early 1790s, native leaders undertook the political work of building a multitribal alliance to resist U.S. expansion. Inspired by prophets like the Shawnee Painted Pole and a Mohawk woman named Coocoochee, who denounced the ways of Europeans and urged unity, tribes from the Southeast to the Great Lakes formed an alliance to drive out the Americans and restore full sovereignty. Although this alliance routed federal forces in 1790–91, a U.S. military expedition broke the movement's back in 1794. Some native leaders made accommodations to U.S. power, signing treaties that ceded land, while others advocated continued resistance. In the early 1810s, a new generation of prophets and politicians, most notably the Shawnee brothers Tecumseh and Tenskwatawa (The Prophet), forged a new alliance, drawing support from several tribes. Although resisters achieved some military successes, U.S. forces, commanded by William Henry Harrison and Andrew Jackson, delivered crushing blows between 1811 and 1814. Harrison's and Jackson's military successes helped them build their political careers, and both eventually became president.

The defeat of the militants set the stage for a policy of removal. Although U.S. officials emphasized assimilation as the preferred route by which tribes would cease to exist, pressures from land-hungry Americans increased momentum to force tribes east of the Mississippi River to Indian Territory. Under the Indian Removal Act of 1830, the government pressed tribes to sign treaties agreeing to abandon their homelands. The politics of removal were complex. In Congress, many Northerners opposed removal (the 1830 legislation passed by a narrow margin). In Indian country, the implementation of removal became a deeply divisive process that aggravated factionalism within tribal communities.

To coerce Cherokees to leave lands recognized under prior treaty, Georgia passed legislation in 1829 extending its jurisdiction over Cherokee lands within its boundaries. The Cherokees challenged Georgia in court. In *Cherokee Nation v. Georgia* (1831) and *Worcester v. Georgia* (1832), the Supreme Court upheld the Cherokees' position that they were a sovereign nation and that Georgia's extension of state law over their territory was unconstitutional. The Court, however, limited tribal sovereignty by defining the Cherokees as a "domestic dependent nation." An earlier decision, *Johnson v. McIntosh* (1823), had also diminished sovereignty by upholding the "doctrine of discovery." This gave European nation-states "absolute title" to the continent's lands, leaving Native American nations only a "right of occupancy." Taken together, these three foundational cases set the parameters of sovereignty under colonialism. Tribes would try to expand the boundaries of practical sovereignty, while facing repeated efforts to reduce or eliminate their autonomy. For tribes forced to relocate, the Court's recognition of limited sovereignty was of little immediate value. In the 1830s thousands of Native Americans died as the government forced them from their homes.

Reservations and the "Peace Policy"

Little time passed before Americans encroached on the lands of the relocated tribes and those already in the West. In the 1840s, slave owners and free settlers poured into Texas, Arkansas, Missouri, and Kansas, while emigrants to Oregon, California, and Utah cut through the Great Plains and beyond. Federal officials began to articulate a "reservation policy." Like removal, this policy, cloaked in paternalism, was designed to take aboriginal lands. In exchange for assistance toward assimilation, tribes would sign treaties confining them to increasingly smaller reservations.

From the government's perspective, the reservation policy was humane. The tribes, however, saw it differently. No tribe truly wanted to part with its land, but many leaders feared the consequences of refusal. Indeed, government officials frequently threatened dire consequences during treaty negotiations. These included genocide, as when Washington territorial governor Isaac Stevens informed Columbia Plateau tribes in 1855 that "if they refused to make a treaty with him, soldiers would be sent into their country to wipe them off the earth." In addition to facing physical annihilation, tribal leaders feared that if they did not agree to reservations, they would lose all their land and be without government assistance at a time when game and other resources were becoming precariously scarce.

Some tribes pursued strategies of accommodation. The Crows, for example, a small people threatened by other tribes, decided to make an alliance with the U.S. military for self-preservation. On the other hand, many tribes (or segments of tribes) opposed treaties altogether and took up arms in defense of their lands. War broke out for this and other reasons, all stemming from the relentlessness of U.S. expansion. During the Civil War, the situation was further complicated by the emergence of two contending colonial powers, the United States and the Confederate States. In Indian Territory, the practice of slavery among the recently removed tribes tilted them toward an alliance with the Confederacy, though factions within these tribes opposed repudiating earlier treaties with the United States.

During the Civil War, the U.S. Army had a free hand in the West and undertook several military operations, including the removal of the Navajos to a bleak reservation at Bosque Redondo in New Mexico and the suppression of the Dakotas' uprising against oppressive reservation conditions in Minnesota. As the war ended, reformers with links to abolitionism pointed to these and other events, especially the 1864 Sand Creek Massacre, in which Colorado militia forces slaughtered over a hundred Cheyennes, to argue for a new "peace policy." The peace policy was not a departure from the reservation policy but rather a call for applying Christian principles and personnel to its implementation and maintenance. In the early 1870s, the peace policy foundered, as Indians rejected its paternalist premises by continuing to defend their land and resisting programs of assimilation. Paralleling their retreat from radical Reconstruction of the South, liberals increasingly advocated warfare and other punitive measures.

Coercive Assimilation

By the late 1870s, with most tribes confined to reservations, the government began several initiatives to promote assimilation. Some involved efforts to destroy non-Christian religious practices, break up communal property, and disrupt existing forms of tribal government. Others entailed efforts to remake Native Americans by educating them and converting them to Christianity.

This program of coercive assimilation was accompanied by legal and judicial attacks on sovereignty. In 1871 Congress abolished treaty making. Although pledging to honor previous treaties and negotiate "agreements" with tribes in the future, this legislation signaled a retreat from recognizing tribes as nations. Through the Major Crimes Act (1885), Congress asserted U.S. legal jurisdiction over Native Americans who committed serious crimes. In *United States v. Kagama* (1886), the Supreme Court upheld this legislation on the grounds that Congress possessed "plenary power" (meaning, in this context, absolute and unlimited power) over tribes. The Dawes General Allotment Act (1887) initiated a final assault on aboriginal lands by outlining the goal of allotting communal lands to individual tribal members and opening what remained to settlers. In 1901 Kiowas filed suit to overturn a congressional act requiring allotment of their reservation in violation of an earlier treaty. In a serious blow to tribal sovereignty, the Supreme Court in *Lone Wolf v. Hitchcock* (1903) upheld a doctrine of unlimited congressional authority to abrogate treaties.

As the reservation system tightened in the late 1880s, a Paiute prophet named Wovoka forecast a cataclysm that would remove or destroy European Americans and renew the earth so that Native American communities could flourish once again. Wovoka's teachings inspired a movement known as the Ghost Dance, which attracted adherents from several tribes in the West. In late 1890, the U.S. Army, falsely claiming that the Lakota Ghost Dancers had turned Wovoka's message into a doctrine of war, sent several thousand troops to suppress the Ghost Dance on the Lakota reservations in South Dakota. This led to the slaughter of more than 300 Lakotas at Wounded Knee in late 1890. Although the Ghost Dance persisted on some reservations into the twentieth century, its political dimensions subsided.

Overt resistance to colonialism continued in the early twentieth century. The Crazy Snake rebellion, named after Chitto Harjo (Muskogee), resisted allotment. But most Native American political activity tacitly accepted allotment and other aspects of colonialism and tried to limit their damaging effects. On the Crow reservation, for example, a new generation of leaders, many educated

Native American boys and girls stand in front of the Indian School in Cantonment, Oklahoma, circa 1909. (Library of Congress)

at the Carlisle Indian Industrial School in Pennsylvania, responded to government efforts to open their reservation to settlement by proposing to divide their land into individual shares to keep property in Crow hands. Another issue was the protection of a new religion in which adherents ritually ingested the peyote cactus. As government officials cracked down on the peyote religion, leaders like Quanah Parker (Comanche) appealed to the United States's ostensible commitment to religious freedom and formed the Native American Church. Other leaders, however, regarded the peyote religion as detrimental to their people's progress. As this example highlights, Native Americans remained divided over the issues they faced.

In theory, the crowning achievement of assimilation was citizenship. Allotment and military service opened routes to citizenship, but it was not until 1924 that the United States granted citizenship to all Native Americans. While citizenship's recognition of equality was in one sense a great advance, in practice citizenship was limited. Just as southern states restricted voting rights of African Americans, so did western states restrict those of Native Americans. In this way, the Native American experience was similar to those of other racialized groups in American society. But for Native Americans, citizenship carried a unique ambivalence because the logic behind it ran counter to tribal sovereignty. Although many Native Americans embraced citizenship, others were indifferent and suspicious.

Indian New Deal and World War II

In the early 1930s, the United States retreated from a policy of coercive assimilation. New ideas favoring cultural pluralism, a greater awareness of the poor conditions of reservations, and the fact that Native Americans had successfully resisted assimilation suggested the need for an "Indian New Deal." The new approach was formalized in the 1934 Indian Reorganization Act (IRA). In some respects, the IRA advanced tribal sovereignty. The legislation ended allotment, allowed tribes to recover lost lands, funded tribal economic development, and encouraged tribes to adopt constitutions and organize governments. Yet, tribal constitutions were subject to government approval and imposed what many Native Americans regarded as alien forms of political organization. Several tribes rejected the IRA, while many of those that approved did so by narrow margins.

U.S. entry into World War II pulled Native American people in different directions. Many tribes, though supportive of the war effort, argued that conscription violated tribal sovereignty. Some individuals resisted the draft, but thousands enlisted, both to defend the United States and serve their tribes in the traditional role of warriors. For most government officials, Native Americans' military service and labor on the home front implied postwar policies to promote assimilation. Tribal leaders, however, thought their people's sacrifices required the United States to redress past injustices and respect tribal sovereignty. In 1944 these leaders organized the National Congress of American Indians (NCAI), the first modern intertribal political organization. The NCAI supported the Indian Claims Commission (established in 1946) and worked closely with tribes on various issues affecting their welfare.

Termination and Revitalization

Despite tribes' efforts to advance their sovereignty, they were thrown on the defensive by a growing movement to terminate the federal government's trust responsibility for Native American people. In 1953 Congress passed legislation allowing for termination, extending state criminal jurisdiction over reservations, and encouraging the relocation of tribal people to urban areas. Two years later, in *Tee-Hit-Ton Indians v. United States*, the Supreme Court invoked the discovery doctrine to hold that the government could take Native American lands without having to pay just compensation under the Fifth Amendment. Although several tribes were terminated and their lands liquidated, termination had the unintended consequence of inspiring tenacious political organizing. In the early 1960s, new organizations like the National Indian Youth Council contested termination. Terminated tribes like the Menominees of Wisconsin, led by Ada Deer, began to lobby for restoration.

These initiatives signaled the emergence of a robust movement for Native American self-determination. The struggle for fishing rights in the Pacific Northwest, the organization of the American Indian Movement (AIM) in 1968, and the occupations of Alcatraz (1969), the Bureau of Indian Affairs (1972), and Wounded Knee (1973) marked the revival of an oppositional politics that had not been seen since early in the century. In the 1970s, Native Americans won several important victories. Congress reversed termination, returned the sacred Blue Lake to the Taos Pueblo tribe, adopted the American Indian Religious Freedom Act, and passed legislation to promote Native American education and child welfare. Congress also enacted the Alaska Native Claims Settlement Act (1971), which established Alaska's Indian, Inuit, and Aleut communities as corporations and recognized their title to 45 million acres of land. In addition to these national developments, Native American people undertook an enormous amount of political work within their communities—urban and reservation—on a broad array of issues, including health care, education, cultural revitalization, economic development, and land restoration.

Since 1980 Native Americans have continued to fight to rebuild their communities and extend self-determination, while remaining subject to U.S. colonialism. Tribal governments have greater authority than in the past to de-

American Indian Movement members and U.S. authorities meet to resolve the 1973 standoff at Wounded Knee, South Dakota. (Jim Mone/Associated Press)

fine their own procedures, establish courts, provide social services, levy taxes, exclude nontribal members, regulate hunting and fishing, and promote economic development. The Native American Graves Protection Act (1990) facilitated repatriation of ancestors' remains and cultural patrimony, while casino revenues under the Indian Gaming Regulatory Act (1988) improved reservation economic conditions and expanded the power of tribes to influence local, state, and national politics. Yet, tribal welfare and sovereignty remain precarious. As Native American people have made gains, they have been subject to "backlash" from groups equating the exercise of their rights with special privilege. Tribal governments remain subject to adverse court decisions and interference from state governments, federal agencies, and Congress. Despite casino revenues, most tribal governments still lack the resources to address daunting social problems. Nonetheless, the local and national political achievements of Native Americans in recent decades suggest that their prospects are brighter than at any time since 1776. Building on a long history of struggles against colonialism, Native Americans continue the political work of restoring the sovereignty they once possessed.

see also race and politics.

FURTHER READING

Deloria, Philip J., and Neal Salisbury, eds. *A Companion to American Indian History*. Malden, MA: Blackwell Publishing, 2002.

Deloria, Vine, Jr., and Clifford M. Lytle. *The Nations Within: The Past and Future of American Indian Sovereignty*. New York: Pantheon, 1984.

Dowd, Gregory Evans. *A Spirited Resistance: The North American Indian Struggle for Unity, 1745–1815*. Baltimore, MD: Johns Hopkins University Press, 1992.

Edmunds, R. David, Frederick E. Hoxie, and Neal Salisbury. *The People: A History of Native America*. Boston: Houghton Mifflin, 2007.

Hoxie, Frederick E. *Parading through History: The Making of the Crow Nation in America, 1805–1935*. Cambridge, UK: Cambridge University Press, 1995.

Iverson, Peter. *"We Are Still Here": American Indians in the Twentieth Century*. Wheeling, IL: Harlan Davidson, 1998.

Prucha, Francis Paul. *The Great Father: The United States Government and the American Indians*. 2 vols. Lincoln: University of Nebraska Press, 1984.

Wilkins, David E. *American Indian Politics and the American Political System*. Lanham, MD: Rowman and Littlefield, 2002.

Wilkins, David E., and K. Tsianina Lomawaima. *Uneven Ground: American Indian Sovereignty and Federal Law*. Norman: University of Oklahoma Press, 2001.

Wilkinson, Charles. *Blood Struggle: The Rise of Modern Indian Nations*. New York: Norton, 2005.

JEFFREY OSTLER

nativism

Fear of "the other," of minority groups seen as alien peoples threatening a dominant population, is present in many lands. *Nativism* is the term used to describe this hostile view of such alleged outsiders. Scholars have identified nativist movements in Nigeria and Australia, Japan and Brazil, Iran, China, Zimbabwe, and across the planet and history. But it is in the United States that the term emerged, and it is there that nativism has had it most profound impact. This should not be surprising, for the United States is the world's preeminent example of a great multiethnic, multireligious, multiracial society. It is the continent-sized "land of immigrants," a democracy that for much of its history has been the great magnet for those seeking a better life in a New World. And so inevitably it also has been the setting for resistance to these waves of newcomers, seen as incapable of being assimilated, as destructive and dangerous to the stable order created by the heirs of the earlier settlers, the "real Americans."

These real Americans, of course, were not Native Americans, dismissed by the first nativists as primitives, aboriginal peoples who must be pushed aside and later fit only for reservations. Native Americans were seen as racial inferiors, a breed apart. Certainly this was also true—and most profoundly the case—with African slaves and their heirs. Surely, African Americans, Native Americans (and some other "people of color") would be the objects of particular fear and contempt across history. They would be the victims of racism. And racism, while linked to nativism, has had its own peculiar characteristics and chronology in the story of America.

But so powerful has been the heritage of racism in this nation that some recent historians have suggested that nativism should be seen only as a relatively minor subtext of the racist past. The objects of nativist animus, it is argued, needed only to calculate how they could use America's real hatred of the feared "other," racism, to overcome their own ethnic and/or religious outsider status. Thus, there are works that describe how the Irish, the Italians, or the Jews "became white." But these works, while useful correctives to simplistic explanations concerning the fate of anti-alien movements, can be misleading if used to denigrate the enormous impact of nativist attitudes and nativist actions on millions of Americans across much of the nation's history. Such attitudes and actions darkened the lives of Catholics for centuries. They also created severe obstacles to social, economic, and political mobility for Irish, Italian, Jewish, and Slavic immigrants—and their descendents—for generations.

Nativism became the dark underbelly of the American dream of equality and opportunity beckoning immigrants to the New World. Yet it was the decline of nativism—at least in the ways it affected the lives of the Catholic and Jewish white ethnic groups who were traditional objects of such hatred—that can offer encouragement, not only for those groups still victimized and marginalized in American society but also for such groups in other nations troubled by religious, ethnic, and racial hostilities.

American nativism, which one scholar has defined as "the intense opposition to an internal minority on the grounds of its allegedly un-American characteristics," affected not only the lives of its victims but also of the victimizers, the nativists. By attacking the "other," some people were able to identify themselves by what they were not; the alien enemy was crucial to their self-image. The common foe, the "un-Americans" in their midst, allowed many anti-aliens to find community, for in polarization there was bonding. Here was a way to overcome other differences inside the favored circle of "real" Americans, people who did not carry the mark of religious or ethnic inferiority. Moreover, by projecting or displacing anger and hatred on the enemy within, nativists could more easily deal with the tragic dissonances in their own lives and in their moment in history.

Yet to view nativism only as a psychological crutch for hostile bullies and unexamined bigots does an injustice to the complexity of this American story. Many anti-aliens perceived real threats to the health and comity of their national community. The newcomers brought wrenching social and economic problems to the New World. Many nativists seriously grappled with the question of what it meant to be an American, and their fears were not merely the product of arrogance, ignorance, and hatred. The history of nativism in America is a complex story that begins with the very dawn of white settlement in the New World.

In Colonial America

The earliest targets of anti-alien hostility were Roman Catholics. Anti-Catholicism was widespread in England for decades before the first colonists arrived in America. It was the product of the rival imperial ambitions of Catholic Spain and France and was a continuous feature of English society across the late sixteenth and seventeenth centuries, after the Elizabethan Acts of Supremacy and Uniformity had put the kingdom permanently in the Protestant camp. The colonists arrived in the wilderness across the ocean having spent their lives with "no-Popery" laws proscribing the role of Catholics.

Particularly in the Massachusetts Bay Colony, where Calvinists would build a "city upon a hill," the goal was a church "purged of Romish corruptions." Catholicism was a destructive element that threatened "God's American Israel." These settlers had despised the Anglican Church because they saw it as a mirror image of the Church of Rome.

In the seventeenth century, the Catholic mass could not be celebrated anywhere except Pennsylvania. All Englishmen save Roman Catholics enjoyed the franchise in several colonies, and there were repeated anti-Catholic demonstrations in many places. In the Bay Colony, Catholics were banished and priests returned only on pain of execution. Even Roger Williams, founder of Rhode Island, the great enemy of religious persecution and the man who had demanded freedom of worship for Quakers, conducted his dispute with Puritan divines of Massachusetts in the terminology of antipapal hatred, writing of the "Romish wolf gorging herself with huge bowls of the blood of saints."

There was no toleration for Catholics in colonial America, and the eighteenth century brought new assaults on religious freedom. In Maryland, founded by a Catholic who had encouraged Catholic settlement before the proprietor's charter was voided and it became another royal colony with an established Anglican church, the governor in 1704 assailed the "Irish Papists" and their "false . . . superstitious worship." In New England, Elisha Williams, a famously learned figure who had supported religious conscience, wrote of "the Pope, who has deluged the Earth with the Blood of Christians and is the most detestable Monster the Earth ever had upon it."

In a land where wars against France and Spain had led to rumors of Catholic conspiracy, the papist was seen as an enemy agent. Nativism became firmly rooted in the conventional wisdom. In communities where children learned to write by use of rhymed couplets beginning with the letter "A," public school primers instructed them to "abhor that arrant Whore of Rome and all her Blasphemies." "Pope Night" festivals showed how the Devil was aligned with the Catholics. Fireside games bore such names as "Break the Pope's Kneck."

It was bizarre that so many felt so threatened by such a tiny minority. There were fewer than 35,000 Roman Catholics, half of them in Maryland, among the 3 million Americans at the end of the colonial period.

But the coming of the Revolution ameliorated the hostility. If anti-Catholic activism in the colonial era served to unite a disparate people, creating a sense of community in a vast and threatening continent, the conflict with England suddenly made all this counterproductive. The Revolution was a great unifying force for "true" patriots; the test of loyalty was whether one supported the new government or the Crown, not whether one practiced Catholicism or some other "false" religion. General George Washington quashed the Pope Day festivals in 1775.

In fact, success in the Revolutionary War seemed to signal an end to anti-Catholic nativism. In 1790 President Washington told clerical and lay leaders in Maryland that he believed America would become an example to the nations of the world in advancing justice and freedom, noting that "your fellow-citizens will not forget the patriotic part which you took in the accomplishment of their Revolution and the establishment of their Government, or the important assistance which they received from a nation [France] in which the Roman Catholic faith is professed." But it was not to be. The next century would bring the most intense nativist activities in American history.

Nineteenth-Century America: Immigration Leads to Nativism

In the period just after the birth of the new United States and through the depression of 1819, immigration to the new nation remained relatively low. But by 1830 conditions had changed. At least 60,000 foreigners a year arrived through the mid-1830s and the numbers escalated in the early 1840s. By 1840 there 660,000 Roman Catholics in the United States, and this number tripled in the next decade. More than a third of the new arrivals were from Ireland.

The newcomers arrived in an expanding nation undergoing political and social upheaval. The Jacksonian era was a time of opportunity but also a disorienting one. In grappling with its challenges, many sought community in zealous new Protestant groups caught up in the revivalism of the age. Soon, anti-Catholic newspapers proliferated, with such titles as *Anti-Romanist*, *Priestcraft Unmasked*, and *Downfall of Babylon, or Triumph of Truth over Popery*. The fear was that Catholics could not be citizens of a democracy because they owed fealty to a foreign sovereign, the "Pope in Rome."

There were widespread clashes between Protestant and Catholic, native and "foreigner." In 1834 the imposing brick Ursuline Convent in Charlestown, Massachusetts, was attacked by an angry mob of Protestant workmen shouting anti-Catholic slogans; furniture was smashed and the vast building sacked and set aflame. The convent burners were acquitted. In New York City, Protestant gangs—the True Blue Americans, the American Guards—fought street battles with Irish rivals.

In these years, Samuel F. B. Morse, inventor of the telegraph, wrote two books warning of an international conspiracy by European Catholics to infiltrate Jesuits into the trans-Mississippi region, with plans to annex the land and deny America expansion to the west. Meanwhile, publications in the East printed Catholic immigration statistics, sounding alarm at an influx of foreign criminals and paupers.

Catholic priests and nuns—such as those in the Ursuline Convent—were seen as particularly despicable deviants, as sadists and murderers. In 1836 a slim volume published in New York became an immediate sensation, the best-selling book in American history (save the Bible) until *Uncle Tom's Cabin*. *The Awful Disclosures of Maria Monk* purported to tell the story of a Protestant girl converted to Catholicism and, after entering a convent, brutally abused by nuns and priests. The work sold 300,000 copies and, with its explicit detail of torture and sexual assault, became a classic in pornographic literature. Yet it was only one of a growing number of "convent books" with similar messages printed during the nineteenth century. And its fabricated tales were widely believed. When nativists gained control of the Massachusetts legislature in the succeeding years, their "nunnery committee" demanded access to convents, digging up cellars in hopes of locating the bleaching bones of babies who had been killed and buried following the rapes of innocent girls by Jesuits secretly brought to the convents by evil nuns.

In this context, nativist party organizations emerged to check the power of the newcomers. The American Republican Party's leaders talked of election fraud, voting by noncitizens, corrupt political machines manipulating the votes of credulous, dull-witted Irish Catholics. When the issue became the "school controversy," that perennial nativist fear of new parochial schools educating children in a doctrine imposed by "a foreign ecclesiastical power," the party played a major role in an 1845 Fourth of July confrontation in Philadelphia. Thousands of nativists clashed with groups of Irish laborers and fire brigades; buildings were set ablaze, cannons exchanged fire, and the city was ravaged by intergroup violence.

All this occurred months before the huge wave of Irish immigration that began in 1847. It was in that year that the Great Famine—the failure of the potato crop, with its devastating impact on millions in Ireland and Europe—sent a huge wave of starving Irish immigrants to America. In 1844 there were 75,000 immigrants; in 1847 the number swelled to 234,000, and by 1851 it reached 380,000. In an eight-year period, 2.75 million newcomers arrived, the vast majority of them Roman Catholic. While many came from Germany, most were from Ireland. And they brought with them what the nativists saw as critical and dangerous social problems.

There was some substance to nativist concerns. The immigrants arrived at port cities in the Northeast in desperate straits. The vessels were filled with the sick and the dying—victims of "ship fever" (a form of typhus), smallpox, cholera, and dysentery. Epidemics erupted in all ports of disembarkation, and quarantine hospitals had to be financed. Most newcomers were postfeudal peasants, people who knew only farming and lacked the capital or skills to head west; they found themselves housed in some of the first (and worst) slums in the history of urban America.

In New York City, Boston, Philadelphia, and other communities where the immigrants settled, crime rates immediately escalated (half of those arrested in New York by 1850 were of Irish ancestry) and state penal institutions had to be expanded. The number of "paupers"—those in need of "pecuniary assistance" or refuge in almshouses—grew apace and there was a striking rise in the number of "truant and vagabond children." *The Report on Insanity and Idiocy in Massachusetts* charted a huge increase of "foreign lunatics" in state asylums. And everywhere the new immigrants settled, the number of "gin houses" and arrests for public drunkenness skyrocketed.

Nativists clearly linked the social problems of the immigrant ethnic group to their ancient fears of religious difference. Irish Catholics were seen as a cancer in the New World. They were penniless alien intruders, sick, drunk, violent, and dangerous. They had come to steal American jobs and bring dirt and chaos to communities. An ignorant and illiterate mob of fist-fighting thugs, the Irish were aggressive and clannish and would stay that way because they were controlled by priests who opposed the public school system.

The response was the creation of new nativist organizations. A series of secret societies were shaped, and from one—the Organization of the Star Spangled Banner—a new political party emerged, bearing a name "real Americans" could rally to: the American Party. But so fearful were its leaders of the secret power of "Jesuitical conspirators" that members were instructed to say "I Know Nothing" if asked about the party.

Because this was the critical decade in which the slavery issue would rip apart so many American institutions, including mainline Protestant churches and the major political parties, the Know-Nothing Party would gain in strength beyond the appeal of its potent nativist rhetoric. As the Whig Party was sundered into northern and southern factions and the Democrats were stretched to the breaking point, many political leaders and members of the older organizations found refuge in a new party insisting that the real division in America was not between those who differed on the questions of free soil and abolition but on the threat of alien immigrants.

The Know-Nothings were briefly the second largest political party in America, their presidential candidate a formidable contender in 1856. But the growth was an illusion. Soon the Know-Nothing Party was split apart by the same intractable forces dividing the nation North and South. By 1860 the party had appeal only in some border states. Fear of the alien "other" had enormous impact in the 1850s, but the great crisis that led to the Civil War swept everything aside—including nativism.

As the Civil War neared its end, Abraham Lincoln, no friend of the nativists, seemed to promise the immigrant Catholic population what Washington had at the conclusion of the Revolutionary War. Perhaps anti-alien hostility would soon fade away. But, as in decades past, nativism would find new life in the years following a great and unifying struggle.

Once again, a floodtide of new immigrants stimulated nativist activism. From 1870 to the middle of the next decade, new settlers headed to a booming, postwar America. Most newcomers were from familiar locales, including large numbers from Germany and Ireland. But by 1887 the "new immigration" began, and by 1900, southeastern European émigrés were by far the dominant element in the huge waves transforming the nation. Three-quarters of the almost 450,000 arrivals in 1900 were from Italy, the Russian Empire, or Austria-Hungary (the Hapsburg Monarchy); by 1907 of the 1.2 million immigrants, 285,000 were from Italy, 258,000 from Russia, 338,000 from the Hapsburg Monarchy—many of them south Slavs or Jews. Between 1880 and 1915, when the Great War in Europe arrested the process, more than 20 million had arrived, the majority "new immigrants." Most were Catholics, many were Jewish, and few spoke English. They represented almost a quarter of the population of a nation that had doubled in size from 50 million to 100 million in those years.

Violent resistance to newcomers flared in some areas. In California, fear of the "Yellow Peril" marked anti-Chinese and anti-Japanese activism. But the émigrés from Asia were a tiny population compared to those arriving from southeastern Europe and settling in the East and Midwest. These new immigrants became the target of hostility by intellectual and social elites as well by as the ordinary folk—merchants, laborers, small farmers—who were the traditional members of anti-alien groups.

Princeton professor Woodrow Wilson contrasted the "men of the sturdy stocks of the north of Europe" with the "more sordid and hopeless elements which the south of Europe was disburdening . . . men out of the ranks where there was neither skill nor energy nor quick intelligence." Other major academic and political figures, some of whom would become leaders of the Progressive movement, shared his contempt. Stanford professor E. A. Ross wrote of "their pigsty mode of life, their brawls and criminal pleasures, their coarse, peasant philosophy of sex." One writer noted that Italians were "largely composed . . . of the most vicious, ignorant, degraded and filthy paupers with an admixture of the criminal element . . . the lowest Irish are far above these creatures." Other prominent writers described Jews as "dirty, bearded, lecherous, foreign degenerates"; this "squat Slavonic" people were "pushy, money-grubbing materialists."

With the huge numbers of new immigrants came poverty, crime, and teeming urban slums—and renewed interest in nativist fraternal organizations. Dozens of anti-alien associations were organized, with such names as Patriotic Order of the Sons of America, the American Patriotic League, the Red, White and Blue Organization, and United Organization of the Pilgrim Fathers. Some had were little more than a few passionate activists, but many had growing memberships and boasted dozens or even hundreds of chapters. One organizaion, the American Protective Association (APA), would become a national phenomenon.

Founded in a small Iowa railroad and mill town in 1887, the APA was created to combat "political Romanism." As it grew through the 1890s, it continued to focus on anti-Catholic themes but also assailed, in the words of one of its publications, the "pauper and criminal riff-raff of Europe . . . every ignorant Dago and Pole, Hun and Slav." APA writers warned of the "Jews who have been brought in to wage war with Rome against America and Americans."

The APA—and the other nativist sects—lost members and influence after 1896. New political and social forces were stirring across the land: the Populist movement and progressive reformers in state and local government as well as in the media. Populism, with its concern for the struggle against predatory economic interests, created a dramatic new cause that made the anti-alien crusade suddenly seem much less significant. Its emergence helped ensure that the APA and the entire resurgent nativism of the post–Civil War era—which never enjoyed the political success of the Know-Nothings—would pass into history.

Although the Populist Party declined in the late 1890s, with the Progressive movement dominating the national scene in the first decade and a half of the new century, it would be a generation before even a modest revival of nativism occurred.

Into the Twentieth Century

The most notable progressive leaders, including presidents Theodore Roosevelt and Woodrow Wilson, believed in the natural superiority of Teutonic, Anglo-Saxon people. They accepted the fashionable views of European writers like Count Gobineau and Houston Stuart Chamberlain as well as the American Madison Grant, who insisted on the inferiority of those "degraded savages" who had arrived at nineteenth-century immigration stations. But the reform agenda of the Progressive movement, with its goal of adjusting capitalism to democracy after the excesses of industrial expansion, made nativism seem irrelevant.

World War I changed that. When America entered the Great War on the side of the Allies in 1917, German Americans suffered. Before the Civil War, it had been Irish, not German, immigrants who were the central focus of the most virulent anti-alien activity. Now, German Americans were accused of poisoning food, spoiling medical supplies, and undermining public support for the war effort. German names were changed, German dishes disappeared from restaurants, German-language newspapers were burned in the streets. Private "patriotic" groups, the Knights of Liberty and the American Protective League, played a role in the harassment of German Americans.

The end of the war in November 1918 brought an end to much of this hysteria. But 1919 was a time of social upheaval in America. Postwar inflation led to massive strikes and brutal repression by corporate managers, some of whom blamed "these foreigners" for the widespread labor unrest. The Bolshevik Revolution in Russia had rekindled fears of radical activists and when a series of anarchist bombs were discovered, the "Red Scare" led to wholesale violations of civil liberties. With President Wilson disabled by a stroke, hundreds of alleged "un-Americans" were arrested in Palmer Raids, named after the attorney general, A. Mitchell Palmer. Palmer, defending his action in an article entitled "Where Do the Reds Come From? Chiefly Imported and So Are Their Red Theories," pointed to the new immigrants from southeastern Europe, "these aliens, not of our sort," particularly a "small clique of autocrats from the East Side of New York." He was referring, of course, to Jewish radicals.

The Red Scare was over by the summer of 1920. Labor unrest receded and the postwar era boom would soon be underway. But nativism did not disappear in the Roaring Twenties. Across much of the decade, anti-Jewish rhetoric was found in the pages of the *Dearborn Independent*, the newspaper purchased by billionaire auto pioneer Henry Ford, a fanatical anti-Semite. Ford's efforts had limited impact; the major nativist development in the 1920s was the growth of the Ku Klux Klan.

The modern Klan, founded in 1915 by fraternal organizer William J. Simmons, had little to do with the post–Civil War Ku Klux Klan (KKK), whose hooded vigilantes repressed black freedmen and helped to restore native white supremacy in the South. After a period of slow growth and little interest, this new Klan grew to enormous size in the 1920s.

Simmons soon lost control of the organization to shrewder promoters. The KKK prospered as an anti-Catholic, anti-Semitic, and anti-ethnic immigrant crusade. Using the white garb and the bizarre titles of the old Klan (the magical "K" for ranks such as Klud, Kluxter, Klabee), the organization soon spread across America. It had strength in the South, but it was stronger still in the Midwest and had many active chapters in several western states as well as some urban areas in the Northeast. The Klan left fragmentary local records and no national archives; estimates of its total membership at the high point of its meteoric rise range from 2.5 to 5 million.

The Klan offered community to many left behind or left out in the boom years of the Roaring Twenties. It was a fraternal movement that sponsored picnics, ballgames, and "konklaves" for the like-minded. It attacked the decline of traditional values in the "modern Sodoms and Gomorrahs" that were the skyscraper cities of the new age, and assailed the immigrant drinking masses violating Prohibition and the urban elites with their depraved sexual practices. The old convent tales found a new readership. Hiram Wesley Evans, the imperial wizard, explained: "We are a movement of the plain people . . . we demand a return to power of the everyday, not highly cultured, not overly intellectualized but entirely unspoiled and not de-Americanized average citizens of the old stock."

There were only a few notable instances of repressive violence involving this KKK. While it had a powerful political presence in some areas and played a role in checking the early presidential aspirations of Al Smith (a Catholic who was governor of New York), the Klan had limited political influence on the national scene. But it attracted many ambitious and unsavory figures, men who saw in it a road to wealth and influence. And it disappeared rapidly after allegations of corruption in some states weakened its appeal. The final blow was a sex scandal involving the most powerful Klan state leader (in Indiana) in mid-decade, which put a lie to the organization's defense of traditional family values. After the Klan's collapse, no powerful new nativist movements would emerge in the twentieth century.

The Decline of Nativism

The Great Depression was not a fertile ground for nativism. Extremist groups that offered to save Americans facing economic ruin by emulating the work of European Fascists, blaming Jews and foreigners for the crisis, attracted only tiny followings.

Then, during World War II and the postwar era, nativism in America seemed to fade away. What explains its decline? The first important factor was the end of unlimited immigration. Since a series of congressional actions passed from 1917 to 1924, over a generation had passed in which the golden door was essentially closed. Millions of newcomers no longer arrived yearly, with their poverty and language difficulties. Earlier arrivals had settled in, and many were beginning to achieve mobility and realization of their own American success story. As assimilation proceeded, the reasons for anti-alien movements withered away.

President Franklin D. Roosevelt also played a key role. He shrewdly appealed to groups that had been victimized in the past by nativists, offering support and political patronage in the difficult Depression decade. It was the "Roosevelt coalition," embracing Catholics, Jews, and a variety of former immigrant subcultures, that not only empowered ethnic political constituencies and "minority" religious groups but celebrated the glories of the melting pot.

The programs of Roosevelt's administration also helped to bury the old hatreds. In earlier eras, the anxieties and dislocations accompanying economic and social upheaval had led many to displace or project their anger onto "the aliens," symbolic scapegoats for the troubles of the moment, the New Deal insisted it was not villains but the vagaries of the capitalist system that had placed so many at economic risk. There was no need this time to blame Catholics or Jews, Irish, Italians, or Asians for the crisis; strong federal policies would save America.

There were also other factors at work. In the pre-war decade, the menace of Hitler helped discredit fashionable racial theories that had influenced elites and others in previous years. The work of a new generation of influential academics, led by anthropologist Franz Boas, assailed the "scientific" racism of Gobineau, Grant, and others. In a series of resolutions passed at national meetings of sociologists, psychologists, and biologists as well as anthropologists, racist ideologies were reviled by a vast cross section of scientific professionals. They demolished the argument that certain people were destined to be inferior, that Anglo-Saxons were intellectually superior, that there were "racial" cultures or racial "moralities." By the 1940s, nativist ideas could no longer be defended in rational discourse.

Another critical factor in the decline of nativism was the impact of World War II. Not only was the war a bonding experience for many Americans, but it also provided a full-employment boom during the conflict and the setting for postwar prosperity, removing some of the economic anxieties in which the old anti-alienism had taken root. More important, perhaps, the war marked the accelerated growth of a more complex business and professional culture that had been emerging in America for years before Pearl Harbor.

Significant changes transformed finance, marketing, law, medicine, advertising, and other specialized fields. Large corporations increasingly were directed not by the risk-taking entrepreneurs who had given them birth but by a new class of managers trained and certified to handle complex problems of a new age. In the war—when it was essential to get the job done right—and in the postwar era, a person's occupational credentials, not religion or ethnicity, increasingly became the central variable in judging acceptability. Skills, not culture, became the standard of admission to elites. And the G.I. Bill allowed many to move more quickly on the path to such status.

The toleration of ethnic diversity widened as strict professional rules took hold. Making it in America more and more became a matter of not who you were but how skilled and educated you appeared to be. In a new age of access and opportunity after the war, barriers to entry into elite colleges and professional schools weakened. Opinion leaders turned to pluralism in their definition of success. Ethnic difference soon seemed to be disappearing everywhere. In food and clothing, in language and even religion, distinctions were blurred and the old animus seemed out of place, even un-American. As the twentieth century neared its conclusion, nativism had all but disappeared. But in the next decade, some would argue it found renewed life in a time of terrorist threats and a new wave of immigration.

Toward a New Millenium: A Return of Nativism?

In the last years of the twentieth century, a few extremist sects with miniscule membership continued to focus on the old hatreds. There were fragmentary Klan chapters, unconnected to the great Klan of the 1920s. Christian identity groups such as Aryan Nations and the Order viewed Jews as children of the Devil who dominated the nation through a Zionist Occupied Government. Their rhetoric had only marginal impact, and only in a few remote areas.

Nativist-inspired restrictions on immigration, in place for over 40 years, were finally eliminated in 1965, with the abolition of the national origins quota system that created overt discrimination against Asian immigrants and a historic preference for western Europeans. But then large numbers of illegal aliens arrived in the 1970s and 1980s, and there were efforts to arrest this flow. Opponents of such modest but restrictive legislation characterized it as grossly nativistic, inspired by "the spirit of the Know-Nothings." However, even large numbers of Hispanic Americans supported the successful passage of the Simpson-Rodino Act in 1986, which sought—unsuccessfully—to deal with illegal immigration through employer sanctions.

Into the new millennium, nativist animus seemed a thing of the past. But the 2001 terrorist attack on 9/11 was followed by the U.S. Patriot Act. New immigration restrictions were put in place. Some Muslim Americans complained of harassment by law enforcement agencies. There were reports that Muslim men and women had been insulted and shunned in the weeks following the attack. Still, with an unpopular war in Iraq dragging on for over five years, and no further terrorist incidents in the United States during this period, fear of widespread anti-Muslim discrimination waned.

Yet, at the same time, there was renewed debate about undocumented aliens. Early in 2008, with the numbers of such immigrants in the nation reaching over 12 million, with thousands of people from Asia, Central America, and—most significantly—from Mexico illegally crossing the southern border daily, immigration became a major political issue. Certain media commentators and members of Congress used inflammatory nativist rhetoric. But many who endorsed immigration restriction avoided and condemned such arguments. Some of the old fears mixed with new concerns: newcomers had broken the law, had not waited to be included in an immigration quota, would not be assimilated and insisted on speaking Spanish, were stealing American jobs, and were illegally using services provided by U.S. taxpayers.

Of course, there were powerful counterarguments by those calling for immigration reform that would not result in draconian sanctions on those already in the United States. And, during the 2008 election campaign, the immigration issue was eclipsed by other concerns. Even the brief touch of nativist rhetoric disappeared from public debate. Nativism, it seemed, was no longer a meaningful issue in America.

See also African Americans and politics; American (Know-Nothing) Party; Asian immigrants and politics; Catholics and politics; European immigrants and politics; immigration policy; Jews and politics; Protestants and politics.

FURTHER READING

Bennett, David H. *The Party of Fear: The American Far Right from Nativism to the Militia Movement.* 2nd ed. New York: Vintage, 1995.

Billington, Ray Allen. *The Protestant Crusade, 1800–1860.* Chicago: Quadrangle Books, 1964.

Brodkin, Karen. *How Jews Became White Folks.* New Brunswick, NJ: Rutgers University Press, 1998.

Gerstle, Gary. *American Crucible: Race and Nation in the Twentieth Century.* Princeton, NJ: Princeton University Press, 2001.

Higham, John. *Strangers in the Land: Patterns of American Nativism, 1860–1925.* 2nd ed. New York: Atheneum, 1963.

Ignatiev, Noel. *How the Irish Became White.* New York: Routledge, 1995.

Roediger, David R. *The Wages of Whiteness.* New York: Verso, 1991.

DAVID H. BENNETT

New Deal Era, 1932–52

By 1932 the United States was in the third year of the worst economic depression in its history. Industrial production stood at half the level of 1929. Nearly one in four Americans was unemployed. For those lucky enough to still be employed, average weekly earnings dropped from $25 to $15. Under such circumstances, the outcome of the 1932 presidential election was never in serious doubt: voters would hold the party in power responsible for the economic debacle. On Election Day, the Democratic challenger, New York State governor Franklin D. Roosevelt, handily defeated the incumbent Republican in the White House, Herbert Hoover, with 57.4 percent of the popular vote and the electoral votes of 42 of the 48 states. The previous summer, accepting the nomination for the presidency, Roosevelt had pledged to his audience to devote his administration to securing "a new deal for the American people." But what a "New Deal" would mean in practice was something neither the voters nor even the candidate himself had a very clear idea of on Election Day.

A Crisis of Abundance

The New Deal is often associated with the ideas of British economist John Maynard Keynes, who in 1932 urged policy makers to recognize that the worldwide economic downturn was "not a crisis of poverty, but a crisis of abundance." Modern capitalism, Keynes argued, had in a sense become too efficient by producing vast quantities of consumer goods that, due to inequalities in income distribution, outstripped effective demand—a "crisis of abundance." In Keynes's view, it was irresponsible for a government to rely on market forces alone to restore prosperity, which might require years of mass suffering and political and economic instability. Instead, he advocated increasing demand by consumers through government spending on public works projects and relief programs. This strategy was known as "pump-priming." It would be costly, and rather than raise taxes (which would decrease demand), Keynes also advocated the government embrace deficit spending.

Yet there was nothing like a coherent economic theory or plan guiding Roosevelt's policy choices. If in time he became a Keynesian in practice, FDR was never a committed one in theory. Raymond Moley, a Barnard College economist, served as a campaign adviser to Roosevelt and briefly as a member of his administration, before leaving over political differences. In a critical memoir of his experiences with Roosevelt, published in 1939, Moley complained about the president's eclectic approach to ending the Depression, noting, "To look upon [Roosevelt's] policies as the result of a unified plan was to believe that the accumulation of stuffed snakes, baseball pictures, school flags, old tennis shoes, carpenter's tools, geometry books, and chemistry sets in a boy's bedroom could have been put there by an interior decorator."

Such criticisms did not bother Roosevelt, a self-assured politician who prided himself on pragmatism, not ideological or intellectual consistency. His willingness to embrace varied and even contradictory policies, keeping those that worked and discarding those that failed, proved a hallmark of his administration.

Two New Deals

Some historians of the 1930s, in an effort to bring at least a measure of order to the "boy's bedroom" concept of Roosevelt's policies, speak of two New Deals: the first an attempt to end the Depression from the top down, the second an attempt to end it from the bottom up. At the risk of oversimplification (because policies and periods overlapped), the first New Deal could be said to have run from Roosevelt's inauguration in March 1933 to mid-1935. It was represented in the policies of the National Recovery Administration, and the Agricultural Adjustment Administration, new federal agencies that encouraged large producers in industry and agriculture to restrict production and fix prices to restore profitability, and thus encourage increased production and the rehiring of laid-off workers. The second New Deal, which came to the fore from 1935 through 1938, was represented in the policies of the Public Works Administration, the Works Progress Administration (WPA), the Civilian Conservation Corps, and the Farm Security Administration. These agencies followed what amounted to a Keynesian strategy of putting money into the pockets of the unemployed through federally sponsored work projects and the like, intended to end the "underconsumption" that since 1929 had kept consumer demand low.

There were important political as well as policy differences between the two New Deals. The language of the early New Deal stressed "unity"—"We Do Our Part" was the slogan of the National Recovery Administration. The language of the later New Deal shifted toward an acknowledgment of the conflicts and divisions in American society; in his 1936 reelection campaign, Roosevelt directed his appeal to the "ill-housed, ill-clothed, ill-fed" of the nation while denouncing his Republican opponents as "economic royalists." Despite this whiff of rhetorical class warfare, and despite the fanatical hatred the president inspired among some wealthier Americans, Roosevelt was no radical. His goal was to save capitalism from its own excesses through the judicious application of a combination of government regulation and economic stimulus.

Revolution or Reform?

Of course, some Americans in the 1930s—Socialists, Communists, and other left-wing activists—did actively seek the downfall of capitalism. The Depression brought them some political gains, at least in the short run. Socialist Party presidential candidate Norman Thomas received nearly 900,000 votes in the 1932 election. Communists led demonstrations of the unemployed that often ended in clashes with the police but also brought them new recruits. And, beginning in 1935, a powerful new trade union federation, the Committee of Industrial Organizations, began organizing mass-production workers in the auto, steel, electrical manufacturing, maritime, and other major industries. The most devoted organizers, and some of the leaders of those new unions, were often radicals of one stripe or another. The new union militancy was certainly one factor that pushed the New Deal "leftward" in the mid-1930s, and helped bring passage of new laws ensuring the right of workers to collective bargaining (the National Labor Relations Act), and securing old age pensions (Social Security) and unemployment insurance.

However, those who hoped that such reforms were merely the prelude to a socialist transformation of the United States (either through peaceful or violent means), would be disappointed. American politics were indeed transformed in the 1930s—but by a realignment, not a revolution. Political scientists use the term *realignment* to describe a decisive and long-term shift in political power from one party or coalition to another in a democratic electoral system. From the mid-1890s through the end of the 1920s, the Republican Party had been the majority party in U.S. politics, winning all but two presidential elections in those years. Roosevelt's 1932 victory, which also saw the Democrats gain control of both houses of Congress for the first time since 1916, ushered in several decades when the Democratic Party took over as the majority party. Roosevelt's sweeping reelection victory in 1936, when he won 60.8 percent of the popular vote, and the electoral votes of all but the two rock-ribbed Republican states of Maine and Vermont, illustrate the extent of the dramatic political changes brought by the Great Depression. Voter turnout increased dramatically in the 1930s, with most of the new voters supporting the Democratic Party. For the first time, white, urban working-class voters in the big industrial states in the Northeast and Midwest, many of them immigrants or the children of immigrants, overwhelmingly backed the Democrats. To give one example, in 1928 Democratic presidential candidate Alfred E. Smith received 19 percent of the vote in the auto-producing city of Flint, Michigan; in 1936 Roosevelt got 72 percent of Flint's vote. Black voters, traditionally suspicious of Democrats (historically the party of white supremacy in the South), gave three-quarters of their votes to Roosevelt in 1936. The white South remained solidly Democratic, as it had since the Civil War. These three broad groups of voters—white workers, blacks, and white Southerners, were the core of the New Deal coalition that propelled the Democrats to the White House and control of both houses of Congress in the 1930s and for some years thereafter.

Second Term Blues

During Roosevelt's second term in office, he secured some significant reforms, including the Fair Labor Standards Act of 1938 that established a minimum wage and a 40-hour workweek and curtailed the employment of child labor. But the pace of reform slowed in the later 1930s, in part because of Roosevelt's own political and fiscal miscalculations. In his first term in the White House, the president had frequently clashed with the conservative majority of the Supreme Court, who declared his National Industrial Recovery Act unconstitutional in 1935. After his reelection, he retaliated with an ill-fated proposal to expand the number of Supreme Court justices, widely condemned as a "court-packing" scheme that failed in Congress (although it did push the Supreme Court to take a more lenient attitude toward the New Deal, as a majority of justices subsequently upheld the constitutionality of the Social Security and National Labor Relations Acts).

In what amounted to a self-inflicted political wound, Roosevelt decided to cut spending in 1937 on social welfare and public works programs. Here was another example of the contradictions at the heart of the New Deal. Despite the sizable sums appropriated for his New Deal programs, Roosevelt was still no Keynesian. He remained a fiscal conservative uncomfortable with the idea of deficit spending. As soon as a more favorable economic climate began to develop, he was determined to balance the budget by getting government out of the role of employer of last resort. And by 1937, New Deal programs like the WPA had succeeded in rolling back the worst effects of the Depression: between 1933 and 1937, the economy expanded by an annual rate of 9 to 10 percent, and the unemployment rate dropped from 25 percent to 14.3 percent of the workforce. But when Roosevelt pushed through cuts in spending for programs like the WPA, it quickly became apparent that the Depression had not yet run its course, and that the private sector remained incapable of provide anything like full employment. Between 1937 and 1938, unemployment jumped back up to 19 percent in an economic downturn dubbed the "Roosevelt recession." His popularity suffered, and he seemed to be losing his political touch.

Foreign Challenges

Yet Roosevelt would go on to serve an unprecedented third term in office and be elected to a fourth one, chiefly because of ominous developments overseas. Nazi leader Adolf Hitler came to power in Germany in 1933. He had rebuilt Germany's military might, and by 1938, was using it to force territorial concessions in central and eastern Europe. The Germans invaded Poland in 1939, precipitating World War II. Meanwhile, in Asia the imperial Japanese government was waging a brutal military campaign to extend its power over mainland China. In 1940 Germany, Japan, and Italy (led by fascist dictator Benito Mussolini, who had his own territorial ambitions) joined together in a military alliance known as the Axis powers.

Although the United States remained officially neutral at the beginning of World War II, Roosevelt was determined to do all he could to shore up the Allied powers, while building up American military forces. In doing so, he finally managed to end the Depression. American factories converted from producing civilian consumer goods to military weapons, and hired millions of formerly unemployed workers, with millions more joining the armed forces. As Keynes wrote from an embattled Britain in an article for an American magazine in July 1940, "Your war preparations . . . far from requiring a sacrifice, will be the stimulus, which neither the victory nor the defeat of the New Deal could give to you, to greater individual consumption and a higher standard of life."

Dr. Win the War

On December 7, 1941, the Japanese attacked Pearl Harbor, and the United States went to war, both in the Pacific Ocean and in Europe. President Roosevelt announced that "Dr. New Deal" was being replaced for the duration by "Dr. Win the War." New Deal agencies like the WPA were shut down. Full employment in defense industries, combined with growing trade union strength, brought dramatic gains in the living standards of American workers, even with wartime rationing and higher taxes.

Many Americans feared that when the war ended the Depression would resume. To forestall such a possibility, Roosevelt oversaw one final expansion of federal social welfare spending. In a 1943 speech, he declared that America's "gallant men and women in the armed services . . . must not be demobilized . . . to a place on the breadline or on a corner selling apples." The following year Congress passed the GI Bill of Rights, which guaranteed financial assistance to returning veterans seeking to pursue an education, purchase a home, or start a business. With over 13 million men and women serving in the U.S. military during the war, that represented a commitment to expanding opportunities for ordinary Americans larger than any undertaken during the New Deal (the WPA, at its height, had never employed more than 3.5 million people).

Truman's Fair Deal

President Roosevelt died on April 12, 1945, just weeks before the Allies prevailed over Nazi Germany. His successor, Harry S. Truman, sought to protect and expand the reform legacy of the New Deal. But in doing so, he faced stiff political opposition. In 1946 American voters signaled their impatience with lingering wartime austerity and government regulation by electing a Republican majority to both houses of Congress. Their success proved short-lived; in a hard-fought campaign in 1948, the Democrats regained control of Congress, and Truman was elected to the presidency in his own right.

In his 1949 State of the Union address, Truman announced plans for a "Fair Deal" that would expand the existing American social welfare state to include new programs like a system of national health insurance. But that proposal went down to defeat, along with other reform measures. Since the late 1930s, southern Democrats (labeled "Dixiecrats") had grown increasingly unreliable as partners in the New Deal coalition, and often made common cause with conservative Republicans. White Southerners feared that a more powerful federal government would inevitably try to extend full civil rights to African Americans in the South (indeed, in 1948 Truman issued an executive order desegregating the armed forces). Increasingly, conflict about race rather than economics became the new dividing line in American politics.

President Truman also had to contend with another world crisis, the cold war between the United States and the Soviet Union. Republicans exploited fears that the Soviets were winning that conflict, supposedly aided by spies and subversives within the Truman administration. In 1952 Truman chose not to run for reelection. Republican presidential candidate Dwight D. Eisenhower swept into office, bringing along with him Republican majorities in the House of Representatives and the Senate. And here is where the durability of the New Deal became apparent, because during his two terms in office neither President Eisenhower nor congressional Republicans made any serious effort to dismantle the social welfare programs instituted under Roosevelt. The New Deal had become a seemingly permanent part of the American political landscape.

See also Democratic Party, 1932–68; Republican Party, 1932–68.

FURTHER READING

Brinkley, Alan. *The End of Reform: New Deal Liberalism in Depression and War*. New York: Knopf, 1995.

Fraser, Steve, and Gary Gerstle, eds. *The Rise and Fall of the New Deal Order, 1930–1980*. Princeton, NJ: Princeton University Press, 1990.

Kennedy, David M. *Freedom from Fear: The American People in Depression and War, 1929–1945*. New York: Oxford University Press, 1999.

Moley, Raymond. *After Seven Years*. New York: Harper and Brothers, 1939.

Rauchway, Eric. *The Great Depression and the New Deal: A Very Short Introduction*. New York: Oxford University Press, 2008.

Zieger, Robert. *The CIO: 1935–1955*. Chapel Hill: University of North Carolina Press, 1995.

MAURICE ISSERMAN

New England

New England is America's most clear-cut region, hanging appendage-like into the North Atlantic. Maine, whose top-heavy bulk dominates the region geographically, is precariously bolted to the nation by only one state, New Hampshire. Maine is thus the only contiguous state that borders but one state. Similarly, the entire six-state region is attached to the United States by a single state, New York. Thus America's only land route to or from New England is through but one state. The only other way in or out of New England is by Canada or by sea.

New England is only about the size of the state of Washington and accounts for only 2 percent of the land mass of America. Fewer than 5 of every 100 Americans live there. Yet in New England, history runs deep: back to the very beginnings of America, the United States, and the New England town meeting, the Western world's first real democracy since the experiment in ancient Athens. In New England, the sinews of culture have been toughened by the natural adversity of a hard land and a still harder sea. Patterns of human events have been defined by rhythms of ethnic settlement that, in microcosm, reflect those of the nation as a whole.

New England is a geography set apart, but its human base and its politics have traditionally been as eclectic as the nation's. Here the boredom and the drama, the growth and the decline, the despair and the hope of the American experiment in self-government are laid bare.

The Connecticut River valley, which splits the region, from the Canadian border to Long Island Sound, marks the complexity of New England in ways political as well as economic. West of the river in Connecticut and Massachusetts, the land is apt to be rolling and hilly in the south, growing more mountainous as one goes north into Vermont. Its towns west of the river are accordingly smaller and more defined and its culture tends to be more rural and radical. From this region of Connecticut came Ethan Allen, who published the first anti-Christian book on the continent. From the hills of western Massachusetts came Daniel Shays and his agrarian revolutionaries. And when convention (in Shays's case, made manifest by an army from eastern Massachusetts) drove these men out, they didn't go west in what was to become the American way of radicalism. They went *north* and stayed on the same side of the river—Allen to agitate in and Shays to hole up in western Vermont.

Although in the north the Connecticut River valley on both sides was settled by more conservative churchgoers from southern New England, by 1840 the river marked important political divisions—mainly, the border between Vermont and New Hampshire. During the presidential election of that year, in what historian Richard McCormick calls "a conundrum for political analysis," Whig William Henry Harrison received a 2 to 1 majority in Vermont and Democrat Martin Van Buren a 3 to 1 majority in New Hampshire. By the end of the twentieth century, no two adjacent American states were more different politically than Vermont, to the west of the river, and New Hampshire, to the east. Vermont's southern border abuts Massachusetts' Berkshire Hills (an extension of Vermont's Green Mountains) where town meetings are still strong and local currencies seek to compete with the dollar. New Hampshire's southern border abuts metropolitan Boston and the northern end of the vast East Coast megalopolis, where cities, casinos, and commerce abound.

Moreover, important divisions exist within the six states themselves. Southeastern Maine is profoundly dissimilar from the thick, wet, and rolling timberlands to the northwest or the fertile open potato fields of Arrostic County to the northeast. Vermont's Green Mountains divided the state's development and politics for a century; today its Northeast Kingdom remains a place apart where one can still find the older Vermont, ungentrified, hard-sledding, sometimes defiant. Northeastern and southwestern Connecticut are cultures apart. Its two major cities are oriented in different directions: Hartford looks toward Boston, New Haven toward New York City. Southern New Hampshire has always been an extension of industrial New England, which thrust itself northward from Boston along an axis of small factory cities like Nashua, Manchester, and the state capital, Concord. Less than an hour north of Concord abruptly rise the White Mountains, cold, lonely, and dangerous. Following them the great northern hardwood forest region stretches uninterrupted to the Canadian border.

Then there is Boston itself; its massive metropolitan presence creating its own region—a cultural overlay, which affects all six states. Boston is to New England what Chicago is to the Midwest—and more. In the little towns of northern New England radios are often set to WTIC hundreds of miles away in Hartford, Connecticut, to hear (almost eerily—so far the distance and so rugged the topography in between) baseball games of the Boston Red Sox. For New England, especially northern New England, there is something important and accurate in the euphemism "Red Sox Nation."

Even so, when Robert Frost—clearly New England's (and perhaps America's) greatest poet of the twentieth century—titled his famous book of poems *North of Boston,* he identified the most important division of all in New England. One is in the north, the other the south. One is old; one is new. One contains the three states north of Boston and the other Massachusetts and the two states below it, Connecticut and Rhode Island. Above the line is postcard New England, below it is urban-industrial New England. In the northern half one is most likely to be "Yankee"; in the southern half one is more likely to be "ethnic."

In 1960 the six-state region of New England contained three of the ten most urban states in America and two of the ten most rural. The two most urban states in America (Rhode Island and Massachusetts) along with the eighth most urban (Connecticut) were in southern New England. Of the two most rural states in the nation, two were in northern New England: Vermont (the most rural) and Maine (the ninth most rural). Political differences—north to south—also prevailed. Before the landslide election of Franklin D. Roosevelt in 1936, Maine was called the bellwether state: "As Maine goes, so goes the nation." In 1936, when Maine and Vermont were the only two states to vote against Roosevelt, the phrase was changed to "As Maine goes, so goes Vermont." At midcentury the three New England states classified as "two-party competitive" were in southern New England, and the three one-party states in northern New England.

By the 1980s, however, along with the completion of the interstate highway system and during the beginnings of the information superhighway, the north-south distinction was fading like a September morning fog along the Connecticut River.

The decline of the north-south division began in earnest with the passage of the Interstate Highway Act of 1958. Since then, the federal government has squeezed four north-south interstate highways into the area north of Boston that hook the two New Englands together. These highways have changed the regional character of northern New England profoundly. A key component of New England's current political culture took the highway north so that many could live rural, clean, and easy lives—and still be within three hours' driving distance of Boston.

New England's Political Past

In its mix of peoples, in the variety of their social and economic arrangements, in the kinds of issues that arise, and in the political expression of all three, New England has long been (in varying degrees and with the inevitable nuisances) a microcosm of America. This development is reflected in the dynamics of its political past. Bernard De Voto called it "the first finished place" in America.

The Revolution began in New England. But New England had begun there a century and a half earlier. Indeed, as much American history transpired in that time as transpired between the adoption of the U.S. Constitution and the end of World War II. Prior to 1789, New England had worked through a westward expansion (from the Atlantic Ocean to the Connecticut River), settled a northern frontier (up the Connecticut to Canada), and endured a series of wars with native populations, which in their viciousness to civilian and combatants alike on both sides make the battle Little Bighorn seem tame. Had the dime novel existed in the mid-seventeenth century, Robert Rogers, not Buffalo Bill, would be the first popular male American frontier hero and Susanna Johnson, not Annie Oakley, the first female hero.

Most of all during this time, before the beginning of the United States, New England planted and then cultivated democracy in North America. The transition from fundamentally democratic economic arrangements like the Mayflower Compact and religious institutions like Puritanism to a secular, liberal institution of governance still operating democratically—the town meeting—was in all its agony, its fits and starts, and its warts and roses the most unique contribution America has made to the science of governance. Indeed, political historians agree that the representative republic fashioned in Philadelphia owes its creation to the mind of Europe as much or more than to the mind of America.

But the Greeks were *not* to New England what the English theorists, especially John Locke, were to America. Moreover, no genetic connection between town meeting and Athens exists. And while the antecedents of the town meeting, especially the English vestry tradition, were obviously European, their transition into a purely political structure was worked out in the wilderness during the settlement of New England. In fact, the origins of the Constitutional Convention can be traced in part to the actions of town meeting democracies in western New England as, indeed, was the American Revolution itself a result of town meetings in eastern New England. When the king's secretary for the colonies, Lord Germaine, heard about the Boston Tea Party, his response was: "This is what comes of their wretched town meetings—these are the proceedings of a tumultuous and riotous rabble, who ought, if they had the least produce, to follow their mercantile employment and not trouble themselves with politics and government, which they do not understand."

The town meeting, this uniquely American institution in which every voting citizen is a legislator and laws are made in face-to-face assemblies of the whole, remained the fundamental governing institution in New England for the first three centuries of its existence. In his classic *The City in History*, Lewis Mumford called the "American failure" to incorporate town meeting democracy "in both the federal and state constitutions" a "tragic oversight in postrevolutionary political development." Thus the most *unique* thing about New England as a political region in America is its town meeting tradition—a tradition that did not spread westward.

The first impediment to the westward expansion of the New England town meeting was the aristocratic New York county system. This roadblock appeared as early as 1644 with the attempt to carry the town meeting across the Long Island Sound and implant it in Hempstead, New York, where it withered and died under the influence of first the Dutch and then the Duke of York. Over a century later, opposition to the county system was an important ingredient in the conflict between Vermont and New York over the latter's land claims. The eastern towns of Vermont, which were more sympathetic to New York than the western towns led by Ethan Allen, became very concerned when the proposed New York county system failed to recognize town meeting government.

The second and ultimately more significant factor in the failure of the New England town meeting to take hold elsewhere in America was the face of the land west of New England. It was too broad, too flanked by distant horizons, lacking the ups and downs, the nooks and crannies of topography that typify most of New England. Where was the natural bumpiness essential to communal governance in village and town? Representation was the solution and face-to-face democracy, even in the places where attempts to transplant it were energetic, did not survive in meaningful measure. In short, most of the Midwest, the middle border, and the Far West were simply physically inhospitable to deliberative, communal enterprise.

Within New England, town meetings remained dominant until the urban industrial revolution took firm hold of the region. Then they began to fall to the one variable they could not accommodate: numerical size. This dynamic had begun modestly in Connecticut in 1784 when Hartford and New Haven adopted city councils within the towns themselves. It continued with a jolt when, in 1822, Boston deliberated for three days to abandon its town meeting. Providence, Rhode Island, followed suit in 1830 and Portland, Maine, in 1832.

Still, town meetings defined the great majority of local governance in New England throughout the nineteenth century, remained strong during the first half of the twentieth century, and continue to govern most small towns in the region. And although the great majority of New Englanders no longer practice town meeting democracy because they live in cities, the spirit of the face-to-face original meaning of democracy pervades the region's consciousness. As late as 1948, a town meeting in a southwestern Connecticut town thwarted an attempt to place the headquarters of the United Nations within its town boundaries.

New England's politics are tied to its past via the town meeting in several other ways beyond the political culture of face-to-face communal decision making. Most important is the structural heritage of the town. Since the town and its town meeting were sacrosanct, they received institutional protection. Towns were given geographical representation *as towns* in the state legislatures. This meant that several New England states violated the democratic principle of "one person, one vote" in the extreme. By 1950, in Vermont and Connecticut, the situation was as bad as it got in America. In both these states, only 12 percent of the population held 51 percent of the seats in the lower body of the legislature. In Rhode Island, 18 percent of the population could control the state senate. Since the towns of New England tended to be so powerful in the legislatures, these bodies felt little need to protect the towns with "home rule" provisions in their state constitutions. Town representation also meant that state legislatures were huge. In 1950, 4 of the 50 state legislatures with more than 200 members were in New England.

Moreover, the constitutions of New England, being examples of late-eighteenth-century constitutions in this, America's "most finished" region, were short, difficult to amend, and gave great power to the legislature. In turn, the legislatures, which represented towns or at least combinations of towns (the counties are very weak in New England), were happy to leave local politics alone. For example, the organizing bases of the political parties themselves were apt to be town-based. There were exceptions, of course, but by the middle decades of the twentieth century (as Duane Lockard put it), the "town meeting and the concomitant emphasis on local autonomy" were still unique New England phenomena.

It is no accident, therefore, that the phrase "all politics is local" was made famous by a New Englander, Thomas Phillip "Tip" O'Neill, who, when he said it, was speaker of the House of Representatives in Washington. By the end of World War II, these localities in New England represented a profound mix of ethnic populations, rural and urban lifestyles, topographical settings, commercial enterprises, and socioeconomic class structures. This complexity was (and remains) manifest in the region's politics. The passion of these politics was most often found in the locality, and the spark that most often triggered it was ethnicity.

Beginning in 1620, New England experienced two centuries of nearly universal Yankee/Puritan homogeneity. But aggressive commercial growth and diversification and the resulting need for labor, followed by the Irish potato famine in the middle decades of the nineteenth century, brought newcomers in increasing numbers and from increasingly varied places. At the same time, many Yankees headed west (often preceded by a trip south in blue uniforms). By 1850 only one in ten New Englanders was foreign born. By 1920 almost 25 percent were. No other region in America had become more ethnically diverse.

Vermont, the coldest, most isolated state of the region and the only one without a seacoast, places the ethnic base of New England and its linkage to politics in sharp relief. Prior to the 1960s, the Democratic Party in New England's (indeed, America's) most rural and most one-party (Republican) state was almost exclusively located in the larger towns and tiny (by national standards) cities. And it was securely tied to ethnic politics. In the city of Winooski, French Canadian Catholic Democrats worked in the mills; in the city of Barre, the Italian Catholic Democrats quarried and carved granite; in other larger towns and little cities, the Irish Catholic Democrats did what they could.

Elsewhere in New England, this urban, ethnic, Catholic base, first united against the "Yankee Stock" and then taking the form of interethnic rivalry, was, throughout the first half of the twentieth century, the prime source of political and partisan conflict in New England. In its intensity and longevity, ethnicity has been to New England what water has been to the West.

In Maine and New Hampshire, the Democratic Party was strengthened by French Canadians and the Irish in the cities. In the southern half of the region, the Democrat-urban-ethnic versus the Republican-rural-suburban relationship was starkly more powerful. By 1950 ethnic names outnumbered Yankee names among Democrat representatives 78 percent to 22 percent in the lower body of Rhode Island's legislature. Among Republican legislators, however, the percentages were Yankees 84 percent and ethnics 16 percent. In Connecticut in 1951, ethnic names outnumbered Yankee names in the lower chamber of the state house 72 percent to 28 percent among Democrats, while, among Republicans, Yankees outnumbered ethnics 84 percent to 16 percent.

Nowhere was ethnic politics more dramatically played out than in Massachusetts. Beginning in 1884, when the Irish Catholic James Michael Curley was elected mayor of Boston, and continuing beyond his career (portrayed in Edward O'Connor's *The Last Hurrah*), the struggle between the Yankee Republicans (most notably represented by the "Boston Brahmins") and ethnic minorities within the Democratic Party dominated politics. By the 1950s, only 9 percent of the Republicans serving in the Massachusetts house of representatives had either Irish or Italian surnames, while 64 percent of the Democrats did. It would be a mistake, however, to believe that the "ethnic" alternative was totally monolithic. The conflict between eastern and western Democrats in Massachusetts, for instance, is reflected in the important division between David Walsh from the western part of the state, who was the first Irish Catholic elected governor, and Curley himself to the east. The rise of the Kennedy family as "Green Brahmins" is symbolized by the graduation of Joseph Kennedy (father of John F. Kennedy) from Harvard University. His subsequent penetration of many Yankee economic and cultural institutions also speaks to the complexity of ethnic politics in Massachusetts and throughout New England.

Political Transition

Locating political watersheds in time is a tricky business, but several factors emerged during the first two decades following World War II that, in (rough) combination, contributed to a new politics in New England.

First, a series of U.S. Supreme Court decisions beginning with *Baker v. Carr* in 1962 forever changed the nature of locality in American state politics, and especially in New England. These decisions demanded that geographical representation in *both* houses of all state legislatures (unlike the U.S. Congress) must be based on the principle of "one person, one vote." This decision democratized state politics in that it gave those living in cities their rightful share of political power. In New England, the decision's effect was to shift power away from places that practiced town-meeting, communitarian, and face-to-face politics to those that practiced big-city, liberal, and representative politics. It also shifted power away from the Republican Party and toward the Democratic Party.

In Connecticut in 1960, the city of Hartford had a population of 177,397 and two seats in the state's house of representatives. The town of Union, with a population of 261, had one seat. In Vermont, the largest city, Burlington, had one seat in the legislature representing 35,531 people and the town of Victory, with a population of 46, also had one. By 1970, however, all this had changed. Local units everywhere received representation based on their population in *both* houses of the legislature. The partisan impact of what was then called "the reapportionment revolution" did not happen overnight and varied from state to state. But no doubt exists that a region in which the partisan balance was often defined in rural-versus-urban terms was significantly affected when the cities got their fair share of the votes in the legislatures. In New England (as elsewhere in America), the partisan advantage was to the Democrats and the cultural advantage was to the cities, and perhaps more importantly to the growing suburbs attached to them.

Second, the New Deal Democratic coalition that dominated national politics—especially in Congress—beginning with the Great Depression and featuring the urban-industrial north in combination with the "Solid South" disappeared when the Deep South shifted sides and began voting Republican in 1964. New England's involvement in this coalition, called "Austin to Boston" ticket balancing (John F. Kennedy and Lyndon Johnson in 1960 and Michael Dukakis and Lloyd Bentsen in 1988), began when the tactic was still strong and ended as it became weaker. As New England has increasingly become a Democrat/liberal region and the national pattern has shifted to a bicoastal/heartland split, the region's national leverage has declined accordingly.

Third, the electronic revolution, which replaced the mechanical urban-industrial revolution, has diminished the importance of planetary variables in politics: rivers, oceans, mountains, valleys, watersheds, soil, and—most important—climate. In short, as air conditioning changed the politics of the Deep South, so too has central heating changed the politics of New England—especially northern New England. Moreover, variables tied to people matter more than variables tied to place. Within states, regions have become less important politically as they have become more culturally homogenized. This has tended to weaken traditional factional patterns within the political parties. This is especially important in New England, where geography traditionally played such an important role in political organization.

Fourth, no pattern has declined more sharply as a result of these changes than ethnic politics. Duane Lockard, in his seminal work on New England politics through the 1950s, proclaimed that ethnic names on the ballot were important only when the quality of the candidates was near equal and the election close. In such cases "the right kind of name" might be "the fillip needed for success." Two decades later, Neal Peirce would write, in regard to Massachusetts, that "everyone seemed to agree that a lot of the juice had been drained out of the old ethnic issue."

Democrats Become Dominant

Against this backdrop, and as the twenty-first century began, more specific sources of conflict had developed that are more typical of politics everywhere in America: energy, land use, an increasingly isolated low-income working class and wider issues of growth and environmental protection. Although these problems add to the decline in the importance of ethnic politics—especially the spatial (urban/rural) distribution of its core components—the current debates over social issues such as civil unions for same-sex couples (first allowed in Vermont) and same-sex marriage (first instituted in Massachusetts) demonstrate that ethnicity (when it is linked to traditional religious identities) still can play a role in New England. Yet whatever the issue, it seems increasingly likely that a solution will need to please Democrats and/or liberal causes.

It was only symbolic at the time but it mattered. In 1972, when 49 of the 50 American states cast their electoral votes for the soon-to-be-disgraced president Richard Nixon, the lone dissenting state was in New England. Soon after the Watergate scandal forced Nixon to resign, bumper stickers appeared on automobiles with Massachusetts license plates reading "Don't Blame Us!"

In national politics, New England had held forth as a bastion of Republicanism after the party's imprint was embedded by America's most profound and enduring political realignment—which itself was caused by the first serious national crisis, the Civil War. Although New England *as a region* had itself posed an early and dangerous secessionist threat to the Union during the War of 1812, New England had subsequently become the epicenter of abolitionism. Antislavery and recurrent economic differences had made it a fierce enemy of the South by 1860; the election of Abraham Lincoln sealed the deal.

It took a century for New England's attachment to the Republican Party to change. The key moment was the election of New Englander Kennedy in 1960. Kennedy's Catholicism reflected the ethnic component of Yankee New England. Prior to Kennedy's victory, the only other time New England exceeded the national percentage for the Democrat candidate for president was in 1928, when the first Catholic to run for president, Alfred E. Smith, lost to Herbert Hoover. Smith actually carried Massachusetts and Rhode Island, the first two New England states in the twentieth century to cast more than half their votes for a Democrat. Yet, despite New England's significant urban base and ethnic diversity, it lagged behind the realignment triggered by the second national apocalypse, the Great Depression—the "New Deal/Solid South/urban-industrial North" Democratic coalition.

Kennedy closed this gap. His victory nationally, however, was based in part on the old (and soon to disappear) north-south alignment of strange political bedfellows. Yet in New England, the old coalition was more a catalyst than a cause. By the end of the twentieth century, the New Deal Democratic Coalition was only a memory. The Republicans had walked off with the Solid South. As they did, New England continued to unify against them. It had cast its lot with the Democrats.

The key to this regional transformation is the northern half of the old "two New Englands." Whereas in 1936, Vermont and Maine would buck the nation as the only two states to vote against Roosevelt, now these two states vote solidly Democratic. Indeed, in the last four presidential elections the six New England states have had in the aggregate 24 chances to cast their votes for the Republican candidate. They did so only once, when New Hampshire cast its votes for George W. Bush in 2000. Of the three northern New England states, only New Hampshire trails behind. Vermont and Maine voted more heavily Democratic than Connecticut in the last four presidential elections, although Rhode Island and Massachusetts (so close in so many ways) tip the Democratic totals in favor of southern New England. Since 1988, of the six New England states, Vermont (which stuck with the GOP without a hitch from 1860 to 1960) now ranks third in its percentage-point differential for Democratic presidential candidates in New England.

In the 1980s, the New England delegation in the U.S. Senate was almost perfectly balanced between Democrats and Republicans. Since 2000 the Democrats have gained only a slight advantage there. In the House, however, Republicans have taken a severe hit since the 1980s. In that decade they averaged 37 percent of the New England delegation. Since the turn of the century this percentage has dropped to 18.

More important, perhaps, is the New England trend in state legislative elections; it clearly favors the Democrats. Of these 1,290 state representatives serving in 2008, 875 (over two-thirds) were Democrats. None of the 12 legislative chambers in New England had a Republican majority. The closest the GOP came to controlling even 1 house of the 12 is in the Maine senate, where they lacked but one seat. In all the other states Democratic majorities are substantial to massive. Even in New Hampshire, the Democrats controlled the state senate 14 to 10, and in the New Hampshire house of representatives, numbering 400 members, they had a 237 to 158 majority.

As is the trend across America, New England voters seem more apt to elect Republicans to governorships than they are to legislative offices. In 61 different gubernatorial elections between 1980 and 2007, New Englanders chose

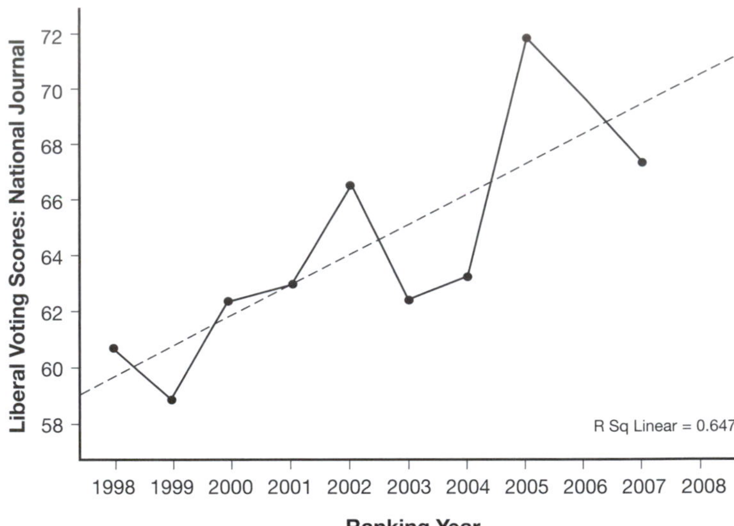

Figure 1. Liberal Voting: New England Senators (1998–2007). Rankings: Percentage of senators voting less liberal than average New England senator on key social, economic, and foreign policy votes.

32 Republicans, 26 Democrats, and 3 independents. Between 2000 and 2007, they chose 9 Republicans and 7 Democrats. Thus, the New England states often experience divided government. In 2007 Connecticut, Rhode Island, and Vermont had Republican governors facing Democratic legislatures.

But the New England shift in partisanship is only part of the story. New England's political ideology is changing as well. Between 1996 and 2006 public opinion polls demonstrate that, while the percentage of Americans identifying themselves as liberals held steady, five of the six New England states increased their liberal scores. In short, New England was significantly more liberal than the nation in 1996 and, by 2006, this gap had widened. Moreover, the percentage of New Englanders identifying themselves as conservatives decreased an average of 6 percentage points while, at the national level, conservatives have declined by only 1 percentage point.

Another, perhaps more poignant, measure of the political character of the New England states is how the region votes in the U.S. Congress, especially in the Senate. The composite voting index of political ideology prepared by the *National Journal* (which combines key votes on social, economic, and foreign policy issues) documents the solid and increasing liberal posture of the New England region. In nine of ten years of voting in the Senate (1998–2007), the New England average for liberalism was above the 60th percentile of all the senators combined. Moreover the New England delegation's liberal position is rising dramatically (see figure 1).

The shift in New England's partisan and ideological balance away from the American mainstream (becoming increasingly liberal) coupled with New England's downward slide in Electoral College votes in national elections may spell an increasing marginalization of New England's influence in national politics. Indeed, it may mean a return to the midpoint of American life (1860–1960), when New England became so Republican it was taken for granted by the prevailing majority.

When the Census of 1790 was taken, New England controlled 29 percent of the electoral votes. The Census of 2000 gave it 6 percent (see figure 2). Electoral votes reflect power in Congress. With the closing of the continent and the statehood of Alaska and Hawaii, New England's share of Senate seats has ceased to decline. But its share of House seats still drops slowly downward. Clearly there is a bottom limit that precludes precipitous losses in the future. Yet it is likely New England will lose another seat with the 2010 Census.

This decline in New England's mathematical share of the republic and its increasing ideological marginalization is revealed by the success rates of presidential and vice presidential candidacies from the region in the last half century. Since the success of Kennedy, none of the ten presidential or vice presidential candidates who (like Kennedy) were both *of* New England and ran *from* New England were successful. Nor were the candidacies of Howard Dean or Mitt Romney, who were born elsewhere but ran from New England. Thus, Kennedy was the last president of the United

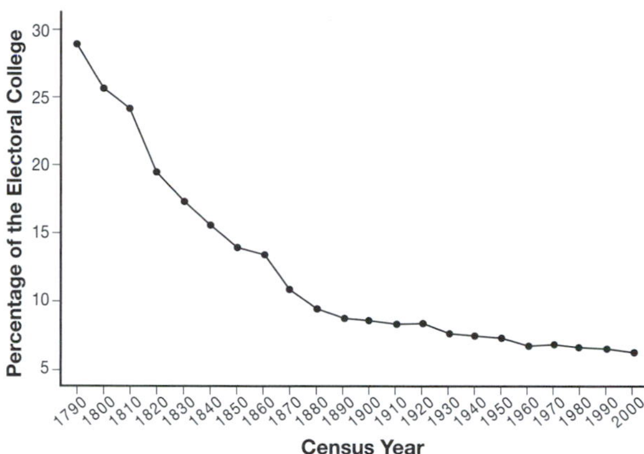

Figure 2. New England's Percentage of the Electoral College Vote.

States who was a child of New England and stayed in New England.

Establishing causality in matters political is a dangerous business. The linkage between the blending of the two New Englands and the region's increasing political homogeneity as a Democratic stronghold is far from clear; nor is the longevity of this new political posture. Most problematic of all is the extent to which regional historical habits and cultural imperatives can withstand the overarching changes (both national and global) caused by third-wave, postindustrial, electronic technology.

What is clear, however, is that if regional values can survive the present technological revolution, then New England's heritage featuring classical liberalism (equal rights for all under law) and classical democracy (citizens making law face-to-face) may be a useful model for the future. No other region in America had as much to do with the formation of the American liberal, national enterprise (its representative and federal republic) as did New England. At the same time, only New England created and preserved America's most profoundly important local institution, the town meeting. Thus, as an architect of the machinery to operate a continental government and provider of a local means to train a citizen base to sustain it, New England's endowment for the future of American democracy is precious indeed.

See also liberalism; state government.

FURTHER READING

Adams, James Truslow. *The Founding of New England.* Boston: Atlantic Monthly Press, 1921.

———. *New England in the Republic 1776–1850.* Boston: Little, Brown, 1926.

———. *Revolutionary New England, 1691–1776.* Boston: Atlantic Monthly Press, 1923.

Brooks, Van Wyck. *The Flowering of New England.* New York: E. P. Dutton, 1936.

———. *New England: Indian Summer 1865–1915.* New York: E. P. Dutton, 1940.

Daniels, Jonathan. *A Southerner Discovers New England.* New York: Macmillan, 1940.

Hale, Judson. *Inside New England.* New York: Harper and Row, 1982.

Hrebenar, Ronald J., and Clive S. Thomas, eds. *Interest Group Politics in the Northeastern States.* University Park: Pennsylvania State University Press, 1993.

Jensen, Merrill, ed. *Regionalism in America.* Madison: University of Wisconsin Press, 1951.

Lockard, Duane. *New England State Politics.* Princeton, NJ: Princeton University Press, 1959.

Milburn, Josephine F., and Victoria Schuck, eds. *New England Politics.* Cambridge, MA: Schenkman, 1981.

Mires, Charlene. "The Lure of New England and the Search for the Capital of the World." *New England Quarterly* 79 (March 1, 2006), 37–64.

Mumford, Lewis. *The City in History.* New York: Harcourt Brace Jovanovich, 1961.

Nelson, Garrison. "Running from New England: Will It Ever Lead the Nation Again?" Paper presented at the conference *The State of New England.* Easton, MA, March 29, 2008.

Peirce, Neal R. *The New England States.* New York: Norton, 1976.

Pierson, George Wilson. "The Obstinate Concept of New England: A Study in Denudation." *New England Quarterly* 28 (March 1955), 3–17.

Pike, Robert. *Tall Trees, Tough Men: A Vivid, Anecdotal History of Logging and Log-Driving in New England.* New York: Norton, 1967.

Sharkansky, Ira. *Regionalism in American Politics.* New York: Bobbs-Merrill, 1970.

Wilson, Harold F. *The Hill Country of Northern New England.* New York: Columbia University Press, 1936.

FRANK M. BRYAN

New Left

Since the time of the French Revolution, people agitating for radical change in the direction of human equality have been known as "the Left." In the United States, from the late nineteenth century through World War II, leftists focused on the problems of economic inequality and exploitation. They identified the industrial working class and its allies as the main agents of progressive change, and ultimately they hoped to replace capitalism with socialism. In the 1960s, however, a new left-wing movement arose in America—as in other wealthy countries, such as England, France, and West Germany—so different from the labor-oriented socialist left that it became known as a "New Left," to distinguish it from what suddenly was called the "Old Left." The New Left enjoyed a meteoric career in American politics, becoming large and disruptive in the late 1960s and then ebbing rapidly as an organized force for political change in the early 1970s.

The New Left was a youth movement, largely middle class and white, whose analysis of American society focused on the political and cultural problems of power and alienation, rather than on economic questions. Compared to the Old Left, the New Left was loosely organized, although it featured one important national organization, Students for a Democratic Society (SDS), which existed from 1960 to 1969. Early on, New Left radicals declined to identify capitalism as American society's affliction and to embrace socialism as the cure, but this reluctance diminished as time passed, and late-1960s radicals expressed a more traditional leftist perspective. The New Left shared with the Old Left an antipathy to imperialism, understood as the control by wealthy nations over the resources and affairs of poor nations, a system that often involved large-scale violence. The New Left viewed racial domination by whites as key to understanding both U.S. society and the wider world, and New Left radicals took inspiration from the African American struggle of the post–World War II era.

Origins

American leftists were few in the late 1950s, and their efforts to recruit new adherents to their creed bore little fruit before 1960. In that year, the Student League for Industrial Democracy (SLID), a small organization with a long history in the non-Communist Left, changed its name to Students for a Democratic Society. "Sit-ins" in 1960 protesting racial segregation spread rapidly at lunch counters in the American South. Also in 1960, a largely African American gathering of civil rights organizers established the Student Nonviolent Coordinating Committee (SNCC), which became the youth vanguard of civil rights militancy. Idealistic young white people around the country found SNCC members compelling as models of moral integrity, devotion to social change, and political courage.

SDS convened a conference on human rights in the North in 1960. Participants had been active in the National Student Association, the Young Men's and Women's Christian Associations, and other groups. The conference featured presentations about poverty, civil rights, and militant nonviolence. For SDS members, the urgency surrounding race relations in the American South had become a lever that might pry open a wide-ranging contemplation of social change throughout the United States. They wished to play a key role in pushing such change forward.

In the early 1960s, New Left activists sometimes talked and wrote as if they mostly wanted American liberals to pursue the liberal agenda—creating equal opportunity and social equity within the structure of American capitalism—with increased zeal. But at other times, the New Left gave the impression that it embraced a different, more destabilizing agenda. Some aspects of conventional liberal politics, as embodied by activists in the Democratic Party, repelled many in SDS from the start. According to the New Left, liberals made too many compromises with powerful conservative forces, such as white southern congressmen, business concerns, and the U.S. military. Liberals seemed like insiders, not outsiders calling for fundamental change. Whether this indictment was fair or not, it proved compelling to many of the most energetic activists among American youth.

New Left radicals wished to see power more widely dispersed in contemporary society. They called their vision of American society "participatory democracy." In their view, most Americans played little or no role in ruling America, or even in ruling their own lives. New Left radicals focused their attention on political structures that, they believed, kept individuals isolated and powerless. These structures included social welfare agencies that monitored the behavior of the poor, corporations and unions that together managed American workers, governments that repressed African Americans, and universities that trained young people to become establishmentarian "yes men." New Left criticisms of bureaucracy as an impediment to freedom sometimes echoed conservative themes. But this was misleading. The New Left supported the very social forces, such as militant African American protest and radical third world nationalism, which conservatives fiercely opposed.

In Search of Insurgencies

New Left activists saw themselves as intellectuals who could support and help to guide insurgencies against the political and social status quo, insurgencies that might force the citadels of power to yield important concessions to the cause of increased political and social democracy. They spent the 1960s in a search for such insurgencies. This roving quest for a battering ram that might smash open the doors of the power structure led radicals to embrace the slogan "The issue is not the issue," which sounded cynical to some, but which expressed the New Left belief that specific controversies were important mainly if they could lead Americans toward a radical perspective on society.

Between 1962 and 1964, SDS members worked as political organizers in poor, mainly urban communities around the country, seeking to build what they called "an interracial movement of the poor" that would agitate for basic changes in how wealth and power were distributed in America. They cared about the problem of poverty, but the key to their activity was a view that the poor, as a politically and socially excluded group, formed a potent force for change. In contrast, the New Left viewed labor unions and the relatively comfortable working class as too deeply invested in "the system" to work for fundamental change. After two or three years, though, SDS members became pessimistic about their strategy and abandoned the effort.

SDS spent most of its energies between 1964 and 1968 organizing university students as a force for change and working against the Vietnam War from a radical left-wing perspective. In 1964 and 1965, when New Left activists were reexamining their priorities, SNCC and other militant black groups became influenced by Black Power thinking, which held that whites should cease involving themselves in the movement for African American freedom. This ensured that the New Left would not fulfill its mission through a deeper participation in any movement of people of color. In these same years, President Lyndon Johnson escalated the U.S. war in Vietnam. These developments set the stage for the direction that the New Left took in the late 1960s.

In the fall of 1964, political protest among white students in California introduced the theme of "student power" to the American scene. The Free Speech Movement (FSM) protested restrictions on dissident political activity on the campus of the University of California in Berkeley, and it sought to expose ties between this major research university and conservative political forces. The FSM established a model that student radicals used to foment confrontations with university administrators for the rest of the 1960s, including a tumultuous series of events at Columbia University in 1968.

Research universities in the cold war era eagerly put themselves at the service of large corporations and the U.S. Department of Defense, so there was plenty of muck for leftists to rake. Demands for greater democracy in the internal workings of universities addressed the longing young people in this era often expressed for greater control over their own lives. New Left radicals hoped to use universities as instructive case studies in the corruption of supposedly idealistic institutions by powerful forces. They hoped to transform universities into engines of dissident thought and action.

Anti-Imperialism and Militancy

Protest against universities' involvement in the military-industrial complex would have commanded less attention in a time of peace, but the late 1960s was a time of war. The New Left came early to protest against the Vietnam War. Unlike many in the Old Left, the New Left disdained the Soviet Union as a progressive force in the world. However, New Left radicals sympathized with the Vietnamese revolution, as with the Cuban revolution and other national-liberation movements, often led by Communists, across the third world. Radicals did not view the Vietnam War as a mistake made by U.S. policy makers. Rather, they concluded that America's cold war rhetoric of uncompromising anticommunism, and its commitment to maintaining the international economic status quo, fated the United States to try to defeat revolution in the third world. In April 1965, after President Lyndon Johnson commenced sustained bombing of North Vietnam and a major U.S. land war in South Vietnam, SDS organized the first major demonstration against the war inside the United States, attracting more than 20,000 people to Washington, D.C.

The New Left's early leadership role in the antiwar movement soon slipped away. The escalation of the war made it a mainstream youth issue, and, after 1968, liberals swamped radicals in the ranks of antiwar protest. New Left thinkers tried, with some success, to persuade their peers that the war's brutality could be explained only through a radical analysis of America's role in the world. Why else would U.S. leaders prosecute such a seemingly disproportionate war, in such a far-off land, if not because they cast America in the role of a global enforcer of the conditions that third world revolutionaries were seeking to change? The New Left's searching attempts to explain the role of the United States in the contemporary world produced a large body of stimulating, often controversial "revisionist" scholarship about the history and nature of the nation's foreign relations. In this area, as in others, the New Left succeeded in carving out a place for dissident, socially critical thought in American intellectual life.

In the late 1960s and early 1970s, some radicals engaged in increasingly militant protest tactics. In the most notorious developments of the New Left's career, small groups, including the so-called Weather Underground, engaged in property destruction, such as sporadic bombings of police stations and the U.S. Capitol. Such groups helped to wreck SDS by demanding its members follow a course that most of them found unattractive, and then splitting the organization, which quickly expired. The importance of SDS by that time is debatable; it had become more a "brand name" than the actual source of youth radicalism. Individual campus chapters organized activities as they saw fit in their local environments. However, even as the ranks of youth radicalism continued to grow, the demise of SDS revealed a crisis of direction within the New Left. The radicals had failed to find a way to push conventional politics sharply to the left, and when they sought to chart a strategy for political change, they displayed a volatility that suggested confusion and frustration.

Evaluations

After SDS dissolved, New Left radicals continued along the path that had emerged by 1965: they worked to expand the presence of radicalism among college-educated, white American youth. This movement's erratic behavior in the late 1960s reflected the embarrassment that some radicals felt over the fact that the contemporary left's primary constituency was a relatively privileged group. The main path of activism for the New Left, from the mid-1960s until the movement disintegrated in the early 1970s, was to cultivate islands of radicalism within a conservative sea. They attempted to live as they thought people would live in a different, better society. This was not a conventional strategy for political change, although many New Left radicals hoped that, in the long term, they would sow the seeds of a new America.

Women within the New Left, frustrated at the sexism they encountered among male comrades who supposedly believed in radical democracy, and inspired by the rising discussion of women's place in American society during the 1960s, found a way out of the New Left's moral discomfiture by working for their own empowerment. Some radical feminists stayed active in the political left, while others abandoned it as irredeemably sexist. Some male radicals reveled in the freer sexuality of the 1960s and 1970s but failed to question either the subjection of women to an inferior social role or the objectification of women that was endemic in American culture. Young feminists had ample cause for complaint. In the 1970s, some women and men tried to sustain and revive the New Left as a radical campaign that embraced feminism, but this effort came too late for the movement, which had entered a terminal phase.

Some view the later years of the New Left as a decline into muddled thinking, moral error, and political irrelevance. Others see the late 1960s and early 1970s as an impressive era in American radicalism, filled with worthy, hopeful experiments, marred by the mistakes of a mere handful of militants. Both views have merit. Alienated from the mainstream political system, lacking a strong organizational framework, and with no political strategy for creating progressive change, it was difficult for the New Left to have a clear impact on other Americans in its later years, and it could not sustain itself as a coherent enterprise. It scattered into innumerable local and individual activities, and soon the phrase "New Left" referred only to a school of political analysis, not to an active movement. On the other hand, the New Left in its later years fulfilled its deepest mission, rather than forsaking its original path. This movement was one expression of the collective experience of Americans of a particular racial, class, and generational identity. Moreover, its failure to upend American society does not distinguish it from the Old Left or from other radical movements in U.S. history. For a time, its members impressed themselves on the awareness of Americans, made many people think deeply about the nature of their society, and left behind a provocative set of questions and answers about that society that far outlived the movement itself.

See also era of confrontation and decline, 1964–80; era of consensus, 1952–64; liberalism; radicalism.

FURTHER READING

Berman, Paul. *A Tale of Two Utopias: The Political Journey of the Generation of 1968*. New York: Norton, 1996.

Evans, Sara. *Personal Politics: The Origins of Women's Liberation in the Civil Rights Movement and the New Left*. New York: Knopf, 1979.

Gosse, Van. *Where the Boys Are: Cuba, Cold War America, and the Making of a New Left*. London: Verso, 1993.

Isserman, Maurice. *If I Had a Hammer . . . : The Death of the Old Left and the Birth of the New Left*. New York: Basic Books, 1987.

Miller, James. *"Democracy Is in the Streets": From Port Huron to the Siege of Chicago*. New York: Simon and Schuster, 1987.

Rossinow, Doug. *The Politics of Authenticity: Liberalism, Christianity, and the New Left in America*. New York: Columbia University Press, 1998.

Sale, Kirkpatrick. *SDS*. New York: Random House, 1973.

DOUG ROSSINOW

Pacific Coast, the

California, Oregon, and Washington had dissimilar political origins and came to statehood in different ways and at different times. Nonetheless, the three states came to share several common political characteristics, notably experiences with progressivism in the early twentieth century, the frequent use of direct democracy in state and local politics since then, and, recently, strong Democratic majorities in most urban areas along the coast and Republican majorities in inland areas.

American Acquisition

Several European nations laid claim to the Pacific Coast. Spanish explorers established settlements in Alta California after 1769, and a Russian settlement in what is now northern California lasted from 1812 to 1841. Spanish, British, and American ships visited the Pacific Northwest in the late eighteenth century. In 1804 President Thomas Jefferson dispatched the Lewis and Clark expedition in part to find a route to the Pacific and strengthen the American claim to the Northwest.

In 1818, the United States and Great Britain created a "joint occupancy" for the Oregon country—everything west of the Rocky Mountains between Alta California and Russian North America. The Adams-Onís Treaty (1819), between the United States and Spain, set the northern boundary of Alta California at the forty-second parallel. Missionaries from the United States began work in the Willamette Valley in 1834, and settlers soon followed along the Oregon Trail. American settlers created a provisional government in 1843, and it functioned as the civil government until 1848.

In the 1844 presidential campaign, Democrats sometimes invoked Manifest Destiny to demand annexation of Texas and the Oregon country. Their candidate, James K. Polk, won the election and began to carry out his party's platform. Some Oregon enthusiasts insisted on "54–40 or Fight," meaning the entire jointly occupied region, but in 1846 the United States and Britain compromised on the forty-ninth parallel. In 1848 Congress organized the region as Oregon Territory.

Congress annexed the Republic of Texas in 1845. The same year, Polk asked Mexico to sell Alta California and Nuevo México to the United States. A major attraction was the Bay of San Francisco, the best natural harbor on the Pacific Coast. The Mexican government refused to sell and continued to claim Texas. War was declared on May 13, 1846.

Earlier, a U.S. Army unit commanded by John C. Frémont had entered California, allegedly on a mapping expedition. By then, northern California included several American and European settlers, some of whom held Mexican land grants. In mid-June 1846, not knowing that war had been declared, American settlers at Sonoma proclaimed a California Republic and raised a crude flag that included a grizzly bear in its design. Soon after, a U.S. Navy detachment sailed into San Francisco Bay with news of the war. The Bear Flaggers, Frémont's troops, and the Navy took control of northern California. Mexicans offered sharper resistance in southern California, but U.S. forces took control there by mid-January 1847.

By the Treaty of Guadalupe Hidalgo (1848), ending the war, the United States purchased all of Alta California and Nuevo México, including all or parts of Texas, New Mexico, Arizona, California, Nevada, Utah, Colorado, and Wyoming, for less than half the price Polk had offered before the war.

In 1849, when gold seekers began to pour into northern California, the region was under Navy control and not yet organized as a territory. A convention soon met to draft a state constitution. The constitution, written in both English and Spanish, included a provision from

Mexican law permitting a married woman to own property in her own name, the first such guarantee in any state constitution. Congress in 1850 approved statehood for California, with its modern boundaries.

Admission of California was hotly contested because the proposed constitution barred slavery, and admission of California as a free state would break the balance between slave states and free states. The Compromise of 1850 included admission of California as a free state among its many provisions but provided only a lull in the regional conflict over slavery.

1850–1900

Both Oregon Territory and the new state of California faced questions regarding land titles. In creating Oregon Territory, Congress voided laws passed by the provisional government, thereby calling into question the validity of land titles. Under pressure from settlers, in 1850 Congress approved the Oregon Donation Land Act, which provided for the award of up to 320 acres per person.

Artists' depictions of California, like the panorama advertised here, attracted large audiences curious about life in the West. (Library of Congress, Rare Book and Special Collections Division)

The land question in California involved Spanish and Mexican land grants, which often were large and vaguely defined. Congress in 1851 set up a commission to review land titles. Over five years the commissioners heard more than 800 claims and confirmed more than 600. Nearly all were appealed through the courts. The legal proceedings dragged on interminably, and many successful applicants sold their land to pay costs. Further complicating matters, squatters settled on some ranchos and refused to leave. Most scholars of the subject have agreed with Henry George, a journalist, who in 1871 called it a "history of greed, of perjury, of corruption, of spoliation and high-handed robbery."

In San Francisco, the largest city in the West, political processes broke down twice in the 1850s. In 1851, responding to a rash of robberies, burglaries, and arson, merchants and ship captains formed a Committee of Vigilance. Despite opposition from city and state officials, the committee constituted itself as an impromptu court and hanged four alleged wrongdoers, whipped one, and banished several. In 1856 the Committee of Vigilance revived and took control of the city, establishing a force of nearly 6,000 well-armed men, mostly merchants and businessmen. City officials, the major general of the militia (William T. Sherman), the governor, and other prominent political figures all opposed the committee, but it disarmed the state militia, hanged four men, and banished about 20. The committee then established a political party and yielded power only after its candidates won the next election.

In California and Oregon Territory, a new approach to Indian reservations evolved in the 1850s. Native Americans in the east had usually been moved westward and given a reservation for each tribe. In the far west, reservations often were established by region, not tribe, and peoples from various tribes were put together regardless of the relations between them. In the 1850s, California officials approved stringent regulations over the many California Indians outside the reservations. California Indians were frequently the victims of random violence. More than one historian has concluded that genocide is the only appropriate term for the experience of California Indians during the 1850s and 1860s, and similar violent episodes took place in Oregon.

In 1853 Congress divided Oregon Territory along the Columbia River and forty-sixth parallel into Oregon and Washington territories. Four years later, Oregonians seeking statehood submitted a constitution and two other questions to voters. The voters approved the proposed constitution, decided by nearly 3 to 1 to ban slavery in the new state, and chose by an even larger margin to bar free African Americans from living in Oregon. Given the close balance in Congress, approval for statehood was uncertain but finally came in 1859.

Slavery roiled politics through the 1850s. Prompted by Democrats with southern proclivities, the California legislature prohibited African Americans from voting, serving on juries, marrying whites, or testifying in state courts, and applied similar restrictions to American Indians and Chinese immigrants. By 1859 California Democrats split into two camps, each led by a U.S. senator. David Broderick's faction opposed slavery; William Gwin's faction had southern sympathies. Tension ran even higher when a Gwin supporter killed Broderick in a duel. In 1860 California voted for Abraham Lincoln, as did Oregon.

When secession led to civil war, the two Pacific Coast states were securely committed to the Union. Though comprising just 2 percent of the Union's population, Californians donated a quarter of all funds raised by the Sanitary Commission, the humanitarian organization that assisted Union troops, and raised more volunteers per capita than any other state. California volunteers helped to rout a Confederate army from New Mexico Territory and occupied much of the West.

During the war, Republicans moved to tie the Union together with iron rails. The Pacific Railroad Act (1862) incorporated the Union Pacific (UP) company to build a railroad westward and permitted the Central Pacific company to build eastward to meet the UP. The Central Pacific was controlled by four Sacramento merchants, all Republicans, including Leland Stanford, who was elected governor in 1861. For a quarter-century, the Central Pacific and its successor, the Southern Pacific (SP), dominated rail transportation in California and elsewhere in the West. Most Californians also understood the SP to be the most powerful force in state and local politics.

In 1871 Newton Booth, a Republican opponent of the SP, won the California governorship just as the Granger movement began to affect state politics. Grangers joined other SP critics in 1873 to create the People's Independent Party, which did well in the elections of 1873 and helped elect Booth to the U.S. Senate in 1875. After 1875, however, the Granger movement quickly faded.

A Granger party also appeared in Oregon, where Republicans had been in control since the early 1860s. Oregon Republican leaders were generally conservative and business-minded, and intraparty conflicts stemmed more from personalities than principles. In 1874, though, Grangers and other farmer groups formed a short-lived Independent Party that showed substantial strength in state legislative elections.

The 1876 presidential election thrust Oregon into national headlines. The Republican, Rutherford B. Hayes, carried Oregon, but national returns showed him trailing Samuel Tilden, the Democrat. Republicans challenged the returns from Louisiana and Florida; if successful, Hayes would have a one-vote majority in the Electoral College. Democrats then challenged one Oregon elector as unqualified; if successful, their ploy would have thrust the election into the House of Representatives, which had a majority of Democrats. Ultimately, a congressional election commission with a Republican majority accepted all of Oregon's electoral votes as Republican, along with the electoral votes of Louisiana and Florida, giving Hayes a one-vote majority.

After 1877, teamster Denis Kearney attracted a political following in San Francisco by condemning the monopoly power of the SP and arguing that monopolists used Chinese workers to drive down wages. He soon led the Workingmen's Party of California (WPC) and provided its slogan, "The Chinese Must Go." The WPC briefly dominated San Francisco politics, winning elections in 1878 and 1879. Oakland and Sacramento also elected WPC mayors.

The WPC's greatest statewide success came in 1878, in elections for a constitutional convention. WPC and Granger delegates comprised a majority and wrote into the new constitution an elected railroad commission to regulate rates and restrictions on Chinese immigrants. The constitution also declared water subject to state regulation and guaranteed equal access for women to any legal occupation and to public colleges and universities. Controversial for its restrictions on corporations, the new constitution nonetheless won a majority from voters. Many of the provisions restricting Asians were invalidated by the courts.

Anti-Chinese agitation also appeared in Oregon and Washington Territory. In 1882 such western opposition to Chinese immigration led Congress to ban further immigration of laborers from China. In the mid-1880s anti-Chinese mobs appeared throughout the West, sometimes associated with the Knights of Labor. In Washington Territory the anti-Chinese movement spawned a short-lived largely unsuccessful reform party.

In California during the 1880s, voters divided closely between the Republicans and Democrats. The SP continued its prominence in state politics—symbolized in 1885

Chinese immigrants work on the North Pacific Coast Railroad at Corte Madera, California, 1898. (Library of Congress)

when Stanford won election to the U.S. Senate amid allegations of vote buying. That decade marked the political apogee of Christopher Buckley, a blind San Francisco saloon keeper who emerged as "boss" of the city's Democrats and a power in state Democratic politics. In 1891 charges of bribery led Buckley to leave the country, and his organization fell apart.

Washington Territory grew slowly until the 1880s, when railroad construction finally connected Puget Sound directly with the Midwest. Washington statehood was delayed not only by slow population growth but also by partisan maneuvering in Congress, where the Democratic majority in the House feared that Washington statehood would mean more Republican electoral votes. When Republicans won secure control of both houses and the presidency in 1888, statehood for Washington followed in 1889.

Populism affected all three states. In 1891 the California Farmers' Alliance launched a state Populist Party, focusing their campaign against the SP. They took 9 percent of the 1892 presidential vote and won one congressional seat and eight seats in the state legislature. Populist candidates later won the mayor's office in San Francisco and Oakland. In the 1896 presidential election, however, Republicans took California by a tiny margin. That margin soon widened. Between 1898 and 1938 no Democrat won the California governorship, and Republicans typically had large majorities in the state legislature, as California became one of the most Republican states in the nation.

In Oregon delegates from farmers' organizations, prohibitionists, and trade unions formed a new party in 1889, and the new party promoted the Farmers' Alliance. By 1892 these groups had aligned with the national Populist Party. The most prominent Populist in Oregon was Governor Sylvester Pennoyer, elected in 1886 as a Democrat and reelected in 1890 as a Democratic-Populist fusionist. In the 1892 presidential election, Oregon cast one of its electoral votes for Populist James B. Weaver because a Democratic-Populist candidate for elector received enough votes to edge out a Republican. Republicans won the other three electoral votes. Populists won some seats in the Oregon legislature in 1892 and 1894 but accomplished little. Republicans swept the Oregon elections in 1896 and usually dominated state politics thereafter.

As in California, Populists made a decent showing in Washington's major cities, and Spokane elected a Populist mayor in 1895. Not until 1896, however, did Populists win more than local elections; that year, in fusion with the Democrats, they carried Washington for William

Jennings Bryan, elected the governor and a majority of the legislature, and then sent a Silver Republican fusionist to the U.S. Senate. The party soon died out, however, and Republicans dominated the Washington statehouse in the early twentieth century.

During the late nineteenth century, women promoted a range of reform issues, including woman suffrage. In 1878 California's U.S. senator Aaron A. Sargent introduced, for the first time, a proposed federal constitutional amendment for woman suffrage. The Washington territorial legislature approved woman suffrage in 1883, but it was ruled unconstitutional by the territorial supreme court in 1888. Woman suffrage came before California voters in 1896, but a large negative vote in San Francisco and Oakland overcame the small favorable majority elsewhere.

1900 through World War II

The three Pacific Coast states moved in similar political directions in the early twentieth century. All experienced progressivism, became more conservative in the 1920s, and moved toward the Democrats and the New Deal in the 1930s.

Much of Oregon progressivism centered on William U'Ren, a Populist turned Republican. U'Ren was attracted to the single-tax proposed by Henry George but concluded that it was unlikely to be adopted without a popular vote, so he began to promote the initiative and referendum (I&R), part of the Populist platform. U'Ren pushed and prodded until voters approved I&R through a constitutional amendment in 1902. Between 1904 and 1914, Oregonians voted on 136 initiatives, approving 49, and I&R became known as the Oregon System. Successful initiatives included a railroad commission, bank regulation, a child labor law, recall, a minimum wage, home rule for cities, and a direct primary. Governor Oswald West, a Democrat elected in 1910, frequently resorted to the initiative when the legislature refused reforms he sought.

When an Oregon law mandating protection for women workers was challenged, the Supreme Court's decision upholding protection, in *Muller* v. *Oregon* (1908), set an important precedent.

Events in Oregon influenced Washington progressives, especially I&R and recall, which were adopted early and used regularly, including recall of the mayors of Seattle and Tacoma in 1911. The Washington legislature also created regulatory commissions for railroads and other industries and established minimum wages for women and children, maximum hours for women, limits on child labor, workman's compensation, and the direct primary.

California came late to progressivism, but legislators finally adopted the direct primary in 1909, which led to the nomination of Hiram Johnson for governor in 1910. Johnson, a Republican, lambasted the SP and won, as did other progressives. The 1911 legislature produced more than 800 new laws and 23 constitutional amendments, including I&R, recall, regulation of railroads and public utility companies, the eight-hour day for women, restrictions on child labor, workman's compensation, and an investigation of corruption and inefficiency in state government.

In 1912 Theodore Roosevelt ran for president as candidate of the new Progressive Party, and he chose Johnson as his running mate. Roosevelt carried six states, including California and Washington.

All three Pacific Coast states were in the vanguard of states adopting woman suffrage. Washington became the fifth state to do so, in 1910. California followed in 1911, and Oregon in 1912.

California experienced another round of progressive reform in 1913, including laws restricting political parties. After 1913 California had more nonpartisan elected offices than any other state. Other legislation that year included reforms promoted by women's groups and the creation of three new commissions: Industrial Welfare (health, safety, and welfare of women and children), Industrial Accidents, and Immigration and Housing (migrant farm labor). The Alien Land Act, prohibiting immigrants ineligible for citizenship (those from Asia) from owning land, was intended in part to embarrass President Woodrow Wilson and the Democrats. Johnson carried the progressive banner into the U.S. Senate in 1917 and served until his death in 1945.

Progressivism transformed politics and government in all three states, adding new functions, especially the regulation of public utilities and protection of workers and consumers. The progressives' assault on political parties transformed the ground rules of state politics. The initiative became an important source of policy making. And women entered the political arena in a significant way.

Many progressives decried any role for economic class in politics, but class-based political groups appeared in all three states. Between 1901 and 1905, in San Francisco the Union Labor party won the mayoralty three times and took other local offices, then returned to power in

1909, despite revelations of earlier corruption. Socialists won local offices in several places; in 1912 Eugene Debs, the Socialist presidential candidate, received 12 percent in California and Washington and 10 percent in Oregon, compared to 6 percent nationwide. The Industrial Workers of the World established a significant presence in the lumbering areas of Oregon and Washington. World War I brought a surge of wartime patriotism, and these radical groups drew strong opposition.

Opposition to radicals continued after the war. In 1919 the Seattle Central Labor Council (unions affiliated with the American Federation of Labor) called a general strike in support of striking shipyard workers. Largely successful, the general strike lasted three days, but conservatives and antilabor groups held it up as an example of the dangers posed by radicals.

Progressivism waned after the war but did not disappear. Hiram Johnson continued as a strong progressive voice in the U.S. Senate and also staunchly opposed the League of Nations. Throughout the 1920s, a large majority of California voters registered as Republicans but divided closely between the progressive and conservative wings, making the Republican primary more important than the general election. Similar patterns appeared in Oregon and Washington, but Republican progressives there rarely mounted significant challenges to conservative dominance. Nonetheless, in 1924 Robert La Follette drew a third of the vote in California and Washington, double his national average, and a quarter of the vote in Oregon, edging the Democrats out of second place in all three states.

The Ku Klux Klan appeared in all three Pacific Coast states in the 1920s. In Oregon the Klan and other groups promoted a 1922 initiative requiring children to attend public school. Passed by a large margin, the law aimed at closing Catholic parochial schools, but the state supreme court declared it unconstitutional in 1924, and the U.S. Supreme Court did the same in *Pierce* v. *Society of Sisters* (1925). Also in 1922, Walter Pierce, a Democrat, received Klan support in his campaign for governor and won by a large margin. A prohibitionist and progressive, committed to public ownership of the electrical industry, Pierce nonetheless got little support from Republican progressives. In Washington in 1924, voters overwhelmingly defeated a Klan-sponsored initiative, modeled on the Oregon law, to require all children to attend public schools. The Klan showed strength in several California cities but played no significant role in state politics.

The Great Depression and the New Deal of Franklin D. Roosevelt revived Democratic fortunes. Roosevelt carried the three states by 57–58 percent in 1932 and 64–67 percent in 1936. During the 1930s, Democrats won U.S. Senate seats in California and Washington and took the governorship in all three states.

The California gubernatorial election of 1934 drew national attention, but electoral politics were pushed out of the headlines earlier that year by the three-state longshore and maritime strikes, which shut down shipping for three months, and by the four-day San Francisco general strike, all of which conservatives blamed on Communists. Upton Sinclair, author of *The Jungle* (1906) and a former Socialist, won the Democratic nomination for governor with a program called End Poverty In California (EPIC). Though voters flocked to register as Democrats, Sinclair lost after a torrent of attacks that broke new ground in negative campaigning. The winner, Republican Frank Merriam, disappointed conservatives by supporting a new income tax and increasing the sales tax. A referendum to repeal the new taxes failed. The 1938 election marked the high point of Communist support for the Democrats, but Democrats' success rested primarily on a base of EPIC organizing and strong support from AFL and CIO unions, brought together by an antilabor initiative. Led by Culbert Olson, their gubernatorial candidate, Democrats swept nearly every statewide office and took a majority of the state assembly. The Senate, however, remained Republican. A broad liberal legislative agenda, including health care for nearly all workers and their families, wages and hours legislation, civil rights, and other initiatives, was defeated. Olson lost in 1942, Democrats in most other races.

Clarence Martin, a Democrat, won the governorship of Washington in 1932. As in California, the state legislature completely revised the tax code, shifting the major revenue source from property taxes to sales, income, and excise taxes. The income tax, however, was ruled unconstitutional. In 1935 leftist, labor, and farm organizations formed the Washington Commonwealth Federation (WCF), drawing inspiration from EPIC. The WCF was so active and successful in pushing Washington to the left that Postmaster General James Farley in 1936 jokingly referred to the "the forty-seven states . . . and the Soviet of Washington." Communist Party members did take an active part in the WCF, and a few were elected to office as Democrats.

In Oregon, Julius Meier, running as an independent candidate, committed to public development of hydroelectric power, won the governorship in 1930 but failed to accomplish his goal. He was succeeded by Charles Martin, a conservative Democrat, who increasingly attacked the New Deal and was not renominated in 1938. Republican governor Charles Sprague, in turn, proved to be such a progressive that he lost his renomination bid in 1942 to a conservative. An Oregon Commonwealth Federation, modeled on the WCF, was less successful than its Washington counterpart.

The New Deal brought important changes to Pacific Coast states. The Bonneville, Grand Coulee, and other dams gave the Pacific Northwest a bonanza of cheap, publicly generated electricity, which stimulated industrial development and prompted the creation of public power districts. New Deal labor policies brought many new members into unions; most voted Democratic and pushed the party to the left. In California Democrats have consistently outnumbered Republicans among registered voters since 1934. Democratic registered voters in Oregon increased sharply in the 1930s, first outnumbered Republicans in the early 1950s, and have consistently outnumbered Republicans since 1958. Similar data does not exist for Washington, but election results suggest a pattern more like California than Oregon.

By the late 1930s and early 1940s, support for the New Deal and the Democrats ebbed, especially among the middle class and farmers, even as war industries contributed to a boom in manufacturing and union membership. Republicans won the Oregon governorship in 1938 and held it and the state legislature until 1956. Republicans won the Washington governorship in 1940 and held it for 12 of the next 16 years, although Democrats usually controlled at least one house of the legislature. In California, the gubernatorial victory of Earl Warren in 1942 launched 16 years of Republican control in Sacramento. Similar patterns appeared in the region's congressional delegations, although Democrats held more seats than before the New Deal.

Since World War II

After World War II, Democrats began to accumulate considerable congressional seniority, notably the two Washington senators, Warren Magnuson (1944–81) and Henry "Scoop" Jackson (1953–83). Both held significant leadership positions, as did Alan Cranston (1969–93) from California. Wayne Morse, from Oregon, first a Republican, then an independent, and finally a Democrat, served from 1945 to 1969. Beginning in the late 1960s, Oregon voters repeatedly returned moderate Republicans to the Senate: Mark Hatfield (1967–97) and Robert Packwood (1969–95), both of whom held leadership positions. Similar patterns characterized some members of the House; two House members, both Democrats, served as Speaker: Thomas Foley, from Washington, who was Speaker from 1989 to 1995, and Nancy Pelosi, from California, who was first elected Speaker in 2007.

The late 1950s marked an important turning point for Democrats. In California, Edmund G. "Pat" Brown won the governorship in 1958, and, for the first time since the 1880s, Democrats controlled both houses of the legislature. Brown and the Democrats enacted a massive water project, a major expansion of higher education, highway construction, and a fair employment practices act. A controversial fair housing act and demonstrations at the University of California, Berkeley, contributed to Brown's defeat for a third term in 1966. In Washington a Democrat, Albert Rosellini, won the governorship in 1956 and, with a Democratic legislature, adopted a long list of administrative reforms and expanded higher education and highways. A Democrat, Robert Holmes, won the governorship in Oregon in 1956 but was defeated in 1958, and Republicans led the state for the next 16 years.

Republicans held the governorships in all three states by the mid-1960s. Elected governor of California in 1966 and reelected in 1970, Ronald Reagan championed conservative values but proved more pragmatic in practice. Promising to "cut, squeeze, and trim" the budget, he made deep cuts in higher education and mental health funding but nonetheless produced the largest budgets up to that time, requiring significant tax increases. He sent the National Guard to Berkeley to suppress demonstrations but signed the most liberal abortion bill in the country. His commitment to cutting taxes and reducing welfare forecast his presidency. Reagan was succeeded by the sometimes enigmatic Edmund G. "Jerry" Brown, son of Pat Brown and a Democrat, but voters then turned to Republicans for the next 16 years.

Daniel Evans won the Washington governorship in 1964, despite a nationwide Democratic landslide, and served three terms. A Republican, he promoted liberal environmental policies, endorsed legal abortions, expanded higher education, and supported an income tax.

In Oregon Democrats took a majority in the state legislature in 1958, for the first time in the twentieth century, but Mark Hatfield, a moderate Republican, won a closely contested election for governor. Hatfield worked to expand higher education and to bring a more diversified economy to Oregon. His successor, Tom McCall, also a moderate Republican, served two terms and initiated policies to clean up the environment and create the first state-level land-use planning system. In 1973 Oregon became the first state to decriminalize possession of small amounts of marijuana, and was followed by California and a few other states.

Recent decades have brought increasing ethnic and gender diversity among elected officials, especially in California. Since 1970 African Americans have served as mayors of Los Angeles, Oakland, San Francisco, and Seattle; Latinos as mayors of Los Angeles and San José; and Asian Americans as mayors of Long Beach, Sacramento, and San José. Asian Americans have served as U.S. senator from California and governor of Washington. Willie Brown, an African American, holds the record as longest-serving Speaker of the California Assembly, and the most recent three speakers include two Latinos and an African American woman. Since 1970 women have served as governors of Oregon and Washington, and California and Washington were the first states to have two women simultaneously serving as U.S. senators. From 1993 to 2004, Washington led the nation in the percentage of women in the state legislature. Women have been elected as mayors of most of the region's major cities. Gays and lesbians have served on city councils and in state legislatures, but not as mayor of a major city, member of Congress, or governor. A dramatic breakthrough in gay and lesbian rights came in 2008, when the California Supreme Court ruled that restricting marriage to heterosexual couples violated the state constitution's guarantee of equal rights. In response, evangelical Christians, Catholics, and Mormons mobilized to pass a constitutional amendment defining marriage as between a man and a women; advocates of same-sex marriage vowed to continue the fight for equal treatment.

The three Pacific Coast states remain distinctive in their reliance on direct democracy. Most elections include a list of initiative measures. California's Proposition 13 of 1978 launched a "taxpayer revolt" that spread to other states, and California's Proposition 45 of 1990 established term limits and inspired similar measures elsewhere, including Washington in 1992. Oregon's Proposition 16 of 1994 legalized physician-assisted suicide; similar initiatives have appeared on the ballot elsewhere but none passed until Washington's measure in 2008. California's Proposition 215 of 1996 legalized marijuana use for medical purposes; voters passed similar measures elsewhere, including Washington. California Republicans used the recall in 1994–95 to punish members of their party for crossing party lines in the legislature, and, in 2003, California voters grabbed international headlines when they recalled Governor Joseph "Gray" Davis and replaced him with movie star Arnold Schwarzenegger.

In California, Proposition 13 also generated a revolution in the *use* of the initiative. In Proposition 98 of 1988, the California Teachers Association used the initiative to mandate funding for public K–14 education. Taken together, Propositions 13 and 98 presented a new version of direct democracy: people could vote not to tax themselves but could mandate expenditure of public funds. By the end of the 1990s, some political observers pointed to the initiative as a central culprit in creating a dysfunctional state government.

During the first decade of the twenty-first century, patterns that began in the 1980s continued to mark state politics in the Pacific Coast. Democratic presidential candidates John Kerry in 2004 and Barack Obama in 2008 carried all three states, and Democrats did well in the 2006 elections, although Schwarzenegger won a second term against a weak Democratic candidate. In Oregon in 2008, Jeff Merkley, a Democrat, defeated incumbent Senator Gordon Smith, one of the last remaining moderate Republicans in Congress. A map of voting behavior in those elections shows all three states with blue (Democratic) counties along the coast, especially in urban areas, and red (Republican) counties, typically more rural and inland. Voting on initiatives and referenda often reflected the same configuration. Thus, interior voters, especially in agricultural areas, behave politically more like voters in agricultural areas in parts of the Midwest or like the voters to their east, in Idaho and Nevada. Coastal and urban voters behave much like urban voters in the northeastern United States.

FURTHER READING

Burton, Robert E. *Democrats of Oregon: The Pattern of Minority Politics, 1900–1956*. Eugene: University of Oregon Press, 1970.

Dembo, Jonathan. *Unions and Politics in Washington State, 1885–1935*. New York: Garland, 1983.

Ficken, Robert E. *Washington: A Centennial History*. Seattle: University of Washington Press, 1988.

Gullett, Gayle Ann. *Becoming Citizens: The Emergence and Development of the California Women's Movement, 1880–1911*. Urbana: University of Illinois Press, 2000.

Johnston, Robert D. *The Radical Middle Class: Populist Democracy and the Question of Capitalism in Progressive Era Portland, Oregon*. Princeton, NJ: Princeton University Press, 2003.

Lower, Richard Coke. *A Bloc of One: The Political Career of Hiram W. Johnson*. Stanford, CA: Stanford University Press, 1993.

Mitchell, Greg. *The Campaign of the Century: Upton Sinclair's Race for Governor of California and the Birth of Media Politics*. New York: Random House, 1992.

Murrell, Gary. *Iron Pants: Oregon's Anti-New Deal Governor, Charles Henry Martin*. Pullman: Washington State University Press, 2000.

Pomeroy, Earl. *The Pacific Slope: A History of California, Oregon, Washington, Idaho, Utah, and Nevada*. Seattle: University of Washington Press, 1965.

Rarick, Ethan. *California Rising: The Life and Times of Pat Brown*. Berkeley: University of California Press, 2005.

Scates, Shelby. *Warren G. Magnuson and the Shaping of Twentieth-Century America*. Seattle: University of Washington Press, 1997.

Tygiel, Jules. *Ronald Reagan and the Triumph of American Conservatism*. New York: Pearson Longman, 2006.

Williams, R. Hal. *The Democratic Party and California Politics, 1880–1896*. Stanford, CA: Stanford University Press, 1973.

ROBERT W. CHERNY

pacifism

Pacifism, the rejection of violence as a means of solving disputes, is a broad doctrine that encompasses a variety of ideas and practices and dates back to the earliest settlements in colonial America. Throughout much of American history, pacifism has been closely associated with religion, particularly the so-called historic peace churches (the Quakers, Mennonites, and Church of the Brethren). Pacifism has found a home in other religions as well.

Arguably, the earliest pacifists in American history were religious dissenters such as Roger Williams and Anne Hutchinson, who were banished in 1635 and 1638, respectively, from the Massachusetts Bay Colony for their heretical beliefs. Other, less prominent dissidents adhered strictly to nonviolent practices, even when they faced death sentences for their beliefs.

Historians such as Peter Brock, Charles Chatfield, and Meredith Baldwin Weddle have explored the history of pacifism in colonial America and found it to be a vibrant tradition that borrowed heavily from transatlantic ideas rooted in the Enlightenment and religious dissent. Some Quakers, such as itinerant eighteenth-century preacher John Woolman, preached against conscription and condemned the use of tax revenues for war purposes. Pennsylvania, with its policies of religious tolerance and separation of church and state, became a haven for a number of colonial pacifist sects.

During the American Revolution, nonviolent resistance, such as boycotts, public protests, petition drives, and other acts of noncooperation, coexisted with more violent forms of anti-British resistance. While pacifists enjoyed only a marginal presence in the Revolution, their cultural bark would prove much more powerful than their political bite, and ultimately helped influence the restrained treatment of Loyalists after the conflict.

Peace movements flourished in antebellum America, dovetailing with the broader landscape of pre–Civil War reform efforts. In 1815 David Low Dodge, a pacifist merchant, founded the New York Peace Society, the first of many such organizations formed during the first half of the nineteenth century. His 1809 tract *The Mediator's Kingdom, not of this world, but Spiritual* inspired the creation of similar groups across the United States. Reverend Noah Worcester, a New Hampshire–born Unitarian and tireless advocate of peace, worked so hard to promote pacifist ideas that he earned the title "father of the American peace movement." Pioneering American antiwar activist William Ladd, also a New Hampshire native, was a sea captain, chaplain, and author. During his life, Ladd was called the "Apostle of Peace." His newspaper, *Harbinger of Peace*, brought a wide variety of pacifists together from several states and territories, and Ladd was one of the founders in 1828 of the American Peace Society. Twenty years later, in 1848, blacksmith Elihu Burritt founded the first secular pacifist organization, the League of Universal Brotherhood.

Much of the antebellum abolitionist movement, while militant, remained nonviolent between the 1830s and the eve of the Civil War. For practical more than doctrinal reasons, abolitionists seldom took up arms against lynchings, mob violence, arson, and shootings carried out by their foes. Influenced by the work of Henry David Thoreau and other pacifist writings of the New England renaissance, abolitionist leaders such as William Lloyd Garrison, Maria Chapman, and Frederick Douglass preached restraint. Still, most abolitionists refused to condemn the violence used by foes of slavery in the 1850s, most notably in Kansas in mid-decade and by John Brown at Harpers Ferry in 1859.

As Thomas Curran documented in *Soldiers of Peace: Civil War Pacifism and the Postwar Radical Peace Movement* (2004), pacifists confronted a number of challenges during the Civil War and ultimately emerged from the conflict somewhat less robust than before. But the Universal Peace Union flourished in the late nineteenth century, attracting thousands of members, and it eventually joined the chorus of anti-imperialist voices in protesting America's involvement in the Spanish-American War (1898).

American pacifism in the twentieth century became increasingly secularized, although religious pacifism remained strong. Antiwar sentiments, robust before World War I, persisted on a smaller scale after President Woodrow Wilson declared war in 1917. More radical antiwar advocates in the Socialist Party and Industrial Workers of the World sometimes endured harsh treatment, such as prison sentences, loss of mail privileges, and in certain cases a loss of citizenship.

Despite the repression of antiwar activists in World War I, the American peace movement reemerged stronger than ever during the interwar period, especially in the Great Depression. The heyday of pre–World War II isolationism also created fertile ground for pacifism, especially on college campuses and in cities. Opinion polls from the era painted a portrait of an American public more receptive than ever to pacifist ideas.

World War II abruptly reversed that situation. Pacifism went into full retreat during the war. Tiny enclaves of pacifists working in government-run Civilian Public Service (CPS) camps or languishing in prison kept the movement alive through the war. In the postwar era, small groups of intrepid "radical pacifists" attempted to breathe new life into the movement. Even though the cold war chilled dissent, pacifists such as A. J. Muste, Bayard Rustin, Dorothy Day, David Dellinger, George Houser continued to organize protests against war and the arms race. This small but committed group developed a more sophisticated and nuanced theoretical framework for pacifism and nonviolent direct action.

Pacifists exercised tremendous influence within the civil rights movement. Arguably, the most famous pacifist in American history was Martin Luther King Jr., who constantly sought to keep the movement nonviolent. The Vietnam War also ushered in another brief golden age for pacifism. The anti–Vietnam War movement, thriving by 1967, was a boon for the American pacifist movement. During the 1960s and early 1970s, it found new life, colorful adherents, and a restored purpose. While pacifists were always a minority within the antiwar struggle, they exercised tremendous influence over the direction and tempo of the movement.

In the last quarter of the twentieth century and opening years of the new millennium, pacifism experienced many setbacks. While it enjoyed a temporary post–Vietnam War resurgence in the early 1980s around the nuclear arms race of the Reagan era and the looming prospect of U.S. intervention in Central America, it was once again in retreat by the 1990s. The antiglobalization movement fanned the embers of pacifism again, however, and it attracted a new, if small, number of followers in the aftermath of the September 11, 2001, terrorist attacks and the war in Iraq launched in 2003. Widening resistance against the Iraq War jump-started several moribund pacifist groups. While pacifism as a protest movement remains tiny, confined mostly to large urban centers, pacifism's core ideas continue to capture the imagination of those Americans who envision a more peaceful future.

See also radicalism; religion and politics.

FURTHER READING

Brock, Peter. *Pacifism in the United States: From the Colonial Era to the First World War.* Princeton, NJ: Princeton University Press, 1968.

Cooney, Robert, and Helen Michalowski. *The Power of the People: Active Nonviolence in the United States.* Culver City, CA: Peace Press, 1977.

Lynd, Staughton, and Alice Lynd, eds. *Nonviolence in America: A Documentary History.* Maryknoll, NY: Orbis Books, 1995.

Tracy, James. *Direct Action: Radical Pacifism from the Union Eight to the Chicago Seven.* Chicago: University of Chicago Press, 1996.

Ziegler, Valarie H. *The Advocates of Peace in Antebellum America.* Bloomington: Indiana University Press, 1992.

ANDREW HUNT

party nominating conventions

Political party conventions perform a number of tasks. They generally meet every four years, several months in advance of a presidential election. The modern convention meets over several days to achieve various procedural and political goals. Leaders compose and approve the party platform, a policy statement including "planks," or specific proposals, on which the party's candidates run, as well as set rules for party procedure. In addition, leaders use the convention to address the party en masse. Minor figures are often given the opportunity to address the convention during the day while most delegates are in meetings; evening addresses, however, are heavily publicized and often delivered by major figures. The keynote speaker is often selected to fulfill some symbolic or political goal. For example, Zell Miller, a Democratic senator from Georgia endorsed George W. Bush at the 2004 Republican convention for president based on his national security credentials. Often a party's rising stars are chosen to deliver prominent addresses. Two such speakers between 1988 and 2004—Bill Clinton and Barack Obama—were subsequently nominated as presidental candidates in their own right. The most visible and historically important task of the convention is the nomination of that party's candidates for president and vice president.

Conventions are composed of delegates, apportioned among various state and territorial party organizations. Delegates vote for presidential and vice presidential nominees and on other procedural matters. Since the early 1970s, delegates of the two major parties have generally been bound to follow the results of state caucuses or primaries when they vote for candidates. Therefore, the identity of each party's eventual nominee is often known weeks or even months before the conventions begin; primaries have historically been held over several months during the first half of the year, and the conventions not until late summer. The events themselves have increasingly become mere formalities, serving primarily as publicized launching pads for the final weeks of the presidential campaign.

Early History

The earliest conventions wielded a great deal of influence. By the early 1830s, the party founded by Thomas Jefferson had dominated American national politics for three decades. Contemporary Democratic political operatives like Martin Van Buren thought of a party as a system of officeholders who dispensed patronage. A caucus of prominent party leaders, therefore, generally selected each presidential candidate. President Andrew Jackson, who had held office since defeating incumbent John Quincy Adams in 1828, however, was a controversial figure, and opposition to him meant that schism and a viable two-party system would soon emerge. The appearance of the political convention facilitated the transformation.

In September 1831, the Anti-Masons—an insurgent northern group particularly powerful in New York that was fearful of what it imagined was a secret yet powerful Masonic influence on politics—organized a national convention. The Anti-Masons were imitating not American politicians (who had never held conventions) but social reformers and benevolent organizations (who had). The Anti-Masons, however, reconceived the system; their party was a mass movement, and a convention was a way to attract popular participation and establish egalitarian (as opposed to the imagined Masonic conspiracy) credentials.

In Baltimore, the Anti-Masons nominated William Wirt, a former attorney general, as their presidential candidate. The convention attracted a great deal of public attention, and mainstream politicians quickly followed suit. Later that year, a group calling themselves National Republicans (disaffected Democrats who hoped to unseat Jackson) met in convention, hoping to gain both popular attention and legitimacy as a viable opposition party; they nominated Senator Henry Clay of Kentucky. Jackson's Democrats, however, did not let Clay's convention stand unmatched. In early 1832, they also met in Baltimore and nominated Jackson for a second term with Van Buren as his running mate. The convention also established the "two-thirds" rule, requiring any candidate to receive that proportion of the party vote and each state's delegation to vote unanimously. Both rules were designed to preserve the influence of the southern states. Democrats repeated the process in 1836, nominating Van Buren in Baltimore, and easily won the election, defeating three opposition candidates. In 1840 Van Buren had settled into the convention system enough to tinker with the format, directing the Democratic convention to issue the first party platform in history.

In 1836 the Whigs failed to organize anti-Jacksonian elements well enough to hold a convention; they were determined not to repeat the error. The 1839 Whig convention was held well in advance of the next election to give the party publicity and time to organize. It was the first convention to see jockeying for position, as the military hero William Henry Harrison outmaneuvered Winfield Scott and Clay for the nomination and then defeated Van Buren in the general election. In 1844, the Democratic convention was deeply divided over the proposed annexation of Texas. The first eight ballots failed to give any candidate the required two-thirds proportion of delegates, including former president Van Buren, who had the support of the majority of delegates but who had alienated the southern wing of the party by opposing annexation. James Polk, a relatively minor party figure and former governor of Tennessee, was unexpectedly nominated on the ninth ballot.

By the 1850s conventions were firmly established as a technique for gaining publicity, interest, and party legitimacy. As the Whig Party flagged, divided between northern and southern factions over the expansion of slavery, disaffected Whigs held mass meetings in Ripon, Wisconsin, and Jackson, Michigan, early in 1854. In June 1856, a national Republican Party was born at a convention in Philadelphia, which appointed a national committee, drew up a platform, and nominated John C. Fremont for president.

On the other hand, the fragmentation of the Democratic convention in 1860 signaled the collapse of that party. At the national convention held in April in Charleston, South Carolina, 50 southern delegates walked out, and after 57 ballots, the convention failed to produce a candidate. Two months later, Democrats met again in Baltimore. Again, southern delegates abandoned the convention; however, in desperation, the remaining delegates nominated Stephen Douglas for the presidency. The southern faction reconvened in Richmond, Virginia, and nominated John Breckenridge. The Republicans met in Chicago in May, and nominated Abraham Lincoln on only the third ballot. Lincoln went on to win the presidency. Four years later, in the midst of the Civil War, Lincoln declared the 1864 Republican convention would be renamed the National Union convention, and invited Democrats who opposed southern secession to attend. The convention nominated one of these men, Andrew Johnson, for vice president.

Conventions in Ascendency

The post–Civil War era saw several transformations in national conventions. Baltimore, then strategically located at the midpoint of the nation, had long been the preferred location; the Anti-Masons had met there, as had the first six Democratic conventions and nearly all the Whig conventions (including the last convention of that party in 1860). After the war, however, the nation began to look west, and the conventions followed shifting patterns of settlement, economy, and transportation. For its first 60 years, from 1856 to 1920, the Republican Party held most of its conventions in the midwestern center of Chicago, only occasionally diverting to Philadelphia (three times, in 1856, 1872, and 1900) and once each in St. Louis (1896), Cincinnati (1876), Minneapolis (1892), and New York (1916). By the early twentieth century, the Democrats were going even farther across the nation, visiting Denver in 1908 and San Francisco in 1920.

The host city increasingly became a strategic selection, chosen to highlight an aspect of a party's campaign or to appeal to a particular region or state. Both parties moved to increase their appeal across the nation. The 1924 Democratic convention took 103 ballots before nominating John Davis, a compromise candidate various party factions could agree upon. In 1936 the convention decided to drop the two-thirds rule. Additionally, the 1940 Republican primary in Philadelphia was the first to be televised, and the dramatic victory of dark-horse businessman Wendall Willkie on the sixth ballot count boosted public interest in the candidate selection process.

The Progressive movement of the early twentieth century also encouraged popular influence at conventions, beginning a series of political reforms to curb the power of convention delegates. Several conventions in the late nineteenth century included bitter candidate battles over delegates and surprise nominees. A 36-year-old representative from Nebraska, William Jennings Bryan, seized the Democratic nomination at a divided Chicago convention in 1896 on the power of his "Cross of Gold" speech, delivered in favor of adding the free coinage of silver to the party platform. Similarly, in 1880 the Republicans took 36 ballots to select dark horse James Garfield of Ohio, nominated primarily as an alternative to unpopular former president Ulysses S. Grant, who was seeking a nonconsecutive third term. In 1910 Oregon became the first state to establish a primary system for apportioning its delegates. By 1912, 11 other states had followed suit. Further, that year former president Theodore Roosevelt challenged incumbent William Howard Taft for the Republican nomination. Roosevelt swept the primaries, winning 9 out of 12, versus Taft's single primary win, and 278 delegates to Taft's 48 (Robert La Follette, another candidate, secured 36 delegates and 2 primaries). Taft, however, controlled the party machinery.

At the convention, Roosevelt was denied more than half the delegates he had won, and Taft easily secured the nomination. Following the tradition of dissatisfied convention dissenters, Roosevelt led his followers from the Republican convention to the Auditorium Theatre, where they voted to establish the Progressive Party, complete with a platform and endorsements for a number of local and state candidates. Both Taft and Roosevelt were defeated by Democrat Woodrow Wilson in the general election, and when Roosevelt refused to attend or accept the Progressive Party's nomination at the 1916 convention, the party dissolved.

Following the tradition of the Anti-Mason Party, several other minor parties have held conventions throughout history both to attract publicity and rally their faithful. The Populist Party, born of an alliance between dissatisfied farmers and part of the union movement in the early 1890s, held a convention every four years between 1892 and 1908, nominating candidates for the presidency and other offices. The Prohibition Party, which primarily opposed the consumption of alcohol but also endorsed other social reforms, gained its widest support in the same period, though it held a convention as early as 1872. The Libertarian Party held a convention in Washington, D.C., every four years from 1972 to 2004, moving to Denver in 2008. Beginning in the 1990s, the Green Party and the Constitution Party also began holding conventions, the Greens most frequently in Los Angeles.

The Rise of Primaries and the Decline of Conventions

After World War II, primaries, though still limited in number, grew increasingly influential as a demonstration of a candidate's ability to attract votes. In 1952 New Hampshire held an early primary, an event that became a tradition. The supporters of former general Dwight D. Eisenhower waged a surrogate campaign that defeated Senator Robert Taft. Though the primary was nonbinding, the defeat weakened the conservative Taft, who had been the presumed front runner for the nomination. Following New Hampshire, Eisenhower demonstrated enough electoral strength in the primaries to defeat Taft on the first ballot at the convention. The former general allowed the convention to choose his running mate, the conservative Richard Nixon of California. Similarly, in 1964 the insurgent conservative senator Barry Goldwater shocked party leaders, defeating Nelson Rockefeller, the governor of New York, as well as William Scranton, the governor of Pennsylvania, whom frantic moderates had convinced to run after Rockefeller's weaknesses became evident. The 1964 convention was bitter, with Rockefeller and his supporters aiming rhetorical barbs at Goldwater and vice versa. But as with Eisenhower, Goldwater—the candidate who triumphed in the primaries—won the nomination on the first ballot.

In the same decade, the Democrats had virtually the opposite experience. In 1968 the party was in turmoil. President Lyndon Johnson, whose rigorous pursuit of the war in Vietnam made him extremely unpopular, declined to run for reelection. In the primaries, two candidates opposed to the war, Robert Kennedy and Eugene McCarthy, struggled for victories, a battle that ended with Kennedy's assassination shortly after winning the California primary on June 4. Many of Kennedy's supporters rallied to either McCarthy or Senator George McGovern; however, despite having not run in any of the 13 primaries, Vice President Hubert Humphrey controlled much of the remaining party organization and easily secured the nomination on the first ballot, outraging many McCarthy and Kennedy supporters. Humphrey maintained his support for the Vietnam War; his nomination was therefore unacceptable to many of the antiwar activists who rallied in the Chicago streets outside the convention. The demonstrations turned brutal when the Chicago police assailed protesters with clubs and tear gas; meanwhile, on the convention floor, Senator Abraham Ribicoff and Chicago Mayor Richard Daley clashed over the behavior of the police. That year, 1968, was the last time a major party held a convention in Chicago until 1996.

After Humphrey's defeat at the hands of Richard Nixon in the general election, McGovern headed a commission that reformed the Democratic nominating system; primaries became vastly more influential and numerous. McGovern himself rode a string of primary victories to the nomination at the 1972 Democratic convention in Miami. McGovern's commission had implemented several new rules, including a delegate quota system that guaranteed a certain number of seats to minority groups. This system was unpopular among such Democratic centers of power as organized labor; McGovern's supporters, however, won a number of credential battles at the convention and easily defeated Senator Henry Jackson for the nomination on the first ballot. However, this was not the end of the convention's troubles. McGovern's selection of a vice president was protracted and poorly run; Senator Thomas Eagleton of Missouri was selected well behind schedule, which meant that the nominees' acceptance speeches were given long after prime television hours. McGovern failed to receive the "bounce" in the polls that generally follows a convention, and overwhelmingly lost the general election to the incumbent Nixon.

Despite the failures of his convention and campaign, McGovern's system of primaries generally worked well. In subsequent years, only in 1980, when Senator Edward Kennedy challenged the incumbent president Jimmy Carter in the Democratic primaries and forced a floor vote at the convention in New York City before conceding, was the identity of the Democratic nominee even theoretically in question when the convention began. In 2008 Senator Hillary Rodham Clinton, who had narrowly lost the race for delegates to Senator Barack Obama, was granted the formality of a floor vote. However, unlike Kennedy, she had already conceded the nomination to Obama.

A similar state of affairs prevailed among Republicans after the 1970s. In 1976, former governor Ronald Reagan of California had managed to force President Gerald Ford into a deadlock; Ford had won more delegates in the primaries, but neither he nor Reagan had secured enough to win the nomination outright at the convention in Kansas City. Reagan, who had the support of the party's conservative wing, bid for the moderates' support by announcing that he would select Senator Richard Schweiker as his running mate. The move backfired, however, and Reagan lost the support of many conservatives. Ford narrowly won the nomination on the first ballot, with 1,187 votes to Reagan's 1,070, but conservatives managed to insert several planks in the party platform, including a call for an amendment to the U.S. Constitution that would outlaw abortion. Since then, the identity of the Republican nominee has been known by the end of the primary season.

Conventions as Spectacle

In recent decades, the conventions have become little more than publicity events. In 2008, for example, Democratic nominee Barack Obama chose to deliver his acceptance speech to the general public in a football stadium, rather than solely to the party delegates in the convention hall. For this reason, the conventions have come under increasing criticism, particularly since both major parties receive public aid to fund the events.

See also campaigning; Democratic Party; elections and electoral eras; political advertising; Republican Party.

FURTHER READING

Chase, James. *The Emergence of the Presidential Nominating Convention, 1789–1832*. New York: Houghton Mifflin, 1973.

Congressional Quarterly. *National Party Conventions, 1831–1972*. Washington, DC: Congressional Quarterly, 1972.

Howe, Daniel Ward. *What Hath God Wrought: A History of the United States, 1815–1848*. New York: Oxford University Press, 2007.

Panagopoulos, Costas. *Rewiring Politics: Presidential Nominating Conventions in a Digital Age*. Baton Rouge: Louisiana State University Press, 2007.

Shafer, Byron. *Bifurcated Politics: Evolution and Reform in the National Party Convention*. Cambridge, MA: Harvard University Press, 1988.

MATTHEW BOWMAN

patronage

Patronage is as old as politics itself. Indeed, since Roman times, different kinds of patronage arrangements have existed in a range of societies, and many theorists have remarked upon their connection to the practice of politics. In writing *The Prince*, for example, Niccolò Machiavelli set out to craft a manual of governance that would encourage his Medici sponsors to transcend relations of patronage in order to construct a more robust form of statecraft that could increase and consolidate their authority. In general, historians, sociologists, and anthropologists have studied patronage as a set of relationships that are personal, reciprocal, asymmetrical, and informal in nature. While today, patronage is often viewed as external to formal political practice, during much of U.S. history, patronage is better thought of as crucial to the functioning of politics and the evolution of governance. It usually encompasses the practice of politicians (or a political party) distributing government jobs or public contracts as rewards to their supporters. Patronage was not something that existed on the margins of American society. Rather, for many years, it was central to its functioning.

The Seventeenth and Eighteenth Centuries

Before the American Revolution, patronage played an important role in the evolution of relations between British colonies in North America and the London metropole, as well as within the colonies themselves. In many colonies, the relationship between the king and the governors was one in which patronage was crucial. Gaining an appointment to the office of governor usually depended on successfully cultivating a set of personal relationships with powerful figures in London. From the perspective of the British monarchy, governorships in the colonies could be distributed to reward and maintain loyalty. (Once appointed, of course, a governor had to maintain his relationships with the crown over a great distance, over which news traveled slowly and irregularly.)

After taking office, a royally appointed governor faced a number of official public duties that were layered with patronage considerations. While maintaining ties with London, in seventeenth- and eighteenth-century British North America, a governor had to balance these external concerns while dealing with colonial legislatures that were becoming increasingly powerful. Before the end of the Seven Years' War in 1763, British colonies were treated with benign neglect by the imperial bureaucracy. During this period colonial legislatures often frustrated governors by gradually claiming a number of important public powers (particularly the power to set and collect taxes) as their own prerogative. Many of the public policy-making activities of colonial legislatures thus pivoted around questions of patronage: Who would be appointed to collect revenues? Where would public works projects be built? To whom would public printing contracts be awarded? How would judicial appointments be handled? How would public lands be distributed? Even appointments to Anglican Church positions in the colonies were dealt with within the framework of patronage.

The resulting colonial political culture in British North America was one of constant jockeying, as elites sought favors from assembly members, who in turn wrangled with colonial governors, who in turn strove to deal with the crown. In many colonies, voting also took on aspects of a patron-client relationship. In Virginia, for example, members of the gentry reluctantly stood for office and solicited the support of yeomen farmers through the practice of "treating," providing free and copious amounts of alcohol in exchange for votes. This common social ritual of deference was satirized in Robert Munford's play *The Candidates* (1770), which featured two elite candidates (named Worthy and Wou'dbe) competing for the support of the common people (one character, a yeoman with a particular enthusiasm for the attentions of the candidates, was named Guzzle).

As the colonies gradually grew apart from Great Britain, much of the rhetoric adopted by citizens of the colonies reflected anxiety and concern over the connection between patronage and corruption in public life. As J.G.A. Pocock has observed, by the time of the American Revolution many Americans came to think that patronage, when wielded by the English monarchy, greatly increased "the incidence in society of individuals whose modes of social and political existence entailed a dependence upon government that made them a menace to their neighbors." In order to secure liberty from tyranny, in the framework of Republican thought, citizens were to be independent from the corrupting influence of patronage. In practice, this warning was not always followed. Alexander Hamilton used the patronage resources of the U.S. Treasury Department to help secure support for the Federalists during the first years of the new nation. In the early national period, friction between Hamilton's Federalists and Thomas Jefferson's Democratic Republicans hardened into the First Party System. Subsequently, American politics between 1789 and 1840 underwent a major transition, from an earlier deferential style of relationships to a politics organized around formal parties, one that focused on mobilizing the electorate in a more egalitarian fashion.

The Nineteenth Century

The rise of mass political parties in the nineteenth century led to an era of strong partisan rivalry with patronage at its core. The Democratic Party, particularly under the leadership of Andrew Jackson, stood astride the political landscape, while the opponents of "King Andrew" labeled themselves Whigs, in a nod to English opponents of the monarchy. Despite their differences, however, both Democrats and Whigs strove to distribute patronage to solidify the loyalties of their supporters. At both the local and national levels, each party rewarded its faithful with jobs. The federal postal system, with its national scope, became a prime site for this exchange, as loyalists contributed funds to the parties with hopes of securing employment from their legislators, who controlled access to postal patronage at the district and state level. The growing departments of War and Treasury presented politicians with job openings as well.

Jackson's "spoils system" reflected a close integration of party structure and the bureaucratic framework of government. Following his election, the president replaced many officials from the previous administration with political loyalists. To the victor, in short, belonged the spoils. These new officeholders, in turn, were required to donate part of their salaries directly to the party—a "political assessment," as it was termed. This constant turnover of administrative positions led Alexis de Tocqueville to note that in the United States a "revolution" in government came with regularity—every four years. It also served to consolidate the power of political party "bosses" while knitting mass political parties (and mass political participation) into the fabric of American life.

This American system of "campaign finance," based on patronage, began to end in the late nineteenth century, with the rise of the cause of civil service reform. Led by urban professionals from the Northeast, merchants concerned about customhouse corruption, and intellectuals, the drumbeat for reform began in the years following the Civil War. Reform-minded Republicans, including Senator Carl Schurz, *Nation* editor Edwin Godkin, and *Harper's Weekly* editor George William Curtis, became active in the National Civil-Service Reform League, seeking to eliminate the blatant corruption of their party under the presidencies of Ulysses S. Grant and James Blaine. The voices of these reformers were unheard until the assassination of President James Garfield in 1881. Garfield was killed by a mentally unbalanced office seeker, Charles Guiteau, whose efforts to obtain a government job had been unsuccessful. In the wake of this shocking event, the U.S. Congress responded in 1883 by passing the Pendleton Civil Service Reform Act, a small, yet important, first step toward curbing patronage in the federal government. The Pendleton Act created the U.S. Civil Service Commission, an important addition to the federal bureaucracy, but at first only a relatively small number of federal jobs were awarded on the basis of merit examinations.

While patronage was crucial to national politics during much of the nineteenth century, it was also a central feature of urban politics. In many American cities, machine politics and the rule of political bosses reflected the social stresses inflicted upon municipalities by the growth of immigration, urbanization, and industrialization. Thus, bosses like New York City's George Washington Plunkitt, of the Tammany Hall machine, held political meetings in neighborhood saloons, provided jobs, and distributed food, clothing, and favors in return for votes and reciprocal "donations" of money. Often sharing the same immigrant background as their working-class constituents, these bosses viewed their position as helping the less fortunate while helping themselves—what Plunkitt referred to as "honest graft." Indeed, Plunkitt observed, "As a rule [the boss] has no business or occupation other than politics. He plays politics every day and night . . . and his headquarters bears the inscription, 'Never closed.'" Not surprisingly, most urban bosses had little patience for the moralistic pieties of reformers, whom they viewed as disconnected from the realities of urban life. Reformers, according to Plunkitt, were delicate flowers, like morning glories: They "looked lovely in the mornin' and withered up in a short time, while the regular machines went on flourishin' forever, like fine old oaks."

The Twentieth Century

Despite the skepticism of urban bosses like Plunkitt, the late nineteenth and early twentieth centuries witnessed the growth of various movements to reform urban politics and curb the power of the patronage system. Responding to the worries of native-born middle-class Americans, reformers and their allies worked to elect leaders who would, unlike the urban bosses, professionalize government and run it like a business. These reformers called for balanced municipal budgets and lower taxes, for citywide instead of neighborhood-based elections, and for newer forms of government incorporating nonpartisan city managers and commissions—all to weaken the power of urban boss rule and enhance the standing of apolitical experts. This movement met with some success, as a number of cities elected reform-minded mayors, as in Cleveland, Ohio (Tom Johnson), Detroit, Michigan (Hazen S. Pingree), and New York City (Fiorello LaGuardia). While patronage was gradually losing its sway in urban politics in the first half of the twentieth century, it remained a factor in a number of cities, including Chicago, under Mayor "Big" Bill Thompson in the 1920s, and Kansas City, Missouri, where the machine of Tom Pendergast remained important into the late 1930s.

At the federal level during the Great Depression, patronage also played an important part in Franklin D. Roosevelt's New Deal. Retaking the White House in 1933 after 12 years of Republican control of the presidency, Democrats were eager for patronage appointments when FDR took office. Office- and favor-seekers, as well as their champions, descended upon the newly created programs of the New Deal, each seeking gains, whether employment for a loyal constituent or a new public works project for their district or locality. James Farley, chair of the Democratic Party and, after Roosevelt's inauguration, the new postmaster general, coordinated the distribution of federal patronage. Relying on the careful record keeping of his assistant, Emil Hurja, Farley kept track of an applicant's loyalty to Roosevelt and sought to award federal largesse in a proportionate fashion. For such conduct, Farley earned the nickname "Jobmaster General" from his critics. As had been the case with politicians in the past, New Dealers also sought to use patronage to reward loyalists and punish opponents. In the ill-fated attempt to push the Judicial Reorganization Act through Congress in 1937, Roosevelt advisor Thomas Corcoran tried to recruit congressional supporters with the carrots of patronage and the promise of federal public works dollars, as well as with the stick of threatened political reprisals.

In 1938–39, continued controversy over public works programs, a central undertaking of the New Deal, brought the twin issues of patronage and civil service reform back into the newspaper headlines. Harry Hopkins, the head of the Works Progress Administration, commanded attention when he reportedly ascribed the success of the New Deal to the fact that it could "tax and tax, spend and spend, and elect and elect." Troubled by the issue of "politics in relief," reform-minded Democrats and conservative Republicans joined together to prevent federal public works monies from being deployed to influence electoral outcomes.

This effort culminated in the passage of the 1939 Hatch Act, named for Senator Carl Hatch, a Democrat from New Mexico. Designed to prevent "pernicious political activities," the act prohibited public funds intended for relief from being used in connection with electoral campaigns and made illegal the use of these funds (and the jobs they provided) to pressure workers to vote for a particular candidate. In these ways, the Hatch Act served as the culmination of earlier civil service reform efforts. At the same time, the increase of federal social spending during the Great Depression also served to weaken the power of local urban bosses, who did not have the resources to compete with the programs of the New Deal. As chronicled in Edwin O'Connor's novel *The Last Hurrah*, the events of the Great Depression, taken together, signaled the end of an era for urban bosses, and for the power of patronage, more generally.

Since World War II, patronage has played a much less important role in American political life. In large part, this decline is related to a decrease in the number of public jobs not controlled by the civil service system. However, the continued presence of certain features of political life has helped to ensure that concerns over patronage have not vanished altogether. For example, the distribution of public spending for items like federal shipyards, the construction of bridges, the maintenance of military bases, and the like, as well as concerns over campaign finance reform, indicate that while patronage's importance has waned substantially, its echoes continue to resonate within the U.S. political system.

FURTHER READING

Allswang, John M. *Bosses, Machines, and Urban Voters: An American Symbiosis*. Port Washington, NY: Kennikat Press, 1977.

Dorsett, Lyle W. *Franklin D. Roosevelt and the City Bosses*. Port Washington, NY: Kennikat Press, 1977.

Hoogenboom, Ari. *Outlawing the Spoils: A History of the Civil Service Reform Movement, 1865–1883*. Urbana: University of Illinois Press, 1961.

Hubbell, Jay B., and Douglass Adair. "Robert Munford's 'The Candidates'." *William and Mary Quarterly* 5 (April 1948), 217–57.

Greene, Jack P. *The Quest for Power: The Lower Houses of Assembly in the Southern Royal Colonies, 1689–1776*. Chapel Hill: University of North Carolina Press, 1963.

John, Richard R. *Spreading the News: The American Postal System from Franklin to Morse*. Cambridge, MA: Harvard University Press, 1995.

McCormick, Richard. *The Party Period and Public Policy: American Politics from the Age of Jackson to the Progressive Era*. New York: Oxford University Press, 1986.

Pocock, J.G.A. *Virtue, Commerce, and History: Essays on Political Thought and History, Chiefly in the Eighteenth Century*. New York: Cambridge University Press, 1985.

Riordan, William L. *Plunkitt of Tammany Hall: A Series of Very Plain Talks on Very Practical Politics*. Boston: Bedford/St. Martin's, 1993.

Smith, Jason Scott. *Building New Deal Liberalism: The Political Economy of Public Works, 1933–1956*. New York: Cambridge University Press, 2006.

Stave, Bruce M. *The New Deal and the Last Hurrah: Pittsburgh Machine Politics*. Pittsburgh, PA: University of Pittsburgh Press, 1970.

JASON SCOTT SMITH

political advertising

Political advertising refers to communications intended to influence the electorate. Advertising has been a feature of virtually all political campaigns in the United States, electoral and otherwise. The dominant media have changed over time, though, as have the relationships between candidates and ad makers.

One can distinguish political advertising from other forms of campaign communication by two criteria. First, political advertising is mediated; speaker and audience are physically separate. Second, the sponsor—typically the campaign, though sometimes a supporter—controls the content and timing of the communication.

Observers commonly categorize a political ad as positive or negative, depending on whether it principally promotes the favored candidate or position or, by contrast, principally denigrates the opposing candidate or position. Since the 1980s, negative ads have grown increasingly prevalent, and journalists and scholars have grown increasingly critical of them.

Printed Materials, Medals, Buttons, Trinkets

Political advocacy is older than the nation. During the 1760s and 1770s, Patriots and Tories—that is, those who opposed British rule and those who favored it—debated events and principles in brief handbills and longer pamphlets. Magnifying their audience, popular handbills and pamphlets passed from hand to hand, and some people read them aloud in taverns and elsewhere. Another medium, the broadside, served as the billboard of the day (printed on one side and posted where passersby could read it).

The landmark pamphlet of the Revolutionary era was *Common Sense,* Thomas Paine's argument for independence. Published on January 10, 1776, *Common Sense* sold 1,000 copies within two weeks, 150,000 copies within a year, and perhaps half a million by the end of the Revolutionary War. *Common Sense,* like many political ads throughout American history, tried to evoke fear. Paine wrote that British soldiers in Boston had murdered families, plundered houses, and left citizens on the brink of starvation. The goals of "tyrant" King George, further, were nothing less than "laying a country desolate with fire and sword, declaring war against the natural rights of all mankind, and extirpating the defenders thereof from the face of the earth."

Pamphlets, broadsides, and other printed material entered American political campaigns around 1800. Some were hyperbolic, if not hysterical. In a pamphlet published in 1798, Timothy Dwight, the president of Yale University, declared that if Thomas Jefferson were elected president in 1800, Jefferson's supporters would burn Bibles and force "our wives and daughters" into prostitution.

Printed materials themselves could become campaign issues. In a letter to the *Gazette of the United States* in 1796, a writer complained that "lies, abuse, and slander" targeting presidential candidate John Adams were being spread by "one hundred thousand" broadsides and other printed sheets, plastered all over "the trees on the road, and the door and gate posts of every house through the country." Another letter writer wondered, "At whose expense is this business conducted?" The sponsor's identity mattered, in part, because self-promotion could suggest unseemly ambition. A North Carolina voter wrote of a congressional candidate in 1800, "The hand bills which he has industriously posted along every road, seem to pronounce to all that he is at least of a suspicious character."

One of the more notorious print ads of the twentieth century promoted Richard Nixon in the 1950 California campaign for U.S. Senate. A legal-sized flyer, the ad listed instances in which Nixon's Democratic opponent, Representative Helen Gahagan Douglas, had voted with Vito Marcantonio, a member of the left-wing American Labor Party. The flyer omitted the fact that on most of the votes Douglas and Marcantonio had followed the Democratic Party line. To underscore the implication that Douglas was a soft-on-communism pinko, the Nixon campaign printed the flyer on pink paper.

Print also provided a vehicle for authorized biographies of candidates. Some historians consider the first biography of a presidential candidate to be a pamphlet published in 1800, *Address to the People of the United States; with an Epitome and vindication of the Public Life and Character of Thomas Jefferson*. Starting in the 1820s, book-length biographies featured in many presidential campaigns. In New York City in 1852, supporters of Franklin Pierce gave away some 5,000 copies of a biography written by Pierce's college classmate, Nathaniel Hawthorne. By the last decades of the twentieth century, though, autobiographies had come to outnumber authorized biographies. Autobiographies of candidates or future candidates include *Six Crises* (1962), by Richard Nixon; *Why Not the Best?* (1976), by Jimmy Carter; and *Looking Forward* (1987), by George H. W. Bush.

Political advertising reached clothing starting in the 1820s. Some voters pinned silk ribbons, lithographed with the candidate's picture or slogan, to their lapels, or wore medallions hanging from ribbons. Changes in technology made lapel-worn advertisements more attractive and less expensive. Medallions of 1860 held tintype photographs, which let voters see the presidential candidates, often for the first time. In 1896 the presidential campaigns produced more than a thousand different buttons, using a new and cheaper manufacturing method.

The cost of buttons dropped further in the 1920s. Today, buttons seem to be losing out to a still-cheaper form, round stickers. Candidates' names, images, and slogans have appeared on other items as well. Nineteenth-century campaigns distributed flasks, bowls, mirrors, belt buckles, toothpick holders, and umbrellas.

Some buttons and other promotional materials reinforced a campaign's positive themes. In 1860 the presidential campaign of "rail-splitter" Abraham Lincoln distributed wooden axes. Campaign gewgaws served as negative advertisements, too. A button opposing Franklin Delano Roosevelt's campaign for a third term in 1940 asserted No Man Is Good Three Times. In other instances, campaign trinkets addressed issues. Tokens distributed in 1860 by presidential candidate Stephen Douglas told slavery opponents to mind their own business: Intervention Is Disunion 1860 / M.Y.O.B.

Like other new forms of advertising, these materials provoked criticism. In 1836 Senator Thomas Hart Benton denounced "derisory manufactures" that were designed "to act on the thoughtless and ignorant through appeals to their eyes and passions."

Since 1896, buttons have allowed voters to wear their politics on their sleeves. (University of Wisconsin-River Falls Archives)

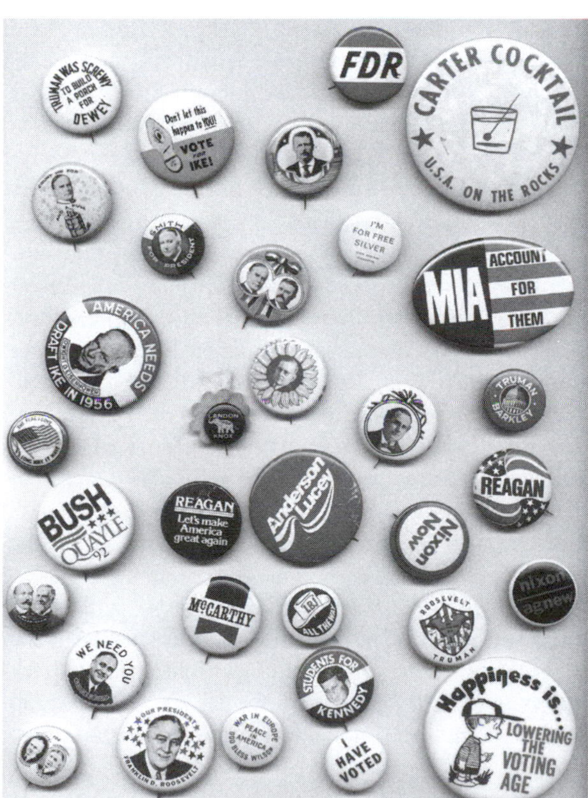

New Creators, New Media

Around the turn of the twentieth century, the landscape of political advertising started to change—not just the media, but the people who created the ads as well. Previously, candidates, their aides, or party officials had developed advertisements. Now, experts in public opinion began to craft ad campaigns, though these professionals might have no connection to the candidate or to politics in general. The influence and visibility of these outsiders steadily increased during the twentieth century.

Outside experts first entered political campaigns as a result of three intertwined developments in the late nineteenth century. New machinery allowed mass production; new railroad lines allowed mass distribution; and new periodicals offered mass communications for disseminating promotional messages through advertisements and news coverage. These developments created a niche for specialists. Corporate executives might know their products, but they did not know the public mind—or so the new experts maintained. Advertising agencies and public relations firms multiplied and flourished.

Public opinion specialists gradually entered politics. Before attaining prominence as a public relations pioneer, Ivy Ledbetter Lee worked for New York City mayor Seth Low's unsuccessful campaign for reelection in 1903 and then for the Democratic National Committee. Albert Lasker headed a major advertising firm, Lord & Thomas, when he oversaw advertising and other communications in the 1920 presidential campaign of Warren G. Harding. By 1952 ad agencies were virtually ubiquitous in presidential politics, and public relations firms played a prominent role as well.

For these companies, political work was a sideline. One group of specialists, political consultants, devoted themselves solely to politics. The first consulting firm, Campaigns Inc., was founded by Clem Whitaker and Leone Baxter in California in 1933. By the 1970s, political consultants had overshadowed ad agencies in presidential campaigns. The consultants themselves became newsworthy, too. Like party bosses of the late nineteenth century, some consultants had the clout to confer legitimacy on candidates.

The rise of promotional experts, market research, and new advertising media both reflected and hastened changes in American politics. Participatory politics of the nineteenth century—rallies, bonfires, well-attended speeches, and other modes of face-to-face campaigning—gradually gave way to campaigns built around advertising. Whereas political parties once orchestrated electoral campaigns, party affiliation gradually became little more than a brand for candidates. Individuals' party loyalties likewise diminished, with more and more voters calling themselves independents. In addition, polls and other forms of market research enabled campaigns to identify the most compelling positions on the most salient issues. As a consequence, party-run, ideology-dominated, participatory-voter campaigns gave way to consultant-run, research-dominated, passive-voter campaigns.

Broadcast advertising contributed substantially to the shift. In the presidential election of 1924, both major-party campaigns bought radio time to broadcast the candidates' speeches. The 1928 campaigns made far heavier use of radio, mostly in one-hour time slots. Whereas the major parties had spent some $100,000 on radio in 1924, expenditures in 1928 exceeded $2 million. As the 1928 campaign approached its end, the *New York Times* proclaimed radio "a new instrument of democratic government," and added that "the town meeting of New England has been made national."

To Franklin D. Roosevelt, radio played to the voter's reason and rationality. "In the olden days," presidential candidate Roosevelt said in 1932, "campaigns were conducted amid surroundings of brass bands and red lights. Oratory was an appeal primarily to the emotions and sometimes to the passions. . . . With the advent of the radio, mere oratory and mere emotions are having less to do with the determination of public questions. . . . Common sense plays the greater part and final opinions are arrived at in the quiet of the home." In 1933 President Roosevelt's "fireside chats" established him as a master of the medium.

In a precursor of television, some presidential candidates starred in short films that were shown in content-hungry movie theaters. Under the guidance of advertising expert Lasker, the Republicans in 1920 produced silent films showing nominee Harding and his supporters. "I do not subscribe to the idea of selling a candidate," Democratic nominee James Cox declared in October 1920, a few weeks before losing the election.

Television and Its Critics

In 1952 television reached some two-fifths of American households, enough to attract attention and money from political campaign. The Democrats spent nearly all of their funds on half-hour segments in which they aired speeches by nominee Adlai Stevenson and his backers. To save money, the Democrats bought late-evening time slots, 10:30 to 11 p.m., which mainly attracted Stevenson diehards. The Republicans, by contrast, devoted much of their money to short commercials, a minute or less, shown in various time slots, which reached undecided voters. Stevenson, though he too had used advertising and promotional specialists, declared that Eisenhower's reliance on ad agencies showed "contempt for the intelligence of the American people."

Since the 1960s, television has dominated political advertising. Many ads try to evoke emotion—either fear, as with Paine's pamphlet *Common Sense,* or national pride.

The reelection campaign of President Lyndon B. Johnson aired the paradigmatic fear ad in 1964, "Daisy." The ad capitalized on Republican nominee Barry Goldwater's suggestion that he might use tactical nuclear weapons in Vietnam. In an open field, a little girl counts as she plucks petals from a daisy. Just before she reaches ten, a stern voice begins a countdown from ten to zero. The girl looks up, the frame freezes, and the camera closes in on the pupil of one of her eyes, until the screen is black. At zero, an atomic bomb explodes. As the mushroom cloud fills the screen, the viewer hears President Johnson say: "These are the stakes—to make a world in which all of God's children can live, or to go into the dark. We must either love each other, or we must die." The ad closes with the voice-over "Vote for President Johnson on November third. The stakes are too high for you to stay home."

One of the most noteworthy national-pride ads, "Morning again in America," aired during Ronald Reagan's campaign for reelection in 1984. To quiet, upbeat music, the ad shows a harbor at dawn, a man going to work, a farmer atop a tractor, a couple getting married, and other images, some in slow motion, each gently fading into the next. The voice-over—Hal Riney, one of the leading TV voices of the 1980s—recites evidence that the country has prospered since Reagan took office. "It's morning again in America," Riney says. "And, under the leadership of President Reagan, our country is prouder, and stronger, and better. Why would we ever want to return to where we were, less than four short years ago?" With the mention of President Reagan's name, the viewer sees a series of Americans raising flags. Reagan himself appears only on the final screen, in a small photo alongside a flag.

As televised ads have come to dominate American political campaigns, critics have increasingly denounced the form. Since the 1980s, academics and journalists have especially targeted negative commercials. According to critics, negative ads diminish trust in government, reduce voter turnout, and spread half-truths and lies.

As critics charge, negative ads have become more prevalent. In some recent presidential elections, negative ads have accounted for nearly 70 percent of advertising. Studies have found, not surprisingly, that challengers are more likely to air negative ads than incumbents are: challengers must make the case for change, which, more often than not, requires criticism of the incumbent. Researchers have also found that negative ads generally address issues rather than personalities. In presidential campaigns, finally, Democrats have aired more negative ads than have Republicans.

Some critics favor a law requiring the candidate to address the camera throughout the duration of every TV ad, on the theory that few candidates would directly associate themselves with attacks on opponents. Congress enacted a weaker version of the proposal in 2002, which requires each commercial in a federal campaign to include the candidate's name and a statement that he or she has approved the ad.

In a related development, news media since the late 1980s have increasingly featured "ad watches," which analyze political ads, especially negative ones, and assess their accuracy. Although scholars continue to debate the point, some studies have found that a televised ad watch can reinforce an ad's misleading message, because some viewers focus on imagery rather than critique.

The Internet and Beyond

The Internet has played an increasingly prominent role in political campaigns since 1992, when Jerry Brown took part in online questions and answers and Bill Clinton's campaign e-mailed supporters. The first campaign Web sites appeared in 1994. Internet-focused political organizations, most notably MoveOn.org, formed later in the 1990s. In 2004 a candidate for the Democratic presidential nomination, Howard Dean, attracted an unprecedented number of volunteers and contributions through a Web site and e-mail lists.

With its capacity for two-way communication, the Internet may help revive the sort of participatory politics that largely died away during the twentieth century. But the Internet appears most effective in reaching a candidate's existing supporters. Broadcasting, by contrast, brings the campaign's message to undecided and antagonistic voters.

From broadsides to Web sites, campaign advertisements have been as varied as campaigns themselves. Nonetheless, a few generalizations can be made. First, old media forms generally exist even after new ones dominate. Buttons, print advertisements, and radio ads live on in an age of television. The basic forms—print, audio, and video—will endure even if, as some anticipate, they increasingly originate online.

Second, political advertisements are controversial, and they always have been. Their producers have been accused of selling candidates like consumer products, manipulating the public, distorting the truth, and demeaning the process. Although losing candidates have always been prominent detractors of political ads, journalists and academics have been vocal critics since the 1980s.

Finally, despite their controversial nature, political ads will not disappear. As long as Americans vote, advocates of candidates and issues will work to persuade them. In the United States political persuasion requires political advertising.

See also campaign consultants; campaigning; Internet and politics; press and politics; radio and politics; television and politics.

FURTHER READING

Ansolabehere, Stephen, and Shanto Iyenbar. *Going Negative: How Political Advertisements Shrink and Polarize the Electorate.* New York: Free Press, 1995.

Diamond, Edwin, and Stephen Bates. *The Spot: The Rise of Political Advertising on Television.* 3rd ed. Cambridge, MA: MIT Press, 1992.

Fischer, Roger A. *Tippecanoe and Trinkets Too: The Material Culture of American Presidential Campaigns, 1828–1984.* Urbana, IL: University of Illinois Press, 1988.

Foot, Kirsten A., and Steven M. Schneider. *Web Campaigning.* Cambridge, MA: MIT Press, 2006.

Jamieson, Kathleen Hall. *Packaging the Presidency: A History and Criticism of Presidential Campaign Advertising.* New York: Oxford University Press, 1984.

Kaid, Lynda Lee, and Christina Holtz-Bacha, eds. *The Sage Handbook of Political Advertising.* Thousand Oaks, CA: Sage, 2006.

Richardson, Glenn W. *Pulp Politics: How Political Advertising Tells the Stories of American Politics.* Lanham, MD: Rowman and Littlefield, 2003.

Sabato, Larry J. *The Rise of Political Consultants.* New York: Basic Books, 1981.
Silbey, Joel H., ed. *The American Party Battle: Election Campaign Pamphlets, 1828–1876.* Cambridge, MA: Harvard University Press, 1999.

STEPHEN BATES

political culture

Germans believe in a national "culture of solidarity." The French profess a faith in *liberté, égalité, fraternité.* Citizens of Thailand cling to elaborate networks of patronage and deference. Americans boast of rugged individualism (which some Europeans derogate as "cowboy culture"). Every nation has a shared set of attitudes, assumptions, aspirations, and norms that are rooted in history and legend. We call this shared vision a people's culture, and it forms the essential backdrop to politics and society.

Culture can be elusive—one historian described cultural studies as nailing jelly to a post. British anthropologist Sir E. B. Tylor proffered a definition in 1871: Culture is "that complex whole which includes knowledge, belief, art, morals, law, customs, and other capabilities and habits acquired by [people] as member[s] of society." Margaret Mead boiled it down to a simple phrase: "Culture is the learned behavior of a society." Clifford Geertz, an anthropologist at Princeton University, offered an even more direct and useful definition: "Culture is simply the ensemble of stories we tell ourselves about ourselves."

Every people has its "ensemble of stories." However, the shape and meaning of those stories is often contested—sometimes fiercely. After all, important events benefit some people and harm others; each group recalls a different tale, draws different lessons, and champions it own version over others.

Do Americans share a set of attitudes and assumptions embedded in myths about the past? Not long ago most social scientists thought so. They described a national consensus stretching back to the American founding. Important books bore titles like Henry Steel Commager's *The American Mind* (published in 1950), Richard Hofstadter's *The American Political Tradition* (1948), and Daniel Boorstein's *The Americans* (1965). Critics occasionally damned the cultural consensus for its suffocating homogeneity, but few questioned its existence or challenged its content.

Today, agreement over a shared American culture has vanished, and three very different perspectives have emerged. First, some scholars insist that the traditional American culture is still going strong. Americans, they argue, remain deeply committed to core values like individualism, political rights, equal opportunity, and a wariness of government power. These add up, say proponents, to a great American Creed originally set down by Thomas Jefferson in the Declaration of Independence. Of course, the people of the United States have never fully lived up to their high-flying ideals, but each generation fights to close the gap between quotidian life and creedal aspirations.

Others mournfully view the American Creed as a fading relic of the past. Centrifugal forces press on our society and bode serious trouble for the grand old culture. Today, the United States "belittles *unum* and glorifies *pluribus*," wrote Arthur Schlesinger Jr. in 1991. Almost 40 million people in the United States (or about one in eight) were born abroad. They cling to foreign values and resist the purifying fire of America's melting pot. Ethnic militancy "nourishes prejudices, magnifies differences and stirs antagonisms." Proponents of this view fret that a fierce politics of identity challenges traditional American culture. "Will the center hold?" asksed Schlesinger. "Or will the melting pot give way to the tower of Babel?"

A third view cheers the diversity. Proponents of this perspective reject the traditional accounts of American political culture. Images of consensus, they argue, chronicled the perspective of wealth and power while ignoring alternative voices. Perhaps the most popular exhibition in the brief against the old school lies in a fear expressed during the 1962 presidential address of the American Historical Association. Carl Bridenbaugh of Brown University warned his colleagues about a gathering storm. Once upon a time, scholars shared a common culture. Now, he fretted, historians were increasingly "products of lower middle class or foreign origins, and their emotions not infrequently get in the way of historical reconstruction. They find themselves in a very real sense outsiders on our past." Bridenbaugh's fears proved prophetic. A new generation of scholars began to read the nation in a fresh way: the real American culture, they argued—and argue still—lies in a rich amalgamation of immigrant voices, African American blues, and songs from the urban alleys. This perspective celebrates the American "Babel" as the welcome sounds of diversity. It sees cultural pluralism as nothing less than the mainspring of national renewal.

The debate continues. Did the Americans really share a political culture? If they had it, did they lose it? If they lost it, should they feel distressed or liberated? The answer is simple and reflects the central fact of every culture: contestation. Yes, the United States has a vibrant political culture. Where many observers go wrong is to search for a static conception celebrated on all sides. American culture is constantly debated and continuously evolving. Each generation of immigrants brings new perspectives to the ensemble of stories. African Americans insist that the black experience lies at the heart of the American experience—challenging past generations that shrugged aside slavery as, in Frederick Jackson Turner's phrase, a mere "incident." Liminal groups of every sort remake American culture as they struggle for legitimacy. The uproar over the national story reminds us that there is nothing inevitable or permanent about the ideas and groups that win a hearing and become part of the mainstream—or those that lose and fall to the margins.

Ironically, a notorious jeremiad got the bottom line exactly right. In a speech to the Republican National Convention of 1992, Patrick Buchanan rattled the mainstream media with his ferocious declaration: "We are . . . in a culture war . . . for the soul of America." He failed to add that the "war" has waxed and waned for 300 years. What is most distinctive and timeless about American political culture is not the desire for freedom or the demand for rights or even the irresistible rise of Wal-Mart across the countryside, but the lively debate over each of those topics and many more. In short, American political culture was and is a constant work in progress.

Like every national culture, debates about the United States turn on a series of great national myths. Each powerfully resonates with at least some of the population. Each carries its own set of lessons. The central question is always the same: How do the stories add up? What do they tell Americans about America?

Consider three classic tales and lessons they bear.

Brave Pilgrims

Perhaps the best-known story that people in the United States tell about themselves begins with a legend made famous by Alexis de Tocqueville: the first Americans sailed away from Old World tyrannies and came to a vast, unpopulated land. In contrast to the people in Europe, those early Americans did not face powerful political or economic elites. Here there were no rigid social classes or repressive political authorities. Instead, as Tocqueville put it, "Americans were born equal instead of becoming so." White men (this story gets a bit shaky once you include women or people of color) faced extraordinary opportunities. The land and its riches awaited them. Anybody could become a success—all it took was a little capital and a lot of work.

In this context, continues the famous American legend, the early settlers soon became unabashed individualists. After all, if success and failure lay in every individual's own hands, there would be no need for government assistance or collective action. European serfs *had* to band together to fight for political rights and economic mobility. But Americans were free from the start.

This story helps explain why Americans are so quick to denigrate their government and to celebrate markets. After all, the legend comes with an unambiguous exhortation repeated down through history: hard work leads to economic success; the poor have no one to blame but themselves. Abraham Lincoln famously recited the upside of the market credo when he declared that any man who was "industrious, honest, sober, and prudent" would soon have other men working for him. He left the inevitable corollary to nineteenth-century preachers like Henry Ward Beecher: "If men have not enough it is from want of . . . foresight, industry and frugality. No man in this land suffers from poverty unless it be more than his fault—unless it be his *sin*."

Band of Brothers (and Sisters)

When contemporary historians began to examine the myths of rugged individualism, they discovered precisely the contrary—a robust collective life. Early Americans lived hard lives on a sparsely populated land and relied on one another for almost everything. When a barn burned down, the neighbors gathered and helped raise a new one. Public buildings—churches and meeting houses—were built by citizens working together. Historian Laura Ulrich Thatcher pored over household inventories and discovered that families even shared ownership of expensive cooking utensils—the lists of family possessions often include one-half or one-third of an iron pot or pan. Forget the legends about individuals on the frontier succeeding or failing on their own. Early Americans relied on their neighbors a great deal. They were communitarians more than individualists, republicans as much as liberals.

A focus on our common life offers a counter to the vigorous individualism and voracious markets that spring out of the first story. American idealists of every political persuasion invoke the nation's fragile, recurring communal values. Conservatives see the American communal legacy as an opportunity to restore "traditional values"; leftists stress our obligations to one another and suggest programs like national health insurance.

At the same time, there is a more troubling aspect embedded in the communal tradition. Defining "us" also identifies "them." In fact, the United States long ago developed a distinctive kind of American outsider—the un-American. The popular communal story, symbolized by the congenial melting pot, imagines a nation constantly cooking up a richer democracy with thicker rights. The darker alternative counters with a less cheerful story: Many Americans have faced repression simply for their ascriptive traits—their race, gender, ethnicity, or religion.

The two visions of community mingle in a long cultural dialectic. Generous American visions of equality and inclusion face off against prejudice and exclusion. The two impulses are evenly matched, Manichean twins wrestling for control of each historical moment. As William Carlos Williams put it in 1925, always poised against the *Mayflower* (a symbol of the quest for freedom) sails a slave ship (symbol of racial repression).

City on a Hill

Still another story goes back to the Puritans sailing to New England in 1630. Those early settlers arrived in the New World facing the essential communal question: Who are we? The Puritans concocted an extraordinary answer: they were the community of Saints. Leadership, in both state and church, went to individuals who could prove that they were pre-ordained for salvation. The saints could vote, hold office, and enjoy full church membership. Citizens who had not demonstrated salvation (through elaborate rituals) were expected to follow the saints; they could not vote, hold office, or become full church members. And the irreparably damned had to be driven from the community—the settlers hung witches, slaughtered Native Americans, and sent heretics packing to Rhode Island. In short, moral standing defined leaders, allocated political privileges, defined the communities, and identified the dangerous "others."

The Puritan legend concludes with a dynamic turn. Even before the settlers landed, Governor John Winthrop delivered one of the most famous sermons in American history. "We shall be as a city on a hill, the eyes of all people are upon us." This strange idea—the tiny settlement at the edge of the Western world was on a mission from God and the eyes of all people were fixed on them—stuck and grew. The American lesson for the world has evolved over time—religious faith, political freedom, unfettered economic markets. But 350 years after John Winthrop delivered his sermon, Sacvan Berkovitch, a scholar specializing in early America, described the "astonishing" consequence: "a population that despite its bewildering mixture of race and creed . . . believe[s] in something called the American mission and . . . invest[s] that patent fiction with all the emotional, spiritual and intellectual appeal of a religious quest."

Each of these three stories packs a different moral charge: Americans are rugged individuals, they wrestle over their common lives, they populate an international exemplar, a city on a hill. These are all the stuff of the national culture. They suggest national norms, serve up fodder for primal debates, and establish a setting for domestic debates, social policies, and international adventures.

Today, however, many political scientists dismiss the entire notion of political culture. Political cultures, they say, change slowly across the generations, while political events move fast. How can a constant (culture) explain a variable (politics)? Besides, the idea of national cultures imposes a kind of determinism on politics. Leftists have grown especially agitated about the ways conservatives have deployed cultural arguments; progressives resist the notion that poverty stems from "a cultural of poverty" (which blames and denigrates poor people regardless of the broader economic circumstances), and they reject efforts to ascribe tensions with the Arab world to a clash of cultures (which lets the United States off the hook for blundering international policies and writes off all the friction as the inevitable "clash between civilizations").

In dismissing the idea of political culture, however, political scientists fall into an old error. Culture is not an unyielding political fact, cast in granite. It is vibrant and dynamic; it reflects a constant debate over what it means to be an American. The stories we tell about ourselves do not belong to either left or right, to the powerful, or the poor. They are, however, formidable weapons. They shape the ways in which people see themselves; they shape the national aspirations.

Still, the critics have a point. National culture cannot offer a complete picture of political developments. It cannot, by itself, explain why the American welfare state looks so different from Sweden's or why Iraqis view the United States with suspicion. Politics also moves through constitutions and laws, leaders and political movements, exogenous shocks and the caprice of chance. Of course, those dynamics are also incomplete. We cannot fully explain political events without understanding political culture. It forms the backdrop for events in every nation. Leaders who seek to reshape welfare programs or remake foreign nations without heeding the national "ensemble of stories" rapidly come to rue their ignorance.

In short, the United States, like every other nation, has a rich national culture that should be read as a perpetual work in progress. Americans have been contesting their ensemble of stories since the first settlers stepped ashore and began to define themselves and their colonies. The battle heats up when the society appears in flux; moments of large-scale immigration, broad economic change, and shifting social relations (especially if they agitate race or gender norms) seem to foment particularly keen culture clashes. Still, every era witnesses its own exuberant debate about what the nation has been, what it is, and what it ought to be.

FURTHER READING

Morone, James. *Hellfire Nation: The Politics of Sin in American History.* New Haven, CT: Yale University Press, 1993.

Schlesinger, Arthur M., Jr. *The Disuniting of America: Reflections on a Multi Cultural Society.* New York: Norton, 1991.

Smith, Rogers. *Civic Ideals: Conflicting Visions of Citizenship in U.S. History.* New Haven, CT: Yale University Press, 1997.

Tocqueville, Alexis de. *Democracy in America.* 1835, 1840. Reprint, Garden City, NY: Doubleday, 1966.

Williams, William Carlos. *In the American Grain.* New York: Harper Brothers, 1925.

JAMES A. MORONE

politics in American film

Movies and politics were bound together from the start of the film industry. From the opening of the first nickelodeon in 1905, silent films represented a new means of political communication that bypassed traditional authorities and spoke directly to millions of viewers. Movies reached a larger and more diverse array of people than any mass medium of the time. By 1910 nearly one-third of the nation's population flocked to the movies each week; ten years later nearly half attended movies, and by the 1930s, admission figures approached 100 percent of the nation's population. Throughout their history, movies simultaneously shaped and reflected the public's understanding of American political culture. Emerging in the midst of the Progressive Era, silent films addressed the most contentious issues of the day—poverty, immigration, racism, sexism, class conflict, child labor, women's rights, birth control, judicial corruption—and offered viewers possible solutions to these vexing problems.

Political films are about more than just politicians, political parties, and organized political activity. They deal with power and power relations, and depict the uses and abuses of power by one individual, group, or class against another. They explore power as practiced in government, society, households, and between individuals. The political focus of American films depended on the nature of an era's problems and the economic state of the motion picture industry itself.

Between 1905 and April 1917, when the United States entered World War I, filmmakers such as Edwin Porter, D. W. Griffith, Lois Weber, Charlie Chaplin, and others made thousands of social problem films that depicted a broad range of controversial issues. These polemical productions often reflected the reformist hopes—and limitations—of progressive thought and its largely middle-class, male view of the world. They deplored extremes in class conditions and denounced both excessive wealth and abject poverty. They condemned individual capitalists but never capitalism. They called for reform but denounced radical solutions. They were sympathetic to the hardships working people suffered at the hands of employers and police but rarely endorsed collective action by the exploited as a means of solving those problems. Nevertheless, these early social problem films raised public consciousness and often helped politicians pass bills aimed at remedying contemporary ills. Likewise, Charlie Chaplin's Tramp, the most popular comic character of the silent era, delighted working-class and immigrant audiences by mocking the power and legitimacy of those who continually gave ordinary Americans a hard time.

Although commercial companies produced the bulk of these films, the low cost of making movies allowed capitalists, reformers, government agencies, and labor and radical organizations to make films intended to shape public perceptions about a wide range of issues. Class-conscious filmmakers on both left and right transformed labor-capital struggles previously hidden from sight into highly visible parts of a new public sphere. Tragedies such as the fire at the New York Triangle Waist Company that left 146 seamstresses dead in March 1911 and the massacre of 24 men, women, and children at John D. Rockefeller's Colorado Fuel and Iron Company in Ludlow, Colorado, on April 20, 1914, were recreated and reinterpreted on the screen. The National Association of Manufacturers produced two films in 1912, *The Crime of Carelessness* and *The Workman's Lesson*, that blamed the aforementioned tragedies on careless employees and portrayed employers, not unions, as the group most concerned with the welfare of workers. Radicals and working-class organizations responded by producing popular melodramas such as *A Martyr to His Cause* (1911), *From Dusk to Dawn* (1913), and *What Is to Be Done?* (1914) that depicted their struggles in a positive light and offered viewers viable alternatives to the politics of both the Democrats and the Republicans.

The outbreak of World War I precipitated dramatic changes in the American movie industry and the politics of American film. In 1914 the United States produced approximately half of the world's movies; by 1919, with European film production in shambles, that figure rose to 90 percent. During the 1920s, Hollywood assumed its modern identity and, in so doing, altered the political character of American film. The geographically scattered array of small- and medium-size producers, distributors, and exhibitors gave way to an increasingly oligarchic, vertically integrated studio system centered in Los Angeles and financed by some of the largest industrial and financial institutions in the nation. By the end of the 1920s, eight major studios controlled over 90 percent of the films made and distributed in the United States.

Far from being a bastion of liberalism, the corporate studio system known as Hollywood pushed the politics of American films in increasingly conservative directions. Looking to increase profits rather than solve controversies, studios abandoned the politically engaged social problem films of the Progressive Era in favor of more conservative "society films" that helped moviegoers forget about the horrors of the war years. Audiences, director William de Mille observed in his autobiography *Hollywood Saga*, wanted films that offered "a sumptuous and spectacular dramatization of the age of jazz, prohibition, and flaming youth." Movies about class conflict, racism, sexism, and exploitation did not disappear from the screen during the 1920s but were fewer in number and rarely appeared in the studio-owned first-run theaters that earned films their greatest visibility and profits.

Anti-Communist films proved an exception to this rule. Between 1917 and 1922, in the wake of the Russian Revolution and ensuing Red Scare, motion picture industry leaders, the *Los Angeles Times* reported on January 3, 1920, joined the government's Americanization campaign to combat "Bolshevism and radicalism" by using "the Power of the Motion-Picture screen to spread anti-Red teachings all over the country." Films such as *Bolshevism on Trial* (1919), *Dangerous Hours* (1920), and *The Stranger's Banquet* (1922) echoed capitalist propaganda that attributed postwar labor unrest to the work of Bolshevik agents and the corrupt labor leaders who aided them. Labor and radical groups such as New York's Labor Film Services, Seattle's Federation Film Corporation, and the American Federation of Labor responded by making feature films and documentaries—including *The Contrast* (1921), *The New Disciple* (1921), *Labor's Reward* (1925), and *The Passaic Textile Strike* (1926)—that promoted their political agenda for the 1920s: union organizing, worker cooperatives, support for continuing strikes, and exposing the lawless actions of employers and their private armies. Federal Bureau of Investigation head J. Edgar Hoover considered these films so dangerous that he assigned secret agents to monitor the activities of radical filmmakers and give extensive summaries of their productions.

Depression, War, and Reaction

The impact of the Great Depression and the high cost of making "talking" pictures in the early 1930s drove many smaller studios and independent groups (like labor filmmakers) out of business. Hard times led surviving studios and independents to move in two political directions, one taken by Warner Brothers, the other by Metro-Goldwyn-Mayer (MGM). No studio was more self-consciously political during the 1930s and early 1940s than Warner Brothers. In addition to making a wide array of social problem films often based on contemporary headlines, Warners attempted to warn the nation of the dangers posed by fascists abroad and by Nazi sympathizers at home. This was no small task: a Gallup Poll taken in November 1936 revealed that

95 percent of Americans opposed U.S. participation in any potential war.

Prohibited by the Production Code Administration (PCA) from making any film that directly attacked foreign leaders, the studio produced antifascist features based on real events. *Black Legion* (1937) told the story of a domestic fascist organization that wrought terror throughout the Midwest during the early 1930s. In 1939 Warners produced the nation's first overtly anti-Nazi film, *Confessions of a Nazi Spy*, which revealed how the FBI broke a Nazi spy ring operating out of New York. When the PCA dropped its prohibition, the studio quickly made a number of antifascist films between Hitler's invasion of Poland in September 1939 and the Japanese bombing of Pearl Harbor in December 1941. Warners' efforts to curry sympathy for the Allies prompted isolationist and anti-Semitic senators Gerald Nye and Bennett Clark to launch an investigation of propaganda in motion pictures in September 1941 that charged "Jewish" Hollywood with warmongering. The investigation ended after the Japanese attack on Pearl Harbor in 1941, when the United States entered the war.

Unwilling to jeopardize lucrative foreign business by producing anti-Nazi films, studios nevertheless released movies offering sympathetic depictions of the various injustices faced by Depression-era Americans. Films like *Modern Times* (1936), *The Grapes of Wrath* (1940), and *The Devil and Miss Jones* (1941) empathized with the plight of individuals but did not explicitly endorse efforts at collective action; nor did they attempt to explain the larger forces responsible for the hardships endured by millions of people. These productions portrayed class and political problems in terms of corrupt individuals rather than a corrupt system. Frank Capra's populist romances *Mr. Smith Goes to Washington* (1939) and *Meet John Doe* (1941) may have made viewers feel good about the ultimate justice of a political system in which David could beat Goliath, but they proposed solutions that had little chance of succeeding against real foes offscreen.

MGM's cinematic ideology proved a stark contrast to the progressive films coming out of the Warner Brothers studio. While Warners repeatedly exposed what was wrong in American life—poverty, corruption, lack of opportunity—MGM turned out lavish productions that stressed the conservative values favored by its head, Republican power player Louis B. Mayer. The patriotic Russian-born mogul who claimed the Fourth of July as his birthday produced political visions brimming with optimism and heralded everything that was right with America. MGM's most successful series—the Andy Hardy films made between 1937 and 1943—created an updated Victorian world where anything was possible as long as one subscribed to family, country, and God. Success was a matter of individual effort and not collective action. Although these may seem like old-fashioned values today, at the time MGM went against the tide of the New Deal's vision of increased reliance on the government. Indeed, films such as *Judge Hardy's Children* (1938) denounced federally owned corporations such as the Tennessee Valley Authority.

Studio domination of American cinema in the early sound era did not signal the end of oppositional filmmaking. During the 1930s and 1940s, leftist film organizations like the Workers' Film and Photo League, Nykino, and Frontier Films produced feature films, documentaries, and newsreels—such as *Millions of Us* (1936), *People of the Cumberland* (1937), and *Native Land* (1942)—that exposed audiences to scenes of strikes, demonstrations, and multiracial organizing efforts they were unlikely to see anywhere else. Yet, with most first- and second-run theaters controlled by studios, these films were pushed to the margins of mass culture.

During Word War II, studios emphasized themes of national unity, harmony, patriotism, and the heroic struggles of men and women fighting abroad. After the war, the rabidly anti-Communist House Un-American Activities Committee (HUAC) quickly forgot Hollywood's vital contribution to the "Good War" and launched an investigation that linked earlier antifascist films with Communist efforts to undermine democracy. Movie industry personnel who helped the war effort by making films that heralded cooperation with the country's Russian allies—*Mission to Moscow* (1943), *The North Star* (1943), and *Song of Russia* (1944)—found themselves accused of being Communists or at least "fellow travelers" who aided them. Dalton Trumbo, John Howard Lawson, and the eight other writers, directors, and producers who refused to answer HUAC questions—known as the Hollywood Ten—were sent to prison for contempt of Congress. Worried that the hearings would taint their industry and hurt profits, studio heads issued a statement in December 1947 requiring loyalty oaths for all employees and pledging to fire any known Communists. Under pressure to prove their own patriotism, studios turned out a series of anti-Communist films—*The Red Menace* (1949), *I Married a Communist* (1949), and *Big Jim McLain* (1952)—that all proved box-office disasters.

Postwar Promises and Problems

Despite setbacks from HUAC, filmmakers nevertheless grappled with controversial issues dealing with the difficulties of postwar readjustment, brilliantly explored in *The Best Years of Our Lives* (1946); the problems of anti-Semitism in *Gentleman's Agreement* (1947) and *Crossfire* (1947); and the persistence of racism in the post-Hitler world in *Pinky* (1949) and *No Way Out* (1950). The Hollywood studio system dominated the world market until the late 1940s and early 1950s, when challenges from the new medium of television and a court decision ordering the separation of studio production and exhibition weakened their near monopolistic hold over the industry.

During the mid-1950s, filmmakers turned their attention to exploring the disparities between the promises and problems of daily life in President Dwight D. Eisenhower's America. Among the spate of juvenile delinquency films released during the decade, *Rebel Without a Cause* (1955) proved the most provocative. Set in a seemingly ideal wealthy suburban community where families lived in homes with white picket fences and teenagers drove their own cars, this story of discontent and death challenged dominant ideas about family, sexuality, gender roles, and the meaning of success.

In the wake of the Supreme Court's momentous 1954 *Brown v. Board of Education of Topeka* decision, which ruled against segregation in U.S. schools, filmmakers increasingly focused on the vexing issue of race. Despite fears of losing 20 percent in revenues because of boycotts by southern exhibitors and moviegoers, studios produced a spate of films that ventured beyond stereotypical portrayals of African Americans as anything other than slaves, domestics, or Pullman porters. While Sidney Poitier starred in popular films such as *Edge of the City* (1957) and *The Defiant Ones* (1958), his close friend, the more radical Harry Belafonte, organized his own film company in 1957 with the goal of using the screen to reshape ideas about race. As he explained to the *New York Times* on March 15, 1959, "I intend to show the Negro in conflicts that stem from the general human condition and not solely from the fact of his race." At a moment when southern blacks were under siege and when most civil rights leaders were clergy, Belafonte's two films, *The World, the Flesh, and the Devil* (1959) and *Odds Against Tomorrow* (1959), offered audiences a model of a secular, tough-minded yet flawed black man who always stood up for himself.

The most politically progressive film of the 1950s did not come out of Hollywood but from a partnership between the International Union of Mine, Mill and Smelter Workers, and the leftist Independent Productions Corporation. Written, directed, and produced, respectively, by prominent blacklisted figures Michael Wilson, Herbert Biberman, and Paul Jarrico, *Salt of the Earth* (1954) used a true story to show how a strike at a New Mexico copper mine transformed the strikers, their families, and their community. The film proved so provocative that conservative politicians denounced it, unions refused to work on it, and exhibitors refused to show it. After a brief run at a small New York theater, the film virtually disappeared until the late 1960s, when it was shown on college campuses across the country.

Cold war fears also prompted the release of a number of allegorical features such as *The Ten Commandments* (1956), in which the struggle between Pharaoh and Moses mirrored the struggle between the Soviet Union and the United States. To make sure audiences understood his intentions, director Cecil B. DeMille appeared in the film's two-minute prologue to explain, "The theme of this picture is whether men ought to be ruled by God's law or whether they are to be ruled by the whims of a dictator like Ramses. Are men the property of the state or are they free souls under God? This same battle continues throughout the world today." In the wake of the Korean War, filmmakers played upon fears of a possible Soviet attack by making science-fiction thrillers—*The Thing* (1951), *Invaders from Mars* (1953), *Invasion of the Body Snatchers* (1956)—in which alien invaders (substituting for "Reds") took over the minds and bodies of helpless Americans. These fantasies continued into the 1960s, when in 1964, following the Cuban Missile Crisis, filmmakers released a number of dramatic (*Fail-Safe* and *Seven Days in May*) and comedic (*Dr. Strangelove*) views of potential nuclear war with the Soviet Union.

Politics in the New Hollywood

In the "new Hollywood" of the 1960s and 1970s, studios struggled to reverse declining box-office receipts by exposing audiences to lively debates about civil rights, black militancy, the Vietnam War, and gender roles. Martin Luther King Jr.'s 1963 March on Washington and the passage of the Civil Rights Act in 1964 inspired a number of integrationist films, many of them starring Sidney Poitier, such as *To Sir, with Love*, *In the Heat of the Night*, and *Guess Who's Coming to Dinner?* (all 1967). Although militant African Americans found Poitier's saintly image hard to take, especially in the midst of calls for black nationalism, many white Americans found the interracial romance in *Guess Who's Coming to Dinner?*

disturbing enough to precipitate violent incidents at a number of theaters in both the North and South.

Angry at the way African Americans were portrayed on the screen, black filmmakers—and later studios eager to replicate their box-office success—created a new genre known as blaxploitation films. Aimed specifically at African American audiences, and especially inner-city youths, features such as *Sweet Sweetback's Baadasss Song* (1971), *Superfly* (1972), and *Cleopatra Jones* (1973) revealed an urban world filled with drugs, money, and violence that had rarely been seen on the screen by white America. Yet, while these films were popular with young African Americans, older leaders worried that they created new negative stereotypes of blacks and, more important, shifted the political focus of their community toward more individualist, self-indulgent activities and away from the collective struggles that marked the civil rights movement of the 1950s and 1960s.

Willing to engage changing ideas about race, Hollywood proved hesitant to confront the war in Vietnam. The first major Vietnam film, John Wayne's *The Green Berets* (1968), which offered a staunch defense of American involvement, did not appear until well into the conflict and came at a time when domestic opposition to the war was growing stronger. Reluctant to be seen as unpatriotic during wartime, studios had far less trouble releasing a number of conspiracy thrillers that questioned the integrity of the government. Given the abuses of power that led to President Richard Nixon's resignation, including his illegal use of government agencies to persecute people on his "enemies list," it is hardly surprising that paranoia about government surveillance and deception emerged as a major theme in films such as *The Conversation* (1974), *The Parallax View* (1974), and *Three Days of the Condor* (1975).

Once the Vietnam War ended in April 1975, producers began turning out antiwar films—*The Deer Hunter* (1978), *Coming Home* (1978), and *Apocalypse Now* (1979)—that questioned American involvement in the conflict. Opening with the Doors' song "This Is the End," *Apocalypse Now* portrayed the war as an exercise in madness—a conflict in which no one was in charge, where troops fought to make the beaches safe for surfing, and where the U.S. Army's rising star officer went mad in the jungles of Vietnam. Although the personal politics of many industry leaders was decidedly liberal, their studios were ultimately in the business of making money, not raising public consciousness. Consequently, as the New Right rose to power in the 1980s, Hollywood produced films like *Red Dawn* (1984), *Missing in Action* (1984), and *Rambo: First Blood Part II* (1985) that helped renew the nation's faith in the military and pave the way for greater public acceptance of military actions taken by presidents Ronald Reagan and George H. W. Bush.

The political activism of the 1960s and early 1970s did, however, inspire films—*The Front* (1976), *The China Syndrome* (1979), *Norma Rae* (1979), *Reds* (1981), and *Matewan* (1987)—that attacked "Red-baiters," warned against the dangers of nuclear power, and offered positive visions of unions and radicals. Left-oriented independent filmmakers supplemented these features with documentaries that presented moving accounts of strikes, organizing efforts, and corporate greed: *Union Maids* (1976), *Harlan County, U.S.A.* (1977), and *Roger and Me* (1989). On the other hand, as conservative movements gained large numbers of new adherents, Hollywood produced films—*F.I.S.T.* (1978) and *Hoffa* (1992)—that disparaged working-class organizations, their leaders, and their goals.

The dramatically changing domestic political climate of the 1970s and 1980s led to conflicting left and right depictions of gender. Influenced by the women's movement, feminist films of the 1970s—*Alice Doesn't Live Here Anymore* (1974), *The Turning Point* (1977), and *An Unmarried Woman* (1978)—showed men and women struggling to see each other in ways that transcended traditional gender roles. For women, this meant being able to choose whatever kind of career or personal status—single, married, divorced, parenting, or childless—they wanted. The 1980s, however, proved a tough decade for strong-minded independent women—on and off the screen. The conservative climate of the Reagan era manifested itself in a spate of antifeminist films that called for a return to more traditional gender roles, for men as well as women. Films like *The War of the Roses* (1989), *The Hand that Rocks the Cradle* (1992), and especially *Fatal Attraction* (1987), which featured Glenn Close as a homicidal career woman gone mad, used fear to send a clear message that straying outside of "normal" behavior led to dire consequences.

The 1990s and Beyond

Cynicism marked American politics and political films of the 1990s and the first decade of the twenty-first century. Democratic president Bill Clinton outmaneuvered Republicans by adopting many of their conservative positions, and Hollywood responded with films that offered disparaging views of electoral politics: *Bob Roberts* (1992), *Wag the Dog* (1997), and especially *Bulworth* (1998). The latter film—written, directed, and starring Warren Beatty—highlighted the hypocrisy of the Democratic Party and the unwillingness of African American voters to hold politicians to their promises. This climate of skepticism helped Michael Moore take the documentary from the margins to the center of American film with three surprising hits—*Bowling for Columbine* (2002), *Fahrenheit 9/11* (2004), and *Sicko* (2006). *Fahrenheit 9/11* returned $111.2 million by October 2004—making it the most commercially successful documentary in American history. Moore's films marked a return to the humorous but biting antiauthoritarian politics of Charlie Chaplin. Like the Tramp, Moore skewered a wide range of powerful individuals and organizations: the National Rifle Association, George W. Bush, Congress, and the American health care system.

The events of September 11, 2001, marked a turning point in American history, yet fears of terrorism made it to the screen well before the destruction of the World Trade Center towers. *Navy Seals* (1990), *True Lies* (1994), and *Executive Decision* (1996) all featured threats by nefarious Middle Eastern forces, while *The Siege* (1998) showed Islamic terrorists plotting an attack on New York City. Unlike the war in Vietnam, Hollywood studios did not wait a decade before dealing with the second Gulf War, begun in March 2003. This time, however, films such as *Home of the Brave* (2006), *Redacted* (2007), and *Stop-Loss* (2008) focused on the difficulties faced by military troops rather than on the government and military leaders who botched the war.

For more than 100 years, movies have served as a powerful means of disseminating ideas to millions of people who eagerly watch on the screen things they might hesitate to read about. People who had little daily contact with unionists, radicals, feminists, politicians, gay men and lesbians, African Americans, Latinos, Asians, and various minority groups were most likely to be influenced by what they saw on the screen—especially if exposed to the same kinds of images repeatedly until they came to assume the appearance of "reality."

In the future, the globalization of Hollywood is likely to diminish the number of films that examine the complex political issues of American life. In 1993 U.S. films generated $13 billion in revenues, $8 billion (61.5 percent) of which came from foreign markets; that percentage of foreign revenue held constant through 2006. With the bulk of profits increasingly coming from abroad, studios are inclined to put out blockbuster action films that contain little dialogue and that non-English speaking audiences throughout the world can understand. Films exploring controversial issues continue to be made, but they tend to focus on political events of international concern (such as terrorism), or, if uniquely American, come out of smaller independent companies. The challenge is to understand how these films—past and present—continue to affect visions of American society and politics.

See also television and politics.

FURTHER READING

Alexander, William. *Film on the Left: American Documentary from 1931 to 1942*. Princeton, NJ: Princeton University Press, 1981.

Belton, John. *American Cinema/American Culture*. New York: McGraw-Hill, 2008.

Bodnar, John. *Blue-Collar Hollywood: Liberalism, Democracy, and Working People in American Film*. Baltimore, MD: Johns Hopkins University Press, 2003.

Booker, M. Keith. *Film and the American Left: A Research Guide*. Westport, CT: Greenwood Press, 1999.

Brownlow, Kevin. *Behind the Mask of Innocence: Sex, Violence, Prejudice, Crime: Films of Social Conscience in the Silent Era*. New York: Knopf, 1990.

Ceplair, Larry, and Steven Englund. *The Inquisition in Hollywood: Politics in the Film Community, 1930–1960*. Urbana: University of Illinois Press, 2003.

Christensen, Terry, and Peter J. Haas. *Projecting Politics: Political Messages in American Films*. Armonk, NY: M. E. Sharpe, 2005.

Guerrero, Ed. *Framing Blackness: The African American Image in Film*. Philadelphia: Temple University Press, 1993.

May, Lary. *The Big Tomorrow: Hollywood and the Politics of the American Way*. Chicago: University of Chicago Press, 2000.

Ross, Steven J. *Working-Class Hollywood: Silent Film and the Shaping of Class in America*. Princeton, NJ: Princeton University Press, 1998.

Ryan, Michael, and Douglas Kellner. *Camera Politica: The Politics and Ideology of Contemporary Hollywood Film*. Bloomington: Indiana University Press, 1990.

STEVEN J. ROSS

politics in the American novel

The political novel in America does not directly follow divisions in party politics, and party politics, in

America, have rarely been influenced by novels or poetry. The American republic was called into being by lawyers, soldiers, and politicians: the national poem—rather than lines by Dante, or J. W. von Goethe, or Aleksandr Pushkin—is the Declaration of Independence (1776). The republic was remade by Abraham Lincoln (1809–65) in his 1863 Gettysburg Address, and remade again by Martin Luther King Jr. (1929–68) in his "I Have a Dream" speech (1963): stirring oratory built upon well-chosen words, with its own civic poetry and richness of language, but in form and content unrelated to novels. Abstract concepts like conservatism and radicalism do little to explain the political novel's career in America.

A more salient contrast is between novels that protest existing social and political conditions and those that protest the ideology or posture of protest. Two lines of literary activity can be traced forward from the nineteenth to the twentieth centuries. One runs from Harriet Beecher Stowe's *Uncle Tom's Cabin* to Upton Sinclair's *The Jungle* to Richard Wright's *Native Son*—the canonical literature of protest, a staple of left-wing culture by the twentieth century; these are books that cry out for political reform or revolution. The other line runs from Nathaniel Hawthorne's *The Blithedale Romance* to Lionel Trilling's *The Middle of the Journey* to Saul Bellow's *Mr. Sammler's Planet*—novels that address the "ideology of protest" and take a skeptical look at literature's quixotic resources and its capacity to transform readers into self-proclaimed knights; these writers worry about literature's power to stir political fantasy and to confuse the grim business of politics with the imaginative pleasures of literature. By the twentieth century, the ideology of protest had been interwoven with the fluctuating fortunes of the American left, though it does not necessarily follow that Hawthorne, Trilling, or Bellow enshrined the political right in their novels. There is a conservative literature of protest. Ayn Rand's popular novels, for example, critiqued New Deal America and its socialist-inflected cultural elite; but the fruits of this particular tree are not as bright or as beautiful, in literary terms, as the fruits from Hawthorne's or Wright's respective trees.

The Literature of Protest

The literature of protest forms a contract with the reader. If the reader assents to the political logic of the novel, this logic should hold for the society at large: the ills chronicled in the political novel are our ills, and we have the power to purge them from ourselves and our polity. Harriet Beecher Stowe (1811–96) exploited this power in the first major protest novel in American literature, *Uncle Tom's Cabin* (1852): some even credited Stowe with "starting" the Civil War, with the spread of the abolitionist movement, and with the election of Abraham Lincoln in 1860. Her novel arose out of mid-century Protestantism, out of the soil of mainstream American culture, a novel conceived in a church and written to redeem a sinful republic. Stowe felt that America was corrupting the virtuous Christian family by condemning whites and blacks to live with slavery. The reader can begin the work of redemption by reading, and over time the political order will honor such Protestant faith in the marriage of moral individual with truthful text. *Uncle Tom's Cabin* resonated with its readers because it traced a motif of Christian redemption. America could simultaneously go forward toward the abolition of slavery and back to the purity of the Christian family, a template of the good society, housed in an Uncle Tom's cabin undefiled by slavery.

As Christianity's hold on American literary culture began to fade in the late nineteenth century, novelists explored other avenues to redemption. Socialism enjoyed cultural and intellectual prestige in America from the 1890s to the 1930s. If America's sins—after the Civil War, in the Gilded Age, and beyond—were the sins of avarice or, in more modern language, the sins of capitalism, they could be redeemed by socialism. The political novelist could be political by making the literary case for socialism. For a relatively short time, this was a potent politicoliterary formula.

Two novels describe the arc of the socialist idea: Edward Bellamy's *Looking Backward* (1888) and Upton Sinclair's *The Jungle* (1906). Bellamy's utopian novel codifies the spirit of nineteenth-century socialism, fascinated by whole-scale alternatives to known societies, excited by the mechanics of technical and industrial development, and optimistic that an age of reason might well be dawning. Bellamy (1850–98) bypassed a competing strain of socialism articulated by Karl Marx (1818–83), the socialism or communism that took its inspiration from class conflict, with a bleak present haunted, as Marx stated in *The Communist Manifesto* (1848), by the "specter" of communism and with revolution the midwife of a wondrous future. In the utopia pictured in *Looking Backward* (1888), voluble residents of the future reflect with amused condescension on the disorganization and backwardness of the late nineteenth century. Bellamy's novel could be read almost as a good-natured capitalist fantasy, as if the profit motive, the appetite for consumer goods, and the American preoccupation with technological progress could be harmonized and private virtue united with a quasi-socialist public good. Redemption, on this pattern, carries no hint of apocalypse, no premonition of "the fire next time." Bellamy's will to protest had very soft edges.

The Jungle (1906), in contrast, has the hard edges of class-conscious socialism. Like Stowe, Sinclair (1878–1968) delves deep into the horrors of American life—in this case, the jungle of American capitalism and of the modern American city. Literary realism serves Sinclair's purposes well: he does not moralize as Stowe does, nor does he speculate in the manner of Bellamy. Instead Sinclair forms his contract with the reader through a barrage of disturbing verisimilitude, lingering in horrific detail over the Chicago stockyards, confronting the reader with the misery of those condemned to work in such places. The French writer Emile Zola (1840–1902) had done the same with his masterful protest novel, *Germinal* (1885), stripping the capitalist world bare of lyricism and its attendant political illusions and immersing the reader in the details of mining work. Sinclair's ideal reader was compelled to find political fortitude in social fact, amassing the strength to resist capitalism's logic by facing the capitalist system directly; the ugliness of Sinclair's literary world—its aesthetic of ugliness—carries a political judgment. The title is a metaphor: the jungle would have to be subdued, tamed, cleared; the job of civilization is at its beginning, given the barbarism of the industrial age, the ancient repression and primitive struggle that capitalism had reintroduced; and the job of civilization is equivalent to the creation of socialism. Sinclair makes his political vision manifest in *The Jungle*: the darkness of the capitalist jungle yields to the socialist light, and socialism will guide America out of its modern underworld. The reader is to be persuaded, at the novel's end, that socialism will prevail.

Native Son (1940) by Richard Wright is a postsocialist novel. The essay that Wright (1908–60) later contributed to the bible of political disillusionment, *The God that Failed* (1950), a compendium of writing by authors who had left the Communist Party, was a melancholy postscript to the radical novel. *Native Son* is alive with social detail, an indictment of American racism for the poverty, and poverty of opportunity, it imposes upon African Americans; but it devotes more novelistic energy to the psychological cataclysm of American racial prejudice. The novel's hero, a young black man, fulfills the expectation of pathology that a racist America had set for him at birth. The pathology of whites, expressed in their disgust for blacks, inverts the ethical lives of African Americans, who harm themselves when doing the "good" that whites ask of them; Wright's hero achieves a kind of ethical stature by killing—and killing brutally. Wright's political world is blurred with uncertainty, and here he differs from classic protest writers like Stowe and Sinclair. The Communists who appear toward the end of the novel are not the agents of redemption. The Christian God has failed long ago, and the radical gods will not succeed. To be a native son of America, white or black, is to circulate in a political predicament (Wright, himself lived much of his adult life in Paris).

After the death of socialism, a fragmentation of political protest set in. The literary Old Left, which cherished high modernism as much as it did the gritty prose of a Communist writer like Mike Gold (1893–1967), gave way to a New Left that was more musical than literary. Bob Dylan (1941–) was a dominant figure for this later generation, a poet and singer with a literary sensibility but not a novelist. In the late twentieth century, Thomas Pynchon (1937–) and Don DeLillo (1936–) fashioned voices of protest, capturing, in novels, a cold war America that was a danger to itself, and each of the various New Left agendas—from the women's movement to the gay rights movement to the environmental movement—had novels to its credit; but these novels were not the lifeblood of the New Left, which dissipated in the 1970s. The literary aspirations of the New Left found their true home not in the novel but in the academic literary criticism of the 1980s and 1990s, to which novels were still important. The passion for political change, the preoccupation with alternatives to the dismal present, and the emotional peaks of vigorous protest all figured in literary scholarship that came to be known as postmodern. Postmodern scholarship, an endeavor from the left, grew in radicalism in the 1980s and 1990s as the political scene itself became more conservative, as if to compensate for the deficits of the Reagan era by rigorously fashioning a theoretical progressivism.

Protesting Protest

The symmetrical opposite of protest would be acquiescence or celebration, but this is the stuff of great literature only in discreet episodes and moments, not as the governing impetus for a novel. Thus, literary alternatives to the protest novel are novels that take up the question of protest, subjecting it to the kind of critical scrutiny that protest novels apply to society at large or to some failing part of it. If outrage is the predominant mood of the protest novel, novels that protest protest are saturated with ambiguity, which is itself a political gesture. Ambiguity can favor political moderation, implying that politics consists of a yes and a no; that both negation and celebration, the will to change and the will to conserve, deserve a hearing in the novel; that the novel is no monologue of discontent but a dialogue, encompassing multiple, conflicting voices; that American democracy demands novels that are pluralist and not, in the language of the *Federalist Papers* (1787–88), the product of faction. Ambiguity can also be a proxy for conservatism, and novels that affirm "the politics of ambiguity" open the door to conservatism in all its mercurial American configurations.

The *Uncle Tom's Cabin* of the antiprotest genre is *The Blithedale Romance* (1852) by Nathaniel Hawthorne (1804–64). It is, typically, a novel of intellectuals and a novel of ideas far more than a novel of social fact, like *The Jungle*. The ideas in question belong to the Transcendentalist movement. Hawthorne depicts a radical world overburdened with world-changing fervor, with models and platforms and programs for reform. The reforming impulse starts with political economy and comes to include domestic habits, speech, and the categories of male and female. Hawthorne rejects the very ambitiousness of such reform, and *The Blithedale Romance* is a tale of political disillusionment. The novel's protagonist joins a utopian community only to realize that it may be worse off than the society or polity it is struggling to improve. Hawthorne uses a tool that "protest novelists" employ sparingly or avoid altogether: mockery. Hawthorne knows that protest must be serious and, to be sustained, must be taken seriously, and he mocks the protester's earnestness, tacitly arguing that politics does not begin and end in social problems, in poverty or inequality, as the politically engaged are likely to believe. Hawthorne detaches politics from abstract idealism and roots political appetite in the individual personality, often in personal problems that are resolved through political engagement. The protagonist of *The Blithedale Romance* settles on the word *aloof* in his reckoning with a utopian experiment that leaves him cold. He is too much the intellectual to be a conservative, and too conservative—too skeptical of the reforming impulse—to stand with the progressive elect.

A twentieth-century variant upon Hawthorne's theme is *The Middle of the Journey* (1947) by Lionel Trilling (1905–75), a novel informed by the epochal Russian Revolution of 1917 and not just by a preoccupation with intellectuals. Here the political stakes are higher than in *The Blithedale Romance*: nineteenth-century dreams of reform are a charming relic of the past; in their place are fearsome twentieth-century ideologies. Right and left both have aspirations to make the world anew. Trilling's friend, the British poet W. H. Auden (1907–73) had labeled the 1930s a "low, dishonest decade," a decade when Adolf Hitler and Joseph Stalin were ubiquitous and when intellectual life traded in passions on the edge of homicide.

In *The Middle of the Journey*, Trilling attacks what he saw as the Stalinism of the 1930s. The novel is set in this decade, when intellectuals arrived at their romance with the Soviet Union and their complicity with Soviet crimes, according to Trilling, via an intoxication with the righteousness of protest. For the sake of ideological balance, *The Middle of the Journey* offers a complex portrait of an American conservative, based on a historical figure, Whittaker Chambers (1901–61), a Soviet spy turned Christian conservative. In an age of zealotry, the conservative has mostly zeal to contribute; left and right are alternating forms of fanaticism. The novel's many ambiguities belong to a liberal spirit that favors self-criticism and even weakness, as opposed to ideological certainty and self-confidence.

Saul Bellow (1915–2005) puts ambiguity to a different political purpose in *Mr. Sammler's Planet* (1970), concluding his novel on an ambiguous note of affirmation and celebrating America's banal moderation. The twentieth century—under its Nazi and Soviet stars—had uprooted all bourgeois certainty, Bellow felt. Modern novelists contributed to this uprooting with their cultural war on the middle class, their protesting of everything, which spread, in the delirious 1960s, to the educated classes. Bellow set his novel in the New York City of the 1970s, a metaphor for Western civilization in crisis, awash in cultural decadence, crime, and sexual perversion. The novelistic consciousness belongs to a world-weary Holocaust survivor. Born in Poland, he had once been an optimistic liberal; trauma turns him into a knower of civilization's frailty who is surely no Republican but who is conservative in his loathing of radical change. He lends the moral authority of his European past to a critique of America's troubled present. The novel ends with the death of the protagonist's nephew, who knows his responsibilities, carrying them out unheroically, without high distinction, grandeur, or protest, but with the knowledge that such responsibilities are the bedrock of the public good. This old-fashioned, middle-class message is embedded in a novel carefully designed to provoke—even outrage—its readers, a political novel immoderate in its plea for moderation.

The left has no premium on American fiction, and with Bellow and Trilling the left has been dissected, picked to pieces, put alongside and at times beneath conservative principles. Yet the left remains the point of political orientation for most American writers and therefore for the political novel in America. Autobiography is the literary métier of the modern conservative movement, beginning with *Witness* (1952) by Whittaker Chambers (1901–61) and continuing with *Breaking Ranks* (1979) by Norman Podhoretz (1930–) and *Radical Son* (1998) by David Horowtiz (1939–). Conservative autobiography has flourished with the many biographical shifts from left to right, a commonplace of twentieth-century political history. Fiction matters to conservatives for the continuity it can offer, for its canonical majesty, circumscribing the contours of Western civilization; immediate political content is peripheral to the project of defending civilization. The left, the godfather of the political novel, has sought a fusion of culture with immediate political content in novels, poems, and films. If the left is to be the sponsor of future political novels, it will have to face the challenge confronting all contemporary novelists—the challenge of connecting novel to reader, of ensuring that literature has a social context outside a few major cities and academia, as the cult of the text fades further and further into the American past. The novel has long been losing a battle against film and television, a gentle irony of the late twentieth and early twenty-first centuries, when—from the Monica Lewinsky scandal to the September 11 terrorist attacks to the 2008 presidential campaign—American politics has never been more novelistic.

See also politics in American film.

FURTHER READING

Baldwin, James. *Notes of a Native Son*. Boston: Beacon Press, 1990.

Buell, Lawrence. *The Environmental Imagination: Thoreau, Nature Writing and the Formation of American Culture*. Cambridge, MA: Harvard University Press, 1995.

Butler, Judith. *Gender Trouble: Feminism and the Subversion of Identity*. New York: Routledge, 1990.

Howe, Irving. *Politics and the Novel*. Chicago: Ivan Dee, 2002.

Jameson, Frederic. *The Political Unconsciousness: Narrative as a Socially Symbolic Act*. London: Routledge, 2002.

Riss, Arthur. *Race, Slavery and Liberalism in the Nineteenth Century*. New York: Cambridge University Press, 2006.

Stauffer, John. *The Black Hearts of Men: Radical Abolitionism and the Transformation of Race*. Cambridge, MA: Harvard University Press, 2001.

Trilling, Lionel. *The Liberal Imagination: Essays on Literature and Society*. New York: New York Review of Books, 2008.

White, Hayden. *Tropics of Discourse: Essays in Cultural Criticism*. Baltimore, MD: Johns Hopkins University Press, 1986.

MICHAEL KIMMAGE

popular music and politics

It is impossible to imagine twentieth-century American culture without the various strands of popular music that have both enlivened and confounded it. To be sure, the industry of American popular music, as we currently understand it, was created in the nineteenth century, before the advent of electronically reproduced sound. Tin Pan Alley, home of the American pop song; race music or the racialized categorization of commercial music based in minstrelsy; the creation of American patriotic music—from "The Star Spangled Banner" to "Dixie" as the national anthem of the confederacy; American folk music, from Shaker hymns to Negro Spirituals; and the cult of "genius" popular composer (Stephen Foster), the popular band leader (John Phillip Sousa) and the prodigiously popular pop singer (Jenny Lind) were all products of the nineteenth century.

Yet in the twentieth century, music has reigned supreme in American cultural life. No other country has been more shaped by its popular music or more entranced and disturbed by the music industry's financial success, the course of its aesthetic expression, and the unpredictable ends of its social possibilities. Historian Jacques Barzun called the transformation in the public reception of music in the twentieth century "a cultural revolution," as amateur passion, unbridled zeal, and wearisome ubiquity characterize the presence of music—particularly popular music—in public life. Popular music became impossible to escape in the twentieth and twenty-first centuries as it fell upon the public in torrents, from the sonic wallpaper of piped-in music heard everywhere from sporting events to the grocery store to the doctor's office, to the music videos of MTV and VH1 that have made the public think that every image or picture requires a soundtrack, to the obsession with portable "personal" music players: there is music not just for every major occasion in life but for every moment of it.

Indeed, American popular music—from ragtime, jazz, and swing, to Broadway show tunes and standards, to country, to blues, rhythm and blues, rock, punk, hip-hop and beyond—is arguably the single most impressive of America's cultural exports and among its most influential. The young everywhere seem to admire American popular music, and that appeal is what gives it such power. Even many stodgy American leaders recognized this in the cold war era when they used popular music as a cultural and ideological tool in the fight against communism. (In the current war on terrorism, Islamic extremists have pointed to American popular music as a sign of decadence and moral corruption, an opinion held by more than a few Americans.)

The dramatic impact of U.S. popular music has resulted from a set of circumstances that are not unique to the United States but are indeed unique in their combination:

- the introduction of recorded sound at the turn of the twentieth century, which transformed the music industry and spread music faster than ever before
- the rising number of immigrants—especially Jewish, and to a lesser extent, Irish immigrants who, because of their status of being not quite the equal of white Protestants and thus frequently condemned to the cultural margins, played an essential role in the creation and marketing of popular music
- a significant population of African Americans—for whom music always had important cultural and social functions—that has helped to shape American musical tastes and dance forms
- the advent of radio, which exposed millions of people to a variety of music
- the advent of the long-playing record album, which changed the way artists conceived of recorded music and the way the music business packaged and marketed it
- the influence of Latin America from musical forms like the tango and the mambo to musicians, including the Cuban bandleader Xavier Cugat, who appeared in a number of American movies in the 1930s and 1940s; Brazilian singer, guitarist, pianist, and songwriter Antonio Carlos Jobim, who helped invent the bossa nova craze of the 1960s; and Mexican American guitarist Carlos Santana, who was among the first to create the genre now known as Latin rock via his blend of rock, salsa, and jazz
- the rise of American urban life at the beginning of the twentieth century, with the resulting expansion of the machinery of American popular culture into music

No country developed such an extensive and intensive commercial "mass" culture as the United States, and music was its centerpiece, as important to Hollywood film as it was to social dance, important as a programmatic art meant to accompany or explain or contain a narrative and as an art form referring purely to itself as music with no narrative references. The power of popular music to arouse an emotional response helps explain its strong appeal to young people and its use as an erotic or romantic stimulant.

Popular Music and Politics

Although little American popular music is explicitly political in the sense of advocating a specific political ideology or interpreting current events in an overtly political way, 1930s leftist folk music by performers like Pete Seeger, Josh White, Woody Guthrie, the Almanac Singers, and others made songs like "United Front," "On the Picket Line," "Jim Crow Train," "Bad Housing Blues," "Hard, Ain't It Hard," "No, No, No Discrimination," and "The Hammer Song" popular. Folk music had a resurgence in the late 1950s through the mid-1960s, with performers like Joan Baez, Bob Dylan, the Chad Mitchell Trio, Odetta, and Phil Ochs making, on occasion, explicitly political music, spurred largely by the civil rights movement and protests against the war in Vietnam. Some of these songs—"I Ain't Marching Anymore," "Blowing in the Wind," "The Times, They Are a-Changin'," "Alice's Restaurant," and "Where Have All the Flowers Gone?"—became famous and commercially successful. But it would be incorrect to characterize the folk resurgence of this period as preoccupied solely or mostly with political music or, more accurately, songs with politicized lyrics. Dylan, for example, influenced other musicians more with his poetic and cryptic lyrics than with any political implications his lyrics may have borne. He liberated the pop song more than he politicized it.

The 1960s folk revival is more rightly understood as a "roots" movement, or an attempt to return to "authentic" American music, which was always the claim for this music by its adherents. This return to the "primitive church," as it were, happens from time to time in American popular music as a revolt against commercialism and the formulaic. (In jazz, bebop was much the same kind of "primitive church" creative reaction to the big band swing that preceded it. In black dance music, rap was a "primitive church" creative reaction to the commercialism of disco.)

Such movements, though, are not purely aesthetic in nature. There is an underlining political impulse that informs most "roots" challenges against what is seen as an illegitimate hegemony that has both stolen the music from its rightful owners and creators and debased it in a process that dilutes or contains the music's original insurgent implications. Bebop as a self-consciously black music created by black musicians is a good example of this sort of roots revolt against the whiteness of swing.

Other overtly political songs appeared occasionally in popular music genres throughout the twentieth century—including jazz singer Billie Holiday's performance of the anti-lynching song "Strange Fruit" in 1939; folk-rock singer Barry McGuire's "Eve of Destruction" in 1965, a song protesting political violence; Mac Davis's "In the Ghetto" (1969), sung by Elvis Presley; and pop-folk singer Tracy Chapman's "Talkin' 'bout a Revolution" in 1988—but never consistently or in large numbers. Not even rap, a music whose appeal was in part based on the reality of the street and implicit protest against the hypocrisy of the status quo, produced many overtly political songs.

Popular music creators never thought it was a good idea to make "political" music as it did not, in most instances, sell well. "If you want to send a message, call Western Union," was the common retort of most music creators and businesspeople when asked about making music with an obvious or clear political slant. (Elvis Presley was reluctant to record "In the Ghetto," a huge hit for him, for that very reason: he did not want to be associated with "message" music.) The assumption was that people listened to popular music for escape or entertainment, not for political indoctrination, to shape their political consciousnesses, or to become politically aware—although, to be sure, people may go to some explicitly political music to have their political beliefs affirmed.

What Is Political Music?

The existence of political music—or, more accurately, politicized popular music—raises two questions. The first is whether politically oriented popular music is largely protest and leftist oriented. Irving Berlin's "God Bless America" (written in 1918 and revised in 1938) is a political song, even though it is clearly not a protest or leftist piece. George M. Cohan's jaunty World War I song "Over There" (1917) is clearly political, as is Sergeant Barry Sadler's "Ballad of the Green Berets" (1966), but neither is leftist nor antiestablishment. The same can be said for more recent patriotic songs like country singer Toby Keith's "Courtesy of the Red, White, and Blue" (2003), Neil Diamond's "America" (1980), Dan Hartman and Charlie Midnight's "Living in America" (1985; sung by James Brown), and Sammy Johns' "America," (1986; sung by Waylon Jennings).

James and Rosamond Johnson's "Lift Every Voice and Sing" (1900), also known at the "black national anthem," is not leftist; its lyrics tell the story of endurance and triumph rather than protest, and it is thus essentially a patriotic song for African Americans. And James Brown's paean to staying in school, "Don't Be a Dropout" (1966), or his antidrug song "King Heroin" (1972), or Chuck Berry's "Back in the USA" (1959) are not ironic or "edgy" in the obvious way that Jewel's "America" (2003) is, but all have political messages. Political popular music is more likely to be patriotic or conventionally bourgeois liberal in its sentiments than leftist in orientation.

In short, what constitutes the political in popular music may be more complex and varied than many people think. The great bulk of political music in the nineteenth century, some of John Phillip Sousa's marching tunes or "The Battle Hymn of the Republic," among other examples, are not protest pieces but patriotic ones.

The second question is whether political music can only be political per se if a song has intelligible lyrics. If political music depends on its lyrics to convey its message, how can any musician be sure that listeners even understand the lyrics, much less the intended message of the words? Studies have discovered that most people do not fully understand the lyrics to most of the songs they like, except for those written for musical shows or films. If listeners misunderstand many of the lyrics they hear, do lyrics really contribute to the emotional impact of a particular tune? Even more important, can instrumental music be political? When jazz saxophonist Sonny Rollins released his 1958 album, "Freedom Suite," how could a listener know from anything except the title (and the artist's accompanying notes) that it was meant as a musical commentary about the civil rights movement? The same might be said for the 1961 tune "Freedom March" by guitarist Grant Green, or saxophonist John Coltrane's 1963 tune "Alabama," which was meant to be a musical commentary on Martin Luther King's bloody Birmingham campaign of that year.

To be sure, a great number of political issues and concerns are implicit in American popular music, sometimes reflecting the politics of the people who created it, but much of it reflects the beliefs and anxieties of the general public or the political strains in the culture. Frequently, American political leaders have used popular music at political rallies, such as Harry Truman using "I'm Just Wild about Harry" when he ran for the presidency in 1948. (Whether Truman knew the song was written by black songwriters Noble Sissle and Eubie Blake is interesting to consider, but it hardly mattered in the way that he used the song because it was not intended to convey any political message other than the positive, rousing use of his name.)

Frequently, however, politicians use popular music to promote cultural and political values and not merely to wind up a crowd at a political rally. For instance, in the 2008 presidential race, Alaska governor Sarah Palin, only the second woman to run on a major party ticket, often used Shania Twain's "She's Not Just Another Pretty Face" to end her rallies, which underscored not only the governor's good looks but also acknowledged her nod to feminism as she wished to be judged as a capable politician. The song attacks sexism while slyly evoking it. Its popularity with working-class whites was also intended to stress the governor's populist aspirations. Many politicians look for a popular song to do just this sort of symbolic work for them when they are running for office.

Race and Censorship

Two particular areas in which politics has had an impact on American popular music are race and censorship. American popular music has been sold by race since the days of minstrelsy; that is, in the United States, there is "black" music and "white" music, and each presumably bears the racial traits of its creators. Blacks were good for rhythm and sensual music; whites were better at harmony and more cerebral music. In the twentieth century, music composed and performed by black artists became a distinct commerical category known as "race music" or "race records," a classification eventually replaced by rhythm and blues, then soul music, and finally black music.

Black music is perhaps easier to recognize than to define. But many African Americans themselves have never been fully comfortable with what they felt to be the exploitation of ethnic content of their music, often wishing to self-consciously reethnicize it (as in the case of soul music or "gangsta" rap), so that whites could not copy it; or blatantly politicize it (as in the case of songs by a host of artists including Curtis Mayfield, Public Enemy, Gil Scot-Heron, and Nina Simone), as something suitable only for a black artist performing before a black audience. Historically, the designation of black music not only characterized and categorized but also stigmatized this music culturally, artistically, and politically.

For much of the twentieth century, black musicians were not permitted to perform "white" music or any nonexplicit racial music. For instance, it was thought that blacks were not culturally or temperamentally suited to compose for strings, to play classical music, or to write or perform "art" music generally. They were denied both jobs and creative outlets (from film scoring to chairs in symphony orchestras), and also were paid less for doing the same work as white musicians. In the racialization of popular music, blacks were not permitted to play "nonblack" music, by and large, because it was thought they could not; on the other hand, whites were thought to be insufficiently intuitive to be able to play black music. "Crossing over" was fraught with all sorts of anxiety: many African Americans have never liked the George and Ira Gershwin/Dubose Heyward opera *Porgy and Bess* (1935)—the most important operatic work written for black performers and probably the most famous opera produced by an American—in part because it was written by whites; and many see such artists as Benny Goodman, called the "King of Swing," and Elvis Presley, the king of rock and roll, as imitators and thieves who profited by stealing black musical idioms and performing them for a larger white audience. Until the 1960s, whites controlled all aspects of the music business: the performance venues, the press and critical apparatus, the record companies, the music publishing houses, and the unions. Some African Americans also have been suspicious of certain black musicians who have had great appeal to white audiences, like rock guitarist Jimi Hendrix and jazzman Louis Armstrong or even less seminal artists like Johnny Mathis, Tracy Chapman, and Richie Havens. Even the black-owned record company Motown went through a period in the late 1960s when many blacks thought the company, led by the great crossover group, the Supremes, made music that sounded "too white."

Popular music has always been subjected to censorship on grounds as diverse as sexual indecency, poor quality (thus, fostering bad taste), moral corruption, and excessive racial or ethnic content (therefore Africanizing or "niggerizing" the culture). Ragtime and especially jazz were condemned on these grounds by the white musical establishment, the white conservative Christians, and black bourgeoisie and black religious groups, who believed either that popular black dance music was low-class, bred crime, and failed to uplift the race or that it was the devil's music and celebrated sin. These factions, with varying amounts of energy, sought to suppress these forms of music by discouraging the young from listening to them and banning their sale or performance when they could.

Such efforts intensified after World War II with the rise of rock and roll, which many thought to be an even more virulent musical disease than jazz or ragtime. Censorship efforts included the banning of rock and roll on certain radio stations, the destruction of rock and roll records in mass demonstrations, and attempts to water down the more explosive or less seemly elements of the music through more traditional arrangements sung by "respectable" performers. In the mid-1980s the Parents Music Resource Center, led by wives of prominent politicians, instigated congressional hearings on the subject of heavy metal and rap song lyrics that it considered obscene. Some critics saw similarities between this effort and the comic book scare of the early 1950s: in both instances, the industries under attack chose to regulate their content through labeling rather than engage in a fight over First Amendment rights. Some blacks thought this was simply another way for the white establishment to attack the "immorality" of black music, although, to be sure, many blacks were made uneasy by the explicit lyrics of many rap songs. Music companies agreed to put warning labels on recordings with song lyrics that contained obscene or pornographic language or violent imagery.

Politics and popular music is a complex subject, for so much beyond the will or inclination of the artist determines what music will be popular in any commercial or aesthetic way: where and how the music is recorded; what instruments are used and the musical abilities of the performers; how the music is distributed, marketed, and sold (the Internet has greatly affected this in recent years); how listeners choose to listen to the music; how successfully the music accommodates some visual representation of itself (music videos have become essential for nearly all popular music in the last 30 years); and how the music is reviewed and criticized. The incredible complexity of the role popular music plays in American life is contradictory enough to ensure that the politics popular music both evokes and is subjected to will always be difficult to measure.

FURTHER READING

Barzun, Jacques. *Music in American Life*. Garden City, NY: Doubleday, 1956.

Gioia, Ted. *The History of Jazz*. New York: Oxford University Press, 1998.

Nicholls, David, ed. *The Cambridge History of American Music*. New York: Cambridge University Press, 2004.

Nuzum, Eric. *Parental Advisory: Music Censorship in America*. New York: HarperCollins, 2001.

Starr, Larry. *American Popular Music: From Minstrelsy to MP3*. New York: Oxford University Press, 2007.

GERALD EARLY

populism

Populism has long been among the more fiercely contested yet promiscuously applied terms in the American political lexicon. It was coined by a Kansas journalist in 1890 as an adjectival form of the People's Party, a radical third party organized in Kansas that blossomed into a national force in 1892. But in the lower case, *populist* soon became a common description for any rebellious movement of ordinary, working Americans. In recent decades journalists have affixed the term *populist* to persons and commodities that seem authentic, unadorned, and to have sprung from common sources. At times, this has included everything from plain-speaking politicians to bargain bookstores, from Bruce Springsteen's recordings to cotton trousers, which, according to their manufacturer, are "steeped in grassroots sensibility and the simple good sense of solid workmanship."

To cut through the confusion, one should define two kinds of populism—first, the historical movement itself; and second, the broader political critique and discourse. But a populism untethered to overtly political concerns is too vague and ubiquitous in American history to be useful as an interpretive category.

The Populist movement arose in the latter third of the nineteenth century, the period historians have traditionally called the Gilded Age. This was a time of rapid industrial and agricultural growth punctuated by sharp economic depressions. Absent state relief measures, increasing numbers of farmers were caught in a spiral of debt and many urban wage earners and their families were left hungry and homeless.

Populism was an insurgency largely made up of small farmers and skilled workers. It was strongest in the cotton states of the Deep South, the wheat-growing states of the Great Plains, and the mining states of the Rocky Mountains. The movement's concerns were primarily economic: during a time of low commodity prices, small agrarian proprietors demanded equal treatment in a marketplace increasingly dominated by industrial corporations, banks, and large landowners. They formed local and state Farmers' Alliances. Craft workers who resisted a cut in their wages and attacks on their trade unions believed that they shared a common set of enemies.

Populist activists proposed a variety of solutions—including nationalization of the railroads, a cooperative marketing system, a progressive income tax, and an end to court injunctions that hampered the growth of strong unions. But when a severe depression began in 1893, Populists focused on the need to inflate the money supply by basing the currency on silver reserves as well as the less plentiful reserves of gold, in hopes of spurring investment and rescuing small producers from an avalanche of debt. Most Populists were white evangelical Protestants who tended to favor prohibition and woman suffrage, "moral" issues that drew a good deal of controversy at the time.

In 1892, thousands of movement activists met to organize a national People's Party. At founding conventions held in St. Louis and Omaha, the great orator Ignatius Donnelly proclaimed, "We meet in the midst of a nation brought to the verge of moral, political, and material ruin. . . . A vast conspiracy against mankind has been organized on two continents and is rapidly taking possession of the world." The Populists, he promised, would bring the nation back to its presumably democratic roots. "We seek to restore the Government of the Republic to the hands of the 'plain people' with whom it originated," he concluded.

This vision was notably silent about racial divisions among the "plain people"; equality was more preached than practiced in the Populist movement. During the late 1880s, Colored Farmers' Alliances had sprung up in several states, and an umbrella group of the same name—led by a white Baptist minister—emerged at the end of the decade. But the Colored Alliance collapsed in 1891 when some of its members, who didn't own land, went on strike against their employers, many of whom were members of the white Farmers' Alliance. White Populists were no more hostile to black citizens than were most other white political actors at the time. In fact, such movement leaders as Thomas Watson of Georgia defended the right of black citizens to vote, in the face of violence by white Democrats in the South. But few white Populists from any region endorsed social integration or questioned the virtues of a past in which most African Americans had been held in bondage.

From its founding until 1896, the People's Party drew a sizable minority of the ballots in a swath of rural states stretching from North Carolina west to Texas and Kansas and north into Colorado and Idaho. In 1892 James Weaver, the party's first presidential nominee, won over a million votes, which translated to 8.5 percent of the popular vote and 22 electoral votes. During the 1890s, hundreds of Populists were elected to local and state offices, and the party boasted 50 members of Congress, some of whom ran on fusion tickets. These results emboldened insurgents and alarmed conservatives in both major parties.

In 1896 the Democrats emerged from a fierce internal battle with a presidential nominee from Nebraska, William Jennings Bryan, who had worked closely with Populists in his own state and was a well-known champion of the third party's demand to remonetize silver. The People's Party then met in its own convention and, after a bitter debate, voted to endorse Bryan. When he was defeated that fall, the party and the movement it led declined into the status of a sect. The party ran its own candidates for president and vice president in 1900, 1904, and 1908, and then disbanded. Only in 1904 did its ticket—led by Thomas Watson of Georgia—draw more than 100,000 votes.

But half a century after their demise, the Populists became the subject of a ferocious, dualistic debate among some of America's most prominent historians and social scientists. From the early 1950s through the 1970s, such scholars as Oscar Handlin, Richard Hofstadter, C. Vann Woodward, Daniel Bell, and Lawrence Goodwyn disputed whether populism was conservative, defensive, and bigoted or the last, best chance for a true smallholders' democracy. One side marshaled quotes from Populists that reeked of anti-Semitism, bucolic nostalgia, and conspiracy theorizing; the other stressed that the insurgents of the 1890s tried to remedy real grievances of workers and farmers and had specific, thoughtful ideas for reforming the system.

As a critique, however, populism predated the movement and survived it, with important alterations. Central to the original critique was an antagonism between a large majority of *producers* and a tiny elite of *parasites*. Such oppositional terms were used by the Country Party in eighteenth-century Britain and became powerful markers in American politics during the early nineteenth century. The producers were viewed as the creators of wealth and the purveyors of vital services; their ranks included manual workers, small farmers, small shopkeepers, and professionals who served such people. This mode of populism offered a vigorous attack on class inequality but one that denied such inequality had any structural causes. Populists have insisted that social hierarchies are artificial impositions of elites and doomed to vanish with a sustained insurgency of the plain people.

Populism represents the antimonopolistic impulse in American history. Populists are generally hostile to large, centralized institutions that stand above and outside communities of moral producers. They have a romantic attachment to local power bases, family farms, country churches, and citizen associations independent of ties to governments and corporations. The populist critique also includes an explicit embrace of "Americanism" that is both idealistic and defensive. In the United States, which most Populists consider a chosen nation, all citizens deserve the same chance to improve their lot, but they must be constantly on guard against aristocrats, empire builders, and totalitarians both within and outside their borders who would subvert American ideals.

The populist critique is usually most popular among the same social groups who originated it during the late nineteenth century: farmers and wage earners who believe the economy is rigged against them. For example, in the 1930s, amid the first major depression since the Populist era, Huey Long and Father Charles Coughlin gained millions of followers among desperate white workers, farmers, and small proprietors by denouncing "international bankers" and calling for a radical redistribution of wealth.

But populist discourse has often floated free of such social moorings. Anyone who believes, or pretends to believe, that democratic invective can topple a haughty foe and that the judgment of hardworking, God-fearing people is always correct can claim legitimacy in the great name of "the People." Thus, in the era of World War I, socialists on the Great Plains remade themselves into champions of the same small farmers they had earlier viewed as anachronisms in an age of corporate capitalism. The organization they founded, the Nonpartisan League, captured the government of North Dakota and came close to winning elections in several other neighboring states. During the 1930s and 1940s, industrial union organizers, including thousands of members of the Communist Party, portrayed themselves as latter-day Patrick Henrys battling such "Tory parasites" as Henry Ford and Tom Girdler, the antiunion head of Republic Steel.

From the 1940s through the 1980s, American conservatives effectively turned the rhetoric of populism to their own ends. During the "Red Scare" following World War II, they accused well-born figures in the federal government, such as Alger Hiss and Dean Acheson, of aiding the Soviet Union. In the 1950s and 1960s, the Right's populist offensive shifted to the local level, where white homeowners in such cities as Detroit and Chicago accused wealthy, powerful liberals of forcing them to accept integrated neighborhoods and classrooms—with no intention themselves of living in such areas or sending their children to such schools. In four presidential campaigns from 1964 to 1976, George Wallace articulated this message when he championed "this average man on the street . . . this man in the steel mill . . . the beautician, the policeman on the beat."

By the time Ronald Reagan was elected and reelected president in the 1980s, the discourse of populism had completed a voyage from Left to Right, although community and union organizers on the left continued to claim they were its rightful inheritors. "Producers" were now widely understood to be churchgoing, home-owning taxpayers with middling incomes; "parasites" were government officials who took revenues from diligent citizens and lavished them on avant-garde artists, welfare mothers, and foreigners who often acted to thwart American interests.

During the 1990s and the first decade of the twenty-first century, fear of the globalized economy spurred a new round of populist discourse. First, activists on both the labor left and the protectionist right accused multinational corporations and international bodies such as the World Bank and the International Monetary Fund of impoverishing American workers. Then the collapse of the financial system in 2008 revived anger at "Wall Street" for betraying the public's trust and driving "Main

Street" into bankruptcy. Economic populists continued to have the power to sting their enemies and, perhaps, stir a desire for social change.

See also agrarian politics; labor and politics.

FURTHER READING

Argersinger, Peter. *The Limits of Agrarian Radicalism: Western Populism and American Politics*. Lawrence: University Press of Kansas, 1995.

Ayres, Edward L. *The Promise of the New South: Life after Reconstruction*. New York: Oxford University Press, 1992.

Brinkley, Alan. *Voices of Protest: Huey Long, Father Coughlin, and the Great Depression*. New York: Knopf, 1982.

Carter, Dan T. *The Politics of Rage: George Wallace, the Origins of the New Conservatism, and the Transformation of American Politics*. New York: Simon and Schuster, 1995.

Goodwyn, Lawrence. *Democratic Promise: The Populist Moment in America*. New York: Oxford University Press, 1976.

Hicks, John. *The Populist Revolt: A History of the Farmers' Alliance and the People's Party*. Minneapolis: University of Minnesota Press, 1931.

Kazin, Michael. *The Populist Persuasion: An American History*. Rev. ed. Ithaca, NY: Cornell University Press, 1998.

McMath, Robert. *American Populism: A Social History*. New York: Hill and Wang, 1994.

Ostler, Jeffrey. *Prairie Populism: The Fate of Agrarian Radicalism in Kansas, Nebraska, and Iowa, 1880–1892*. Lawrence: University Press of Kansas, 1993.

Woodward, C. Vann. *Tom Watson, Agrarian Rebel*. New York: Macmillan, 1938.

MICHAEL KAZIN

presidency, the

The establishment of a national executive empowered to act independently of the legislature was one of the Constitutional Convention's most consequential, and disquieting, innovations. The Revolution had targeted executive power as a threat, and both the states and the national government had kept it weak and subordinate. The supremacy of the representative assembly was a principle widely viewed as emblematic of the new republican experiment. The Constitution, however, rejected that principle. By creating a presidency equal in standing to the national Congress and by fortifying the new national executive with unity, energy, and institutional security, the framers pushed to the fore a very different conception of self-government.

In one sense, this innovation marked a clear retreat from the radical thrust of the Revolution. It is hard to miss the model of kingship behind the singular figure that the Constitution vests with "the executive power." The president commands armies, suppresses insurrections, receives foreign emissaries, and pardons almost at will. The office stands watch over the legislature, its veto power potent enough both to protect its own independence and to check the programmatic impulses of simple majorities. This was, for all appearances, a conservative position designed to preserve order, manage affairs, and bring a measure of self-control to the government as a whole.

In another sense, however, the American executive drew upon and extended the principles of the Revolution. The presidency stands apart from the Congress but not from the people. As the decision to vest executive power in a single person focused responsibility for the high affairs of state, the selection procedure ensured that individual's regular accountability to a national electorate. Provisions for a fixed term and a separate national election established the presidency as the equal of the Congress, not only in the powers at its disposal but also in its popular foundations. Overall, the construction of separate institutions each balanced against the others and each accountable to the same people underscored the sovereignty of the people themselves over any and all institutional expressions of their will.

How, and with what effect, this new arrangement of powers would work was far from clear. The few broad strokes with which Article II of the Constitution constructed the presidential office are indicative of the delicate political circumstances of its creation and of the strategic value of keeping its implications ambiguous. There is no counterpart in Article II to the crisply punctuated list of powers expressly vested in the Congress by Article I, section VIII. By the same token, the more implicit and open-ended character of the powers of the presidency gave freer reign to interpretation and the exigencies of the moment. It imparted to the office an elastic quality that incumbents were invited to exploit by their own wits.

A few issues became apparent early on. One was that the scope of presidential power would be fiercely contested. The administration of George Washington ventured bold initiatives in foreign policy, domestic policy, and law enforcement, and it backed them up with strong assertions of presidential prerogative. But each brief issued on behalf of the power and independence of the executive office provoked a strong reaction, and together they became a rallying cry for opposition. No less clear was the portentous character of the transfer of power from one president to another. John Adams's initial decision to retain Washington's cabinet aimed to assure stability and continuity in government operations across administrations, but it could not be sustained without severely handicapping the president in his efforts to exercise the powers of his office on his own terms. As Adams ultimately discovered, a president cannot maintain control of his own office if he does not first secure control over the other offices of the executive branch. The election of a new president would thenceforth bring in its train the formation of a new administration, with all that it implied for the disruption of established governing arrangements and the perturbation of governing coalitions.

Behind these early revelations loomed another: that presidential elections and presidential administrations would orient American national politics at large. Providing a focal point of responsibility for the state of the nation, the president spurred political mobilization, the articulation of national issues, and the reconfiguration of political cleavages. Ironically, an office designed with an eye to bringing order and stability to national affairs became a magnet for popular controversies and an engine of change.

Institutional Development

Most of what we know of the presidency today is a product of latter-day embellishments. Two historical processes, in particular, figure prominently in its development: the democratization of the polity and the nationalization of the affairs of state.

The democratization of the polity was first expressed institutionally in the form of party development, and this gave rise in the nineteenth century to a party-based presidency. The emergence of two national parties in the 1790s distilled rival interests across great geographical distances and coordinated their actions for presidential elections. The Twelfth Amendment, ratified in 1804, formally separated the election of president and vice president and thus facilitated the formation of a national party ticket. The emergence of nominating conventions in the 1830s brought state party organizations together for the purposes of articulating a common platform and selecting candidates for the national ticket that would rally coalition interests.

Through innovations such as these, the presidency was connected organizationally to local bases of political support and integrated into national politics. Parties eased constitutional divisions of power by providing a base of common action among like-minded partisans in the presidency and the Congress. Just as importantly, the president lent support to his party base by distributing the offices at his disposal in the executive branch to its constituent parts at the local level. The spoils system, which rotated executive offices with each transfer of power and filled them with partisan supporters of the new incumbent, complemented the convention system. As the convention tied the president to local party organizations, the spoils tied local party organizations to the president. Each side had powerful incentives to support the other, and the tenacious community of interests that was formed helped to hold America's contentious democracy together as it sprawled across a continent.

The presidency was recast again over the early decades of the twentieth century. The growing interdependence of interests in industrial America and the heightened stakes of world affairs for national security rendered the prior integration of presidency into a locally based party politics increasingly anachronistic. Progressive reformers sought to break down the community of interest that had animated the party presidency and to construct in its place powerful national bureaucracies capable of managing the new problems posed by industrialization and world power. At the same time, presidents asserted leadership more directly. They began to take their case to the people. The hope was that by rallying public opinion behind their policy proposals, they would catalyze concerted action across the dispersed and divided institutions of the Washington establishment.

With presidents and national bureaucracies assuming a more prominent role in governing, the office of the presidency itself was refortified. The passage of the Executive Reorganization Act in 1939 and the establishment of the Executive Office of the President (EOP) gave incumbents new resources for managing the affairs of state. Agencies of the EOP such as the Bureau of the Budget (later the Office of Management and Budget), the Council of Economic Advisors, and the National Security Council were designed by Congress with two concerns in mind: to help the president tackle national problems holistically and to assure Congress that the president's recommendations for national action were based on the candid advice of trained professionals and policy experts.

In recent decades, institutional developments have supported greater claims on behalf of independent presidential action. In the 1970s primary elections displaced national party conventions as the chief mechanism for candidate selection. This has encouraged candidates for the office to build national political organizations of their own. A personal political organization is then carried over by the party nominee into the general election, and it is transferred again by the successful candidate into the offices of the White House. One effect has been to weaken the mutual control mechanisms of the old party-based presidency. Another has been the downgrading of the statutory agencies in the EOP, which progressive reformers had relied upon to institutionalize neutral advice, interbranch coordination, and information sharing. The locus of presidential power has shifted into the inner sanctums of the White House itself, where the incumbent's personal control is least likely to be contested and where the strategic orientation revolves almost exclusively around the president's own political priorities. The reforms of earlier generations, which relied on extraconstitutional devices to ease the separation of powers and integrate the presidency into the rest of the government, are giving way to new assertions on behalf of the unitary executive—assertions that accentuate the separation of powers, expand the legitimate domain of unilateral action, and delimit the reach of checks and balances.

Institutional Power and Political Authority

Though reformers may have believed that bolstering the institution of the presidency would make for more effective political leadership, the connection between institutional development and political performance remains weak. More resources have not ensured more effective leadership; great performances dot the presidential history in a seemingly random fashion. This has led many observers to stress the importance of character, personality, and skill in the exercise of presidential power, and appropriately so: as the purview of American national government has expanded and the office of the presidency has grown more resourceful, incumbent competence has been placed at a premium.

Still, it is hard to discern any coherent set of personal attributes that distinguishes politically effective leaders from politically ineffective ones. Franklin Roosevelt and Lyndon Johnson both possessed extraordinary political skills. But while one reconstructed the standards of legitimate national action, the other self-destructed. Andrew Jackson and Andrew Johnson were rigid, vindictive, and divisive leaders. But one succeeded in crushing his opponents while the other was crushed by them. A long look back over this history suggests that the variable political effectiveness of presidential leadership is less a matter of the personal attributes of the incumbent than of the political contexts in which he is called upon to act.

One of the more striking patterns to be observed in presidential history is that the leaders who stand out both for their political mastery in office and their reconstructive political effects were immediately preceded by leaders who are widely derided as politically inept and out of their depth: John Adams and Thomas Jefferson, John Quincy Adams and Andrew Jackson, James Buchanan and Abraham Lincoln, Herbert Hoover and Franklin Roosevelt, Jimmy Carter and Ronald Reagan. In each historical pairing, we first find a president whose actions in office seemed self-defeating and whose chief political effect was to foment a nationwide crisis of legitimacy; next we find a president whose actions in office proved elevating and whose chief effect was to reset the terms and conditions of legitimate national government. On further inspection, it will be observed that the first president in each pair led to power a governing coalition whose commitments were well established but increasingly vulnerable to identification as the very source of the nation's problems. The second president in each pair led to power an untested political insurgency. Each used his powers to define the basic commitments of that insurgency and secure them in a new governing coalition. Difficult as it is to distill a shared set of personal attributes that clearly distinguishes the incumbents on one side of these pairings from those on the other, the common political circumstances faced on each side are unmistakable.

This pattern points back to fundamental attributes of the presidential office, qualities that have held sway despite the dramatic developments to be observed over time in the accoutrements of institutional power. The most telling of these is the one first revealed in the transfer of power from George Washington to John Adams: the inherently disruptive political impact of the election of a new president and installation of a new administration. In one way or another, new presidents shake things up. The constitutionally ingrained independence of the office, the provision for separate elections at regular intervals to fixed terms, the institutional imperative that each new incumbent assert control over the office in his own right—all this has made the presidency a persistent engine of change in the American political system. It is precisely because all presidents change things in one way or another that the power to change things has been less of an issue in the politics of leadership than the authority that can be found in the moment at hand for actions taken and changes instigated. Unlike institutional power, which has developed in stages over the long course of American history, authority of this sort can shift dramatically from one president to the next.

It is not surprising that incumbents affiliated with established interests have a harder time sustaining authority for their actions than do incumbents who come to power from the opposition. The opposition stance plays to the institutional independence of the presidential office and supports its inherently disruptive political effects; affiliation compromises independence and complicates the meaning of the changes instigated. This difference is magnified when, as in the case of our starkly contrasting historical pairs, the political commitments of the dominant governing coalition are being called into question by events on the ground. Affiliated leaders like the Adamses, Buchanan, Hoover, and Carter could neither forthrightly affirm nor forthrightly repudiate the political interests to which they were attached. Actions that reached out to political allies served to cast the president as a symptom of the nation's growing problems while actions that charted a more independent course tended to alienate the president from his base of political support. Lacking the political authority to secure firm ground for their actions, these presidents found themselves in an impossible leadership situation. In turn, Jefferson, Jackson, Lincoln, Franklin Roosevelt, and Reagan drew great advantages from the political disaffection created by the hapless struggles of their predecessors. Leading to power an insurgency defined largely by its forthright repudiation of an old establishment, they were able to rearticulate first principles, to sustain freedom of action across a broad front, and, ultimately, to locate a common ground of new commitments that their supporters would find authoritative.

Historically, the weaker the political ties binding presidents to established standards of action, the stronger the president has been in tapping the independence of his office and delivering on its promise of a new beginning. How, then, will recent developments in the institution of the presidency come to bear on this general rule? On the one hand, we might expect that as all presidents become more independent in the resources at their disposal, any limitations imposed by the political affiliations they bring into office will diminish. On the other hand, as these new resources become more self-contained and detached from those of other institutional actors, we may also discover new limits on the presidency's capacity to play its vital historical role in the renewal and reinvigoration of the American polity as whole. In the past, the presidents who effectively reconstructed the terms and conditions of legitimate national government did not just break old bonds; they also forged new ties that knit the system back together. Whether a reintegration of that sort remains possible is an open question.

See also cabinet departments; Constitution, federal.

FURTHER READING

Arnold, Peri E. *Making the Managerial Presidency: Comprehensive Reorganization Planning, 1905–1996*. Lawrence: University Press of Kansas, 1998.

Calabresi, Steven G. "Some Normative Arguments for the Unitary Executive." *Arkansas Law Review* 48 (1995), 23–104.

Ceaser, James W. *Presidential Selection: Theory and Development*. Princeton, NJ: Princeton University Press, 1979.

Howell, William G. *Power without Persuasion: The Politics of Direct Presidential Action*. Princeton, NJ: Princeton University Press, 2003.

Mansfield, Harvey C. *Taming the Prince: The Ambivalence of Modern Executive Power*. New York: Free Press, 1989.

Milkis, Sidney M. *The President and the Parties: The Transformation of the American Party System since the New Deal*. New York: Oxford University Press, 1993.

Moe, Terry M. "The Politicized Presidency." In *The New Direction in American Politics*, edited by John E. Chubb and Paul E. Peterson, 235–71. Washington, DC: Brookings Institution, 1985.

Neustadt, Richard E. *Presidential Power and the Modern Presidents: The Politics of Leadership from Roosevelt to Reagan*. New York: Free Press, 1991.

Schlesinger, Arthur M., Jr. *The Imperial Presidency*. Boston: Houghton Mifflin, 1973.

Skowronek, Stephen. *The Politics Presidents Make: Leadership from John Adams to Bill Clinton*. Cambridge, MA: Belknap Press of Harvard University Press, 1997.

Thach, Charles C. *The Creation of the Presidency, 1775–1789: A Study in Constitutional History*. Baltimore, MD: Johns Hopkins University Press, 1922.

Tulis, Jeffrey K. *The Rhetorical Presidency*. Princeton, NJ: Princeton University Press.

STEPHEN SKOWRONEK

presidency to 1860

The seventeenth and eighteenth centuries marked the transition from a powerful to a tamed executive branch of government, first in Great Britain and then in the United States. In the 1600s, England began the long, slow, and often violent process of wresting power away from the king and placing authority in the hands of the Parliament. This transition led to both the democratization of the polity and the control of executive power. The American Revolution of 1776 furthered this process by placing the executive branch within the constraints of a constitution (1787), a separation-of-powers system, the rule of law, and checks and balances. While the French Revolution that followed (1789) unleashed the best and the worst of democratic sentiments, it was to serve as a warning against unchecked power in the hands of the masses. The American Revolution occurred in the middle of these transitions and drew lessons from both the British and the French. From the British, Americans were convinced that the divine right of kings and executive tyranny had to give way to a controlled executive, and from the French experience, they learned that unleashing democracy without the rule of law and checks and balances could lead to a different but also quite dangerous form of tyranny.

The American experiment in empowering as well as controlling executive powers within a web of constitutional and political constraints led to the creation of a rather limited presidency. Yet over time, this executive branch would grow and expand in power and responsibility; both necessity and opportunity would allow for the growth of presidential power.

The Rise of the Presidency

As the United States became a world power, it also became more of a presidential nation. In the early years of the republic, however, with few international responsibilities and fewer foreign entanglements, the presidency would be a rather small institution, with limited powers, whose holders would struggle to establish a place of power within the new system of government.

Of the framers' handiwork at the Constitutional Convention, the presidency was the least formed and defined of the three governing institutions. Thus, while the office may have been invented by the framers, it was brought to life by George Washington and his successors.

The framers were concerned that this new president not become a tyrant or monarch. Having fought a revolution against the hereditary monarchy of Great Britain, they wanted to create an executive branch that, as its name implies, would preside, enact laws passed by the Congress, manage the government's business, and be but one element of a three-part government. Designed to promote deliberation and not efficiency, this new government would not have an all-powerful figure at its head. But could such a government work in practice?

The Presidency in Practice

George Washington, the towering figure of his era, was, as first president (1789–97), a precedent setter. He was a man who could have been king, yet chose to be president. At the time of his inauguration, the American experiment was just that—an experiment; thus, everything that Washington did mattered. As he noted at the time, "I walk on untrodden ground." Whatever Washington did would have an impact on what was to follow. One of the reasons the Constitutional Convention was willing to leave Article II, which created a presidency, somewhat vague and ill-defined was that the delegates knew Washington would occupy the office first, and they so trusted his republican sensibilities that they allowed him to set the tone for what the presidency would become.

Washington's goal was to put the new office on a secure footing, create conditions in which a republican executive could govern, give the office some independence, and establish the legitimacy of the new republic. This was no small order. He attempted to be a national unifier at a time when divisions were forming in the new nation. His major effort toward this goal was to bring Alexander Hamilton and Thomas Jefferson, two bitter personal and ideological rivals, together in his first cabinet. This worthy goal would fail, however, and the clash between these two rivals was instrumental in forming the nation's first political parties.

Washington exercised independent authority over treaty making, declared neutrality in the war between France and England, and asserted independence from Congress in managerial matters within the executive branch. For Washington, the president was not to be a messenger boy for Congress but instead an independent officer with powers and prerogatives. But if Washington set precedents for the ill-defined office, could he trust his successors to exercise such ambiguous authority with honor and dignity? The ambiguity that allowed him to invent an office could also potentially be used by less skilled men, with less character, to less benign ends.

John Adams followed Washington into the presidency (1797–1801), and his term in office was marked by internecine warfare between the president and members of his own Federalist Party. Adams's disappointing presidency led to the shift in power from the Federalists to the Jeffersonians in the hotly contested election of 1800.

Party Leadership and Prerogative

The next president to add markedly to the powers of the office was Thomas Jefferson (1801–9), who set an important precedent in that his inauguration marked the first of what would be many peaceful transfers of power from one party to another. Jefferson wanted to deceremonialize the presidency and make it a more republican institution. He did away with bowing, replacing the regal custom with the more democratic handshake; he abolished the weekly levee (a reception); ended formal state dinners; and abandoned the custom of making personal addresses to Congress. Jefferson also used the cabinet as an instrument of presidential leadership and exerted control over Congress by exploiting opportunities for party leadership.

When the opportunity to purchase the Louisiana Territory from France presented itself, Jefferson believed that he did not have the authority to act and had his cabinet draw up a constitutional amendment to give him such authority. But time was short, and an amendment might take months, if not years, to pass. Jefferson was confronted with a stark choice: act on his own questionable authority or lose one of the great opportunities for promoting the nation's security and expanding its borders. Jefferson acted. It was one of the most important, if constitutionally questionable, acts in presidential history.

Perhaps Jefferson's greatest contribution to presidential leadership was his linking of that which the framers separated: the president and Congress. Jefferson exercised a form of hidden-handed legislative leadership by inviting important members of his party in Congress to the White House for dinners, after which he would chart out a legislative strategy and agenda for his fellow party members to push through Congress. It was an effective tool of leadership and one that subsequent presidents exercised with mixed success.

The next three presidents faced something of a congressional backlash. James Madison (1809–17), James Monroe (1817–25), and John Quincy Adams (1825–29) had mixed success as presidents. The one key to the rise of presidential power in this era occurred during the Monroe administration, when, seeing European powers eyeing territories in the Americas, the president announced the Monroe Doctrine, a warning to European states to abandon imperial ambitions in the Americas. Monroe issued this declaration on his own authority, and it helped increase the foreign policy powers of the presidency.

The President and the Rise of Democracy

The next president, Andrew Jackson (1829–37), was one of the most cantankerous and powerful men ever to occupy the White House, and he became president at a time of great social change in America. By the 1820s, most states no longer required men to own property in order to vote, and nearly comprehensive white male suffrage had arrived. Jackson recognized the potential implications of this momentous change and exploited it to his advantage. He claimed that, as the only truly nationally elected political leader in the nation, he was elected to speak for the people. By making the president the voice of the people, and linking presidential power to democracy, Jackson greatly added to the potential power of the office. Merging the presidency with mass democracy, Jackson used what he saw as his mandate to lead (some might say bully) the Congress. Such a link between the people and the president was something the framers feared, believing that this could lead a president to manipulate public opinion and emerge as a demagogue, destroying the possibility of true statesmanship and deliberative government.

The Rise of Congress

After Jackson, a series of weaker presidents followed, and Congress reasserted its constitutional prerogatives. This became a pattern in American history: a strong president, followed by congressional reassertion, followed by a strong president, a backlash, and again strong congressional leadership. The three presidents after Jackson—Martin Van Buren (1837–41); William Henry Harrison (1841), who died after a month in office; and John Tyler (1841–45), the first vice president to assume office on the death of a president)—faced strong congressional leadership and were limited in what they could achieve.

James Polk (1845–49), however, changed that pattern. He demonstrated that a determined president could, in effect, start a war (the Mexican-American War). Polk was able to manipulate events along the Texas-Mexican border coaxing the Mexican force to attack, and by initiating aggressive action, preempt the Congress and force it to follow his lead. This initiative was yet another tool of presidential leadership added to the arsenal of presidential power.

Several weaker presidents followed Polk, as the nation became swept up in sectional rivalry and the issue of slavery. Rather than presidential government, this was an era of congressional dominance. Presidents Zachary Taylor (1849–50), Millard Fillmore (1850–53), Franklin Pierce (1853–57), and James Buchanan (1857–61) were weak presidents in a difficult age.

The Impact of War on the Presidency

James Buchanan is an especially interesting case in presidential weakness. Sectional difficulties were heating up, and the slavery issue was causing deep divisions between the North and the South. Many southern states were threatening nullification, if not outright secession, from the Union. Despite the grave threat to the nation's future, Buchanan did not believe he had the constitutional authority to prevent the southern states from seceding, and his self-imposed restraint meant that the rebellious states would meet little resistance. Buchanan saw slavery as a moral evil, but he conceded to the South a constitutional right to allow slavery to exist. He tried, but failed, to chart a middle course. Although a strong unionist, Buchanan's limited conception of presidential power prevented him from taking the steps necessary to stem the breakup of the nation.

Buchanan was a strict constitutional constructionist; he believed the president was authorized to take only those actions clearly spelled out in the Constitution. This conception of the office severely limited Buchanan's efforts to stem the tide of secession. In his last message to the Congress, delivered on December 3, 1860, Buchanan stated, "Apart from the execution of the laws, so far as this may be practical, the Executive has no authority to decide what shall be the relations between the Federal Government and South Carolina. . . ." Less than three weeks later, South Carolina seceded from the Union.

Buchanan left his successor, Abraham Lincoln, a seemingly unsolvable crisis. He told the incoming president, "If you are as happy, Mr Lincoln, on entering this house as I am in leaving it and returning home, you are the happiest man in this country." Lincoln, however, was animated by the challenge. His presidency (1861–65) would reinvent the office and take its power to new heights.

The Evolution of the Presidency

The presidency was invented at the end of the era of the aristocracy, yet before the era of democracy had fully arrived. The framers of the U.S. Constitution created a republican form of government with limited powers, under the rule of law, within a constitutional framework, with a separation of powers system. From 1789 to 1860 the presidency they invented proved viable, resilient, and—at times—quite effective. The evolution of the presidency from idea to reality, from blank slate to robust office, resulted in the creation of a new office that achieved stability and independence. This experiment in governing was built on and grounded in the Constitution, but that document was only its starting point. In reality, the presidency was formed less by the Constitution and more by the tug-of-war over power between the president and Congress as politics played out over the first 70 years of the republic. In this sense, the presidency was created in practice more that at the drafting table.

The presidency before 1860 did not need to be large, powerful, or imperial. The United States was a relatively small nation, somewhat geographically isolated from the troubles of Europe, with few entangling alliances and no position of world leadership. As a secondary world power, the United States did not have to flex its military muscle or make its presence known across the globe. This allowed the presidency to develop free from the pressures of global responsibilities.

Likewise, the domestic demands placed on the federal government were more limited in this period than they are today. The federal government did less, and less was expected of it. The media was localized and, prior to the advent of radio (and then television and the Internet), tools of communication were limited. But, although the presidency was "small" as an institution, the seeds were planted in this era for the rise and growth of presidential power that was to follow. That growth would await the advent of the twentieth century, and the rise of the United States as a world military, political, and economic superpower.

See also era of a new republic, 1789–1827; Jacksonian era, 1828–45.

FURTHER READING

Genovese, Michael A. *The Power of the American Presidency, 1789–2000*. New York: Oxford University Press, 2001.

Ketcham, Ralph. *Presidents above Party: The First American Presidency, 1789–1829*. Chapel Hill: University of North Carolina Press, 1984.

Milkis, Sidney M., and Michael Nelson. *The American Presidency: Origins and Development, 1776–2002*. Washington, DC: CQ Press, 2003.

Riccards, Michael P. *The Ferocious Engine of Democracy: A History of the American Presidency*. Vol. 1. Lanham, MD: Madison Books, 1995.

MICHAEL A. GENOVESE

presidency, 1860–1932

The presidential elections of 1860 and 1932 brought to power two of America's most important presidents: Abraham Lincoln and Franklin D. Roosevelt. These two elections also marked the beginning and the end of an era in which Republicans dominated the office of president. The power of the presidency ebbed and flowed during the period from 1860 to 1932, depending on the personality and ambitions of the officeholder and the challenges of his times.

The Civil War and Reconstruction: 1860–76

In 1860 Abraham Lincoln, the candidate of the Republican Party, founded just six years earlier, won the presidency as the only antislavery contender in a crowded field. Lincoln opposed the expansion of slavery beyond its existing boundaries, which many slaveholders regarded as tantamount to abolition. Consonant with the party's emphasis on activist government and economic development, Lincoln's platform also called for homestead legislation to promote western settlement, protective tariffs, and internal improvements. Although he won only 40 percent of the popular vote, he carried every northern state. The new president would have the cheerless task of presiding over the near dissolution of the nation itself. Even before Lincoln took the oath of office on March 4, 1861, seven southern states had seceded from the Union. On April 12, 1861, the Civil War began with the bombardment of Fort Sumter in South Carolina.

As a wartime leader, Lincoln became the most activist president to that time in U.S. history, expanding the powers of the presidency and the importance of the national government. Lincoln assumed broad powers to quell what he believed was a lawless domestic insurrection. When he issued the Emancipation Proclamation that freed all slaves still held by the Confederacy, he committed the federal government for the first time to a decisive stand against slavery. He summoned the militia to defend the Union, ordered a blockade of the Confederacy's ports, expanded the regular army beyond its legal limit, and spent federal funds without congressional approval. He suspended the writ of habeas corpus, which now meant that persons could be imprisoned without charges, and authorized army commanders to declare martial law in areas behind the lines. The Lincoln administration also instituted a graduated income tax, established a national banking system, facilitated the settlement of western lands, and began the nation's first draft of soldiers.

Lincoln won reelection in 1864, aided by Union victories in the fall of that year. He would not, however, survive to preside over postwar Reconstruction, a task that would fall to lesser leaders. After Lincoln's assassination in mid-April 1864, Andrew Johnson, a Democrat and the former wartime governor of Tennessee, assumed the presidency. Lincoln had put Johnson on his ticket in 1864 to present a united front to the nation. Johnson's tenure as president marked a significant decline in presidential power and prestige.

Johnson and the Republican Congress battled over Reconstruction policy, with Congress gaining the upper hand. Congress enacted civil rights laws, the Fourteenth Amendment guaranteeing "equal protection under the law," and the Fifteenth Amendment, which prohibited the denial of voting rights on grounds of race, color, or previous servitude. Congress authorized the stationing of federal troops in the South to enforce Reconstruction. In 1868 Johnson became the first president impeached by the U.S. House of Representatives. The primary charge against him was that he had violated the Tenure of Office Act, which forbade him from firing cabinet members without the approval of the Senate. Conviction in the Senate failed by a single vote. However, Johnson's political career was over, and a Republican, war hero Ulysses S. Grant, won the presidency in 1868. Johnson's impeachment strengthened the hand of Congress relative to the presidency, but it also discredited the use of impeachment as a political weapon.

Grant proved to be a weaker president than he had been a general. He assumed office with no program of his own; he followed the precedents set by the Republican Congress. Despite a lack of enthusiasm for black equality, Grant supported measures to sustain and extend Reconstruction. He continued the circulation of paper money, reduction of the federal debt, protection of industry through tariffs, and subsidization of the railroads. But Reconstruction was already unraveling during Grant's first term. Although the shell of federal power kept the South in Republican hands, the party that identified with black aspirations was unable to gain the support of white Southerners and thereby maintain its hold on the majority-white South.

Grant easily won reelection in 1872, but the advent of an economic depression in 1873 dashed his hopes for a bright second term. With Grant lacking ideas for reviving the economy, Congress acted on its own to expand the currency. But Grant, a president committed to the ideal of sound money, vetoed the legislation, leading to a paralysis of policy that endured through the end of the depression in 1878. Widespread corruption pervaded the Grant administration, which was also ineffectual in sustaining Reconstruction. By the end of Grant's second term, white supremacist "Redeemers" had gained control of every southern state with the exceptions of Florida, Louisiana, and South Carolina.

The Gilded Age: 1877–1900

The disputed presidential election of 1876 marked the end of Reconstruction and another low point in the powers of the presidency. Although Democratic candidate Samuel J. Tilden, the governor of New York, won the popular vote against Republican governor Rutherford B. Hayes of Ohio, the outcome of the election turned on disputed Electoral College votes in Florida, South Carolina, and Louisiana, the three states in which Republicans still retained power. With the U.S. Constitution silent on the resolution of such disputes, Congress improvised by forming a special electoral commission that ultimately consisted of eight Republicans and seven Democrats. The commission voted eight to seven on party lines to award all disputed electoral votes to Hayes, which gave him the presidency.

Hayes fulfilled his campaign promises to govern from the center and serve only a single term in office. By the time of the next presidential election, the nation had divided sharply into a solidly Democratic South that systematically moved to disfranchise black voters and a predominantly Republican North. The years from 1876 to 1892 were marked by a sharp regional division of political power growing out of Civil War alignments and a national stalemate between Republicans who dominated the North and Democrats who controlled the "redeemed" South. The Republican Party was also deeply divided between reformers and leaders, known as the Stalwarts, who were intent upon exploiting the political system for private gain. The Republican convention of 1880 held 35 ballots before nominating a dark horse candidate and mild reformer, Representative James A. Garfield of Ohio. In a gesture of conciliation to the Stalwarts, he chose as his running mate Chester A. "Boss" Arthur, who had held the key patronage position of customs collector of the Port of New York. The Democrats countered with former Civil War general Winfield Scott Hancock.

Garfield's hairbreadth victory over Hancock, by some 2,000 popular votes, began a series of four consecutive presidential elections in which the major party candidates were separated by an average of just 2 percent of the popular vote. Garfield had served less than four months as president before succumbing to an assassin's bullet. The newly inaugurated Chester Arthur disappointed his Stalwart friends by steering a middle course as president. Ironically, one of his crowning achievements was to sign into law the Pendleton Act of 1883 that established the federal civil service system. Arthur, however, had endeared himself to neither wing of the GOP and, in 1884, became the only sitting president in U.S. history to be denied his party's renomination.

In 1884, with the victory of New York governor Grover Cleveland, the Democrats gained the White House for the first time in 24 years. Cleveland's presidency harkened back to Andrew Jackson. Like Jackson, Cleveland believed in limited government, states' rights, sound money, fiscal responsibility, free trade, and a president who protected the public from the excesses of Congress. Cleveland vetoed several hundred special pension bills for Union veterans and their dependents. In 1887 he also vetoed the Dependent Pension Bill, which would have mandated payments to most disabled veterans regardless of whether their disabilities resulted from wartime service. During his first term, Cleveland exercised the presidential veto more than twice as many times as all his predecessors combined.

In his reelection bid, Cleveland prevailed in the popular tally, but lost his home state of New York and with it the Electoral College. Republican president Benjamin

Harrison sought to restore to his party the activism of Lincoln, with mixed success. Among his achievements was the McKinley Tariff of 1890, which substantially increased tariff rates. Harrison and other Republicans of the Gilded Age presented tariff protection as a comprehensive economic policy that would nurture industry, keep wages high, and strengthen domestic markets for agricultural goods. Harrison also gained passage of a pension bill similar to the legislation that Cleveland had vetoed. By 1893 pension payments would account for nearly half of the federal budget, and pensions would constitute the only substantial federal relief program until the New Deal of the 1930s. Congress also enacted the Sherman Anti-Trust Act, which outlawed corporate combinations or conspiracies "in restraint of trade or commerce." Harrison failed, however, to steer new civil rights laws through Congress, and the Sherman Act proved ineffective in restraining the concentration of industry.

In 1892 Cleveland defeated Harrison in a rematch of the 1888 election and became the only American president to serve two non-consecutive terms. Cleveland's election appeared to foreshadow a dramatic shift of party power in favor of the Democrats. The party seemed finally to have transcended the sectionalism of Civil War politics by combining its lock on the solid South with a revived ability to compete in the North. Cleveland's second term, however, proved to be a disaster for both the president and his party. He would spend nearly all of his four years in office on a futile effort to combat the worst economic depression to date in the history of the United States. President Cleveland, captive of his commitment to hard money and limited government, refused to consider reforming the financial system, increasing the money supply, or providing relief for the unemployed. His only solution to the economic calamity was to maintain a currency backed by gold, which only exacerbated the monetary contraction that had depressed investments, wages, and prices.

Cleveland declined to run for a third term, and his party's nominee, William Jennings Bryan, repudiated the president's policies. Bryan began the transition to a Democratic Party committed to activist government. Bryan embraced such reform proposals as the free coinage of silver to inflate the currency, a graduated income tax, arbitration of labor disputes, and stricter regulation of railroads. Bryan also helped introduce the modern style of presidential campaigns by giving stump speeches across the nation in 1896. In turn, the Republicans, who vastly outspent the Democrats, pioneered modern fundraising techniques.

Bryan lost in 1896 to Republican William McKinley, who benefited as president from the end of the depression in 1897. In domestic policy, McKinley steered new protective tariffs through Congress but otherwise followed a largely stand-pat approach to domestic matters. As president, however, he assumed the stewardship of a foreign empire and an expanded role in foreign affairs. As a result of winning the Spanish-American War of 1898, the United States acquired Puerto Rico, the Philippines, and several Pacific islands. It also established a protectorate over the Republic of Cuba. Although the United States would not endeavor to extend its formal empire of overseas territories in later years, it would frequently intervene in foreign nations to promote its values and interests. McKinley also expanded the powers of the presidency as he pioneered the steering of public opinion through a systematic program of press relations and speaking tours.

The Progressive Era: 1901–20

In 1900 McKinley won a rematch with Bryan, but in September 1901 he became the third president in 40 years to fall victim to an assassin. His successor—Theodore Roosevelt—was a man of different personality and ideas. Roosevelt was a showman with substance. During the remainder of McKinley's term and a second term of his own, Roosevelt transformed the presidency, the nation, and the Republican Party. As president, Roosevelt was both a big-stick diplomat abroad and a reformer at home. He altered the agenda of the Republican Party by adding a progressive domestic agenda to the expansionist policies of his predecessor, William McKinley. Roosevelt would become the first president to champion the use of federal power to protect the public interest and to curb abuses of the new corporate order. Ultimately, he would became the leader of progressive movements throughout the nation that worked toward improving social conditions, purifying American civilization, ending corrupt political practices, conserving resources, and regulating business. Roosevelt believed that reform was necessary to ameliorate the harshest consequences of industrial society and to thwart the appeal of radical groups.

Roosevelt also expanded the margins of presidential power. Prior presidents had typically deferred to constitutional ambiguities insofar as executive powers and privileges were concerned, preferring to err on the side of caution—and, by extension, weakness. Roosevelt, however, believed that he could do anything in the public interest that was not specifically prohibited by the Constitution. He intervened in disputes between labor and capital, used executive orders to conserve federal lands, attacked corporate monopolies in court, mediated foreign disputes, and aggressively acquired the territory needed to build the Panama Canal. His presidency not only served as a template for future ones but fittingly began what has been called the American century.

After retiring from the presidency, Roosevelt anointed a handpicked successor, his secretary of war, William Howard Taft, who thwarted Bryan's third bid for the presidency. But in 1912 Roosevelt was so disappointed with the moderate Taft that he unsuccessfully challenged the incumbent for the Republican Party's presidential nomination. The disappointed Roosevelt launched a third-party campaign that split the GOP and handed the election to Democratic candidate Woodrow Wilson, the progressive governor of New Jersey.

During his two terms in office, Wilson continued the liberal transformation of the Democratic Party that Bryan had begun in 1896. Under his watch, the federal government reduced tariffs, adopted the Federal Reserve System, established the Federal Trade Commission to regulate business, inaugurated social welfare programs, and joined much of the Western world in guaranteeing voting rights for women. Wilson also continued America's increasing involvement abroad and led the nation victoriously through World War I.

Like Theodore Roosevelt, Wilson also redefined the presidency, making the office both more powerful and active than before. Wilson was more engaged than any prior president in crafting legislation and steering it through Congress. A month after his inauguration, he addressed a special session of Congress to press for tariff reform, becoming the first president since John Quincy Adams in the 1820s to appear as an advocate before the legislature. Wilson also restored the practice of delivering the State of the Union address in person to Congress—a practice that Thomas Jefferson had discontinued after his election in 1800. Wilson also seized the initiative in foreign affairs. He attempted to broker peace between warring factions in World War I, and when that effort failed, led the nation into war. With his Fourteen Points, Wilson also articulated an ambitious vision for a postwar era marked by open covenants of peace, arms reductions, freedom of the seas, fair trade, self-determination for all people, and an international organization to keep the peace.

The Conservative Ascendancy: 1921–32

America's postwar future belonged not to Woodrow Wilson but to conservative Republicans. Wilson failed to gain acceptance in the United States or abroad for his ambitious peace plans, and his poor health precluded any hope for a third-term campaign. In the presidential election of 1920, Republican Senator Warren Harding of Ohio prevailed on a platform that promised a "return to normalcy" for Americans tired of liberal reform, war, and waves of Catholic and Jewish immigrants from southern and eastern Europe. Republicans would win all three presidential elections of the 1920s by landslide margins and maintain control over Congress during the period. Republican presidents and congresses of the 1920s would slash taxes, deregulate industry, restrict immigration, try to enforce Prohibition, and increase protective tariffs. In 1928, when Commerce Secretary Herbert Hoover decisively defeated New York Governor Alfred E. Smith—the first Catholic presidential candidate on a major party ticket—many believed the Democratic Party was on the verge of extinction.

The tide turned after the stock market crash of 1929 began the nation's longest and deepest depression. Unlike Grant and Cleveland, Hoover responded vigorously to the economic downturn. He held conferences of business leaders, sought to boost farm prices through federal purchases of commodities, and expanded federal public works projects. He assented to the formation of the Reconstruction Finance Corporation, which made low-interest loans to banks, railroads, and insurance companies. But he opposed federal regulation of business and vetoed legislation enacted by Democrats and progressive Republicans in Congress for direct aid to individuals and families—the so-called federal dole. The Depression failed to respond to his remedies, which Americas believed were inadequate to the challenges of the times. Franklin D. Roosevelt, the Democratic governor of New York, trounced Hoover in the presidential election of 1932, which ended conservative control of national government and marked the beginning of a new era of liberal politics in the United States.

See also assassination, presidential; Civil War and Reconstruction; conservative interregnum, 1920–32; Democratic Party; Reconstruction; Republican Party; sectional conflict and secession, 1845–65.

FURTHER READING

Brands, H. W. *T. R.: The Last Romantic*. New York: Basic Books, 1997.

Clements, Kendrick A. *The Presidency of Woodrow Wilson.* Lawrence: University of Kansas Press, 1992.

Donald, David. *Lincoln.* New York: Simon and Schuster, 1995.

Foner, Eric. *A Short History of Reconstruction, 1863–1877.* New York: Harper and Row, 1990.

Lichtman, Allan. *The Keys to the White House.* Lanham, MD: Rowman and Littlefield, 2008.

McGerr, Michael E. *The Decline of Popular Politics: The North, 1865–1928.* New York: Oxford University Press, 1986.

Riccards, Michael P. *The Ferocious Engine of Democracy: A History of the American Presidency.* Vol. 1. Lanham, MD: Madison Books, 1997.

ALLAN J. LICHTMAN

presidency, 1932–2008

Presidential Power and Responsibility

From 1932 to 2004, the powers and responsibilities of the presidency expanded together with the size and scope of the federal government. In 1932 the federal government spent less than $5 billion, including only about $700 million on the military. About 100 employees worked in the White House. In 2004 the federal government spent more than $2 trillion, the military budget hit $400 billion, and 1,800 people worked in the White House. Yet even as the federal bureaucracy has exploded, the modern president has become a celebrity figure, prized for his ability to inspire and lead the American people. Presidential success, moreover, has not always followed from presidential power. To the contrary, modern presidents have often fallen victim to the overreach that accompanies the arrogance of power.

The presidency from 1932 to 2004 can be partitioned into two distinct eras. From 1932 to 1980, presidents took the lead in establishing the modern liberal state. From 1980 to 2004, conservative presidents put their distinctive stamp on government in the United States.

The Origins of the Liberal State

In 1928 Herbert Hoover became the third consecutive Republican to win a landslide election to the presidency. But after 1929, Hoover battled the baleful consequences of a worldwide depression that resisted every remedy he tried. During the Hoover years, the Democratic opposition established the precedent of the permanent political campaign, with no pause between elections or deference to the presidency. Patrick Hurley, Hoover's secretary of war and political advisor, lamented that "our political opponents tell the story [and] we are on the defensive." Henceforth, every American president would be compelled to engage in a perpetual campaign.

Liberal Democrat Franklin Roosevelt's smashing victory over Hoover in 1932 profoundly changed both the presidency and the nation. During the new administration's first 100 days, conservatives watched in dismay as Roosevelt seized command of the legislative agenda more decisively than any prior president. He steered through Congress 15 major bills that addressed the banking crisis; got lawmakers to repeal Prohibition; created substantial relief and public works programs; and established recovery programs for agriculture and industry. Roosevelt became the first president to sell his policies to the public through fireside chats on the radio and freewheeling, twice-weekly press conferences. He had the ability both to inspire Americans with soaring rhetoric and to make ordinary folk believe that he, their patrician leader, truly understood and could help solve their problems.

After Roosevelt won a second decisive victory in 1936, he completed a political realignment that established the Democrats as the nation's majority party, sustained by a coalition of African Americans, Catholics, Jews, union members, and southern white Protestants. Scholars have aptly noted that FDR's reforms were incremental, modestly funded, and designed to rescue the capitalist economy. Nonetheless, Roosevelt's New Deal was a transforming moment in American life. It challenged old structures of power, threw up new ones, and created new social roles and opportunities for millions of Americans who worked for government, labored in offices and factories, or farmed for a living. It advanced American pluralism by offering jobs and power to Catholics and Jews and a few African Americans without disrupting local traditions. President Roosevelt shifted the center of American politics by taking responsibility for steering the economy, promoting social welfare, regulating labor relations, and curbing the abuses of business. Henceforth, Americans would expect their president, Democrat or Republican, to assure prosperous times, good jobs, high wages, and aid for those unable to fend for themselves.

The Cold War Presidency

During an unprecedented third term, Roosevelt led the nation into a world war that ended America's isolation from political entanglements abroad. The president assumed broad emergency powers during the war, and new federal agencies like the War Production Board foreshadowed the creation of America's military-industrial complex. It was not Franklin Roosevelt, however, but his successor, Harry S. Truman, who brought World War II to a successful conclusion. After FDR's death in April 1945, Truman became the first vice president to assume the presidency in the midst of a major war. Truman was shocked, nervous, and unprepared for the presidency. He told reporters, "I felt like the moon, the stars, and all the planets had fallen on me." Truman, however, had a very personalized view of history that idealized great men overcoming impossible odds. He acted decisively to use the atomic bomb to end World War II and led the nation into the cold war and the Korean War.

Like his celebrated predecessor, Truman expanded the powers of the presidency. He steered through Congress legislation that created the Central Intelligence Agency, the Joint Chiefs of Staff, the Department of Defense, and a National Security Council within the Executive Office of the President. He began the first program for screening the loyalty of federal employees. He entered the Korean War without a declaration of war or even token approval from Congress. Under Truman, America developed a military structure to sustain its global strategic and economic responsibilities and an "invisible government" that wielded global power with little scrutiny from Congress or the public. As libertarian Lawrence Dennis said in 1947, whether Republicans or Democrats held the presidency, America's "holy war on communist sin all over the world commits America to a permanent war emergency." Hereafter, "the executive has unlimited discretion to wage undeclared war anywhere, anytime he considers our national security requires a blow to be struck for good agin sin."

Amid the burdens of a stalemated war in Korea, a series of administration scandals, and challenges to his anti-Communist credentials by Senator Joseph McCarthy of Wisconsin and other Republicans, Truman declined to seek a third term. In 1952, Democrats nominated Illinois governor Adlai Stevenson. Among Republicans, war hero Dwight David Eisenhower competed for the Republican nomination against Senator Robert Taft of Ohio. In Eisenhower's view, a Taft presidency would threaten national security because the senator still clung to isolationist ideas that would undo the collective security measures that contained communism and deterred World War III. In the last national convention to resolve a deadlock between candidates, Eisenhower won the nomination and eventually the presidency only after the convention voted to seat his Texas delegation, rather than a competing delegation pledged to Taft.

Although mocked as a president who loved golf and loathed governing, Eisenhower carefully directed the policies and decisions of his administration, often keeping his influence hidden rather than overt. More than any prior president, Eisenhower relied on a chief of staff—Sherman Adams—as a gatekeeper and on the work of executive agencies such as the National Security Council. He also made extensive use of executive privilege to shield staff members from congressional oversight. Politically, Eisenhower promised to steer a middle course that weaved "between conflicting arguments advanced by extremists on both sides of almost every economic, political, and international problem that arises." He worked to balance the federal budget and control inflation. He believed in protecting the private economy from government meddling but also refused to roll back liberal reforms. He ratified Truman's approach to collective security and sought to contain communism without trampling civil liberties at home.

Eisenhower achieved considerable personal popularity, but his middle-way approach failed to break the Democrats' hold on the loyalty of voters and the control of Congress. In 1960 Democrat John F. Kennedy won election as America's first Catholic president. Kennedy's campaign, with its creative use of television, polling, image making, and a personal organization that was independent of the regular party machinery, also pointed to the future of American politics.

The Expansion and Crisis of the Liberal State

Kennedy was the first president since Franklin Roosevelt to inspire Americans with his rhetoric. Unlike later presidents, he spoke idealistically of shared sacrifice and the need for ordinary Americans to contribute to the common good, as envisioned in his most memorable line: "Ask not what your country can do for you, ask what you can do for your country." Kennedy steered the nation through the Cuban Missile Crisis, negotiated the first arms control treaty with the Soviets, and began the process that led to the end of segregation in America. Kennedy also accelerated the arms race with the Soviet Union and expanded America's commitment to far-flung areas of the world. However, Kennedy might not have led the United States to escalate the Vietnam War. Shortly before his assassination in late November 1963, he was working on a plan that contemplated withdrawing one thousand troops initially and extracting most American forces from Vietnam by 1965.

If Kennedy was cool and detached, his successor Lyndon Johnson was engaged and passionate. Johnson could talk endlessly about politics and had little interest in anything else. He also had a burning ambition to make his mark on the world and to help the less privileged. Johnson used his physical size to influence others and achieve his aims. It was not unusual for Johnson to stand inches away from another, bodies touching and eyes locked. The "Johnson treatment" was almost hypnotic. Yet he could just as easily alienate anyone who rebuffed him or refused his gifts.

After crushing conservative Republican Barry Goldwater in the presidential election of 1964, Johnson used his legislative skills to engineer a major expansion of the liberal state. Johnson imbedded the struggle for minority rights within the liberal agenda and, in another departure from the New Deal, he targeted needs—housing, health care, nutrition, and education—rather than groups such as the elderly or the unemployed.

But Johnson could not focus solely on domestic reform. Two days after his inauguration, Ambassador Maxwell Taylor cabled from Vietnam, "We are presently on a losing track and must risk a change. . . . The game needs to be opened up." The pugnacious president would not display unmanly personal and national weakness, encourage Communist aggression, and damage America's credibility by running from a fight. He began an air and ground war in Vietnam and ultimately dispatched some 550,000 American troops to the small Asian nation. Johnson promised the nation victory but privately told his cabinet that at best America could achieve a "stalemate" and force a negotiated settlement. Ultimately, the gap between inflated expectations and minimal achievements in Vietnam led to Johnson's "credibility gap" with the American people. In 1967 a frustrated president pleaded with his generals to "search for imaginative ideas to put pressure to bring this war to a conclusion"—not just "more men or that we drop the Atom bomb." Without military answers to the problems, on March 31, 1968, a dispirited Johnson told a national television audience that, rather than seeking reelection, he would work on bringing peace to Vietnam.

In 1962 Richard Nixon, after losing elections for the presidency and the governorship of California, said, "You won't have Nixon to kick around anymore, because, gentlemen, this is my last press conference." Six years later, Nixon completed the most improbable comeback in American history by narrowly winning the presidential election of 1968. Yet, from the early days of his presidency, Nixon exhibited the fear and suspicion that ultimately doomed a presidency marked by such accomplishments as the passage of pathbreaking environmental laws, the opening of relations with mainland China, and the deescalation of the cold war. Nixon told his staff that they were engaged in a "deadly battle" with eastern businessmen and intellectuals. He said, "No one in ivy league schools to be hired for a year—we need balance—trustworthy ones are the dumb ones." Jews were especially "untrustworthy. . . . Look at the Justice Department. It's full of Jews." Few business leaders "stood up" for the administration "except Main Street biz." Nixon brooded over his enemies in the press—"75 percent of those guys hate my guts"—and complained about needing to "keep some incompetent blacks" in the administration. "I have the greatest affection for them, but I know they ain't gonna make it for 500 years."

After engineering a landslide reelection in 1972, Nixon planned to bring the federal budget and bureaucracy to heel by refusing to spend funds appropriated by Congress and reorganizing government to expand presidential power. This power grab failed, however, as the Watergate scandal shattered Nixon's second term. Watergate involved far more than the botched break-in at Democratic Party headquarters in the Watergate complex in Washington, D.C., in June 1972. As moderate Republican senator Edward Brooke of Massachusetts said, "Too many Republicans have defined that dread word 'Watergate' too narrowly. It is not just the stupid, unprofitable break-in attempt. . . . It is perjury. Obstruction of justice. The solicitation and acceptance of hundred of thousands of dollars in illegal campaign contributions. It is a pattern of arrogance, illegality and lies which ought to shock the conscience of every Republican."

After Nixon resigned in August 1974, Democrats swept the midterm elections and sought to curb what they saw as a runaway presidency. They limited the president's war-making powers, expanded congressional input on the budget, and placed new restrictions on the CIA and the FBI. Such measures largely failed to return the balance of governmental power to Congress. Nonetheless, President Gerald Ford, whom Nixon had appointed vice president under authority of the Twenty-Fifth Amendment to the Constitution after the resignation of Spiro Agnew in 1973, struggled to govern after pardoning Nixon for Watergate-related crimes. However, conservative Republicans began rebuilding in adversity. They formed the Heritage Foundation to generate ideas, the Eagle Forum to rally women, new business lobbies, and Christian Right groups to inspire evangelical Protestants.

The Triumph of Conservatism

Although Democrat Jimmy Carter defeated Ford in 1976, he failed to cure an economy suffering from "stagflation" (an improbable mix of high unemployment, slow growth, and high inflation). Under Carter's watch America also suffered humiliation abroad when he failed to gain the release of hostages taken by Islamic militants in Iran. In 1980 conservative Republicans found an appealing candidate in Ronald Reagan, the former Hollywood actor and two-term governor of California. Reagan decisively defeated Carter in 1980, running on a forthright conservative platform. He promised to liberate Americans from the burdens of taxation and regulation, rebuild the nation's defenses, and fight communism with new vigor.

As president, Reagan delivered on most of his promises. He cut taxes, reduced regulation, and shifted government spending from domestic programs to the military. Like Roosevelt and Kennedy, Reagan emerged as a "Great Communicator," able to inspire Americans with his words and style. During his first term, Reagan restored luster to a tarnished presidency and optimism to the nation. As journalist Bob Greene wrote, Reagan "manages to make you feel good about your country. . . . All those corny feelings that hid inside of you for so long are waved right out in public by Reagan for everyone to see—and even while you're listing all the reasons that you shouldn't fall for it, you're glad you're falling. If you're a sucker for the act, that's okay."

Reagan cruised to easy reelection in 1984 after a troubled economy recovered during the election year. To borrow a metaphor from Isaiah Berlin, most modern American presidents are foxes who know a little about everything, poke their noses everywhere, and revel in detail. Reagan, however, was a hedgehog who knew a few things but knew them very well and left the management to others. Reagan's detached style helped him weather the Iran-Contra scandal of 1986–87 that stemmed from the sale of arms to the terrorist state of Iran and the illegal diversion of the profits to the Contra fighters who were battling a left-wing government in Nicaragua. Although the "Reagan revolution" in domestic policy stalled during the second term, he achieved a major breakthrough in foreign policy, despite antagonizing his conservative supporters. Conventional thinkers on the right or left failed to understand how Reagan could weave together seemingly contradictory ideas. He was a warrior against evil and a man of peace who dreamed of banishing nuclear weapons from the Earth. He was a leader of principle and a pragmatist who understood better than his right-wing critics how the world had changed since 1980. In the teeth of conservative opposition, Reagan steered through the Senate a landmark treaty to eliminate nuclear missiles in Europe that he negotiated with reformist Soviet leader Mikhail Gorbachev. In 1988 Reagan foreshadowed the end of the cold war when he said that the Soviet's "evil empire" was from "another time, another era."

It was Reagan's successor, George H. W. Bush, who presided over the collapse of the Soviet Empire. Bush took office with no guarantees that communism would collapse without bloodshed. He seemed shy and awkward but not overmatched, at least in foreign affairs. His realistic, steady-hand diplomacy prodded events forward without provoking a Soviet backlash. Bush drew a contrast between himself and the flamboyant Reagan when he said that, although conservatives told him to "climb the Berlin Wall and make high-sounding pronouncements . . . [t]he administration . . . is not going to resort to such steps and is trying to conduct itself with restraint." Not a single Soviet soldier fired a shot to preserve communism in Eastern Europe in 1989. The Soviet Union crumbled in 1991; the same year that Bush led a multinational coalition that liberated Kuwait from the Iraqi armies of Saddam Hussein.

In 1992, however, Bush's success in foreign policy could not overcome a sluggish economy, his lack of vision in domestic policy, and the appeal of his Democratic challenger, Bill Clinton. Clinton positioned himself as a "new kind of Democrat" armed, like Eisenhower, with a "third-way philosophy" that purported to transcend left and right.

However, the future of the Clinton administration turned on a battle over the president's plan to guarantee health care coverage to all Americans. Representative

Dick Armey of Texas privately told Republicans that the health care debate was "the Battle of the Bulge of big-government liberalism." If the GOP could defeat Clinton's health care plan, he said, "It will leave the President's agenda weakened, his plan's supporters demoralized, and the opposition emboldened. . . . Historians may mark it as the end of the Clinton ascendancy and the start of the Republican renaissance."

Armey proved to be a reliable prophet. Republicans won the health care battle and regained control of both houses of Congress in 1994 for the first time in 40 years. The elections established Republicans as the majority party in the South, polarized the parties along ideological lines, and forestalled any major new liberal initiatives by the Clinton administration. While Clinton won reelection in 1996 and survived impeachment by the Republican-controlled House of Representatives, his party failed to regain control of Congress during his tenure or to win the presidential election of 2000.

The Implosion of Conservatism

Although president-elect George W. Bush lost the popular vote in 2000, his advisors rejected advice that Bush govern from the center. Dick Cheney, who was poised to become the most influential vice president in American history, said, "The suggestion that somehow, because this was a close election, we should fundamentally change our beliefs I just think is silly." Even before the al-Qaeda terrorist attacks of September 11, 2001, Bush had moved domestic policy to the right and adopted a more aggressive, unilateralist approach to foreign affairs than his Democratic predecessor.

President Bush narrowly achieved reelection in 2004. However, his years in office revealed deep contradictions within his conservative movement. With the rebuilding of Iraq, a conservative administration that disdained social engineering assumed the most daunting such project in American history. Similarly, the president built a form of big government that contradicted conservatives' rhetorical defense of limited government, states' rights, fiscal responsibility, and individual freedom. Although conservatives had once rallied against the excessive presidential powers under Roosevelt, Truman, and Johnson, Bush greatly expanded executive prerogatives through unprecedented secrecy in government, expanding the domestic surveillance of Americans, exercising political control over the legal and scientific agencies of government, and aggressively using executive signing statements to reserve the option to override provisions of federal law. More forthrightly than any prior president, he asserted America's right to wage preemptive war against potential enemies. President Bush's terms in office exposed a paradox at the heart of the modern presidency. Although his tenure was a high watermark in presidential power, it also added to a deep-seated distrust of the presidency that had begun with Johnson's deceptive war and continued through the Watergate and Iran-Contra scandals and the impeachment of President Clinton. The Bush era ended with the election of Democrat Barack Obama, America's first African American president, who entered the presidency with a solidly Democratic U.S. House and Senate.

See also conservative ascendancy, 1980–2008; era of confrontation and decline, 1964–80; era of consensus, 1952–64; New Deal Era, 1932–52.

FURTHER READING

Dallek, Robert. *Hail to the Chief: The Making and Unmaking of American Presidents*. New York: Oxford University Press, 2001.

Gould, Lewis L. *The Modern American Presidency*. Lawrence: University of Kansas Press, 2003.

Leuchtenburg, William. *In the Shadow of FDR: From Harry Truman to Ronald Reagan*. Ithaca, NY: Cornell University Press, 1983.

Lichtman, Allan J. *The Keys to the White House, 2008 Edition*. Lanham, MD: Rowman and Littlefield, 2008.

Riccards, Michael P. *The Ferocious Engine of Democracy: A History of the American Presidency, from Theodore Roosevelt to George W. Bush*. New York: Cooper Square Press, 2003.

Shenkman, Richard. *Presidential Ambition: How the Presidents Gained Power, Kept Power, and Got Things Done*. New York: HarperCollins, 1999.

ALLAN J. LICHTMAN

press and politics

The press has played a major role in American politics from the founding of the republic. Once subordinate to politicians and the major parties, it has become increasingly independent, compelling politicians and elected officials to develop new strategies to ensure favorable publicity and public support.

Newspapers in the colonial era were few in number and very different from what they would later become. Operated by individual entrepreneurs who produced a variety of printed materials, newspapers included little political news. Instead, their few columns were devoted to foreign news and innocuous correspondence that would not offend colonial officials or the wealthy patrons on whom printers relied for much of their business.

This began to change during the Revolutionary era, when printers were drawn into the escalating conflict with Great Britain. Adversely affected by the Stamp Act, many printers opened their columns to opponents of British rule and eventually became champions of American independence. Others sided with the British and often found themselves the objects of popular wrath. After the war most printers returned to publishing uncontroversial items, but an important precedent had been set. Politicians and elected officials recognized that they could use the press to win support for favored causes, and ordinary Americans now saw newspapers as a medium through which they might gain knowledge about public affairs and become active citizens. Believing that a free press could spur public enlightenment and political engagement, Congress passed laws that reduced periodical postal rates and encouraged publishers to share and reprint their correspondence.

By the early 1790s, then, most Americans considered newspapers vital to the health of the republic, providing a medium through which politicians and the public could communicate, learn about issues, and develop policies that were shaped by rational, informed debate.

Almost immediately, however, the appearance of a very different kind of journalism confounded this expectation. Sparked by divergent plans for the future of the new republic, competing factions emerged within George Washington's administration and Congress, and by the mid-1790s each faction had established partisan newspapers championing its point of view. These publications were subsidized through patronage, and, though they had a limited circulation, the material they published was widely reprinted and discussed, and contributed to the establishment of the nation's first political parties, the Federalists and the Democratic-Republicans.

Newspapers like Philip Freneau's *National Gazette*, the most prominent Democratic-Republican organ, crafted distinctly partisan lenses through which readers were encouraged to view the world. Specializing in gossip, innuendo, and ad hominem attacks, these newspapers sought to make readers fearful about the intentions of their opponents. The strategy was quite effective at arousing support and mobilizing voters to go the polls—after all, the fate of the republic appeared to be at stake. But it hardly made the press a fount of public enlightenment, to the dismay of many an observer.

The rabid and unexpected partisanship of the 1790s culminated in the passage by the Federalist-dominated Congress of the Sedition Act (1798), which was designed to throttle the most intemperate journalistic supporters of the Democratic-Republicans by criminalizing "false, scandalous, and malicious writing" that defamed government officials. Though resulting in relatively few prosecutions, the law sparked an uproar that benefited Thomas Jefferson and his allies and created a groundswell of support for the principle of freedom of the press. In the wake of Jefferson's election to the White House, the act's sponsors were unable to extend its life and it expired in March 1801.

The partisan press expanded in the early 1800s and reached the peak of its influence during the age of Jackson. Publishers, eager for government printing contracts, allied themselves with leading politicians and devoted their columns to publicizing their candidacies and policy aims. Newspaper publishers were particularly important in promoting Andrew Jackson, serving in his kitchen cabinet, and enabling him to develop a national following. Jackson's rise to power prompted a dramatic polarization of newspapers, a divide that was essential to the emergence of the Democrats and the Whigs, truly national parties that were organized down to the grass roots.

Political parties were not the only organizations to establish newspapers. Religious denominations and reform societies also founded newspapers and journals of opinion and advocacy to attract supporters and influence public opinion. Evangelical groups were especially enterprising in their use of newspapers and other printed tracts to win converts and promote piety, and in the 1820s and 1830s these efforts often spilled over into broader campaigns to improve public morality. By constructing a network of affiliated publications that extended through much of North and by developing narrative themes that were at once sensational and didactic, the religious and reform newspapers of the early 1800s were important pioneers of modern journalism and popular culture.

The most controversial reform organs were abolitionist newspapers like William Lloyd Garrison's *The Liberator*, which was launched in 1831 and inspired many similar publications. Making use of the communications infrastructure developed by the religious press, abolitionist newspapers spread throughout the North and were sent en masse to cities and towns in the South in hopes of kindling opposition to slavery in the region. To suppress their dissemination, pro-slavery activists broke into post offices and seized and burned any copies they found. While this tactic was effective at minimizing the spread of antislavery sentiment, it angered and alarmed many Northerners, bolstering abolitionist claims that the republic was imperiled by the tyrannical designs of the "Slave Power."

Despite their effectiveness in helping to build national parties and raising public awareness of social and political issues, the partisan press and reform press were widely criticized, and their limitations paved the way for a new kind of publication, a commercial mass-circulation press that first appeared in the 1830s. Inexpensive, widely accessible, and written in a colorful style designed to entertain as well as inform, newspapers like the *New York Sun* sparked a revolution in journalism as publishers, impressed by the commercial potential of an unabashedly popular journalism, rushed to establish similar publications. By opening their papers to advertising, publishers of the "penny press" discovered a lucrative source of revenue and freed themselves from dependence on political parties and patrons. They acquired an incentive to expand their readership to include working-class people, who had never been targeted by newspaper publishers, and to plow their profits into new technologies that allowed them to enlarge their publications and vastly increase the range of topics they covered.

Filling their columns with material of general interest, publishers like James Gordon Bennett, founder of the *New York Herald*, invented the modern concept of "news." And while much of it was about politics, when Bennett and his rivals expanded coverage of other realms they diminished the prominence and centrality of political news, which became one of many different kinds of reportage. The penny press also treated political news differently, and, as it gained readers, its perspective on politics and public affairs became more influential. Most publishers recognized the strength of partisanship, and supported one party or another. Yet, because commercial imperatives encouraged publishers to reach across lines of class, ethnicity, and party, they often confined their partisanship to editorials, where it was less likely to offend.

This is not to say that the commercial mass-circulation press was objective. Editors and publishers—until after the Civil War, they were usually one and the same—had strong points of view and were not squeamish about inserting them into news reports. But their reliance on advertising allowed editors to aspire to a new role as tribunes of the public. In many instances, this meant standing by their party; in others, however, it meant criticizing it. Publishers like Bennett or Horace Greeley relished opportunities to display their independence and commitment to the public interest, a gambit inspired as much by commercial intent—the desire to attract a broad readership—as by disgust for the excesses of partisanship.

The trend toward a less partisan brand of political reporting was reinforced by the establishment of wire services like the Associated Press, which provided members with news from Washington and state capitals and eschewed partisanship out of commercial necessity. Under the influence of such services, by the 1880s, most political reporting had become standardized and largely descriptive, consisting of transcripts of speeches, legislative hearings, and official pronouncements. Most of this material was gathered by salaried wire service and newspaper correspondents, not, as in years past, by freelance correspondents who also worked for elected officials or the major parties. Just as their employers viewed themselves as independent of party, so too did increasing numbers of reporters, a trend that accelerated in the early 1900s when big-city newspapers became large business, and journalists began to think of themselves as professionals.

But the commercial orientation of the mass-circulation press also pulled journalists in another direction, toward an emphasis on entertainment values. In the 1880s and 1890s, determined to attract more immigrant and working-class readers, publishers like Joseph Pulitzer and William Randolph Hearst created an even more popular and entertaining brand of journalism that emphasized scandal, personalities, and a wide variety of human-interest material. Political news in their publications became increasingly sensational, as editors focused on exposé of corruption and mounted highly publicized crusades. A similar imperative affected magazine journalism, inspiring the muckraking campaigns of *Cosmopolitan* and *McClure's*. Spurred by recognition that much of the public was sincerely concerned about social problems, the sensational press played a key role in building support for reform. By transforming politics into entertaining yet sordid morality tales, however, they also may have encouraged public cynicism and disengagement from politics.

Many middle-class and upper-class Americans were appalled by the new journalism, and, in response to its rise, Adolph Ochs transformed the *New York Times* into a more sober and "informational" alternative. In the early 1900s, other papers followed Ochs's lead, creating a new divide between a popular journalism directed at lower middle-class and working-class readers and a self-styled "respectable" press that was targeted at the educated and well-heeled. But publishers of respectable newspapers, in response to consumer demand, were soon compelled to publish features and human-interest stories as well, blurring the differences between the two kinds of journalism. Indeed, by the 1920s, the most salient distinction between the sensational press and the respectable press was the relative restraint that the latter displayed when covering many of the same stories. Even in the respectable press, political news was designed to entertain as well as inform, an increasingly difficult mission now that newspapers had to compete for the public's attention with motion pictures and other forms of popular culture.

The commercial transformation of journalism had a major impact on politicians and government officials. Not surprisingly, it forced them to present themselves in a less partisan light. Seizing the opportunities created by the spread of human-interest journalism, politicians sought to appear as "practical idealists," party members who were nonetheless sensitive to broader concerns and willing to break with their party if necessary. To that end, politicians began to hire press secretaries and public relations advisors, usually former journalists who knew how to exploit the conventions of news gathering to gain favorable coverage for their clients. The federal government also began to employ public relations and advertising techniques, most notably in its effort to build public support for American involvement in World War I. Led by George Creel, an acclaimed journalist, the government's campaign sparked an orgy of hyperpatriotism, demonstrating how mass-mediated propaganda could mold public opinion and potentially influence the democratic process.

Alarmed by the ease with which politicians, the government, and economic elites could use the press to get free publicity, journalists began to produce more interpretive and objective forms of news, particularly of topics like politics. This important trend was inspired by a belief that the world was too complex to be understood by readers, and that the job of the press was to digest, analyze, and interpret events and developments so that the public could make sense of them. Newspapers hired columnists like Walter Lippmann and Dorothy Thompson to provide "expert" commentary on political events. Their columns were disseminated by syndicates to newspapers around the country, enabling them to reach a nationwide audience. Interpretive news also became a staple of the weekly newsmagazine *Time*. Founded in the early 1920s, it exerted a wide influence on newspaper as well as magazine journalism. The commitment of print media to interpretive news was reinforced by the spread of radio. As radio became the principal medium through which most Americans heard about late-breaking news, newspapers and magazines redoubled their emphasis on more detailed coverage.

By the 1940s, the press had become a vital institution, providing the public with information about candidates and elected officials, covering primary campaigns and nominating conventions, and offering regular reports on the vastly expanded operations of federal, state, and local government. The lens through which most of this news was filtered was the commercial, feature-oriented, largely nonpartisan perspective pioneered by the cheap popular press and further refined by more respectable organs and the major wire services. Despite persistent differences in tone among newspapers and magazines—differences attributable to their intended audiences—the political news that most Americans read was relatively standardized, a blend of interpretive reporting, analyses, commentary, and "personalized" features. Much of it was quasi-official in origin, inspired by the efforts of politicians and government officials to attract publicity or direct attention to a particular issue. More often than not, this was because the routines of news gathering encouraged close contact between journalists and official sources, an arrangement that made the news media a reliable platform for establishment points of view.

The spread of television in the 1950s did little to alter the situation. To display their commitment to the public interest, the major networks and local stations produced news and public affairs programming, covering events like the 1954 Army-McCarthy hearings and airing documentaries on issues like civil rights, the alienation of youth, and the arms race. However, it wasn't until the expansion of the nightly network news broadcasts to 30 minutes in the early 1960s, and a similar increase in local news programming, that television became the main source of political news for most Americans. Making use of new video and satellite technologies that enabled extensive coverage of the era's tumultuous events—from the Kennedy assassination to the Watts uprising to the debacle in Vietnam—television news broadcasts began to attract more viewers, sparking a gradual yet inexorable decline in newspaper readership. The centrality of television news became even more pronounced in the 1980s and 1990s with the rise of cable television and the popularity of news channels such as CNN.

The public's growing reliance on television for news had significant repercussions. No less than in the print media, advertising and entertainment values came to dominate television at every level, encouraging network officials to decrease coverage of politics and make what little they offered more superficial and entertaining. Under pressure to make the news "pay," a trend brilliantly satirized in the movie *Network* (1976), television journalists were forced to produce more human-interest stories and sharply limit airtime devoted to political stories that were overly complex or considered boring. With less airtime devoted to politics, politicians and elected officials gradually learned to express themselves in compact "sound bites," a technique that placed a premium on wit and personality and further degraded public discourse. This shift was particularly evident in coverage of election campaigns. Aware of the power of television, candidates and their campaign managers in the 1960s made increasing use of modern advertising and public relations methods, a process in which candidates' personalities were literally sold to the public. This trend was reinforced in the 1970s, when electoral reforms heightened the importance of primary elections, which the mass media, led by the major networks, transformed into highly publicized "horse races."

Beginning in the late 1960s, the press became increasingly aggressive and adversarial. Disconcerted by recognition that government and military officials had lied about the situation in Vietnam, journalists began to seek a wider range of sources and question official reports in a spirit not seen since the early 1900s. Journalists came to see themselves as public watchdogs responsible for exposing malfeasance and providing Americans with the truth. The publication of the Pentagon Papers, a top-secret history of the Vietnam War that was leaked to the *New York Times*, and the aggressive investigative reporting of the *Washington Post* that precipitated the Watergate scandal were perhaps the most famous manifestations of this trend. But it influenced many newspapers, magazines, television news departments, and individual journalists, inspiring them to express critical views of important institutions, including some of the large corporations for which they worked. To foster public debate, newspapers established op-ed pages and expanded their roster of columnists, making editorial pages less uniform and predictable. By the early 1980s, however, much of the mainstream press had backed away from this adversarial stance. Chastened by charges of liberal bias, journalists went out of their way to appear fair to conservatives, and in the 1990s, eager to display their balance, they zealously contributed to the right's persecution of Bill Clinton.

The post-1960s era also witnessed a tremendous increase in alternative sources of political news, as journalists sought new platforms to produce in-depth and adversarial reportage. These alternatives included underground newspapers, political magazines specializing in advocacy journalism, politically oriented network and cable talk shows like *The McLaughlin Group*, *Crossfire*, and *The Daily Show*, and innumerable political Web sites and blogs. Many of these sources specialized in ideologically inspired, openly subjective reporting and commentary, creating a new field where news and opinion were hopelessly blurred. Often targeted at true believers rather than a broad audience, they vastly enlarged the parameters of political discourse and made it easier for citizens to gain access to diverse views. This was clearly an advance over the more limited, elite-driven discourse that prevailed from the 1920s through the early 1960s, particularly given the ability of government and the corporate behemoths that own the major media to exploit the conventions of journalism to project their own self-interested versions of reality.

But it is an open question whether the welter of often fiercely partisan and ideologically driven sources of political news in America serves—or will ever serve—the larger cause of public enlightenment. Can a mode of discourse that is designed at least in part to entertain, in a popular culture marketplace that is fragmented into increasingly specialized niche markets, ever contribute to inclusive, constructive debate? Or will it reach its logical conclusion and become another species of show biz?

See also Internet and politics; radio and politics; television and politics.

FURTHER READING

Baldasty, Gerald J. *The Commercialization of News in the Nineteenth Century*. Madison: University of Wisconsin Press, 1992.

Ewen, Stuart. *PR! A Social History of Spin*. New York: Basic Books, 1996.

Fallows, James. *Breaking the News: How the Media Undermine American Democracy*. New York: Pantheon, 1996.

Leonard, Thomas C. *The Power of the Press: The Birth of American Political Reporting.* New York: Oxford University Press, 1986.

Nord, David Paul. *Communities of Journalism: A History of American Newspapers and Their Readers.* Chicago: University of Illinois Press, 2001.

Overholser, Geneva, and Kathleen Hall Jamieson, eds. *Institutions of American Democracy: The Press.* New York: Oxford University Press, 2005.

Ponder, Stephen. *Managing the Press: Origins of the Media Presidency, 1897–1933.* New York: Palgrave Macmillan, 1999.

Schudson, Michael. *The Good Citizen: A History of American Civic Life.* Cambridge, MA: Harvard University Press, 1998.

Starr, Paul. *The Creation of the Media: Political Origins of Modern Communications.* New York: Basic Books, 2004.

CHARLES L. PONCE DE LEON

Progressive parties

Progressive parties emerged in 1912, 1924, and 1948. These were three distinct political parties, each with its own political organization, reform agenda, and voting constituency. Yet all three wrestled with a common set of problems: adjusting American democratic processes in response to the changes wrought by industrialization, urbanization, and immigration; establishing the proper role of the state in the management of the nation's increasingly complex economy; and meeting the demands of economically and politically marginalized groups as they mobilized to claim their rights as American citizens and to expand the very definition of what exactly these rights entailed. Viewed sequentially, the different constituencies, platforms, and electoral fortunes of each Progressive Party provide a way to trace the changing definitions and shifting boundaries of *progressive* reform over time.

The Progressive (Bull Moose) Party of 1912

The Progressive Party of 1912 remains one of the best-known third parties in American history, largely because of the outsized personality of its standard-bearer, the trust-busting, big game-hunting, former president Theodore Roosevelt. After all, it was Roosevelt who, speaking in anticipation of the Progressives' 1912 campaign, famously declared himself "as fit as a bull moose," thereby giving the Progressive Party its nickname. The electoral fortunes of the Progressive Party of 1912 depended heavily upon the power of Roosevelt's unique political persona.

Regardless of Roosevelt's prominence, however, the Progressive Party of 1912 emerged as a consequence of long-standing structural and ideological divisions within the Republican Party, divisions that Roosevelt did not create. Progressive insurgents within Republican ranks—a loose coalition of midwestern congressional leaders and middle-class urban reformers—long advocated a series of economic, social, and political reforms designed to use the power of the federal government to curb the influence of big business, reinvigorate American democratic institutions, and protect workers and consumers, all in response to the advent of the urban-industrial economy that transformed life in the United States during the late nineteenth and early twentieth centuries. But conservative, Old Guard Republicans—the Northeastern financial and industrial elites who controlled the party—blocked the progressives' calls for reforms and preserved the party's traditional commitments to pro-corporate policies and party patronage. This fissure within Republican ranks split wide open during the presidency of William Howard Taft (1909–13), as Taft repeatedly sided with the conservative Old Guard and against the party's progressive wing. Unable to wrest control from the Old Guard, progressives sought to build an independent party strong enough to relegate the Old Guard Republicans to permanent third-party status, and the Progressive Party of 1912 was born of this split.

Theodore Roosevelt, did not create the split between the progressives and the Old Guard, but he did transform the progressives' entrenched yet inchoate discontent into a national political movement. Roosevelt did this by articulating a far-reaching reform program, dubbed the New Nationalism, that provided the basis for the Progressive Party's platform in 1912. As outlined by Roosevelt in countless speeches between 1910 and 1912, the New Nationalism was a sweeping appeal for democratic reforms, protective legislation for workers and consumers, and increased governmental regulation of the nation's economy. Borrowing heavily from reform proposals widely circulated during the Progressive Era, the New Nationalism contained full-throated endorsements of the referendum, initiative, and recall, the direct election of U.S. Senators, woman suffrage, a workmen's compensation law, protective legislation for women workers, the prohibition of child labor, and graduated income and inheritance taxes. Roosevelt also added a reform of his own to the Progressive canon by calling for a dramatic expansion in the power of the federal government to manage the nation's economy through the creation of a permanent federal bureaucracy designed to oversee large interstate corporations. Yet, for all of these sweeping proposals, Roosevelt's New Nationalism was also an inherently conservative philosophy. Convinced of the need for social and economic reforms, Roosevelt nevertheless remained profoundly suspicious of what he viewed as dangerous radical movements emanating from the working class. He urged all Americans to set aside their material self-interest and transcend class and ethnic identities in favor of "a spirit of broad and far-reaching nationalism." The New Nationalism, then, was a program of reform designed to be undertaken by those Roosevelt identified as judicious, level-headed, and moderate Americans—exactly the kind of people who flocked to the Progressive Party in 1912.

The delegates who gathered in Chicago on August 5, 1912, to nominate Roosevelt and his running mate, Governor Hiram Johnson of California, embodied the New Nationalism's peculiar mixture of boldness and moderation. Although joined in Chicago by a handful of Roosevelt loyalists and a larger number of midwestern agrarian Progressives, the Progressive Party of 1912 was predominantly a party of middle-class urban reformers dismayed by the changes wrought upon American society as a result of industrialization, immigration, and urbanization.

On the one hand, these middle-class Progressives possessed a bold, crusading zeal for reform. Contemporary accounts describe the Progressive Party's Chicago convention as akin to a religious revival. Delegates sang "Onward, Christian Soldiers" and other hymns, furiously waved yellow handkerchiefs symbolic of woman suffrage, cheered wildly as Jane Addams seconded Roosevelt's nomination, and interrupted Roosevelt's acceptance speech—aptly titled "A Confession of Faith"—almost 150 times with raucous applause.

On the other hand, the Progressive Party's base in the native-born, well-educated, white-collar Protestant and urban middle class circumscribed its vision of reform. The platform may have proclaimed that "the first essential in the Progressive program is the right of the people to rule," but the Progressives had a rather narrow definition of "the people." Theirs was not a labor party or a party of farmers. Nor was it a party of recent immigrants, African Americans, or other minorities. Middle-class Progressives did not make cross-class alliances with organized labor or reach out successfully to recent immigrants. And Roosevelt and the Progressive Party pursued a "lily-white" strategy that excluded southern blacks in an effort to woo southern white voters. The largely middle-class Progressive Party of 1912 claimed to eschew interest-group politics in favor of the New Nationalism, but, in so doing, it blinded itself to the class, racial, and ethnic biases inherent in its own program.

The election results in November 1912 revealed the strengths and limitations of the Progressive Party's message and its foundation in the urban middle class. Roosevelt finished an impressive second behind the victorious Democratic Party candidate, Woodrow Wilson. In an embarrassing third-place finish, Taft and the Old Guard won only 23 percent of the popular vote, just 2 states, and only 8 electoral votes. Roosevelt and the Progressives won 27.4 percent of the popular vote nationwide, 6 states, and 88 electoral votes—the strongest electoral showing in the history of American third parties.

A closer look at the election results suggests the contours of Progressive support. Roosevelt polled 35 percent of the popular vote in the nation's largest urban areas, well ahead of the 27.4 percent he won overall. One historian of the party has noted that areas of Progressive strength correlated with urban areas experiencing high rates of growth—presumably areas that contained large percentages of middle-class professionals. But the Progressives fared poorly in heavily Catholic and Jewish precincts, among the most recent immigrants, and among working-class voters in general, particularly in such immigrant-heavy industrial states as Connecticut, Massachusetts, New Jersey, New York, and Rhode Island. The so-called lily-white strategy also proved to be a failure. The Progressives polled especially poorly in the South. These areas of electoral weakness underscored the limitations of the Progressive Party's middle-class reform program.

The Progressive Party of 1924

Whereas urban middle-class reformers dominated the Progressive Party of 1912, the Progressive Party of 1924 was a class-based coalition party consisting of farmers and organized labor. A number of Socialist Party members and progressive intellectuals provided the effort with intellectual energy and political organization. The 1924 Progressives fought for a more activist state to meet the specific needs of workers and farmers. This sui generis attempt to forge a national-level farmer-labor coalition outside the Republican and Democratic parties proved to be a relative disappointment. But such efforts at coalition-building anticipated the class-based interest-group politics characteristic of the Democratic Party coalition during the New Deal era of the 1930s.

The 1924 Progressive coalition of organized labor, farmers, Socialists, and intellectuals emerged from the dashed hopes of the World War I era. Each of these groups watched as gains made during the war disappeared early in the postwar era. Organized labor endured a withering public reaction to a mass strike wave in 1919 and then the return of a conservative, probusiness Republican administration to the White House one year later. Farmers experienced a severe postwar agricultural depression and a bitter harvest of bankruptcies, foreclosures, and abandoned farms. Progressive intellectuals and Socialists stood aghast as the Red Scare of 1919–20 demonstrated that the expanded powers of the wartime state could easily be seized by the most conservative forces in American society. It was thus a shared sense of disaffection that led representatives of these four groups to organize.

In February 1922, representatives from the Railroad Brotherhoods, the Socialist Party, midwestern farmers belonging to such organizations as the Non-Partisan League, and a handful of veterans of the 1912 Progressive Party met in Chicago to form the Conference for Progressive Political Action (CPPA). The CPPA initially adopted a wait-and-see approach to fielding a third-party candidate in the presidential election of 1924. But when the Republicans renominated President Calvin Coolidge, a pro-business, laissez-faire conservative, and the Democrats selected John W. Davis, a corporate lawyer with strong ties to Wall Street, it became clear to the CPPA that no home existed for progressives in either major party. On July 4, 1924, more than a thousand CPPA delegates met in Cleveland to organize a third-party effort. Delegates to the convention—mostly from the ranks of the Railroad Brotherhoods or members of the Non-Partisan League—announced the creation of the Progressive Party of 1924, promptly named Wisconsin senator Robert M. La Follette as the party's candidate for president, and attempted to draft a platform faithful to the party's nascent farmer-labor coalition.

The 1924 Progressive Party, in its attempt to forge a farmer-labor coalition, crafted a platform that differed subtly but significantly from the one adopted by the 1912 Progressives. Both parties envisioned a more activist state with the authority to manage the economic and social problems wrought by industrialization. Whereas the middle-class Progressives of 1912 emphasized moderation in reform, the transcendence of class differences, and enlightened administration by middle-class reformers, the Progressives of 1924 sought to directly empower workers and farmers to fight for their own economic and social interests. The platform adopted by the 1924 Progressive Party, for example, called for a series of union friendly measures, including nationalization of the railroads and utilities and, significantly, the right of all workers to organize and bargain collectively. The 1924 platform also outlined a program to meet the needs of struggling farmers, including a program of expanded farm credit, federal financial assistance for agricultural cooperatives, and government-mandated reductions in railroad rates. Finally, the Progressives of 1924 emphasized a stridently anticorporate message that reflected long-standing midwestern agrarian distrust of large interstate corporations. Rather than regulate the big corporations, the 1924 Progressives wanted to use the power of the state to dismantle them. This antimonopoly message, alongside the outright appeals for class-based policies, clearly distinguished the platform of the 1924 Progressives from the New Nationalism of 1912.

The Progressive Party of 1924 was plagued by a number of challenges common to third parties in the American political system, including fund-raising difficulties and daunting organizational obstacles at the state and local levels. But its gravest problem was the failure of the farmer-labor coalition to materialize at the ballot box. In spite of the Progressives' attempt to advance a balanced platform that touched upon the needs of both farmers and organized labor, agrarian concerns dominated the platform and campaign. Agrarian enthusiasm for the strict antimonopoly policy, to cite one important example, was not shared by the labor elements in the coalition. The decision to nominate La Follette only underscored the imbalance. A renowned orator with a fierce sense of both his own righteousness and that of the causes he championed, by 1924 "Fighting" Bob had spent two decades in the Wisconsin Senate laboring tirelessly for progressive reform. But La Follette's brand of progressivism was distinctly midwestern and oriented toward agrarian issues. Whether he could win sizeable support from the ranks of organized labor remained uncertain in the months leading up to the general election.

The results of the 1924 general election indicate La Follette's failure to reconcile the farmer and labor elements within Progressive ranks. The Progressives performed strongly only in the agricultural Midwest and West. La Follette won just his home state of Wisconsin, but he finished a strong second to Coolidge in the Dakotas and Minnesota, strongholds of the Non-Partisan League, and also in California, Idaho, Iowa, Montana, Oregon, Washington, and Wyoming. Labor support was not entirely absent. The American Federation of Labor abandoned its traditionally nonpartisan stance and endorsed La Follette. And the Progressive Party did run second in many precincts throughout such industrial states as Illinois, Michigan, Ohio, Pennsylvania, New Jersey, and New York. In the end, however, labor's support was simply too tepid for the Progressives to mount a serious challenge to either of the major parties.

The 1924 Progressives finished with 16.6 percent of the popular vote nationwide and just 13 electoral votes, all from Wisconsin. This showing placed the Progressives in distant third place behind the victorious Republican Calvin Coolidge (54 percent of the popular vote) and Democrat John Davis (28.8 percent). It was also far short of the 27.4 percent polled by Roosevelt's Progressive Party just 12 years earlier.

Although La Follette's 16.6 percent of the popular vote ranks as the third-highest popular vote total for a third party in the twentieth century, his failure to achieve a stronger farmer-labor coalition disappointed organizers. By mid-1925 the AFL had returned to its traditional nonpartisan stance, La Follette had died of heart failure, and the CPPA—still the organizational arm of the party—was meeting only intermittently before disbanding for good in 1927. Nevertheless, the Progressive Party of 1924 marked an early example of political interest-group politics and a view of an activist state that would gain fruition in the New Deal Era.

The Progressive Party of 1948

Led by Henry A. Wallace, outspoken New Deal liberal and former secretary of agriculture and vice president under President Franklin Roosevelt, the Progressive Party of 1948 emerged as a movement among liberals and left-wing activists. They had hoped that the post–World War II era would bring a return to New Deal reform at home and lasting peace through liberal internationalism abroad. But to many on the left, President Harry Truman squandered the postwar opportunity by beating a hasty retreat from New Deal domestic policies and by engaging in an unnecessarily militaristic foreign policy toward the Soviet Union that helped precipitate the cold war. The fact that he inherited the presidency upon Roosevelt's death in April 1945 only heightened the sense that Truman had violated a sacred trust. In response to such perceived betrayals, the most progressive elements of the New Deal coalition, including the leaders of several militant labor unions and progressive farm organizations, civil rights activists, a handful of old New Deal liberals, and an assortment of other leftists, including current and former Communists, convened in late December 1946 to form the Progressive Citizens of America (PCA). The Progressive Party of 1948 emerged from the organizational work undertaken by PCA activists.

Foreign policy figured prominently in the decision to organize the Progressive Party of 1948. This clearly distinguished the Progressive Party of 1948 from the earlier Progressive efforts focused almost entirely on domestic reform.

As vice president during World War II, Wallace emerged as the leading champion of a progressive postwar foreign policy. In order to promote peace and prosperity, Wallace argued, America needed to embark on an outward-looking foreign policy to spread American ideas, goods, and technologies abroad—while avoiding militarism, imperialism, and unilateralism. International disputes were best left to a strong United Nations.

Given these views, Wallace quickly became uneasy with the direction of Truman's foreign policy, which he considered to be far too militaristic toward the Soviet Union. Wallace argued instead for a U.S.-Soviet relationship based on negotiation and mutual coexistence. He sharpened his criticisms as Truman and his advisors pursued policies that are now synonymous with the cold war. In March 1947, Truman justified U.S. military aid to distant countries facing Communist revolutions by articulating what became known as the Truman Doctrine. Three months later the Truman administration announced the creation of the Marshall Plan, a U.S.-financed reconstruction program for Western Europe. Wallace criticized the militarism and unilateralism he detected in both policies, deriding them as "programs which give guns to people when they want plows." Wallace moved into an open break not only with Truman but with the Democratic Party itself. On December 29, 1947, he announced his decision to mount a third-party candidacy.

The Progressives' objections to cold war foreign policy stemmed in part from their belief that a militaristic foreign policy would hinder the effort to resurrect progressive, New Deal–style policies at home. The platform adopted by the Progressive Party at its July 1948 convention in Philadelphia articulated this holistic vision: "peace, freedom, and abundance—the goals of the Progressive Party—are indivisible." The Progressives' "peace" plank, of course, conformed to Wallace's vision of foreign affairs. But the "freedom" and "abundance" planks concentrated on domestic issues and envisioned a breathtaking expansion in the American progressive reform tradition. The freedom component contained prophetic demands for civil rights and civil liberties. Progressives called for an end to discrimination against African Americans and other minorities, an end to segregation in the armed forces, an antilynching law, anti-poll-tax legislation, and a constitutional amendment guaranteeing equal rights for women. The abundance plank demanded economic democracy through such measures as nationalized health insurance, expanded Social Security, federal housing subsidies, and regional economic planning on the Tennessee Valley Authority model. With these demands, the Progressives of 1948 articulated a reform program far more ambitious than either of the two earlier Progressive parties.

The Progressive Party of 1948 initially seemed to jeopardize Truman's reelection. National polls taken shortly after Wallace announced his candidacy measured his support at 11.5 percent. In New York, Illinois, and California, Wallace appeared poised to win enough votes to throw the election to Truman's Republican challenger, Thomas E. Dewey.

But Wallace and the Progressives suffered steady erosion in support throughout the year. Nothing proved more damaging than the politics of anticommunism. Both the PCA and the Progressive Party of 1948 provided a political home to many current and former American Communists; they were particularly energetic political organizers. Wallace also refused to disavow the Communist presence in his party organization he considered as red-baiting. This was a principled argument but not one that could be won given the political climate in 1948, particularly given the Progressives' views on American foreign policy. Wallace was widely condemned as a Communist "dupe," a "pink," and a "fellow traveler."

Press coverage of Wallace and the Progressives vacillated between hostility and outright contempt, and Wallace's popular support withered accordingly. But the Communist issue also deprived Progressives of crucial support among liberal activists. Some New Deal liberals agreed with the politics of anticommunism and formed Americans for Democratic Action (ADA) in January 1947 as an alternative to the Communist-influenced PCA. Truman may have been a disappointment to these ADA liberals, but Wallace became a pariah. The ADA attacked Wallace and the Progressives on the Communist issue throughout 1948. Whereas Roosevelt took the better half of the Republican Party with him during the Bull Moose charge of 1912, Wallace was unable to unite even the liberal activist wing of the New Deal coalition. In the end, the politics of anticommunism crippled the 1948 Progressive Party.

Even a spirited campaign could not prevent the 1948 election from becoming a disaster for the Progressive Party. Wallace logged tens of thousands of miles on the campaign trail and spoke before large and enthusiastic crowds, such as the 48,000 supporters who attended a September rally at Yankee Stadium. Wallace himself privately estimated that he could garner at least 3 to 5 million votes—enough to establish the Progressives as a force within the Democratic Party that could be was strong enough to exert a leftward pull on Truman. But on Election Day the Progressives won just 1,157,000 votes, an anemic 2.38 percent of the popular vote. Only in New York and California did the Progressive vote total exceed 4 percent. They won only 30 precincts nationwide, mostly African American, Jewish, or Hispanic districts in New York City and Los Angeles.

The Progressive Party had a negligible impact on the 1948 election. At best, the Progressives' presence on the ballot may have pushed Truman to chart a more liberal course in domestic policies. But the judgment of history should be more kind. If the Progressives of 1948 struggled at the ballot box, it was because the issues they raised were not easily addressed. Wallace and the Progressives fought for an issue that eventually marked liberalism's greatest triumph in the postwar era—civil rights—and against postwar liberalism's greatest compromise—acquiescence to belligerent anti-Communist policies at home and abroad.

The Progressive Parties and the American Reform Tradition

The varied constituencies, platforms, and electoral fortunes of the Progressive parties of 1912, 1924, and 1948 are suggestive of the broader history of American progressive reform politics in the first half of the twentieth century. Theodore Roosevelt and the 1912 Progressives polled a large percentage of the vote because the New Nationalism appealed to many middle-class Americans and because Roosevelt could count on support from large portions of the Republican electorate hostile to the

Old Guard. Progressive reform was, in a sense, middle-of-the-road politics in 1912. La Follette's Progressives of 1924 instinctively tried to organize a class-based party among two economic groups—workers and farmers—who were especially aggrieved during America's transformation into an urban and industrial nation. Although this effort was a disappointment in 1924, Franklin Roosevelt's Democratic Party coalition of the 1930s demonstrated the power latent in an alliance of politically active workers and farmers. Roosevelt harnessed this power to win elections and enact many of the economic reforms sought by the earlier Progressive parties. The anemic showing of Wallace and the 1948 Progressives paradoxically marked the end of one reform era but the beginning of another. The 1948 Progressives' forceful demand for civil rights and their trenchant questioning of America's proper role in world affairs offered a glimpse at issues destined to occupy the next generation of progressive reformers.

See also New Deal Era, 1932–52; progressivism and the Progressive Era, 1890s–1920.

FURTHER READING

Blum, John Morton. *The Republican Roosevelt.* Cambridge, MA: Harvard University Press, 1954.

Culver, John C., and John Hyde. *American Dreamer: The Life and Times of Henry A. Wallace.* New York: Norton, 2000.

Gable, John Allen. *The Bull Moose Years: Theodore Roosevelt and the Progressive Party.* Port Washington, NY: Kennikat Press, 1978.

McKay, Kenneth Campbell. *The Progressive Movement of 1924.* New York: Columbia University Press, 1947.

Markowitz, Norman D. *The Rise and Fall of the People's Century: Henry A. Wallace and American Liberalism, 1941–1948.* New York: Free Press, 1973.

Thelen, David P. *Robert M. La Follette and the Insurgent Spirit.* Boston: Little, Brown and Company, 1976.

KEVIN POWERS

progressivism and the Progressive Era, 1890s–1920

Progressivism was both an idea and a movement. It arose because many Americans believed that their existing institutions, which had been organized around individual liberty and limited government, could no longer function in an increasingly urban, industrial, and ethnically diverse society. Advocates of progressivism sought to reorder the nation's institutions to produce more order, efficiency, stability, and a sense of social responsibility. They believed that Americans would guarantee progress toward a democratic future by moving away from individualism toward social responsibility. As a movement, progressivism was the struggle of individuals and groups to promote and institutionalize reform. Order, efficiency, stability, and social responsibility meant different things to different Americans, so there was no single progressive movement or single set of proposed reforms. But progressivism succeeded in implementing government regulation of the economy and changing the relationship of Americans to their government and to one another.

Progressivism and Discontent

In the years following the Civil War, discontented groups of Americans founded new political parties and workers' organizations, joined local voluntary organizations and the woman suffrage movement, and enlisted in socialist and anarchist movements. All of these groups challenged fundamental premises of American politics. By the middle of the 1890s, such widespread discontent made many Americans fear the collapse of democracy unless society and its institutions were reformed.

The origins of progressivism coincided with a new intellectual movement and technological innovations. Across the Western world, thinkers and academics were arguing that lived experience should decide the worth of existing institutions and structures. New academic disciplines of social science appeared in European and American universities, attracting students across the transatlantic divide to study new fields, such as economics, that emphasized how rational and scientific investigation of social structures would yield the information needed to justify and direct reform. Some of these universities were now admitting female students. Though their numbers were limited, these women would greatly advance progressivism.

Such technological innovations as electricity, railway transportation, the Bessemer converter that transformed iron into steel, steel-frame construction, and massive industrial plants with machinery that sped up the pace of work, among others, were changing everyday life and forms of work. The Columbian Exposition held in Chicago in 1893 celebrated the genius of American inventors and manufacturers. The displays of new technology and economic advances celebrated capitalist industrial production and tied progress to the human ingenuity that would tame and conquer nature. These innovations, however, were implemented with little thought to the conditions of life and work they produced, and with minimal government regulation or oversight. The exposition, moreover, coincided with an economic depression that left many Americans homeless, unemployed, and on the verge of starvation. The contrast between the glittering exposition and the conditions on the streets of cities across the country spurred new organization among Americans already concerned with the direction of the country.

Progressivism and Political Reorganization

By the end of the century, journalists and writers called "muckrakers" were investigating and publicizing the problems of American society. One of the most vexing problems they attacked was the "corrupt bargain" between business and government. For decades, businessmen had curried favors from government officials in order to advance their economic endeavors. In return, politicians and officeholders solicited and accepted bribes. In a climate where economic progress was considered sacrosanct, business received a relatively free hand to conduct its own affairs. Moreover, many businessmen were big contributors to the Republican Party, which reciprocated by passing legislation favorable to them. The money pouring into the party made it the country's most powerful party on the federal level. Republicans controlled the presidency between 1860 and 1912, interrupted only by Democrat Grover Cleveland's two terms.

Progressives argued that government should serve the public good. This "corrupt bargain" allowed private interests, including the leading party politicians, to benefit at the public's expense. Progressives' insistence that the state must protect and promote this public good challenged lingering sentiments about negative liberty (freedom from government) and self-guiding markets. Progressives demanded legislation to give government new powers, reform of the party and electoral systems, and new constitutional amendments.

Their successes crafted a moderate regulatory state. Congress regulated the power of business to engage in monopolies and trusts, created the Federal Reserve System to oversee the country's monetary system, and enacted laws regulating the production of food and drugs. New agencies such as the Federal Trade Commission were organized to oversee adherence to these laws. To help finance the regulatory state, the Sixteenth Amendment to the Constitution gave Congress power to levy an income tax. Progressives charged that giving state legislatures the power to appoint U.S. senators had led to collusion among businessmen, state legislators, and their appointees. The Seventeenth Amendment thus mandated the popular election of senators to Congress.

Individual states passed new political measures, and municipal governments were overhauled. Wisconsin became the first state to require the direct primary for nominating candidates, and Oregon adopted the initiative and referendum to give voters more voice in determining state legislation. Other states quickly followed. Some cities reduced the size of their city councils, gave mayors more power, eliminated district-based ward systems in favor of at-large council membership, municipalized some public services, and enacted public safety measures. Such reforms aimed to minimize the role of political parties, eliminate the franchise system by which public services were awarded to the highest private bidder, and replace party politicians with professionals whom progressives believed would be better equipped to bring order, efficiency, honest government, and protections to the chaotic industrial city.

Progressives also expanded the power of the presidency. Presidents Theodore Roosevelt (1901–8) and Woodrow Wilson (1912–20) each made the presidency more active and powerful in promoting a national progressive agenda. Roosevelt had coined the derisive term "muckraker," but his tours of poverty-stricken urban areas as police commissioner of New York City (1895–97) with the crusading newspaper reporter Jacob Riis convinced him that the uncurbed power of the wealthy few, especially industrialists, threatened democracy. Money influenced politics and allowed business to use the police power of the state to thwart all labor initiatives. As president, Roosevelt used the existing Sherman Anti-Trust Act (1890) to break up monopolies and trusts. He oversaw new legislation to regulate railroad rates and food and drug production and expanded the role of the executive branch by creating new cabinet positions and broadening the powers of others. He was the first president to use his office to compel industry to resolve a major labor strike, that of coal miners in 1902. His administration took the first steps toward developing a national conservation policy. Roosevelt justified this innovative use of presidential power with the progressive idea that the president was "the steward of the public welfare."

His successor, Republican William Howard Taft, attacked monopolies and trusts even more vigorously but did not share Roosevelt's ideals. Taft fought trusts because he believed they restrained free trade, not to promote the public welfare. Unhappy progressive Republicans such as Senator Robert LaFollette (Wisconsin) founded the National Progressive Republican League to contest the Taft regulars. When the party renominated Taft in 1912, they organized the Progressive Party and nominated Roosevelt for president. Progressive women were drawn to this party, even though most still could not vote, because it promised that it would govern in the public interest and would back woman suffrage. The Democrats nominated Woodrow Wilson, and the 1912 race became a contest over the future of progressivism.

Wilson won as the Republican vote split between Taft and Roosevelt. In his first two years in office, Wilson demonstrated his progressive credentials by helping secure new banking, currency, and trade regulations and new antitrust legislation. Wilson managed to keep his southern base intact by promising not to expand the powers of the federal government at the expense of states' rights and by ignoring other progressive demands to promote racial equality and woman suffrage.

Roosevelt and Wilson confronted a U.S. Senate and Supreme Court hostile to government regulation. The Seventeenth Amendment helped to change the makeup of the Senate, and both presidents took a hands-on approach to dealing with Congress. Since progressivism professed a faith in democracy, both men also appealed directly to the people during their presidencies. Each man used Congress's constitutional power to regulate interstate commerce to secure regulatory measures. Wilson was able to appoint leading progressive lawyer Louis Brandeis to the court. Brandeis promoted the progressive idea of social realism: legal rulings should be made on the basis of factual information presented to the courts in the social context of the problem. Although few other jurists of the time so readily accepted social realism, the idea gradually gained a place in legal decisions.

Progressivism and Social Reorganization

Many progressives were motivated by an ideal of collective responsibility for resolving social problems. Settlement house founder Jane Addams argued that democratic governments could not ignore social problems or leave them to the mercy of private charity. She and other progressives proposed that certain social goods, including housing, transportation, parks, recreation areas, health, sanitation, and public education, should not be left to the vagaries of the marketplace. Ideas of social politics owed as much to a transatlantic exchange of ideas as they did to American innovation. Academics, settlement house workers, and professionals in law, economics, finance, and even religion journeyed to Europe to study, investigate, and exchange ideas with leading progressive thinkers there.

The specifics of social politics—for instance, how far and by what means to remove social goods from the marketplace—were contested. As head of the federal Children's Bureau, Julia Lathrop declared that a democratic state must abolish poverty altogether. Catholic priest Father John A. Ryan wanted government to guarantee a living wage to male workers who could then support their families. African Americans Ida B. Wells-Barnett and W.E.B. DuBois used the ideas and language of progressivism to fight for racial equality, arguing that there could be no true democracy without racial democracy.

Social politics inspired tens of thousands of women across the country to join settlement houses and organize local and national voluntary associations that investigated social conditions and demanded that government solve them. These women were in the forefront of demanding that government provide adequate housing, decent public schools, and health and sanitation programs; promote public safety; and end the use of child labor. Fundamental to their progressivism was the idea that the middle class must learn to experience the lives of the poor, the working class, and immigrants in order to foster social responsibility. Working-class and African American women formed similar organizations.

A distinguishing feature of women's progressivism was class-bridging organizations such as the National Women's Trade Union League and the National Consumers' League, which promoted protective labor legislation and abolition of child labor. In 1908 the Supreme Court had accepted, in *Muller v. Oregon*, Brandeis's argument—based on statistics gathered by the women of the National Consumers' League—that excessive strenuous work harmed women's health and that the state thus had a reason to regulate their hours of labor. But the Court refused to extend such protection to male workers, citing the "right to contract" implied by the Fourteenth Amendment. The Senate passed the Keating-

Owen Child Labor Act in 1916 to outlaw the "awful blot" of child labor, but the Court overturned the law as a violation of state powers to regulate labor.

Progressivism generated other new organizations through which like-minded individuals worked to enact reform. Men formed city clubs and municipal leagues. Activist women banded into the General Federation of Women's Clubs. Black and white Americans founded the National Association for the Advancement of Colored People (NAACP). Through such organizations, progressivism formulated a new interest-group politics that voters believed gave them more access to government.

Progressivism and Internationalism

From the 1890s through World War I, progressives often justified territorial expansion and conquest. Most viewed Native Americans as being at odds with white European economic, religious, and social practices. While some progressives advocated compulsory "civilizing," by removing Indian children from their parents, others sought less repressive means by which to integrate them into the broader society. Whichever method used, Native Americans' lands were appropriated to foster white settlement and their customs undermined as part of progressive reordering of society.

Most progressives also justified overseas imperialism. The economic justification was that this would create a more orderly and efficient world in which to do business. It was usually accompanied by a sense of Anglo-Saxon superiority. While some progressives were motivated by a more benign ideal that imperialism could bring education and progress, others simply believed that American superiority gave the United States the right to control the world.

Ideas about gender also underlay progressive imperialism. As women moved into public life and demanded suffrage as both a democratic right and as necessary to promote both domestic and international progressivism, political figures such as Theodore Roosevelt worried that American manhood was being undermined. Nothing could prove manhood, he believed, as much as war, conquest, and making the United States the economic and political powerhouse of the world.

International progressivism did have another side, however. Figures such as Addams and LaFollette promoted an ideal of universal social responsibility to bring order and peace to the world. The international membership of the Women's Peace Party (founded 1915) and its successor, the Women's International League for Peace and Freedom, encouraged such thinking. If domestic progressivism could make Americans take responsibility for each other, then its international dimension could draw the peoples of the world into a broad alliance to defeat poverty and end armed conflict. But, in 1919, the Versailles Peace Conference and the U.S. Senate's refusal to ratify the treaty and join the new League of Nations dashed such hopes.

The Twilight of Progressivism

World War I severely limited the continuation of progressivism. One strain of progressivism had argued that only the right populace could guarantee a good democracy. This idea justified immigration exclusion, antisocialist hysteria, and narrowly defining what it meant to be American. Wartime hysteria heightened such thinking and institutionalized the concept of "100 percent Americanism." Anyone who opposed the war or who supported radical ideologies or groups was labeled un-American and subjected to persecution. The so-called science of eugenics proposed that humans had inbred racial traits that could be measured to determine who would make good democratic citizens. By the 1920s, new laws restricted immigration and enforced new naturalization requirements. Caught in this racialist thinking were African Americans whose progressive activities and participation in the war effort were not rewarded with racial democracy.

Progressivism as a massive movement died out after the war, but its ideals and effects did not. It had never pretended to overturn capitalism but to reform it to cause less harm to Americans. Progressivism's ideals of social responsibility and the need for government regulation were institutionalized into American politics to provide a balance against the forces of the unrestrained marketplace.

See also foreign policy and domestic politics, 1865–1933; interest groups; press and politics; Progressive parties.

FURTHER READING

Addams, Jane. *Democracy and Social Ethics*. New York: Macmillan, 1902.

———. *Peace and Bread in Time of War*. New York: Macmillan, 1922.

Flanagan, Maureen A. *America Reformed: Progressives and Progressivisms, 1890s–1920s*. New York: Oxford University Press, 2007.

Keller, Morton. *Regulating a New Society: Public Policy and Social Change in America, 1900–1933*. Cambridge, MA: Harvard University Press, 1994.

Muncy, Robyn. *Creating a Female Dominion in American Reform, 1890–1935*. New York: Oxford University Press, 1991.

Rauchway, Eric. *Murdering McKinley: The Making of Theodore Roosevelt's America*. New York: Hill and Wang, 2003.

Rodgers, Daniel. *Atlantic Crossings: Social Politics in a Progressive Age*. Cambridge, MA: Harvard University Press, 1998.

Schechter, Patricia. *Ida B. Wells-Barnett and American Reform, 1880–1930*. Chapel Hill: University of North Carolina Press, 2001.

Spain, Daphne. *How Women Saved the City*. Minneapolis: University of Minnesota Press, 2001.

Unger, Nancy. *Fighting Bob LaFollette: The Righteous Reformer*. Chapel Hill: University of North Carolina Press, 2002.

MAUREEN A. FLANAGAN

Prohibition and temperance

From its beginnings in the 1820s through its demise in the 1930s, the temperance movement and its descendant, the Prohibition movement, had a tremendous impact on American politics. Temperance and Prohibition helped to both create and disrupt the Second Party System that existed roughly from 1828 to 1854, and proved a staple (and difficult) issue of party politics during the Gilded Age.

The temperance movement brought women into politics before they had the vote. During the Progressive Era, the Prohibition movement created the first single-issue pressure group, a model of influencing politics that was widely imitated. Prohibition also created the only constitutional amendment directly aimed at the personal habits of the people. National Prohibition presented challenges to the political order. After repeal of the amendment, temperance and Prohibition faded as issues. The birth of neoprohibitionism at the end of the twentieth century sidestepped federal politics as it pressured states into raising the legal drinking age and enforcing harsher laws against drunk driving.

The temperance movement began as a reaction to the alcoholic republic of the late eighteenth and early nineteenth centuries. Americans consumed alcohol at a tremendous rate in this period. For instance, it is estimated that between 1800 and 1830, adult Americans consumed 6.6 to 7.1 gallons of pure alcohol annually, compared to a current annual consumption rate of 2.8 gallons. Alcohol was part of daily life and public culture. Temperance advocates blamed all manner of social disorder on the consumption of drink. Alcohol, they argued, directly caused poverty, disease, crime, political corruption, and family disruption. Many Americans, especially those of Anglo-Saxon and old immigrant stock, saw liquor as an unmitigated evil that needed to be outlawed. Many Christians, inspired by the Second Great Awakening, joined the movement, whose members abstained from liquor and tried to persuade others to do the same.

The Second Party System

From the 1830s through the 1840s, many antiliquor agitators moved beyond moral suasion to embrace political means. The first steps toward politicizing temperance came in New England communities where temperance advocates promoted the policy of no license—that is, they pressured local authorities to stop granting licenses to liquor retailers, removing what they saw as a public sanction of the trade. In some states, such struggles were decided through the ballot in what became known as local option elections (a method, while much altered, that still exists). States, by law, authorized the people of any township, county, city, or precinct to decide in a special election to allow or deny liquor sales in their locality. Liquor merchants, as well as advocates of laissez-faire policies and opponents of reform, mobilized against these efforts.

Such divisions fed into the emerging Second Party System. At first, the Whigs tended to support the temperance advocates' legal solutions while the Democrats opposed them. As immigration increased, bringing both Germans and Irish with established drinking cultures to the United States, the political divisions took on ethnic and religious dimensions, and these immigrants (especially the Catholics among them) tended to favor the Democratic Party. But over time, the rigid divisions between parties over temperance started to erode.

The parties in the 1840s viewed antiliquor measures as both appealing and dangerous. For instance, after Whig-dominated state governments passed laws that restricted the sale of liquor to large bulk orders (in effect imposing a ban on retail alcohol sales), they were turned out of office. Afterward, Whig politicians tried to avoid adopting extreme temperance policies, but only at the risk of alienating some of their supporters. Similarly, Democrats, seeing how popular temperance policies were with some voters, would advocate them, to the disgust of a significant number of their supporters. In short, temperance started out as a defining issue between the parties but became a contested issue within both parties.

By the 1850s, such conflicts led to new political organizations and alliances. Temperance movements throughout the country came together around the Maine Law (named after the first state to adopt it in 1851), which essentially prohibited the manufacture and sale of alcohol within a state. In all, 13 northern states attempted to adopt such laws, and in almost every case, the laws passed. Most of the Maine Laws were quickly repealed, however, as the political alliances that had created them proved to be unstable. The emergence of a new political party system centered on the slavery issue took Prohibition out of politics for almost a generation.

The Gilded Age

At the opening of the Gilded Age (around 1870), drinking had a new venue, the saloon—a primarily male institution, a fact that made its respectability automatically suspect. Even so, saloons existed almost everywhere, spread by the practice of many brewers of establishing their own street-level retailing venues. Throughout the period, the Prohibition Party and the Woman's Christian Temperance Union (WCTU) agitated for national constitutional Prohibition. By the end of the period, six states prohibited the sale of alcohol, and almost every state allowed local option elections on liquor sales. At this time, the Democrats and the Republicans preferred to avoid the issue of Prohibition. Republicans pushed alternative policies of high license (which imposed all sorts of restrictions on liquor merchants), while Democrats preferred to leave the matter up to voters in local option elections. In turn, the leading temperance organizations denounced the major political parties and saw the corruption of politics (symbolized by the saloon) as one of the main evils spawned by the legal manufacture and sale of liquor.

The Prohibition Party was the leading male temperance organization of the Gilded Age. Because it asked men to abandon other party affiliations, in an age where party affiliations were extremely strong, the party remained at the margins of power. Its members came primarily from the temperance wing of the Republican Party, and it had effective organizations only in the Northeast and the Midwest. Throughout its history, the Prohibition Party splintered over whether it should embrace other issues, such as woman suffrage or railroad regulation; in some election cycles it did (thus dividing its members) and in others it did not, but then lost voters to organizations that focused on issues other than liquor. Indeed, the emergence of populism, and a host of new political issues, including regulating the money supply and controlling corporations, ended the Prohibition Party's electoral appeal. By the middle of the last decade of the nineteenth century, the party was widely perceived to be a failure.

Conversely, the female temperance organization of the same period was seen as a great success. The WCTU was the largest female reform organization of the Gilded Age. It was the first national women's reform movement directed and controlled solely by women. Under the leadership of Frances Willard from 1879 to 1898, this largely white, middle-class Protestant women's organization kept the Prohibition issue alive when the political structure was hostile to the antiliquor reform—and convinced a generation of women that they should seek the right to vote. The WCTU pioneered highly effective lobbying techniques (keeping in Washington the first woman lobbyist, Margret Dye Ellis), and in the areas seen as within women's sphere, such as education or the sexual protection of minors, the WCTU was quite successful, especially at the state level. Less successful were the WCTU's attempts to build political coalitions, first with the Prohibition Party and later with the Populist Party and the Knights of Labor. It is only when the WCTU began working with a new Prohibition organization, the Anti-Saloon League, that the temperance advocates could compel the major parties to pass more restrictions on alcohol, culminating in national Prohibition.

The Progressive Era

In the 1890s, antiliquor Protestants built the first national interest group mobilized to shape public policy: the Anti-Saloon League. The league's strength came from its mobilization of millions of church members who opposed the sale of liquor. It grew from the grass roots and built a professional hierarchy of organizers, lobbyists, and power brokers. Through its organization and extensive media empire, the league commanded its supporters to vote the way it told them to, and most did. The league adopted an "omnipartisan" strategy—that is, it supported any politician regardless of party if that politician would support the league's proposals. The Anti-Saloon League cared only about how a politician voted, not how he acted or what he believed. Thus, Warren G. Harding,

New York City Deputy Police Commissioner John A. Leach, right, watches agents pour beer into the sewer following a raid during the height of Prohibition. (Library of Congress)

a known drinker and gambler, always had league support. The league limited its proposals strictly to liquor issues and to policies that would garner support from voters. As its name implied, it first took aim at the unpopular saloon, supporting such restrictions as the high license, although by the turn of the new century, its favored tool was local option elections. When a state adopted that policy, the league then focused on statewide Prohibition.

At first, the Anti-Saloon League concentrated its operations in the states. Working with both major parties, it dried out large parts of the nation through local option and state Prohibition during the first decade of the twentieth century. At the same time, its lobbyists established an effective presence in Washington, where they sought federal legislation (in alliance with other groups, most notably the WCTU) based on the commerce power and taxing power designed to help dry states effectively carry out their Prohibition policies. Its leaders—William Anderson, Purley Baker, Joseph Cannon, Edwin C. Dinwiddie, and Wayne Wheeler—became familiar and feared faces in Washington.

By 1913, after a major victory in congressional passage of the Webb-Kenyon Act, which prohibited the interstate transportation of liquor intended to be used contrary to the receiving state's law, the league launched its campaign for national Prohibition. By 1917 the league and the WCTU persuaded Congress to send the Prohibition Amendment to the states for ratification. They were aided by the anti-German hysteria of World War I (which weakened the brewers, the movement's most effective opponents), as well as the emergency rationale to preserve grain for food (not alcoholic beverages) and to uplift the morals of the people. League organization and political power resulted in speedy ratification and the passage in 1919 of the Volstead Act, which set up the Prohibition enforcement system. On January 16, 1920, national Prohibition went into effect.

National Prohibition proved troubling to both political parties, especially by the middle of the 1920s, when repeal sentiment began to grow. The Prohibitionists, led by the Anti-Saloon League, tied their fortunes to the Republican Party, which welcomed their support at first. But as Prohibition became increasingly unpopular, Republicans tried unsuccessfully to distance themselves from the policy. For example, President Herbert Hoover's Presidential Commission (known widely as the Wickersham Commission after its chairman, George Wickersham) floated several revision proposals in the course of its life, only to be pulled back to the Prohibitionist line by the time it issued its report.

Meanwhile, the Democratic Party was bitterly divided over the issue, with its southern wing strongly supporting Prohibition and its urban, ethnic, northern wing supporting repeal. Thus, the "wet" presidential candidate Alfred E. Smith was saddled with a bone-dry platform plank in the 1928 election. The lobbying of repeal groups, the diminution in size and strength of temperance groups, and the increasing unpopularity of the Prohibition regime (in tandem with a widely accepted view that Prohibition, not alcohol, bred lawlessness and political corruption) culminated in support from both parties for modification or repeal in the 1932 election. Thus, within 14 years of its adoption, the Eighteenth Amendment was repealed through the Twenty-First Amendment.

From National Prohibition to Neoprohibitionism

Repeal took Prohibition out of partisan politics. Even as he proclaimed the passing of national Prohibition, President Franklin D. Roosevelt declared the nation should return to true temperance, not to the old-time saloon. Thus, the Federal Alcohol Act of 1933 prohibited distillers or brewers from owning retail outlets. The Twenty-First Amendment's second clause also returned almost complete control over liquor to the states, where the sale of liquor proved easier to regulate than prohibit. Within four years of the amendment's adoption, 43 of the 48 states had legalized the sale of all liquor. By 1959 there were no Prohibition states left, although several states preserved the policy in local option systems. To prevent the return of the old, much-vilified saloon, virtually all the states adopted either a government monopoly system or a state-controlled license system of distribution. These systems controlled the number of liquor licenses granted in communities, regulated the environment in which liquor could be consumed in a public venue, and made liquor issues questions of bureaucratic politics, not partisan ones.

From the 1930s through the 1970s, an odd alliance of those who saw drink as evil and sinful, bootleggers who profited by bringing liquor into dry areas, and those who did not want liquor stores or bars in their neighborhoods made the United States a patchwork of regions where liquor was sold without restriction, sold only by the drink, or not sold at all.

An unintended consequence of this patchwork was the emergence of driving while intoxicated. Drinking and driving was perceived as a societal problem as early as the 1950s but did not gain strong advocates against it until the 1980s, when it became associated with related issues of underage drinking.

The key advocacy group, at the state and federal levels, was Mothers against Drunk Driving (MADD). As a group, MADD had inherent advantages. First, it was a victims' group, with personalized stories—My child was killed by a drunk driver, what are you doing to do about it? Second, it quickly gained powerful allies, most notably the insurance industry, the liquor industry (prompted in part by fear of stricter liquor regulations), and car manufacturers (fearful of requirements for more safety devices on cars). MADD, like earlier advocates, started with local and state action. Its first actions were to track judges and others in their sentencing of drunk drivers (and to obtain harsher sentences, either through mandatory sentencing laws or a change of judges) and to push for state laws that lowered the blood alcohol level that legally defined intoxication. In these and later efforts, the group avoided partisan politics in favor of lobbying and leveraging the administrative state. Through its actions, the 1984 Highway Act included provisions that withheld highway funds to any state that had a legal drinking age lower than 21. At the time, legal drinking ages varied among the states, but by 1988, with virtually no political struggle, the legal drinking age in all states was 21.

The control of drink bedevilled party politics from the 1820s to the 1930s. The Prohibition movement mobilized women's mass political power before suffrage and gave birth to the single-issue pressure group. After repeal, temperance and Prohibition faded as issues, only to be reborn in a far different form in the late twentieth century as neoprohibitionism.

See also Gilded Age, 1870s–90s; populism; progressivism and the Progressive Era, 1890s–1920.

FURTHER READING

Foster, Gaines M. *Moral Reconstruction: Christian Lobbyists and the Federal Legislation of Morality, 1865–1920.* Chapel Hill: University of North Carolina Press, 2002.

Kerr, K. Austin. *Organized for Prohibition: A New History of the Anti-Saloon League.* New Haven, CT: Yale University Press, 1985.

Kyvig, David E. *Repealing National Prohibition*. 2nd ed. Kent, OH: Kent State University Press, 2000.

Pegram, Thomas R. *Battling Demon Rum: The Struggle for a Dry America, 1800–1933*. Chicago: Ivan R. Dee, 1998.

RICHARD F. HAMM

Protestants and politics

Protestant movements have been important in almost every period of American political history, yet Protestant political influence has varied greatly depending on times, places, and circumstances. Protestants were more dominant during the Civil War—when they accounted for over 90 percent of the nation's places of worship—than they have been in the "culture wars" of recent times, when much higher numbers of Roman Catholics, Jews, Muslims, and secularists share the religious landscape. Region is also a constant variable. Since the 1880s, Protestant interests have remained more important in the South, which retains a substantial Protestant majority, than in other parts of the country where Protestant churches have become relatively weaker. Changes within Protestantism also matter. In the nineteenth century, mainstream Congregationalists, Presbyterians, Methodists, and Episcopalians enjoyed a widely recognized educational and cultural authority; more recently, the numbers of Pentecostals, independents, and megachurches have burgeoned, yet they have also had to compete with much stronger cultural rivals. Above all, race has significantly complicated American Protestant politics. To this day, most black Protestants are similar to white Protestants in their traditional religious beliefs and conservative moral convictions, but they differ dramatically in both political opinions and political allegiance.

Yet when the United States is viewed from afar—especially by visitors from abroad—the general Protestant imprint on political history is unmistakable. In 1775, at the onset of the American Revolution, Edmund Burke reminded Parliament that the colonies were naturally wary about the arbitrary exercise of British power because they were "protestants; and of that kind, which is the most adverse to all implicit submission of mind and opinion."

A century and a half later, a visiting Frenchman, André Siegfried, concluded that Protestantism was still the "only national religion" of the United States. To Siegfried, Protestantism had become a matter of cultural style more than explicit beliefs. He felt that Calvinism, broadly defined to take in the religious activism of the nineteenth century as well as the original legacy of the Puritans, still dominated the public: "Every American is at heart an evangelist, be he a [Woodrow] Wilson, a [William Jennings] Bryan, or a [John D.] Rockefeller. He cannot leave people alone, and he constantly feels the urge to preach."

More recently, Sébastien Fath, a French sociologist and historian who is himself an active Baptist layman, has argued that Protestant heritage is the best explanation for the importance of American holidays like Thanksgiving, the prominence of religious language in political speech making, the public deference afforded to figures like the evangelist Billy Graham, the individualistic approach to moral questions, the sense of national destiny under providence, and the checkered responses to terrorism.

In *Democracy in America*, Alexis de Tocqueville spelled out how he thought Protestantism had shaped the nation's political course. During his visit to the United States in the 1830s, Protestant churches enjoyed an almost complete monopoly over the nation's formal religious life. In Tocqueville's view, the conundrum was why religion—which, because of the Constitution's separation of church and state, "never mixes directly in the government of society"—nonetheless had to be considered "the first of their political institutions." His explanation centered on how Protestant faith had aligned itself with republican principles of liberty: "if [religion] does not give them the taste for freedom, it singularly facilitates their use of it." His final judgment was comparative: in Europe, he had "seen the spirit of religion and the spirit of freedom almost always move in contrary directions. Here [in the United States] I found them united intimately with one another: they reigned together on the same soil."

The sociopolitical connections that Tocqueville described also differentiate the American story from Protestant histories elsewhere. Unlike Germany, Switzerland, the Netherlands, England, and Scotland, where Protestant churches were long established by law, American Protestantism thrived where church and state were separated. Unlike Protestants in Catholic and Orthodox Europe, Protestants in the United States have enjoyed mainstream status. Unlike Protestant movements that sprung up during the twentieth century in the Southern Hemisphere, American Protestants have enjoyed material wealth and cultural authority. The opinions of foreign observers and the comparative differences with Protestants elsewhere in the world both point to the same conclusion: to explain the place of Protestantism in American politics it is necessary to heed the specifics of American history.

The Founding Era

During the American Revolution, Protestants were divided. Many Anglicans, along with a few from other denominations, remained loyal to the mother country. The substantial numbers of Quaker, Mennonite, Moravian, and Brethren pacifists in the 13 colonies clung to their principles and refused to align with either warring side. Yet what became the majority position joined together Protestant religion and patriotic politics so strongly that some observers could see little difference between the two. Joseph Galloway, a prominent Pennsylvania legislator who became a loyalist, wrote that the general colonial insurrection was led by "Congregationalists, Presbyterians, and smugglers." Behind this perception was the confluence of a Puritan tradition that had been revived through colonial religious awakenings and a republican tradition that was flourishing in opposition to British court politics. The Puritan inheritance featured a moral approach to public life alongside a belief that God covenanted with nations on the basis of their religious actions. Oppositional—or Real Whig—opinion also took a moral approach to politics, but focused on preventing the corruption that the Whigs believed came from unchecked centralized power.

In the heat of the Revolution, the Puritan and Whig viewpoints came together. Both contained what historian Edmund Morgan once called "a distinctly bearish view of human nature"—in Puritan terms, a consequence of Adam and Eve's "original sin," and in Whig terms, a consequence of the inherently corrupting character of governmental authority. Both felt that personal liberty and civic health had to be supported by collective virtue. If the Puritans defined virtue as God's triumph over sin and the Whigs defined it as honest public dealing by altruistic gentlemen, there was enough common ground for an alliance against what seemed to be the schemes of Parliament and the heavy-handed assaults on liberty authorized by George III.

Once this link was forged, the fight against British political oppression could be seen as the fight against sin itself. Thus, as tensions rose with the mother country, a Connecticut Congregationalist likened Parliament to the Pharaoh in Exodus 1:8, "which knew not Joseph," and ministers from several denominations described Parliament as the apocalyptic "Beast" from Revelation, chapter 13. During the conflict, patriot preachers often referred to American events as replicating biblical precedents—for example, some compared the patriot victory at Saratoga, New York, to the triumph of Hezekiah over the Assyrians.

Tom Paine's tract *Common Sense* (1776) exploited these politicoreligious parallels by using biblical illustrations from the story of King Saul to show how Scripture supported republican politics. A similar message came in a famous sermon of May 17, 1776, from John Witherspoon, the president of Princeton College. Witherspoon's address, "The Dominion of Providence over the Passions of Men," defended resistance to leaders who transgressed justice, liberty, and common humanity, and proclaimed God's ability to bring good out of the unrestrained excesses of Britain's tyranny. In a thanksgiving sermon at the end of the war on December 11, 1783, Witherspoon said what many others, like Paine, Thomas Jefferson, Ben Franklin, and George Washington, also believed, that "the separation of this country from Britain had been of God." Paine, the free-thinking deist, and Witherspoon, the traditional Presbyterian clergyman, were not very close in theological or ethical beliefs. Yet in the political crises of the war, their convictions came together to support the drive for national independence. Later, this conjunction of political and religious opinion would lend a sacred aura to U.S. political principles and convince many Protestants that the nation's long-term health depended on their own vigilance.

A few patriotic African Americans, like Lemuel Haynes of New England, also felt that a divine mandate supported the patriotic cause. But, unlike most of his white contemporaries, Haynes also expanded the standard mix of Whig principles and biblical language into an attack on slavery. Other African Americans reversed the application of the Bible. The slave David George of South Carolina, for instance, referred to his manumission by British troops as an "Exodus."

By the time warfare gave way to nation building, Protestant public influence was less obvious than when ministers had preached for independence. Although Protestant allegiance to Scripture made the Bible the era's most widely read and quoted book, it exerted less direct influence on constitutional political theory than on the country's cultural mores. Political principles drawn from John Locke, European republican traditions, and practical American experience were more obviously important for the Constitution and the Bill of Rights.

Protestants were divided on how to organize church and state. Many Congregationalists and Episcopalians, along with a few Presbyterians, looked for broad government funding, usually along the lines proposed by Patrick Henry of Virginia, who favored a "general assessment" whereby individual taxpayers designated particular churches to receive their tax revenues. A strong coalition of sectarian Protestants and Enlightenment political leaders fought off this proposal in Virginia. They also succeeded at putting into the Constitution's First Amendment the principle that the federal government could neither authorize "an establishment of religion" nor prohibit "the free exercise thereof." As promoted by Baptists like Isaac Backus of Massachusetts and John Leland of Virginia, alongside noted founders like Thomas Jefferson and James Madison, this federal stance was soon accepted by the states as well.

A Second Founding: 1790s–1830s

The early history of the United States witnessed a great surge of evangelical Protestantism preceded by numerous local revivals during the Revolutionary era that went mostly unnoticed by national elites. For their part, these elites expected American religious life to follow historical precedents. Leaders of the colonies' largest churches—Episcopal, Presbyterian, Congregational—expected that some form of favored treatment would replace formal establishment. A few champions of the Enlightenment, like Thomas Jefferson, thought that Unitarianism, deism, or some other kind of "reasonable religion" would come to dominate the country. What actually developed was a new style of Protestant Christianity that first altered religious life and then gradually began to affect politics. During the presidential election of 1800, many leaders of the older Protestant denominations campaigned actively against Jefferson for what they called his "infidelity." When Jefferson as president proved inoffensive to the churches, Protestant leaders mostly retreated from active political involvement. This retreat lasted for about a generation.

Meanwhile, religious life at the grass roots was undergoing a transformation. Methodists under the leadership of Bishop Francis Asbury, Baptists guided by countless local preachers, and "Disciples" and "Christians" inspired by Thomas Campbell and Barton Stone were busy preaching the salvation of souls, organizing congregations, and recruiting young men (and a few young women) to serve as itinerants. For some Baptists and the Methodists, especially under Asbury's tutelage until his death in 1816, politics faded almost entirely away. For other Baptists and followers of Campbell and Stone, the Christian message was thoroughly mixed with a republican ideology zealous for the liberty of local congregations and scrupulously alert to the corruptions of power.

The style of public religious life in the new United States followed the bottom-up course of the Methodists, Baptists, and "Christians" rather than the top-down course foreseen by leaders of the traditional churches. Between 1790 and 1860, the U.S. population increased eightfold; the number of Baptist churches increased fourteenfold; the number of Methodist churches twenty-eight-fold, and the number of "Disciples" and "Christian" churches of the Restorationist Movement rose from none in 1790 to over two thousand in 1860.

Gradually the more traditional churches also took on the new religious style. It was republican insofar as it internalized the fear of unchecked authority and the commitment to private virtue that drove the ideology of the political founders. But it was also "Christian republican"; the energetic itinerants promoted not classical manliness but humility in Christ. This religion did not trust in ascribed authority or inherited bureaucracies but in achieved authority and ad-hoc networking. It was populist or democratic in championing the ability of any white man to assume leadership in any religious assembly. It also gave supreme authority to Scripture, which trumped all other religious authorities and which was open for all to read and interpret for themselves.

Above all, the religion that came to prevail in the nineteenth century was voluntaristic, keyed to innovative leadership, proactive public advocacy, and entrepreneurial goal setting. Voluntary societies organized for preaching the Christian message, distributing Christian literature, encouraging Christian civilization, and networking philanthropic activity came into their own after about 1810. The most important were founded by interdenominational networks of evangelicals for evangelical purposes, like the American Board of Commissioners for Foreign Missions (1810), the American Bible Society (1816), and the American Education Society (1816). The period's dynamic evangelicalism established an enduring template for the future. Other religious movements that differed greatly in belief and practice from Protestant evangelicals would flourish in the United States by adopting, to at least some degree, many of the free-form, populist, and voluntaristic traits that evangelical Protestants pioneered.

Religious voluntarism became more broadly influential when religious practices came to inspire mobilization on behalf of social and political causes. By the 1830s, national parties reemerged as voluntary societies that organized local campaigns and national conventions on the model of religious revivals and religious societies. Increasingly, religious concerns influenced the political agenda by pushing to the fore issues like Cherokee removal, temperance reform, Sunday movement of the mail, and—preeminently—slavery.

Highs and Lows: 1830s–80s

The extraordinary impact of Protestants on national politics in the antebellum years and through the Civil War rested on the extraordinary expansion of evangelical Protestantism earlier in the century. By the 1830s and 1840s, the religious situation was changing rapidly, especially with the increase of Roman Catholic immigration from Germany, Ireland, and other European countries. Yet because Protestants had adapted so well to the ideology and social circumstances of the new nation, this period witnessed the most comprehensive Protestant impact on politics in American history. In the 1830s, the issues of Indian policy, temperance reform, and moving the mails on Sunday brought Protestants back into the political arena.

Of these contested issues, temperance reform went deepest. From the early nineteenth century on, temperance societies made up an important component of the American voluntary empire. But not until the 1840s did voluntary persuasion spill over into direct political action; the 1846 Maine Law enacting Prohibition became a model for how to channel private reform into public legislation.

Strong Protestant associations with the Whig, Liberty, Free Soil, American (Know-Nothing), and Republican parties—along with a reciprocating Catholic loyalty to the Democratic Party—made all of the era's national elections and many local contests occasions of religious tension. The country's most consistent Whig, and then Republican, voters were northern Protestants, with Congregationalists, Episcopalians, Presbyterians, and Methodists providing near unanimous support. Baptists and other sectarian Protestants in the North leaned to the Whigs and Republicans. Many southern Protestants were also Whigs, until sectional division over slavery drove these voters to the Democratic Party. Catholics of all ethnic backgrounds were strong for the Democrats against the Whigs and became even more ardent in opposing the Republican Party.

The ideological affinity that drew Protestants, especially in the North, to the Whigs and Republicans was congruity between political activism and evangelical voluntarism. As depicted by historian Daniel Walker Howe, the Whigs and evangelical Protestants shared a common approach to public life: self-realization linked to care for community, personal liberty coordinated with self-discipline, "moral responsibility" existing alongside "moral conditioning"—in sum, "the balancing of freedom and control." Inner ties between evangelicals and Whigs help explain why Abraham Lincoln, though never a church member and more "church friendly" than an active Christian, enjoyed such strong support from northern Protestants in his two Republican campaigns for president (in 1860 and 1864). For many Whigs/Republicans and evangelicals, as for Lincoln, the progress of American society and the development of American religion took place expressly under the providential hand of God. Some sectarian Protestants, especially Baptists and especially in the South, along with a few members of Lutheran and Reformed churches who found "Yankee meddling" obtrusive, objected to this vision and turned to the Democratic Party (or, in the election of 1860, the Constitutional Union Party).

Protestant support for Whig political culture became more overt as evangelical revivalism became more political. For Charles Grandison Finney, the era's most notable revivalist, salvation from sin took on overt political implications. In his much reprinted *Lectures on Revival* (1835), Finney boldly claimed that "politics are part of the religion in such a country as this." In his view, slavery was not as important as personal salvation but it was nonetheless vital to realize that "slavery is, pre-eminently, the *sin of the church*."

Disputes over slavery eventually involved all American churches. During the antebellum years, African Americans in the North formed their own religious bodies, like the African Methodist Episcopal Church, and took the first steps in political organization that, more than a century later, would directly influence national politics. In 1833 Protestants of several types took the lead in forming the American Anti-Slavery Society, which became a notable voice for abolition, defined as a moral obligation under God. More northern

Protestants, however, were probably emancipationists rather than abolitionists. They worried about slavery and hoped for its eventual demise but looked for a long-term, gradual remedy rather than an immediate end to the institution. Protestant backing for the American Colonization Society (founded in 1816), which proposed "returning" blacks to Africa, fit neatly with emancipationist goals.

In the South after 1830, northern abolitionist attacks on slavery and the increasing politicization of all regional differences stimulated a fresh religious defense of slavery in which learned Presbyterians and Baptists, like the Reverend William Stringfellow of Virginia, took the lead. They based their defense on the obvious acceptance of slavery in the Bible, both Old and New Testaments. The argument that abolitionists both ignored Scripture and threatened national stability with a flood of slaves unprepared for the duties of citizenship also won considerable support, in the North as well as the South.

Many Northerners, however, including Theodore Dwight Weld, a convert to Finney's revivalism, and Francis Wayland, the Baptist president of Brown University, responded that "the spirit of the Bible" had always moved toward liberty. They argued that biblical slavery for the ancient Hebrews and under the Romans was very different from the chattel slavery found in the United States. A few authors, like the independent Kentucky minister John G. Fee and the African American reformer Frederick Douglass, pointed out that, in the Bible, almost all slaves were members of white races.

Religious strife over slavery had momentous institutional consequences. In 1844–45, the main Baptist and Methodist denominations split over the issue. Among the Methodists, especially, subsequent contentions over assets of the publishing house and boundaries between the northern and the southern churches became a festering source of bitter sectional conflict. To observers, the schisms, which took place in organizations with a major presence throughout the nation, were an ominous portent, as when Henry Clay said in 1852, "I tell you this sundering of the religious ties which have hitherto bound our people together, I consider the greatest source of danger to our country."

In the immediate run-up to the Civil War, Harriet Beecher Stowe's landmark novel *Uncle Tom's Cabin* (1852) inspired antislavery readers with a vision of Protestantism defined by its power to free. Stowe's brother, Henry Ward Beecher, pastor of Brooklyn's prestigious Plymouth Congregational Church, ardently preached abolition, took paid assignments to speak for the Republican Party, and during the war, visited Britain as an unofficial ambassador for the Union. His southern counterpart, the much-respected Presbyterian minister James Henley Thornwell of South Carolina, published carefully argued sermons and treatises defending the moral character of the Confederacy. During the war, chaplains served sacrificially in both armies; the United States Christian Commission pioneered in providing nonmilitary assistance to northern troops; both president Abraham Lincoln and Jefferson Davis repeatedly enlisted the churches for special days of fasting and thanksgiving; and the struggle took on the character of a religious war.

The Civil War marked the high tide of Protestant political influence in American history. In the immediate aftermath, many northern churches sent volunteers into the South, especially to educate freed slaves. But for the most part, Protestant concerns shifted from national reform to private religious nurture. After emancipation, African Americans did form several new denominations and strengthened denominations that had existed before the war. But for public purposes, Protestant energies flagged. As Reconstruction came to an end after the presidential election of 1876, white Protestants either actively supported or passively accepted the imposition of white political control in the South. By the 1890s, some white Protestants even advanced religious arguments to sanction the regime of lynching, while only a very few in the North protested. The American Anti-Slavery Society disbanded in 1870. Former advocates of reform like Henry Ward Beecher spoke out more actively for North-South reconciliation than for racial justice.

The evangelist D. L. Moody, as emblematic for his postbellum era as Charles Finney had been for the antebellum period, from the mid-1870s on agreed to segregate his preaching services in the South. Along with large segments of the Protestant world, Moody's heightened stress on personal piety seemed to entail a decrease of interest in social conditions. Moody and his supporters represented a wide swath of white Protestant religion in speaking much about sins of the flesh, little about sins of greed, and almost never about sins of social domination. In national elections, white Protestants in the South voted overwhelmingly for Democrats, black and white Protestants in the North voted consistently Republican, and black Protestants in the South were gradually, and then systematically, prevented from voting at all.

Readjustments: 1890s–1940s

Between the end of Reconstruction and the end of World War II, organized religion gradually receded as a force in American politics. Protestant personalities, however, played a large role in both the Populist and Progressive movements, and Protestant factors came directly to the fore in the crusade for Prohibition, support for World War I, continuing opposition to Roman Catholicism, and various efforts at social reform.

William Jennings Bryan, a three-time Democratic nominee for president (1896, 1900, 1908) and secretary of state from 1913 to 1915, was an active Presbyterian who used politics to promote public morality defined by both Christian and American ideals. For Bryan, the Populist desire to protect the farmer, the wage laborer, the women and children working in factories, and the hard-pressed debtor represented moral as well as political imperatives. Yet Bryan's reformist campaigns on behalf of ordinary Americans never gained wide success. They failed in part because the racist Democratic regimes in the South made all Democrats suspect to the rest of the nation, and in part because many Democrats—especially in the South—were suspicious of Bryan's appeal to government action for social change.

With the election of Woodrow Wilson in 1912 and in 1916, the Progressive Era enjoyed its most visible successes. Under President Wilson, who like Bryan was an active Presbyterian layman, reforms that became law—the national income tax, probation, and women's suffrage—reflected some of the goals of the Social Gospel. This informal movement mobilized northern, more liberal Protestants trying to address the humanitarian crises attending the nation's massive and rapid industrialization. Their leaders included Washington Gladden, a pastor in Columbus, Ohio, who once had the temerity to refuse a donation from John D. Rockefeller, and Walter Rauschenbusch, whose experiences as a pastor in a New York City slum led to a landmark book in 1907, *Christianity and the Social Crisis*. In many cities, the Salvation Army, a holiness sect that came from Britain in 1880, offered the most effective hands-on responses to unemployment, poverty, family fracture, alcoholism, poverty, and unwanted or neglected children.

Although the energies of Populist and Progressive Protestants were not insubstantial, they fell far short of meeting the needs of a rapidly changing nation. When President Wilson's effort to turn World War I into a springboard for worldwide democracy faltered, Protestant reforming efforts seemed to deflate as well. White Protestants offered no serious resistance against the persistence of racism and lynch laws, the Red Scare that followed the war, the consumerist materialism that swept the country in the "Roaring Twenties," and the punitive restrictions on immigration legislated in 1925.

The temperance crusade that led to the Eighteenth Amendment, or Prohibition, in 1919 represented a last gasp of the "evangelical united front." The drive for Prohibition had been carried into the twentieth century by the Women's Christian Temperance Union, founded in the early 1870s under the effective leadership of Frances Willard, and by the ecumenical Anti-Saloon League (1895). By the 1920s, the front was busily dividing into mutually antagonistic submovements. Besides the fundamentalist-modernist controversy, the rise of Pentecostalism, the growing strength of ethnic Protestant churches, and the emergence of Catholicism as a public force fragmented religious energy in American political life. Prohibition's relative lack of success, combined with its failure to sustain popular support, indicated that the religious forces behind it had become relatively marginal.

The 1928 presidential election brought Protestants momentarily back into the political spotlight. As a sign that ancient Protestant-Catholic antagonisms still could exert a political impact, Democratic support for the presidential run of Catholic Alfred E. Smith dipped dramatically in the strongly evangelical South, especially in those areas with large Baptist populations. But from the perspective of the 1930s and 1940s, the 1928 election was an anomaly. Protestants remained a large and active constituency in the American body politic, but they no longer seemed a potent political force.

Reassertions: 1950s–Present

The civil rights movement once again made Protestantism important for American politics. Broadly theistic themes had resurfaced in public life during World War II, which both Winston Churchill and Franklin D. Roosevelt called a battle for "Christian civilization." Even more, the cold war enlisted public religiosity as an ally in the struggle against "godless communism"—for example, by adding "under God" to the Pledge of Allegiance in 1954. But African Americans, in the campaign for equitable treatment under the law, provided the spark that made hard-edged religious faith politically significant again.

Leaders of the movement, like Martin Luther King Jr., had been trained by teachers who for more than a generation combined elements of Mahatma Ghandi's pacifism and the socialism of A. Philip Randolph with traditional Protestant emphases on the justice of God and the power of the Holy Spirit. In his "I Have a Dream" speech in Washington, D.C., on August 28, 1963, King illustrated the public leverage that such teaching could generate when combined with the rhetorical power of classic African American preaching. Yet the success of the movement depended not only on the sophisticated convictions of leaders but on a Christian faith that remained close to the ardent supernaturalism of the autonomous black denominations and, beyond them, of slave religion. Annell Ponder and Fannie Lou Hamer were only two of the movement's countless foot soldiers whose identification with Jesus Christ sustained them through beatings, imprisonment, and public humiliation.

Civil rights legislation became the law of the land when well-publicized violence against self-sacrificing civil rights proponents compelled the federal government to act. In turn, the success of the civil rights movement precipitated a thorough realignment in national political power and a dramatic alteration in the nation's public ethos. The realignment took place when voting was reconfigured in support of civil rights reforms or in reactions against those reforms. The alteration in ethos took place when other groups followed the path of civil rights activists and began to use religious or quasi-religious convictions as reasons to pursue their political goals.

Among the unintended consequences of the mobilization of Christian language for civil rights was the use of very similar language by those who later mobilized to form the New Christian Right. Biblical phrases, traditional Christian verities reworked for contemporary problems, energetic organization on the model of religious voluntary associations, and selective use of Christian imperatives—all followed the path taken by civil rights reform.

Charges of rampant "big government," which from segregationists were a smoke screen for white supremacy, became more honestly debatable for a much larger population when they responded to other federal reforms. For example, the early civil rights movement coincided with new federal initiatives in science education that were part of the effort to catch up with Soviet Union's space exploration program. These curricular changes offended some communities who objected to the promotion of evolution, particularly to the use of tax dollars for public education that seemed to question what parents wanted their children to learn about God's presence in the world.

Soon thereafter, the courts began vigorously to adjudicate aspects of religion and public life that had hitherto been mostly left to the states. These included prohibition of prayer and of Bible reading in the public schools (1962–63), and the *Roe v. Wade* decision that legalized abortion in 1973. At first, Protestants paid little attention, since many considered abortion a "Catholic issue." But improving relations between a few Protestants and Catholics, along with effective antiabortion advocacy by some white evangelicals, especially the theologian Francis Schaeffer, soon made opposition to abortion a foundation of the New Christian Right.

By the late 1960s and early 1970s, white evangelicals, even in the South, had mostly accepted the inevitability of civil rights for blacks, and some even became advocates of the new order. Expansion of the federal government was another matter, however. Many evangelicals regarded busing for school desegregation, the equal rights amendment, and the expansion of gay rights as illegitimate extensions of civil rights reforms. Many also complained about "activist" judges who enforced church-state separation strictly.

Some commentators have suggested that concern over the Massachusetts Supreme Court ruling in 2003 that permitted gay marriage helped tilt the election of 2004 to George W. Bush. If so, this shows a clear link between recent political divisions and early civil rights activities—but with civil rights understood broadly as the groundwork for a "rights revolution" promoted by the nation's courts rather than narrowly as a struggle for racial justice. Where evangelical Protestants made up only 24 percent the vote for Richard Nixon's run for president in 1960, by 2004 they made up 40 percent of George W. Bush's total.

The relative success of the civil rights movement in ending enforced segregation in the South also allowed "natural" political instincts finally to overcome the "artificial" results of the Civil War. As long as religion-backed white supremacy prevailed in the South—as long as Democratic allegiance in the South was protected by resentment against Republicans for "the war of northern aggression"—it was impossible for the small-government and largely Protestant ideology of white Southerners to make common political cause with the small-government and substantially Protestant ideology of northern Republicans and those in the West. Once legally enforced racism was out of the picture, however, it was much easier for the Republican Party to mount an appeal in the white South. Once segregation became illegal, the promotion of a political agenda that championed personal responsibility, traditional values, and Judeo-Christian morality—in exploratory fashion by Barry Goldwater in his 1964 candidacy, with great effect by Ronald Reagan in 1980 and 1984, and with sustaining force by George W. Bush and his chief political advisor, Karl Rove, in 2000 and 2004—enjoyed a broad national appeal, except in those parts of the country where other political goals had become paramount.

This brief account cannot explore the many nuances of Protestant political history. Smaller groups like Quakers, Mennonites, and Seventh-day Adventists, as well as denominations with large regional concentrations like Lutherans in the Upper Midwest, have not always followed the political path of the large Protestant constituencies. But for almost all Protestants throughout the course of American history, traditional Protestant emphases—including lay appropriation of Scripture, the urgency of personal moral judgments, and the perception of close ties between personal morality and public well-being—have deeply affected U.S. political as well as religious history.

See also abolitionism; Catholics and politics; civil rights; Prohibition and temperance; religion and politics.

FURTHER READING

Campbell, David E., ed. *A Matter of Faith: Religion in the 2004 Presidential Election*. Washington, DC: Brookings Institution, 2007.

Carwardine, Richard J. *Evangelicals and Politics in Antebellum America*. New Haven, CT: Yale University Press, 1993.

Chappell, David L. *A Stone of Hope: Prophetic Religion and the Death of Jim Crow*. Chapel Hill: University of North Carolina Press, 2004.

Engeman, Thomas S., and Michael P. Zuckert, eds. *Protestantism and the American Founding*. Notre Dame, IN: University of Notre Dame Press, 2004.

Fath, Sébastien. *Dieu bénisse l'Amérique: La Religion de la Maison-Blanche* [God Bless America: The Religion of the White House]. Paris: Éditions du Seuil, 2004.

Fox-Genovese, Elizabeth, and Eugene D. Genovese. *The Mind of the Master Class: History and Faith in the Southern Slaveholders' Worldview*. New York: Cambridge University Press, 2005.

Goen, C. C. *Broken Churches, Broken Nation: Denominational Schisms and the Coming of the Civil War*. Macon, GA: Mercer University Press, 1985.

Guth, James L., John C. Green, Carwin E. Smidt, Lyman A. Kellstedt, and Margaret M. Paloma. *The Bully Pulpit: The Politics of Protestant Clergy*. Lawrence: University Press of Kansas, 1998.

Handy, Robert T. *Undermined Establishment: Church-State Relations in America, 1880–1920*. Princeton, NJ: Princeton University Press, 1991.

Hatch, Nathan O. *The Democratization of American Christianity*. New Haven, CT: Yale University Press, 1989.

Howe, Daniel Walker. *The Political Culture of the American Whigs*. Chicago: University of Chicago Press, 1979.

Kazin, Michael. *A Godly Hero: The Life of William Jennings Bryan*. New York: Knopf, 2006.

Kleppner, Paul. *The Third Electoral System, 1853–1892: Parties, Voters, and Political Cultures*. Chapel Hill: University of North Carolina Press, 1979.

Marty, Martin E. *Righteous Empire: The Protestant Experience in America*. New York: Dial Press, 1970.

Miller, Randall M., Harry S. Stout, and Charles Reagan Wilson, eds. *Religion and the American Civil War*. New York: Oxford University Press, 1998.

Morgan, Edmund S. "The Puritan Ethic and the American Revolution." *William and Mary Quarterly* 24 (January 1967), 3–43.

Noll, Mark A. *Race, Religion, and American Politics from Nat Turner to George W. Bush: A Short History*. Princeton, NJ: Princeton University Press, 2008.

Noll, Mark A., and Luke E. Harlow, eds. *Religion and American Politics: From the Colonial Period to the Present*. New York: Oxford University Press, 2007.

Payne, Charles M. *I've Got the Light of Freedom: The Organizing Tradition and the Mississippi Freedom Struggle*. Berkeley: University of California Press, 1995.

Siegfried, André. *America Comes of Age: A French Analysis*. New York: Harcourt Brace, 1927.

Silk, Mark, and Andrew Walsh, eds. Religion by Region Series. 8 vols. Walnut Creek, CA: Alta Mira Press, 2004–7.

Tocqueville, Alexis de. *Democracy in America*. Edited and translated by Arthur Goldhammer. New York: Library of America, 2004.

Witherspoon, John. *The Selected Writings of John Witherspoon*. Edited by Thomas Miller. Carbondale: Southern Illinois University Press, 1990.

Wuthnow, Robert. *The Restructuring of American Religion: Society and Faith since World War II*. Princeton, NJ: Princeton University Press, 1988.

MARK A. NOLL

public opinion polls

The current American political process is nearly unimaginable without public opinion polls. These surveys measure not only the relative standing of candidates for office but also citizens' views on myriad social and political issues. Attempts to record political opinion are as old as the nation. But such polls, at least in their contemporary guise, date only from the mid-1930s, when George Gallup, Elmo Roper, and Archibald Crossley championed the ability of scientific sampling methods to reveal the "pulse of democracy." The modern public opinion poll—along with its ramifications for U.S. politics and civic life—was born of their success.

Interest in elucidating citizens' political sentiments stretches far back into the American past, as well as that of most republican nations. Since at least the eighteenth century, when the term *public opinion* first surfaced, representative governments have claimed to be able to locate—as well as listen and respond to—the will of the people. As James Madison argued in 1791, the "opinion of the majority" was the "real sovereign in every free government." Public opinion, whether deemed virtuous, unruly, or in need of enlightened guidance, became part of the rhetorical arsenal of rulers and elites who claimed to speak in its name. Collective opinion about public affairs was also thought to exercise a shaping force on citizens. In the words of political philosopher John Locke, "the law of opinion, the law of reputation, the law of fashion . . . is heeded more than any divine law or any law of the state."

In the United States, where democratic rule and political legitimacy were firmly tied to majority will, assessing the national mood was a favorite pastime of journalists, politicians, and social commentators long before Gallup appeared on the scene. Political scientist Susan Herbst has observed that "technically sophisticated attempts to quantify popular sentiment trailed far behind theorizing and discussion of it."

Starting in the nineteenth century, rudimentary political surveys, whether for entertainment or electoral gain, were undertaken by reporters, party loyalists, and ordinary citizens. In the 1820s, partisan newspapers began conducting straw polls as a means of both calculating and swaying political contests. "Straws," named for the way a straw held up in the wind could determine which way it was blowing, were haphazard instruments for gauging opinion, with passengers on a train or people encountered during a phase of a political campaign polled as the entire sample. Regardless, these quantitative surveys were popular news features into the twentieth century, encouraging a "horse race" approach to reporting elections that continues to the present.

Origins of the Modern Opinion Poll

A conjunction of statistical and social scientific innovations, commercial demands, and journalistic trends led to more systematic public opinion surveys in the first decades of the twentieth century and ultimately to the "scientific" polling of the 1930s. The estimation of standard errors based on sample size was crucial to pollsters' ability to extrapolate from the views of a small group of respondents something like national public opinion on a given issue. Equally significant were developments in the burgeoning field of market research, which sought ever more precise gauges of consumer desires and, in the process, supplied the techniques and personnel for political research. Finally, media interest in public opinion as news guaranteed that the polls would have both audiences and financial backers.

But the rise of modern political polling also required the entrepreneurial skills of Gallup and his colleagues. All of them got their start (and remained) in private commercial research and aspired to extend sample survey techniques to other arenas. In the lead-up to the 1936 presidential election, Gallup, along with Roper and Crossley, publicly challenged the best-known straw poll of the day, conducted by the *Literary Digest*. The *Digest* poll had correctly predicted the winner of the past five elections. But in 1936, even though it tallied over 2 million mail-in ballots, the poll incorrectly called the election for Republican Alfred Landon. Gallup et al., on the other hand, surveyed significantly fewer but more representative individuals and correctly forecast the election, if not the actual percentage of votes (Gallup was off by 7 points), for Franklin D. Roosevelt. Their victory gave instant credibility to scientific opinion polls, based on careful cross sections of the national population—what Gallup called the "miniature electorate."

Gallup and Roper, and soon a corps of other "pollers," were not content to confine their efforts to electoral contests. Indeed, many believed that election polls, although good for business and for legitimating their techniques in the public eye, were socially useless. The real goal was, in Gallup's words, "charting virtually unexplored sectors of the public mind": polling citizens on social and political issues that never made it onto a ballot. With this aim in mind, Gallup's American Institute for Public Opinion (AIPO) was established in 1935 to conduct a "continuing poll on the issues of the day." By 1940 its reports of Americans' opinions, on topics ranging from working women to U.S. entrance into World War II, were syndicated and carried by 106 newspapers. Roper's Fortune Survey, also created in 1935, had a similar goal, if never as wide a following.

James Bryce, author of *The American Commonwealth*, suggested in 1888 that public opinion ought to be "the real ruler of America," but lamented the lack of "machinery for weighing or measuring the popular will from week to week or month to month." In his many tracts promoting polling techniques, Gallup portrayed his new technology as the fulfillment of Bryce's vision.

By this light, opinion polls were more than a method for gathering information. They were a civic instrument, able to revitalize democracy—the spirit, if not the form, of the New England town meeting—in an increasingly complex, bureaucratic nation. Polls would achieve this goal by opening up a direct channel between "the people" and those in power, bypassing unreceptive legislators, political machines, and pressure groups. "As vital issues emerge from the fast-flowing stream of modern life," pledged Gallup, public opinion polls would "enable the American people to speak for themselves." Roper similarly described polls as "democracy's auxiliary ballot box." In short, the new polls would make ordinary citizens articulate—and their leaders responsive—in an age of mass organization.

In the years after 1936, other individuals, notably Samuel Lubbell, Lou Harris, and Mervin Field, would enter the polling arena, as would government agencies and major survey research organizations such as the National Opinion Research Center (1941), Columbia University's Bureau of Applied Social Research (1944), and the Survey Research Center at the University of Michigan (1946). Technical improvements in sampling and survey design ensued, although they did not prevent spectacular failures in polling techniques. The polls' confident prediction that Thomas Dewey would prevail over Harry Truman in the presidential election of 1948 was the best known of these failures, triggering a major investigation by the Social Scientific Research Council and much soul-searching by pollsters, social scientists, journalists, and market research clients.

The relative ease with which polling's 1948 crisis passed, however, suggested the growing dependence of various sectors of U.S. society on Gallup's techniques. Opinion polling, along with the allied field of market research, expanded dramatically in the 1960s and beyond, as interest groups, political consultants, and television and news organizations got into the polling business. By the mid-1960s, opinion surveying had spread throughout the world. The Gallup Poll had 32 affiliates and conducted polls in nearly 50 countries. In the early twenty-first-century United States, several hundred polling organizations existed on national, state, or local levels. Quantitative reports based on the aggregation of individual responses had largely displaced older ways of gauging citizens' views, among them public hearings, petitions, rallies, and letter-writing campaigns.

Polling's Critics

Gallup's rosy view of the democratic potential of opinion surveys was never fully embraced by his contemporaries, nor by later observers of the polls. Multiple criticisms were leveled at public opinion polls from their inception and recurred loudly during each new election cycle.

Some critiques were political and came from those who had something to lose or gain from poll numbers. Legislators on both sides of the aisle in the 1930s and 1940s looked skeptically at the new electoral polls, citing bias and distortion. (Early polls often did overestimate Republican support, making Franklin Roosevelt suspect that Gallup was on the opposing party's payroll.) Beginning in 1932, there were regular proposals in Congress to investigate or regulate the polls, and Gallup himself came under congressional scrutiny in 1944.

Ordinary citizens also denounced what they considered to be slanted or inaccurate polls. But their chief complaint concerned the practice of scientific sampling. To many Americans, the notion that national opinion could be distilled from as few as 1,000 respondents was not simply counterintuitive but undemocratic. Given the regular claims of polling's founders to represent the citizenry, many individuals were puzzled—or offended—by the fact that their opinions were not included in the surveys. Especially in the early decades of scientific polling, some were even moved to write to Gallup and Roper to ask why they hadn't been questioned. Despite the ubiquity of polls in American life today, widespread distrust of their central methodology persists. Over half of Americans surveyed in 1985, for example, claimed not to believe in the representativeness of random sampling.

Some of the most important challenges to the polls came from those who worried that data publicizing majority views would have negative effects in the public arena, due to either the overt manipulation or subtle influence of opinion data. Many legislators, commentators, and citizens from the 1930s onward decried the purported sway of polls over politicians or individual opinions—the latter the so-called bandwagon effect. Although Gallup dismissed this possibility, some studies, including those in the 1940s by sociologist Paul Lazarsfeld, suggested that published survey data could indeed influence voters, favoring candidates who were ahead in the polls. In a later iteration of this theme, scholars found that public opinion research could create a "spiral of silence," dampening minority voices through social pressure.

Other critiques were technical in nature. Pollsters' early method of choosing respondents, particularly their use of a discretionary system of "quota" sampling, was one area that came under fire. After the fiasco of 1948, most moved to the more costly procedure of "probability," or random, sampling, where every individual had an equal likelihood of being polled. Academic survey researchers then and now have pointed to other vexing problems with obtaining valid poll results. Among the most important of these are interviewer bias (the potential for the social background of the interviewer and/or respondent to affect responses) and question-wording effects (the fact that Americans register dramatically different levels of support for "welfare" versus "assistance to the poor," for example).

Still, other criticisms issued from commentators who found poll results like Gallup's a poor stand-in for something as complex and changeable as "public opinion." They argued that tallying individual, anonymous responses to standardized questions fundamentally obscured how opinion was forged. Political scientist Lindsay Rogers, who in 1949 coined the term *pollster* (partly for its resonance with the word *huckster*), was a vehement early critic of this stripe. In an influential 1948 argument, sociologist Herbert Blumer faulted the polls for severing opinions from their social context: the institutions, groups, and power relations that helped to shape them. Other critics, returning to concerns raised earlier in the century by political commentator Walter Lippmann, wondered whether Gallup's vision of direct democracy via polls was desirable—that is, whether citizens were capable of wise, informed opinions about complicated public issues.

A host of recent detractors, including French sociologist Pierre Bourdieu, further argued that polls do not neutrally report public views but rather generate entirely new entities: "nonattitudes" born of queries about topics that individuals have little knowledge of or interest in; political debates that would not otherwise be on the public agenda; and even the illusion of an opinionated public. In this view, "public opinion"—as revealed by polls—is an artifact of a particular measurement technique and often benefits interested elites such as politicians and journalists rather than the citizenry at large. Arguing that polls have had a disproportionate role in agenda-setting, such critics have urged paying attention to "don't know" responses and refusals to learn more about what public opinion polls obscure and whom they serve.

In the late twentieth century, frustration with the limitations of polls, and especially their seeming failure to enrich political discourse, led to multiple experiments with polling formats as well as a movement for "deliberative polling," led by political scientist James Fishkin. Proponents claimed that when citizens were provided with briefing materials on issues and had time to discuss their opinions face to face with others, reasoned collective judgments would result.

Certainly, many parties over the years have welcomed poll data for measuring public preferences as well as the potential to inform political discussion. Polls have clarified major differences between majority sentiment and political leaders. Longitudinal survey data have allowed new windows on ordinary citizens' political beliefs and affiliations, documenting, for instance, Americans' remarkably stable policy preferences over time. One recent study concludes that U.S. opinion surveys reveal a "rational public" and, furthermore, that public policy aligns with majority views in approximately two out of three instances. But the range and extent of critiques over the last 70 years suggest that Gallup's and Roper's ambitious hopes for polls as the "pulse of democracy" have not yet been realized.

Polls and Civic Life

Notwithstanding such challenges, modern opinion polls and their creators have exercised tremendous influence in American life. Ultimately, Gallup's surveys managed not only to transform political reportage but also to change politics itself. Polling techniques quickly penetrated the corridors of Congress and the White House. Franklin D. Roosevelt, an early convert to survey data, began receiving three-page summaries of public opinion in 1941; by 1942 these reports were often 20 pages in length. Roosevelt, significantly, monitored polls less to learn the public's views and more to shape them and garner support for specific policies. Two of the administration's unofficial pollsters, Hadley Cantril and Gerard Lambert (famous for a successful Listerine advertising campaign), were careful to include in all their analyses suggestions as to "how the attitude reported might be corrected."

In this, Roosevelt was hardly alone: from the 1930s onward, every president save Harry Truman relied on confidential surveys of opinion, whether to evaluate campaign strategies or claim an independent base of support for his views. Such uses of private polling accelerated over the decades: pollster Lou Harris played a key role in John F. Kennedy's presidential campaign; Richard Nixon employed (and suppressed) polls to gain advantage over his political opponents; and Bill Clinton made pollster Stanley Greenberg part of his "war room" of advisors (and, by one account, spent nearly $2 million on polls in a single year).

In addition to presidential administrations, members of Congress, governors, and mayors now regularly consult or commission polls. Politicians may disavow "poll-driven" politics, but their actions speak louder than their words. George W. Bush ran for president in 2000 stating, "we take stands without having to run polls and focus groups to tell us where we stand"—and then spent $1 million on polls the following year. It is clear that opinion polling has become a permanent feature of U.S. governance, coloring campaign strategies and political advertisements, public statements, and policy making. Even despite recent, well-publicized flaws in pre-election and exit polls (which, it should be noted, are typically the best designed and most comprehensive kinds of polls, as compared to social issue polls), quantitative opinion surveys are here to stay.

Historically, public opinion has had many different shades of meaning. In 1965 Harwood Childs, founder of the *Public Opinion Quarterly*, was able to list some 50 competing definitions for the term. One sign of Gallup's astonishing success is today's ready conflation of poll data and public opinion: the near-complete merging of the people's will and a specific statistical technique for measuring it.

See also political culture.

FURTHER READING

Althaus, Scott L. *Collective Preferences in Democratic Politics: Opinion Surveys and the Will of the People*. New York: Cambridge University Press, 2003.

Berinsky, Adam J. *Silent Voices: Public Opinion and Political Participation in America*. Princeton, NJ: Princeton University Press, 2004.

Bishop, George F. *The Illusion of Public Opinion: Fact and Artifact in American Public Opinion Polls*. New York: Rowman and Littlefield, 2005.

Bourdieu, Pierre. "Public Opinion Does Not Exist." In *Communication and Class Struggle*, edited by Armand Mattelart and Seth Siegelaub. New York: International General, 1979.

Converse, Jean. *Survey Research in the United States: Roots and Emergence, 1890–1960*. Berkeley: University of California Press, 1987.

Eisinger, Robert M. *The Evolution of Presidential Polling*. New York: Cambridge University Press, 2003.

Fishkin, James S. *The Voice of the People: Public Opinion and Democracy*. Reprint ed. New Haven: Yale University Press, 1997.

Ginsberg, Benjamin. *The Captive Public: How Mass Opinion Promotes State Power*. New York: Basic Books, 1986.

Herbst, Susan. *Numbered Voices: How Opinion Polling Has Shaped American Politics*. Chicago: University of Chicago Press, 1993.

Igo, Sarah E. *The Averaged American: Surveys, Citizens, and the Making of a Mass Public*. Cambridge, MA: Harvard University Press, 2007.

Page, Benjamin I., and Robert Y. Shapiro. *The Rational Public: Fifty Years of Trends in Americans' Policy Preferences*. Chicago: University of Chicago Press, 1992.

Robinson, Daniel J. *The Measure of Democracy: Polling, Market Research, and Public Life, 1930–1945*. Toronto: University of Toronto Press, 1999.

SARAH E. IGO

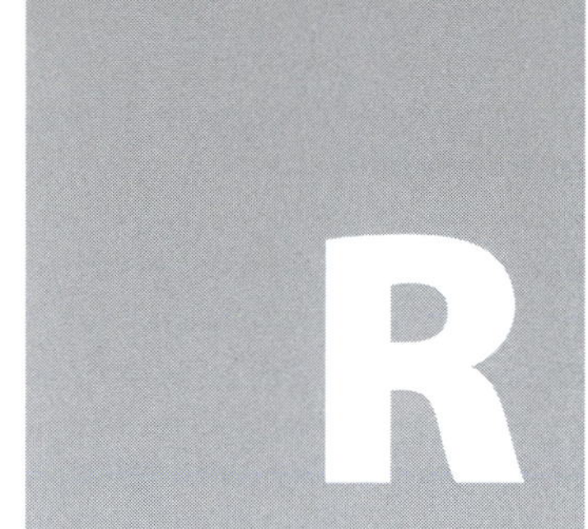

race and politics to 1860

Between the American Revolution and the Civil War, the politics of race and of slavery danced around one another, colliding here, overlapping there, changing over time, always related but never quite identical. Before 1820 northern politics had a strong current of antislavery sentiment based on the principle that blacks and whites were equally entitled to the same fundamental rights. Between the two great antebellum sectional crises—that of the Missouri Compromise of 1820 and of the Compromise of 1850—a more virulent proslavery racism prevailed. But with the Mexican American War, debates about slavery—and with it, antiracist politics—revived. The Republican electoral triumph of 1860 brought these two competing traditions into direct collision.

Slavery and Antislavery in the Age of Revolution

The antislavery radicalism of the Revolutionary years neither died nor dissipated in the 1790s. On the contrary, it was not until 1799 that New York passed a gradual emancipation law, followed five years later by New Jersey. Far from the bedraggled leftovers of a once formidable antislavery politics, the emancipations in New York and New Jersey were signal achievements of an antislavery coalition that became better organized and more ideologically coherent after 1790. Nor were these the only successes of early American antislavery politics. Throughout the North, gradual emancipation laws were reinforced by state and local statutes that weakened what remained of slavery. Slave trading was banned, fugitive slave catchers were thwarted, slave marriages were legalized, and slaves were permitted to own property. What was left of "slavery" had been transformed into something more closely approximating apprenticeship. Yet even those remaining "slaves" who fought for the United States during the War of 1812 were emancipated.

Despite increasingly stiff resistance from slaveholders, antislavery politics remained vital at the national level. The new federal government quickly readopted the Ordinance of 1787, banning the migration of slaves into the Northwest Territories. Long before the 1808 nationwide ban on the Atlantic slave trade went into effect, Congress prohibited slave trading in the southwestern territories and imposed stiff regulations that thwarted it in eastern seaports as well. Once the Atlantic trade itself was banned, Congress passed a series of increasingly aggressive enforcement laws culminating in the declaration of the trade as "piracy" in 1820.

Yet by then, slavery's opponents looked back on the republic's first 30 years and saw a series of defeats at the hands of a slaveholding class that had grown more, rather than less, powerful. Antislavery politicians had tried but failed to impose a tax on slave imports before 1808. Instead, as the deadline for closing the Atlantic slave trade approached, Georgia and South Carolina opened the floodgates and imported tens of thousands of African slaves into the United States. Northern congressmen had tried to restrict the migration of slaves into the southwestern territories but were again thwarted by an increasingly powerful and belligerent slaveholding bloc in Congress. Antislavery politicians likewise failed in their efforts to inhibit the growth of slavery in the territories acquired under the Louisiana Purchase. Indeed, so aggressive had proslavery forces become that in the immediate aftermath of the War of 1812 they made a serious effort to overturn the restriction on slave imports in the states that had been carved out of the northwestern territories. Opponents of the institution who had once hoped that the Revolution's "contagion of liberty" would lead to the steady disappearance of the institution instead looked back a generation later and saw the opposite. A cotton boom had breathed new life into the slaveholding class, making the southern states the most economically and politically potent force in the new nation. Slavery was expanding far more rapidly than was freedom, and with it grew a new domestic slave trade that duplicated many of the horrors of the illegal Atlantic trade.

By 1820 slaveholders and their opponents had honed their arguments in a debate that was already 30 years old. Racial equality was always an issue in these early struggles over slavery, but it was assumed rather than highlighted. Antislavery politicians almost always insisted that blacks and whites were equally entitled to the universal rights promised in the Declaration of Independence and to the same privileges and immunities of citizenship guaranteed by the Constitution. Their commitment to gradualism rested on the environmentalist assumption that, although slavery had left its victims unprepared for immediate emancipation, blacks were ultimately equal to whites in their innate capacity to assume the responsibilities of citizenship. In that sense, antislavery politics was always fundamentally antiracist.

By contrast, slavery's defenders insisted on the right of property in slaves and the right of slave states to be left alone by the federal government, but they also claimed that blacks alone, by virtue of their racial inferiority, were suitable for slavery. In this sense, the proslavery argument was intrinsically racist—not because racism led logically to the defense of slavery but because the defense of slavery led logically to the question of *who* should be enslaved. And the proslavery answer was always the same: Africans and their descendants.

Racial Politics and the Defeat of Revolutionary Antislavery

But the logic of proslavery racism had a way of spilling beyond its initial purpose. If Africans and African Americans were racially destined for slavery, it followed that free blacks were destined for inferiority as well. In 1790 Congress passed a citizenship law restricting naturalization to whites. By the end of the eighteenth century, individual states began stripping free blacks of the right to vote. Tennessee did this in its 1799 constitution; Ohio disfranchised African Americans in 1803. In 1814 New York required blacks to prove their freedom before they could vote. But it was not until the disastrous defeat of antislavery politics in the Missouri Crisis that racism moved into the center of American politics. In 1821 both Missouri and New York paved the way for a generation of racially inflected politics in which slavery's defenders used attacks on free blacks as a means of silencing antislavery lawmakers. In one state after another, constitutions were rewritten to grant all white men the right to vote while at the same time stripping black men of the same right or at least severely restricting it. In 1821 New York abolished property qualifications for voting and office holding for white men while simultaneously imposing a steep property qualification—lands valued at at least $250—on black men. Some states banned black voting altogether. Missouri, meanwhile, led the way in discriminatory citizenship laws, declaring, in its 1821 constitution, that free blacks could not move into the state—thus depriving them of one of the basic privileges of citizenship, the right of mobility.

All across America, states and localities rushed to impose harsh and demeaning racial discriminations on free blacks. They banned racial intermarriage; they prohibited blacks from serving on juries; they used politics to depoliticize African Americans, excluding blacks from public office and severely restricting—if not outright banning—them from voting. In lockstep with the spread of legal inequality came an explosion of private discriminations. Black and white passengers were segregated from one another in streetcars, ferries, and railroad cars. Theaters relegated blacks to "nigger balconies." Cemeteries separated black and white funeral plots. In this, at least, there were few regional distinctions, for racial segregation became the way of life for free blacks in the North as well as the South. For black abolitionists like Frederick Douglass, racial discrimination represented "the spirit of slavery," extending its influence beyond the borders of the slave states.

The Democratic Party was the primary vehicle for this ascendant racial politics. A coalition of northern plebeians and southern slaveholders, the Democratic Party unified its northern and southern wings under the banner of white supremacy. Even so, the impetus behind racial politics was essentially negative. It did not foreground racial politics so much as it made antislavery politics impossible. New York's 1821 constitution is an example of this. Many African Americans had already been stripped of the vote by earlier statutes requiring blacks to prove their freedom before they could cast their ballots. There is evidence suggesting partisan motives for imposing a property qualification: New York Jeffersonians were internally divided, and they used racial demagoguery both to unify their own party and to wipe out the remnants of the Federalists. Martin Van Buren saw what was happening in his home state of New York and helped develop it into a nationwide strategy for uniting the northern and southern wings of an emerging Democratic Party.

It worked. Having used white supremacy to shut down the threat of antislavery politics that had loomed so large in the Missouri crisis, The Democracy (as the Democratic Party was then known) was free to focus on other issues. As a result, the most important political battles of the next generation were waged over who would gain and lose from economic development. Racial politics unified the party faithful by purging the system of the potentially disruptive impact of antislavery politics.

Colonization and Its Opponents

The colonization movement was yet another symptom of the relative weakening of antislavery politics. The idea itself was not new. As early as the 1780s, Thomas Jefferson suggested that the abolition of slavery had to be accompanied by systematic efforts to "colonize" freed blacks somewhere outside the United States. Blacks were so different from whites, so clearly inferior, Jefferson argued, that even though they were entitled to the same right to freedom as all other human beings, they could never live in America as the equals of whites. The idea achieved new prominence with the founding of the American Colonization Society (ACS) in 1816, and from that moment until the Civil War, colonization remained a remarkably popular "solution" to the problem of slavery among political elites.

On the surface, the founding of the ACS seemed to reflect a broadening of the same sentiment that was sparking a revival of antislavery politics after the War of 1812. But antislavery leaders saw the emergence of colonization as a disastrous failure. Unlike the earliest abolitionists, colonizationists assumed that blacks could never be equal citizens in the United States. Thus the emergence of the ACS foreshadowed the triumph of racial politics. In theory, colonization could appeal to racism and antislavery sentiment at the same time. Its emergence, at the very moment that the struggle between proslavery and antislavery politicians was coming to a head, reflected the persistence of the dream of ridding the nation of slavery but also the ascendance of the dream of ridding the country of blacks.

A handful of prominent African Americans agreed that blacks and whites could never live together as equals and that the best solution was for blacks to emigrate to Sierra Leone, Liberia, or perhaps to the black republic of Haiti. But most black Americans objected to such proposals. Shortly after the founding of the ACS, 3,000 blacks in Philadelphia rallied to express their vehement opposition to colonization. They were only marginally more interested in voluntary emigration, despite the strenuous efforts by the government of Haiti and prominent black Americans like James Forten and Richard Allen to encourage emigration to the Caribbean island. Instead, most African Americans, born and raised in the United States, chose to remain and wage the struggle for equality in the land of their birth.

Opposition to colonization became the rallying cry among a new generation of black abolitionists. In 1827 they founded the nation's first black newspaper, *Freedom's Journal*, which combined attacks on colonization with equally vehement denunciations of northern racism and southern slavery. As the journal's editor warmed to the idea of colonization to Africa, *Freedom's Journal* lost its appeal to African American readers and ceased publication in 1829. But over the next several decades, black newspapers appeared in cities all across the North. At the same time, blacks organized a series of conventions that, like the newspapers, openly protested the rising tide of racism in the North and the expansion of slavery in the South. Disfranchisement had wiped out much of the black electorate, but it did not put an end to black politics.

Radicalization of the Debate

White militants like William Lloyd Garrison, inspired by their black predecessors, made opposition to colonization a keystone of a radical abolitionist movement that emerged in the late 1820s in the wake of the recent disastrous defeat of antislavery politics. And like the antislavery politics that it replaced, radical abolitionism was almost by definition antiracist—whatever the particular prejudices of individual reformers. By the 1830s, the racial climate had changed, however, and with it the salience of abolitionist antiracism. Just as the Democratic Party had fused racial inequality to the defense of slavery, many abolitionists now demanded racial equality along with the abolition of slavery. For obvious reasons, black abolitionists were especially inclined to link antislavery with the struggle for racial equality, but white radicals now agreed that the struggle against slavery in the South was indissolubly linked to the struggle against racial discrimination in the North. It was this racial egalitarianism, more than antislavery, that made radical abolitionism *radical*.

Thus, as politicians used race to squeeze antislavery out of the mainstream, the debate over slavery became more polarized than ever. Proslavery intellectuals helped inspire an "American school" of ethnography dedicated to developing scientific proofs of the innate inferiority of the African "race." Meanwhile, radical abolitionists argued that the same principle of human equality that made slavery immoral made racial inequality illegitimate as well. By the 1830s, the politics of race were explicitly bound with the politics of slavery at every point along the ideological spectrum.

Revival of Antislavery Politics

One of the goals of radical abolitionists was to force antislavery back onto the national political agenda. First they tried flooding the South with antislavery propaganda, but President Andrew Jackson shut them down by telling his postmaster general not to deliver such mail. More successful was the abolitionist effort to bombard Congress with petitions asking for the abolition of the slave trade, and then slavery, in Washington, D.C. This campaign precipitated the notorious "gag rule" whereby Congress automatically tabled all antislavery petitions in the hopes of thwarting any discussion of slavery in either the House of Representatives or the Senate. The debate over the gag rule erupted in 1835 and dragged on for nearly a decade. By the time the rule was abandoned, antislavery politics was coming back to life.

One reason for this was the revival of party competition in the 1830s, stimulated by opposition to President Jackson. This anti-Jackson, or Whig, party was, like the Democratic Party, national in its appeal. The prominence of Southerners in the Whig coalition thereby ensured that it would not be an antislavery party. Moreover, the Whigs' "American System" assumed that slavery had a permanent place in a nationally integrated economy. Yet, like the Federalists of an earlier generation, the Whigs were more likely than the Democrats to attract those northern politicians who were opposed to slavery. The reemergence of party competition in the 1830s thus created more space for antislavery politicians to survive within the political mainstream than had been the case in the late 1820s. But Whig antislavery was weak and was channeled primarily into empty encomia to colonization. For antislavery politics to revive, pressure would have to be administered from outside the two-party system.

The revival began in 1840 with the launch of the Liberty Party, which picked up steam in the 1844 presidential election. The Liberty Party was a coalition of abolitionists committed to racial equality and pragmatists who hoped to revive antislavery politics by focusing primarily on the issue of slavery's expansion. Thus, from the earliest moments of its revival, antislavery politics revealed an impulse to separate the issue of slavery from the issue of race. The potential of this strategy soon became clear. The war with Mexico gave antislavery politics a critical boost, leading to the formation of the Free Soil Party in 1848. With that, the focus of antislavery politics shifted away from both colonization as well as racial equality and toward halting the further expansion of slavery into the western territories. There was a racist argument for the notion of "free soil": the claim that the western territories should be reserved for whites. But there was also an egalitarian argument, a conviction that the federal government should place its finger on the scales in favor of universal freedom, for blacks and whites alike, by preventing slavery from expanding beyond its present limits.

The collapse of the Whig Party in the wake of the Compromise of 1850 paved the way for the triumph of antislavery politics when it was replaced, in the northern states, by a new Republican Party committed to free soil ideals. The Republicans nominated their first presidential candidate in 1856 and went on to victory in 1860.

Race and Antislavery Politics

This second generation of antislavery politics was similar to its pre-1820 predecessor in important ways, but different as well—and one of the crucial differences had to do with its relationship to the politics of race. The first generation of antislavery politicians tended to assume that blacks and whites were equally entitled not merely to the presumption of freedom but to the same voting rights and the same privileges and immunities of citizenship as well. They could take this position, in part, because race was not yet a major theme in American politics. Politicians assumed rather than highlighted their disagreements over racial equality. A generation later, the situation was very different. Antislavery politicians in the 1840s and 1850s also assumed that blacks and whites were entitled to the same basic rights—life, liberty, and the pursuit of happiness—something proslavery Democrats flatly denied. At the same time, however, Republicans in the 1850s denied that, in opposing slavery, they necessarily supported racial equality. This position opened the Republican Party to a wide spectrum of racial attitudes—from antislavery racists to radical egalitarians.

The most successful spokesman for this position was Abraham Lincoln. By the late 1850s, Lincoln repeatedly dismissed racial equality as a "false issue." The great issue facing the nation was slavery not racial equality, he argued. White voters disagreed, not over the question of racial equality but over the question of slavery. And in any case, Lincoln added, questions of racial equality were matters to be handled by individual states and thus had no bearing on national political campaigns. Republicans in the Massachusetts legislature might support both racial equality and discrimination against immigrants, while Republicans in the Illinois legislature favored racial discrimination while supporting the rights of immigrants. In either case, Lincoln argued, racial and ethnic discriminations were state matters and had no bearing on the antislavery principles of the Republican Party nationwide.

This explicit separation of race from slavery understandably alienated many abolitionists, but it succeeded in releasing American politics from the stranglehold of proslavery racism. Thus without actually advocating racial equality, the Republican Party broke the back of racial politics by insisting that race and slavery were two different issues and that slavery was the only issue that mattered.

Nevertheless, just as the racist logic of proslavery politics—"the spirit of slavery"—was felt in the spread of laws discriminating against African Americans, the egalitarianism at the core of antislavery politics had the reverse effect. Despite the wide spectrum of opinion about racial equality among Republicans, party victories in the North resulted in the first sporadic reversals of the racial legal structure put in place a generation earlier. Massachusetts abolished segregated schools, for example. Republicans in the New York legislature put an equal suffrage amendment on the ballot in 1860. But it was not until the Republicans took control of Congress and the presidency that a nationwide rollback of the racial regime was begun.

This rollback was largely stimulated by the demands of the Civil War. Once emancipation became Union policy, white Northerners questioned: "What shall be done with the Negro?" The answer that emerged, tentatively at first, was a repudiation of more than a generation of racial politics. The Lincoln administration declared that free blacks were citizens and were equally entitled to the associated privileges and immunities. Republicans opened the U.S. Army to blacks for the first time since the 1790s. Shortly after the war ended, they passed the landmark Civil Rights Act of 1866. Eventually, Republicans endorsed voting rights for the former slaves and enacted constitutional amendments against racial qualifications for voting that effectively abolished discriminatory voting laws in the northern as well as the southern states. With the triumph of antislavery politics, came a reversal—incomplete but nonetheless significant—of the racial politics of the proslavery Democracy.

See also abolitionism; slavery; voting.

FURTHER READING

Earle, Jonathan. *Jacksonian Antislavery and the Politics of Free Soil, 1824–1854.* Chapel Hill: University of North Carolina Press, 2004.

Foner, Eric. *Free Soil, Free Labor, Free Men: The Ideology of the Republican Party Before the Civil War.* New York: Oxford University Press, 1970.

Forbes, Robert Pierce. *The Missouri Compromise and Its Aftermath: Slavery and the Meaning of America.* Chapel Hill: University of North Carolina Press, 2007.

Gellman, David N. *Emancipating New York: The Politics of Slavery and Freedom, 1777–1827.* Baton Rouge: Louisiana State University Press, 2006.

Hammond, John Craig. *Slavery, Freedom, and Expansion in the Early American West.* Charlottesville: University of Virginia Press, 2007.

Mason, Matthew. *Slavery and Politics in the Early American Republic.* Chapel Hill: University of North Carolina Press, 2006.

Oakes, James. *The Radical and the Republican: Frederick Douglass, Abraham Lincoln, and the Triumph of Antislavery Politics.* New York: Norton, 2007.

Quarles, Benjamin. *Black Abolitionists.* New York: Oxford University Press, 1969.

Sewell, Richard H. *Ballots for Freedom: Antislavery Politics in the United States, 1837–1860.* New York: Oxford University Press, 1976.

Zilversmit, Arthur. *The First Emancipation: The Abolition of Slavery in the North.* Chicago: University of Chicago Press, 1967.

JAMES OAKES

race and politics, 1860–1933

The politics of race went through more than one revolution during the seven decades after 1860. Consider three moments at the beginning, middle, and end of the period: In 1860 the prospect that the presidency would be occupied by a member of a political party committed merely to banning slavery from territories where it did not then exist was enough to provoke the Deep South into violent rebellion. On the eve of the Civil War, according to the Supreme Court's *Dred Scott v. Sandford* decision, people of African descent could never become American citizens and had "no rights which a white man was bound to respect." Yet in September 1862, the preliminary Emancipation Proclamation signaled the end of more than two centuries of slavery in America. By the middle of the period, in 1895–96, African American rights that had expanded dramatically in the 1860s were contracting: South Carolina held a state constitutional convention openly aimed at disfranchising black men; Tuskegee Institute head Booker T. Washington publicly promised in the "Atlanta Compromise" that southern blacks would accept racial segregation; and the Supreme Court, in *Plessy v. Ferguson*, announced that segregation was constitutional. In 1930 the first African American member of Congress from the North, Chicago's Oscar De Priest, was elected to his second term in office; the National Association for the Advancement of Colored People (NAACP) helped defeat the Supreme Court nomination of John J. Parker for his role in excluding blacks from the Republican Party in North Carolina; and NAACP-affiliated attorneys were litigating their second case in a successful 20-year legal campaign to outlaw the white primary.

Sudden advances, counterrevolutions, and periods of incremental change in both directions characterized this turbulent, contradictory, complex period. Race relations varied from time to time and place to place, and issues and institutional features of governments that had nothing inherently to do with race often determined racial policy outcomes. Racial politics can only be understood if it is not separated from other concerns, tensions, and actions.

Violence and Freedom

Secession freed the Republican Party, and then the slaves. As long as southern whites threatened to break up the Union if Northerners moved against slavery, Republican policy was itself enslaved. Once secession was declared, southern slaveholders resigned from Congress, and Fort Sumter was fired upon, the Union inevitably became the enemy of slavery instead of its protector. After securing the border states militarily, the Republicans were free to ban the interstate slave trade, to authorize the federal government, for the first time, to hire African Americans to work for the national government, and to declare escaped slaves "contraband of war" instead of returning them to their owners as the 1850 Fugitive Slave Act required.

Slaves forced the issue, fleeing toward Union lines as soon as Union armies approached and demanding to work to feed themselves and to fight to restore a nation purified of its original sin of slavery. The longer the Civil War went on and the more white northern soldiers were killed or badly wounded, the less resistance there was to enrolling black soldiers. Once they began fighting for Union forces after the Emancipation Proclamation took permanent effect in January 1863, complete abolition was ensured. Approximately 180,000 African Americans served in the army and navy, about 12 percent of the total number of soldiers and sailors, and they died at the same ghastly rates as whites did. For Northerners, granting and preserving the rights of African Americans who had fought for the Union—especially protecting them from attacks by former secessionists—took on, for a time after the conclusion of the war, the character of a patriotic duty.

White Southerners, however, acted as though the Civil War had settled nothing except the impracticality of secession and the nominal abolition of slavery. After Abraham Lincoln's assassination and the succession of his vice president, Tennessee Democrat Andrew Johnson, southern states passed "black codes" that denied African Americans the right to buy or lease real estate, sign yearly labor contracts, serve on juries, testify against whites in court, and vote. Blacks were excluded from public schools, black orphans were "apprenticed" to their former owners, and black "servants" were required to labor from sunup to sundown for their "masters." White Southerners also demanded that a delegation of former Confederate officers and politicians be seated immediately in Congress.

But the Republicans who controlled Congress refused to admit the erstwhile rebels and took decisive control of Reconstruction. When Johnson vetoed a bill extending the Freedmen's Bureau, which provided food to destitute Southerners of both races, supervised labor contracts, and started schools where ex-slaves could be educated and courts where their concerns could be adjudicated, Republicans in Congress overrode his action, as they did his veto of the 1866 Civil Rights Act. That act began to carry out the implications of the Thirteenth Amendment (ratified in 1865), which Republicans interpreted as doing much more than abolishing slavery. In their expansive interpretation, one resurrected by the U.S. Supreme Court a century later, the Thirteenth Amendment allowed Congress in the Civil Rights Act to outlaw racial discrimination, even in such private contracts as those for housing and admission to private schools, as "badges and incidents of slavery." Seceding states were required to ratify the Thirteenth Amendment as a condition for their readmission to the Union. After enacting the Civil Rights Act, Republicans, over unanimous northern Democratic opposition in Congress, passed the Fourteenth Amendment, which even more securely constitutionalized civil rights, seeking explicitly to guarantee privileges and immunities, due process, and equal protection for all.

In the critical 1866 election campaign, Johnson demagogically lambasted Congress, northern Democrats endlessly race-baited, and white Southerners rioted in Memphis and New Orleans, killing 89 African Americans in full view of the national press. Northern voters reacted to Johnsonian and southern Democratic overreaching by giving the Republicans a landslide, which turned Reconstruction more radical. Ten southern states were placed under temporary military rule, forced to enfranchise African American men and to rewrite their constitutions, and readmitted to Congress only after ratifying the Fourteenth Amendment and much more liberal state constitutions. Because Johnson persisted in trying to subvert the antiracist settlement, he was impeached, almost convicted, and, for all intents and purposes, rendered innocuous.

The United States was the only large slaveholding society that quickly enfranchised freedmen, and the eagerness and skill with which they took to politics surprised and dismayed their former masters, who had expected docility and incompetence. Even in the face of Ku Klux Klan violence, African American voter turnout in the 1860s and 1870s often surpassed 80 percent. Buttressed by the presence of federal troops, by the Fifteenth Amendment, which mandated racially impartial suffrage nationally, and by official jobs for their supporters, the new southern governments launched statewide education systems, encouraged the building and rebuilding of railroads, passed civil rights laws, and protected the rights of laborers, renters, and small farmers. Even after the Reconstruction governments fell, African Americans continued to enjoy the rights to legally marry, worship as they wished, form private clubs, receive (usually inferior) educations at public expense, and, often, to patronize public accommodations such as restaurants, theaters, and railroads, on a nonsegregated basis—if they could afford to pay. Absolute segregation of public places in the South arrived only toward the turn of the century, and it was a matter of law, not of custom.

Disfranchisement by Stages

White southern Democrats fought back against the southern Republican governments with the most extensive peacetime violence in American history. The bloodiest were Louisiana Democrats who, according to a congressional investigation, killed 1,081 persons, mostly black, in the six months before the presidential election of 1868. But violence did not, by itself, doom Reconstruction or account for the ultimate nullification of the Fifteenth Amendment. Murder was most effective as a political tactic if it targeted key political leaders and exploded in the period just before a crucial election. Yet in nine of the dozen southern counties where the best-known violent incidents took place, African Americans somehow managed to poll nearly their full vote for the Republicans in the presidential election that succeeded the incident.

After northern voters reacted to the 1873 depression, bitter northern ethnoreligious conflicts, and widespread tales of corruption by electing a Democratic majority in the House of Representatives in 1874, congressional Republicans managed in their last few months in power to enact the 1875 Civil Rights Act, which mandated the integration of public accommodations, but they failed to pass a strong voter protection bill because Democrats filibustered against it in the House until it was too late for the Senate to act. Although the GOP rebounded to win the second closest presidential election in U.S. history in 1876, part of the price for settling disputes over the election outcome was an implicit promise to stop using the army to protect southern Republicans. Partisanship, economic and nonracial moral issues, and political strife between separate groups of a heterogeneous "white" society, as well as issues of race and Reconstruction per se, brought about what became known as the "Compromise of 1877," which marked what historians traditionally viewed as the end of Reconstruction.

Yet, as is shown in figure 1, which charts the number of black members of Congress and the state legislatures elected from 1868 through 1900 from the 11 states that formed the Confederacy, blacks were not eliminated from politics after 1877. In fact, the number of African

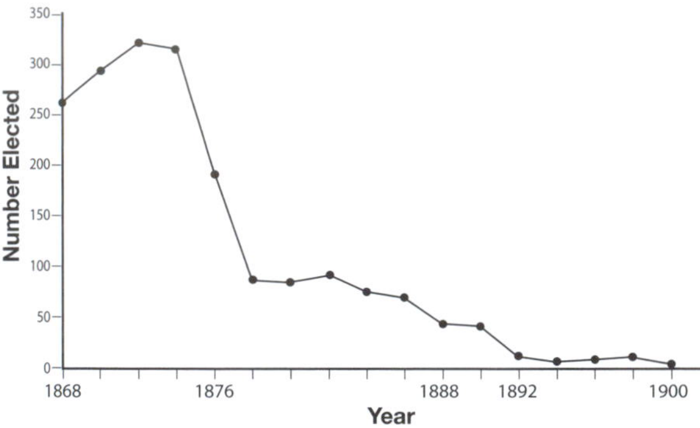

Figure 1. Black Members of Congress and State Legislatures

Americans elected to legislative office from the South was higher in 1882 than in any subsequent year until 1974, and from 1878 to 1890, the decline in black office holding was palpable, but gradual. Moreover, even where they could not elect black candidates, which was usually their first preference, blacks could often still vote for sympathetic whites. In 1880, three years after President Rutherford B. Hayes symbolically confined U.S. troops to their barracks in the South, an estimated two-thirds of the adult male African Americans were recorded as voting, and two-thirds of that group managed to have their votes recorded for Republican James A. Garfield, whom they had nearly all, no doubt, supported for president. The high black turnout in this election, which was greater than overall national participation a century later, was not atypical, nor did Democrats allow it only because presidential elections were less important to them than those closer to home. An average of six out of ten African Americans voted in the most heavily contested gubernatorial races in each of the 11 states during the 1880s, despite the fact that none of these elections took place on the same day that voters cast ballots for president. Of those blacks who voted, at least 60 percent supported the Republican, Greenback, or other anti-Democratic candidates in each state. Even in the 1890s, after several states had restricted suffrage by law, nearly half of the African American population is estimated to have voted in key gubernatorial contests, although the Populist-Democratic battles were sufficiently severe that Democrats pushed fraud to new levels.

Five principal tactics were used to reduce and, finally, to eliminate black political strength—no single one sufficient by itself, but all working together and, roughly, following a predictable sequence: violence, fraud, structural discrimination, statutory suffrage restriction, and constitutional disfranchisement. Corresponding to these tactics were four approximate stages in the attack on black voting rights after Reconstruction: the Klan stage, in which fraud and violence predominated; the dilution stage, characterized by structural legal changes; the disfranchisement stage, where the last legal underpinnings of the real "Solid South" were put into place; and the lily white stage, the aim of which was to crush any elevation of blacks above the distinctly secondary political status into which the disfranchisement measures had forced them, and to reduce—from very slim to none—any chances of African Americans being elected or appointed to office or exercising any political muscle whatsoever.

Violence was not only a dangerous weapon for a conservative establishment to use, for it invited retaliation from desperate victims, but it was also less effective than fraud perpetrated by election officials and their superiors. Southern election fraud in the late nineteenth century, as often a matter of boasting in the South as it was a matter of outrage in the North, far surpassed voting fraud at any other time or place in American history. For instance, Louisiana senator and former governor Samuel D. McEnery stated in 1898 that his state's 1882 election law "was intended to make it the duty of the governor to treat the law as a formality and count in the Democrats." William A. Anderson, author of the 1894 election law in Virginia, admitted that elections under his law were "crimes against popular government and treason against liberty." A delegate to the 1901 Alabama constitutional convention reported that "any time it was necessary the black belt could put in ten, fifteen, twenty or thirty thousand Negro votes." A leader of the 1890 Mississippi constitutional convention declared that "it is no secret that there has not been a full vote and a fair count in Mississippi since 1875," which was the last election until 1967 in which African Americans voted at all freely in the state. Like violence, fraud was most potent if ramped up during crucial elections—for instance, referenda on ratifying discriminatory amendments to state constitutions, as in Alabama in 1901, where, according to the official returns, nearly 90 percent of those in counties with black populations of at least 70 percent supported a new constitution whose advertised purpose was black disfranchisement.

Supplementing fraud were structural changes in election laws, such as gerrymandering election district boundaries; drawing election districts with very different population sizes; switching from district to at-large elections, which made it more difficult to elect members of groups that formed a majority in a part of a city, but only a minority in the whole city; abolishing local elections entirely; annexation or deannexation of territory to add white or subtract black areas from a jurisdiction; requiring officeholders to post bonds too high to meet for anyone who lacked wealthy friends; shifting or consolidating polling places to confuse voters or require them to travel many miles to the polls; and impeaching Republican or other anti-Democratic officials, often on transparently specious grounds. All these measures cut black and Republican office holding at the local, state, and national levels without actually disfranchising voters.

Other laws did reduce individual voting: poll taxes, which in some states had to be paid for every year after a person reached 21 years of age before one could vote, discouraged the poor of both races from voting, but especially the generally poorer blacks. Registration laws could be devised to prune the electorate by compelling registration months before every election, especially at a central location during working hours; demanding copiously detailed information, which sometimes had to be vouched for by witnesses, before a voter could register; allowing registration boards sufficient discretion to enable them to pad or unfairly purge the rolls; disproportionate representation for the Democrats on such boards; requiring voters unaccustomed to keeping records to produce registration certificates at voting places; or permitting widespread challenges to voters at the polls. The then infamous South Carolina "eight-box" law of 1882 required election officials to shift separate ballot boxes for each of eight offices around during the voting to make it impossible for a literate friend to put an illiterate's tickets in the correct order before he entered the polling place, and prohibited anyone but state election officers, all but one or two of whom seem to have been Democrats, from assisting unlettered voters. After 1888, when states began to require ballots to be supplied only by governments, secret ballot laws, employed in eight southern and many northern states with the intent and effect of disfranchising illiterates, could be designed to be so long and complex as to disfranchise all but the well educated and those whom the election officials chose to help.

Along with violence, fraud, and structural measures, such laws reduced Republican and inhibited Populist representation enough to create legislative majorities in favor of state constitutional disfranchisement. Conventions or referenda then wrote into more permanent form poll taxes and literacy or property tests for registration, often with temporary exemption clauses to allow illiterate (white) voters to register if they could demonstrate to a registrar's satisfaction that they understood parts of the Constitution or laws when they were read to them, or if their ancestors could have voted before 1867 (before southern blacks were enfranchised), or if they or their ancestors had served in the military (including, of course, the Confederate States Army). These were referred to as the "grandfather" and "fighting grandfather" clauses. Constitutional disfranchisement effectively moved fraud one step back, delegating it to registration officials instead of those at the polls. It also reduced widespread unfavorable publicity about white southern election cheating, which had invited national intervention, such as the Lodge Elections Bill of 1890, defeated only by another Senate filibuster, and made legal attacks on white election supremacy more difficult to mount.

Why the Solid South?

The Solid South created by disfranchisement laws—effectively outlawing political party competition, almost entirely excluding southern African Americans from political participation, proudly starving governmental services for poor people—lasted for a half century. Did whites in other regions of the country allow this system to be constructed and maintained because they lost interest in equality during and after the 1870s or increasingly drew a hard white line that treated all people of European origins as identical and all of African origins as naturally inferior, to be excluded from civil society? Or did Reconstructionists, thwarted by the structural peculiarities of the governmental system and adverse judicial decisions, turn north, shifting their focus from national to state governments, lowering their sights, but pursuing the same goal of racial equality closer to home?

Northern laws and litigation on racial discrimination in public accommodations and schools suggest that Reconstruction was not so much abandoned as redirected. After the Supreme Court overturned the 1875 national Civil Rights Act in 1883, most of the northern legislatures that had not earlier passed state public accommodations laws quickly did so. Thereafter, equal access to northern trains, streetcars, restaurants, and places of amusement was largely a matter of right, although the legalities were not always observed. In fact, even in the South until the turn of the nineteenth century, streetcars and many railroads were not rigidly segregated.

Moves by states, cities, or private companies to require segregation on streetcars were resisted by black boycotts, sometimes lasting for many months, in more than 25 southern cities.

It took a longer time for every nonsouthern state except Indiana with a black population of 1 percent or more to pass laws requiring most or all public schools to stop restricting the admissions of African Americans. From Massachusetts in 1855, to California in 1880, to New York in 1901, blacks and their white allies fought for equal status by petitioning school boards, filing legal cases, and pressing state legislatures for laws granting every child access to what were then known as "common schools." African Americans contested and won more cases on racial discrimination in public education in the decade of the 1880s, after the nominal end of Reconstruction, than in any other decade before the 1940s. In fact, they filed nearly 100 such cases in 20 states and the District of Columbia in the nineteenth century and prevailed in a majority of them. Nineteenth-century arguments and tactics before school boards and legislatures prefigured those of the twentieth-century civil rights movement, just as the doctrines and rhetoric in some of the legal opinions in the nineteenth-century school cases paralleled those a century later.

If agitation for those rights—in the North, at least—did not cease after 1876, and northern public opinion, as indexed by legislative action, continued to support black rights, why did the legal disfranchisement of southern African Americans succeed? There were three reasons: partisanship, the filibuster, and adverse decisions by the Supreme Court. First, since African Americans remained almost unanimously committed to the Republican Party—the party of Lincoln, emancipation, and Reconstruction—until well after disfranchisement, northern Democrats opposed any efforts to guarantee southern blacks the right to register, vote, and have their votes counted as cast. If southern blacks could vote freely, the fortunes of the Democratic Party nationally were likely to be permanently depressed. Accordingly, not a single Democratic member of Congress voted for any civil or voting rights measure from 1865 through 1900. That this pattern was motivated by partisanship, and not merely by racial animosity, is shown by the fact that an appreciable number of Democrats in northern state legislatures supported school integration and public accommodations bills, especially during the 1880s.

Rabid Democratic partisanship was especially on display in the bitter struggles over the national election bills in 1875 and 1890, when they relentlessly talked to death measures to protect individuals while voting, as well as to oversee registration, voting, and vote counting. Guarding the fundamental right to vote from violence, intimidation, and fraud amounted—the Democrats and much of the nation's press shrieked—to "force bills." Largely to counter these filibustering tactics, Republicans in the House changed the body's rules in 1889–90 to end unlimited debate, and these "Reed Rules," named for House Speaker Thomas B. Reed, not only facilitated the passage of the Lodge Elections Bill in that branch of the national legislature but also fundamentally changed the nature of the House forever. Never again would a minority of the House be able to block the chamber's business until the majority gave up and dropped a bill or severely compromised it. Yet the Senate, during that same congressional session, failed to adopt a proposal by Senator Nelson W. Aldrich that was similar to the Reed Rules. Democrats filibustered the Lodge Bill for 33 days, the longest filibuster in history up to that time, and the bill was finally set aside by a single vote. Since the Senate has not yet followed the House's lead on antifilibuster rules, every civil rights or voting rights proposal through the 1960s had to face the prospect or reality of having to break a filibuster to pass the Senate. As a consequence, between 1875 and 1957, not a single civil rights bill passed in Congress.

How different the history of race and politics in America might have been if both chambers in 1875 or 1890 or even later had adopted antifilibuster rules. If the "Force Bill" of 1875 had passed in time to protect voters from violence, intimidation, and fraud in the 1876 elections, and to prevent the overthrow of state authority, which were the objects of the bill, Hayes would easily have been elected president, Republicans would have continued to control many Deep South governments, and the decisions of southern white voters and leaders to abandon the Republicans as a lost, dangerous cause might well have been reversed. Republican rule in the Deep South would have begun to seem normal, and the developmental sequence of violence, fraud, structural changes, legislative disfranchisement, and constitutional disfranchisement would have been interrupted near the beginning.

Even if the less far-reaching Lodge Bill of 1890 had passed, which would have required breaking the Senate filibuster, southern African Americans would have been able to register more freely and have their votes more nearly counted as cast. If states had nonetheless passed disfranchisement measures, the effects of those laws would have been diminished because federal observers would have been available to restrain local registrars from applying racially separate and unequal standards to prospective voters. And if a serious southern Republican vote had persisted, national Republicans would have had an incentive to follow up the Lodge Bill with other, more comprehensive voting rights laws. Instead of a downward cycle leading to the practically complete disfranchisement of southern blacks by 1910, there might well have been an upward cycle, with less fraud, less structural discrimination, and fewer and more fairly administered restrictions on suffrage. The antilynching bills of the 1920s and 1930s and the anti–poll tax bills of the 1940s would have passed, and there would have been major efforts to extend northern integration laws nationally long before the 1964 Civil Rights Act. No revolutions in sentiment, interest, or cultural mores were required for those policy revolutions to occur—just a change in the operations of Congress to allow majority rule.

Of course, such laws might have been derailed by the Supreme Court, the least democratic of the national government's three branches, designed with life tenure to ensure the greatest possible independence from the pressures of partisan politics or public opinion. In a confusing and often contradictory line of cases, the Supreme Court, during this period, wavered in protecting or allowing Congress to protect African American political rights. In opinions in *U.S. v. Reese* and *U.S. v. Cruikshank* that were delayed from 1874 to 1876, while the debate on the "force bill" was taking place, Chief Justice Morrison R. Waite, President Grant's *seventh* choice for the position, ruled provisions of the 1870–72 Enforcement Acts unconstitutional or largely unenforceable. Ignoring the Fourteenth Amendment, which does not mention race and which was repeatedly invoked during congressional debates as a basis for the Enforcement Acts, Waite declared that the only constitutional justification for the acts was the Fifteenth Amendment, and that either the acts or the indictments pursuant to them were insufficiently direct in their references to race to satisfy the Fifteenth Amendment.

Thus, in Reese, the refusal of a Lexington, Kentucky, tax collector to accept payment of the poll tax from an African American did not, according to the Court, infect with a racial purpose the actions of election officials who disfranchised him for failure to show a poll tax receipt. And in *Cruikshank*, Louisianians who perpetrated the largest racial mass murder in American history (the Colfax Riot of 1873), went free because Waite split off the beginning sections of the act, which explicitly mentioned race, from the later sections, which only indirectly referred to race.

As a consequence of these two decisions, the existing federal voting rights enforcement machinery was severely weakened. Nothing in the decisions themselves, however, prevented Congress from passing new laws that made the connection between racial discrimination and the protection of voting rights more explicit, and later Court decisions viewed the Fourteenth Amendment's equal protection and due process clauses more expansively, allowing Congress to guard the fundamental rights of citizens where the states did not.

As with the receptiveness of northern legislatures and courts to antisegregation appeals during the decade after the supposed end of Reconstruction, Supreme Court decisions of the 1880s seemed to invite a renewed movement for racial reform. In *Ex parte Siebold* (1880), *Ex parte Clarke* (1880), and *Ex parte Yarbrough* (1884), the high court interpreted Congress's plenary power under Article I, Section IV to regulate the "times, places and manner of holding elections" to Congress broadly enough to allow it to guarantee peaceable assembly and restrict fraud and violence. These decisions inspired Republicans to frame the 1890 Lodge Bill without fear that it would be declared unconstitutional. Moreover, in the 1880 jury exclusion case of *Strauder v. West Virginia* and the 1886 Chinese laundry case of *Yick Wo v. Hopkins*, the Supreme Court struck down racially discriminatory laws not related to voting in such expansive language as to suggest that the justices had not entirely forgotten the original purposes of the Reconstruction Amendments, after all. Despite the Court's narrow construction of the powers of the federal government in *The Civil Rights Cases* (1883), the other, more moderate decisions allowed some scope for national action to protect minority rights if Republicans took firm control of the government again, as they did in 1889 for the first time since 1875.

After the failure of the Lodge Bill, however, the Supreme Court shifted direction again. In *Williams v. Mississippi* in 1898, the Court denied disfranchised blacks a remedy by very strictly construing its earlier decision in *Yick Wo*. Counsel for the Chinese laundryman had shown that a San Francisco ordinance was adopted with both the intent and effect of discriminating against Chinese. While Henry Williams's African American lawyer, Cornelius J. Jones, quoted extensively from the Mississippi disfranchising convention of 1890 to demonstrate its racist intent, he apparently took the exclusion of blacks from the Greenville voter, and, therefore, jury rolls to be proof enough of the state constitution's discriminatory impact. The Court's crabbed reading of *Yick Wo* cost Williams, convicted of murder by an all-white jury, his life. Yet when Wilford H. Smith, an African American lawyer representing disfranchised Alabama blacks in *Giles v. Harris* (1903), presented extensive evidence of the new state constitution's discriminatory effects, as well as its intent, the Court, in a decision written by the "liberal" Oliver Wendell Holmes, declared that the judiciary could do nothing, because suffrage was a "political question."

After southern blacks were safely disfranchised, the Court reversed itself again, entirely ignoring *Williams* and *Giles* when ruling in *Guinn and Beal v. U.S.* (1915) that the Oklahoma grandfather clause was unconstitutional. Chief Justice Edward Douglass White, a former member of the "conservative" faction of the Democratic Party in Louisiana, which had opposed the grandfather clause in that state's constitutional convention in 1898, did not endanger white supremacy directly in *Guinn*, because eliminating the escape clause for Oklahoma whites would not thereby actually allow any African Americans to vote. Once William Howard Taft, whose presidential administration had originally brought the *Guinn* case, became chief justice in 1921, the Court went further, ruling the Texas white primary unconstitutional as a violation of the Fourteenth Amendment in *Nixon v. Herndon* (1927), in the first of several NAACP challenges to the discriminatory practice. When Texas repealed its explicit racially restrictive policy in law and delegated the setting of primary participation standards to the State Democratic Executive Committee, the Supreme Court struck down that subterfuge, too, in *Nixon v. Condon* (1932).

The Court, many of whose appointees over the period were Democrats or Republicans chosen without racial policies foremost in mind, failed to protect African American political rights when they needed protection most. But they allowed some scope for potential congressional action, and toward the end of the period, were beginning to move toward unraveling the web of laws and rules that kept southern blacks powerless. Had Chief Justice Salmon P. Chase, the father of antislavery constitutionalism, lived as long as his two predecessors instead of dying when more than 20 years younger than John Marshall and Roger Brooke Taney, or had the brilliant radical Republicans Roscoe Conkling and George Franklin Edmunds (both members of the Thirty-Ninth Congress that had passed the major Reconstruction measures) not turned down appointments to the Court, the course of race and politics during the era might have been very different.

Politics Migrates

While institutional rules and interests made national action to bring about racial equality in politics difficult after 1875, the American system of federalism allowed for some antidiscriminatory legislation and some growth in African American political power at the state level outside of the South. Although the Democratic administration of Woodrow Wilson—the first southern-born president elected since the antebellum period—segregated national government employees for the first time and publicly endorsed the major racist propaganda film in American history, *The Birth of a Nation*, other nonsouthern Democrats began to compete for black votes at the local and state levels by offering jobs, candidate opportunities, and favorable policies, an opening that would finally begin to pay off for the party during the administration of Franklin D. Roosevelt.

African American political opportunity in the North was both facilitated and inhibited by demographic trends. As racial conditions in the South deteriorated, many ambitious black Americans moved north, providing a core of leadership for potential movements similar to the core of northern blacks who had moved south during Reconstruction. The northward migration of talent began before, and proceeded during, the "Great Migration" of the era of World War I and the 1920s, when the inhibition of emigration from Europe and the mushrooming of war industries fostered the relocation of perhaps a million and a half African Americans from the South to the North and to western cities. The white backlash against the massive increase of black populations in many cities sometimes turned violent and nearly always sparked increased discrimination against African Americans in schools, jobs, and, especially, housing. But the corresponding black backlash against the rise in discrimination fed black activism, led by the NAACP, which had been founded after riots in Springfield, Illinois, in 1908. African Americans' growth in numbers and their forced concentration in ghettoes in states where they could vote and organize freely meant that the black side in the continuing conflicts would be potent. The legal legacy of Reconstruction, the constitutional amendments and the egalitarian northern state laws and state and national judicial decisions, and the memory of Reconstruction political activism (very different and much stronger in the black than in the white community), provided a foundation for racial equality in politics that was manifestly much stronger than in 1860, a launching pad for the many civil rights movements to come.

See also African Americans and politics; Asian immigrants and politics; voting.

FURTHER READING

Binder, Sarah A. *Minority Rights, Majority Rule: Partisanship and the Development of Congress*. New York: Cambridge University Press, 1997.

Brown, Thomas J. *Reconstructions: New Perspectives on the Postbellum United States*. New York: Oxford University Press, 2006.

Foner, Eric. *Forever Free: The Story of Emancipation and Reconstruction*. New York: Knopf, 2006.

Hahn, Steven. *A Nation under Our Feet: Black Political Struggles in the Rural South from Slavery to the Great Migration*. Cambridge, MA: Harvard University Press, 2006.

Jacobson, Matthew Frye. *Whiteness of a Different Color: European Immigrants and the Alchemy of Race*. Cambridge, MA: Harvard University Press, 1998.

Klinkner, Philip A., with Rogers M. Smith. *The Unsteady March: The Rise and Decline of Racial Equality in America*. Chicago: University of Chicago Press, 1999.

Kousser, J. Morgan. *Colorblind Injustice: Minority Voting Rights and the Undoing of the Second Reconstruction*. Chapel Hill: University of North Carolina Press, 1999.

———. "'The Onward March of Right Principles': State Legislative Action on Racial Discrimination in Schools in Nineteenth-Century America." *Historical Methods* 35 (Fall 2002), 177–204.

Schickler, Eric, and Gregory Wawro. *Filibuster: Obstruction and Lawmaking in the U.S. Senate*. Princeton, NJ: Princeton University Press, 2007.

Upchurch, Thomas Adams. *Legislating Racism: The Billion Dollar Congress and the Birth of Jim Crow*. Lexington: University Press of Kentucky, 2004.

J. MORGAN KOUSSER

race and politics since 1933

Barack Obama's 2008 election as president of the United States was a singular moment in African American history, comparable to the arrival of the first African slaves in colonial Virginia, the founding of the African Methodist Episcopal (AME) Church in Philadelphia in 1793, Abraham Lincoln's 1863 Emancipation Proclamation, the U.S. Supreme Court's 1954 *Brown v. Board of Education of Topeka* decision, and the passage of the 1964 Civil Rights Act and the 1965 Voting Rights Act. More directly, it represents the culmination of 75 years of political history during which rising levels of African American support for the Democratic Party and the accompanying shift of defenders of the racial status quo from the Democratic to the Republican Party remade the American political landscape.

Race, Politics, and the New Deal

It was during the Depression of the 1930s that black voters first began to migrate from the "party of Lincoln" to the Democratic Party. From the Civil War through the 1920s, region, race, and ethnicity had marked the divide between the two major political parties. The Republicans were the party of white native-stock Northerners and those African Americans, primarily in the North, who were able to exercise their right to vote, while the Democrats were the party of the white South and of "white ethnics" (Catholic and Jewish immigrants of European descent and their descendants) in the industrial North.

The growing influence of urban political machines within the national Democratic Party, and the increasing influence of "white ethnic" voters and politicians within those machines, was the one countervailing trend to racialism in post–World War I politics. By 1930, 56.2 percent of the U.S. population lived in urban areas. This trend culminated in the Democrats' nomination of Alfred E. Smith, the Irish Catholic governor of New York, as the party's standard-bearer in the 1928 presidential election, an achievement as momentous in its time as Obama's nomination was in 2008. But while Smith's nomination portended the increasing integration of European immigrant communities into the mainstream of American politics, his defeat in the face of widespread anti-Catholic prejudice demonstrated the continuing power of nativism in the country's politics.

Four years later, another Democratic governor of New York, Franklin D. Roosevelt, swept to victory over the incumbent Republican president, Herbert Hoover. Coming three years into the most severe economic depression in U.S. history and after 12 years of Republican rule in Washington, Roosevelt's victory was in one sense unremarkable. The Democratic Party remained, as it had been under Al Smith, an alliance of northern urban political machines and southern segregationists. What made

Roosevelt's victory possible was the growing disaffection from the Republicans of native-stock middle-class and working-class voters in the Northeast, the Midwest, and California. One group of traditional Republican voters not drawn to Roosevelt's call for a "New Deal" for American families were African American voters. Black voters in most major cities voted for Hoover in 1932 by margins of more than two to one.

However, the New Deal quickly reorganized the racial and ethnic divisions within American politics in three significant ways. First, the Roosevelt administration's policies built for the Democrats an unassailable base among lower- and middle-income voters outside the South. Galvanized by Roosevelt's promise of government assistance to those most affected by the collapse of American industrial economy, working-class voters who had previously divided their votes between the two major parties along ethnic and religious lines flocked to the Democratic Party. In 1936 Roosevelt swept to reelection with nearly 61 percent of the vote.

As significant to shifts in working-class views on race, nation, and identity was the rapid growth in union membership in the 1930s, particularly following the founding of the Committee on Industrial Organizations (CIO) in 1935 as an industrial alternative to the craft unions in the American Federation of Labor (AFL). The impact of the CIO's organizing drive on race relations within the working class was contradictory. On the one hand, the effort to organize every worker in a factory irrespective of differences of job, skill, race, ethnicity, or religion cast class unity—rather than hierarchies of race, religion, or ethnicity—as the key to advancing workers' interests in a capitalist economy. And, in fact, the CIO organized many minority and women workers whom the AFL had ignored. Yet, central to the CIO's appeal was also the labor organization's representation of the ideal American worker as white and male. The result was a working-class nationalism that for the first time fully included white Catholic and Jewish workers, while implicitly suggesting that minority and women workers were marginal to the cause of labor.

Second, the New Deal solidified the alliance between the southern and northern wings of the Democratic Party. To win the support of southern Democrats, however, Roosevelt had to assure white Southerners that New Deal programs would be administered in ways that would not disrupt race relations in the region. Most important, the Roosevelt administration allowed state and local officials to control the implementation of most New Deal programs. For example, the Civilian Conservation Corps and the Works Progress Administration both operated segregated employment projects in the South. Most devastating to the interests of African American workers was the Roosevelt administration's decision in 1935 to accede to the demands of key southern congressional leaders to exclude farm and domestic workers from the provisions of the Social Security Act. As a result, 65 percent of black workers were excluded from Social Security's unemployment and retirement provisions.

Nor were the New Deal's racial inequities limited to the South. The New Deal policies with perhaps the longest-lasting disparate racial impact came in the area of housing. The Federal Housing Administration (FHA) was established in 1934 to rescue the private housing industry by providing mortgage guarantees to lenders willing to provide long-term mortgages to home buyers. As criteria for these mortgages, the FHA adopted standards from the real estate industry that favored white neighborhoods over integrated and predominately minority areas, suburban communities over urban neighborhoods, and owner-occupied single-family homes over multifamily structures and rental properties. The full import of this policy would not be evident until after World War II. New Deal housing programs would, in effect, subsidize the postwar boom in all-white suburbs while steering private housing investment away from the middle- and working-class urban neighborhoods that became the only housing option for ever-increasing numbers of southern black migrants.

Despite the racial inequities built into the New Deal, the third and final component of the New Deal coalition was in place by the end of the 1930s. In 1936 Roosevelt won more than 60 percent of the black vote in every major city except Chicago. Roosevelt's popularity with black voters was the product of two distinct aspects of his first two terms in office. First, large numbers of African Americans became, for the first time, recipients of government assistance. To be included among the beneficiaries of Roosevelt's New Deal was both a matter of survival in those hungry years and thrilling to a people so long treated as undeserving of the rights and privileges of American citizenship.

Second, and as important to black voters as these substantive benefits of the New Deal, was the symbolic value of Roosevelt's appointment of an unprecedented number of African Americans to high positions in his administration. While it would be another 30 years before an African American would be elevated to a position in the cabinet, Roosevelt's so-called "Negro Cabinet"—

made up of well-educated professionals appointed to the position of "Adviser for Negro Affairs" in the various agencies of the federal government—was a source of tremendous pride to black voters. These voters were also deeply impressed by Eleanor Roosevelt's determined and very visible commitment to racial equality. The most dramatic emblem of the first lady's commitment came in 1939 when she publicly resigned her membership in the Daughters of the American Revolution after the nativist and elitist women's patriotic organization refused to allow Marian Anderson, the African American opera singer, to perform in the organization's Constitution Hall in Washington. Mrs. Roosevelt instead arranged for Anderson to perform at the Lincoln Memorial for a national radio audience, a concert that became the high-water mark of African American inclusion in the New Deal.

World War II and the Double-V

Even as a majority of African American voters switched allegiance to the Democratic Party during the 1930s, it would be another decade before the party would formally commit itself to a civil rights agenda. During the 1940s, African American activists and their allies codified the "civil rights" strategy of achieving racial equality through legislation and judicial rulings that guaranteed government protection of individual rights. Three factors enabled civil rights activists to make much more significant demands on the administrations of Roosevelt and Harry S. Truman during the 1940s. First was the rapid growth in the African American population in the North as wartime labor shortages and growth in defense industry employment reinvigorated black migration from the South following the lull of the Depression years. In this decade, the black population living outside the South grew by 65 percent, to a total of 12.8 million people. Second, the rise of Nazism in Europe discredited theories of racial supremacy within the United States, particularly among liberal elites within the Democratic Party. Third, and most important, were the efforts of civil rights advocates to take advantage of the wartime social and political context to pressure the federal government and the Democratic Party to more directly address structures of racial discrimination within American society.

What one black newspaper would call the "Double-V" campaign (victory over fascism abroad and victory over racism at home) began when A. Philip Randolph, president of the all-black Brotherhood of Sleeping Car Porters, called for a black-only march on Washington, D.C., in June 1941 to demand the desegregation of the armed forces and equal treatment for black workers in the nation's defense industries. Concerned that such a march would undercut popular support for his efforts to aid the European allies, Roosevelt convinced Randolph to call off the march in return for an executive order banning racial discrimination in defense employment. The resulting President's Fair Employment Practices Committee (FEPC) became the focus of the activists' wartime efforts to improve employment opportunities for African American workers. In 1944, for example, the FEPC ordered the Philadelphia Transit Company to promote eight black maintenance workers to the position of trolley conductor. When the company's white workers responded with a wildcat strike that shut down the transit system, the secretary of the Navy had to order troops into Philadelphia to run the trolleys.

It was during the 1940s that the National Association for the Advancement of Colored People (NAACP) transformed itself from a primarily middle-class and northern organization into a truly national and mass-based one. Membership in the NAACP during the war grew from 54,000 to more than 500,000. Particularly significant was the growth of the organization's membership in the South during these years. The NAACP's southern chapters served as a training ground for a generation of local leaders who went on to play crucial roles in the civil rights mobilizations of the 1950s and 1960s, including Modjeska Simmons and Septima Clark in South Carolina, E. D. Nixon and Rosa Parks in Alabama, and Medgar Evers and Amzie Moore in Mississippi.

Also crucial to the increase in southern civil rights activism was the U.S. Supreme Court's ruling in *Smith v. Allwright* (1944), which outlawed the Democratic Party's use of all-white primary elections across the South. As Charles Payne has argued, the decision spurred black southern voter registration, particularly in urban areas. The percentage of southern blacks registered to vote grew from less than 5 percent in 1940 to 12 percent in 1947 and 20 percent in 1952. Black voters in Atlanta and other cities were able to use their increased voting power to play a moderating influence in certain local elections.

The Civil Rights Movement in Cold War America

It was, however, developments in the North during the 1940s that provided the NAACP with new opportunities to pursue its civil rights agenda in the political arena. In 1948 Henry Moon, the NAACP's public relations director, published *Balance of Power: The Negro Vote*, in which he argued that black voters in the urban North now held the balance of power between the two political parties in national elections and that for the first time since Reconstruction African American voters had the ability to demand significant civil rights reforms in return for their votes. Clark Clifford, President Truman's chief political advisor, reached a similar conclusion as he look forward to the 1948 presidential election. Clifford concluded that unlike Roosevelt's four campaigns, southern support for the Democratic candidate would not be sufficient in 1948, but that an effective appeal to northern African American voters could return Truman to the presidency even if he lost some southern votes in the process.

To win northern black votes, however, Truman would have to fend off a challenge from Henry Wallace, his predecessor as Roosevelt's vice president and the candidate of the left-wing Progressive Party. Truman thus appointed a blue-ribbon commission in 1946 to study civil rights issues. The President's Committee on Civil Rights issued its report, titled *To Secure These Rights*, in 1947. The report laid out an agenda of actions that all three branches of the federal government should take to protect the rights of the nation's racial minorities. While the report's recommendations had little chance of being adopted by Congress, they did form the basis for Truman's groundbreaking appeal for the votes of northern blacks. Most dramatically, and in response to threats from A. Phillip Randolph to organize a civil disobedience campaign against the Selective Service system, Truman issued Executive Order 9981 on February 2, 1948, mandating the desegregation of the armed forces. The results of the 1948 election proved both Moon and Clifford to have been right. South Carolina Democratic governor Strom Thurmond won four Deep South states as the candidate of the States' Rights Democratic Party. But in the North, African American voters largely rejected Henry Wallace's candidacy and provided the margin of victory for Truman's upset defeat of the Republican nominee, Thomas E. Dewey.

With southern Democrats effectively blocking federal civil rights legislation, northern civil rights activists turned their focus to passing civil rights legislation at the state and local level. Between 1945 and 1964, 28 states passed Fair Employment Practices (FEP) laws. But as important as these legislative victories were, they could not mask the fact that racial discrimination remained pervasive in the North. Thus, the northern FEP laws did little to change the informal hiring policies and exclusionary union practices that kept African American workers locked out of many white- and blue-collar occupations. And while the Supreme Court declared in 1948 that racial covenants were unenforceable in court, the suburban housing boom remained closed to African Americans as federal mortgage guarantors, housing developers, and white home buyers continued to favor white-only communities. Civil rights activists also faced increasing political opposition from other elements of the New Deal coalition to their efforts to address persistent racial inequities in northern communities. In the 1949 mayoral election in Detroit, for example, Albert Cobo, a conservative Republican, defeated the United Auto Workers–endorsed candidate on a platform of opposition to the building of public housing projects in white neighborhoods. As historians Arnold Hirsch and Thomas Sugrue have shown, black families seeking to move into all-white neighborhoods in cities like Chicago and Detroit were often greeted with racial violence.

Historians continue to debate the impact of the cold war on the civil rights movement. Manning Marable and Martha Biondi have argued that the stigmatization of left-wing politics during the period of McCarthyism greatly hampered civil rights efforts in part because of the prominence of left-wing figures like Paul Robeson among advocates of civil rights, in part because defenders of racial segregation were able to use the charge of communism to discredit all advocates of racial equality, and in part because organizations like the NAACP became extremely cautious politically in order to distance themselves from radicalism. In contrast, Mary Dudziak has argued that the cold war helped civil rights activists to advance their cause because of the pressure it placed on the nation's political leaders to demonstrate to the emerging nations of the third world that capitalist democracies were better able to deliver on the promise of racial equality than was the Soviet bloc.

Perhaps more detrimental to the cause of civil rights during the 1950s than cold war anxieties about the threat of internal subversion was the widespread belief among political leaders that the nation had entered a period of political consensus. The notion of consensus politics was rooted in two beliefs—first, that the country had solved most of its domestic problems, and second, that internal political unity was required to defeat the Communist threat. In this view, whatever social inequities remained in American society (among which most advocates of consensus politics would have included racial issues) would gradually disappear as the capitalist economy continued to grow, while efforts to speed the process of social change (through, for example, aggressive efforts to implement civil rights reforms) would only divide the country and weaken its resolve in the struggle against communism. As a result, the 1950s were characterized both by historic civil rights achievements rooted in an idealistic view of the United States as the world's foremost defender of individual liberty and equal rights under law and by the failure of government officials to fulfill the promise of those achievements for fear of the reaction of the white majority. Thus, the Supreme Court ruled in the 1954 *Brown v. Board of Education* case that school segregation is unconstitutional. But with southern Democrats promising "massive resistance" to the *Brown* decision, President Dwight Eisenhower refused to vigorously enforce the decision. Moreover, the Supreme Court ruled just one year later that school desegregation should take place with "all deliberate speed," thus opening the door to two decades of southern efforts to sustain dual school systems. In a similar fashion, the U.S. Congress passed its first major piece of civil rights legislation since Reconstruction, the Civil Rights Act of 1957, just days before Eisenhower was forced to send federal troops to enforce a federal court order requiring the integration of Central High School in Little Rock, Arkansas. By the time of its passage, however, the enforcement provisions of the act, which sought to increase the number of African American voters in the South, had been so watered down that leading southern Democratic senators declared its passage a victory for their side.

The 1960s

Thirty-two years after Al Smith lost his bid to become the first Catholic president of the United States, John F. Kennedy defeated Richard Nixon in the 1960 presidential election. Twice during the campaign, Kennedy felt it necessary to give speeches declaring his commitment to the separation of church and state. What was not in question, however, was Kennedy's status as a white American. In contrast to previous generations of European Catholic immigrants and their descendants who were seen as racially distinct from native-stock white Americans, Kennedy, like his contemporaries Frank Sinatra and Joe DiMaggio, became a symbol of the quintessential American experience in a nation of immigrants.

African American voters again played a crucial role in the 1960 presidential election. Nine months earlier, the student sit-in movement to protest segregated lunch counters had spread rapidly across the South. That fall, civil rights protest became an issue in the presidential campaign when Martin Luther King Jr. was arrested for leading a sit-in in Atlanta and was subsequently sentenced to four months in a south Georgia prison camp. Nixon refused to intervene, hoping to gain the votes of white Southerners upset by the civil rights plank in Democratic Party platform. Kennedy, in contrast, placed a call to King's wife, Coretta Scott King, to express his concern. Within days, Kennedy campaign officials had successfully petitioned Georgia officials for King's release. On the Sunday before the election, the Kennedy campaign distributed a flyer to black churches across the nation announcing the endorsement of King's father, Martin Luther King Sr. In one of the closest presidential campaigns in American history, black votes provided the margin of victory for Kennedy in a number of northern states.

Civil rights issues were not a priority for Kennedy when he entered the White House in 1961. Rather, his central focus was on foreign policy. Within months, however, the efforts of civil rights protesters—particularly the interracial teams of "freedom riders" who sought to ride interstate buses across the South—would force Kennedy to address the question of southern race relations. In an effort to defuse the sense of crisis generated by nonviolent protest, the Kennedy administration initially sought to encourage civil rights activists to shift their focus to voter registration on the theory that a growing black electorate in the South would lead the region's politicians to moderate their positions on racial issues.

In June 1963, however, as nonviolent protest campaigns continued to roil southern cities and as voter registration drives in the rural South were met with racist violence, Kennedy submitted to Congress civil rights legislation banning segregated public accommodations and employment discrimination. Support for the Kennedy civil rights bill was a central feature of the August 1963 March on Washington, even as activists affiliated with the student wing of the movement pressed unsuccessfully for the march to explicitly criticize the president for failing to do enough to protect civil rights workers in the South from racist violence.

Still, little progress had been made on the civil rights bill by the time of Kennedy's tragic assassination in November 1963. It would take a Southerner, Kennedy's successor Lyndon Johnson, to overcome southern opposition and steer the civil rights bill through Congress. During his 23 years in Congress, including six as Senate majority leader, Johnson had been an ardent New Dealer and, for a Southerner, a moderate on civil rights issues. Now he pledged "to take the dead man's program and turn it into a martyr's cause." On June 11, 1964, the Senate voted for the first time to end a southern Senate filibuster against a civil rights bill and, on July 1, Johnson signed the Civil Rights Act of 1964 into law.

The act was only part of Johnson's agenda of social and political reform, however. In his first State of the Union address in January 1964, Johnson called for the most prosperous nation in the world to wage "a war on poverty." Then, in May, he pledged to use the nation's material wealth to build a "Great Society" based on "an abundance and liberty for all . . . an end to poverty and racial injustice . . . [and] the desire for beauty and the hunger for community." Johnson's vision of the Great Society was rooted in two seemingly contradictory views of American society—the first of a great country ready to use its wealth to help those with the least, the second of a nation flawed by racism but willing to confront its failings in pursuit of justice for all. Johnson promoted the war on poverty and the Great Society both as efforts to provide assistance to the poor of all races and as essential to fulfilling the call of the civil rights movement to end racial injustice.

In the short run, Johnson would parlay these twin imperatives into a remarkable streak of legislative and political victories. In the summer of 1964, Congress passed the Economic Opportunity Act—the centerpiece of Johnson's antipoverty initiative—which would provide nearly $3 billion in government funds for local antipoverty programs over the next three years. That fall, not only did Johnson win a landslide victory over his Republican opponent, Barry Goldwater, but the Democrats swept to the party's largest majorities in both the House and the Senate in the post–World War II period. This majority enabled Johnson to push a legislative agenda through Congress over the next two years that rivaled the reforms of the New Deal. Most significant was the Voting Rights Act of 1965, which established for the first time, federal oversight over the voter rolls in the ten southern states that had historically denied the vote to African Americans. Educational programs were enacted for low-income children, including the preschool program Head Start; Medicare and Medicaid, health insurance programs for the elderly and the poor; immigration reform; mass transit programs; and consumer safety and environmental safety legislation.

By the fall of 1966, there were signs of declining support for Johnson's reform agenda. Civil rights protests, urban race riots, and rising urban crime rates combined to weaken white support for the president's agenda of racial reform and poverty reduction, while the growing cost of the Vietnam War and rising inflation strengthened the voices of conservative critics of taxes and government spending. Republicans picked up 50 seats in the 1966 congressional elections, effectively bringing a halt to Johnson's Great Society agenda and setting the stage for the resurgence of Republicans in national elections.

Historians have tended to see the 1960s as the moment when the national Democratic Party committed itself fully to the cause of civil rights, the Republican Party began to capture the allegiance of white southern voters, and the New Deal coalition of white southern, black, and northern white working-class voters began to collapse. This analysis must be qualified in three ways. First, racial issues in the urban North had begun to lead middle- and low-income white voters to abandon the Democrats in local elections as early the late 1940s. Second, Republicans had begun in the 1950s to pursue a strategy of capturing the votes of white southern Democrats rather than seeking to compete with the Democrats for the votes of African Americans and other supporters of civil rights.

Third, the most important factor in the shift of white voters toward the Republican Party, in the South and in the industrial states of the Northeast and the Midwest, was only tangentially related to the civil rights reforms of the 1960s. Rather, Republican candidates in presidential and congressional elections benefited from the growing importance of white suburban voters, relative to both northern urban and southern rural voters, within the American electorate. By the late 1960s, suburban voters—many of them the children of New Dealers—were increasingly hostile to the perceived cost (in taxes) of government programs designed to address racial and economic equality as well as to any efforts by the federal government and courts to force local communities to adopt policies (in areas like zoning and public schooling) designed to lessen racial segregation in the North. Suburban voters were also attracted to Republican calls for lower taxes and for a vigilantly anti-Communist foreign policy.

The splintering of the New Deal coalition was most evident in the 1968 presidential election. While Richard Nixon received only about 500,000 more votes than his Democratic opponent, Hubert Humphrey, he won the Electoral College by more than 100 votes. Humphrey's defeat was in part the result of the loss of support for Democrats among white southern voters. Nixon swept the Upper South, South Carolina, and Florida for a total of 65 electoral votes, while Alabama's Democratic governor George Wallace, running as a third-party candidate, won five Deep South states and a total of 45 electoral votes. However, the Democratic standard-bearer might still have won the election had Wallace not cut severely into his support among white northern working-class voters who felt abandoned by the Democratic Party's civil rights policies. The Alabama governor campaigned extensively in the North, drawing large crowds to campaign rallies during which he received appreciative applause for his attacks on elitist liberals for insisting that poor whites integrate their schools even as those liberals sent their own children to exclusive private schools. In six northern states, the Wallace vote more than doubled Nixon's margin of victory over Humphrey.

Racial Codes and the Rise of the New Right

These fissures within the New Deal coalition did not immediately add up to Republican dominance of American politics. Nixon won the 1968 election with only 43.4 percent of the vote. Moreover, Democrats remained in firm control of both houses of Congress despite Nixon's landslide reelection in 1972. Not until 1994 would Republicans win majorities in both houses of Congress. Throughout this period, Democrats remained competitive in southern congressional elections, particularly when they campaigned on New Deal–style populist economics that appealed to middle- and lower-income white as well as black voters.

Nixon's victory in the 1968 presidential campaign began a streak in which Republicans won seven of the next ten presidential elections. While largely conceding the more formal aspects of the civil rights revolution—a "color-blind" legal system, school desegregation, equal access to public accommodations—Republicans proved adept at using racial codes to promote key aspects of their conservative policy agenda to white voters across the economic spectrum. Racial coding was most pronounced in Republican efforts to stigmatize liberal policies in the areas of school desegregation, welfare, affirmative action, and immigration.

Nixon most effectively used racial codes to express sympathy for white anxieties about court-ordered school desegregation plans. In his 1968 campaign, Nixon won broad support in upper-income suburban districts across the South by affirming his support both for the Supreme Court's *Brown* decision and for local control over public schooling. He thus managed to distance himself simultaneously from southern segregationists like Wallace and from civil rights activists and federal judges who were advocates of what he called "forced integration." Over the next decade, the Supreme Court would uphold a series of federal court rulings that required the use of mandatory busing schemes to achieve school integration in both southern and northern urban school districts. In all of these cases, the courts found that a constellation of government policies—from the gerrymandering of school boundaries to housing and zoning policies designed to maintain residential segregation—had served to perpetuate school segregation despite the Court's ruling in the *Brown* case. And yet, each case gave conservative politicians from Charlotte, North Carolina, to Boston the opportunity to position themselves as defenders of legitimate white working-class interests—explicitly, of the right to keep their children in neighborhood schools and implicitly, of the right to keep those schools exclusively white.

Racial coding was equally effective for Republicans on the issue of welfare. Central to the conservative attack on excesses of the Great Society programs of the 1960s was the argument that the growth in government assistance to the poor constituted little more than a transfer of income from "hardworking" taxpayers to African American and Latino beneficiaries deemed too lazy to work. The majority of welfare recipients were, of course, white. Moreover, antipoverty programs contributed to a 50 percent decline in the poverty rate in the United States between 1960 and 1980. While books like conservative sociologist Charles Murray's *Losing Ground: American Social Policy, 1950–1980* (1984) argued that income assistance programs promoted dependency on government by providing a disincentive to work, conservative opposition to welfare focused less on policy debates than on stories of welfare recipients as "cheats" and "frauds." Anecdotal narratives of Cadillac-driving "welfare queens" who used multiple aliases to collect excessive benefits were central to Ronald Reagan's emergence as a leader of the conservative movement during the 1970s. While he rarely referred to specific individuals, Reagan's references to neighborhoods like Chicago's South Side invariably marked welfare cheaters as African American.

Opposition to welfare remained a central feature of Republican appeals to white lower- and middle-income voters into the 1990s. In an effort to inoculate his candidacy against charges of liberal elitism, Democrat Bill Clinton built his 1992 presidential campaign around a pledge "to end welfare as we know it." Still, opposition to welfare remained at the top of the Republicans' 1994 "Contract with America," the manifesto on which Republican congressional leaders based their successful campaign to wrest control from the Democrats of both houses of Congress for the first time in 40 years. In 1996 the Republican Congress passed and President Clinton signed a reform bill that transformed welfare from an entitlement meant to serve everyone who qualified for aid into a time-limited program with stringent requirements and a five-year cap on benefits.

Also central to the Republican critique of the racial excesses of liberalism was affirmative action. The origins of affirmative action lay in the response of civil rights activists and liberal government officials to the failure of antidiscrimination laws to substantively desegregate local labor markets. Private-sector employers found that a minimal adjustment in their hiring procedures—and, in some cases the employment of a token few minority employees—quickly brought them into compliance with fair employment laws. Debate over whether employers could and should be required to take action to increase their employment of minority workers bore fruit in March 1961, when President Kennedy issued an executive order requiring federal agencies and contractors to take "affirmative action" to remove racially discriminatory barriers to employment.

Over the next decade, federal officials responded to increasingly militant civil rights protests against continued discrimination in private-sector hiring, particularly in the construction trades, with a series of policy experiments designed to establish affirmative action's parameters and procedures. In 1969 a federal court upheld the constitutionality of the Philadelphia Plan in the building trades, and the Nixon administration extended its requirements to all federal contracts worth more than $50,000. Women were added to the affirmative action requirements in 1971, and many state and local governments adopted similar plans.

President Nixon seems to have decided to support affirmative action both in hopes of winning support from the black business and professional classes and as part of a strategy to promote divisions between the labor (that is, white working class) and black wings of the Democratic Party.

Opposition to affirmative action would not become a central feature of Republican appeals for white working- and middle-class votes until Reagan's 1980 presidential campaign. Reagan and the emergent conservative wing of the Republican Party argued that affirmative action constituted reverse discrimination against whites, particularly those from lower- and middle-income communities, and thus violated the civil rights movement's commitment to building a colorblind society. The most dramatic instance of the Republicans' use of affirmative action to draw working-class white votes came in the U.S. Senate election in North Carolina in 1990, when Senator Jesse Helms used a last-minute television ad (in which the viewer saw only the hands and flannel sleeves of a white worker opening a letter informing him that the job he "needed" had been given to a "minority") to win a come-from-behind victory over Harvey Gantt, his African American opponent.

In the legal arena, the charge of reverse discrimination was advanced, with some success, in the name of whites who claimed to have been denied educational or economic opportunity on the basis of their race—most prominently Allen Bakke, Jennifer Gratz, and Barbara Grutter, the plaintiffs in the 1977 and 2005 Supreme Court cases that defined how universities can and cannot use affirmative action procedures in admissions. Within the political realm, many of the leading opponents of affirmative action were black and Latino conservatives. Figures like Supreme Court Justice Clarence Thomas, economists Thomas Sowell and Glen Loury, Republican activist Linda Chavez, and political essayists Shelby Steele and Richard Rodriguez argued that affirmative action violated Martin Luther King Jr.'s call for people to be judged according to the content of their character and not the color of their skin, and that it reinforced the view that racial minorities were incapable of competing on equal terms with whites. In 1995 Ward Connerly, a University of California trustee and Republican Party activist, emerged as the most prominent black opponent of affirmative action when he led a successful referendum campaign in California to ban the use of racial and gender preferences in all state government programs and contracts. Over the next decade, Connerly would lead similarly successful campaigns in Washington, Florida, Michigan, and Nebraska.

Black and Latino conservatives did not limit their political activism and advocacy to affirmative action, offering free market, self-help, and faith-based policy prescriptions on issues from poverty and the rising number of female-headed single-parent households to failing schools and insufficient economic investment in the inner cities. While Republican efforts to increase the party's share of the black and Latino vote produced only minimal results, advocates of self-help, entrepreneurship, and traditional religious and social values enjoyed growing influence in black and Latino communities in the post–New Deal era.

Race and the Politics of Immigration

Bilingual education provides another example of the ways in which racial politics infused conservative efforts to discredit federally funded domestic programs. In 1968 Congress passed the Bilingual Education Act, which provided the first federal funding for bilingual education programs. But it was not until the early 1970s that federal education officials began to require that school districts provide bilingual educational programming to non-English speakers as a mechanism for promoting both immigrant educational achievement and ethnic and racial pride.

In the ensuing decades, the debate over bilingual education has proceeded on two separate, if overlapping, tracks. While educators debate whether bilingual transitional or monolingual immersion programs are the best mechanism for enabling immigrant children to simultaneously learn English and keep up with their English-speaking classmates, conservative activists, led in the 1980s by Reagan administration Secretary of Education William Bennett, have criticized bilingual education for promoting ethnic pride and multicultural identities over assimilation into American society. A direct result of the furor of bilingual education was the emergence of the "English-only" movement, which won passage of legislation declaring English to be the sole official language of the United States in 26 states between 1984 and 2007.

By the early 1990s, English-only campaigns were largely superseded by a broader conservative backlash against immigration, particularly that from Mexico and Central and South America. The policy agenda of anti-immigration activism has been to prevent undocumented immigrants from entering the country and to deny government services to those already in the United States. For example, California's Proposition 187, enacted with 59 percent of the vote in 1994, would have denied social services, public health care, and public education to undocumented immigrants had it not been overturned in the courts. But while anti-immigration groups like the Federation for American Immigration Reform have long denied any racial motivation to their agenda, popular animus against Latino immigrants, whether legal or undocumented, has driven much of the demand for immigration reform over the last two decades. Latino immigrants are accused of being fundamentally different from previous generations of immigrants, of failing to learn English and assimilate into "American culture," and of taking jobs from American workers. In 2004, for example, Harvard political scientist Samuel Huntington published "The Hispanic Challenge," an extended essay later developed into a book, in which he argued that "Mexicans and other Latinos have not assimilated into mainstream U.S. culture, forming instead their own political and linguistic enclaves—from Los Angeles to Miami—and rejecting the Anglo-Protestant values that built the American dream."

Within the Republican Party, however, opinion was split over whether to pursue an anti-immigration agenda or to campaign for Latino votes. One the one hand, California governor Pete Wilson was a strong supporter of Proposition 187, and the 1994 Contract with America promised to disqualify even legal immigrants from public assistance programs. Other Republicans argued that the party should make it a priority to reach out to upwardly mobile and socially conservative Latinos in states like Florida and Texas. For example, the Nixon administration's initial support for bilingual education emerged from a desire to appeal to Latino voters. And Nixon did in fact double his share of the Latino vote to about 33 percent between 1968 and 1972. Similarly, support from Latino voters and a moderate position on immigration issues were instrumental in George W. Bush's emergence as a national political leader during his years as governor of Texas as well as to his narrow victories in the 2000 and 2004 presidential elections.

African American and Latino Politics in the Post–Civil Rights Era

Despite conservative gains since the 1960s, the final decades of the twentieth century were also marked by the unprecedented growth in the number of African American and Latino elected officials. By 2000 the combined total of black and Latino elected officials at all levels of governments exceeded 13,000. The majority of these politicians of color were elected to office in the "black belt" regions of the rural South and in California and Texas, the two states with the largest Latino populations.

It was in the nation's big cities, however, that black and Latino politicians were most visible. From 1967, when Carl Stokes and Richard Hatcher became the first African Americans elected mayor of major cities (Cleveland, Ohio, and Gary, Indiana, respectively) to Antonio Villaraigosa's election as the first Latino mayor of modern-day Los Angeles in 2005, urban politicians of color have sought to use election to public office as a mechanism for addressing the continued economic and social underdevelopment of minority communities in the United States. It was, in fact, this vision of black urban governance—particularly as practiced by Chicago's first and so far only African American mayor, Harold Washington—that first attracted Barack Obama to electoral politics. In the 1960s and 1970s, this strategy of winning control over city government was rooted in a view of the federal government as a willing and essential ally in efforts to revive the nation's urban economies. But even as the national political culture grew more conservative and the fulcrum of political power shifted from cities to the suburbs, many politicians of color maintained their vision of elective office as a mechanism for the collective uplift of their communities.

See also African Americans and politics; Asian immigrants and politics; civil rights; Latinos and politics.

FURTHER READING

Biondi, Martha. *To Stand and Fight: The Struggle for Civil Rights in Postwar New York City*. Cambridge, MA: Harvard University Press, 2003.

Chafe, William. *Unfinished Journey: America since World War II*. 6th ed. New York: Oxford University Press, 2006.

Countryman, Matthew J. *Up South: Civil Rights and Black Power in Philadelphia*. Philadelphia: University of Pennsylvania Press, 2006.

Davies, Gareth. *See Government Grow: Education Politics from Johnson to Reagan*. Lawrence: University of Kansas Press, 2007.

Dillard, Angela. *Guess Who's Coming to Dinner Now? Multicultural Conservatism in America*. New York: New York University Press, 2002.

Dudziak, Mary. *Cold War Civil Rights: Race and the Image of American Democracy*. Princeton, NJ: Princeton University Press, 2002.

Gilmore, Glenda. *Defying Dixie: The Radical Roots of Civil Rights, 1919–1950*. New York: Norton, 2008.

Hirsch, Arnold. *Making the Second Ghetto: Race and Housing in Chicago, 1940–1960*. Cambridge, UK: Cambridge University Press, 1983.

Hornsby, Alton. *Black Power in Dixie: A Political History of African-Americans in Atlanta*. Gainesville: University Press of Florida, 2009.

Huntington, Samuel P. *Who Are We? The Challenges to America's National Identity*. New York: Simon and Schuster, 2005.

Katznelson, Ira. *When Affirmative Action Was White: An Untold History of Racial Inequality in Twentieth-Century America*. New York: Norton, 2006.

Lassiter, Matthew D. *The Silent Majority: Suburban Politics in the Sunbelt South*. Princeton, NJ: Princeton University Press, 2006.

MacLean, Nancy. *Freedom Is Not Enough: The Opening of the American Workplace*. Cambridge, MA: Harvard University Press, 2008.

Marable, Manning. *Race, Reform, and Rebellion: The Second Reconstruction and Beyond in Black America, 1945–2006*. 3rd ed. Jackson: University Press of Mississippi, 2007.

Moon, Henry. *Balance of Power: The Negro Vote*. Reprint ed. Westport, CT: Greenwood Press, 1977.

Murray, Charles. *Losing Ground: American Social Policy, 1950–1980*. 10th anniversary ed. New York: Basic Books, 1994.

Payne, Charles M. "'The Whole United States Is Southern!': *Brown v. Board* and the Mystification of Race." *Journal of American History* 91 (June 2004), 83–91.

Sugrue, Thomas J. *The Origins of the Urban Crisis: Race and Inequality in Postwar Detroit*. Princeton, NJ: Princeton University Press, 1998.

———. *Sweet Land of Liberty: The Forgotten Struggle for Civil Rights in the North*. New York: Random House, 2008.

Weiss, Nancy J. *Farewell to the Party of Lincoln: Black Politics in the Age of FDR*. Princeton, NJ: Princeton University Press, 1983.

MATTHEW J. COUNTRYMAN

radicalism

The term *radicalism* comes from the Latin word *radix*, meaning "root." Radicalism seeks to locate the root causes of social injustice and extirpate them, to overturn existing social structures and replace them with forms more conducive to equality, cooperation, dignity, inclusion, and freedom. An amorphous concept, radicalism denotes a disposition, an emancipatory and egalitarian élan, rather than a precise program. Although radicalism has sometimes been taken to denote "extremism" and therefore to include a political right that propounds order and hierarchy, the far right, which aims to reconstitute privileges rather than uproot them, is better designated as reactionary. Radicalism is also distinct from gradualism or liberalism, although that stops neither radicals from seeking reforms nor vigorous reformers from styling themselves "radical liberals."

Radicalism is innately controversial. Its admirers value its creativity, courage, and adherence to principle, while opponents view it as rash, impractical, and fanatical. Radicalism is further characterized by a willingness to employ tactics outside approved channels. Although radicals rarely consider themselves beholden to existing law or authority, the association of radicalism with violence and destruction is not entirely warranted, since radicals have primarily engaged in peaceful protest, suasion, and civil disobedience.

Radicals typically scrutinize everyday life with the intention of transforming self and culture as much as state and society. No one philosophy, however, defines radicalism. What counts as "radical" changes over time, and radicals differ in visions, priorities, and strategies. Affection for American democracy has motivated many radicals, such as the poet Walt Whitman, who heard America singing yet wrote at the end of his life, "I am as radical now as ever." Other radicals have spoken from a position of profound alienation from their country. Radicalism has served as a catalyst, dramatizing problems, disrupting routines, and introducing preposterous notions that in time come to seem commonsensical. Many radical propositions, however, have gone down to defeat, and America has frequently vilified its radicals. Radicalism, in short, has existed both at the center and at the margins of American political life.

Early American Radicalism

Although Native American resistance to European settlement might be viewed as the origin of American radicalism, uprisings motivated by defense of tradition, such as Pontiac's pan-Indian rebellion of 1763, could just as readily be classified as ardent conservatism. Colonial radicals, moreover, rarely extended solidarity to Indian resistance. Nathaniel Bacon's Virginia Colony uprising of 1676 united poor white farmers, indentured servants, free blacks, and slaves in attacking indigenous tribes before turning on wealthy planters and burning Jamestown to the ground.

The Puritans, Quakers, and other religious nonconformists who populated the English colonies were radicals by the norms of the countries they left behind. They, in turn, produced their own antinomian heretics, such as Roger Williams, advocate of separation of church and state, and Anne Hutchinson, who challenged clerical authority. The Protestant emphasis on individual conscience and morality would inform much of the subsequent history of American radicalism—as would rationalist challenges to authoritarian religion.

With the coming of the American Revolution, Crispus Attucks, Patrick Henry, Samuel Adams, the Sons of Liberty, and "mobs" protesting the Stamp Act, Sugar Act, and other parliamentary measures were radicals, pushing events past a mere imperial-colonial adjustment toward separation and a republic based on consent of the governed. Thomas Paine's *Common Sense* (1776) lambasted monarchy, aristocracy, and hereditary rule itself, giving voice to a transatlantic radicalism of cordwainers, tailors, coopers, and other skilled artisans suspicious of decadent, parasitical classes. The Declaration of Independence's pronouncement that "all men are created equal" and endowed with "certain inalienable rights" was decidedly radical for its day, as was Thomas Jefferson's aphorism, "the tree of liberty must be refreshed from time to time with the blood of patriots and tyrants."

This political culture of egalitarianism and libertarianism generated some revolutionary aftereffects, such as the uprising of indebted Massachusetts farmers led by Daniel Shays in 1786. Fearful that a headstrong democracy would threaten property rights, the Constitutional Convention in 1787 created an elite Senate, executive, and judiciary to check the popular House. Set aside was the unicameral legislature preferred by Paine, who had departed for England and France, where he would defend the French Revolution. Anti-Federalist dissent compelled passage of a constitutional Bill of Rights, but Pennsylvania's Whiskey Rebellion of 1794 showed lingering qualms about federal legitimacy.

By the early nineteenth century, artisanal radicalism took on new qualities as apprentices and journeymen began to worry over the "aristocratical" designs of their masters, who were fast becoming capitalist employers. This producer radicalism, fed by fear of "wages slavery," informed calls by the Working Man's Party of 1829–32 for free public education and restriction of the working day to ten hours. Thomas Skidmore's *The Rights of Man to Property* (1829) called for "a General Division of property," a sign that radicals would increasingly aspire to equality of condition.

America was the seedbed of world socialism in the early nineteenth century, its vast expanses of land making utopian experimentation affordable. The first agrarian colonies sought spiritual perfection, from the Shakers in upstate New York to the German Pietists at Amana, Iowa. These were followed by secular acolytes of the British industrialist Robert Owen and French philosopher Charles Fourier. The colony Frances Wright established in 1826 at Nashoba, Tennessee, sought to prove emancipation from slavery viable, but its interracial sexuality scandalized polite society, as would the "complex marriage" of John Humphrey Noyes's Oneida community. Utopian colonies often sundered apart or attracted drones. Robert Dale Owen, though a dedicated socialist, described New Harmony, Indiana, as "a heterogeneous collection of radicals, enthusiastic devotees of principle, honest latitudinarians and lazy theorists, with a sprinkling of unprincipled sharpers thrown in."

The antebellum period was effervescent with evangelical revival and moral reform causes such as temperance, phrenology, and penal reform. George Henry Evans and Horace Greeley advocated a radical measure—free land—that reached fruition in the Homestead Act of 1862. The paramount property question of the hour, however, was slavery. Radicals were first to demand the immediate end of slavery rather than gradual emancipation. Driven by conviction, and sometimes attacked physically, they set out to shock a nation into action. In *An Appeal to the Coloured Citizens of the World* (1829), the Bostonian free black David Walker called upon slaves to rise up, violently if necessary, a path taken independently by Virginia slave Nat Turner in 1831.

Abolitionism fostered further radicalisms. As Sojourner Truth and other female antislavery orators defied prejudices against women speaking in public, relations between men and women became issues for radical reconsideration. Elizabeth Cady Stanton, Lucretia Mott, and others joined at Seneca Falls, New York, in 1848 to draft a Declaration of Sentiments calling for equal rights for women to property ownership, education, and suffrage on the grounds that "all men and women are created equal." Similarly, Henry David Thoreau's discourse on civil disobedience, a cornerstone of radical pacifist thought, arose from his tax resistance to the Mexican-American War of 1846–48, which was widely seen as a war for slavery's expansion.

Alarmed that a "slave power" extended to the federal level, abolitionists worried for the soul of the republic. Enraged by the Constitution's tacit sanction of slavery, William Lloyd Garrison burned copies of it in public. In 1852 Frederick Douglass asked, "What, to the American slave, is your 4th of July? I answer: a day that reveals to him, more than all other days in the year, the gross injustice and cruelty to which he is the constant victim." Douglass declined to join John Brown's 1859 armory seizure at Harpers Ferry, West Virginia, but the failed insurrection portended the coming Civil War. Only the carnage of Blue and Gray, combined with a massive slave exodus, made possible the Thirteenth, Fourteenth, and Fifteenth Amendments, transforming the Constitution and ending slavery.

Apex of Working-Class Radicalism

Radical republicanism, utopianism, agrarianism, and producerism remained vibrant through the Gilded Age, present in one manner or another in Tennessee Claflin and Victoria Woodhull's free love-advocating *Weekly*, a mélange of currency reform proposals, the cooperative ventures of the Knights of Labor, Edward Bellamy's millenarian novel *Looking Backward, 2000–1887* (1888), the single-tax on land advocated by Henry George, and 1890s farmer populism directed at monopolistic railroads and banks. Some anarchists proposed to spark worker revolt by violent provocation, but such incidents as the Haymarket affair of 1886 and the assassination of President William McKinley in 1901 instead brought opprobrium and repression, enhancing the appeal of alternative radical approaches premised on mass action.

As industrial militancy reached its pinnacle between the 1870s and 1940s, radicals increasingly looked to working-class self-activity to achieve the socialization of production. At first this view was mainly limited to German-American immigrant circles, even though Karl Marx and Friedrich Engels published articles in English in the *New York Tribune* between 1852 and 1861. Marxist theory acquired wider credence in the late nineteenth century, as mass socialist parties flourished in Europe and economic downturns and strike waves lent plausibility to the prospect that the world's workers would overthrow a crisis-prone capitalism. By the early twentieth century, Marxism was the lingua franca of the American Left, and anarcho-syndicalism, revolutionary socialism, and communism reached their respective heights.

Anarcho-syndicalism sought a stateless society and eschewed electoral politics, but differed from individualist anarchism by emphasizing revolution at the point of production. In a preamble written by Daniel De Leon, a Marxist, the largely anarcho-syndicalist Industrial Workers of the World (IWW), or "Wobblies," founded in 1905, called for "abolition of the wage system." The IWW's 1912 "Bread and Roses" textile strike of mostly Jewish and Italian women at Lawrence, Massachusetts, enthused Greenwich Village radicals such as Max Eastman, Randolph Bourne, and John Reed writing in *The Masses,* a freewheeling magazine that supported Margaret Sanger when she distributed literature about contraception in violation of the 1873 Comstock Act.

The Socialist Party was supported by millions at the polls from its founding in 1901 until 1920. Its standard-bearer, Eugene V. Debs, received 6 percent of the vote for president and more than 1,200 Socialists were elected to office, from Oklahoma to Ohio, in 1912. New York Representative Meyer London, one of two Socialists elected to Congress, advocated in his first address to the House in 1915 "an inheritance tax that would make it impossible for unfit men by the mere accident of birth to inherit millions of dollars in wealth and power." Socialist pressure could prompt reform, as when the depiction of Chicago meatpacking in Upton Sinclair's novel *The Jungle* (1906) compelled signing of the Meat Inspection Act and Pure Food and Drug Act by President Theodore Roosevelt.

Economic determinism led many Socialists to ignore or accommodate racist lynching and segregation. It was Socialists Mary White Ovington and William English Walling, however, who helped create the National Association for the Advancement of Colored People in 1909. Black radicals responded variously to rising racism. Ida B. Wells advocated armed self-defense and exodus from the South, Marcus Garvey espoused black nationalism, and trade unionist A. Philip Randolph sought class solidarity. Even as blacks were disfranchised, the provocative tactics of woman suffragists, including radical hunger-striker Alice Paul, helped win ratification of the Nineteenth Amendment in 1920.

Socialists and Wobblies alike opposed World War I and were consequently battered by wartime repression and the "Red Scare" of 1919. Emma Goldman and other immigrant radicals were deported, Debs imprisoned. "The notion that a radical is one who hates his country," countered H. L. Mencken in 1924, "is naïve and usually idiotic. He is, more likely, one who likes his country more than the rest of us, and is thus more disturbed than the rest of us when he sees it debauched."

The 1929 stock market crash and Great Depression brought a resurgence of labor and the left. Dynamism shifted to the Communist Party, emulators of the 1917 Russian Revolution and the Soviet Union. Communist Party members led demonstrations by the unemployed, helped organize basic industry, and challenged racism, inspiring numerous Americans to join or work closely with them, including Woody Guthrie, Representative Vito Marcantonio, Elizabeth Gurley Flynn, W.E.B. Du Bois, and Paul Robeson. However, the Communist Party's authoritarian structure and zig-zagging political line, corresponding to every shift of Soviet foreign policy under Joseph Stalin, led others to criticize communism as a bureaucratic phenomenon. Small bands of dissenting radicals, from A. J. Muste's American Workers Party to Leon Trotsky's followers, argued that socialism required not merely state ownership but workers' control, which the Stalinist dictatorship had destroyed. This anti-Stalinist left, including Norman Thomas's Socialist Party and Dwight Macdonald's *Politics*, joined with radical pacifist conscientious objectors to World War II, including Dorothy Day's *Catholic Worker*, in criticizing racial segregation in the military and use of the atomic bomb. Such alternative perspectives found little traction, however. During the Popular Front of 1935–39 and World War II, liberals and Communists marched arm-in-arm against fascism, interrupted only by such inconvenient events as the Nazi-Soviet Non-Aggression Pact of 1939.

"Communism is Twentieth Century Americanism," Earl Browder declared during the Popular Front. Conservative southern Democrats and Republicans demurred, branding Communists "un-American" subversives. Red-baiting escalated in the postwar period, as the cold war began. The last gasp of the Popular Front came in former Democratic vice president Henry Wallace's 1948 Progressive Party campaign, which was hounded by charges of Communist influence. Security oaths and congressional investigations purged hundreds of Communists and other radicals from unions, government, Hollywood, and universities. Severely bruised, the American Communist Party limped along until 1956, when most of its remaining members quit in disillusionment after Nikita Khrushchev confirmed Stalin's record of mass murder, and the Soviet Union invaded Hungary, suppressing the attempt to reform communism in that country.

The New Left and After

The Montgomery bus boycott of 1955–56 signaled a rebirth of movement activity and an opening for radicalism. By 1960 a youthful New Left with dreams of "participatory democracy" was stirring in the Student Non-Violent Coordinating Committee (SNCC) and Students for a Democratic Society (SDS). The new radicals conceived of politics in moral and existential terms, typified by Mario Savio's call during Berkeley's 1964 Free Speech Movement to "put your bodies upon the gears and upon the wheels, upon the levers, upon all the apparatus."

Issues of race and war pitted the New Left against the liberal Democratic establishment. Sit-ins, Freedom Rides, and marches were met by brutal segregationist response, tarnishing the image of the United States abroad and compelling passage of the Civil Rights Act of 1964 and Voting Rights Act of 1965. The Vietnam War generated an equally powerful crisis. SDS called the first antiwar demonstration in Washington in 1965, and by decade's end, huge mobilizations were mounted, complemented by radical G.I. resistance. Radical pacifism revived, espoused by the likes of David Dellinger and Catholic priests Daniel and Philip Berrigan, although many other radicals opposed the war out of opposition to empire rather than all instances of violence. War and race intertwined as Martin Luther King Jr. challenged Chicago residential segregation, opposed the Vietnam War as a diversion from the needs of the poor at home, and was assassinated in 1968 while supporting Memphis garbage strikers, setting off riots nationwide.

By 1968 the revolutionary enthusiasm was contagious. Vietnam's Tet Offensive set off worldwide upheavals, East and West, from Prague to Paris to Mexico City. Emulating Malcolm X and third world guerrillas, Stokely Carmichael, the Black Panther Party, and other Black Power militants advocated armed struggle and cultural pride. Jerry Rubin and Abbie Hoffman, as "Yippies," fused radical politics with the counterculture's sex, drugs, and rock 'n' roll. Women liberationists objected to the 1968 Miss America pageant in Atlantic City, New Jersey, as a "degrading mindless-boob-girlie symbol," putting the spotlight on a movement that would assert reproductive rights and challenge male chauvinism in the home, workplace, and culture. Street fighting between New York City police and Stonewall Inn patrons produced the Gay Liberation Front in 1969. The cultural revolution in race, gender, and sexual norms unleashed by the 1960s radicalization would produce far-reaching and unfolding changes in American consciousness across the next several decades.

As a coherent political movement, however, the New Left did not endure. As radicals moved from protest to resistance to revolution, some decided to "Bring the War Home" by planting bombs. Confrontation could dramatize injustice, as when the American Indian Movement occupied Bureau of Indian Affairs headquarters in Washington in 1972, but one-upmanship and factional prejudice took hold as radicals misjudged the moment. One reason for New Left unreality was its distance from the American working class. C. Wright Mills and Herbert Marcuse dismissed labor for its quiescence. To many young radicals, labor unions evoked "corporate liberal" compromise or the musty Old Left, if not racist whites. By 1970 the New Left realized that students alone could not remake the world, but the belated turn to the working class too often took the form of sterile Maoist posturing, despite sounder rank-and-file projects initiated by proponents of "socialism from below."

By the mid-1970s, the New Left had disintegrated. As national politics turned rightward and labor declined, New Left themes lived on in 1980s direct-action groups like the AIDS Coalition to Unleash Power (ACT UP) and Earth First! Laments about a fragmentary "identity politics" became commonplace, although left-of-center electoral coalitions still could succeed, as when Vermont sent socialist independent Bernie Sanders to Congress in 1990 and the Senate in 2006. The Soviet bloc's demise in 1989–91 fostered a general presumption that socialism was discredited, but the 1994 Zapatista rebellion in Mexico inspired new forms of anticapitalist opposition to corporate globalization. These culminated in the 1999 Seattle protests against the World Trade Organization and the millions of votes cast in 2000 for Green Party candidate Ralph Nader, critic of the Democratic and Republican parties as a "corporate duopoly."

Radical opposition to empire revived in the years following September 11, 2001, in youthful opposition to the Iraq War. Species consciousness nearly rivaled class consciousness in radical circles, as antisystemic criticism of global warming generated reconsiderations of industrial society itself. American radicalism, though much reduced in strength from its early twentieth-century apex, continued its search to identify the fundamental causes of social injustice and irrationality and to find ways to root them out.

See also abolitionism; anarchism; communism; Greenback-Labor Party; labor parties; pacifism; populism; socialism.

FURTHER READING

Aronowitz, Stanley. *The Death and Rebirth of American Radicalism.* New York: Routledge, 1996.

Bialer, Seweryn, ed. *Radicalism in the Contemporary Age.* 3 vols. Boulder, CO: Westview, 1977.

Buhle, Mari Jo, Paul Buhle, and Harvey J. Kaye, eds. *The American Radical.* New York: Routledge, 1994.

Goldberg, Harvey, ed. *American Radicals: Some Problems and Personalities.* New York: Monthly Review Press, 1957.

Kelley, Robin D. G. *Freedom Dreams: The Black Radical Imagination.* Boston: Beacon, 2002.

Lens, Sidney. *Radicalism in America.* New York: Crowell, 1966.

Lynd, Staughton. *The Intellectual Origins of American Radicalism*. New York: Pantheon, 1968.

McCarthy, Timothy Patrick, and John McMillian, eds. *The Radical Reader*. New York: New Press, 2003.

Symes, Lillian, and Travers Clement. *Rebel America: The Story of Social Revolt in the United States*. New York: Harper and Brothers, 1934.

Young, Alfred E., ed. *Dissent: Explorations in the History of American Radicalism*. Dekalb: Northern Illinois University Press, 1968.

CHRISTOPHER PHELPS

radio and politics

Connections between radio and politics were formed at the very beginning of radio broadcasting: the first scheduled broadcast, by Westinghouse's KDKA in Pittsburgh on November 2, 1920, was of the election returns that made Warren Harding president of the United States. As radio developed during the 1920s and 1930s, it contributed significantly not only to political campaigning and advertising styles but also to the politics of industry regulation, congressional oversight, and free speech. Consequently, radio was of central importance in politics during the interwar years, but its influence declined after 1945 as first television and then the Internet replaced it as the "hot" medium of political communication. The radio age began in 1920 amid bold predictions of a new age of citizenship and political debate, but within a decade, radio had become a powerful reinforcer of the two-party system, the commercialized consumer economy, and powerful politicians and businessmen.

Radio and Regulation

When KDKA began the radio age, only 0.02 percent of American families owned a radio. Ten years later, 45 percent of the nation's 30 million households included a radio, and by 1940 80 percent of Americans lived in homes with a radio. By then, radio had assumed its place as a bright star of the interwar consumer economy, enjoying growth even during the Great Depression. This explosive growth led to rapid organization of the industry, which saw radio broadcasting become commercialized and networked between 1920 and 1928. By 1930, American listeners could tune in to more than 600 radio stations; 120 were affiliated with either the National Broadcasting Company (NBC) or the Columbia Broadcasting System (CBS); the great majority of stations were sustained by the sale of advertising. Two other radio networks, the Mutual Broadcasting System and the American Broadcasting Company, emerged in 1934 and 1940, respectively. In 1940 nearly 60 percent of the nation's 765 broadcast radio stations were affiliated with a network, and by then radio was the second largest advertising medium in the nation, with annual revenues of nearly $200 million.

Radio's rapid growth forced significant changes in public policy. The limitations of the radio spectrum meant that First Amendment freedom of the press could not apply to it. Nonregulation led inevitably to overcrowding, interference, and unreliable signals for broadcasters, advertisers, and audiences. The first attempt at radio regulation, the Radio Act of 1912, which Congress passed before broadcasting began, did not attempt to organize the infant industry. After broadcasting began, Congress legislated twice, in the Radio Act of 1927 and the Communications Act of 1934, to create an assertive regulatory regime through which broadcasters were licensed by a powerful Federal Radio Commission (FRC) in 1927 and then the Federal Communications Commission (FCC) after 1934. Of particular importance to political broadcasting was Section 17 of the Radio Act of 1927, repeated as Section 315 of the Communications Act of 1934, which required stations that offered or sold radio time to one candidate in a political contest to offer or sell time to all candidates in that contest. Stations were also prohibited from censoring political broadcasts.

The FRC and then the FCC were soon captured by the very broadcasters they were supposed to regulate. Attempts to require stations to devote fixed amounts of time to educational programming were defeated by industry lobbying, as were proposals to require broadcasters to provide free airtime to all candidates during election campaigns. Under FRC and FCC oversight, radio was dominated by commercial networks, which preferred to sell time to advertisers than to give time to political, civic, or educational groups. Although NBC and CBS were willing to provide free time to presidents, senators, and congressmen and to sell time to those parties and candidates that could afford it, network and unaffiliated broadcasters were reluctant to allow their facilities to become vehicles of political debate and engagement. Yet broadcasters remained acutely aware that their very existence depended upon FRC and FCC licensing powers and congressional goodwill.

As radio broadcasting developed into a highly capitalized industry dominated by three networks, it evolved a complex and subtle triangular web of understandings between broadcasters, politicians, and regulators that buttressed the networks' position and protected advertising and private ownership. Radio's connections to political culture became more important through its rapid application to election campaigning, political advertising, and government publicity. Most broadcasters, mindful of the need to maintain regulatory and legislative goodwill, donated and sold airtime to candidates and parties throughout radio's golden age. The growing interdependence between politicians and radio also blurred regulatory and legislative boundaries; lawmakers were the broadcasters' regulators but also their customers. Politicians soon found that they needed broadcasters' goodwill as much as radio required legislative and political protection.

Radio and Political Advertising and Campaigning

Political candidates and parties were quick to realize radio's potential to expand their electoral reach. At first, parties and candidates simply purchased radio time to broadcast speeches made to audiences in meeting halls. These "advertisements" were between 30 and 60 minutes long and showed little awareness of the possibilities of the new medium. By bringing political speeches into American homes, however, radio allowed previously excluded groups, such as women and the elderly, to hear political candidates and discussions.

NBC and CBS also provided free coverage of the Democratic and Republican national nominating conventions. In 1932 NBC devoted 46 hours to the Democratic Convention alone, costing the network more than $590,000 in lost advertising revenue—a cost that NBC described as its contribution to the nation's political education. Requests by the Socialist and Communist Parties for similar treatment were ignored. NBC and CBS also provided their facilities, subject to their commercial commitments, to incumbent federal legislators, administrators, and presidents. In 1935 NBC stations aired talks by 239 federal legislators and administrators in 560 broadcasts. The networks also attempted to apportion their time fairly to these requests, favoring the congressional majority party of the day. Minor parties, and those unrepresented in the federal legislature, were frozen out of network airtime between elections.

The two major parties spent $90,000 combined on broadcasting speeches during the 1924 presidential campaign. In 1928, however, radio campaigning became much more sophisticated—and expensive. Both major parties took giant strides in their use of radio, making 1928 the first true radio presidential campaign. In that year, NBC and CBS charged the parties $10,000 per hour for their coast-to-coast facilities, and the GOP and Democrats bought nearly $1 million of airtime. Radio costs in 1928 were the single largest component of both parties' publicity budgets. Both sides had radio bureaus, and both organized sophisticated radio campaigns with coordinated advertising directed to specific groups of voters. Each national election campaign of the 1930s rested more heavily on radio advertising than its predecessor. In 1932 CBS and NBC devoted more than 120 hours and 210 programs on their national networks to broadcasts by the two major parties, in 1936 the Republicans and Democrats spent a combined total of $1.5 million on radio advertising time, and in 1940 the two parties spent $2.25 million between them on radio.

Although Franklin D. Roosevelt's "fireside chats" are the most famous examples of radio politics before World War II, Roosevelt was not the first "radio president." That title properly belongs to Herbert Hoover, who made nearly 80 broadcasts between his two election campaigns. Hoover talked more often on radio during his four years in the White House than FDR did in his first term. Hoover made radio history in 1928, when he became the first presidential candidate to speak on radio without the presence of a live audience. But, once elected, he reverted to the older format of broadcasting live speeches instead of delivering addresses purely to a radio audience. Hoover tended to equate quantity of broadcasting with quality and paid little attention to his speaking technique.

Roosevelt was a much more effective radio political speaker and campaigner. Unlike Hoover, FDR polished his radio style and worked within network radio's scheduling and commercial imperatives. He was also careful not to overexpose himself on the airwaves, delivering only 16 fireside chats during his first two years as president and 31 during his 12-year tenure. Radio audience measurement techniques, developed during the 1930s, revealed that FDR's radio audience ranged from 10 percent of radio homes for a speech broadcast in June 1936 to 79 percent for his fireside chat soon after Pearl Harbor. Roosevelt saw radio as a way to bypass what he believed was the Republican bias of the major newspapers. Radio also offered him a means of public communication that did not reveal his physical disability.

Inspired by Roosevelt's example, New Dealers used radio to publicize their activities throughout the 1930s. Publicity offices within federal departments grew rapidly after 1932, and their use of radio to inform Americans of their policies increased dramatically. During the first four months of 1937, for example, federal agencies broadcast 88 radio programs on network radio, including question-and-answer sessions, dramatizations, and programs to explain the activities of a vastly expanded federal government. New Deal critics also noted that radio had become a powerful tool through which the Democratic administration could reassure listeners—and voters—of its unrelenting efforts on their behalf.

Politicians away from Washington, D.C., also took advantage of the new possibilities presented by radio to project themselves beyond their local strongholds. Father Charles E. Coughlin used radio sermons in 1926 to swell his diminishing congregation in a Detroit suburb. Through use of network radio, and his increasingly strident political commentary, Coughlin became a national radio star by 1930. Under pressure from the Hoover administration, CBS cut Coughlin from its network in 1931, but he continued to broadcast his increasingly anti-Semitic commentaries on unaffiliated stations throughout the 1930s. In 1934 Coughlin received more mail than any other American, including the president, and in 1936 his listeners sent in more than $320,000 in donations. In his prime during the early 1930s, the Radio Priest spoke to a weekly audience of 10 million. In Louisiana, Governor and later U.S. Senator Huey P. Long used radio to become a national political figure. Long's senatorial status after 1930 allowed him access to national radio networks, which he used to create a national constituency and to advocate his own plans to combat the Depression. From funds confiscated from millionaires, Long promised every American family a car, a washing machine—and a radio. "Between the team of Huey Long and the priest we have the whole bag of crazy and crafty tricks," New Deal leader General Hugh Johnson warned in 1935, ". . . with the radio and the newsreel to make them effective."

Radio played a central role in the most celebrated state election campaign of the 1930s. In 1934 radical novelist Upton Sinclair ran for governor of California on the End Poverty in California (EPIC) platform, which promised the unemployed work in idle factories and ownership of what they produced. Sinclair's opponents undertook an integrated and well-funded campaign against him, using newsreels, billboards, newspapers, and radio. The radio campaign, conducted by the Lord and Thomas advertising agency, produced serials and advertisements warning Californians of an army of hoboes allegedly heading for their state and of the catastrophic consequences of Sinclair's ideas for California's future prosperity. In its heavy use of visual and radio advertising, the successful anti-EPIC campaign presaged modern electioneering techniques and was an early example of the close integration of radio and other publicity methods that increasingly characterized political campaigns.

Enthusiasts of radio politics tended to equate information with education and education with engagement. "Of all the miracles that this age has witnessed," a speaker at one World Radio Convention declared, "radio is the most marvellous. It has taken sound, which moved with leaden feet, and given it to the wings of morning. We are now like Gods. We may speak to all mankind." Radio could blanket the nation with reasoned debate on political issues and contests, and millions of Americans would find political issues and discussion more accessible and attractive. During the 1920s, commentators were overwhelmingly optimistic about these changes. But in the 1930s, as radio lost its novelty and as Adolf Hitler, Father Coughlin, and Huey Long demonstrated its power to assist demagoguery as much as democracy, more sober assessments of radio politics emerged.

Assumptions about the power of radio to influence public opinion, so prevalent during the first decade of radio broadcasting, were questioned by the work of social scientists during the 1930s and 1940s. Researchers led by Paul Lazarsfeld at Columbia University studied groups of voters to gauge the effect of radio advertising during elections. Their conclusions were sobering for those who believed in a "radio revolution" in politics, but comforting to those who feared that voters might be unduly influenced by the new medium. Radio, Lazarsfeld concluded, was more effective in reinforcing voter choices than in changing them. It preached best to the converted but also had some influence in mobilizing nonvoters. Radio enabled politicians to communicate to listeners in homes rather than to partisans in halls, but it did not produce more gullible voters or more pliable citizens.

Radio's Decline

World War II marked the end of radio's golden age, and of its greatest influence on U.S. political institutions and actors. Wartime censorship, more active regulation, and the arrival of broadcast television robbed radio of its novelty as a glamorous new medium that exercised profound influence over American entertainment and politics. Television, which inherited the statutory and regulatory framework established for radio, replaced radio as the advertising and publicity medium of choice for state and federal governments, political parties, and candidates. In order to survive in the post-television age, radio broadcasters focused on narrower audience segments, while national television networks emphasized mass commercialized entertainment over older conceptions of civic education that had been so influential on the early development of radio.

During its golden age, radio was considered the most influential of all mass media, and its pervasiveness made it far more important to political institutions and political process than either the telegraph or the telephone. Radio exercised powerful influence on the ways in which candidates, officeholders, parties, and governments addressed their electorates. The high cost of network radio time, and its rigorous scheduling and technical requirements, ushered in a more professional approach to campaign organization and strategy. By 1940 both major parties, and most broadcasters, had developed expertise in radio politics that proved to be readily transferable to television after World War II.

See also Internet and politics; political advertising; press and politics; television and politics.

FURTHER READING

Barnouw, Erik. *A History of American Broadcasting in the United States*. 3 vols. New York: Oxford University Press, 1966–1968.

Brinkley, Alan. *Voices of Protest: Huey Long, Father Coughlin, and the Great Depression*. New York: Vintage Books, 1983.

Chester, Edward W. *Radio, Television, and American Politics*. New York: Sheed and Ward, 1969.

Craig, Douglas B. *Fireside Politics: Radio and Political Culture in the United States, 1920–1940*. Baltimore, MD: Johns Hopkins University Press, 2000.

Fones-Wolf, Elizabeth. *Waves of Opposition: Labor and the Struggle for Democratic Radio*. Urbana: University of Illinois Press, 2006.

Loviglio, Jason. *Radio's Intimate Public: Network Broadcasting and Mass-Mediated Democracy*. Minneapolis: University of Minnesota Press, 2005.

McChesney, Robert W. *Telecommunications, Mass Media and Democracy: The Battle for the Control of U.S. Broadcasting, 1928–1935*. New York: Oxford University Press, 1993.

Smulyan, Susan. *Selling Radio: The Commercialization of American Broadcasting, 1920–1934*. Washington, DC: Smithsonian Institution Press, 1994.

Starr, Paul. *The Creation of the Media: Political Origins of Modern Communications*. New York: Basic Books, 2004.

DOUGLAS CRAIG

Reconstruction Era, 1865–77

Reconstruction, once defined as the period immediately following the Civil War, is now generally understood as an interlocking web of political, social, and economic transformations that followed the wartime destruction of slavery and lasted until the withdrawal of federal military support for the last Republican state governments in the former Confederacy in 1877. Among the most important political developments were the virtual revolution in southern life, the consolidation of national citizenship, and the forces that arose to limit those projects.

From Johnson's Policies to Radical Reconstruction

Wartime Reconstruction of the South began as officials and slaves in the Union-occupied slave states wrestled with the messy end of slavery. Emancipation had emerged from the crucible of war, and many Americans (President Lincoln included) believed that ex-slaves, on the whole, did not merit political citizenship. But the Emancipation Proclamation, the mass enlistment of black troops, and the success of free-labor experiments—such as the collective farm at Davis Bend, Mississippi, and the coastal lands General William T. Sherman allocated under Special Field Order No. 15—gave freed people's claims to citizenship greater weight.

Freed people began to make these claims during the war and its immediate aftermath. They held political meetings in cities and contraband camps across the occupied South. They challenged employers in hearings before agents of the newly established federal Bureau of Refugees, Freedmen, and Abandoned Lands (the Freedmen's Bureau). Whether through local initiatives or, later, under the aegis of the Union Leagues, previously disparate social groups began to come together: ex-slaves' formerly clandestine political culture and the restricted organizational life of antebellum free black people met with the political and economic ambitions of northern missionaries, entrepreneurs, and activists (people known by their contemporary enemies and later detractors as "carpetbaggers"), as well as with the hopes and fears of some southern whites (similarly dubbed "scalawags"). Meanwhile, several states under Union occupation held wartime elections and established new governments; of these, only Tennessee's would achieve lasting recognition.

With the ratification of the Thirteenth Amendment in December 1865, slavery came to a final, formal end even in the Union slave states of Kentucky and Delaware. To Lincoln's successor, Andrew Johnson, this change seemed sufficient. He appointed provisional governors, and with his approval, southern electorates forged new governments; for a time, it seemed the former slave states would be reconstructed on the basis of white male citizenship. In the winter of 1865–66, these southern state governments began to pass laws, known as "black codes," that severely limited freed people's freedom of mobility and were designed to force them into low-wage agricultural labor. Johnson pardoned leading former Confederates, and he vetoed both the Civil Rights Act—passed by Congress in 1866 to overturn the black codes—and a bill reauthorizing the Freedmen's Bureau. In a step emblematic of this version of Reconstruction, the newly reformed legislature of Georgia elected former Confederate vice president Alexander Stephens to the U.S. Senate.

Congressional Republicans, who controlled more than two-thirds of each house, pushed back: they refused to seat congressional delegates from most ex-Confederate states, they passed the Civil Rights and Freedmen's Bureau Bills over Johnson's veto, and in the spring of 1867 they rejected Johnson's program of Reconstruction in toto, establishing a new framework for readmission. The Reconstruction Acts of 1867 divided ten of the eleven Confederate states, all but Tennessee, into five military districts and set guidelines for their readmission that effectively enfranchised black men. Federal officials registered black and white men over 21 for the election of delegates to new constitutional conventions; those conventions wrote constitutions that included the principle of manhood suffrage. The new southern electorates created under the Reconstruction Acts helped elect Johnson's successor, former Union commanding general Ulysses S. Grant, in 1868. President Johnson's resistance to the acts—particularly his removal of federal officials supportive of Congress's purposes—led Congress to pass the Tenure of Office Act and to impeach Johnson for its violation, though he was not convicted and removed from office. In an effort to safeguard the principles of the Civil Rights Act, Republican legislators also passed a somewhat altered version of that law as a new constitutional amendment and made the ratification of that amendment a precondition for the readmission of the states now under military rule.

Radical Reconstruction transformed the U.S. Constitution. The Fourteenth Amendment (ratified in 1868) established that national citizenship belonged to all persons born within the United States, without regard to race or prior status; that this citizenship conveyed certain rights, including the "equal protection of the laws" and certain unspecified "privileges and immunities"; that states could not interpose their own limitations or qualifications; and that states would lose representation in Congress to the extent that they denied voting rights to their adult male population. In other words, it made national citizenship paramount—at least in theory. The Fifteenth Amendment (passed in 1869, ratified in 1870) extended the principle of race-neutral suffrage by prohibiting—rather than simply penalizing—disfranchisement on the basis of race, color, or previous condition of servitude. Together with various federal enforcement acts, the Fifteenth Amendment sought to ensure that the most essential expression of political citizenship—the right to vote—would not be abridged on account of race.

The Transformation of Southern Politics

The southern Republican coalition that took shape in 1867 and 1868 brought new voices into southern political life. Freed people's collective mobilization for new constitutional conventions brought hundreds of thousands of men to vote for the first time in 1867; it also mobilized black women, who—though denied the franchise—attended meetings, voiced political opinions, and sometimes insisted that men take women's wishes into account when voting. The freed people's political goals included basic liberal freedoms: their desire to reconstitute their families, move freely, seek the protection of the law, secure an education, and be secure in their property. But the southern Republican coalition brought together a variety of competing and divergent interests. White Southerners who had owned few or no slaves did not necessarily support universal public education, which would inevitably be funded by taxes on land; they often balked at the idea that people just freed from slavery should sit on juries, hold local offices, or determine the outcome of elections. Northern emigrants and antebellum free people of color, whose experiences and interests often were quite different than those of ex-slaves, played disproportionately large roles in the party leadership.

Most seriously, freed people and their northern Republican allies had somewhat different visions for the postbellum economy. Republicans had begun by seeking to guarantee the end of slavery and the creation of loyal governments committed to free labor in the ex-Confederate states; with these steps they became participants in a political revolution, sometimes dubbed Radical Reconstruction, that would transform nearly 4 million slaves into citizens with political, economic, and civil rights. Congressional "radicalism" mainly took the form of economic liberalism: since the early days of the federal wartime occupation, most federal policies and philanthropic activities had sought to transform the freed people into agricultural wage laborers. In the capital-poor world of the postwar South, this effectively meant labor on annual contracts, with supplies advanced but most wages deferred until after the harvest. But freed people's political, social, and economic visions were not limited to the orthodoxies of contractual wage labor. They sought ownership of land, not perpetual employment under contracts. They wanted the freedom to deploy labor flexibly within households and, when possible, limited women's participation in the market for agricultural labor. These tensions shaped Republican policies and offered fracture points for those who saw advantages in splitting the coalition. Democrats, who attracted few black voters, early on sought to identify the Republican Party as the representative only of black and northern interests. Their 1868 platform accused Republicans of seeking to "secure negro supremacy."

In states where the antebellum slave population had constituted a majority—South Carolina, Louisiana, and Mississippi—freed people and antebellum free people of color demanded and finally obtained meaningful roles in state and local government. The states' new constitutions removed property restrictions and apportionment by wealth, created free common schools for all children, and enacted property legislation for married women. The systematic redistribution of ex-slaveholders' land had failed to win wide support in Congress, but South Carolina created a land commission to purchase and sell small plots, boosting black landholding there well above the low regional average.

Republican black men—freeborn and freed Southerners, as well as Northerners—served southern constituencies at every level, from justice of the peace to U.S. senator. In Mississippi, Hiram Revels, a minister, was elected to fill the Senate seat vacated by Jefferson Davis in 1861, 1 of 16 black men who would ultimately serve in Congress during the era. With the exception of South Carolina's lower house, the new legislatures had white majorities. Republican leaders divided over economic policies and along axes of race, region, antebellum status, and wealth. Numerous fractures developed, with some Republicans making coalitions with opposition factions, often called Conservatives. In these states, Republican coalitions that included significant numbers of whites governed until the mid-1870s, against considerable opposition in the forms of vigilante violence and of real or feigned outrage at the corruption that marked so much of the period's politics across lines of region and party.

In states where whites made up larger percentages of the population, ex-slaves played smaller roles in the Republican Party then did northern- and southern-born whites. Governments in these states passed civil rights bills and supported black male suffrage and public schools, sometimes (as in Florida) building them from the ground up; they also invested heavily (and often corruptly) in railroads. In many states Democrats or Conservatives gained legislative majorities early, and in a few states Reconstruction as a state policy virtually ended before it began. In 1868 white conservatives in Georgia moved rapidly to expel black representatives from the state legislature. Though they reversed course when their action caused Congress to refuse to seat the state's delegation, Democrats took control of the state after the 1870 elections. By then they also controlled North Carolina's legislature and one house of Alabama's. Virginia's Republicans fractured from the start, allowing Conservatives to triumph in 1869 and bring the Commonwealth back into the Union without ever having a Republican government.

But state-level Reconstruction was not the beginning and end of the story. Power at the local level—especially in black-majority constituencies in white-majority states—could also matter enormously. For freed people, local voting rights and jury service meant being able to withstand the worst abuses of their opponents. Where they continued to exercise these rights, black men or those sympathetic to their interests might oversee contractual or criminal disputes; people who had been defrauded, assaulted, or raped could hope for equal justice. White Democrats sometimes took aim at these areas, for example, by gerrymandering black voters into a small number of districts or by stripping black-majority cities of their right to self-government.

Paramilitary Politics and the End of Southern Reconstruction

Paramilitary violence played a significant role in Reconstruction politics, mainly to the advantage of Republicans' foes. The Ku Klux Klan, formed in Tennessee in the winter of 1865–66, was the most famous and widespread organization to take up arms against the Republican Party and freed people's political activity. Similar paramilitary forces of former Confederates and their younger male relations organized across the region, terrorizing Republican voters, organizers, and officeholders, seeking to paralyze black constituencies and to discourage whites from allying with blacks. The Klan had its own oath-bound hierarchy, but it functioned fundamentally in the interest of the reconstituted state Democratic parties, holding down Republican turnout through intimidation and murder, seizing effective control of local courts and law enforcement, and making Democratic victories possible even in areas with substantial black populations.

Serious Klan violence during the 1868 election campaign helped provide the impetus for the Fifteenth Amendment; it also led to a series of federal laws designed to protect voting rights. Efforts to counter the Klan by legal means were generally ineffective, but more forceful responses carried their own risks. North Carolina governor William Holden organized a militia to put down Klan activity in the election of 1870 and was impeached for his pains, effectively ending Reconstruction in the state. Republican government in Arkansas and Texas fought the Klan effectively for a time with forces of black and white men. Federal anti-Klan activity peaked in 1871 with the reoccupation of part of South Carolina and the trials of hundreds of Klansmen under new anti-Klan laws. White supremacist terror diminished in the short run but resumed in earnest after the 1872 election.

In the states still under Republican government after 1872, white supremacist paramilitaries sought to polarize state politics and drive a wedge between black Republicans and their white allies by provoking racialized military conflict with state militias, which by this point consisted mainly of all-black units. In these contests, black militiamen were generally overmatched, and governors often chose to withdraw their forces, fearing a massacre. Well-publicized battles between black militiamen and white paramilitaries between 1873 and 1876 (e.g., in Hamburg and Ellenton, South Carolina, and Colfax and New Orleans, Louisiana) helped fracture politics along racial lines and make democratic governance virtually impossible. Federal intervention on behalf of Republican elected officials and militiamen protected some individuals but did not deter paramilitary violence; such intervention, especially in removing Democratic contestants from the Louisiana legislature in 1874, also supported Democratic charges that Reconstruction was little more than federal "bayonet rule."

The recapture of state governments by Democrats changed the terms of political conflict: black agricultural and domestic laborers, now politically all but powerless, could no longer demand laws that protected their interests. Instead, various groups of whites battled over lien, railroad, and homestead exemption laws based on differences of economic or sectional interest; ex-slaves could no longer participate actively in these contests. Supporters of these counterrevolutions lauded the "redemption" of their states from "radical and negro misrule." The destruction of Reconstruction's local legacies proceeded unevenly, leaving some islands of comparative black freedom and autonomy even in states now governed by white Democrats. Despite decades of Democratic gerrymandering, intermittent paramilitary activity, discriminatory registration laws, and constitutional changes, some of these areas continued to elect black officeholders and convention delegates until the end of the nineteenth century. White Republicanism survived in some upland areas and remained important in counties and localities but played a major part in state politics only when dissident whites (sometimes allying themselves with blacks) mounted third-party insurgencies in the 1880s and 1890s.

Reconstruction beyond the South

After 1870 few Northerners made the defense of black citizenship rights a priority. Northern Republicans rhetorically celebrated the victory over slavery and the enfranchisement of black men, and a handful of white-majority northern constituencies elected black men to office. Northern white supremacy took various forms, from white laborers' fears of an influx of southern freed people to the scientific racism promoted by leading scholars. Most white Northerners had persistently rejected calls for abolition before the war, and even after 1865, white popular majorities in state after northern state rejected referenda calling for black male suffrage, though there were only about 250,000 nonwhite citizens in the non-slaveholding states in 1860.

Many Republicans believed that, rather than making expensive and expansive federal commitments in the South, the country needed to subsidize the conquest and settlement of the West. Secession made possible a flood of Republican legislation in 1862, including legislation to fund transcontinental railroads and homesteads on the federal domain. Between 1867 and 1871, as railroad building and homesteading continued, the U.S. government signed a series of treaties establishing large Indian territories in the trans-Mississippi West. But railroad workers, settlers, and miners continued to encroach on the remaining Indian lands, and conflict between Indians and the U.S. military escalated. By the mid-1870s U.S. forces defeated most Plains tribes, who were forced to accept treaties granting them smaller reservations. The Fourteenth Amendment's exclusion of "Indians not taxed" from its protections left them without legal recourse.

The wartime development of a new national banking system facilitated the growth of ever-larger enterprises, but, in the 1870s, Republicans abandoned the flexible currency of the war years in favor of the demonetization of silver and a commitment to return to the gold standard by decade's end. The postwar years witnessed a rush of speculative investment, especially in railroads, virtually unimpeded by federal regulation or oversight, and corruption became widespread at every level of government and in every region. This, together with opposition to Grant's efforts to annex Santo Domingo, helped precipitate an unsuccessful Liberal Republican Party challenge to Grant's reelection in 1872. Corruption—notably the Crédit Mobilier scandal, which implicated many high officials in railroad construction fraud—also led to business failures, a financial panic, and a profound economic depression that began in 1873. During the depression years Republican hard-money policies inspired the rise of alternative economic visions and the Labor Reform Party and the Greenback Party. As economic struggles weakened Republican dominance, Democrats gained control of the U.S. House of Representatives in 1874, further weakening the ability of Republican radicals to promote southern Reconstruction.

The Fall and Rise of Reconstruction

The Supreme Court played an important role in undoing Reconstruction's political revolution. In the *Slaughter-House Cases* (1873), the Court upheld a state-chartered butchering monopoly in New Orleans against the claims of other butchers, ruling 5 to 4 that the rights of national citizenship, as defined by the amended federal constitution, extended only to a few specific protections, including the right to peaceable assembly, protection on the high seas and abroad, and access to navigable waterways. Similarly narrow rulings in *U.S. v. Reese* (1875) and *U.S. v. Cruikshank* (1875), cases emerging from violence against southern Republicans, held that the right to vote was a state not a federal matter and that the Fourteenth Amendment's guarantee of equal protection of the laws granted protection only against state governments' violations; against other individual and collective violations of those principles, the Court held, the federal government was powerless. The last legislative act of congressional Reconstruction—the Civil Rights Act of 1875—sought to reenlarge the now minimal inventory of citizenship rights by prohibiting discrimination on the basis of race on juries and in railroads, theaters, hotels, and (in its early versions) schools. The final project of Charles Sumner, longtime antislavery senator from Massachusetts, the act passed only after his death and in a truncated form. The Supreme Court in 1883 struck down this law as well.

Only a handful of states enacted full or partial suffrage for women during Reconstruction; political citizenship remained closely tied to military service and male household authority. Advocates of women's voting rights had hoped their movement would succeed alongside the movement to enfranchise black men, but they were dismayed by the inclusion of the word "male" in the Fourteenth Amendment and were dealt a grievous blow by the omission of "sex" from the excluded categories of discrimination in the Fifteenth Amendment. During the election of 1872, many women, including Susan B. Anthony, Sojourner Truth, and black Republicans in the South, challenged their exclusion at the polls by casting or seeking to cast ballots; Anthony was among those arrested for those actions. In one resulting case, *Minor v. Happersett* (1874), the Supreme Court ruled that though women were indeed citizens, voting was a state matter and not among the "privileges and immunities" of national citizens.

Reconstruction as a federal project ended following the contested national election of 1876. Democratic factions in South Carolina and Louisiana, determined to seize power, provoked violent conflicts with black officeholders and state militias that essentially militarized state politics; these states' elections were marred by extensive violence and fraud. Nationally, Democratic presidential candidate Samuel Tilden won a popular majority and seemed poised to defeat Republican Rutherford B. Hayes in the Electoral College, but Republicans claimed victory in South Carolina, Louisiana, and Florida, which together would give them a narrow electoral majority. With the election results in these states subject to bitter dispute, a deadlock ensued. Throughout the winter and early spring, Washington powerbrokers sought to hammer out a compromise and select a president, while rival governments claimed legitimacy in Columbia and New Orleans. A convoluted agreement finally developed, under which the Republicans gained the presidency and Democrats won the remaining southern state governments, a bargain lubricated with levee and railroad subsidies as well as pledges not to prosecute violators of election laws. In April 1877, after Hayes's inauguration, the federal government withdrew its forces, Republican governments crumbled, and Reconstruction as a federal policy came to an end.

Reconstruction's political legacies took many forms. In some parts of the South, black and white Republicans continued to exert political power through and even beyond the end of the century, sometimes making alliances with Populists and other third-party challengers to Democratic rule. Meanwhile, fables of Reconstruction as a period of "radical and negro misrule" became an article of faith among southern Democrats and many other white Americans, ultimately mutating into a tale of black men's sexual designs on white women (as depicted in D. W. Griffith's 1915 film *The Birth of a Nation*). During and especially after World War II, however, black Southerners and northern allies vigorously challenged their political and civil disabilities, and the Supreme Court slowly reversed its earlier course and began to apply the Reconstruction amendments in ways that supported African American political and civil rights. This period is therefore sometimes called the Second Reconstruction.

See also Civil War and Reconstruction; Confederacy; race and politics, 1860–1933; slavery; South since 1877; voting.

FURTHER READING

Bensel, Richard F. *Yankee Leviathan: The Origins of Central State Authority in America, 1859–1877*. New York: Cambridge University Press, 1991.

Brown, Elsa Barkley. "Negotiating and Transforming the Public Sphere: African-American Political Life in the Transition from Slavery to Freedom." *Public Culture* 7 (Fall 1994), 107–46.

DuBois, W.E.B. *Black Reconstruction in America, 1860–1880*. 1935. Reprint ed. New York: Free Press, 1998.

Foner, Eric. *Reconstruction: America's Unfinished Revolution, 1863–1877*. New York: Harper and Row, 1988.

Hahn, Steven. *A Nation under Our Feet: Black Political Struggles in the Rural South from Slavery to the Great Migration*. Cambridge, MA: Harvard University Press, 2003.

STEPHEN KANTROWITZ

regulation

Enduring and valued traditions of American regulation predate the constitutional republic launched in 1789. They include the governance of markets and firms and their advertising and manufacturing practices; of individuals, their expression, their sexuality, and other features of their daily behavior; of families, their homes and property, and their consumption patterns; of land, air, and water and their use and conservation. These patterns are not fully consensual but have been contested thoroughly, not mainly over whether there should be more or less regulation, but over which form regulation should take and who should do the regulating. All this contestation aside, regulation is as deeply rooted within the fabric of American government as liberty itself. Indeed, Americans have long viewed regulation the way that Alexander Hamilton did in the Federalist Papers and his early financial writings—as protective of liberty. It is only recently in U.S. political history that regulation has been interpreted as an intrusion into a separate, private sphere.

"Regulation" in twenty-first-century politics often connotes the rule of a marketplace, the rule of the state over purely economic activity. Yet for much of American history, and in ways that continue into the present, this reading narrows what was a much broader phenomenon. The distinction between "economic regulation," "social regulation," and "moral regulation" was one that eighteenth- and nineteenth-century Americans would have been hard pressed to identify. Like the hues in a child's watercolor painting, the moral, the social, the financial, the spiritual, the private, the public, and the communal realms bled into one another.

Early American Regulation

The marketplaces of eighteenth- and nineteenth-century America were literally made by state regulation and government rules. The price system, standards and minimal expectations of quality and security, and the structure of exchange were created and fashioned by government action. It was government laws, not exogenous market conventions, that required prices to be visibly published for perusal by the citizen (this requirement remains, invisibly but significantly, in state and local laws governing numerous transactions today). Governments elaborated standards of construction for business, of packaging for products, of licenses for entry into health and medicine, of hair cutting, of machine repair, and of numerous other occupations. Market clerks and government auctioneers—themselves employed by state and local authorities—presided over market activity. In creating and sustaining marketplaces, these public institutions served multiple purposes; they were "common carriers" of the varied aims of the public. Market-constituting regulation stemmed from the common-law philosophy of a "well-regulated" society, incorporating values of fairness, of consumer protection, of the transparency of the marketplace. These concerns echoed centuries of accumulated tradition and philosophy and reflected longstanding republican traditions of popular sovereignty, particularly in their focus on "the people's welfare" as the "highest law" of the land (*Salus populi extrema lex*).

Strong restrictions on property and its uses were a central feature of early American regulation. Fire safety regulations constrained the store of gunpowder, the piling of wood, and the construction of new homes. Until the 1870s, these regulations were virtually immune to judicial challenge, and even then they persisted through many legal disputes well into the twentieth century. In their public safety and public health regulations, cities and counties prohibited standing water, compelled the removal of dead animals, and enjoined citizens from burning all manner of objects on their private property.

Another stable theme of early American regulation lay in the fusion of moral regulation and economic regulation. Decades before and after the temperance movements of the 1800s, state and local governments achieved a vast regulation of alcohol: its production, sale, distribution, and consumption. These laws governed public morality even as they deeply shaped the congeries of markets that composed the alcoholic beverage industry.

The moral basis of economic regulation also emerged in the symbolic logic of "adulteration." The idea of adulterated commodities held that a product's misrepresentation in the marketplace was a matter not simply of economic fraud but of moral and spiritual corruption. Adulteration linked nineteenth-century product regulation to the governance of alcohol, of gambling and lotteries, and of pornography and sexuality. Notions of adulteration as a form of corruption (and not simply a failure of market information) were central to state pure food laws and, later, laws regulating the manufacture and dispensation of medicines. Concerns about adulteration also drove and shaped the evolution of occupational licensing; not only products but also services and labor could be immorally represented. Under these laws, local and state governments hired more inspectors and built administrative bodies for regulating everything from steamboats to meatpacking facilities to proprietary medicine firms.

The main constraint on American regulation lay in federalism. Capacities for regulation developed largely in states and localities and much less in the national government. This disjuncture flowed partially from the commerce clause of Article I, Section IV of the U.S. Constitution; federal regulation was often justified on the basis that the national state could uniquely govern patterns of commerce among the states. The primary exceptions to national regulatory weakness rested in areas where the American state had developed administrative capacity. In the national postal system, Americans were already accustomed to the regulation of markets whose products coursed by the million through that system. When Victorian reformers led by postal official Anthony Comstock turned their attention to the regulation of vice and morals, they achieved the Comstock Law of 1872 and the Anti-Lottery Acts of 1890 and 1895. These statutes and their enforcement projected the power of national government into the everyday sexuality of millions of women and men, and the latter brought an end to the most profitable gambling concern of the nineteenth century: the Louisiana Lottery Company. They also changed the structure of the regulatory state; newly emboldened postal inspectors launched a massive postal fraud campaign, which issued over 20,000 fraud orders from 1910 to 1924. Postal regulators averaged 3,500 arrests and 2,000 convictions annually by the 1920s, with targets ranging from Texas oil companies to patent medicine outfits.

Growth of Federal Regulation

With the Meat Inspection Act of 1885, the U.S. Department of Agriculture began to acquire vast authority over the nation's livestock farms, stockyards, slaughterhouses, and meat-processing plants; the agency hired thousands of inspectors, creating the largest regulatory apparatus outside of the postal system.

Robust patterns of economic activity had always crossed state boundaries, but the size and rapidity of interstate commerce grew substantially in the nineteenth century, aided by federal policy itself—the postal system, land grants to railroads, the forcible opening of cheap land by the U.S. Army. The coming of a new industrial age (and with it, a growing concentration of capital and political power in fewer and fewer firms) meant that market developments outran the capacity of states and localities to monitor and govern them. The emblematic case came in railroads. Midwestern and western state legislatures passed a number of strong statutes regulating railroad pricing and safety in the 1870s and 1880s. The federal government followed in 1887 by creating a hybrid (and characteristically American) form of regulatory institution: the independent regulatory commission. The Interstate Commerce Commission (ICC) was governed not by a single individual but by a min-legislature, a five-person commission with voting and staggered terms. The ICC's powers grew slowly, often in contest with the federal courts, which were not eager to relinquish their regulatory powers to "expert commissions." Yet with a series of statutes culminating in the National Transportation Act of 1920, the ICC assumed plenary authority (involving issues of pricing, safety, planning, and cost structure) over rail and truck transport in the United States.

The independent commission found expression in other modes of regulation as well, most notably in the Federal Trade Commission Act of 1914. The FTC's primary architect was Louis Brandeis, often called the "patron saint" of the American regulatory tradition. Along with the Department of Justice, the FTC was responsible for regulating large corporations. In the republican political tradition and in the "fair trade" and pro-competition vision of Brandeis, antitrust and corporate regulation served explicitly political purposes: to combat the concentration of economic and hence political and social power within large, unaccountable, and ungovernable organizations. As the American antitrust regime entered the New Deal, policy became less politically focused and more economically driven, captivated by the concept of "consumer surplus" and its maximization.

Other federal regulations of the Progressive and New Deal Eras also arrived in commission form. These include the Federal Power Commission (1920), today the Federal Energy Regulatory Commission (FERC); the Federal Radio Commission (1927), renamed the Federal Communications Commission (FCC) in 1934; the Securities and Exchange Commission (SEC) (1934); the National Labor Relations Board (NLRB) (1935); the Atomic Energy Commission (AEC) (1946), now the Nuclear Regulatory Commission (NRC) (1975); and the now-defunct Civil Aeronautics Board (1938).

In these and other realms, federal and state regulators cooperated as often as they battled for turf. Comstock's anti-vice crusades depended heavily on the willing support and subsidy given by state and local law enforcement officials, and the vice-suppression societies of major American cities. State regulators formed associations among themselves for the exchange of information, for professional fraternity, and for the making of model statutes. Two of the most notable of these adventures in "cooperative federalism" were the National Association of Railroad and Utility Commissioners (NARUC) and the National Association of Food and Drug Officials. These bodies sponsored model laws that were pivotal in shaping twentieth-century regulation and that served as templates for legislative activity at the federal level.

The Consumer Revolution in Regulation

The institution-building impulse of the Progressive and New Deal Eras marked a significant expansion of the regulatory state at the national level. Yet slowly, and profoundly, it continued a transformation of ideals in American regulation. Increasingly, in the ideology, law, and administration of American governance, the object of policy was less the people's welfare than consumer welfare. Regulation was meant less to protect the American as citizen and more to protect the American as consumer. This language had its roots in nineteenth-century jurisprudence and political economy, and it slowly engendered a policy world characterized by rights-based claims, individually focused analysis, and welfare-maximizing goals.

The Progressive-New Deal legacy is colossal. The federal government experimented with industrial licensure in the National Recovery Act. It counseled an expansion of trade practices and advertising by the Federal Trade Commission. It continued and bolstered Progressive Era programs of conservation in forestry, natural resources, and land management. The Agricultural Adjustment Acts of 1933 and 1938 created extensive patterns of regulation over agriculture, many of which persist to this day. The Glass-Steagall legislation separated commercial banking from investment banking and created the Federal Deposit Insurance Corporation (FDIC). For every regulation observed, countless other, more radical and more conservative ideas were floated.

Twentieth-century regulation was characterized by institutions and ideals that flowed from multiple traditions of philosophy, ideology, law, and policy administration. Republican regulation of the "well-ordered society" was displaced by "liberal" regulation (what political philosopher Michael Sandel has called "the procedural republic") as analysis and justification purely in terms of costs and benefits have taken over. This is one of the crucial shifts in regulation in America in the twentieth century; its primary concern with Americans as consumers and not citizens. Independent regulatory commissions were created alongside regulatory bodies in large executive departments. Regulators combined statistical and economic tools with older patterns of legal analysis and enforcement.

Yet the republican face of early American regulation has not died out. Moral claims about regulation still echo in twenty-first-century politics, not least because American political elites and regulators are still responsive to them. The regulation of telecommunications has been concerned with concentration of ownership, minority representation, and the advancement and standardization of technology, but it has persistently returned to issues of indecency in broadcast radio and television. Antitrust and trade regulation have been motivated not merely by issues of efficiency but also of fairness.

Another forceful metaphor of twentieth- and twenty-first-century American regulation—one that harkens back to the symbolic logic of adulteration in the late 1880s and early 1900s—is protection. Even the mantra of "consumer protection" legislation—from labor and health rules, the governance of consumer products, environmental policy—implied that there were values other than rights and efficiency that were being served by the American regulatory regime. Indeed, the protection metaphor was transformed and recycled in the 1950s, 1960s, and 1970s, precisely at the time that American citizenship became defined ever more upon the principles of consumption and leisure. Cold war America saw new initiatives in environmental protection, most notably the Clean Air Act of 1970 and the establishment of the Environmental Protection Agency (EPA) that same year. The Occupational Safety and Health Act of 1970 created the federal Occupational Safety and Health Administration (OSHA), which regulates workplace safety in a complex web of overlapping relationships and jurisdictions with state labor safety agencies. The Consumer Products Safety Commission was created in 1972, empowered with the authority to recall products.

The 1960s and 1970s also witnessed growing patterns of regulation by the rule making of federal agencies, even though the Administrative Procedures Act of 1946 was supposed to have constrained such practices. Scholars began to size up American regulation by tallying the number of pages published in each year's *Federal Register*. Where formal rule making through administrative procedures has become cumbersome for agencies, they have shifted to issuing guidance documents that are not binding but nonetheless have a powerful shaping influence on behavior. Federal regulatory agencies have also become adept at using advisory committees composed of outside experts in order to gather information and to gain legitimacy for their policies.

Deregulation and the Reemergence of Regulation

The closing of the twentieth century was marked by a reimagining of regulation and a campaign for deregulation. Three forces—the growing political power of business, the emergence of policy and academic critiques focusing on the self-corrective power of the marketplace, and the broad distrust of government among American citizens—fueled the rollback of regulation. All sectors of regulation were affected—especially in airlines, where President Jimmy Carter joined with congressional Democrats and his appointee Alfred Kahn to eliminate federal price regulation, eventually terminating the Civil Aeronautics Board. Antitrust regulation was increasingly constrained by the notion that monopolistic markets might still be "contestable"; hence monopolies might limit their pricing out of the possibility that a presently invisible firm might enter the marketplace. The 1990s witnessed the deregulation of transportation (including the elimination of the ICC in 1995) and of telecommunications (1995), and a more moderate deregulation of health and pharmaceuticals. A new law in 1999 repealed the Glass-Steagall Act, allowing investment banks and commercial service banks to consolidate operations. New agency rules were subject to cost-benefit analysis, a practice centered in the president's Office of Management and Budget. In this conservative political age, the national government became the restrainer, not the enabler, of state and local governance.

The governance of medical products constitutes the one sphere of regulation for which American institutions have served as an exemplar of strength and a global model. The U.S. Food and Drug Administration (FDA), empowered in the New Deal legislation of 1938 and again in 1962 following the thalidomide tragedy, has created institutions, procedures, and scientific and technical concepts that have been copied worldwide. It is a small agency with a remarkably big power: the authority to veto the marketability of any new drug product, medical device, or vaccine. Its regulation of pharmaceuticals has powerfully structured the global clinical research industry, cleaving modern medical research into four distinct phases of experiment. Its regulation of "safety" and "efficacy" has literally defined the terms on which medical and pharmaceutical innovation operates worldwide.

In reality, the experiment of American government writ large is one of regulation—the regulation of racial relations, of sexuality, of the poor, of firearms and other weapons, of labor relations, of personal space. Yet the republican past, while faded, still lives with us. In the wake of numerous corporate accounting scandals in the early twenty-first century, Congress passed the Sarbanes-Oxley Act, which regulates corporate accounting on a template not merely of rights and efficiency but of "responsibility." The mortgage-lending crisis of 2007 and 2008 has led to calls for similar regulation of the lending industries. These and other regulatory initiatives have been introduced not for efficiency reasons, but out of senses of abuse, consumer protection, and the like. And with the financial and global economic crises of 2008 and 2009, new regulatory visions and organizations are being created. The language of regulation—the terms used to justify it, attack it, implement it, constrain it—is revealing and marks the enduring legacy of American regulation as well as its most contested transformations.

See also consumers and politics; economy and politics; health and illness; Prohibition and temperance; transportation and politics.

FURTHER READING

Carpenter, Daniel. *The Forging of Bureaucratic Autonomy: Reputations, Networks and Policy Innovation in Executive Agencies, 1862–1928.* Princeton, NJ: Princeton University Press,

Clarke, Sally. *Regulation and the Revolution in United States Farm Productivity.* New York: Cambridge University Press, 1994.

Derthick, Martha, and Paul J. Quirk. *The Politics of Deregulation.* Washington, DC: Brookings Institution, 1985.

Hawley, Ellis W. *The New Deal and the Problem of Monopoly: A Study in Economic Ambivalence.* New York: Fordham University Press, 1995.

Law, Marc. "The Origins of State Pure Food Regulation." *Journal of Economic History* 63 (December 2003), 1103–30.

McCraw, Thomas. *Prophets of Regulation.* Cambridge, MA: Harvard Belknap Press, 1984.

Novak, William. *The People's Welfare: Law and Regulation in Nineteenth-Century America.* Chapel Hill: University of North Carolina Press, 1996.

Skowronek, Stephen. *Building a New American State: The Expansion of National Administrative Capacities, 1877–1920.* New York: Cambridge University Press, 1982.

DANIEL CARPENTER

religion and politics to 1865

To see how breathtaking the changes were in the relationship between religion and politics from the nation's founding to 1865 and how easily American Protestants, the dominant religious group, accommodated them, one only need consider the way American Presbyterians did a quick about-face on the duties of the civil magistrate. In 1787 the Synod of New York and Philadelphia, then the highest body in the American Presbyterian Church, appointed a committee to prepare a revised edition of the Westminster Confession of Faith and Larger and Shorter Catechisms for the proposed establishment of the General Assembly and its constitution. This revision rejected the understanding of the civil magistrate's duties to maintain and protect the "true" religion that was common throughout the Protestant world during the sixteenth and seventeenth centuries, and enshrined in the original documents of the Westminster Assembly. In so doing, American Presbyterians modified their understanding of church and state in ways that at the time fellow Presbyterians in Scotland, Canada, Northern Ireland, and Australia would have found objectionable and perhaps even a betrayal of the genius of Calvinism. In fact, when English Parliament convened the Westminster Assembly during the Civil War of the 1640s, only Anabaptists and other radicals could have countenanced the kind of arrangement affirmed in the American revisions.

The case of American Presbyterians reversing the patterns of 15 centuries of church-state relations in the West is one example of the surprising ways that Protestants in the new nation reconciled themselves to what appeared to be a secular national government. As revolutionary as the new relationship between church and state was from a European perspective, it became palatable to Protestants in the United States for a variety of reasons. On the one hand, American framers were not hostile to but supported Christianity, at least of a generic kind. At the same time, Protestant leaders adopted the ideology of independence in ways that gave the American experiment redemptive significance. On the other hand, church leaders would eventually learn that by severing ties to the state faith they could be even more influential than when regulated by the state. Indeed, the American Revolution unleashed religious motivations for political activism in ways barely imaginable in the late eighteenth century. But by the middle decades of the nineteenth century, when the United States began to experience greater religious diversity and conflict, the benefits of religious activism for the American republic looked much less obvious than they appeared during the heady days of the 1770s.

Christian Republicanism

One of the Presbyterian ministers who had a hand in revising the Westminster Confession was also the only clergyman to sign the Declaration of Independence. John Witherspoon, the president of the College of New Jersey (now Princeton University), was a well-respected Presbyterian pastor who also trained graduates who would support the revolutionary cause. During his tenure at the college, only 5 of its 355 graduates would remain loyal to the British crown. This earned Witherspoon's school the nickname "seminary of sedition." His educational labors as well as his service as a member of the Continental Congress made him one of the colonies' leading patriots.

Witherspoon's service to the revolution went beyond teaching and politics to enlisting Christianity for the cause of independence. One sermon in particular, "The Dominion of Providence over the Passions of Men," demonstrated the convergence of Protestant theology and revolutionary politics that allowed for such a harmonious relationship between America's believers and the nation's framers. Witherspoon delivered this sermon on Friday, May 17, 1776, a day of prayer called by Congress. In this oration, published the next month in Philadelphia during the meetings of the Continental Congress, Witherspoon articulated one of the chief themes that aligned Christianity and Enlightenment political thought: the sacred cause of liberty. He believed that the cause of America was one predicated on justice and liberty, and that it conformed to the truth about human nature. It also showed that religious and civil liberty were inextricably linked. Both the temporal and the eternal happiness of Americans depended on their gaining independence from England. In fact, religion prospered the most in those nations that enjoyed political liberty and justice.

Witherspoon's logic not only typified a large swath of Protestant colonists but also reflected a similar attitude toward religion even among America's less than orthodox founders. When he deduced that the most zealous advocates of liberty were also the ones who were most active in promoting true religion, Witherspoon was asserting, in Christian idiom, the classical republican view that tied the prospects of liberty to the virtue of citizens. This Christian republicanism, according to Mark A. Noll, featured two ideas. First was the fear of the abuse of illegitimate power and second was an almost millennial belief in the benefits of liberty. For Protestants like Witherspoon—and the Revolution found its greatest clerical support from Calvinists in the Presbyterian and Congregationalist denominations—the best form of government was one that best preserved freedom, which would, in turn, nurture human flourishing. The flip side of this view was that any form of tyranny would be abusive both for persons and society. The critical contrasts in Christian republicanism, consequently, were virtue versus corruption, and liberty versus slavery. Protestants like Witherspoon conceded that liberty could also be abused. But this was why religion was all the more essential to a republican form of government. Virtue promoted freedom, and vice produced tyranny and social disorder. For the Protestants who supported the cause of freedom, religion was the only way to guarantee the kind of virtue on which freedom depended.

Christian republicanism was not only the logic of Protestant colonists, however. The American framers also believed that liberty required a virtuous citizenry and that virtue generally stemmed from religion. Thomas Jefferson was no favorite of many Calvinists who supported his Federalist opponents, but even he did not hesitate to affirm the new nation's need for religion, such as in his 1801 inaugural address as president. There he declared, "Let us, then, with courage and confidence pursue our own federal and republican principles. . . . enlightened by a benign religion, professed, indeed, and practiced in various forms, yet all of them including honesty, truth, temperance, gratitude, and the love of man; acknowledging and adoring an overriding Providence, which by all its dispensation proves that it delights in the happiness of man here and his greater happiness hereafter."

Jefferson's faith in providence was a far cry from orthodox Protestantism. But it was not explicitly hostile to Christianity, especially with the qualifications supplied by clergy like Witherspoon. Jefferson himself maintained "a more beautiful or precious morsel of ethics I have never seen" than the teachings of Jesus. Similar affirmations of faith came from Jefferson's political opponents, such as

John Adams, who was not much more orthodox in his Christian affirmation than the Virginian. In 1813 Adams wrote to Jefferson that "The general principles, on which the Fathers achieved independence, were . . . the general Principles of Christianity, in which all these Sects were United. . . ." The basis for Adams's positive assessment of Christianity drew directly on the fusion of Protestant and republican thought; religion and virtue supplied the only true foundation for a republican form of government and political liberty.

To be sure, these appeals to Christianity by American statesmen not known for their doctrinal precision should not be read, as American Protestants have sometimes interpreted them, as an indication of U.S. Christian origins. Nor is it clear that Protestants like Witherspoon were theologically within their rights to endorse the Revolution on Christian or Protestant grounds. But the lure of Christian republicanism to both the orthodox and heterodox patriots is significant for understanding why the American Revolution avoided an anticlerical or antireligious thrust. The widespread claim that republicanism and liberty depended upon virtue, and its corollary that tyranny was fundamentally incompatible with virtue, provided all the leverage believers and skeptics needed to find a place for religion in the new republic. As long as that connection existed, the orthodox could look on the skeptical as friendly to the churches and believers; and at the same time, as long as believers promoted virtue—as opposed to dogma—as the necessary ingredient for liberty's success, the skeptical among the framers could regard the churches and their members as benevolent partners in the enterprise of founding a free and well-ordered republic.

Disestablishment and Revival

Religious complications to the American founding emerged almost as soon as George Washington secured the terms of peace from Lord Cornwall at Yorktown. In the debates leading up to the Constitution, Protestants did not worry that the federal government required no religious tests for office or refused to establish Christianity as the state's religion. The federal government's powers were so restricted that the Constitution's lack of religious provisions were thoroughly in keeping with the expectation that state governments would oversee the lion's share of general welfare within their borders. Furthermore, the framers regarded the maintenance of established churches at the state level as an appropriate outworking of the relations between state and federal sovereignty. Even so, older fears of the Church of England gaining a foothold through the creation of an American bishop, which had contributed to some churches' support for independence from Great Britain, led Protestants eventually to question the wisdom of ecclesiastical establishments also at the state level. Consequently, while Protestants may not have objected to a federal Constitution free from religious tests, some were less than content with religious regulations within their own states.

The processes by which established churches in Virginia and Massachusetts lost their privileged status are instructive for understanding how the logic that informed federal developments could trickle down to the local level. In Virginia, revivalist Protestantism and Enlightenment political theory combined to undermine the Episcopal establishment inherited from the colonial era. Revivalist dissatisfaction with church-state patterns in Virginia went back to the Great Awakening of the mid-eighteenth century, when itinerant evangelists had been imprisoned for upsetting the social order because of their ministry outside the bounds of the Episcopal order. What is more, all ministers not in the Episcopal Church were required to assent to 34 of the Church of England's Thirty-Nine Articles in order to lead worship legally. Even then, only Episcopal priests were allowed to perform marriages. At the same time, citizens were taxed by local vestries to pay for the services of the Episcopal churches. Dissenters, of course, relied on the generosity of their own congregations.

The arguments against preferential treatment for Episcopalians took two forms. On the one hand, dissenting Protestants deduced that by incorporating a particular denomination the state had usurped Christ's own rule within the church. For instance, Virginia Presbyterians adopted a resolution in 1776 that called on the legislature to overturn all religious establishments, and to abolish taxes that violated liberty of conscience. Disestablishment would properly define the true relationship between civil and ecclesiastic authority. It would also do justice to Christ's own status as the sole legislator and governor of the church. Baptists argued in a similar vein and urged the Virginia assembly to recognize that because Christ's kingdom was not of this world it could not properly be regulated by the state. Baptists also argued that favoring one denomination above all others was unjust and at odds with Virginia's bill of rights.

On the other hand, the language of rights echoed a less Christian and more libertarian argument about freedom of thought. The Virginia Bill for Establishing

Religious Freedom (1786), written by Jefferson, appealed to the politics of liberty even if it also claimed to know the mind of the Creator. This bill, which proved influential on debates leading to the First Amendment of the U.S. Constitution, asserted the principle of freedom of thought and disdained any attempt to coerce beliefs or ideas by legislation or state power. In fact, to bind anyone's conscience was a violation of the law of nature as well as the law of liberty. Although the language of the Virginia legislation clearly appealed to dissenting Protestants when it insisted that God did not intend to propagate Christianity by state coercion, its appeal to human reason was different from Baptist and Presbyterian arguments for religious freedom. In the latter case, revivalist Protestants were more likely to claim the sincerity of faith or the religion of the heart than freedom of thought on behalf of religious freedom and ecclesiastical disestablishment. Even so, the logic of revivalism and the Enlightenment combined in Virginia to place religious faith in the category of freedom of thought and expression. Those who advocated either a rational religion or a zealous Protestantism joined hands to conclude that the civil magistrate had no appropriate power to intrude into the arena of privately held beliefs and opinions.

Disestablishment of the Congregationalist churches in Massachusetts, the state-church system that lasted the longest of any—until 1833—stemmed less from the logic of freedom of expression than from internal conflicts within the churches themselves. The state's constitution of 1779 did provide for religious freedom but also, in Article III, empowered towns to raise taxes in support of teachers of religion—in other words, pastors—who would produce the instruction necessary for a religious and virtuous citizenry. This provision allowed the Congregationalist churches to continue to receive state support because of the preponderance of Congregationalists in the state.

But the Congregationalist churches encountered a double threat from opposite sides of the Protestant spectrum that threatened their established position. Baptists voiced objections to a system that forced them to pay taxes to support Congregationalist ministers. Like their counterparts in Virginia, New England Baptists were also supporters of revivalism and, in some cases, had run afoul of the established order by conducting religious services without legal permission. On the other side of the spectrum were liberal Congregationalists, the forerunners of Unitarianism, who continued to receive state support despite objections from Trinitarian Congregationalists, who believed the legislature should fund only orthodox faith. (The division between the two parties became so great when Unitarians in 1805 took control of theological instruction at Harvard University that orthodox rivals in 1808 founded Andover Seminary to counter the spread of false teaching from Cambridge.)

These two sets of circumstances—a dissenting group of Protestants who objected to a state church and a theological rift within the established church itself—generated a series of court cases during the 1820s and forced Massachusetts to abandon tax support for the standing Congregationalist order. Even so, Massachusetts absorbed disestablishment with relative ease by relying on the public school system, created by school reformer Horace Mann, to provide the religious instruction that the state needed.

The Second Great Awakening

Disestablishment could have been a threat to Protestantism in the United States had the sort of anticlericalism experienced in France accompanied the American form of separating church and state. But because political leaders typically couched disestablishment in the language of neutrality to all Protestant denominations, the process of disentangling church and state proved to be a tremendous boon to spiritual vitality in the United States (and continues to account for the ironic combination of America's secular political order and its unprecedented levels of religious observance among western societies). By weaning the church from the financial nurture of the state, church leaders needed to draw support directly from the faithful. This environment gave an advantage to the most entrepreneurial of denominations in the new competition for adherents and financial support. In particular, Methodists and Baptists, who had already learned to exist without state aid, benefitted indirectly from religious disestablishment because of skills honed in the work of itinerancy and promoting revivals. In fact, disestablishment was a boon to revivalistic Protestantism.

Of course, revivalism was not new to America. The First Great Awakening (1740s), led by the revivalist George Whitefield with support from the likes of Jonathan Edwards and Gilbert Tennent, had already popularized the practice of itinerancy—that is, the traveling evangelist who preaches anywhere, including fields, town markets, and meeting houses without regard for church etiquette or legal sanctions. For Methodists and Baptists, however, the practice of conducting revivals and recruiting new members was not the exception but the rule. Indeed, the zeal for holiness and conversion that Methodist and Baptist forms of Protestantism encouraged sprang directly from the logic of conversion and the subsequent demand for holy living. In contrast to formal and apparently stuffy clergy trained in universities and colleges, revivalism opened the ministry to a host of lay itinerants adept at speaking the language of people well outside the influence of the older and established churches. In turn, these itinerants also provided the building blocks of a denominational structure that emerged in the early nineteenth century for Methodists and Baptists with loosely established networks and associations. These institutional forms gave a collective identity to populist denominations that stretched from the eastern seaboard to the expanding western frontier both in the North and the South.

Membership statistics from the era underscore the capacity of revivalism to adapt and thrive in the new circumstances of disestablishment. The most aggressively revivalist denominations grew the fastest, leaving the older and more established ones behind. Congregationalists and Presbyterians at the time of the American Revolution, for example, constituted approximately 40 percent of religious adherents in the United States (20 and 19 percent, respectively), while Baptists (17 percent) and Methodists (3 percent) were only half the size of the Calvinist denominations at the time of the Declaration of Independence. But after the war for independence and the new church-state order took form, Methodists and Baptists outpaced their Protestant competitors. In 1850 Methodists were the largest denomination, at 34 percent of American Protestants, and Baptists were the next largest American Protestant church with a membership of 20 percent of the Protestant whole. In contrast, by 1850 Congregationalists had fallen to 4 percent, and Presbyterians to 12 percent. The reasons for the growth among Methodists and Baptists and the decline of Calvinistic denominations are numerous. But the dynamic of disestablishment combined with the innovation and expansionist impulses of revivalism were crucial to the change in fortunes of these denominations. The success of Methodists and Baptists also demonstrated an unintended consequence of separating church and state—namely, that without the support and especially the oversight of government, churches could flourish in ways previously unimaginable.

Revivalism and Reform

Even if the Congregationalist and Presbyterian religions suffered in popularity during the antebellum period, they made up for numerical inferiority with associational superiority. After 1820, the United States was awash in a sea of voluntary societies that further complicated the relationship between religion and politics. Not only did disestablishment create a religious vacuum that revivalist-inspired Protestants filled with amazing efforts to plant churches on the expanding western frontier, but the lack of political and social structures in the new nation created an opening for religiously inspired political activism. Protestants in the Northeast, especially New England Congregationalists, responded with a vast array of voluntary associations designed to Christianize the new nation in a variety of ways. Most of these organizations received support and inspiration from the religious zeal of the Second Great Awakening, a series of revivals during the 1820s and 1830s whose principal agent was Charles Grandison Finney. These revivals and the reforms they animated gave the new society a semblance of order. They were not simply a religious but also a social response to unsettled and expanding conditions. In effect, the voluntary associations of the Second Great Awakening, also known as the Benevolent Empire, became the mechanism for civilizing life on the frontier with the "proper" ways of the East.

Some of these voluntary associations were more explicitly religious than social or political. For instance, Congregationalists, with help from northern Presbyterians, established organizations for the inexpensive production and distribution of religious materials such as Bibles and tracts. Other associations provided means for the education of clergy and for supporting the establishment of new churches in the Northwest Territory. But religious voluntary societies encouraged a widespread perception of the United States as a republic that conformed to Christian ideals. This conviction led to a number of humanitarian efforts to reform prisons, hospitals, establish schools, and train teachers for schools. A desire for a wholesome, well-ordered, and devout society also prompted revivalistic Protestants to insert themselves into the political process.

Sometimes the religious zeal of revivalistic Protestants had a direct influence on public policy and the electoral process. Some Protestant social crusades were of a limited duration and particular to a specific region of the country. Some started and gained momentum in the antebellum era only to see their greatest influence in a later period. And some substantially changed the face of party politics. In each case, the Protestant political muscle showed that disestablishment could lead to entanglements of religion and politics far thornier than the architects of separating church and state had ever contemplated.

In the category of Protestant political reforms that were limited to a specific time and place stand both the Sabbatarian-inspired opposition to Sunday mails and the Anti-Mason movement. Opposition to post offices staying open on Sundays surfaced as early as 1809, when Hugh Wylie, the postmaster of Washington, Pennsylvania, and an elder in the Presbyterian Church, was disciplined by his church for keeping the post office open on the day of Christian worship. The U.S. postmaster general, Gideon Granger, responded, in 1810, by orchestrating legislation that required all of the nation's 2,300 post offices to remain open for business seven days a week. The issue of Sunday mails resurfaced at the time of the Second Great Awakening when Protestants formed the General Union for the Promotion of the Christian Sabbath, which launched a petition campaign to persuade Congress to repeal the 1810 Postal Act, in addition to calling for a boycott of all businesses that operated on Sundays. The effort generated over 900 petitions. But the arguments, many of which appealed to the nation's Christian origins, failed to change federal law. The chairman of the Senate Committee on the Post Office and Post Roads, Richard M. Johnson, argued persuasively against the petitions, and post offices continued to remain open on Sundays throughout the nineteenth century.

Anti-Masonry also emerged from Protestant objections to church members belonging to secret societies and from widespread fears of conspiracy that such secrecy encouraged. In the minds of many Protestants, secret societies were pagan in origin, smacked of Roman Catholic hierarchy, and undermined true religion. In 1826 the cover-up of the murder of a defector from the Masonic Order led to the creation of America's first powerful third party. Anti-Masons called on American voters to drive Masons out of elected office. For them, Freemasonry was a privileged elite that lacked accountability to the nation's republican institutions. Their antagonistic platform was hardly a stable foundation for a successful party. Even so, the Anti-Masonic Party ran its own candidate for president in 1832, William Wirt, and proved disruptive to the National Republican Party's fortunes in the North.

Eventually the populism of Anti-Masonry would find an outlet in the Whig Party's opposition to Andrew Jackson's apparent disregard for legal and constitutional norms. For Whigs, Jackson's expropriation of Indian land violated a proper Christian regard for existing treaties, and his banking policies constituted a swindling of the American republic by disregarding the obligations of contracts.

In contrast to these brief and focused episodes of partisan politics inspired by Protestant devotion, temperance was a social reform that began during the middle decades of the nineteenth century and would not succeed on a national level until the early twentieth century. Again, the reasons drew heavily on Protestant understandings of self-control and biblical commands against drunkenness. The organizational spirit of the Second Great Awakening generated numerous voluntary associations with active local societies, large membership, and many tracts and journals. During the 1840s, an argument for moderation and against drunkenness turned into a brief for total abstinence as the only solution to the nation's lack of temperance. New associations emerged that reflected this shift in rationale: the Independent Order of Good Templars, the Sons of Temperance, the Templars of Honor and Temperance and, after the Civil War, the Anti-Saloon League, and the Prohibition Party.

Demand for abstinence led to the first legislation to ban the sale and distribution of alcohol. In 1851 Maine took the lead in passing laws to ban the sale of alcohol except for medicinal and manufacturing purposes. By 1855, 12 states had passed similar measures. Prohibition proved to be a divisive issue and spawned a number of independent parties and political candidates at the state level, especially in Ohio and New York but also in Delaware and Maryland. Neither Whigs nor Democrats were skillful enough to shepherd evangelical temperance demands for party gains. In fact, evangelical dissatisfaction with both Whigs and Democrats over temperance fueled the appeal in the 1850s of the American Party.

Dissolution of the Second-Party System

As volatile as temperance, Anti-Masonry, and Sabbatarianism were for American politics during the antebellum era, antislavery and anti-Catholicism proved that the separation of church and state was incapable of adjudicating the demands of either religious-inspired reforms or Protestant-based defenses of a republican order. The radical antislavery movement emerged among revivalist Protestants during the 1830s, citing slavery as the gravest example of the young nation's compromise with sin. Charles Finney, the greatest revivalist of the era, spoke out vociferously against slavery and added vigor to an emerging abolitionist movement. But the demands for immediate emancipation proved divisive among even those who opposed slavery. Some abolitionists split from the American Colonization Society in 1838 and then the American Anti-Slavery Society a few years later. Voluntary societies were not the only casualties; Methodists and Baptists split along sectional lines in 1844 over demands to condemn slavery.

With its failure to unite Protestants, the antislavery movement found other political outlets that stemmed more from rising sectionalism than from moral rectitude. Free-soil spokespersons and Northerners opposed to the expansion of slavery in the West became prominent allies of the movement. In turn, third parties emerged that sapped the electoral strength of both the Whigs and the Democrats. The Liberty Party significantly hurt the Whigs by attracting enough votes to prevent the election of Henry Clay in 1844. The Democrats were not immune from antislavery attempts, at least in the North. The Free Soil Party upended the Democrats in 1848 and pointed forward to the emergence of the Republican Party.

If Protestants lost the chance to rally around the antislavery cause in the pursuit of righteous politics, the increasing presence of Roman Catholics in the United States gave them another opportunity for unity. But anti-Catholicism, which turned primarily on older arguments about the affinity between Protestantism and republicanism, further unraveled the two-party system dominated by Whigs and Democrats. Protestant hostility was steeped in religious disputes and wars going back to the English Civil War of the 1640s and Whig hostility to the Stuart monarchy fueled antagonism to Roman Catholicism. During the 1830s and 1840s, anti-Catholicism became politically explicit as white American Protestants reacted to economic uncertainty and political upheaval.

In 1845 the founding of the Order of the Star Spangled Banner tapped these hostilities. Originally a secret society whose aim was to prevent immigrants and Roman Catholics from holding elected office, this association eventually blossomed into the Know-Nothing Party, nicknamed for its response to questions about the party and efforts to maintain its secrecy. Between 1854 and 1855, the party was one of the fastest growing in the United States, and it tapped voters in both the North and the South. By 1856 it had adopted the name the American Party and had sapped enough of the Whig Party's support for many to think the American Party's presidential nominee, Millard Fillmore, might have a chance in the general election. But again the issue of bringing slavery into the territories could not prevent the American Party from splitting, with many of its northern members deserting to the Republican Party.

Although evangelicals faulted the American Party for its initial secrecy and intolerance of foreign-born Americans, anti-Catholicism was an important piece of a religiously inspired defense of republicanism. In fact, Roman Catholicism shared qualities with slavery and alcohol that it made anti-Catholicism a plausible prejudice for those committed to antislavery and temperance. Native Protestants easily associated drinking with Roman Catholics because the cultures from which many of the new immigrants came—those of Ireland and Germany—encouraged the consumption of alcohol, not to mention that Rome had never countenanced a policy of abstinence. Protestants also noted resemblances between slavery and Roman Catholicism because of the latter's hierarchical system of church government and the obedience that Rome demanded (at least on paper) of church members. Protestantism was considered the most republican form of Christianity while Rome stood for thralldom and dependence.

The net effect of religion on America's Second Party System was to show the inadequacies of the arrangement if not to unravel it all together. Religious-based reforms inspired new parties during the three decades before the Civil War that often wooed away voters from the Whigs and Democrats. In addition, the moral dilemma of slavery caused splits within the established parties along regional lines. In 1852 Whigs, Democrats, and the Free Soil Party each supported their own candidates in the presidential election. In 1856 the third party to run alongside Whigs and Democrats was the Republican Party. And in 1860, four candidates ran for the presidency—two Democrats (northern and southern), one Constitutional Union, and one Republican. By 1860 the Whigs no longer existed and the Democrats were seriously divided. Economic and political circumstances would have made the longevity of the Whig-Democrat system unlikely. But religion added significantly to the political instability that the parties and their candidates tried to negotiate.

Divided Allegiances

In the years between the Declaration of Independence and the outbreak of the Civil War, the United States emerged as a formally secular political order that was informally one of the most religious societies in the West. Although apparently in fundamental tension, secular politics and religious zeal turned out to be almost directly proportional. The disestablishment of Christianity, what some have called de-Christianization, was actually immensely useful for the popularity of religion in the United States. And yet, the religious fervor that Americans displayed between 1776 and 1865 did not prove as advantageous for America's political leaders. At times, faith could perform remarkable assistance in American public life. But it also proved especially difficult to govern and invariably competed with the major political parties for Americans' allegiance. Ironically, by conceding that religion is a private matter that government should not coerce, America's founders also established conditions that allowed religion to be even more politically potent than it was in those states where the churches were still established.

See also Catholics and politics; Protestants and politics.

FURTHER READING

Abbott, John C., and Russell H. Conwell. *Lives of the Presidents of the United States of America.* Portland, ME: H. Hallett and Company, 1882.

Carwardine, Richard J. *Evangelicals and Antebellum Politics.* New Haven, CT: Yale University Press, 1993.

Curry, Thomas J. *The First Freedoms: Church and State in America to the Passage of the First Amendment.* New York: Oxford University Press, 1986.

Goen, C. C. *Broken Churches, Broken Nation: Denominational Schisms and the Coming of the Civil War.* Macon, GA: Mercer University Press, 1985.

Guelzo, Allen C. *Abraham Lincoln: Redeemer President.* Grand Rapids, MI: Eerdmans, 1999.

Hamburger, Philip. *The Separation of Church and State.* Cambridge, MA: Harvard University Press, 2002.

Hatch, Nathan O. *The Democratization of American Christianity.* New Haven, CT: Yale University Press, 1989.

Howe, Daniel Walker. *The Political Culture of American Whigs.* Chicago: University of Chicago Press, 1973.

Isaac, Rhys. *The Transformation of Virginia, 1740–1790.* Chapel Hill: University of North Carolina Press, 1982.

Johnson, Curtis D. *Redeeming America: Evangelicals and the Road to the Civil War.* Chicago: Ivan R. Dee, 1993.

Kramnick, Isaac, and R. Laurence Moore. *The Godless Constitution: The Case against Religious Correctness.* New York: Norton, 1997.

McLoughlin, William G. *New England Dissent, 1630–1833: The Baptists and the Separation of Church and State.* 2 vols. Cambridge, MA: Harvard University Press, 1971.

Noll, Mark A. *America's God: From Jonathan Edwards to Abraham Lincoln.* New York: Oxford University Press, 2002.

Smith, Timothy L. *Revivalism and Social Reform: American Protestantism on the Eve of the Civil War.* Revised ed. Baltimore, MD: Johns Hopkins University Press, 1980.

D. G. HART

religion and politics, 1865–1945

Religious institutions were among the most influential forces shaping American culture and society from 1865 to 1945. Every major religious group experienced tremendous growth in numbers and institutional might in this period even as Protestantism, the largest and most influential religious group in 1864, lost its prominence in the public arena after 1920.

American Religion on the Eve of the Civil War

By the beginning of the Civil War, the power of religion in America was perhaps best expressed in its theological and political ideals and its cultural influence rather than its actual numerical dominance. Only about 25 percent of Americans were members of religious institutions at the time of the Civil War, and the majority of those belonged to Protestant institutions. Nevertheless, most Americans—Protestants, Catholics, and those belonging to smaller groups like Jews, spiritualists, and others—adhered to a fairly uniform set of assumptions. Beyond a simple belief in God, most assumed God was a personal being involved in the intricacies of human life who intended that humans adhere to moral certainties that were easily discerned through revelation or common sense, and that life as a member of a family, community, and nation connected to God's providence. Moreover, even though only about one-fourth of Americans were formal members of religious institutions, far more attended local congregations, read religious literature, attended schools that promoted religious belief, or were conversant in biblical or Christian theological ideas. Even Native Americans, who practiced non-European religions, interacted with Christianity in degrees ranging from conversion to syncretism to rejection.

If religious Americans of European origin held to these general theological assumptions, most also believed America—and, most important, its Republican or Democratic political ideals and institutions—marked the highest stage of God's providential development of human beings. For religious Americans—in the North or the South; slave or free; Protestant, Catholic, Jew, theosophist, or do-it-yourselfer—the lineaments of religious belief, philosophy, political and economic activity, family, and community were almost seamless. To be religious was to be American; to be American was to be religious.

As those who believed God's providence established the United States as a "city on a hill," religious Americans were also aware of the difficulties in discerning and then living up to that providential plan. Seen most clearly in the antebellum dispute over slavery but also in the anti-Catholicism (among Protestants), anti-Mormonism, and temperance movements, as well as other causes that enlisted the debate and activity of religious Americans, commitments to common sense–based certainty and patriotic millennialism drove Christians into conflict that ranged from anti-Catholic violence to the Civil War itself.

Post–Civil War Structural Developments

By 1865, then, Americans still held to these essential theological and political ideals but faced both the consequences of having pushed those ideals to bloodshed as well as the need to address an emerging American landscape that would look increasingly different from the one in 1860. Specifically, religious Americans addressed and adapted themselves and their institutions to the most important historical trends of this period: migrations of people westward within America, and immigration into America from overseas; urbanization; industrialization; war and the emergence of America as a world power; and new patterns of thought such as pragmatism, theological liberalism/modernism, and evolution.

Shaping such connections among religion, politics, and society between 1865 and 1945 was the striking and unprecedented numerical growth among religious groups in America, which was marked by growing institutional predominance with centralization and professionalization, increasing diversity in terms of new religious belief, ethnicity, and schisms within older religious groups, and new theological, philosophical, and social ideas emerging from the engagement with urbanization and new intellectual patterns. Because of such growth in real numbers and influence, if it was not the case before the Civil War, it became increasingly the case afterward that America was, if not a "Christian nation," then certainly a nation of believers.

In 1865 the majority of American churchgoers remained affiliated with Protestant denominations, and this remained true up to 1945, as these denominations grew at extraordinary rates. Methodists, the largest Protestant denomination in 1860 with about 2 million members, grew to about 5.5 million members in 1900 and then to just under 12 million in 1950. Baptists grew from 1 million to 4.5 million to 15 million in that same period, passing Methodists as the largest Protestant denomination. Other Protestant denominations such as the Lutherans, Presbyterians, Episcopalians, Congregationalists, and Disciples of Christ grew in similar scale.

At the same time, however, non-Protestant or groups on the fringes of Protestantism grew in like manner, challenging Protestant hegemony. Roman Catholics, for example, became the largest single Christian religious body in the nation before the Civil War, with just under 5 million adherents. Catholic numbers exploded due to post–Civil War immigration to approximately 10 million by 1900 and well over 20 million by 1950. Likewise, Holiness and Pentecostal denominations (Church of God in Christ, Church of God–Cleveland Tennessee, Church of the Nazarene, Assemblies of God, and others) emerged at the turn of the century; drawing on older traditions of moral certitude, a belief in the human perfection, and the experience of religious ecstasy, along with speaking in tongues and healing, they forged a movement that by the end of the twentieth century was probably the most pervasive and dynamic Christian body worldwide, claiming 100 million and possibly as high as 500 million adherents. This movement would provide the backbone of the religious right of the late twentieth century. Like Pentecostals, Eastern Orthodoxy (primarily Russian and Greek), the Church of Jesus Christ of Latter-Day Saints, and eastern religions (especially Buddhism and Confucianism), grew between 1865 and 1945, but did so especially after 1945.

The late nineteenth and early twentieth centuries also saw the emergence of spiritualist and adventist groups. Though these groups were often rooted in antebellum patterns of thought, groups such as the Christian Science movement of Mary Baker Eddy, the Jehovah's Witnesses, the Theosophical Society of Madame H. P. Blavatsky, Mesmerism, and other mind cures or loosely Christian adventists prospered in the twentieth century and, in some cases, especially overseas. Sometimes, as in the case of Christian Science and its *Christian Science Monitor*, these groups exerted a political and social influence beyond their actual number of adherents.

American Judaism also prospered and grew in this period. Before the 1890s, most American Jews were of German origin and clustered in cities such as Cincinnati, Ohio, or Charleston, South Carolina. These were often Reform Jews who mitigated the strictures of the Torah according to American cultural, political, and social customs. Immigration from Eastern Europe, and especially Russia, brought the number of Jews in the United States to nearly 1 million by 1900, and then to about 5 million by 1950. These Eastern European Jews saw immigration as a means to exercise their religious practices freely; hence, many of these immigrants established conservative or orthodox synagogues as they sought initially to be faithful Jews rather than assimilated Americans.

Finally, Native American religious belief systems declined in the number of adherents throughout the second half of the nineteenth century through Christian missionary activity, persecution, and privatization of Native American lands under the 1887 Dawes Severalty Act or syncretism with or conversion to Christianity. One prominent example of such syncretism was the Ghost Dance movement of the Plains Indians, which, as taught by the Piute prophet Wovoka, merged Christian patterns of millennialism with traditional Native American religious beliefs, teaching that participation in a series of rituals (the Ghost Dance) would hasten a millennial world as well as happiness in the here and now. The movement was suppressed by the 1890s, most infamously at the Wounded Knee Massacre of 1890. Native American religion experienced revival, however, under the Indian Reorganization Act of 1934, which not only restored tribal lands and governance but encouraged the practice of traditional religions.

Immigration and Nativism

As noted, the swell of immigration that lasted from the 1870s to the 1920s from China (until the Exclusion Act of 1882), Japan, and Europe led to tremendous growth among certain groups—Roman Catholics, Jews, and Lutherans especially. But immigration had other consequences as well, for as many immigrants connected ethnicity to religion, some religious groups experienced fragmentation along ethnic lines. For example, Swedes, Norwegians, and other immigrants from Scandinavia established their own Lutheran bodies, while Catholics from Poland, Portugal, Austria, Italy, Germany, Bohemia, and elsewhere solidified their own parish identities and regularly fought with the established Irish leadership for control; one extreme example was the establishment of the Polish National Catholic Church in 1904. Jewish immigration also led to fragmentation as Jewish synagogues aligned themselves along three lines: Reform (generally Americanized Jews from previous immigrations), Conservative, and Orthodox (the latter two made up largely of immigrants arriving after 1890).

Another way that ethnicity connected to religion was in the way some Protestants connected Roman Catholicism (and, later in the early twentieth century, Judaism) to ethnicity in periodic outbreaks of nativism. As far back as the Puritan era, many Protestants had opposed, sometimes with violence, Catholics on theological and—especially in the antebellum period—political grounds, arguing that Catholic allegiance to the Papacy threatened the basis of American Democracy. After the Civil War, this theological or political anti-Catholicism—most often expressed in struggles over public funding for Catholic education—combined with fears of urbanization and xenophobia in the form of nativism. Nativists, many of whom were explicitly Protestant, blamed immigrants—especially Catholic and Jewish immigrants—for the vices of cities, local political corruption (bossism), radical political ideas, and a perceived shift in America away from its Protestant culture. Nativist activity was especially prominent in the 1890s and 1920s and expressed institutionally through the American Protective Association (APA) in the late nineteenth century and the Ku Klux Klan in the 1920s.

Progressivism, Modern Organization, and the Social Gospel

As all these religious groups grew in number they also organized themselves along the lines of the emerging corporate culture of the late nineteenth and early twentieth centuries, borrowing the language and concepts of centralization and efficiency to create some of the most prominent and powerful institutions in the country. Protestant denominations, Roman Catholic dioceses, Spiritualists, Buddhists, and even Native Americans (who formed the Native American Church in 1918 to legally protect the use of peyote) centralized the governance of their own institutions, professionalized their clerical ranks, established colleges, graduate schools, and seminaries or divinity schools, and funneled money into clerical pensions and especially missionary activities at home and abroad and to social services. Much of this centralization took place within denominational structures already in place; Protestant denominations, Mormons, Adventists, Jehovah's Witnesses, and others funded missionaries, especially to China and Asia in the twentieth century; Roman Catholics founded the Catholic Foreign Missionary Society in 1911 in Maryknoll, New York, which focused on Central and South America. Catholics also established the National Catholic Welfare Conference (originating in 1917 as the National Catholic War Council), which, under Monsignor John A. Ryan, voiced the needs of the poor among Catholics. Missionary activities, especially in China, the Philippines, and Central and South America, dovetailed in friendly or hostile ways with growing American military and commercial interests abroad.

Along with denominational initiatives, organizations such as the Federal Council of Churches (1908) and the Synagogue Council (1926) established organizational ties across institutions. More important, though, organizations outside denominational and church institutions also organized with great efficiency and impact. Rooted in the volunteer societies of the antebellum period, national religious groups formed to address specific problems or to engage in missionary work. Some of the most prominent were the Young Men's (and Women's) Christian Associations (YMCA and YWCA), which strove to protect young men and women from the vices of city life; the Student Volunteer Movement, founded by John R. Mott, which sent young college graduates overseas as missionaries; the Women's Christian Temperance Union (WCTU) led by Frances Willard; the Knights of Columbus, which provided mutual aid for Roman Catholics; the Salvation Army, from England; the Catholic Worker movement (1933) of Dorothy Day and Peter Maurin, countless rural and urban holiness, Pentecostal, and apostolic groups that preached the Gospel in farming communities or storefront churches and also provided assistance to the poor; and the organizations, conferences, and schools that grew up around the most prominent independent preachers of the period such as Dwight L. Moody and Billy Sunday. These groups and personalities often competed with denominations in terms of loyalty and impact.

Even though the memberships of most religious bodies included more women than men, those that were extensions of denominations and churches, as well as most independent organizations, retained an almost completely male leadership and clergy. There were exceptions to this such as Christian Science and some holiness/Pentecostal groups. Women often organized or held prominent roles in organizations and missionary endeavors existing alongside these churches; the WCTU or Catholic Worker movement are prominent examples. The early twentieth century saw some movement toward ordination of women among Protestants, but most movement in this direction occurred after 1945. The Catholic Sisters, however, were at the heart of Catholic educational life and benevolence.

At the turn of the century, much of the activity of these and other institutions focused on alleviating the "social problem"—meaning urban poverty, political corruption (especially at the local level), and labor unrest. While in the antebellum period, volunteer societies had addressed issues like abolition and temperance, between the 1880s and the end of World War I, Protestants and many Catholics adopted what has come to be called the Social Gospel (though at the time religious leaders used the name "Applied Christianity").

For religious Americans, the "social problem," which came to prominence with Jacob Riis's *How the Other Half Lives* (1891) and Henry George's *Progress and Poverty* (1879), involved urban poverty and its attendant vices, which were often associated with Catholic or Jewish immigrants. For this reason, some Social Gospel advocates were implicitly or explicitly nativist or promoted Anglo-Saxon superiority (Josiah Strong and his *Our Country* [1885], for example).

Often, too, the social problem was connected to the specter of "class warfare," the assumption being that if economic conditions in American cities fell to the point of "European conditions," America would find itself in a war between the middle class and the politically radicalized "masses." To stay the advance of such a class war, many religious Americans turned to older forms of benevolence—assisting the poor, fighting alcohol consumption, and so on. Those who adopted the Social Gospel, however, employed the new social science of sociology; social scientific theories of education, liberal, or modernist theology; and forms of social evolution—in short, progressivism—to forge a systemic approach to urban poverty, education, and work. Social Gospel advocates like Walter Rauschenbusch, Washington Gladden, and Richard T. Ely wanted clerics trained in the social sciences to use political and educational means to alter systems of vice, oppression, and urban corruption in order to end the social problem. In their minds, such political and otherwise practical endeavors would introduce the Kingdom of God—a new social and political system based on love and justice—to the world. This movement was especially prominent in cities outside the South and in Protestant divinity schools.

Even though Protestants were more visible in organizing activities associated with the Social Gospel, Catholics, too, engaged in such thought, often with a more radical edge. Based on the criticism of capitalism and call for social justice in Pope Leo XIII's 1891 encyclical letter *Rerum Novarum* (Of New Things), which was restated in 1931 when Pope Pius XI issued *Quadragesimo Anno* (In the Fortieth Year), groups like the Catholic Worker movement put social action in place that was in some ways more radical that Protestants. The Catholic Worker movement associated with radical political and intellectual movements and explicitly challenged a belief in capitalism.

After World War I, as intellectuals gradually dismissed many of the progressive ideals touting human progress and perfectibility through education and reform, the ideals of the Social Gospel gave way in seminaries, universities, and divinity schools, at least among Protestants, to the theological "Neo-Orthodoxy" of the 1930s and 1940s. This Neo-Orthodoxy, which drew on the thinking of Swiss Theologian Karl Barth and Americans Reinhold Niebuhr and H. Richard Niebuhr, professed little confidence in human perfection, stressing instead, and in different ways, the transcendent gap between God (or philosophical ideals) and the mire of the human condition.

Fragmentation, Schism, and the Fundamentalist-Modernist Controversy

The growth and centralization of institutional life also brought about fragmentation and schism among Protestants just as pressures from immigration brought schism to American Judaism and Catholicism. In the late nineteenth century, many Protestants, especially in the Upper South and Midwest, drew on the same fears about centralization and hierarchy that had earlier produced groups like the Disciples of Christ and Primitive Baptists. Many rural practitioners worried that the new institutions favored leaders from larger urban churches, while others worried that centralized plans for setting amounts and distributing missionary funds were inherently antidemocratic. Often these concerns coupled with theological emphases on holiness, antimissionary Calvinism, or religious ecstasy to produce a number of separatist groups that formed their own denominations. Already mentioned are the holiness and Pentecostal groups, black and white, that formed with these emphases; other important Protestant groups included Landmark Baptists and the Churches of Christ, which split from the Disciples of Christ. Similar struggles in ethnic churches pitted those who wished to retain Old World languages and theological emphases against those who more openly embraced the English language and American intellectual and political ideals. Such tensions were especially strong among certain Lutherans and Dutch Calvinists. Catholics, too, struggled between allegiance to the worldwide church with it Eurocentric emphases, practices, and ideals, and allegiance to American ideals such as congregational autonomy and the separation of church and state. This struggle in America often paralleled European struggles between liberal and ultramontane leaders and theologians. Supporters of Ultramontane Catholicism, drawing on Pope Pius IX's *Syllabus of Errors* (1864), generally condemned political liberalism and the separation of church and state.

The major Protestant denominations in the North (Presbyterians, Methodists, remained separated as northern and southern bodies until 1983 and 1939, respectively) experienced schism most acutely in the fundamentalist-modernist controversy that extended roughly from the Presbyterian heresy trial of Charles A. Briggs in 1892 to the Scopes Trial of 1925. Other denominations, because they were decentralized (such as the Lutherans) or more uniform theologically (as with southern denominations and Roman Catholics), avoided this schism over the control of denominations.

The fundamentalist-modernist controversy involved some elements of the concerns over centralization but focused more on theological and intellectual innovations that were sweeping the nation and on who would control denominational machinery—in particular, the governance of overseas missionaries and the divinity schools and seminaries.

Theological modernism emerged out of Europe—especially Germany—as well as from Unitarian and theologically experimental institutions of higher education in the United States. It challenged a number of traditional assumptions about the origins and content of the Old and New Testaments and especially the relationship of theology to science and philosophy. Higher criticism of the Bible challenged traditions of authorship and dating in biblical documents along with the historical verifiability of biblical events and persons. For many, higher criticism of the Bible undercut the claims of authority that Christians believed it held. Other thinkers challenged theological claims of Christian exclusivity in light of increasing knowledge of world religions. And the introductions of Darwinism, philosophical positivism, historicism, ethical pragmatism, and the ideas of Karl Marx, Sigmund Freud, and others challenged traditional views concerning the unity of theology, philosophy, and science. Unlike the challenges to religion itself from science, skeptics, or atheists, modernist theology attempted to adapt modern thought and criticism to the basic tenets of Christianity in order to save it by modernizing it. Modernist thinkers also generally adopted social scientific views about human nature and society consistent with the Social Gospel. The impact of modernism was strongest in northern and midwestern denominations. Southern Protestants were more uniformly resistant to modernism, while the Roman Catholic hierarchy also resisted it.

As theological modernists became increasingly vocal and gained leadership in northern Protestant denominations, traditionalists began to challenge them. The first challenge to gain widespread notoriety was the trial of Charles A. Briggs in 1892. Briggs, a northern Presbyterian and professor of biblical literature at New York's Union Seminary, was tried and acquitted of heresy by the Presbytery of New York for accepting certain tenets of higher criticism. At the same time, conservatives attempted to wrest control of missionary activities, fearing that modernists saw missions as an extension of the Social Gospel and therefore a program for social service rather than for preaching the gospel.

As the opponents to modernism coalesced, their leaders became known as "fundamentalists," so named for a series of books called *The Fundamentals*, published from 1910 to 1917 and edited by A. C. Dixon and R. A. Torrey. Although conservatives, led by figures such as Dixon, Torrey, and J. Gresham Machen of Princeton Seminary eventually lost control over their denominations (many left to form their own), fundamentalism became a larger cultural and religious movement by the early 1920s. It fought not only theological modernism but the Social Gospel, Bolshevism, and—especially—evolution, all of which, taken together, were seen as leading to atheism and the destruction of American society. Along with being theologically conservative, many in the movement also expressed a belief in divine healing and holiness as well as dispensational premillennialism, which taught that the world would continue to get worse as Satan ruled the present dispensation of time; only when God removed Christians from the world would Jesus return, redeem the earth, and establish the millennium through direct intervention. This belief system ran counter to the earlier nineteenth-century postmillennialism that expected human beings to work with God in perfecting the earth and establishing the millennium—a belief that had prompted countless nineteenth-century reform movements, including abolitionism.

This stage of the fundamentalist movement peaked at the 1925 Scopes Monkey Trial in Dayton, Tennessee, in which William Jennings Bryan battled Clarence Darrow over John T. Scopes's right to teach evolution in the schools. Bryan, arguing for the prosecution against Scopes, won the legal battle in Dayton, but fundamentalists lost the war for American culture, as media personalities such as H. L. Mencken and Reverend Henry Emerson Fosdick cast fundamentalists as rural yokels attempting to point Americans in a backward direction. Fundamentalist Protestants continued, however, to prosper, establishing radio ministries, Bible colleges, missionary endeavors, publications, and other institutions. Their numbers grew and their institutions strengthened throughout the middle of the twentieth century, even though their public voice was restricted largely to radio preaching. They were poised, however, to reappear with Billy Graham in the 1950s and later with conservative political movements.

African American Christianity

Much of what characterized white religious activity also characterized that of African-American Christianity, but with some important exceptions. In the North, free blacks had formed their own denominations in the antebellum period, mostly in cities like Philadelphia and New York. The two most important were the African Methodist Episcopal (AME) and the African Methodist Episcopal Zion (AMEZ) churches, both of which experienced growth rates similar to other religious groups between 1865 and 1945.

Southern black religion developed in the crucible of slavery, so although the southern blacks shared certain beliefs with whites and northern blacks—conversion, baptism, and in some cases ecstatic worship—the historical context of slavery meant many shared beliefs took on profoundly different meanings. Furthermore, in the South, the black church became the central social and political institution for the developing African American community and culture.

Although introduced to Christianity by whites, slaves quickly made it their own as they developed the "secret institution"—secret meetings held in "brush harbors" beyond white control. These secret meetings provided sanctuary as slaves developed their own rituals and beliefs, selected their own leaders, and found release through religious ecstasy. Slaves also synthesized Christianity in varying degrees with African and Caribbean religious beliefs.

After 1865, African Americans quickly established churches free, as much as possible, from white control. Black Baptists, who developed into the largest body of black Christians, formed their own state conventions immediately after the Civil War, though they continued to utilize help from southern and northern whites (and eventually formed the National Baptist Convention). Black missionaries from the AME and AMEZ churches established congregations throughout the South, while southern whites helped draw some blacks into their own separate, white-controlled denominations such as the Colored Methodist Episcopal Church. Catholic Parishes in the South typically followed this latter pattern.

As with white denominations in this period, such growth involved conflict that almost always had racial overtones. The two primary axes of conflict were between urban, middle-class blacks and rural blacks on the one hand, and conflict between blacks and northern and southern whites on the other. Many middle-class urban African Americans who attempted to earn cultural, social, and political equality through "respectability" produced increasing class tensions in the late nineteenth century within and among different churches as they saw poor, uneducated, and often rural blacks with their ecstatic worship and uneducated preachers as a hindrance to racial uplift. These class-related tensions fueled both intradenominational (localists versus denominational centralizers) and interdenominational warfare—especially between the more middle-class AME/AMEZ churches and the more rural Baptists. In terms of black/white tensions, blacks often needed northern whites' resources but resented white control and paternalism. Also, southern whites offered blacks land, money, and education, but such benevolence was not only coupled with paternalism but white supremacy.

African American churches also became enclaves against the subtle or overt horrors of postbellum racism as they continued to nurture black leadership and to provide relief, mutual aid, and secondary and higher education. At the same time, the church functioned as the primary public sphere for black men and women in southern society through education, preaching, and moral reform designed to gain equality with whites. Black women were often at the forefront of these endeavors. Especially before the imposition of legal vote restriction and Jim Crow in the 1890s, for black men, and especially black preachers, the church provided the primary base for political involvement and mobilization aimed at securing suffrage and civil equality. Like white Protestants, blacks coupled their conceptions of spiritual freedom and equality with republican notions of individual and social freedom and American millennialism. This would become evident in the civil rights movement of the 1950s and 1960s.

By the turn of the century, black Baptists and various other independent congregations practiced a Pentecostal style of worship and ecstasy. Many African Americans also accepted the practices of healing, the second blessing, and the Baptism of the Holy Spirit common to Pentecostalism. By the middle of the twentieth century, black Pentecostal groups were the second largest group of black Christians behind the Baptists.

Loss of a Mainstream Protestant Political Voice

Through the twentieth century, even as white Protestant churches and denominations grew in number and strengthened denominational infrastructures, and influenced ideas, social patterns, laws (Prohibition), and the like, Protestantism also experienced an increasing alienation from and lack of influence in the public arenas it had dominated in the nineteenth century. It would be hard to call this phenomenon "secularization" in light of the institutional and numerical growth among not just Protestants but religious groups generally in this period. But in the realm of politics, arts, literature, and higher education, Protestant leaders gave way to other, often nonreligious ones. Partly because of the general cultural and intellectual assault on progressivism and the Social Gospel, partly as fallout from the Scopes trial, and partly from new models and criteria for professional achievement and celebrity, by the 1920s, Protestant ministers and theologians disappeared from state dinners and no longer oversaw large reform movements. They yielded to figures like Walter Lippmann, thinkers like John Dewey, and popular novelists regarding the moral instruction of the public, and turned public education over to teachers trained under Dewey's educational ideas and secular leaders in institutions of higher education (exceptions would include Reinhold Niebuhr, Billy Graham, and by the 1960s, Dr. Martin Luther King Jr.). All the while, Protestants shared the American public stage with Catholics, Jews, and village atheists like Mencken and Darrow. Ironically, even as Protestants, Catholics, and religious Americans in general experienced tremendous growth numerically and institutionally between 1865 and

1945, Protestants, who in 1860 held pervasive cultural and social sway over the nation, saw their influence decline.

See also Catholics and politics; Jews and politics; Protestants and politics.

FURTHER READING

Albanese, Catherine L. *A Republic of Mind and Spirit: A Cultural History of American Metaphysical Religion*. New Haven, CT: Yale University Press, 2007.

Carpenter, Joel. *Revive Us Again: The Reawakening of American Fundamentalism*. New York: Oxford University Press, 1997.

Dolan, Jay. *The American Catholic Experience*. South Bend, IN: University of Notre Dame Press, 1992.

Gaustad, Edwin Scott, and Philip L. Barlow, eds. *New Historical Atlas of Religion in America*. New York: Oxford University Press, 2001.

Handy, Robert T. *A Christian America*. New York: Oxford University Press, 1971.

Harvey, Paul. *Freedom's Coming*. Chapel Hill: University of North Carolina Press, 2005.

Hutchison, William R. *Between the Times: The Travail of the Protestant Establishment in America, 1900–1960*. New York: Cambridge University Press, 1989.

Marsden, George M. *Fundamentalism and American Culture*. New York: Oxford University Press, 1980.

Marty, Martin. *Modern American Religion*. 3 vols. Chicago: University of Chicago Press, 1986.

McGreevy, John T. *Catholicism and American Freedom: A History*. New York: Norton, 2003.

Wacker, Grant. *Heaven Below*. Cambridge, MA: Harvard University Press, 2001.

Wuthnow, Robert. *The Restructuring of American Religion*. Princeton, NJ: Princeton University Press, 1988.

JOE CREECH

religion and politics since 1945

The United States in the second half of the twentieth century was, paradoxically, both very secular and very religious. Like most other industrialized democracies, it conducted its daily business in a pragmatic and down-to-earth way. At the same time, however, most of its citizens believed that an omnipotent God was watching over them. While the church membership rate in Western Europe had dwindled to just 4 or 5 percent, in the United States it was still over 50 percent. American religion and politics, meanwhile, were linked in complex ways, even though the First Amendment to the Constitution specified their separation.

No aspirant to high political office could be indifferent to religious questions, and every school board in the country had to wrestle with the problem of what religious symbols and activities they should allow on their campuses without displeasing the Supreme Court. The evangelist Billy Graham befriended every president between Harry Truman and George W. Bush, and all of them valued his goodwill. As recently as 2007, the governor of Georgia held a meeting on the steps of his state capitol, during a drought, to beseech God for rain.

European sociologists early in the twentieth century predicted a continuous process of secularization for industrial societies, and the experience of most nations vindicated them. Why was the United States such an exception? Numerous theories were offered at the time. One was that the United States had such a diverse population, drawn from so many immigrant groups (voluntary and unfree), that religion was used to hold on to the vestiges of an older identity. Rural Italian immigrants, for example, had to turn themselves into urban industrial workers when they came to America and had to learn English, but they could still be Roman Catholics. A second theory was that a highly mobile population sought a proxy form of community and found it by joining churches as they moved from one city to the next. A third was that church-state separation, which denied state support to any church, forced religious leaders to act like businessmen, seeking out "customers" and making sure they offered a "product" to the liking of their clients; otherwise they would not get paid. A fourth, often advanced during an upsurge in religiosity in the 1950s, was that the fear of annihilation in a nuclear war was so intense that it drove anxious men and women back to churches and synagogues for reassurance. All these theories could find empirical support; together they went far to explain the anomalous American situation.

The Cold War

Many Americans perceived the cold war as a conflict of both political and religious significance, in which the United States, champion of religion, confronted "godless communism." Emphasizing that America stood not just for democratic capitalism but also for religious freedom was a way of sharpening and clarifying the face-off. Among the organizations advocating militant anti-Communist policies in the 1950s was the Christian Anti-Communist Crusade, whose leader, Fred Schwartz, regarded communism as a substitute religion, a horrible parody of Christianity. President Dwight Eisenhower inspired some observers and amused others by declaring that America itself made no sense without "a deeply held religious faith—and I don't care what it is!" This was a way of affirming a point that was later made more formally by sociologist Robert Bellah: that America has a civil religion in addition to its citizens' many particular religions. Eisenhower also authorized the inclusion of the phrase "under God" in the Pledge of Allegiance and the stamping of "In God We Trust" on currency.

The fact that America's defense policy was based on nuclear deterrence added an apocalyptic dimension to the cold war. A nuclear war could do the kind of world-shattering damage that until then only God had been able to accomplish—and that he had promised Noah he would never do again after the great flood. Nuclear weapons themselves occasioned an anguished religious debate. Twenty-two Protestant theologians from the Federal Council of Churches declared that the bombing of Hiroshima and Nagasaki in August 1945 was "morally indefensible." The editors of the *Catholic World* agreed, adding that America had "struck the most powerful blow ever delivered against Christian civilization and the moral law." The hardheaded neo-orthodox theologian Reinhold Niebuhr, a man highly respected among foreign policy makers, wrote in *The Irony of American History* (1952) that America had created for itself an intolerable paradox. Posing as the defender of Christian civilization, it was able to make good on the commitment only by threatening to use a weapon so fearsome, and so indiscriminate, that it would make a mockery of its users' claim that they believed in a righteous and loving God.

Civil Rights

The cold war standoff persisted through the 1950s as the United States underwent dynamic changes. None was more significant than the civil rights movement, whose activist phase began in late 1955 with the Montgomery bus boycott. Energized by the Supreme Court's school desegregation decision in *Brown v. Board of Education* (1954), the Montgomery Improvement Association persuaded African Americans not to ride the city's segregated buses until the company changed its seating policy. Martin Luther King Jr., a Baptist minister, took command of the boycott and guided it to victory after nearly 13 months. A native of Atlanta whose father was also a prominent minister, King developed a superb preaching style. Boycott meetings in Montgomery were closely akin to religious revivals; hymn singing and his passionate sermons strengthened the boycotters' sense of unity and determination to persist.

King went on to become a leader of the nationwide civil rights movement, which succeeded in prompting Congress, over the next decade, to abolish all legally enforced racial segregation and to guarantee the vote to African Americans for the first time since Reconstruction. He had the knack of linking immediate circumstances in the South to transcendent questions of religious significance, a skill demonstrated in his "Letter from Birmingham Jail" (1963), which compared his work to that of Jesus and St. Paul in the early Christian communities. It is no coincidence that King and nearly all the other early civil rights movement leaders (Ralph Abernathy, Fred Shuttlesworth, Jesse Jackson, and others) were clergymen. Ministers enjoyed high status in the segregated African American community and often brokered agreements between whites and blacks. King, moreover, knew how to appeal to whites as well as blacks in a language drenched in biblical imagery—both races honored the scriptures. The fact that he was also able to achieve a high level of nonviolence gave his group, the Southern Christian Leadership Conference, the moral high ground, and worked effectively on the consciences of white voters.

Religion and Politics

The success of the civil rights movement was to have profound consequences not just for African Americans but also for the two main political parties. The Democrats' electoral base had long been the white Solid South, but as southern blacks began to vote Democrat after the Voting Rights Act of 1965, growing numbers of southern whites began to switch their allegiance to the Republican Party. Party politics was also changed in 1960 by the election of a Roman Catholic, John F. Kennedy, to the presidency. The only other Catholic to run for the presidency up to that time, Al Smith, had been soundly beaten in the election of 1928, partly because southern whites, most of them evangelical Christians, had refused to vote for a Catholic. Anti-Catholicism had a long history in America by 1960, some of it lowbrow bigotry, symbolized by episodes of anti-Catholic rioting in nineteenth-century cities. It could also be refined and well read, however, as Paul Blanshard's best-selling *American Freedom and Catholic*

Power (1949) bore witness. Blanshard, whose book was favorably reviewed in all the mainstream media, argued that Catholics' loyalty to an absolute monarch, the pope, overrode their loyalty to the nation, making them dubious citizens. He even suggested that Catholics, like Communists, were an internal fifth column, threatening the future of the republic. Kennedy, in the run-up to the 1960 election, appeared before a meeting of evangelical Protestant ministers in Houston and denied having divided loyalties. He later joked to advisors that it was unreasonable for Blanshard and others to suspect him of disloyalty because he was such a bad Catholic!

During the Kennedy administration, the Supreme Court, under the leadership of Chief Justice Earl Warren, who was already controversial because of the *Brown* decision, issued its findings in several church-state cases: *Engel v. Vitale* (1962), *Murray v. Curlett* (1963), and *School District of Abington Township v. Schempp* (1963). The Court ruled that collective prayers in public school classrooms, then widespread, were a violation of the First Amendment. So, too, were Bible reading and recitation of the Ten Commandments. The cases had been brought by an alliance of Unitarians, Jews, and atheists, who wanted to strengthen the wall of separation between church and state. Most other religious groups protested against this breach of American tradition, with some arguing that it would give comfort to the Communists and diminish the religious dimensions of the cold war. Numerous draft constitutional amendments appeared before Congress in the following years, trying to reinstate school prayer, but none won the necessary two-thirds majority. At almost the same time (1961), however, the Supreme Court upheld the conviction of Abraham Braunfeld, who claimed his free exercise of religion was abridged by the state of Pennsylvania. An orthodox Jew, Braunfeld closed his furniture store on Saturdays, but the state's Sunday closing laws forbade him to open it then, putting him at an unfair business disadvantage. The Court ruled against him, decreeing that Sunday closing laws served a compelling secular interest, even if their origin could be found in a religious practice.

In the following decades, however, the trend in church-state cases was toward an increasingly emphatic dissociation. In 1983 the Supreme Court even considered a case, *Lynch v. Donnelly*, involving government-owned illuminated Christmas displays—it decided to permit them if nonreligious items like candy canes, Santa Claus, and red-nosed reindeer were there, but to object if the exhibit comprised only a Christian crèche.

Vietnam

Soon after President Kennedy's death, the American escalation in Vietnam began. In the early days of American involvement, a Catholic doctor, Tom Dooley, who had served there in the 1950s, regarded the war as a battle between Christian South Vietnam and the Communist North; at first Cardinal Francis Spellman of New York and the American Catholic hierarchy agreed. Doubts about the "domino theory," however, along with the lack of a clear military objective and unease about the viability and integrity of the South Vietnamese ally, led to antiwar protests. Religious observers from many different traditions began to think of the war as power politics at its dirtiest—sacrificing Vietnam and its people because the risk of fighting the cold war in Europe was too great. Roger LaPorte, a young Catholic activist, set fire to himself on the steps of the United Nations in 1965 to protest the war. An interfaith organization, Clergy and Laity Concerned about Vietnam (founded in 1966), agreed to put aside its members' religious differences in its campaign to end the war. It organized protests and sent a delegation to Secretary of Defense Robert McNamara, led by Rabbi Abraham Heschel, William Sloane Coffin (Protestant), and Daniel Berrigan (Catholic).

Berrigan, a Jesuit priest, also led a group of religious antiwar activists in invasions of two Selective Service offices in the Baltimore area. They poured blood over draft files in the first and set fire to files in the second with homemade napalm, then stood waiting to be arrested, explaining to local journalists the symbolic significance of their actions. Berrigan was convicted but went underground rather than to prison. For a year he was the romantic hero of the religious resistance, showing up unexpectedly to preach in different churches, then disappearing again before the police or FBI could arrest him.

Vietnam also raised anew question of religious conscientious objectors (COs). During World War II the judiciary had permitted members of the historic peace churches, Quakers, Mennonites, and Jehovah's Witnesses, to register as COs and to perform alternative service rather than enter the army. This rule persisted, but now, large numbers of draftees from other traditions also claimed that their consciences forbade them from serving in Vietnam. Such objectors found the Supreme Court partially sympathetic to their point of view in a 1970 decision that permitted objections based on "a deeply held and coherent ethical system," even if it had no explicit religious element. On the other hand, the Court added in a case the following year, CO status would not be granted to protesters against only some wars: it had to be all or nothing.

American Judaism

Another conflict, the 1967 Six-Day War between Israel and its Arab neighbors, had a very different effect on American religious history. It galvanized American Jews into a renewed sense of pride, identity, and concern for their community. Jews, only about 3 percent of the American population in 1945—most of them children or grandchildren of immigrants—had been preoccupied with assimilation, often trying to minimize the distinctive elements of their way of life. Except among a handful of Orthodox communities, mainly in the New York area, Jews tended to blend in rather than stand out in the 1950s and early 1960s. Many opted to join Conservative synagogues, to keep kosher tradition at home but not elsewhere, not to wear distinctive garments like the *kippah* in public, and at times even to placate their fretful children in December by celebrating Christmas. Intermarriage rates between Christians and Jews rose steadily.

Three trends changed this trajectory toward assimilation. First was Israel, which since its creation in 1948 had to fight for its existence. Israel's leaders hoped that well-to-do American Jews would migrate there, bringing their wealth, education, and skills. Most declined to do so, but they did lobby on behalf of Israel, made sure its point of view was well represented in Congress, and sent financial contributions. Second was the rediscovery of the Holocaust. Many Jews' first instinct had been to forget about it—very little literature discussed it in the 1950s—but after Hannah Arendt's *Eichmann in Jerusalem* (1963) it became a central issue in American Jewish education and self-definition; her book was followed by a flood of Holocaust-related literature. Third was the Six-Day War itself, which, though it ended victoriously for Israel, showed that Jews still faced terrifying enemies eager to annihilate them. In the aftermath, contributions to Israel and American Jews' decision to migrate there rose sharply. Modern Orthodoxy began to develop in the late 1960s and 1970s, a form of Judaism that permitted full engagement in American life without compromising religious distinctiveness and observance. Ensuring American Jews' support, meanwhile, remained a high priority among Israeli politicians. It led to a controversy, which continues to the present, over whether "the Jewish lobby" is a disproportionately powerful element in American political life and whether it prompts the American government to act in ways that are more beneficial to Israel than to the United States itself.

Abortion Politics

The 1960s witnessed great social turbulence and a rapid shift in public mores, many of which had religious and political implications. The women's movement, for example, lobbied for the abolition of gender discrimination in employment and raised a variety of questions under the previously unfamiliar category of "sexual politics."

One was the issue of abortion, which has convulsed American religious and political life ever since. The Supreme Court ruled in *Roe v. Wade* (1973) that women could legally obtain abortions in the first trimester of a pregnancy and, with some restrictions, in later stages of pregnancy. The decision overturned laws in all 50 states. It delighted feminists who had been working for revision of restrictive abortion laws, in line with their belief that women should have the right to choose whether or not to give birth. But it horrified those believers who considered an unborn fetus to be a human being and who saw the ruling, in effect, as authorizing the killing of children. Subsequent decisions of the Court, notably *Planned Parenthood v. Casey* (1992), upheld the *Roe* precedent but had the effect of embittering political and judicial life; advocates of each side found it difficult to sympathize with the other.

The first antiabortion activists were Catholics. Some lobbied for legal restrictions or a constitutional amendment; others undertook direct action, picketing abortion clinics and trying to persuade pregnant women to carry their babies to term, offering them and their babies material and psychological support. In the 1980s, the movement became more radical; Randall Terry's Operation Rescue brought large numbers of "pro-life" evangelical Protestants into direct activism side by side with Catholics, a combination that would have been unlikely prior the 1960s. Operation Rescue worked across denominational lines and tried to get large numbers of its members arrested at the Democratic convention of 1988 in Atlanta, packing the jails as a symbolic way of bringing attention to the issue. In the 1990s a trio of the most extreme activists, Michael Griffin, Paul Hill, and Shelley Shannon, assassinated abortion providers in the firm belief that God authorized this drastic step. The effect of their attacks was almost certainly counterproductive, horrifying not only most American citizens but also the majority of religious pro-lifers, who were explicitly dedicated to the sanctity of life.

The New Christian Right and Left

This turn to activism bore witness to an important trend in the 1970s, the return of evangelicals and fundamentalists to active politics. Ever since the Scopes trial of 1925, most fundamentalists (Protestants who thought of the Bible as literally true and accurate, the direct and dependable word of God) had withdrawn from public life. Many of them were dispensational premillennialists, believers that the second coming of Jesus was very close and that it was more important to turn to Jesus individually than to work on transforming society. In the 1970s, dismayed by sexual permissiveness, unfamiliar new roles for women, legal abortion, and what seemed like the breakdown of the family, they began to return to political life, joining Christian lobbies like Jerry Falwell's Moral Majority. Their theorist was the theologian Francis Schaeffer, who urged them to contest what he thought of as the growing power of evil in the world. They were also goaded into action by what was, to them, the disappointing presidency of Jimmy Carter: A born-again evangelical Christian, Carter should have been solidly behind their program but in practice seemed too willing to accept the orthodoxy of the Democratic Party on gender and family questions. He was also an advocate of détente with the Soviet Union, despite its persecution of Russian Christians and Jews.

The New Religious Right drew the lion's share of media attention in the late 1970s and early 1980s, not least because it contributed to the defeat of Carter and the election of an outspoken conservative, Ronald Reagan. It would be quite wrong, however, to imagine that religion was, as a whole, a conservative force in American life. Religious feminists had begun to transform gender roles inside churches and synagogues, while religious anti-Vietnam activists could be found, a few years later, working in poverty programs and in the "sanctuary" movement, helping Nicaraguan and Salvadoran refugees in the Southwest, or working in the environmental movement. Stewardship of God's creation was, in the view of many Christians, a religious imperative.

This way of looking at nature also prompted a renewed assessment of nuclear weapons. They remained in the 1980s, as in the 1950s, the basis of America's defense policy, but a growing religious antinuclear movement considered them utterly incompatible with civilization and common decency. The National Conference of Catholic Bishops wrote a pastoral letter on the issue, "The Challenge of Peace: God's Promise and Our Response" (1983), condemning the targeting of Soviet cities and coming close to opposing any policy that condoned the use of nuclear weapons. Once a dependable bloc of anti-Communists, the bishops were now staking out new territory, openly critical of their government. Many of the Protestant churches wrote comparable letters. One Methodist bishop, John Warman of Harrisburg, Pennsylvania, signed his denomination's letter and told a journalist: "You cannot boil seven million human beings in their own juices and then speak of Christian love. It would be far better for us to trust the God of the Resurrection and suffer death than to use such a weapon."

Other Christians dissented sharply; Michael Novak, a lay Catholic and political conservative, wrote "Moral Clarity in the Nuclear Age" (1983), a book-length answer to the bishops that filled an entire special issue of *National Review*. Invoking the tradition of "just war theory," as had the bishops, he argued that nuclear weapons were actually instruments of peace. Paradoxically, the government *used* them by *not* firing them, merely threatening to do so, and in this way assured the maximum of deterrence with the minimum of destruction.

Religious Celebrities

Everyone can be grateful that the cold war ended without an exchange of nuclear missiles. The Soviet empire in Eastern Europe began to unravel in 1989, the Berlin Wall came down, Germany was reunified, and in 1991 Soviet communism itself came to a peaceful end.

Several individuals who played prominent roles in this world-changing sequence of events became political-religious celebrities in America. One was Lech Walesa, the Gdansk dockyard worker whose Solidarity movement created a new center of legitimacy inside Communist Poland in the 1980s and made him a luminous figure to human rights activists. The Catholic faith had the same kind of function for Solidarity as evangelical Christianity had had in the American civil rights movement, binding members together and empowering them to resist unjust power. A second individual who became prominent in America was Karol Wojtyla, who in 1978 was elevated to the papacy and chose the name Pope John Paul II. Also Polish, and the former archbishop of Krakow, Wojtyla's life and work demonstrated that Christianity, even when persecuted, could outlast communism. His visits to America drew vast crowds of Catholics and non-Catholics alike.

Several other religious figures also played symbolically important roles in movements to resist political oppression. One was the Russian novelist Alexander

Solzhenitsyn, a Russian Orthodox exile in America from 1975, who gave the commencement address at Harvard in 1978; another was the Anglican South African bishop Desmond Tutu, a leading antiapartheid activist. A third was the Dalai Lama, religious leader of the Tibetan community in exile, who embodied Buddhist resistance to the Chinese conquest of Tibet. All were revered in America and helped discredit the regimes against which they campaigned.

The Changing Religious Landscape

By 1990 historians and sociologists were observing seismic shifts in American religious life. First was the steady decline in membership and influence of "mainstream" Protestant churches. Presbyterians, Congregationalists, Episcopalians, and Lutherans, who had once dominated the religious landscape, faced dwindling congregations, whereas the Assemblies of God, Disciples of Christ, Southern Baptists, and independent Christian churches enjoyed rapid increases. These growing congregations, many under the leadership of charismatic evangelical leaders, imposed tough rules on their members, expecting them to tithe (give a tenth of their pretax income to the church) and follow exacting codes of personal conduct. They provided foot soldiers for the Moral Majority and for its successor, the Christian Coalition, and campaigned hard for seats on school boards, city councils, and state assemblies.

A second shift was the increasing politicization of religious life. The sharpest divisions had once been between denominations, but now separation was deepest between the religious left and the religious right, often with representatives of both points of view in the same denomination. Princeton sociologist Robert Wuthnow charted this shift in his influential book *The Restructuring of American Religion* (1988).

Denominational conferences squabbled over theological and doctrinal questions, and over whether to regard scripture as inerrant. The wider public felt the effect of these disputes in renewed attacks on the teaching of Darwinian evolutionary theory. Evangelicals on school boards argued that school science curricula should include "Creation science," an approach to human origins that was consonant with the creation narrative in Genesis. They were aware, however, that the Supreme Court would reject that approach if they made its religious provenance explicit. Proponents therefore claimed that they were indeed advancing a genuine science, rather than a religious point of view in religious dress. The Institute for Creation Research in San Diego backed up this claim. Their antagonists, an alliance of nonfundamentalist Christians, Jews, and academic scientists, countered that creation science was a bogus form of special pleading, and that the evolutionary hypothesis alone could explain the nature of life on Earth. Several southern states passed laws in the 1980s that were hospitable to creationists, only to see them rejected by the courts on First Amendment grounds. Evangelical activists on school boards also tried to stop sex education classes or else convert them into advocacy seminars on sexual abstention.

At the same time, independent Christian schools thrived as places where evangelical teachings on creation and sexuality could be central to the curriculum. In southern states, many of these schools were attractive to white parents who disparaged the effects of public school desegregation.

A more radical alternative was homeschooling. The homeschooling movement had begun among advocates of the 1960s counterculture, who protested the repressive and conformist nature of public education. Ironically, it was overtaken by Christian homeschoolers who thought public education was too secular, undisciplined, ideologically biased against religion, and tended to expose students to excessive peer pressure. Homeschool organizations lobbied successfully for state laws entitling them to educate their children at home so long as they met basic standards of literacy and numeracy.

New Religions

These developments bore witness to the continuing energy and diversity of American religious life. So did the growth of new religions, hundreds of which had sprung up throughout American history. Many lasted only a few years, but a few, like the Mormons, the Jehovah's Witnesses, and the Nation of Islam, struck a resonant chord among citizens and became permanent parts of the religious landscape. The sharp divisions in American national life during the 1960s, 1970s, and 1980s prompted the creation of a new crop of religions, a few of which had political implications. Some put such psychological pressure on their members that anxious relatives sought government prevention or regulation of what they perceived as brainwashing. Other groups demanded the handing over not just of a tenth but of all a member's property. Some sheltered illegal sexual practices.

Two dramatic incidents illustrated these dangers. The first was the fate of the People's Temple, under the leadership of Jim Jones. It began as a Christian Pentecostal church in Indianapolis and was the city's first fully racially integrated congregation. The church moved to rural California in 1964, when Jones became convinced that nuclear war was imminent. Then it became involved in San Francisco politics when Jones's preaching proved effective at reforming drug addicts. Finally, Jones, under investigation for financial and sexual irregularities and convinced that he was the target of government persecution, moved the People's Temple to a settlement that became known as Jonestown, in Guyana, South America. The parents of some members asked a California congressman, Leo Ryan, to investigate the church, and his arrival at Jonestown in November 1978 triggered a horrific finale. A group of Jones's men ambushed and killed Ryan, then the whole community—900 men, women, and children—drank cyanide-poisoned Kool-Aid in a mass suicide ritual, something they had practiced in the foregoing months.

The second incident involved the Branch Davidians, a splinter group from the Seventh-Day Adventists, which was led by charismatic preacher David Koresh. Koresh, like Jones, had sexual relationships with a variety of the group's members. When rumors surfaced in 1993 that his partners included children, the Federal Bureau of Alcohol, Tobacco, and Firearms raided the compound in Waco, Texas. The group fought back, FBI armored cars rolled in, and the two sides exchanged gunfire and tear gas for several days. The entire compound eventually caught fire and burned to the ground, killing 103 people, including at least 17 children. Public reaction was sharply divided; to some citizens drastic action against cults was necessary. Others saw the government's heavy-handedness as disgraceful and disproportionate. This second view gained credibility when it later emerged that Timothy McVeigh—who two years later blew up a federal building in Oklahoma City—had been convinced by the Waco affair that the federal government was at war with ordinary citizens.

Increasing religious diversity included not just new sects and cults but also the arrival in America of larger numbers of non-Judeo-Christian peoples than ever before. The Immigration Reform Act of 1965 abolished racial and geographical discrimination in immigrants' point of origin and opened the way for large-scale immigration from Africa and Asia. America's wealth and political stability, along with First Amendment protection to all religions, made it an extremely desirable destination. Buddhist, Hindu, and Muslim communities grew in many cities, while scholars hurried to study them and to widen the ideal of American inclusiveness. For many of these immigrants from societies where restriction and intolerance were the norm, America was a pleasant surprise. Some American Muslims took the view that the United States was the ideal place in which to practice Islam. The international situation, however, tended to work against this easy accommodation. Surges of anti-Islamic prejudice coincided with such events as the Iranian Revolution and hostage crisis (1978–80), the first Gulf War (1990–91), and the attack on the World Trade Center and Pentagon (2001). After the latter event, politicians, led by President George W. Bush, took the view that the United States would protect all forms of religious practice, Islam included, but would make unceasing war on militarized forms of Islamic fundamentalism.

The Catholic Child Abuse Scandal

Balancing the two imperatives specified in the First Amendment—free exercise and no establishment—has never been easy, as a new scandal made clear at the beginning of the twenty-first century. Journalistic investigations uncovered widespread sexual abuse of children and teenagers by Catholic priests, and evidence showed that it had been going on for a long time. Church authorities had earlier reacted to reports of predatory priests not by turning them over to the law—which would cause scandal and discredit—but by reassigning them to new parishes with a promise of reform. The reform rarely worked, and abuse recurred. The Catholic Church was sued successfully by victims and their families, and it sustained catastrophic losses and was forced to sell assets to cover the cost of judgments against it. The scandal raised the possibility that religious freedom had provided cover for misconduct, and that closer scrutiny would have prevented it, just as closer scrutiny of cults could have prevented the tragedies of Jonestown and Waco. The cost of scrutiny would also be high, however, both financially and in the erosion of civil liberties.

The scandal in the Catholic Church bore witness to the inextricable mixing of religion and politics in American life. As the twenty-first century began, the United States remained the most religiously diverse nation in the world, and the most religiously active among the Western industrial democracies. Its hospitality to religions of all kinds, and the prosperity of these groups, took visible form in the shape of beautiful new churches, synagogues, temples, and mosques. America maintained a high degree of religious freedom, offered tax exemption to all alike, and tried to ensure that all enjoyed free exercise. It was reasonable to anticipate that this state of affairs would persist.

See also Catholics and politics; Jews and politics; Muslims and politics; Protestants and politics.

FURTHER READING

Allitt, Patrick. *Religion in America since 1945: A History*. New York: Columbia University Press, 2003.

Bellah, Robert. "Civil Religion in America." *Daedalus* 96 (Winter 1967), 1–21.

Capps, Walter. *The New Religious Right: Piety, Patriotism, and Politics*. Columbia: University of South Carolina Press, 1990.

Chidester, David. *Salvation and Suicide: An Interpretation of Jim Jones, the People's Temple, and Jonestown*. Bloomington: University of Indiana Press, 1988.

Fox, Richard W. *Reinhold Niebuhr: A Biography*. San Francisco: Harper and Row, 1987.

Frankel, Marvin. *Faith and Freedom: Religious Liberty in America*. New York: Hill and Wang, 1994.

Garrow, David. *Bearing the Cross: Martin Luther King, Jr. and the Southern Christian Leadership Conference*. New York: Vintage, 1988.

Gray, Francine DuPlessix. *Divine Disobedience: Profiles in Catholic Radicalism*. New York: Knopf, 1970.

Marty, Martin. *Modern American Religion, Volume 3: Under God, Indivisible, 1941–1960*. Chicago: University of Chicago Press, 1996.

Risen, James, and Judy Thomas. *Wrath of Angels: The American Abortion War*. New York: Basic Books, 1998.

Silk, Mark. *Spiritual Politics: Religion and America since World War II*. New York: Simon and Schuster, 1988.

Tabor, James. *Why Waco? Cults and the Battle for Religious Freedom in America*. Berkeley: University of California Press, 1995.

Wertheimer, Jack. *A People Divided: Judaism in Contemporary America*. New York: Basic Books, 1993.

Wuthnow, Robert. *The Restructuring of American Religion: Society and Faith since World War II*. Princeton, NJ: Princeton University Press, 1988.

PATRICK ALLITT

Republican Party

During its century and a half as a major political organization, the Republican Party has undergone significant shifts in its ruling ideology and electoral base. Created in 1854 in response to the Kansas-Nebraska Act as a way of opposing the expansion of slavery into the territories, the Republican Party, for the first 50 years of its existence, favored the broad use of national power to promote economic growth. During the early twentieth century, as the issue of government regulation emerged in the national debate, Republicans became identified with opposition to such supervision of the economy. That stance defined the party's position on economic questions for the next six decades.

By the 1960s, the Republicans slipped away from their traditional posture in favor of the rights of African Americans and sought new support from alienated white voters in the previously Democratic South. The party grew more conservative, opposing abortion rights and other manifestations of cultural liberalism. In foreign policy, Republicans have been, by turns, expansionists from 1890 to 1916, isolationists in the 1930s and 1940s, and militant anti-Communists during the cold war. A firm belief that they were the natural ruling party and that the Democrats carried the taint of treason and illegitimacy have been hallmarks of Republican thinking throughout the party's history.

The first phase of Republican history extended from the party's founding through the presidential election of 1896. In 1854 antislavery Northerners, former Whigs, and some dissenting Democrats came together to create a new party that took the name "Republican" from the Jeffersonian tradition. After the Republican presidential candidate, John C. Fremont, lost in 1856, the Republican Party won the White House in 1860 behind Abraham Lincoln, who led the nation through the Civil War. Republican strength was sectional, with its base in the Northeast and the upper Middle West. The Middle Atlantic states were a contested battleground with the Democrats.

To wage that conflict, the Republicans in power enacted sweeping legislation to impose income taxes, distribute public lands, and create a national banking system. Party leaders also pushed for a constitutional amendment to abolish slavery, and the more intense or "radical" Republicans called for political rights for the freedmen whom the war had liberated from bondage.

Lincoln's assassination in 1865 brought to power his vice president, Andrew Johnson, a former Democrat with little sympathy for Republican ideology or the plight of former slaves in the South. The result was a contest between the mainstream of the party for some degree of political rights for African American men and a president who opposed such innovations. Throughout Reconstruction and beyond, the Republicans sought to build an electoral base in the South of black and white voters sympathetic to government support for economic growth. The effort was protracted and sincere; the results were disappointing. By the mid-1870s, the South had become solidly Democratic, with the Republicans a minority party in most of the states below the Mason-Dixon Line.

During Reconstruction, the Republicans did achieve the passage of the Fourteenth and Fifteenth Amendments to the Constitution to provide citizenship and voting rights to former slaves. These significant contributions attested to the party's sincerity on the issue, but the will to extend equality further in the 1880s and 1890s proved lacking. Republicans slowly relinquished their interest in black rights and turned to questions of industrialization and economic expansion at the end of the nineteenth century.

The protective tariff became the hallmark of Republican ideology during this period. Using the taxing power of the government to provide an advantage to domestic products appealed to the entrepreneurial base of the Republicans as well as to labor. The tariff offered a vision of benefits diffused throughout society in a harmonious manner. In the hands of such leaders as James G. Blaine and William McKinley, the doctrine of protection also took on a nationalistic character as a way of achieving self-sufficiency in a competitive world. Charges soon arose that the tariff was nothing more than a rationale for economic selfishness. As businesses grew larger and industrialism took hold in the United States, Republicans were seen as the party of producers and identified with capitalist aspirations. Measures such as the McKinley Tariff of 1890 and the Dingley Tariff of 1897 raised tariff rates. Republicans argued that protection brought prosperity and that Democratic free-trade policies imperiled the nation's economic health.

Throughout the late nineteenth century, Republicans and Democrats battled on even electoral terms. Then, in the 1890s, the Grand Old Party (as it had become known) emerged as the nation's dominant political organization. With the election of Benjamin Harrison in 1888, the Republicans controlled Congress and the presidency. Their activist program in the 51st Congress (1889–90) brought a voter backlash that led to a Democratic victory in the 1892 presidential contest. The onset of the economic downturn in 1893 discredited the Democrats under President Grover Cleveland and gave the Republicans their opportunity. The congressional elections of 1894 produced a Republican sweep in the House of Representatives and opened an era of dominance for the party.

Years of Ascendancy: 1896–1932

The presidential election of 1896, which brought William McKinley to the White House, confirmed the emergence of a national Republican majority. For most of the next four decades, the party held an electoral advantage. Under McKinley, Theodore Roosevelt, and William Howard Taft, the Republicans acquired an overseas empire, broadened government power over the economy, and took a few steps toward limiting the power of corporations. By 1912, however, as Roosevelt and Taft split the party, the Republicans moved rightward and generally opposed the expansion of government regulatory authority.

During the eight years that Woodrow Wilson and the Democrats were in power, from 1913 to 1921, the emphasis on Republican conservatism intensified. The 1916 presidential campaign between Wilson and Charles Evans Hughes anticipated the ideological divisions of the later New Deal on domestic questions. In that contest, the Republican candidate opposed organized labor, federal regulation of child labor, and farm credit legislation. Wilson won reelection largely on the issue of American neutrality in World War I. As the country swung to the right during the war and the Democratic electoral coalition broke up, Republicans made big gains in the 1918 congressional elections. The landslide victory of Warren G. Harding two years later confirmed that Republican dominance of national politics had returned after an eight-year interruption.

The presidencies of Harding, Calvin Coolidge, and Herbert Hoover, from 1921 to 1933, represented a high point of Republican rule. Under Harding and Coolidge, income tax cuts stimulated the economy and helped fuel the expansion of that decade. Government regulation receded, labor unions were weakened, and social justice laws died in Congress. As long as prosperity continued, the Democrats seemed an impotent minority. The Republicans still had no base in the South, despite efforts of the presidents to break that monopoly. Outside of Dixie, Republicans dominated the political scene. In 1928 Hoover won a decisive triumph over Democrat Al Smith, as if to confirm the Republican mastery of national politics.

The onset of the Great Depression of the 1930s undermined the Republican position just as the depression of the 1890s had the Democrats. President Hoover's failure to provide real relief for the unemployed during the hard times of 1931–33 doomed his reelection chances. The Democrats selected Franklin D. Roosevelt as their presidential candidate in 1932, and his promise of a New Deal produced a landslide victory for his party. The Republicans were then to experience 20 years without presidential power.

Against the New Deal Coalition: 1932–68

During the 1930s and 1940s, the Grand Old Party struggled to find an answer to Roosevelt and the Democrats. In the three elections in which they faced the incumbent president (1936, 1940, and 1944), the Republicans sought to moderate their conservatism and appeal to the broad middle of national politics. They continued this strategy in 1948 when Thomas E. Dewey ran against Harry S. Truman. Each time they lost.

In Congress and in the nation at large, the Republicans were more explicit about their conservatism. They opposed the social programs and deficit spending of the Roosevelt and Truman administrations. On issues of foreign policy, the party was isolationist during the 1930s and anti-Communist in the 1940s and 1950s. Believing that the Democrats had a predisposition to help the nation's enemies, the Republicans readily assumed that Roosevelt and Truman were soft on the Communist "menace." The leading symbol of this point of view became Senator Joseph R. McCarthy of Wisconsin, whose crusades against Communists in government delighted many Republicans between 1950 and 1954. Republicans of this stripe hoped that Senator Robert A. Taft of Ohio (known as "Mr. Republican") would be the Republican nominee in 1952 and oust the Democrats after what McCarthy called "20 years of treason."

In 1952 the Republicans, after a bitter convention, nominated Dwight D. Eisenhower, a military hero whose election was more certain than Taft's would have been. Finally regaining power after 20 years, the Republicans found their 8 years in power with Eisenhower rewarding at first but frustrating in the long run. The president governed to the right of center but did not embark on crusades to roll back the programs of the New Deal. He called his point of view "modern Republicanism." Eisenhower's popularity brought his reelection in 1956, but, by then, Republicans were a minority in Congress again. As the 1960 election approached, Vice President Richard M. Nixon sought to extend the Eisenhower legacy while party conservatives went along grudgingly.

After Nixon's narrow defeat by John F. Kennedy, conservative Republicans sought to recapture control of the party through the presidential candidacy of Senator Barry M. Goldwater of Arizona. In 1964, Goldwater defeated the moderate alternative, Governor Nelson A. Rockefeller of New York, and his forces controlled the national convention in San Francisco. Goldwater's candidacy was an electoral disaster. He carried only his home state and five states in the South, as Lyndon B. Johnson secured a landslide victory.

In terms of Republican history, however, Goldwater's candidacy proved a sign of things to come. Although a majority of Republicans in the House of Representatives and the Senate helped to pass the Civil Rights Act of 1964, the party appealed to white Southerners as an alternative to the more liberal and racially integrated national Democrats. The movement of southern Democrats into Republican ranks accelerated in the three decades after 1964. In another electoral portent, an actor turned politician named Ronald Reagan gave a very successful fundraising speech at the end of the Goldwater campaign. Soon Reagan would enter national politics himself.

After the disaster of 1964, the Republicans regrouped. Soon the Democrats under Lyndon Johnson became bogged down in an unpopular war in Vietnam. Racial tensions mounted within the United States, and a reaction against the party in power ensued. Republicans made gains in Congress during the 1968 elections, and Nixon again emerged as the leading Republican candidate for the White House. He united the party behind his candidacy and gained the nomination despite a last-minute challenge from Ronald Reagan. Nixon went on to win the presidency in a narrow victory over Democrat Hubert Humphrey and independent Alabama governor George Wallace.

Conservative Dominance: 1968–2004

Nixon's presidency proved a troubled episode for the Grand Old Party. At first, he seemed to have found the way to marginalize the Democrats. The strategy of winding down the war in Vietnam proved popular, and Republicans capitalized on divisions in the opposition party to achieve a landslide triumph of their own in the 1972 presidential election. Nixon crushed the Democratic candidate, George McGovern.

The triumph was not to last. The Watergate scandal, covered up during the election, burst into full view in 1973 and led to Nixon's resignation in August 1974 in advance of impeachment and removal. Nixon's legacy to the party was mixed. He had strengthened its southern base, but his moderate social policies and foreign policy opening to China put off many conservatives. That wing of the party looked to Reagan as its champion. Nixon's successor, Gerald R. Ford, won the presidential nomination in 1976 over Reagan, but then lost the election to Democrat Jimmy Carter in the fall. Reagan was the party's nominee in 1980.

Reagan beat the weakened Carter in that election, and the Republicans also regained control of the Senate. During the eight years that followed, Reagan became a Republican icon for his policies of lowering taxes, advocating an antimissile defense system, and bringing down the Soviet Union. The reality was more complex, since Reagan also raised taxes, the missile system did not work, and the fall of the Soviet Union that came after he left office was not his achievement alone. Yet, because of his landslide reelection victory in 1984, Reagan remained the electoral standard by which future Republicans were measured.

Reagan's successor, George H. W. Bush, had a rocky single term. Having pledged during the 1988 campaign not to raise taxes, Bush never recovered when he reached a budget deal in 1990 that imposed new taxes. He lost to Democrat Bill Clinton in the 1992 presidential contest. Clinton's first two years were difficult, and the Republicans made big gains in the 1994 elections. They took back the Senate, and under the leadership of Newton "Newt" Gingrich, they recaptured the House for the first time in 40 years, with a "Contract for America" as their program. Gingrich proved to be better at campaigning than governing; yet the Republicans, now dominant in the South, retained their congressional majority for 12 years. In 1998 the majority party in Congress impeached President Clinton for lying under oath and other alleged crimes, but the Senate acquitted him.

The 2000 election brought Governor George W. Bush of Texas, son of George H. W. Bush, to the White House. Although he lost the popular vote, Bush won a disputed election in the Electoral College. The terrorist attacks of September 11, 2001, and Bush's initial response to them lifted the new president to high poll ratings. Republicans gained in the 2002 elections and, for the next four years, controlled all branches of the federal government. Bush won reelection in 2004, defeating Democrat John Kerry.

Yet in that period, the Grand Old Party experienced striking changes. The party of small government expanded the size of the federal establishment to unprecedented levels. The champions of lower spending brought government expenditures to record heights. Proud of their record as administrators, the Republicans under Bush mismanaged wars in Iraq and Afghanistan, permeated the federal government with partisan cronies, and produced record budget deficits. Bush's poll rating sank, and his unpopularity spilled over to other members of his party.

Social conservatives wanted a government that regulated private behavior; pro-business conservatives hoped for a government that would keep taxes low and diminish regulations. Disputes over immigration and control of the borders further divided the GOP. By the end of the first decade of the twenty-first century, it was unclear what constituted the ideology of the Republican Party. After a century and a half in American politics, the Republicans faced a crisis over their identity that would shape how they performed during the century to come.

FURTHER READING

Brennan, Mary. *Turning Right in the Sixties: The Conservative Capture of the GOP.* Chapel Hill: University of North Carolina Press, 1995.

Calhoun, Charles W. *Conceiving a New Republic: The Republican Party and the South, 1869–1900.* Lawrence: University Press of Kansas, 2006.

Gienapp, William E. *The Origins of the Republican Party, 1852–1856.* New York: Oxford University Press, 1987.

Gould, Lewis L. *Grand Old Party: A History of the Republicans.* New York: Random House, 2003.

Pollack, Sheldon. *Refinancing America: The Republican Antitax Agenda.* Albany: State University of New York Press, 2003.

Rees, Matthew. *From the Deck to the Sea: Blacks and the Republican Party.* Wakefield, MA: Longwood Academic, 1991.

Reinhard, David W. *The Republican Right since 1945.* Lexington: University Press of Kentucky, 1983.

Weed, Clyde. *The Republican Party during the New Deal.* New York: Columbia University Press, 1994.
Zak, Michael. *Back to Basics for the Republican Party.* Chicago: Thiessen, 2001.

LEWIS L. GOULD

Republican Party to 1896

The Republican Party emerged in the 1850s and soon became one of the nation's two major parties. It began as a coalition of elements set loose by the collapse of America's Second Party System. In the previous two decades, the Whigs and the Democrats had divided principally over such economic issues as the tariff, the Bank of the United States, and internal improvements. But as the question of territorial expansion grew more salient, the vexatious issue of slavery, especially the extension of the institution westward, made it difficult for leaders of both those parties to keep their organizations united across sectional lines. The Whigs' staggering loss in the 1852 election dealt a devastating blow to that party, whose constituent elements—anti-Catholic and anti-immigrant nativists, temperance advocates, and antislavery Northerners—concluded that the party had become an ineffectual vehicle to achieve their ends.

The climactic crisis for the Second Party System came with the controversy over the Kansas-Nebraska Act of 1854, which repealed the Missouri Compromise ban on slavery in most of the Louisiana Purchase territory. Conflict between northern and southern Whigs over this law completed the destruction of their party as a significant national entity, although a remnant limped along for the next few years. Though sponsored by Illinois Democrat Stephen Douglas and endorsed by the Democratic administration of Franklin Pierce, the Kansas-Nebraska Act tore a gash through the Democratic Party, whose unity its northern and southern leaders had maintained for many years only with great difficulty. The Nebraska issue dominated the congressional elections of 1854. In states across the North, the Democrats confronted an array of variously configured coalitions that included old Free Soilers, anti-Nebraska Democrats, antislavery Whigs, temperance supporters, and nativists. These anti-Democratic "parties" fought under various names: Anti-Nebraska, Fusion, Opposition, and People's Party. In only two states, Michigan and Wisconsin, did they take the name *Republican.* Whatever the label, the new coalitions achieved phenomenal success, winning a plurality of seats in the new House of Representatives.

As time passed, more of these northern state coalitions adopted Republican as a fitting name to cast the party as a relentless opponent of corruption and tyranny and a defender of liberty and civic virtue. In 1854, however, the Republican Party did not emerge either full blown or as the sole alternative to the Democrats. Some Whigs still harbored hope for a reversal of their party's ill fortunes, but more problematic for the new Republican strategists was the anti-Catholic and nativist Know-Nothing movement, which claimed to have elected 20 percent of new House members from districts scattered throughout the country, especially in New England. Know-Nothingism proved attractive not only to Americans who resented the presence of immigrants and "papists" and their supposed subservience to the Democratic Party but also to those who saw nativist issues as a way to deflect attention from the potentially Union-rending slavery question. The task of those who strove to make the Republicans the principal anti-Democratic party was to fashion an approach to public questions that would co-opt the Know-Nothings while preserving the allegiance of the various northern antislavery elements that had made up the fusion movement of 1854.

In 1856 the nativists fielded a presidential candidate, former president Millard Fillmore, under the American Party banner and garnered 22 percent of the popular vote and 8 electoral votes from Maryland. The Republicans, now campaigning generally under that name, nominated John C. Frémont and put forth a combative platform focused on opposition to slavery expansion, and particularly condemning the outrages committed by proslavery forces in the battle for control of Kansas Territory. Frémont posted a remarkable showing for the party's first run for the White House. Running only in the North, he won 33 percent of the national popular vote and 114 electoral votes to Democrat James Buchanan's 45 percent of the popular vote and 174 electoral votes. In the free states, significantly, Frémont outpolled Fillmore by more than three to one. Had Frémont won Pennsylvania plus either Indiana or Illinois, he would have been the first Republican president. Republican leaders recognized that future success depended on converting or reassuring enough nativists and conservatives on the slavery question to win these key northern states.

Events in 1856 and the ensuing years moved the slavery question to center stage in the struggle against the Democrats. These included not only the Kansas turmoil but also the vicious caning of Massachusetts Republican senator Charles Sumner by a South Carolina congressman, the Supreme Court's *Dred Scott* decision declaring unconstitutional the Missouri Compromise ban on slavery in a territory, and calls by southern leaders for a reopening of the African slave trade and for a federal code sustaining slavery in the territories. Although these developments served to underscore Republicans' warnings of the threats posed by an aggressive "slave power," the new party designed its campaign strategy in 1860 not only to retain the support of men who gave priority to that issue but also to attract as broad an array of voters in the North as possible.

The party's platform in 1860 took a balanced approach on slavery, denouncing the *Dred Scott* decision and denying the power of Congress or a legislature to legalize slavery in any territory, but also upholding the individual states' right to decide the slavery question for themselves, and condemning John Brown's attempt to spark a slave revolt at Harpers Ferry. Aiming to appeal to men on the make, the party endorsed an economic package that included a protective tariff, internal improvements, and a homestead law. In an effort to woo German Americans, who formed a critical bloc in key states, the Republicans eschewed nativism and called for the protection of the rights of immigrants and naturalized citizens. Most important, in choosing their presidential nominee, they turned aside candidates such as William Seward and Salmon Chase, deemed too radical on slavery, and selected the newcomer Abraham Lincoln, whose record on the issue appeared more conservative. Hopelessly riven, the northern and southern Democrats chose separate nominees, Stephen A. Douglas and John C. Breckinridge, while a nativist remnant and other conservatives offered a fourth ticket headed by John Bell. In the popular vote, Lincoln led with only 39.6 percent of the vote. In the Electoral College he swept the entire free-state section except for New Jersey, which he split with Douglas, who came in last behind Breckinridge and Bell.

Civil War and Reconstruction

Despite Lincoln's victory, his party still stood on shaky ground. It failed to win a majority in either house of Congress, and only the departure of Southerners after their states had seceded enabled Republicans to assume control. They proceeded to pass most of their legislative agenda, but in the face of prolonged bad news from the military front during the Civil War, the Democrats remained alive and well and actually gained House seats in the 1862 midterm elections. Lincoln also confronted severe critics in his own party, and, in the summer of 1864, he doubted he could win reelection. At their convention, the Republicans even changed their name to the National Union Party to attract pro-war Democrats. At last, Union battlefield successes muffled the carping, and Lincoln defeated Democrat George McClellan.

That the Republicans' first president was a man of Lincoln's greatness, who guided the nation safely through its darkest hour, contributed mightily to establishing the party as a permanent fixture on the American political landscape. Ever after, Republicans could rightly claim the mantle of saviors of the Union and liberators of the slaves. In the wake of Lincoln's death, however, reconstructing the Union proved enormously difficult. In 1864 the party had put a Tennessee War Democrat, Andrew Johnson, on the ticket, and, when he succeeded to the presidency, he broke with Congress and the Republicans and did all in his power to block their efforts to remodel the South. After a titanic struggle, Republicans added the Fourteenth and the Fifteenth Amendment to the Constitution to uphold blacks' civil rights and the right of black men to vote. To reorder the southern political landscape, Republicans encouraged the creation of a new wing of the party in the South comprising blacks, southern white Unionists, and Northerners who had moved south. Against this tenuous coalition, conservative white Democrats posed a fierce, sometimes violent, opposition. Although congressional Republicans passed enforcement legislation and Johnson's Republican successor, Ulysses S. Grant, occasionally intervened militarily, state after state in the South fell under Democratic control.

In the North, moreover, the Republicans suffered divisions, especially spurred by so-called Liberal Republicans who opposed Grant's southern policy, his acceptance of probusiness policies such as the protective tariff, and his handling of the touchy subject of federal appointments. In 1872 Grant easily defeated liberal Republican (and Democratic) nominee Horace Greeley, but, during his second term, a series of scandals tainted his administration and hurt his party. Economic collapse after the panic of 1873 compounded the Republicans' woes. In 1874, the Democrats took the House of Representatives for the first time since before the war. Only after a prolonged and bitter controversy following the indeterminate outcome of the 1876 election was Republican Rutherford B. Hayes able to win the presidency.

Political Equilibrium

During Hayes's term, the Democrats secured control of the last southern states formerly held by Republicans, and the nation entered a prolonged period of equilibrium between the two major parties. From the mid-1870s to the mid-1890s, the Republicans and Democrats were nearly equal in strength nationwide. The Democrats had a firm grip on the Solid South, while Republicans enjoyed support nearly as solid in New England and the upper Midwest. But neither of these blocs held enough electoral votes to win the presidency, and each election in this period turned on the outcome in a few key swing states, most notably New York and Indiana. Moreover, the national government was nearly always divided in this era. The Democrats usually controlled the House, and the Republicans usually controlled the Senate. Rarely did one party hold both houses and the presidency. These circumstances obviously made governing difficult.

Although close elections underscored the need for party unity, Republicans nonetheless continued to suffer divisions. Most Liberal Republicans returned to the party fold, but as independents, later dubbed "mugwumps" (after an Indian word for leader), they continued to push for civil service reform and chastised party leaders whose probity they suspected. In several states the party was rent by factions, often based on loyalty to particular party leaders. This factionalism reached a head in the convention of 1880, where "stalwarts" hoping to restore Grant to the presidency battled against the adherents of former House speaker James G. Blaine, labeled "half-breeds" by their enemies for their alleged lukewarm commitment to the party's older ideals. The delegates eventually turned to a dark horse, James A. Garfield, a half-breed, and nominated for vice president a stalwart, Chester A. Arthur, who succeeded to the White House after Garfield's assassination.

In presidential election campaigns during this period, Republicans faced a strategic dilemma. Some insisted they should work to mobilize a united North, including the swing states, by emphasizing the righteousness of the party's position on black rights and by denouncing political oppression in the South—a tactic their opponents and many later historians disparaged as "waving the bloody shirt." Other party leaders argued that the party should strive to break its dependence on winning New York and other doubtful northern states by trying to detach states from the Democratic Solid South, primarily through economic appeals and the promise of prosperity for a new South.

In 1884 presidential nominee James G. Blaine took the latter course, pursuing a conciliatory campaign toward the South and emphasizing the benefits of Republican economic policies, especially the protective tariff, to the southern states and the nation at large. This strategy dovetailed with the party's increasing solicitude for the nation's industries and for workers threatened by foreign competition. Blaine lost every former slave state, and with his narrow defeat in New York, he lost the presidency to Democrat Grover Cleveland. But Blaine received 49 percent of the vote in Virginia and 48 percent in Tennessee. Had he carried those two states, he would have secured a victory without any of the northern doubtful states, including New York.

Republicans had won every presidential election from 1860 to 1884, and in 1888 they faced the unaccustomed prospect of campaigning against a sitting president. GOP leaders could not, as in the past, turn to federal employees as a ready contingent of campaign workers and contributors, but they could tap a large corps of party cadres eager to regain what they had lost. In addition to the regular party organization of national, state, and local committees, they created a structure of thousands of Republican clubs around the country ready to do battle.

In 1888 Republican nominee Benjamin Harrison, like Blaine, emphasized the tariff issue, though not entirely omitting civil rights questions. He defeated Cleveland. Like Blaine, Harrison carried none of the former slave states but ran well in the upper South. In the congressional elections the Republicans won enough House seats from the upper South to take control of the new Congress. Thus, for the first time since the Grant years, the GOP held both the presidency and the two houses. In one of the most activist Congresses of the nineteenth century, the party passed a host of new laws, including the McKinley Tariff, the Sherman Anti-Trust Act, the Sherman Silver Purchase Act, the Meat Inspection Act, and the Forest Reserve Act, and it came close to enacting strict new protections for black voting in the South. In addition, legislatures in key Republican states passed "cultural" regulations such as temperance laws and restrictions on the use of foreign languages in private schools. Despite these accomplishments, all the activism alarmed an essentially conservative electorate still enamored of Jeffersonian ideals of limited government. Voters turned against the Republicans overwhelmingly in the 1890 midterm congressional elections and in 1892 put Cleveland back in the White House joined by a Democratic Congress.

The New Majority Party

Soon after Cleveland took office, the panic of 1893 struck, and the economy spiraled downward into the deepest depression of the century. The GOP blamed the Democrats, and Cleveland's bungling of tariff and currency legislation underscored the Republicans' charge that the Democrats' negative approach to governing failed to meet the needs of a modernizing economy. In the 1894 congressional elections, Republicans crushed their opponents in the largest shift in congressional strength in history. Two years later Republican presidential nominee William McKinley campaigned as the "advance agent of prosperity," emphasizing the tariff issue and condemning Democrat William Jennings Bryan as a dangerous radical whose support for the free coinage of silver threatened to destroy the economy. McKinley won in a landslide, and, with a Republican Congress, he proceeded to enact a new protective tariff and other probusiness measures. McKinley was a popular chief executive. During his term, the economy rebounded, largely for reasons unrelated to government policy. But the Republicans took credit for prosperity and positioned themselves as the nation's majority party for more than three decades.

McKinley was the last Civil War veteran to serve in the White House. His victory in 1896 marked the culmination of the party's drift away from sectional issues as the key to building a constituency. After the Democrats secured their grip on the South in the late 1870s, some Republicans touted issues such as nativism and temperance to build a following in the North on the basis of cultural values. But Blaine, Harrison, and McKinley recognized the futility of this sort of exclusionary politics. Instead they emphasized economic matters such as tariff protectionism tempered by trade reciprocity, plus a stable currency, to fashion a broad-based coalition of manufacturers, laborers, farmers, and others who put economic well-being at the center of their political concerns. As a result, the Republicans held the upper hand in American politics until the Great Depression demonstrated the inadequacy of their economic formula.

See also American (Know-Nothing) Party; Democratic Party; Free Soil Party; nativism; slavery; Whig Party.

FURTHER READING

Calhoun, Charles W. *Conceiving a New Republic: The Republican Party and the Southern Question, 1869–1900*. Lawrence: University Press of Kansas, 2006.

———. *Minority Victory: Gilded Age Politics and the Front Porch Campaign of 1888*. Lawrence: University Press of Kansas, 2008.

Engs, Robert F., and Randall M. Miller, eds. *The Birth of the Grand Old Party: The Republicans' First Generation*. Philadelphia: University of Pennsylvania Press, 2002.

Foner, Eric. *Free Soil, Free Labor, Free Men: The Ideology of the Republican Party before the Civil War*. New York: Oxford University Press, 1970.

———. *Reconstruction: America's Unfinished Revolution, 1863–1877*. New York: Harper and Row, 1988.

Gienapp, William E. *The Origins of the Republican Party, 1852–1856*. New York: Oxford University Press, 1987.

Gould, Lewis L. *Grand Old Party: A History of the Republicans*. New York: Random House, 2003.

Holt, Michael F. *The Political Crisis of the 1850s*. New York: Norton, 1978.

Morgan, H. Wayne. *From Hayes to McKinley: National Party Politics, 1877–1896*. Syracuse, NY: Syracuse University Press, 1969.

Richardson, Heather Cox. *The Greatest Nation of the Earth: Republican Economic Policies during the Civil War*. Cambridge, MA: Harvard University Press, 1997.

Williams, R. Hal. *Years of Decision: American Politics in the 1890s*. Prospect Heights, IL.: Waveland Press, 1993.

CHARLES W. CALHOUN

Republican Party, 1896–1932

In the history of the Republican Party, the years between the election of William McKinley in 1896 and the defeat of Herbert Hoover in 1932 stand as a period of electoral dominance. To be sure, Woodrow Wilson and the Democrats interrupted this period with eight years of power from 1913 to 1921. That shift occurred in large measure because the Republicans themselves split, first between Theodore Roosevelt and William Howard Taft in 1912 and then, to a lesser extent, over World War I in 1916. For all these 36 years, however, the electoral alignment that had been established during the mid-1890s endured. The Republican majority that emerged during the second term of President Grover Cleveland and the Panic of 1893 lasted until another economic depression turned Hoover and the Republicans out of office.

The coalition that supported the Republicans during this period rested on capitalists, predominantly in the Northeast and Midwest; Union veterans; skilled workers; and prosperous, specialized farmers who identified with the tariff policies of the party. German Americans also comprised a key ethnic voting bloc for the Republicans. African American voters in the North, although still a small contingent, regularly endorsed Republican candidates. In those states that were more industrialized, the Republicans tended to be stronger and their majorities more enduring. Outside of the Democratic South, Republicans enjoyed wide backing from all segments of society.

The Republican triumph during the 1890s rested first on voter alienation from the Democrats. Cleveland and his party had not been able to bring relief and recovery from the economic downturn that began during the spring of 1893. The resulting social unrest that flared in 1894 contributed to the perception that the Democrats lacked the capacity to govern. These causes helped the Republicans sweep to victory in the congressional elections of 1894, when the largest transfer of seats from one party to another in U.S. history took place. The Republicans gained 113 seats in the U.S. House of Representatives and the Democrats suffered serious losses in the Northeast and Midwest, a growing bastion of Republican strength. The third party, the Populists, failed to make much headway with their appeal to farmers in the South and West.

The Republican Appeal

The Republican appeal rested on more than just criticism of the Democrats. The main ideological position of the party was support for the protective tariff. Republicans believed that raising duties on foreign imports encouraged the growth of native industries, provided a high wage level for American workers, and spread economic benefits throughout society. The Grand Old Party also associated prosperity with the benefits of protection. According to Republicans, the Democratic Party, with its free-trade policies, was a menace to the economic health of the country. By 1896 William McKinley of Ohio was the politician most identified with protection as a Republican watchword.

As the 1896 election approached, McKinley emerged as the front-runner for the nomination. With his record in the House of Representatives and his two terms as governor of Ohio, McKinley was the most popular Republican of the time. His campaign manager, Marcus A. Hanna, an Ohio steel magnate, rounded up delegates for his candidate and easily fought off challenges from other aspirants. McKinley was nominated on the first ballot at the national convention. He then defeated the Democratic nominee, William Jennings Bryan, in the most decisive presidential election victory in a quarter of a century.

Republican fortunes improved during the McKinley administration. The Dingley Tariff Law (1897) raised customs duties and became associated with the prosperity that returned at the end of the 1890s. The success in the war with Spain in 1898 brought the United States an overseas empire. These accomplishments identified the Republicans with national power and world influence. In the 1898 elections, the Grand Old Party limited Democratic gains. McKinley then defeated Bryan in a 1900 rematch with a larger total in the electoral vote and in the popular count. By the start of the twentieth century, the electoral dominance of the Republicans seemed assured. As his second term began, McKinley pursued a strategy of gradual tariff reduction through a series of reciprocity treaties with several of the nation's trading partners. In that way, the president hoped to defuse emerging protests about high customs duties.

The Age of Theodore Roosevelt

The assassination of McKinley in September 1901 brought Theodore Roosevelt to the White House. In his first term, Roosevelt put aside McKinley's tariff reciprocity initiative in the face of Republican opposition. Instead, he assailed large corporations (known as "trusts"), settled labor disputes, and promised the voters a "square deal" as president. In 1904 the Democrats ran a more conservative candidate, Alton B. Parker, as a contrast to Roosevelt's flamboyance. The strategy failed, and Roosevelt won by a large electoral and popular vote landslide. Elected in his own right, the young president wanted to address issues of government regulation that an industrial society now faced. While his party enjoyed big majorities in both houses of Congress, these Republican members were less enthusiastic about government activism and regulation than Theodore Roosevelt.

During his second term, Roosevelt persuaded Congress to adopt the Hepburn Act to regulate the railroads, the Pure Food and Drug Act to safeguard the public, and inspection legislation to address the problem of diseased and tainted meat. He pursued conservation of natural resources and legislation to protect workers and their families from the hazards of an industrial society. These measures bothered Republicans who were now doubtful that government should be overseeing the business community as Roosevelt desired. When the issue of regulation arose, conservative Republicans believed that the government's role should be minimal. By the time Roosevelt left office in March 1909, serious divisions existed within his party over the issue of government power.

To succeed him, Roosevelt selected his secretary of war, William Howard Taft, as the strongest Republican in the 1908 election. Taft defeated William Jennings Bryan in a race where ticket-splitting helped Democrats put in office a number of state governors. The Republicans still enjoyed substantial majorities in Congress, but there was restiveness among the voters over the party's congressional leaders, Speaker Joseph G. Cannon of Illinois and Senator Nelson W. Aldrich of Rhode Island. At the same time, the transition from Roosevelt to Taft was unpleasant. Surface harmony hid tensions between the two men over Taft's cabinet choices and the future direction of the party.

In their 1908 platform, the Republicans had pledged to revise the tariff. Taft sought to fulfill that promise during the spring of 1909. Long-simmering disagreements over the tariff broke into public view when the Payne Bill, named after the chair of the Ways and Means Committee, Sereno E. Payne, reached the Senate. The House had made reductions in duties. Senator Aldrich, who lacked a secure majority, made concessions to other senators that drove rates up again. Midwestern senators, known as insurgents, rebelled and fought the changes. In the ensuing conference committee, Taft secured some reductions in the rates of what became known as the Payne-Aldrich Tariff Law. Hard feelings lingered within the party about the result.

During Taft's first year in office, while Roosevelt was on a hunting trip in Africa, controversy erupted between his friend Chief Forester Gifford Pinchot and Secretary of the Interior Richard A. Ballinger over conservation policy. The ouster of Pinchot accelerated Roosevelt's feeling that he had made a mistake in selecting Taft. When he returned from his journey, Roosevelt plunged into Republican politics with a philosophy of "new nationalism," which called for more presidential power and government regulation of the economy. Roosevelt's tactics contributed to the Republican disunity that marked 1910. The Democrats regained control of the House in that fall's elections and the GOP lost ground as well in the Senate. Taft's prospects for 1912 seemed bleak.

The Crisis of 1912

By the eve of 1912, relations between Taft and Roosevelt had deteriorated to the point where the former president was on the verge of challenging the incumbent. Brushing aside the candidacy of Robert M. La Follette of Wisconsin, Roosevelt entered the race in February 1912. A bitter battle for delegates ensued during the spring, which led to a series of primary elections, most of which Roosevelt won. Taft controlled the party machinery and came to the national convention with a narrow but sufficient lead in delegates. After Taft men used their power to renominate the president, Roosevelt decided to form his own party. The Republican division had now become open warfare.

Roosevelt bested Taft in the fall election with his new Progressive Party. However, the Democrats, behind the candidacy of Woodrow Wilson, won the White House as well as majorities in both houses of Congress. The success of Wilson in enacting the New Freedom Program of lower tariffs, banking reform, and antitrust legislation showed that the Democrats could govern. Still, the Republicans looked to the 1914 elections as a test of whether the country was returning to its usual political allegiances. The outbreak of World War I in August 1914 changed the political landscape. The Democrats urged voters to rally behind Wilson. Nonetheless, Republicans regained seats in the House while Democrats added seats in the Senate. Prospects for Wilson's reelection in 1916 seemed doubtful, but the Republicans had to find a winning presidential candidate.

The impact of World War I clouded Republican chances as the 1916 election approached. Some eastern party members wanted a more assertive policy against Germany's submarine warfare toward neutral nations. If that meant war, they supported it as a way of helping Great Britain and France. In the Midwest, where German Americans formed a large voting bloc among Republicans, sentiment for war lessened. The party had to find a way to oppose Wilson's neutrality strategy without alienating voters who wanted to stay out of war. Theodore Roosevelt, now edging back toward the GOP, was the leading exponent of pro-war views. Nominating him seemed unwise to party elders.

Their alternative was Charles Evans Hughes, a former governor of New York who was chief justice on the Supreme Court. Hughes had not been involved in the elections of 1912 and was seen as a fresh face who could win.

The Republicans nominated him, only to learn that the jurist lacked charisma and campaign skills. Hughes never found a winning appeal against Wilson and the Democrats, who proclaimed that the president "kept us out of war." The election was close, but after days of counting the returns, Wilson eked out a narrow victory.

When Wilson later took the United States into World War I, the coalition that brought him victory in 1916 broke up. The Republicans capitalized on popular discontent with higher taxes, a growing government bureaucracy, and inefficiency in the war effort. Wilson's call for the election of a Democratic Congress to sustain him in October 1918 outraged the GOP. Even with victory in sight in Europe, voters ended Democratic control of both houses of Congress. Republican electoral supremacy, outside of the South, had reasserted itself.

The Harding Years

Republicans, under the direction of Senate leader Henry Cabot Lodge, then blocked Wilson's campaign to approve the Treaty of Versailles, which would have taken the United States into the League of Nations. By early 1920, it was evident that the Republicans were likely to win the presidency, and a crowded field of candidates emerged to compete for the prize. Few took seriously the chances of Warren G. Harding, a one-term Republican senator from Ohio. After three intellectually formidable candidates in Roosevelt, Taft, and Hughes, the party was ready for a less threatening nominee. The affable Harding was the second choice of many delegates at the national convention. Despite the legend that he was designated in a "smoke-filled" room by Senate leaders, Harding won the nomination because of his good looks, availability, and adherence to party orthodoxy; the delegates chose Calvin Coolidge of Massachusetts as his running mate. The election of 1920 was no contest. Harding swamped the Democratic nominee, James Cox, also of Ohio, with nearly 61 percent of the vote. Only the South stayed in the Democratic column.

Harding's brief presidency was undistinguished, though not as bad as historical legend has it. Two high points were the adoption of a federal budget for the first time and the Washington Naval Conference of 1922 to reduce armaments. By 1923, however, the administration faced a looming scandal over money exchanged for leases to oil lands in California and Wyoming that became known as Teapot Dome. Worn out by the exertions of his office and suffering from a serious heart condition, Harding died while on a tour of the country in August 1923.

Calvin Coolidge pursued pro-business policies with a greater fervor than Harding. The new president gained from the disarray of the Democrats, who were split on cultural issues such as Prohibition and the Ku Klux Klan. Coolidge easily won nomination in his own right. In the 1924 election, he routed the Democrats and brushed aside the third-party candidacy of Robert M. La Follette. The Republicans seemed to have regained the position of electoral dominance they had enjoyed at the turn of the century. With the economic boom of the 1920s roaring along, their ascendancy seemed permanent.

After Coolidge chose not to run for another term, the Republicans turned to his secretary of commerce, Herbert Hoover, in 1928. In a campaign based on the cultural and religious divide within the country, Hoover bested the Democratic Party nominee, Alfred E. Smith of New York. Smith's Catholicism helped Hoover carry several states in the South. Prosperity was also an essential ingredient in Hoover's triumph.

The End of Republican Dominance

Within a year of his election, the economic environment soured. The stock market crash of 1929 and the depression that ensued over the next three years tested the resilience of the Republican coalition. When Hoover proved incapable of providing relief for the unemployed, his assurances of an imminent return of prosperity seemed hollow. The Republicans lost seats in the congressional elections of 1930. Soon it was evident that the nation had lost faith in Hoover, too. The defeat he suffered at the hands of Franklin D. Roosevelt in 1932 was an electoral landslide. Democrats now dominated both houses of Congress as well.

Beneath the wreckage, Republicans retained the allegiance of some 40 percent of the voters. However, they had failed to address the economic inequities of the nation during the 1920s or to propose effective solutions to the plight of farmers, industrial workers, and the disadvantaged. They had the power to do so but chose instead not to offend the business interests at the heart of their party. For these lapses, they would spend two decades out of the White House and a decade and a half out of control of Congress.

Until the 1930s, the Republicans held the allegiance of African American voters, both North and South. The Grand Old Party continued its rhetorical devotion to black rights against the racist policies of the Democrats, but it did little to advance the interests of African

Americans. Under Taft, Harding, and Hoover, some Republicans proposed abandoning blacks and appealing to white southern Democrats. By 1932 sufficient disillusion existed among African Americans about Republicans that an opening for the Democrats existed if that party changed its segregationist stance.

From the heady days of the late 1890s, when Republicanism seemed the wave of the nation's political future, through the challenges of the Roosevelt-Taft years, the Republican Party had at least engaged some of the major issues and concerns of the time. After eight years of Wilson, however, the conservatism of the GOP lost its creative edge and became a defense of the status quo. As a result, the party encountered a well-deserved rebuke during the depths of the Great Depression in 1932.

See also Democratic Party, 1896–1932; Gilded Age, 1870s–90s; Progressive parties; progressivism and the Progressive Era, 1890s–1920.

FURTHER READING

Blum, John Morton. *The Republican Roosevelt*. Cambridge, MA: Harvard University Press, 1954.

Ferrell, Robert H. *The Presidency of Calvin Coolidge*. Lawrence: University Press of Kansas, 1998.

Gould, Lewis L. *Four Hats in the Ring: The Election of 1912 and the Birth of Modern American Politics*. Lawrence: University Press of Kansas, 2008.

———. *Grand Old Party: A History of the Republicans*. New York: Random House, 2003.

———. *The Presidency of Theodore Roosevelt*. Lawrence: University Press of Kansas, 1991.

Haynes, John Earl, ed. *Calvin Coolidge and the Coolidge Era*. Washington, DC: Library of Congress, 1998.

Hoff-Wilson, Joan. *Herbert Hoover: Forgotten Progressive*. Boston: Little, Brown, 1975.

Margulies, Herbert F. *Reconciliation and Revival: James R. Mann and the House Republicans in the Wilson Era*. Westport, CT: Greenwood Press, 1996.

LEWIS L. GOULD

Republican Party, 1932–68

The FDR Eclipse

The GOP began the 1930s as the nation's majority party. Winner of eight of the ten presidential elections dating back to 1896, it held a coalition comprising eastern probusiness conservatives, who controlled the party purse strings, and reform-minded midwestern and western progressives, who identified more with middle-class Americans. But during the Great Depression, the mainstays of Republican dominance—a surging economy and stock market—lay prostrate. Another usual source of GOP political strength, the protectionism embodied in the Smoot-Hawley Tariff of 1930, only worsened the economic quagmire. By decade's end, amid economic despondency, Franklin D. Roosevelt had welded together a new Democratic coalition that crushed the Republican supremacy.

The contrast between the 1928 and 1932 presidential elections demonstrated the GOP's devastation. In 1928 Herbert Hoover won 41 states; four years later, he claimed just 6, all in the Republican Northeast and New England. While the party in power usually loses ground in midterm elections, the Democrats increased their congressional majority in 1934. Worse for Republicans, their small minority splintered between pro–New Deal progressives and conservatives who opposed FDR, although feebly. The 1936 election brought Republicans more despair. Not only did Roosevelt pummel its nominee, Governor Alf Landon of Kansas, who won just Maine and Vermont, but his victory transcended geographical lines. He claimed the traditionally Republican regions of the Northeast and Midwest, as the GOP hemorrhaged members; liberals, African Americans, urbanites, and farmers abandoned it to join the New Deal coalition.

But Roosevelt's hubris following his 1936 triumph enabled Republicans to regain some footing. When the president clumsily proposed "packing" the Supreme Court with up to six more justices to ensure against having his programs ruled unconstitutional, the overwhelmingly Democratic Congress defied him. Roosevelt's blunder and an economic downturn in 1937, which critics dubbed the "Roosevelt recession," allowed Republicans to band together with conservative southern Democrats, forming a coalition on Capitol Hill to oppose Roosevelt and later Harry Truman.

Southern members of Congress fought Roosevelt partly because his programs expanding the federal government's powers and spending reawakened their traditional sympathy for states' rights. The New Deal also provoked a fundamental shift in the Republican Party's philosophy. Heir to the Hamiltonian tradition supporting a strong central government, Republicans began to espouse limited federal powers and states' rights, positions they advocated more emphatically in the coming decades. Despite cooperating with Republicans, southern Democrats declined to switch parties, for that would have cost them seniority and committee chairmanships. They stayed put, and although the GOP gained seats in the 1938 midterms, it remained in the congressional minority.

Republicans also squabbled, revealing deep party fissures. By 1940 they were divided between internationalists and isolationists. With war consuming Europe and Asia, isolationists wanted to steer clear of the conflict, while internationalists favored aid to allies. An even deeper breach was between Northeast and Middle Atlantic Republicans, who tightly controlled the party, and western progressives, who resented the eastern establishment's power. These splits helped Wendell Willkie, an Indiana native and former president of an electric utility, to win the 1940 GOP nomination, beating out rivals like establishment favorite Thomas Dewey of New York. Willkie was an unusual candidate, and his elevation showed the dearth of Republican leaders. A political novice, he had been a Democrat until 1938. To balance Willkie's internationalism, Republicans picked as his running mate isolationist Senator Charles McNary of Oregon. Although Willkie received more votes than Hoover or Landon did against FDR, the president won an unprecedented third term. In the 1944 election, Roosevelt's margin of victory over GOP nominee Dewey was slimmer still, but wartime bipartisanship reduced Republican chances of making inroads against the Democrats.

A Surge of Strength and Modern Republicanism

When Roosevelt died in 1945, Republican fortunes appeared to change. Truman had far fewer political gifts than FDR, and in the 1946 midterm elections, Republicans scored their greatest gains of the twentieth century, picking up a total of 67 seats in Congress—55 in the House and 12 in the Senate—to win control of both houses of Congress. Jubilant Republicans brandished brooms to symbolize their sweeping victories, and *Newsweek* declared, "An Era Begins," anticipating a long Republican reign on Capitol Hill. The 80th Congress stamped a permanent conservative imprint, passing the anti-labor Taft-Hartley Act and the Twenty-Second Amendment, which limited the president to two terms. But the new Congress proved unable to roll back New Deal programs, and GOP dominance proved short-lived.

In the election of 1948, the strong Democratic coalition helped Truman pull off an upset of Thomas Dewey, and Democrats retook control of Congress. But the president soon suffered setbacks. In 1949 the Soviet Union exploded its first atomic bomb; Communists won control of China, prompting charges that Truman "lost" the world's largest nation to a growing Red tide. The Korean War, which began in 1950, exacerbated fears of worldwide Communist gains. Republican Senator Joseph McCarthy of Wisconsin capitalized on the Red Scare by charging that a large conspiracy of Communist spies had infiltrated America's government. Cold war anxieties and the issue of anticommunism provided a winning theme for Republicans and united the party's moderates, libertarians, and social and moral conservatives.

The new unity boded well for the 1952 election, but the run-up to the contest again revealed party friction. Conservatives wielded considerable strength, yet in both 1944 and 1948, Dewey, an eastern moderate, won the nomination. In 1952 the leading conservative contender was Senator Robert Taft of Ohio, President William Howard Taft's son. But Taft suffered a severe charisma deficit and generated no widespread appeal. Moreover, he had an isolationist bent, favoring a decreased U.S. commitment to NATO and opposing the Marshall Plan, America's successful economic aid program for Western Europe. These views alarmed Taft's potential rival for the GOP nod, General Dwight Eisenhower, the World War II hero and NATO commander.

A late 1950 meeting with Taft proved critical in propelling Eisenhower into politics. Before conferring with the senator, he had drafted a letter declaring himself out of the 1952 race, intending to make it public if he found Taft's diplomatic views palatable. But Taft refused to commit to NATO and internationalism. After the meeting, Eisenhower destroyed the letter.

The importance of American internationalism was just one factor inducing Eisenhower to run. Growing federal budget deficits jarred his sense of fiscal integrity. The string of five consecutive Democratic presidential victories made him fear the two-party system's collapse if the Republicans lost again. Supporters entered him in the GOP primaries, and he won the nomination. But Taft controlled party machinery, and the Republican platform reflected conservative views more than Eisenhower's moderation, denouncing Truman's foreign policy of containment and the 1945 Yalta agreements for immuring Eastern Europe behind the iron curtain. Conservatives advocated a more aggressive stance, "rollback," which meant forcing Communists to yield ground and free captive peoples.

The 1952 elections allowed Republicans to taste success for the first time in more than 20 years. Eisenhower soundly defeated the Democratic nominee, Governor Adlai Stevenson of Illinois. Significantly, he made inroads into the Solid South, winning four states there and establishing a beachhead in a region that proved fertile ground for Republicans. His coattails also extended to Congress. The GOP gained control of the House and had equal strength with Senate Democrats, where Vice President Richard Nixon's vote could break a tie.

In 1956 Eisenhower read *A Republican Looks at His Party*, a book written by his undersecretary of labor, Arthur Larson. A centrist, Larson considered New Deal activism excessive but believed modern times demanded a greater government role in areas like labor and social insurance. The president praised the book for encapsulating his own political philosophy. What Eisenhower called "modern Republicanism" embraced internationalism and fiscal conservatism yet accepted a more active government role in social services than conservatives could stomach. Disdaining conservatives out to shrink or even end Social Security, he wrote, "Should any political party attempt to abolish social security and eliminate labor laws and farm programs, you would not hear of that party again in our political history."

Eisenhower proved a popular president. His approval ratings averaged 66 percent during his eight-year tenure, and the prosperity of the 1950s allowed Republicans to shuck their image as the party of the Great Depression. In 1956 Eisenhower beat Stevenson more handily than four years earlier. He exulted, "I think that Modern Republicanism has now proved itself, and America has approved of Modern Republicanism."

But Eisenhower's popularity was personal and never translated to a broader party appeal. During the 1954 midterms, Democrats regained control of Congress and in 1956, picked up one more seat in each house. In the 1958 midterms, Democrats rode a wave of worries over a recession, national security, and lack of progress in areas like space exploration, concerns made palpable in 1957 when the Soviet Union launched the world's first satellite, *Sputnik*. They pasted the GOP, gaining 48 seats in the House and 13 in the Senate. Many Republican elected during these years—especially in the House, which remained Democratic until 1995—spent their entire Capitol Hill careers in the minority.

Restless Conservatism

Republican conservatives were restive. The party's failure to make gains against Democrats was frustrating, and they howled in protest at Eisenhower's budgets, which grew despite his attempts to restrain spending. Blaming modern Republicanism for the increases, they derided it as a political philosophy that advanced government programs on only a smaller scale than what Democrats liked—a "dime store New Deal," as Republican Senator Barry Goldwater of Arizona called one GOP program. They resented Taft's being passed over as a presidential nominee, and his death in 1953 left them bereft of a leader. They failed to limit the president's foreign policy powers when the Bricker amendment, which would have constrained them, was defeated. An image of extremism sullied fringe conservatives, such as members of the John Birch Society, the extremist anti-Communist group founded in 1958, whose leader even charged that Eisenhower was a Communist agent. Indeed, the battles over many of Eisenhower's domestic and international views within the party explain why, despite a successful two-term presidency, he never won the reverence within the GOP that Ronald Reagan later did.

Moderates got another crack at the Democrats when the GOP nominated Nixon in 1960. Although the Californian had built a reputation as a harshly anti-Communist conservative in Congress, as vice president he identified himself with Eisenhower's moderation. His razor-thin loss to Senator John Kennedy in the presidential election gave conservatives more heft to advance one of their own.

They gained strength, especially in the South and West, regions ripe for right-wing thought. In the West, the spirit of individualism and freedom from personal restraints meshed with the ideal of limited government. Westerners distrusted the federal government, and its vast western land ownership irritated residents. In the South, Democratic support for the civil rights movement drove white conservatives out of the Democratic Party and into a new home, the GOP. These Sunbelt regions also enjoyed an economic boom, and their financial contributions—including from Texas oilmen—registered a growing impact in the party. The GOP, once too weak even to field congressional candidates in the South, began to bring in big names and even cause conversions. In 1961 Texas Republican John Tower won Lyndon Johnson's Senate seat; in 1964 Democratic Senator Strom Thurmond of South Carolina switched to the Republicans, and Governor John Connally of Texas later followed suit.

Conservatives determined to get their chance in 1964, nominating Barry Goldwater to run against President Johnson. To many moderates, Goldwater's views were extreme. He urged a tough stand against the USSR, favored voluntary Social Security, and opposed the Civil Rights Act of 1964, because he feared it would lead to hiring quotas. Moderates fought him. Liberal New York governor Nelson Rockefeller ran against Goldwater in the 1964 primaries, and after Rockefeller withdrew, Pennsylvania governor William Scranton jumped in. In defeat, Scranton sent Goldwater a harsh letter denouncing "Goldwaterism" for "reckless" foreign policy positions and civil rights views that would foment disorder. The letter killed any possibility of a unifying Goldwater-Scranton ticket, and the bitter clash between moderates and conservatives persisted to the national convention, where conservatives booed Rockefeller. The intraparty fight left the nominee wounded; Goldwater recalled, "Rockefeller and Scranton cut me up so bad there was no way on God's green earth that we could have won." Other moderates rebelled. Rockefeller and Governor George Romney of Michigan declined to campaign for Goldwater, and Arthur Larson even endorsed LBJ.

Badly trailing Johnson in polls, Goldwater hoped to garner at least 45 percent of the popular vote. Instead, he received just 38.5 percent. Democrats gained 2 Senate seats and 37 House members, making Congress even more Democratic. So thorough was the Republican Party's repudiation that pundits expressed doubts about its viability.

Goldwater later reflected, "We were a bunch of Westerners, outsiders, with the guts to challenge not only the entire Eastern establishment—Republican and Democratic alike—but the vast federal apparatus, the great majority of the country's academics, big business and big unions. . . ." Therein lay an important facet of Goldwater's effort. He laid the groundwork for a future conservative upsurge by energizing the party's southern and western forces, which began to wrest control of the party from the eastern establishment. His ideological brand of conservatism provided rallying cries for Republicans: lower taxes, small government, states' rights, anticommunism, and an emphasis on law and order. His crusade also enlisted the participation of fresh faces in politics, including actor Ronald Reagan, who filmed an eloquent television spot endorsing Goldwater. The humiliation of 1964 also prodded Republicans to find better leadership. In 1965 House Republicans elected Michigan congressman Gerald Ford minority leader, providing more effective resistance to Johnson policies, while new Republican National Committee chairman Ray Bliss also helped rebuild the party.

Significantly, Goldwater won ten southern states in 1964. He emphasized campaigning "where the ducks are," so he hunted for votes in the South. There, white conservatives, traditionally states' rights supporters, viewed federal support for civil rights as big government intrusion. Desiring more local control over issues involving integration, taxes, and church, they began drifting from the Democrats and moored themselves to the GOP.

The Southern Strategy

Republicans rebounded in the 1966 midterms to win 50 congressional seats, 47 in the House and 3 in the Senate. Richard Nixon rode the wave of renewed GOP energy, capturing the 1968 nomination and fashioning an electoral strategy that used two overarching issues, the Vietnam War (he called for "an honorable settlement") and "law and order."

The war had generated protests nationwide, and riots in cities plus student uprisings shattered the country's sense of stability. The unrest disturbed middle-class Americans, and polls showed that a majority of respondents felt that LBJ had moved too quickly on civil rights. An independent candidate, Alabama governor George Wallace, played on such sentiments by charging that communism lay behind the civil rights movement.

Nixon's appeal was more subtle. Promising law and order, he addressed patriotic "forgotten Americans" who quietly went to work and spurned the demonstrations that rocked the nation. His vice presidential pick reinforced his message: as Maryland governor, Spiro Agnew had taken a strong stand against urban rioters. Agnew's presence on the ticket plus Nixon's strong stand on crime and opposition to forced busing for integrating schools all capitalized on race as a political issue. Burgeoning suburbs, home to millions of middle-class Americans, welcomed Nixon's message, and the suburbs drew strength away from old Democratic political machines in cities. Meanwhile, in the South a momentous reversal occurred. White conservatives there switched to the GOP, while African Americans nationwide deserted the party of Abraham Lincoln. In 1960, Nixon won 30 percent of the African-American vote; eight years later, he received little more than 10 percent.

Nixon's "southern strategy" helped him win the election, beating Vice President Hubert Humphrey by a slim popular margin. Had third-party candidate Wallace not won five southern states, Nixon would have gained them. His appeal to issues involving race, crime, and war cracked the core of the New Deal coalition, attracting traditional Democratic voters such as blue-collar workers. He also pulled the South more firmly into the Republican fold. After a century as solidly Democratic, the region became reliably Republican. Although Nixon failed to carry either house of Congress, his party had made much headway since the 1930s. Struggling for decades, it gained enough strength by 1968 to win the White House while making new regional inroads. For Republicans, the doleful days of the Great Depression seemed a part of the past. After a third of a century as the minority party and a disastrous defeat in 1964, Republicans had built the foundation for a promising future.

See also era of consensus, 1952–64; New Deal Era, 1932–52.

FURTHER READING

Brennan, Mary. *Turning Right in the Sixties: The Conservative Capture of the GOP.* Chapel Hill: University of North Carolina Press, 1995.

Donaldson, Gary. *Truman Defeats Dewey*. Lexington: University Press of Kentucky, 1999.

Edwards, Lee. *Goldwater: The Man Who Made a Revolution.* Washington, DC: Regnery Publishing, 1995.

Goldwater, Barry. *The Conscience of a Conservative*. Shepherdsville, KY: Victor Publishing, 1960.

Gould, Lewis. *Grand Old Party: A History of the Republicans.* New York: Random House, 2003.

———. *1968: The Election That Changed America.* Chicago: Ivan Dee, 1993.

Grantham, Dewey. *The Life and Death of the Solid South: A Political History*. Lexington: University of Kentucky Press, 1988.

Larson, Arthur. *A Republican Looks at His Party.* New York: Harper and Brothers, 1956.

Ritchie, Donald. *Electing FDR: The New Deal Campaign of 1932*. Lawrence: University Press of Kansas, 2007.

Rutland, Robert A. *The Republicans: From Lincoln to Bush.* Columbia: University of Missouri Press, 1996.

Stebenne, David. *Modern Republican: Arthur Larson and the Eisenhower Years.* Bloomington: Indiana University Press, 2006.

YANEK MIECZKOWSKI

Republican Party, 1968–2008

When former vice president Richard M. Nixon became the Republican Party nominee for president in 1968, the GOP was deeply divided between its moderate and conservative wings. Moderates such as New York governor Nelson Rockefeller had supported racial equality and federal spending on education, health care, and welfare. Conservatives like Senator Barry Goldwater of Arizona opposed what they called "big government" and "tax-and-spend" policies, and they championed limited government, individualism, and self-reliance.

Goldwater's 1964 presidential nomination seemed to have shifted the momentum to the conservative wing until his landslide defeat by President Lyndon B. Johnson in the general election. But the conservative wing eventually rebounded with renewed strength in the 1980s under the leadership of Ronald Reagan. The revived conservative movement that turned into a juggernaut in the 1980s was a result of a variety of factors, including a reaction against the social upheavals of the 1960s and 1970s, as well as the gradual political realignment of the South.

Nixon: The Southern Strategy and a New Foreign Policy

Many Southerners had become dissatisfied with high taxes, government regulations, federal civil rights legislation, and what they saw as the dismantling of traditional institutions, such as church and family. Goldwater appealed to these Southerners and other Americans upset with the direction of U.S. politics. Despite his loss, the 1964 election marked the first time since Reconstruction that most Southerners had voted Republican. This achievement set the stage for what became known as Richard Nixon's "southern strategy" for regaining the White House in 1968.

The 1968 presidential race touched on many sensitive issues. Public concerns ignited over the conflict in Southeast Asia, the civil rights movement, inner-city riots, and the violent antiwar protests on college campuses throughout the nation. Nixon faced off against Democratic nominee Vice President Hubert Humphrey and third-party candidate George Wallace.

Nixon won 301 electoral votes and 43.4 percent of the popular vote. Humphrey received 191 electors and 42.7 percent. Nixon won the popular vote by approximately 500,000 votes. It was a narrow victory, with a margin that was almost as small as John F. Kennedy's against

Nixon in 1960. Wallace garnered 13.5 percent of the vote and 46 electors.

For Republicans, Nixon's victory meant the beginning of the demise of the New Deal liberal coalition and the emergence of a political realignment. In *The Emerging Republican Majority*, Kevin Phillips argued that "a liberal Democratic era ha[d] ended and that a new era of consolidationist Republicanism ha[d] begun." Yet the evidence for realignment was not so clear.

Indeed, from 1968 until the 1990s, Republicans dominated presidential elections, while Democrats maintained strong majorities in the House of Representatives. It was the beginning of an era of divided government, which emerged from the increase of registered independents, the weakening of political parties, and the rise of split-ticket voters. Since 1968, Republicans have won seven out of eleven presidential elections, losing only four times to Democrats—to Jimmy Carter in 1976, Bill Clinton in 1992 and 1996, and Barack Obama in 2008. In Congress, from 1968 until 1994, Republicans gained a majority in the Senate only once and for only six years, from 1981 until 1987. Republicans served as the minority party in the House for 40 straight years, from 1954 until 1994.

To be sure, Republicans learned well their role as a minority party, at least until they captured both houses of Congress in 1994, the year of the so-called Republican revolution. Nevertheless, Republican presidents, beginning with Nixon, faced Democratic-controlled Congresses and had to come to terms with the concept of "separated institutions sharing powers." As a result, some GOP presidents moved their policies to the center of the political spectrum.

In the 1970 midterm elections, Republicans won two seats in the Senate but lost nine seats to the Democrats in the House. Nixon characterized the outcome as a victory for Republicans because usually the president's party loses many more congressional seats in midterm elections. However, the true test of the party's strength, and its ability to build a coalition big enough to win another presidential election, would occur two years later.

Nixon's 1972 reelection campaign relied on personal loyalists instead of party leaders at the national, state, and local levels. Former senator Bob Dole of Kansas, then the chair of the Republican National Committee, stated, "The Republican Party was not only not involved in Watergate, but it wasn't involved in the nomination, the convention, the campaign, the election or the inauguration." Isolated from his party, but possessing a favorable foreign policy record, Nixon campaigned tirelessly.

Leading up to the 1972 election, conservatives had mixed feelings about Nixon's social, economic, and foreign policy record. Nixon's policies in health care, affirmative action, and the environment estranged him from conservatives. He proposed a national health insurance program, approved affirmative action programs for federal workers, and signed into law legislation establishing the Environmental Protection Agency.

Yet Nixon made some policy decisions that pleased conservatives. For example, he rejected congressional attempts to reduce defense spending. He removed many antipoverty programs passed under Johnson's Great Society, including Model Cities, Community Action Activities, and aid to depressed areas. Nixon pushed for tough crime laws. He also ordered officials at the Department of Health, Education, and Welfare to not cut off funding to school districts that failed to comply with the Supreme Court's desegregation order.

In an effort to court the vote of disaffected white Southerners, Nixon spoke out against court-ordered busing and lamented the moral decline in America. He denounced the Supreme Court's decision in *Swann v. Charlotte-Mecklenburg Board of Education*, which upheld busing laws and allowed federal courts to oversee the integration process. The issue of busing caused many working-class Americans to join Nixon and the GOP. To gain the Catholic vote and the support of religious conservatives, Nixon bemoaned the loss of traditional moral values and condemned abortion and the removal of prayer in public schools.

Nixon's foreign policy accomplishments enhanced his stature. A longtime staunch anti-Communist, Nixon surprised his critics when he reached out to China and when he sought détente with the former Soviet Union. His trip to China in 1972 was a success. Intending to drive a wedge between China and the Soviet Union, Nixon successfully negotiated a trade agreement and thereby opened China to Western markets. Achieving relations with China empowered Nixon during his trip to Moscow that same year. Nixon and the Soviet premier Leonid Brezhnev met and formulated a Strategic Arms Limitations Treaty (SALT I), which imposed limits on both countries' nuclear weapons. Though the treaty did not do much in the area of arms reduction, the meeting itself was enough to temporarily ease U.S.-Soviet tensions. Nixon's opening to China and his trip to Moscow enhanced his credibility among American voters.

Nixon's 1972 opponent was Senator George McGovern of South Dakota. As a liberal Democrat, one of McGovern's biggest problems was that most voters in America still remembered the urban riots and violent protests on college campuses that occurred in the late 1960s and early 1970s.

Nixon won by the largest margin in history—60.7 percent of the popular vote to McGovern's 37.5 percent. The electoral margin between the two was 520 to 17. In the congressional elections, Republicans lost 1 seat in the Senate and gained 12 in the House. However, the momentum for Republicans would soon change after the 1972 election because of scandals in the White House.

Vice President Spiro Agnew resigned after revelations of his involvement in bribes and tax evasion while governor of Maryland. Then the Watergate scandal began to consume the Nixon presidency. On June 17, 1972, five men had broken into the Democratic National Committee's headquarters, located in the Watergate Hotel in Washington, D.C. Although Nixon dismissed the break-in by people associated with his reelection campaign as a "third rate burglary," the president's role in the cover-up led to his resignation on August 8, 1974. Nixon's vice president, Gerald R. Ford, appointed previously to replace Agnew, succeeded to the presidency.

Ford's Accidental Presidency

Ford was an unlikely person to rise to the presidency, as he had never aspired to an office higher than the House of Representatives and was contemplating retiring from public life when Nixon chose him to replace Agnew. As president, Ford moved quickly to win public trust—an essential goal given public cynicism toward government and political leaders in the wake of Watergate. Although Ford initially succeeded in that task, he lost enormous support from the public when he issued a controversial pardon for Nixon a mere month after taking office. The combined effects of Watergate and the Nixon pardon on public perceptions were disastrous for the GOP. The party lost 49 seats in the House of Representatives and 3 seats in the Senate in the 1974 midterm elections. The president himself never recovered politically from the pardon and lost his bid for election to the presidency in 1976.

Ford's brief tenure highlighted the ideological rift in the GOP. He appointed Nelson Rockefeller as his vice president, an action that infuriated conservatives who had long battled the politically moderate New Yorker for control of the GOP. Ford further alienated the Right with his support for détente with the former Soviet Union. Former California governor Ronald Reagan challenged Ford's quest for the 1976 GOP nomination, and the two ran a close race right up to the party's convention. Ford prevailed, but not before he had suffered much political damage. In the general election, Ford lost to Democratic nominee Jimmy Carter, a former one-term governor of Georgia whose improbable campaign for the presidency stunned political observers.

By the time Carter assumed the presidency in 1977, the Republicans were hugely outnumbered by the Democrats in Congress. The GOP held a mere 143 seats in the House (versus 292 for the Democrats) and 38 in the Senate (against 61 Democrats and 1 independent). The GOP did gain 15 House seats in the 1978 midterm elections, as well as 3 seats in the Senate. Public disaffection with Carter created an opportunity for the GOP to stage a political comeback.

Reagan and the Rise of the New Right

The conservative wing of the Republican Party gained strength during Carter's term. Conservatives reached out to working- and middle-class voters with appeals for lower taxes, deregulation, and reduced social spending, and they courted religious voters by criticizing liberal abortion laws and the elimination of school prayer. Many conservative Catholics and evangelical Protestants set aside their theological differences and joined the ranks of the Republican Party. A movement known as the New Right brought together a new coalition of voters for the GOP. The New Right stood for traditional institutions (family and church), traditional moral values (antigay, antiabortion, and progun), and states rights (limited government).

Some conservative Democrats joined the GOP. Many became known as "neoconservatives," and they were distinctive in their emphasis on strong defense and U.S. intervention abroad along with their preference for progressive domestic policies. Together, the New Right and neoconservatives set in motion a conservative juggernaut, which became palpable in the 1980 election of Reagan. The conservatism of Reagan revolutionized the Republican Party. What Reagan had done to the party was to revitalize the type of conservatism that Barry Goldwater advocated in the 1960s.

Reagan's 1980 campaign held Carter and Democrats responsible for high inflation, high interest rates, and for the long hostage crisis in Iran. Reagan believed that the federal government had become too large and powerful, that it had assumed too much social and economic responsibility. In his first inaugural address, Reagan told Americans, "government is not the solution to our problems; government is the problem."

Reagan won 51 percent of the popular vote, carried 44 states and 489 electoral votes compared to Carter's 49. In addition to winning the White House, Republicans picked up 32 seats in the House, which was short of a majority, but which marked the largest gain of seats in the House during a presidential election since 1920. Of greater importance was the Republican victory in the Senate. Republicans won 12 seats and took control of the Senate. Republicans had not been the majority party in the upper house since 1955. Overall, the outcome of the 1980 election demonstrated a significant shift in the political landscape.

After taking office in 1981, Reagan pushed his conservative agenda. Cutting domestic programs, deregulating the economy, reducing taxes, and building up the military were some of his key initiatives. Reagan proposed cutting the Food Stamp and School Lunch programs. He proposed loosening many environmental regulations. Reagan perpetuated Carter's deregulation of the airline industry, and he objected to the Federal Communications Commission (FCC) regulating the cable television networks industry. In foreign affairs, Reagan sought to put an end to the spread of communism. In doing so, he rejected the policies of containment and détente. He accepted the use of military intervention in and economic aid to non-Communist countries, a policy known as the "Reagan Doctrine." To improve national security—and perhaps to bankrupt the Soviet Union—Reagan oversaw the largest military buildup during peacetime in American history.

By the 1984 presidential election, Reagan had increased his popularity among the American electorate. One reason was that the economy had rebounded during his first term. He had achieved major tax cuts and convinced the Federal Reserve to loosen its grip on the money supply. Another reason for Reagan's popularity had to do with his decisions in foreign policy. He labeled the former Soviet Union the "evil empire" and launched his Strategic Defense Initiative (SDI), better known as "Star Wars." He aided anti-Communist groups in their fight against oppressive regimes. Reagan's speeches also imbued Americans with optimism about their future.

The 1984 GOP platform was a document of conservative principles. It contained promises to pass an antiabortion amendment, a balanced budget amendment, and a law that would reform the federal tax code. In the general election, Reagan defeated former vice president Walter Mondale. Reagan won 59 percent of the popular vote and 525 electoral votes. In Congress, the GOP lost only 2 seats in the Senate and gained a small number in the House.

In his second term, Reagan had his share of difficulties. Republicans lost six seats in the Senate in the 1986 midterm election and, consequently, their majority status. Reagan could not, as he had promised, balance the budget. The federal deficit surged well over $200 billion in 1986 and dropped down thereafter to $150 billion, a result attributed to both economic growth and tax reform. A big victory for Reagan occurred in 1986, when he signed a tax reform bill into law. The new law simplified the tax code by setting uniform rates for people with similar incomes, and it eliminated many tax deductions. However, in the same year, the Iran-Contra scandal broke.

Top White House officials, including Lieutenant Colonel Oliver North and Admiral John Poindexter, had illegally sold arms to Iran in exchange for the release of American hostages. The proceeds of the arms deal were sent surreptitiously to a rebel group, called the Contras, who were trying to overthrow the Communist regime in Nicaragua. Leading up to the 1988 elections, the scandal did not hurt the Republican Party as much as Democrats would have liked. In the final two years of Reagan's presidency, other events overshadowed Iran-Contra.

In 1987 Reagan's conservative Supreme Court nominee Robert Bork failed to win confirmation. In December 1987, Reagan and the Soviet premier, Mikhail Gorbachev, signed the Intermediate-range Nuclear Forces (INF) treaty. Unlike SALT I, which limited the number of nuclear weapons, the INF treaty eliminated an entire class of nuclear weapons. Most Americans lauded Reagan's foreign policy decisions. They believed his agreement with Gorbachev and his May 1988 trip to Moscow signaled the beginning of the end of the cold war. Despite record federal budget deficits, Reagan left the presidency—and his party—in relatively good shape for the 1988 election.

The One-Term Presidency of George H. W. Bush

In 1988 the GOP nominated Vice President George H. W. Bush for the presidency, and he campaigned on the promise to continue Reagan's policies. He also pledged not to support new taxes. Bush beat Democratic nominee governor Michael Dukakis of Massachusetts, winning 40 states and 54 percent of the popular vote. However, while Republicans held on to the presidency, the Democrats kept their majorities in Congress.

Bush's middle-of-the-road views widened the gap between moderates and conservatives. For example, in 1990 he signed into law the Americans with Disabilities Act and an extension of the Clean Air Act. The savings-and-loan bailout, spending on the Gulf War, as well as welfare and Medicare payments increased the strain on the federal budget. As a result, the deficit rose, and Bush was compelled to break his pledge not to raise taxes.

In response, Pat Buchanan, a conservative columnist, challenged Bush for the GOP nomination in 1992. Buchanan forcefully spoke out against abortion, gay rights, and sexual tolerance, and he advocated the restoration of prayer in public schools. Although Buchanan's challenge failed, he had weakened Bush politically and embarrassed the party with an overheated prime-time speech at the Republican National Convention.

The Clinton Era and the Gingrich-led Republican Revolution

The Democrats nominated Governor Bill Clinton of Arkansas. The general election also included a billionaire third-party candidate, Ross Perot, who garnered 19 percent of the vote. Clinton won with merely 43.3 percent of the popular vote. Within two years, however, voters started to view Clinton negatively because of his proposed tax increases and proposed universal health care program.

In the 1994 midterm election, sensing an electorate disgruntled over low wages and the loss of traditional moral values, conservative Republicans, led by Representative Newt Gingrich of Georgia, devised a series of campaign promises. Under the rubric of the Contract with America, the promises included tax cuts, welfare reform, tougher crime laws, congressional term limits, an amendment to balance the budget, and a return of power and responsibility to the states. Some 300 Republican candidates signed the contract in a public ceremony on the steps of the U.S. Capitol. Republicans won control of both houses of Congress. They had not enjoyed a majority in the House in 40 years.

Yet, after failed attempts to enact the Contract with America, the public soon became disgruntled with the GOP in Congress, so much so that the 1996 presidential nominee Bob Dole distanced himself from Gingrich and others associated with the Republican revolution. Clinton ably defined the GOP "revolutionaries" as political extremists and easily won reelection, although he failed to win a majority of the vote with Perot again on the ballot.

The George W. Bush Era

In the 2000 campaign, Texas governor George W. Bush faced off against Vice President Al Gore. Bush called himself a "compassionate conservative," which was a campaign stratagem designed to attract independents and moderates without sacrificing conservative support. Bush promised to restore dignity to the White House, a reference to President Clinton's personal scandals and impeachment. After the polls closed on November 7, it was clear that Gore had won the popular vote by a narrow margin, a little over 500,000 votes. Not so clear was the winner of the Electoral College. The election came down to Florida. The winner of Florida's 25 electoral votes would become president-elect. For over a month, Florida remained undecided because of poorly designed ballots in Palm Beach County. As recounts by hand were taking place, Gore's legal team convinced the Florida Supreme Court to rule that the results of a hand count would determine the winner. On December 12, Bush's legal team appealed the decision to the U.S. Supreme Court. In a 5 to 4 decision, the Supreme Court stopped recounts on the premise that they violated the equal protection clause of the Fourteenth Amendment. Bush thus won Florida and with it the presidency.

In his first year in office, Bush signed into law a bill that lowered tax brackets and cut taxes by $1.35 trillion over a ten-year period. In education, his No Child Left Behind Act required standardized national tests for grades three through eight. He proposed a school voucher program that would allow children to leave failing schools and attend schools of their choice—including private, parochial schools—at the expense of taxpayers. He also banned federal funding for research on stem cell lines collected in the future.

Bush's leadership would be put to the test on September 11, 2001, when terrorists attacked the World Trade Center and the Pentagon. He reminded Americans of their resiliency and assured them the United States would seek and punish the terrorist group responsible for the attacks. His approval ratings soared, and the GOP gained seats in Congress in the midterm elections in 2002.

Bush won the 2004 election against Senator John Kerry of Massachusetts with 51 percent of the popular vote and 286 votes in the Electoral College. In Congress, Republicans increased their majorities, winning four more seats in the Senate and five more in the House. The success of the Republican Party was, in part, a result of a strategy to focus on the registration of conservative voters, especially in key battleground states, such as Florida, Ohio, Iowa, and Pennsylvania. To mobilize conservatives in those states, Republicans emphasized social issues, such as abortion, stem cell research, and gay marriage.

However, by the 2006 midterm elections, Bush's popularity had fallen significantly due to the bungled U.S. military intervention in Iraq and the government's slow response to hurricane Katrina in the Gulf States. Bush's mismanagement of Katrina lowered public confidence in the national government. Moreover, in the month preceding the election, a number of scandals within the GOP had become public. House Majority Leader Tom Delay of Texas violated the campaign finance laws of Texas. He later resigned his seat in the House. Representative Mark Foley of Florida resigned due to sexual misconduct.

Democrats won majorities in both houses of Congress. They interpreted their victory as a mandate to end the war in Iraq. Bush continued to prosecute the war, and shortly after the elections he requested more money from Congress to fund the troops. The unpopular war and Bush's low approval ratings increased Democrats' prospects of taking back the White House in 2008.

The 2008 Elections: Democrats Take Back Control of Washington

The 2008 GOP nomination contest failed to attract much enthusiasm from conservatives. The leading candidates—former Massachusetts governor Mitt Romney, former Arkansas governor Mike Huckabee, and Senator John McCain of Arizona—were all seen by conservative activists as too politically moderate. McCain eventually won the nomination, and to shore up conservative support, he chose as his vice presidential running mate the staunchly conservative governor of Alaska, Sarah Palin.

Amid the collapse of the U.S. financial sector under a Republican administration and a national surge in support for the Democratic Party, McCain lost the election to first-term senator Barack Obama of Illinois. In Congress, the Democrats picked up 21 seats in the House of Representatives and at least 8 seats (one race was undecided at the time of this writing) in the U.S. Senate. For the first time since 1993, Republicans were clearly the minority party.

See also Conservative ascendancy, 1980–2008; Era of confrontation and decline, 1964–80.

FUTHER READING

Ceaser, James W., and Andrew E. Busch. *The Perfect Tie: The True Story of the 2000 Presidential Election*. Lanham, MD: Rowman and Littlefield, 2001.

Fenno, Richard F. *Learning to Govern: An Institutional View of the 104th Congress*. Washington, DC: Brookings Institution Press, 1997.

Gregg, Gary L., and Mark J. Rozell, eds. *Considering the Bush Presidency.* New York: Oxford University Press, 2004.

Jeffrey, Harry P., and Thomas Maxwell-Long, eds. *Watergate and the Resignation of Richard Nixon*. Washington, DC: Congressional Quarterly Press, 2004.

Phillips, Kevin P. *The Emerging Republican Majority*. New Rochelle, NY: Arlington House, 1969.

Small, Melvin. *The Presidency of Richard Nixon.* Lawrence: University Press of Kansas, 1999.

MARK ROZELL AND KYLE BARBIERI

republicanism

Republicanism is a political philosophy that exerted a profound cultural influence on the life and thought of Americans living in the Revolutionary and antebellum eras (1760–1848). This unique view of government and society originated during the crisis in Anglo-American relations that resulted in the independence of the 13 colonies and the creation of a new nation.

English Commonwealthmen

Responding to actions of the British government during the 1760s and 1770s, colonial American spokesmen drew extensively on the libertarian thought of English commonwealthmen. Epitomized by John Trenchard and Thomas Gordon's *Cato's Letters* and James Burgh's *Political Disquisitions*, the publications of these dissenting radicals railed against the urgent danger posed by the systematic corruption they attributed to Robert Walpole's ministry (1721–42). The parliamentary government emerging under Walpole appeared to them to maintain the facade of constitutional procedures while actually monopolizing the whole of governmental powers within his cabinet. In their minds, Walpole's machinations were destroying the balance among king, lords, and commons that constituted the very strength of the British constitution. Believing in a separation of powers among the three constituent elements of the government, commonwealthmen urged parliamentary reforms such as rotation in office, the redistribution of seats, and annual meetings to restore the proper constitutional balance. Beyond that, their concern for freedom of thought and the sovereignty of the people led them to speak out passionately against the increasing corruption and tyranny they believed to be infecting English society and government. Pairing liberty with equality, Trenchard and Gordon's *Cato's Letters* and Burgh's *Disquisitions* proclaimed the preservation and extension of liberty to be all important. Since the greatest danger to the liberty and the equality of the people came from their leaders, all citizens must maintain a constant vigilance to prevent governmental officials from being corrupted by power and stealthily usurping liberty away from the people. In their minds all men were naturally good; citizens became restless only when oppressed. Every man should, therefore, act according to his own conscience, judge when a magistrate had done ill, and, above all, possess the right of resistance. Without such a right, citizens could not defend their liberty.

Revolutionary Republicanism

While revolutionary leaders in America made extensive use of such conceptions, the ideas of these commonwealthmen did not cross the Atlantic intact. Americans adapted beliefs regarding consent, liberty, equality, civic morality, and constitutions to their specific and concrete needs, so that even when the same words were used and the same formal principles adhered to, novel circumstances transformed their meanings. Consequently, revolutionary leaders, believing that history revealed a continual struggle between the spheres of liberty and power, embraced a distinctive set of political and social attitudes that gradually permeated their society. A consensus formed in which the concept of republicanism epitomized the new world they believed they were creating. This republicanism called for a constant effort on the part of all American citizens to protect the realm of liberty (America) from the ceaseless aggression of the realm of power (Great Britain) under the guidance of gentlemen of natural merit and ability.

Above all, republicanism rested on a self-reliant, independent citizenry. The sturdy yeoman—the equal of any man and dependent upon none for his livelihood—became the iconic representation of American republicanism. Americans believed that what made republics great or what ultimately destroyed them was not the force of arms but the character and spirit of the people. Public virtue, the essential prerequisite for good government, became all important. A people practicing frugality, industry, temperance, and simplicity were sound republican stock; those who wallowed in luxury were corrupt and would corrupt others. Since furthering the public good—the exclusive purpose of republican government—required a constant sacrifice of individual interests to the greater needs of the whole, the people, conceived of as a homogeneous body (especially when set against their rulers), became the great determinant of whether a republic lived or died. Thus republicanism meant maintaining public and private virtue, social solidarity, and vigilance against the corruptions of power. United in this frame of mind, Americans set out to gain their independence and to establish a new republican world.

By the end of the eighteenth century, the American commitment to republicanism had grown even stronger than it had been in 1776. Its principal tenets—a balance between the separate branches of government and a vigilance against governmental power—had been inscribed in the U.S. Constitution and Bill of Rights. America had indeed become republican, but hardly in the manner intended by its early leaders. Economic and demographic changes taking place at an unparalleled rate had begun to work fundamental transformations within the new nation. Geographic expansion spawned incredible mobility, and great numbers of Americans, becoming increasingly involved in the market economy, strived to gain all the advantages they could from their newly acquired social and economic autonomy.

Revolutionary republicanism, rather than constraining these activities, seemed rather to encourage them and to afford them legitimacy. The emphasis placed on equality in revolutionary rhetoric stimulated great numbers of previously deferential men to question all forms of authority and to challenge distinctions of every sort. Rather than generating an increased commitment to order, harmony, and virtue, republicanism appeared to be fostering an acquisitive individualism heedless of the common good and skeptical about the benevolent leadership of a natural elite. Postrevolutionary America, instead of becoming the New World embodiment of transcendent classical values, appeared increasingly materialistic, utilitarian, and licentious: austerity gave way to prosperity; virtue appeared more and more to connote the individual pursuit of wealth through hard work rather than an unselfish devotion to the collective good. No longer a simple, ordered community under the benign leadership of a natural elite, America seemed instead to be moving toward being a materialistic and utilitarian nation increasingly responsive to both the demands of the market and the desires of ordinary, obscure individuals.

The rapid democratization and vulgarization that took place in American society during the last decades of the eighteenth century helped create a far more open and fluid society than had been anticipated by most revolutionary leaders. Indeed, the transformations taking place in American society through these years were so complex and indeliberate, so much a mixture of day-to-day responses to a rapidly changing socioeconomic environment, that most Americans were unaware of the direction that such changes were taking them and their society. Their commitment to republicanism, however, allowed them to continue to imagine themselves as members of a virtuous, harmonious, organic society long after the social foundations of such a society had eroded. The fact that republican language became increasingly disembodied from the changing cultural context made self-awareness that much more difficult. Such language allowed—even impelled—citizens to view themselves as committed to the harmony, order, and communal well-being of a republican society while actively creating an aggressive, individualistic, and materialistic one.

Most Americans clung to a harmonious, corporate view of their society and their own place in it, even while behaving in a materialistic, utilitarian manner in their daily lives. Thus, while rapidly transforming their society in an open, competitive, modern direction, Americans idealized communal harmony and a virtuous social order. Republicanism condemned the values of a burgeoning capitalistic economy and placed a premium on an ordered, disciplined personal liberty restricted by the civic obligations dictated by public virtue. In this sense, republicanism formalized or ritualized a mode of thought that ran counter to the flow of history; it idealized the traditional values of a world rapidly fading rather than the market conditions and liberal capitalistic mentality swiftly emerging in the late eighteenth century. As a result, Americans could—and did—believe simultaneously in corporate needs and individual rights. They never, however, had a sense of having to choose between two starkly contrasting traditions—republicanism and liberalism. Instead, they domesticated classical republicanism to fit contemporary needs while amalgamating inherited assumptions with their liberal actions.

Jeffersonian Republicanism

The kind of society that would emerge from the increasingly egalitarian and individualistic roots being formed in the late eighteenth century was unclear when Thomas Jefferson assumed the presidency in 1801. Even by that time, the perception of personal autonomy and individual self-interest had become so inextricably intertwined that few of Jefferson's supporters had any clear comprehension of the extent to which entrepreneurial and capitalistic social forces were shaping American life. Under the pressure of such rapidly changing conditions, the autonomous republican producer—the yeoman integrally related to the welfare of the larger community—gradually underwent a subtle transmutation into the ambitious self-made man set against his neighbors and his community alike. Consequently, by incorporating as its own the dynamic spirit of a market society and translating it into a political agenda, the party of Jefferson had unself-consciously developed a temper and a momentum that would carry it beyond its original goals. Indeed, even by 1800, personal independence no longer constituted a means by which to ensure virtue; it had itself become the epitome of virtue. The process by which this took place was complicated, often confused, and frequently gave rise to unintended consequences. It ultimately resulted, nonetheless, in profound changes in American culture in the nineteenth century.

Republicanism in the hands of the Jeffersonians—the foremost advocates of the persuasion—spawned a social, political, and cultural movement that quite unintentionally created the framework within which liberal commitments to interest-group politics, materialistic and utilitarian strivings, and unrestrained individualism emerged. Simultaneously, however, republicanism also fostered a rhetoric of unselfish virtue—of honest independence devoted to the communal welfare—that obscured the direction in which American society was moving. By promoting the desire for unrestrained enterprise indirectly through an appeal to popular virtue, the Jeffersonians helped produce a nation of capitalists blind to the spirit of their enterprise. Consequently, their movement enabled Americans to continue to define their purpose as the pursuit of traditional virtue while actually devoting themselves to the selfish pursuit of material wealth. Irresponsible individualism and erosive factionalism replaced the independent producer's commitment to the common good. Still, free enterprisers, who by the 1850s would include publicly chartered business corporations, fell heir to the republican belief that an independent means of production sufficiently attached a citizen's interests to the good of the commonwealth. Entrepreneurial fortunes became investments in the general welfare. The entrepreneur himself, freed by the American belief in virtuous independence, could proceed unencumbered by self-doubts in his attempt to gain dominion over a society of like-minded individuals who could only applaud his success as their own.

The triumph of Thomas Jefferson initiated a brief period—a "Jeffersonian moment"—when the virtues of both republicanism and eighteenth-century liberalism merged into a cohesive political philosophy offering the bright promise of equal social and economic advancement for all individuals in a land of abundance. That the moment was brief stands less as a critique of the individuals who combined to bring Jefferson to the presidency than it is a comment on the forces that impelled them, forces over which they had little control and, perhaps, even less understanding. Just at the time when an ideology translated the realities of the American environment into a coherent social philosophy, those very realities carried American society far beyond the original goals of the Jeffersonian movement as they transmuted eighteenth-century American republicanism into nineteenth-century American democracy.

Republican Historiography

If the protean nature of republicanism obscured such transformations by providing a sense of harmony and comfort to great numbers of late-eighteenth- and early-nineteenth-century Americans, no such cordiality and consensus characterizes scholarly attempts to come to grips with republicanism as a historical concept. Indeed, since first receiving formal analytic and conceptual identity in the early 1970s, republicanism has been at the epicenter of strife and contention among historians of the early national period. Even though the concept had become omnipresent in scholarly literature by the mid-1980s (in the terms *republican motherhood*, *artisan republicanism*, *free labor republicanism*, *pastoral republicanism*, *evangelical republicanism*, and others), a good many scholars, particularly social historians, remained convinced that the emphasis on republicanism obscured far more than it clarified about early American society. For them the scholarly concentration on republicanism occluded vast domains of culture—religion, law, political economy, and ideas related to patriarchy, family, gender, race, slavery, class, and nationalism—that most scholars knew were deeply entangled in the revolutionary impulse.

The greatest challenge to republicanism, however, came not from social historians but from scholars wedded to the concept of liberalism. For these individuals, Americans of the Revolutionary era manifested aggressive individualism, optimistic materialism, and pragmatic interest-group politics. In their minds, John Locke's liberal concept of possessive individualism, rather than Niccolò Machiavelli's republican advocacy of civic humanism, best explained American thought and behavior during the years after 1760.

The intellectual conflict that emerged between advocates of republicanism and those of liberalism ushered in years of sterile debate. An entirely unproductive "either/or" situation resulted: either scholars supported republicanism or they espoused liberalism. Fortunately, in realizing that partisans of both republican and liberal interpretations had identified strands of American political culture that simply could not be denied, a great many historians transcended this tiresome dialogue. Replacing it with a "both/and" mode of analysis, these scholars have revealed the manner in which republicanism, liberalism, and other traditions of social and political thought interpenetrated one another to create a distinctive and creative intellectual milieu. Over time a "paradigmatic pluralism" emerged: scholars employing a "multiple traditions" approach emphasized concepts drawn from natural rights, British constitutionalism, English opposition writers, contract theory, Protestant Christian morality, Lockean liberalism, and republicanism. Such work has resulted in a far more sophisticated understanding of early American culture.

The multiple traditions approach to early American history provides scholars with significant insights of inestimable value in their efforts to analyze this vital era. The first and perhaps most important of these is that no single concept—whether republicanism, liberalism, or Protestant Christianity—provides a master analytical framework for understanding revolutionary America. Each of these concepts comprised a multitude of arguments developed in different contexts to solve different problems and to articulate different ideals. Whatever conflicts or contradictions might seem apparent among them could always be held in suspension by the interpenetration of ideas and mutual reinforcement. While republicanism can clearly no longer be considered *the* key to understanding early American history, it certainly remains *a* vital constituent element in the political culture of revolutionary America. If no longer a conception of transcendent meaning, republicanism remains a discourse deeply embedded in the central issues facing Americans in the late eighteenth and early nineteenth centuries—a time in which a distinctive pattern of social and political thought incorporating republican, liberal, and religious ideas emerged in response to these issues. Each of these clusters of ideas comprised a vital part of the larger meaning Americans brought to particular disputes in the years of the early republic. To abstract one set of ideas—whether republican, liberal, or religious—from this intellectual fabric not only impairs an understanding of this distinctive pattern of thought, but obscures the special character—the very uniqueness—of the early republic.

See also democracy; era of a new republic, 1789–1827; liberalism; war for independence.

FURTHER READING

Appleby, Joyce. *Capitalism and a New Social Order: The Republican Vision of the 1790s.* New York: New York University Press, 1984.

Bailyn, Barnard. *The Ideological Origins of the American Revolution.* Cambridge, MA: Harvard University Press, 1967.

Gibson, Alan. "Ancients, Moderns and Americans: The Republicanism-Liberalism Debate Revisited." *History of Political Thought* 21 (2000), 261–307.

Kloppenberg, James. "Premature Requiem: Republicanism in American History." In *The Virtues of Liberalism*, 59–70. New York: Oxford University Press, 1998.

———. "The Virtues of Liberalism: Christianity, Republicanism, and Ethics in Early American Political Discourse." *Journal of American History* 74 (1987), 9–33.

Kramnick, Isaac. *Republicanism and Bourgeois Radicalism: Political Ideology in Late Eighteenth-Century England and America.* Ithaca, NY: Cornell University Press, 1990.

Pocock, J.G.A. *The Machiavellian Moment: Florentine Political Thought and the Atlantic Republican Tradition.* Princeton, NJ: Princeton University Press, 1975.

Rahe, Paul A. *Republics Ancient and Modern: Classical Republicanism and the American Revolution.* Chapel Hill: University of North Carolina Press, 1992.

Robbins, Caroline. *The Eighteenth-Century Commonwealthmen: Studies in the Transmission, Development, and Circumstances of Liberal Thought from the Restoration of Charles II Until the War with the Thirteen Colonies.* Cambridge, MA: Harvard University Press, 1959.

Rogers, Daniel T. "Republicanism: the Career of a Concept." *Journal of American History*, 79 (1992), 11–38.

Shalhope, Robert E. *The Roots of Democracy: American Thought and Culture, 1760–1800.* Boston: Twayne, 1990.

Smith, Rogers M. "Beyond Tocqueville, Myrdal, and Hartz: The Multiple Traditions in America." *American Political Science Review* 87 (1993), 549–66.

Wood, Gordon S. *The Creation of the American Republic, 1776–1787.* Chapel Hill: University of North Carolina Press, 1969.

ROBERT E. SHALHOPE

Revolutionary War

See war for independence.

Rocky Mountain region

While the political history of the Rocky Mountain region—Montana, Wyoming, Colorado, Idaho, Utah, Nevada, Arizona, and New Mexico—does not lack stories of partisan division and struggle, a greater share of that history challenges the assumptions and conventions of party loyalty and identification. Over a century and a half, the desires for economic development and federal money have acted as incentives to pay little attention to the usual boundaries of party. A proliferation of factions and interest groups has often muddled efforts to define and patrol the usual lines of partisanship. Reinforced by an enthusiasm for individualism and independence, electoral success has frequently coincided with eccentric personality and temperament in the candidate. In the Rockies, traditional party activists have often found themselves a demoralized people, bucking a trend toward the hybrid and the maverick.

For all the electoral success awarded to eccentrics who set their own courses, the political history of the region in the last century tracks the usual arrangement of eras and phases in American political history. And yet the region's citizens gave those familiar eras a distinctive or even unique inflection. Moreover, the U.S. Constitution enhanced the national impact of the Rockies, since states with comparatively sparse populations were awarded the same number of senators as eastern states with dense populations. Thus, a number of senators from the Rocky Mountain states have exercised consequential power in national and international decisions.

In the invasion, conquest, mastery, and development of the interior West, an initially weak federal government acquired greater authority, force, and legitimacy. The history of the Rockies is rich in case studies of agencies and institutions of the federal government exercising a remarkable force in the political life (not to mention the social, cultural, economic, and emotional life) of the region. Under the Department of State until 1873 and then under the Department of the Interior, the territorial system oversaw the progression (sometimes quite prolonged and halting) to statehood. Even after statehood, the residents of the Rockies found themselves subject to the rules, regulations, and sometimes arbitrary authority of agencies in the executive branch, many of them clustered in the Department of the Interior: the Office (later Bureau) of Indian Affairs, the U.S. Army (both the combat forces and the Army Corps of Engineers), the U.S. Geological Survey, the Bureau of Reclamation, the Forest Service, the National Park Service, the Fish and Wildlife Service, the Bureau of Land Management (a hybrid itself of the venerable General Land Office and the more junior Grazing Service), the Atomic Energy Commission, the Department of Energy, and the Environmental Protection Agency.

Many of the activities of federal agencies in the Rockies focus on the management, use, preservation, and regulation of the region's mountains, canyons, and deserts. In national politics, the issues that have come to occupy the category of "the environment" have fluctuated in the attention paid to them, sometimes dipping below visibility. In the Rockies, policies governing water, land, and wildlife have long held a place at the center of political life; the region has thus functioned as a political seismograph, recording dramatic shifts in attitudes toward nature. This is a region in which indigenous peoples retain important roles in local, state, and national politics, as do the "other" conquered people—the descendants of Mexicans who lived in the territory acquired by the United States in the Mexican-American War. In this case and in the case of Asian immigrants, western race relations are often intertwined with international relations, with the terms of treaties and the actions of consuls stirred into the struggles of civil rights. The great diversity of the population meant that the civil rights era had many dimensions, as Indians, Mexican Americans, Asian Americans, and African Americans pursued similar, though sometimes conflicting, agendas of self-assertion.

Early Native American Political Systems and Conflicts

Diversity, variation, and complex negotiations between and among peoples set the terms for Rocky Mountain politics long before the arrival of Europeans. Decentralized governance characterized the nomadic groups of the northern Rockies as well as the Southwest, with the band far more established as the unit of loyalty than any broader tribal identity. Kinship set the terms of cohesion and obligation, and leaders rose to authority by repeated demonstrations of their courage and wisdom.

The arrival of Spanish explorers, soldiers, settlers, and missionaries near the end of the sixteenth century initiated a long-running struggle for imperial dominance. As the more rigid and hierarchical systems of Europeans encountered the widely varying structures of leadership among native peoples, the comparatively simple dreams of empire produced far more tangled realities. One particularly ironic and awkward outcome was the rise of a vigorous slave trade in the Southwest, as Utes, Navajos, and Apaches traded captives from other tribes to Spanish settlers; centuries later, under U.S. governance, the campaign for the abolition of the interior West's version of slavery extended well beyond the abolition of the much better known practices of the American South.

The Spanish introduction of horses into North America unleashed a cascade of unintended and unforeseen rearrangements in the balance of power. With the horse, Indian people took possession of a new mobility for trading, raiding, hunting, and warfare. The spread of the horse unsettled the balance of power between the newly mounted native people and their would-be European conquerors. When the Navajos and Apaches, as well as the Utes and Comanches (nomadic people to the north of the New Mexican settlements) took up the horse, both Pueblo Indians and Spanish settlers found themselves living in communities where the possibilty of a raid was a constant source of risk and vulnerability.

The opportunities for bison hunting and migration offered by the horse brought new peoples into the region, and thereby accelerated the contests for turf and power. By the time of European contact, these groups would become known as the Cheyenne, Arapaho, Sioux, Crow, Blackfeet, Shoshone, Gros Ventre, and Nez Perce. In the northern and central Rockies, while people with a shared language, similar religious beliefs, and a sense of common origin gathered together annually for ceremonies, they spent most of the year divided into bands who dispersed for hunting and gathering through much of the year. Tribes varied widely in the formality and informality of their designation of leaders. In many groups, men rose to leadership through constant and repeated demonstration of generosity and courage. For most tribes, decisions rested on consensus emerging from long discussion. Over the next centuries, the political diversity and complexity of the native groups, as well as their democratic forms of decision making, would perplex European and American newcomers to the Rocky Mountains. Non-Indian explorers, emissaries, or military leaders, who arrived expecting to meet a group and identify a man or men who carried the authority to make lasting decisions for all, had come to the wrong place.

Centralized, imperial authority held sway only intermittently in locations remote from capitals and home offices. Disunity and opposing factions within the colonial society could set the empire's plans to wobbling as effectively as resistance from the indigenous communities.

The Mexican Period and Fluid National Boundaries

Mexican independence in 1821 introduced even greater complexity to an already complicated and precarious political landscape. One of the most consequential actions of the new nation was the opening of the northern borderlands to trade with Americans, a change in policy of great political consequence. As merchants began traveling back and forth between Santa Fe, New Mexico, and St. Louis, Missouri, the United States acquired the chance to have a commercial presence, initially tolerated and welcomed, in Mexican terrain. But the Santa Fe trade presented the possibility of a conquest by merchants, and Mexican authorities struggled to limit the intrusions of the legal and illegal aliens of their day.

Thus, by the 1820s, the future of sovereignty in the Rocky Mountains was an unsettled domain. It was one thing to sit in distant offices and trace lines of sovereignty on a map, and quite another to give substance and meaning to those lines. No other section of the United States experienced so many changes in national boundaries and came under so many governmental jurisdictions. In the first half of the nineteenth century, maps of the Rockies recorded claims by six nations: Spain, France, Mexico, Britain, the United States, and the independent republic of Texas. The former Spanish territories—from the southwest corner of Wyoming through the western half of Colorado, and the bulk of what would become Utah, Nevada, Arizona, and New Mexico—remained under Mexican control after independence. The purchase of the Louisiana Territory from the French placed the central and northern Rockies under the sovereignty of the United States. Between 1836 and 1850, Texas claimed portions of New Mexico, Colorado, and even a sliver of Wyoming. Meanwhile, the area now called Idaho fell under the joint occupation of Great Britain and the United States until awarded to the United States by treaty in 1846. These "official" Euro-American boundaries, moreover, existed in not particularly splendid isolation from the most important dimension of power on the ground: the authority of the Indian tribes.

The aridity, elevation, and difficult terrain of much of the Rockies further challenged the aspirations of empire. The area seemed, as early explorers bluntly noted, ill-suited to conventional American agricultural settlement. Given the aridity in the interior West, it seemed possible that Americans would find that they had no need or desire to assert power over areas like the Great Salt Lake Basin, since there seemed to be no imaginable economic use to which to put them. And yet Americans still hoped that explorers would uncover other resources that would inspire settlers and lead to the political incorporation of this territory into the nation. Still, the pursuit of beaver pelts, the key resource of the 1820s and 1830s, did not offer much of a foundation for a new political order. As it did elsewhere on the continent, the fur trade brought Euro-Americans and Indian people into a "middle ground" of shifting power, with no obvious answer to the question of who was in charge.

In 1846, the joint occupancy of the Northwest came to an end, assigning the Oregon territory to the United States. The Mexican-American War dramatically rearranged the lines of sovereignty to the advantage of the United States. In 1848 the Treaty of Guadalupe Hidalgo transferred more than one-third of Mexico's land to the Americans. Hundreds of one-time Mexican citizens found themselves reconstituted as residents of the United States. In a promise that, in the judgment of some latter-day activists, still awaits full delivery, Article IX of the treaty declared that the Mexicans in the acquired territories ". . . who shall not preserve the character of citizens of the Mexican Republic . . . shall be incorporated into the Union of the United States, and be admitted at the proper time (to be judged of by the Congress of the United States) to the enjoyment of all the rights of citizens of the United States."

With the Gadsden Purchase of 1853, the United States achieved its lasting borders. The value of the territory of the Rocky Mountains was undemonstrated and unrecognized; it had simply been necessary to acquire this land in order to span the continent from sea to sea. In the 1840s, the movements of Americans—overland travelers on their way to California and Oregon, and then, in the late 1850s, gold seekers drawn to discoveries in Colorado and Nevada—began to give on-the-ground meaning to U.S. territorial claims. And yet the undiminished powers of Indian tribes still rendered the U.S claims both hollow and precarious.

Civil War, Reconstruction, Territories, and Indian Conquest

The discovery of gold and silver put to rest any lingering doubt that the territory of the Rockies might not be worth the trouble of political incorporation. In many sites in the mountains, collections of individualistic strangers improvised methods of governance that would, at the least, formalize mining claims and property rights. The political unit of the mining district tied small camps together and established procedures for platting out the district's boundaries, defining claims, setting up law-enforcement and court systems, and establishing water rights, most often through the system known as prior appropriation, or "first in time, first in right." Settlers also sought recognition, organization, and aid from the federal government.

For white Americans newly arrived in Colorado, the onset of the Civil War brought a heightened sense of vulnerability to Indian attack, since the new settlements depended on an overstretched and ill-defended supply line to the Midwest, and the resources and attention of the Union Army were directed to the war in the East. The primary feature of the Civil War era in the Rocky Mountain region was thus an escalation of Indian-white violence, as militia and volunteer forces reacted forcefully to threats and suspicions. With the shift of federal attention away from the West, at the Bear River Massacre in Utah, at the Sand Creek Massacre in Colorado, and in the campaign against the Navajo, the conduct of white soldiers and volunteers was often extreme and unregulated.

The Confederate Territory of Arizona (the southern half of the New Mexico Territory) represented the one foothold of the rebellion in the West. Operating out of Texas, Confederate troops entered New Mexico, took Santa Fe, and headed north to take the Colorado gold mines, but then met defeat from a Colorado militia at Glorieta Pass. With this battle, the question of the loyalty of the Rocky Mountain states was put to rest.

The post–Civil War era in the Rockies gained its shape and structure from three major projects: creating territories and then determining when they had reached the condition that justified the awarding of statehood; designing and installing systems for allocating property in minerals, land, water, and transportation routes; and conquering (sometimes through direct military engagements and sometimes through more subtle processes of negotiation and escalating economic dependence) the Indian people of the region and confining them to reservations under treaties that, even if negotiated under terms of surrender and defeat, nonetheless turned out to provide a basis for a reassertion of Indian self-governance a century later.

Mining towns like Black Hawk, Colorado, shown here circa 1878, developed in the Rocky Mountain region after discoveries of gold or silver. (Charles Weitfle/Miningbureau.com)

In the post–Civil War era, the political circumstances of the West both resembled and differed from the political circumstances of the South. In the Reconstruction enterprise of providing the vote to African American men, the West led the South. African Americans in Colorado tied the cause of black suffrage to the cause of statehood, and enlisted influential senators to their cause. The Territorial Suffrage Act of 1867 granted the vote to African American men in the territories, two months before the first Reconstruction Act gave freedmen the vote in the former Confederacy.

In their greatest era of common experience, the South and the West were the targets and subjects of the attentions, plans, and reforms of ambitious northern Republicans. If the word *Reconstruction* sums up this experience for the South, historian David Emmons has argued, the similar process for the West might more accurately be called Construction. In the South, Republicans undertook to reconstruct a comparatively well-defined social and political order, while in the West, without a comparable, well-established elite like the southern planters, the Republicans had the opportunity to construct a new political and economic order from the foundation. Under the terms of territorial government, American citizens found their assumed rights of self-government temporarily (for New Mexico and Arizona, this "temporary" status endured for over 60 years) diminished and restricted. They could elect their territorial legislators, and they could send a nonvoting delegate to Congress, but the federal government appointed the governor and (perhaps even more important) the judges. Those who chafed under this regime and longed for statehood often found that their cause had become thoroughly entangled in national tussles over slavery, race, and partisan dominance in Congress.

Through most of the territorial period, Republicans held the presidency, and Democrat Grover Cleveland did not make a consistent practice of using his patronage power to replace Republicans with Democrats in territorial positions. At first glance, this situation may have seemed to give an advantage to Republicans in shaping the partisan leanings of the territories under their governance. But territorial government was so unpopular, and the governors so often resented and disliked, that the Republican advantage in appointments over the territorial period may actually have worked in favor of the Democrats, or at least did them little injury. Historian Earl Pomeroy has reported that Democrats in Montana in 1877 privately acknowledged that they were happy to have a Republican governor, noting that "it will keep the [Republican] party divided and we will stand a much better show to defeat them in the elections." Even though denunciation of appointed officers as outsiders was a standard refrain, appointing a local man to office did not necessarily increase the supply of goodwill. The legacy of territorial status lingered in the minds, hearts, and certainly the rhetorical reserves of Westerners, enhancing resentment of the federal government and reinforcing a sense of powerlessness and victimization. As Pomeroy has observed, the "political complexions" of the Rocky Mountain states came out of the territorial period stamped as "unpredictable, insurgent."

Tension over the control exercised by Congress and presidential appointees was most sustained in Utah, as northern Republicans undertook to eliminate Mormon polygamy, which they had initially paired with slavery as one of the "twin relics of barbarism." Before the creation of the Utah Territory, and in the years in which Mormon Church leader Brigham Young held the office of governor, the Mormon homeland of Deseret was a theocracy, a state of affairs that troubled the souls of northern Republicans even as they themselves were guided in many of their own political undertakings by Protestant Christianity. With a sequence of increasingly forceful antipolygamy laws, the federal government undertook a purposeful campaign to end Mormon political and cultural distinctiveness, including congressionally mandated disenfranchisement of Utah territory women in 1887. The Woodruff Manifesto in 1890, renouncing polygamy, was a key step in Utah's progression toward legitimacy and statehood. How to shift the distinct politics of Utah to the partisan rivalries of the nation as a whole was far more complicated and orchestrated with considerably less explicit exercise of church authority. Given the long campaign of persecution of the church by the Republican Party during the territorial period, the Mormons' eventual shift to a strong Republican affiliation offered its own telling demonstration that political categories have shown, in this region, a remarkable capacity for reconfiguration and realignment.

Along with territorial government, a second major arena for the process of "constructing" the West involved the federal government's allocation of property rights in transportation routes, land, minerals, and water. The remoteness and isolation of the region made the building of railroads a major concern of settlers; by ending the struggle over whether the route of the transcontinental railroad would serve the interests of the North or the

South, the secession of the Confederacy opened the way for the Pacific Railroad Act of 1862, providing crucial government aid. In a similar way, secession cleared the way for the passage of the Homestead Act in 1862, followed by a complicated stream of legislation trying to adapt the homestead principle to the difficult terrain of the Rockies. The 1872 Mining Law took the local improvisations of the mining West and built them into federal legislation, guaranteeing free access of prospectors and miners to the public domain and omitting a royalty that would have directed a portion of the revenue from mining to the public treasury. The allocation of water presented the greatest challenge to federal hopes of bringing order to the West; under the doctrine of prior appropriation, a tangle of water rights already held status in the region well before Congress or the executive branch could try to establish a national policy.

In the last half of the nineteenth century, the most unambiguous display of federal power occurred in the final campaigns of conquest against Indian people. After the Civil War, the West became the main arena for the military campaigns of the U.S. Army. Military forts and posts, already significant, gained in importance as economic drivers for the region. In 1849, jurisdiction over the Office of Indian Affairs transferred from the Department of War to the newly established the Department of Interior. This shift of agencies gave institutional form to the contest between civilians and the military in setting the direction of Indian relations.

In the region of the Rockies, Indian peoples tried every imaginable strategy to respond to the imposition of American power. Even as the Sioux and Cheyenne fought against George Armstrong Custer in the battle at Little Big Horn, Crow Indians allied themselves with Custer as scouts and auxiliaries. In the Southwest, the Army used Apache scouts to find and pursue other Apaches who had refused to surrender. In their dealings with the Americans, native peoples chose various combinations of alliance and resistance, and those choices meant stress and strain for Indian communities. All these strategies led to the negotiation (and sometimes imposition) of treaties shrinking the tribes' land holdings, designating reservations for their confinement, ending their mobility, prohibiting their religious practices, and subordinating tribal leadership to the arbitrary powers of appointed agents of the Office of Indian Affairs. And yet the treaties also recorded a formal recognition of the tribes and their rights, providing the foundation for the U.S. Supreme Court's recognition of tribal sovereignty a century later.

In this era of constructing the region, voters responded with enthusiasm to the idea of governmental support for economic development, and with that priority front and center, the warmth of support could shift easily and rapidly from Republican to Democratic and back again. The category of "booster of the economy" trumped party affiliation. In states like Nevada, Colorado, or Montana, with the mining industry at the center of the economy, the state legislatures had a way of selecting (sometimes with an incentive, encouragement, or bribe provided by the aspiring officeholder) the heads of mining companies to serve in the Senate. In any individual state or territory, citizens sparred and struggled over the material benefits and advantages delivered by political success, but these contests were rarely guided by political principle. A term coined by historian Kenneth Owens, *chaotic factionalism*, goes a long way toward capturing the reality of political conduct in the Rockies in the last half of the nineteenth century. The term works equally well when applied to Indian tribes, making difficult choices between resistance and accommodation; to the agencies and officials of the federal government; *and* to the region's Euro-American settlers, almost infinitely divided by nationality, class, and competing occupations and professions.

Rocky Mountain Style Populism and Progressivism

In the 1890s, populism diminished the "chaotic" part of "factionalism" for at least a few years. Responding to the serious economic troubles of that decade, the People's Party posed a genuine challenge to northeastern political and economic dominance, as a sectional party with a complicated mix of southern and western dimensions. Fusion politics—loose, temporary alliances across party lines—spurred campaigns that emphasized issues and candidates over party loyalty. The 1896 campaign of Democrat William Jennings Bryan marked the high point of fusion politics in the interior West. Bryan's pro-labor and pro-silver Populist Party/Democratic Party coalition earned the popular and electoral votes of every western state except California and Oregon. The election also highlighted the limits of Rocky Mountain electoral power, since states with such sparse populations yielded just a fraction of the electoral votes Bryan would have needed to win the presidency. Carrying the Rockies still meant losing nationwide.

Demanding federal intervention and protections against burdensome railroad shipping rates and arbitrary charges for the storage and marketing of grain, farm families were the backbone of Midwestern and southern populism. In the Rockies, the activism of miners and their unions gave rise to a more inclusive and class-conscious form of populism. Rocky Mountain populism brought together a coalition of farmers, workers, and small businesspeople. This large voting bloc helped elect more Peoples' Party candidates in the mountain states than in any other region. Populist goals moved well beyond economic protections for farmers to include passage of the nation's first eight-hour day laws and protections for union organizing. Populist support for women's suffrage spurred the enactment of that radical measure, and thus gave additional clout to the voting power of the People's Party in Colorado, Utah, and Idaho. The Populist enthusiasm for "direct democracy" also fired up voter interest in election campaigns in the Rockies. Electoral reforms like the voter initiative and referendum, and the direct election of senators, were not unique to the Mountain West, and yet, embraced by voters, they quickly became the hallmark of elections and lawmaking in the region during and after the 1890s.

Four of the Rocky Mountain states—Wyoming (1869 territory, 1890 state), Colorado (1893 state), Utah (1870 territory, until congressional disenfranchisement in 1887; 1896 state), and Idaho (1896 state)—led in the cause of women's voting rights in the United States. Arizona women voted by 1912, joined by women in Nevada and Montana in 1914, all well in advance of the passage of the Nineteenth Amendment in 1920. Voting rights in all of the interior mountain states were achieved through popular referenda, demonstrating a remarkable willingness to experiment on the part of male voters. Strong and active mining unions, as well as the influential Populist Party, proved receptive to efforts of persuasion and recruitment by activist women. Women's unmistakable importance in the household economies of farming and ranching carried a symbolic power that, in itself, made a case for suffrage.

The Mountain West also led the nation in women's party and electoral activism. From 1896 to 1910, when no additional states granted suffrage, an era that eastern suffragists and historians have dubbed "the doldrums," women in the first four Rocky Mountain suffrage states seized their new powers. Spurred on by the belief that western politics offered a greater openness to experimentation, suffrage leaders in the Rocky Mountain states often reached across dividing lines of place, race, ethnicity, creed, and economic circumstance to win both men and women to their cause. In many states of the region, early women activists and voters embraced "nonpartisanship," furthered third-party movements and independent candidates, promoted public referenda to circumvent entrenched and lethargic state legislators, and won early electoral reforms like primary election laws opening up the nomination process to wider constituencies. Partisan women in the interior West also worked to open up the party machinery to broader participation, with Mountain West women emerging as the nation's first female elected officials, well into the Progressive and New Deal Eras.

Even though the Populist Party had faded in membership and influence by 1900, many of the innovations it had placed on the political agenda came to fruition during the Progressive Era. The legacy of western populism, ongoing labor activism, women's independent voting patterns, and the sweeping national reform movement known as progressivism combined to produce a whirlwind of political reforms in the Rockies. Since participants in this movement were sometimes Republicans, sometimes Democrats, and sometimes members of the Progressive Party, this era made its own contribution to the muddling of partisan identity in the region.

The fact that the Progressive Era coincided with the era of labor wars in the Rockies made a reckoning with the tensions of industrial labor relations unavoidable. Under the militant leadership of the Western Federation of Miners, unions spread in the precious-metal mining districts, especially in Colorado, Idaho, Utah, and Montana. At the same time, organizers for the United Mine Workers went into action in Utah, Colorado, and New Mexico to establish union locals in coal mining communities. Strikes often edged into violence, as miners clashed not only with company guards but also with state troops. The repetitious pattern of state intervention of the military on behalf of mining companies produced political repercussions regionally and nationally. Created by Congress in 1912, the Commission on Industrial Relations led by Frank Walsh held highly visible hearings on Colorado's Ludlow Massacre. In 1914 a strike against the Colorado Oil and Fuel Company, owned by John D. Rockefeller Jr. exploded in a long run of violence involving strikers, their families, mine guards, and the Colorado National Guard. When Rockefeller and labor activist Mother Jones both testified at the Walsh Commission hearings, the intensity of labor struggles in the Rockies preoccupied the nation.

Beyond strikes, the members of mining and other labor unions in the mountain states joined the political fray in state legislatures, electoral campaigns, and voter initiatives. The eight-hour workday, workers' compensation acts, unemployment relief, and laws protecting union organizing came relatively early in the Rocky Mountain states. The nation's first eight-hour day law for miners in the nation was passed (and upheld by the U.S. Supreme Court) in the Utah legislature in 1899. The peaceful, effective, and legal political activity of unionists in the Rocky Mountain region contrasted dramatically with the "pure and simple" unionism of the eastern leadership of the American Federation of Labor. The pursuit of progressive unionism also portrayed union members as good citizens and voters, quite different from the violent terrorists that newspapers of the time often made them out to be based on the actions of a few hard-boiled radical union leaders.

Water and Progressivism in the Semi-Arid Rockies

Urban progressivism gained a foothold in Denver, Colorado; Salt Lake City, Utah; Boise, Idaho; and Albuquerque and Santa Fe, New Mexico. Middle-class women reformers played a direct and visible role as enfranchised citizens in western urban reform movements, which by and large matched the national pattern of concerns for public education, civil service laws, juvenile courts, child labor laws, public transportation franchises, public health, and sanitation. Water supply added a regional variation to the Progressive agenda, as urbanites responded to the challenges of aridity. In Denver, women's groups joined forces with men's civic associations and union leaders to demand public control of the city water system, resulting in the creation of the Denver Water Department, a quasi-public agency with an enormous impact on the allocation and distribution of water in the Rockies. Over the next century, Denver Water would be a central case study in the mounting friction between urban and rural interests, as conflicting visions of the region's political and economic future came to focus on the supply of water.

In Progressive minds, the storage and diversion of water in dams and canals fell under the category of conservation, since water left in streams and rivers seemed wasted and thus in need of "conserving" for productive use. Nevada Democratic U. S. senator Francis Newlands led the campaign for the Newlands Reclamation Act in 1902, setting up the framework for the Reclamation Service (later, the Bureau of Reclamation) to build dams and reservoirs to supply water to farms and ranches. The passage of the Reclamation Act has posed a puzzle for historians: Why did senators and congressmen, representing eastern and Midwestern regions with agricultural sectors, vote in favor of a federal program to aid their competitors in the arid West? Historian Don Pisani has solved this riddle with a finding of relevance to the big picture of the region's political history: the passage of the Reclamation Act offers prime evidence of "the West's increasing power in Congress," produced by the admission, in the 1890s, of North and South Dakota, Montana, Washington, Idaho, Utah, and Wyoming, with those seven additional states having two senators each. The West now "had the power to block important legislation in the Senate," and recognition of that power "explains the passage of the Reclamation Act."

In both the Progressive and New Deal Eras, enthusiasm for dam building was widespread, in a dramatic contrast to lamentations in the mid- and late twentieth century over the disturbance of free-flowing rivers. Considerably more controversial was the revolution in federal management of the public domain, as policy shifted from disposal (the transfer to private ownership) to the permanent reservation of lands under federal control. With much of his hearty public image derived from his hunting expeditions in the Rockies, President Theodore Roosevelt and his chief forester Gifford Pinchot were the iconic proponents of this enormous change. Progressive conservation launched a process that remapped the Rockies, with half or more of land recategorized as public, not private, property.

To many Westerners, ranging from the heads of large mining and timber corporations to small-scale ranchers, the creation of the Forest Service and the National Park Service seemed not an exciting and enterprising invention of a new form of land management, but a resurgence of the familiar colonialism of the territorial period. The struggle, both rhetorical and material, between the authority of the states and the authority of the federal government would remain central to regional political life, even as economic change revealed that landscapes reserved from extractive activity could provide equally valuable economic opportunities in recreation and tourism.

During World War I and into the 1920s, the efforts at political cooperation between the middle class and workers took a downturn, as anti-immigrant and antilabor political movements gained force. A mob in Bisbee, Arizona, forcefully deported over a thousand striking miners to a remote desert town in New Mexico in 1917; in Montana, alarm over the speeches and actions of the Industrial Workers of the World came to reshape the basic terms of national civil liberties. During the war, the Sedition Act of 1798 had come back into play as prosecutors around the country used it to bring charges against people who criticized the war or the government. Wanting more power to police than the 1798 law provided, Democratic senator Henry Myers of Montana proposed a bill in Congress in August 1917 that gave the terms of sedition a very broad definition, including criticism of the government during wartime; when it failed to pass at the national level, the Montana legislature "recycled" it, passing it in 1918. With the national mood toward dissent souring, Senator Myers then returned to Washington, D.C., and proposed the bill again. This time, it passed with only minor changes.

The Mountain West's Imprint on New Deal Politics and Policy

Already of inestimable importance in the Rockies, the role of the federal government expanded in the Depression, as federal funding provided the investments once derived from private capital. The operations of the New Deal proved compatible with the enthusiasm of western political leaders for economic development. The landslide victory of Franklin D. Roosevelt throughout the West in 1932 and in subsequent elections, moreover, reconfirmed the power of personality in the region's political culture. Warm feelings toward Roosevelt were validated and reconfirmed as the Rocky Mountain states received a disproportionately large flow of federal dollars per capita. The interior mountain states' regional average was between one-third and one-half more than the next highest region, the Pacific states, and double that received by the states in the Great Plains. One form of federal funding had a lasting impact on the region's landscape, providing an important foundation for the growing tourism economy. Teams of the Civilian Conservation Corps (CCC) cleared hundreds of mountain trails, built roads and bridges, and even carved a spectacular public amphitheater, near Denver, out of solid red rock.

Representatives from the Rocky Mountain states had an important impact in the area of federal agricultural policy and aid programs. Most notably, the Taylor Grazing Act of 1934, sponsored by Colorado's Democratic congressman, Edward P. Taylor, rescued the region's cattle industry from extinction during the drought-ridden 1930s by regulating grazing on federal land. In the next quarter century, the Grazing Service would be merged with the General Land Office to become the Bureau of Land Management, the federal agency with the ironic combination of the largest territory with the lowest profile and funding.

At the other end of the spectrum of visibility and fame, Hoover Dam remains the most telling monument

Hoover Dam was completed in 1935 on the border between Arizona and Nevada. (Library of Congress)

to the centrality of Depression-era federal funding in the Rocky Mountain West. As much as the dam has come to stand for New Deal achievements, its very existence was made possible by its pre–New Deal namesake, Herbert Hoover, and his work as secretary of commerce in negotiating the Colorado River Compact of 1922. The compact, as an interstate agreement signed by all the western states through which the river flowed, was itself a political innovation. By the early 1920s, uncertainty over the provisions for allocating the waters of the Colorado River put the economic well-being of all the neighboring states at risk. Called together by Secretary of Commerce Hoover, representatives from Arizona, California, Colorado, Nevada, New Mexico, Utah, and Wyoming all signed on to a plan to divide the flow of the river between the Colorado River's upper and lower basins. Even though the agreement assumed a much greater and steadier flow of water than the river actually delivered, the compact provided the legal foundation for construction of Hoover Dam and the massive system of dams and reservoirs along the Colorado.

The Military in the Mountain West

In the 1940s, the Mountain West had both an extraordinary range of federally controlled open spaces in remote locations and an extraordinary enthusiasm on the part of local communities for jobs arising from federal projects. The match between these qualifications and the needs of the American military was an obvious one. The technology involved may have been innovative and novel, but these military installations in the West echoed and even revived the pattern of the nineteenth century, when Army forts had played an important role in providing markets for farmers, ranchers, and merchants. World War II and the cold war led to a resurgence in the importance of the military in the region, with new military posts and bases, as well as contractor-operated defense plants. The majority of the strategically remote Japanese American internment camps dotted the interior West. The Manhattan Project made Los Alamos, New Mexico, into the vital center of the new nuclear age. As the cold war arms race gathered momentum, the interior West won the competition for many of the key facilities in nuclear weapons production: the Nevada Nuclear Test Site north of Las Vegas, the Idaho National Engineering Labs near Twin Falls, the Sandia Laboratory in Albuquerque, and the Rocky Flats nuclear weapons plant near Denver. All of these research and production facilities generated contaminated material and waste requiring permanent storage, and after considerable controversy, the Waste Isolation Pilot Project near Carlsbad, New Mexico, came into operation in 1999. The passage of time would make the legacy of these enterprises into yet another source of tense relations between Westerners and the federal government, as communities worried about the dangers of radioactivity in the soil, water, and air, and workers from the plants asked for a reckoning with the health impacts of their jobs.

Defense projects brought millions of dollars and hundreds of new residents into the region during and after World War II. In ways both directly and indirectly related to those projects, the cold war reconfigured both the western infrastructure and political landscape. Justified by the needs of national security, the Highway Act of 1956 transformed transportation through the region. In the mid-twentieth century, the Bureau of Reclamation went into overdrive, designing, funding, and operating a new network of dams and diversions. Here, too, cold war justifications played their part; the interior West's greatest champion of water projects, Democratic congressman Wayne Aspinall from western Colorado, was also an outspoken cold warrior, drawing anti-Communist rhetoric into the arguments he made for more dams. The massive Central Arizona and Central Utah Projects represented both the enthusiasm of the interior West's residents for federally subsidized economic development and the ambitions of the Bureau of Reclamation at their peak.

The Politics of Post–World War II Demographic Shifts and Environmentalism in the Rocky Mountain West

Central to the political changes of World War II and the cold war was the push for greater power and representation on the part of Indians, Mexican Americans, Asian Americans, and African Americans. The civil rights movements of the Rockies were thus multiple and varied, ranging from the reclaiming of treaty rights by Indian tribes to the protesting of segregation, on the part of both Mexican Americans and African Americans, in the Denver school system, with Asian Americans contesting both discrimination and relegation to the status of "model minority." All these campaigns for rights took place in the context of a region shaped by waves of migration and immigration, leaving the legitimacy of any group or individual always open to dispute, as were the roles of insider and outsider. Tensions over population growth thus sometimes pitted groups of white Americans against other white Americans, as "old-timers" and "newcomers" squared off in an ongoing dispute of who was a deserving resident of the Rockies and who was an unwelcome intruder. In that context, with citizens already squabbling intensely among each other, the issue of immigration policy—and especially the status of Mexican immigrants—could be the subject of heated debate while also registering as just another one of many disputes over who deserved the status of rightful Rockies resident.

While the region held no particular advantage over any part of the nation in its progression toward racial inclusiveness and equity in the political process, the history of Denver's election of mayors is nonetheless striking, with the Latino Federico Peña serving from 1983 to 1991, followed by the African American Wellington Webb. In the same spirit, when the state of Idaho became the home of pernicious white supremacy groups, citizens of the state rallied with a number of organizations, monuments, and governmental resolutions, denouncing racism and defending human rights. Idaho's Malicious Harassment Act of 1983, adding force to the prosecution of "crimes based on religious and racial hatred," was, as Stephen Shaw has described it, "the product of bipartisan effort in the Idaho legislature and especially between a Democratic governor and a Republican attorney general."

In the second half of the twentieth century, an extraordinary reorientation of public opinion and legislation brought on a political earthquake that has not stopped shaking voters and elected officials in the interior West. For more than a century, the discovery and development of natural resources, and the use of land and water to support expanding human settlement, had the enthusiastic support of most Westerners. As the national movement known as environmentalism played out, with particular impact in the interior West, it dramatically shifted the very direction of progress and improvement. In the minds—and votes—of many, the direction ascribed to progress reversed, as population growth and economic development were recast, not as the hope of the region but as its bane and burden. As articulate, powerful, and well-funded organizations, exemplified by the successful voter initiative rejecting Colorado's bid for the 1976 Winter Olympics, campaigned for the preservation of natural ecosystems, a new political alignment came into being.

The most consequential element of this change was the passage of an extraordinary package of environmental laws in the 1960s and 1970s, ranging from the Wilderness Act of 1964 to the Endangered Species Act of 1973. Without the active and committed support of both Republican and Democratic members of Congress (and the signature of Republican president Richard Nixon), most of these laws would have remained pipe dreams. But as they went into effect, the memory of their bipartisan origins faded from public awareness. Astute Republican office seekers in the Rockies seized the opportunity presented by the friction and frustration arising from the implementation of environmental laws. With an agile dismissal of recent history, they built an image of the Republican Party as the standard-bearer for the right of local Westerners to use natural resources, free of burdensome regulations and restraints imposed by the imperial East. In the Rockies, as elsewhere in the nation, Democrats became more and more identified as the party allied with federal oversight and environmental causes, and Republicans became more and more identified as the party supporting the traditional forces for development, extraction, and growth, a configuration without particularly deep roots in time.

Of the many environmental laws passed in the 1970s, the Federal Land Policy and Management Act (FLPMA) of 1976—the organic act that belatedly established the specific powers and mission of the Bureau of Land Management (BLM) 30 years after its birth—had the greatest effect in stirring up local resistance. The FLPMA gave the BLM (cynically nicknamed the "Bureau of Livestock and Mining") a much broader, "multiuse" mandate, with recreational and ecological values now included in the BLM's mandate, along with extractive uses. In areas where locals had come to take for granted their right to graze livestock, make mining claims, and build roads on public lands, the FLPMA evoked strong resentment. In the late 1970s, the Sagebrush Rebellion, calling for the transfer of federal lands to state ownership, as well as relief from federal grazing, mineral, water, and environmental regulations, became a force in several legislatures in the region. Nevada set the precedent with a resolution in 1979 with Assembly Bill 413 mandating the transfer of BLM lands to the state, and Arizona, New Mexico, Utah, and Wyoming passed similar laws. In the manner of such campaigns, Sagebrush Rebels championed the cause of small-scale ranchers, loggers, or miners. While many of their troubles stemmed from changes in the national and even international economy rather than from federal intrusion, many of the reforms they sought also suited the purposes of extractive corporations operating on a vastly larger scale. Senator Orrin Hatch of Utah introduced the Western Lands Distribution and Regional Equalization Act—a Sagebrush Rebellion bill—in Congress in the fall of 1979, but the election of Ronald Reagan in 1980 took the wind out of the sails of the Sagebrush Rebellion, with the installation of a presidential administration that declared official sympathy and support for the rebels.

Rocky Mountain Federalism: Late Twentieth-Century National and Local Politics

Since the 1970s, the majority of the region's electoral votes have gone to Republican presidential candidates, tempting pundits to declare that the region had become solidly and definitively conservative. And yet the region's voters often chose Democrats as governors, senators, and congresspeople. The case study of Idaho makes this point dramatically: widely characterized as extremely conservative, the voters of Idaho four times elected Democrat Cecil Andrus as governor. Utah's history makes the same point: between 1965 and 1985, Democrats (Calvin Rampton, followed by Scott Matheson) held the post of governor. Gubernatorial elections have never ceased to follow a pattern of committed variability: in 2000, all eight of the Rocky Mountain states had Republican governors, but by 2006 five had chosen Democrats as governors. The region's defiance of clear and steady political categorization, and the reluctance of many voters to see themselves as consistent party loyalists, continued into the twenty-first century.

The Republican Party, meanwhile, faced a number of tough challenges in self-definition. To some degree, this involved the national split between social conservatives and fiscal conservatives. But the energy boom of the 1990s and the early twentieth-first century opened new rifts in the center of the party. Beginning in the 1990s, a big boom in natural gas production in the Rockies strained Republican unity, as oil and gas developers struggled with opposition from ranchers and sportsmen. A shared identification of all these people as "conservatives" did nothing to reduce this conflict.

While some Rocky Mountain residents gave unswerving support to the cause of environmental preservation and some gave equally single-minded support to the extraction of natural resources, a much larger percentage of the region's residents occupied a category one could call "the muddled majority," with attitudes that were far more characterized by hybridity than by purity. This majority tried to accommodate its desire for the resources produced by extraction to the changing economic valuation of nature, as recreation, tourism, second homes, and the attraction of intact landscapes to employers and employees became increasingly powerful forces in local and state economies.

As a practice called cooperative conservation emerged in response to this complicated set of issues, the political world of the Rockies presented an instructive and telling laboratory for experiments in the evolving meaning of federalism. In many arenas, the relationship between federal authority and local governments came up for renegotiation and redefinition. Over a century and a half, the region had emerged with a proliferation of jurisdictional lines laying out the turf of numerous federal agencies, state agencies, municipalities, counties, tribes, and special districts with jurisdiction over matters like electricity and water supply. Nearly every law, regulation, or policy required some degree of coordination between these various jurisdictions, demanding considerable political inventiveness in finding methods of negotiation and collaboration across these lines, and in allocating authority and responsibility among various levels of governance. In many western communities, a new tradition of "stakeholder" coalitions or "watershed" associations came into play as representatives of agencies and various interest groups met to work out agreements for the management of local natural resources. From the Malpai Borderlands Group in southern New Mexico and Arizona north to the Clark Fork Basin Committee in Montana, the Rockies saw a proliferation of groups attempting to avoid the usual channels of contention and litigation, and, in the words of Matt McKinney and William Harmon, "to integrate the interests of affected parties" through "collaboration and consensus building." Without any particular awareness of the connection between them, the descendants of white settlers had happened onto a process of decision making that bore a similarity, coincidental but still striking, to the consensus-based practices of the Native American tribes who originally lived in the region.

The Weak Parties of the Rockies: A Persistent Pattern

In the first decade of the twenty-first century in the state of Colorado, one-third of registered voters chose "unaffiliated" over identification with either major party. In all the states of the Rockies, even many voters who went ahead and registered as Democrats or Republicans showed, in their voting, the region's trademark flexibility and inconsistency. How can the persistent pattern of weak party identification and independent voting be explained?

First, economic development, often with federal support, has been the key concern of the region's citizens, and Democrats and Republicans have both pursued this goal. In the early twenty-first century, environmental preservation may be primarily identified with Democrats, but Democrats from the region have a strong record in supporting projects in economic development, whatever their effect in environmental disruption. Democratic congressman and senator Carl Hayden was the leading force behind the giant Central Arizona Project, bringing water to the state's cities, a project loyally supported by the noted conservationist, Democratic congressman Morris Udall.

Second, for many of the most pressing and immediate western issues, the positions of the major parties had little bearing or relevance. In matters ranging from the allocation of water for urban or agricultural use to land-use planning in growth-burdened counties, from the challenges of fighting wildlands fire to the mediation of conflicts between the recreational economy and the extractive economy, the political platforms of both parties bore a striking resemblance to Mother Hubbard's very bare cupboard.

Third, in many parts of the Rocky Mountain West, high rates of mobility have both introduced and minimized the possibility of big changes in political behavior. In the late twentieth century, the Rockies had the highest population growth rates in the country. Yet, even if many of those newcomers arrived with far more settled party loyalties than those held by longer-term residents, the newcomers did not come in organized phalanxes, equipped to swing into action and to substitute their ways for local tradition. Moreover, in recent decades, for many of the new residents, the charm of natural landscapes has been a major factor in the decision to relocate, leaving them solid reasons to join the "muddled majority," with loyalties split between continued economic growth and the preservation of natural amenities.

And, fourth, the persistent and omnipresent western myth, of a region populated by hardy folk characterized by an unbreakable spirit of independence and self-determination, has exercised an unmistakable power over voters—with consequential results. The myth's inability to achieve a high score in historical accuracy has not in any way reduced the certainty that it inspires in its believers, nor its political power. With surprisingly undiminished power, this myth can be counted on to validate and celebrate the region's party-defying mavericks. Resting on the inseparability of myth from reality, the political history of the Rocky Mountain states offers constant reminders of the extraordinary subjectivity that guides human self-perception and self-appraisal in the terrain of politics.

See also Great Plains; Native Americans and politics; territorial governments.

FURTHER READING

Bloom, John Porter. *The American Territorial System.* Athens: Ohio University Press, 1973.

Donnelly, Thomas C. *Rocky Mountain Politics.* Albuquerque: University of New Mexico Press, 1940.

Emmons, David M. "Constructed Province: History and the Making of the Last American West." *Western Historical Quarterly* (Winter, 1994).

Enyeart, John P. *"By Laws of Their Own Making": Political Culture and the Everyday Politics of the Mountain West Working Class, 1870–1917.* Dissertation, University of Colorado, Boulder, 2002.

Goldstein, Marcia Tremmel. *"Meet Me at the Ballot Box": Women's Innovations in Party and Electoral Politics in Post-Suffrage Colorado, 1893–1898.* Dissertation, University of Colorado, Boulder, 2007.

Goodwyn, Lawrence. *Democratic Promise: The Populist Movement in America.* New York: Oxford University Press, 1976.

Kantner, John. *Ancient Puebloan Southwest.* Cambridge, UK: Cambridge University Press, 2004.

Kazin, Michael. *The Populist Persuasion: An American History.* Revised ed. Ithaca, NY: Cornell University Press, 1998.

Lamar, Howard Roberts. *The Far Southwest, 1846–1912: A Territorial History.* New Haven, CT: Yale University Press, 1966.

Limerick, Patricia Nelson. *The Legacy of Conquest: The Unbroken Past of the American West.* New York: Norton, 1987.

Lowitt, Richard, ed. *Politics in the Postwar American West.* Norman: University of Oklahoma Press, 1995.

McKinney, Matt, and William Harmon. *Western Confluence: A Guide to Governing Natural Resources.* Washington, DC: Island Press, 2004.

Mead, Rebecca J. *How the Vote Was Won: Woman Suffrage in the Western United States, 1868–1914.* New York: New York University Press, 2004.

Owens, Kenneth. "Patterns and Structure in Western Territorial Politics." *Western Historical Quarterly* (October, 1970).

Pisani, Donald. *Water and American Government: The Reclamation Bureau, National Water Policy, and the West, 1902–1935*. Berkeley: University of California Press, 2002.

Pomeroy, Earl. *The Territories and the United States, 1881–1890: Studies in Colonial Administration*. Seattle: University of Washington Press, 1969.

Rosales, Francisco A. *Chicano!: The History of the Mexican-American Civil Rights Movement*. Houston, TX: University of Houston, Arte Publico Press, 1997.

Shaw, Stephen. "Harassment, Hate, and Human Rights in Idaho." In *Politics in the Postwar American West*, edited by Richard Lowitt, 94–105. Norman: University of Oklahoma Press, 1995.

Smith, Daniel A. *Tax Crusaders and the Politics of Direct Democracy*. New York: Routledge, 1998.

Taylor, Quintard. *In Search of the Racial Frontier: African-Americans in the American West, 1598–1990*. New York: Norton, 1998.

Thomas, Clive S., ed. *Politics and Public Policy in the Contemporary American West*. Albuquerque: University of New Mexico Press, 1991.

White, Richard. *"It's Your Misfortune and None of My Own": A History of the American West*. Norman: University of Oklahoma Press, 1991.

Wilkinson, Charles. *Blood Struggle: The Rise of Modern Indian Nations*. New York: Norton, 2005.

PATRICIA NELSON LIMERICK
AND MARCIA TREMMEL GOLDSTEIN

sectional conflict and secession, 1845–65

Sectional conflict, or growing tensions between northern and southern states, mounted from 1845 to 1860 as the main fault lines in American politics shifted from a partisan division (Whigs versus Democrats) to a geographical one (North versus South). In broad terms, a majority of northern and southern voters increasingly suspected members of the other section of threatening the liberty, equality, and opportunity of white Americans and the survival of the U.S. experiment in republican government; specific points of contention between northern and southern states included the right of a state to leave the federal union and the relationship between the federal government and slavery. Constitutional ambiguity and the focus of both the Whig and Democratic parties on national economic issues had allowed the political system to sidestep the slavery issue in the early nineteenth century, but the territorial expansion of the United States in the 1840s forced Congress to face the question of whether or not slavery should spread into new U.S. territories. The pivotal event that irreversibly injected slavery into mainstream politics was the introduction of the Wilmot Proviso in Congress in August 1846. The slavery extension issue destroyed the Whig Party, divided the Democratic Party, and in the 1850s, enabled the rise of an exclusively northern Republican Party founded to oppose the westward expansion of slavery. When Republican candidate Abraham Lincoln won the presidential election of 1860, his victory precipitated the immediate secession of seven states, the eventual secession of four more states, and a Civil War that lasted from 1861 to 1865.

The Slavery Extension Issue

Beginning with the annexation of Texas in 1845, the rapid acquisition of western territories stoked sectional conflict by forcing Congress to face the question of slavery's expansion into those new territories. In prior decades, the two dominant national parties, the Whigs and the Democrats, relied on the support of both northern and southern constituencies and courted voters by downplaying slavery and focusing on questions of government involvement in the economy. Before 1845, expansion, much like support for tariffs or a national bank, was a partisan rather than sectional issue, with Democrats championing and Whigs opposing the acquisition of territory, but the annexation of Texas set in motion of series of events that would eventually realign loyalties along sectional contours.

A Mexican state from the time of Mexican independence in 1821, Texas was settled largely by white American Southerners who chafed against the Mexican government's abolition of slavery in 1829 and broke away to form the Republic of Texas in 1836. The 1836 Treaty of Velasco between the Republic of Texas and General Antonio Lopez De Santa Ana of Mexico named the Rio Grande as the border between Texas and Mexico. But the Mexican Congress refused to ratify that boundary because the Nueces River, far to the North of the Rio Grande, had been the southern limit of Texas when it was a Mexican state, and redrawing the border at the Rio Grande gave thousands of miles of Mexico's northern frontier (the present-day southwest) to Texas. Almost immediately, Americans in Texas began to press for the admission of Texas into the Union. When the United States annexed Texas in 1845, it laid claim to land between the Nueces River and the Rio Grande, which Mexico still regarded as part of Mexico, thus provoking a boundary dispute between the United States and Mexico. American president James K. Polk, an ardent Democrat and expansionist, ordered U.S. troops under General Zachary Taylor to the banks of the Rio Grande, where they skirmished with Mexican forces. Pointing to American casualties, Polk asked Congress to approve a bill stating that a state of war existed between Mexico and the United States, which Congress passed on May 12, 1846.

Militarily, the Mexican-American War seemed like an easy victory for the United States, but international context and domestic politics helped make the war a spur to sectional disharmony. According to the Treaty of Guadalupe Hidalgo, negotiated on February 2, 1848, and announced by President Polk to be in effect on July 4 of that year, the United States was to assume debts owed by the Mexican government to U.S. citizens and pay the Mexican government a lump sum of $15 million, in exchange for which it would receive Texas to the Rio Grande, California, and the New Mexico territory (collectively known as the Mexican Cession). Public opinion was shaped in part by differing American reactions to the revolutions of 1848 in Europe, with some Americans interpreting the European blows for liberal democracy as mandates for the expansion of American-style democracy via territorial acquisition, while others (primarily in the North) viewed conquest as the abandonment of democratic principles. Reaction was even more acutely influenced by developments within the Democratic Party on the state level. While the annexation of Texas and the war with Mexico were generally popular among the proexpansion Democratic Party in the northern as well as southern states, fear that the party was being turned into a tool for slaveholders began to percolate with the annexation of Texas and intensified in response to the war with Mexico. In New Hampshire, for example, loyal Democrat John P. Hale denounced Texas annexation and broke with the state organization to form the Independent Democrats, a coalition of antislavery Democrats, dissatisfied Whigs, and members of the Liberty Party (a small, one-issue third party formed in 1840) that grew strong enough to dominate the New Hampshire legislative and gubernatorial elections of 1846. In New York, Pennsylvania, and Ohio, some Democratic voters grew increasingly worried that President Polk had precipitated the war with Mexico specifically to expand slavery's territory. In hopes of quelling such fears, Pennsylvania Democratic congressman David Wilmot irrevocably introduced slavery into political debate in August 1846 with the Wilmot Proviso.

Wilmot introduced his proviso when Polk asked Congress for a $2 million appropriation for negotiations with the Mexican government that would end the war by transferring territory to the United States. Wilmot added an amendment to the appropriations bill mandating that "neither slavery nor involuntary servitude shall ever exist" in the territories gained from Mexico. The proposed amendment did not end slavery anywhere (slavery was illegal under Mexican law in the territories in question), but it did attempt to curb slavery's extension, and from that time on, the slavery expansion question dominated congressional debate and fueled sectional conflict. With the support of all northern Whigs and most northern Democrats, and against the opposition of all southern Democrats and Whigs, the Wilmot Proviso passed in the House of Representatives but failed in the Senate.

Outside of Washington, D.C., the impact of the Wilmot Proviso escalated in 1847 and 1848. By the spring of 1847, mass meetings throughout the South pledged to oppose any candidate of any party who supported the Proviso and pledged all-southern unity and loyalty to slavery. In the North, opinion on the Proviso was more divided (in politically powerful New York, for example, the Democratic Party split into the anti-Proviso Hunkers and pro-Proviso Barnburners). But the same strands that had come together to form the Independent Democrats in New Hampshire in 1846 began to interweave throughout the North, culminating in the Buffalo National Free Soil Convention of 1848, a mass meeting attended by delegates elected at public meetings throughout the northern states.

An incongruous mix of white and black abolitionists, northern Democrats who wanted no blacks (slave or free) in the western territories, and disaffected Whigs and Democrats, the Buffalo convention created a new political party, the Free Soil Party, based on a platform of "denationalizing slavery" by barring slavery from western territories and outlawing the slave trade (but not slavery) in Washington, D.C. Adopting the slogan, "Free Soil, Free Speech, Free Labor, and Free Men," the Free Soil Party nominated former Democrat Martin Van Buren as its candidate for the 1848 presidential election. Van Buren did not win (Zachary Taylor, a nominal Whig with no known position on the slavery extension issue became president), but he did get 10 percent of the popular vote. In addition, 12 Free Soil candidates were elected to the U.S. House of Representatives. In Ohio, 8 Free Soilers went to the state legislature, where they repealed Ohio's discriminatory "black laws" and sent Free Soiler Salmon P. Chase to the Senate. In all, the emergence of the Free Soil Party weakened the existing two-party system even as it signaled growing northern disinclination to share the western territories with slaves and slaveholders.

The growth of Free Soil sentiment in the North worried many moderate southern voters, who grew alarmed that the nonextension of slavery beyond its current limits would eventually place the slaveholding states in a minority in the Union as more free states entered and tipped the current balance. A radical group of southern separatists known as the Fire Eaters and led by men such as William Yancey, Edmund Ruffin, and Robert Barnwell Rhett, gained influence as moderates' concern over permanent minority status grew. The Fire Eaters succeeded in convincing all slaveholding states to send delegates to a formal southern convention to meet in Nashville, Tennessee, on June 3, 1850, where delegates would discuss strategies for combating growing hostility to slavery, including secession from the Union. The Nashville Convention asserted the southern states' commitment to slavery and assumed the rights of a state to secede if its interests were threatened, but the convention also affirmed that slavery and southern interests were best served within the Union, as long as Congress met a series of conditions. Conditions included rejection of the Wilmot Proviso, a prohibition against federal interference with slavery in Washington, D.C., and stronger federal support for slaveholders attempting to reclaim slaves who had escaped to free states. The convention agreed to reconvene after Congress had resolved the slavery extension issue to determine if the solution met its conditions.

While opinion hardened in House districts, Congress tackled the question of slavery's fate in the Mexican Cession. Four possible answers emerged. At one extreme stood the Wilmot Proviso. At the opposite extreme stood the doctrine, propagated by South Carolinian and leading southern separatist John C. Calhoun, that "slavery followed the flag" and that all U.S. territories were de facto slave territories because Congress lacked the right to bar slavery from them. A possible compromise, and third possible approach, was to extend the Missouri Compromise line all the way to the Pacific, banning slavery from territories north of the 36° 30′ line, and leaving territories south of that line open to the institution; this approach would permit slavery in the Mexican Cession. A final possibility (the favorite of many northern Democrats) was to apply the principle of "popular sovereignty," which would permit voters living in a territory, and not Congress, to determine if slavery would be allowed in the territory; noted adherents such as Lewis Cass and Stephen Douglas did not specify if voters would determine slavery's fate at the territorial or statehood stage.

The Nashville Convention and the urgent press to admit California to the Union following the discovery of gold in 1849 forced Congress to cobble together the Compromise of 1850. An aging Henry Clay, whose brand of compromise and Whig Party were both wilting as the political climate relentlessly warmed, submitted an omnibus compromise bill that admitted California as a free state, barred the slave trade in Washington, D.C., threw out the Wilmot Proviso, and enacted an unusually harsh Fugitive Slave Law. Clay's bill pleased nobody, and was soundly defeated. Illinois Democrat Stephen Douglas separated the individual provisions and scraped together the votes to get each individual measure passed in what has become known as the Compromise of 1850. In reality, the measure represented a truce more than a compromise. The passage of the individual measures, however contentious, satisfied most of the demands of the Nashville Convention and depressed support for secession. Conditional unionist candidates, or candidates who advocated remaining in the Union as long as conditions like those articulated at Nashville were met, did well in elections throughout the South in 1850 and 1852.

Despite the boost that the Compromise of 1850 gave to conditional unionism in the South, two provisions of the Compromise prevented lasting resolution. One was the Fugitive Slave Law. While Article IV of the U.S. Constitution asserted the rights of masters to recapture slaves who fled to free states, the Fugitive Slave Law included new and harsher provisions mandating the participation of northern states and individuals in the recapture process and curtailing the rights of alleged fugitives to prove they were not runaways. The severity of the law and the conflict it created between state and federal jurisdiction led to controversy. Harriet Beecher Stowe published *Uncle Tom's Cabin*, a novel that gained great popularity in the North but was banned in the South. The New England states, Wisconsin, Ohio, and Michigan passed personal liberty laws allowing state citizens to refrain from participating in slave recaptures if prompted by personal conscience to refrain. Rescue cases like those of Anthony Burns in Massachusetts and Joshua Glover in Wisconsin captured headlines and further strained relations between northern and southern states.

The second problem with the Compromise of 1850 was that it did not settle the question of slavery's expansion because it rejected the Wilmot Proviso without offering an alternative, an omission whose magnitude became apparent when Kansas Territory opened to white settlement in 1854. Fearing that southern congressmen would impede the opening of Kansas because slavery was barred there by the Missouri Compromise (which prohibited slavery in the Louisiana Purchase above the 36° 30′ latitude), Democratic senator Stephen Douglas of Illinois introduced the Kansas-Nebraska Act, which threw out the Missouri Compromise and opened Kansas and Nebraska Territories to popular sovereignty.

The result was that violence erupted between proslavery and free-state settlers in Kansas. Proslavery advocates from Missouri initially gained the upper hand and, in an election in which 6,318 votes were cast despite the presence of only 2,905 legal voters in Kansas, elected a proslavery convention. In 1857 the convention drafted the Lecompton constitution, which would have admitted Kansas to the Union as a slave state and limited the civil rights of antislavery settlers, and sent it to Washington for congressional approval over the objections of the majority of Kansans.

The "Slave Power Conspiracy" and "Black Republicans"

The violence in "Bleeding Kansas" and the obvious unpopularity of the Lecompton constitution did more than just illustrate the failure of popular sovereignty to resolve the slavery extension issue. Kansas further weakened the Second Party System by speeding the collapse of the Whig Party, facilitating the emergence of the Republican Party, and deepening divisions within the Democratic Party. Crippled by its inability to deal effectively with the slavery question, the Whig Party steadily weakened and for a brief time, the anti-immigrant American Party (or Know-Nothings) appeared likely to become the second major party. But when the Know-Nothings failed to respond effectively to the Kansas-Nebraska Act, they lost support among Northerners.

Meanwhile, Free-Soil Democrats, former Whigs, and veterans from the Liberty and Free Soil parties united within several northern states to form a new party explicitly pledged to prevent the westward expansion of slavery. The new party allegedly adopted its name, the Republican Party, at a meeting in Ripon, Wisconsin. Discontented Democrats like Salmon Chase, Charles Sumner, Joshua Giddings, and Gerritt Smith helped to knit the newly emerging state organizations into a sectionwide party by publishing "An Appeal of the Independent Democrats in Congress to the People of the United States" in two newspapers the day after the introduction of the Kansas-Nebraska Bill. The appeal criticized slavery as immoral and contrary to the principles of the nation's founders, and it portrayed the question of slavery in Kansas and other territories as a crisis of American democracy because a "slave power conspiracy" was attempting to fasten slavery on the entire nation, even at the cost of suppressing civil liberties and betraying the principles of the American Revolution.

The violence in Kansas seemed to support charges of a slave power conspiracy, especially in May 1856, when proslavery settlers sacked the abolitionist town of Lawrence, Kansas—just one day before South Carolina congressman Preston Brooks marched onto the Senate floor to beat Massachusetts senator Charles Sumner into unconsciousness in retaliation for Sumner's fiery "Crime against Kansas" speech, which portrayed proslavery Southerners generally—and one of Brooks's relatives particularly—in an unflattering light. "Bleeding Sumner and Bleeding Kansas" made Republican charges that a small number of slaveholders sought to dominate the nation and suppress rights persuasive to many northern voters in the 1856 election; Republican candidate John C. Frémont lost to Democrat James Buchanan, but he carried the New England states, Ohio, Michigan, Wisconsin, and New York, and Republican candidates won seats in Congress and state offices in the North.

In 1857, a financial panic, the Supreme Court's *Dred Scott v. Sanford* case, and the Lecompton constitution built Republican strength in the North while the Democratic Party fractured. Dred Scott, a slave taken to Illinois and Wisconsin Territory by his master and then brought back to slavery in Missouri, sued for his freedom on the grounds that residency in states and territories where slavery was illegal made him free. Chief Justice Roger B. Taney's decision against Scott declared that blacks could not be citizens, even though several northern states recognized them as such, and that in fact they had "no rights which the white man is bound to respect"; it also held that Congress could not outlaw slavery in any U.S. territory, and that slaveholders retained the right to take slaves wherever they pleased. By denying the right of Congress, territorial governments, or residents of a territory to ban slavery from their midst, Taney's decision seemed to support Republican charges that southern oligarchs sought to fasten slavery onto the entire nation regardless of local sentiment. When President James Buchanan (a Pennsylvanian thought to be controlled by southern Democrats) tried unsuccessfully to force Congress to ratify the Lecompton constitution and admit Kansas as a slave state over the objections of the majority of Kansans, the Democratic Party splintered. Even Stephen Douglas faced stiff competition for his Senate seat in 1858. In a series of debates throughout Illinois, Douglas faced Republican candidate Abraham Lincoln, who articulated the slave power conspiracy theme and outlined a platform of opposition to the extension of slavery. Because the Democrats retained a slim edge in the state legislature and state legislatures (not the popular vote) selected senators, Douglas retained his Senate seat. But the wide press coverage of the Lincoln-Douglas debates gained a national audience for Lincoln and his views.

The fast but exclusively northern growth of the Republicans alarmed Southerners who saw themselves as potential victims of a "Black Republican" conspiracy to isolate slavery and end it, sentence the South to subservient status within the Union, and destroy it by imposing racial equality. With conditional unionism still dominant throughout much of the South, many southern leaders called for firmer federal support for the Fugitive Slave Law, federal intolerance for state personal liberty laws, and a federal slave code mandating the legality of and federal protection for slavery in all U.S. territories as prerequisites for southern states remaining in the Union. The Fire Eaters added the demand for the reopening of the African slave trade, even as they increasingly insisted that southern states could preserve their rights only by leaving a Union growing more hostile to the institution on which the South depended. Fears of a "Black Republican" conspiracy seemed to be realized in 1859 when John Brown seized the federal arsenal at Harpers Ferry, Virginia, in hopes of overthrowing slavery by inspiring slave insurrection throughout the South. Brown failed and was executed for treason in December 1859, but a white Northerner marching South to arm slaves embodied white Southerners' grimmest fears that the growing strength of the Republican Party could only lead to violent insurrections.

Election, Secession, and War

The Democratic Party split deepened in 1860, setting the stage for the election of a Republican president. In January 1860, Mississippi senator Albert Brown submitted resolutions calling for a federal slave code and an expanded role for Congress in promoting slavery. The Alabama State Democratic Convention identified the resolutions as the only party platform it would support in the presidential election; several additional southern state delegations also committed themselves to the "Alabama Platform." Northern Democrats espoused popular sovereignty instead. When the National Democratic Convention assembled in Charleston, South Carolina, it split along sectional lines.

As the Democratic rift widened in 1859–60, the Republican Party faced the decision of how best to capitalize on its opponents' dissent. Should it nominate a well-known candidate like senator and former New York governor William Seward, who was seen as a radical because of famous speeches declaring that slavery was subject to a "higher law" than the Constitution (1850) and that the slave and free states were locked in an "irreconciliable conflict" (1858)? Or should it nominate a more moderate but lesser-known candidate? After four ballots, the Republican convention in Chicago settled on Abraham Lincoln, a less prominent politician whose debates with Douglas and a February 1860 New York City address about slavery and the founders had helped introduce him to a national audience. The convention also adopted a platform that decried John Brown and advocated economic measures like a homestead act, but its most important plank consisted of its opposition to the expansion of slavery.

The 1860 presidential campaign shaped up differently in the North and South. Southern Democrats nominated John Breckinridge, who ran on the Alabama platform. He vied for southern votes with John Bell of the newly created Constitutional Union Party, a party that appealed to moderate Southerners who saw the Alabama platform as dangerously inflammatory and instead supported the maintenance of slavery where it was but took no stand on its expansion. In the North, Democrat Stephen Douglas and his platform of popular sovereignty opposed Republican candidate Abraham Lincoln and the Republican nonextension platform. No candidate won a majority of the popular vote. Stephen Douglas captured the electoral votes of New Jersey and Missouri. John Bell carried Virginia, Kentucky, and Tennessee. John Breckinridge won every remaining slave state, and Abraham Lincoln, with 54 percent of the northern popular vote (and none of the southern popular vote) took every remaining free state and the election.

Anticipating Lincoln's victory, the South Carolina legislature stayed in session through the election so that it could call a secession convention as soon as results were known. On December 20, 1860, the convention unanimously approved an ordinance dissolving the union between South Carolina and the United States. By February 1, 1861, Mississippi, Florida, Alabama, Georgia,

Louisiana, and Texas had also seceded in response to the election results. The secession ordinances all made clear that Lincoln's election on a nonextension of slavery platform and northern failure to uphold the Fugitive Slave Clause entitled southern states to leave the Union. Delegates from the seven states met in Montgomery, Alabama, to form the Confederate States of America, draft a provisional constitution, select Jefferson Davis and Alexander Stephens as provisional president and vice president, and authorize the enrollment of 100,000 troops.

The states of the Upper and Border South, where Constitutional Unionist candidate John Bell had done well, resisted Deep South pressure to secede immediately, and instead waited to see if Lincoln's actions as president could be reconciled with assurances for slavery's safety within the Union. Yet they also passed coercion clauses, pledging to side with slaveholding states if the situtation came to blows. Congress considered the Crittenden Compromise, which guaranteed perpetual noninterference with slavery, extended the Missouri Compromise line permanently across the United States, forbade abolition in the District of Columbia without the permission of Maryland and Virginia, barred Congress from meddling with the interstate slave trade, earmarked federal funds to compensate owners of runaway slaves, and added an unamendable amendment to the constitution guaranteeing that none of the Crittenden measures, including perpetual noninterference with slavery, could ever be altered. The Crittenden Compromise failed to soothe conditional unionists in the South while it angered Republican voters in the North by rejecting the platform that had just won the election. Stalemate ensued.

The Fort Sumter Crisis pressured both Lincoln and the states of the Upper South into action. When Lincoln took office in March 1861, all but four federal forts in seceded states had fallen. Fort Sumter in Charleston Harbor remained in Union hands but was short of supplies. South Carolina officials warned that any attempt to resupply the fort would be seen as an act of aggression. Believing that he could not relinquish U.S. property to a state in rebellion, nor could he leave U.S. soldiers stationed at Fort Sumter to starve, Lincoln warned Confederate president Davis and South Carolina officials that a ship with provisions but no ammunition would resupply Fort Sumter. In the early morning hours of April 12, 1861, South Carolina forces bombarded Fort Sumter before the supply ship could arrive; Fort Sumter surrendered on April 14. Lincoln called for 75,000 volunteers to serve for 90 days to put down the rebellion. In response, Virginia, Arkansas, North Carolina, and Tennessee seceded. The border slave states of Delaware, Kentucky, Maryland, and Missouri remained in the Union, though each state except Delaware contained a significant secessionist minority.

Fought from 1861 to 1865, the Civil War settled the question of slavery's extension by eventually eliminating slavery. The war also made the growth of federal power possible, although dramatic growth in the federal government would not really occur until the later Progressive and New Deal Eras. Conflicts between state and federal sovereignty would persist in U.S. political history, but the Civil War removed secession as a possible option for resolving those conflicts.

See also Civil War and Reconstruction; Confederacy; Reconstruction Era, 1865–77; slavery.

FURTHER READING

Earle, Jonathan H. *Jacksonian Antislavery and the Politics of Free Soil, 1824–1854*. Chapel Hill: University of North Carolina Press, 2004.

Foner, Eric. *Free Soil, Free Labor, Free Men: The Ideology of the Republican Party Before the Civil War.* New York: Oxford University Press, 1971.

Gienapp, William E. "The Crisis of American Democracy: The Political System and the Coming of the Civil War." In *Why The Civil War Came*, edited by Gabor S. Boritt. New York: Oxford University Press, 1996.

———. *The Origins of the Republican Party, 1852–1856.* New York: Oxford University Press, 1987.

Howe, Daniel Walker. *What Hath God Wrought: The Transformation of America, 1815–1848.* New York: Oxford University Press, 2007.

Potter, David. *The Impending Crisis, 1848–1861.* New York: Harper and Row, 1976.

Richards, Leonard L. *The California Gold Rush and the Coming of the Civil War.* New York: Knopf, 2007.

Rothman, Adam. "The 'Slave Power' in the United States, 1783–1865." In *Ruling America: A History of Wealth and Power in a Democracy*, edited by Steve Fraser and Gary Gerstle. Cambridge, MA: Harvard University Press, 2005.

Sewell, Richard H. *Ballots for Freedom: Antislavery Politics in the United States, 1837–1860*. New York: Oxford University Press, 1976.

Stampp, Kenneth M. *America in 1857: A Nation on the Brink.* New York: Oxford University Press, 1990.

Wilentz, Sean. *The Rise of American Democracy: Jefferson to Lincoln*. New York: Norton, 2005.

CHANDRA MANNING

segregation and Jim Crow

Jim Crow is the system of racial oppression—political, social, and economic—that southern whites imposed on blacks after the abolition of slavery. *Jim Crow,* a term derived from a minstrel-show routine, was a derogatory epithet for blacks. Although the system met its formal demise during the civil rights movement of the 1960s, its legacy is still felt today.

Political White Supremacy

During Reconstruction (1865–77), recently enfranchised southern blacks voted in huge numbers and elected many black officeholders. During the final decades of the nineteenth century, however, black voting in the South was largely eliminated—first through fraud and violence, then through legal mechanisms such as poll taxes and literacy tests. Black voter registration in Alabama plummeted from 180,000 in 1900 to 3,000 in 1903 after a state constitutional convention adopted disfranchising measures.

When blacks could not vote, neither could they be elected to office. Sixty-four blacks had sat in the Mississippi legislature in 1873; none sat after 1895. In South Carolina's lower house, which had a black majority during Reconstruction, a single black remained in 1896. More importantly, after disfranchisement, blacks could no longer be elected to the local offices that exercised control over people's daily lives, such as sheriff, justice of the peace, and county commissioner.

With black political clout stunted, radical racists swept to power. Cole Blease of South Carolina bragged that he would rather resign as governor and "lead the mob" than use his office to protect a "nigger brute" from lynching. Governor James Vardaman of Mississippi promised that "every Negro in the state w[ould] be lynched" if necessary to maintain white supremacy.

Economic White Supremacy

Jim Crow was also a system of economic subordination. After the Civil War ended slavery, most southern blacks remained under the economic control of whites, growing cotton as sharecroppers and tenant farmers.

Laws restricted the access of blacks to nonagricultural employment while constricting the market for agricultural labor, thus limiting the bargaining power of black farmworkers. The cash-poor cotton economy forced laborers to become indebted to landlords and suppliers, and peonage laws threatened criminal liability for those who sought to escape indebtedness by breaching their labor contracts. Once entrapped by the criminal justice system, blacks might be made to labor on chain gangs or be hired out to private employers who controlled their labor in exchange for paying their criminal fines. During planting season, when labor was in great demand, local law enforcement officers who were in cahoots with planters would conduct "vagrancy roundups" or otherwise "manufacture" petty criminals.

Some black peons were held under conditions almost indistinguishable from slavery. They worked under armed guard, were locked up at night, and were routinely beaten and tracked down by dogs if they attempted to escape. Blacks who resisted such conditions were often killed. In one infamous Georgia case in the 1920s, a planter who was worried about a federal investigation into his peonage practices simply ordered the murder of 11 of his tenants who were potential witnesses.

While southern black farmers made gains in land ownership in the early twentieth century, other economic opportunities for blacks contracted. Whites repossessed traditionally black jobs, such as barber and chef. The growing power of racially exclusionary labor unions cut blacks off from most skilled trade positions. Black lawyers increasingly found themselves out of work, as a more rigid color line forbade their presence in some courtrooms and made them liabilities to clients in others. Beginning around 1910, unionized white railway workers went on strike in an effort to have black firemen dismissed; when the strike failed, they simply murdered many of the black workers.

Social White Supremacy

As blacks lost their political clout and white racial attitudes hardened, racial segregation spread into new spheres of southern life. Beginning around 1890, most southern states required railroads to segregate their passengers, and laws segregating local streetcars swept the South soon after 1900. Many southern states also segregated restaurants, theaters, public parks, jails, and saloons. White nurses were forbidden to treat black hospital patients, and white teachers were forbidden to work in black schools. Banks established separate deposit windows for blacks. Beginning in 1910, southern cities adopted the first residential segregation ordinances.

Segregation statutes required that accommodations for blacks be equal, but in practice they never were. Blacks described Jim Crow railway cars as "scarcely fit for a dog to ride in"; the seats were filthy and the air was fetid. Convicts and the insane were relegated to these cars, which white passengers entered at will to smoke, drink, and antagonize blacks. Such conditions plainly violated state law, yet legal challenges were rare.

Notwithstanding state constitutional requirements that racially segregated schools be equal, southern whites moved to dismantle the black education system. Most whites thought that an education spoiled good field hands, needlessly encouraged competition with white workers, and rendered blacks dissatisfied with their subordinate status. In 1901 Georgia's governor, Allen D. Candler, stated, "God made them negroes and we cannot by education make them white folks." Racial disparities in educational funding became enormous. By 1925–26, South Carolina spent $80.55 per capita for white students and $10.20 for blacks; for school transportation, the state spent $471,489 for whites and $795 for blacks.

Much social discrimination resulted from informal custom rather than legal rule. No southern statute required that blacks give way to whites on public sidewalks or refer to whites by courtesy titles, yet blacks failing to do so acted at their peril. In Mississippi, some white post office employees erased the courtesy titles on mail addressed to black people.

Violent White Supremacy

Jim Crow was ultimately secured by physical violence. In 1898 whites in Wilmington, North Carolina, concluded a political campaign fought under the banner of white supremacy by murdering roughly a dozen blacks and driving 1,400 out of the city. In 1919, when black sharecroppers in Phillips County, Arkansas, tried to organize a union and challenge peonage practices, whites responded by murdering dozens of them. In Orange County, Florida, 30 blacks were burned to death in 1920 because 1 black man had attempted to vote.

Thousands of blacks were lynched during the Jim Crow era. Some lynching victims were accused of nothing more serious than breaches of racial etiquette, such as "general uppityness." Prior to 1920, efforts to prosecute even known lynchers were rare and convictions virtually nonexistent. Public lynchings attended by throngs of people, many of whom brought picnic lunches and took home souvenirs from the victim's tortured body, were not uncommon.

National Endorsement

Jim Crow was a southern phenomenon, but its persistence required national complicity. During Reconstruction, the national government had—sporadically—used force to protect the rights of southern blacks. Several factors account for the gradual willingness of white Northerners to permit white Southerners a free hand in ordering southern race relations.

Black migration to the North, which more than doubled in the decades after 1890 before exploding during World War I, exacerbated the racial prejudices of northern whites. As a result, public schools and public accommodations became more segregated, and deadly white-on-black violence erupted in several northern localities. Around the same time, the immigration of millions of southern and eastern European peasants caused native-born whites to worry about the dilution of "Anglo-Saxon racial stock," rendering them more sympathetic to southern racial policies. The resurgence of American imperialism in the 1890s also fostered the convergence of northern and southern racial attitudes, as imperialists who rejected full citizenship rights for residents of the new territories were not inclined to protest the disfranchisement of southern blacks.

Such developments rendered the national government sympathetic toward southern Jim Crow. Around 1900, the U.S. Supreme Court rejected constitutional challenges to racial segregation and black disfranchisement, made race discrimination in jury selection nearly impossible to prove, and sustained the constitutionality of separate-and-*un*equal education for blacks. Meanwhile, Congress repealed most of the voting rights legislation enacted during Reconstruction and declined to enforce Section II of the Fourteenth Amendment, which *requires* reducing the congressional representation of any state that disfranchises adult male citizens for reasons other than crime.

Presidents proved no more inclined to challenge Jim Crow. William McKinley, who was born into an abolitionist family and served as a Union officer during the Civil War, ignored the imprecations of black leaders to condemn the Wilmington racial massacre of 1898, and his presidential speeches celebrated sectional reconciliation, which was accomplished by sacrificing the rights of southern blacks. His successor, Theodore Roosevelt, refused to criticize black disfranchisement, blamed lynchings primarily on black rapists, and proclaimed that "race purity must be maintained." Roosevelt's successor, William Howard Taft, endorsed the efforts of southern states to avoid domination by an "ignorant, irresponsible electorate," largely ceased appointing blacks to southern patronage positions, and denied that the federal government had the power or inclination to interfere in southern race relations.

Decline of Jim Crow

A variety of forces contributed to the gradual demise of Jim Crow. Between 1910 and 1960, roughly 5 million southern blacks migrated to the North, mainly in search of better economic opportunities. Because northern blacks faced no significant suffrage restrictions, their political power quickly grew. At the local level, northern blacks secured the appointment of black police officers, the creation of playgrounds and parks for black neighborhoods, and the election of black city council members and state legislators. Soon thereafter, northern blacks began influencing national politics, successfully pressuring the House of Representatives to pass an antilynching bill in 1922 and the Senate to defeat the Supreme Court nomination of a southern white supremacist in 1930.

The rising economic status of northern blacks facilitated social protest. Larger black populations in northern cities provided a broader economic base for black entrepreneurs and professionals, who would later supply resources and leadership for civil rights protests. Improved economic status also enabled blacks to use boycotts as levers for social change. The more flexible racial mores of the North permitted challenges to the status quo that would not have been tolerated in the South. Protest organizations, such as the National Association for the Advancement of Colored People (NAACP), and militant black newspapers, such as the *Chicago Defender*, developed and thrived in the North. Because of a less rigid caste structure, blacks in the North were less likely to internalize racist norms of black subordination and inferiority.

Jim Crow was also being gradually eroded from within. Blacks moved from farms to cities within the South in search of better economic opportunities, eventually fostering a black middle class, which capitalized on the segregated economy to develop sufficient wealth and leisure time to participate in social protest. Many blacks in the urban South were economically independent of whites and thus could challenge the racial status quo without endangering their livelihoods. In cities, blacks found better schools, freer access to the ballot box, and a more relaxed code of racial etiquette. Because urban blacks enjoyed better communication and transportation facilities and shared social networks through black colleges and churches, they found it somewhat easier to overcome the organizational obstacles confronting any social protest movement.

World Wars I and II had profound implications for Jim Crow. Wars fought "to make the world safe for democracy" and to crush Nazi fascism had ideological implications for racial equality. In 1919, W.E.B. Du Bois of the NAACP wrote: "Make way for Democracy! We saved it in France, and by the Great Jehovah, we will save it in the United States of America, or know the reason why." Blacks who had borne arms for their country and faced death on the battlefield were inspired to assert their rights. A black journalist noted during World War I, "The men who did not fear the trained veterans of Germany will hardly run from the lawless Ku Klux Klan." Thousands of black veterans tried to register to vote after World War II, many expressing the view of one such veteran that "after having been overseas fighting for democracy, I thought that when we got back here we should enjoy a little of it."

World War II exposed millions of Southerners, white and black, to more liberal racial attitudes and practices. The growth of the mass media exposed millions more to outside influence, which tended to erode traditional racial mores. Media expansion also prevented white Southerners from restricting outside scrutiny of their treatment of blacks. Northerners had not seen southern lynchings on television, but the brutalization of peaceful black demonstrators by southern white law enforcement officers in the 1960s came directly into their living rooms.

Formal Jim Crow met its demise in the 1960s. Federal courts invalidated racial segregation and black disfranchisement, and the Justice Department investigated and occasionally prosecuted civil rights violations. Southern blacks challenged the system from within, participating in such direct-action protests as sit-ins and freedom rides. Brutal suppression of those demonstrations outraged northern opinion, leading to the enactment of landmark civil rights legislation, which spelled the doom of formal Jim Crow.

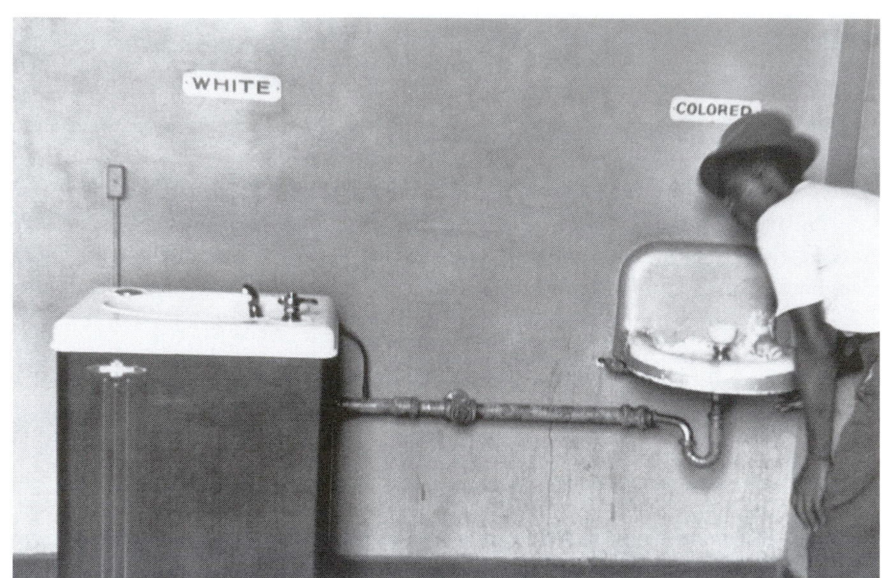

Segregated water fountains, North Carolina, 1950. (Elliott Erwitt/Magnum Photos)

Jim Crow's Legacy

Today, racially motivated lynchings and state-sponsored racial segregation have largely been eliminated. Public accommodations and places of employment have been integrated to a significant degree. Blacks register to vote in roughly the same percentages as whites, and more than 9,000 blacks hold elected office. The previous two secretaries of state have been black.

Blacks have also made dramatic gains in education and employment. The difference in the median number of school years completed by blacks and whites, which was 3.5 in 1954, has been eliminated almost entirely. The number of blacks holding white-collar or middle-class jobs increased from 12.1 percent in 1960 to 30.4 percent in 1990. Today, black men with college degrees earn nearly the same income as their white counterparts.

Yet not all blacks have been equally fortunate. In 1990 nearly two-thirds of black children were born outside of marriage, compared with just 15 percent of white children. Well over half of black families were headed by single mothers. The average black family has income that is just 60 percent and wealth that is just 10 percent of those of the average white family. Nearly 25 percent of blacks—three times the percentage of whites—live in poverty. Increasing numbers of blacks live in neighborhoods of extreme poverty, which are characterized by dilapidated housing, poor schools, broken families, juvenile pregnancies, drug dependency, and high crime rates.

Residential segregation compounds the problems of the black urban underclass. Spatial segregation means social isolation, as most inner-city blacks are rarely exposed to whites or the broader culture. As a result, black youngsters have developed a separate dialect of sorts, which disadvantages them in school and in the search for employment. Even worse, social segregation has fostered an oppositional culture among many black youngsters that discourages academic achievement—"acting white"—and thus further disables them from succeeding in mainstream society.

Today, more black men are incarcerated than are enrolled in college. Blacks comprise less than 12 percent of the nation's population but more than 50 percent of its prison inmates. Black men are seven times more likely to be incarcerated than white men. The legacy of Jim Crow lives on.

See also African Americans and politics; South since 1877; voting.

FURTHER READING

Ayers, Edward L. *Promise of the New South: Life after Reconstruction*. New York: Oxford University Press, 1992.

Dittmer, John. *Black Georgia in the Progressive Era 1900–1920*. Urbana: University of Illinois Press, 1977.

Fairclough, Adam. *Better Day Coming: Blacks and Equality, 1890–2000*. New York: Viking Penguin, 2001.

Gilmore, Glenda Elizabeth. *Gender and Jim Crow: Women and the Politics of White Supremacy in North Carolina, 1896–1920*. Chapel Hill: University of North Carolina Press, 1996.

Klarman, Michael J. *From Jim Crow to Civil Rights: The Supreme Court and the Struggle for Racial Equality*. New York: Oxford University Press, 2004.

Litwack, Leon. *Trouble in Mind: Black Southerners in the Age of Jim Crow*. New York: Vintage Books, 1998.

McMillen, Neil R. *Dark Journey: Black Mississippians in the Age of Jim Crow*. Urbana: University of Illinois Press, 1989.

Myrdal, Gunnar. *An American Dilemma: The Negro Problem and Modern Democracy*. 2 vols. New York: Harper and Bros., 1944.

Woodward, C. Vann. *The Strange Career of Jim Crow*. 3rd revised ed. New York: Oxford University Press, 1974.

Wright, George C. *Life behind a Veil: Blacks in Louisville, Kentucky 1865–1920*. Baton Rouge: Louisiana State University Press, 1990.

MICHAEL J. KLARMAN

Senate

The framers of the U.S. Constitution viewed the Senate as a check on the more passionate whims of the House of Representatives. Known as the "greatest deliberative body," the Senate has traditionally valued procedure over expediency, thereby frustrating action-oriented House members and presidents. Despite its staid reputation, however, the Senate has produced many of American history's most stirring speeches and influential policy makers. Indeed, the upper chamber of Congress has both reflected and instigated changes that have transformed the United States from a small, agrarian-based country to a world power.

In its formative years, the Senate focused on foreign policy and establishing precedents on treaty, nomination, and impeachment proceedings. Prior to the Civil War, "golden era" senators attempted to keep the Union intact while they defended their own political ideologies. The Senate moved to its current chamber in 1859, where visitors soon witnessed fervent Reconstruction debates and the first presidential impeachment trial. Twentieth-century senators battled the executive branch over government reform, international relations, civil rights, and economic programs as they led investigations into presidential administrations. While the modern Senate seems steeped in political rancor, welcome developments include a more diverse membership and bipartisan efforts to improve national security.

The Constitutional Convention

Drafted during the 1787 Constitutional Convention, the Constitution's Senate-related measures followed precedents established by colonial and state legislatures, as well as Great Britain's parliamentary system. The delegates to the convention, however, originated the institution's most controversial clause: "The Senate of the United States shall be composed of two Senators from each State, chosen by the Legislature thereof. . . ." Although delegates from large states supported James Madison's Virginia Plan, which based Senate representation on state population, small-state delegates wanted equal representation in both the House and the Senate. Roger Sherman sought a third option: proportional representation in the House and equal representation in the Senate. Adopted by the delegates on July 16, Sherman's Connecticut Compromise enabled the formation of a federal, bicameral legislature responsive to the needs of citizens from both large and small states.

Compared to the representation issue, the measure granting state legislatures the right to choose senators proved less divisive to convention delegates. Madison dismissed concerns that indirect elections would lead to a "tyrannical aristocracy," and only James Wilson argued that senators chosen in this manner would be swayed by local interests and prejudices. By the late nineteenth century, however, corruption regarding the selection of senators triggered demands for electoral reform. Ratified in 1913, the Seventeenth Amendment established direct election, allowing individual voters to select their senators.

As outlined in Article I of the Constitution, the Senate's primary role is to pass bills in concurrence with the House of Representatives. In the event that a civil officer committed "high crimes and misdemeanors," the Constitution also gives the Senate the responsibility to try cases of impeachment brought forth by the House. And, under the Constitution's advice and consent clause, the upper chamber received the power to confirm or deny presidential nominations, including appointments to the cabinet and the federal courts, and the power to approve or reject treaties. The Senate's penchant for stalling nominations and treaties in committee, though, has defeated more executive actions than straight up-or-down votes.

Within a year after the Constitutional Convention concluded, the central government began its transition from a loose confederation to a federal system. In September 1788, Pennsylvania became the first state to elect senators: William Maclay and Robert Morris. Other legislatures soon followed Pennsylvania's lead, selecting senators who came, in general, from the nation's wealthiest and most prominent families.

The Early Senate

The first session of Congress opened in the spring of 1789 in New York City's Federal Hall. After meeting its quorum in April, the Senate originated one of the most important bills of the era: the Judiciary Act of 1789. Created under the direction of Senator Oliver Ellsworth, the legislation provided the structure of the Supreme Court, as well as the federal district and circuit courts. Although advocates of a strong, federal judiciary system prevailed, the bill's outspoken critics indicated the beginning of the states' rights movement in the Senate, a source of significant division in the nineteenth century.

Between 1790 and 1800, Congress sat in Philadelphia as the permanent Capitol underwent construction in Washington, D.C. During these years, the first political parties emerged: the Federalists, who favored a strong union of states, and the anti-Federalists, later known as Republicans, who were sympathetic to states' rights. The parties aired their disputes on the Senate floor, especially in debates about the controversial Jay Treaty (1794) and the Alien and Sedition Acts (1798).

Negotiated by Chief Justice John Jay, the Jay Treaty sought to resolve financial and territorial conflicts with Great Britain arising from the Revolutionary War. In the Senate, the pro-British Federalists viewed the treaty as a mechanism to prevent another war, while the Republicans, and much of the public, considered the treaty's provisions humiliating and unfair to American merchants. By an exact two-thirds majority, the treaty won Senate approval, inciting anti-Jay mobs to burn and hang senators in effigy.

Partisan battles erupted again in 1798, when the Federalist-controlled Congress passed four bills known as the Alien and Sedition Acts. Meant to curtail Republican popularity, the legislation, in defiance of the First Amendment, made it unlawful to criticize the government. Ironically, the acts unified the Republican Party, leading to Thomas Jefferson's presidential election and a quarter-century rule by Senate Republicans.

The Federalist-Republican power struggle continued in the new Capitol in Washington. In 1804 the Senate, meeting as a court of impeachment, found the Federalist U.S. district court judge John Pickering guilty of drunkenness and profanity and removed him from the bench. The following year, the Senate tried the Federalist Supreme Court justice Samuel Chase for allegedly exhibiting an anti-Republican bias. Chase avoided a guilty verdict by one vote, which restricted further efforts to control the judiciary through the threat of impeachment.

Prior to the War of 1812, foreign policy dominated the Senate agenda. Responding to British interference in American shipping, the Senate passed several trade embargoes against Great Britain before declaring war. In 1814 British troops entered Washington and set fire to the Capitol, the White House, and other public buildings. The Senate chamber was destroyed, forcing senators to meet in temporary accommodations until 1819. In the intervening years, the Senate formed its first permanent committees, which encouraged senators to become experts on such issues as national defense and finance.

When the war concluded in 1815 without a clear victor, the Senate turned its attention to the problems and opportunities resulting from territorial expansion. As lands acquired from France, Spain, and Indian tribes were organized into territories and states, senators debated the future of slavery in America, the nation's most divisive issue for years to come.

The Antebellum Senate

In 1820 the 46 senators were split evenly between slave states and free states. The Senate considered numerous bills designed to either protect or destroy this delicate balance. Legislation regulating statehood produced the Missouri Compromise (1820–21), the Compromise of 1850, and the Kansas-Nebraska Act (1854). While the compromises attempted to sustain the Union, the Kansas-Nebraska Act, with its controversial "popular sovereignty" clause, escalated the conflict between slave owners and abolitionists.

Senate historians consider the antebellum period to be the institution's golden era. The Senate chamber, a vaulted room on the Capitol's second floor, hosted passionate floor speeches enthralling both the public and the press. At the center of debate stood the Senate's "Great Triumvirate": Henry Clay, Daniel Webster, and John C. Calhoun.

As Speaker of the House, Clay had overseen the formation of the Missouri Compromise, which stipulated that Missouri would have no slavery restrictions, while all territories to the north would become free states. Later, as senator, Clay led the opposition against President Andrew Jackson's emerging Democratic Party. In 1834 he sponsored a resolution condemning Jackson for refusing to provide a document to Congress. Although the first (and only) presidential censure was expunged in 1837, it sparked the rise of the Whig Party in the late 1830s.

Webster, one of the greatest American orators, defended the importance of national power over regional self-interest, declaring in a rousing 1830 speech, "Liberty and Union, now and forever, one and inseparable!" His views challenged Vice President Calhoun's theory of nullification, which proposed that states could disregard laws they found unconstitutional. By the time Calhoun became a senator in 1832, the Senate had divided between those who promoted states' rights and those with a nationalist view.

The Mexican-American War inflamed the issue of slavery. Led by Calhoun, the Senate blocked adoption of the House-sponsored Wilmot Proviso (1846) that would have banned slavery in the territories won from Mexico. Fearing a national crisis, Clay drafted new slavery regulations. When Calhoun, now gravely ill, threatened to block any restrictions, Webster responded with a famous address upholding the Missouri Compromise and the integrity of the Union.

After Calhoun's death in March 1850, the atmosphere in the Senate chamber grew so tense that Henry S. Foote drew a pistol during an argument with antislavery senator Thomas Hart Benton. After months of such heated debates, however, Congress passed Clay's legislation. As negotiated by Senator Stephen A. Douglas, the Compromise of 1850 admitted California as a free state, allowed New Mexico and Utah to determine their own slavery policies (later known as popular sovereignty), outlawed the slave trade in Washington, D.C., and strengthened the controversial fugitive slave law.

Webster and Clay died in 1852, leaving Douglas, as chairman of the Senate Committee on Territories, to manage statehood legislation. Catering to southern senators, Douglas proposed a bill creating two territories under popular sovereignty: Nebraska, which was expected to become a free state, and Kansas, whose future was uncertain. Despite the staunch opposition of abolitionists, the bill became law, prompting pro- and antislavery advocates to flood into "Bleeding Kansas," where more than 50 settlers died in the resulting conflicts.

Opponents of the Kansas-Nebraska Act formed the modern Republican Party, drawing its membership from abolitionist Whigs, Democrats, and Senator Charles Sumner's Free Soil Party. In 1856 Sumner gave a scathing "crime against Kansas" speech that referred to slavery as the wicked mistress of South Carolina senator Andrew P. Butler. Three days after the speech, Butler's relative, Representative Preston S. Brooks, took revenge in the Senate chamber. Without warning, he battered Sumner's head with blows from his gold-tipped cane. The incident made Brooks a hero of the South, while Sumner, who slowly recovered his health, would become a leader of the Radical Republicans.

The Civil War and Reconstruction

In the late 1850s, to accommodate the growing membership of Congress, the Capitol doubled in size with the addition of two wings. The new Senate chamber featured an iron and glass ceiling, multiple galleries, and a spacious floor. It was in this setting that conflicts with the Republican-majority House led to legislative gridlock, blocking a series of Senate resolutions meant to appease the South. In December 1860, South Carolina announced its withdrawal from the Union. One month later, in one of the Senate's most dramatic moments, the Confederacy's future president, Jefferson Davis, and four other southern senators resigned their seats, foretelling the resignation of every senator from a seceding state except Andrew Johnson, who remained until 1862.

Following the fall of Fort Sumter in April 1861, Washington, D.C., was poised to become a battle zone. A Massachusetts regiment briefly occupied the Senate wing, transforming it into a military hospital, kitchen, and sleeping quarters. Eventually, thousands of troops passed through the chamber and adjacent rooms. One soldier gouged Davis's desk with a bayonet, while others stained the ornate carpets with bacon grease and tobacco residue.

Now outnumbering the remaining Democrats, congressional Republicans accused southern lawmakers of committing treason. For the first time since Senator William Blount was dismissed for conspiracy in 1797, Senate expulsion resolutions received the required two-thirds vote. In total, the Senate expelled 14 senators from the South, Missouri, and Indiana for swearing allegiance to the Confederacy.

Within the Republican majority, the Senate's Radical Republican contingent grew more powerful during the war. Staunch abolitionists formed the Joint Committee on the Conduct of the War to protest President Abraham Lincoln's management of the army. Radicals demanded an end to slavery and investigated allegations of government corruption and inefficiency. They also passed significant domestic policy laws, such as the Homestead Act (1862) and the Land Grant College Act (1862).

When a northern victory seemed imminent, Lincoln and the congressional Republicans developed different plans for reconstructing the Union. In December 1863, the president declared that states would be readmitted when 10 percent of their previously qualified voters took a loyalty oath. Radicals countered with the Wade-Davis Bill requiring states to administer a harsher, 50 percent oath. Lincoln vetoed the legislation, outraging Senator Benjamin F. Wade and Representative Henry W. Davis.

In the closing days of the war, the Senate passed the Thirteenth Amendment abolishing slavery. After Lincoln's assassination in April 1865, the new president, former senator Andrew Johnson, infuriated congressional Republicans when he enabled Confederate politicians to return to power and vetoed a bill expanding the Freedmen's Bureau, which assisted former slaves. Republicans, in turn, enacted the Fourteenth Amendment, providing blacks with citizenship, due process of law, and equal protection by laws.

Chaired by Senator William P. Fessenden, the Joint Committee on Reconstruction declared that the restoration of states was a legislative, not an executive, function. Accordingly, Congress passed the Reconstruction Acts of 1867, which divided the South into military districts, permitted black suffrage, and made the adoption of the Fourteenth Amendment a condition of state readmittance. To protect pro-Radical civil officials, Republicans proposed the Tenure of Office Act, requiring Senate approval before the president could dismiss a cabinet member.

Johnson violated the act by firing Secretary of War Edwin M. Stanton, and the House of Representatives impeached him on February 24, 1868. A week later, the Senate convened as a court of impeachment, and on May 16, 35 senators voted to convict Johnson, 1 vote short of the two-thirds majority needed for removal. The case centered on executive rights and the constitutional separation of powers, with 7 moderate Republicans joining the 12 Democrats in voting to acquit.

While Johnson retained his office, he was soon replaced by Ulysses S. Grant, the Civil War general. Marked by corruption, the Grant years (1869–77) split the congressional Republicans into pro- and antiadministration wings. The party was weakened further when representatives and senators were caught accepting bribes to assist the bankrupt Union Pacific Railroad. And after two senators apparently bought their seats from the Kansas legislature, much of the press began calling for popular Senate elections to replace the indirect election method outlined by the Constitution.

Meanwhile, Republicans still dominated southern state legislatures, as most Democrats were unable to vote under Radical Reconstruction. In 1870 Mississippi's Republican legislature elected the first black U.S. senator, Hiram R. Revels, to serve the last year of an unexpired term. Another black Mississippian, Blanche K. Bruce, served from 1875 to 1881. (Elected in 1966, Edward W. Brooke was the first African American to enter the Senate *after* Reconstruction.)

The 1876 presidential election ended Radical Reconstruction. Although the Democrat, Samuel J. Tilden, won the popular vote, ballots from Florida, Louisiana, and South Carolina were in dispute. To avert a constitutional crisis, Congress formed an electoral commission composed of five senators, five representatives, and five Supreme Court justices, who chose Republican Rutherford B. Hayes by a one-vote margin. As part of the Compromise of 1877, Republicans agreed to end military rule in the South in exchange for Democratic support of the Hayes presidency.

The Gilded Age and the Progressive Era

During the late nineteenth century, corruption permeated the public and private sectors. While the two major parties traded control of the Senate, the Republicans divided between those who wanted institutional reform and those in favor of retaining political patronage, the practice of dispensing government jobs in order to reward or secure campaign support.

New York senator Roscoe Conkling epitomized the problem of patronage. In the 1870s, he filled the New York Custom House with crooked friends and financial backers. Moderates from both parties called for a new method to select government workers. In 1881 a disturbed patronage seeker assassinated President James A. Garfield. The act motivated Democratic senator George H. Pendleton to sponsor legislation creating the merit-based civil service category of federal jobs.

In 1901 William McKinley's assassination elevated progressive Republican Theodore Roosevelt to the White House, while Republicans once again dominated the Senate. As chairman of the Republican Steering Committee, as well as the Appropriations Committee, William B. Allison dominated the chamber along with other committee chairmen. In a showdown between two factions of Republicans, Allison's conservative Old Guard blocked progressives' efforts to revise tariffs. Despite the continued opposition of conservatives, however, Roosevelt achieved his goal of regulating railroad rates and large companies by enforcing Senator John Sherman's Antitrust Act of 1890.

Prior to World War I, Progressive Era reformers attempted to eradicate government corruption and increase the political influence of the middle class. The campaign for popular Senate elections hoped to achieve both goals. In 1906 David Graham Phillips wrote several muckraking magazine articles exposing fraudulent relationships between senators, state legislators, and businessmen. His "Treason of the Senate" series sparked new interest in enabling voters, rather than state legislatures, to elect senators. But although the Seventeenth Amendment (1913) standardized direct elections, the institution remained a forum for wealthy elites.

In 1913 reform-minded Democrats took over the Senate, as well as the presidency under Woodrow Wilson, resulting in a flurry of progressive legislation. Wilson's Senate allies, John Worth Kern and James Hamilton Lewis, ushered through the Federal Reserve Act (1913), the Federal Trade Commission Act (1914), and the Clayton Antitrust Act (1914). As chairman of the Democratic Conference, Kern acted as majority leader several years before the position was officially recognized, while Lewis served as the Senate's first party whip. As such, he counted votes and enforced attendance prior to the consideration of important bills.

World War I and the 1920s

Following Europe's descent into war in 1914, domestic concerns gave way to foreign policy, and Wilson battled both progressive and conservative Republicans in Congress. On January 22, 1917, Wilson addressed the Senate with his famous "peace without victory" speech. Shortly thereafter, a German submarine sank an unarmed U.S. merchant ship, and the president urged Congress to pass legislation allowing trade vessels to carry weapons. Noninterventionist senators, including progressive Republicans Robert M. La Follette and George W. Norris, staged a lengthy filibuster in opposition to Wilson's bill, preventing its passage. Furious, Wilson declared that a "little group of willful men" had rendered the government "helpless and contemptible." Calling a special Senate session, he prompted the passage of Rule 22, known as the cloture rule, which limited debate when two-thirds (later changed to three-fifths) of the senators present agreed to end a filibuster.

The 1918 elections brought Republican majorities to both houses of Congress. As the Senate's senior Republican, Massachusetts senator Henry Cabot Lodge chaired the Foreign Relations Committee and his party's conference. Angered by the lack of senators at the Paris Peace Conference (1919), the de facto floor leader attached 14 reservations to the war-ending Treaty of Versailles, altering the legal effect of selected terms, including the provision outlining Wilson's League of Nations (the precursor to the United Nations), which Lodge opposed. The Senate split into three groups: reservationists, irreconcilables, and pro-treaty Democrats, who were instructed by Wilson not to accept changes to the document. Unable to reach a compromise, the Senate rejected the treaty in two separate votes. Consequently, the United States never entered the League of Nations and had little influence over the enactment of the peace treaty.

In the 1920s, the Republicans controlled both the White House and Congress. Fearing the rising numbers of eastern Europeans and East Asians in America, congressional isolationists curtailed immigration with the National Origins Act of 1924. Senators investigated corruption within the Harding administration, sparking the famous Teapot Dome oil scandal.

Two years after the Nineteenth Amendment gave women the right to vote, Rebecca Latimer Felton, an 87-year-old former suffragist, served as the first woman senator for just 24 hours between November 21 and 22, 1922. Felton considered the symbolic appointment proof that women could now obtain any office. The second female senator, Hattie Wyatt Caraway, was appointed to fill Thaddeus Caraway's seat upon his death in 1931. She became the first *elected* female senator, however, when she won the special election to finish her husband's term in 1932. Caraway won two additional elections and spent more than 13 years in the Senate.

In 1925 the Republicans elected Charles Curtis as the first official majority leader, a political position that evolved from the leadership duties of committee and conference chairmen. Curtis had the added distinction of being the first known Native American member of

Congress (he was part Kaw Indian) and was later Herbert Hoover's vice president.

The New Deal and World War II

The 1929 stock market crash signaled the onset of the Great Depression and the end of Republican rule. Democrats swept the elections of 1932, taking back Congress and the White House under Franklin Roosevelt, who promised a "new deal" to address the nation's economic woes. The first Democratic majority leader, Joseph T. Robinson, ushered through the president's emergency relief program, while other senators crafted legislation producing the Federal Deposit Insurance Corporation, the Tennessee Valley Authority, the Social Security Administration, and the National Labor Relations Board.

In 1937 the Senate majority leader worked furiously to enlist support for Roosevelt's controversial Court reorganization act, designed to expand the Supreme Court's membership with liberal justices. Prior to the Senate vote, though, Robinson succumbed to a heart attack, and the president's "Court-packing" plan died with him. The debate over the bill drove a deep wedge between liberal and conservative Democrats.

In the late 1930s, another war loomed in Europe. Led by Republican senators William E. Borah and Gerald P. Nye, Congress passed four Neutrality Acts. After Germany invaded France in 1940, however, Roosevelt's handpicked Senate majority leader, Alben W. Barkley, sponsored the Lend-Lease Act (1941), enabling the United States to send Great Britain and its allies billions of dollars in military equipment, food, and services. The monumental aid plan invigorated the economy, ending the Depression, as well as American neutrality.

During the war, little-known senator Harry Truman headed the Senate's Special Committee to Investigate the National Defense Program. Elected as Roosevelt's third vice president in 1944, Truman assumed the presidency when Roosevelt died three months into his fourth term. The new president relied heavily on Senate support as he steered the nation through the conclusion of World War II and into the cold war.

The Cold War Senate

The Senate assumed a primary role in shaping the mid-century's social and economic culture. In 1944 Senator Ernest W. McFarland sponsored the Servicemen's Readjustment Act. Better known as the GI Bill, the legislation provided veterans with tuition assistance and low-cost loans for homes and businesses. In 1947 the Republicans regained Congress and passed the antilabor Taft-Hartley Act (1947) over Truman's veto. The act restricted the power of unions to organize and made conservative senator Robert A. Taft a national figure. Responding to the Soviet Union's increasing power, the Foreign Relations Committee approved the Truman Doctrine (1947) and the Marshall Plan (1948), which sent billion of dollars of aid and materials to war-torn countries vulnerable to communism.

The Senate itself was transformed by the Legislative Reorganization Act (1946), which streamlined the committee system, increased the number of professional staff, and opened committee sessions to the public. In 1947 television began broadcasting selected Senate hearings. Young, ambitious senators capitalized on the new medium, including C. Estes Kefauver, who led televised hearings on organized crime, and junior senator Joseph R. McCarthy from Wisconsin, whose name became synonymous with the anti-Communist crusade.

In February 1950 Republican senator McCarthy made his first charges against Communists working within the federal government. After announcing an "all-out battle between communistic atheism and Christianity," he gave an eight-hour Senate speech outlining "81 loyalty risks." Democrats examined McCarthy's evidence and concluded that he had committed a "fraud and a hoax" on the public. Meanwhile, Republican senator Margaret Chase Smith, the first woman to serve in both houses of Congress, gave a daring speech, entitled "A Declaration of Conscience," in which she decried the Senate's decline into "a forum of hate and character assassination."

Nevertheless, McCarthy continued to make charges against government officials, and as chairman of the Permanent Subcommittee on Investigations, he initiated more than 500 inquiries and investigations into suspicious behavior, destroying numerous careers along the way. In 1954 McCarthy charged security breaches within the military. During the televised Army-McCarthy hearings, the army's head attorney, Joseph N. Welch, uttered the famous line that helped bring about the senator's downfall: "Have you no sense of decency?" On December 2, 1954, senators passed a censure resolution condemning McCarthy's conduct, thus ending one of the Senate's darker chapters.

A new era in Senate history commenced in 1955, when the Democrats, now holding a slight majority, elected Lyndon B. Johnson, a former congressman from Texas, to be majority leader. Johnson reformed the committee membership system but was better known for applying the "Johnson technique," a personalized form of intimidation used to sway reluctant senators to vote his way. The method proved so effective that he managed to get a 1957 civil rights bill passed despite Senator Strom Thurmond's record-breaking filibuster, lasting 24 hours and 18 minutes. In the 1958 elections, the Senate Democrats picked up an impressive 17 seats. Johnson leveraged the 62–34 ratio to challenge President Dwight D. Eisenhower at every turn, altering the legislative-executive balance of power.

Johnson sought the presidency for himself in 1960 but settled for the vice presidency under former senator John F. Kennedy. Although popular with his colleagues, the new majority leader, Mike Mansfield, faced difficulties uniting liberal and conservative Democrats, and bills affecting minority groups stalled at the committee level. Following Kennedy's assassination in November 1963, Democrat Hubert H. Humphrey and Republican Everett M. Dirksen engineered the passage of Johnson's Civil Rights Act of 1964. They did so by first securing a historic cloture vote that halted a filibuster led by southern Democrats Robert C. Byrd and Richard B. Russell. Johnson and Mansfield then won additional domestic policy victories, including the Voting Rights Act (1965) and the Medicare/Medicaid health care programs (1965).

The president's foreign policy decisions, however, would come to haunt him and the 88 senators who voted for the 1964 Tonkin Gulf Resolution. Drafted by the Johnson administration, the measure drew the nation into war by authorizing the president to take any military action necessary to protect the United States and its allies in Southeast Asia. As the Vietnam War escalated, Senator John Sherman Cooper and Senator Frank F. Church led efforts to reassert the constitutional power of Congress to declare war, culminating in the War Powers Resolution of 1973, which required congressional approval for prolonged military engagements.

Although the Democrats lost the presidency to Richard M. Nixon in 1968, they controlled the Senate until 1981. In 1973 the Senate Select Committee on Presidential Campaign Activities investigated Nixon's involvement in the cover-up of the 1972 break-in at the Democratic Party's National Committee office in the Watergate complex. Chaired by Senator Samuel J. Ervin, the select committee's findings led to the initiation of impeachment proceedings in the House of Representatives. In early August 1974, prominent Republicans, including Senate Minority Leader Hugh Scott, Senator Barry Goldwater, and House Minority Leader John Rhodes, informed Nixon that he did not have the party support in either house of Congress to remain in office. Rather than face a trial in the Senate, Nixon resigned prior to an impeachment vote in the House.

The Modern Senate

From 1981 to 1987, the Republicans controlled the Senate and supported White House policy under President Ronald Reagan. During this period, the Senate began televising floor debates. Televised hearings, however, continued to captivate followers of politics, especially after the Democrats regained the Senate in 1987 and conducted hearings on the Reagan and George H. W. Bush administrations.

In 1987 the House and Senate held joint hearings to investigate the Iran-Contra affair. Later that year, senators grilled conservative Supreme Court nominee Robert Bork, before defeating his appointment. Nominated for defense secretary in 1989, retired Republican senator John G. Tower suffered a humiliating rejection from his former Senate colleagues, and in 1991 Clarence Thomas survived the Judiciary Committee's scrutiny of his Supreme Court nomination despite allegations of sexual harassment by his former staff member Anita Hill.

In 1992, the "Year of the Woman," female candidates won elections nationwide, including five seats in the Senate, with Carol Moseley Braun serving as the first African American woman senator. President Bill Clinton's early domestic policy initiatives, such as the Family and Medical Leave Act (1993), reflected the influence of mothers serving in Congress. In 1994, however, the "Republican revolution" brought the Senate under conservative rule, and Republicans thwarted Clinton's legislative agenda while they investigated his public and personal activities.

In December 1998, the House of Representatives passed two articles of impeachment against Clinton: lying under oath and obstruction of justice regarding a 1994 sexual harassment case and an affair with the White House intern Monica Lewinsky. With Chief Justice William H. Rehnquist presiding, the Senate convened as a court of impeachment in January 1999. Although several Democratic senators voiced objections to Clinton's behavior, on February 12 every Democrat, as well as a few moderate Republicans, voted for his acquittal.

The 1990s closed with a divided Senate, bruised from in-fighting and media reports criticizing the influence of lobbyists in Washington. While it did not reduce candidate spending, the 2002 McCain-Feingold Campaign Finance Bill limited "soft money" contributions and regulated the broadcast of issue ads. The bipartisan effort demonstrated that Republican and Democratic senators could work together to achieve common goals, although they rarely chose to do so.

The September 11, 2001, terrorist attacks provided an opportunity to unite the Senate in support of national security policies. Shortly after 9/11, Congress adopted the controversial USA Patriot Act, increasing federal law-enforcement and intelligence-gathering capabilities to the possible detriment of civil liberties. The October 2001 anthrax attack on the Hart Senate Office Building prompted senators and staffers to work together to eliminate vulnerabilities in the Capitol complex. But soon tensions escalated, as senators sparred over the ongoing war in Iraq.

Despite instances of acrimony throughout its history, the Senate has maintained a more cordial environment than the much larger House of Representatives. Institutional rules keep tempers in check, although lapses in demeanor occur. However strained, friendships "across the aisle" do exist and are helpful in forging compromises prior to important votes. In the years ahead, the Senate will continue to shape American society as long as thoughtful deliberation remains the institution's most distinguishing feature.

See also House of Representatives; presidency; Supreme Court.

FURTHER READING

Baker, Richard A. *200 Notable Days: Senate Stories, 1787 to 2002*. Washington, DC: U.S. Government Printing Office, 2006. Downloadable as "Historical Minute Essays" from http://www.senate.gov, Art & History page.

———. *The Senate of the United States: A Bicentennial History*. Malabar, FL: R. E. Krieger, 1988.

Baker, Richard A., and Roger H. Davidson, eds. *First among Equals: Outstanding Senate Leaders of the Twentieth Century*. Washington, DC: Congressional Quarterly Press, 1991.

Byrd, Robert C. *The Senate, 1789–1989*. Washington, DC: U.S. Government Printing Office, 1988–1994.

Gould, Lewis L. *The Most Exclusive Club: A History of the Modern United States Senate*. New York: Basic Books, 2005.

Harris, Fred R. *Deadlock or Decision: The U.S. Senate and the Rise of National Politics*. Oxford, UK: Oxford University Press, 1993.

Hibbing, John R., and John G. Peters, eds. *The Changing World of the U.S. Senate*. Berkeley: IGS Press, Institute of Governmental Studies, University of California at Berkeley, 1990.

Zelizer, Julian E., ed. *The American Congress: The Building of Democracy*. Boston: Houghton Mifflin, 2004.

JANE ARMSTRONG HUDIBURG

slavery

Slavery was deeply entrenched in the early United States, and its overthrow is one of the epic stories of the nation's history. It is tempting to believe that the problem of slavery was destined to haunt American politics from the very moment that the Declaration of Independence announced that "all men are created equal" and "endowed by their Creator with certain unalienable rights" including liberty, but those words might have remained dead on the page if both black and white Americans opposed to slavery had not struggled together to give them an antislavery meaning in the political arena. From the end of the American Revolution onward, the ebb and flow of the slavery controversy in politics can be roughly divided into four general periods: the republican era, leading up to the Missouri Compromise; the Jacksonian era, from the Missouri Compromise to the Mexican-American War; the years of sectional crisis, from the Mexican War to the secession of the southern states; and the final chapter, of Civil War and emancipation.

Many Northerners in the 1840s and 1850s thought that a "slave power" had come to dominate American politics. Although some historians have dismissed that idea as a paranoid fantasy, slaveholders actually did wield political power from the start to protect their controversial interest in human property. Accommodating slaveholders' concerns, the framers of the U.S. Constitution included three clauses that offered thinly veiled protections to slaveholders: the Three-Fifths Clause mandated that the enslaved population count in a fractional ratio for purposes of determining representation in the U.S. House of Representatives; the Fugitive Slave Clause prevented "persons bound to labor" from acquiring their freedom by virtue of escaping to another state; and the Slave Trade Clause prevented the U.S. Congress from prohibiting the importation of foreign slaves until 1808.

The Three-Fifths and Slave Trade Clauses were not pure concessions to slaveholders. Southern delegates wanted slaves to count fully for purposes of representation, and while the slaveholders from South Carolina and Georgia wanted to protect slave importation, many in the Upper South would have preferred an immediate ban. Although American slaveholders united to defend their claims to human property (as in the Fugitive Slave Clause), they disagreed among themselves over an array of secondary issues relating to slavery (as in the debates over slave importation before 1810 and again in the 1850s). In the framing of the Constitution, they compromised for the sake of union.

The Republican Era: 1789–1821

The northern and southern states followed different paths in the republican era that followed the American Revolution. Slavery slowly disappeared in the North through judicial fiat, state legislation mandating gradual emancipation, private acts of manumission, and the sale of slaves to the South. Free black communities emerged in northern towns and cities from Boston to Philadelphia, where they endured legal discrimination and customary prejudice and, with few exceptions, were relegated to the lowest rungs of the economic ladder. Free black northerners banded together in "African" mutual aid societies and independent churches, which were the earliest stronghold of radical abolitionism in the United States.

But in the southern states, slavery weathered the republican storm. Manumission significantly increased the free black population in Maryland and Virginia before new legal restrictions made it more difficult for owners to free their slaves. As tobacco and rice growers regained their economic footing on the Atlantic seaboard, burgeoning demand for short-staple cotton in the industrial centers of British textile manufacturing gave a powerful boost to the use of slave labor in the southern interior from the Carolina upcountry to the lower Mississippi River valley. The number of slaves in the country doubled between 1790 and 1820, and several new slave states (Kentucky, Tennessee, Louisiana, Alabama, and Mississippi) joined the Union. Thirty years after the ratification of the Constitution, those who hoped that slavery would evaporate in the new United States were sorely disappointed.

During this early republican period, the two main points of contention over slavery at the national level were the regulation of U.S. participation in the Atlantic slave trade and the status of slavery in new territories. Thomas Jefferson's first draft of the Declaration of Independence had accused King George III of waging "cruel war against human nature itself" by protecting the slave trade; the Continental Congress cut the accusation out of the final version. Most of the states prohibited foreign slave importation after independence, although South Carolina's temporary lifting of its state ban in 1804 allowed traders to import tens of thousands of African slaves before Congress exercised its constitutional power to end slave importation in 1808. Highly publicized cases of slave smuggling into the Gulf South after the War of 1812 prompted Congress to pass a series of reforms between 1818 and 1820 that authorized the U.S. Navy to suppress illegal slave trading on the African coast and defined such trading as piracy punishable by death. But not until the Civil War, with the execution of Nathaniel Gordon in 1862, was capital punishment used as a sentence in the United States for participation in the illegal slave trade. Congress also tried to stop U.S. citizens from participating in the slave trade between Africa and foreign countries beginning with an anti–slave trade law in 1794, but fragmentary evidence suggests that the legislative effort to stop such activity was ineffective. Despite British naval and diplomatic pressure, Atlantic slave trading persisted as a shadowy sector of the American economy well into the nineteenth century.

More controversial was the issue of slavery's western expansion. The Continental Congress prohibited slavery in the Northwest Territory in 1787 but allowed it in the territory south of the Ohio River, implicitly drawing a line between free and slave territories in the trans-Appalachian West. In 1798 and in 1803, Congress debated the status of slavery in the Mississippi and Orleans territories, respectively, allowing slaveholding but not foreign slave importation in both places.

Three decades of simmering conflict over the geographic extension of slavery boiled over in 1819 when Missouri, a slave-owning territory, applied for statehood. For the first time, northern opponents of slavery blocked the introduction of a state rather than a territory, raising a new and explosive constitutional question. Thomas Jefferson called it "a firebell in the night." Led by Congressman Rufus King of New York, northeastern representatives in the House tapped into a genuine wellspring of antislavery sentiment among their constituents, for whom slavery was now a potent metaphor for oppression rather than a day-to-day reality. They saw the prospect of slavery flourishing in the "empire of liberty" west of the Mississippi as a betrayal of American ideals. But unionism prevailed. The Missouri Compromise welcomed Missouri as a slave state and Maine as a free state, thereby preserving sectional balance in the U.S. Senate, and drew a line between free and slave territories elsewhere in the Louisiana Purchase at 36° 30′ latitude. For a generation, this agreement bought sectional peace on the question of slavery's expansion.

The Jacksonian Era: 1822–45

The Missouri crisis also revealed the danger of antagonistic sectional interests in national politics. One solution, as New York's "little magician" Martin Van Buren recognized, was to forge a national political coalition around the shared interests of people in the northern and southern states. Rising to power with the election of the slave-owning planter and military hero Andrew Jackson in 1828, Van Buren's Democratic Party pursued an *anti*-antislavery position consistent with its principles of limited government. The Democrats refused to continue federal support for the gradual emancipationist African Colonization Society, which had been granted a de facto subsidy through the 1819 slave trade law. The Democrats sustained a "gag rule" in the House of Representatives from 1836 to 1844 that prevented debate on petitions relating to slavery. As proponents of a strong national government and moral reform, the northern wing of the Whig Party was less ideologically hostile to antislavery than the Democrats. (Returning to Congress as a Massachusetts Whig, John Quincy Adams became the leading opponent of the gag rule in the House.) Yet for the Whigs, too, the task of winning national elections required the muffling of antislavery tendencies so as not to alienate its southern constituency. The Jacksonian two-party system thus repolarized national politics around issues other than slavery.

Yet the progress of antislavery ideas and organizations in northern civil society made it difficult for the two-party system to keep the lid on the slavery issue. The slave population continued to increase and, although the United States had legally withdrawn from the Atlantic slave trade, a new interstate slave trade carried enslaved people from the Upper South to the Deep South. The image of slave traders marching coffles of chained slaves through the District of Columbia became a staple of abolitionist propaganda. The American Colonization Society (ACS) and its program for gradual emancipation came under intense fire from both port and starboard. Free black Northerners and their radical white abolitionist allies assailed the ACS as a proslavery trick, while proslavery ideologues in the South regarded it as impractical at best and, at worst, a Trojan horse of state-sponsored abolition.

As the promise of gradual emancipation faded, some white Northerners sought a clean break with slavery. Inspired by perfectionist ideas emanating from the Second Great Awakening, a radical abolitionist movement sprang up in the 1830s under the banner of William Lloyd Garrison's Boston-based newspaper, the *Liberator*. The radical abolitionists regarded slavery as a terrible sin, advocated immediate emancipation, and rejected the colonization of freed people outside the United States. After Garrison and other leading abolitionists organized the American Anti-Slavery Society (AAAS) in 1833, state and local chapters proliferated in the northern states, much to the horror of southern slaveholders and their "doughface" northern allies.

The abolitionist movement launched two campaigns in the mid-1830s that tested the American political system's tolerance for antislavery dissent. The first came in 1835, when the wealthy New York merchant Lewis Tappan orchestrated a scheme to use the national postal system to flood the southern states with AAAS propaganda, including a children's gazette called *The Slave's Friend*. Angry mobs seized the offending literature from many southern post offices and burned it on the pretext of protecting public safety, prompting abolitionists to protest against interference with the mail and the violation of free speech. Buoyed by the publicity garnered through the postal campaign, the AAAS launched a petition drive designed to demonstrate northern support for the abolition of slavery and the slave trade in the District of Columbia. It was this petition drive that provoked the House of Representatives to initiate the gag rule.

The end of the decade witnessed a schism in the abolitionist movement, pitting those who wanted to press the slavery issue in the political arena against the Garrisonian faction, who wanted nothing to do with politics whatsoever. (Garrison would eventually denounce the U.S. Constitution as a "covenant with death.") Supported by the splinter group American and Foreign Antislavery Society, the political wing of abolitionism launched the Liberty Party in 1840, running former ACS agent James Birney as a candidate for president. Although Birney won only 7,000 votes in 1840 and 62,000 votes in 1844, the Liberty Party did articulate an antislavery alternative to the Jacksonian party system.

Events beyond the nation's borders bolstered Jacksonian-era antislavery. Abolitionists celebrated British West Indian emancipation in the 1830s, even though the

British government paid £20 million to slaveholders. In 1839 northeastern abolitionists rallied to the defense of a group of Africans who had commandeered a Spanish slaver, the *Amistad*. The Africans were captured by a U.S. naval vessel off the coast of Long Island, New York, as they tried to sail back to Sierra Leone. Their case was litigated all the way to the U.S. Supreme Court, which ruled, in 1841, that they had been illegally enslaved in violation of Spanish law and treaty obligations. Later that year, a ship called the *Creole* carrying slaves from Richmond, Virginia, to New Orleans was also commandeered by its human cargo, who sailed the vessel to the Bahamas, where they were liberated. In a striking contrast to the *Amistad* case, the United States demanded that the slaves be returned to their owners. Joshua Giddings, an antislavery Whig representative from Ohio, introduced a resolution declaring the slaves' revolt to be legal and the government's effort to recover them dishonorable. He was censured by the House, resigned his seat, and was promptly reelected by his constituents.

As the British stepped up their campaign against the Atlantic slave trade, the United States steadfastly refused to allow the Royal Navy to search American vessels suspected of "blackbirding." Instead, the Webster-Ashburton Treaty of 1842 committed the United States to maintaining a naval patrol off the West African coast to "act in concert and cooperation" with the British navy in the suppression of the Atlantic slave trade. The results were unimpressive, as American naval vessels in the West Africa Squadron captured only 36 slavers between 1843 and 1861.

Until the mid-1840s, Whigs and Democrats avoided the issue of slavery's expansion. When Texas won independence from Mexico in 1836, Democratic leaders initially deflected pressure to annex the new republic. After Van Buren's defeat in 1840, William Henry Harrison, a Whig, would undoubtedly have kept Texas at arm's length, but his untimely death catapulted the idiosyncratic Virginian John Tyler to the presidency. After Tyler clashed with his own party, he seized on Texas annexation as a way to rally southern Democrats behind him. In 1844 Secretary of State John C. Calhoun, who openly feared British abolitionist influence in Texas, negotiated an annexation treaty that was defeated by an alliance of Whigs and northern Democrats in the Senate. The leading candidates for the presidency—Martin Van Buren for the Democrats and Henry Clay for the Whigs—came out against annexation. Southern Democrats retaliated against Van Buren by denying him the party's nomination, which was extended to a relatively obscure former governor of Tennessee, James K. Polk, who supported the annexation of Texas as well as the acquisition of the Oregon Territory with a northern border of 54°40′. Polk edged out Clay in the general election, Texas entered the Union as a slave state the following year, and, shortly after, a boundary dispute with Mexico flamed into war.

Some historians suggest that the Liberty Party's 15,000 votes in New York tipped the 1844 election to Polk, thus initiating a chain of events that returned slavery to the center of American politics—just not in the way that Liberty Party supporters had imagined. This great "what if?" supposes that Clay would have won those 15,000 votes in the absence of the Liberty Party, when it is at least plausible that those voters would have stayed home rather than cast a ballot for the slave-owning Kentuckian. Blaming the Liberty Party also overlooks other factors, from electoral fraud to the Democrats' popularity among immigrants, that contributed to Clay's defeat.

Slavery and the Sectional Crisis: 1846–60

The Mexican-American War was both a partisan and a sectional issue. Whigs opposed the war; many Northerners regarded it as a land grab for the southern "Slave Power." Three months into the war, David Wilmot, a Pennsylvania Democrat, moved to deflect this criticism by proposing to prohibit slavery in any territory acquired from Mexico. (It should be noted that Mexico abolished slavery in 1829, so Wilmot's measure would simply have preserved the legal status quo.) The Wilmot Proviso, as it became known, passed the House with nearly unanimous support from northern congressmen in both parties, but it failed in the Senate, where southern power was stronger. Congress put the proviso through the same paces in 1847, and the war ended with no agreement on the status of slavery in the vast territory acquired in the Treaty of Guadalupe Hidalgo, which the Senate ratified early in 1848.

Committed to prohibiting slavery wherever constitutionally permissible, a coalition of Democratic "Barnburners," Conscience Whigs, and holdovers from the Liberty Party organized the Free Soil Party, nominating Van Buren for president and Charles Francis Adams for vice president. The Free Soil Party won more than 290,000 votes (14 percent of the popular vote in the North), with its strongest support coming in the ticket's home states of New York and Massachusetts. The party did not win any electoral votes, and its effect on the outcome of the election was murky, but it did contribute to a crucial shift in the emphasis of antislavery politics toward concern for the rights of free white Northerners rather than the wrongs done to southern slaves.

Thirty years after the Missouri crisis, another storm gathered around the issue of slavery. To slaveholders' chagrin, the Whig president Zachary Taylor, a Louisiana slaveholder, supported the admission of gold-mad California as a free state. The status of slavery in the rest of the Mexican cession remained in dispute. Antislavery Northerners wanted to abolish slavery in the District of Columbia, while proslavery Southerners wanted more rigorous enforcement of the Constitution's Fugitive Slave Clause. Some radical southern politicians went so far as to threaten disunion if the North did not accede to their demands. After Congress rejected an "omnibus" bill designed by Clay to resolve all these issues at once, the torch passed to Illinois Democratic senator Stephen A. Douglas, who broke up the various elements of Clay's bill and navigated each one separately through Congress.

The so-called Compromise of 1850 passed, even though only a small band of compromisers supported the whole package. They allied with a sectional bloc to form a slim majority on each measure. The territorial issue was solved by admitting California as a free state while effectively adopting the principle of "popular sovereignty" elsewhere in the New Mexico and Utah territories. This solution blunted the appeal of the Free Soil Party. Most Barnburners returned to the Democratic Party, and the Free Soil vote dropped by almost 50 percent from 1848 to 1852. Congress also banned the slave trade but not slave owning in the District of Columbia; the district's slave traders moved their pens outside the city and carried on business as usual.

The most controversial piece of legislation was the new Fugitive Slave Act. It was designed to counteract northern states' "personal liberty laws," which gave free black Northerners due process protections and, in many cases, prohibited state officials from participating in the recovery of fugitive slaves. The Fugitive Slave Act created a new cadre of federal "commissioners" with the authority to arrest runaway slaves and return them to their owners. The commissioners had a financial incentive to determine that seized persons belonged to those who claimed them. Northerners could be deputized by the commissioners to help enforce the law and were subject to fines and punishment if they refused.

These terms inflamed antislavery public opinion in the North. Abolitionists pledged civil disobedience and resistance, and many black Northerners fled to Canada. Dozens of alleged fugitives were captured in the year following the passage of the law, and, in a few celebrated incidents, vigilance committees tried to rescue them. The most famous case occurred in Boston in 1854, when the administration of President Franklin Pierce deployed federal troops to safeguard the return of a fugitive slave named Anthony Burns to Virginia. The "Slave Power" had camped in the North. Harriet Beecher Stowe's *Uncle Tom's Cabin*, written as a protest against the law, was serialized in Gamaliel Bailey's antislavery newspaper *The National Era* in 1851–52 and became a worldwide best-seller. Southern slaveholders were taken aback. They viewed the return of fugitive slaves as a solemn constitutional obligation, and they were aghast at northern antislavery appeals to a "higher law than the Constitution," in the explosive words of New York's Whig senator William Seward.

Despite the furor over the Fugitive Slave Act, it was the revival of the territorial issue that killed off the Second Party System. In 1854, hoping to win support for his preferred transcontinental railroad route, Douglas introduced legislation to organize the Kansas and Nebraska territories and allow the people of each to decide the status of slavery for themselves. Although the Utah and New Mexico territories had been organized on the principle of popular sovereignty four years earlier, Douglas's extension of the principle to Kansas and Nebraska proved explosive because it meant overturning the Missouri Compromise. The Kansas-Nebraska bill divided both major parties along sectional lines, but with enough support from pro-Douglas northern Democrats it passed. If the Democrats split over Kansas and Nebraska, the Whigs fell apart. Southern Whigs had been trounced by the Democrats in the 1852 and 1853 elections, and the Kansas-Nebraska debates finally convinced them to cut loose from the northern wing of their party. Riding a wave of anti-immigrant sentiment, the Know-Nothing Party enjoyed some popularity in local and state elections in 1855 and 1856 as an alternative to the Whigs, but it crashed on the politics of slavery just as the Whigs had done.

Antislavery backlash against the Kansas-Nebraska legislation coalesced in the Republican Party, which emerged in the 1856 elections as the leading rival to the Democrats in the North. Running on a platform that condemned "the twin relics of barbarism—Polygamy, and Slavery," John Frémont, the Republican presidential candidate, won 11 northern states and almost 40 percent of the electoral vote.

Radical southern politicians, often known as "fire-eaters," advocated an aggressively proslavery agenda through the 1850s. Some fire-eaters hoped to force the Democratic Party to give in to proslavery interests; others hoped to create a new southern party and ultimately sever the slave states from the Union. Their platform included rigid enforcement of the Fugitive Slave Act, a federal slave code to protect slaveholders' special property rights, the extension of slavery into the western territories, the annexation of Cuba, support for filibusters in Central America, and the reopening of the African slave trade to the United States. They promoted southern nationalism with calls for railroads, colleges, and a literature unique to the South. Proslavery ideologues painted the abolitionists as fanatics and slavery as humane. Asserting that southern slaves were treated well, they taunted northern and British abolitionists for ignoring the dire plight of wage workers. Some pointed to the emerging utopian socialist movement as proof of the failure of free society.

The sectional crisis deepened in the late 1850s. First, popular sovereignty in the Kansas territory led to a debacle. Violence erupted between proslavery and antislavery factions, punctuated in May 1856 by the murder of five men at Pottawatomie Creek by John Brown and his sons. The violence spilled onto the floor of the Senate, where Preston Brooks, a representative from South Carolina, caned Massachusetts senator Charles Sumner for insulting his cousin, South Carolina senator Andrew Butler, during a speech on the atrocities in Kansas. When pro- and antislavery forces in Kansas submitted rival state constitutions to Congress in 1858, President James Buchanan supported the proslavery version, but Douglas saw it as fraudulent and opposed it. An alliance of Douglas Democrats and Republicans in the House defeated the proslavery constitution, outraging southern Democrats. The Supreme Court added fuel to the fire early in 1857, ruling in *Dred Scott v. Sandford* that the due process clause of the Constitution prevented Congress from prohibiting slavery in the territories. The decision undermined Douglas's preferred solution of popular sovereignty; Abraham Lincoln and many other Republicans thought that it paved the way for the nationalization of slavery.

Then, in the fall of 1859, John Brown attempted to seize the federal armory at Harpers Ferry, Virginia, and incite a slave insurrection. Federal troops under Robert E. Lee quashed the revolt. Brown was captured, tried, and executed for treason. Widespread northern admiration for Brown after his hanging convinced many white Southerners that the Union was an empty shell.

Slavery dominated the election of 1860. Nominating the relatively obscure Lincoln as its presidential candidate, the Republican Party opposed any expansion of slavery into the western territories. In a bid to expand support in the Lower North, the Republicans also broadened their economic agenda to include a protective tariff, a homestead act, and federal aid for internal improvements. The Democrats fractured, with Douglas at the head of a northern ticket pledged to support popular sovereignty and Kentucky's John Breckenridge at the head of a southern ticket determined to protect slavery in federal territory. Conservative former Whigs organized the Constitutional Union Party with the bold platform of upholding the Constitution and enforcing the law. They nominated John Bell of Tennessee for president and Edward Everett from Massachusetts for vice president in a last-ditch effort to hold the country together by ignoring the divisions over slavery.

Lincoln won a majority of the popular vote in the North and the electoral votes of every northern state except New Jersey, which he split with Douglas. Breckenridge won the Lower South, plus Delaware and Maryland. Bell won Virginia, Kentucky, and Tennessee, while Douglas won only Missouri. The upshot was that Lincoln won the presidency without a single electoral vote from the slave states; a northern party had risen to national power on an antislavery platform. Despite Lincoln's assurances that the Republicans would not seek to abolish slavery in the states where it already existed, many white Southerners believed that Lincoln's election portended the death of slavery in the Union one way or another.

Secession, the Civil War, and Emancipation: 1861–65

Secession was intended to protect slavery, but it had the opposite effect. By leaving the Union and daring the North to stop them, southern secessionists invited a terrible war that led, by its own logic, to emancipation. "They have sowed the wind and must reap the whirlwind," reflected William Tecumseh Sherman in the middle of the Civil War. Seven states in the Lower South seceded between late December 1860 and early February 1861, and another four joined the Confederacy in the two months after Fort Sumter. The decision to secede was fiercely contested within the South. Opposition tended to come either from ultraconservative planters who valued prudence above all, or from the spokesmen for regions that had little stake in slavery, such as western

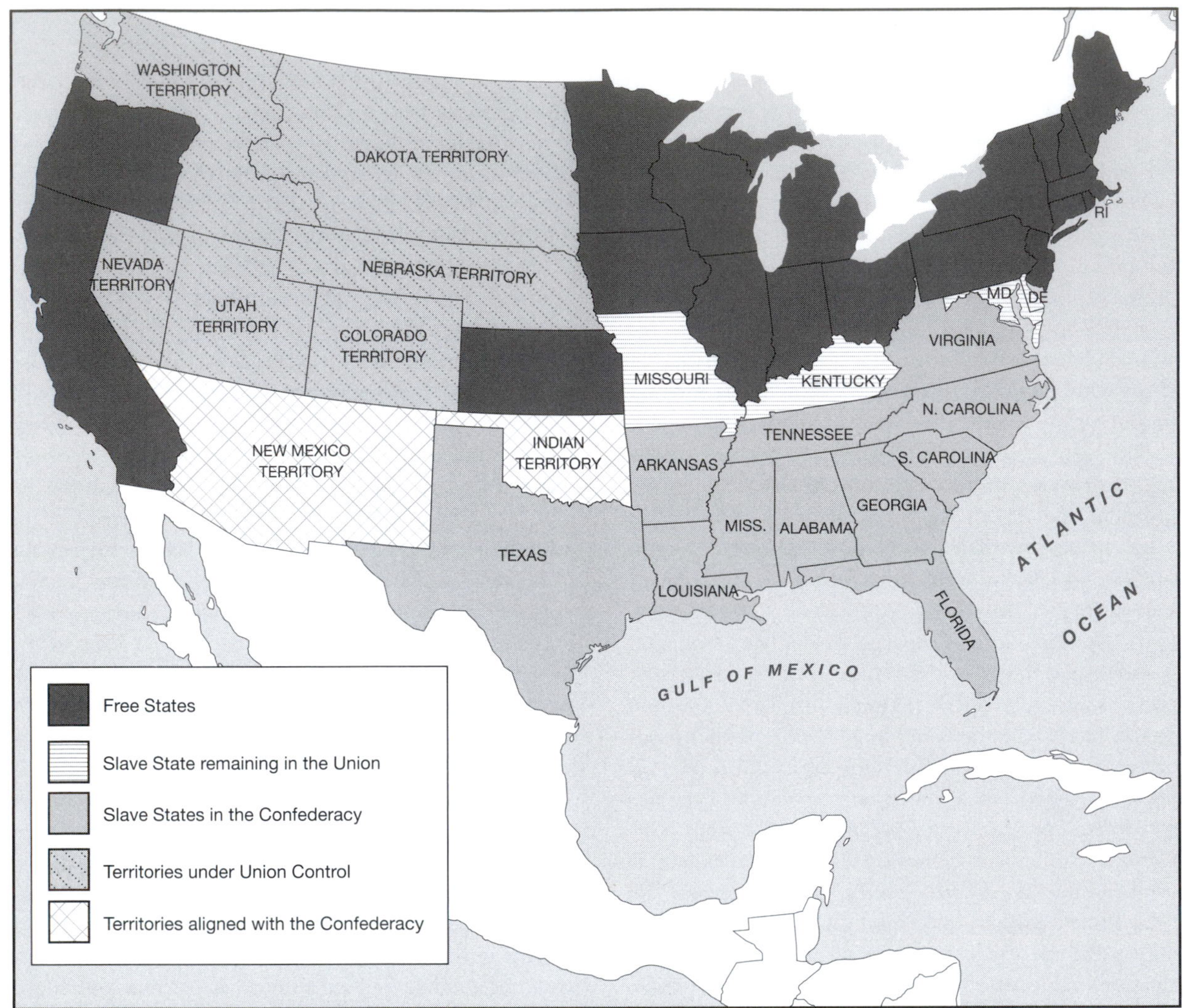

Slave and Free Areas, 1861

Virginia, eastern Tennessee, and northern Alabama. Four border slave states (Delaware, Maryland, Kentucky, and Missouri) remained in the Union, providing some counterweight to abolitionist pressures during the war. But with the slaveholders' power greatly diminished and the Democrats in a minority, Lincoln and the Republican Congress implemented an antislavery agenda: admitting Kansas as a free state, recognizing Haiti, prosecuting illegal Atlantic slave traders, and abolishing slavery (and compensating slaveholders) in the District of Columbia.

At the beginning of the war, however, Lincoln was careful to honor his promise not to challenge slavery in the states where it existed. He did not think that secession abrogated the Constitution's protections for slavery in the states. Moreover, keeping the loyalty of northern Democrats and white men in the border slave states required political caution. So when General David Hunter took it upon himself in May 1862 to declare all the slaves in South Carolina, Georgia, and Florida free, Lincoln revoked the order, earning the wrath of northern abolitionists.

Union policy nevertheless moved toward emancipation. It was spurred on by enslaved people themselves, who risked life and limb to make their way to the Union Army. General Benjamin Butler was the first to turn slaves' status as property against their owners, declaring fugitives to be "contraband of war" in May

1861 and putting them to work at Fortress Monroe in Virginia. Invoking military necessity, the Union continued to counterpunch against slavery, passing a Confiscation Act in August 1861 that freed slaves who were employed in the service of the Confederacy, then passing a Second Confiscation Act in July 1862 that freed the slaves of persons actively engaged in the rebellion. The Emancipation Proclamation continued this trajectory, freeing slaves in all territories still in rebellion as of January 1, 1863. Although it is true that the Emancipation Proclamation did not free a single person at the moment it was promulgated, it did have the momentous effect of transforming the Union Army into an instrument of emancipation as the war dragged on. Moreover, the Proclamation authorized the employment of black men in the army and navy, even if black soldiers would still have to wrestle their own government for equal pay with white soldiers and the opportunity to see combat. Lincoln's resounding victory over McLellan and the Republican landslide in Congress in the election of 1864 confirmed the war's abolitionist turn. Slavery crumbled in the Union as well as in the Confederacy. Unionist governments in Arkansas and Louisiana abolished slavery in 1864, as did Maryland; Missouri and Tennessee followed suit early in 1865. In January of that year, the House approved a constitutional amendment abolishing slavery, but it was not until December that the Thirteenth Amendment was ratified.

The end of slavery raised crucial questions about the status of the country's 4 million freed people: Would they be citizens? What rights would they have? What did society and government owe to them? Emancipation did not end the labor problem that gave rise to slavery in the first place, nor did it wipe away the stain of racism that slavery left behind. As in other postemancipation societies in the Atlantic world, former slaveholders replaced slavery with an array of coercive labor practices ranging from debt peonage to convict labor. Freed people faced a ferocious campaign of racist terror and violence waged by former Confederates embittered by military defeat and the upheaval of social and political Reconstruction. The reaction against emancipation practically eviscerated the Fourteenth and Fifteenth Amendments until the black freedom movement after World War II ended Jim Crow. Unmoored from the struggle against chattel slavery, antislavery rhetoric has drifted through American politics like a ghost ship, reappearing out of the fog in struggles over prostitution, unions, women's rights, communism, and the reserve clause in baseball.

It is impossible to tally the whole cost of slavery and its vicious legacies to the United States, but the reckoning continues. In July 2008, the U.S. House of Representatives passed a nonbinding resolution apologizing for "the fundamental injustice, cruelty, brutality, and inhumanity of slavery and Jim Crow." As William Faulkner wrote, "The past is never dead. It's not even past." Today the United States and the world community confront new manifestations of slavery in its modern guises of "human trafficking" and severe forms of sex and labor exploitation.

See also abolitionism; African Americans and politics; civil rights; Civil War and Reconstruction; sectional conflict and secession; segregation and Jim Crow.

FURTHER READING

Anbinder, Tyler. *Nativism and Slavery: The Northern Know Nothings and the Politics of the 1850s*. New York: Oxford University Press, 1992.

Ashworth, John. *Slavery, Capitalism, and Politics in the Antebellum Republic*. Cambridge, UK: Cambridge University Press, 1995.

Berlin, Ira, Barbara J. Fields, Steven F. Miller, Joseph P. Reidy, and Leslie S. Rowland. *Slaves No More: Three Essays on Emancipation and the Civil War*. Cambridge, UK: Cambridge University Press, 1992.

Cooper, William J. *The South and the Politics of Slavery, 1828–1856*. Baton Rouge: Louisiana State University Press, 1978.

DuBois, W.E.B. *The Suppression of the African Slave Trade to the United States of America, 1638–1870*. New York: Oxford University Press, 2007.

Earle, Jonathan Halperin. *Jacksonian Antislavery and the Politics of Free Soil, 1824–1854*. Chapel Hill: University of North Carolina Press, 2004.

Fehrenbacher, Don Edward. *The Dred Scott Case: Its Significance in American Law and Politics*. New York: Oxford University Press, 1978.

———. *The Slaveholding Republic: An Account of the United States Government's Relations to Slavery*. New York: Oxford University Press, 2001.

Foner, Eric. *Free Soil, Free Labor, Free Men: The Ideology of the Republican Party before the Civil War*. Oxford: Oxford University Press, 1995.

———. *Reconstruction: America's Unfinished Revolution, 1863–1877*. 1st ed. The New American Nation series. New York: Harper and Row, 1988.

Forbes, Robert Pierce. *The Missouri Compromise and Its Aftermath: Slavery and the Meaning of America*. Chapel Hill: University of North Carolina Press, 2007.

Freehling, William W. *The Road to Disunion*. New York: Oxford University Press, 1990.

Holt, Michael F. *The Rise and Fall of the American Whig Party: Jacksonian Politics and the Onset of the Civil War*. New York: Oxford University Press, 1999.

Mason, Matthew. *Slavery and Politics in the Early American Republic*. Chapel Hill: University of North Carolina Press, 2006.

Potter, David Morris. *The Impending Crisis, 1848–1861*. New York: Harper and Row, 1976.

Richards, Leonard L. *The Slave Power: The Free North and Southern Domination, 1780–1860*. Baton Rouge: Louisiana State University Press, 2000.

Siddali, Silvana R. *From Property to Person: Slavery and the Confiscation Acts, 1861–1862*. Baton Rouge: Louisiana State University Press, 2005.

Stewart, James Brewer. *Holy Warriors: The Abolitionists and American Slavery*. Revised ed. New York: Hill and Wang, 1996.

Vorenberg, Michael. *Final Freedom: The Civil War, the Abolition of Slavery, and the Thirteenth Amendment*. Cambridge Historical Studies in American Law and Society. Cambridge, UK: Cambridge University Press, 2001.

Wilentz, Sean. *The Rise of American Democracy: Jefferson to Lincoln*. New York: Norton, 2005.

ADAM ROTHMAN

Social Security

Social Security refers to the program of old-age insurance, subsequently broadened to include survivors (1939) and disability insurance (1956), that President Franklin D. Roosevelt initiated on August 14, 1935, by signing the Social Security Act. Old-age insurance began as a federally administered program in which the government collected equal contributions of 1 percent of the first $3,000 of an employee's wages from employers and employees, and paid pensions to the employees on their retirement. Since 1951 the program has experienced enormous growth, and in 2005 some 48,445,900 Americans, more than the combined populations of California and New Jersey, received benefits from the Social Security program. That year the program collected more than $700 billion from payroll taxes—about as much revenue as the gross domestic product of the Netherlands—and spent a little more than $500 billion on benefits.

Legislative Origins

In June 1934, President Roosevelt asked Labor Secretary Frances Perkins to chair a cabinet-level Committee on Economic Security that, together with a staff headed by two Wisconsin state government officials, made the crucial decision to recommend a federal social insurance program for old age, financed through payroll taxes. The president contrasted this contributory approach favorably with other currently popular plans, such as Francis Townsend's proposals to pay everyone over age 60 a pension of $200 dollars a month. When the president's plan was introduced to Congress in January 1935, the old-age insurance portions of the legislation (the proposed legislation contained many features, including federal aid to the states for public assistance and a state-run unemployment compensation program) received an indifferent reception. Congressmen objected to the fact that the program would not pay regular benefits until 1942 and would exclude those already past retirement age. Members from predominantly agricultural districts realized that old-age insurance meant almost nothing to their constituents who, because the program was limited to industrial and commercial workers, would not be eligible to participate. The president, bolstered by the favorable results of the 1934 elections, resisted congressional attempts to abandon social insurance in favor of noncontributory welfare grants to the elderly and to permit those with liberal private pension plans to withdraw from Social Security.

Getting Established: 1936–50

Social Security surfaced as a campaign issue in 1936, when Republican candidate Alfred Landon criticized the program as "unjust, unworkable, stupidly drafted, and wastefully financed." In response to his criticism, President Roosevelt agreed to a plan, passed by Congress in 1939, to reduce the amount of money held in reserve to finance benefits, to initiate benefits earlier than planned, and to include special benefits for workers' wives and for the dependents of workers who died before retirement age. The 1939 amendments contained the implicit assumption that men participated in the labor force and women did not. Dependent wives but not dependent husbands received spousal benefits, and a benefit went to widows of covered workers but not to widowers. Widows received only three-quarters of a basic benefit. Not until 1983 were these gender distinctions lifted from the law.

Despite the 1939 amendments, Social Security did not gain great popularity. Instead, it remained a relatively neglected program. In 1940, for example, even before the nation's entrance into World War II, the United States spent more on veterans' payments and workers' compensation than it did on old-age and survivors' insurance. Even in the area of old-age security, social insurance—a federal program—played a distinctly secondary role to welfare—a state and local program. The average monthly welfare benefit was $42 in 1949, although with considerable variance from state to state, compared with an average Social Security benefit of $25. As late as 1950, more than twice as many people were on state welfare rolls receiving old-age assistance as were receiving retirement benefits from the federal government under Social Security. Throughout the 1940s, Congress felt little pressure to expand the program and, as a consequence, repeatedly refused to raise payroll taxes, increase benefit levels, or expand coverage.

The situation changed with the 1950 amendments, which expanded coverage and raised benefits. The amendments were the result of a report by an advisory committee in 1948 that argued that the nation could either rely on welfare, which the council portrayed as demeaning since it required recipients to prove they were poor and induced a state of dependency, or on social insurance, which, according to the council, reinforced "the interest of the individual in helping himself."

On August 28, 1950, after lengthy congressional hearings, the recommendations of the advisory council became law. The 1950 amendments raised average benefits by 77 percent and broke the impasse over Social Security taxes. Congress agreed to raise the tax level to 3 percent and to increase the taxable wage base (the amount of earnings on which taxes were paid) from $3,000 to $3,600. In addition, the amendments brought new groups, such as self-employed businessmen, into the Social Security system. The ranks of Social Security supporters included labor unions and liberal Democrats, whose standing was boosted in 1948 with President Truman's surprising reelection, the revival of Democratic control of Congress, and the election of Social Security supporters such as Paul Douglas of Illinois. These factors helped change the congressional mood from indifference to a willingness to expand the system.

The Golden Age of Social Security

Stalled in the 1940s, Social Security became a popular program in the 1950s. Expanded coverage encouraged more congressmen to take an interest. Prosperity enabled the program to collect more money than Depression-era planners had predicted. As a result, increased benefits were legislated in 1952, 1954, 1956, and 1958. Social Security surpassed welfare in popularity and in the generosity of its benefits. The only real test the program faced came with the election of Dwight D. Eisenhower in 1952. He expressed an interest in looking at alternatives to Social Security, and he was encouraged by the Chamber of Commerce, representatives from the insurance industry, and some Republican congressmen. By 1954, however, Eisenhower had decided to reject the advice to change the system to a flat benefit paid out to everyone. In September 1954, the president proposed and secured passage of a law preserving the existing system, raising benefit levels, and extending Social Security coverage to farmers.

During Eisenhower's first term, the creation of disability benefits became the major issue in Social Security politics. Liberals wanted to expand the system to pay benefits to people who had dropped out of the labor force before the normal retirement age because of a functional limitation or impairment. Conservatives worried that disability was a vague concept whose adoption would lead to a precipitous rise in expenditure and discourage the more constructive alternative of rehabilitation. On this matter, the Democrats defeated the Republicans by a one-vote margin in the Senate in July 1956. Social Security expanded to encompass benefits for disabled workers 50 years or older. Four years later Congress removed the age restriction.

By 1958 the cutting edge issue had shifted from disability to health insurance. Proponents of expansion wanted to use the Social Security system as a means of funding insurance to cover the costs of hospital care for Social Security beneficiaries. They argued that retirement benefits could never be raised high enough to cover the catastrophic costs of illness. President Eisenhower, emphasizing health insurance coverage that relied on private insurance companies, opposed this expansion, as did the influential Democratic congressman Wilbur Mills of Arkansas and Senator Robert Kerr, Democrat from Oklahoma. Despite President John F. Kennedy's advocacy of what became known as Medicare, the legislation stalled in Congress and interrupted the pattern of regular Social Security benefit increases. It took the masterful efforts of President Lyndon B. Johnson in 1965 to break the impasse. Only after the creation of Medicare and Medicaid in 1965 did Social Security politics resume its normal course.

Indexing and Modern Dilemmas

A major development in 1972—automatic indexing of Social Security benefit increases to the cost of living—once again changed the course of Social Security politics. The idea of indexing benefits, rather than leaving them to Congress, came from President Richard M. Nixon. The president saw Social Security as an issue where the majority Democrats could always outbid the minority Republicans and take credit for benefit increases. Nixon argued that it would be better to establish a rational structure that related benefit increases to changes in the cost of living and reduced congressional temptation to raise benefits above what the nation could afford. Not surprisingly, Ways and Means Committee Chairman Wilbur Mills resisted the idea, effectively blocking it in 1969 and 1970. As members of Congress became more sympathetic to the indexing idea, Mills acquiesced to a plan that permitted automatic cost-of-living adjustments, but only if Congress failed to raise benefits in a discretionary manner. Because of disagreements between the House and the Senate, largely over the matter of welfare reform, the process took until the summer of 1972 to resolve. In the end, Congress agreed to cost-of-living adjustments on Mills's terms. The Democratic Congress outbid the Republicans on the level of Social Security benefits. Where Nixon hoped for a 5 percent increase, Mills and his colleagues legislated one of 20 percent.

This change made the program vulnerable to the unfavorable economic conditions of the 1970s. High unemployment cut down on tax collections and induced more people to retire; inflation drove up benefit levels. In June 1974, the trustees who oversaw Social Security announced that the program was "underfinanced in the long range." A slower rate of population growth meant a higher future percentage of aged people in the population and a heavier future burden for Social Security. Support for Social Security remained high, but the system faced a new vulnerability

Social Security survived its vulnerable period between 1975 and 1983 because of the many beneficiaries invested in its survival but also because it contained built-in legislative protection. As a result of the 1972 amendments, benefit levels were protected against inflation, without Congress having to do anything.

President Jimmy Carter's advisors convinced him to take action to ensure that Social Security met its obligations. Congress ignored most of the president's recommendations (such as raising the level of employer taxes) and instead raised the level of wages on which workers and their employers paid Social Security taxes, and increased tax rates. Passage of a modified version of Carter's bill showed that Congress was willing to go to great lengths to preserve the basic Social Security system. Carter's advisors assured him that the 1977 amendments had "fixed" Social Security in both the short and long runs.

The economic recession of the late 1970s soon undid the projections of program planners and once again pointed the way to a crisis. As the actuaries duly reported, there was the possibility that Social Security would not be able to meet its obligations and pay full benefits in 1983.

Once again, Congress—which included a House under Democratic control—and the Reagan administration joined forces to "save" the program and preserve its basic structure. The Reagan administration began with an aggressive stance on Social Security, seeking among other things to reduce the size of early retirement benefits (legislated in 1956 for women and 1961 for men). Democrats tended to favor tax increases, Republicans benefit cuts. Interested in sharing the blame, each side hesitated to take action without the tacit approval of the other.

President Reagan and House Speaker Tip O'Neill decided to remove the issue from public scrutiny, at least until after the 1982 elections. In December 1981, Reagan appointed a bipartisan commission, the National Commission on Social Security Reform, to propose solutions to the system's problems. The commission held a number of ceremonial meetings, waiting to see how the 1982 elections turned out. The election results gave the commission no easy outs, since neither party gained a victory decisive enough to provide a comfortable working majority to deal with the issue.

After the election, President Reagan and House Speaker O'Neill of Massachusetts used their surrogates on the commission to negotiate a deal. Each side kept a running score sheet that listed the potential savings from each item, all the time hoping roughly to balance tax increases and benefit costs. In the spirit of reaching a deal, the Democrats accepted a permanent six-month delay in the annual cost-of-living adjustment—in effect a 2 percent reduction in benefits. The Republicans acquiesced to small increases in Social Security taxes achieved by initiating already legislated payroll tax increases earlier than scheduled. The Congress in 1983 honored the terms of the compromise. Politicians on both sides of the aisle celebrated the rescue of Social Security, and Ronald Reagan signed the 1983 Social Security Amendments with pomp and circumstance.

The Modern Era

Conservatives believed that the crisis leading to the 1983 amendments illustrated the vulnerability of the system and the unwillingness of Congress to take steps to put a permanent end to the problems. Liberals pointed to the apparently robust shape of the Social Security trust funds as proof that the amendments had, in effect, resolved the issue. Advocates in conservative think tanks like Cato and the Heritage Foundation tried to make people aware of Social Security's long-term liabilities and its inability to provide windfall gains to later entrants into the system (such as the baby boom generation and its echo). They also touted governmental sanctioned alternatives that relied on individual and private-sector administration, such as individual retirement accounts (IRAs) and 401(k)s—a parallel private universe for Social Security, equivalent to the private health insurance on which most Americans relied.

When Social Security reform returned to the political agenda in the 1990s, the result of changed actuarial assumptions about real wage growth and the future of the economy, conservatives were able to offer more fundamental alternatives than simply tinkering with the present system. Evidence that the latest crisis in Social Security would be handled differently from previous ones came when an advisory council met in 1994 through 1996. This officially sanctioned group, one of the sort that usually reinforced the conventional bureaucratic wisdom, could not agree on a single recommendation and instead gave official sanction to privatization as one of three solutions to the Social Security financing problem.

When George W. Bush came into office, he expected to solve the long-term financing problem and point the way to a fundamental reform of Social Security. In 2000, as a candidate, Bush said he wanted to give younger workers the chance to put part of their payroll taxes into what he called "sound, responsible investments." Interspersed with the political rhythms of the post-9/11 era, the president continued his initiative. In his 2004 State of the Union address, Bush said, "We should make the Social Security system a source of ownership for the American people."

After the 2004 election, the president brought the Social Security campaign to center stage, announcing that it would be a priority of his administration. If nothing were done, Bush argued, the system would run out of money. That set the stage for a call to action in the 2005 State of the Union address. According to the president, Social Security was a great moral success of the past century but something different was required for the new millennium. The president followed up with a full-scale publicity campaign.

Despite his unprecedented effort, Bush gained no political traction as he faced serious technical and political obstacles. One problem, broadly stated, was how to move from one system to another. Benefits for people already receiving Social Security needed to be preserved while simultaneously moving to a private system—a difficult and costly transition. Meanwhile, the shortfall in the program's long-range financing provided continuing pressure on all parties to find some common ground.

See also welfare.

FURTHER READING

Altman, Nancy J. *The Battle for Social Security: From FDR's Vision to Bush's Gamble.* Hoboken, NJ: Wiley, 2005.

Beland, Daniel. *Social Security: History and Politics from the New Deal to the Privatization Debate.* Lawrence: University of Kansas Press, 2005.

Derthick, Martha. *Policymaking for Social Security.* Washington, DC: Brookings Institution Press, 1979.

EDWARD D. BERKOWITZ

socialism

Socialist attempts to redirect the political culture of the United States proved to be a difficult task—one that, while never succeeding, did on occasion achieve a certain success even in failure. The fertile earth of the New World produced a variety of political fruits, but none was as potent as the idea that this American earth itself was, as Irving Howe once said, "humanity's second chance." In this rendering, it was the American Revolution that secured for the nation its exceptional status, and, in the process, dismissed the socialist premise of a required second revolution as misguided or malicious. Understandings of nineteenth-century socialism varied: preindustrial agricultural communes coexisted with urban industrial workers contesting employers in the factory. They shared, however, a concern to democratize decision making in the society and the workplace and to share more equitably the profits from those enterprises. Whatever the specific expression, the socialist experience in America would prove to be, at its best, a bittersweet experience.

The first phase of socialist experimentation in America was primarily communitarian. Reflecting impulses that motivated many of the continent's initial European settlers, these self-defined socialists separated from the developing capitalist society to form communities that would serve, in their reengineered social and personal relations, as beacon lights to the majority of their countrymen they considered lost souls in a materialist diaspora. Influenced by certain European utopian socialists (Charles Fourier and Count Henri de Saint-Simon, especially), by the deep religious currents already evident in American life, and by incipient social reformers such as Robert Owen and Edward Bellamy, these communities proliferated throughout the United States. Most prevalent in the nineteenth and early twentieth centuries, this tradition revived again in the 1960s in the communes organized by so-called hippies seeking personal authenticity in collective life apart from an overly commercialized culture.

Whatever the benefits for individual participants, the majority of these utopian communities were short-lived. John Humphrey Noyes (1811–86), who led the Oneida Community near Utica, New York, explained in his 1870 history of the movement that those communities organized along secular utopian lines failed more quickly than those created from a shared religious belief. Noyes hoped that the latter efforts possessed greater prospects of introducing socialism through "churches . . . quickened by the Pentecostal Spirit." Although the evangelical spirit would influence American socialism, it would not be the singular element in organizing the socialist movement that Noyes imagined.

Transition to Industrial Capitalism

From an international perspective, 1848 marks a turning point in both the idea and practice of socialism. The European revolutions fought that year against the continent's monarchial regimes ignited a variety of dissenting movements; *The Communist Manifesto* by Marx and Engels, published that year, offered an interpretative analysis of the turmoil that emphasized the oppressive class distinctions imposed by the inner logic of the capitalist economic system. A decidedly antiutopian "scientific" socialism emerged from this European cauldron. In Marx's view, working people—the oppressed class created by capitalism—would be the collective agent that would overthrow industrial capitalism. These socialists rejected liberal reform efforts and declared, as a scientific fact, the coming transformation to socialism and, following that, to communism—the state of full human freedom and equality. Not surprisingly, their attempted revolutions and their repression by European authorities led to large-scale migrations by activists and sympathizers to other European countries and to America.

From the start of their American experience, the expectations of European socialist immigrants encountered a difficult reception. In sharp contrast with their European past, America's "universal" suffrage (for white men) was a fundamental aspect of citizenship. As the ballot was preeminently an individual right, its possession validated a core belief in individualism, in the expectation of social mobility, and in the superiority of American democratic governance. While not all Americans held these beliefs with equal intensity, these principles were, as Alexis de Tocqueville and many others noted, a fundamental component of American political consciousness.

As newly arrived socialists entered the workforce and sought to join the nascent trade union movement in the three decades after 1848, many despaired of the "backwardness" of the American working people. The individualistic aspirations of these workers led most to ignore appeals to a collective class consciousness as they avidly engaged in mainstream political activity, often closely aligned with employers. Most confusingly, American working people seemed to embrace the promise of American life. Friedrick Sorge, Marx's representative in America, harshly dismissed these interrelated strands of the political culture as a "delusion [that] transforms itself into a sort of creed." Yet, after almost two decades working in the American wilderness, Sorge reported to Marx in 1871 that, despite the enormous industrial growth that Marx held was the precondition for class consciousness, American "workingmen in general . . . are quite unconscious of their own position toward capital" and thus "slow to show battle against their oppressors. . . . "

But if American working people did not endorse an orthodox Marxist analysis, neither did they simply acquiesce to the demands of employers. In the three decades after Sorge's report, an intense series of strikes occurred nationwide. Strikers protested the transformation of work inherent in the change from an artisan to an industrial system of production, with the consequent loss of control by local communities of their daily lives, and the dramatically widening income gap between workers and employers. State and federal troops were deployed to break these strikes in iron mining and steel production, in coal mining, in railroad operations, and in other industries. Working people sought new approaches to gain their demands. Politically independent labor parties sprouted up across the nation, and the labor movement, while still small, began to solidify. The socialist movement also changed, softening Sorge's rigid view, and became more inclusive of America's particular political attitudes. Not insignificantly, its most prominent leader was deeply attuned to the possibilities of American democratic ideals.

The Socialist Party of America (SPA) was founded in 1901, but it had been in formation for some years before. Itself a coalition of beliefs and opinions, the SPA sought to define socialism in a manner consistent with the promise of democracy in both economic relations and politics. It ran candidates for political office, supported striking workers as well as the vote for women, and sought civic benefits such as the extension of sewer pipes and electricity to working people's neighborhoods. The party also held that socialism would ultimately come to America through electoral means. This emphasis on vying for votes within the dominant political structure rather than advocating an openly revolutionary program generated a split within the SPA, one that would become most evident during World War I.

Eugene Victor Debs (1855–1926) led this movement from its inception until his death. Although many socialist intellectuals considered his appreciation of Marx's theory deficient, he was the single national SPA leader who could appeal to its varied constituencies: new immigrants, native-born workers, intellectuals, and reformers. Debs, a native of Terre Haute, Indiana, ran for the presidency on the SPA ticket five times between 1900 and 1920 (he was ill in 1916). In 1912 Debs received 6 percent of the national vote, the highest percentage ever recorded by a socialist candidate. Eight years later, imprisoned in Atlanta Federal Penitentiary for his opposition to American involvement in World War I, Debs nonetheless received almost 1 million votes. The core of Debs's analysis, and the source of his appeal, was his understanding of socialism as the fulfillment of American democratic ideals in an era of industrial capitalism. It was the corporation, he argued—with its enormous financial and political power that could influence decisions in communities across the nation—that systematically violated the "truths" the Declaration of Independence held to be "self-evident." To democratize industrial capitalism, to share with its workforce decision making as well as the benefits and profits of its work, was a central aim of Debs's agitation.

Two issues particularly generated tension within the ranks of the SPA prior to World War I. Many male socialists dismissed agitation for woman suffrage because, they held, it detracted from the party's focus on economic issues; many also objected to any enhancement of a more visible role for women within the party. Undaunted by this resistance, a group of activist women within the SPA, many with ties to either the trade unions and/or progressive reformers, worked to include a woman's right to vote within the socialist agenda; in the process they created a network of activist socialist women. In major strikes in New York City (1909); Lawrence, Massachusetts (1912); and Patterson, New Jersey (1913), as editors and writers, trade union activists, and advocates for birth control, socialist women found a public voice and organized many. Their male comrades, however, changed slowly—when they changed at all. The values of nineteenth-century American culture that objected to a female presence in the presumed male public sphere permeated the ranks of its socialist critics as well.

Racial tension also divided the party. Victor Berger (1860–1929), the Milwaukee socialist leader and one of two socialists elected to the U.S. Congress, symbolized one position. Berger dismissed attempts to organize African Americans and publicly embraced the most racist stereotypes of African American men as a threat to white "civilization." Debs, on the other hand, although not without his own racial prejudices, refused to speak to segregated audiences of socialists and publicly joined with the National Association for the Advancement of Colored People in 1916 to condemn D. W. Griffith's hate-filled film about post–Civil War Reconstruction, *The Birth of a Nation*. Relatively few black Americans joined the SPA, but one who did made a major impact on the movement and the nation in the decades to come.

Asa Philip Randolph (1889–1979) came to New York in 1911, studied economics and politics at the City College of New York, and soon joined the SPA. He led an organizing drive among elevator operators in New York, founded and edited the *Messenger*, a socialist magazine aimed at the black community, and spoke out unceasingly for labor rights, racial equality, and opposition to American involvement in the war. In 1925 he became the leader of the Brotherhood of Sleeping Car Porters, a union of African American men who staffed the nation's railway sleeping cars. Randolph led a difficult fight against two opponents simultaneously: to gain recognition for the union from employers and to win admittance into the American Federation of Labor, the nation's major union grouping in the 1920s. In the process, the Brotherhood became the black community's national "telegraph" system. As porters crisscrossed the nation as they worked, they created an effective communications system that spread news of atrocities, of protest and organization, and of cultural developments to African Americans in diverse and dispersed communities. In the decades to come, Randolph's vision, one that integrated civil rights, trade union recognition, and civil liberties for all Americans, would play a major role in the civil rights movement and other social justice causes.

The postwar years took a toll on the SPA. It suffered a major split in 1919 when those influenced by the 1917 Russian Revolution split to form two revolutionary Communist parties; it was further weakened by the imprisonment of many of its activists, victims of the wartime resurgence of a narrowed patriotism that legitimized the repression of dissent. Debs, too, was not the same. Physically weakened after prison, he found that neither his oratory nor the substance of his message carried the force they once possessed. Americans, including many working people, accepted the permanence of the corporate structure, sought benefits from it where they could, and carefully chose when they might directly challenge their employers.

Socialism and Liberalism

The decades after 1920 were difficult for the SPA. The party's new leader, Norman Thomas (1884–1968), an ordained Presbyterian minister, was a committed socialist and pacifist who lacked the broad popular appeal Debs had possessed. Thomas ran six times for the presidency between 1928 and 1948, and never surpassed Debs's 1920 total.

But the problem was not simply one of personality. Factional fighting repeatedly split the SPA from within, as the impact of the Great Depression, the momentarily powerful appeal of communism, and diminishing membership (especially among working people) sharply weakened the party. Even more devastating to the SPA's expectations was the revival of liberalism in the person of Franklin D. Roosevelt (1882–1945) and the New Deal program he instigated. Thomas would soon claim that the New Deal almost completely absorbed the SPA platform, and the majority of its working-class voters. This was largely true because neither Thomas nor the SPA were able to convince working people that the pragmatic thrust of New Deal liberalism embodied reforms that represented no serious challenge to industrial capitalism. Thomas and his colleagues were persistent advocates of civil liberties, civil rights, and trade unions, but increasingly found themselves hard pressed to effectively distinguish their approach from liberalism. Thomas's 1939 opposition to America's involvement in the emerging war—a position consistent with his long-held pacifism—created additional difficulties in appealing to liberal voters.

By 1945, the socialist movement in America was a shadow of its former self. Its strongest institutional base was a handful of unions with headquarters in New York City who were already transferring their allegiance to the New Deal and the Democratic Party. Beyond that, the movement possessed isolated outposts of strength in communities across the country but, with the exception of Milwaukee, Wisconsin, there were few areas of institutional strength. What complicated the situation further for socialists was the reality that a majority of a generation's politically progressive young people had, since the 1930s, gravitated toward liberalism and the legacy of the New Deal—and not to their party.

Not all followed that path, however. During the 1950s, Michael Harrington (1928–89), a Midwestern Catholic trained by the Jesuits at the College of the Holy Cross, emerged as one of the most promising socialists of the postwar generation. Grounded in a Catholic social justice tradition, including close ties with Dorothy Day and the Catholic Worker movement, Harrington evolved into a creative Marxist thinker. His approach to socialism reflected a sensibility similar to Debs's, while his intellectual engagement far surpassed most in the American socialist tradition. His first book, *The Other America* (1962), startled the nation and helped convince President John F. Kennedy to create a poverty program. In his later books, Harrington provided an intelligent, radical analysis of American political culture, the economic crisis of "stagflation" in the 1970s, and of the potential that yet resided in a democratic socialist approach.

From the vantage point of Norman Thomas's generation, Harrington represented a new generation of socialists; but to the emerging New Left protestors of the 1960s, he was decidedly old guard. Harrington himself, along with others in the SPA, cemented this perception with an early dismissive critique of the New Left's philosophy, strategy, and culture. In the 1970s, however, following the New Left's experiment with violent direct action, Harrington led a revived movement ultimately known as the Democratic Socialists of America (DSA). Struggling to maintain a socialist perspective, the DSA worked closely with the progressive wing of the Democratic Party, as events well beyond its control further diminished the prospects for socialism itself. The rise of modern conservatism enabled the election of President Ronald Reagan in 1980, a campaign in which the candidate won the enthusiastic support of many of the white working people who had once formed the foundation of both the SPA and the Democratic Party. That this occurred at a time when membership in American trade unions began its precipitous decline (nearly 30 percent of the nonagricultural workforce in 1980 to just over 12 percent in 2008) made the socialist predicament all the more painful.

Nor did the strategy of joining with progressive liberals bear immediate fruit. In the face of the conservative ascendancy, liberalism itself changed, becoming more centrist and supportive of an increasingly global corporate economy. Reagan's famous 1987 challenge to Soviet leader Mikhail Gorbachev to "tear down this wall" (while speaking in front of the Berlin Wall, which symbolized the divisions of the cold war) was perhaps a public ringing of socialism's death knell. Two years later, on November 9, 1989, the wall itself came down. In America, socialism's appeal, always a minor note in the nation's politics, all but disappeared as an institutional presence.

American Socialism's Legacy

The reasons for socialism's failure in the United States are numerous, and many are noted above. But to focus solely on them is to miss the contributions to American democratic thought that even this failed movement achieved. Debs and the early SPA's emphasis on democracy in the workplace broadened the nation's understanding of its democratic ideals and asserted the dignity and respect due working people if the country was to maintain its democratic ethos. It defended as well American civil liberties in time of war and fear and, with the actions and sacrifices by Debs and many others, kept alive the tradition of protest so central to maintaining a democracy. In the era of Thomas, that emphasis on preserving civil liberties remained strong, and broadened to include civil rights activity as well. The problem of effectively defining socialism apart from liberalism in the public arena was not solved in these years, nor would it be in the Harrington era. But Harrington brought to public debate an incisive intellectual analysis and a deep moral perspective that spoke more to core democratic values than to any orthodox version of Marxist thought. Like Debs before him, if with greater intellectual command and less oratorical power, Harrington framed potential solutions to America's deeper problems within its democratic traditions in ways that challenged conservatives and liberals alike. In short, the historical experience of socialism in America was to serve as a persistent reminder (and an occasionally successful advocate) of the potential that yet lies in the American tradition of democratic citizenship.

See also communism; democracy; labor movement and politics; liberalism; New Left.

FURTHER READING

Buhle, Mari Jo. *Women and American Socialism, 1870–1920*. Urbana: University of Illinois Press, 1981.

Guarneri, Carl J. *The Utopian Alternative: Fourierism in Nineteenth-Century America.* Ithaca, NY: Cornell University Press, 1991.

Harrington, Michael. *The Other America: Poverty in the United States.* Baltimore, MD: Penguin, 1962.

Harris, William H. *Keeping the Faith: A. Philip Randolph, Milton P. Webster, and the Brotherhood of Sleeping Car Porters, 1925–1937.* Urbana: University of Illinois Press, 1991.

Howe, Irving. *Socialism and America.* San Diego, CA: Harcourt Brace Jovanovich, 1985.

Isserman, Maurice. *The Other American: The Life of Michael Harrington.* New York: Public Affairs Press, 2000.

Noyes, John Humphrey. *History of American Socialisms.* 1870. Reprint ed. New York: Dover, 1966.

Pfeffer, Paula F. *A. Philip Randolph: Pioneer of the Civil Rights Movement.* Baton Rouge: Louisiana State University Press, 1990.

Salvatore, Nick. *Eugene V. Debs: Citizen and Socialist.* Urbana: University of Illinois Press, 1982.

Sorge, Friedrick. "To the General Council . . ." In *A Documentary History of American Industrial Society. Vol. IX: Labor Movement, 1860–1880,* edited by John R. Commons et al. Cleveland: Arthur Clark Company, 1910.

Swanberg, W. A. *Norman Thomas, The Last Idealist.* New York: Scribner's, 1976.

NICK SALVATORE

South since 1877, the

For nearly a century following the Civil War, the South was the most economically backward and politically repressive region of the United States. One-crop agriculture reigned throughout much of the region. The levels of southern poverty had few parallels inside American borders. And a system of racial segregation gave rise to a political system that was democratic in name only. It was only in the 1960s that the region began to lose its distinctiveness. Economic transformations brought income levels closer to the national average, the civil rights movement remade the region politically and culturally, and the conservatism of white Southerners converged in unexpected ways with that of other white Americans.

The antebellum period and the Civil War set the stage for the political distinctiveness of the late-nineteenth-century South. Secession and the formation of the Confederacy covered over countless political divisions in the South before the war. A notable split that survived the conflict was between the political priorities of the lowland plantation belt and upland areas dominated by yeoman farmers. This political rivalry would ebb over time, yet remained relevant well into the twentieth century.

The Civil War transformed the South most obviously by ending slavery, yet its impact could be seen in countless other ways. One out of ten white adult males in the South died during the war, and one out of every three white families lost a male relative. The economic consequences were equally dramatic. During the 1860s, the South's share of the nation's wealth fell from 30 to 12 percent. The region's largest and most important cities lay in ruins. Nine thousand miles of railroad lines were rendered useless; two-thirds of southern shipping capacity was destroyed. The most devastating economic impact of the war was also its greatest moral achievement: with emancipation, southern slave owners who dominated the region's politics and economy lost over $3 billion that they had invested in human chattel.

From Reconstruction to Jim Crow

Such death and devastation created monumental challenges for postwar reconstruction. In some areas of the South, it was hard to say when the war actually ended, so intense was the political terrorism carried out against white and black Republicans. Reconstruction governments faced a daunting set of tasks. They rebuilt destroyed infrastructure, promoted railroad development, established the region's first public school system, and created a network of basic public institutions to deal with the sick and suffering. The higher taxes and public debts that ensued only further enflamed political resentment among former Confederates, fueling biased charges of incompetence and greed and setting the stage for conservative white Southerners to return to power. Tragically, this southern nationalist view of the alleged failures of biracial Republican-controlled governments came to dominate the memory of the postwar period for most white Americans, Southerners and Northerners alike.

The presidential election of 1876 marked the end of efforts to remake the South after the Civil War and the beginning of the region's rough century of political, economic, and cultural peculiarity. The Democratic nominee that year, Samuel Tilden of New York, won 184 electoral votes, one short of a majority. Republicans disputed the count in three southern states: Florida, Louisiana, and South Carolina. Rival canvassing boards sent in conflicting returns; in South Carolina and Louisiana, competing state governments appeared. Congress established a special Electoral Commission to investigate the disputed elections and report its findings. The panel split along party lines in favor of the Republican nominee, Rutherford B. Hayes of Ohio. The House voted to accept the report in March 1877, but only after southern Democrats brokered a deal with Republicans that included promises for help with southern railroads, levee construction along the Mississippi, and a southern Democratic cabinet appointment. Few of the pledges were kept save for the most significant one: the withdrawal of the remaining federal troops from the South. One month into his presidency, Hayes recalled military units from the state houses in Louisiana and South Carolina. Republican governments there abruptly collapsed.

The Compromise of 1877 doomed two-party politics in the region. Democrats ruled the Solid South until the 1960s. For much of that period, white Southerners dominated the Democratic Party. Until 1936, when the Democrats dispensed with the two-thirds rule for presidential nominees, no candidate could win the Democratic nomination without southern backing. The South's dominance placed Democrats in a subordinate position nationally. From 1860 to 1932, Democrats elected only two presidents, Grover Cleveland and Woodrow Wilson. Neither candidate ever won a majority of the national popular vote.

By the 1890s, what threat there was to Democratic dominance in the South came not from Republicans but from Populists. The People's Party drew on widespread unrest among farmers in the South and West that could be traced to the Panic of 1873. Its antecedent was the Farmers' Alliance, an economic movement that began in 1876 in central Texas. In an era of economic consolidation, the alliance represented small-scale producers and derided the brokers, merchants, railroad executives, and bankers who profited from the crops that farmers grew. The late 1880s were a boom time for the alliance, which by 1890 counted 852,000 members in southern states alone. Half of all eligible people joined the alliance in the states of Arkansas, Florida, Mississippi, and Georgia.

The Farmers' Alliance's frustration with the two major parties boiled over in the early 1890s. The failure of the Democrats to address what they felt were systemic economic problems, such as low agricultural prices and the availability and high cost of credit, led to the formation of the People's Party in 1892. It supported a range of policies that included the expansion of the currency, government ownership of the railroads, and a graduated income tax. Southerners played prominent roles in the effort. Leonidas Polk of North Carolina, who had served as president of the National Farmers' Alliance since 1889, was thought to be the leading candidate for the Populist presidential nomination. Polk died unexpectedly, however, in the summer of 1892. The eventual nominee, James B. Weaver, was a former Union general who did little to inspire Southerners.

Populists were a phantom presence in some parts of the South, but in others their challenge to the Democrats was fierce. Thomas Watson of Georgia, who had been elected to the House of Representatives as a Democrat in 1890, ran as a Populist two years later. Watson's candidacy was notable for his efforts to win black votes. He condemned lynching at a time when Georgia led the nation in the malevolent practice. When an African American Populist received a lynching threat, Watson called out over 2,000 armed whites to defend him. Watson lost narrowly, however, as he would again in 1894 amid widespread charges of election fraud. In 1896 the Democrats successfully co-opted the party's most politically tame but symbolically important issue, the free, or unlimited, coinage of silver. After the Democrats nominated the 36-year-old William Jennings Bryan, the Populists followed suit. Bryan proved to be enormously popular in the South. With the Democrats seeming to have regained their footing and the economic crisis of the 1890s on the wane, the South was solid once again.

One consequence of the Populist threat was that southern Democrats took steps to deter future challengers. New voting laws denied suffrage rights to many poor whites and almost all African Americans. This disfranchisement campaign began before the Populist threat—Mississippi kicked off the effort in 1890 with its new state constitution—but agrarian radicalism gave it fresh impetus. The dramatic impact of the new southern constitutions could be seen in Louisiana. As late as 1897, Louisiana counted 294,432 registered voters, 130,344 of whom were African American. Three years later, after the adoption of a new constitution, total registration numbered 130,757, with only 5,320 black voters.

The Supreme Court removed any barriers to the process in 1898 in the case of *Williams v. Mississippi*. The Court held that Mississippi's voting provisions themselves were not discriminatory. Experience soon showed, however, that they could be used by officials to exclude black voters. The new laws troubled few whites outside of the region. Some actually envied the efforts as the kind of thing needed to deter machine politics in northern cities. Others viewed southern disfranchisement in light of American involvement in the Philippines, as essential to preserving "white civilization" in the midst of darker races.

The disfranchisement campaign coincided with a turn toward radical racism that could be seen throughout the region. Southern states passed a wave of Jim Crow legislation that certified in law what often had been the custom of racial segregation. The new laws asserted white supremacy in new public spaces where racial etiquette was not inscribed. Not surprisingly, some of the first Jim Crow laws involved segregation on railroad cars—one of the most important and ubiquitous of public spaces in the late nineteenth century. In fact, the Supreme Court decision in 1896 that provided federal sanction of Jim Crow, *Plessy v. Ferguson*, involved a law segregating rail cars in Louisiana. The most vicious side of the Jim Crow system could be seen in a surge in racial violence. In the 1880s and 1890s, lynching was transformed from a frontier offense committed in areas with little established police authority to a racialized crime perpetrated largely by southern whites to terrorize the black community. In the 1890s, 82 percent of the nation's lynchings took place in 14 southern states.

Jim Crow voting laws suppressed voter participation among whites and blacks alike. This fact, combined with one-party rule, gave rise to one of the more curious figures in American political history—the southern demagogue. In the one-party South, intraparty factions developed around dominant personalities or well-established cliques rather than around political platforms. Candidates distinguished themselves more by the force of their personality than by the distinctiveness of their ideas. With little of the population participating in elections, few issues of substance or controversy came up in southern politics, certainly no issues that threatened white supremacy. Rural forces dominated southern politics; county fairs, courthouse steps, and country barbecues were grand theaters for the demagogues' histrionic speechifying. Among the more notorious were "Pitchfork" Ben Tillman and Cole Blease of South Carolina, James K. Vardaman and Theodore Bilbo of Mississippi, Tom Watson and Eugene Talmadge in Georgia, and Jeff Davis of Arkansas. None was more charismatic than Huey Long of Louisiana, who went further than most in making good on the populist rhetoric and activist pledges to working people that typified demagogic appeals.

In the first few decades of the twentieth century, citizens moved by the Progressive Era's spirit of pragmatic reform and public activism found plenty of problems to work on in the South. Progressives combated issues such as underfunded public schools, child labor, the convict lease system, and public health problems born of the region's intense poverty, like pellagra and hookworm. White Southerners took pride in the election of the southern-born Democrat Woodrow Wilson in 1912. Wilson showed his fidelity to southern racial mores by instituting segregation in federal offices in the nation's capital. Despite the reforms of the Progressive Era, the South remained for most Americans a uniquely backward region. H. L. Mencken's description of the South as the "Sahara of the Bozarts" sufficed for most. No incident sealed this image more completely than the Scopes trial in 1925, which pitted William Jennings Bryan against Clarence Darrow in a dispute over a Tennessee law barring the teaching of evolution in public schools. National reporters flocked to the tiny town of Dayton, Tennessee, to report on fundamentalist Southerners at war with the modern world. The image of an intensely rural and religiously backward region lived on through much of the twentieth century.

A New Deal for the South

The election of Franklin D. Roosevelt in 1932 transformed southern life and politics. Roosevelt had a special relationship with the region, born of the considerable time he spent at a treatment center for polio victims that he founded in Warm Springs, Georgia. The new president had seen southern poverty firsthand. In the 1930s, the region's over-reliance on agriculture and its handful of low-wage, low-skill industries created levels of neglect shocking even for Depression-era Americans. In 1938 Roosevelt famously declared the South "the nation's number one economic problem." A major goal of his presidency was to integrate the South more fully into the nation's economy.

The central problem for New Deal reformers was how to turn poor rural people into modern middle-class consumers. The Tennessee Valley Authority (TVA), an unprecedented public works project, was one solution. The federal government built an elaborate series of dams along the lower Tennessee River. Auxiliary programs repaired eroded landscapes and resettled rural families from depleted homesteads to modern, model farms. Most importantly, the TVA provided inexpensive electrical power that dramatically improved the quality of life for thousands of rural Southerners and attracted new industries to the region.

The New Deal also addressed economic problems more broadly. The Agricultural Adjustment Act (AAA), one of Roosevelt's first reforms, revolutionized southern farming. In an attempt to stem overproduction, the federal government paid farmers to take fields and livestock out of production. The subsidies spelled the end of sharecropping, the unique system of labor organization that had developed after emancipation as a compromise between former masters and slaves. It also began a decades-long shift toward agricultural mechanization and the flight of agricultural workers, white and black alike, from the region. Few southern laborers benefited more directly from the New Deal than the region's industrial workers. The Federal Labor Standards Act (FLSA) created a national minimum wage. A mere 25 cents an hour at initial passage, the standard actually doubled the wages of African American tobacco laborers. With increases built in for subsequent years, the legislation boosted incomes in numerous southern industries and created incentives for factory owners to modernize their plants.

Yet the New Deal's benefits were political as well as material. With Roosevelt's landslide victory in 1932 came a Democratic majority that dominated Congress for the next half century. This put conservative southern Democrats in positions of unprecedented power. In 1933 Southerners headed seven out of the nine most influential Senate committees. It also allowed them to check some of the New Deal's more liberal impulses. For example, Roosevelt refused to back federal antilynching legislation, much to the chagrin of his progressive supporters. He knew that doing so would alienate powerful Southerners, jeopardizing their support for other New Deal priorities.

Southern representatives were indeed among the most passionate supporters of the New Deal, yet as early as Roosevelt's second term, the forces that would eventually drive conservative Southerners out of the Democratic Party were already at work. Some white Southerners were suspicious of what they felt was Roosevelt's penchant for centralized power, made explicit in his court-packing plan. Others complained that too many New Deal dollars were going toward northern cities. In 1937 North Carolina senator Josiah Bailey was the driving force behind the Conservative Manifesto, a list of grievances against Roosevelt's alleged drift toward collectivism. Roosevelt himself deepened the rift with conservative Southerners when he intervened in the 1938 midterm elections. He used one of his regular trips to Warm Springs as an opportunity to campaign against two of the regions most powerful conservatives, Walter George of Georgia and Ellison "Cotton Ed" Smith of South Carolina.

The most significant wedge between the white South and the New Deal was race. In the 1930s, Roosevelt's gestures to African Americans were small and largely symbolic. The tiniest of nods, however, was enough to convulse some white Southerners. Cotton Ed Smith walked out of the 1936 Democratic National Convention after an invocation delivered by a black minister. In 1941 Roosevelt's support for black civil rights moved beyond mere symbols when he signed an executive order creating the Fair Employment Practices Committee (FEPC). The order came only after intense lobbying by African Americans who threatened to march on Washington if Roosevelt did not act, and the committee's powers were relatively feeble. Still, the decision was a monumental victory for African Americans, a historic break of white Southerners' veto power over national civil rights policy. The FEPC instantly became the bete noire of white Southerners; legislative efforts after the war to make it permanent elicited charges of statism and racial coddling run amuck.

The South and World War

World War II marked a turning point in southern racial politics. The fight against Nazism cast Jim Crow racial practices in a harsh light and gave new impetus for movements toward equality. In the 1940s, NAACP membership increased by a factor of ten. A Supreme Court decision during the war opened new paths to the polls for some African Americans. In 1944 the Court struck down the "white primary," a discriminatory voting scheme that barred black voters from participating in Democratic Party elections, which in most southern states was the only election that mattered. This decision, along with the abolition of the poll tax in several southern states, cleared the way for the registration of thousands of black voters in the peripheral and Upper South, along with some urban areas in the lower South. In Atlanta, for example, a federal court decision allowed for the registration of 21,244 black voters in 1946. These new voters instantly constituted over a quarter of Atlanta's registered voters and transformed the city's political dynamics. Newly enfranchised black voters helped elect moderate, business-oriented white leaders, who, in turn, quietly brokered the token desegregation of neighborhoods and public spaces.

In the 1940s, black Southerners were not just leaving the South to go to war; many left for urban areas in the North and the West. This was not the first time that African Americans had left the region—a small migration had taken place during Reconstruction, and roughly half a million blacks left during World War I. But the migration that followed World War II was unprecedented. Of the 6.5 million African Americans that left the South between 1910 and 1970, 5 million exited after 1940. This migration coincided with the collapse of plantation agriculture, and it transformed racial politics nationally. Southern migrants filled African American urban neighborhoods and elected some of the first black representatives to Congress since Reconstruction. These black voters also became important swing voters in large, highly contested industrial states in the Northeast and Midwest.

Many of the African American soldiers who returned to the South after the war were determined to secure the freedoms at home for which they had fought abroad. One such serviceman was Medgar Evers of Mississippi, who had served in France. When he and other African American veterans attempted to vote in the 1946 Democratic primary in Decatur, Mississippi, an armed white mob turned them away. Deterred only temporarily, Evers went on to become the field secretary for the NAACP in Mississippi, working tirelessly to organize African American protest in his home state until June 1963, when he was shot and killed by a racist fanatic.

The armed deterrence in Mississippi was not uncommon. Emboldened African American soldiers heightened racial anxieties among whites during and in the immediate aftermath of the war. This unrest was not specific to the South. Race riots broke out in several northern and southern cities in 1943; the largest was in Detroit, where 25 African Americans and 9 whites were killed. But in some rural areas of the South, racial tensions took an old familiar form. In July 1946 a lynch mob in Monroe, Georgia, killed 4 young African Americans, 2 men and 2 women. The spike in racial violence led President Harry Truman to form a commission to study racial problems. Its 1947 report, *To Secure These Rights*, became a blueprint for federal civil reforms that would come over the next two decades.

The following year, Truman went further, setting the stage for a historic presidential election. In February 1948 he announced his support for ending racial discrimination in the armed services. Clark Clifford, Truman's campaign advisor, urged him to take a strong civil rights stand because the support of southern states was a given; the key to the election, Clifford argued, was northern industrial areas where urban African American voters could help swing the election for the Democrats. Clifford's strategy succeeded, but only by the narrowest of margins. At the Democratic National Convention in Philadelphia that summer, the Alabama and Mississippi delegations walked out over the party's civil rights stand. Individual delegates from other southern states joined them to form the States' Rights Democratic Party.

Strom Thurmond, the governor of South Carolina, accepted the presidential nomination of the "Dixiecrats," the nickname given to the splinter group by a waggish reporter. Thurmond himself never used the term, insisting that his campaign was not a regional but a national effort that drew on long-standing conservative Democratic principles. In truth, the campaign's support came mainly from white voters in the Black Belt, Deep South counties with the largest African American population and the most racially polarized politics. With little money and an inexperienced campaign staff, Thurmond ended up winning only four states—Alabama, Mississippi, Louisiana, and South Carolina. Yet in the larger sweep of southern history, the States' Rights Democrats represented a turning point in the region's politics by initiating the slow drain of white Southerners from the Democratic Party.

The Era of Massive Resistance

The 1950s was a decade of political retrenchment across the region. The cold war contributed to this trend. Segregationist Southerners denounced civil rights activists as either outright Communists or tools of the Communist conspiracy. Senator James Eastland of Mississippi chaired the Senate Internal Security Subcommittee, which regularly called witnesses to testify about alleged links between the civil rights movement and politically subversive organizations. Southern state legislatures held similar hearings that investigated civil rights organizations with alleged ties to subversive organizations or in some cases became the basis for new laws that helped to deter civil rights organizations.

More than anything, however, the Supreme Court's 1954 decision in *Brown v. Board of Education*, striking down school segregation laws, precipitated white Southerners' organized resistance to racial change. The Ku Klux Klan experienced a third wave of revival in the region, following the Reconstruction period and its resurgence in the 1920s. Organized resistance also took a more middle-class form with the Citizens' Council, which began in 1954 in the Mississippi Delta. The councils styled themselves as a modern political interest group, replete with a monthly publication and a series of television programs featuring interviews with policy makers. Council leaders denounced violence publicly, but they often turned a blind eye or even subtly encouraged violence by working-class whites. This grassroots organizing underwrote high-profile acts of resistance during the late 1950s and early 1960s. In 1957 Governor Orval Faubus of Arkansas, who up to that point was viewed as a racial moderate, defied federal authorities in blocking the entrance of African American students into Little Rock's Central High School. Three years later, white resistance to school desegregation in New Orleans led to violent clashes throughout the city. In 1962 Governor Ross Barnett of Mississippi led his state into a constitutional showdown with President John Kennedy over the admission of the African American James Meredith to the University of Mississippi.

The most charismatic and talented leader of massive resistance was Governor George Wallace of Alabama. Wallace began his career as an economic populist and racial moderate, following the path of his mentor, James "Big Jim" Folsom. In his race for governor in 1958, Wallace misjudged the intensity of white recalcitrance after the *Brown* decision and lost in a close election. Afterward, he vowed to political friends never to be "out-nigguhed" again.

After Wallace won the governorship in 1962 on a hard-line segregationist platform, he had a Klansman draft his inaugural address. Wallace defied Kennedy administration officials in 1963, standing "in the schoolhouse door" to symbolically block the admission of African American students to the University of Alabama. In 1964 he became the face of the white backlash against civil rights when he ran surprisingly well in Democratic presidential primaries in Wisconsin, Indiana, and Maryland. Four years later, running as the candidate of the American Independent Party, Wallace narrowly missed out on his goal of throwing the election into the House of Representatives. Wallace lost North Carolina and Tennessee by statistically insignificant margins; a win in either of those states accompanied by a shift of less than 1 percent of the vote from Richard Nixon to Hubert Humphrey in New Jersey or Ohio would have been enough to do the trick. He was reelected as governor in 1970 in a notoriously racist campaign. In May 1972 he was a leading candidate in a chaotic race for the Democratic presidential nomination. Wallace was shot while campaigning in Maryland. He survived the shooting but was relegated to a wheelchair for the rest of his life, all but ending his national political aspirations.

Yet Wallace's impact could be measured in other ways. In one sense, Wallace helped "southernize" national politics. His parodying of government bureaucrats, liberal elites, and anti-American political activists gave a populist bent to the post–World War II American conservative movement. Up to that point, conservatism consisted largely of a loose coalition of corporate executives, renegade intellectuals, and anti-Communist hardliners. Wallace, however, pioneered appeals to white working-class and lower middle-class Americans, pleas that worked equally well outside the South. Wallace was elected governor of Alabama twice more, in 1974 and 1982, and he returned to his racially moderate, economic populist roots. By that time, however, the antigovernment slogans that had sustained his national aspirations had been taken up by a new generation of ideological conservatives in the Republican Party.

Sunbelt Politics

For many people, Lyndon Johnson summed up the conventional wisdom on the southern GOP in the 1960s. On the night he signed the 1964 Civil Rights Act, Johnson lamented to an aide, "I think we just delivered the South to the Republican Party for a long time to come." Yet white racism was not the only factor spurring two-party politics in the South. Urban Southerners showed their distaste for one-party rule in the 1950s, when a majority of the region's city dwellers twice voted for the modern Republicanism of Dwight Eisenhower. Business-oriented, racially moderate urban and suburban Southerners were an important source for the growing southern GOP. Federal court decisions in the early 1960s that upheld the principle of "one man, one vote" gave a boost to moderate metropolitan Southerners. Thanks to outdated apportionment laws, rural interests had dominated southern politics for years. Under the county unit system in Georgia, for example, each county was assigned "units" that ranged from two units for the smallest county to six for the largest. As a result, residents of rural counties held political power far beyond their proportion of the state population. A vote in tiny Echols County, Georgia, was worth 99 times as much as a vote in Atlanta.

Metropolitan Southerners joined urban and suburban citizens of other expanding areas across the Southwest and far West to make up what commentators came to describe as the Sunbelt. From the 1960s through the end of the century, southern states from the Carolinas to California were the most economically dynamic areas of the country. Southern state industrial programs attracted new industries through a mix of tax breaks and other economic subsidies, and southern legislatures passed right-to-work laws that suppressed union membership. Cold war military spending benefited the Sunbelt disproportionately; military contracts poured into southern states like Texas, Florida, and Georgia. Powerful southern congressmen directed other defense dollars into their home districts. These new Sunbelt jobs attracted college-educated middle- and upper middle-class migrants to the region. The 1960s was the first decade since the 1870s that more people moved into the South than out of it. Many of these new Southerners settled in expanding suburban neighborhoods. From 1960 to 1968, the suburbs of Houston grew by 50 percent, New Orleans 45.5 percent, Washington 39.2 percent, and Atlanta 33.6 percent. During the 1960s, per capita income increased in the South 14 percent faster than anyplace else.

These new Sunbelt residents were a natural fit for the Republican Party. Yet, despite the dynamic social and economic changes in the region, southern GOP advances in the 1960s and 1970s were surprisingly mixed. Republican presidential candidates did well across the region, but the party struggled in state and local elections. One reason was that the hard-line conservatives who built the southern parties were still a minority within a national party in which moderate and liberal Republicans played a major role. Also, in many parts of the South, Republican candidates struggled to shed an image as the party of the country club set.

Most important to Democratic perseverance, however, was the 1965 Voting Rights Act, which restored voting rights to thousands of African American voters across the region. African Americans first started to drop their historic allegiance to the party of Lincoln during the New Deal, and thanks to liberal Democrats' passionate support for civil rights, these new southern black voters almost uniformly identified as Democrats. In southern states with African American populations that ranged from a quarter to well over a third of the total population, successful Republicans had to amass supermajorities among white voters.

From these electoral dynamics were born the New South Democrats: progressive, racially moderate, practical-minded politicians who assembled coalitions of working-class whites, black voters, and urban liberals. Prominent examples included Reubin Askew and Lawton Chiles of Florida, Jimmy Carter and Sam Nunn of Georgia, Dale Bumpers and David Pryor of Arkansas, John West and Richard Riley of South Carolina, and Bill Waller and William Winter of Mississippi.

No politician better symbolized the regional and national potential of New South Democrats than Jimmy Carter, the Georgia governor who vaulted into national politics in the wake of the Watergate crisis. Carter pursued centrist policies that angered the liberal wing of his party. He insisted on a balanced budget and attempted to cut spending and jobs programs that were bedrocks for liberal Democratic constituencies. He appointed a staunch advocate of deregulation as head of the Civilian Aeronautics Board and signed legislation that deregulated a number of industries. But Carter's major failure was one of timing—he presided over the White House during a period when the historic post–World War II economic boom petered out. His talk of limits and the need for Americans to scale back was rooted in his Southern Baptist faith, his sense of humility and stewardship. Political opponents, however, easily parodied it as rudderless leadership and weak-kneed defeatism.

A notable aspect of Carter's politics was his open discussion of his religious faith. It reflected his genuine personal devotion, but it also played into his appeal as the post-Watergate antipolitician—a man who would never lie to the American people. It was ironic then that Carter, who spoke sincerely of his personal relationship with Jesus Christ, would come to be so vehemently opposed by other southern Christian conservatives. White Southerners played prominent roles in what came to be known as the Religious Right. Jerry Falwell helped establish the Moral Majority in 1979, a conservative Christian advocacy group that was credited with playing a major role in Ronald Reagan's successful presidential campaign in 1980. Pat Robertson headed the Christian Broadcasting Network in Virginia Beach, Virginia, which became a focus of Religious Right broadcasting in the 1970s and 1980s. Jesse Helms of North Carolina was the leading voice in the Senate for conservative Christian concerns.

By the 1980s, the Religious Right was a key constituency in Ronald Reagan's conservative coalition. Reagan's charisma and Hollywood glamour won over countless white Southerners. No figure did more in encouraging white Southerners to shift their political identity from the Democratic to the Republican Party. Reagan articulated in a genial way the reaction against social and political liberalism that had been such a defining part of the region's modern politics. For the most conservative white Southerners, Reagan's election provided a sense of vindication that their opposition to the transformations of the 1960s was not so misguided after all. Southern Republicans played leadership roles in the dominant conservative wing of the party. Most prominently, in the 1994 midterm elections, Newt Gingrich of Georgia orchestrated the Republicans' Contract with America, a set of conservative policy positions that was credited with helping the GOP gain control of the House of Representatives for the first time in 40 years.

Despite Republican successes, moderate southern Democrats continued to exert a powerful influence on national Democratic Party politics. Bill Clinton showed the lingering power of the moderate New South model when he teamed with fellow Southerner Al Gore to become the first twice-elected Democratic president since Franklin Roosevelt. He did so following the same centrist path that Jimmy Carter had blazed in the 1970s. Clinton declared that the era of big government was over, signed the North American Free Trade Agreement, and backed a welfare reform bill that alienated liberals in his own party. He might have continued to provide moderate pragmatic leadership for the Democrats—the only path that had provided any significant electoral gains for the party since the 1960s—

had the final years of his presidency not been marred by personal scandal.

By the twentieth-first century, the South remained a source of consternation for progressive political forces, the seeming heart of Republican-dominated "red America." Some Democrats counseled their party to hand the region over to the Republicans, to "whistle past Dixie," and focus on liberal ideas that would appeal to voters in more traditionally progressive areas of the country. Other Democrats argued that Southerners were no different from other Americans, that they were motivated by the same concerns about economic security, health care, and education. That position was bolstered in the 2008 presidential election, when Barack Obama carried Virginia, North Carolina, and Florida—made possible by a huge turnout of African American voters.

In the roughly 135 years since the end of Reconstruction, the South underwent enormous transformations. The differences between the region and the nation had eroded enough to lead many to question what, if anything, remained distinctive about the South. And yet within national politics, many Americans still found it relevant to talk about the South as a discrete entity, a place with a unique past that continued to shape its politics in subtle yet powerful ways.

See also Democratic Party; race and politics; Reconstruction; segregation and Jim Crow.

FURTHER READING

Ayers, Edward. *The Promise of the New South*. New York: Oxford University Press, 1992.

Bartley, Numan. *The New South, 1945–1980*. Baton Rouge: Louisiana State University Press, 1995.

Bartley, Numan, and Hugh Davis Graham. *Southern Politics and the Second Reconstruction*. Baltimore, MD: Johns Hopkins University Press, 1975.

Black, Earl, and Merle Black. *Politics and Society in the South*. Baton Rouge: Louisiana State University Press, 1995.

———*The Rise of Southern Republicans*. Cambridge, MA: Belknap Press, 2002.

Crespino, Joseph. *In Search of Another Country: Mississippi and the Conservative Counterrevolution*. Princeton, NJ: Princeton University Press, 2007.

Key, V. O. *Southern Politics in State and Nation*. New York: Knopf, 1949.

Lassiter, Matthew. *The Silent Majority: Suburban Politics in the Sunbelt South*. Princeton, NJ: Princeton University Press, 2005.

Schulman, Bruce. *From Cotton Belt to Sunbelt: Federal Policy, Economic Development, and the Transformation of the South, 1938–1980*. New York: Oxford University Press, 1991.

Tindall, George. *The Emergence of the New South, 1913–1945*. Baton Rouge: Louisiana State University Press, 1967.

Woodward, C. Vann. *Origins of the New South, 1877–1913*. Baton Rouge: Louisiana State University Press, 1951.

JOSEPH CRESPINO

Spanish-American War and Filipino Insurrection

John Hay, then secretary of state, called it the "splendid little war." Almost 100 years after its start, historian Walter LaFeber called it the first modern war of the twentieth century for the United States. The Spanish-American War, and the more than decade of fighting that followed in the Philippines, reflected the tremendous growth in U.S. power in the late nineteenth century and the changing nature of domestic and international politics involving the United States. This war also provided the occasion for introducing some of the policies that shaped the U.S. polity as it moved into the twentieth century. The Spanish-American War was particularly influential in six areas: (1) development of ideas and practice of the modern presidency, (2) modification of traditional U.S. military doctrine, (3) reflection of new approaches to democratic politics and public opinion, (4) opportunities for state building, (5) creation of layers of empire, and (6) new struggles over the nature of American identity.

The Course of War

Cubans organized as early as the 1860s to achieve independence from Spain. Interest in Cuba was strong because of U.S.-owned sugar and tobacco plantations, but Americans were also altruistically sympathetic to the Cuban cause. Mass-circulation newspapers and U.S. labor organizations supported the Cubans, increasingly so through the 1890s, as Spanish repression of the Cuban independence movement became harsher.

President William McKinley, elected on the Republican ticket in 1896, was cautious but determined to support U.S. interests. He felt compelled in early 1898 to send the USS *Maine* to Havana harbor, where a few weeks later, it blew up. The "yellow press," led by William Randolph Hearst's *New York Journal*, issued the battle cry "Remember the Maine." Congress declared war in April 1898, but the U.S. fleet had already begun moving into position near Spanish possessions in both the Caribbean (Cuba and Puerto Rico) and the Pacific (Philippines). The small and undertrained U.S. Army was augmented by numerous enthusiastic volunteers, including the famous Rough Riders, organized by Teddy Roosevelt, who benefited from admiring publicity. The navy performed better than the army, but both performed better than the Spanish, and the fighting was over within a few weeks, costing the United States few dead, and most of those from disease rather than battle. During the war, the United States annexed Hawai'i. As a result of the war, although not until 1902, Cuba became independent. Puerto Rico, Guam, and the Philippines became U.S. colonies, technically called "unincorporated territories."

Filipinos also had been fighting for their independence from Spain. While initially working with U.S. forces or tolerating their presence, Filipino independence fighters soon realized U.S. liberation from Spain would not mean independence, and they took up arms against U.S. soldiers. This part of the war was costly for the United States, with more than 70,000 U.S. troops in the islands at the peak of the conflict and U.S. deaths of more than 4,000. At least 20,000 Filipinos were killed as a direct result of fighting. The Philippine Insurrection, which Filipinos call the Philippine-American War, officially lasted until 1902. Fighting continued in various parts of the islands until 1913, especially in the southern island of Mindanao, which has never fully acquiesced in any kind of rule from Manila, the capital of the Philippines.

Powerful President

The narrative above is factual and familiar but obscures more than it reveals. McKinley appears passive in it, reacting to popular media and events in both Cuba and Congress. This image of McKinley prevailed for years among scholars, many of whom repeated Theodore Roosevelt's claim that he had the backbone of a chocolate éclair. Timing of the declaration of war suggests otherwise, however. Both a majority in Congress and many mass-circulation newspapers had been advocating war for months before McKinley submitted his carefully crafted request for a declaration of war. McKinley drafted the declaration so that it allowed him to pursue almost any policy he wanted, subject only to the promise in the Teller Amendment not to annex Cuba.

The president was more than merely astute, however. First, he was thinking in an integrated manner about U.S. global interests and was working to coordinate the consequences of the war to serve a variety of U.S. interests, including maintaining an open system in China for U.S. trade and investment, sufficient control over areas such as Cuba where U.S. investment was substantial and growing, and creation of types of control in both Asia and the Caribbean in concert with the loose, minimally bureaucratic character of twentieth-century U.S. imperialism.

Second, McKinley used new technology effectively to increase his own power. Both the telegraph and telephone allowed him rapid, personal contact with other U.S. officials and the military in the field. He used these advantages to communicate directly and left less of a paper trail than previous presidents, which had the effect of decreasing freedom of action by subordinates while also making it more difficult for historians to trace the ultimate authority for decisions. Finally, McKinley and his closest personal advisors were men who believed in applying principles for the efficient organization of large corporations to running the government. They worked to continue professionalizing, organizing, and making government bureaucracy more effective. This too increased the power of the executive, especially at the expense of the still amateur and small congressional staffs. With or without the Spanish-American War, McKinley would have worked to increase executive power; the war gave him a large canvas on which to work.

Modern Military

The military, both navy and army, naturally was the government entity initially most affected by the war. The traditional narrative emphasizes the effectiveness of the U.S. Navy, which while not yet impressive in comparison with the British Navy, had several able advocates who had successfully promoted acquisition of modern and far-ranging ships. Alfred Thayer Mahan epitomizes this group who saw a larger, better trained navy as essential to projecting U.S. power into the world's oceans in support of increased U.S. commerce and control. The U.S. Navy handily demonstrated its superiority over the Spanish, even defeating a Spanish fleet at such far reaches as the Philippines. The battle in Cuba, for which the Spanish were more prepared, went scarcely better for them. The Spanish-American War confirmed for these navy advocates that they had been right; the acquisition of far-flung colonies provided them with continuing justification for a large and modern navy.

The U.S. Army generally looks less capable in accounts of the Spanish-American War. Its tiny size of less than 30,000 in 1898 meant that the war could not be fought without calling on thousands of volunteers, no doubt eager but ill-trained, and the militias, perhaps less eager and trained for different tasks. Logistics proved embarrassingly poor: U.S. soldiers lacked proper clothes for the tropics, were fed poisonously bad food, and died of disease or poorly treated wounds in greater numbers than from battle. The "splendid little" part of the war, the fighting against Spain, revealed an army poorly prepared for the type of fighting required. The next task was less splendid and little; the U.S. Army was called on to subdue Cubans and Filipinos who had different ideas than did U.S. officials about what the end of the Spanish-American War meant. This fighting often was characterized by brutality, as both regular army and militia employed tactics of repression or even extermination they had learned fighting against Native Americans, and which all too often resembled what the Spanish had done to their former subjects. Simultaneously, however, the army was the first to carry out the "benevolent" components of U.S. rule, including improving sanitation, building infrastructure, and opening schools. Violence and benevolence were intertwined, as they usually are in imperial projects. The U.S. Army began to develop nation-building capacities that have characterized its mission up to the present day.

New Approaches to Politics

The long buildup to a declaration of war allowed plenty of political maneuvering and public involvement, allowing the display of key developments in late-nineteenth- and early-twentieth-century domestic political organization. A familiar part of the story of the Spanish-American War is the way the "yellow press" promoted sympathy for Cubans. These mass-circulation newspapers continued the American tradition of a partisan press but depended on technological developments and increased literacy to present ever more realistic, if also lurid and emotional, images to an entranced public. The press did not create the war, but it did create conditions in which Americans enthusiastically accepted a war arguably remote from the interests of ordinary citizens. Public opinion was led in directions that served a variety of interests.

As the importance of political parties began to wane in the early twentieth century, presidents and newspaper publishers began to appeal directly to the mass public, unmediated by the party hierarchy. President McKinley went on a speaking tour with the stated purpose of gauging public support for acquiring a colony in the Philippines but with the hidden intent of promoting public support for that action. Much of the language used in these public appeals and discussions about the war and the responsibilities stemming from it reflected concerns about honor and manliness. Cubans, and later Filipinos, needed chivalrous rescuers; the Spanish deserved punishment for their misdeeds from honorable soldiers; American men could bravely demonstrate their willingness to sacrifice on the battlefield. Roosevelt's Rough Riders, volunteers from all walks of life from the most rough-and-tumble to the most elite, epitomized for many the benefits of testing American men in battle. At the turn to the twentieth century, American men were less likely than in preceding decades to vote and participate actively in party politics, more likely to work in large, hierarchical organizations, and to learn about the world through the medium of mass-circulation newspapers. Politicians used these developments to shape public attitudes about the war and the consequences of it.

Building the American State

Although the war itself was relatively short and easily won, it posed logistical challenges to an underdeveloped U.S. state. Both the war and the overseas colonies acquired as a consequence provided officials with opportunities to build U.S. state institutions. The military was the most dramatic example. The navy began to develop more far-reaching capacities in the years leading up to the war, and the army followed suit during and after the war. Both branches acquired permanent overseas responsibilities. The logistical requirements of permanent deployment outside the continental United States help explain trends toward professionalization, bureaucratization, and growth of both the army and navy in the early twentieth century. The decision to locate the Bureau of Insular Affairs, the government agency charged with governing the colonies, in the War Department further increased that department's growth. Even in ways not explicitly related to fighting the war or governing the colonies, U.S. governmental institutions took on new responsibilities as a result of the war, including some related to immigration and the conduct of foreign relations.

Layers of Empire

A key outcome of the Spanish-American War was the acquisition of overseas territories, arguably for the first time in U.S. history. The United States became an imperial power, owning colonies it had no intention of incorporating into the nation as states. It newly ruled over Hawai'i, Puerto Rico, Guam, and the Philippines directly. The United States also exercised a large amount of indirect control over Cuba through the mechanism of the Platt Amendment, a U.S. law whose substance was written into the Cuban constitution. It placed limits on Cuban sovereignty regarding financial affairs and the nature of Cuba's government, mandated U.S. ownership of a base at Guantanamo, and forced Cuban acquiescence in U.S. intervention to guarantee these measures.

The U.S. empire was a layered one. Cuba experienced effective control, but indirectly. Hawai'i was governed as an incorporated territory, theoretically eligible for statehood, but its racial mix made that an unappealing prospect for many Americans. Hawai'i did not become a state until 1959. Guam was ruled directly by the U.S. Navy—which used it as a coaling station—and it remains part of the United States, governed by the Office of Insular Affairs in the Department of the Interior. Both the Philippines and Puerto Rico were governed directly as colonies through the Bureau of Insular Affairs, but their paths quickly diverged. Puerto Rico developed close links with the United States through revolving migration, economic and tourism ties, and increased political rights for its citizens. Puerto Rico is still part of the United States, as the Commonwealth of Puerto Rico. The Philippines developed more modest and ambiguous relations with the United States, since Filipinos had restricted migration rights, and U.S. economic investment in the islands was limited. The Philippines achieved independence in 1946. The layered and decentralized nature of the U.S. empire developed out of the particular legal and political processes used to decide how to rule over territories acquired in the Spanish-American War. These decisions were widely and publicly debated in the early twentieth century, as Americans wrestled with the changing nature of territorial expansion involving overseas colonies.

Debating the American Identity

The Spanish-American War and the resulting acquisition of colonies prompted heated debates in the United States about what it meant to be American. These debates may well be among the most important consequences of the war for the nation. One set of agruments revolved around whether the United States should acquire overseas colonies, and if so, how they should be governed. A vocal and prominent anti-imperialist movement had many older leaders, representatives of a fading generation. Most politicians of the day advocated acquiring the colonies as demonstration of U.S. power and benevolence.

Still, there remained a contentious debate about the status of these new territories, legally settled only by the U.S. Supreme Court in the Insular Cases, beginning in 1901 with *Downes v. Bidwell* and confirmed subsequently by almost two dozen additional cases. The 1901 decision found that Puerto Rico was "not a foreign country" but "foreign to the United States in a domestic sense." In other words, not all laws or constitutional protections extended to unincorporated territories such as Puerto Rico and the Philippines. Many Americans were disturbed by these decisions, finding no provision in the Constitution that anticipated ruling land not intended to be part of the United States. They worried that an important part of U.S. political identity was being discarded.

Overriding those concerns, however, was a strong desire on the part of almost all white Americans to avoid the racial implications of incorporating places like the Philippines and especially Cuba into the body politic. Jim Crow segregation was established by the 1890s, and colonial acquisitions promised to complicate an already contentious racial situation in the United States. Cuba was filled with what many commentators called an "unappealing racial mix" of descendants of Spaniards, indigenous peoples, and Africans brought to the island as slaves. U.S. politicians had no desire to bring the racial politics of Cuba into the nation; so Cuba was not annexed. The Philippines was almost as problematic: Filipinos might be the "little brown brothers" of Americans, but in the end they were Asians, including many ethnic Chinese. During these years of Chinese exclusion, the status of Filipinos, U.S. nationals eligible to enter to the United States but not eligible to become citizens, was contested and contradictory. Movement toward granting independence seemed a good way to exclude Filipinos altogether. Puerto Ricans were, apparently, white enough. When they moved to the continental United States, they could naturalize as U.S. citizens, and in 1917, citizenship was extended to all Puerto Ricans. Regarding these groups, however, racial politics complicated both colonial governance and conceptions of U.S. identity.

Hostilities between Spain and the United States were brief and minor, but this splendid little war changed the United States into a colonial power; provided opportunities for the growth of executive government agencies, both the presidency itself and some departments; highlighted developments in mass media and party politics; and opened new lines of debate about the meaning of American identity.

See also foreign policy and domestic politics, 1865–1933; press and politics; race and politics; territorial government.

FURTHER READING

Brands, H. W. *Bound to Empire: The United States and the Philippines.* New York: Oxford University Press, 1982.

Hoganson, Kristin L. *Fighting for American Manhood: How Gender Politics Provoked the Spanish-American and Philippine-American Wars.* New Haven, CT: Yale University Press, 1998.

Kramer, Paul A. *The Blood of Government: Race, Empire, the United States and the Philippines.* Chapel Hill: University of North Carolina Press, 2006.

LaFeber, Walter *The American Search for Opportunity, 1865–1913.* Cambridge, UK: Cambridge University Press, 1993.

Perez, Louis A. "Incurring a Debt of Gratitude: 1898 and the Moral Sources of United States Hegemony in Cuba." *American Historical Review* 104 (April 1999), 356–98.

ANNE L. FOSTER

sports and politics

Artists across the centuries have been drawn to the athlete in action and repose. "What a piece of work is man!" Hamlet mused. "[I]n form and moving how express and admirable! [I]n action how like an angel!" The athletic form, the silkiness of an athlete's movements, the twitch of muscle and fiber, has been the gold standard of beauty since at least the ancient Greeks. But observers have ascribed meaning to beauty, and politics to meaning. In the abstract, the athletic body and sports are void of politics and ideology, but politicians and ideologues have long employed athletes and athletics to buttress their agendas. In twentieth-century America, journalists, politicians, and millions of citizens used sports to affirm the American way of life, validate democracy, and promote social change. Far from being delightful games—amusing, meaningless pastimes—sports have become essential to understanding political life.

As far back as the mid-nineteenth century, prizefighters and gamblers were involved in politics. Prizefighting's illegality often forced fighters and spectators to travel to rural locations for a bout, and state and local governments prosecuted many fighters, using various riot acts. Prizefighting also became associated with local Democratic machines, as bosses like William Tweed in New York hired fighters to serve as ballot enforcers on Election Day. One fighter, John Morrissey, rode his success as a pugilist to the U.S. Congress, where he served two terms (1867–71). In general, Democratic politicians, often seen as defenders of ethnic immigrants, supported prizefighting while Republicans generally fought to further restrict the sport.

During the Reconstruction era, African Americans were systematically excluded from professional baseball. Although one black player did compete in the National Association of Base Ball Players, by 1876 a new National League had organized with a formal "color ban." In 1883, however, Moses Fleetwood Walker signed a contract with Toledo of the American Association. By the late 1880s, white players and managers like Adrian "Cap" Anson of the Chicago White Sox refused to compete with or against black players. It would take until 1947 before another black man, Jackie Robinson, played in the major leagues.

Affirming the American Way of Life

The modern Olympic Games, though designed to be apolitical and promote internationalism, have always included political wrangling and expressions of nationalism. Few Games were more politicized than the 1936 Olympics in Berlin. Prior to the Games, Adolf Hitler's Nazi regime passed the Nuremberg Laws that deprived German Jews of their citizenship. These laws, coupled with Germany's policies regarding Jewish athletes, led Americans on the American Olympic Committee (AOC) to threaten a boycott of the Games. Despite opposition from the AOC president, Avery Brundage, a 1935 Gallup poll revealed that 57 percent of Americans favored withdrawal from the Games. A proposed boycott resolution failed by two-and-a-half votes at the 1935 Amateur Athletic Union (AAU) convention, leading to the resignation of the AAU president, Jeremiah Mahoney, who supported the boycott.

Hitler used the Olympic Games as an opportunity to unveil the "New Germany" to the world. Foreign journalists sat in a new, state-of-the-art, 100,000-seat track and field stadium, covered torchlight ceremonies and festivals, and were greeted by thousands of smiling children. Before the Olympics, Hitler's German Labor Front ordered Berliners to take down anti-Semitic signs, not overcharge their guests, be friendly toward the foreign press, and keep the city clean—all in promotion of Nazism. Seemingly oblivious of Nazi repression, foreign journalists wrote home about the "Miracle of Germany." As historian Benjamin Rader noted, the 1936 Berlin Games showed that "more than ever before, nations perceived their athletes as their representatives in a struggle for international power and glory."

During the cold war, the Americans and the Soviets used the Olympics to validate democracy and state socialism, respectively. For Americans, the Games were international battles between East and West, communism and capitalism, repression and freedom. American decathlete Bob Mathias recalled that the cold war increased the pressure on American athletes because the Russians "were in a sense the real enemy. You just love to beat 'em. You just had to beat 'em." Athletes representing Communist-bloc nations also felt the need to elevate their performances for the glory of their states. In the 1952 Helsinki Games, Czechoslovakian Emil Zatopek entered the marathon after winning the 10,000-and 5,000-meter races, a daunting combination.

To Americans like Brundage, the Soviets were everything the Americans were not: they polluted the Games by allowing professional athletes to compete, populated the International Olympic Committee with bloc-voting Communist Party members, and condoned steroid use. The latter point became abundantly clear in 1954, when John Ziegler, a U.S. team physician, noticed remarkable physical growth among Soviet weightlifters. As it turned out, Soviet athletes had been given pure testosterone to improve their performance in the strength events: track and field, boxing, wrestling, and weightlifting. Though Ziegler later developed the first anabolic steroid, Soviet drug use helped lead Russia to an impressive 98 medals in the 1956 Melbourne Games, compared to 74 for the United States. Only through artificial enhancers, the American press argued, were the Soviets able to defeat the United States.

Tensions between the two nations ran high again in 1979 after the Soviets invaded Afghanistan. This event led President Jimmy Carter to consider a boycott of the 1980 Games to be held in Moscow. With the winter Games scheduled for Lake Placid, New York, in February, Carter waited until after that event to announce his plans. The winter Games witnessed a major international victory for the United States when its young and inexperienced hockey team defeated a heavily favored Russian team. The American team sang "God Bless America" in the locker room after the game, despite many of the players not knowing the lyrics. Sporadic chants of "USA, USA" broke out in Lake Placid, and television commentator Al Michaels labeled the victory a miracle. In the eyes of many Americans, the win was a triumph for democracy and hard work.

Validating American Democracy

In addition to affirming the American way of life, sports have also served as a cauldron of democracy. Throughout the twentieth century, the integration of American sports often preceded the integration of schools, public transportation, hospitals, and public facilities. At the same time that African Americans could not eat at the same lunch counter with whites, they could watch Joe Louis win the heavyweight boxing crown, Althea Gibson win at Wimbledon, and Jackie Robinson star for the Brooklyn Dodgers. Though black athletes faced constant discrimination on the field and off, by the 1960s, blacks competed equally with whites in all major sports.

Prior to 1908 only one African American man, George Dixon, held a national boxing title, albeit in the bantam and featherweight divisions. In the early 1900s, Jack Johnson emerged as a black fighter capable of winning the heavyweight crown. Johnson consistently defied white America by dating white women, smiling in the ring, and taunting his white opponents. In Australia in 1908, he defeated Tommy Burns in impressive fashion to capture the world heavyweight title. Immediately, promoters began searching for a "Great White Hope" to challenge Johnson. Finally, Jim Jeffries, the champion before Burns, agreed to fight Johnson in Reno, Nevada, in what the press billed as a contest between white "civilization and virtue" and black "savagery and baseness." White journalists predicted that Jeffries would win, claiming that black boxers had thick skulls, weak stomachs, and small brains. Johnson soon proved that such journalists were poor anthropologists.

Johnson's fifteenth-round knockout victory over Jeffries led to public celebrations in black communities throughout the United States. In such cities as Chicago and Atlanta, white racists assaulted blacks who openly cheered Johnson's win. Fearing more riots, local and state governments banned the film of the Johnson-Jeffries fight from playing in American theaters. His victory even led to the passage of miscegenation laws in a number of states. In 1913, believing he was a threat to white supremacy, the federal government charged Johnson with violating the Mann Act, a seldom-used Progressive Era reform that attacked "white slavery" prostitution by making it illegal to transport women across state lines for immoral purposes. Johnson, who usually professed no ideology, was viewed as a racial symbol by both black and white. In a time of segregation a black man reigned supreme over the boxing world.

After Johnson lost his title to Jess Willard in 1915, it took 22 years for another African American to become heavyweight champion. If Johnson was loud and threatening to whites, Joe Louis was the direct opposite: quiet, polite, and unassuming. His trainer Jack Blackburn and managers John Roxborough and Julian Black carefully crafted Louis's image. In public, Louis was always clean-cut, and he rarely smiled and did not pose in photographs with white women. But in the ring, Louis was just as dominating as Johnson. In 1935 he defeated the Italian champion and former heavyweight champion Primo Carnera as Benito Mussolini invaded Ethiopia. One year later, Louis suffered a devastating twelfth-round knockout by the German boxer Max Schmeling, whom Hitler hailed as a great symbol of his Nazi regime. Louis rebounded in 1937, knocking out James J. Braddock to capture the heavyweight crown and setting up a rematch with Schmeling.

Two months before the second fight, Hitler annexed Austria. Thus, before the rematch, Louis took on the symbolic role of America's hero defending democracy and the free world against German aggression and Nazism. President Franklin D. Roosevelt met with Louis to discuss the political implications of the fight, and a Nazi Party official announced that Schmeling's winnings would be used to build German tanks. On June 22, 1938, an estimated two-thirds of the American people tuned in on the radio to hear the fight. What they heard was a rout as Louis knocked out Schmeling in just two minutes and four seconds. The press wrote that the win was a great victory for America. After Pearl Harbor, Louis volunteered to join the U.S. Army, serving as a symbol of American racial harmony and openness (even though all the armed forces were segregated), in contrast to the racism and secrecy of the Axis powers.

While Louis represented African Americans in the boxing ring, baseball remained completely segregated into the mid-1940s. A gentleman's agreement among the owners ensured that no African American players would compete in the major leagues. In 1945, however, Brooklyn Dodgers president Branch Rickey began scouting the Negro Leagues in search of the perfect black player to cross the color line. He found his man in Jackie Robinson, an army veteran who had experienced interracial competition while at UCLA. In exchange for a contract, Robinson agreed not to respond, verbally or physically, to any racially motivated abuse. After spending a year with the Montreal Royals, Brooklyn's minor league team, Robinson made his debut with the Dodgers in 1947. Although he helped lead the Dodgers to their first pennant in six years, he was also a target for racists. Some players slid into Robinson with their spikes up, threw at his head while he batted, and yelled racial slurs. He received death threats and was forced into segregated accommodations while on the road with the team.

Despite the controversy, Robinson was named Rookie of the Year and became a major draw at ballparks. Five teams set attendance records in 1947, and by the 1950s, most teams had black players. By the spring of 1949, Robinson began to speak up politically. In July he testified before the House Un-American Activities Committee against Paul Robeson, who argued that African Americans would not fight in a war with the Soviet Union. For the rest of his life, Robinson was an outspoken critic of segregation and eventually served as an advisor to Governor Nelson Rockefeller of New York.

Into the 1950s and 1960s, tennis remained a lily-white sport—most big tournaments were held in country clubs where blacks could not become members. But in the summer of 1950, four years before the *Brown v. Board of Education* decision, Althea Gibson competed in several United States Lawn Tennis Association (USLTA) events. She became the first African American to play in the USLTA National Championships (now called the U.S. Open) in 1950, and in 1951 she became the first black player to enter Wimbledon. A winner of five Grand Slam titles between 1956 and 1958, Gibson's crowning achievement came with her Wimbledon victory in 1957. She also served America's cold war aims by playing a series of goodwill exhibition matches in Southeast Asia on a State Department tour between 1955 and 1956. A versatile athlete, Gibson also became the first African American woman professional golfer in 1964.

While Gibson won at Wimbledon in 1957, Arthur Ashe became the first black man to win the U.S. Open in 1968. He later went on to win the Australian Open in 1970 and Wimbledon in 1974. Ashe became politically active in the late 1960s, specifically opposing South African apartheid. His trip to South Africa in 1973 was a major accomplishment that demonstrated that sports could help to break down a racist regime.

Sports as a Vehicle for Social Change

Sports have often served as a vehicle for social change. Inspired by the Black Power movement of the late 1960s and 1970s, black athletes increasingly demanded equal rights, on the field and off. Activist Harry Edwards, boxer Muhammad Ali, basketball player Bill Russell, and others used sports as a platform to demand social justice.

In 1960 boxer Cassius Clay seemed like an unlikely person to challenge the status quo. Hailing from Louisville, Kentucky, Clay defeated an experienced Russian fighter to win the gold medal in the light-heavyweight division at the 1960 Olympic Games in Rome. When asked by a Russian journalist about race relations in the United States, Clay replied, "Tell your readers we got qualified people working on that, and I'm not worried about the outcome." Four years later, Clay took a different position. Clay's good looks, exuberant personality, and propensity to run his "Louisville lip" ensured ample media attention for the young fighter. Before beating Sonny Liston for the heavyweight title in 1964, Clay had already labeled himself "the greatest."

After capturing the crown, Clay shocked fans and reporters by renouncing what he called his slave name and taking the name Muhammad Ali. He also joined the Nation of Islam, a militant religious group that opposed racial integration. Ali's 1965 title defense against Floyd Patterson took on special meaning, as the fight was billed as a contest between a newly converted Catholic (Patterson) and a Black Muslim (Ali). Ali successfully defended his title with a twelfth-round knockout.

Ali became a larger political symbol when he was drafted into the army in 1966. He famously remarked, "I ain't got no quarrels with them Viet Congs," and filed for an exemption as a contentious objector. Denied the exemption, Ali was indicted for draft evasion, and the New York Athletic Commission suspended his boxing license. All this made Ali a hero to those who opposed the war, including working-class African Americans, and an unpatriotic militant to those who supported the actions in Southeast Asia.

In 1967 and 1968, Edwards, a professor of sociology at San Jose State College, initiated a movement to boycott the 1968 Olympic Games to protest worldwide racial discrimination. Edwards's organization sought to expose human rights violations in the United States, show how the U.S. government exploited black athletes, and create social responsibility among black students. Boston Celtics center Bill Russell, UCLA basketball star Lew Alcindor, CORE director Floyd McKissick, and Martin Luther King Jr. all spoke out on behalf of Edwards's movement. Ultimately, the movement divided the black community, and most black athletes who qualified for the Games chose to compete. On October 16, 1968, however, two black sprinters, Tommie Smith and John Carlos, put on black gloves and raised their fists in the air as they received their Olympic medals in Mexico City. The clear display of Black Power led Avery Brundage to bar both men from the Olympic Village.

Like many African American athletes, women athletes have also used sports as a vehicle for achieving social change. Resistance to women's participation in sports at the intercollegiate level first gave way as a result of the cold war. U.S. officials hoped that the creation of a Women's Advisory Board in 1958 would improve the success of American women athletes in international competitions. Later, the feminist movement of the 1960s sparked women to demand the same opportunities as men, and those opportunities included institutional support for varsity sports programs. Though the National Collegiate Athletic Association organized its first set of national championships for women's sports in 1969, it was not until passage of Title IX of the Educational Amendments Act in 1972 that colleges and high schools across the country were forced to commit more resources to women's sports. By 1980 funding for women's sports had grown from less than 1 percent to just over 10 percent of the total national intercollegiate budget. Far from sexually integrating sports programs beyond physical education classes, Title IX advocated a "separate but equal" doctrine similar to the official racial policy of the United States prior to the Supreme Court's 1954 decision in *Brown*.

By the end of the twentieth century, sports had fully muscled their way onto the American political landscape. Professional sports had become big businesses, and so had college sports and the Olympic Games. On the fields and diamonds, the courts and courses, millionaire athletes competed for ever-larger fortunes. Off the playing fields, labor unions, agents, television executives, and team owners divided up the multi-trillion-dollar sports pie. In the halls of Congress, legislators debated steroid and antitrust issues. In newspapers, magazines, and books, and on television, commentators opined on the role sports have played and continue to play in the national dialogue about race. And in an age of globalism, American sports have become one of the nation's most marketable commodities, symbols not only of American capitalism but of democracy and cultural imperialism as well.

FURTHER READING

Gorn, Elliot, ed. *Major Problems in American Sport History: Documents and Essays*. Boston: Houghton Mifflin, 1997.

Guttmann, Allen. *The Olympics: A History of the Modern Games*. Urbana: University of Illinois Press, 1992.

Rader, Benjamin G. *American Sports: From the Age of Folk Games to the Age of Televised Sports*. 5th ed. Upper Saddle River, NJ: Prentice Hall, 2004.

Roberts, Randy, and James S. Olson. *Winning Is the Only Thing: Sports in America since 1945*. 2nd ed. Baltimore, MD: Johns Hopkins University Press, 1991.

Sammons, Jeffrey T. *Beyond the Ring: The Role of Boxing in American Society*. Urbana: University of Illinois Press, 1990.

Wiggins, David K. *Glory Bound: Black Athletes in a White America*. Syracuse, NY: Syracuse University Press, 1997.

RANDY ROBERTS AND ERIC ALLEN HALL

state constitutions

State constitutions are more easily amended and address a broader range of issues than the U.S. Constitution and, as a consequence, have often played an important role in American political development. On many occasions, the relative flexibility of state constitutions has permitted political reforms to be more easily adopted by states, and only implemented later, if at all, at the federal level. At times also, the greater range of issues addressed in state constitutions, which is due in part to the nature of the federal system and in part to conscious choices made by state constitution makers, means that many political issues have been regulated primarily or even exclusively by state constitutions. This importance of state constitutions can be seen throughout the course of the American regime but is particularly evident in the founding era, Jacksonian era, Progressive Era, and after the reapportionment revolution of the 1960s.

The Founding Era

Eleven of the original thirteen states adopted constitutions prior to the drafting of the U.S. Constitution (Connecticut and Rhode Island retained their colonial charters until 1818 and 1842, respectively), and it was through drafting these state constitutions that Americans first developed principles of constitutionalism and republicanism that were then adopted at the federal level.

State constitution makers were the first to grapple with the appropriate process for writing and adopting a constitution. The first state constitutions drafted in early 1776 in New Hampshire and South Carolina were intended to be temporary. However, drafters of subsequent state constitutions came to view them as enduring charters. Meanwhile, some of the early state constitutions were drafted by legislators or by officials who were not selected specifically for the purpose of constitution making. Eventually, though, it came to be understood that constitutions should be written by delegates who were chosen for this express purpose and who assembled in a convention. A similar evolution took place in the understanding of how a constitution should be approved. Although the earliest state constitutions took effect by proclamation of the drafters, this changed when the Massachusetts Constitution of 1780 was submitted for popular ratification. Not only have state constitution makers generally followed this process in drafting and revising the 146 documents that have been in effect in the 50 states, but this was also the model that federal constitution makers followed in holding a convention in 1787 and submitting their work for ratification by the 13 states.

State constitution makers also had extensive opportunities in the 1770s and 1780s to debate the means of designing governing institutions that would best embody republican principles, and these debates influenced the design of the federal constitution in various ways. Some of the first state constitutions were quite democratic in form. The outstanding example was the Pennsylvania constitution of 1776, which established a unicameral legislature whose members stood for annual election and were subject to term limits and whose work could not be vetoed by the executive. As state constitution making progressed, and as concerns arose over the ineffective performance of governing institutions, efforts were made to limit legislatures and secure a greater degree of deliberation, such as by adopting bicameralism, lengthening legislators' terms, eliminating term limits, and creating a strong executive. The New York constitution of 1777 was the first to adopt a number of these features; the Massachusetts constitution of 1780 went even further in embodying these developments; and, by the time that Pennsylvanians adopted a revised constitution in 1790, they had eliminated many of the more democratic features of the 1776 document. When delegates assembled at the federal convention of 1787, they drew heavily from the state constitutional experience.

The Jacksonian Era

The Jacksonian era brought calls for the democratization of both state and federal governing institutions. Though some changes were made at the federal level, the changes were even greater in the states, and these changes frequently took the form of constitutional amendments. In particular, states retained responsibility for most issues of governance during the nineteenth century, including efforts to expand the suffrage, which required changes in state law, and frequently in state constitutions. Moreover, the flexibility of state constitutions, in contrast to the rigidity of the federal amendment process, meant that certain institutional reforms, such as the popular election of judges, were only adopted at the state level.

In terms of the suffrage, the principal developments during this period were the elimination of freeholder and taxpayer requirements for voting, and these changes were frequently achieved through state constitutional amendments. Additionally, although federal acts would later remove from state discretion other voting qualifications—such as those regarding race, sex, and age—states were the innovators in each of these areas, both during the Jacksonian era and in later years. Thus, New England states permitted blacks to vote well before the Fifteenth Amendment. Wyoming, followed by numerous other states, permitted women to vote long before the Nineteenth Amendment. And Georgia and Kentucky enfranchised 18-year-olds several decades prior to ratification of the Twenty-Sixth Amendment. Moreover, states have retained control over other suffrage requirements, such as those concerning citizenship and felony conviction. Therefore, battles over suffrage requirements continued to be waged to a great degree in state constitutional forums long after the federal government began to establish national suffrage requirements in the Reconstruction era. In fact, although Reconstruction-era state conventions were required by federal law to enfranchise African Americans, these gains were mostly reversed by state conventions in the 1890s that adopted various disenfranchising mechanisms.

State constitution makers during the Jacksonian era also made attempts to democratize governing institutions. Not a single federal amendment was ratified between passage of the Twelfth Amendment in 1804 and the Thirteenth Amendment in 1865. State constitutions, though, were easier to amend, and amendment procedures were made even more flexible during this period. Some states went so far as to require that a popular referendum be held periodically on whether to hold a new constitutional convention.

As a result, constitutional reformers were able to experiment with alternative institutional arrangements at the state level. Some constitutions imposed procedural restrictions on the legislature, such as requiring that bills be read three times and contain a single subject accurately reflected in the title. There were also substantive restrictions on the legislature, such as prohibiting the incurring of debt or the lending of state credit. A number of states also moved during this period to adopt a plural executive of sorts: a wide range of executive department heads were subject to popular election, along with the governor. Most notably, beginning with Mississippi's adoption in 1832 of popular elections for all state judges and accelerating in the 1840s, states increasingly provided for an elected judiciary. State constitution makers also democratized governing institutions by changing inequitable apportionment plans that had long privileged older tidewater regions over growing piedmont and mountain regions. The Ohio Constitution of 1851 was the first to provide for an apportionment board that removed the decennial task of redistricting from the legislative process. This approach was later emulated by several other states.

The Progressive Era

Among the chief concerns of Progressive reformers was securing protection for workers in the face of obstructionist legislatures and courts. The flexibility of state amendment processes enabled reformers to adopt numerous constitutional changes introduced to bypass legislatures or overturn court decisions.

Progressive reformers pushed for a variety of protective measures for workers—including an eight-hour day, minimum wage, workers' compensation, and child labor regulations. But they experienced mixed success in getting these measures approved by legislators and then sustained by the courts. Even when Congress and state legislatures did enact protective laws, federal and state courts occasionally invalidated them. The only federal constitutional amendment formally proposed in this area was a child labor amendment, but it failed to be ratified by the requisite number of state legislatures and so never took effect. Reformers had more success securing enactment of state provisions to protect workers. Some amendments were intended to bypass legislatures, by mandating an eight-hour day or prohibiting child labor. Other state constitutional changes sought to overturn court decisions, by declaring that the legislature was empowered to pass a minimum-wage law or establish a workers' compensation system or enact other protective measures, regardless of state court rulings to the contrary.

Progressive reformers also tried to restructure governing institutions they viewed as insufficiently responsive to public opinion and overly susceptible to special-interest influence. The only structural change adopted at the federal level in the early twentieth century was direct senatorial elections, as a result of passage of the Seventeenth Amendment. But state reformers had more success. The South Dakota constitution was amended in 1898 to provide for the popular initiative and referendum, and during the twentieth century half of the states adopted similar reforms. A third of the states provided for the constitutional initiative. The Ohio constitution was amended in 1912 to permit judicial review to be exercised only by a supermajority of the state supreme court judges, and two other states soon adopted similar provisions. A number of states in the first two decades of the twentieth century also adopted the recall of judges and other public officials.

The Reapportionment Revolution

After a long period in the mid-twentieth century of relative inattention to constitutional revision, the U.S. Supreme Court's reapportionment decisions in the early 1960s led to a significant number of changes in state constitutions. States had to bring their redistricting laws into compliance with the Court's rulings, and constitution makers took the opportunity to modernize other state governing institutions as well. They also added rights provisions that had no counterpart in the federal constitution. For example, several states provided for a right to privacy or a prohibition against sex discrimination. Other states guaranteed a right to a clean environment. Victims' rights clauses were added to other state constitutions.

Much of the renewed interest in state constitutions in the late twentieth century was generated not by amendments but as a result of liberal state court interpretations of state bills of rights. When the Supreme Court under chief justices Burger and Rehnquist proved less aggressive than the Warren Court in interpreting the federal Bill of Rights in an expansive fashion, state judges began to provide redress for civil liberties claimants. Thus, the U.S. Supreme Court declined to recognize a federal constitutional right to equal school financing, but a number of state supreme courts found such a right in their state constitutions. And whereas the U.S. Supreme Court declined to rule that the death penalty violated the federal cruel and unusual punishment clause, as long as it was administered in a proper fashion, several state supreme courts interpreted their state bills of rights as prohibiting capital punishment in all circumstances. Then, at the turn of the twenty-first century, several state courts interpreted their bills of rights as guaranteeing a right to same-sex civil unions or same-sex marriage. Although state amendment processes permitted citizens to eventually adopt constitutional amendments overturning some of these state court rulings, many of these decisions were left undisturbed, ensuring that state constitutions will be a continuing battleground in civil liberties debates in the years to come.

See also Constitution, federal; state government.

FURTHER READING

Adams, Willi Paul. *The First American Constitutions: Republican Ideology and the Making of the State Constitutions in the Revolutionary Era*. Chapel Hill: University of North Carolina Press, 1980.

Dealey, James Q. *Growth of American State Constitutions from 1776 to the End of the Year 1914*. Boston: Ginn and Company, 1915.

Dinan, John J. *The American State Constitutional Tradition*. Lawrence: University Press of Kansas, 2006.

Dodd, Walter F. *The Revision and Amendment of State Constitutions*. Baltimore, MD: Johns Hopkins Press, 1910.

Elazar, Daniel J. "The Principles and Traditions Underlying State Constitutions." *Publius* 12 (Winter 1982), 11–25.

Fritz, Christian G. "Fallacies of American Constitutionalism." *Rutgers Law Journal* 35 (Summer 2004), 1327–69.

Gardner, James A. *Interpreting State Constitutions: A Jurisprudence of Function in a Federal System*. Chicago: Chicago University Press, 2005.

Kruman, Marc W. *Between Authority and Liberty: State Constitution Making in Revolutionary America.* Chapel Hill: University of North Carolina Press, 1997.

Lutz, Donald S. "The Purposes of American State Constitutions." *Publius* 12 (Winter 1982), 27–44.

Scalia, Laura J. *America's Jeffersonian Experiment: Remaking State Constitutions, 1820–1850.* DeKalb: Northern Illinois University Press, 1999.

Sturm, Albert L. *Thirty Years of State Constitution-Making, 1938–1968.* New York: National Municipal League, 1970.

Tarr, G. Alan. *Understanding State Constitutions.* Princeton, NJ: Princeton University Press, 1998.

Tarr, G. Alan, Robert F. Williams, and Frank P. Grad., eds. *State Constitutions for the Twenty-first Century.* 3 vols. Albany: State University of New York Press, 2006.

JOHN DINAN

state government

History texts have traditionally depicted the evolution of the American republic as progressing from the disunion of the Confederation era to the consolidation of the twentieth century, with state subordination ensured by the triumph of the national regime in the Civil War. According to this scenario, state governments survived in the shadow of policy makers in Washington, D.C., who gradually whittled away at the residual powers of lawmakers in places like Albany and Sacramento. Yet one of the most significant, though often overlooked, features of American political history is the persistent and powerful role of state governments in the lives of citizens. The United States is and always has been a federal republic; its very name makes clear that it is a union of states. Throughout its history the states have provided the lion's share of government affecting the everyday life of the average American. The professors who write the history texts work at state universities; their students are products of the public schools established, supervised, and to a large degree funded by the states. Every day of the year state police disturb the domestic tranquility of speeders driving along highways built and owned by the states. The municipalities that provide the water necessary for human survival are creations of the states, and these water supplies are subject to state supervision. Though the American nation is united, it is not a seamless polity. In the twenty-first century state government remains a ubiquitous element of American life.

From the Revolution to the 1890s

The original 13 states of 1776 were heirs to the governmental traditions of the colonial period. The first state constitutions retained the office of governor, though they reduced executive powers and granted the bulk of authority to a legislative branch that most often consisted of two houses. The federal Constitution of 1787, however, clearly limited the authority of these seemingly all-powerful legislatures. It declared federal laws, treaties, and the federal Constitution itself supreme over state laws. Yet it left the plenary power to govern with the states, creating a national government of delegated powers. The Tenth Amendment ratified in 1791 reinforced this fact. All powers not granted to the federal government nor specifically forbidden to the states were reserved to the states and the people thereof.

During the first 80 years of the nation's history, democratization gradually transformed the structure of state government as the people's role expanded and legislative supremacy eroded. Property or taxpaying qualifications gave way to white manhood suffrage, legislative appointment of executive and judicial officials yielded to popular election, and voter approval of constitutional amendments and revisions became a prerequisite in most states. Meanwhile, the rise of political parties imposed a limited degree of partisan discipline on legislators. They were no longer responsible only to their constituents but also had to answer to party leaders.

During these same years, state governments expanded their functions, assuming broader responsibility for economic development, education, and treatment of the disabled. Internal improvement programs with ambitious blueprints for new roads, rail lines, and canals drove some states to the brink of bankruptcy but also produced a network of artificial waterways in the Northeast and Midwest. Most notably, New York's Erie Canal funneled western commerce through the Mohawk Valley and ensured that the Empire State would wield imperial sway over much of the nation's economy. State governments also funded new universities as well as common schools, laying the foundation for their later dominance in the field of education. State schools for the blind and deaf and asylums for the insane reflected a new confidence that human disabilities could be transcended. Moreover, states constructed penitentiaries to punish and reform malefactors.

Reacting to legislative activism and the public indebtedness incurred by ambitious transportation schemes, mid-nineteenth century Americans demanded a curb on state authority. From 1843 to 1853, 15 of the 31 states drafted new constitutions, resulting in new limits on state debt and internal improvements. In addition, they restricted local and special legislation that was flooding state legislatures and benefiting favored interests. As suspicion of state-chartered business corporations mounted, wary Americans sought constitutional guarantees against legislative giveaways that might enrich the privileged few at the expense of the general public.

Union victory in the Civil War confirmed that the states were not free to withdraw from the nation at will, and the Reconstruction amendments to the federal Constitution seemingly leveled additional blows at state power. Henceforth, the Constitution prohibited the states from depriving persons of life, liberty, or property without due process of the law or denying anyone equal protection of the laws. In addition, states could not limit a person's right to vote on the basis of race, color, or previous condition of servitude. The United States Supreme Court, however, interpreted the guarantees of racial equality narrowly, allowing the states maximum leeway in discriminating against African Americans. By the early twentieth century, most southern states had disenfranchised most blacks through such devices as literacy tests and poll taxes and had enacted a growing array of segregation laws that mandated separate accommodations for African Americans in schools, on transportation lines, and other facilities. The Civil War had decided that states could no longer impose slavery on blacks, but by 1900 state governments had full authority to ensure that African Americans suffered second-class citizenship.

When confronted with the expanding volume of state economic regulatory legislation, the federal Supreme Court was not always so generous toward the states. In 1869 Massachusetts created a state railroad commission with largely advisory powers; it investigated and publicized the practices of rail companies. Illinois pioneered tougher regulation when, in the early 1870s, it authorized a rail commission with the power to fix maximum rates and thereby protect shippers from excessive charges. Twenty-four states had established rail commissions by 1886; some replicated the advisory function of the Massachusetts body while others, especially in the Midwest, followed the rate-setting example of Illinois. That same year, however, the United States Supreme Court limited state regulatory authority to intrastate rail traffic, reserving the supervision of interstate rates to the federal government. It thereby significantly curbed state power over transportation corporations.

To further protect the public, legislatures created state boards of health, with Massachusetts leading the way in 1869. During the next two decades, 29 other states followed Massachusetts's example. The new agencies were largely restricted to the investigation of health conditions and collection of data. By the last decade of the century, however, a few state boards were exercising veto powers over local water and sewerage projects, ensuring that municipalities met adequate health standards.

Activism and the Automobile

In the early twentieth century, state activism accelerated, resulting in even greater intervention in the economy. From 1907 through 1913, 22 states embarked on regulation of public utilities, extending their rate-fixing authority not only to railroads but to gas, electric, streetcar, and telephone services. Meanwhile, state governments moved to protect injured workers by adopting worker compensation programs; between 1910 and 1920, 42 of the 48 states enacted legislation guaranteeing employees compensation for injuries resulting from on-the-job accidents.

The early twentieth century not only witnessed advances in state paternalism but also changes in the distribution of power within state government. During the late nineteenth century, critics increasingly lambasted state legislatures as founts of corruption where bribed lawmakers churned out nefarious legislation at the behest of lobbyists. The criticisms were exaggerated, but owing to the attacks, faith in the legislative branch declined. Exploiting this popular distrust, a new breed of governors presented themselves as tribunes of the people, who unlike legislators, spoke not for parochial or special interests but championed the commonweal. Charles Evans Hughes in New York, Woodrow Wilson in New Jersey, Robert La Follette in Wisconsin, and Hiram Johnson in California all assumed unprecedented leadership in setting the legislative agenda, posing as popular champions who could prod state lawmakers into passing necessary reforms.

Further reflecting popular skepticism about legislative rule was the campaign for initiative and referendum procedures at the state level. In 1897 South Dakota adopted the first initiative and referendum amendment to a state constitution, allowing voters to initiate legislation and approve it by popular vote. The electorate could thereby bypass an unresponsive legislature. Moreover, voters could demand a referendum on measures passed by the legislature, and a majority of the electorate could thus undo the supposed misdeeds of their representatives. Twenty states had embraced both initiative and referendum by 1919, with Oregon and California making especially frequent use of the new procedure.

Among the issues troubling early-twentieth-century voters was state taxation. Traditionally, states had relied on the property tax, which placed an inordinate burden on land-rich farmers. Seeking to remedy this situation, Wisconsin in 1911 adopted the first effective state graduated income tax for both individuals and corporations. It proved a success, and 13 states had enacted income taxes by 1922, accounting for almost 11 percent of the state tax receipts in the nation.

During the early twentieth century the advent of the automobile greatly expanded the role of state government and further necessitated state tax reforms. Throughout most of the nineteenth century, the construction and maintenance of roads had remained almost wholly a local government responsibility. In the 1890s, however, the growing corps of bicyclists lobbied for better roadways. Responding to this pressure, state legislatures began adopting laws that authorized funding for highways that conformed to state construction standards. Nineteen states had established state road agencies by 1905. Over the following two decades, the burgeoning number of automobile owners forced the other states to follow suit, resulting in a sharp increase in highway expenditures. In 1916 and 1921 Congress approved some funding for state highway programs, but the states still shouldered the great bulk of road financing and construction. From 1921 through 1930 state governments appropriated $7.9 billion for highways; federal aid accounted for only $839 million of this total.

To fund this extraordinary expansion of state responsibility, legislatures embraced the gasoline tax. In 1919 Oregon adopted the first gasoline levy, and over the next ten years every other state followed. This tax on fuel consumption was easy to administer, highly lucrative, and popular with motorists, who were willing to pay for better roads.

From the Depression to the Present

With the onset of economic depression in the 1930s, however, the states confronted a new financial crisis. Unable to collect property taxes from cash-strapped home and business owners and faced with mounting relief expenditures, local authorities turned to the state governments for help. State legislators responded by adopting yet another new source of revenue, the retail sales tax. Mississippi led the way in 1932, and by the close of the 1930s, 23 states imposed this new levy. As early as 1936, it was second only to the gasoline tax as a source of state tax revenue. A massive influx of federal money also helped states improve services and facilities. For example, the federal Civilian Conservation Corps was instrumental in the development of state park systems.

State governments used their new sales tax revenues to bail out local school districts. From 1930 to 1940 the states' share of school funding almost doubled from 16.9 percent to 30.3 percent. Throughout the early twentieth century, states had gradually imposed stricter standards on local districts, centralizing control over public education. The financial crisis of the 1930s, however, accelerated the pace, as states were forced to intervene and maintain adequate levels of schooling.

The Great Depression also stirred new interest among the states in economic development. This was especially true in the South, where leaders tried to wean the region from its dependence on agriculture and to lure industrial plants. In 1936 Mississippi adopted its Balance Agriculture with Industry program, permitting local governments, subject to the approval of a state board, to issue bonds to finance the construction of manufacturing facilities. Meanwhile, the Southern Governors Conference, founded in 1937, lobbied the federal Interstate Commerce Commission to revise its rail charges and thereby eliminate the rate discrimination hampering the development of southern manufacturing.

After World War II the southern states fought a two-front war, defending their heritage of racial segregation while taking the offensive on economic development. First, the Supreme Court and then Congress began putting teeth in the guarantees of racial equality embodied in the Reconstruction amendments to the Constitution. The Court held state segregation laws unconstitutional, and, in the Voting Rights Act of 1965, Congress dismantled southern state restrictions on black voting. Adding to the North-South clash of the postwar era, however, was the southern economic counteroffensive. Southern governors led raiding parties on northern cities, promoting their states to corporate executives tired of the heavily unionized northern labor force and attracted to more business-friendly climes.

During the last decades of the twentieth century, northern governors responded with economic initiatives of their own. By the 1980s states were not only attempting to steal industrial plants from other parts of the country but were also embarking on high-technology incubator programs aimed at fostering innovative growth industries. Governors preached high-tech venture capitalism and promoted each of their states as the next Silicon Valley. Moreover, economic promotion trips to both Europe and Asia became regular events on governors' schedules; German and Japanese moguls welcomed one business-hungry state executive after another. With overseas trade offices and careful calculations of state exports and potential foreign markets, state governments were forging international links. State governments were no longer simply domestic units of rule but also international players.

Educational demands were meanwhile pushing the states to assume ever larger obligations. The state share of public education funding continued to rise, reaching 46.8 percent in 1979–80. Moreover, states funded the expansion of existing public universities as well as the creation of new four-year campuses and systems of two-year community colleges. To pay their mounting education bills, states raised taxes, and most of those that had not previously adopted sales or income levies did so.

With heightened responsibilities, the states seemingly needed to upgrade their governmental structures. In the 1960s the Supreme Court mandated reapportionment of state legislatures; representation was to be based solely on population. Moreover, in the 1960s and 1970s there were mounting demands for professionalization of the state legislatures. Historically, state legislators were part-time lawmakers who met for a few months each biennium, earning a modest salary for their service. During the last decades of the twentieth century, annual legislative sessions became the norm, and, in the largest states, law making became a full-time job, with state legislators acquiring a corps of paid staff. Reacting to the increasing number of entrenched professional legislators, a term-limits movement swept the nation in the early 1990s. Twenty-two states had approved term limits for lawmakers by 1995, restricting them to a maximum service of 6, 8, or 12 years.

In the early twenty-first century state governments were confronting everything from stem cell research to smart-growth land-use planning. The United States remained very much a union of states, jealous of their powers and resistant to incursions by the national regime. State governments survived as significant molders of the policies governing the everyday lives of the nation's 300 million people.

See also state constitutions.

FURTHER READING

Campbell, Ballard C. "Public Policy and State Government." In *The Gilded Age: Essays on the Origins of Modern America*, edited by Charles W. Calhoun, 309–29. Wilmington, DE: SR Books, 1996.

———. *Representative Democracy: Public Policy and Midwestern Legislatures in the Late Nineteenth Century*. Cambridge, MA: Harvard University Press, 1980.

Dealey, James Quayle. *Growth of American State Constitutions from 1776 to the End of the Year 1914*. Boston: Ginn and Company, 1915.

Fosler, R. Scott, ed. *The New Economic Role of American States: Strategies in a Competitive Economy*. New York: Oxford University Press, 1988.

Lipson, Leslie. *The American Governor: From Figurehead to Leader*. Chicago: University of Chicago Press, 1939.

Patterson, James T. *The New Deal and the States: Federalism in Transition*. Princeton, NJ: Princeton University Press, 1969.

Ransone, Colman B., Jr. *The Office of Governor in the United States*. Tuscaloosa: University of Alabama Press, 1956.

Ritter, Charles F., and Jon L. Wakelyn. *American Legislative Leaders, 1850–1910*. New York: Greenwood Press, 1989.

Sharkansky, Ira. *The Maligned States: Policy Accomplishments, Problems, and Opportunities*. New York: McGraw-Hill, 1972.

Teaford, Jon C. *The Rise of the States: Evolution of American State Government*. Baltimore, MD: Johns Hopkins University Press, 2002.

JON C. TEAFORD

suburbs and politics

The United States became a suburban nation during the second half of the twentieth century, according to conventional wisdom, popular consciousness, and scholarly consensus. The most dramatic transformation took place during the two decades after World War II, when the percentage of suburban residents doubled from one-sixth to one-third of the population. Federal policies that promoted both single-family homeownership and racial segregation subsidized the migration of millions of white families from the central cities and the countryside to suburbia, the location of about 85 percent of new residential construction in the postwar era. In 1968 suburban residents cast a plurality of ballots for the first time in a presidential election. In a period of social unrest in cities and on college campuses, Republican candidate Richard Nixon reached the White House by appealing to the "great majority" of "forgotten Americans" who worked hard, paid their taxes, and upheld the principles of the "American Dream." By 1992 suburban voters represented an outright majority of the American electorate, more than the urban and rural populations combined. During a period of economic recession and downward mobility for blue-collar workers, Democratic presidential nominee Bill Clinton reclaimed the political center with a time-honored populist appeal that championed the "forgotten, hard-working middle-class families of America."

The bipartisan pursuit of swing voters of "middle America" reveals the pivotal role played by the rise of suburban power in national politics since the 1950s. The broader story of suburban political culture in modern U.S. history also includes public policies that constructed sprawling metropolitan regions, the grassroots influence of homeowner and taxpayer movements, and the persistent ideology of the white middle-class nuclear family ideal. A clear-cut definition of the "suburbs" is elusive because the label simultaneously represents a specific yet somewhat arbitrary census category (everything in a metropolitan statistical area outside of the central city limits), a particular form of land-use development (the decentralized sprawl of single-family houses in automobile-dependent neighborhoods physically separated from shopping and employment districts), and a powerful set of cultural meanings (the American Dream of homeownership, upward mobility, safety and security, and private family life in cul-de-sac settings of racial and economic exclusion). Residents of suburbs have long defined themselves in cultural and political opposition to the urban-industrial center, from the growth of commuter towns along railroad lines in the mid-1800s to the highway-based "edge cities" and exurbs of the late twentieth century. Although scholars emphasize the diversity of suburban forms and debate the extent to which many former bedroom communities have become urbanized, the utopian imagery of the nineteenth-century "garden suburb" maintains a powerful sway. Suburban politics continues to revolve around efforts to create and defend private refuges of single-family homes that exclude commercial functions and the poor while achieving a harmonious synthesis between the residential setting and the natural environment.

Suburban Growth and Residential Segregation

Beginning in the late 1800s and early 1900s, the quest for local autonomy through municipal incorporation and zoning regulations emerged as a defining feature of suburban political culture. Garden suburbs outside cities such as Boston and Philadelphia incorporated as separate municipalities in order to prevent urban annexation and maintain local control over taxes and services. The 1898 merger that created the five boroughs of New York City stood as a rare exception to the twentieth-century pattern of metropolitan fragmentation into autonomous political districts, especially in the Northeast and Midwest (pro-urban laws continued to facilitate annexation of suburbs in a number of southern and western states). Municipal incorporation enabled affluent suburbs to implement land-use policies of exclusionary zoning that banned industry and multifamily units from homogeneous neighborhoods of single-family homes. The concurrent spread of private racial covenants forbade ownership or rental of property in particular areas by "any person other than of the white or Caucasian race." By the 1920s, real estate developers and homeowners associations promoted restrictive covenants in most new subdivisions, often specifically excluding occupancy by African Americans, Asians, Mexicans, Puerto Ricans, American Indians, and Jews. The NAACP repeatedly challenged the constitutionality of racial covenants during the early decades of the modern civil rights movement, but the Supreme Court continued to permit their enforcement until the *Shelley v. Kraemer* decision of 1948.

By 1930 one-sixth of the American population lived in the suburbs, with public policies and private practices combining to segregate neighborhoods comprehensively by race and class. From the local to the national levels, suburban politics revolved around the protection of white middle-class family life through the defense of private property values. Following the turn to restrictive covenants, the National Association of Real Estate Boards instructed its members that "a realtor should never be instrumental in introducing into a neighborhood a character of property or occupancy, members of any race or nationality, or any individual whose presence will clearly be detrimental to property values in the neighborhood." During the depths of the Great Depression, the federal government established the Home Owners Loan Corporation, which provided emergency mortgages in single-family neighborhoods while "redlining" areas that contained industry, multifamily housing units, and low-income or minority residents. The National Housing Act of 1934 chartered the Federal Housing Administration (FHA), which insured low-interest mortgage loans issued by private banks and thereby revolutionized the market for suburban residential construction. The FHA also endorsed restrictive racial covenants and maintained the guideline that "if a neighborhood is to retain stability, it is necessary that properties shall continue to be occupied by the same social and racial classes." Between 1934 and 1960, the federal government provided $117 billion in mortgage insurance for private homes, with racial minorities formally excluded from 98 percent of these new developments, almost all of which were located in suburbs or outlying neighborhoods within city limits.

During the sustained economic boom that followed World War II, suburbs became the primary residential destination for white-collar and blue-collar families alike, although neighborhoods remained stratified by socioeconomics as well as segregated by race. Suburban development became a powerful validation of the New Deal social contract, embodied in President Franklin Roosevelt's promise that the national state would secure "the right of every family to a decent home." The GI Bill of 1944 offered interest-free mortgages to millions of military veterans and enabled many white working-class and middle-class families to achieve the suburban dream of a detached house with a yard. The federal government also subsidized suburban growth through interstate highways and other road-building projects that connected bedroom communities to downtown business districts and accelerated the decentralization of shopping malls and office parks to the metropolitan fringe. The number of American families that owned their own homes increased from 40 to 60 percent between the 1940s and the

Aerial view of Levittown, New York, 1953. (Library of Congress)

1960s, the period of the great white middle-class migration to the suburbs.

In 1947 the corporate-designed Levittown on Long Island became the national symbol of this new suburban prosperity, an all-white town of 70,000 residents marketed as "the most perfectly planned community in America." Social critics mocked Levittown and similar mass-produced developments for their cookie-cutter houses and the allegedly bland and conformist lifestyles of their inhabitants. But defenders credited the suburbs with achieving "the ideal of prosperity for all in a classless society," the epitome of the consumer-based freedoms that would assure the victory of the United States in the cold war, as Vice President Richard M. Nixon proclaimed in the 1959 "kitchen debate" with Premier Nikita Khrushchev of the Soviet Union.

Suburbs under Siege

The suburban political culture of the 1950s celebrated consensus, consumer affluence, and a domestic ideology marked by rigid gender roles within the heterosexual nuclear family. On the surface, in the television family sitcoms and mass-market magazines, postwar America seemed to be a place of white upper-middle-class contentment, with fathers commuting to corporate jobs while stay-at-home mothers watched their baby boomer youth play with toys advertised by Walt Disney and other large corporations. In the presidential elections of 1952 and 1956, a substantial majority of voters twice rejected the reformist liberalism of Adlai Stevenson for the moderate conservatism of President Dwight D. Eisenhower, later labeled "the great Republican hero of the suburban middle class" by GOP strategist Kevin Phillips.

But this consensus ideology of 1950s suburban prosperity existed alongside a growing crisis of domesticity that would soon explode in the social movements of the 1960s. Sociologist William Whyte characterized white-collar managers from the affluent suburbs as the collective "Organization Man," a generation that had sacrificed individuality to the demands of corporate conformity. Betty Friedan critiqued the "feminine mystique" for promoting therapeutic rather than political solutions to issues of sex discrimination and proclaimed: "We can no longer ignore that voice within women that says: 'I want something more than my husband and my children and my home.'" In 1962 Students for a Democratic Society called for a new left that rejected the utopian promises of suburban tranquility: "We are people of this generation, bred in at least modest comfort, housed now in universities, looking uncomfortably to the world we inherit."

In the 1960s and 1970s, the greatest challenge to suburban political autonomy came from the civil rights campaign for school and housing integration. A growing white backlash greeted these efforts to open up the suburbs, signaled by the passage of Proposition 14 by California voters in 1964. Three-fourths of the white suburban electorate supported this referendum to repeal California's fair-housing law and protect the private right to discriminate on the basis of race in the sale and renting of property. The open-housing movement, which had been attacking policies of suburban exclusion for half a century, gained new urgency with the race riots that erupted in American cities in the mid-to-late 1960s. During the summer of 1966, Martin Luther King Jr. led open-housing marches into several of Chicago's all-white suburbs, but the violent reaction of white homeowners did not persuade Congress to pass a federal open-housing law.

In 1968 the National Advisory Commission on Civil Disorders (Kerner Commission) issued a dire warning that the United States was divided into "two societies; one, largely Negro and poor, located in the central cities; the other, predominantly white and affluent, located in the suburbs and outlying areas." The Kerner Report also placed blame for the urban crisis on public policies of suburban exclusion: "What white Americans have never fully understood—but what the Negro can never forget—is that white society is deeply implicated in the ghetto. White institutions created it, white institutions maintain it, and white society condones it." Congress responded by passing the landmark Fair Housing Act of 1968, which banned discrimination on the basis of race, color, religion, and national origin in the sale and renting of property.

The political backlash against the civil rights movement galvanized white voters in working-class and middle-class suburbs alike. In 1966 Republican candidate Ronald Reagan won the California gubernatorial election by denouncing fair-housing legislation, calling for "law and order" crackdowns against urban criminals and campus protesters, and blaming liberal welfare programs for squandering the tax dollars of mainstream Americans. In 1968 Richard Nixon's pledge to defend middle–American homeowners and taxpayers from the excesses of liberalism carried white-collar suburbs across the nation and made inroads among blue-collar Democrats. During his first term in office, Nixon vigorously defended the principle of suburban autonomy by opposing court-ordered busing to integrate public schools and by resisting inclusionary zoning to scatter low-income housing throughout metropolitan regions. "Forced integration of the suburbs," Nixon declared in 1971, "is not in the national interest." In his 1972 reelection campaign, Nixon won 49 states by uniting working-class and middle-class white voters in a populist antiliberal alliance that he labeled the "silent majority." In the 1980s, Ronald Reagan strengthened the Republican base in the suburbs by blaming the Democrats for economic recession, welfare cheaters, racial quotas, court-ordered busing, urban crime, and high taxes imposed on the hard-working majority to pay for failed antipoverty programs. Capitalizing on grassroots movements such as the California property tax revolt of 1978, Reagan dominated the suburban electorate by a 55-to-35 margin in 1980 and a 61-to-38 landslide in 1984.

Suburban Diversity

Reagan's victories in the 1980s represented the culmination of a suburban-driven realignment that ultimately destroyed the political base of New Deal liberalism, but the temporary triumph of Republican conservatism soon gave way to new forms of suburban diversity and heightened levels of electoral competitiveness. In 1985 a group of moderate Democrats formed the Democratic Leadership Council (DLC) to expand beyond the party's urban base by becoming "competitive in suburban areas" and recognizing that "sprawl is where the voters are." In the 1992 presidential election, Bill Clinton won by turning the DLC agenda into a campaign to honor the values of America's "forgotten middle class, . . . like individual responsibility, hard work, family, community." Clinton championed programs such as universal health care to address middle–American economic insecurity while neutralizing the GOP by promising to cut middle-class taxes, enact welfare reform, and be tough on crime. Clinton won a plurality of suburban votes in the three-way elections of 1992 (41 to 39 percent) and 1996 (47 to 42 percent), while maintaining the traditional Democratic base in the central cities. At the same time, the Democratic resurgence reflected the increasing heterogeneity of American suburbia, home to 54 percent of Asian Americans, 49 percent of Hispanics, 39 percent of African Americans, and 73 percent of whites at the time of the 2000 census (based on the 102 largest metropolitan regions). By century's end, some political strategists were predicting an "emerging Democratic majority" based on the party's newfound ability to appeal to white swing voters in the middle-class suburbs (a fiscally and culturally moderate electorate) and to capture the high-tech, multiracial metropolises of the booming Sunbelt.

Republican George W. Bush reclaimed the suburban vote by narrow margins in 2000 (49 to 47 percent) and 2004 (52 to 47 percent), but the dynamics of recent elections suggest the problematic nature of viewing contemporary metropolitan politics through the stark urban/liberal versus suburban/conservative dichotomy that took hold in the 1950s. Republican "family values" campaigns have mobilized the outer-ring suburbs that are home to large numbers of white married couples with young children, and Bush won 97 of the nation's 100 fastest-growing exurban counties in the 2000 election. Democrats have found new bases of support in older inner-ring suburbs, many of which are diversifying as racial and ethnic minorities settle outside the city limits, as well as with middle-income women and white-collar professionals who dislike the cultural agenda of the religious right.

Suburban political culture is also in flux in other ways that challenge the partisan divisions that emerged during the postwar decades. The bellwether state of California, which led the national suburban backlash against civil rights and liberal programs in the 1960s, now combines an anti-tax political culture with a massive prison-industrial complex, a multiracial electorate with a deeply conflicted stance toward immigration, and some of the nation's most progressive policies on environmental regulation and cultural issues.

Perhaps the most important consequence of the suburbanization of American politics is the way in which the partisan affiliations of voters has often mattered less than the identification of suburban residents as homeowners, taxpayers, and school parents. Regardless of which party controls Washington, America's suburbs have proved to be quite successful at defending their property values, maintaining middle-class entitlement programs, resisting policies of redistributive taxation, preventing meaningful racial and economic integration, and thereby policing the cultural and political boundaries of the American Dream.

See also cities and politics.

FURTHER READING

Baxandall, Rosalyn, and Elizabeth Ewen. *Picture Windows: How the Suburbs Happened.* New York: Basic Books, 2000.

Cohen, Lizabeth. *A Consumers' Republic: The Politics of Mass Consumption in Postwar America.* New York: Knopf, 2003.

Connelly, Marjorie. "How Americans Voted: A Political Portrait." *New York Times*, November 7, 2004.

Fogelson, Robert M. *Bourgeois Nightmares: Suburbia, 1870–1930.* New Haven, CT: Yale University Press, 2005.

Freund, David M. P. *Colored Property: State Policy and White Racial Politics in Suburban America.* Chicago: University of Chicago Press, 2007.

Frey, William. "Melting Pot Suburbs: A Census 2000 Study of Suburban Diversity." Washington, DC: Brookings Institution, June 2001. Downloadable from http://www.brookings.edu/~/media/Files/rc/reports/2001/06demographics_frey/frey.pdf.

Greenberg, Stanley B. *Middle Class Dreams: The Politics and Power of the New American Majority.* Revised ed. New Haven, CT: Yale University Press, 1996.

Jackson, Kenneth T. *Crabgrass Frontier: The Suburbanization of the United States.* New York: Oxford University Press, 1985.

Lassiter, Matthew D. *The Silent Majority: Suburban Politics in the Sunbelt South.* Princeton, NJ: Princeton University Press, 2006.

McGirr, Lisa. *Suburban Warriors: The Origins of the New American Right.* Princeton, NJ: Princeton University Press, 2001.

Meyer, Stephen Grant. *As Long as They Don't Move Next Door: Segregation and Racial Conflict in American Neighborhoods.* Lanham, MD: Rowman and Littlefield, 2000.

Nicolaides, Becky M., and Andrew Wiese, eds. *The Suburb Reader.* New York: Routledge, 2006.

Schneider, William. "The Suburban Century Begins." *Atlantic Monthly* (July 1992), 33–44. Downloadable from http://www.theatlantic.com/politics/ecbig/schnsub.htm.

Self, Robert O. *American Babylon: Race and the Struggle for Postwar Oakland.* Princeton, NJ: Princeton University Press, 2003.

Wiese, Andrew. *Places of Their Own: African American Suburbanization in the Twentieth Century.* Chicago: University of Chicago Press, 2004.

MATTHEW D. LASSITER

suffrage

See voting; woman suffrage.

Supreme Court

There is no doubt that the U.S. Supreme Court has influenced the politics of the country. As a public body, the Court is a highly visible part of the federal government. This has always been so, even when the justices met briefly twice a year in the drafty basement of the Capitol. Yet the idea that the Court itself is a political institution is controversial.

The justices themselves have disputed that fact. Indeed, the Court has gone to great pains to avoid the appearance of making political decisions. In *Luther v. Borden* (1849), the Court adopted a self-denying "prudential" (judge-made) rule that it would avoid hearing cases that the legislative branch, or the people, could decide for themselves, the "political questions." In 1946 Justice Felix Frankfurter reiterated this principle in *Colegrove v. Green*. Because it did nothing but hear and decide cases and controversies brought before it, and its decisions affected only the parties in those cases and controversies, Alexander Hamilton assured doubters, in the *Federalist Papers,* No. 78, that the High Court was "the weakest branch" of the new federal government.

There are other apparent constraints on the Court's participation in politics that arise from within the canons of the legal profession. Judges are supposed to be neutral in their approach to cases, and learned appellate court judges are supposed to ground their opinions in precedent and logic. On the Court, the high opinion of their peers and the legal community allegedly means more to them than popularity.

Conceding such legal, professional, and self-imposed constraints, the Court is a vital part of U.S. politics for three reasons. First, the Court is part of a constitutional system that is inherently political. Even before the rise of the first national two-party system in the mid-1790s, the Court found itself involved in politics. The Court declined to act as an advisory body to President George Washington on the matter of veterans' benefits, asserting the separation of powers doctrine. In 1793 the Court ordered the state of Georgia to pay what it owed a man named Chisholm, an out-of-state creditor, causing a constitutional crisis that prompted the passage of the Eleventh Amendment. Those kinds of political frictions—among the branches of the federal government and between the High Court and the states—continue to draw the Court into politics.

After the advent of the national two-party system, partisanship became institutionalized, with the result that appointments to the Court have always been political. Nominees often have political careers before they agree to serve. They are almost always members of the president's political party. The role the Senate plays in consenting to the president's nominations (or, in slightly under one-fourth of the nominations, refusing to consent), further politicizes the Court, for the Senate divides along party and ideological lines in such votes. The confirmation debates and, after 1916, the hearings, are riven with politics, and once on the Court, the justices' political views are often remarkably accurate predictors of their stances in cases that involve sensitive issues. The controversies surrounding President Ronald W. Reagan's nomination of Robert Bork and President George H. W. Bush's nomination of Clarence Thomas are recent examples of this observation.

Similarly, once on the Court the justices do not necessarily abandon their political aspirations. Salmon P. Chase, Stephen J. Field, Charles Evans Hughes, Frank Murphy, and William O. Douglas all wanted to be president of the United States, and Chief Justice William Howard Taft was an ex-president when he assumed the center chair. Felix Frankfurter and Abe Fortas continued to advise their respective presidents while on the bench.

Finally, the output of the Court has a major impact on the politics of the day. While it is not always true that the Court follows the election returns, it is true that the Court can influence them. In the first 60 years of the nineteenth century, slavery cases fit this description. Even after the Thirteenth Amendment abolished slavery, politically sensitive civil rights cases continued to come to the High Court. Labor relations cases, taxation cases, antitrust cases, and, more recently, privacy cases all had political impact.

Even the self-denying stance the Court adopted in political questions was subject to revision. In a famous footnote to *Carolene Products v. U.S.* (1938), the Court announced that it would pay particularly close attention to state actions that discriminated against "discrete and insular minorities" precisely because they were not protected by democratic "political processes." In the 1940s, the Court struck down state laws denying persons of color the right to vote in election primaries. Later decisions barred states from drawing legislative districts intended to dilute the votes of minority citizens. By the 1960s, the Court's abstinence in political questions had worn thin. In a series of "reapportionment cases," the Court determined that states could not frame state or congressional electoral districts unfairly. The High Court's rulings, sometimes known as the "one man, one vote" doctrine, remade state and federal electoral politics.

The Early Period

Perhaps the most appropriate way to demonstrate the Court's complex institutional politics is to describe its most prominent cases. The very first of the Court's great cases, *Marbury v. Madison* (1803) involved political relations within government, the partisan composition of the Court, and the political impact of a decision. It began when the Republican Party of Thomas Jefferson and James Madison won control of the presidency and both houses of Congress in what Jefferson called the revolution of 1800.

The Jeffersonian Republicans wanted to purge the judiciary of their rivals, the Federalists, and eliminate many of the so-called midnight appointments. In the coming years, Congress would impeach and remove Federalist district court judge Timothy Pickering and impeach Federalist Supreme Court justice Samuel Chase. Into this highly charged partisan arena came the case of William Marbury.

Marbury was supposed to receive a commission as a justice of the peace for the District of Columbia. However, when he was the outgoing secretary of state, John Marshall failed to send the commission on, and the incoming secretary of state, James Madison, with the assent of President Jefferson, did not remedy Marshall's oversight. When Marbury did not get the commission, he filed suit with the clerk of the Supreme Court under the provisions of the Judiciary Act of 1789, which gave the Court original jurisdiction in such matters.

Thus, the case went directly to the Court. The issue, as Marshall, who was now chief justice, framed it, was whether the Court had jurisdiction over the case. He intentionally ignored the political context of the suit. It seems obvious that the issue was political, but in a long opinion for that day (26 pages), Marshall wrote for a unanimous Court that the justices could not issue the writ because it was not one of the kinds of original jurisdiction given the Court in Article III of the Constitution. The Constitution controlled or limited what Congress could do, and prohibited the Congress from expanding the original jurisdiction of the Court. Congress had violated the Constitution by giving this authority to the Court. In short, he struck down that part of the Judiciary Act of 1789 as unconstitutional.

The power that Marshall assumed in the Court to find acts of Congress unconstitutional, and thus null and void, was immensely important politically within the government structure, for it protected the independence of the Court from Congress, implied that the Court was the final arbiter of the meaning of the Constitution (the doctrine of judicial review), and reminded everyone that the Constitution was the supreme law against which every act of Congress had to be measured. Although critics of *Marbury* decried judicial tyranny and asserted that the opinion was colored by Marshall's party affiliation, a political challenge to Marshall's opinion was not possible because it did not require any action. Marbury went away empty-handed.

Marbury managed to keep the Court out of politics in a formal sense, though it was deeply political; the "self-inflicted wound" of *Dred Scott v. Sanford* (1857) plunged the Court into the center of the political maelstrom. What to do about slavery in the territories was a suppurating wound in antebellum national politics. By the late 1850s, the controversy had destroyed one national party, the Whigs, and led to the formation of a new party, the Republicans, based wholly in the North and dedicated to preventing the expansion of slavery.

Against this background of intensifying partisanship and sectional passion, the Supreme Court might have elected to avoid making general pronouncements about slavery and stick to the facts of cases, narrowing the precedent. However, in 1856 newly elected Democratic president James Buchanan asked the Court to find a comprehensive solution to the controversy when Congress deadlocked over the admission of Kansas as a slave state. A Democratic majority was led by long-term chief justice Roger B. Taney of Maryland, a dedicated states' rights Democrat who had been Andrew Jackson's reliable aide in the war against the second Bank of the United States.

Dred Scott was the slave of U.S. Army doctor John Emerson, and was taken with him from Louisiana to posts in free states and free territories. In 1843 Emerson returned to a family home in Missouri, a slave state, and Scott went with him. In 1846, three years after Emerson's death, for himself and his family, Scott sued for his freedom. After two trials and four years had passed, the Missouri trial court ruled in his favor. The Missouri Supreme Court reversed that decision in 1852. Northern personal liberty laws, the response to the Fugitive Slave Act of 1850, angered Missouri slaveholding interests, and the new policy that the state's supreme court adopted in *Scott* reflected that anger.

But Scott's cause had also gained new friends, "free soil" and abolitionist interests that believed his case raised crucial issues. Because Emerson's estate had a New York executor, John Sanford, Scott could bring his suit for freedom in federal court under the diversity clause of the Judiciary Act of 1789. This litigation could only go forward if Scott were a citizen, but the federal circuit court sitting in St. Louis decided to hear the suit. In 1854, however, the federal court agreed with the Missouri supreme court: under Missouri law, Scott was still a slave.

The U.S. Supreme Court agreed to a full dress hearing of Scott's appeal in 1856. Oral argument took four days, and the Court's final ruling was delayed another year, after the presidential election of 1856. Joined by six of the other justices, Taney ruled that the lower federal court was correct: under Missouri law, Scott had no case. Nor should the case have come to the federal courts, for Scott was not a citizen. The law behind this decision was clear, and it was enough to resolve the case. But Taney added two dicta, readings of history and law that were not necessary to resolve the case but would, if followed, have settled the political questions of black citizenship and free soil.

Taney wrote that no person of African descent brought to America to labor could ever be a citizen of the United States. Such individuals might be citizens of particular states, but this did not confer national citizenship on them. In a second dictum, Taney opined that the Fifth Amendment to the Constitution, guaranteeing that no man's property might be taken without due process of law, barred Congress from denying slavery expansion into the territories. In effect, Taney retroactively declared the Missouri Compromise of 1820, barring slavery in territories north of 36° 30′ north latitude, unconstitutional.

The opinion was celebrated in the South and excoriated in the North. Northern public opinion, never friendly to abolitionism, now found the possibility of slavery moving north frightening. Abraham Lincoln used it to undermine his rival for the Illinois Senate seat, Stephen Douglas. Lincoln lost the race (Douglas and the Democrats controlled the legislature), but he won the debates and found an issue on which to campaign for president in 1860.

In his first inaugural address, President Lincoln issued a subtle warning to the holdover Democratic majority on the Court, and to Taney in particular. The will of the people, embodied in the electoral victory of the Republicans, would not tolerate a Court that defended secession. The justices took the hint. They agreed to the blockade of the Confederate coastline and accepted the administration view that the Confederacy did not legally exist. By the end of the war, Lincoln was able to add enough Republicans to the Court, including a new chief justice, Salmon Chase, to ensure that Republican policies would not be overturned. For example, the majority of the Court found that "greenbacks," paper money issued by the federal government to finance the war, were legal tender.

The Industrial Age

The Reconstruction amendments profoundly changed the constitutional landscape, giving the federal government increased supervision over the states. Insofar as the High Court had already claimed pride of place in interpreting the meaning of the Constitution, the Thirteenth, the Fourteenth, and the Fifteenth Amendments, along with the Civil Rights Acts of 1866, 1870, 1871, and 1875, should have led to deeper Court involvement in the politics of the South. Instead, the Court's repeated refusal to intervene reflected the white consensus that nothing further could be done to aid the newly freed slaves in the South, or the black people of the North, for that matter.

The so-called voting rights cases were inherently political because they touched the most basic rights of citizens in a democracy—the right to participate in the political process. In these cases, the Court deployed the first kind of politics, the politics of federalism, in response to the third kind of politics, the wider politics of party. By 1876, the Radical Republican impulse to enforce an aggressive Reconstruction policy had spent itself. In the election of 1876, the Republican nominee, Rutherford B. Hayes, promised that he would end the military occupation of the former Confederate states, in effect turning over state and local government to the "Redeemers," former Confederate political leaders, and leaving the fate of the former slaves to their past masters.

In *U.S. v. Hiram Reese* and *U.S. v. William Cruikshank et al.*, decided in 1875 and 1876, the Court found ways to back the Redeemers. In the former case, a Kentucky state voting registrar refused to allow Garner, an African American, to pay the poll tax. The motive was as much political as racial, as the state was Democratic and the party leaders assumed that every black voter was a Republican. A circuit court had dismissed the prosecutor's indictments. The High Court affirmed the lower court. In the latter case, a mob of whites attacked blacks guarding a courthouse in New Orleans. Again the federal circuit court had found the indictments wanting. The High Court agreed.

Was the Court concerned about the political implications of the two cases? They were heard in 1875, but the decision was not announced until the next year. In his opinion for the Court in *Cruikshank*, Chief Justice Morrison R. Waite introduced the concept of "state action," a limitation on the reach of the Fourteenth Amendment's due process and equal protection clauses. The New Orleans mob was not an agent of the state, so the Fourteenth Amendment and the civil rights acts did not apply. The door was now wide open for the Redeemers to pass Jim Crow laws, segregating public facilities in the South, and deny freedmen their rights using supposedly neutral restrictions like literacy tests for voting as well as "whites only" primaries for the most important elections—those in the Democratic primary. Outright discrimination received Court approval in the case of *Plessy v. Ferguson* (1896), in which "equal but separate" laws, more popularly known as "separate but equal," became the rule of the land.

The politicization of the High Court in the Gilded Age, a period of rapid industrialization, was nowhere more apparent than in a trio of highly political cases that arrived at the Court in 1894 and 1895. The first of the cases arose when the federal government prosecuted the E. C. Knight sugar-refining company and other refining operations, all part of the same sugar trust, for violation of the 1890 Sherman Antitrust Act.

Chief Justice Melville Fuller wrote the opinion at the end of 1894. Congress had the power to regulate interstate commerce but, according to Fuller, the refineries were manufacturing plants wholly within the states of Delaware, Pennsylvania, and New Jersey, and thus not subject to federal law. The Court, by a vote of 8 to 1, had refused to let the progressives in the government enjoin (legally stop), combination of the sugar refineries. It was a victory for the monopolies and the politicians they had lobbied. By the same lopsided vote, in *In Re Debs* (1895) the Court upheld a lower-court injunction sought by the federal government against the American Railway Union for striking. It too was a triumph for conservative political forces.

The third time in which the Fuller Court delved into the great political causes of the day was an income tax case. Democratic voters in rural areas favored the reintroduction of an income tax. The tax Congress passed during the Civil War expired in 1872. In 1894 Congress passed a flat 2 percent income tax on all incomes over $4,000—the equivalent of about $91,000 in 2005 dollars. Defenders of the sacredness of private wealth were aghast and feared that the measure brought the nation one step closer to socialism. In *Pollock v. Farmers Loan and Trust Company* (1895), Fuller and the Court agreed and set aside the entire act of Congress, not just the offending corporate provisions.

All three of the High Court's opinions angered the Populists and other reformers. William Jennings Bryan, the former congressman who captured the Democratic Party nomination in 1896, won over a much divided convention, in part, with an attack on the Court's dismissive view of the working man. But Bryan sounded like a dangerous extremist in a decade filled with radicalism. Better financed, supported by most of the major newspapers, the Republicans and McKinley won a landslide victory, with 271 electoral votes to Bryan's 176.

During U.S. participation in World War I, nothing could have been more political than the antiwar protests of 1917–18, and the Court handled these with a heavy hand. Here the Court acted not as an independent check on the other branches of the federal government, upholding the Bill of Rights, but as the handmaiden of the other branches' claims to wartime powers. In such cases, the Court was political in the first sense, as part of the larger operation of the federal government.

When pro-German, antiwar, or radical spokesmen appeared to interfere with the draft by making speeches, passing out leaflets, or writing editorials, or when they conspired to carry out any act that might interfere with the draft, the federal government arrested, tried, and convicted them under the Espionage Act of 1917. The High Court found no protection for such speech in the First Amendment. As Justice Oliver Wendell Holmes Jr. wrote in upholding the conviction of Socialist Party leader Eugene V. Debs, Debs's avowed Socialist commitments could not be tolerated by a nation at war. The government had to protect itself against such upsetting speech. Holmes would reverse himself in *U.S. v. Abrams* (1919), but antigovernment political speech in time of war did not receive protection from the Court under the First Amendment until the Vietnam War.

Liberalism Triumphant

In the New Deal Era, the Court thrust itself into the center of the political arena. By first upholding federal and state intervention in the economy, then striking down congressional acts, and then deferring to Congress, the Court proved that external political considerations could be as powerful an influence as the justices' own political views. The New Deal, from 1933 to 1941, was, in reality, two distinct political and economic periods. Most of the more controversial programs from the first New Deal, like the National Recovery Administration, the Court (led by the conservative quartet of George Sutherland, Willis Van Devanter, Pierce Butler, and James C. McReynolds, joined by Owen Roberts) struck down, under the substantive due process, doctrine it originally announced in the case of *Lochner v. New York* (1905).

With the Depression largely unaffected by the first New Deal, Franklin Roosevelt's administration and Congress enacted more egalitarian reforms in 1935. Among these were programs to provide jobs (the Works Progress Administration), the Social Security Act, the Rural Electrification Administration, and the National Labor Relations Act. The last of these finally ended the antilabor injunction, in effect overruling the Court's attempts to protect it. The stage was set for a constitutional crisis between Roosevelt and the Court. In 1937, however, Justice Roberts shifted his stance, joining, among others, Chief Justice Charles Evans Hughes to uphold the constitutionality of the Social Security Administration, the National Labor Relations Board, and other New Deal agencies. What had happened to change the constitutional landscape?

One factor could have been Roosevelt's plan to revise the membership of the Court. Congress had done this before, adding justices or (at the end of the Civil War) reducing the number of justices. Roosevelt would have added justices to the Court for every justice over the age of 70, in effect "packing it" with New Deal supporters. From their new building, dubbed "the marble palace" by journalists, all the justices disliked the packing plan. No one knew what Roosevelt's plan would bring or if Congress would accede to the president's wishes. In fact, the Senate quashed the initiative. But by that time the High Court had shifted its views enough to let key measures of the second New Deal escape, including Social Security, collective bargaining for labor, and minimum wage laws.

With the retirement of one conservative after another, Roosevelt would be able to fill the Court in a more conventional way with New Deal supporters. From 1937 to 1943, turnover in the Court was unmatched. The new justices included Hugo Black, Stanley Reed, Felix Frankfurter, William O. Douglas, Frank Murphy, James F.

Byrnes, Robert Jackson, and Wiley Rutledge. All, to one degree or another, believed in deference to popularly elected legislatures.

After World War II, the cold war and the so-called second Red Scare again required the Court to step carefully through a political minefield. At the height of the cold war, the House Un-American Activities Committee and the Senate's Permanent Subcommittee on Investigations, led by Senator Joseph McCarthy of Wisconsin, sought to uncover Communists in government posts. A wider scare led to blacklists of former Communists and their alleged conspirators in Hollywood, among New York State school teachers, and elsewhere.

Here the Court's majority followed the election returns in such cases as *Dennis v. United States* (1951). The case arose out of Attorney General Tom Clark's orders to prosecute the leaders of the Communist Party-USA (CPUSA) for violating the 1940 Smith Act, which forbade any advocacy or conspiracy to advocate the violent overthrow of the government. Although this was only one of many cases stemming from the "Foley Square Trials" in the federal district court in New York City, the High Court had yet to rule on the First Amendment issues involved.

Chief Justice Fred Vinson warned that the government did not have to wait to act as the Communist Party organized and gathered strength. The Smith Act was clear and constitutional—and the Communist Party, to which Dennis and the others indicted under the act belonged, had as its policy the violent overthrow of the government. Justices Hugo Black and William O. Douglas dissented.

In so doing, they initiated a great debate over whether the Court should adopt an absolutist or more flexible interpretation of the Bill of Rights. Black's dissent was that the First Amendment's declaration that Congress shall make no law meant "no law." Conceding some power to the government, Douglas, an author himself, would be the first to grant that printed words could lead to action, and he made plain his dislike of the Communists' required reading list. But, he reasoned, "If the books themselves are not outlawed, if they can lawfully remain on library shelves, by what reasoning does their use in a classroom become a crime?" Within a decade, Douglas's views would triumph.

The Rights Revolution and Reaction

Civil rights again thrust the Court into the center of political agitation, except this time it spoke not in political terms but in moral ones. The civil rights decisions of the Warren Court elevated it above the politics of the justices, and the politics of the men who put the justices in the marble palace. Earl Warren, chief justice during this "rights revolution," came to personify the Court's new unanimity. He was first and foremost a politician. His meteoric rise in California politics, from humble beginnings to state attorney general, and then governor, was accompanied by a gradual shift from conservative Republicanism to a more moderate, centrist position—one that favored government programs to help the poor and regulation of business in the public interest. In return for Warren's support at the 1952 national convention, newly elected President Dwight D. Eisenhower promised him a place on the Court. The first vacancy was the chief justiceship, and Eisenhower somewhat reluctantly kept his word.

Warren did not have a distinguished civil rights or civil liberties record in California. During World War II, he had been a strong proponent of the forced relocation of Japanese Americans from their homes on the West Coast to internment camps. But on the Court he saw that the politics of civil rights and the Fourteenth Amendment's plain meaning required the end of racial discrimination in schools, public facilities, and voting.

There can be no doubt that the Court's decisions in *Brown v. Board of Education* (1954), *Cooper v. Aaron* (1958), and subsequent school desegregation cases had a major political impact. Certainly southern members of Congress recognized that impact when they joined in a "manifesto" denouncing the Court for exceeding its role in the federal system and the federal government for its intrusion into southern state affairs. President Eisenhower was so disturbed by the Court's role in the rights revolution that he reportedly said—referring to Warren and Justice William J. Brennan—that his two worst mistakes were sitting on the Supreme Court.

In more recent times, the nomination process itself has become the beginning of an ongoing politicization of the Court. The abortive nominations of the Nixon and Reagan years proved that the presidency and Congress at last considered the Court a full partner—with the result that every nominee was scrutinized more carefully. There would be no more Earl Warrens, at least in theory. The effect was a hearing process that had become a national spectacle of partisan politics.

The focal point of that spectacle has been another of the Court's decisions—*Roe v. Wade* (1973). Every candidate for the Court is asked where he or she stands on this case that legalized abortion for most pregnancies. Oddly enough, it was President Nixon's Court, which he had constructed in reaction to the Warren Court's rulings on criminal procedure, that produced this ruling.

Chief Justice Warren Burger knew the importance of *Roe v. Wade* and its companion case, *Doe v. Bolton*, from the moment they arrived in 1971 as two class-action suits challenging Texas and Georgia abortion laws, respectively. In both cases, federal district court panels of three judges struck down the state laws as violating the federal Constitution's protection of a woman's privacy rights, themselves a politically charged issue after the Court's decision in *Griswold v. Connecticut* (1965), which struck down a Connecticut law banning the distribution of birth control materials, largely on privacy grounds.

The majority of the justices agreed with the lower courts but labored to find a constitutional formula allowing pregnant women to determine their reproductive fates. Justice Harry Blackmun, a Nixon appointee, was assigned the opinion for the majority, and based the right on the due process clause of the Fourteenth Amendment, though he clearly had more interest in the sanctity of the doctor-patient relationship than in the rights of women. His formulation relied on the division of a pregnancy into trimesters. In the first of these, a woman needed only the consent of her doctor. In the second and third trimesters, after the twentieth week, the state's interest in the potential life allowed it to impose increasingly stiff regulations on abortions.

The 7-to-2 decision invalidated most of the abortion laws in the country and nationalized what had been a very local, very personal issue. *Roe* would become one of the most controverted and controversial of the Court's opinions since *Dred Scott*, to which some of its critics, including Justice Antonin Scalia, would later compare it. For women's rights advocates it was a decision that recognized a right, but only barely, with qualifications, on a constitutional theory ripe for attack. Opponents of abortion jeered a decision that recognized a state interest in the fetus but denied that life began at conception. They would mobilize against the desecration of religion, motherhood, and the family that they felt the decision represented. The position a nominee took on *Roe* became a litmus test. Congressional and presidential elections turned on the abortion rights question, as new and potent political action groups, in particular religious lobbies, entered the national arena for the first time to battle over *Roe*.

If more proof of the place of the Court in American politics were needed, it came at the end of the hotly contested 2000 presidential election campaign between Albert Gore Jr. and George W. Bush. As in *Marbury*, *Bush v. Gore* (2000) exemplified all three of the political aspects of the Court's place in U.S. history. First, it was a federalism case. Second, the division on the Court matched the political background of the justices. Finally, no case or opinion could have a more obvious impact on politics in that it determined the outcome of a presidential election.

To be sure, there was a precedent. In 1877 another hotly contested election ended with a decision that was clearly controversial, and five justices of the High Court played the deciding role in that case as well, voting along party lines to seat all the electors for Republican Rutherford B. Hayes and none of the electors for Democrat Samuel J. Tilden as part of the commission set up to resolve the dispute. But in *Bush v. Gore*, the disputed results in the Florida balloting never reached Congress. Instead, the justices voted to end the Florida Supreme Court–ordered recount and declare Bush the winner in Florida, and thereby the newly elected president. The majority disclaimed any partisan intent.

Whatever stance one takes on *Bush v. Gore*, the case, like those before it, offers proof that the Court has a role in the institutional politics of the nation, that the members of the Court are political players themselves, and that the Court's decisions can dramatically affect the nation's political fate.

See also House of Representatives; presidency; Senate.

FURTHER READING

Abraham, Henry. *Justices, Presidents, and Senators*. Rev. ed. Lanham, MD: Rowman and Littlefield, 1999.

Greenberg, Jan Crawford. *Supreme Conflict: The Inside Story of the Struggle for Control of the United States Supreme Court*. New York: Penguin, 2007.

Hall, Kermit, et al., eds. *The Oxford Companion to the Supreme Court of the United States*. 2nd ed. New York: Oxford University Press, 2005.

Hoffer, Peter Charles, Williamjames Hull Hoffer, and N.E.H. Hull. *The Supreme Court: An Essential History*. Lawrence: University Press of Kansas, 2007.

Neely, Richard. *How Courts Govern America*. New Haven, CT: Yale University Press, 1981.

O'Brien, David M. *Storm Center: The Supreme Court in American Politics.* 7th ed. New York: Norton, 2005.
Rosen, Jeffrey. *The Supreme Court: The Personalities and the Rivalries That Defined America.* New York: Times Books, 2007.
———. *The Most Democratic Branch: How the Courts Serve America.* New York: Oxford University Press, 2006.
Tomlins, Christopher, ed. *The United States Supreme Court: The Pursuit of Justice.* Boston: Houghton Mifflin, 2005.
Toobin, Jeffrey. *The Nine: Inside the Secret World of the Supreme Court.* New York: Doubleday, 2007.

WILLIAMJAMES HULL HOFFER

tariffs and politics

From the Colonial Period to the Civil War

The tariff bridges economics and politics. As a tax on imports, it juggles local, sectional, national, and international agendas; it divides and subdivides political parties; it conflates profit with policy; it blurs the public and private spheres; it tests political and economic theory. Tariff politics reflects the opportunities and challenges of each historic era, thereby mirroring both national aspirations and national anxieties. Because tariffs have never been proven to either promote or retard economic development, they provide a fascinating window on America's political struggles.

Trade has been central to American political discourse since colonial times. Exchange between Europeans and Native Americans determined the survival of the original settlements and their development as trading posts. Mercantilism, as embodied in England's Navigation Acts, defined the colonies as sources of raw materials and markets for finished goods. While fulfilling this commercial mandate, the colonies also pursued economic self-sufficiency and, consequently, resented economic restrictions.

Eager to raise revenue after the Seven Years' War, which ended in 1763, but stung by colonial protests against direct taxes like the Stamp Act, England turned to indirect taxes via modest tariffs. Low import duties on slaves and on luxuries such as sugar and tea were accompanied by low export duties on raw materials such as wood and wool. Minimal as they were, these taxes offended the colonists. In practice and in principle, they highlighted the disadvantages of political and economic imperialism.

Colonial opposition to taxation without representation created common cause against trade laws. From the 1764 Sugar Act to the 1774 Coercive Acts (which the colonists called the Intolerable Acts), protests mounted and economic policy became markedly political. Petitions to Parliament, boycotts, riots, and tea parties consolidated colonial opposition. Significantly, the First Continental Congress refused to import, export, or consume British goods. Trade clarified the case for revolution.

After the Revolution, the states acquired authority over import and export duties. This decentralized approach reflected the spirit of the 1781 Articles of Confederation, replete with its weaknesses. As a result, the Constitutional Convention of 1787 revisited the issue. Recognizing the need for better coordination and more revenue, the Founding Fathers took tariff-making powers away from the states and gave them to the nation. The tariff issue was so important that it comprised the first and third of the enumerated powers of Congress. Control over commerce was critical to redefining the political power of the central government, and it was no accident that George Washington wore homespun at his inauguration.

Immediately, tariff policy became tariff politics. The first act of Congress was the Tariff of 1789, a revenue-raising measure providing minimal protection to domestic industries with an average duty of 8.5 percent. Engineered through Congress by James Madison, it struck a compromise between nascent northern manufacturing interests, southern agricultural interests, and northern commercial interests. The heated debate over duties on goods and foreign ships was the first open sectional confrontation in the newly united nation and the first step toward party conflict.

Treasury Secretary Alexander Hamilton crystallized the issues with an ambitious four-point program for economic growth, stability, and independence. His 1791 *Report on Manufactures* advocated using the tariff to promote industrial development by protecting infant industries against competing foreign manufacturers. Hamilton's vision of a mixed economy bolstered by centralized power produced the Federalist Party. By contrast, James Madison and Thomas Jefferson feared federal power and the use, or abuse, of tariffs to shape the economy. They drew upon classical free-trade theory, even though they did not want to remove all tariff barriers.

Nonetheless, as slaveholding Southerners, they understood that taxing British manufactured imports would benefit the North at the expense of the South, which depended on England to buy the agricultural goods that fueled the plantation economy. Implicit was a broader anxiety about federal intrusion into states' rights, especially regarding slavery. For the emerging Jeffersonian Democratic-Republican Party, low tariffs for revenue meant less central government and more local autonomy. The tariff was not just a cold calculus of cash.

During the next decade, tensions with England grew over restrictions on American trade, seizure of American ships, and impressment of American sailors. President Jefferson tried to avoid armed war by engaging in a trade war marked by the 1808 Embargo Act. It failed to curtail British smuggling, but succeeded in exacerbating sectional conflict while simultaneously stimulating nationalistic fervor. By 1812 the "War Hawks" had achieved their goal and, for three years, hostilities with England trumped trade.

The combined effect of the Embargo of 1808 and the War of 1812 was to promote northern manufactures and strengthen their cry for protection. After the war, England dumped large quantities of surplus manufactured goods on the American market at low prices, thereby undercutting American-made products. Consequently, even Southerners supported higher tariffs, not only to raise much-needed revenue, but also to aid domestic manufactures in the interest of national defense. For a rare moment, unity prevailed.

The Tariff of 1824 signaled a new era of divisive tariff politics by raising duties to an average of 30 percent on a wide variety of goods. Senator Henry Clay of Kentucky defended the increases as part of an "American System" whereby domestic industry would turn raw materials and agricultural products into finished goods for sale in the home market. However, his Hamiltonian appeal to national economic integration rang hollow to southern planters and northern shippers, both of whom relied on foreign trade and resented sacrificing their own economic interests to Clay's political ambitions.

Pre–Civil War tariff politics bordered on the absurd when, in 1828, low-tariff advocates supported high duties in order to pit interest against interest and defeat pending tariff legislation. Instead, the bill passed with an average duty of 45 percent, backed by an odd coalition of bedfellows willing to accept protection in any form. They were led by Senator Daniel Webster of Massachusetts, whose new support for protection reflected the rise of manufacturing in his state. The aborted scheme is often viewed by historians as a political ploy for Andrew Jackson's election, that is, less for the promotion of manufactures than for "the manufacture of a President of the United States."

The resulting tariff was so inconsistent and so extreme that it was called the "Tariff of Abominations," the first of several emotional labels for supposedly dull, dry tariff bills. It inspired John C. Calhoun, formerly a senator but now Andrew Jackson's vice president, to anonymously write the *South Carolina Exposition and Protest*, based on Jefferson's 1798 claim that states could nullify an act of Congress considered inimical to the general welfare. Nullification moved from theory into practice after Congress passed another tariff in 1832 reducing some rates but raising others. Becoming the first vice president to resign, Calhoun returned to South Carolina and was reelected senator to speak for the South.

A national crisis ensued. Set against the backdrop of rising abolitionist sentiment, the tariff became a test case for states' rights. At Calhoun's urging, South Carolina declared the 1828 and 1832 tariffs null and refused to collect tariff duties. Much to everyone's surprise, President Jackson, a southern slaveholder himself, responded with a Nullification Proclamation that affirmed the supremacy of national law, dismissed nullification as unconstitutional, and resolved to resist South Carolina by force if necessary. Conflict was averted in 1833, when Clay negotiated and Calhoun accepted a compromise that would reduce tariff duties to 20 percent by 1842. The episode underlined the importance of the tariff to presidential politics, sectional antagonism, and American political theory. No wonder it was considered a prelude to Civil War.

The tariff issue continued to fester. In 1842 Congress restored so many duties that Southerners dubbed the new act the "Black Tariff." However, prosperity and surplus revenues justified tariff rates as low as 23 percent in 1846. They remained low until the depression of 1857–60 revived the cry for protection. Although the tariff was not the primary cause of the Civil War, it certainly exacerbated sectionalism. Indeed, with the South out of Congress and wartime expenses mounting, northern legislators systematically raised customs duties in every session, reaching an average of 35 percent by 1865. After the war, Republicans resisted tariff revision despite the reduced need for revenue. The result was conflict over priorities in an era of rapid economic change.

From the Industrial Revolution to the New Deal

The tariff was intensely controversial in the Gilded Age. At issue was the impact of industrialization on prices and wages, markets, and monopolies. Whereas Republicans promoted protection in terms of prosperity and patriotism, most Democrats attacked tariffs as tools of greed and exploitation. Protectionist Democrats complicated matters by derailing their party's efforts to reform the tariff. Lobbyists worked both sides of the aisle.

From the Liberal Republican movement of 1872 through Grover Cleveland's two presidencies, tariff reformers criticized the manipulation of public policy for private profit. They ridiculed the practice of protecting "infant industries" that were really trusts, protested against the influx of foreign "pauper labor," and cited the government's surplus revenue as proof that tariffs were excessive. In 1887 Cleveland called protection an "indefensible extortion and a culpable betrayal of American fairness and justice." During the Gilded Age, the tariff reflected the pitfalls as well as the possibilities of prosperity and progress.

Responding to criticism, Republicans created the 1882 Tariff Commission, which acknowledged the need for reform. However, the Tariff of 1883 made no reforms and was so inconsistent that it was dubbed the "Mongrel Tariff." The presidential election of 1888 was the only one in U.S. history to revolve around the tariff question, which became the vehicle for assessing the impact of industrialism on American life. In the end, the low-tariff Democrats were outmaneuvered and outspent by the high-tariff Republicans. Benjamin Harrison's Electoral College victory over Grover Cleveland, who won the popular vote, begat the 1890 McKinley Tariff, named after its author, the archprotectionist senator from Ohio, William McKinley. The new bill raised rates to an average of 49 percent. However, anger over the resulting rise in consumer prices cost the Republicans the election of 1892.

With Democrats back in control and Cleveland back in the White House, the 1894 Wilson-Gorman Tariff slightly reduced customs duties. Three years later, when the Republicans regained power and William McKinley became president, tariff duties rose again. Levying an average duty of 52 percent, the 1897 Dingley Tariff set the highest rates thus far in U.S. history and, due to 14 years of Republican dominance, lasted the longest. Meanwhile, imperialism provided new resources and new markets for economic expansion.

Concerns about rising prices and gigantic trusts compounded by panics in 1904 and 1907 revived opposition to tariffs during the Progressive Era. In 1909 midwestern insurgent Republicans, led by Wisconsin's Robert M. La Follette, waged a bitter Senate fight against protection. They failed, but the tariff was hotly contested during the election of 1912. Pressured by Democratic tariff reformer Woodrow Wilson, Congress reduced duties to 26 percent, the lowest levels since the Civil War. A new income tax offset the lost revenue. The low 1913 Underwood Tariff survived nine years only to be eviscerated in 1922, when the high Fordney-McCumber Tariff raised average duties back up to 33 percent. Ironically, World War I revived economic nationalism just as the United States was expanding its international role.

The 1930s marked a turning point in American tariff politics. At first, protectionism prevailed when, epitomizing the influence of pressure groups on tariff policy, the 1930 Smoot-Hawley Tariff raised average rates higher than ever, to 52.8 percent. But after other nations responded with retaliatory tariffs, and a worldwide depression devastated international trade, Smoot-Hawley became (and remains) a synonym for disaster. Change came under the Democratic administration of President Franklin D. Roosevelt and his secretary of state, former Tennessee congressman Cordell Hull, who embraced the Wilsonian belief that international trade would further world peace.

Building on aspects of the 1890, 1909, and 1922 tariffs, the president was authorized to negotiate reciprocal trade agreements without the approval of Congress. Republicans opposed this expansion of executive power, but the bill passed in 1934 by a strict party-line vote. Dominated by the State Department until 1962, when Congress shifted power to the Commerce Department, tariffs were gradually reduced by 80 percent. As presidential control over trade steadily expanded, tariff policy making became more administrative than legislative, defined less by politicians than by nonpartisan experts in the U.S. Tariff Commission, created in 1916, and by a U.S. trade representative, created in 1962 within the executive branch.

The Modern Era

Reflecting the nation's superpower status after World War II, U.S. tariff policy was increasingly shaped by foreign policy. Of course, tariffs always had international implications, but they were primarily determined by domestic economic priorities. Now tariffs also became a factor of cold war politics—a bulwark against the spread of communism and a tool for rebuilding Europe and Japan. The favorable balance of trade and a burgeoning economy bolstered America's confidence that it could lead the world in liberalizing trade without losing control over its own economic future.

This international commitment was evident when the 1947 General Agreement on Tariffs and Trade (GATT) was forged in Geneva, Switzerland, not in Washington, D.C. Despite continuing controversy over the president's new powers, Congress passed a series of Trade Expansion Acts from the 1940s through the 1960s. In 1974 the U.S. Tariff Commission was renamed the U.S. International Trade Commission (ITC). By that time, average tariff rates were a mere 8.5 percent, returning to where they began in 1789 and moving toward the virtual free trade level of 3 percent by 2008.

Yet, from the start, the supposedly solid support for free trade was qualified. Market realities demanded escape clauses for retaliating against countries that established non-tariff barriers (NTBs) to trade and quotas or antidumping laws for restricting imports that threatened domestic industries. Unable to prevent trade-induced unemployment, in 1962 Congress began aiding affected workers to adjust and retrain; it also helped affected businesses retool.

By the 1970s, America's international status was no longer secure. The Vietnam War, an oil crisis, inflation, a recession, and a trade deficit undermined the nation's self-confidence. As Japanese goods displaced American goods and the "steel belt" became the "rust belt," protectionism spread. Congress set more limits on executive power over trade agreements, assumed more control of the Tariff Commission, and paid more attention to NTBs, such as foreign import quotas.

Traditional party positions on trade had largely been reversed. Although many Democrats remained committed to international trade, others called for protection against low-wage foreign labor and low-cost foreign products. Facing competition not only from Japan, but also from other East Asian countries and Europe, U.S. labor unions along with the textile, oil, chemical, and steel industries decided that trade liberalization was a "Gattastrophe."

Meanwhile, the traditionally protectionist Republican Party advocated freer trade as big farmers and major corporations sought wider access to world markets. Of course, neither party was unified on trade policy because lobbying and local economic interests cut across party lines. Moreover, trade policies that might benefit one economic interest, like domestic steel producers or sugar growers, might hurt another interest, like domestic steel and sugar users. As always, political party divisions on trade were complex and porous.

Trying to balance these conflicting concerns, advocates of the proposed North American Free Trade Agreement (NAFTA) with Canada and Mexico claimed that profits made by companies expanding abroad would benefit the United States through inexpensive imported consumer goods and domestic jobs created by foreign demand for American products. Although NAFTA was the child of Republican presidents Ronald Reagan and George H. W. Bush, it was endorsed by Bill Clinton, a centrist New Democrat. Clinton's 1992 campaign slogan, "It's the economy, stupid," captured the connection between politics and pocketbooks.

In the 1992 presidential election, it was maverick businessman turned independent candidate Ross Perot who warned against exporting American jobs through generous trade agreements that continued to give concessions abroad without providing protection at home. Ultimately, NAFTA was ratified in 1993 due to support from Republicans and southern Democrats. After a Republican midterm electoral sweep in 1994, Congress approved the GATT, which created the World Trade Organization (WTO).

However, Clinton himself argued with Japan over trade issues, and concerns about trade policy led Congress to rescind the president's fast-track authority. First granted in 1975, this compelled Congress to approve or disapprove trade agreements without changes within 90 days of submission. Although this power was restored in 2002, it was revoked again in 2007, a testimony to the ongoing tensions between the legislative and executive branches over trade policy.

In the early twenty-first century, many Americans still believed that the nation could withstand foreign competition and benefit from freer trade. They were encouraged by a steadily growing gross national product, vast world markets, record corporate profits, cheap consumer goods, and a net gain of jobs. President George W. Bush faced only weak opposition in Congress when he signed free trade agreements with Australia, South Korea, and countries in South and Central America.

At the same time, concerns were growing about trade deficits, de-industrialization, income polarization, and illegal immigration, not to mention the outsourcing of both blue- and white-collar jobs. Critics complained about rules that protected American pharmaceutical companies against importation of cheaper foreign medicines but did not protect American consumers against importation of dangerous toys and poisonous pet food. Anger mounted at countries that sent limitless exports to the United States but that limited imports from the United States. Farmers guarded their government subsidies. Support spread for "fair trade," or "managed trade," to establish international labor, safety, and environmental standards. The multilateralism that had shaped the global economy and dominated U.S. trade policy for 60 years was being reassessed.

Globalization redefined the relationship between producer and consumer, nationalism and internationalism, short- and long-term benefits. Changes in public policy, compounded by revolutions in transportation and communication, created an unprecedented level of international commercial integration. The situation was complicated by the fact that U.S. companies built factories abroad or used foreign parts and foreign raw materials, while foreigners built factories in the United States and invested in the American economy. Domestic and foreign interests were increasingly intertwined. On the one hand, globalization meant economic distress for segments of America's middle and working classes. On the other hand, it presented economic opportunity for other segments of America's agricultural, manufacturing, technology, and financial service interests. With both sides asking the government for support, trade was as personal and as political as ever.

Throughout U.S. history, the debate over international economic exchange has been controversial. Time and again, the issues go beyond profits, prices, wages, and markets to include matters of state: the role of government in the economy, constitutional powers, sectional interests, party politics, and foreign policy. In this sense, Bill Clinton was only half right. It's not simply the economy; it's the political economy, stupid.

See also economy and politics; foreign policy and domestic politics; taxation.

FURTHER READING

Destler, I. M. *American Trade Politics*. Washington, DC: Institute for International Economics; and New York: Twentieth Century Fund, 1992.

Dobson, John M. *Two Centuries of Tariffs: The Background and Emergence of the U.S. International Trade Commission*. Washington, DC: U.S. International Trade Commission, 1976.

Eckes, Alfred E., Jr. *Opening America's Markets: U. S. Foreign Trade Policy since 1776*. Chapel Hill: University of North Carolina Press, 1995.

Irwin, Douglas A. *Free Trade under Fire*. Princeton, NJ: Princeton University Press, 2002.

Kaplan, Edward S. *American Trade Policy, 1923–1995*. Westport, CT: Greenwood Press, 1996.

Kunz, Diane B. *Butter and Guns: America's Cold War Economic Diplomacy*. New York: Free Press, 1997.

Ratner, Sidney. *The Tariff in American History*. New York: D. Van Nostrand, 1972.

Stanwood, Edward. *American Tariff Controversies in the Nineteenth Century*. Boston: Houghton Mifflin, 1903.

Taussig, Frank W. *The Tariff History of the United States*. New York: Putnam, 1931. First published in 1892.

JOANNE REITANO

taxation to 1913

Taxation before 1913 was very different from what it has been ever since. The obvious change came about with ratification of the Sixteenth Amendment, which sanctioned the federal income tax ("The Congress shall have power to lay and collect taxes on incomes, from whatever source derived. . . ."), whose implications unfolded over the ensuing decades. Before then, two features of the tax system were quite different: (1) the federal government relied overwhelmingly on the tariff, a tax on imports, instead of its current mix of income taxes, Social Security taxes, and so on; and (2) states and especially local governments probably did most of the taxing throughout the period. Nineteenth-century figures are sketchy, but by 1913, the states and the nation's many local governments (counties, cities, townships, school districts, etc.) levied two-thirds of all U.S. taxes. By the late twentieth century, the federal government was levying two-thirds.

It is ironic that economic historians have had to struggle to estimate the size of local tax burdens in precisely the period when they were most important. The result, however, is that we know much more about how taxes were enacted, how they worked, and how people argued about them than about how much money they raised.

Federal Taxes

Before the adoption of the Constitution, the national government could not tax. Under Article VIII of the Articles of Confederation, Congress had to finance the Revolutionary War by asking the states to tax. This arrangement, known as the "requisition" system, was disastrous. One problem was that the states simply could not raise enough money through their tax systems, which had been designed in the colonial era, when Britain paid most defense costs. Another problem was the unrealistic rule in the articles for distributing taxes among the states. Article VIII directed Congress to set a quota for each state according to the value of its real estate ("land and the buildings and improvements thereon"). Unable to find a practical way to assess real estate, Congress ignored this rule and set arbitrary quotas based loosely on population (there was no census either). Meanwhile, Congress tried and failed to amend Article VIII to authorize an "impost," a tax on imports that would have been far more practical. Shays's Rebellion (1786), caused in large part by a massive tax that Massachusetts imposed to pay its requisition quotas and other war debts, dramatized the inadequacy of the requisition system.

The U.S. Constitution was adopted for many reasons, but the most immediate need was to establish a national government that could tax. The framers succeeded at this, though at the cost of vague and complex language that caused long-term problems. The Constitution empowered Congress to "lay and collect taxes, duties, imposts, and excises" as long as they were "uniform throughout the United States" and not levied on exports. But in one of the main compromises to accommodate slavery—the three-fifths clause—they inserted another rule. Congress could levy "direct taxes" only if these taxes were apportioned to the states by population (counted by the three-fifths rule). This provision ignored the reality that some states were richer than others, but, remarkably, it did not generate much discussion in either the Philadelphia convention or the ensuing ratification debates. The prevailing assumption was that "direct taxes" would be property taxes of one kind or another, but nobody seemed to think the term was important enough to define precisely.

The reason the direct tax provision drew so little attention is that the real plan was for the federal government to rely on import taxes—like the "impost" that could not be added to the Articles of Confederation. Import taxes were the easiest taxes to collect because they were paid only at ports by small groups of merchants, who then shifted the costs silently into consumer prices. This plan was successful. From the adoption of the Constitution until the War of 1812, import taxes always raised at least 85 percent of federal tax revenue. From 1817 until the outbreak of the Civil War, they were the *only* federal taxes.

But there were complications. In the 1790s and 1810s, Congress also levied other taxes, most notoriously the 1791 whiskey excise that provoked the Whiskey Rebellion of 1794. As the wars of the French Revolution disrupted international trade and came to involve the United States (the 1798 "Quasi-War" with France, the War of 1812 with Britain), Congress levied several other excises as well as apportioned "direct" taxes on property (land, houses, and slaves). One of the excises, a tax on carriages, generated a permissive judicial interpretation of the Constitution's direct tax provision. In *Hylton v. U.S.* (1796), the Supreme Court ruled that a carriage tax was an excise that only had to be uniform rather than a direct tax that had to be apportioned.

The more important complications involved import taxes. The original impost plans were for flat 5 percent levies on almost all imported goods. In the first session of the first Congress, however, tax policy became economic policy, as the impost changed into the tariff—a tax designed not only to raise money but also to "protect" domestic manufacturing by raising the prices of competing foreign products. Protective tariffs, which the United States continued to levy until after the Great Depression of the 1930s, had several critical characteristics. First and most obviously, they subsidized domestic business by letting firms in "protected" industries raise their prices. Tariff supporters justified the subsidies by arguing that the young republic's "infant industries" should be protected against cheaper European (British) goods to promote the growth of American manufacturing. Opponents pointed to another key characteristic: protective tariffs subsidized producers at the expense of consumers, or, more precisely, of producers whose goods were not protected. This category included most American farmers. Unsurprisingly, the leading opponents of protective tariffs lived in the South and West.

Tariff politics also often became rather sordid. Not only did the producers of particular goods scramble to win high rates for their own industries, but debates usually featured intensive logrolling ("I'll vote for yours if you'll vote for mine") and, on occasion, sophisticated partisan manipulations such as high tariffs targeted key blocs of voters. One notorious example was the 1828 "tariff of abominations" that provoked the nullification crisis (1830), in which South Carolina claimed that states could nullify federal laws within their own borders. After 1828, however, the trend was tariff reduction, highlighted by the Walker tariff of 1846.

As productive as tariffs were, they could not finance anything as expensive as the Civil War. The Confederacy, for its part, could not tax imports at all once the U.S. Navy established a blockade of its ports—breached only by "runners" that were small, fast, and unlikely to tarry at custom houses. Nor could the Confederacy tax effectively in other ways. This failure, in turn, undermined its bond sales and doomed its currency to hyperinflation. The Union was a different story. Where the Confederacy raised only 5 percent of its war costs from taxes, the Union raised 20 percent, an achievement that strengthened its credit and supported the value of its "greenback" currency.

The essence of Union tax policy was for the government to try everything. There was a high tariff, a comprehensive excise program, an apportioned direct tax on real estate, and even a small progressive income tax—most interesting for its lack of confidentiality. As the *Chicago Tribune* explained, printing the returns of the richest local taxpayers, "we have been actuated by no motive to gratify a morbid curiosity, but solely by a desire to assist the Gov't in obtaining its dues. No man who has made a correct return will object to the publication, and no man who has made a false return has a right to object." Local governments also taxed to recruit soldiers and help support families in their absence.

Most federal taxes were abolished after the end of the war, though the exceptions were significant. One was the excise on whiskey, which produced an impressive scandal known as the Whiskey Ring. The ring consisted of federal collectors, distillers, and other officials in the big midwestern cities, who not only stole vast amounts of tax revenue but siphoned much of it directly into the coffers of the Republican Party. A long investigation culminated in a series of raids in 1875 that led to more than 100 convictions.

The critical holdover, however, was the high and ever more highly protective tariff. By the late nineteenth century, with tariff supporters unable to make claims about "infant industries," the case for high tariffs switched to protecting the "American standard of living" (higher wage rates). Still, the real case was partisan. Republicans used high protective tariffs to build a powerful and lasting coalition across the North, with protection appealing to many workers while the surplus revenues the tariffs produced—plowed into generous pensions for Union veterans—appealed to many farmers. The tariff so dominated the political rhetoric of Republicans and Democrats that the Populists, in their 1892 Omaha Platform, condemned "a sham battle over the tariff" intended "to drown the outcries of a plundered people" by ignoring what they saw as the real issues.

The 1894 Wilson-Gorman Tariff Act included a small income tax. The idea was to offset some of the tariff costs that Southerners and Westerners paid disproportionately with a tax that would fall heavily on the richer Northeast. Although the Supreme Court had approved the Civil War income tax in *Springer v. U.S.* (1881), rejecting a claim that it was a direct tax that had to be apportioned to the states by population, the Court saw the 1894 version differently. In *Pollock v. Farmers' Loan and Trust Company* (1895), the justices decided that income taxes were indeed direct taxes. Since apportionment by population would have defeated the purpose of income taxation—it actually would have produced higher tax rates in poor states than rich states—the Court ruled the income tax unconstitutional. After a long campaign, the Sixteenth Amendment, adopted in 1913, authorized what would later become the quintessential federal tax.

State and Local Taxes

While the tariff was the critical federal tax before 1913, property taxes were the mainstay of state and local government. Today, American property taxes are levied almost exclusively on real estate. Before the 1910s, however, they were usually levied on both real estate and various forms of "personal property"—"tangible" items such as livestock, vehicles, jewelry, and lavish furniture; "intangible" (paper) assets such as corporate stocks and bonds; and, before the Civil War, human "property" in the form of enslaved African Americans.

By the late nineteenth century, these taxes on real and personal property were called "general property taxes." In language that was as familiar then as the language of income tax deductions and brackets is today, many state constitutions required general property taxes to be "uniform" and "universal." A general property tax was uniform if every form of taxed property was assessed the same way and taxed at the same rate, regardless of who owned it (individual or corporation). The tax was universal if it was levied on all forms of property instead of only on certain items (except a few specified exemptions). Because in practice no taxes could fulfill these mandates to the letter—no assessors could find "all" property or assess the holdings of banks and railroads the same way as those of farmers and country storekeepers—general property taxes were highly vulnerable to legal challenge, especially by wealthy taxpayers and large corporations.

But before the late nineteenth century, there was much more variation. Surveying the state tax systems in 1796, Treasury Secretary Oliver Wolcott Jr. found them "utterly discordant and irreconcileable." The main differences were between North and South. Most northern states had levied versions of the general property tax since before 1776 (or statehood in the West). Until the 1850s, however, many southern states taxed only specific items, and often in idiosyncratic if not downright primitive ways, such as levying one flat sum on each acre of land without assessing its value. Indeed, one reason Congress could not use the real estate apportionment of the Articles of Confederation was that the southern governments had never before valued real estate. The costs of the Revolutionary War prompted innovations in the South, but most were scaled back or abandoned at war's end.

The tricky aspect of early southern taxes was their handling of slaves. In the early republic, many states supplemented their property taxes with poll taxes. In the North, these taxes were highly regressive, as flat sums levied on each male adult regardless of his income or wealth. In the South, however, poll taxes were often levied on free male adults and holdings of enslaved adults of both sexes. This practice meant that southern "poll taxes" actually combined poll taxes on free men with property taxes on slaveholders. As states slashed or abolished poll taxes in the antebellum years (although some retained or later resurrected them), southern states treated slave taxes more forthrightly as property taxes.

By the 1850s, most states were taxing the value of real estate, livestock, financial assets, slaves in the South, and other items such as commercial inventories, vehicles, and jewelry. In the North, this property was included under the general rubric "all property," with the state and local governments imposing rates on each taxpayer's total. In the South, the taxed items usually were specified in detail and often with elaborate schedules of rates for particular items. After the Civil War, however, southern states replaced these systems with general property taxes like those of the North—a change small farmers experienced as massive tax hikes since the loss of the old slave tax revenue raised the rates on land, livestock, and other items.

Urban growth contributed to rising local tax burdens in the late nineteenth century, as the cities professionalized services such as police and fire protection, improved what had been jerry-rigged water and sewerage systems, took the enforcement of building codes and health regulations more seriously, and added amenities such as street lights and parks. But expanding public education probably drove much of the rise in local taxes. Some jurisdictions provided more than others—schools were better and more plentiful in cities than rural areas and in the North than in the South. These distinctions affected relative tax burdens, as local communities weighed the benefits of better services against the costs of higher taxes.

By the 1880s and 1890s, the general property tax was in crisis. While part of the problem was the high cost of local government (sometimes hiked further by political corruption), the real problem was that economic development rendered the tax obsolete. Because of industrialization and urbanization, much if not most of the nation's wealth was held in "intangible" (paper) assets that were hard for assessors to find. As a result, farmers whose property was highly visible—livestock and machinery were harder to hide than stock certificates—objected that urban elites were not paying their share. In fact, however, as urban and rural assessors tried to protect their constituents, competitive underassessments created a chaos of often ridiculously low figures as well as widespread fraud.

Gradually, the states abolished general property taxation and, in particular, the taxation of "personal property." In the new systems, adopted in the early twentieth century, states often relied on income, corporation, and inheritance taxes, while local governments levied property taxes only on real estate. In the 1930s, many state and local governments added sales taxes, producing the system of state and local taxation that is familiar today.

See also economy and politics; tariffs and politics; taxation since 1913.

FURTHER READING

Bensel, Richard Franklin. *The Political Economy of American Industrialization, 1877–1900*. Cambridge, UK: Cambridge University Press, 2000.

Brownlee, W. Elliott. *Federal Taxation in America: A Short History*. New York: Cambridge University Press, 2004.

Dewey, Davis Rich. *Financial History of the United States*. 12th ed. New York: Longmans, Green, 1939.

Edling, Max M. *A Revolution in Favor of Government: Origins of the U.S. Constitution and the Making of the American State*. New York: Oxford University Press, 2003.

Einhorn, Robin L. *American Taxation, American Slavery*. Chicago: University of Chicago Press, 2006.

Seligman, E.R.A. *Essays in Taxation*. 10th ed. New York: Macmillan, 1925.

Taussig, F. W. *The Tariff History of the United States*. 8th ed. New York: Putnam, 1931.

Thornton, J. Mills, III. "Fiscal Policy and the Failure of Radical Reconstruction in the Lower South." In *Region, Race, and Reconstruction: Essays in Honor of C. Vann Woodward*, edited by J. Morgan Kousser and James M. McPherson, 349–94. New York: Oxford University Press, 1982.

Wallis, John Joseph. "American Government Finance in the Long Run: 1790–1990." *Journal of Economic Perspectives* 14 (2000), 61–82.

Yearley, C. K. *The Money Machines: The Breakdown and Reform of Governmental and Party Finance in the North, 1860–1920*. Albany: State University of New York Press, 1970.

ROBIN L. EINHORN

taxation since 1913

Introduction of Income Taxation

The modern era of taxation in the United States began in 1913 with the introduction of the nation's first permanent income tax. During the twentieth century, that tax would become the most important fiscal vehicle for (1) expanding government, (2) centralizing government at the federal level, (3) regulating the economy, and (4) redistributing the costs of government according to the principle of "ability to pay."

The Sixteenth Amendment, which expressly permitted federal income taxation, was ratified in 1913. Later that year, Congress included an income tax within the Underwood-Simmons Tariff legislation. Bipartisan support for income taxation was broad, but the income tax measure enacted was only modest. Virtually none of the major proponents of income taxation, including President Woodrow Wilson, believed that the income tax would become a major, let alone the dominant, permanent source of revenue within the federal tax system. The Republicans who supported income taxation adhered to protectionist orthodoxy and wanted to retain tariffs (taxes on imports) and "sin taxes" (taxes on alcoholic beverages and tobacco) at the heart of federal taxation. And the Democratic drafters of the 1913 legislation regarded the revenue capacity of the tax as far less important than its ability to advance economic justice, through both redistribution of the tax burden and attacking monopoly power. In the first several years of the income tax, only the wealthiest 2 percent of American households paid income taxes.

World War I

The intervention of the United States in World War I, however, transformed the income tax. The disruption of international trade during the war meant that the United States had to reduce its reliance on customs duties. The massive financial scale of the American war effort required the federal government to find new taxes that did far more than just replace customs revenues.

Options were limited. Sin tax revenues were large, accounting for nearly half of all federal tax revenues. But they were not nearly large enough, and expanding the systems for assessing and collecting sin taxes into a system for imposing general taxes on consumption was impossible in the brief period of time (roughly a year and a half) the United States was at war. It was also impossible to expand the fledgling income tax into a system for collecting large revenues from middle- and low-income Americans by setting personal exemptions at low levels and levying high rates on wages and salaries. The federal government lacked the capacity to assess and collect taxes on the Americans—two-thirds of the labor force—who worked on farms or in small, usually unincorporated, nonfarm businesses. During World War I, the federal government did not know who these people were and had no means of readily discovering their identities. The only taxes that raised huge revenues from these Americans were property taxes, and co-opting property taxation for wartime finance faced daunting problems: the interest of states and localities in maintaining control over their powerful revenue engine; the constitutional requirement that a direct tax be allocated to the states on the basis of population; and the extreme difficulty of reconciling the enormous variations in property assessments across the nation.

The impossibility of developing mass-based systems of consumption, income, or property taxation meant that the federal government had only one option—taxing the incomes of wealthy individuals and corporations. This approach allowed the Treasury and Congress to conscript corporations in the army of tax assessors. With corporate data in hand, the Treasury could easily assess the incomes of many of the wealthiest individuals and also tax corporate profits. Within this category of taxation, the Wilson administration had many options and chose a "soak-the-rich" approach, imposing extremely progressive taxes on both corporate and individual incomes. This approach made the American tax system the most progressive in the industrial world. Under the Revenue Act of 1918, the progressive rates of excess-profits taxation ranged from 30 to 65 percent on profits above a "normal" rate of return, which a board of Treasury experts determined. (In contrast, Great Britain took the more conservative approach of taxing profits that were above prewar levels.) Most of the remaining revenue came from a highly progressive income tax on the wealthiest individuals. In 1918 the wealthiest 1 percent of households paid marginal tax rates that ranged from 15 to 77 percent.

The Wilson administration and Congress hoped that such taxes would become a permanent part of the revenue system. They intended the excess-profits tax to act, in the words of one Treasury staffer, "as a check upon monopolies or trusts earning exorbitant profits." The excess-profits tax accounted for about two-thirds of all federal tax revenues during the war, enabling the federal government to cover roughly 30 percent of wartime expenditures through taxes—a larger share of total revenues than in any of the other combatant nations.

The wartime tax program of the Wilson administration, however, contributed to its political downfall. During the congressional elections of 1918, the investment banking community and the leaders of the Republican Party launched an assault, calling for major tax relief from the problem of "bracket creep" (inflation pushing people into higher tax brackets). The Republicans captured both houses of Congress and set the stage for the victory of Warren G. Harding and the "return to normalcy" in the presidential election of 1920. Repeal of the excess-profits tax and reduction of the top marginal rate on individual income to 58 percent followed in 1921.

The progressive income tax itself survived, however. It did so, in part, because both Republicans and Democrats valued the capacity of the tax to fund new programs such as the building of highways. But it was also because Woodrow Wilson, through his handling of wartime finance, had reinforced and enhanced Americans' belief in the justice of taxing according to "ability to pay." In deference to the power of this ideal and to protect the important new source of revenue for domestic programs, Andrew Mellon, the influential secretary of the treasury from 1921 to 1932, cast his support behind preservation of the progressive income tax.

The Great Depression and New Deal

The Great Depression created pressures on the federal government to resume expansion of its taxing capacity and the centralization of fiscal power at the national level. During the early, and most severe, period of the Depression, the federal government reacted to weak tax revenues with major increases in tax rates. Support for them was, to a significant extent, bipartisan. In 1932 Republican president Herbert Hoover initiated the largest peacetime tax increases in the nation's history to close the federal budget deficit, reduce upward pressure on interest rates, and thus stimulate economic recovery. The Revenue Act of 1932 raised personal and corporate income tax rates across the board and restored the top marginal rate to nearly World War I levels. In 1933 Hoover's Democratic successor, Franklin D. Roosevelt, effectively raised consumption taxes through the repeal of Prohibition. The old sin tax on alcoholic beverages, which had remained in the tax code, provided revenue for federal coffers and helped fund the relief and recovery programs of the early New Deal.

As the New Deal continued, Roosevelt turned increasingly to tax reform, which Republicans generally resisted. In 1935 the growing "Thunder on the Left," particularly Huey Long's Share Our Wealth movement, pushed Roosevelt into proposing a tax program that included a graduated tax on corporations and an increase in the maximum income tax rate on individuals. FDR justified this program in terms of both its equity and its ability to liberate the energies of individuals and small corporations, thereby advancing recovery. Congress gave Roosevelt most of what he wanted, including an undistributed profits tax—a graduated tax on the profits that corporations did not distribute to their stockholders. More than any other New Deal measure, this tax aroused hostility from large corporations, and they retaliated by entering the political arena in search of support outside the business community. In 1938 Roosevelt was vulnerable, weakened by the recession of 1937–38 and his disastrous fight to restructure the Supreme Court. A coalition of Republicans and conservative Democrats repealed the tax on undistributed profits.

In 1935 Roosevelt's reform agenda led to another new tax, a payroll tax shared equally between employers and employees to fund the Old Age and Survivors Insurance Program under the new Social Security system. The payroll tax was regressive, although less regressive than the consumption taxes that European governments typically used to finance social welfare expenditures. The incongruity between this regressive initiative and Roosevelt's reforms of income taxation might suggest that he was little more than a cynical manipulator of the powerful symbolism of taxation. But he conceived of Social Security as an insurance system. In his mind, taxpayers received the benefits for which they had paid. Roosevelt's concept was shared by much of the American public, and it lent the payroll tax a popularity that enabled Roosevelt and Congress to expand it significantly in 1939.

During the 1930s, state and local governments also increased taxes to make up for a weakening tax base and finance a growing demand for welfare services. Local governments continued to rely primarily on property taxes, and state governments generally adopted or expanded sales taxes and taxes designed to make users of automobiles and trucks pay the cost of highways. Increasing these taxes offset to some degree the growing progressiveness of the federal tax system, but federal tax revenues grew much more rapidly than those at the state and local levels and continued to do so during World War II. By 1950 state and local tax revenues constituted only 31 percent of the nation's total tax revenues, compared with 71 percent in 1913, at the beginning of the modern tax era.

World War II

World War II created an opening for Roosevelt to continue reform in the realm of taxation. Roosevelt and his military and financial planners assumed that the cost of fighting World War II would be even greater than that of World War I, and they wanted to cover an even larger share of wartime expenses with taxes in order to contain inflation. They needed a tax that would reach far more Americans than had the tax measures of World War I, particularly since Democrats in Congress were unwilling to support high levels of corporate taxation for fear of the kind of backlash that had crushed the Wilson administration.

Roosevelt rejected heavy reliance on consumption taxation as too regressive and favored, instead, a broad-based income tax that would also have a highly progressive rate structure. The broad base, which had been impossible to implement earlier, was now practical because of the information-gathering capability created to collect payroll taxes for the Social Security system and because of a great expansion of corporate employment. Under the new tax system, which included mechanisms for withholding taxes, the number of individual taxpayers grew from 3.9 million in 1939 to 42.6 million in 1945, and federal income tax collections over the period leaped from $2.2 billion to $35.1 billion. In 1944 and 1945, individual income taxes accounted for roughly 40 percent of federal revenues, whereas corporate income taxes provided about a third—only half their share during World War I. And current tax revenues paid for approximately half of the costs of the war.

Mass taxation had become a central element of federal taxation. At the same time, the income tax reached its pinnacle of progressivity. By the end of the war, the marginal rate of taxation on personal income had risen to 94 percent (on dollars earned over $200,000), higher than at any other time in the history of American income taxation. The rates were high enough that, even with the broad base of taxation, in 1945 the richest 1 percent of households produced 32 percent of the revenue yield of the personal income tax.

Issues since 1945

In contrast with Wilson's tax program of World War I, Roosevelt's wartime tax regime survived the war's aftermath essentially intact. This reflected a general agreement by the two major political parties on the need to maintain a large federal government and to keep the World War II revenue system as the means of financing it. Of particular political value was the fact that the new tax regime was generally able to fund the expansion of both domestic and foreign programs, including national defense and prosecution of the cold war, without requiring any legislated tax increases, thus avoiding the unpleasant task of picking losers. Both economic growth and long-term inflation, working through the expansion of the tax base, provided an elastic source of new revenues. In fact, that elasticity enabled the federal government to make periodic, substantial tax cuts.

The convergence on tax policy involved restraint by Republicans in seeking consumption taxation and an acceptance by them of greater taxation of large incomes than they had found palatable before World War II. Republican leaders recognized the political appeal of "ability to pay" and, until the 1990s, did not seriously entertain shifting to a consumption-tax system. For their part, Democrats largely abandoned taxation as an instrument to mobilize class interests. Most dramatically, they abandoned the antimonopoly rhetoric of World War I and the New Deal and adopted instead a more benign view of corporate power.

Republican and Democratic leaders also agreed that there were two major problems with high marginal rates of taxation and, at least through the presidential administration of Ronald Reagan, they often lent bipartisan support to rate reform. The first problem was that the rates, which were the most progressive within the advanced industrial nations, created economic disincentives for wealthy Americans to save and invest. The Kennedy-Johnson tax cuts in 1964 began the work of reducing the high marginal rates, and then the Reagan tax reforms (both the Economic Recovery Act of 1981 and the Tax Reform Act of 1986) continued the reductions, bringing them down to roughly 36 percent.

The second problem was that the high marginal rates tended to undermine the goal of broadening the economic base for taxation. They created incentives for taxpayers to seek "tax expenditures"—loopholes in the form of special deductions and exemptions. The "tax expenditures," in turn, created economic distortions by favoring one form of income over another, made the tax code mind-numbingly complex, and weakened the public's faith in the fairness of the income tax and government in general. The most comprehensive and successful effort to close loopholes was the Tax Reform Act of 1986.

Bipartisan agreement on tax reform broke down quickly, however. Both Republicans and Democrats abandoned any interest in ridding the tax code of tax expenditures. In fact, each party developed a list of new tax loopholes and enacted many of them into law. On the one hand, President George H. W. Bush revived the idea of preferential taxation of capital gains. On the other hand, President Bill Clinton returned to a soak-the-rich policy and, in 1993, led in significantly raising rates on the wealthiest Americans. Meanwhile, he "plumped" for numerous tax preferences for middle-class Americans. The tax cuts of President George W. Bush further increased the complexity of the tax code. One of the goals of these cuts was to advance the transformation of the progressive income tax into a system of regressive consumption taxation. Bush was not able to accomplish this, but his cuts did weaken the revenue capacity of the income tax and thereby the fiscal strength of the federal government. At the end of his administration, the tax rate in the United States (all taxes as a percentage of national income) was lower than in any other major industrial nation, except for Japan. And the surpluses in the federal budgets of the years of the Clinton administration had been replaced by huge deficits that threatened to have major consequences for the future economic health of the nation.

See also economy and politics; tariffs and politics; taxation to 1913.

FURTHER READING

Brownlee, W. Elliot. *Federal Taxation in America: A Short History*. 2nd ed. Washington, DC, and Cambridge, UK: Wilson Center Press and Cambridge University Press, 2004.

———, ed. *Funding the Modern American State, 1941–1996*. Washington, DC, and Cambridge, UK: Wilson Center Press and Cambridge University Press, 1996.

———. "The Public Sector." In *The Cambridge Economic History of the United States*, vol. 3, edited by Stanley L. Engerman and Robert E. Galman, 1013–60. Cambridge, UK: Cambridge University Press, 2000.

Daunton, Martin. *Just Taxes: The Politics of Taxation in Britain, 1914–1979*. Cambridge, UK: Cambridge University Press, 2002.

King, Ronald F. *Money, Time, and Politics: Investment Tax Subsidies and American Democracy*. New Haven, CT: Yale University Press, 1993.

Leff, Mark. *The Limits of Symbolic Reform: The New Deal and Taxation*. Cambridge, UK: Cambridge University Press, 1984.

Ratner, Sidney. *Taxation and Democracy in America*. New York: Farrar, Straus, and Giroux, 1980.

Stein, Herbert. *The Fiscal Revolution in America*. Chicago: University of Chicago Press, 1969.

Steinmo, Svan. *Taxation and Democracy: Swedish, British, and American Approaches to Financing the Modern State*. New Haven, CT: Yale University Press, 1993.

Steuerle, C. Eugene, *Contemporary U.S. Tax Policy*. Washington, DC: Urban Institute, 2004.

Witte, John. *The Politics and Development of the Federal Income Tax*. Madison: University of Wisconsin Press, 1985.

Zelizer, Julian E. *Taxing America: Wilbur D. Mills, Congress, and the State, 1945–1975*. New York: Cambridge University Press, 1998.

W. ELLIOT BROWNLEE

television and politics

Although television as a broadcast medium was technologically viable prior to World War II, after the war it became a commercial reality capable of delivering regular programming to entertain and inform audiences in their own homes. Radio, the most popular mass medium at the time, was quickly displaced as the primary outlet for mass entertainment in American households, as families adopted television at an unprecedented rate—from 8,000 homes in 1946 to 26 million (over half of all households) by 1954. In what is now called the network era of television broadcasting, national television programming was produced by only four commercial broadcast networks—NBC, CBS, ABC, and DuMont (which failed in the mid-1950s)—and public television, which first became available in the late 1960s. Television, therefore, quickly became a centralized source of storytelling, a means through which millions of Americans ritually attended to and understood their nation and their own citizenship.

The Network Era: Broadcasting Politics to Mass Audiences

In the network era, politics was primarily represented through three programming forms, all produced by network news divisions: the evening newscast, political talk shows, and documentary newsmagazines. When nightly dinnertime newscasts first appeared in 1948, they were 15-minute narrated theatrical newsreels edited for television. Not until the late 1950s did the networks dedicate sufficient resources to newsgathering operations. Although the longer-format 30-minute newscast did not appear until 1963, with the start of the nightly *Huntley-Brinkley Report* on NBC in 1956 and the *CBS Evening News* with Walter Cronkite in 1962, television began to offer the viewing public an identifiable and trustworthy personality in the role of the news anchor, a person who presented and interpreted the day's events. Such a role conferred a special status on that individual. Cronkite, once listed as America's "most trusted figure" in an opinion poll, established (if not unwittingly recognized) his role in defining political reality through his trademark nightly sign-off, "And that's the way it is." Network news anchors became the central defining feature of each network's status as institutional mediators between the public and political authorities, with the real or perceived power to influence public opinion. After viewing Cronkite's critical on-air determination that "the bloody experience of Vietnam is a stalemate," for example, President Lyndon Johnson is reported to have said, "If I've lost Cronkite, I've lost middle America."

Political talk shows first appeared on television in 1947, when NBC started broadcasting *Meet the Press*, a weekly program in which politicians and government officials answered questions from a panel of journalists. This format became the prototype for political talk shows for years to come, including CBS's similarly styled *Face the Nation*, which debuted in 1954. As the names of both programs suggest, the networks intended them to represent the public and its interest through their journalistic, interrogational style. The names also highlight the network conception that political talk should be conducted by political "experts" as embodied by journalists (as opposed to philosophers, scholars, or civic activists). Similar shows in the network era included *Agronsky and Company* (PBS, 1969), *Washington Week in Review* (PBS, 1969), *This Week with David Brinkley* (ABC, 1981), and *The McLaughlin Group* (PBS, 1982). What these programs demonstrated over time was not necessarily that they were accessible forums through which the public could understand the issues of the day or see politicians held accountable; instead, they were public spaces through which policy makers talked to one another, signaled their forthcoming actions, justified and rationalized past behavior, and generally enunciated what, in essence, became a working political consensus (often derisively called "inside the Beltway" thinking).

In the early network years, television news divisions embraced the documentary form that had been popularized in film. Famed CBS reporter Edward R. Murrow, who had made his name reporting for radio during World War II, introduced the prime-time news documentary series *See It Now* (1951–58), which covered a variety of political and social issues. Murrow's most celebrated show detailed the tactics behind Senator Joseph McCarthy's anti-Communist crusade (since dubbed *McCarthyism*), and included Murrow's own criticism of the senator. Murrow's use of his television platform, combined with his reputation as an honorable and trustworthy reporter, was an important step toward McCarthy's eventual censure and downfall.

The news documentary form gained more prominence and political importance in the early 1960s when the networks offered several prime-time documentary series, including *NBC White Paper*, *CBS Reports*, and *ABC CloseUp*. In what is now deemed the golden age of documentary television in the United States, this programming included such famous reports as "The U-2 Incident" (government deception in an international spying case), "Harvest of Shame" (the poverty of migrant workers), and "Yanqui No!" (anti-U.S. feelings in Latin America). As the networks suspended much of their documentary output over time, the tradition of documentary television series largely became the responsibility of public television broadcasters (such as PBS's *Frontline*). The networks would find the newsmagazine a more popular and profitable format (comprised of reporting that is much less politically ambitious, while focused on villains who are more clearly defined). CBS developed *60 Minutes* in 1968, which was followed by a host of imitators over the years, including *20/20* (ABC, 1978) and *Dateline* (NBC, 1992).

Through the network era and even beyond, network news divisions continued to be the foremost arbiters of public life, serving as the nexus for citizen knowledge, understanding, and engagement with politics through television. From coverage of institutional political processes, domestic and international crises and events, and social movements to rituals of memory and mourning that mythologized "Americanness," television news helped audiences make sense of politics.

Television transformed modern campaigns and elections in numerous ways. The medium allowed candidates not only to reach mass audiences but also to craft their own image in voters' minds without depending on journalists and other media "gatekeepers" to do it for them. One primary means of such image construction was spot advertising. In 1952 Dwight D. Eisenhower was the first presidential candidate to learn the power of television advertising. Eisenhower chose to run a series of spot ads during entertainment programming, while his opponent, Adlai Stevenson, did not. Historians tend to agree that the ads helped create a warm and friendly persona for Eisenhower, who went on to win the presidency. Since that time, television advertising has become the dominant form of communication between candidates and voters. In contemporary elections, television advertising accounts for between 50 and 75 percent of a campaign's expenditures and is also one of the primary reasons that modern campaigns are so enormously expensive.

Yet candidates used television to do more than shape their own image; they also constructed a negative image of their opponent. Although voters consistently say they deplore negative advertising, studies have shown repeatedly that negative spots are effective in shaping public opinion. Negative advertising also often attracts (free) news media attention, as Lyndon Johnson's famous "Daisy" ad did in 1964. The ad attacked Johnson's Republican opponent, Barry Goldwater, by showing a young girl picking the petals off a daisy while a missile launch countdown sounded in the background, followed by the image of a nuclear explosion. The ad contrasted Goldwater's stated willingness to use small nuclear weapons with the innocence of childhood. Although the ad ran only a few times, its controversial nature assured that it would gain broader circulation through commentary in the news media, while suggesting that Goldwater was too dangerous to be commander in chief.

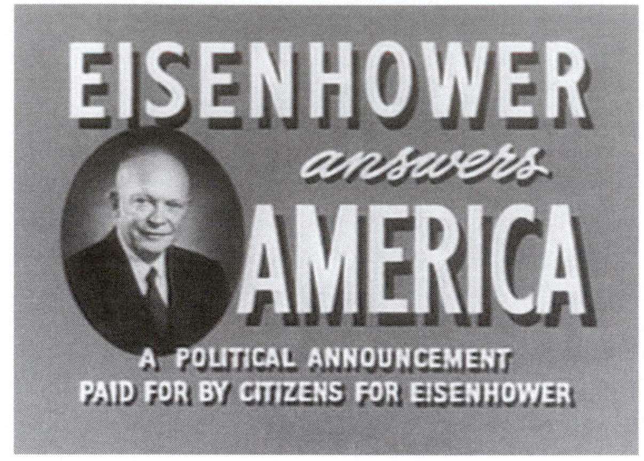

One of the first political advertising campaigns to appear on television, the "Eisenhower Answers America" commercial of 1952 included a short question and answer session between voters and presidential candidate Dwight D. Eisenhower. (Dwight D. Eisenhower Library)

Candidates also tailored their image by crafting campaign appearances to attract news media attention. Derided as "pseudoevents" for their fabricated nature, these events were choreographed more for the television audience at home than the audience present at the event itself. The need for expertise in crafting such imagery in ads and public events led to the rise of political professionals in modern campaigns—pollsters, marketers, and other consultants—adept at information management. The writer Joe McGinnis was one of the first to examine the role of political professionals in campaigns, detailing the rise of this new class of political operatives and their efforts on behalf of Richard Nixon's campaign for president in *The Selling of the President 1968*. Ronald Reagan, a former Hollywood actor and corporate spokesman, realized the need for a tightly controlled media image. He hired California media consultant Michael Deaver, who was widely viewed as a master innovator of modern presidential image making and central in crafting Reagan's popular appeal.

In 1960 presidential candidates began a formal process of debates in front of television cameras. The debate that year between Democrat John F. Kennedy and Republican Richard Nixon also suggested the potential effects that television might have on the process. The intimate scrutiny that the television cameras offered of the two candidates—a young, handsome, and cool Kennedy contrasting with a hot, sweaty, and less-clean-shaven Nixon—was seen as crucial in voters' perceptions of the two candidates. Voters who listened to the debate on radio told pollsters that they thought Nixon fared better, while more television viewers came to the opposite conclusion. The Kennedy-Nixon debate looms large in the historical imagination for suggesting that television performances and imagery are perhaps as important (if not more so) than candidates' policy positions. Although televised presidential debates did not occur again until 1976, such debates have become routine in presidential contests. Over the years, the demands of the commercial medium tended to dictate length, style, and even the allowable number of participants in the general election debates, with third-party candidates often excluded. Television, therefore, did not simply broadcast the event but instead actually composed it.

News coverage of politics extends, of course, beyond campaigns and elections into governance itself. Network television offered extensive "gavel-to-gavel" coverage of important congressional hearings, from the 1954 Army-McCarthy hearings (investigating charges of Communist infiltration of the U.S. Army), the 1973–74 Watergate hearings (surrounding executive misconduct by the Nixon administration), the 1987 Iran-Contra Affair hearings (investigating illegal arms sales to Iran), and the 1991 Anita Hill–Clarence Thomas hearings (examining the sexual harassment allegations by law professor Hill against U.S. Supreme Court nominee Thomas during his confirmation hearings). Such televised events not only offered insight into important political proceedings, but they also became riveting dramas for the millions of Americans who ritually tuned in to watch at home. The hearings often mirrored and pronounced larger political and social issues (the cold war, government secrecy, gender and racial politics), while simultaneously producing great television entertainment.

President Lyndon B. Johnson's controversial "Daisy Ad," broadcast on September 7, 1964, begins with a young girl counting petals on a flower and shifts to a man's voice counting down to the detonation of a nuclear bomb. The next image is of the mushroom cloud of an atom bomb. Johnson's voice then states, in part, "These are the stakes! To make a world in which all children can live." (Lyndon B. Johnson Library)

Television has had a special relationship to the office of the president. The U.S. Congress, with its 535 members, as well as the agencies and departments that comprise the federal bureaucracy, are much more difficult for television reporters to cover—or at least make into compelling stories. Hence, news networks quickly recognized that the president—as symbolic leader of the nation and the singular most powerful politician in Washington, D.C.—made for a good story and good television. The Eisenhower administration was the first to allow cameras to cover presidential press conferences (1955), while John F. Kennedy was the first president to conduct a live television press conference in 1961. Kennedy's easygoing and humorous style was well suited for television, and he is generally regarded as the first president to master communication through the medium. Ronald Reagan and Bill Clinton showed similar skill in succeeding years.

The president's State of the Union address is another moment at which television amplified the power of the presidency; all of the major networks interrupt prime-time programming to carry the speech live. Television has also provided a direct link between the president and the nation in moments of peril, crisis, or extraordinary news. These have included Lyndon Johnson's announcement in 1968 that he would not seek a second term in office; Richard Nixon's resignation from office in 1974; George H. W. Bush's and George W. Bush's declarations of war in the Middle East in 1999 and 2003, respectively; Bill Clinton's apology for lying about his extramarital affairs; and George W. Bush's address to the nation after the terrorist attacks of September 11, 2001.

Television is also an important ritual site of mourning, remembrance, and nationhood during national tragedies. The assassinations of John F. and Robert F. Kennedy, the state funeral of Ronald Reagan, the Oklahoma City bombing, the 9/11 tragedy, and other events became moments at which television news not only provided information and images of the events but offered a collective site of mourning and tribute to the fallen. At these moments, television played its most defining role in crafting a sense of nationhood among the imagined community of citizens. This role also extended to major domestic and international events. Through its coverage of cold war summits, urban riots, and school massacres, or of the terrorist attacks at the 1972 Munich Olympics and the 1979–80 Iran hostage crisis, television news became a primary site through which the public learned about and felt connected to these events.

Television's role in mediating wars has been a source of great concern for politicians, military leaders, and citizens alike. The Vietnam War, in particular, is generally considered America's first television war. While network news coverage was supportive of the U.S. mission during the early years of the conflict, some critics blamed the continued broadcast of images of the war zone, antiwar protesters, and flag-draped coffins of dead soldiers for deterring the war effort by eroding public support for it. Indeed, the idea that the media "lost" the war became so prevalent among U.S. military personnel that the Pentagon instituted a vast array of media management techniques that they deployed in the 1991 Gulf War, including limits on how reporters could cover the war and how the military would conduct it. American television reporters and networks proved remarkably compliant to the military's information management techniques—agreeing, for example, to participate in press pools. Numerous studies have found that media coverage, especially that of national and local television news, was favorable to the point of providing a crucial "cheerleading" role that helped garner and maintain public support for the war.

Television news has also played a strategically important role in its coverage of social movements, at times offering sympathetic images that helped mobilize for change. At other times, though, television has helped marginalize and discredit such groups. The civil rights movement, the anti–Vietnam War movement, the women's movement, and the gay rights movement have all felt the effects of television not only on their success and failures, but also on how each movement should conduct itself. Social movements use television to achieve much-needed publicity and visibility while striving to achieve legitimacy for their cause. National news networks were effective, for example, in broadcasting the dramatic and bloody conflicts of desegregation battles in the Deep South, thereby attracting enormous sympathy and support from citizens and legislators elsewhere in the nation.

In dealing with television, however, movements have come to recognize it as a double-edged sword. To improve their chances for positive coverage, activists have learned to supply attractive or appealing imagery, requisite conflict and drama, messages condensed into sound bites, and access to spokespersons—all of which may simplify the movement and its message, create tensions and disagreements within the leadership, or lead it to engage in activities simply to attract attention. Yet the history of such coverage has shown that television reporters have tended to focus on extreme and angry voices (radicals vowing to use violence), irrelevant matters (the hairy legs of feminists), and negative imagery (the pierced nipples of gay men), all while marginalizing the movement ideologically by counterpoising such images and voices with "normal" "mainstream," or "reasonable" individuals. In short, television offers the mass publicity necessary to bring about change, but news reporters have proven willing to discard norms of objectivity if it makes for sensational programming.

Yet news divisions were not the only ways in which television dealt with political and social issues. Entertainment programming often provided another point of reference, a place in which cultural struggles were also taken up in different narrative ways. For instance, as civil rights legislation was debated in Congress, a young Bill Cosby portrayed a Rhodes scholar and agent of espionage in the television drama *I Spy* (NBC, 1965–68). National discussions about affirmative action, welfare, and integration played out on shows such as *All in the Family* (CBS, 1971–79) and *Good Times* (CBS, 1974–79), while programs such as *Julia* (NBC, 1968–71) and the miniseries *Roots* (ABC, 1977) offered more honest (in terms of the history of slavery and continuing racism) and nonstereotypical portrayals of African Americans. Issues such as abortion, equal rights, and female politicians were taken up in *Maude* (CBS, 1972–78). Even mainstream comedy programs such as *The Smothers Brothers Comedy Hour* (CBS, 1967–69) and *M*A*S*H* (CBS, 1972–83) were able (sometimes successfully, sometimes not) to include antiwar messages during the Vietnam era. Television—including entertainment programming—is a cultural forum in which political and social issues are taken up and discussed, though rarely resolved. Television has also played an important role in shaping people's understanding of public institutions such as the courts, police, and hospitals, as the networks have supplied a seemingly endless array of police, lawyer, and doctor dramas in prime time.

The Cable Era: Audience Fragmentation and Narrowcasting Politics

In the late 1970s and early 1980s, cable television emerged as a programming alternative to network television. Although the broadcast networks continued to shape the presentation of politics on television, cable began whittling away at the numbers of people who regularly watched network programming. While the economics of network television relied on a mass audience, cable television fragmented the audience into narrower demographic slices. Channels that appealed primarily to men, women, youth, and other groups began to appear, while programmers also devoted channels to specific genres such as sports, cartoons, music, news, and religion. For political life, perhaps the most important of these were C-SPAN (Cable Satellite Public Affairs Network) and CNN (Cable News Network).

C-SPAN appeared in 1979 as a noncommercial, nonprofit television network dedicated to covering the proceedings of the U.S. House of Representatives, later expanding its coverage to the Senate in 1986. Funded largely by the cable industry, the channel dedicated itself to long-form public affairs programming. Over the years, C-SPAN has expanded to several channels and covers a wide variety of government, electoral, and public policy activities, with only 13 percent of its coverage now dedicated to the House of Representatives, but it remains one of the few places for extensive and unfiltered coverage of government proceedings unimpeded by opinionated talk and analysis that dominate network news coverage of most political events.

In 1982 Atlanta businessman Ted Turner introduced CNN as the first 24-hour cable news network. Although unprofitable in its early years, CNN redefined the viewing audience's relationship to television news by late in the 1980s. No longer was it necessary for people to catch one of the three network newscasts at dinnertime or the late evening slots at 10 or 11 p.m.; CNN let audiences watch news when it was convenient for them. Although its ratings (viewership numbers) are minuscule in comparison to the network newscasts, its ability to provide continuous and extended coverage of breaking news events (such as the fall of the Berlin Wall, the Chinese democracy movement at Tiananmen Square, and the floods following hurricane Katrina) has made cable news an indispensable resource. CNN became the "go-to" channel during the 1991 Gulf War, as it provided continuous coverage of the Iraqi and American invasions of Kuwait. But the constant need for new material has led critics to claim that the network helped facilitate U.S. government propaganda efforts in that war by beaming live military press briefings unfiltered by editors. Furthermore, scholars began using the term *telediplomacy* to highlight how instantaneous satellite messages (such as those between the Bush administration and Saddam Hussein's regime) might supplant traditional channels of diplomatic communication, especially in times of crisis. In the mid-1990s, critics also began referring to the "CNN effect," surmising that the amount of television imagery broadcast has a direct effect on government action or inaction toward crises around the world. Extended coverage of, for example, starving children in Ethiopia or "ethnic cleansing" in Bosnia is more likely to create public pressure on policy makers to take action than when little or no television coverage exists.

Cable news competitors MSNBC and the Fox News Channel appeared in 1996. Fox News vaulted to the lead of cable news ratings in the early years of the twenty-first century as a conservative ideological alternative to the supposed "liberal" mainstream media. Although Fox branded itself as "fair and balanced," its reporting was widely seen as overtly partisan (Republican). Fox also transformed the presentation of news through its ESPN-style visual graphics and spectacular audio displays while also largely using opinionated talk shows (instead of news reports) to fill its 24-hour programming schedule. The result was that while cable news channels did provide continuing coverage of political events, they also focused most of their attention (because of its ease of production and inexpensive nature) on political talk rather than reporting.

Cable programmers have also ushered in a different variety of political talk on television. Whereas the network talk show model depended on experts and political insiders to do the talking, cable began offering talk shows populated by political outsiders. CNN's *Larry King Live*, which began in 1985, became a site for a less-interrogational style of political talk. From 1993 to 1996, Comedy Central aired a political talk show (which later aired on ABC from 1997 to 2002) hosted by comedian Bill Maher called *Politically Incorrect*, which included a variety of guests from the world of entertainment, music, sports, and publishing—few of whom had any expertise in politics. From 1994 to 2002 on Home Box Office (HBO), Dennis Miller, another comedian, discussed political and social issues with a celebrity guest and fielded phone calls from viewers. In short, cable outlets challenged the network model that tacitly sanctioned certain people—but not others—to talk about politics. While the Sunday morning network talk shows still drew viewers, audiences could also look to nonexperts like radio host Sean Hannity, former infotainment host Bill O'Reilly, and former sportscaster Keith Olbermann for alternative forms of political talk in the cable universe.

Other forms of public affairs programming traditionally handled by the networks increasingly became the province of cable programmers. Beginning with the Republican convention in 1952, for instance, the networks gave party nominating conventions extensive coverage during prime time. The networks saw these conventions as news events and reported them as such. But as the news value of such party meetings subsided (due to changes in party election procedures in the 1970s), the networks reduced the amount of coverage dedicated to them, letting cable news, public television, and C-SPAN offer more extensive coverage. While cable coverage may have proven more thorough than the networks ever provided (such as C-SPAN's gavel-to-gavel coverage of the conventions), the move to cable nevertheless signaled the diminished stature of such ritualistic political events for both the broadcast networks and their mass audiences. The network move suggested that only political events with specific news value, as defined by the networks—not other forms of political communication based on ritual or communal connection to politics—deserved attention. Similarly, presidential debates during primary seasons are now largely carried by cable news outlets. And as the noncommercial public television network PBS came under increased attack by Republicans for what they saw as liberally biased or indecent programming, cutting-edge political documentaries became more readily available on HBO and other cable channels. In short, the competitive environment of television in the cable era resulted in a division of duties between networks and cable channels, with the networks increasingly pushing politics and public affairs away from mass viewership and more into a niche market for the politically interested and aware.

The Postnetwork Era: Interactivity and Public Engagement

Since the rise of the Internet in the 1990s, digital technologies have transformed how people use and view television. Music videos, for instance, were once produced solely for television broadcast. But citizens could now produce their own music videos comprised of both new and existing television images—such as, in 2008, Obama Girl's "I've Got a Crush on Obama" and Will.i.am's pro–Barack Obama ode "Yes We Can"—and circulate them on the Internet, outside the confines of broadcasting's regime. Similarly, citizens were able to mix together snippets of political candidates' interviews on news and talk shows to produce mash-up videos that demonstrate inconsistencies, distortions, and incoherent statements—to produce an alternative interpretation of the candidate. While television imagery was still central to politics, the distribution of production away from centralized institutions affected how political meaning was established in the postnetwork era.

What accompanied this citizen empowerment was a tremendous decline in viewership of television news by young people, many of whom turned to other sources for their news and information. With their departure, and the declining viewership of other demographic groups, the status and authority of network news as primary arbiters of political life rapidly decreased. Certainly the Internet was central to this migration, but so too were alternate sites for information and entertainment on television, such as the Comedy Central's faux news and pundit shows, *The Daily Show with Jon Stewart* (1996–) and *The Colbert Report* (2005–), respectively. As the mainstream news media were misled by the information management efforts of the Bush administration in the run-up to the Iraq War (while also refusing to aggressively challenge such efforts), satirical television programs such as these questioned and challenged the dominant thinking.

Entertainment television further expanded its political programming in the post-network era. Broadcast networks found that dramas and sitcoms about political institutions such as *The West Wing* (NBC, 1999–2006), *J.A.G.* (CBS, 1995–2005), *Spin City* (ABC, 1996–2002), and *24* (CBS, 2001–) could be quite successful with viewing audiences. Similarly, cable networks like Comedy Central flourished by providing biting political and social satire in programs such as *That's My Bush!* (2001) and *Lil' Bush* (2007–8)—the first programs dedicated to ridiculing a sitting president—as well as *South Park* (1997–). Subscription cable channels such as HBO produced daring programs such as *The Wire* (2002–8), a fictional series that examined Baltimore's underground drug economy and the failure of political and social institutions to deal with the intransigent problems of urban decay.

In sum, television in the postnetwork era, like the Internet and other new media technologies, became a place for new narratives of politics and new forms of citizen engagement with political life. Television transformed American politics, and continued to play an important—yet changing—role in the public's relationship to representative democracy.

See also Internet and politics; press and politics; radio and politics.

FURTHER READING

Alterman, Eric. *Sound and Fury: The Making of the Punditocracy*. Ithaca, NY: Cornell University Press, 1999.

Curtin, Michael. *Redeeming the Wasteland: Television Documentary and Cold War Politics*. New Brunswick, NJ: Rutgers University Press, 1995.

Dayan, Daniel, and Elihu Katz. *Media Events: The Live Broadcasting of History*. Cambridge, MA: Harvard University Press, 1992.

Diamond, Edwin, and Stephen Bates. *The Spot: The Rise of Political Advertising on Television*. Cambridge, MA: MIT Press, 1984.

Frantzich, Stephen, and John Sullivan. *The C-SPAN Revolution*. Norman: University of Oklahoma Press, 1996.

Gitlin, Todd. *The Whole World Is Watching: Mass Media in the Making and Unmaking of the New Left*. Berkeley: University of California Press, 1980.

Hallin, Daniel. *The "Uncensored War": The Media and Vietnam*. New York: Oxford University Press, 1980.

Hertsgaard, Mark. *On Bended Knee: The Press and the Reagan Presidency*. New York: Farrar, Straus and Giroux, 1988.

Hollihan, Thomas A. *Uncivil Wars: Political Campaigns in a Media Age*. 2nd ed. New York: Bedford/St. Martins, 2008.

Jones, Jeffrey P. *Entertaining Politics: New Political Television and Civic Culture*. Lanham, MD: Rowman and Littlefield, 2005.

Kellner, Douglas. *The Persian Gulf TV War*. Boulder, CO: Westview, 1992.

McGinniss, Joe. *The Selling of the President, 1968*. New York: Pocket Books, 1970.

Mickelson, Sig. *From Whistle Stop to Sound Bite: Four Decades of Politics and Television*. New York: Praeger, 1989.

Rapping, Elayne. *Law and Justice as Seen on TV*. New York: New York University Press, 2003.

Robinson, Piers. *The CNN Effect: The Myth of News, Foreign Policy and Intervention*. New York: Routledge, 2002.

Thelen, David. *Becoming Citizens in the Age of Television: How Americans Challenged the Media and Seized Political Initiative During the Iran-Contra Debate*. Chicago: University of Chicago Press, 1996.

JEFFREY P. JONES

temperance

See Prohibition and temperance.

territorial government

The U.S. government has administered territories that make up almost three-quarters of the land area of the nation, and its continued possession of territories gives the United States the largest territorial area of any country in the world. The United States governed territories at its founding under the Northwest Ordinance, and it administers them at present in the Caribbean and Pacific. Spanning this vast amount of space and time, U.S. presidents, the courts, and especially the U.S. Congress established territorial governments and set territorial policies. By the same token, because of the lengthy period over which the United States has administered its territories and the size of its territorial possessions, few general rules apply to the U.S. territorial system as a whole.

Only two clauses of the U.S. Constitution discuss territories. Article IV, Section III, Clause 2, states explicitly that "The Congress shall have Power to dispose of and make all needful Rules and Regulations respecting the Territory or other Property belonging to the United States; and nothing in this Constitution shall be so construed as to Prejudice any Claims of the United States, or of any particular State." Clause 1 of Article IV, Section III touches implicitly on the territories: it allows Congress to admit new states into the Union as long as states are not created out of other states or formed by combining all or parts of other states "without the Consent of the Legislatures of the States concerned as well as of Congress." Such language assumed that the new states would be formed out of already existing U.S. territory (or property).

The United States always had territories. Since 1783, the United States had sovereignty over the Trans-Appalachian West, an area roughly double the size of the original states, inclusive of Vermont which was assumed to be part of the Union although it was not an original state. The U.S. government acquired the Trans-Appalachian West from Great Britain according to the terms of the 1783 Treaty of Paris. But the entire tract belonged solely to the U.S. government, rather than to any state or group of states, under the terms of the ratification of the Articles of Confederation. Maryland had insisted that before it would approve the articles (which had to be ratified unanimously), the states with claims on the Trans-Appalachian West (Connecticut, Virginia, North Carolina, South Carolina, and Georgia, in particular) first had to surrender those claims to the U.S. government. The states agreed, surrendering their claims over a period of years. The result was that the fledgling U.S. government now controlled the vast lands beyond the Allegheny (and Appalachian) Mountains and up to the banks of the Mississippi River, as the "public domain."

The Constitution said little about the territory of the United States, and the Trans-Appalachian West attracted little discussion in Philadelphia, because Congress had already taken action. Under the Articles of Confederation and Perpetual Union, Congress had passed the Land Ordinance of 1785, which established a grid system for surveying the lands of the public domain, held that government land was to be sold at auction for no less that one dollar an acre, and mandated that the land be sold either in townships of 36 square miles for groups of settlers or in single sections (640 acres) for individual buyers. More significantly, during that same summer in Philadelphia, Congress, under the Articles of Confederation, passed the Northwest Ordinance on July 8, 1787, for the purpose of establishing territorial government in the area north and west of the Ohio River.

The Northwest Ordinance and Its Legacy

The purpose of both the Land Ordinance and the Northwest Ordinance was for the United States to develop the vast public domain through policies that would encourage settlement and then political incorporation into the Union through the formation of territorial governments. The U.S. government would thus be able to transform what white European Americans saw as unproductive and unpopulated wilderness into economically productive and politically contributing regions of an expanded republic. But the territories were to be under the authority of the federal government until they were ready for statehood.

Thomas Jefferson, James Monroe, and Nathan Dane drafted the Northwest Ordinance with this premise in mind: the Northwest Territory was to be administered "for the purpose of the temporary government." Congress could then decide "at as early periods as may be consistent with the general interest" to admit the territories as states, annexed on an "equal footing" with the existing states of the Union. The Northwest Ordinance was to be a covenant between the European Americans who had emigrated beyond the existing several states proper and those who still lived in those states. The founders assumed that the persons in the Northwest Territory were other European Americans, suitable for eventual citizenship in one of the states of the Union.

The Northwest Ordinance explicitly stated that its first four articles were "articles of compact, between the original states and the people and states of the said territory." Articles I and II, foreshadowing the Bill of Rights, protected the civil liberties of territorial residents by guaranteeing the free expression of religion, the rights to habeas corpus and trial by jury, the prohibition of cruel and unusual punishment, the unlawful deprivation of property, and infringements on contracts.

James Madison, George Mason, and other founders meeting in the summer of 1787 in Philadelphia recognized that they could not restrict European Americans from emigrating farther westward and deeper into the South. Rather than trying to restrict Americans from moving farther west and south, and rather than risking alienating their fellow Americans from the newly formed United States—and possibly inciting them to affiliate with Britain or Spain, instead—the founders sought to induce their fellow Americans to stay within the United States by becoming residents of newly formed territories that over time could become states within the Union.

The Northwest Ordinance thus set the terms for the temporary administration and government of the old Northwest until such time that the territories had "grown up" enough to become states. It divided the area north and west of the Ohio River into administration districts, each of which had to proceed through a three-stage process before becoming a state. The first stage was the creation of a district government under Congress's sole authority, wielded through an appointed governor, a secretary, and three judges (after 1789, when Congress, acting under the new U.S. Constitution, "repassed" the Northwest Ordinance and stipulated that the U.S. president was to make the appointments). The second stage, reached once the district had 5,000 adult white male inhabitants, consisted of the establishment of a territorial government composed of a locally elected legislature, a governing council, and three judges. All elected officers also had to fulfill minimum property requirements. The governor had near-total power; he had absolute veto power over the legislature and could convene or dismiss the legislature at will. The third stage was achieved once the territory had achieved a recommended population of 60,000 persons (*not* an absolute requirement per the terms of the Northwest Ordinance) and once it had set up a republican government under a written constitution. The organized territory could then petition Congress for statehood.

The Northwest Ordinance acquired near-constitutional status, despite its application only to the old Northwest. There were several reasons for its great legacy. The drafting and passage of the Northwest Ordinance and Land Ordinance preceded the drafting and ratification of the Constitution, so by implication, the Constitution did not need to address the matters of the territories or political expansion of the United States in any detail. In addition, rules about how the public domain was to be disposed and settled carried immense stakes for more than a few of the founders, who had invested heavily in the public lands—whether individually, or indirectly by investing in land companies. The land issue was highly contentious and since it had been a sticking point with respect to the states' approval of the Articles of Confederation, the founders were understandably reluctant to take on the topic in the Constitution. Instead, they could leave decisions on the public domain and the territories for future Congresses, presidents, and judges to settle.

The principal reason for the lasting impact of the Northwest Ordinance, though, was the immensity of subsequent U.S. expansion; the founders scarcely envisioned the geographic scope that the nation would eventually encompass. With the Louisiana Purchase of 1803, the acquisition of West Florida (1811) and East Florida (1819), the 1846 Oregon Cession, the 1848 Mexican Cession, the 1867 purchase of Alaska, and other additions, the total area of the U.S. acquisitions reached 1.2 billion acres.

It remained for Congress to divide the new tranches of public domain into districts and territories, decide on territorial policies, and annex them as states—if often with different borders than when the territories were first drawn up. Congress established 74 separate territories of different boundaries and duration, eventually resulting in the creation of 31 states. Neither could the founders have imagined that the United States would possess territories spanning continental North America and reaching into the Caribbean Sea (Puerto Rico, the U.S. Virgin Islands) and Pacific Ocean (Guam, the Philippines, Hawai'i, American Samoa, and the Northern Marianas). Nor could the founders have known that territorial acquisitions would continue from 1787 (with the establishment of the Northwest Territory) until 1975 (with the addition of the Northern Marianas), and that the United States, 230 years after the Declaration of Independence, would still have five territories in its possession.

The precedent set by the Northwest Ordinance thus applied not only to the five states created from the Northwest Territory but served as the template for the addition of the dozens of other territories forged out of the new areas periodically acquired by the U.S. government. With the Constitution providing little direction for the government of territories, the processes specified in the Northwest Ordinance continued to be applied throughout the nineteenth century and into the twentieth, as the new U.S. territories transitioned into states. The United States grew from 16 states in 1800 to 23 states in 1820, 26 states in 1840, 33 states in 1860, 38 states in 1880, 45 states in 1900, and 48 states in 1920. The last two states, Alaska and Hawai'i, were added in 1959.

The Insular Territories

The historical trajectory of U.S. territorial development was disrupted after the Spanish-American War. None of the territories the United States acquired after 1898, except Hawai'i, were later annexed as states, nor did the islands acquired in 1898 and 1899 (Puerto Rico, Guam, the Philippines, and American Samoa) or in the twentieth century (the U.S. Virgin Islands in 1917, and the Northern Marianas, a United Nations trust territory of the Pacific Islands administered by the United States and annexed in 1975), become states. (The territories already existing in 1898—Oklahoma, New Mexico, Arizona, and Alaska—did, of course, become states). The present U.S. territories are not in a designated transition period toward statehood; they are not likely to be annexed as states in the foreseeable future, and it is highly unlikely that they will be let go to become independent states or the possessions of other powers.

Hawai'i, annexed three days after the close of the Spanish-American War, was controlled politically and dominated economically by a small white ruling class (*haoles*), a situation that none of the other new island territories shared. With its white ruling class, its value as a naval station and midoceanic port, and its sugarcane production, Hawai'i was much more acceptable to the U.S. Congress as a territory—and, much later, as a state—than were the other U.S. possessions in the Caribbean and the Pacific islands, which were densely populated with nonwhite residents.

The Supreme Court ratified this new direction in U.S. territorial history. In a series of closely decided and controversial decisions known as the Insular Cases, the Court ruled that the United States could exert sovereignty over territories that were not fully incorporated into the nation and not fully protected by the provisions of the Constitution. Congress could rule these nonincorporated territories under the sweeping authority of the territory clause to "make all needful Rules and Regulations respecting the Territory or other Property belonging to the United States." Congress could also impose tariffs on trade going to and from the island territories and the states proper; it could deny territorial inhabitants trial by jury; and it could withhold other guarantees and protections of the U.S. Constitution and its amendments. It was Congress's perogative to choose whether to extend all rights and privileges guaranteed by the Constitution to its territories.

No longer did territorial governments have to be temporary or serve under transition periods until statehood, in contrast to the precedent set by the Northwest Ordinance. Instead, the United States could keep a "conquered country indefinitely, or at least until such time as the Congress deemed that it should be either released or retained," as Justice Edward Douglass White wrote in his concurring opinion in *Downes v. Bidwell.* Justice White, along with a majority of justices on the Supreme Court, U.S. presidents from William McKinley onward, most policy makers, many political and legal scholars, and most of the American public, agreed that the new island territories could be kept permanently as territories, according to the best interests of the United States, since as they saw it the inhabitants of the new territories were not suited to become members of the American polity. The Court and most Americans further agreed that the United States could divest itself of its territories, something it could not do with the states. And Congress did precisely that when it released the Philippines from territorial status in 1946.

Congress and Territorial Government

Throughout U.S. history, Congress oversaw the administration of the territories and set territorial policy. Congress governed the territories by passing "organic acts" for the establishment of territories with organized governments. The dozens of territorial organic acts took remarkably consistent form, and many of the differences among them were minor—at least until the addition of the U.S. island territories.

Each of the organic acts defined territorial boundaries; each specified that the U.S. president was to appoint the principal officers in the territory (the governor, secretary, and judges), and to set their terms and salaries; and each established court systems and judicial jurisdictions. Each also mandated that a nonvoting congressional delegate be selected for the U.S. House of Representatives, with a limited term in office (with the exception of the territories of Alaska and Hawai'i), and each either determined the location of the territory's capital city or authorized the territorial legislature or territorial governor to decide the location of the territorial seat of government (with the exception of the organic acts for the territories of Florida, Arizona, and Hawai'i).

The territorial acts specified, too, that only free white adult males could vote or hold office, with the exceptions of the territorial acts for Arkansas, Montana, Wyoming, and the island territories, including Hawai'i. The territories of Montana (1864) and Wyoming (1868) were established during and after the Civil War, however, and were the last two territories formed out of the area to become the lower 48 states (with the exception of Oklahoma, which became a state in 1907). Since the Caribbean and Pacific territories had predominantly nonwhite populations, restricting suffrage and office holding to adult white males would have made little sense.

For the most part, the territorial acts avoided mention of slavery. The Northwest Ordinance prohibited slavery, but only the territorial acts establishing Indiana Territory (1805) and the organic acts for the Philippines (1902) and for Puerto Rico (1917) also explicitly prohibited slavery. Slavery in the territories was determined, instead, by the Constitution's prohibition on importing slaves after 1808, and by the Missouri Compromise restricting slavery to areas below 36° 30′ latitude. A few of the territorial acts followed Stephen Douglas's principle of popular sovereignty and allowed the territories (e.g., New Mexico, Utah, Kansas, and Nebraska) to decide whether they would become free or slave states at the time of their annexation. In the instance of Kansas and Nebraska, though, Congress's organic act stipulated that the territories had to recognize the Fugitive Slave Act—the only territorial governments for which Congress made such an explicit requirement.

Although some territorial acts specified that the Constitution and all the laws of the United States were to apply in full, most simply assumed this to be the case. Congress explicitly extended the Constitution and the laws of the United States to the territories in its organic acts only when the territories in question—New Mexico, Utah, Colorado, Nevada, North and South Dakota, Wyoming, Puerto Rico, Hawai'i, and Alaska—were created under conditions that elicited Congress's caution: New Mexico had a majority Hispanic population; Utah was populated largely by Mormons; Colorado, Nevada, and the Dakotas were organized in 1861, during the Civil War, and Wyoming was organized in 1868, shortly afterward; Puerto Rico and Hawai'i had majority non-European-American populations; and Alaska had a miniscule white population and majority indigenous population of Inuit and other Eskimos.

In addition, the organic acts establishing the territories of the midwestern and western United States, from Oregon (established in 1848) through Oklahoma (1890), required progressively more of their new territorial governments. They mandated that land sections be reserved for schools, for instance, and that congressional funds be dedicated for the erection of public buildings such as capitols or libraries in the territorial capitals. Other acts specified the construction of prisons. In Oklahoma Territory, Congress limited the use of railroad bonds and railroad scrip, directed that homestead titles in Oklahoma be given to U.S. citizens only, and specified that any treasury appropriations be explicitly explained and defined.

When Congress established territorial governments in Hawai'i (1898), Puerto Rico (1900, and then again in 1917), Alaska (1912), and the Philippines (1916), however, it departed from an earlier practice; it did not require that the chief territorial officers be appointed by the U.S. president. Nor did Congress at the time call for these territories to assign delegates with term limits to U.S. House of Representatives. That would only come later; the Northern Marianas did not send a nonvoting territorial delegate to Congress until so approved by the 110th Congress in 2008.

Congress and Territorial Policy

Besides establishing the fundamentals of territorial government, Congress set public policies on numerous issues that affected the security, wealth, and political development of the territories. Congress set—and continues to set—territorial policy with respect to commerce (taxes, tariffs, shipping regulations, etc.), military affairs (military spending, troop levels, troop movements and positioning, the construction of forts, naval bases, and other military installations), communications (railroads, telegraphy, telephony, television, etc.), and other issues. Throughout much of U.S. territorial history, too, Congress set policies on Indian affairs, slavery, and the disposal of government lands that affected all the territories—and often the states as well.

Much of this policy making revolved around money, since Congress subsidized much territorial development.

Congress funded the exploration and mapping of the territories by the U.S. Army Topographical Corps (and later the Army Corps of Engineers), which conducted surveys, mapped terrain and waterways, and planned road, canal, and railroad routes. Congress also paid for the construction of outposts for the U.S. military, given that the territories often featured desirable ports (New Orleans, San Francisco, Honolulu, San Juan, Manila Bay, Guam, Pago Pago) and provided choice sites for the construction of forts, arsenals, and other military establishments. As the United States added to its public domain, so too did the number of forts in the territories (including camps, barracks, arsenals, and river defenses) grow—although not in every instance—from 8 in 1800, to 12 in 1820, 12 in 1830, 13 in 1845, 69 in 1870, and 57 in 1885.

Forts and naval stations also constituted favorable locations for the conduct of trade and as sites for towns and cities. Furthermore, in the Midwest, on the Great Plains, and in the Mountain West, U.S. military personnel were able to assist westward migrants (and thereby facilitate further settlement) by providing information on travel routes; assisting sick and exhausted overland travelers; furnishing crucial supplies, including guns and ammunition; and providing refuge against Indian attacks. The U.S. territories and the public domain may have constituted a buffer between existing states and hostile Indians or foreign powers, but they also promoted the economic growth of the nation.

Emigrants to the new areas could engage in farming, ranching, mining, shipping, and other productive activities. Congress encouraged these activities in several ways. For one, it enacted liberal immigration policies throughout most of the eighteenth and nineteenth centuries, thereby allowing the United States to increase its population quickly. Many of these new immigrants either settled immediately in the west or emigrated west within a generation, given the additional space and opportunities the territories afforded them. Congress also helped territorial development by providing postal service—and thus transportation—to its territories by stagecoach, and then by rail at below cost. The 21,000 total post-road miles in the United States in 1800 (inclusive of the states and the territories) doubled to 44,000 by 1815. That doubled again to 94,000 miles by 1825, and came to a total of 144,000 miles by 1845. These roads connected the large and growing number of post offices in the states and territories.

While the overwhelming majority of post offices were in the states, many were in the territories. The number of post offices in U.S. territories grew from 10 in 1800 to 177 by 1820, 374 by 1830, and 346 by 1845. In 1885 the territories had 2,519 post offices, up from 532 in 1870. As Alexis de Tocqueville expressed in amazement, "the district of Michigan" already had "940 miles of post roads," and "[t]here were already 1,938 miles of post roads through the almost entirely wild territory of Arkansas." Whereas the United States had 74 post offices per 100,000 residents in 1838, Britain had just 17, and France had just 4. For the Americans living in the territories and on the frontier, especially, mail was the "soul of commerce" and critical to their economic and political future.

Congress further subsidized the development of the territories through land grants. While the Homestead Act of 1862 may be the best-known subsidy in the western states, more important by far were the number and scale of Congress's railroad land grants during the mid-nineteenth century. These checkerboard grants, totaling more than 100 million acres, facilitated rail service in territories and across the continent; they encouraged movement and land speculation that often preceded significant human settlement or other economic activities. The railroad land grants provided faster and better transportation and communication, and promoted far more economic activity, than the railroads would have provided absent government subsidies.

The cumulative effect of Congress's policies with respect to the railroads, the post, and the military was to lay the foundation so that others—such as farmers, ranchers, miners, bankers, and businessmen—would populate the public domain, settle in the territories, form territorial governments, and eventually join the United States as full citizens.

Congress's Plenary Power

Residents of the territories had little recourse if they thought that Congress did not do enough to protect them from Indian violence, survey and administer land sales, or provide for mail service. If Congress set the key policies that affected the residents of the territories, it was not electorally accountable to them—even if they predominantly consisted of European Americans. Members of Congress were elected by voters in the states and in the congressional districts created within the states, with the result being that the residents of the territories were effectively disenfranchised, without a voice in their political and economic futures—whether such persons were white American émigrés, enslaved or free African Americans, Mormons, American Indians, Puerto Ricans, or the Chamorros of Guam and the Northern Mariana Islands.

For some territorial residents, this disenfranchisement was relatively short-lived; it took Kansas just seven years to become a state after becoming an organized territory (1854–61), and nine years for Missouri (1812–21) and Minnesota (1849–58). Other territorial residents experienced much longer periods of disenfranchisement: New Mexico, for instance, with its dominant Hispanic population, was annexed as a territory in 1850 but not annexed as a state until 1912; Utah, with its Mormon population, was annexed as a territory in 1850, but not admitted as a state until 1896 (after it renounced polygamy in 1890); and Hawai'i, with its Polynesian and Asian population, was annexed in 1898 but not admitted as a state until 1959. The island residents of Puerto Rico, Guam, and the other current U.S. territories (all formally U.S. citizens except for American Samoans) remain without effective representation in the U.S. House of Representatives, Senate, or Electoral College.

Congress has therefore been able to set territorial policy according to its interpretation of the U.S.'s "general interest." The definition of that interest depended on party alignment, sectional balance, and the dominant interests of the day. Congress created districts and territories, drew up territorial boundaries, and decided exactly when to annex territories as states as it judged most expedient. In particular, Congress could decide when to form territorial governments and when to retain territorial governments, delaying their annexation as states.

For the 31 states that had formerly been territories, it took an average of 40 years between the time the area came under U.S. sovereignty and the time Congress annexed the area as a state. Since neither the Constitution nor the Northwest Ordinance set a time frame for admitting qualified territories as states once they petitioned for annexation, Congress used its own discretion to decide when territorial governments could become states. Sometimes the lengthy struggle for statehood was a matter of ethnicity, as with the delays in admitting Oklahoma and its Indian population (1803–1907) and New Mexico and its dominant Hispanic population (1848–1912). Other times, the delays were caused by low territorial populations, as in the Dakotas (1803–1889), Arizona (1848–1912), and Alaska (1867–1959).

Another cause for delay was slavery. Congress in the antebellum United States timed the annexation of states to balance the number of free states and slave states; it accordingly admitted some states in successive years to retain the balance in the U.S. Senate, such as Illinois (1818), Alabama (1819), Maine (1820), Missouri (1821), Arkansas (1836), Michigan (1837), Florida (1845), and Iowa (1846). Congress admitted "battle born" Nevada in 1864 despite its relatively low population (30,000 to 40,000) because it anticipated support from the territory for President Lincoln, the Republican Party, and their wartime policies.

After 1898, however, questions of timing became moot, since Congress and the U.S. government decided that the island territories would remain territories; territorial governments were no longer temporary. The present-day U.S. Caribbean and Pacific territories have their own elected legislatures, executive branches, and court systems—the rulings of which may be appealed to the U.S. federal courts—but the U.S. Congress and executive branch decide trade policy (e.g., fishing and customs laws), set citizenship and immigration requirements, make telecommunications policies, and oversee criminal proceedings. The constitution of the commonwealth of Puerto Rico forbids capital punishment, for instance, yet Puerto Ricans may still be executed in mainland U.S. prisons for capital crimes committed under federal law.

Executive Influence

Congress may have had plenary power over the U.S. territories, but the executive branch was often able to exert its own considerable influence. One form such influence took was the U.S. president's appointment of territorial governors—at least in the cases of the continental "incorporated" territories—unlike the elected governors of the later island territories. The territorial governors could dominate their legislatures through their powers of absolute veto and their authority to convene or dismiss the territorial legislatures. They could decide if and when to hold censuses and referenda so as to determine when their territories could enter the second stage of territorial government, and if and when to hold elections for delegates for a constitutional convention. Furthermore, the governors had significant authority in their multiple roles as the commanders of the local militia, superintendents of Indian affairs in the territory, and overseers of the disposal of public lands (even if Congress set the overall land policy).

Territorial governors, as a general rule, were ambitious men who saw their roles as stepping-stones to higher office and better positions. Despite the governors' relatively low salaries and scarce resources, many of them were popular with their territorial residents and seen as political assets by U.S. presidents. Territorial governors served on average more than three years in office, a tenure almost as long as the average for the elected governors of the states. Among the most famous of the governors were later U.S. president William Henry Harrison (governor of the Indiana Territory), William Clark of the Lewis and Clark expedition (governor of the Missouri Territory), secretary of war and presidential candidate Lewis Cass (governor of the Michigan Territory), explorer and presidential candidate John C. Frémont (governor of the Arizona Territory), and the prominent Federalist and former president of the Continental Congress, Arthur St. Clair (governor of the Northwest Territory).

Scarce funding from Congress and general neglect of the territories, however, meant that territorial governors could not, as a practical matter, rule autocratically. Congress was notoriously stingy about funding land offices, providing sufficient resources for Indian affairs and internal improvements, and granting enough personnel to execute other governmental policies in the territories. As a result, territorial governors had to work with other key individuals and dominant economic interests in the territories, such as railroad companies, banks and other investors, mining companies, and large eastern or foreign landowners. Conversely, governors who did not work closely with the prominent individuals and dominant interests in the territories were typically ineffective (e.g., Governor St. Clair of the Northwest Territory). The logic of territorial government led to a government brokered by the established individuals, major economic actors, and other principal interests of a territory—in effect, to oligarchical territorial government.

U.S. presidents also governed the public domain through the military. Military governments were often the product and continuation of conquests, such as that of General Andrew Jackson in Florida or General Stephen W. Kearny in New Mexico and Arizona, until such time that Congress was able to pass organic acts and establish formal territorial governments. Florida was under military government from 1819 to 1822, for instance; Louisiana was under military rule from 1803 to 1804; New Mexico from 1846 to 1851; and Puerto Rico from 1898 to 1902. (The U.S. Army also managed the Panama Canal Zone while it was leased to the United States.) The U.S. Navy administered and governed Guam from 1898 until 1952, American Samoa from 1899 to 1952, and the U.S. Virgin Islands from 1917 to 1931.

The Many Systems of the Territorial System

There was no single system for the government of the territories of the United States, just as there is no one principle that orders the history of the United States' government of its territories. The brevity of the territorial clause made it inadequate for administering the public domain and led to the lasting precedent set by the Northwest Ordinance. Yet the Northwest Ordinance, for all of its long-lasting impact, did not serve as a blueprint for the government of the later island territories.

Territorial government was shaped by slavery and the Civil War, Indian policy and U.S. strategic concerns, Mormonism and disregard for other than European-American populations, economic interests and trade policies, and a host of other factors. Whereas the territories were once as close to the states as the Pennsylvania-Ohio and Georgia-Florida boundaries, they later became more distant geographically, separated by thousands of miles of land or sea. The result is that territorial government changed considerably, from the tighter control of the first U.S. territories to the less direct control of the later continental territories. The government of the Philippines, for instance, achieved increasing autonomy through the territorial acts of 1902, 1916, 1937 (when the Philippines became a "commonwealth"), and 1946 (when it achieved formal independence). Similarly, the Puerto Rican government, officially organized by the Foraker Act of April 2, 1900, was amended by the Jones Act of March 2, 1917 (which provided Puerto Rico with three separate branches of government and granted Puerto Ricans U.S. citizenship), and then Public Law 600 of July 4, 1950 (which conferred commonwealth status on Puerto Rico and enabled Puerto Ricans to draft their own constitution).

But such changes in U.S. territorial government did not depend on the Constitution, existing federal laws, or the territory in question. The ultimate control exercised by the U.S. Congress, executive branch, and Supreme Court was the by-product of other issues: economic development and industrial growth; sectoral rivalry and party politics; U.S. foreign policy interest and grand strategy; and considerations of citizenship and American identity.

See also Alaska and Hawai'i; Great Plains; Midwest; Pacific Coast; Rocky Mountain region.

FURTHER READING

Bloom, John Porter, ed. *The American Territorial System.* Athens: Ohio University Press, 1973.

Carter, Clarence Edwin, and John Porter Bloom, eds. *Territorial Papers of the United States*. 28 vols. Washington, DC: U.S. Government Printing Office, 1934–.

Dick, Everett. *The Lure of the Land: A Social History of the Public Lands from the Articles of Confederation to the New Deal*. Lincoln: University of Nebraska Press, 1970.

Eblen, Jack Ericson. *The First and Second United States: Governors and Territorial Government, 1784–1912*. Pittsburgh, PA: University of Pittsburgh Press, 1968.

Goetzmann, William H. *Army Exploration in the American West, 1803–1863*. Lincoln: University of Nebraska Press, 1979.

Goodrich, Carter. *Government Promotion of American Canals and Railroads 1800–1890*. New York: Columbia University Press, 1960.

Grupo de Investigadores Puertorriquenos, *Breakthrough from Colonialism*. 2 vols. Rio Piedras: Editorial de la Universidad de Puerto Rico, 1984.

Leibowitz, Arnold H. *Defining Status: A Comprehensive Analysis of United States Territorial Relations*. Dordrecht, Netherlands: Martinus Nijhoff, 1989.

Meinig, Donald William. *The Shaping of America: A Geographical Perspective on 500 Years of History*. 3 vols. New Haven, CT: Yale University Press, 1986, 1993, 1998.

Onuf, Peter S. *Statehood and Union: A History of the Northwest Ordinance*. Bloomington: Indiana University Press, 1987.

Pomeroy, Earl S. *The Territories and the United States 1861–1890*. Seattle: University of Washington Press, 1969.

Robbins, Roy M. *Our Landed Heritage: The Public Domain, 1776–1970*. 2nd ed., rev. Lincoln: University of Nebraska Press, 1976.

Sparrow, Bartholomew H. *The* Insular Cases *and the Emergence of American Empire*. Lawrence: University Press of Kansas, 2006.

Utley, Robert M. *Frontiersmen in Blue: The United States Army and the Indian, 1848–1865*. New York: Macmillan, 1967.

BARTHOLOMEW H. SPARROW

think tanks

For more than a century, policy experts have been understood as neutral, credible, and above the rough and tumble of policy making. Progressive reformers early in the twentieth century turned to the burgeoning social sciences for salvation. Reformers believed that the new ranks of policy experts trained at universities would be capable of usurping patronage politics; experts would develop *real* solutions to the social and economic instabilities that stemmed from the Industrial Revolution. Many would be housed at think tanks, public policy research organizations with origins in the early twentieth century. American politics and society would be better informed and much improved as a result of experts' efforts.

In the early twentieth century, the training of new policy experts became a central focus of reformers, with the creation of schools for policy analysts at leading universities and of agencies within government departments that produced research and evaluations for decision makers. Scholars observed these developments and contributed to the prevailing understanding of experts in American policy making: as important background voices that bring rational, reasoned analysis to long-term policy discourse based on the best evidence available.

For much of the last century, this assessment was basically accurate; experts fulfilled these mandates. By the beginning of the twenty-first century, however, the ranks of real-life policy experts scarcely conformed to the promise of making policy choices clearer and more rigorous and decisions necessarily more rational. These experts were based at a growing number of think tanks in Washington, D.C., and in state capitals across the country, and it was as common for think tanks to reflect clear ideologies and values as commitments to objectivity or neutrality.

Think tanks have contributed to a transformation in the role of experts in American policy making. Many experts now behave like advocates. They are not just visible but highly contentious as well. They more actively market their work than conventional views suggest; their work, in turn, often represents preformed points of view rather than even attempts at neutral, rational analysis.

These developments apply particularly to a group of identifiably ideological and mostly conservative think tanks that have emerged since the 1970s. Assessed from various angles, conservative ideology has had substantial influence over the direction of the U.S. policy agenda. Even when Democrats have regained their electoral strength, ideas about limited government, unfettered free markets, and strong heterosexual families remain influential in debates over everything from tax policy and business regulation to education reform and civil rights. Conservative ideology has been advanced by a conservative infrastructure of nonprofit organizations led by think tanks.

Early National Think Tanks

The first think tanks embodied the promise of neutral expertise. They formed as the social science disciplines of economics, sociology, and political science became established fields of inquiry and as confidence grew in the uses of expertise as a means for correcting social problems. Through the first half of the twentieth century, think tanks largely sought to identify government solutions to public problems through the detached analysis of experts. Think tank scholars wrote on topics relevant to policy makers but typically maintained a distance from political bargaining in the final stages of the policy-making process. This analytic detachment was a behavior to which researchers held fast and which fostered an effective relationship between experts and policy makers. Between 1910 and 1960, think tanks often influenced how government operated. The Brookings Institution, formed in Washington, D.C., in 1916, informed the creation of the Bureau of the Budget early in the century. The RAND Corporation, formed in Santa Monica, California, in 1948, developed systems analysis for the Department of Defense. The influence of these think tanks was significant, and their research served political purposes. But the policy process did not compel experts to become directly involved in partisan battles. Experts were mobilized by policy makers to prescribe possibilities for change.

Through the first two-thirds of the twentieth century, while think tanks at times produced politically contentious research, their input was sought and generally respected by policy makers. Although think tanks were not the only source of expertise, they were prominent, consistent, and visible providers.

Through the 1950s and 1960s, the ideas and expertise produced by think tanks generally reflected a near consensus that developed among elites about the need for government management of social and economic problems. Even when policy entrepreneurs of a conservative bent established new think tanks, they usually followed prevailing organizational norms, hiring academically trained staff and avoiding any appearance of having links to a single political party.

The Ascendance of Conservative Ideology

By the end of the 1960s, as government grew larger, the desirability and possibility of achieving social change through government programs began to be challenged. Some of the problems themselves—notably civil rights for African Americans and the Vietnam War—were highly divisive. Increasingly, critics described the government as ineffective and overextended, both at home and abroad. Combined inflation and unemployment in the 1970s—"stagflation"—contributed further to the decline of confidence in "expertly devised" government programs as well as to doubts about Keynesian principles generally.

The growth of government fueled organization among those who disapproved of it. Conservatives, by the 1970s, were united by strong opposition to communism and a shared belief that government resources were better channeled toward the nation's defense and the fight against communism than to what they viewed as bloated and ineffective domestic programs. A group of relatively small, politically conservative foundations and wealthy individuals provided support for applying these principles to public affairs. More than a dozen conservative foundations and individuals formed a nucleus of support of conservative organizations that emerged through the 1970s and 1980s, think tanks prominent among them. The explicit intent of these efforts was to destabilize the pro-government convictions that had dominated American politics since the New Deal. Avowedly ideological, contentious, and politicized ideas and expertise became tools in these endeavors.

The formation of the Heritage Foundation in 1973 was a turning point. Heritage was the first of a new breed of think tanks that combined what Kent Weaver described as "a strong policy, partisan, or ideological bent with aggressive salesmanship and an effort to influence current policy debates." The political entrepreneurs who started the Heritage Foundation sought to create a highly responsive apparatus that could react quickly to hostile proposals in Congress. By the late 1970s, as Lee Edwards observed in his history of the Heritage Foundation for its twenty-fifth anniversary, "an increasingly confident Heritage Foundation set an ambitious goal: to establish itself as a significant force in the policy-making process and to help build a new conservative coalition that would replace the New Deal coalition which had dominated American politics and policy for half a century."

Through the 1970s and 1980s, advocacy-oriented think tanks modeled after the Heritage Foundation proliferated. Some of the older institutions, like the American Enterprise Institute, founded in 1943, adapted to become more advocacy oriented. Most were conservative, but liberal and centrist organizations emerged as well. The staffs of these organizations tended to be ideologically homogeneous, and their leaders used research as vehicles to advance their underlying ideologies.

The Influence of Think Tanks

By 2007 more than 300 think tanks were active in national and state policy making. Yet, despite their numbers, the nature and extent of their influence were in question. Although think tanks can make their work influential among experts, in practice, the orgaizations too often focus their efforts on producing commentary about urgent policy decisions rather than intervening at earlier stages of policy making.

Thus, think tanks' commentary often serves as little more than ammunition for policy makers who need public justification for their preferred policy choices. In fact, specific estimates of the financial costs of new initiatives or the benefits of legislation are much more influential during the final stages of policy debates. Research that explores the foundations of a growing problem and possibilities for addressing it are also often important, creating a context for future changes in policy.

While the recent focus by think tanks on producing media commentary has not enhanced their immediate policy influence, it has damaged the collective reputation of policy experts generally. Policy research today is frequently evaluated more in terms of its ideological content and accessibility to audiences than by the quality of its content.

The War of Ideas

Conservatives, in particular, view think tanks from the perspective that ideas and values motivate—rather than result from—research. In their view, all research is ideological insofar as ideas inform the questions that the so-called neutral researcher asks. There is no such thing as disinterested expertise. Instead, as James Allen Smith observed, there are "permanent truths, transcending human experience, [that] must guide our political life." These truths motivate research, and research is a means to a more important end: realizing the ideas that are a reflection of these truths. The staff of ideological think tanks act as agents of ideologies rather than independent analysts.

Conservatives are diverse in their viewpoints but believe, at a fundamental level, that ideas have power. And ideas not only are but *should be* more powerful than expertise. One engages in (or supports) policy research for the same reasons one supports political advocacy: because both contribute to the larger causes of shifting the terms of debate in American policy making and to amplifying the power of conservative ideas. Conservative think tanks have thus advanced a plan to privatize Social Security in the 1970s and promoted it relentlessly for 25 years, until it appeared on the "mainstream" policy agenda of President George W. Bush in 2004.

Until 2007 conservative think tanks outnumbered liberal think tanks by two to one. Research-based think tanks of no identifiable ideology—many of them the older institutions like Brookings—still reflected the greatest number of think tanks, but the ranks of ideological think tanks were growing the fastest. The aggressive advocacy of the new organizations has affected think tanks of all stripes. Most think tanks—old and new, ideological and not—have increased their investments in communications and public affairs over the past two decades. Many have switched from producing books and longer studies to producing more short policy briefs, the types of products that are easily and quickly digested by decision makers and journalists.

The race between conservative and liberal think tanks has tightened. In the wake of the 2004 election, foundations and individual donors demonstrated a fresh interest in supporting new liberal think tanks. Since then, the Center for American Progress has become a sizable presence in Washington, and other, smaller think tanks have emerged on the liberal left. In the years ahead, observers should track both the competition among ideological think tanks and the struggle between those organizations and their seemingly nonideological brethren.

See also conservatism; patronage.

FURTHER READING

Edwards, Lee. *The Power of Ideas*. Ottawa, IL: Jameson Books, 1997.

Kingdon, John W. *Agendas, Alternatives, and Public Policies*. 2nd ed. New York: HarperCollins, 1995.

Lasswell, Harold D. "The Policy Orientation." In *The Policy Sciences*, edited by Daniel Lerner and Harold D. Lasswell, 3–15. Stanford, CA: Stanford University Press, 1951.

Merriam, Charles E. *New Aspects of Politics*. Chicago: University of Chicago Press, 1970.

Rich, Andrew. *Think Tanks, Public Policy, and the Politics of Expertise*. New York: Cambridge University Press, 2005.

Smith, James Allen. "Think Tanks and the Politics of Ideas," in *The Spread of Economic Ideas*, edited by David C. Colander and A.W. Coats. New York: Cambridge University Press, 1989

ANDREW RICH

third parties

See American (Know-Nothing) Party; conservative third parties since the New Deal; Free Soil Party; Greenback-Labor Party; labor parties; Libertarian Party; Liberty Party; populism; Progressive parties.

transnational influences on American politics

After more than 50 years in elected office and 10 years as speaker of the U.S. House of Representatives, Thomas "Tip" O'Neill encapsulated his wisdom about government in a single phrase: "All politics is local." In the words of his biographer, John A. Farrell, O'Neill's commitment to the needs of his Boston-area constituents made him one of the paragons for the twentieth-century transformation in American society: "As a young man with a passion for politics, O'Neill had watched and learned as Franklin D. Roosevelt employed the modern science of government to blunt the devastating effects of the Depression. . . . O'Neill fought Rooseveltian battles in Massachusetts, pushing for higher state payments to the elderly, new hospitals for the sick and mentally ill, a fair employment practices act for the state's African Americans, and the grand, ambitious public works and highway projects that transformed the face of the commonwealth in the postwar years. He believed that government was the means by which a people came together to address their community's ills, to right wrongs and craft a just society." This was traditional local "boss" politics, dominated by ethnic identity, personal favors, and appeals to the "common man." This was American democracy in action.

This was also transnational politics in practice. For all the appeals to a special local set of interests, every major policy issue that O'Neill and his counterparts addressed had an international dimension. From state payments to the elderly to public works projects, U.S. government legislation reflected the influence of events, personalities, and ideas in foreign societies. The same could be said about basic policies, even at the most local level, during the prior two centuries. American politics have never existed in a national vacuum; they have always been part of a wider space that crosses the Atlantic and Pacific Oceans, as well as the Rio Grande and the northern border with Canada.

The nature and weight of transnational influences have, of course, varied over time. Particular moments in the nation's history—the 1780s, the 1840s, the 1920s, and the 1960s—witnessed a remarkable density in personal connections between prominent political actors at home and their counterparts abroad. Other moments of more inward focus in the United States—the 1830s, the 1870s, and the 1930s—saw less explicit discussion of foreign political relationships. Nonetheless, even the latter decades were transnational, as Americans continued to import products, ideas, and people in large numbers. Many politicians have contested the appropriate degree of American involvement with the wider world, but no one of any prominence has ever really advocated for complete U.S. separation. American politics have always been transnational politics.

"Isolationism," in this sense, was more a polemical label than an accurate description for a particular point of view. Politicians who at one time called themselves "isolationists"—Robert La Follette, Arthur Vandenberg, and Gerald Nye, among others—were themselves the products of transnational influences on the United States. La Follette, for example, had traveled extensively in Russia and Europe. His progressive politics reflected his observations of state welfare programs overseas. Even the "isolationists" were also transnational political actors.

We can best understand the diverse transnational influences on American politics from the eighteenth century to the present by dividing these influences into roughly two areas: *war* and *public activism*. Although these topics often overlap in practice, it is helpful to examine how each reflects a series of particular and recurring transnational connections across numerous decades. These topics neglect many other areas of foreign influence that have received extensive attention from historians—commerce, popular culture, immigration, and technology, among others. Focusing on war and public activism, however, highlights some of the most significant ways in which the sources and practices of American politics changed in connection with developments abroad. The experiences of Americans in foreign societies, and American perceptions of those societies, had an enormous influence on the definition of the nation and the formulation of its policies. The U.S. experience in both war and public activism was deeply conditioned by transnational personal and institutional relations.

War

In one way or another, the United States has been at war for most of its history. These wars have included battles with foreign powers on or near American-claimed territory, continental conflicts over land control and political authority, and military interventions against adversaries overseas. In each of these contexts, war has exposed American politics to transnational experiences and ideas.

The American Revolution was typical of this process. During the late 1770s and early 1780s, the rebelling colonists aligned with France and Spain to fight against continued British control of North America. The alliance converted a group of domestic revolutionaries—provincials, in the eyes of the British—into international ambassadors for American nationalism. Benjamin Franklin, John Jay, and John Adams (as well as his precocious son, John Quincy Adams) spent most of the conflict in Europe, negotiating for foreign support. Despite their explicit rejection of traditional European aristocratic politics, these men became diplomats at the courts of monarchs. They were succeeded, after the Treaty of Ghent in 1783, by another generation of American diplomats—particularly Thomas Jefferson, who served at the court of the Bourbon monarch on the eve of the French Revolution.

These diplomatic experiences made the American revolutionaries into worldly politicians. Although they rejected traditional Old World politics, they learned to practice them for radical purposes. Franklin and Adams, in particular, made numerous deals to procure military aid and trade from European states. They also made and broke alliances to serve the needs of an emerging independent government. Their definition of an American republic was self-conscious of the place the new nation would occupy as a small and weak state in a world filled with much more powerful, aggressive empires. Their support for a strong central government, under the Constitution, was a political calculation about the foreign threats the new United States would face, and the need to prepare for international competition. Key constitutional innovations, especially the creation of the presidency, reflected the influence of monarchy and its unifying institutions on the republican revolutionaries in Philadelphia.

George Washington's famous Farewell Address in 1796 was a testament to the formative influence of European diplomacy and institutions on American politics. At a moment of intensive conflict between the United States and France and Great Britain (both of whom were at war), Washington advised citizens that "nothing is more essential than that permanent, inveterate antipathies against particular nations, and passionate attachments for others, should be excluded; and that, in place of them, just and amicable feelings towards all should be cultivated." This was a classic call for American adherence to a political balance of power—avoiding moral crusading and carefully steering clear of permanent bonds that could implicate the nation in unwanted conflicts. Following from Niccolò Machiavelli more than Jefferson or Madison, Washington defined the United States as a practitioner of raison d'état, the pursuit of the "national interest" through secular and flexible maneuver between different coalitions of power. Washington and his successors in the White House spoke of "temporary alliances" with republican and nonrepublican states, not isolation or ideological consistency in policy making. They were European-influenced realists who practiced power politics for the defense and promotion of American ideals.

This realism kept the United States out of foreign revolutions, despite rhetorical urges to the contrary. The French, Haitian, and Latin American revolutions of the late eighteenth and early nineteenth centuries received no significant support from the American government. In Haiti, the administration of Thomas Jefferson was overtly hostile to the creation of a regime that challenged European authority under African leadership. The United States was a revolutionary nation, but its definition of acceptable revolution included attachment to European-inspired notions of good government and realist traditions of the balance of power in foreign policy.

Every subsequent war, especially those outside of North America, reinforced these principles and increased other foreign influences on American politics. In the Civil War, both the Union and Confederate armies—the largest military institutions built within the United States to that date—studied and implemented European fighting methods. Confederate general Robert E. Lee adopted Napoleonic tactics for maneuver and surprise in battle. Union general Ulysses S. Grant used centralized methods of resource and manpower mobilization to build a fighting force that could take grave casualties but still annihilate its enemies. Neither Lee nor Grant fought like any of their American predecessors; both fought a modern European war on American soil. Many European observers in Germany, France, and Great Britain studied the Civil War as a testing ground for their ideas of war in an age of more powerful Machiavellian states. The "American way of war," like the American approach to international relations, was also European in origins, and soon global in scope.

Beyond military strategy, President Abraham Lincoln also adopted a strongly European-influenced argument against slavery in the cause of the Union. British politicians of the eighteenth and early nineteenth centuries pursued the global abolition of slavery for the purpose of empowering free labor markets. This position received reinforcement from the French Revolution's Declaration of the Rights of Man. Ending slavery—or at least eliminating any foreign support for the institution of slavery—became a widely embraced political duty outside North America on the eve of the Civil War.

Lincoln shared many antislavery views, but he avoided taking a categorical position on the issue as long as possible. Once it became clear in course of the Civil War that he could not find a political compromise between North and South to preserve the Union, Lincoln invoked British and French antislavery positions to justify the use of violence against the slaveholding Confederacy. The Emancipation Proclamation, signed by Lincoln on January 1, 1863, freed the slaves in the Confederate states and pledged that "the Executive Government of the United States, including the military and naval authority thereof, will recognize and maintain the freedom of such persons."

Lincoln issued the Emancipation Proclamation to enlist the freed slaves against the Confederacy. He also used this document to attract antislavery opinion in Europe to the Union side. The latter consideration was crucial. The British government, in particular, had strong economic interests connected to the cotton trade from the Confederate states. It also had geopolitical interests in North America that would be served by a weak and divided American nation. Lincoln and his secretary of state, William Henry Seward, feared that British recognition and support for the Confederacy would undermine, and perhaps defeat, Union aims. The Emancipation Proclamation countered this possibility by appealing directly to British and other foreign audiences to embrace the Union as the force against slavery. Lincoln alienated moderates in the United States with this document, but he appealed to foreign constituencies that he needed on his side. The Emancipation Proclamation and the "second American Revolution" that it came to represent were strongly connected to European politics. Although the battles occurred on American soil, the Civil War was a transnational conflict.

American politics in both world wars fit the same pattern. The two defining political moments of the conflicts for the United States—President Woodrow Wilson's announcement of his Fourteen Points on January 8, 1918, and President Franklin D. Roosevelt's signature on the Atlantic Charter of August 14, 1941—reflected important connections between domestic aims and foreign influences. Both documents had a deep and simultaneous impact on citizens at home and abroad. They contributed to a "liberal" and "modernizing" set of politics that crossed national boundaries.

Wilson's Fourteen Points, articulated in his speech to a joint session of Congress, began by explaining that the United States had sent its soldiers to fight on European soil for the first time "because violations of right had occurred which touched us to the quick and made the life of our own people impossible unless they were corrected and the world secure once and for all against their recurrence. . . . All the peoples of the world are in effect partners in this interest, and for our own part we see very clearly that unless justice be done to others it will not be done to us."

To combat threats from abroad and assure that the world was "made safe for democracy," Wilson espoused long-standing European ideas about international law and organization. Drawing on the experiences of the European states that had formed transnational cooperative institutions—including the Central Commission for the Navigation of the Rhine (founded in 1815), the Superior Council for Health (founded in 1838), and the First Geneva Convention on the treatment of war wounded (founded in 1864)—Wilson proposed a new international organization for peace. During the negotiations outside of Paris at the end of World War I, this idea became the basis for the League of Nations—the most important effort at global governance and war prevention in the early twentieth century.

The U.S. Senate vetoed American membership in the League of Nations for fear that it would restrict American independence, but the League remained influential in American politics. Under Wilson's successors, especially President Herbert Hoover, the United States continued to support the creation of a "civilized" system of international law to regulate aggression among states. In addition, the United States participated in the growing range of international exchanges of people, ideas, and technology operating in parallel with the League of Nations. The power of the U.S. federal government grew with the creation of a Department of Commerce in 1913 that managed and promoted these activities. Through federal grants of aid, legal encouragement, and foreign negotiations the U.S. government became what one historian calls a "promotional state," much more akin to its European counterparts than to its pre-twentieth-century American predecessors. The end of World War I contributed to a stronger federal role in American society and deeper transnational ties to local businesses and communities.

These developments underpinned the New Deal—a domestic and international "war" on poverty and economic dislocation during the Great Depression. President Franklin D. Roosevelt solidified the transnational strains of American politics when, in the summer of 1941 (months before the Japanese attack on Pearl Harbor), he hinged the future of American freedom and prosperity on the defeat of fascism. Meeting with British prime minister Winston Churchill off the coast of Newfoundland, Roosevelt signed the Atlantic Charter that committed both Great Britain and the United States to "common principles" for a "better future for the world." These common principles included the "final destruction of Nazi tyranny," and the creation of a new international peace "which will afford to all nations the means of dwelling in safety within their own boundaries, and which will afford assurance that all the men in all lands may live out their lives in freedom from fear and want." Domestic and international liberty, according to this formulation, were interdependent.

Roosevelt defined America's national purpose in the Great Depression and World War II as an extension of the Wilsonian goal of making the world safe for democracy. He reorganized American society along these lines, under the direction of a now dominant federal government. Similarly, Roosevelt defined foreign threats—political extremism, economic autarchy, and interstate violence—as core challenges to America's national purpose. Citizens of the United States were mobilized to fight for their freedom *as a single nation* on an unprecedented scale. American society never looked back. Historian Michael Sherry identifies the Great Depression and World War II as the formative moment for a militarized, outward-looking political culture in the United States. The European-inspired realism of Benjamin Franklin and John Adams had, over the course of 150 years, evolved into a form of federal dominance in American society unanticipated by any of the nation's founders. This new role for Washington reflected influences and threats from abroad, as much as those at home.

American politics during the cold war deepened this phenomenon. From the last days of World War II through the collapse of the Soviet Union in 1991, U.S. leaders consistently emphasized the need to keep the nation mobilized for conflict with Moscow and other communist challengers. New institutions, including the Office of the Secretary of Defense and the Central Intelligence Agency, emerged to manage domestic resources, monitor threats, and control dissent. The National Security Act of 1947 concentrated power more centrally in the White House with the creation of the National Security Council and the reduction of congressional oversight for security matters. As a consequence, the United States prepared for and fought numerous conflicts after 1947, but the president never again sought a formal declaration of war.

The perceived threat of foreign communism was ever-present in American society. It motivated a change in the size and scope of the American military as it became a permanent global force with bases on every continent and nuclear weapons ready for immediate use. It transformed universities as the U.S. government used its financial and legal leverage to make the academy more helpful in addressing pressing policy challenges. Most significant, perceptions of communism transformed the terms of political debate. To win election to office—Republican or Democrat—one had to appear "tough" on communism and committed to a broad global agenda for the United States. Domestic cold war politics were international anti-Communist politics.

The figures who came to dominate the American political scene in this context were not the usual suspects from elite families and white Anglo-Saxon pedigrees. Men of this background remained powerful, but not as exclusively as before. The international dimensions of the cold war placed a new premium on anti-Communist cosmopolitanism—a knowledge of foreign societies, a personal biography rooted in struggle against foreign extremism, and a hypernationalism born of immigration to America as a "savior" nation. Henry Kissinger and Zbigniew Brzezinski are prime examples of this phenomenon. European immigrants who came to the United States fleeing Nazi terror, they emerged as powerful, unelected policy makers promising to help the United States manage a world of dangerous threats and difficult balance of power decisions. Kissinger and Brzezinski espoused American ideals, but they consistently counseled the country to curtail its cherished hopes and act more like a "normal" state, accepting "lesser evils" in its friends and combating "greater evils" in its enemies.

The same political rhetoric, and many of the same personalities, carried on into the post–cold war era in American politics. Iraq and Islamic fanaticism replaced the Soviet Union and communism as the overriding threats in American debates. Mobilizing the nation for combat at home and abroad became the guiding principle, yet again, for the government after the September 11, 2001, terrorist attacks on the United States. As the Truman administration created the National Security Council during the onset of the cold war, the administration of President George W. Bush founded the Department of Homeland Security as a response to terrorism in the new century. Pervasive perceptions of foreign threats, in a time of perpetual war, set the terms of American political debate. Transnational influences were now central to the most local discussions of authority, economy, and survival. The war at home and abroad continued.

Public Activism

The intersection between the foreign and the domestic in war had a close analogue among public activists—including social reformers, local organization leaders, prominent intellectuals, and public demonstrators. Especially during the twentieth century, public activists in the United States drew on ideas, strategies, and tactics from abroad. They frequently thought of themselves as part of larger global transformations in society. Most significant, activists often had personal connections to foreign countries, derived from birth, family, study, and travel. American activists were transnational translators, synthesizers, and innovators at the same time.

The transnational scope of public activists was also somewhat broader than that of the politicians more deeply involved in war and daily policy making. Figures like Franklin, Lincoln, Wilson, Roosevelt, and Kissinger focused their energies on Europe above all other non-American areas of the world. For them, the transnational was largely trans-European. Activists in the twentieth century, however, had a more transglobal perspective. They came from and interacted with a broader geography in their daily politics. They often looked self-consciously beyond Europe to other societies for alternative reform inspirations. Europe mattered to American activists, but over the course of the twentieth century it became less central to them than it was to their counterparts in policy-making institutions.

Advocates of substantial reforms in American race relations were most explicit about their desire to look beyond Europe. Founded in 1816 by a mix of northern abolitionists and Southerners fearful of slave violence, the American Colonization Society helped to transport more than 10,000 freed slaves to the West African territory of Liberia. With the end of the Civil War and the promise of African American suffrage during Reconstruction, support for the emigration of freed slaves largely evaporated. Nonetheless, the controversial work of the American Colonization Society was the beginning of a "return to Africa" movement that would animate public discussions of the "race problem" in the United States for the next century, especially among those who believed that blacks and whites could live in peace only if they were separated. According to this logic, African Americans would live freer and happier lives if they were back on a continent populated by people who looked like them and presumably shared similar traditions. This was often a well-intentioned effort, but its separatist logic was adopted by a range of political activists, for a variety of purposes, in later decades.

Marcus Garvey was perhaps the most influential and transnational figure in the early twentieth century to espouse a separatist African American agenda. Born in Jamaica and widely traveled throughout Central America and Western Europe, Garvey came to the United States as a penniless immigrant in 1916. Within a few years he organized and led the largest transnational black organization of the twentieth century: the United Negro Improvement Association (UNIA), which would open chapters in more than a dozen countries, including many parts of Latin America and Africa. The organization emphasized self-reliance, racial autonomy, and black nationhood. According to Garvey, descendants of Africa should take pride in their past and work together for the common advancement of their race. He called for a transnational organization of blacks to create a single nation under his leadership and the UNIA.

Garvey's aims became most explicit in August 1920 when he organized the monthlong International Convention of the Negro Peoples of the World at Madison Square Garden in New York City. Elected "provisional president of Africa" by the assembly, Garvey oversaw the writing and approval of the "Declaration of Rights of the Negro Peoples of the World," which demanded that "the governments of the world recognize our leader and his representatives chosen by the race to look after the welfare of our people under such governments." As a transnational sovereign, the UNIA called on "the various governments of the world to accept and acknowledge Negro representatives who shall be sent to the said governments to represent the general welfare of the Negro peoples of the world." Africa should be protected for Africans, according to the declaration, and the UNIA asserted that, on other continents blacks would "demand complete control of our social institutions without interference by any alien race or races." Announced in New York amid signs of growing American intolerance to dissent, this was a bold and transnational vision of African American power as part of a global racial movement.

Garvey and the UNIA never achieved their goals, but they contributed to a remarkable transnational outpouring of reform ideas and initiatives among activists with diverse interests. The most prominent African American intellectual of the period, W.E.B. DuBois, strongly disagreed with Garvey on many points, but he shared the UNIA's commitment to a global movement for racial reform. Speaking at the first Pan-African Convention in London on July 25, 1900, DuBois famously proclaimed, "The problem of the twentieth century is the problem of the color line, the question as to how far differences of race—which show themselves chiefly in the color of the skin and the texture of the hair—will hereafter be made the basis of denying to over half the world the right of sharing to utmost ability the opportunities and privileges of modern civilization." DuBois did not call for a common black nation with a single leader, but he did link the local with the international when he asked in his London speech, "may the conscience of a great nation rise and rebuke all dishonesty and unrighteous oppression toward the American Negro, and grant to him the right of franchise, security of person and property, and generous recognition of the great work he has accomplished in a generation toward raising nine millions of human beings from slavery to manhood. . . . Let the nations of the world respect the integrity and independence of the free Negro states of Abyssinia, Liberia, Haiti, and the rest, and let the inhabitants of these states, the independent tribes of Africa, the Negroes of the West Indies and America, and the black subjects of all nations take courage, strive ceaselessly, and fight bravely, that they may prove to the world their incontestable right to be counted among the great brotherhood of mankind."

DuBois's "brotherhood of mankind" was a clarion call for many activists focused on issues other than race—including poverty, urban blight, health, and children's welfare. A generation of reformers, generally labeled "progressives" by historians, conceptualized the problems of the United States in transnational terms that resonated with the arguments voiced by both Garvey and DuBois. These progressives self-consciously drew on what they envisioned as an international dialogue among activists about how to improve society through rational, determined, and cooperative action. Like Garvey and DuBois, they formed countless organizations that crossed borders for this purpose, they participated in a widening web of "exchanges," and, most important, they embraced the experimental application of foreign ideas to local problems. In Wisconsin, for example, a group of intellectuals and politicians came together to author what they called the "Wisconsin Idea"—a mix of remarkably creative and cosmopolitan reform initiatives inspired by local problems in an agrarian and industrializing community. Borrowing from the British, Germans, French, and others, Wisconsin activists pioneered worker's compensation insurance, unemployment benefits, public education, and social security. They did not assert a sense of common racial consciousness across boundaries, but they did nurture an enduring commitment to transnational reform rooted in local needs.

This dream did not die with the Great Depression and World War II but attracted the attention of a new generation of young activists in the 1960s. Unlike their predecessors, the New Left did not endorse rational planning or state-building efforts. Instead, it focused on the transnational participatory spirit that had animated Garvey and DuBois, as well as their progressive counterparts. Activists in the 1960s emphasized a common experience of youth across societies confronting paternalistic, militaristic, and unjust institutions of power that needed rapid change from below. Inspired by "liberationist" movements in the third world, the euphoria of mass demonstrations, and a new feeling of relevance, young people on every continent demanded far-reaching change. They pushed for an end to foreign wars, attention to hidden suffering within modern societies, and more egalitarian politics. They argued that this was a truly worldwide agenda that must begin within each state.

Students for a Democratic Society (SDS), the most prominent New Left organization in the United States during the 1960s, put this argument in apocalyptic terms. Its "Agenda for a Generation" (also known as the "Port Huron Statement") announced: "Although mankind desperately needs revolutionary leadership, America rests in national stalemate, its goals ambiguous and tradition-bound instead of informed and clear, its democratic system apathetic and manipulated rather than 'of, by, and for the people.' . . . Our work is guided by the sense that we may be the last generation in the experiment with living. But we are a minority—the vast majority of our people regard the temporary equilibriums of our society and world as eternally functional parts. In this is perhaps the outstanding paradox: we ourselves are imbued with urgency, yet the message of our society is that there is no viable alternative to the present."

SDS and the many other activist groups that emerged in the 1960s did not achieve their desired changes in policy, and they did not create a cohesive generation of reformers. They did, however, transform local and international attitudes. American society and many of its counterparts abroad became more sensitive and accepting of racial, gender, and various ethnic differences. Concern for human rights also grew in public attitudes, if not always in policy practice. Most significant, transnational borrowings of ideas and programs became more common and more accepted. To think locally after the 1960s meant to think about localities across societies. This basic attitude transferred from the New Left demonstrators of the 1960s to the environmental, feminist, and antiglobalization activists of the late twentieth century. The 1960s endure in the contemporary imagination as the moment of transnational political activism that all subsequent movements seek to capture in one way or another.

Looking Outward

Tip O'Neill was correct; all politics is local. The local, however, has always included deep and diverse connections to practices, ideas, and influences that are not American in origin. From the American Revolution to the demonstrations of the 1960s, American politics have been transnational politics. The experiences of war and public activism have reflected this phenomenon; they have also increased its intensity. During nearly every military conflict and nearly every burst of reform the United States became more, not less, connected to its counterparts near and far. The nation globalized long before people used the term.

If there is a general direction to American history, it is outward, not inward. If there is a general lesson from American history, it is that political change requires familiarity with a landscape far beyond the borders of the 50 states. These were O'Neill's politics, as they were the politics of his heroic predecessors in Boston and his modern successors from the Sun Belt South. In order to do more for one's constituents, one must do more for their transnational hopes and interests.

FURTHER READING

Dawley, Alan. *Changing the World: American Progressives in War and Revolution.* Princeton, NJ: Princeton University Press, 2003.

Declaration of Rights of the Negro Peoples of the World, August 15, 1920. http://www.pbs.org/wgbh/amex/garvey/filmmore/ps_rights.html.

Farrell, John A. *Tip O'Neill and the Democratic Century.* Boston: Little, Brown, 2001.

Gaines, Kevin. *American Africans in Ghana: Black Expatriates and the Civil Rights Era.* Chapel Hill: University of North Carolina Press, 2006.

Gilbert, Felix. *To the Farewell Address: Ideas of Early American Foreign Policy.* Princeton, NJ: Princeton University Press, 1961.

Grant, Colin. *Negro with a Hat: The Rise and Fall of Marcus Garvey.* New York: Oxford University Press, 2008.

Horn, Gerd-Rainer. *The Spirit of '68: Rebellion in Western Europe and North America, 1956–1976.* Oxford: Oxford University Press, 2007.

Iriye, Akira. *Cultural Internationalism and World Order.* Baltimore, MD: Johns Hopkins University Press, 2000.

Leffler, Melvyn P. *A Preponderance of Power: National Security, the Truman Administration, and the Cold War.* Stanford, CA: Stanford University Press, 1992.

Port Huron Statement of Students for a Democratic Society, June 15, 1962. http://www2.iath.virginia.edu/sixties/HTML_docs/Resources/Primary/Manifestos/SDS_Port_Huron.html.

Rodgers, Daniel T. *Atlantic Crossings: Social Politics in a Progressive Age.* Cambridge, MA: Belknap Press of Harvard University Press, 1998.

Rosenberg, Emily. *Spreading the American Dream: American Economic and Cultural Expansion, 1890–1945.* New York: Hill and Wang, 1982.

Sherry, Michael S. *In the Shadow of War: The United States since the 1930s.* New Haven, CT: Yale University Press, 1995.

Suri, Jeremi. *Power and Protest: Global Revolution and the Rise of Détente*. Cambridge, MA: Harvard University Press, 2003.

Wilson, Woodrow. Speech to a joint session of Congress, January 8, 1918. http://www.yale.edu/lawweb/avalon/wilson14.htm.

JEREMI SURI

transportation and politics

A remarkable number of new transportation technologies emerged in the United States and other industrialized nations during the nineteenth and early twentieth centuries, including long-distance stagecoach lines, river steamboats and oceangoing steamships, steam and electric railways, automobiles and all-weather highways, and commercial aviation. Each new mode of transportation invariably elicited a variety of political responses.

Perhaps nothing better illustrates the intimate relationship between transportation and American politics than the oddly shaped and geographically roundabout route chosen for transcontinental stagecoach service inaugurated in the late 1850s; for the first time it became possible to cross the United States from coast to coast by land using only commercial transportation. The Butterfield Overland Stage linked the cities of San Francisco and St. Louis, Missouri, by way of such frontier outposts as El Paso, Texas; Tucson, Arizona; and Los Angeles, the most populous of which could claim only a few thousand residents. From Fort Smith, in far western Arkansas, Butterfield ran a branch line east to Memphis, Tennessee, to serve the home state of Postmaster General Aaron Brown, who oversaw the federal mail contracts that funded much of the expense of operating a stage line across so much unpopulated space.

Mail Contracts

It would be impossible to overestimate the importance of income from federal mail contracts in underwriting the cost of new modes of transportation across vast sections of the United States in the nineteenth century. Mail subsidies were the lifeblood of most long-distance stage lines serving the West, so much so that in the early 1860s, the western "stagecoach king" Ben Holladay maintained one of his several homes near Capitol Hill in Washington, D.C., to cultivate a cordial relationship with members of the U.S. Congress who periodically voted on mail contracts.

Mail contracts also subsidized the operation of many a steamboat plying the navigable waters of the United States, most notably along 3,000 sparsely settled miles of the Missouri River as it meandered between St. Louis and the frontier outpost of Fort Benton, Montana—a transportation hub aptly named for Missouri senator Thomas Hart Benton, one of the strongest supporters in Congress of transportation links across the West. During his 30-year career in the Senate, Benton promoted federally subsidized transportation links not merely between Missouri and the West Coast but extending all the way to China and India.

Much of what Benton (1782–1858) proposed on the floor of the Senate (between 1821 and 1851) and in other public forums was too visionary to be realized in his lifetime, but mail contracts did subsidize the first steamship service between the East and West coasts, by means of a 48-mile portage across the Isthmus of Panama, that commenced just *before* word of gold precipitated a mad rush of travelers to California in 1849.

Long after stagecoach and steamboat transportation had been relegated to the remotest corners of the United States in the early twentieth century, the railroad passenger trains that superseded them depended on federal mail contracts, and increasingly so in the late 1940s and 1950s as the number of rail passengers declined steadily. Many of the trains carried dedicated Rail Post Office cars in which highly trained clerks sorted the mail en route, the schedules of mail-carrying trains being determined largely by the needs of the U.S. Post Office Department. Thus, when the Post Office cancelled all "mail by rail" contracts in late 1967, passenger train service effectively collapsed in all but the most scenic portions of the United States. Had it not been for federal dollars to support Amtrak, implemented in May 1971, long-distance rail passenger service across the United States would very likely have disappeared.

Railroads

Railroads, from their technological infancy in the United States in the early 1830s, had been enmeshed in politics. The money required to build and equip a single mile of railroad often dwarfed the cost of an entire fleet of steamboats and stagecoaches, and thus it was natural for railroad builders in all parts of the United States to seek municipal, state, and federal support. Politics and railroad building often went hand in hand, especially in the sparsely settled Trans-Mississippi West. To encourage construction of the railroad lines needed to develop the region, Congress provided various forms of help, all in addition to the promise of mail contracts once the trains began running. The aid included loans, financial subsidies, and enormous grants of federal land. The federal land grant program to support railroad construction ended in the 1870s as a result of scandals that blackened the reputation of Congress—"the finest that money could buy," to paraphrase Mark Twain—and during the next decade, the politics of railroads evolved from finding ways to underwrite construction and maintain operations to devising ways to regulate them, beginning with the Interstate Commerce Commission in 1887.

In contrast to the federal government, various states had begun to regulate railroads as much as 30 years earlier, in the 1850s. The early state regulations involved matters mainly of safety and service. The initial federal regulations were largely for show in order to placate various political pressure groups, such as the Grangers, an agrarian protest group originating in the Midwest, which claimed railroad rates were exorbitant and service poor. Not until the early twentieth century, during the Progressive Era, did federal regulation of the railroads acquire real teeth.

Responding to aggressive displays of railroad power in a nation that, by 1900, had no alternative modes of transportation apart from the boats that served its coastlines and inland waterways, governments at all levels steadily piled on regulations. It was once claimed that the Interstate Commerce Commission alone had written more than a trillion regulations involving all aspects of railroad service, a number that is surely an exaggeration but nonetheless expresses the growing frustration of railroad executives in the 1920s and 1930s.

The boom in railroad travel in the United States during World War II, which witnessed the highest passenger loads in the history of the industry, was followed by the bust of the 1950s, when despite the railroads' efforts to streamline and speed up their best passenger trains the number of passengers using them continued to drop. In the mid-1950s, airlines for the first time surpassed railroads in terms of the volume of passenger traffic. At almost the same time, Congress passed the Federal Aid Highway Act of 1956 in order to create a new system of superhighways. The railways, by contrast, seemed to languish. One of the nation's largest railroads, the Pennsylvania Central, went bankrupt in 1970. Two other giants, the Rock Island and the Milwaukee Road, went bankrupt in 1975 and 1977, respectively. Rail industry executives complained loudly about unfair competition, but it seemed that no one was listening.

Highways

In the 1820s and 1830s, Democrats and Whigs had battled over how much the federal government should underwrite the cost of internal improvements. The Whigs favored spending government dollars to further the nation's growing network of canals and roads. One showcase project was the National Road, an improved highway that reached west from Maryland and across the agricultural heartland of Ohio and Indiana. The road never reached its stated goal of St. Louis, however, before the Panic of 1837 dried up tax revenues at all levels of government and thus discouraged support for internal improvements. From 1838 to 1916, the federal government conspicuously avoided direct involvement in road-building projects, and the laissez faire interpretation of the U.S. Constitution provided the necessary justification for its hands-off approach.

Ironically, just as the number of government regulations seemed to increase exponentially during the years after 1900—including emergency federal operation of the nation's railroads during World War I and its immediate aftermath—government subsidized and lightly regulated highways emerged to challenge railroad power. Competition from a growing number of private automobiles first made a noticeable impact on local passenger trains in midwestern farm states around 1916, a year that also saw the birth of the first congressionally subsidized highway construction program since the 1830s and the end of federal support for the National or Cumberland Road. In the 1920s and 1930s, Congress and state governments poured billions of dollars into building a national highway network. In good times and bad, state and federal appropriations to build and maintain an ever improving network of highways remained popular with voters—especially after 1919, the year states first discovered that a tax on gasoline was a relatively painless way to raise the necessary revenue.

Much of the newfound constitutional justification for federal involvement in highway construction during the twentieth century was based on the argument that good roads and highways were needed to maintain a strong national defense. The argument appeared frequently in public discussions of funding superhighways during the cold war years of the 1950s and 1960s, but it actually antedated that era by several decades. As early as 1916, when the Mexican revolutionary Pancho Villa and his ragtag troops were widely perceived to threaten America's southwestern borderlands, Congressional proponents of the landmark legislation passed that year argued that highways would provide an additional way to move troops quickly if needed to defend that remote and sparsely settled portion of the United States.

The numbers assigned to the original network of corridors—like U.S. Route 66, which sliced diagonally across the American West from Chicago to Los Angeles; U.S. Route 1, which runs parallel to the coastline from Maine to Florida; and U.S. 101, which does the same along the West Coast—date from meetings that federal and state highway officials held in the mid 1920s. The designation *U.S.* was not just an abbreviation for United States but also for Uniform System. But the evolution of modern transportation in the United States, which probably dates from the landmark completion of the Erie Canal in 1825 or the opening of the first section of the Baltimore and Ohio Railroad five years later, is essentially the product of an inexact, ever changing, and sometimes volatile mix of technological and financial expertise, legislative and legal calculation (and sometimes chicanery), as well as various forms of popular education that over nearly two centuries included everything from fiery stump speeches and lengthy public debates to slick industry advertising and self-promotional propaganda, with winners and losers determined at the voting booth.

The national defense argument remained popular; in the mid-1950s Congress debated whether America needed to build a new system of super highways to relieve the growing congestion of federal highways first built in the 1920s. President Dwight D. Eisenhower was a strong backer of the new superhighway proposal and, in 1956, signed legislation to underwrite construction of the Interstate Highway system, one of the largest appropriations for public works in American history.

As for rules governing interstate highway commerce, Congress approved federal regulation of America's fast-growing intercity truck and bus industries in 1935. Rail executives had complained bitterly that their heavily regulated industry could not compete with new modes of transportation that went almost unfettered, except for state safety and licensing requirements. Over-the-road trucks offering door-to-door delivery service rapidly snatched away money that railroads made by moving personal goods or delivering less-than-full-carload freight. Buses and passenger railroads fought over slices of a rapidly shrinking revenue pie. After the 1920s, by far the greatest number of Americans traveled over the nation's network of all-weather roads and highways in the comfort of their own private automobiles.

Use of the ever-expanding road and highway network became the birthright of every American, a concept periodically reaffirmed in political discussions and legislative debates. By the early 1930s the road was the most conspicuous and widely used "common ground" in the United States, and it made absolutely no difference whether users drove humble Fords and Chevrolets or lordly Duesenbergs and Packards.

Aviation

The first successful flight of Wilbur and Orville Wright took place in December 1903. The next summer, the largest city west of the Mississippi River, St. Louis, basked in the international limelight that came with hosting a world's fair, a tradition that dated back to London in the early 1850s. All world's fairs served to showcase the latest technological achievements of a nation or of Western civilization generally. But not a single airplane was displayed at the St. Louis fair in 1904; Americans were not yet "air-minded" and would not become so for at least another quarter century. Neither they nor the world at large had any idea what the Wright brothers' brief flight portended. Not until young Charles A. Lindbergh piloted *The Spirit of St. Louis* nonstop from New York to Paris in 1927 to win a $25,000 prize and instant worldwide fame did America begin to accept the idea of aviation. *Time* magazine selected Lindbergh as its first Man of the Year and, largely as a result of the publicity his solo flight across the Atlantic generated, Wall Street became aware of the financial gain commercial aviation might offer. After a series of false starts dating back to 1914, commercial aviation in the United States effectively got off the ground in 1929 with 48-hour coast-to-coast service that used an awkward combination of air travel during daylight hours and rail sleeping cars at night. One of the new coast-to-coast carriers, Transcontinental and Western Airlines (later simply TWA), conspicuously advertised itself as the "Lindbergh Line" for added cachet.

Associating the airline with the trusted Lindbergh name was intended to inspire public confidence in a largely untested industry. Ironically, Transcontinental and Western soon compiled one of the worst safety records in an industry that during the first half of the 1930s suffered a succession of newsworthy accidents that shook public confidence in commercial aviation. The legendary Notre Dame University football coach Knute Rockne died in a TWA crash in 1931; another TWA crash killed Senator Bronson Cutting of New Mexico in 1935. The loss of Senator Cutting probably did more than any other aviation-related death to motivate members of Congress to adopt strict federal regulation of the airline industry in 1938. Starting in 1938, the federal government regulated the fares, routes, and schedules of domestic interstate airlines. By treating them as a public utility, federal officials sought to guarantee them a reasonable rate of return. Much to the benefit of the airline industry, the legislation also sought to instill confidence in passengers. As significant as the landmark regulatory legislation was, it was clear that the fortunes of America's commercial air carriers depended to an extraordinary degree on a favorable political and legislative environment.

By the late 1930s, all forms of commercial interstate transportation in the United States, including gas and oil pipelines, were regulated by various federal commissions, agencies, and boards. Some industries, most notably commercial aviation, prospered under the heavy but highly protective hand of federal regulators. Not a single major airline went bankrupt during the years of federal regulation. Other transportation industries, most notably the railroads, stagnated and lost almost all incentive for meaningful innovation. In the late 1930s, when a few American railroads dared enter the business of commercial aviation, federal regulators blocked them. By contrast, north of the border, the Canadian Pacific Railway added both an airline and many luxury hotels to its portfolio.

Deregulation

In the 1970s, a Democratic Congress reversed the course Uncle Sam had been following since 1887 and started to deregulate all forms of American transportation. Senators Edward Kennedy of Massachusetts and Howard Cannon of Nevada gave their names to the 1978 legislation that deregulated the airline industry. The expectation in the halls of Congress and in the airline industry was that unfettered competition would cause ticket prices to fall but profits to rise. Ticket prices did fall, and more Americans than ever were flying, but not much else worked as expected. More than a hundred new airlines joined the competition, and almost all of them failed a short time later. Some established carriers added dozens of new routes, but the overexpansion proved unwise and caused the first bankruptcies the major carriers had ever experienced. In the end, flying within the United States was probably cheaper than it had ever been, but the once glamorous experience of flying was also immeasurably cheapened. Many smaller communities lost commercial air service altogether.

Federal deregulation of the intercity truck and bus industries commenced in 1980, as did the rapid loosening of federal control over railroads. West Virginia congressman Harley Staggers gave his name to 1980 legislation that significantly unfettered the railroads. The result was almost the opposite of that which would befall the airline industry. Railroads abandoned thousands of miles of lightly used track (too many miles, they later learned) and pared freight train crews; the big railroads merged and merged again until just four super railroads dominated traffic across the United States, two on either side of the Mississippi River. More efficient than ever, railroads saw profits soar in the early twenty-first century to unprecedented heights. As savvy investors purchased railroad stocks, it was clear that North American railroads were enjoying good times.

The Changing Landscape

As a result of terrorism, sharply rising fuel costs, and vigorous competition that made it difficult to raise ticket prices, airline profits—even for the biggest and best-known names in the industry—took a nosedive. Purchasers of the common stock of most major U.S. carriers saw their investments wiped out by bankruptcy courts. Those same dollars if invested instead in one of the big four railroads (CSX, Norfolk Southern, Union Pacific, and Burlington Northern Santa Fe) would have doubled or tripled in value.

One advantage contributing to the comeback of America's big railroads was the rising price of oil, which made automobiles, intercity trucks, and airliners increasingly expensive alternatives. Both CSX and Norfolk Southern sponsored televised coverage of the 2008 election returns, and both used the occasion to highlight for a national audience the efficiency of their freight trains versus highway transportation.

Transportation can be described as the "great enabler." In whatever form, it has enabled changes that transformed the landscape, the economy, the politics, and even the basic social habits of Americans. Something as simple as enjoying fresh fruit in Montana, Michigan, or Minnesota in midwinter represents the triumph of good transportation over distance and time, enabling oranges from groves in Florida or California, for example, to travel in refrigerated railcars and trucks to breakfast tables in distant corners of the nation. A morning orange is a simple pleasure, but it also epitomizes the complex history of transportation; it is the remarkable result of two centuries of public discussion and dissent, vigorous partisan political debate, slick corporate advertising, and personal disappointments mixed with individual dreams realized, technological breakthroughs that displaced less efficient and adaptable modes of transportations, and financial goals both realized and unrealized.

See also regulation.

FURTHER READING

Bailey, Elizabeth E., David R. Graham, and Daniel P. Kaplan. *Deregulating the Airlines*. Cambridge, MA: MIT Press, 1985.

Chandler, Alfred D., Jr. *The Railroads: The Nation's First Big Business*. New York: Harcourt, Brace, 1965.

Ely, James W., Jr. *Railroads and American Law*. Lawrence: University Press of Kansas, 2001.

Flink, James J. *America Adopts the Automobile, 1895–1910*. Cambridge, MA: MIT Press, 1970.

Heppenheimer, T. A. *Turbulent Skies: The History of Commercial Aviation*. New York: Wiley, 1995.

Kolko, Gabriel. *Railroads and Regulation, 1877–1916*. Princeton, NJ: Princeton University Press, 1965.

Martin, Albro. *Enterprise Denied: Origins of the Decline of American Railroads, 1897–1917*. New York: Columbia University Press, 1971.

Petzinger, Thomas, Jr. *Hard Landing: The Epic Contest for Power and Profits that Plunged the Airlines into Chaos*. New York: Three Rivers Press, 1996.

Rae, John B. *The Road and the Car in American Life*. Cambridge, MA: MIT Press, 1971.

Rose, Mark H. *Interstate: Express Highway Politics, 1941–1956*. Lawrence: University Press of Kansas, 1979.

Stover, John F. *American Railroads*. 2nd ed. Chicago: University of Chicago Press, 1997.

Usselman, Steven W. *Regulating Railroad Innovation: Business, Technology, and Politics in America, 1840–1920*. New York: Cambridge University Press, 2002.

CARLOS A. SCHWANTES

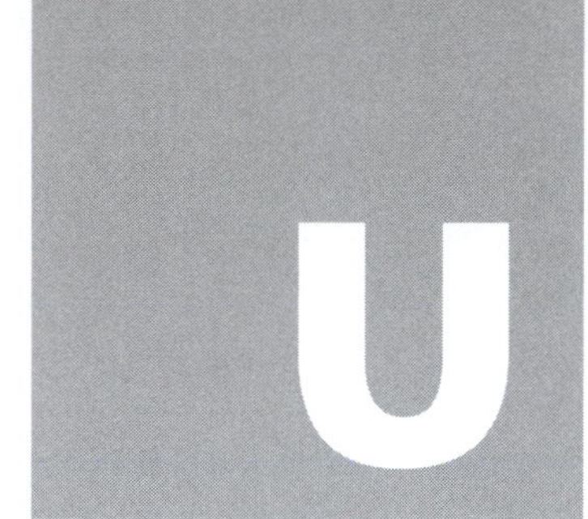

United Nations

The United Nations is one of the most hotly debated institutions in American politics. Critics portray it as corrupt, ineffective in preventing wars, and a threat to American interests. Supporters argue that such cooperation among nations is necessary in an interconnected world, that the United Nations has had a positive impact around the globe, and that in crisis, it brings world leaders together to talk through their differences. Some conservatives argue that the United States should leave the United Nations altogether, while liberals argue for greater investment in it. The debate between those who wish the United States to act independently in its own national interests and those who see U.S. interests tied to international and global interests has surged back and forth for more than a century. The first crisis occurred at the time of World War I.

World War I and the League of Nations

World War I produced death and destruction on a scale never seen before. Year after year, millions died in harrowing circumstances. By 1918 the Austro-Hungarian, Russian, Turkish, and German empires were all destroyed.

Many people in power and in the general public, especially in the United States, believed it was essential to create a political process to prevent another catastrophic war. Most Americans were very much opposed to the centuries-old feuding of Europe's empires and vowed to avoid being ensnared in such foreign entanglements.

In 1917 President Woodrow Wilson, a Democrat, led the United States into the war on the side of Britain and France, and antiwar protestors suffered lengthy jail sentences. Wilson proposed a 14-point program for a lasting peace. The final point of the 14 was to create a new organization, called the League of Nations, to preserve the peace. Its main tool was economic sanctions, which required a consensus of all member states to be enforced.

The organization was crippled from the start, however, when the United States, having invented the League, refused to join it. After the war, many Americans were alarmed at the prospect of never-ending engagement in foreign disputes and favored isolation. Leading senators in opposition to the League prevented the U.S. Senate from ratifying the treaty, a procedure essential for the United States to make treaties.

Britain and France, exhausted and embittered by the war, felt that Wilson had foisted the League upon them. They could not carry forward the farsighted goals of the League without the help of the United States. A turning point came in 1932, when Britain and France, at a world disarmament conference, humiliated the then progressive German government by refusing to disarm equally with Germany. The German government returned home to face a public convinced that military force and a strong nation were the only ways to revive Germany, and Adolf Hitler took full advantage.

Having rejected disarmament, the British and French then showed no will to fight when Japan, Italy, and Germany began to break international agreements and take over the land and peoples of other states. By the time Hitler attacked Poland in 1939, the League of Nations had lost all credibility. Nevertheless, some of its organizations for combating slavery, drugs, and the exploitation of labor continued under the new United Nations after World War II.

Origins and Structure

The United Nations was distinct from the League of Nations in three main respects. First, it grew from the alliance that ultimately won World War II. These allied countries were motivated by the prospect of building a better world, and the new organization began life on the wave of victorious enthusiasm. Second, the United Nations was not one organization but a system of economic, security, legal, and social structures. Third, the critically important security organization of the United Nations had the power to force other states to act and to go to war but also gave the victorious five nations the power to prevent the institution from taking action, especially military action. These five—China, France, Russia, the United Kingdom, and the United States—have permanent seats on the UN Security Council and a veto over any decision.

The alliance that would become the foundation of the UN system we know today was created by U.S. president Franklin D. Roosevelt and British prime minister Winston Churchill three weeks after the Japanese bombing of Pearl Harbor. That winter Roosevelt held a long secret conference with Churchill at the White House. On January 1, 1942, they launched the 26-member United Nations to increase support for the fight; bring in the Soviet Union, which was fighting the Nazi armies on the Eastern front without help; and neutralize any sympathy for Hitler's anticommunism among the American public. China and India were part of the alliance, which pledged to fight together until victory and to advance a postwar human rights agenda that would include democratic freedoms, social security, labor rights, and free trade. In the twenty-first century, this agenda seems liberal, but at the time, the war leaders regarded it as necessary to motivate people to fight and build for the future. War was widely regarded as a product of poverty, competition for resources, financial chaos, and arms races. It is for these reasons that in August 1941, Churchill and Roosevelt issued the Atlantic Charter, an eight-point manifesto that included the statement that nations had to abandon using armed force in international affairs.

After the Declaration by the United Nations, the term *United Nations forces* appeared daily in official documents, the media, and popular culture. In December 1942, the United Nations made one of the first international statements condemning the mass murder of Jews in Poland. And at the end of the war in Europe, President Harry S. Truman informed the American people that Germany had surrendered to the United Nations. Roosevelt and his partners were determined to create new global organizations to prevent a third world war. In 1943 the United Nations created interim organizations:

Leaders of the Atlantic Charter Conference, August 10–12, 1941, attend church services on the deck of HMS *Prince of Wales*, in Placentia Bay, Newfoundland. President Franklin D. Roosevelt (left) and Prime Minister Winston Churchill are seated in the foreground. (Naval Historical Center)

the UN War Crimes Commission, the UN Relief and Rehabilitation Administration, and the UN Food and Agriculture Commission. By using the same name for the military and political effort, Roosevelt took an integrated, internationalist approach that aimed to avoid the public rejection of the United Nations that the League of Nations had suffered.

The wartime United Nations created world financial organizations and the UN we know today. In 1944 the UN Monetary and Financial Conference (UNMFC) created the World Bank and the International Monetary Fund. Today the UNMFC is better known as the Bretton Woods Conference, so named for the site at which it took place in New Hampshire. Similarly, the 1945 conference that created the UN organization we know today is popularly known as the San Francisco Conference and officially called the United Nations Conference on International Organization (UNCIO). At the time, the creation of the United Nations we know today was the crowning glory of the UN political and war effort. Article 3 of the UN Charter states that the first original members of the UN are those who signed the UN Declaration in January 1942. Fifty-one states came to the UNCIO, as did a huge nongovernmental lobby that achieved some amendments to the proposals the great powers had made at the Dumbarton Oaks and Yalta Conferences. One nongovernmental achievement was the explicit mention of women in the UN Charter, which has provided the basis for many global women's initiatives over the last half-century.

In the late 1940s, the rivalry between the Western and Communist worlds escalated into the cold war. From then on, neither side wanted to remind people that they had been allies in World War II. During this period, the term *Allies* referred to the non-Soviet forces that had fought Hitler, and since then, the wartime United Nations that preceded the San Francisco Conference has been forgotten.

The contemporary United Nations is made up of two main bodies, the Security Council and the General Assembly. The Security Council consists of five permanent members (the "P5")—China, France, Russia, the United Kingdom, and the United States—as well as ten members with three-year terms.

The Security Council has the power to make international law and take military action, but this power is subject to the veto of any one of the five permanent members. Also, under Article 51 of the UN Charter, states have a right to defend themselves militarily. These features, along with the use of majority voting in the General Assembly, are major differences between the United Nations and the League of Nations, which needed consensus before it could act. The Soviet Union used the veto power in 1946, when it tried to prevent the West from bringing fascist Spain into UN membership, and many times after that. In recent years, the United States has used the veto most often, sometimes in defense of Israel.

The General Assembly includes all member states, controls the budget, and organizes the general work of the United Nations, which focuses on using economic and social measures to reduce the risk of war. The original wartime organizations evolved into 22 subsidiary or associated bodies, including the World Court; the World Health Organization; the UN Educational, Scientific and Cultural Organization (UNESCO); the Conference on Trade and Development; the Development Program; and other organizations aimed at helping children and refugees.

The Cold War and Decolonization

The cold war dominated global politics by the 1950s. This confrontation prevented the United Nations from taking action as each side canceled out the other in Security Council debates. The United Nations also provided a global political forum at which people not aligned with either side could be courted for their support and provided a nonviolent arena for competition and dialogue at a time when a U.S.-Soviet war could have resulted in a nuclear holocaust.

American debates on the country's role in the United Nations shifted with the rise of McCarthyism in the 1950s, when people who favored progressive causes faced being fired from their jobs and socially excluded in the fight against communism.

The Korean War (1950–53) was fought by the U.S.-led United Nations on one side and North Korea and the People's Republic of China on the other. The Soviet Union, apparently surprised by North Korea's initial invasion of South Korea, was boycotting the Security Council at the time and was not present to veto UN action. China's seat on the Security Council was held by the pro-American government based in Taiwan. Some 50,000 of the more than 3 million war dead were U.S. military personnel. The war froze East-West relations until the later 1960s. One product of a thaw in relations was the 1970 UN Nuclear Non-Proliferation Treaty, which is considered a foundation of international security.

Increasing numbers of new states have changed the character of the United Nations as it has grown to 192 members. This has occurred in two waves, the first in the 1950s and 1960s as the British and French empires collapsed, and then in the 1990s, after the collapse of communism and the fragmentation of the Soviet Union and of other nations—notably, Yugoslavia—into smaller sovereign states. These new states have tended to favor the political opponents of the empires that governed them; states in Africa and Asia looked to the Soviets and, since 1991, people emerging from Russian domination have looked to the West as a model to follow.

In the first wave of new state creation, many of the new states adopted socialist or communist policies and were hostile to their former Western colonial masters. Led by India, Yugoslavia, and Indonesia, many of the newly liberated states rejected both the capitalist and Communist systems to forge a third world movement of nonaligned states. The Suez Crisis of 1956, the war in Congo in the 1960s, and the Vietnam War were all key points in the political history of these years. People in the third world expressed desperation at the economic conditions they perceived as imposed on them by capitalism, and this produced hostility to the U.S. business-focused approach. As a result, U.S. politicians came to regard the United Nations as hostile to the United States, a perception that continues to this day. In the 1980s, President Ronald Reagan withdrew the United States from membership in UNESCO because of what he deemed its leftist policies. Nevertheless, public opinion polls in the United States continue to show support for the nation's membership in the United Nations (above the 50 percent mark into the twenty-first century, down from the above 80 percent level of support in 1945).

Into the Twenty-First Century

The collapse of communism produced a brief renaissance for the United Nations in the 1990s. For decades Western leaders had blamed the Communists for the inability to get UN action, so with the collapse, came a great expectation that the United Nations would be empowered to act. In 1990 Iraq leader Saddam Hussein's occupation of Kuwait led to strong UN support for the expulsion of his troops from that country by military force, which was accomplished in 1991. Peacekeeping operations expanded rapidly after 1990. Whereas in 1987, there were some 10,000 UN peacekeepers on missions around the world, by 1995 the number had grown to more than 70,000. These peacekeepers are all sent by member states—the United Nations itself has no forces, and despite the intentions of the founders, very little military planning staff, and no troops on standby in the forces of its member nations. This lack of capacity represents the will of the member states. For example, during the Korean War of the 1950s and in the war in Iraq of 1990–91, the United States provided its full military capacity, but usually there is no such commitment from member states and resistance to the development of a UN capacity that might rival U.S.-favored organizations such as NATO. Consequently, UN military missions are inevitably slow to assemble and tend to be poorly organized.

UN peacekeeping has a bad name in U.S. politics. The long, violent conflicts in Bosnia, Rwanda, Somalia, and more recently Darfur, indicate to many the weakness of the world body. In Rwanda, in 1994, hundreds of thousands died in ethnic violence. The UN and U.S. involvement in the east African state Somalia marked a rapid turnaround in U.S. political attitudes in 1992–93. President George H. W. Bush deployed 25,000 combat troops to Somalia to help restore order. Shortly after taking office, President Bill Clinton reduced the U.S. military presence there to a few thousand; in the fall of 1993, however, he both refused armored support for U.S. troops and authorized a raid by U.S. Rangers that ended in 18 U.S. dead, a large number in the politics of the time. Clinton was anxious to reduce the negative political impact, so the mission was portrayed as a UN rather than a U.S. action.

In Bosnia, UN peacekeepers were unable to stop ethnic cleansing and were denied a mandate and power to attack aggressors. With U.S. public and elite opinion divided and cautioned by the debacle in Somalia, the United States left the matter to the Europeans and the United Nations, while denying them aid from the North Atlantic Treaty Organization. Finally, when the conflict appeared out of control and domestic concern had grown, the United States led military action and a negotiated settlement. For many, the situtation in Bosnia underlined the reality that whatever the legal niceties at the United Nations, only the United States had the muscle to impose peace in the world. The image of America as the reluctant sheriff gained ground in U.S. politics, while in other parts of the world, the image of the United States as police for the powerful had greater resonance.

UN conferences gathered momentum after the end of the cold war. The Earth Summit in Brazil in 1992 on environmental issues set the new standard and led to others, including the 1997 meeting in Kyoto, Japan, that created the first global agreement to combat climate change. UN-sponsored disarmament agreements banned chemical weapons (the Chemical Weapons Convention in 1993) and the testing of nuclear weapons (the Comprehensive Test Ban Treaty in 1996).

The terrorist attacks on the United States on September 11, 2001, were a defining moment at the start of the new century. The UN Security Council offered its immediate support and endorsed U.S. military action to overthrow the Taliban regime in Afghanistan. Despite its previous hostility to the United Nations, the administration of President George W. Bush sought a closer relationship and rejoined UNESCO.

The run-up to the war in Iraq and subsequent events have once again seen the United Nations portrayed in U.S. politics as either villain or weakling. Prior to the U.S.-led invasion in 2003, UN inspectors seeking weapons of mass destruction in Iraq were criticized as being dupes of Saddam Hussein. Despite stating that the United States needed no "permission slip" from the United Nations to attack Iraq, President Bush sought first one and then a second Security Council resolution to pressure Iraq, arguing that the UN's failure to support the United States made it as useless as the League of Nations in the 1930s. Some Democrats contend that the pursuit of the first resolution was merely an attempt to secure centrist votes in the November 2002 midterm congressional elections, and the second was never seriously pursued. In retrospect, the Bush administration argued that earlier resolutions and the right of preemptive self-defense provided the backing of international law for its actions. UN supporters pointed to the wisdom of the majority of nations on the Security Council who refused to support what they saw as a disastrous war.

UN member states provided funds for a budget of $20 billion in 2008, excluding the IMF and the World Bank, while the United States has accumulated unpaid dues to the United Nations of some $1.5 billion, the lion's share of overdue payments. By way of comparison, the $20 billion budget is about half that of the single U.S. state of Virginia, while the UN agency responsible for controlling nuclear proliferation, the International Atomic Energy Agency, has just $200 million to spend. The United Nations also lacks permanent peacekeeping forces or

UN Peacekeeping Forces from Thailand in East Timor, July 23, 2002. UN peacekeeping operations expanded rapidly after 1990. (Antonio Dasiparu/AFP/Getty)

even a headquarters and communications unit comparable to that of most of its member states.

Reform is a term much used in discussions of the United Nations. Some debate focuses on issues of corruption and ineffectiveness; for some states such as India, Germany, and Japan, the issue is to secure a permanent seat on the Security Council. The term *UN reform*, therefore, does not describe a single agenda. The U.S. nationalist agenda includes removing those members of the United Nations alleged to be undemocratic or inhumane from any influence, cutting the budget, and introducing standards of efficiency drawn from the corporate sector. Others in the United States seek greater resources for peacekeeping and other missions. Internationally, many states believe that either the veto should be done away with or expanded to other major states, such as India.

As Mark Twain put it, "any jackass can kick a barn down, but it takes a carpenter to build one." As new crises arise, the familiar arguments will resume between those who see the United Nations as an ally of liberal causes that should not impede U.S. goals and those who regard it as a necessity in an interdependent world.

See also foreign policy and domestic politics since 1933; Korean War and cold war; New Deal Era, 1932–52.

FURTHER READING

Kennedy, Paul. *Parliament of Man: The Past, Present, and Future of the United Nations*. New York: Vintage, 2007.

Plesch, Dan. *America, Hitler and the UN*. London: I.B. Tauris, 2010.

United Nations. *Basic Facts about the United Nations*. New York: United Nations Pubilcations, 2004.

United Nations Information Organisation. *The United Nations Today and Tomorrow*. London: His Majesty's Stationery Office, 1945.

Weiss, Thomas G., David P. Forsythe, Roger A. Coate, and Kelly-Kate Pease. *The United Nations and Changing World Politics*. Boulder, CO: Westview Press, 2007.

DAN PLESCH

V

veterans

American military veterans were important political actors even before the United States became a nation. All of the American colonies except Connecticut, Delaware, and Quaker Pennsylvania provided pensions for wounded veterans, with South Carolina even holding out the possibility of freedom as a benefit for enlisted slaves. And when it came to pensioning disabled veterans, as the Continental Congress did in 1776, there was ample precedent in the kingdoms of Europe—France, Britain, Prussia, and Russia all had national military hospitals and rudimentary disability pension systems in place by 1780. But the place of the veteran in a self-conscious republic was different and has evolved in unique ways since the Revolution.

When it came to "service pensions"—stipends paid simply on the basis of past military service—some early congressmen balked. In a republic, they argued, military service was a duty of citizenship. Service pensions represented the entering wedge for standing armies and political patronage, creating dependence and (since service pensions were typically limited to officers) invidious distinctions of rank. But under wartime pressures, Congress promised all troops lump-sum payments at the war's end (1778), and Continental officers half-pay pensions for life (1780). When officers of General George Washington's army encamped at Newburgh, New York, demanded full pensions or a cash equivalent as the price of their disbandment, Congress defused the situation with the Commutation Act of 1783, which provided officers with five years' full pay instead of half-pay pensions for life. Noncommissioned indigent veterans, however, would not be pensioned until the Service Pension Act of 1818, and full-service pensions did not arrive until 1832. State militiamen, who made up much of the estimated 232,000-man Revolutionary Army, were excluded from federal benefits entirely. Thus, at its outset the U.S. pension system drew distinctions between officers and men, federal and state troops, and three classes of the deserving: war invalids, indigent "dependents," and soldiers whose only claim to benefits was service.

Continental Army veterans also received warrants for large tracts of land in the public domain, mainly in the Old Northwest Territory and the Southwest Territory, under acts of 1776 and 1780, while land-rich states such as Virginia and New York made grants of their own. Eventually, title to 2,666,080 acres was issued on the basis of Revolutionary War claims. But conflicting state land claims, wars with Native American nations, and a law that, for a time, restricted sales to 4,000-acre parcels made land warrants of small value to most veterans until the late 1790s, by which time most had been sold to speculators. The same thing happened to officers' commutation certificates: by the time the federal government emerged from default in 1791, many officers had sold their certificates for as little as twelve and a half cents on the dollar.

Attitudes toward Continental veterans gradually evolved from republican worries about vice and patronage to widespread sympathy for their suffering in old age that made the 1818 pension act possible. But Revolutionary War service did not lead to public office (after George Washington, it took eight presidential elections before a military veteran was even nominated), and the few public Revolutionary commemorations tended toward the civic and classical rather than the military: Washington appears in a toga atop Baltimore's Washington Monument (1829), while the Bunker Hill Monument in Charlestown, Massachusetts (1843), is a simple classical obelisk. The Society of the Cincinnati, an officers-only veterans' hereditary order that had provoked fears of aristocracy at its founding in 1783, had declined to only six northeastern state chapters by 1832.

The short wars of the early nineteenth century did little to alter this picture. Individual veterans such as William Henry Harrison and Zachary Taylor parlayed military service into political careers, but veterans as such did not organize—there was no recognizable "veteran vote." A tiny Society of the War of 1812 led a fitful existence from 1853 into the 1890s, when it became a hereditary order; the National Association of Mexican War Veterans was not formed until 1874 and lasted barely into the twentieth century. Veterans of both wars continued to benefit from federal land grants and invalid pensions, but dependent and service pensions came to War of 1812 veterans only in 1871 and to Mexican War veterans in 1887 (dependent) and 1907 (service). The pensioning of Mexican War volunteers was politically difficult because so many of them were Southerners who later fought for the Confederacy. The law finally enacted in 1887 excluded those whose wounds had been sustained in Confederate service and those politically disbarred by the Fourteenth Amendment.

Veterans in Politics

The Civil War marked a watershed in the relation of veterans to society and politics. Union veterans created mass organizations to lobby for their interests, the most powerful of which was the Grand Army of the Republic (GAR), organized in 1866. Nearly all northern towns had GAR posts, which functioned as centers of sociability, providers of charity, and promoters of a conservative brand of American patriotism in schools and on public holidays such as Memorial Day (first proclaimed nationally by GAR commander in chief John Logan in 1868). The GAR pushed the federal government and the states to erect soldiers' homes (12 did so by 1888); won land grants and special treatment under the Homestead Act for veterans; persuaded some northern states to give Union veterans preference in hiring; and lobbied ceaselessly for the expansion of the Pension Bureau, whose new building (1882; now the National Building Museum) was the largest public space in Washington until 1971.

The largest impact of the Union veterans was on pension legislation, mainly the Arrears Act (1879) and Dependent Pension Act (1890). The latter granted a pension to nearly all Union veterans at a time when many were still in their fifties. By 1891 military pensions accounted for one dollar of every three spent by the federal government, and at the high point of the Civil War pension system in 1902, 999,446 persons, including widows and orphans, were on the rolls. By 1917 the nation had spent approximately $5 billion on Union Army and Navy pensions. Civilian reformers such as E. L. Godkin attacked the "unmanliness" of those who accepted service pensions and the many frauds riddling the system, especially under the administration of Benjamin Harrison and his profligate pension commissioner, James Tanner.

With more than 400,000 members at its height in 1890, the GAR had the political muscle to make itself heard. It created an organized bloc of voters in the North for which both parties—but mainly Republicans—contended by increasing pension benefits, authorizing expensive monuments (such as Grand Army Plaza in Brooklyn, New York, and the Soldiers and Sailors Monument in Indianapolis, Indiana), and sponsoring "patriotic" state laws such as those requiring schoolhouses to fly the American flag. The pension system also created reciprocal benefits for the Republican Party, because the need for revenue to pay pension benefits justified the high tariffs Republican industrialists sought. At the same time, by putting money into the hands of Union veterans, Republicans created a loyal voting constituency. Especially before the extremely close election of 1888, Democrats charged that the important swing states of Indiana, Ohio, and Pennsylvania were being flooded with expedited pension payments.

In the South, Confederate veterans organized late and at least partly in reaction to the GAR. Barred from federal entitlements, they obtained pensions and soldiers' homes from most southern states, though such benefits were usually modest and limited to the disabled or indigent. Georgia's Confederate disability pensions, for example, averaged only 44 percent of the federal rate in 1900. The United Confederate Veterans (UCV), founded in 1889, presided over a veterans' culture that shifted ground from intransigence in the 1870s to a romantic "lost cause" sensibility in the 1890s that even Union veterans could accept with some reservations. In 1913 Union and Confederate veterans held a highly publicized reunion at Gettysburg, where President Woodrow Wilson declared the Civil War "a quarrel forgotten."

The Spanish-American War produced only 144,252 veterans and two significant organizations: the United Spanish War Veterans (1904), which soon faded, and the Veterans of Foreign Wars (VFW), founded in 1913. Unlike the GAR and UCV, the VFW admitted veterans of subsequent wars, a policy that has allowed it to persevere into the present. On the other hand, the VFW policy of limiting membership to overseas veterans initially hampered the organization in competition with the more inclusive American Legion (founded in Paris in 1919). The Legion quickly became the most popular organization among the approximately 4 million American veterans of World War I. It adopted the GAR's internal structure of local post, state department, and national encampment; consulted with aging GAR members on political strategy; and continued the Grand Army's program of flag ritualism and "patriotic instruction."

In other ways, however, the situation facing World War I veterans was markedly different. Whereas the soldiers of 1865 had come back mostly to farms, those of 1919 returned primarily to cities, where joblessness was acute and vocational training scarce. When Interior Secretary Franklin Lane in 1919 proposed the traditional remedy of land grants, he discovered that most arable public land had already been given away. Instead, like other belligerents (notably Germany and Britain), the United States began moving away from the nineteenth-century model of land grants, pensions, and warehousing veterans in hospitals and toward a model of physical rehabilitation and vocational training. All veterans' programs were finally consolidated in the Veterans Bureau (1921), which in 1930 became the Veterans Administration (VA).

The pension system of 1919 also differed significantly from the expensive, politically partisan, and fraud-riddled Civil War regime. Instead of a system of entitlements, the War Risk Act of 1917 allowed World War I soldiers to pay small premiums in return for life insurance and future medical care. However, its early administration was corrupt, and veterans' hospitals proved too few in number and unable to cope with late-developing disabilities such as shell shock. World War I veterans never did receive service pensions, and were eligible for non-service-related disability pensions only briefly, from 1930 to 1933. Instead, politicians opted for "adjusted compensation," a bonus approved in Congress in 1924 and payable in 1945, designed to make up for wartime inflation and lost earnings. Veterans were seriously divided on the propriety of the bonus, even after Depression hardships drove 20,000 of them to march on Washington, D.C., in 1932 as a Bonus Army demanding its immediate payment. Although troops led by General Douglas MacArthur violently expelled the veterans from Anacostia Flats, the bonus was finally paid in 1936.

The worldwide labor and political strife following 1918 sharpened the hard edge of veteran nationalism. Faced with revolution in Russia, chaos in Germany, a general strike in Seattle, and race riots in cities such as Chicago, the American Legion came out immediately against "Bolshevism," which it defined broadly to include every organization from the Communist Party to the League of Women Voters. Legion members helped break strikes of Kansas coal miners and Boston police in the summer of 1919, and from the 1920s through the 1950s, they made war on "Reds." Legionnaires helped bring a House Un-American Activities Committee into existence in 1938 and aided FBI probes of subversion thereafter. The Legion was strongest in small cities and among prosperous members of the middle class; like the GAR, it left racial matters largely to localities, which in practice usually meant segregated posts.

World War II and After

By the time the 12 million veterans of World War II began to return home, the New Deal had institutionalized social welfare spending. Thus, despite the unprecedented scope of the GI Bill, officially titled the Servicemen's Readjustment Act of 1944, few commentators expressed the worries about fraud and dependence that dogged earlier veterans' relief. Drafted by former Legion commander Harry Colmery, the GI Bill provided World War II veterans with free college educations and medical care, unemployment insurance for one year, and guaranteed loans up to $4,000 to buy homes or businesses. Other legislation guaranteed loans on crops to veterans who were farmers, reinstituted vocational training, and tried to safeguard the jobs of those returning from war. GI Bill educational and vocational benefits proved so popular that they were extended to veterans of Korea and Vietnam and to peacetime veterans in the Veterans Readjustment Benefits Act (1966). By the 1970s, the VA was spending more than all but three cabinet departments; it achieved cabinet status in 1989. By 1980 benefits distributed under the GI Bill totaled $120 billion.

Unlike previous wars (but like subsequent conflicts in Korea and Vietnam), World War II was fought mainly by conscripts, which may have made taxpayers more willing to compensate veterans for their "forced labor." These veterans were slightly younger and better educated than World War I veterans and demobilized into considerably less class and racial strife. For the first time, they also included significant numbers of women (the 150,000 members of the Women's Army Corps and 90,000 Naval WAVEs), who qualified for GI Bill benefits. Still, most of the returnees joined older veterans' groups rather than forming new ones: Legion membership, which had fluctuated between 600,000 and

1 million before 1941, reached a record 3.5 million in 1946, while VFW membership rose from 300,000 to 2 million. Among liberal alternative groups founded in 1945, only AMVETS reached 250,000 members.

Politically, World War II ex-soldiers did not vote as a recognizable bloc, but veteran status was an enormous advantage to those seeking office. Joseph McCarthy, for example, was elected to the Senate as "Tail Gunner Joe," while magazine articles trumpeted John F. Kennedy's heroism aboard his boat, PT-109. Every president from Dwight Eisenhower to George H. W. Bush (except Jimmy Carter, a postwar Naval Academy graduate) was a World War II veteran, a string unmatched since the late nineteenth century. In the postwar years, it became normal for the president to address the annual American Legion convention. Culturally, World War II veterans received heroic treatment in movies such as *The Longest Day* (1962) and in a neoclassical World War II Memorial (2004) that stands in stylistic contrast to the bleaker Vietnam (1983) and Korean War (1995) memorials on the Mall in Washington, D.C.

The Korean and Vietnamese conflicts produced none of the triumphalism that followed World War II. Although the VA continued to grow—its 2009 budget request was for $93.7 billion, half of it earmarked for benefits—the Legion and VFW struggled throughout the 1960s and 1970s to attract new veterans whose attitudes toward war and nationalism were ambivalent. After the Vietnam War, which the older organizations supported fiercely, young veterans felt alienated from a society that often ignored or pitied them. In 1967 they formed the first significant antiwar veterans group, the Vietnam Veterans Against the War (VVAW; after 1983, the Vietnam Veterans of America, VVOA). With fewer than 20,000 members, the VVAW publicized war atrocities and lobbied for American withdrawal. In the 1980s, more Vietnam veterans began to join the Legion and VFW, bringing those groups up to their 2008 memberships of approximately 3 million and 2.2 million, respectively. The treatment of veterans suffering from post-traumatic stress disorder/(PTSD) and exposure to defoliants in Vietnam became important issues for these organizations, often bringing them into conflict with the Defense Department.

In the years since Vietnam, relations between veterans and society have changed in several ways. Subsequent military actions in Grenada, Bosnia, Kuwait, and Iraq have been carried out by volunteer forces, making military experience more remote from the day-to-day lives of most Americans. About 15 percent of those serving in the military are now women, a fact that may eventually change the traditional veteran discourse about war as a test of masculinity—the dedication of the first memorial to military service women at Arlington National Cemetery in 1997 marked the change. And the gradual passing of the World War II generation has produced a wave of nostalgia for veterans of that war similar to the one that engulfed Civil War veterans toward the end of their lives.

See also armed forces, politics in the.

FURTHER READING

Dearing, Mary R. *Veterans in Politics: The Story of the G.A.R.* Baton Rouge: Louisiana State University Press, 1952.

Gawdiak, Ihor, et al. *Veterans Benefits and Judicial Review: Historical Antecedents and the Development of the American System.* Washington, DC: Federal Research Division, Library of Congress, 1992. Downloadable from http://handle.dtic.mil/100.2/ADA302666.

Gerber, David A., ed. *Disabled Veterans in History.* Ann Arbor: University of Michigan Press, 2000.

Glasson, William H. *Federal Military Pensions in the United States.* New York: Oxford University Press, 1918.

Jensen, Laura S. *Patriots, Settlers and the Origins of American Social Policy.* New York: Cambridge University Press, 2003.

McConnell, Stuart. *Glorious Contentment: The Grand Army of the Republic, 1866–1900.* Chapel Hill: University of North Carolina Press, 1992.

Pencak, William. *For God and Country: The American Legion, 1919–1941.* Boston: Northeastern University Press, 1989.

Resch, John P. *Suffering Soldiers: Revolutionary War Veterans, Moral Sentiment, and Political Culture in the Early Republic.* Amherst: University of Massachusetts Press, 1999.

Starr, Paul. *The Discarded Army: Soldiers after Vietnam.* New York: Charterhouse, 1973.

Wecter, Dixon. *When Johnny Comes Marching Home.* Cambridge, MA: Houghton Mifflin, 1944.

STUART MCCONNELL

Vietnam and Indochina wars

Apples and Dominoes

The makers of U.S. foreign policy after World War II often used analogies to explain to the American people the need for cold war commitments. In 1947, trying to justify to a skeptical Congress an outlay of economic and military aid to Greece and Turkey, Undersecretary of State Dean Acheson warned of the consequences of even a single Communist success in southeastern Europe: "Like apples in a barrel infected by the corruption of one rotten one, the corruption of Greece would infect Iran and all to the East." By 1954 the cold war had gone global, and much of the foreign policy concern of President Dwight Eisenhower was focused on Southeast Asia and particularly Indochina (the states of Vietnam, Laos, and Cambodia), where the French were engaged in a struggle to restore their colonial status, despite the clear preference of most Indochinese to be independent of outsider control. The Vietnamese independence movement was led by Ho Chi Minh, a Communist of long standing.

Contemplating U.S. military involvement on the side of the French, Eisenhower told a press conference why Americans should care about the fate of Vietnam. "You have a row of dominoes set up and you knock over the first one, and what will happen to the last one is the certainty that it will go over very quickly. . . . The loss of Indochina will cause the fall of Southeast Asia like a set of dominoes." Communism would not stop with just one or two victories. The loss to communism of strategically and economically important Southeast Asia would be a serious setback.

As U.S. involvement in the Vietnam War grew over the years, resulting in the commitment of hundreds of thousands of ground troops and the lavish use of airpower over North and South Vietnam after early 1965, the domino theory that underpinned it evolved. John F. Kennedy, who inherited from Eisenhower a significant financial commitment to the South Vietnamese government of Ngo Dinh Diem and discovered that U.S. military advisors and Central Intelligence Agency officers were hard at work on Diem's behalf, publicly professed his faith in the domino theory. By the time Lyndon Johnson succeeded to the presidency, following Kennedy's assassination in November 1963, Johnson's foreign policy advisors, most of them inherited from Kennedy, had concluded that the dominoes were perhaps less territorial than psychological. Withdrawal from Vietnam would embolden America's enemies and discourage its friends everywhere. The United States would lose credibility if it abandoned South Vietnam—no one, not even the European allies, would ever again take the Americans' word on faith. The final domino was not, as one official put it, "some small country in Southeast Asia, but the presidency itself"; the American people would not tolerate a humiliating defeat (the word *defeat* always carried the modifier *humiliating*) in Vietnam and would cast out any president judged responsible for having allowed it to occur.

Political Constraints

American presidents faced a dilemma each election cycle during the war in Vietnam. As Daniel Ellsberg, a Pentagon advisor turned antiwar advocate, put it, presidents could not commit large numbers of American soldiers to combat in Southeast Asia, yet at the same time they were not supposed to lose the southern part of Vietnam to communism. All-out war was politically unacceptable. The perception that the United States had abandoned its friends to totalitarianism and reneged on its word was equally unacceptable. A president's political effectiveness therefore depended on a war that could not be lost, but one whose costs remained low enough, in blood and treasure, to keep the American people from growing restive.

Sensing this, the presidents who confronted in Vietnam the rise of a nationalist-Communist independence movement attempted to keep the American role in the conflict out of the public eye. The war must be fought, said Secretary of State Dean Rusk (1961–69) "in cold blood," by which he meant not remorselessly but with restraint. The first U.S. commitment, to what was then a French-backed regime in the south that was supposed to be an alternative to the popular Ho Chi Minh, was a small portion of aid provided by the administration of Harry Truman in 1950, mainly obscured by the far more visible war in Korea. Despite his warning about the dominos falling, Eisenhower also limited U.S. involvement in Vietnam, shouldering aside the French after 1954 and sending funds and advisors to help Diem, but refusing to order airstrikes, send in combat troops, or otherwise stake his reputation on the outcome of the conflict. "I am convinced," wrote the president, "that no victory is possible in that type of theater."

Kennedy, too, refused to commit U.S. combat troops to Vietnam. He did secretly insert several hundred Special Forces to help train the South Vietnamese army. But he resisted pleas by some advisors, in early 1961, to intervene with force in Laos, and spurned recommendations by others to send a Marine "task force" to confront the Communists militarily. Even Johnson, who would authorize the introduction of over half a million troops into the war, tried to escalate quietly, never declaring war, seldom making a speech on the war, and issuing such announcements as there were about the escalations on Saturday afternoons, so as to avoid the full attention of the media.

American Public Opinion and the War

At first, and in good part because of his efforts to keep the war off the front pages, Johnson enjoyed high approval ratings for his policy of quiet but determined escalation. Gallup pollsters had asked a couple of questions about Indochina during 1953 and 1954, as French struggles hit the newspapers, then left the subject altogether until the spring of 1964, when they cautiously inquired, "Have you given any attention to developments in South Vietnam?" Just 37 percent of respondents said they had. That August, after Congress passed the Tonkin Gulf Resolution, which granted the president the latitude to conduct the war in Vietnam as he wished, Gallup asked what the country "should do next in regard to Vietnam." Twenty-seven percent said, "[S]how [we] can't be pushed around, keep troops there, be prepared," 12 percent wanted to "get tougher" using "more pressure," and 10 percent said, "[A]void all-out war, sit down and talk." The largest percentage of respondents (30 percent) had "no opinion."

By February 1965, the month in which the Johnson administration decided to begin systematically bombing targets in North Vietnam, over nine-tenths of those polled had heard that something was going on in Vietnam. Sixty-four percent thought the United States should "continue present efforts" to win the war, and of this group, 31 percent were willing to risk nuclear war in the bargain. (Just 21 percent thought that would be unwise.) Only late in 1965 did pollsters begin to ask whether Americans approved or disapproved of the president's handling of the war. Fifty-eight percent approved, just 22 percent did not. It is worth noting that in Gallup's annual poll seeking the world's "Most Admired Man" (women were measured separately), Johnson topped the list for three years running through 1967.

Johnson's anxieties about the war were growing nonetheless. The conflict was intrinsically vicious: once he committed U.S. combat troops to the fight, in March 1965, casualties began to mount. Johnson was also worried about the domestic political implications of a protracted, indecisive struggle, and even more a failure of nerve that would allow the Vietnamese Communists to take over South Vietnam and thereby revive talk that the Democratic Party was the refuge of appeasers, with himself as Neville Chamberlain. Above all, Johnson needed congressional and popular support for the legislation known collectively as the Great Society, his ambitious effort to undo racism and poverty in the United States. He worried most about the right wing. "If I don't go in now and they show later that I should have," he confided in early 1965, "they'll . . . push Vietnam up my ass every time." So he went in incrementally, hiding the war's true cost and hoping to keep it on low boil while his reform agenda went through, anticipating that his level of commitment would be enough to keep the right satisfied, yet not too much to antagonize the left, which, by early 1965, had begun to object to the escalating conflict.

By mid-1966, Americans were evenly divided over whether they approved or disapproved of the war; 15 months later, by 46 percent to 44 percent, those polled said that the country had "made a mistake sending troops to fight in Vietnam." In the meantime, the 1966 midterm elections favored the Republicans, who had ably exploited fears of urban violence, an indecisive war, and a protest movement by young people who seemed, to many Americans, unruly and unpatriotic.

Rising Protests, and the Tet Offensive

By the fall of 1967, American political culture had been affected by the emergence of the antiwar movement. Starting in the early 1960s with scattered concerns about the escalating war, then catalyzed by Johnson's decisions to bomb and send troops in early 1965, the movement grew rapidly on college campuses, incorporating those who believed the war an act of American imperialism, pacifists, scholars of Asian history and politics, seekers of righteous causes, those who believed sincerely that Vietnam was a wicked war, and many who worried that they or someone they loved would be drafted and sent to the killing fields of Southeast Asia. Large as antiwar demonstrations had become by late 1967—100,000 people rallied against the war in Washington that October—it was never the case that most Americans were protesters or that most Americans sympathized with them.

Yet the protests unnerved Johnson and undeniably affected the nation's political discourse. The president was afflicted by taunts outside the White House: "Hey, hey, LBJ, how many kids did you kill today?" Members of Congress found, at best, confusion about the war among their constituents, and, at worst, open anger about a conflict that seemed to be escalating without cause or explanation. Family members of key Vietnam policy makers asked increasingly sharp questions about the war at the dinner table, and the estrangement of friends who had turned against the war caused much grief; Secretary of Defense Robert McNamara's wife and son developed ulcers as a result of the strain.

Late in 1967, concerned about his slipping poll numbers and the war's possible damage to his domestic program, Johnson called his field commander home to reassure the public. General William Westmoreland was an outwardly confident man who believed that the killing machine he had built would grind the enemy down with superior training, firepower, and sheer numbers. The end of the war, Westmoreland told the National Press Club on November 21, "begins to come into view." Optimism reigned throughout South Vietnam. Victory "lies within our grasp—the enemy's hopes are bankrupt." Early January poll numbers bounced slightly Johnson's way. Then, in the middle of the night on January 30, the start of the Tet holiday in Vietnam, the National Liberation Front (NLF), sometimes known as the Viet Cong, and North Vietnamese soldiers launched a massive offensive against American and South Vietnamese strongholds throughout the south. Countless positions were overrun. The beautiful old capital of Hué fell, and thousands of alleged collaborators with the Saigon government were executed. Tan Son Nhut airbase, just outside Saigon, was shelled. Even the grounds of the American embassy were penetrated by enemy soldiers. The body count, the ghoulish measure of progress in the war demanded by Westmoreland's strategy of attrition, rose dramatically on all sides.

In the end, the enemy failed to achieve its military objectives. The U.S. embassy grounds were retaken within hours. Tan Son Nhut remained secure, along with Saigon itself. Hué was restored to the South Vietnamese government, though only after days of brutal fighting and subsequent revenge killings. The southern-based NLF was badly cut up, its forces having been used as shock troops during the offensive. North Vietnamese officials admitted years later that they had overestimated their ability to administer a crushing blow to the South Vietnamese and American forces during Tet.

In the United States, however, the Tet Offensive seemed to confirm Johnson's worst fears that an inconclusive, messy war would irreparably damage his political standing. It did no good to point out that the enemy had been beaten. Had not Westmoreland, and by extension Johnson himself, offered an upbeat assessment of South Vietnam's prospects just weeks earlier? Had not Americans been assured, time after time, that their military was invincible, its rectitude unquestionable? The war came home in direct ways—the upsurge in the number of American casulties; television coverage of a South Vietnamese policeman summarily executing an NLF suspect on a Saigon street; the twisted logic of a U.S. officer who said, of the village of Ben Tre, "we had to destroy the town in order to save it." Mainstream media reflected new depths of popular discouragement. In March, when Gallup asked whether the time had come for the United States to "gradually withdraw from Vietnam," 56 percent agreed, and only 34 percent disapproved of the idea. Altogether, 78 percent believed that the country was making no progress in the war.

The Unmaking of Lyndon Johnson

Johnson's first impulse was to toughen his rhetoric and stay the course. If the generals wanted more troops, they could have them. Secretary McNamara left the administration and was replaced by Johnson's old friend and presumed supporter Clark Clifford. But the erosion of public support for the war now undercut official unity in Washington. Clifford conducted a quick but honest analysis of the situation in Vietnam and concluded that the military could not guarantee success, even with a substantial infusion of troops. Advisors who had previously urged a sustained commitment now hedged: former secretary of state Acheson, a noted hard-liner, told Johnson that American "interests in Europe" were in jeopardy, in part because the nation was hemorrhaging gold at an alarming rate. On March 12, the president was nearly beaten in the New Hampshire presidential primary by the low-key Eugene McCarthy, who challenged Johnson's Vietnam War policies. The close call left Johnson despondent and concerned about a bruising primary campaign. To the surprise of even close friends, Johnson announced on March 31 that he would not seek reelection but would instead dedicate himself full time to the pursuit of a negotiated peace in Vietnam.

The war had wrecked Johnson and now tore apart his party. The Democrats split following Johnson's withdrawal from the campaign. Some backed McCarthy. Many flocked to the candidacy of Robert Kennedy, who had turned against the war, but whose assassination on June 6 ended the dream that the Democrats would unite under a popular, socially conscious, antiwar leader. George McGovern entered the fray as a stand-in for Kennedy,

CHINA
NORTH
VIETNAM
Hanoi
Haiphong
BURMA
MEKONG RIVER
LAOS
GULF OF TONKIN
HAINAN
Demilitarized Zone
Demarcation Line, July 1954
Khe Sanh
Hué
Da Nang
THAILAND
MEKONG RIVER
SOUTH
VIETNAM
KAMPUCHEA
(CAMBODIA)
TONLE SAP
SOUTH CHINA SEA
GULF OF SIAM
Tan Son Nhut
Saigon
Ben Tre
MEKONG
DELTA
CA MAU
PENINSULA
Ho Chi Minh Trail
U.S. base
0
100
200 miles
0
100
200
300 kilometers

Southeast Asia and the Vietnam War

but he lacked Kennedy's charisma and connections. At its chaotic convention in Chicago that August, in which protesters clashed with Mayor Richard Daley's notoriously unsympathetic police (and came off second best), the party nominated Johnson's vice president, Hubert Humphrey. Loyal to Johnson, who nevertheless maligned him repeatedly, Humphrey at first clung to the discredited policy of toughness on Vietnam. But when polls showed that he was running behind the Republican nominee Richard Nixon (who claimed to have a "secret plan" to end the war) and only slightly ahead of right-wing independent George Wallace (who guaranteed a military victory in Vietnam if the Communists refused to come to heel), Humphrey shifted his position. He would, he said, stop bombing the north. His tone moderated. Despite what had seemed long odds, in the end Humphrey nearly won, falling just 200,000 votes short of Nixon in the popular tally.

The Nixon-Kissinger Strategy, and War's End

Nixon had managed to rise from the political dead by cobbling together a coalition of white Americans fed up with disorder in the streets, militant blacks, militant students, and the indecisive war. Many of those previously loyal to the Democratic Party built by Franklin Roosevelt now defected to the Republicans. They included Catholics, ethnic voters in suburbs, and southern whites who were conservative on social issues but not quite ready to stomach the extremism of Wallace. They were part of what Nixon would call "the great silent majority," whom he presumed wanted "peace with honor" in Vietnam, whatever that meant.

Nixon and his national security advisor, Henry Kissinger, set out to recast diplomacy and liquidate the war. They employed a two-track approach. They would escalate the bombing of enemy targets and initiate attacks in third countries (Cambodia and Laos) in order to demonstrate to Hanoi their determination not to be bullied. At the same time, they would attempt to negotiate an end to hostilities, in part by pursuing détente with the Soviet Union and China. Nixon coldly gauged that most of the domestic, political cost of the war resulted from the death of American soldiers. He therefore proposed to substitute Vietnamese lives for American ones, through a program called "Vietnamization." Nixon continued bombing, but he also funded an expansion of the South Vietnamese army (ARVN) and equipped it with the latest weapons. And in late 1969, he began to withdraw U.S. troops, reducing the need to draft more young men and thus removing the most toxic issue around which the antiwar movement had gathered.

Still the protests did not end. People remained angry that the war dragged on, that Americans and Vietnamese continued to die in great numbers. The expansion of the American war into Cambodia and Laos brought renewed fury. The continued opposition to Nixon's policies, information leaks concerning a secret campaign to bomb Cambodia in 1969, and the disclosure, by Daniel Ellsberg, of the secret *Pentagon Papers* study in 1971, inspired Nixon to establish the clandestine White House "Plumbers," whose job it was to wiretap the telephones of the administration's self-construed enemies and even to burgle offices in search of incriminating information. The capture of a Plumbers' team at the Watergate complex in Washington in June 1972 ultimately led to the unraveling of the Nixon presidency. The attempt to cover up illegal behavior would be traced to the Oval Office.

A peace treaty was signed in Vietnam in January 1973. Both North and South soon violated its terms. Weakened by the Watergate scandal, Nixon was unable to prevent Congress from closing the valve on U.S. support for the South Vietnamese government. And in the summer of 1973, Congress passed the War Powers Act, designed to prevent presidents from conducting war as high-handedly as Johnson and Nixon had done, at least without disclosure to the legislature. Nixon was forced to resign in August 1974. When, the following spring, the North Vietnamese launched a powerful offensive against South Vietnam, and the ARVN largely crumbled, the new president, Gerald Ford, and Henry Kissinger, now secretary of state, tried to get Congress to loosen the purse strings on military aid to the besieged Saigon regime.

But Congress, and the majority of Americans, had had enough. They felt they had been lied to about the war, and they refused to trust Ford. Stung by Vietnam, many Americans now turned inward, shunning the kinds of foreign policy commitments they had seemed to accept so readily during the first three decades of the cold war. Americans had grown skeptical about what critics called, in the aftermath of Vietnam, the "imperial presidency," which acted without proper, constitutional regard for the wishes of the other branches of government or the temper of the people. The Vietnam War thus reshaped international and domestic politics, albeit temporarily. The continued usurpations of power by presidents since 1975 remind us that the supposed lessons of Vietnam—greater caution and humility in foreign affairs, greater transparency at home in the process by which war is undertaken—did not endure.

See also era of confrontation and decline, 1964–80; era of consensus, 1952–64; Korean War and cold war.

FURTHER READING

Kimball, Jeffrey. *Nixon's Vietnam War.* Lawrence: University of Kansas Press, 1998.

LaFeber, Walter. *The Deadly Bet: LBJ, Vietnam, and the 1968 Election.* Lanham, MD: Rowman and Littlefield, 2005.

Logevall, Fredrik. *Choosing War: The Lost Chance for Peace and the Escalation of War in Vietnam.* Berkeley: University of California Press, 1999.

McNamara, Robert S., with Brian VanDeMark. *In Retrospect: The Tragedy and Lessons of Vietnam.* New York: Vintage, 1995.

Rotter, Andrew J., ed. *Light at the End of the Tunnel: A Vietnam War Anthology.* 2nd ed. Wilmington, DE: Scholarly Resources Publishers, 1999.

Schulzinger, Robert D. *A Time for Peace: The United States and Vietnam, 1941–1975.* New York: Oxford University Press, 1997.

Sheehan, Neil. *A Bright Shining Lie: John Paul Vann and America in Vietnam.* New York: Vintage, 1988.

Small, Melvin. *Johnson, Nixon, and the Doves.* New Brunswick, NJ: Rutgers University Press, 1988.

Young, Marilyn B. *The Vietnam Wars 1945–1990.* New York: HarperCollins, 1991.

ANDREW J. ROTTER

voting

The right to vote in the United States has a complex history. In the very long run of more than 200 years, the trajectory of this history has been one of expansion: a far greater proportion of the population was enfranchised by the early twenty-first century than was true at the nation's birth. But this long-run trend reveals only part of the story: the history of the right to vote has also been a history of conflict and struggle, of movements backward as well as forward, of sharply demarcated state and regional variations. It is also the story, more generally, of efforts to transform the United States into a democracy: a form of government in which all adults—regardless of their class, gender, race, ethnicity, or place of birth—would have equal political rights. That history took nearly two centuries to unfold, and in key respects, it continues unfolding to the present day.

Democracy Rising

The seeds of this history were planted in the late eighteenth century, as the new American nation was being forged out of 13 former colonies. The Founding Fathers were staunch believers in representative government, but few, if any, of them believed that all adults (or even all adult males) had the "right" to participate in choosing the new nation's leaders. (Indeed, it was unclear whether voting was a "right" or a "privilege," and the word *democracy* itself had negative connotations, suggesting rule by the mob.) The founders had diverse views, but most believed that participation in government should be limited to those who could establish their independence and their "stake" in the new society through the ownership of property. Many agreed with William Blackstone's view that people "in so mean a situation that they are esteemed to have no will of their own" would be subject to manipulation if they had the franchise, while others feared that such persons might exercise their will too aggressively. Neither the original Constitution, ratified in 1788, nor the Bill of Rights, ratified in 1791, made any mention of a "right to vote."

After some internal debate, the men who wrote that Constitution, meeting in Philadelphia in 1787, decided not to adopt a national suffrage requirement: they left the issue to the states. This was a momentous decision—it meant that the breadth of the right to vote would vary from state to state for most of the nation's history, and the federal government would have to struggle for almost two centuries to establish national norms of democratic inclusion. Yet this decision was grounded less in principle than in pragmatic political considerations. By the late 1780s, each state already had a suffrage requirement, developed during the colonial era or during the first years of independence. The designers of the Constitution worried that any national requirement would be opposed by some states—as too broad or too narrow—and thus jeopardize the process of constitutional ratification. In *Federalist* 52, James Madison wrote, "One uniform rule would probably have been as dissatisfactory to some of the States as it would have been difficult to the convention." The only allusion to the breadth of the franchise in the Constitution was in Article I, section II, which specified that all persons who could vote for the most numerous house of each state legislature could also participate in elections for the House of Representatives.

Thus, at the nation's founding, suffrage was far from universal, and the breadth of the franchise varied from one state to the next. The right to vote was limited to those who owned property (ten states) or paid taxes of a specified value (New Hampshire, Georgia, and Pennsylvania)—only Vermont, the fourteenth state, had no such test. African Americans and Native Americans were expressly excluded by law or practice in South Carolina, Georgia, and Virginia. In New Jersey alone were women permitted to vote, and they lost that right in 1807.

Within a short time, however, popular pressures began to shrink the limitations on the franchise: the first two-thirds of the nineteenth century witnessed a remarkable expansion of democratic rights. These changes had multiple sources: shifts in the social structure, including the growth of urban areas; a burgeoning embrace of democratic ideology, including the word *democracy*; active, organized opposition to property and tax requirements from propertyless men, particularly those who had served as soldiers in the Revolutionary War and the War of 1812; the desire of settlers in the new territories in the "west" to attract many more fellow settlers; and the emergence of durable political parties that had to compete in elections and thus sometimes had self-interested reasons for wanting to expand the electorate. As a result of these social and political changes, every state held at least one constitutional convention between 1790 and the 1850s.

In most states, enough of these factors converged to produce state constitutional revisions that significantly broadened the franchise. By the 1850s, nearly all seaboard states had eliminated their property and taxpaying requirements, and the new states in the interior never adopted them in the first place. The abolition of these formal class barriers to voting was not achieved without conflict: many conservatives fought hard to preserve the old order. Warren Dutton of Massachusetts argued that, because "the means of subsistence were so abundant and the demand for labor great," any man who failed to acquire property was "indolent or vicious." Conservatives like New York's chancellor James Kent openly voiced fears of "the power of the poor and the profligate to control the affluent." But most Americans recognized that the sovereign "people" included many individuals without property. "The course of things in this country is for the extension, and not the restriction of popular rights," Senator Nathan Sanford said at the 1821 New York State Constitutional Convention.

A number of states in the interior expanded the franchise in another way as well: to encourage new settlement, they granted the franchise even to noncitizens, to immigrants who had resided in the state for several years and had declared their "intention" to become citizens. In the frontier state of Illinois, for example, one delegate to the 1847 constitutional convention argued that granting the vote to immigrants was "the greatest inducement for men to come amongst us . . . to develop the vast and inexhaustible resources of our state." Increased land values and tax revenues would follow. In the course of the nineteenth century, more than 18 states adopted such provisions.

However, the franchise did not expand for everyone. While property requirements were being dropped, formal racial exclusions became more common. In the 1830s, for example, both North Carolina and Pennsylvania added the word *white* to their constitutional requirements for voting. By 1855 only five states—all in New England—did not discriminate against African Americans. "Paupers"—men who were dependent on public relief in one form or another—suffered a similar fate, as did many Native Americans (because they were either not "white" or not citizens).

Still, the right to vote was far more widespread in 1850 or 1860 than it had been in 1790; and the reduction of economic barriers to the franchise occurred in the United States far earlier than in most countries of Europe or Latin America. The key to this "exceptional" development, however, resided less in any unique American ideology of inclusion than in two peculiarities of the history of the United States. The first—critical to developments in the North—was that property and taxpaying requirements were dropped before the industrial revolution had proceeded very far and thus before an industrial working class had taken shape. Massachusetts and New York, for example, dropped their property requirements in the early 1820s, before those two states became home to tens of thousands of industrial workers. (In Rhode Island, the one state where debates on suffrage reform occurred after considerable industrialization had taken place, a small civil war erupted in the 1830s and 1840s, when two rival legislatures and administrations, elected under different suffrage requirements, competed for legitimacy.) In contrast to Europe, apprehensions about the political power—and ideological leanings—of industrial workers did not delay their enfranchisement. The second distinctive feature of the American story was slavery: one reason that landed elites in much of the world feared democracy was that it meant enfranchising millions of peasants and landless agricultural laborers. But in the U.S. South, the equivalent class—the men and women who toiled from dawn to dusk on land they did not own—was enslaved and consequently would not acquire political power even if the franchise were broadened.

Indeed, the high-water mark of democratic impulses in the nineteenth-century United States involved slavery—or, to be precise, ex-slaves. In an extraordinary political development, in the immediate aftermath of the Civil War, Congress passed (and the states ratified) the Fifteenth Amendment, which prohibited denial of the right to vote to any citizen by "the United States or by any State on account of race, color, or previous condition of servitude." The passage of this amendment—a development unforeseen by the nation's political leadership even a few years earlier—stemmed from the partisan interests of the Republican Party, which hoped that African Americans would become a political base in the South: an appreciation of the heroism of the 180,000 African Americans who had served in the Union Army, and the conviction that, without the franchise, the freedmen in the South would soon end up being subservient to the region's white elites.

The Fifteenth Amendment (alongside the Fourteenth, passed shortly before) constituted a significant shift in the involvement of the federal government in matters relating to the franchise—since it constrained the ability of the states to impose whatever limitations they wished upon the right to vote—and was also a remarkable expression of democratic idealism on the part of a nation in which racism remained pervasive. Massachusetts senator Henry Wilson argued that the extension of suffrage would indicate that "we shall have carried out logically the ideas that lie at the foundation of our institutions; we shall be in harmony with our professions; we shall have acted like a truly republican and Christian people."

Hesitations and Rollbacks

Yet in a deep historical irony, this idealism was voiced at a moment when the tides of democracy were already cresting and beginning to recede. Starting in the 1850s in some states and accelerating in the 1870s, many middle- and upper-class Americans began to lose faith in democracy and in the appropriateness of universal (male) suffrage. An unsigned article in the *Atlantic Monthly* noted in 1879:

> Thirty or forty years ago it was considered the rankest heresy to doubt that a government based on universal suffrage was the wisest and best that could be devised . . . Such is not now the case. Expressions of doubt and distrust in regard to universal suffrage are heard constantly in conversation, and in all parts of the country.

The sources of this ideological shift were different in the South than they were elsewhere, but class dynamics were prominent throughout the nation. In the Northeast and the Midwest, rapid industrialization coupled with high rates of immigration led to the formation of an immigrant working class whose enfranchisement was regarded as deeply undesirable by a great many middle-class Americans. The first political manifestation of these views came in the 1850s with the appearance and meteoric growth of the American (or Know-Nothing) Party. Fueled by a hostility to immigrants (and Catholics in particular), the Know-Nothings sought to limit the political influence of newcomers by restricting the franchise to those who could pass literacy tests and by imposing a lengthy waiting period (such as 21 years) before naturalized immigrants could vote. In most states such proposals were rebuffed, but restrictions were imposed in several locales, including Massachusetts and Connecticut.

The Know-Nothing Party collapsed almost as rapidly as it had arisen, but the impulse to limit the electoral power of immigrant workers resurfaced after the Civil War, intensified by huge new waves of immigration and by the numerous local political successes of left-leaning and prolabor third parties, such as the Greenback Labor Party and several socialist parties. "Universal Suffrage," wrote Charles Francis Adams Jr., the descendant of two presidents, "can only mean . . . the government of ignorance and vice: it means a European, and especially Celtic, proletariat on the Atlantic coast; an African proletariat on the shores of the Gulf, and a Chinese proletariat on the Pacific." To forestall such a development, proposals were put forward, sometimes with success, to reinstitute financial requirements for some types of voting (for municipal offices or on bond issues, for example) and to require immigrants to present naturalization papers when they showed up at the polls. Gradually, the laws that had permitted noncitizens to vote were repealed (the last state to do so, Arkansas, acted in 1926), and by the 1920s, more than a dozen states in the North and West imposed literacy or English-language literacy tests for voting. (New York, with a large immigrant population, limited the franchise in 1921 to those who could pass an English-language literacy requirement; the law remained in place until the 1960s.) Many more states tightened residency requirements and adopted new personal registration laws that placed challenging procedural obstacles between the poor and the ballot box. In the West, far more draconian laws straightforwardly denied the right to vote to any person who was a "native of China."

In the South, meanwhile, the late nineteenth and early twentieth centuries witnessed the wholesale disfranchisement of African Americans—whose rights had supposedly been guaranteed by the passage of the Fifteenth Amendment. In the 1870s and into the 1880s, African Americans participated actively in southern politics, usually as Republicans, influencing policies and often gaining election to local and even state offices. But after the withdrawal of the last northern troops in 1877, southern whites began to mount concerted (and sometimes violent) campaigns to drive African Americans out of public life. In the 1890s, these "redeemers" developed an array of legal strategies designed expressly to keep African Americans from voting. Among them were literacy tests, poll taxes, cumulative poll taxes (demanding that all past as well as current taxes be paid), lengthy residency requirements, elaborate registration systems, felon disfranchisement laws, and confusing multiple box balloting methods (which required votes for different offices to be dropped into different boxes). These mechanisms were designed to discriminate without directly mentioning race, which would have violated the Fifteenth Amendment. "Discrimination!" noted future Virginia senator Carter Glass at a constitutional convention in his state in 1901. "That, exactly, is what this Convention was elected for—to discriminate to the very extremity of permissible action under the limitations of the Federal Constitution, with a view to the elimination of every negro voter who can be gotten rid of." These strategies were effective: in Louisiana, where more than 130,000 blacks had been registered to vote in 1896, only 1,342 were registered by 1904. Once the Republican Party was so diminished that it had no possibility of winning elections in the South, most states simplified the practice of discrimination by adopting a "white primary" within the Democratic Party. The only meaningful elections in the South, by the early twentieth century, were the Democratic primaries, and African Americans were expressly barred from participation.

This retrenchment occurred with the tacit, if reluctant, acquiescence of the federal government. In a series of rulings, the Supreme Court upheld the constitutionality of the disfranchising measures adopted in the South, because they did not explicitly violate the Fifteenth Amendment. Meanwhile, Congress repeatedly debated the merits of renewed intervention in the South but never quite had the stomach to intercede. The closest it came was in 1890, when most Republicans supported a federal elections bill (called the Lodge Force bill), which would have given federal courts and supervisors oversight of elections (much as the Voting Rights Act would do in 1965); the measure passed the House but stalled in the Senate. As a result, the South remained a one-party region, with the vast majority of African Americans deprived of their voting rights for another 75 years. In both the North and (far more dramatically) the South, the breadth of the franchise was thus narrowed between the Civil War and World War I.

Half of the Population

While all of this was transpiring, a separate suffrage movement—to enfranchise women—was fitfully progressing across the historical landscape. Although periodically intersecting with efforts to enfranchise African Americans, immigrants, and the poor, this movement had its own distinctive rhythms, not least because it generated a unique countermovement of women opposed to their own enfranchisement who feared that giving women the vote could seriously damage the health of families.

The first stirrings of the woman suffrage movement occurred the late 1840s and 1850s. Building on democratizing currents that had toppled other barriers to the franchise, small groups of supporters of female suffrage convened meetings and conventions to articulate their views and to launch a movement. The most famous of these occurred in 1848 in Seneca Falls, New York, hosted by (among others) Elizabeth Cady Stanton—who would go on to become one of the movement's leaders for many decades. With roots in the growing urban and quasi-urban middle class of the northern states, the early suffrage movement attracted critical support from abolitionists, male and female, who saw parallels between the lack of freedom of slaves and the lack of political (and some civil) rights for women. Indeed, many leaders of this young movement believed that, after the Civil War, women and African Americans would both be enfranchised in the same groundswell of democratic principle: as Stanton put it, women hoped "to avail ourselves of the strong arm and the blue uniform of the black soldier to walk in by his side." But they were deeply disappointed. The Republican leadership in Washington, as well as many former abolitionists, displayed little enthusiasm for linking women's rights to the rights of ex-slaves, and they thought it essential to focus on the latter. "One question at a time," intoned abolitionist Wendell Phillips. "This hour belongs to the negro." As a result, the Fifteenth Amendment made no mention of women (and thus tacitly seemed to condone their disfranchisement); even worse, the Fourteenth Amendment explicitly defended the voting rights of "male" inhabitants.

Women also suffered a rebuff in the courts. In the early 1870s, several female advocates of suffrage—including Susan B. Anthony, a key leader of the movement—filed lawsuits after they were not permitted to vote; they maintained that the refusal of local officials to give them ballots infringed their rights of free speech and deprived them of one of the "privileges and immunities" of citizens, which had been guaranteed to all citizens by the Fourteenth Amendment. In 1875, in *Minor v. Happersett*, the Supreme Court emphatically rejected this argument, ruling that suffrage did not necessarily accompany citizenship and thus that states possessed the legal authority to decide which citizens could vote.

Meanwhile, activists had formed two organizations expressly designed to pursue the cause of woman suffrage. The first was the National Woman Suffrage Association, founded by Stanton and Anthony in 1869. A national organization controlled by women, its strategic goal was to pressure the federal government into enfranchising women across the nation through passage of a constitutional amendment akin to the Fifteenth Amendment. The second was the American Woman Suffrage Association, which aimed to work at the state level, with both men and women, convincing legislatures and state constitutional conventions to drop gender barriers to suffrage. For two decades, both organizations worked energetically, building popular support yet gaining only occasional victories. A federal amendment did make it to the floor of the Senate but was decisively defeated. By the late 1890s, several western states, including Utah and Wyoming, had adopted woman suffrage, but elsewhere defeat was the norm. In numerous locales, small victories were achieved with measures that permitted women to vote for school boards.

In 1890 the two associations joined forces to create the National American Woman Suffrage Association (NAWSA). Gradually, the leadership of the movement was handed over to a new generation of activists, including Carrie Chapman Catt, who possessed notable organizational skills and a somewhat different ideological approach to the issue. Older universalist arguments about natural rights and the equality of men and women were downplayed, while new emphasis was given to the notion that women had distinctive interests and that they possessed qualities that might improve politics and put an end to "scoundrelism and ruffianism at the polls." Nonetheless, opponents of woman suffrage railed at the idea, denying that any "right" to vote existed and calling the suffrage movement (among other things) an attack "on the integrity of the family" that "denies and repudiates the obligations of motherhood." Organized opposition also came from some women, particularly from the upper classes, who felt they already had sufficient access to power, and from liquor interests, which feared enfranchising a large protemperance voting bloc.

Resistance to enfranchising women also stemmed from a broader current in American politics: the declining middle- and upper-class faith in democracy that had fueled the efforts to disfranchise African Americans in the South and immigrant workers in the North. As one contemporary observer noted, "the opposition today seems not so much against *women* as against any more voters at all." In part to overcome that resistance, some advocates of woman suffrage, in the 1890s and into the early twentieth century, put forward what was known as the "statistical argument": the notion that enfranchising women was a way of outweighing the votes of the ignorant and undesirable. In the South, it was argued, the enfranchisement of women "would insure . . . durable white supremacy," and, in the North, it would overcome the "foreign influence." Elizabeth Cady Stanton, among others, joined the chorus calling for literacy tests for voting, for both men and women—a view that was formally repudiated by NAWSA only in 1909.

Still, successes remained sparse until the second decade of the twentieth century, when the organizational muscle of NAWSA began to strengthen and the movement allied itself with the interests of working women and the working class more generally. This new coalition helped to generate victories in Washington, California, and several other states between 1910 and 1915. In the latter year, reacting in part to the difficulties of state campaigns—and the apparent impossibility of gaining victories in the South—Catt, the president of NAWSA, embraced a federal strategy focused on building support in Congress and in the 36 states most likely to ratify an amendment to the federal Constitution. Working alongside more militant organizations like the Congressional Union and the National Woman's Party, and drawing political strength from the growing number of states that had already embraced suffrage, NAWSA organized tirelessly, even gaining a key victory in New York with the aid of New York City's Tammany Hall political machine.

The turning point came during World War I. After the United States declared war in the spring of 1917, NAWSA suspended its congressional lobbying, while continuing grassroots efforts to build support for a federal amendment. More influentially, NAWSA demonstrated the importance of women to the war effort by converting many of its local chapters into volunteer groups that sold bonds, knitted clothes, distributed food, worked with the Red Cross, and gave gifts to soldiers and sailors. This adroit handling of the war crisis, coupled with ongoing political pressure, induced President Woodrow Wilson, in January 1918, to support passage of a suffrage amendment "as a war measure." The House approved the amendment a day later—although it took the Senate (where antisuffrage southern Democrats were more numerous) a year and a half to follow suit. In August 1920, Tennessee became the thirty-sixth state to ratify the Nineteenth Amendment, and women throughout the nation could vote.

Democracy as a National Value

The passage of the Nineteenth Amendment was a major milestone in the history of the right to vote. Yet significant barriers to universal suffrage remained in place, and they were not shaken by either the prosperity of the 1920s or the Great Depression of the 1930s. African Americans in the South remained disfranchised, many immigrants still had to pass literacy tests, and some recipients of relief in the 1930s were threatened with exclusion because they were "paupers." Pressures for change, however, began to build during World War II, and they intensified in the 1950s and 1960s. The result was the most sweeping transformation in voting rights in the nation's history: almost all remaining limitations on the franchise were eliminated as the federal government overrode the long tradition of states' rights and became the guarantor of universal suffrage. Although focused initially on African Americans in the South, the movement for change spread rapidly, touching all regions of the nation.

Not surprisingly, such a major set of changes had multiple sources. World War II itself played a significant role, in part because of its impact on public opinion. Americans embraced the war's explicitly stated goals of restoring democracy and ending racial and ethnic discrimination in Europe; and it was not difficult to see—as African American political leaders pointed out—that there was a glaring contradiction between those international goals and the reality of life in the American South. That contradiction seemed particularly disturbing at a time when hundreds of thousands of disfranchised African Americans and Native Americans were risking their lives by serving in the armed forces. Accordingly, when Congress passed legislation authorizing absentee balloting for overseas soldiers, it included a provision exempting soldiers in the field from having to pay poll taxes—even if they came from poll tax states. In 1944 the Supreme Court—partially populated by justices appointed during the New Deal and comfortable with an activist federal government—reversed two previous decisions and ruled, in *Smith v. Allwright*, that all-white primaries (and all-white political parties) were unconstitutional. Diplomatic considerations—particularly with regard to China and other allies in the Pacific—also led to the dismantling of racial barriers, as laws prohibiting Asian immigration, citizenship, and enfranchisement were repealed.

During the cold war, foreign affairs continued to generate pressure for reforms. In its competition with the Soviet Union for political support in third world nations, the United States found that the treatment of African Americans in the South undercut its claim to be democracy's advocate. As Secretary of State Dean Acheson noted, "the existence of discrimination against minority groups in the United States is a handicap in our relations with other countries." The impetus for change also came from within the two major political parties, both because of a broadening ideological embrace of democratic values and because the sizable migration of African Americans out of the South, begun during World War I, was increasing the number of black voters in northern states. Meanwhile, the postwar economic boom took some of the edge off class fears, while the technological transformation of southern agriculture led to a rapid growth in the proportion of the African American population that lived in urban areas where they could mobilize politically more easily. The changes that occurred were grounded both in Washington and in a steadily strengthening civil rights movement across the South and around the nation.

This convergence of forces, coupled with the political skills of Lyndon Johnson, the first Southerner elected to the presidency in more than a century, led to the passage in 1965 of the Voting Rights Act (VRA). The VRA immediately suspended literacy tests and other discriminatory "devices" in all states and counties where fewer than 50 percent of all adults had gone to the polls in 1964. It also authorized the attorney general to send examiners into the South to enroll voters, and it prohibited state and local governments in affected areas from changing any electoral procedures without the "preclearance" of the civil rights division of the Justice Department. (This key provision, section 5, prevented cities or states from developing new techniques for keeping African Americans politically powerless.) The VRA also instructed the Justice Department to begin litigation that would test the constitutionality of poll taxes in state elections. (Poll taxes in federal elections had already been banned by the Twenty-Fourth Amendment, ratified in 1964.) The VRA, in effect, provided mechanisms for the federal government to enforce the Fifteenth Amendment in states that were not doing so; designed initially as a temporary, quasi-emergency measure, it would be revised and renewed in 1970, 1975, 1982, and 2006, broadening its reach to language minorities and remaining at the center of federal voting rights law.

Not surprisingly, six southern states challenged the VRA in federal courts, arguing that it was an unconstitutional federal encroachment "on an area reserved to the States by the Constitution." But the Supreme Court, led by Chief Justice Earl Warren, emphatically rejected that argument in 1966, maintaining that key provisions of the VRA were "a valid means for carrying out the commands of the Fifteenth Amendment." In other cases, the Supreme Court invoked the equal protection clause of the Fourteenth Amendment to uphold bans on literacy tests for voting and to strike down poll taxes in state elections. In the latter case, *Harper v. Virginia*, the Court went beyond the issue of poll taxes to effectively ban—for the first time in the nation's history—all economic or financial requirements for voting. Wealth, wrote Justice William O. Douglas in the majority opinion, was "not germane to one's ability to participate intelligently in the electoral process." In subsequent decisions, the Court ruled that lengthy residency requirements for voting (in most cases, any longer than 30 days) were also unconstitutional.

Three other elements of this broad-gauged transformation of voting rights law were significant. First was that in the late 1940s and early 1950s, all remaining legal restrictions on the voting rights of Native Americans were removed. Although the vast majority of Native Americans were already enfranchised, several western states with sizable Native American populations excluded "Indians not taxed" (because they lived on reservations that did not pay property taxes) or those construed to be "under guardianship" (a misapplication of a legal category designed to refer to those who lacked the physical or mental capacity to conduct their own affairs). Thanks in part to lawsuits launched by Native American military veterans of World War II, these laws were struck down or repealed.

The second development affected a much broader swath of the country: the Supreme Court, even before the passage of the Voting Rights Act, challenged the ability of the states to maintain legislative districts that were of significantly unequal size—a common practice that frequently gave great power to rural areas. In a series of decisions, the Court concluded that it was undemocratic "to say that a vote is worth more in one district than in another," and effectively made "one person, one vote" the law of the land.

The third key change was precipitated by the Vietnam War and by the claim of young protesters against that war that it was illegitimate to draft them into the armed services at age 18 if they were not entitled to vote until they were 21. Congress responded to such claims in 1970 by lowering the voting age to 18. After the Supreme Court ruled that Congress did not have the power to change the age limit in state elections, Congress acted again in 1971, passing a constitutional amendment to serve the same purpose. The Twenty-Sixth Amendment was ratified in record time by the states.

The post–World War II movement to broaden the franchise reached its limit over the issue of felon disfranchisement. Most states in the 1960s deprived convicted felons of their suffrage rights, either for the duration of their sentences or, in some cases, permanently. Many of these laws, inspired by English common law, dated back to the early nineteenth century and were adopted at a time when suffrage was considered a privilege rather than a right. Others, particularly in the South, were expressly tailored in the late nineteenth century to keep African Americans from registering to vote.

The rationales for such laws had never been particularly compelling, and in the late 1960s they began to be challenged in the courts. The grounds for such challenges, building on other voting rights decisions, were that the laws violated the equal protection clause and that any limitations on the franchise had to be subject to the "strict scrutiny" of the courts. (Strict scrutiny meant that there had to be a demonstrably compelling state interest for such a law and that the law had to be narrowly tailored to serve that interest.)

The issue eventually reached the Supreme Court, in *Richardson v. Ramirez* (1974), which decided that state felon disfranchisement laws were permissible (and not subject to strict scrutiny) by a phrase in the Fourteenth Amendment that tacitly allowed adult men to be deprived of the suffrage "for participation in rebellion, or other crime." The meaning of "or other crime" was far from certain (in context it may have been referring to those who supported the Confederacy), but the Court interpreted it broadly in a controversial decision. In the decades following the ruling, many states liberalized their felon disfranchisement laws, and permanent or lifetime exclusions were consequently imposed in only a few states by the early twenty-first century. During the same period, however, the size of the population in jail or on probation and parole rose so rapidly that the number of persons affected by the disfranchisement laws also soared—reaching 5.3 million by 2006.

The significant exclusion of felons ought not obscure the scope of what had been achieved between World War II and 1970. In the span of several decades, nearly all remaining restrictions on the right to vote of American citizens had been overturned: in different states the legal changes affected African Americans, Native Americans, Asian Americans, the illiterate, the non–English speaking, the very poor, those who had recently moved from one locale to another, and everyone between the ages of 18 and 21. Congress and the Supreme Court had embraced democracy as a national value and concluded that a genuine democracy could only be achieved if the federal government overrode the suffrage limitations imposed by many states. The franchise was nationalized and something approximating universal suffrage finally achieved—almost two centuries after the Constitution was adopted. Tens of millions of people could vote in 1975 who would not have been permitted to do so in 1945 or 1950.

New and Lingering Conflicts

Yet the struggle for fully democratic rights and institutions had not come to an end. Two sizable, if somewhat marginal, groups of residents sought a further broadening of the franchise itself. One was ex-felons, who worked with several voting rights groups to persuade legislators around the country to pass laws permitting those convicted of crimes to vote as soon as they were discharged from prison. The second group consisted of noncitizen legal residents, many of whom hoped to gain the right to vote in local elections so that they could participate in governing the communities in which they lived, paid taxes, and sent their children to school. Noncitizens did possess or acquire local voting rights in a handful of cities, but the movement to make such rights widespread encountered substantial opposition in a population that was increasingly apprehensive about immigration and that regarded "voting and citizenship," as the *San Francisco Examiner* put it, as "so inextricably bound in this country that it's hard to imagine one without the other." Indeed, many Americans believed that ex-felons and noncitizens had no legitimate claim to these political rights—although they were common in many other economically advanced countries.

More central to the political life of most cities and states were several other issues that moved to center stage once basic questions about enfranchisement had been settled. The first involved districting: the drawing of geographic boundaries that determined how individual votes would be aggregated and translated into political office or power. Politicians had long known that districting decisions (for elections at any level) could easily have an impact on the outcome of elections, and partisan considerations had long played a role in the drawing of district boundaries. The equation changed, however, when the Supreme Court's "one person, one vote" decisions, coupled with the passage of the Voting Rights Act, drew race into the picture. This happened first when (as expected) some cities and states in the South sought to redraw district boundaries in ways that would diminish, or undercut, the political influence of newly enfranchised African Americans. The courts and the Department of Justice rebuffed such efforts, heeding the words of Chief Justice Earl Warren, in a key 1964 districting case, that "the right of suffrage can be denied by a . . . dilution of the weight of a citizen's vote just as effectively as by wholly prohibiting the free exercise of the franchise."

Yet the task of considering race in the drawing of district boundaries involved competing values, opening a host of new questions that federal courts and legislatures were to wrestle with for decades. What was the appropriate role for race in districting decisions? Should districting be color-blind, even if that meant that no minorities would be elected to office? (The courts thought not.) Should race be the predominant factor in drawing boundaries? (The courts also thought not.) In jurisdictions where African Americans constituted a sizable minority of the population, should legislatures try to guarantee some African American representation?

(Probably.) Should the size of that representation be proportional to the size of the African American population? (Probably not.) Did nonracial minorities—like Hasidic Jews in Brooklyn—have similar rights to elect their own representatives? (No.) The courts and legislatures muddled forward, case by case, decade by decade, without offering definitive answers to questions that were likely insoluble in the absence of a coherent theory of representation or a widely accepted standard of fairness. Between 1970 and the beginning of the twenty-first century, the number of African Americans, Hispanics, and Asian Americans elected to public office rose dramatically, but clear-cut, definitive guidelines for districting without "vote dilution" remained out of reach.

A second cluster of issues revolved around the procedures for voter registration and casting ballots. Here a core tension was present (as it long had been) between maximizing access to the ballot box and preventing fraud. Procedures that made it easier to register and vote were also likely to make it easier for fraud to occur, while toughening up the procedures to deter fraud ran the risk of keeping legitimate voters from casting their ballots. By the 1970s, many scholars (as well as progressive political activists) were calling attention to the fact that, despite the transformation of the nation's suffrage laws, turnout in elections was quite low, particularly among the poor and the young. (Half of all potential voters failed to cast ballots for presidential elections, and the proportion was far higher in off-year elections.) Political scientists engaged in lively debates about the sources of low turnout, but there was widespread agreement that one cause could be found in the complicated and sometimes unwieldy registration procedures in some states. As a result, pressure for reforms mounted, generally supported by Democrats (who thought they would benefit) and opposed by Republicans (who were concerned about both fraud and partisan losses). Many states did streamline their procedures, but others did not, and, as a result, Congress began to consider federal registration guidelines.

What emerged from Congress in the early 1990s was the National Voter Registration Act, a measure that would require each state to permit citizens to register by mail, while applying for a driver's license, or at designated public agencies, including those offering public assistance and services to the disabled. First passed in 1992, the "motor voter bill" (as it was called) was vetoed by President George H. W. Bush on the grounds that it was an "unnecessary" federal intervention into state affairs and an "open invitation to fraud." The following year, President Bill Clinton signed the measure into law, placing the federal government squarely on record in support of making it easier for adult citizens to exercise their right to vote. Within a few years, the impact of the bill on registration rolls had been clearly demonstrated, as millions of new voters were signed up. But turnout did not follow suit in either 1996 or 1998, suggesting that registration procedures alone were not responsible for the large numbers of Americans who did not vote. During the following decade, some Democratic activists turned their attention to promoting registration on election day as a new strategy for increasing turnout.

Meanwhile, Republican political professionals sought to push the pendulum in the opposite direction. Concerned that procedures for voting had become too lax (and potentially too susceptible to fraud), Republicans in numerous states began to advocate laws that would require voters to present government-issued identification documents (with photos) when they registered and/or voted. The presentation of "ID" was already mandated in some states—although the types of identification considered acceptable varied widely—but elsewhere voters were obliged only to state their names to precinct officials. Although Democrats and civil rights activists protested that photo ID laws would create an obstacle to voting for the poor, the young, and the elderly (the three groups least likely to possess driver's licenses), such laws were passed in Georgia and Indiana in 2005, among other states. After a set of disparate rulings by lower courts, the Indiana law was reviewed by the Supreme Court, which affirmed its constitutionality in 2008 in a 6-to-3 decision. Although the Court's majority acknowledged that there was little or no evidence that voting fraud had actually occurred in Indiana, it concluded that requiring a photo ID did not unduly burden the right to vote. In the wake of the Court's decision, numerous other states were expected to pass similar laws. How many people would be barred from the polls as a result was unclear. In Indiana's primary election in the spring of 2008, several elderly nuns who lacked driver's licenses or other forms of photo ID were rebuffed when they attempted to vote.

Conflict over the exercise of the right to vote could still be found in the United States more than 200 years after the nation's founding. Indeed, the disputed presidential election of 2000, between Al Gore and George W. Bush, revolved in part around yet another dimension of the right to vote—the right to have one's vote counted, and counted accurately. Perhaps inescapably, the breadth of the franchise, as well as the ease with which it could be exercised, remained embedded in partisan politics, in the pursuit of power in the world's most powerful nation. The outcomes of elections mattered, and those outcomes often were determined not just by *how* people voted but also by *who* voted. The long historical record suggested that—however much progress had been achieved between 1787 and 2008—there would be no final settlement of this issue. The voting rights of at least some Americans could always be potentially threatened and consequently would always be in need of protection.

See also civil rights; race and politics; woman suffrage.

FURTHER READING

DuBois, Ellen. *Feminism and Suffrage: The Emergence of an Independent Women's Movement in America, 1848–1869*. Ithaca, NY: Cornell University Press, 1999.

Hayduk, Ron. *Democracy for All: Restoring Immigrant Voting Rights in the United States*. New York: Routledge, 2006.

Keyssar, Alexander. *The Right to Vote: The Contested History of Democracy in the United States*. New York: Basic Books, 2000.

Kousser, J. Morgan. *The Shaping of Southern Politics: Suffrage Restriction and the Establishment of the One-party South, 1880–1910*. New Haven, CT: Yale University Press, 1974.

Manza, Jeff, and Christopher Uggen. *Locked Out: Felon Disenfranchisement and American Democracy*. New York: Oxford University Press, 2006.

Sneider, Allison. *Suffragists in an Imperial Age: U.S. Expansion and the Woman Question, 1870–1929*. New York: Oxford University Press, 2008.

ALEXANDER KEYSSAR

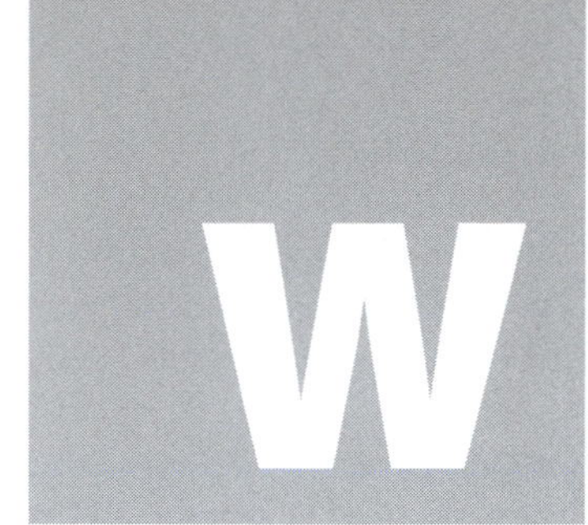

war and politics

War and politics have always been entwined in American history. Politicians and pundits often complained that politics intruded upon war or war upon politics; generals should wage war without second-guessing by politicians, some demanded. The very phrase "war and politics" treats the two as separate if linked entities. But instead they mutually constitute each other, especially if "war" is understood expansively as all activities, institutions, and attitudes involving military power. War defined American politics, not merely intruded upon it, just as politics defined war. This relationship was not unchanging, however. It became more consequential to Americans and the world as the scale of American wars and military prowess grew.

Political Control

The enmeshment of war and politics was inevitable: modern states exist in part to wage war, and war is an extreme form of politics. Some Americans hoped that the United States would be an exception, having witnessed European monarchies and dictatorships deploying war to address personal, imperial, ideological, or racial ambitions. But American exceptionalism was impossible.

The relationship began with the nation's founding. Imperial and local politics sparked the war for American independence, and the nation owed its political existence to war. The Constitution set the terms of enmeshment by giving political authorities control of war and its institutions. Only Congress could declare war and fund it even if war were undeclared (undeclared wars erupted almost from the start). It also had power "to raise and support armies," "maintain a navy," and "make rules" for the armed forces. Its power of the purse was striking (beyond what most European legislatures possessed). Congress could not dictate deployment, strategy, and tactics, but it could set the fiscal terms that made those things possible. The president was made "commander in chief of the army and the navy" and of state militias "when called into the actual service of the United States" but not commander in chief of all government or of the nation, as some presidents and other political figures later presumed. The Constitution was notably briefer about the president's war powers than about those of Congress. Whether brevity established an implicit check on presidential power or a tacit blank check for it periodically roiled American politics. Civilian secretaries of war and the navy (superseded after 1947 by a secretary of the new Department of Defense) headed cabinet departments, although their authority varied widely. Civilians also headed other agencies, proliferating in modern times, that had war-related functions, from the State, Justice, and Treasury departments at the nation's founding to the Veterans Administration (1930), Central Intelligence Agency (1947), and the Department of Homeland Security (2003). Americans phrased these arrangements as imposing "civilian" control of the military, but "civilian" often meant "political."

Most military officers accepted political control, even if they chafed at the decisions, forces, and strategies that politicians provided. Among advantages for officers, civilian supremacy made politicians—often more determined than officers to initiate war or wage it aggressively—more responsible for the controversial decisions and ghastly mistakes that war usually entails. Civilian supremacy prevailed in political dramas, as when Abraham Lincoln fired generals in the Civil War and President Harry Truman fired General Douglas MacArthur during the Korean War (an act condemned by some cold warriors as an intrusion on war making by politicians with a defeatist or subversive mentality). Some officers challenged political control during the cold war by favoring a nuclear first strike on the Soviet Union or

China, conducting unauthorized spy missions, or broadcasting a Christian political agenda. But they were few and their damage to political control was minimal.

War and the State

War was key to the creation of the American state—the activity it most expansively and expensively undertook. War justified its general scale and many of its specific measures, such as a federal income tax (imposed during the Civil War, reestablished in 1913, and greatly expanded during World War II), a welfare system pioneered through veterans benefits, and scientific and medical innovations by the armed forces. "War is the health of the State," the radical critic Randolph Bourne declared in attacking America's entry into World War I. Conservatives sometimes suspected much the same, as when they asserted that President Franklin D. Roosevelt sought to use rearmament and war to consolidate the New Deal and the Democratic Party's hegemony (though World War II undermined both). Americans also expressed their political debt to war by justifying state initiatives as warlike in character: in 1933 FDR wanted the nation to respond to the Depression "as if invaded by a foreign foe"; later presidents waged "war" on crime, disease, drugs, and other challenges. Appeals to war as a model for national action overrode Americans' chronic suspicions of an activist state. They also made war an even more political category.

Similarly, Americans imagined war as serving political purposes, not just the nation's defense or expansion. War, it was said, would Americanize immigrants serving as soldiers (a favorite idea in World War I), crush subversive people and ideas, enhance social mobility (the military is "the greatest equal opportunity employer around," President George H. W. Bush boasted in 1991), revive a flagging economy, spur technological development, and unite a fractious nation. Americans rarely assumed that the perils and benefits of war involved combat alone.

The actions and institutions of war propelled the nation's development. Military force subdued Native Americans and conquered new lands. The Civil War aside, U.S. wars before at least 1941 were efforts at national aggrandizement, not survival; the Mexican-American War (1846–48) secured vast territories in the American West; the Spanish-American War of 1898 expanded America's power and holdings in the Caribbean and the Pacific. The armed forces also promoted development by undertaking exploration, charting canal and railroad routes, building dams and ports, and cultivating technical expertise when the nation lacked other technological institutions (the U.S. Military Academy at West Point was the nation's first engineering school, among its functions). The military's developmental role was often highly visible, as with its building of the Panama Canal (completed in 1914) and its promotion of nuclear, aviation, space, and computer technologies (the Internet had origins in a Defense Department program). Sometimes the military remained in the background except during disaster, as in 2005, when hurricane Katrina spotlighted the Army Corps of Engineers, the politically astute builder of much of America's infrastructure. In these ways, the role of the armed forces was political as well as military.

War and politics also intersected in the scramble for military spending and the resulting connections between civil and military institutions. The desire of local authorities—mayors, legislators, businessmen—for military bases and contracts is an old story, though its scale swelled in the twentieth century. Often it meant overriding the military's judgment about where to erect a base, whether to develop a weapon, or which company should build it. Many politicians who decried civilian interference in other military matters were masters of military pork. Especially in the twentieth century, military spending directed resources, population, and political influence toward southern and western states. From the start, the armed forces used civilian institutions for research, weapons, supplies, and services, and civilians went to work for the military while officers retired to jobs in defense or other businesses. The use of private organizations for quasi-military operations, an old practice by states and especially evident in America's post-9/11 military conflicts, further blurred the line between "civilian" and "military."

War and politics were also enmeshed in how Americans understood citizenship. African Americans' Civil War military service helped underwrite the citizenship they acquired, in theory, during and after the war. Through America's post-9/11 conflicts, noncitizens' military service guaranteed their citizenship. Since service was overwhelmingly a male activity—coerced during periods of conscription—citizenship was gendered in this way as in others. Beyond legal citizenship, war reshaped political and social citizenship. Military service in World War II strengthened citizenship for millions of Americans of eastern and southern European descent. Colin Powell, a career officer and Joint Chiefs of Staff chairman, became the highest-ranking African American in government as secretary of state (2001–5). The second woman in a cabinet post was Oveta Culp Hobby, World War II commander of the Women's Army Corps and then secretary of health, education, and welfare (1953–55). Military service lubricated upward mobility and social change, especially as measured by prominent figures. Likewise, those barred from military service or denied equality in it felt treated as lesser citizens—hence the long struggle over racial desegregation of the armed forces, ordered by Truman in 1948; conflicts over women's place in military service; and the 1993 battle over "gays in the military."

Veterans also had housing, health, education, and employment benefits lacked by most Americans, even as critics regarded those benefits as puny or badly managed. Veterans' elevated status was hardly a constant. Anxiety periodically erupted that veterans, especially of combat situations, would return damaged, disruptive, or dangerous. White Southerners feared demobilized black Union troops, and freed slaves feared ex-Confederates in the Ku Klux Klan. Anxiety surged during World War II—one reason for the famous 1944 GI Bill, or Servicemen's Readjustment Act, which gave unprecedented benefits to most of the war's 16 million veterans. Anxiety resurfaced when Vietnam War veterans were often diagnosed with post-traumatic stress disorder. Still, the sense of veterans as especially entitled or deserving citizens generally prevailed, as evident in the number of presidential candidates who were veterans. Those candidates were especially successful when regarded as heroes in victorious wars—Washington, Jackson, Harrison, Taylor, Grant, Theodore Roosevelt, Eisenhower, Kennedy—although military service was no guarantee of electoral victory, as Nixon in 1960, Dole in 1996, Kerry in 2004, and McCain in 2008 learned.

War and the Presidency

The presidency underlines how war and politics constituted each other. War or its apparent threat underwrote the presidency's expanding powers, both legal and illegal. Major crises, none more so than 9/11, produced presidential claims that constitutional provisions, international laws, and humanitarian norms should be altered, suspended, or reinterpreted. War also brought greater power for individual presidents, though less often lasting glory. Many Americans suspected presidents of using war for political gain, but presidents usually achieved little that endured. Those who secured lasting luster—Lincoln and Franklin D. Roosevelt—died before the emergence of the sour aftermath war usually presents. Woodrow Wilson's presidency crumbled after World War I; Republicans seized the White House in 1921. Truman and the Democrats barely survived World War II's aftermath and then succumbed to the Korean War; a Republican, General Dwight D. Eisenhower, became president in 1953. The Vietnam War and their handling of it destroyed the presidencies of Lyndon Johnson and Richard Nixon (his abuse of war powers shaped the Watergate crisis of 1973–74). Difficult wars readily damaged presidents, as George W. Bush found in the Iraq War, but even a triumphant Gulf War gave no lasting political traction to his father, defeated in 1992 by Bill Clinton. By the same token, three of the four post-1945 presidents who served two full terms—Eisenhower, Reagan, and Clinton—avoided costly war making and remained popular. War was as fickle in its political ramifications as in its conduct and global consequences, often overwhelming the state's ability to control it and ensnaring presidents.

When war went badly, accusations of unwarranted political interference usually intensified. After Japan's attack on Pearl Harbor on December 7, 1941, with American forces in retreat or defeat, critics charged that Roosevelt had connived to bring the United States into World War II or even to allow Japan's attack to proceed. But few complained about political intrusion when later operations pushed by Roosevelt and his civilian advisors succeeded—the invasion of France in 1944, the bombing of Nazi Germany and Imperial Japan, and the use of the atomic bomb in August 1945. Likewise, suspicion of politicians' meddling intensified after 1945, when U.S. wars in Korea, Vietnam, Iraq, and elsewhere had dubious or disastrous outcomes. Success quieted suspicion. Failure stoked it.

So did uncertainty. The cold war arms race, portending a possible nuclear cataclysm, sparked diverse suspicions. Nationalist conservatives charged that politicians denied the military the tools of victory given how the metaphoric "button" of push-button warfare lay under the president's thumb. Cold war liberals suspected that generals like Air Force chief of staff Curtis LeMay schemed to control the button. The growth of a vast civilian bureaucracy aggravated suspicions. Complaints about the number-crunching oversight of the military imposed by Secretary of Defense Robert McNamara (1961–68) prepared the ground for accusations that civilians, especially McNamara and Johnson, hamstrung their generals. Left to their own devices, accusers charged, the generals might have won the Vietnam War.

Faith in a wise officer corps able to win wars ignored institutional realities, however. Top officers disagreed about whether and how to wage war, especially given their intense service rivalries: the Air Force, Navy, Army, and Marine Corps usually had competing schemes for victory, with each also divided within. Indeed, those differences invited or compelled civilian superiors to "intrude"—to meddle, mediate, or mandate. No fount of secret wisdom, the uniformed military mirrored, though inexactly, divisions about war elsewhere in the body politic.

As formal declarations of war ceased after World War II, Americans could readily imagine a distinction between war and politics. The last protracted debate about entering war came before Pearl Harbor, after which power to initiate war lay with the presidency, positioning itself as above politics, not with Congress, the more obviously (though substantively no more) political body. To varying degrees, military actions were undertaken by presidents operating in haste, secrecy, and deception—hardly circumstances conducive to freewheeling debate. Congress trailed behind with various measures, usually approved overwhelmingly, that authorized operations. Hence political contests erupted about the conduct and consequences of wars more than their initiation, especially since most wars seemed dissatisfying or disastrous. As earlier, civilians and service personnel, and voices abroad, charged U.S. forces and leaders with illegal, excessive, or misguided use of force or torture against enemy soldiers, civilians, and captives.

The practice of politicians and pundits criticizing presidents and generals was bipartisan, however partisan at any moment. Many Democrats tried to shield the White House from criticism when their party held the presidency. Many turned against Nixon later in the Vietnam War and George W. Bush in the Iraq War. Likewise, Republicans, often defenders of presidential prerogative and military wisdom, second-guessed Clinton's use of force amid Yugoslavia's disintegration in the 1990s.

War and politics were above all interwoven because the United States waged war frequently. It became a foremost participant in the militarization of the modern world. Perhaps no state waged war more often, even though, or perhaps because, the cost in American lives was light (the Civil War aside), compared to that of its enemies and allies, even in a losing war like Vietnam's. If the Founding Fathers hoped that war would play only an episodic role in American politics, the episodes became so numerous as to be nearly continuous, though often the incidents were not declared or widely recognized as wars (as in Nicaragua in the 1920s and Beirut in 1983).

Efforts to portray war and politics as distinct arenas were not persuasive, but they did express a desire to restrain the course by which war defined much of American life. Americans partook of the appeals and benefits of war, but they also remained suspicious of them.

See also Caribbean, Central America, and Mexico, interventions in, 1903–34; Civil War and Reconstruction; Korean War and cold war; Iraq wars; Mexican-American War; Vietnam and Indochina wars; war for independence; War of 1812; World War I; World War II.

FURTHER READING

Bacevich, Andrew. *The New American Militarism: How Americans Are Seduced by War.* New York: Oxford University Press, 2005.

Gillis, John R., ed. *The Militarization of the Western World.* New Brunswick, NJ: Rutgers University Press, 1989,

Huntington, Samuel P. *The Soldier and the State: Theory and Politics of Civil-Military Relations.* Cambridge, MA: Belknap Press, 1957.

Kerber, Linda K. *No Constitutional Right to Be Ladies: Women and the Obligations of Citizenship.* New York: Hill and Wang, 1998.

Kohn, Richard H. "How Democracies Control the Military." *Journal of Democracy* 8.4 (1997), 140–53.

———. ed. *The United States Military under the Constitution of the United States, 1789–1989.* New York: New York University Press, 1991.

Millis, Walter. *Arms and Men: A Study in American Military History.* New York: Putnam, 1956.

Sherry, Michael S. *In the Shadow of War: The United States since the 1930s.* New Haven, CT: Yale University Press, 1995.

Weigley, Russell F. *The American Way of War: A History of United States Military Strategy and Policy.* New York: Macmillan, 1973.

MICHAEL SHERRY

war for independence

Politics shaped the eight-year war for independence by the English colonies on the North American mainland (1775–83). In 1774 Britain decided to press its ten-year effort, against persistent and sometimes violent American resistance, to tighten imperial control of the colonies. When the British garrison in America was reinforced and its commander, Thomas Gage, appointed royal governor of Massachusetts, the colonies convened a "Continental" Congress in Philadelphia to coordinate resistance.

From Resistance to War

Few colonists expected or wanted war, but almost all opposed British policies, and preparations began by training the militia, a civilian military force established by law in all colonies except Pennsylvania. Britain had made Boston, the apparent heart of American resistance, its primary target for tough measures, and war began there in April 1775. British troops marching out of Boston to destroy a reported cache of arms met a small band of local militia, someone fired, and fighting continued through the day along the march route back to the town. As the news spread, thousands of New England militia rushed to Boston, blockading the British garrison, which was soon reinforced by troops and warships. In June, Gage tried to destroy a fortified rebel position near the town, on Bunker's Hill. The rebels gave way after repeated frontal attacks, but the British troops suffered heavy losses.

By declaring the colonies in rebellion, King George III unleashed his army and navy against the Americans. Congress, concerned by wavering in the colonies south of New England, accepted the proposal of John Adams, a Massachusetts delegate, to appoint a Virginia delegate with military experience, George Washington, to command the militia force around Boston and to rename it the Continental Army. The king's proclamation of rebellion, and the appointment of a Virginian to command the army, did much to unify the American effort.

Local committees, urged on by Congress, prepared for open warfare against the world's strongest military power. American reinforcements marched to Boston through the summer, and Congress authorized an invasion of Canada through the Hudson-Champlain corridor, aimed at denying British forces a base for attack on the American frontier. Appealing to the French-speaking settlers of Canada as liberators, the invaders enjoyed success at first, but had faltered by the New Year, and then collapsed when ice melted on the St. Lawrence, and British reinforcements sailed up the river.

The stalemate at Boston ended when the British decided to evacuate the town in March 1776 and to move operations to New York City, where the Hudson River offered a highway deep into the American interior. Washington believed that defending New York was politically necessary to sustain morale, especially in the uncertain middle colonies (New York, New Jersey, and Pennsylvania), but with no navy and an inexperienced army, the complex geography of the New York port area made his mission almost impossible, though the repulse by South Carolina militia of a British seaborne attack on Charleston was encouraging. As new troops from the southward arrived, Washington raced to train them and prepare defenses around the heights of Brooklyn on western Long Island. Gage's successor, William Howe, spent all summer on Staten Island building up a force of about 25,000, including hard-bitten mercenaries hired in Germany. Howe belonged to an aristocratic family affiliated with the parliamentary opposition, critical of the government's handling of the American problem. Rumors at the time, and some historians since, have suggested that Howe, who had personally led the attack at Bunker's Hill, lacked the stomach for killing English colonists who claimed their rights under the British Constitution.

From War to Independence

Congress, aware after a year of fighting that all-out war was about to begin, declared the rebellious colonies in July 1776 to be the independent United States. When Howe began to embark his army in late August and move toward Long Island, Washington hoped for a fight like that at Bunker's Hill in 1775. Instead, Howe flanked the American position and inflicted a crushing defeat on the Continental Army. But he stopped short at the Brooklyn bastion, where fleeing American soldiers had assembled, and prepared to lay siege. That night, in fog and darkness, Washington took his men across the river to Manhattan, where he rallied them for a gradual retreat up the island. Howe, not for the last time, pursued slowly, and the Americans even struck back once from the heights of Harlem, slowing but not stopping the British army. Washington stood again in late October at White Plains in Westchester County; again Howe won the battle but failed to destroy the American army. Washington then divided what was left of his force and took the larger part across the Hudson into New Jersey.

American morale, military and civilian, was at low ebb in the last weeks of 1776. Declaring independence had heartened many but had decisively alienated others who had supported American rights but would not break the British connection. These "Loyalist" Americans, estimated at a half-million throughout the former colonies, perhaps a quarter of the total white population, were especially numerous in the mid-Atlantic States. Another half-million Americans, slaves mostly in the South, often ran away to the British whenever possible; a smaller number of African Americans, about 5,000, served as soldiers on the American side. As Washington's men straggled across New Jersey, with the British in cautious pursuit, popular support for Congress and the army virtually collapsed in that state.

At the Delaware River, Washington crossed into Pennsylvania with winter setting in. Rumors ran that he would soon be replaced by one of two former British officers who had joined the American cause, Charles Lee or Horatio Gates. Many, even those close to Washington, thought he had lost his grip and credibility. His letters begged Lee to join him quickly with the soldiers left east of the Hudson, and they show more desperation than determination. Instead of joining, Lee let himself be captured by a British patrol. Congress, fleeing Philadelphia for the safety of Baltimore, did not replace Washington and even granted him dictatorial powers to direct the war for six months. His choices were limited: disband the army and withdraw to resist in the western hills or gamble on a counterattack. He chose the latter. With some support from the Pennsylvania militia, he crossed the icy river in late December with soldiers who had spent the past year learning war the hard way, surprising and destroying a German brigade at Trenton, then withdrawing into Pennsylvania. Howe reacted quickly, and almost trapped Washington when he boldly recrossed into New Jersey. But Washington escaped to surprise and destroy another brigade at Princeton before heading for the protective hills of northern New Jersey.

The unexpected victories at Trenton and Princeton rallied the American cause, gave Washington solid support in Congress, and won notice and credit overseas, where Congress was seeking help. Colonial stocks of munitions, plus some captured ones, were enough for the first year, but foreign aid was vital to continuing the war. France was a historic enemy, but it was the only European power likely to help the rebellious British colonies. Benjamin Franklin of Pennsylvania, with a wealth of experience abroad and already known in Europe as a rustic genius, arrived in France just as Washington struggled on the Delaware. Clandestine shipments of French military supplies to America were already underway, but Franklin would seek more as well as money and ships.

Saratoga and the Alliance with France

The year 1777 was decisive. The British planned to invade from Canada and to use most of their New York force to take the rebel capital of Philadelphia. Congress let Washington enlist three-year volunteers to rebuild his army, with which he tried to defend Philadelphia. His defeated army crept back to a winter camp at Valley Forge, not far from the occupied capital. Gates, in the north, managed to stall the invading army from Canada at Saratoga, on the upper Hudson, and compel it to surrender. Washington's tenacity, plus American victory at Saratoga, induced France to ally with the United States and go to war with Britain early in 1778.

Congress rejected proffered British concessions, Howe was recalled and replaced by Henry Clinton, and British leaders revised their strategy. France was now the main enemy, and the American war had to be coordinated with the protection of the valuable West Indies. British troops evacuated Philadelphia and concentrated at New York, with its great, accessible port. Washington's army stood just out of reach in the Hudson Highlands. From 1778 onward it was a war of attrition, of political will as much as of military force. The House of Commons angrily grilled the recalled Howe on why the Americans had not been crushed. Congress hoped for a miracle, and grew weaker as its leading members returned to their states and rampant inflation sapped the Continental paper money that had served to mobilize resources during 1775–77. With no power to tax, Congress could only resort to begging the states to support their own troops. The British meanwhile turned the war toward the South, where large slave populations, strong pro-British Native American tribes on the frontier, and a reported abundance of Americans fed up with the war seemed to beckon, while the navy could shuttle more readily between the mainland and the West Indies.

British Shift Southward

In late 1778, a small British force invaded Georgia, easily took Savannah, and reestablished royal government. A year later, Clinton himself sailed from New York, with a much larger force, to invade South Carolina. For the first time the British attempted to exploit the military potential of Loyalists. Loyalist regiments recruited in the North were part of the invading force, and, as the British advanced, they organized Loyalist militia to hold and secure areas cleared of rebels. Charleston fell to a siege in May 1780, yielding 5,000 American prisoners; news of the victory caused a sensation in England. Congress sent Gates to the rescue. In command, he risked the small force left to him against a bigger, better disciplined British force at Camden in August and was destroyed, his reputation in tatters.

Washington, safe in the highlands, refused to move. He saw the British troops and ships departing New York for the South as an opportunity and resisted pleas from old friends like Governor Thomas Jefferson of Virginia to help the South. British forces were raiding freely into the Chesapeake and up its rivers, and in the Carolinas the war seemed lost. In mid-1780 Washington expected the arrival in Rhode Island of a French expeditionary force of more than 4,000 regular soldiers. His aim was to combine forces, and with the aid of the French navy to attack New York, destroy its depleted garrison, and win the war. When the French arrived, their commander was dubious, and, in September, a leading American general, Benedict Arnold, defected to the enemy. At the New Year, the Pennsylvania Continental troops mutinied for their pay and the promise of discharge after three years, and later New Jersey troops did the same. The French believed that the American effort would collapse after 1781, and many American observers agreed.

Under pressure, Washington sent his best general, Nathanael Greene, to take command in the South after the defeat of Gates at Camden. Even before Greene arrived in late 1780, however, the war had begun to turn against the British. Undefended by any regular force against British occupation, South Carolinians turned to a hit-and-run insurgency with small bands under local leaders who sought to hurt the British but especially to punish the Americans who had joined them. Exceptionally vicious, chaotic warfare erupted in the Carolinas 1780–81, pitting neighbors against neighbors. It was the civil war, Americans against Americans, implicit in the new British strategy. One large Loyalist force wandered too far westward into modern Tennessee, where it was surrounded by a rapidly assembled group of American militia and massacred. Greene understood what was happening, and worked well with the insurgent leaders. He avoided battle whenever possible but led British forces under Lord Cornwallis, left in command when Clinton returned to New York, on an exhausting chase northward over the hills and valleys of the Carolinas. When Cornwallis followed Greene, Loyalist militia could not hold their "liberated" areas against insurgent attack.

Decision at Yorktown

Failing to catch Greene, Cornwallis finally sought refuge in the Virginia tobacco port of Yorktown in mid-1781. He expected supplies, reinforcements, and perhaps evacuation. Instead a French fleet appeared off Chesapeake Bay. Engaging the British fleet, it fought and won a battle for control of the sea off Yorktown. Washington, disappointed that the French navy was not coming north to support an attack on New York, joined the French regulars in Rhode Island in a rapid march to Virginia, where Cornwallis soon found himself in a giant trap. With skilled French engineers pushing the siege forward every day, Cornwallis, cut off by land and sea, surrendered his army on October 19.

Military victory at Yorktown did not win the war, but news of Yorktown in Parliament brought down the wartime government, replaced by men who were opposed to the war. Desultory skirmishing occurred around occupied Charleston and New York; bitter feuds meant continued violence in the Carolina backcountry; and fighting continued in parts of the West. The British army and navy went on fighting the French. French troops and ships in America sailed away from Virginia to defend the West Indies, and, in the United States, something like a tacit armistice held, while the politicians in London and Paris spent two years negotiating a final peace.

The years 1778–83 were difficult for Congress. The French alliance, which many Americans saw as a guarantee of victory, sowed conflict and mistrust in Congress. Suspicion of wily Europeans who might make peace at American expense, skeptism toward the clever colleagues sent abroad to represent American interests, and mistrust of one another all played out in a body steadily weakened by loss of power to the states, a failing currency, and the ongoing departure of its most capable members. Only under direct French pressure did Congress finally ratify the Articles of Confederation in early 1781, one of the lowest points of the war, creating a weak central government out of an ad hoc convention of states. Washington was a mythic national hero when peace finally came in 1783, but Congress was given little credit for its part in achieving American independence.

Final Reckoning

In the Treaty of Paris, the United States gained international recognition, a western boundary on the Mississippi, and an end to the burdens as well as the benefits of membership in the empire. Britain kept Canada, and France saw that its ally Spain got back some of what it had lost in 1763: Florida, the Gulf Coast, and effective control of the Mississippi River. Americans were happy as the British army sailed home, but their economy was in ruins, and many were aggrieved that the impact of war had fallen so unevenly on regions and individuals, with only a feeble national government to address those grievances. American losers in the war were thousands of Loyalists, abandoned by the British; Native Americans, most of whom had sided with the Crown against rapacious American frontiersmen; and African Americans, who received little for service to either side. A few thousand black people were freed for their military service, but thousands more who had fled to the British for protection were re-enslaved, and a more rigorously enforced slave system took hold in the postwar Southern states.

A mythic version of the war became part of American political culture: unprepared citizen-soldiers, defeated at first but surviving, tenaciously holding their own against the best the Old World could throw at them, and winning through great hardships to ultimate victory. The national myth tended to neglect the crucial role played by the French alliance, and ignored the widespread popular apathy and considerable resistance by "loyal" Americans. If the myth faulted any Americans, they were the Congressmen and state officials who had played "petty politics" despite national peril.

See also Declaration of Independence; era of a new republic, 1789–1827.

FURTHER READING

Calhoon, Robert M. *The Loyalists in Revolutionary America, 1760–1781.* New York: Harcourt Brace Jovanovich, 1973.

Calloway, Colin G. *The American Revolution in Indian Country: Crisis and Diversity in Native American Communities.* New York: Cambridge University Press, 1995.

Dull, Jonathan R. *A Diplomatic History of the American Revolution.* New Haven, CT: Yale University Press, 1985.

Ferling, John. *Almost a Miracle: The American Victory in the War of Independence.* New York: Oxford University Press, 2007.

Fischer, David Hackett. *Washington's Crossing.* New York: Oxford University Press, 2004.

Gilbert, Felix. *To the Farewell Address: Ideas of Early American Foreign Policy.* Princeton, NJ: Princeton University Press, 1961.

Higginbotham, Don. *The War of American Independence: Military Attitudes, Policies, and Practice, 1763–1789.* New York: Macmillan, 1971.

Mackesy, Piers. *The War for America, 1775–1783.* Cambridge, MA: Harvard University Press, 1964.

Middlekauf, Robert. *The Glorious Cause: The American Revolution, 1763–1789.* Rev. ed. New York: Oxford University Press, 2005.

Rakove, Jack N. *The Beginnings of National Politics: An Interpretive History of the Continental Congress.* Baltimore, MD: Johns Hopkins University Press, 1979.

Royster, Charles. *A Revolutionary People at War: The Continental Army and American Character, 1775–1783.* Chapel Hill: University of North Carolina Press, 1979.

JOHN SHY

War of 1812

The War of 1812 was officially fought over the rights of neutral carriers and the impressment of American seamen. Because the conflict failed to win any formal concessions from Britain, Federalist critics condemned the war as an unnecessary failure. Their judgment omitted all reference to Federalist activities prior to and during the conflict. The Federalists' resistance to war with Britain helped provoke it, while their efforts to obstruct its conduct forced their retirement from national politics at its conclusion. Most Americans at the time thought the Federalist leadership, not the Republicans, had failed the nation.

Origins of the War of 1812

Following its Revolution, the United States acquired a new central government with powers analogous to those of Europe's nation-states. When the Atlantic World plunged into war after 1792, the conflict proved a blessing for the infant American state in one respect. No better way existed for the federal government to establish its authority than by solving national problems that the individual states had been unable to address. Shays's Rebellion in 1787 had revealed the obstacles the states faced in dealing with the Revolutionary War debt. The earnings derived from the transfer of Europe's seaborne commerce to America's neutral vessels ensured that Alexander Hamilton's ambitious plan for funding the debt would succeed. But war between France and Britain also entailed risks, because good relations with one of the great powers meant bad relations with the other. The U.S. accommodation with Britain after 1794 soured relations with France, igniting a limited naval war between 1798 and 1800. John Adams succeeded in bringing the

"Quasi-War" to a conclusion shortly before the presidential election of 1800, but the taxes accompanying the conflict contributed to Thomas Jefferson's presidential victory and the election of a Republican Congress.

The defeated Federalists worried that the Republicans would compromise the nation's neutrality by allying with France. The Federalists had courted Britain during the 1790s, because most federal revenue derived from taxes on British imports. They counted on France's hostility to neutralize the enmity Americans bore Britain after the Revolutionary War. Federalist leaders, especially in New England, feared the Republicans would promote bad relations with Britain to maintain their power. But, except for a few dissident minorities outside the Northeast, the nation increasingly identified with the Jeffersonian Republicans. Jefferson's success in acquiring the Louisiana Territory from France strengthened the New Englanders' sense of isolation, because everyone assumed new states formed from the western territories would vote Republican. This assessment appeared to be confirmed by Jefferson's landslide reelection in 1804.

However, escalation of the European war after 1805 clouded the Republicans' prospects. Lord Nelson's naval victory at Trafalgar and Napoleon's triumphs on the Continent made each belligerent supreme in one arena but unable to strike its adversary in the other. In 1806 Britain proclaimed a paper blockade—that is, one too extensive for any navy systematically to enforce—of the adjacent French coast in an effort to surmount this difficulty. Napoleon countered with a paper blockade of the British Isles. When Britain responded by ordering vessels making for Europe to enter a British port and pay British duties, Napoleon decreed any vessel that did so or was visited by a British warship to be a lawful prize. Jefferson reacted to the aggressions of both Great Powers with a general embargo on American shipping and exports. Though the measure hurt the American economy, it seemed preferable to war with either or both of the offending powers. But war with Britain seemed most likely because, six months earlier, a British frigate had attacked the USS *Chesapeake* to remove four alleged deserters.

Federalists led by Senator Timothy Pickering of Massachusetts contended the embargo favored France at Britain's expense. Pickering claimed Napoleon had forced the embargo on Jefferson to complete France's "continental system" of isolating Britain and to provoke war between the United States and Britain. Congressional sponsorship for such views emboldened the Federalist legislature of Massachusetts to urge wholesale resistance to the embargo. Though the Republicans warned that the only alternative to the embargo was war, the Federalists assumed they were bluffing. They knew the Republicans feared war was incompatible with republicanism because the French Republic had recently evolved into a military dictatorship under the pressure of the European wars. War would also reverse the progress the Republicans had made in retiring the Revolutionary debt. Though some Americans prepared to risk an appeal to arms, the majority preferred peace. The Federalists sought to split the Republican congressional majority by supporting a dissident Republican, Dewitt Clinton, as Jefferson's successor, rather than James Madison. Though a majority of the Republican congressional caucus backed Madison, it also modified the embargo to apply only to France and Britain instead of declaring war against either or both powers. The policy, known as nonintercourse, affected France more than Britain because the latter's naval supremacy allowed it to procure American commodities in neutral ports while denying French vessels comparable access.

Both Napoleon and the British minister in Washington, David Erskine, saw nonintercourse as a capitulation to Britain. Napoleon responded by ordering the sequestration, a conditional form of confiscation, of all American vessels entering ports under his control. Erskine sought to consolidate British advantage by proposing that the United States and Britain lift their trade restrictions against each other, conditional upon nonintercourse remaining in effect against France. To unify the badly divided nation, Madison accepted Erskine's offer, only to have the British government repudiate it and replace Erskine with the pugnacious Francis Jackson. Ambassador Jackson accused the Madison administration of entering the Erskine Agreement knowing it would be repudiated in order to provoke antagonism against Britain. Federalists then took the part of the British government against the Republican administration. This convinced Madison and his Republican followers that the Federalists were a disloyal minority bent on subverting America's republican institutions.

Other matters besides Britain's commercial restrictions troubled Anglo-American relations. To maintain its blockade of France, the British navy continued impressing American seamen. At the same time, British commercial interests took advantage of the collapse of Spanish authority in the New World following Napoleon's attempt to place his brother on the Spanish throne in 1808. Madison feared that British attempts at political control would soon follow. West Florida, which extended to New Orleans, looked particularly ripe for British appropriation if the United States did not act first. Madison bided his time until the indecisive Eleventh Congress passed a law (Macon's Bill Number 2) that offered France an arrangement resembling the Erskine Agreement but directed against Britain. When Napoleon accepted, Madison issued orders for the peaceful occupation of West Florida by American forces. Madison would not have pursued such a course had he and other Republican leaders not concluded that Britain, backed by Federalist partisans, constituted the principal threat to the republic's future.

Declaring War against Britain

Mobilizing a Republican majority for war with Britain proved difficult. In addition to Republican misgivings about militarism, the administration faced unwavering Federalist opposition. But the 12th Congress proved more determined than the 11th Congress to avenge the humiliations that Federalists, in conjunction with Britain, had inflicted on the nation. The impressment of American seamen also solidified public opinion behind the war hawks. Still, the Republicans could not brand the Federalists as official enemies because doing so worked at cross-purposes with unifying the republic.

Nor could they get France to stop seizing American vessels, as Napoleon had promised to do in responding to Macon's Bill Number 2. The emperor was much more interested in provoking a war between the United States and Britain than in America's trade. Because the British government used France's actions to justify its commercial restrictions, Napoleon continued promising much but delivering little. He did not formally revoke France's decrees until May 1812, and then with a decree that bore a bogus date of April 1811. France's behavior emboldened Britain to insist that its enemy's decrees be repealed, as they affected Britain's and America's commerce, before British restrictions would be lifted. That made Britain seem more unreasonable than France, but the difference was not enough to silence the Federalists, who continued adamantly to oppose war with Britain. A minority, however, pushed for war with both powers as a way of preventing war with either of them. The Republicans replied weakly that France had done something to satisfy American demands while Britain had done nothing.

Madison called on Congress to begin military preparations in November 1811. Since invading Canada was the only way the United States could strike at Britain, war had to be declared in the spring to allow time for operations before the ensuing winter. But neither the preparations for hostilities nor the diplomatic maneuvering surrounding the declaration observed these requirements. An initial war loan fell far short of its goal, partially because of Federalist opposition, while the administration waited in vain for an answer to its latest ultimatum to Britain.

One of King George III's periodic fits of insanity, combined with the assassination of Prime Minister Spencer Perceval, slowed the British response. The retreat of Russian forces before Napoleon's invasion of that nation together with economic difficulties exacerbated by nonintercourse eventually led Britain to lift its restrictions affecting American commerce on June 23, 1812. But Congress had declared war four days earlier. Had the news arrived sooner, it might have averted hostilities. Madison responded coolly to proposals for a truce, however, once he learned of Britain's action. The political difficulties of unifying the Republicans led him to fear the effect the combined intrigues of the British and the Federalists would have on the Republicans. Had the British also been ready to abandon impressment, peace would have followed. But anger over impressment had become so widespread that Madison needed more than commercial concessions from Britain to suspend hostilities.

Federalist Opposition to the Conduct of the War

The administration soon regretted its hard line as, aside from several indecisive victories at sea, the war began disastrously. In August William Hull surrendered a large garrison at Detroit without firing a shot, while two other attempts to invade Canada collapsed ingloriously. News of Napoleon's retreat from Russia followed these defeats. While Madison only wanted commercial cooperation from France, he had counted on Napoleon holding his own against Britain and the other European powers. Instead France grew weaker as Britain grew stronger. Madison readily accepted the czar's offer of mediation early in 1813, only to have Britain reject it.

These setbacks failed to make Congress easier to manage, thanks in part to the use the Federalists made of France's fraudulent repeal of its decrees. Freshman representative Daniel Webster proposed resolutions to the special congressional session of May–July 1813 that demanded full disclosure of the administration's dealings with France prior to declaring war on Britain. Congressional Republicans passed responsibility for an-

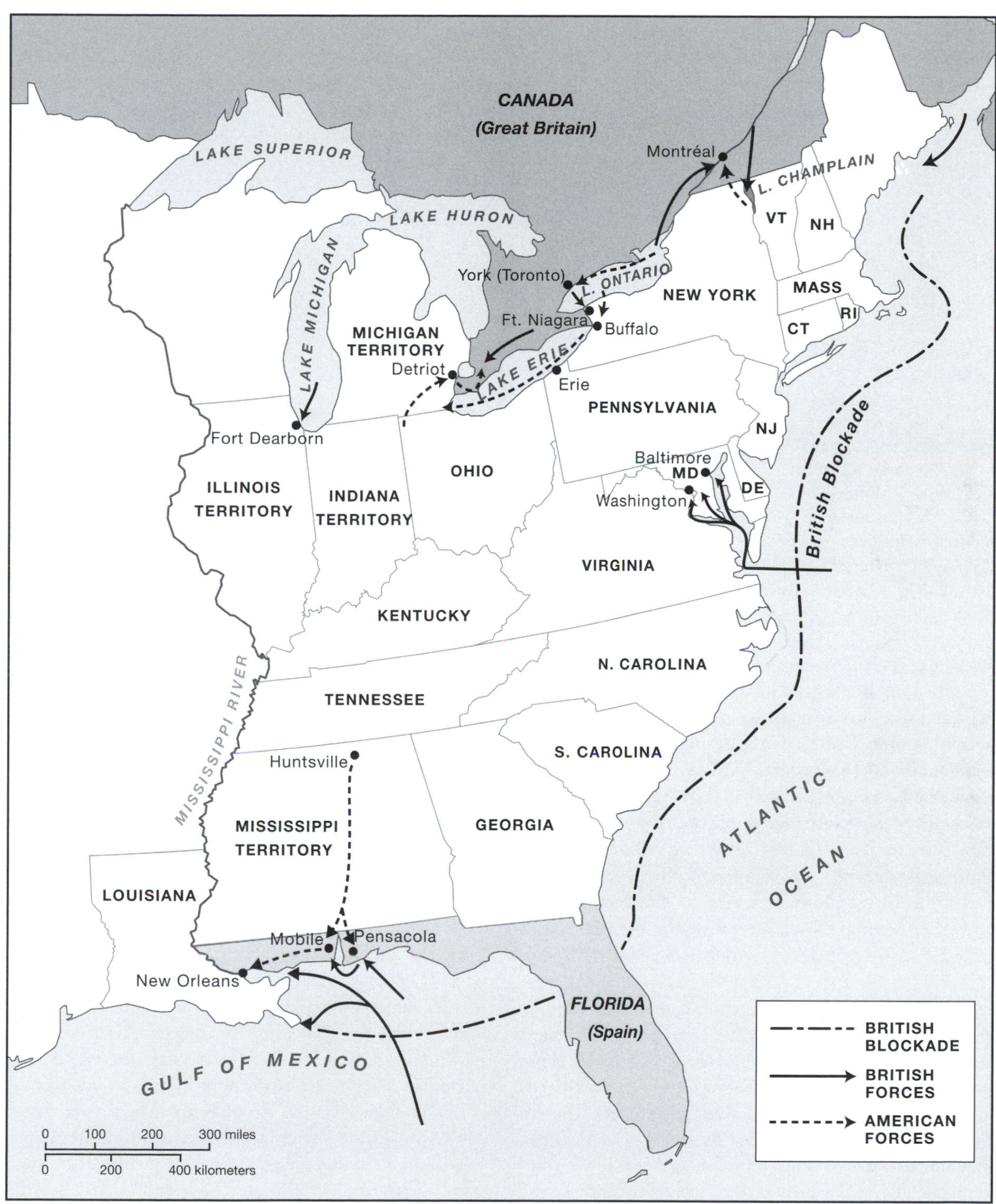
CANADA
(Great Britain)
LAKE SUPERIOR
LAKE HURON
LAKE MICHIGAN
L. ONTARIO
LAKE ERIE
L. CHAMPLAIN
Montréal
York (Toronto)
Ft. Niagara
Buffalo
Erie
Detriot
Fort Dearborn
Baltimore
Washington
Huntsville
Mobile
Pensacola
New Orleans
MICHIGAN TERRITORY
ILLINOIS TERRITORY
INDIANA TERRITORY
OHIO
PENNSYLVANIA
NEW YORK
VT
NH
MASS
RI
CT
NJ
MD
DE
VIRGINIA
KENTUCKY
N. CAROLINA
TENNESSEE
S. CAROLINA
GEORGIA
MISSISSIPPI TERRITORY
LOUISIANA
MISSISSIPPI RIVER
FLORIDA
(Spain)
British Blockade
ATLANTIC OCEAN
GULF OF MEXICO
BRITISH BLOCKADE
BRITISH FORCES
AMERICAN FORCES
0 100 200 300 miles
0 200 400 kilometers

Major Campaigns of the War of 1812

The Taking of the City of Washington in America

View from the Potomac River of Washington, DC, under attack by British forces in the War of 1812 in an engraving published October 14, 1814. (Library of Congress)

swering this challenge to Secretary of State James Monroe. His long document justifying the administration's actions failed to silence the Federalist claim that the administration had let itself be maneuvered into war by Napoleon. The Federalists also hoped to obstruct the war effort by insisting that it be financed by direct taxes. They expected this would destroy the Republicans' popularity, as direct taxes had destroyed theirs during 1799–1800.

The British government agreed to direct negotiations after U.S. Admiral Oliver Perry won decisive control over Lake Erie in September 1813. But Napoleon's abdication in April 1814 freed the British government from any pressure to conclude at a speedy peace. Instead it directed all British military power against the United States. The new strategic situation made reconstituting a national bank, whose charter had been allowed to expire in March 1811, a national priority for the American government. Though the Federalists supported a national bank in principle, they insisted that its notes be redeemable for specie (precious metals), while Boston's Federalist banks were busy engrossing the nation's specie supply. Britain had absolved eastern New England from its blockade of the American coast until April 1814, making Boston the creditor for the rest of the nation. Boston's banks then called on the state banks outside New England to redeem their notes in specie, which they proved unable to do. The ensuing banking crisis obstructed the government's coordination of military operations and thus contributed to the burning of Washington at the end of August. The British also seized a third of Maine's coastline. Such developments did not provide an auspicious setting for the peace negotiations with Britain beginning in Europe. Never had the republic seemed in more peril.

Instead of helping to defend the nation, New England's Federalist leadership tried to turn that peril to its own advantage. While the governor of Massachusetts put out feelers to his counterpart in Nova Scotia soliciting British military intervention, the state's legislature called for a regional convention to meet at Hartford. Federalists were prepared to go to such extremes because reports of Britain's initial peace terms made it clear the Republicans would reject them. Though American forces had repelled a British invasion at Plattsburgh, the Federalists knew a large enemy force was moving against New Orleans. Its seizure would put the western two-thirds of the nation at Britain's mercy. Meeting in December 1814, the Hartford Convention framed a set of constitutional amendments designed to enhance the Federalists' power in the nation. The amendments were to be presented to Congress for acceptance along with the demand that New England be allowed to defend itself. Everyone understood that New England would conclude a separate peace with Britain if the rest of the nation refused to submit to the Federalist minority.

Resolution

The commissioners carrying the Hartford Convention's demands arrived in Washington at the same time as news of the conclusion of a peace in Europe based on the *status quo ante bellum* and of Andrew Jackson's victory over the British at New Orleans. These two events transformed the fortunes of the republic overnight, making the Federalists look like a disloyal minority bent on humiliating the nation. The Hartford commissioners had no choice but to retreat in disgrace. The republic had unexpectedly survived despite all that the Federalists had done to prostrate it before Britain. But Federalist leaders did more than disgrace themselves in the eyes of other Americans. They also destroyed their power base in the New England states. Their policies had assumed the weakness of the republic compared to a powerful monarchy like Britain.

Within a year of the peace, Madison could predict that the nation would be debt free by 1835. A vigorous postwar recovery removed the last thread of justification for Federalist actions. Few realized that the European rivalries fueling the division between Federalists and Republicans had also come to an end. Their disappearance left what survived of the Federalist leadership without a rallying cause in their home states. By the mid-1820s hardly any remnants of the party remained.

See also Democratic Party, 1800–1828; era of a new republic, 1789–1827; Federalist Party; war and politics.

FURTHER READING

Adams, Henry. *History of the United States of America during the Administrations of James Madison.* New York: Library of America, 1986.

Banner, James M., Jr. *To the Hartford Convention: The Federalists and the Origins of Party Politics in Massachusetts, 1789–1815.* New York: Knopf, 1970.

Brown, Roger. *The Republic in Peril: 1812.* New York: Columbia University Press, 1964.

Buel, Richard, Jr. *America on the Brink: How the Political Struggle over the War of 1812 Almost Destroyed the Young Republic.* New York: Palgrave, 2005.

Cress, Lawrence D. "'Cool and Serious Reflections': Federalist Attitudes towards the War of 1812." *Journal of the Early Republic* 7 (1987), 123–45.

Hill, Peter P. *Napoleon's Troublesome Americans: Franco-American Relations, 1804–1815.* Dulles, VA: Potomac Books, 2005.

Mason, Matthew. "'Nothing Is Better Calculated to Excite Division': Federalist Agitation against Slave Representation during the War of 1812." *New England Quarterly* 75 (2002), 531–61.

McCaughey, Robert A. *Josiah Quincy 1772–1864: The Last Federalist.* Cambridge, MA: Harvard University Press, 1974.

Perkins, Bradford. *Prologue to War: England and the United States 1805–1812.* Berkeley: University of California Press, 1961.

Spivak, Burton. *Jefferson's English Crisis: Commerce, Embargo, and the Republican Revolution.* Charlottesville, VA: University Press of Virginia, 1979.

Stagg, J.C.A. *Mr. Madison's War: Politics, Diplomacy, and Warfare in the Early Republic, 1783–1830.* Princeton, NJ: Princeton University Press, 1983.

Watts, Steven. *The Republic Reborn: War and the Making of Liberal America.* Baltimore, MD: Johns Hopkins University Press, 1987.

RICHARD BUEL JR.

welfare

Origins and Meaning of "Welfare"

Welfare originated as a positive term in the early twentieth century. It signified attempts to professionalize and modernize old practices of relief and charity. This positive connotation of welfare and "welfare state" lasted through the New Deal of the 1930s and even into the 1940s. It came under attack in two stages. During the cold war, in the late 1940s and 1950s, opponents associated welfare with European socialism and un-American ideas. Then, in the 1960s, as unmarried women of color with children began to dominate public assistance rolls, welfare acquired the combined stigmas of race, gender, and illicit sex.

This narrow, pejorative use of the term welfare obscures its true meaning and inhibits understanding of the American welfare state. In the original sense—as used from the early twentieth century through post–World War II years—the terms welfare and welfare state referred to a collection of programs designed to assure economic security for all citizens by guaranteeing the fundamental necessities of life. The welfare state is how a society ensures against common risks—unemployment, poverty, sickness, and old age—that in one way or another confront everyone.

The American welfare state confronts universal problems with a distinctive architecture—much broader and more complex than is usually realized. It is not usefully described as either public or private. Instead, its economy is mixed, and its composition reflects American federalism—the division of powers between the federal government and the states. This American welfare state consists of two main divisions, with subdivisions within each. Each subdivision is rooted in a different location in American history and, to some extent, has followed its own trajectory over time.

Public Assistance

The first division is the public welfare state. Its subdivisions are public assistance, social insurance, and taxation. Public assistance, the oldest form of welfare, consists of means-tested programs. Its origins lie in the Elizabethan poor laws, which the colonists brought with them in the seventeenth century. Embodied in "outdoor relief," aid given to people in their homes rather than in an institution, public assistance has a long and controversial history. Although subject to state law, public assistance, with a few exceptions, was administered locally, usually by counties. In the early twentieth century, state governments introduced a new form of public assistance, "mothers' pensions," small amounts of money given to a limited number of worthy widows. During the Great Depression of the 1930s, the federal government introduced two public assistance programs paid for with matching state-federal funds. They were Old Age Assistance, by far the largest until it was eliminated by the growth of Social Security, and Aid to Dependent Children, a federalization of state mothers' pensions, which later became Aid to Families with Dependent Children (AFDC), or what most Americans referred to as welfare, and, in 1966, Temporary Aid to Needy Families (TANF), which replaced AFDC.

A fierce critic of public assistance, President Richard Nixon surprised both his supporters and critics by proposing to replace AFDC with the Family Assistance Plan, a variant of a negative income tax. Opposed by conservatives, who objected in principle, and welfare rights advocates, who thought its benefits inadequate, the plan died. Instead, in 1974 Congress bundled public assistance for the indigent elderly, blind, and disabled, into a new program, Supplemental Security Income.

In 1996 welfare reform legislation—the Personal Responsibility and Work Opportunity Reconciliation Act–passed overwhelmingly in both the House and Senate with bipartisan support and was signed into law by President Bill Clinton on August 22. The legislation capped a long process of negotiation between Clinton and Congress and drew on widespread hostility to public assistance. The legislation, which reoriented public assistance toward what was called the transition to work, abolished the quasi-entitlement to public assistance embodied in AFDC. Its overarching goal was to move people from public assistance into a job in the regular labor market. States could meet this goal by contracting out welfare administration to private firms.

The TANF program has two major components. Both are block grants to states that are intended to help families leave welfare. One gives cash to families in need to support their children while they look for work, and discourages them from having more children outside of marriage. The other component bundles together money for major child-care programs for low-income families.

Two features of the new legislation attracted the most attention. One was time-limited public assistance, which mandated a maximum lifetime benefit of five years, although states were permitted to set shorter limits. The other feature took benefits away from legal immigrants who had been in the United States less than five years; again, states could impose even harsher restrictions on immigrants than the federal government. (Prodded by President Clinton, Congress restored some of these benefits to immigrants in 1997 and 1998.) One other important aspect of the bill was its emphasis on enforcing payment of child support by absent fathers.

The most dramatic change following the new legislation was a rapid drop in the welfare rolls by more than half. Supporters of welfare reform hailed this decline as testimony to the bill's success. With little debate, Congress inserted even tougher work requirements into the legislation's reauthorization, included as part of the Deficit Reduction Act that was signed by President George W. Bush on February 8, 2005. Many observers, however, were not sure that the drop in the welfare rolls resulted only from the new rules or that it should be the measure of the success of welfare reform. The decline, which had begun before the passage of the 1996 bill, reflected three major influences: job growth in a strong economy, individuals either discouraged from applying or sanctioned off the rolls, and work incentives in the legislation. Moreover, leaving welfare did not mean escaping poverty. Many of the jobs held by former public assistance recipients paid poorly, lacked health and retirement benefits, and did not offer avenues for advancement. A large proportion of poor women with children exchanged public assistance for working poverty.

Social Insurance and Taxation

Social insurance, whose origins lie in nineteenth-century Europe, is the second subdivision in the American welfare state. Social insurance programs are not means tested. They provide benefits to everyone who meets certain fixed criteria, such as being 65 years of age or older. They are based on a rough insurance analogy, because potential beneficiaries pay premiums in advance. They have been either state or federal-state programs. Always much more generous than public assistance, social insurance benefits have increased at a more rapid rate over time. The result is that the gap between them and public assistance has progressively widened. The first form of social insurance in the United States was workers' compensation, introduced by most states in the early twentieth century. Few states developed old-age or unemployment insurance. Federal social insurance emerged in a burst with the Social Security Act of 1935, which introduced a complicated federal-state program of unemployment insurance and a federal program of old-age insurance known as Social Security. At first these programs were very restrictive. Social Security excluded agricultural and domestic workers and did not pay benefits, which initially were very low, until 1940. Although social insurance and unemployment insurance originally discriminated against African Americans and women, expansions of coverage have reduced inequities in benefits. Overall, Social Security has been the most effective federal public social program in American history.

Over time, Social Security's coverage expanded, benefit levels increased, disability benefits were added, and in the 1970s, benefits were pegged to inflation. In the burst of social spending during the Great Society years, from the mid-1960s through the early 1970s, Congress passed a major extension to social insurance: Medicare, health insurance for the elderly, along with Medicaid, a medical public assistance program for the poor. By the late 1970s, largely as a result of Social Security's benefits, the elderly, who in 1960 had a poverty rate three times that of any other age group, were less likely to be poor than any other segment of the American population. At the same time, Medicare and Medicaid transformed access to medical care for the elderly and poor.

A third division of the public welfare state is taxation. Low-income people receive benefits indirectly through tax credits given to businesses and real estate developers to create jobs and housing. But the most important program is the Earned Income Tax Credit. Started in 1975, the EITC was expanded greatly under President Clinton in the 1990s. It supplements the income of workers whose earnings fall below a predetermined level. The EITC costs more than AFDC ever did or than TANF does now. It has, however, been effective in boosting people from slightly below the poverty line to just above it.

The Private Welfare State

The private welfare state has two main subdivisions. The first of these consists of charities and social services, which have a long and varied history. Some stretch far back in American history; others are much newer. Contrary to myths this private welfare state has never been adequate to relieve the needs of individuals and families without sufficient health care, income, or housing. In the 1960s, federal legislation funded the expansion of social services. As a result, the character of nominally private agencies and social services changed, because they began to receive a large share of their budgets from federal, state, and local governments. American governments operate relatively few services themselves. Instead, they run social services by funding private agencies. Without government funds, most private agencies would close their doors. In effect, they have become government contractors.

The second subdivision in the private welfare state consists of employee benefits. More than six of ten Americans receive health insurance through their employers. Many receive retirement pensions as well. Although a few businesses and governments provided pensions before World War II, employee benefits developed into mass programs only in the 1940s and 1950s. Fought for by trade unions, they received government sanction in 1949 from the National Labor Relations Board, which required employers to bargain over (though not to provide) employee benefits. Employee benefits fit within the framework of the welfare state because they have been encouraged by the federal government (which allows employers to deduct their cost from taxes) and are regulated by federal legislation. Without them, the public welfare state would have assumed a very different form. In recent decades, the percentage of workers covered by health insurance and retirement benefits has decreased. Employees pay much more for their health care than in the past and receive it through some variant of managed care. In the private sector, most pensions now require defined contributions, which leave future benefits to the vagaries of individual investment decisions and the market, rather than, as in the past, offering defined benefits, which guaranteed the income employees were to receive in retirement.

With these employee benefits added to its economy, the United States appears less of a welfare laggard compared to other developed nations. When nations are arrayed in a hierarchy according to public social spending, the United States and Japan are at the bottom, widely separated from the top. However, when private social welfare is added, the rank order remains the same but the distance is greatly reduced. Including benefits distributed through the tax code would shrink it even more. What is unique about the United States welfare state is the distinctive way in which it delivers its benefits.

In the 1980s, public social policy coalesced around three great objectives that began to redefine the American welfare state. The first objective was the war to end dependence—not only the dependence of young unmarried mothers on welfare but all forms of dependence on public and private support and on the paternalism of employers. The second objective was to devolve authority; that is, to transfer power from the federal government to the states, from states to counties, and from the public to the private sector. The third aspect was the application of market models to social policy. Everywhere, the market triumphed as the template for a redesigned welfare state. Used loosely and often unreflectively as the organizational model toward which public programs should aspire, the market model emphasized competition, privatization, and a reliance on supply and demand to determine policies and priorities. Examples include the replacement of AFDC with TANF and the shift to managed health care and defined contribution pensions; other examples are found everywhere throughout the public and private welfare states.

None of the forces redefining the welfare state originated in the 1980s, but in those years they burst through older tendencies in public policy and combined to form a powerful and largely bipartisan tide. With only a few exceptions, political arguments about the welfare state revolved more around details than great principles. An exception was the battle over the future of Medicare and Social Security that escalated during the administration of President George W. Bush. Conservatives wanted to move both programs toward privatization, which would fundamentally change the model on which they were built, but massive public opposition prevented Bush's plans for Social Security from reaching the floor of Congress.

Bush had partial success reforming Medicare. On December 8, 2003, he signed the controversial Medicare Modernization Act, which introduced a prescription drug benefit known as Medicare Part D. Instead of a uniform benefit administered by Medicare, the Bush scheme relied on private insurers to offer plans that fit the program's guidelines. The legislation forbade Medicare to negotiate directly with drug companies for lower prices, as the Veterans Administration did. It exempted low-income seniors from premiums, moving those eligible for Medicaid into the new drug program, and it reduced premiums for others with near-poverty incomes. But it handed extra dollars to insurance companies for seniors enrolled in Medicare Advantage Plans (managed-care plans that combined medical and prescription benefits). Medicare paid these private health plans about 12 percent more than it would cost to care for the same patients in the traditional Medicare program. Private insurers reaped a windfall from the requirement that Medicaid recipients enroll in the plans. The Democratic congressional majority proved unable to lift the prohibition on negotiating drug prices or to scale back the advantages granted private insurers. It did not even attempt to alter the complicated prescription drug plan that left many seniors still paying thousands of dollars for their medications each year.

By 2007 living-wage ordinances had passed in many cities; elections in several states showed strong support for an increased minimum wage; the lack of universal and affordable health insurance had become the number-one domestic issue; and the presidential campaign of John Edwards had focused national attention on poverty for the first time in decades. These developments held out hope for improving the economic security of the working poor and the accessibility of health care for the nonelderly. But the prospects for a reversal of the trends that had redefined and attenuated the nation's welfare state remained dim.

See also Social Security.

FURTHER READING

Berkowitz, Edward D. *The American Welfare State: From Roosevelt to Reagan.* Baltimore, MD: Johns Hopkins University Press, 1991.

Esping-Andersen, Gosta. *The Three Worlds of Welfare Capitalism.* Princeton, NJ: Princeton University Press, 1990.

Gordon, Colin. *Dead on Arrival: The Politics of Health Care in Twentieth-Century America.* Princeton, NJ: Princeton University Press, 2003.

Gordon, Linda. *Pitied But Not Entitled: Single Mothers and the History of Welfare, 1890–1935.* New York: Free Press, 1994.

Howard, Christopher. *The Hidden Welfare State: Tax Expenditures and Social Policy in the United States.* Princeton, NJ: Princeton University Press, 1997.

Katz, Michael B. *In the Shadow of the Poorhouse: A Social History of Welfare.* 10th ed. New York: Basic Books, 1996.

———. *The Price of Citizenship: Redefining the American Welfare State.* Philadelphia: University of Pennsylvania Press, 2008.

Piven, Frances Fox, and Richard A. Cloward. *Poor People's Movements: How They Succeed, Why They Fail.* New York: Pantheon, 1977.

Reese, Ellen. *Backlash against Welfare Mothers: Past and Present.* Berkeley: University of California Press, 2005.

Skocpol, Theda. *Protecting Soldiers and Mothers: The Political Origins of Social Policy in the United States.* Cambridge, MA: Harvard University Press, 1992.

MICHAEL B. KATZ

Whig Party

The Whig Party was a formidable force in the antebellum United States. From the late 1830s until the early 1850s, roughly half of the American electorate was made up of Whigs. The party won two of the four presidential elections in which it participated—in 1840 and 1848. Because the two Whigs who were elected president—William Henry Harrison and Zachary Taylor—died in office and were succeeded by their vice presidents, John Tyler and Millard Fillmore, four Whigs ultimately held the office.

The Beginnings

Some of the best-known politicians of the day were Whigs, including Henry Clay and the great orator Daniel Webster. During his congressional career, John Quincy Adams consistently acted with the Whigs although he first ran as an Anti-Mason. Leaders of the party included influential Southerners such as Robert Toombs and Alexander Stephens. The greatest educational reformer of the day, Horace Mann, was a Whig, as was William H. Seward, and Abraham Lincoln had a long association with the party. The two best-known congressional leaders of Radical Reconstruction, Charles Sumner and Thaddeus Stevens, had started their political careers as Whigs.

In 1824 all presidential candidates were Republican and deeply involved with the administration of the last of the Virginia dynasty, James Monroe. Andrew Jackson was a U.S. Senator from Tennessee, John Quincy Adams was the secretary of state, William Crawford was the secretary of the treasury, Clay was the speaker of the House of Representatives, and Calhoun, who became vice president, was the secretary of war. When no one received a majority of the electoral votes, the election was thrown into the House of Representatives. The choice of Adams, who came in second in the popular vote, created the movement to make Jackson president in 1828.

The merger of the Albany Regency, the Richmond Junto, and the Nachez Junto, local political cliques at the time, was the beginning of the Democratic Party. The Adams supporters were not as inept as often portrayed, but an alliance of the Jackson and Crawford forces of 1824 could have easily outvoted them. Political organization was moving toward modern parties, but on different rates at different levels. Most important in the North was the Anti-Masonic movement, which opposed the influence of secret societies in state politics and was one of the precursors of the Whigs.

A more general source of the future Whig Party was those who supported the Adams administration, who formed the National Republicans to oppose Jackson in 1832. They held a national convention and nominated Clay for president. These proto-Whigs advocated what they called the American System, a plan to establish a national bank, a protective tariff, federal support for internal improvements, and the colonization of freed blacks in Africa.

In 1833 and 1834, people began to use the term *Whig* to describe the anti-Jackson opposition. The name referred to the English Whigs, who had been associated with the parliamentary opposition to the king from the late seventeenth century to the mid-nineteenth century. The American Whigs originated as a party of congressional opposition to the imperial executive, "King Andrew."

In preparation for the election of 1836, the Democratic Republicans held a convention to anoint Martin Van Buren as Jackson's successor. There was no Whig convention, because there was as yet no national Whig Party. Anti-Jackson groups ran a variety of candidates for president and vice president. Four opposition candidates received electoral votes for president: William Henry Harrison, from Ohio; Daniel Webster, from Massachusetts; Hugh Lawson White, from Tennessee; and Willie P. Mangum, from North Carolina. White, who received 26 electoral votes, openly denied he was a Whig, and Mangum, who received South Carolina's 11 electoral votes, had not agreed to run. The organizational confusion made the election of 1836 the only election in American history in which the Senate had to choose the vice president when none of the four candidates received a majority of the electoral vote.

Coming Together

As the Democratic and Whig parties coalesced in the late 1830s, debates emerged in the states about which could legitimately use "democratic" in its label. By 1840 the two major parties had taken on the official names of the American Democracy and the Democratic Whigs.

The Whigs had held their first party convention in 1839. Henry Clay was the obvious presidential candidate, but the New Yorkers, led by Seward and Thurlow Weed, blocked his nomination and put forth Harrison, who had won 73 electoral votes in 1836. To balance the ticket, the convention chose John Tyler from Virginia.

Because a Democratic editor accused Harrison, a retired general and presidential aspirant in 1836, of wanting to stay at home in his "log cabin" and drink "hard cider," the election has been tainted with this image and the idea that the Whigs did nothing but stage gigantic parades and mouth empty speeches. Yet these political activities brought mass participation to American politics. Voter turnout skyrocketed: more than 80 percent of the white adult men went to the polls. The result was a stunning victory for the Whig candidate.

Who Were the Whigs?

Historians have often asked, "Who were the Whigs?" The partisan battle was neither a simple matter of the rich against the poor, nor one between immigrants and the native-born. The Whigs won two presidential elections, held House majorities in the 27th and 30th Congresses, and did well in practically all of the states from the late 1830s to the early 1850s. Several studies have shown that ethnoreligious affiliation affected partisan perspectives in both sections. Groups such as Irish Catholics were overwhelmingly Democratic, while the various white, Anglo-Saxon Protestant descendents of the Puritans inspired by the Second Great Awakening in the North were heavily Whig. In the South, local conditions often determined the way these factors played themselves out in politics. Where the few free African Americans could vote, they tended to oppose the followers of Jackson until, in most states, the Jacksonians disenfranchised them. While many Democrats were extraordinarily rich—in the northern cities merchants, in the South plantation owners—Whigs tended to control the economically dynamic areas in both sections. Above all, the Whigs differed essentially from their opponents about the proper role of the state in governing economic and moral behavior. It was a matter of attitude. The poor, up-by-your-bootstraps men were primarily Whigs.

During these years, congressional behavior represented a distinctly partisan pattern. Even at the state level, in elections, legislative behavior, and constitutional conventions, partisan conflict reflected attitudes that mirrored differences on federal policy. From Maine to Mississippi, the Whigs emphasized the positive role of government by creating the "credit system"—charter in private- and state-related banks to create not only most of the money supply of the country but also to make loans to farmers and small businessmen—building roads and canals, supporting public education, and generally encouraging morality in public life. In contrast, the Democrats distrusted the actions of the legislatures and viewed the governors as "tribunes of the people" with the power to veto the excesses of government; they embraced laissez faire in all aspects of life.

The election of 1840 took place in the midst of a depression; the contrasting economic proposals of the parties were salient. The Democrats, who wrote the first real party platform in American history, emphasized their commitment to laissez faire and state's rights. The Whigs did not write a platform, but Whig speakers made the party's position clear. Clay began the campaign with a three-hour speech that emphasized banking and monetary policy. Webster spoke in the South and Virginian John Minor Botts toured the North, spreading similar ideas. Harrison—the first presidential candidate to speak widely—echoed the same Whig themes.

After Harrison caught pneumonia and died a month after his inauguration, the presidency fell to Tyler. Congressional Whigs looked toward sweeping economic change by reviving a national bank to control credit and currency, increasing the tariff to encourage domestic production, altering land policy to distribute revenues to the states for the development of internal improvements, and passing a federal bankruptcy law. The central pillar of the Whig economic program, called the "Fiscal Bank of the United States," passed Congress in August, but Tyler vetoed it as overextending the power of the federal government to create banking corporations. After negotiations with Tyler, the Whigs pushed through a slightly revised measure, but Tyler vetoed this as well.

Tyler's vetoes alienated most Whigs. The entire cabinet resigned except Webster, who was in the midst of negotiating the Webster-Ashburton Treaty with England. While this was ostensibly over boundary disputes between the United States and Canada in both Maine and Minnesota, it also touched on other conflicts between Great Britain and the United States, ranging from extradition of criminals to cooperation in ending the African slave trade.

Attempts by Clay and the congressional Whigs to provide for the distribution of the proceeds of land sales to aid the states in providing internal improvements and to revise the tariff did lead to legislation in 1841 and 1842, yet in both cases they were forced to compromise. As Tyler remade and remade again his cabinet, he moved closer to the Democrats. Eventually Calhoun, who had returned to the Democratic Party, served as his secretary of state and oversaw the annexation of Texas, which Tyler thought would revive his presidential prospects and his historical memory.

Slavery

The slavery question was more troubling for the Whigs than for the Democrats and was the rock upon which their ship would eventually founder. From the mid-1830s on, northern Whigs opposed what they called "the slave power"—the political power exercised by southern planters. Led by John Quincy Adams, northern Whigs fought the "gag rules" that restricted congressional consideration of antislavery petitions. While a few southern Whigs did eventually vote to end the gag, this issue separated northern and southern Whigs who voted together on economic matters.

Under the Tyler administration, the question of annexing the territory that would become Texas posed another problem for the Whigs. Secretary of State Abel Upshur of Virginia secretly negotiated a treaty with the Texans to annex the Republic of Texas. When the treaty became public, both northern and southern Whigs bitterly opposed it. They argued that it would create sectional discord because dividing the area into five new slave states could give the South control of the Senate and the Texans' boundary demands could lead to war with Mexico. While the Whigs' argument proved correct on both counts (an increase in sectionalism and a war with Mexico), the Democrats generally embraced annexation and expansion.

After the annexation treaty was defeated, Tyler moved to annex Texas in an unconventional way, by a joint resolution of Congress, which passed in a sharply partisan vote. Against vigorous Whig opposition, the administration of Tyler's Democratic successor, James K. Polk, also moved to institute the Democratic economic agenda. Polk resisted any internal improvements at federal expense and vetoed several acts to improve rivers and harbors in the Great Lakes region, thus alienating some Midwestern Democrats.

Most important, however, by ordering General Zachary Taylor to move his troops in Texas to the Rio Grande, Polk precipitated the events that led to the U.S. war with Mexico. Whigs were forced to support the declaration of war, although a southern Whig, Garrett Davis, said, "It is our own President [Tyler] who began this war." Abraham Lincoln, then a young congressman from Illinois, called on the president to show Congress "the spot" on "American soil" where "American blood" had been "shed," as Polk had stated in his war message.

Moral reformers were more likely to be Whigs than Democrats. In relation to the slavery question, most of the gradualists, who advocated the colonization of free blacks in Africa or Latin America, were Whigs, as were most immediate Abolitionists. Those who wished to use the government to deal with social dependents, either in prisons or public schools, were Whigs. Supporters of women's rights and antibellum pacifism also tended to be Whigs, although some atheist pacifists were Democrats. While it is always difficult to define the American middle class, the Whigs were more likely than their opponents to represent bourgeois values.

The salience of the slavery issue in American politics in the 1840s would eventually destroy the Whig Party and ultimately lead to the Civil War. During the debate on a bill to fund the Mexican-American War, Pennsylvania Democrat David Wilmot introduced an amendment that would exclude slavery from any territories acquired from Mexico. While the Whigs split along sectional lines over the Wilmot Proviso, the party did extremely well in the elections immediately following its introduction.

The Proviso, injected into the election of 1848 by the Free Soil Party, grew out of a conflict in the New York State Democratic Party between supporters of Van Buren and his opponents. The national Democratic convention refused to seat the delegations of either faction and nominated Lewis Cass of Michigan on a platform that denied the power of Congress to act on slavery in the territories. The Van Burenites walked out and then dominated the Free Soil convention in August, which nominated Van Buren for president with Charles Francis Adams, son of the former president, as his running mate.

The Whigs held their convention in Philadelphia that June and passed over Clay in favor of a hero of the Mexican-American War, Zachary Taylor, with the conservative New Yorker Millard Fillmore as his running mate. Taylor's slaveholding and the Whigs' refusal to write into their platform any position on slavery in the territories alienated some Northerners. Many, such as the "Conscience Whigs" of Massachusetts, joined the Free Soil movement. Party leaders hoped that southern Whigs would be satisfied by the fact that Taylor owned a large plantation in Louisiana. He was able to retain national support, gaining the electoral votes of eight slave states and seven free states. Because Van Buren received 10.3 percent of the popular vote, Taylor won with a plurality of 47.3 percent, although he received a majority of electoral votes, 163 versus 127 for Cass. The Whig was able to win because the Free Soilers split the New York Democratic vote. Having made their point, the New York Free Soilers, following their leader, moved back into the Democratic fold. The Free Soil Whigs, however, had permanently broken with their party.

The attempt of the new president to organize California and New Mexico kept the issue of slavery in the territories alive. After the discovery of gold at Sutter's Mill in 1848, the population of California jumped to over 100,000. In the fall, Californians wrote a constitution banning slavery and establishing a state government. Taylor recommended to Congress that California immediately be admitted to the Union. This, along with an earlier speech the president made in Pennsylvania that opposed the expansion of slavery, and his enforcement of the law against a filibustering expedition in Latin America, alienated southern Whigs from their president.

At the end of January, Senator Clay put forth a series of resolutions addressing the difficult questions facing Congress that became the basis for the Compromise of 1850. Because of Clay's initiative and Webster's powerful speech on March 7 favoring compromise, this was long credited as a Whig measure, but Clay's "Omnibus" failed due to opposition from President Taylor. After Taylor's sudden death, which made the pro compromise Millard Fillmore president, the Illinois Democrat Stephen A. Douglas was able to shepherd the five acts that constituted the "compromise measures" through Congress in September. The roll call vote revealed a Whig Party in disarray.

The Decline

The sectional split in the party led many Whigs in the Cotton South to join state "union" parties, which served as a stepping-stone for the movement of some former Whigs into the Democratic Party. Yet most southern Whigs, particularly those in the Upper South, remained loyal to the party and participated in the presidential election of 1852. In their convention that year, the sectional split was apparent in both the choice of the candidate and the platform. President Fillmore, the candidate of most southern Whigs, was rejected in favor of General Winfield Scott, but the platform supported the compromise measures of 1850 over the opposition of antislavery Northerners. Although Scott made a respectable showing in the South and won the electoral votes of Kentucky and Tennessee, sizable numbers of southern Whigs stayed home.

In the North, ex-Whigs, who had voted for the Liberty Party and the Free Soil Party, made up a majority of the voters for the Free Democrat, John P. Hale, who received nearly 5 percent of the popular vote. While Scott got more popular votes than any previous Whig candidate, in part because of the growth of the population, he was overwhelmed in both the popular (50.8 percent to 43.9 percent) and electoral (254–42) vote by Franklin Pierce.

The Whig Party was finally destroyed in the North by the emergence of the nativist Know-Nothings (the American Party) in local elections in 1853 and sectional furor over the Kansas-Nebraska Act in 1854. Most southern Whigs in 1856 joined the American Party, and most Northerners moved into the Republican Party, although a sizable number remained Know-Nothings until the party final split over slavery. In 1856 a rump group of Whigs met in Baltimore and nominated Fillmore, who had previously been put forth by the American Party. This was to be the last formal act of the Whig Party.

Its early death made the once vibrant party of Clay, Webster, Adams, Seward, and Lincoln a mystery to modern Americans. The Whigs gave the nation not only some of the most important politicians of the Civil War era, such as Radical Republicans like Thaddeus Stevens and Charles Sumner who defined Reconstruction, but also the economic policy that, enhanced by a commitment to civil rights, became the "blueprint for modern America" when enacted by the Republicans during the Civil War and Reconstruction. In the period often called the era of Jacksonian Democracy, many historians have caricatured the Whigs. Since the mid-twentieth century, American historians have shown clearly that the development of American democracy has involved not only heroes of the Democratic Party, like Jefferson and Jackson, but their opponents as well.

See also American (Know-Nothing) Party; Free Soil Party; Liberty Party.

FURTHER READING

Benson, Lee. *The Concept of Jacksonian Democracy: New York as a Test Case*. Princeton, NJ: Princeton University Press, 1961.

Curry, Leonard P. *Blueprint for Modern America: Nonmilitary Legislation in the First Civil War Congress*. Nashville, TN: Vanderbilt University Press, 1968.

Formisano, Ronald P. *The Birth of Mass Political Parties: Michigan, 1827–1861*. Princeton, NJ: Princeton University Press, 1971.

———. *The Transformation of Political Culture: Massachusetts Parties, 1790s–1840s*. New York: Oxford University Press, 1983.

Holt, Michael F. *The Rise and Fall of the American Whig Party: Jacksonian Politics and the Onset of the Civil War*. New York: Oxford University Press, 1999.

Howe, Daniel Walker. *The Political Culture of the American Whigs*. Chicago: University of Chicago Press, 1979.

Remini, Robert V. *Daniel Webster: The Man and His Times*. New York: Norton, 1997.

———. *Henry Clay: Statesman for the Union*. New York: Norton, 1991.

Shade, William G. *Democratizing the Old Dominion: Virginia and the Second Party System, 1824–1861*. Charlottesville: University Press of Virginia, 1996.

Silbey, Joel H. *The Shrine of Party: Congressional Voting Behavior, 1841–1852*. Pittsburgh, PA: University of Pittsburgh Press, 1967.

Van Deusen, Glyndon G. *William Henry Seward: Lincoln's Secretary of State, the Negotiator of the Alaska Purchase*. New York: Oxford University Press, 1967.

Wyllie, Irvin G. *The Self-Made Man in America: The Myth of Rags to Riches*. New York: Free Press, 1954.

WILLIAM G. SHADE

woman suffrage

The movement for woman suffrage is at once the historical foundation of American feminism and, along with the labor movement and the movement for black political and civil rights, one of the formative processes in the history of American democracy. Begun in the wake of Jacksonian franchise expansion, and reaching its formal victory in the late years of American progressivism, the struggle for women's political rights is best understood less as a sustained campaign than as a series of distinct but cumulative movements, each with its own philosophies, strategies, constituencies, and leaders. The antebellum reform era, Reconstruction, late-nineteenth-century populism, and twentieth-century progressivism each witnessed its own characteristic campaign for women's voting rights.

Antebellum Women's Rights

The initial exclusion of women from political rights was barely necessary to articulate, so obvious did it seem to all. In speaking of "persons" and "citizens," the laws and constitutions of the early republic did not need to specify males; the identity of political personhood and maleness was generally assumed. The political virtue necessary for the trustworthy exercise of franchise rights was understood to require a level of rationality and personal independence that men, and only men, had. Women were too emotional, too economically dependent, too immersed in the private world of family to be imaginable as active public citizens; and besides, husbands represented their wives as fathers did their children in the larger family of the republic. The only exceptions to the widespread assumption that popular voting rights were thoroughly male in character were in church balloting, where women members participated, and during a brief, almost accidental episode of women voting—so long as they were unmarried and propertied—in New

Jersey in the late eighteenth century. Once discovered, the legislature remedied its error, and New Jersey women slipped back with their sisters in other states into political invisibility.

The accepted date for the first clearly articulated demand for woman suffrage is 1848, made at the Seneca Falls, New York, women's rights convention. The timing links the origins of woman suffrage advocacy to expansions in the franchise for all white men, regardless of property holding, which took place in the previous decades. Following the expansion of the white male franchise, political parties began to multiply, and popular involvement in partisan politics grew rapidly. The most controversial reform movement in the country, abolitionism, made its influence felt in party politics in 1848 with the establishment of the Free Soil Party. These and similar political moves in temperance reform made women's interest in politics immediate and compelling, as well as a matter of egalitarian principle.

The first women to call for equal rights to the franchise did so as part of a broader demand for greater opportunities and equal rights: access to higher education, admission to all professions and trades, independent economic rights for married women, and the formal recognition of religious leadership and moral authority. In the words of the 1848 Seneca Falls Declaration of Sentiments, "Woman is man's equal—was intended to be so by the Creator, and the highest good of the [human] race demands that she should be recognized as such." Of all these demands, woman suffrage was the most controversial. Electoral politics not only was an exclusively male activity but also was thought to be corrupt and self-serving, which offended the moral sensibilities of the reform-minded women at the Seneca Falls convention. The author of the woman suffrage resolution, 33-year-old Elizabeth Cady Stanton, instead saw the right to vote as fundamental because it laid the basis for the political power to realize all their other demands. Her case for woman suffrage was supported by the one man at the Seneca Falls convention who also suffered disfranchisement: Frederick Douglass.

This controversy over woman suffrage led antebellum women's rights advocates to focus on other demands, in particular full economic rights for married women. In some ways, this was a necessary precursor to full-fledged suffrage agitation, because the nearly universal condition of adult women was marriage, and so long as women lacked legal individuality and economic rights within that relationship, the case for their political empowerment was difficult to make. In addition, while changes in women's economic rights could be made legislatively, enfranchisement had to occur through constitutional change—at that point state by state, a much more daunting prospect. Nonetheless, substantial numbers of women's signatures on petitions were submitted in the 1850s in at least one state, New York, on behalf of their full franchise rights.

Reconstruction and National Action

During the Civil War, Elizabeth Stanton and Susan B. Anthony, leaders of the antebellum movement in New York, were already calling for a reconstitution of the American nation on the basis of "civil and political equality for every subject of the Government," explicitly including "all citizens of African descent and all women." The demand for political equality rose to the summit of the women's rights agenda in the years immediately following the war, in the wake of the commitment of the Radical wing of the Republican Party to establish the full national citizenship of ex-slaves and the federal voting rights of African American men. During Reconstruction, the constitutional locale for suffrage expansion shifted from the states to the national level, as evidenced by the Fourteenth and Fifteenth Amendments to the federal Constitution. This assertion of citizenship at the national level and the precedent for establishing a broad franchise in the U.S. Constitution connected the demand for woman suffrage with the resurgent nationalism of the postwar period. In this context, women's rights agitation became a movement with a wider constituency, with political equality at its forefront.

In 1866, along with Lucy Stone of Massachusetts, Stanton and Anthony formed the American Equal Rights Association to link the struggles of woman and black suffrage and influence the constitutional amendment then under debate in the direction of broad, universal rights. Passage and ratification of the Fourteenth Amendment offered woman suffragists both hope and discouragement. On the one hand, the first article defined national citizenship quite broadly, as "all persons born or naturalized in the United States." On the other hand, the second article, which established penalties against any states that persisted in disfranchising citizens, explicitly excluded women. For the first time, the U.S. Constitution employed the adjective "male" to modify the noun "citizens." The Fifteenth Amendment, which explicitly

Men look in the window of the National Anti-Suffrage Association headquarters, circa 1911. (Library of Congress)

prohibited disfranchisement on the basis of "race, creed or color," similarly ignored discriminations of "sex."

At first Stanton and Anthony pressed for another amendment to the federal Constitution, to prohibit the states from denying the right to vote "on account of sex," modeled exactly on the wording of the Fifteenth Amendment. They formed a society, the National Woman Suffrage Association (NWSA), and organized women from New York to California (but not in the former Confederacy) to campaign for political rights. Accusing this new organization of threatening the victory of black suffrage (for the Fifteenth Amendment was not yet ratified), a second group of women's rights activists, under the leadership of Stone and her husband, Henry Blackwell, founded the American Woman Suffrage Association (AWSA), which held back from national constitutional demands in favor of state campaigns to establish women's voting rights.

For a brief period, from about 1870 to 1875, the NWSA set aside its campaign for a new constitutional amendment in favor of pressing Congress and the courts to accept an innovative interpretation of the Fourteenth Amendment that would include woman suffrage. Ignoring the second section of the Amendment, they focused on the first section's broad definition of national citizenship and argued that women were persons, hence national citizens. What other content could there be to national citizenship, their reasoning continued, than that of political enfranchisement? This strategic "New Departure," as NWSA labeled it, was pursued through a bold campaign of direct-action voting during the 1872 presidential election. Women activists went to the polls by the hundreds, asserting their right to vote on the basis of this constitutional construction. And, amazingly, while many failed to cast their ballots, some were allowed to vote.

One of these was Susan B. Anthony, who talked a hapless election official into accepting her vote (for Ulysses S. Grant). Within days, in one of the most famous incidents in the history of the suffrage movement, Anthony was arrested by federal marshals for the crime of "illegal" voting. Ward Hunt, the judge assigned to her case, recognized its political explosiveness. He instructed the jury to find her guilty but did not execute the fine or penalty, thus preventing her from invoking habeas corpus and appealing her case up the judicial hierarchy. In 1875 the case of Missourian Virginia Minor brought the suffragists' New Departure argument before the U.S. Supreme Court. Minor had been prohibited from voting and sued the St. Louis election official, Reese Happersett, for violation of her rights. In *Minor v. Happersett*, a brief but devastating decision, the Court ruled that while women were indeed national citizens, citizenship did not carry with it the inherent right to vote, which was instead a privilege bestowed by government on those deemed reliable and worthy to wield it. The *Minor* decision sent the woman suffrage movement back to the strategy of securing a constitutional amendment specifically to enfranchise women. A bill for such an amendment was first introduced into the U.S. Senate by Republican Aaron Sargent of California in 1878. The *Minor* decision also put the Court's stamp on a narrow construction of the postwar amendments, and a highly conservative theory about voting rights in general, consistent with other decisions undercutting suffrage for freedmen.

The Turn of the Century

During the last quarter of the nineteenth century, woman suffragism changed both as a popular movement and as a political demand. The expansion of white middle-class women's public activities—in higher education, women's clubs, and voluntary social welfare activities—created an enlarged constituency. Unlike the advocates of the antebellum period, these women were not generally radical, not particularly committed to a broad agenda of women's emancipation, and interested in political participation less for principle than to gain leverage for their particular reform concerns. These changes in constituency overran the old antagonisms between AWSA and NWSA, and in 1890 the two groups came together in the National American Association of Woman Suffrage (NAWSA), the largest, most inclusive suffrage organization for the next 30 years.

Meanwhile, in the electoral arena, the growth of radicalism was challenging electoral politics. Rural and small-town people, fed up with the seemingly identical positions of the two major parties and feeling squeezed by the growth of national corporate power, formed third parties and won offices in state legislatures and governors' mansions in the Midwest and West. The demand for woman suffrage was resurrected in these "People's Parties," not as it had been advanced in the 1860s but as constitutional change at the state level. In Colorado in 1893 and Idaho in 1896, voters not only swept Populist candidates into office but also voted amendments to their state constitutions enfranchising women. Women were able to vote in all elections held in these states, including those for president and U.S. Congress. Similar amendments to the Kansas and California state constitutions failed. But a second front in the battle for woman suffrage had now opened. By 1911, women in six states, all of them west of the Mississippi, were exercising their right to vote and thus becoming a force in national politics.

Progressivism: The Movement's Final Phase

Within a decade the base of the woman suffrage movement had shifted from rural areas to cities and to wage-earning and college women. This last phase of the movement was a crucial element of progressive reform. Much more attuned to the politics of class developments than ever before, twentieth-century suffragists made their case for political rights in terms of amelioration of working women's conditions, protection of poor mothers from the pressures of the labor market, and the contributions that women could make to government social and economic welfare programs. This shift in constituency had an impact on suffragist tactics. Suffrage activism became decidedly modern in tone and argument. Women activists marched in the streets (or drove their cars) in disciplined formation, used new media such as movies and advertising to advance their cause, and—perhaps most important—confidently entered the halls of legislatures to advocate for their cause.

Populist radicalism had disappeared from the political scene, but some of its causes—including woman suffrage—reappeared on the left (or progressive) wing of the Republican Party. Following the pattern of populist suffragism, progressive suffragists concentrated on state venues, in their case industrial powerhouses such as New York, Pennsylvania, Massachusetts, and Ohio. In parallel fashion, the Reconstruction-era campaign for an amendment to the federal Constitution was revived. In March 1913, suffragists marched in the streets of Washington, D.C., one of the first national demonstrations of this type, to demand that Congress pass legislation for a woman suffrage amendment to the federal Constitution. This led to the formation of a new suffrage organization, the Constitutional Union, initially a division of NAWSA. Leaders Alice Paul and Lucy Burns were both college graduates and veterans of the British suffrage movement, whose members used more militant tactics. Personal, generational, and political differences separated them from the leadership of NAWSA, which still concentrated on lobbying politicians.

While the militants profited from the strategic agility of a small, cadre-based structure, the giant NAWSA had to hold together a tremendous diversity of women. In the context of early twentieth-century politics, the most

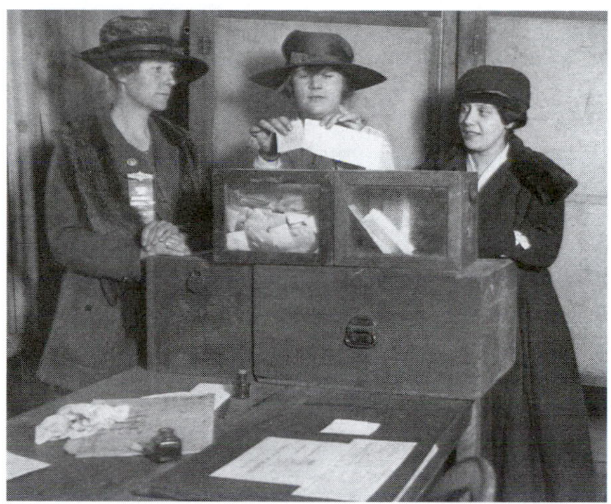

Three suffragists cast votes in New York City circa 1917. (Library of Congress)

explosive of these potential divisions had to do with race. The southern white women who worked within the Democratic Party were consistently shadowed with charges that a woman suffrage amendment would enfranchise black women and bring back the horrors of "black Republicanism." Black woman suffrage advocates, who had been made unwelcome in NAWSA as early as 1899, were no more hospitably received among the militants, as Alice Paul considered the issue of racial discrimination a distraction from her cause. But whereas NAWSA was tied to a nonpartisan approach, lest the Republican and Democratic commitments of their different regional white constituencies come into conflict, the militants plunged directly into the national partisan fray.

Starting in 1914, when congressional legislation for a woman suffrage amendment began to make progress, the militants pressured the national Democratic Party to take up their cause. During the election of 1916, the Congressional Union renamed itself the National Woman's Party. Its organizers traveled throughout the West urging enfranchised women to vote against the Democrats to penalize the party, especially President Woodrow Wilson, for not making women's voting rights a party measure. In the short run, this strategy failed. Wilson was reelected, and within a month of his inauguration, the United States entered the Great War.

The final political maneuvers that led to the passage of congressional woman suffrage legislation played out in this context. Wilson, beholden to the southern wing of his party, initially wanted no part of the campaign for a federal amendment. However, as he turned his attention to his postwar plans, he saw the need for women's political support. In 1918 he finally declared his support for a federal amendment. Even then, antisuffragists fought intense battles against the inevitable. Legislation passed the Senate in January 1919. The ratification process took another 16 months. In the end, the state that took the Nineteenth Amendment over the top and into the Constitution was Tennessee, one of the few southern states with two-party politics that suffrage advocates could mobilize.

Much ink has been spilled over the question of which wing of the Progressive Era suffrage movement, the NWP militants or the NAWSA moderates, was responsible for victory. During and immediately after the war, women were being enfranchised all over North America and Europe, and the ratification of the Nineteenth Amendment to the U.S. Constitution was part of this process. From an even wider framework, the credit goes not to a single organization or leader but to 75 years of building support among diverse constituencies of women, sufficient political will, and sophisticated arguments for women's political equality with men.

While the passage of the Nineteenth Amendment did not lead to an immediate and dramatic change in voting patterns, neither did it terminate women's political activism. Groups of women substituted policy and reform goals for their previous efforts to win the vote. Notably, NAWSA became the U.S. League of Women Voters. However, the 1920s was a conservative decade, and women voters found it difficult to advance many of their progressive goals. Within a decade, women's voting had become so normal that younger women barely remembered the long and hard fight to win it.

See also feminism; voting; women and politics.

FURTHER READING

Baker, Jean, ed. *Sisters: The Lives of America's Suffragists.* New York: Hill and Wang, 2005.

Cott, Nancy F. *The Grounding of Modern Feminism.* New Haven, CT: Yale University Press, 1989.

DuBois, Ellen Carol. *Feminism and Suffrage: The Emergence of an Independent Women's Movement in America, 1848–1869.* Ithaca, NY: Cornell University Press, 1978.

———. *Harriot Stanton Blatch and the Winning of Woman Suffrage.* New Haven, CT: Yale University Press, 1997.

———. *Woman Suffrage and Women's Rights.* New York: New York University Press, 1998.

Flexner, Eleanor. *Century of Struggle: The Woman's Rights Movement in the United States*. Revised ed. Cambridge, MA: Belknap Press, 1975.

Ginzburg, Lori. *Unitidy Origins: A Study of Antebellum Women's Rights in New York*. Chapel Hill: University of North Carolina Press, 2005.

Marilley, Susan. *Woman Suffrage and the Origins of Liberal Feminism in the United States, 1820–1920*. Cambridge, MA: Harvard University Press, 1997.

Mead, Rebecca. *How the Vote Was Won: Woman Suffrage in the Western United States, 1868–1914*. Cambridge, MA: Harvard University Press, 2006.

Terborg-Penn, Rosalyn. *African American Women in the Struggle for the Vote, 1850–1920*. Bloomington: Indiana University Press, 1998.

Wheeler, Marjorie Spruill. *New Women of the New South: The Leaders of the Woman Suffrage Movement in the Southern States*. New York: Oxford University Press, 1993.

ELLEN CAROL DUBOIS

women and politics to 1828

Women in early America played a critical role in securing the nation's independence and shaping the evolution of the first political parties. In recent decades, historians have embraced an expanded definition of politics that illuminates the ways in which women participated, both formally and informally, in the political process. This more capacious understanding of politics has made it possible to trace significant developments in women's involvement in political affairs and discern important changes in women's relationship to the state from the time of the American Revolution to the election of Andrew Jackson.

The Colonial Experience

Prior to the American Revolution, the 13 British colonies in North America shared a common culture with Britain that denied most women formal legal and political rights. The doctrine of *femme covert*, or coverture, pertained. Single women were assumed to be under the guardianship of their fathers; married women were assumed to be under the protection of their husbands. As a result, most women could not own property, make contracts, sue, or be sued in court. Only widows and other unmarried adult women were exempted from these strictures. It was also assumed that women should defer to men and not involve themselves in matters of government or politics. Political participation at this time was restricted to property-owning men. As in Britain, most of the colonies required men to own a certain amount of property before they were allowed to vote or hold public office. Because women lacked property rights, they, like men who did not own land, could not exercise the franchise.

Beginning in the early eighteenth century, attitudes toward women began to change in important ways. Enlightenment thinkers in western Europe began to popularize the notion that women's intellectual inferiority resulted not from a lack of any innate mental capacity but because they did not have access to an adequate education. Women were not inherently incapable of intellectual achievement; they simply had not had the same educational opportunities as men. With more education, they might well equal men's intellectual accomplishments. The gradual acceptance of this notion led to a growth in educational opportunities for women in British America. Over the course of the eighteenth century, more and more women learned to read. Although few women in the colonies received more than a rudimentary formal education, by the time of the American Revolution, a majority of white women possessed basic literacy skills. Beginning around 1750, an explosion in print culture also gave women easier access to a variety of printed publications, including newspapers, magazines, novels, and political tracts. These materials allowed women to engage in the larger political debates of the time.

The American Revolution

The American Revolution transformed women's relationship to the state. As tensions with Britain mounted, colonial leaders knew that if they were to succeed in resisting unjust British policies, they must mobilize large sections of the population, including artisans, small farmers, free blacks, lower-class white men, and women. From the time of the Stamp Act of 1765 until the Declaration of Independence, leaders used print culture—poems, plays, broadsides, and newspapers—to rally women behind the Patriot cause.

Women took up the issue in their own ways. The Daughters of Liberty, a female counterpart to the male Sons of Liberty, publicly announced their refusal to drink British tea and wore garments made of homespun material. Some women held patriotic spinning bees to increase the production of domestic cloth, signed nonimportation agreements in which they refused to purchase British goods, or boycotted merchants who violated the ban on imported goods. One woman in particular, Mercy Otis Warren of Massachusetts, took up her pen in support of the cause and published poems and satirical plays that fanned the flames of dissent. Throughout the decade leading up to independence, women's participation helped solidify colonial resistance to Britain and strengthen popular commitment to the Patriot cause.

During the war itself, women found other ways to express their patriotic sentiments. Some knit stockings for the troops; others made shirts. Still others collected money for the badly underfunded Continental Army. In 1780 Esther DeBerdt Reed organized a group of women in Philadelphia that went door to door to solicit funds for supplies. Over the course of one month, the women collected more than $300,000 in Continental dollars. Women in New Jersey, Maryland, and Virginia soon undertook similar campaigns.

Women contributed to the war effort in more personal ways as well. When men went away to conduct the business of government or serve on the field of battle, women maintained the home front. During their husbands' absences, women such as Abigail Adams took on male responsibilities, including managing crops, hiring servants, overseeing slaves, keeping the books, and disciplining their children. Most women had little prior experience in handling these tasks. Their willingness to undertake these new challenges made it possible for men to be away from home for extended periods. In addition, a small number of women, including Margaret Corbin and Deborah Sampson, actually took up arms and fought alongside men against the British. A much larger group of women sacrificed for their country in a different way—their husbands and sons were killed or wounded in the war, leaving them widowed or without male support.

Post-Revolutionary Experimentation

In the wake of the Revolution, both men and women acknowledged the importance of women's efforts in securing victory over the British. A newly politicized understanding of women's role emerged, a notion that historians have called "republican motherhood." Through their experiences in the Revolution, women had defined a political role for themselves. Even in their traditional capacities as wives and mothers, they contributed to the nation's political life in the ways that were most appropriate to their sex.

One way in which women could contribute was by inculcating republican virtue in their husbands and children. Women needed to be educated in order to inspire future citizens with the values that would sustain republican government: virtue, patriotism, and dedication to the common good. An educated citizenry was particularly important in a republic where the people governed themselves. In the first decades following the American Revolution, more than 400 ladies' academies were founded to provide young women with new venues for formal instruction. As more women gained access to formal education, their intellectual opportunities expanded. By the middle of the nineteenth century, white women's literacy was on par with that of white men.

The American Revolution also witnessed the country's earliest experiment in woman suffrage. In 1776 New Jersey, along with most of the other states in the union, wrote its first state constitution. As was typical for the time, electors had to possess a certain amount of property in order to be allowed to vote. Written in a gender-neutral fashion, the New Jersey constitution did not explicitly limit the franchise to men, but simply restricted the franchise to "inhabitants" possessing the requisite amount of property. This formulation opened up the possibility for women to vote. In 1790 and 1797, the New Jersey legislature went a step further and clarified the constitution's meaning, passing state election laws that referred to voters as "he" and "she." Because men and women with property were taxed, women, it was said, should be allowed to vote on the same terms as men. As a result, qualified women could and did vote in both state and federal elections. Yet, because of the strictures of coverture, only single women who were prosperous enough to meet the property requirement—mostly wealthy widows—could cast ballots. No more than a few hundred women voted in any given election. Nonetheless, the practice was highly controversial, and, in 1807, the New Jersey legislature stripped both women and free blacks of the franchise.

Although no other state followed New Jersey's lead in enfranchising women, the emergence of the first political parties opened up other venues for women's participation in politics. Just as women in eighteenth-century France and Britain created glittering salons, so too did American women sponsor gatherings at their homes that attracted leading political and intellectual figures of the young United States. More than simply social gatherings, these events were deliberate efforts to bring together individuals with different, or even competing, political agendas. When the national capital was in New York and Philadelphia, elite women—including Mrs. Robert Morse, Mrs. Henry Knox, Elizabeth Powel, and Anne Willing Bingham—hosted such events. After the capital was relocated to Washington, D.C., First Lady Dolley Madison's White House salons became famous for providing a respite from the vituperative political atmosphere pervading the country. Madison, however, was an extremely effective political operator in her own right. At these gatherings, she promoted her husband's political program, arranged patronage positions for her friends and relatives, and brought warring male partisans into conversation with one another. Like other *salonnières*, Madison facilitated the creation of social bonds that advanced the smooth functioning of government and, at the same time, promoted her and her husband's interests.

Beyond the capital, both political parties began to court women's approval and vie for their support. Both elite and non-elite women began to demonstrate party allegiance. Federalist women who supported Washington and Hamilton wore golden eagles on their dresses or black rosettes on their hats. In contrast, female Democratic-Republicans who supported Jefferson and Madison might sport liberty caps or wear tricolored cockades. So intense were partisan divisions that some women chose friends, servants, and even prospective husbands primarily on the basis of their party affiliation. Leaders of both parties also encouraged women to show their support by attending partisan functions, especially Fourth of July celebrations. These public demonstrations of support both affirmed the party's widespread basis of popularity and indicated women's moral approval of a given party's agenda. Because women could not vote or hold public office, their interest in politics was regarded as purer and nobler than that of men. Since the very existence of political parties was regarded with suspicion, women's presence at party events conferred a kind of moral sanction on men's partisan activities.

Male political leaders also sought to rally women behind their party's policies in times of national crisis. During the "Quasi-War" with France in 1798, Jefferson's Embargo of 1807–8, and the War of 1812, women were asked to show their support for a party's policies through their actions. In 1798 Federalist women, anticipating the possibility of war with France, presented hand-sewn flags to their local militias in public ceremonies. During the embargo, Jeffersonian women held spinning bees and made homespun cloth rather than buy goods from abroad. During the War of 1812, Republican women, like their Revolutionary-era predecessors, made socks, shirts, and mittens for the troops. Significantly, however, Federalist women who opposed the governing party's policies often chose to do nothing. Their actions revealed important changes in the nature of women's political participation since the time of the American Revolution. Women were no longer patriots, rallying behind their country for the sake of the common good. Now they were partisans, whose actions deepened the tensions between political parties.

Women and Social Reform

By the 1820s, women's participation in party politics had diminished significantly. The Federalist Party was moribund as a national force, leaving the Republicans to dominate the electoral scene. With less competition, party leaders had less need to mobilize nonvoters for party events and activities. In addition, Jeffersonians succeeded in their state-by-state campaign to eliminate property qualifications for voting, and expanded the franchise to include virtually all white males. As a result, partisans increasingly focused attention on those who mattered most to their electoral success: white male voters. Women and other nonvoters had little role to play in this kind of political structure.

Women, however, increasingly discovered other means by which to contribute to the polity, outside the realm of party and electoral politics. Beginning in the 1790s, elite women in many places throughout the country had begun to establish charitable societies and benevolent organizations to help the underprivileged, spread Christianity, and provide moral uplift for those in need. Some societies sheltered widows, established schools, or aided orphans. Other groups collected money to buy Bibles for the poor, funded overseas missionaries, provided clothing and wood for poor families, or assisted those in prison. Significantly, women provided the leadership for these groups. Many societies were founded and run exclusively by women, who drafted the bylaws, conducted the meetings, handled the finances, and decided whom their organization should fund. When issues arose that required dealing with male government officials, women often handled the negotiations themselves.

These organizations quickly grew in number and scope. By 1830 New York supported 18 ladies' societies;

Boston had 17. Many more groups emerged throughout the country, in the South as well as the North, in rural areas and big cities. Although women in the organizations used political means and tactics to achieve their goals, they vehemently insisted that their goals were social, not political, in nature. They disavowed connection with party politics and denied any affinity with male politicians. Despite their denials, however, the women had succeeded in pursuing politics by another means.

In the post–Revolutionary era, women also began to see the utility of another political tool at their disposal, the petition. For women in eighteenth-century Britain and colonial America, the petition had been one of the few means through which they could directly communicate with their government. After the Revolution, more women throughout the United States began to send petitions to their state assemblies or to Congress, seeking redress for a variety of grievances. Initially, most of these petitions sought compensation for property losses suffered during the Revolutionary War or requested pensions based on a husband's military service. Over time, however, women began to use petitions as vehicles of social reform, demanding aid for the dispossessed, the enactment of temperance laws, or an end to slavery. Through petitioning, and their widespread involvement with social reform movements, women became more comfortable with the notion of participatory politics. They claimed their right to act as citizens and to demand satisfaction of their grievances from the government.

Especially after 1830, women came to see the limits of petitioning and of their ability to change society if they did not possess the most potent political weapon, the vote. By the 1840s and 1850s, small groups of women began to form groups specifically to advance women's causes, including the right to vote. Although the process took decades to come to fruition, the American Revolution established the principles, and created the foundation, for women's later forms of political involvement.

See also voting; woman suffrage.

FURTHER READING

Allgor, Catherine. *Parlor Politics: In Which the Ladies of Washington Help Build a City and a Government.* Charlottesville: University Press of Virginia, 2000.

Boylan, Anne M. *The Origins of Women's Activism: New York and Boston, 1797–1840.* Chapel Hill: University of North Carolina Press, 2002.

Branson, Susan. *These Fiery Frenchified Dames: Women and Political Culture in Early National Philadelphia.* Philadelphia: University of Pennsylvania Press, 2001.

Kerber, Linda K. *Women of the Republic: Women and Ideology in Revolutionary America.* Chapel Hill: University of North Carolina Press, 1980.

Norton, Mary Beth. *Liberty's Daughters: The Revolutionary Experience of American Women, 1750–1800.* Glenview, IL: Little, Brown, 1980.

Zagarri, Rosemarie. *Revolutionary Backlash: Women and Politics in the Early American Republic.* Philadelphia: University of Pennsylvania Press, 2007.

———. *A Woman's Dilemma: Mercy Otis Warren and the American Revolution.* Wheeling, IL: Harlan Davidson, 1995.

ROSEMARIE ZAGARRI

women and politics, 1828–65

Between 1828 and 1865, the first movement emerged to demand legal and political rights for women. While the women's rights movement during this period was small, it directly agitated for a new relationship between women and the state. Much of the impetus for these demands came from women's experience in a broad array of reform movements and, by the 1850s, the popular idea that political agitation was replacing moral suasion as a route to change. While the road from women's reform efforts to women's rights is a central component of the story of women and politics between 1828 and 1865, it is also important to recognize that a large number of women participated in political activities informally during this period, even if they were formally denied the right to vote.

Although women had freely expressed political opinions in the late eighteenth century, and single women with property in New Jersey had even been granted the right to vote between 1776 and 1806, by the early nineteenth century, "female politicians" were increasingly scorned, and respectable women were urged to keep their opinions within their households. The increasingly competitive nature of politics, arising with the First Party System in the 1790s and the Second Party System in the 1820s, was deemed an inappropriate arena for respectable females, as two new political parties, the Democrats and the Whigs, competed for votes beginning in the 1830s.

One state after another rewrote their constitutions in the first half of the nineteenth century, and in almost all cases, they extended the franchise to white men who did not own property, creating a large and boisterous electorate that needed to be both courted and entertained by a new breed of politicians anxious to secure office. Old patterns of hierarchy and deference were demolished as a new democratic order took place around stump speaking, torchlight parades, and elections. The results were stunning: in 1824, only 30 percent of adult white men voted in presidential elections, but by 1840 the figure was closer to 80 percent.

Even though women could not vote, many attended political rallies and parades, particularly within the Whig Party. Women could be found lining political parade routes in cities as diverse as New York, San Francisco, and New Orleans. Some women even rode in parades, dressed in white to symbolize purity or liberty. They also made banners for their candidates and cooked food for rallies. In all of these activities, women were seen as symbols of a higher moral order that rose above the grimy competition of a political campaign. They signaled the presence of disinterested virtue: supporters who were committed not so much to winning but to the social good. When women ennobled campaigns in this way, they were not so much active agents in the political contests erupting around them as they were passive spectators and symbols of political ideals.

Not all women were content to be nonpartisan symbols, however. Lucy Kenney, of Fredericksburg, Virginia, began her political career as a Democrat but switched her allegiance to the Whigs in the middle of the 1830s. She had been paid well by Andrew Jackson to write political pamphlets supporting him and was willing to work for his successor, Martin Van Buren. But Van Buren would not pay her more than $1 for her work, and Kenney indignantly switched her loyalties to the better-paying Whigs. Eliza Runnell, another partisan Democrat, accused Kenney of having been "transfigured from an angel of peace, to a political bully" as the election of 1840 heated up. Other women whipped up public support for their candidates at political rallies, particularly in the South and the Midwest. Although it was not common for women to speak at political rallies, that did not stop Mary Ann Inman from introducing the chief speaker to a crowd of 5,000 in Tennessee.

During the antebellum era, women supported not only political candidates but also broader political causes. Some of the most politically active women in the United States in this period championed the filibustering activities of adventurers such as William Walker, one of the most famous filibusters of the nineteenth century, who raised a private army and used it to overthrow the government of Nicaragua in 1855. Walker had plenty of backing from women in the United States as he attempted to set up his new government. Jane McManus Cazneau of Texas, for example, made sure the *New York Sun* followed Walker's campaign, and she traveled to Nicaragua in time to see Walker inaugurated president there. Anna Ella Carroll of Maryland chastised President Franklin Pierce in print when he refused to recognize Walker's ambassador to the United States. Sarah Pellet returned from visiting Nicaragua and took to the lecture circuit in New Orleans in an attempt to rally people to Walker's cause. Whether speaking or writing, such women took a forceful public stand on the military and political adventures of some of their countrymen who were seeking to expand U.S. influence beyond its borders.

While women were present in the swirl of party politics and the debates on U.S. expansion, they more commonly expressed themselves in public through their participation in reform associations. Soon after the Revolution, women formed organizations to help the poor in an expression of civic-mindedness. These new organizations constituted mini-governments, as women wrote constitutions for their groups, gathered and distributed economic resources, decided on membership, and took stands on political issues. As the Great Awakening encouraged a rising spirit of evangelicalism in the early nineteenth century, women created new organizations such as missionary societies to promote the spiritual salvation of the unconverted both at home and abroad. By the end of the 1820s, religious concerns had expanded into debates about social and political issues, including Native American removal, temperance, and antislavery. Women who became involved in organizations and agitation connected with such issues couched their concerns in spiritual and domestic terms, but it was clear that their agendas had political ramifications as well.

Hundreds of women signed petitions to Congress in 1829 and 1830 to protest Andrew Jackson's policy of Native American removal. They were largely inspired by the protests of the American Board of Commissioners for Foreign Missions, a missionary group that worked to convert the Native American population. Women from Maine to Ohio mobilized to protest the forced removal of Cherokee people from their lands. They carefully worded their petitions to defend their signatures as an assertion of moral concern rather than political right. Female petitioners claimed that they spoke to defend the spiritual lives of Indians and to protect their domestic environments—arenas that were widely acknowledged to be the appropriate concern of women. Despite these disclaimers, however, the petitions were met with howls of outrage in Congress, as proremoval senators expressed disgust at what they charged was inappropriate feminine behavior.

The ruckus caused by antiremoval petitions, however, was small compared to the storm caused by the antislavery movement that drew a large number of female followers. Free blacks in the North had set up antislavery societies to demand an immediate end to slavery during the 1820s, and in 1832, the abolitionist William Lloyd Garrison carried that critique to the white community. Black women in Salem, Massachusetts, organized the first female antislavery society in 1832, a move that was repeated by both black and white women in other cities of the North during the following years. Some of these groups were integrated, others were not, and even within the integrated groups, African American women were denied leadership positions.

As women in the antislavery societies organized during the 1830s, they raised large sums of money through antislavery fairs, where they sold handmade items and used that money to fund antislavery newspapers, public events, and petitioning campaigns. Thousands of women signed the petitions to Congress that were circulated to protest slavery. Women, along with men, petitioned against the admission of Texas, a slave state, to the Union and against slavery in the District of Columbia. Lydia Maria Child became the editor of the widely read *National Anti-Slavery Standard*. Abolitionists such as Sarah and Angelina Grimke became well-known speakers, drawing large numbers of men as well as women to their powerful public testimonies on the evils of slavery.

The abolitionist movement provoked outrage throughout the country. Not only did it challenge the property rights of Southerners and the political stability of the nation, it also raised the specter of a racially integrated society—something that most white Americans abhorred. Female abolitionists, like their male colleagues, faced physical threats and vitriolic attacks in the press for their activities. Women in the movement were challenged not only for their abolitionist principles but also for behavior unbecoming of respectable women.

As antislavery advocates confronted these attacks, some argued that women should not alienate potential supporters by taking positions of leadership in the antislavery movement or by speaking in public. The "woman question," as the issue became known, was a key element in the split that took place in the movement in 1840. The minority wing, which argued that the inequality women faced should be part of the broader antislavery vision, retained control of the name of the organization, the American Anti-Slavery Society. Those who advocated a more traditional role for women in reform activities formed the American and Foreign Anti-Slavery Society. Women in both of these organizations, however, continued to be involved in reform activities that most of their neighbors would deem "political."

Temperance organizations were less controversial and more widespread than antislavery ones. Indeed, men dominated the temperance movement during the 1820s and into the 1830s. By the end of the 1830s, however, women were forming their own independent or auxiliary organizations. Temperance reformers focused their attention on personal reform, urging individuals to sign pledges that they would abstain from liquor.

Women who were involved in reform activities in the 1830s and 1840s, whether to protest slavery, Native American removal, alcohol, or other issues, would have argued that they were pursuing a path of moral suasion rather than political involvement. Regardless of the political ramifications, they saw themselves as trying to persuade neighbors and political representatives to do the right thing, rather than exercising a political right in the boisterous and partisan culture of party politics. Like many of the male reformers they worked with, they believed their cause would be sullied if they stooped to engage party politics; instead, they believed they could achieve their aims by converting others to the proper moral principles necessary for a just and peaceful world.

By the end of the 1840s, however, many of these reform efforts were engaging the political process much more directly. The Liberty Party was established in 1840 with an antislavery platform. The Free Soil Party, established in 1848 and largely incorporated into the Republican Party in 1854, challenged the expansion of slavery. Temperance advocates began to agitate for laws outlawing alcohol rather than simply promoting individual pledges not to drink. By the 1850s, reform movements were increasingly moving from strategies of moral suasion to strategies of direct political action. Women who were committed to reform recognized the growing importance of direct political participation.

It was within this context that the first women's rights movement emerged in the United States. The issue of women's rights had been surfacing in the antislavery movement at least since the mid 1830s, when Angelina and Sarah Grimke had passionately defended their right to speak out against slavery. Several hundred of these activists took the issue an important step further, however, when they met in Seneca Falls, New York, in 1848. Listing the grievances of women in the Declaration of Sentiments (modeled on the Declaration of Independence), the organizers presented a list of resolutions to the convention for debate on the rights of women. These rights included not only the right to speak in church and in public and the right to participate in trade and commerce equally with men but also the right to vote. This was by far the most controversial proposition presented, one that shocked many of the delegates and passed only after the famous abolitionist Frederick Douglass rose to defend the demand. Once the resolution had passed, however, it became the defining issue of the movement. Women demanded that the expansion of the franchise include them. Given the growing politicization of the other causes they championed, it was a demand that had become increasingly significant. And since participation in the political order had moved from household heads to individuals, the demand that women be recognized also made logical sense.

Women's rights supporters met yearly during the 1850s to debate the issues associated with their cause. Their numbers were quite small, but the movement was recognized throughout the United States and western Europe, even if it often faced derision. In the United States, critics caricatured woman's rights supporters as manly. Opposition was particularly vociferous in the South, where the movement was associated with abolitionism. Indeed, the overt demand by women for the right to participate in party politics may have dampened the enthusiasm that some southern women had shown for their parties in previous years. In Virginia, women in 1856 spoke less frequently in the presidential election campaign than they had in 1852.

With the coming of the Civil War in 1860, women's rights advocates temporarily put aside their cause. In the North, women such as Elizabeth Cady Stanton helped to form the Woman's National Loyal League, which supported the war effort as well as a petitioning campaign for a constitutional amendment to end slavery. Although Stanton urged the Loyal League to make women's rights one of its issues, she failed to persuade the majority of members. Women's political participation during the war thus continued in the same manner that existed before the war. Women followed the political and military conflict engulfing the nation, organized to provide assistance to soldiers, and pressured government officials for changes in policies. Occasionally, women of both the North and the South took up spying for their governments.

Thus, by the end of the Civil War, women had successfully organized in a wide variety of arenas to pressure local, state, and national governments for change. Women continued to be denied access to most forms of participation in the government, most specifically the right to vote. But they had developed alternative organizational strategies for engaging in politics.

See also abolitionism; Prohibition and temperance; voting; woman suffrage.

FURTHER READING

Ginzberg, Lori. *Women and the Work of Benevolence: Morality, Politics, and Class in the Nineteenth-Century United States.* New Haven, CT: Yale University Press, 1990.

Isenberg, Nancy. *Sex and Citizenship in Antebellum America.* Chapel Hill: University of North Carolina Press, 1998.

May, Robert E. "Reconsidering Antebellum U.S. Women's History: Gender, Filibustering, and America's Quest for Empire." *American Quarterly* 57, no. 4 (2005), 1155–88.

Varon, Elizabeth. *We Mean to Be Counted: White Women and Politics in Antebellum Virginia.* Chapel Hill: University of North Carolina Press, 1998.

Zaeske, Susan. *Signatures of Citizenship: Petitioning, Antislavery, and Women's Political Identity.* Chapel Hill: University of North Carolina Press, 2003.

TERESA MURPHY

women and politics, 1865–1920

Women's participation in politics increased dramatically between 1865 and 1920. By 1913 many municipalities had given women the right to vote on schools and local taxes, and ten states allowed women to vote for president and other government officials. Voting, however, was not the only way women participated in politics in this era. Before the Civil War, women's extensive nonpartisan organizational networks worked for moral and political reforms, such as temperance, antiprostitution, the abolition of slavery, and improvements in women's economic and political status. After 1865 women took on new causes, strengthening their old voluntary associations and creating new ones, some of which, by the 1890s, had become national organizations. Over time women used their nonpartisan associations as a means for moving into political arenas once dominated by men.

Only a few of the women who advocated causes through their voluntary associations thought that by doing so they were entering politics in the traditional sense of the term. According to tradition, politics meant seeking office for its own sake, distributing favors, and making compromises in order to "win" for one's side. Most nineteenth-century women thought they were above or unsuited for that kind of activity. Yet as soon as an organization of women identified a goal, campaigned in public to win support for it, and advocated a law or public policy to achieve it, the women not only had to interact with politicians but became "political" themselves. Thus, decades before the ratification in 1920 of the Nineteenth Amendment, which gave all women the right to vote, thousands of American women were already involved in politics.

Women's Voluntary Associations as Agents of Political Change

Women's nonpartisan political causes after 1865 ranged across a wide spectrum. Some were associated with the Reconstruction amendments, which gave political rights to male freed slaves but not to any women. Later in the century, women became deeply involved in the progressive movement, which sought a greater role for government on behalf of the public's welfare. Other causes were more conservative in nature, focusing on preserving traditional features of American society. Yet others sought to resolve the era's most controversial issues, such as civil liberties for racial and ethnic minorities, votes for women, collective bargaining rights for labor, and the public's right to free expression.

In the immediate post–Civil War period, the achievement of voting rights for women was highest on the agenda for politically active women. The suffrage movement split over the Reconstruction amendments, which explicitly limited the franchise to men. Arguing that it was more important to give the vote to freedmen, some suffragists formed the American Woman Suffrage Association to pursue votes for women state by state. A more radical group, led by Elizabeth Cady Stanton and Susan B. Anthony, formed the National Woman Suffrage Association to pursue voting rights as citizens under the Fourteenth Amendment. In the late 1860s and early 1870s, in a massive campaign of civil disobedience, women across the country attempted to vote, an action that led to Anthony's trial for illegal voting. Activist Victoria Woodhull took a different tack, declaring to Congress that voting was a "right" of national citizenship, not a privilege accorded by the states. Virginia Minor, from St. Louis, Missouri, took her citizenship claim all the way to the U.S. Supreme Court, but lost in 1875. Despite increasingly narrow judicial interpretations of citizenship rights granted by the Reconstruction amendments, in succeeding years women continued to attempt to register to vote.

By the 1870s, temperance—the movement to control if not eliminate national consumption of alcoholic beverages—had also become a national woman's campaign. The Woman's Christian Temperance Union (WCTU) was its most popular organizational expression. The WCTU was founded in Ohio in 1874, and by 1900 had a membership of some 200,000. Frances Willard, WCTU president from 1879 to 1898, was most responsible for setting the organization's course. Convinced that temperance was essential to protecting the home, she pursued laws to restrict the manufacture, sale, and importation of alcoholic beverages. Arguing that such laws alone would not stop people from drinking, Willard also called on society to address related problems, such as poverty, adulterated food and drugs, the lack of labor unions, and women's subordinate status in both the economy and politics. To achieve both Prohibition and woman suffrage, at one point she tried to bring together the Populist Party, the Knights of Labor, and the WCTU. Near the end of her life, Willard became convinced that socialism was the only way to bring about a just society.

The suffrage movement ended its division in 1890, forming the National American Woman Suffrage Association (NAWSA) and eventually enlisting some 10,000 members in campaigns for the vote. In succeeding years its leaders—Stanton, Anthony, Anna Shaw, Alice Paul, and Carrie Chapman Catt—interacted continually with politicians. They lobbied state and federal legislators to pass resolutions in favor of votes for women and pressured party officials to include woman suffrage planks in their platforms. They testified before legislative committees on suffrage and on other women's rights issues. During elections they organized rallies and marches and canvassed neighborhoods for support. In 1915 Alice Paul broke away from NAWSA and formed the National Woman's Party (NWP) in 1917. The party adopted the militant political techniques of the British "suffragettes," including civil disobedience and holding the political parties in power responsible for the failure to pass woman suffrage. For their picketing of the White House during World War I, some NWP members were sent to jail, where their treatment (which included forced feedings) brought wide publicity to the cause.

Other national women's groups in this era included the National Consumers' League (NCL), founded in 1899, and the Women's Trade Union League (WTUL), founded in 1903. Both organizations had tangible political impact. The NCL led the movement to win protections against unsafe goods, outlaw child labor, and regulate factory labor practices. Under the leadership of Florence Kelley, a former resident of Chicago's famous Hull House social settlement and the state of Illinois's first appointed factory inspector, the NCL won its initial victories with the passage of state laws regulating women's working hours. In the wake of the devastating fire at the Triangle Shirtwaist Factory in New York City in 1911, WTUL leaders Margaret Dreier Robins, Mary Dreier, and Rose Schneiderman spearheaded official investigations that led to the passage of dozens of factory health and safety regulations. Both organizations also worked for a minimum wage and for the establishment of federal agencies focused on the welfare of women and children. Two agencies, the Children's Bureau and the Women's Bureau, founded in 1912 and 1920, respectively, were headed by women.

Although less successful legislatively in the early 1900s than temperance and labor reformers, women active in early civil rights movements paved the way for later progress. Memphis-born African American journalist Ida B. Wells-Barnett devoted herself to national and international campaigns against lynching. After moving to Chicago, she founded black female suffrage clubs and integrated the state suffrage movement. Wells-Barnett and Mary Church Terrell were the only black women among the founders of the National Association for the Advancement of Colored People (NAACP), for many years the nation's largest and most visible civil rights organization. White women also helped found the NAACP, most notably Hull House founder Jane Addams and settlement worker Mary White Ovington. Ovington, who came out of an abolitionist family tradition, was a key member of the biracial inner circle of NAACP founders and remained active on the board for almost 40 years. Although male lawyers dominated the organization's leadership, many women founded branches, such as music teacher and clubwoman Nettie Asberry of Tacoma, Washington.

Other important women's organizations founded in this era were the General Federation of Women's Clubs, the Council of Jewish Women, the National Association of Colored Women, and the Young Women's Christian Association. Also initiated were patriotic women's groups based on lineage and dedicated to promoting civic nationalism, such as the Daughters of the American Revolution and the United Daughters of the Confederacy. All of these organizations developed political agendas of varying kinds. Some took up progressive causes, such as pure food and drugs, municipal sanitation and pure water systems, controls on air pollution, and laws to improve or build low-cost housing for urban workers. Others were more conservative, hoping to slow down some of the changes overtaking American society; their agendas included setting quotas on immigration, launching Americanization programs, and opposing racial integration.

Women's organizations were deeply involved in many of the era's controversial political issues. In the 1870s and 1880s, women participated on both sides of the debates over whether plural wives should be allowed to vote in Utah. When journalist and public speaker Kate Field investigated Mormon marriages in the state and then toured with a popular lecture against polygamy, Mormons sent plural wives to Washington, D.C., to counter her arguments. Arguing that votes for women would destabilize the institution of marriage, some women were active in the campaign against suffrage. The "Antis," as they were called, founded local, state, and national leagues to lobby legislators against woman suffrage and engaged suffragists in debate at public meetings.

Women's groups across the political spectrum also used the importance of women's domestic responsibilities to advocate pro-natalist public policies. Insisting that women's primary role lay in reproduction, they favored both welfare for mothers and children and campaigns to reduce infant and maternal mortality as well as greater controls on marriage and divorce, bans on abortion and contraception, and support for the science of eugenics.

Wars aroused some women into political action. In 1887, mindful of how war hurt families, the WCTU established a Department of Peace and Arbitration. In the 1890s and early 1900s, women participated in movements opposing imperialistic expansion by world powers, including the United States. Because the United States was denying American citizenship to the native people of the Philippines after the Spanish-American War of

1898, Boston pacifist Lucia Mead actively opposed the American takeover of the former Spanish colony. The outbreak of World War I in 1914 led to another burst of peace activism on the part of women. On August 29, 1,500 suffragists and anti-imperialists, dressed in black and carrying a large banner of a dove, marched down New York City's Fifth Avenue to the slow beat of a muffled drum. Jane Addams and Carrie Chapman Catt then organized a Woman's Peace Party. Lawyer Crystal Eastman, a pioneer in developing workers' compensation in New York and a militant suffragist, founded a more radical Woman's Peace Party of New York that continued to demonstrate against the war even after the United States joined the conflict in 1917. In 1915 Addams and industrial physician Alice Hamilton traveled to The Hague to attend an International Congress of Women that urged an armistice as well as continuous mediation among the belligerent states. A Second International Congress of Women held in 1919 in Zurich led to the founding of the Women's International League for Peace and Freedom (WILPF), which opposed the continuing occupation of Haiti and Nicaragua by U.S. Marines and issued the first criticisms of the Versailles Treaty.

From Voluntary Associations to Partisan Politics

Women's experience in voluntary associations trained them in political skills, such as how to run large meetings, speak in public, and interact with government and political party officials. Success at winning significant reforms, including pure food and drug laws, controls on the liquor trade, rights for labor, factory regulation, and the vote, raised their confidence as agents of political change. By the time suffrage arrived, women with voluntary association experience began to move into partisan politics and government office.

A number of women had entered partisan politics even before they had the right to vote. Suffragist Victoria Woodhull presented herself as a presidential candidate in 1872 under the banner of the Equal Rights Party. The National Equal Rights Party put attorney Belva Lockwood forward as presidential candidate in 1884 and 1888. In 1892 Judith Ellen Foster, Iowa lawyer, temperance crusader, and ardent Republican, formed the Women's National Republican Association. Over the next 18 years, it organized Republican women's clubs and campaigning for GOP candidates across the nation. Mary Elizabeth Lease, a midwestern temperance and woman suffrage activist, stumped for the Populists between 1890 and 1896, for Socialist Eugene Debs in 1908, and for Progressive Theodore Roosevelt in 1912. Jane Addams, widely known for her work at Hull House, won her first political appointment in 1895, when she became garbage inspector for Chicago's nineteenth ward; in 1912 she seconded Theodore Roosevelt's nomination for president

Women suffragists picket in front of the White House, February 1917. (Library of Congress)

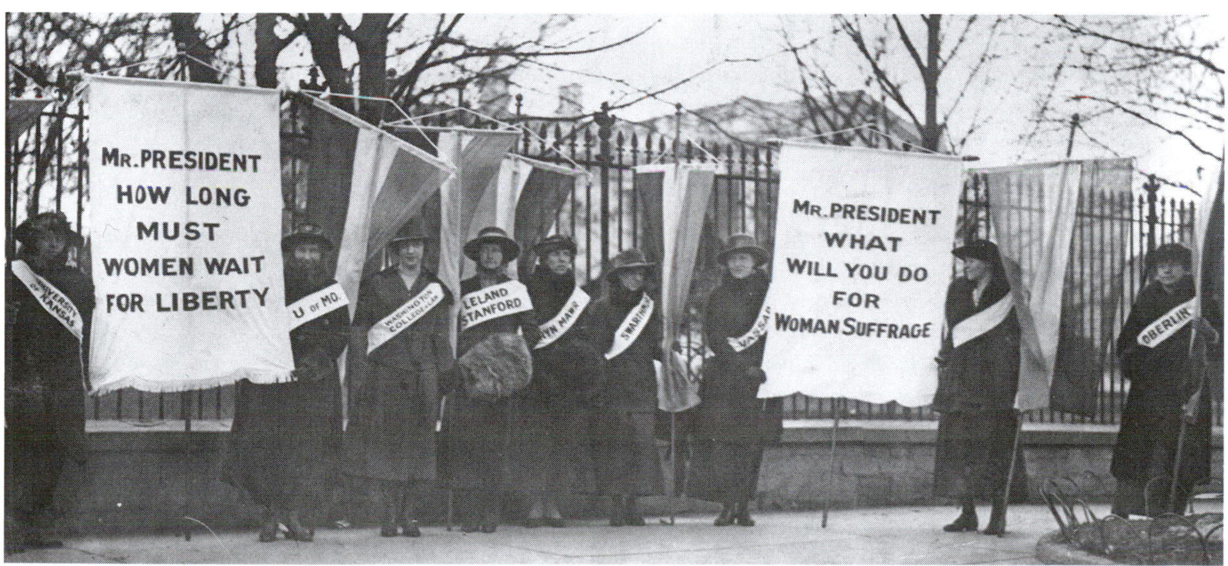

at the Progressive Party National Convention and campaigned for the party's candidates. From her base in New York City, lawyer and social investigator Frances Kellor created and then directed the Progressive Party's research and propaganda arm, the National Progressive Service.

After Illinois women became enfranchised in 1913, Ida B. Wells-Barnett used her Alpha Suffrage Club in Chicago's second ward to help bring about the election of the city's first black alderman, Oscar S. DePriest. In 1915, working from a base in the Woman's Socialist Union of California, Los Angeles journalist Estelle Lawton Lindsey became the first woman elected to the governing council of a major U.S. city. In 1916 Jeannette Rankin, a suffragist from Montana, ran for Congress as a progressive Republican, campaigning for a federal woman suffrage amendment, child protection laws, and Prohibition; she won, but her vote against U.S. entry into World War I in 1917 led to her defeat when she ran for the U.S. Senate. After organizing women to vote for Alfred E. Smith when he ran for governor of New York in 1918, social and labor reformer Belle Moskowitz rose to an executive position on the Democratic National Committee. Frances Perkins got her start in politics as a Consumers' Society lobbyist for industrial safety laws; in 1919 Governor Smith appointed her to the state's Industrial Commission, from which President Franklin D. Roosevelt elevated her into his cabinet in 1933.

These are only some examples of the many women who made the transition from nonpartisan to partisan politics in the late 1800s and early 1900s. While only a few of them gained high political positions, they set precedents for others. As time went on, women's increasing opportunities for professionalization opened up more paths into officeholding and political influence. Women lawyers brought their professional skills to bear on advocacy issues, used their bar associations and civic action leagues to gain footholds in local political party organizations, and eventually ran for elective posts or won appointive office. Women physicians pursued public health issues, advocating health reforms and winning supervisory posts in municipal and state government. Some of the women who had earned distinction in social settlement work and reform gained access to positions of political influence as well, either through winning prestigious professorships, like Alice Hamilton at the Harvard Medical School, or Julia Lathrop, who, as the head of the U.S. Children's Bureau, became the first woman to direct a federal agency.

Women in Radical Politics

For most middle-class women interested in politics, winning the vote was key to their full participation in politics. Some working-class women felt the same way and participated actively in the woman suffrage movement. A radical few took a different path to the exercise of political power: direct agitation. Mary Harris ("Mother") Jones, who inspired miners to strike for better wages and working conditions, cofounded the Industrial Workers of the World (IWW). Russian-born Emma Goldman, who attracted a large and enthusiastic following as a writer and lecturer, advocated anarchism, free speech, birth control for women, and resistance to the draft during World War I. Accused of complicity in the assassination of President William McKinley and jailed multiple times over the course of her career, she suffered deportation to Soviet Russia during the Red Scare of 1919.

Other radical women in this period included fiery labor agitator Elizabeth Gurley Flynn, who began to make public speeches in 1906, speaking out for socialism and the IWW, participating in strikes and free speech demonstrations, and helping to found the American Civil Liberties Union in 1920. Popular Socialist lecturer and journalist Kate Richards O'Hare ran unsuccessfully for Congress from Kansas in 1910. Arrested under the Espionage Act of 1917 for speaking out against participation in World War I, O'Hare spent several years in jail. In 1912 Margaret Sanger began challenging the so-called Comstock Law of 1873, which outlawed sending "obscene" material, including information about contraception, through the U.S. mail. Indicted in 1914 for disseminating *The Woman Rebel,* a monthly newspaper advocating the right to practice birth control, and jailed in 1916 for opening the nation's first clinic devoted to that purpose, Sanger became the leader of the movement that eventually legalized birth control.

Women's Changing Attitudes toward Politics

In the period between the end of the Civil War and the ratification of the Nineteenth Amendment, women's involvement in politics took a variety of forms. Women worked for suffrage, world peace, legislative action on both progressive and conservative fronts, and radical change. They engaged in direct political action as voters, agitators, candidates for elective office, and holders of administrative posts. To pursue any public cause, women had to take political action. As New York City settlement worker and child advocate Lillian Wald expressed it, "When I went to New York, and was stirred to participate in community work . . . I believed that politics concerned itself with matters outside [women's] realm and experience. It was an awakening to me to realize that when I was working in the interests of those babies . . . I was really in politics."

Thus, even in a period when most American women were denied the vote, thousands of them either rejected the prevailing Victorian idea that women should confine their activities to the private sphere, or they used their domestic roles to justify moving into the public sphere. As Kate Kirkman, a Nashville, Tennessee, civic activist, expressed it in 1897, "woman's work" was "[w]hatever may be necessary to preserve the sanctity of the home and ensure the freedom of the State." While women disagreed just as much as men did on exactly what these goals might mean and how to achieve them, they knew that engagement in politics was their essential first step.

See also feminism; voting; woman suffrage.

FURTHER READING

Bordin, Ruth. *Woman and Temperance: The Quest for Power and Liberty, 1873–1900*. New Brunswick, NJ: Rutgers University Press, 1990.

Edwards, Rebecca. *Angels in the Machinery: Gender in American Party Politics from the Civil War to the Progressive Era*. New York: Oxford University Press, 1997.

Fitzpatrick, Ellen. *Endless Crusade: Women Social Scientists and Progressive Reform*. New York: Oxford University Press, 1990.

Gustafson, Melanie Susan. *Women and the Republican Party, 1854–1924*. Urbana: University of Illinois Press, 2001.

Lovett, Laura L. *Conceiving the Future: Pronatalism, Reproduction, and the Family in the United States, 1890–1938*. Chapel Hill: University of North Carolina Press, 2007.

Morgan, Francesca. *Women and Patriotism in Jim Crow America*. Chapel Hill: University of North Carolina Press, 2005.

Norgren, Jill. *Belva Lockwood: The Woman Who Would Be President*. New York: New York University Press, 2007.

Perry, Elisabeth Israels. *Belle Moskowitz: Feminine Politics and the Exercise of Power in the Age of Alfred E. Smith*. New York: Oxford University Press, 1987.

Scott, Anne Firor. *Natural Allies: Women's Associations in American History*. Urbana: University of Illinois Press, 1991.

Sklar, Kathryn Kish. *Florence Kelley and the Nation's Work*. New Haven, CT: Yale University Press, 1995.

Wexler, Alice. *Emma Goldman: An Intimate Life*. New York: Pantheon Books, 1984.

ELISABETH ISRAELS PERRY

women and politics, 1920–70

On August 26, 1970, thousands of women in cities across the country thronged the streets in celebration of the fiftieth anniversary of the ratification of the Nineteenth Amendment, which granted women the right to vote. The Women's Strike for Equality march, one of the largest demonstrations for women's rights in U.S. history, represented a new era in the history of women's reform, in which long-standing assumptions about men and women would crumble and institutions, laws, and policies would be redesigned to reflect a new gender order. The 1920 passage of the Nineteenth Amendment also marked a turning point in women's history, although voting rights for African American women in the southern states would not be secured until the 1965 Voting Rights Act ended almost a century of black male and female disenfranchisement in that region.

Women's Political Power in the Wake of the Nineteenth Amendment

Winning the constitutional right to vote for the vast majority of American women was a milestone in the history of women's political citizenship. Yet women had voted in several states before 1920, when full political rights for women, including equal access to officeholding and representation in the two major political parties and in government, were far from secure. The first woman in the U.S. House of Representatives, Jeannette Rankin, a Republican from Montana, entered Congress in 1917, and, in her first vote that same year, she recorded her opposition to U.S. entry into World War I. But few women followed Rankin into high-ranking elected political office in the 1920s and 1930s. Those who did were termed the "widow contingent" because with a few exceptions—such as Mary T. Norton, Democratic congresswoman from New Jersey, and Ruth Hanna McCormick, Republican congresswoman from Illinois—they had succeeded their ill or dying husbands into office. Both the Democratic and the Republican National Committee set up "Women's Divisions" in the early 1920s, but these separate divisions did little to further women's advancement into influential party offices. Still, both Women's Divisions, along with the Democratic and Republican clubs that formed outside the formal party structure, encouraged women's political education, voting, and party volunteer work. Former National Association of Colored Women

(NACW) leaders Mary Church Terrell and Hallie Q. Brown helped organize a large network of active local black women's Republican clubs in northern urban cities and eventually founded the National League of Republican Colored Women in 1924. In part because of the failure of the Republican Party to enact federal antilynching legislation, several prominent black women, most notably Alice Dunbar-Nelson, switched party allegiance and actively campaigned for Democratic candidates in the federal election of 1924. By 1932, as Evelyn Brooks Higginbotham noted, "the honeymoon had ended between black women and the Republican party." Nevertheless, black women voters remained in the Republican column in national elections until 1936.

In the decades after winning suffrage, the percentage of women who registered and voted consistently fell below that of men. The absolute numbers of women voters would surpass that of men in 1964, but women continued to vote at a lower rate than men until 1980. As with many newly enfranchised groups, it would take time for women to exercise their voting rights. Women's right to vote was established by law but not yet by custom or norm. Some women continued to oppose woman suffrage; others failed to vote because of the intimidation of family members or the larger community. Still others remained ambivalent about mainstream electoral politics and its efficacy as an avenue of political persuasion.

Prior to suffrage, women often exercised their political power in different ways than did men; the sources of their political authority were distinct as well. These distinctive patterns and beliefs continued into the post-suffrage era. The largest woman suffrage organization, the National American Woman's Suffrage Association, headed by Carrie Chapman Catt, disbanded after winning suffrage, and many of its members moved into the National League of Women Voters (NLWV). The NLWV encouraged women to vote and involve themselves in party politics, but it also kept alive an older political tradition by positioning women as above and apart from partisan politics and uniquely suited to pursue a disinterested, selfless agenda.

Shortly after the founding of the NLWV in 1920, its president, Maud Park Wood, set up the Women's Joint Congressional Committee (WJCC) to coordinate women's lobbying at the national level. The vast majority of women's groups joined, including Progressive Era organizations such as the National Consumers' League (NCL), the Women's Trade Union League (WTUL), the National Association of Colored Women (NACW), and the General Federation of Women's Clubs (GFWC), as well as newer groups like the Women's International League for Peace and Freedom (WILPF) and the National Federation of Business and Professional Women's Clubs (NFBPWC). The WJCC, like the NLWV, was a hydra-headed creature. Realizing that no single issue united women as had suffrage, it allowed for a range of political agendas from its member organizations. It also relied on the rhetoric of public service and claimed authority based on women's distinctive experiences while at the same time it lobbied for more women in public and party office. This approach, however, with its emphasis on gender separatism, was losing adherents in the larger society as well as among women reformers. The tension between integration and separatism had always existed in the women's movement, but it intensified in an era in which a growing number of women saw gender integration and equal treatment as both possible and desirable.

In the 1920s, the WJCC and its member organizations pursued the social reform agenda first articulated by Progressive Era reformers like Jane Addams, Florence Kelley, and Julia Lathrop. These women, born in the 1870s and 1880s and among the first generation of women to be college educated, devoted themselves to creating institutions and public policies that would heal class divisions and ameliorate the problems of the poor, the majority of whom were women and children. Along with a younger generation of women they had mentored in the prewar suffrage, consumer, and labor movements, these women played key roles in the passage of the first federal social welfare legislation, the 1921 Sheppard-Towner Act, which set up prenatal and infant health centers across the country. Yet a combined assault from business and self-styled patriot groups cut into the public and congressional support for the WJCC coalition. In addition, as fear of a "woman's voting bloc" waned after the 1924 election revealed women's diverse political preferences, so did the WJCC's lobbying power. The Sheppard-Towner legislation expired in 1929, and the child labor amendment to the Constitution—one of the key goals of the WJCC in the 1920s—was voted down by the states, at times by public referendum.

Not all women shared the WJCC's priorities in the 1920s. Facing the growing threat of a revitalized Ku Klux Klan, a movement in which white women were deeply involved, the NACW put its energy into coalition work with the National Association for the Advancement of Colored People (NAACP) and expressed disappointment at the WJCC's failure to see antilynching legislation as a "woman's issue." Jane Addams increasingly shifted her energies to the WILPF, founded in 1915 to study the causes of war and to work for permanent peace. The Daughters of the American Revolution (DAR), once a former WJCC ally, turned against it by the mid-1920s, accusing it of being un-American because it favored expanding federal powers and remained too closely allied with the peace initiatives of the WILPF. The battle over temperance also continued as a high priority for many women. Following the ratification in 1919 of the Eighteenth Amendment, banning the sale and consumption of alcohol, some joined efforts to repeal the amendment, which ended in victory in 1933. Other women fought a rearguard action in its defense, continuing to claim that alcohol consumption fueled poverty, vice, and family dissolution.

In the 1930s, with Franklin D. Roosevelt in office, the social welfare wing of the women's movement achieved much of its political agenda. Facing pressure from First Lady Eleanor Roosevelt and the Democratic Party Women's Division chair, Molly Dewson, the president appointed a number of women to public office, including Frances Perkins, who as secretary of labor became the first female cabinet member. Women like Perkins were critical in the design and passage of the Social Security Act, which established old-age pensions, unemployment insurance, and new federal income guarantees for the poor, including mothers and children; the Wagner Act, which protected worker rights to bargain collectively with employers; and the Fair Labor Standards Act, which restricted child labor and established minimum wage and hour provisions for industrial workers.

Social Reform in the Post–World War II Decades

The number of female governmental political appointments inched upward during World War II but dropped again in the war's aftermath. In the 1950s and 1960s, however, slow but steady progress in integrating party and governmental ranks occurred, laying the basis for more rapid advances in the 1970s. Former actress Helen Gahagan Douglas ably represented her blue-collar Los Angeles district in Congress throughout the 1940s, only to be defeated by Richard Nixon in a 1950 Senate campaign that was notable for his anti-Communist smear tactics. By the 1960s, congressional ranks had opened to Martha Griffiths (Democrat of Michigan), Frances Bolton (Republican of Ohio), Edith Green (Democrat of Oregon), Katharine St. George (Republican of New York), among others. And in 1965, Patsy Takemoto Mink (Democrat of Hawai'i) became the first woman of color and the first woman of Asian-Pacific-islander descent in the House. A handful of women also moved into the Senate, including Margaret Chase Smith (Republican of Maine). Elected first to the House in 1940, and then to the Senate in 1948, her long and successful congressional career continued into the 1970s.

In 1953 Democratic National Committee (DNC) officials dissolved the DNC's Women's Division amidst protest by female party activists who claimed women were being scapegoated for the loss to the Republicans in 1952. Women had shown a slightly larger preference for Eisenhower in 1952, provoking the debate, but this gender gap in national party preference vanished quickly. Women's voting patterns in national elections were virtually indistinguishable from those of men from 1920 until 1980, when a sizable number of Democratic men shifted their allegiance to the Republican Party and women did not.

In the decades following World War II, as in earlier eras, women's political influence was expressed most powerfully outside traditional party avenues. The separatist social welfare network of women reformers declined, but a new generation of women reinvigorated progressive grassroots social reform through their leadership in the labor, civil rights, human rights, and peace movements. In part because these were new movements, and at times marginal ones, women were welcomed as members and even as leaders.

The labor movement had risen dramatically in the 1930s, offering a vision of interracial and interclass solidarity, avid political advocacy for state regulation, and social benefits and a new openness to a range of political perspectives. In the 1920s, the primary worker-based reform and radical organizations, the American Federation of Labor, the Socialist Party, the Communist Party, and the Industrial Workers of the World (IWW), each pursued separate agendas. In the mid-1930s, however, many Socialists and Communists decided to work within the new labor federation, the Congress of Industrial Organization (CIO), helping organize the millions of mass-production and other low-income workers who would be the basis of labor's power in the postwar era. Women flooded into the new movement, and some—such as Ruth Young of the United Electrical Workers Union, Myra Wolfgang of the Hotel Employees and Restaurant Employees Union, and Caroline Davis, Lillian Hatcher, and Millie Jeffrey of the United

Automotive Workers—moved into key secondary positions of leadership.

By the 1940s, a formidable women's labor movement existed that included close to 3 million women in unions, a million homemakers in women's labor auxiliaries, and a dynamic national network of women labor officials. Through their participation in the U.S. Women's Bureau reform network, women labor officials allied with like-minded women leaders of the National Council for Negro Women (NCNW)—founded in 1935 by Mary McLeod Bethune and later led by Dorothy Height—the American Association of University Women, the YWCA, and other groups. Throughout the 1940s and 1950s, at the height of the supposed era of domesticity and gender conservatism, this coalition pushed for equal pay for equal work; an end to unfair discrimination on the basis of race, sex, marital status, and nationality; improved labor standards legislation; universal day care and other supports for working mothers.

In the early 1960s, under the Kennedy and Johnson administrations, many women's movement goals were realized, including the establishment of the 1961 President's Commission on the Status of Women, passage of the 1963 Equal Pay Act and the 1964 Civil Rights Act, and, in 1966, extension of the Fair Labor Standards Act to cover the majority of workers. Esther Peterson, a longtime labor activist and former lobbyist for the AFL-CIO whom Kennedy appointed assistant secretary of labor in 1961, was instrumental in these victories, as was the lobbying of women's, labor, and civil rights organizations.

Women of color were key public actors and social change advocates in the postwar decades. Black men held the top leadership positions in such African American civil rights organizations as the Southern Christian Leadership Council (SCLC), the NAACP, and the Student Non-Violent Coordinating Committee (SNCC). But the majority of participants were female, in part due to the movement's close connection to organized religion. Ella Baker, Rosa Parks, Fannie Lou Hamer, and others provided indispensable inspiration and intellectual leadership to the movement. Spanish-speaking women helped sustain the work of the League of United Latin American Citizens (LULAC), the oldest Hispanic advocacy organization, and the Mexican-American Legal Defense and Education Fund (MALDEF), set up in 1968. Josefina Fierro de Bright served as the first executive secretary of the Congress of Spanish-Speaking People, a national Latino civil rights organization founded in 1939.

African American and Spanish-speaking women also led and were the majority constituency in the welfare rights movement. Johnnie Tillmon, a mother of six, became executive director of the National Welfare Rights Organization, founded in 1966, and spoke compellingly about the rights of mothers to care for their children and the social value of the mother-work of all women. In the labor movement, African American women like Addie Wyatt of the United Packinghouse Workers Union and Maida Springer-Kemp of the International Ladies' Garment Workers' Union rose to prominence, as did Mexican-American Dolores Huerta, who became vice president of the United Farm Workers of America.

A surprising number of black women ran for public office. Shirley Chisholm, for example, who in 1968 became the first black woman elected to Congress, ran for the Democratic nomination for the presidency in 1972. During seven terms representing her Brooklyn, New York, district in the House, Chisholm effectively championed the concerns of women and minority groups. Her book *Unbought and Unbossed* (1970) chronicles her life in public office.

Disagreement over the equal rights amendment (ERA) ran deep among women in the post–World War II decades. The ERA, a proposed constitutional amendment calling for equal rights for men and women, encountered bitter hostility from the social reformers linked to the U.S. Women's Bureau after the National Woman's Party (NWP) introduced it in Congress in 1923. Women like Mary Anderson, the director of the U.S. Women's Bureau, feared the ERA would jeopardize the legality of the considerable body of woman-only state labor laws that social reformers had worked hard to win. The battle over the ERA raged for nearly a half century, exacerbated by class and other differences. Before the 1970s, conservative Republicans and business groups joined the NWP in backing the ERA, in part because they saw it as a way of overturning labor standards legislation. In contrast, ERA opponents found allies in the progressive wing of the Democratic Party and among organized labor. Eleanor Roosevelt and other prominent women reformers dropped their opposition to the ERA in the postwar decades, but many continued to fight the ERA until the early 1970s when, following the 1969 administrative ruling of the Equal Employment Opportunity Commission and subsequent federal court decisions, the last of the sex-based laws were either repealed or redrafted.

Foreign policy issues divided women as well. With the renewal of cold war hostilities at the end of World

War II, women's political alliances depended in part on how they envisioned achieving global security and how they viewed the Soviet Union. When Henry Wallace ran for president on the Progressive Party ticket in 1948 calling for friendly relations with the Soviet Union, he won only a tiny fraction of the vote. Women, however, comprised a large percentage of his supporters and held some of the top positions in his campaign. Some women such as former IWW organizer Elizabeth Gurley Flynn also held leadership positions in the Communist Party USA. Communist sympathizers as well as anti-Communist Socialists, liberals, and New Dealers—both women and men—faced vitriolic attacks on their integrity and national loyalty by Senator Joseph McCarthy (Republican of Wisconsin) and other lawmakers at the height of the cold war in the late 1940s and 1950s.

The United Nations, established in 1945, remained one of the few forums during the cold war in which all the global powers participated. U.S. women helped establish the UN Commission on the Status of Women in 1947. In 1948 the UN General Assembly passed the Universal Declaration of Human Rights (UDHR). Eleanor Roosevelt chaired the UN Commission that formulated the declaration's call for the economic, political, and social rights of all peoples.

The 1960s: Realignments and Redefinitions

Although the two major political parties jockeyed for power in the 1940s and 1950s, they often agreed on many basic political principles and used similar rhetoric in their appeals to voters. A majority within both parties saw the need for a social safety net for the elderly and the poor, embraced the traditional family as crucial to societal well-being and stability, and heralded their commitment to preserving religious freedom, democratic governance, and containing the spread of communism. In 1964, however, a conservative faction within the Republican Party challenged the dominant moderate wing of the party and nominated Barry Goldwater as the Republican candidate for president. He was overwhelmingly defeated, but the New Right, as the conservative movement came to be called, continued to gain strength, as evidenced by the 1966 election of Ronald Reagan as governor of California and his subsequent 1980 election as president. Republican clubwomen, organized in the National Federation of Republican Women (NFRW), an auxiliary group of volunteers that sought to distance themselves from the more moderate women party officials close to the Republican National Committee (RNC), were a major constituency behind Goldwater and within the New Right. Their emphasis on a moral politics, averse to compromise and distrustful of partisan loyalty, echoed some aspects of an older presuffrage women's political culture. Phyllis Schlafly, a leader of the New Right whose book *A Choice Not An Echo* (1964) helped nail down Goldwater's nomination, would eventually take her conservative followers out of the NFRW and build a powerful antifeminist movement in the 1970s based on opposition to the equal rights amendment, abortion rights, gay rights, and the drafting of women into the military. A substantial number of Republican women, however, continued to identify as liberal or moderate Republicans in the 1960s and 1970s and remained sympathetic to a women's rights agenda.

The largest women's movement of the 1960s, often termed "second-wave feminism," happened largely outside the Republican Party. The new feminism of the 1960s had multiple roots and, like all big-tent mass movements, sheltered an array of organizations and political ideologies. Many 1960s feminists were veterans of the postwar labor, civil rights, and peace movements. Some had been inspired by the radical politics of the Communist Old Left and the New Left student movements that emphasized free speech and participatory democracy. One of the most influential organizations, the National Organization for Women (NOW), was founded in 1966 initially by labor and Democratic Party activists who had been angered by the Johnson administration's unwillingness to enforce the new prohibitions on sex discrimination in employment in Title VII of the Civil Rights Act. Led by Betty Friedan—author of *The Feminine Mystique* (1963), a best-selling exposé of the plight of middle-class housewives and the constraints of conventional femininity—NOW sought equal opportunities for women in every sphere and lobbied vigorously for governmental policies such as affirmative action and day care. Other new feminists, chiefly younger, college-educated women, started consciousness-raising groups, founded radical journals, and organized street protests. Some groups focused on the politics of reproduction and women's bodies, others explored women's sexuality. Still other groups debated strategies for transforming patriarchal society and ending the sexual division of labor. The new feminism of the 1960s, building on the social movements and individual pioneers who had preceded it, laid the foundation for the economic and political breakthroughs of the 1970s and beyond.

See also civil rights; feminism; labor movement and politics; Progressive parties; voting; welfare; woman suffrage.

FURTHER READING

Blee, Kathleen. *Women of the Klan: Racism and Gender in the 1920s.* Berkeley: University of California Press, 1992.

Carroll, Susan J., and Richard L. Fox, eds. *Gender and Elections: Shaping the Future of American Politics.* Cambridge, UK: Cambridge University Press, 2006.

Cobble, Dorothy Sue. *The Other Women's Movement: Workplace Justice and Social Rights in Modern America.* Princeton, NJ: Princeton University Press, 2004.

Cott, Nancy. *The Grounding of Modern Feminism.* New Haven, CT: Yale University Press, 1987.

Freeman, Jo. *A Room at a Time: How Women Entered Party Politics.* Lanham, MD: Rowman and Littlefield, 2000.

Gustafson, Melanie, Kristie Miller, and Elisabeth Israels Perry, eds. *We Have Come to Stay: American Women and Political Parties, 1880–1960.* Albuquerque: University of New Mexico Press, 1999.

Harvey, Anna L. *Votes without Leverage: Women in American Electoral Politics, 1920–1970.* New York: Cambridge University Press, 1998.

Hartmann, Susan. *From Margins to Mainstream: Women and Politics since 1960.* Philadelphia: Temple University Press, 1989.

Higginbotham, Evelyn Brooks. "Politics to Stay: Black Women and Party Politics in the 1920s." In *Women, Politics, and Change.* Edited by Louise A. Tilly and Patricia Gurin, 199–220. New York: Russell Sage Foundation, 1990.

Materson, Lisa G. *For the Freedom of Her Race: Black Women and Electoral Politics in Illinois, 1877 to 1932.* Chapel Hill: University of North Carolina Press, 2009.

Muncy, Robyn. *Creating a Female Dominion in American Reform 1890–1935.* New York: Oxford University Press, 1991.

Nadasen, Premilla. *Welfare Warriors: The Welfare Rights Movement in the United States.* New York: Routledge, 2005.

Orleck, Annelise. *Common Sense and a Little Fire: Women and Working-Class Politics in the United States, 1900–1965.* Chapel Hill: University of North Carolina Press, 1995.

Ransby, Barbara. *Ella Baker and the Black Freedom Movement: A Radical Democratic Vision.* Chapel Hill: University of North Carolina Press, 2003.

Ruiz, Vicki. *From Out of the Shadows: Mexican Women in Twentieth-Century America.* New York: Oxford University Press, 1999.

Rupp, Leila J. *Worlds of Women: The Making of an International Women's Movement.* Princeton, NJ: Princeton University Press, 1997.

Rymph, Catherine E. *Republican Women: Feminism and Conservatism from Suffrage through the Rise of the New Right.* Chapel Hill: University of North Carolina Press, 2006.

Tilly, Louise A., and Patricia Gurin, eds. *Women, Politics, and Change.* New York: Russell Sage Foundation, 1990.

Ware, Susan. *Beyond Suffrage: Women in the New Deal.* Cambridge, MA: Harvard University Press, 1981.

White, Deborah Gray. *Too Heavy a Load: Black Women in Defense of Themselves.* New York: Norton, 1999.

Wilson, Jan Doolittle. *The Women's Joint Congressional Committee and the Politics of Maternalism, 1920–1930.* Urbana: University of Illinois Press, 2007.

DOROTHY SUE COBBLE

women and politics since 1970

Women have made tremendous strides since 1970 in political participation and in successful advocacy of women's issues, but they have not achieved complete equity, especially in holding political office. The lack of such equity can be explained by the fact that women held so few offices in 1970. Therefore they could make substantial gains and still constitute a relatively small percentage of the members in various legislative bodies.

Filling the Pool, 1970–89

The beginning of this period saw a number of changes owing to the reinvigoration of feminism in the late 1950s that, taken together, constitute a watershed. First, although voter turnout historically had been lower among women than men, in 1968 this pattern changed so that by the early twenty-first century women formed a majority of the voting public, as they constituted a slight majority of the population. Second, on August 26, 1970, the fiftieth anniversary of women's winning the right to vote at the national level, thousands of women in large and small cities around the country took to the streets to demonstrate in the largest mobilization of women in U.S. history. Third, in 1971 activists formed the National Women's Political Caucus, the first national organization to recruit and groom women to run for office. And fourth, in 1971, in *Reed v. Reed,* the U.S. Supreme Court for the first time applied the equal protection clause of the Fourteenth Amendment to gender discrimination. The preceding decade had also seen breakthroughs for women of color: in 1965 Hawai'i's Patsy Mink was elected to the House of Representatives, the first woman of color to serve in Congress, and in 1969 Shirley Chisholm became the first African American woman in Congress. The 92nd Congress, elected in 1970, included 15 women, 2 in the Senate and 13 in the House, an improvement over the 11 women in the 91st Congress.

All of this ferment quickly began to bear fruit in the form of pathbreaking legislation. Of great symbolic value was Congress's passage of the equal rights amendment (ERA) in 1972. Though the amendment failed to gain ratification in the requisite number of states, the ERA attested that a majority in Congress was willing to legislate on behalf of women and to the growing sophistication of such women's advocacy groups as the National Organization for Women, founded in 1966.

Of greater substantive value was the passage of Title IX of the Education Act Amendments, also in 1972. Tying federal funding for a particular institution to the cessation of discrimination against women, Title IX had a revolutionary impact on women's access to professional schools and to athletic achievement. Title IX ultimately helped bring more women into the legal profession, one of the main suppliers of candidates for political office. Before Title IX, female students had been a tiny minority in law schools, but in subsequent decades, their enrollment grew to 50 percent and higher in many law schools. Moreover, as women joined the faculties of colleges and universities in larger numbers, with a push from affirmative action and Title IX, they began to challenge the curriculum in many disciplines, thereby rendering the higher education of young women less devoid of female role models and of analysis of the female experience than had previously been the case. Another significant development during this period was the U.S. Supreme Court decision *Roe v. Wade* in 1973, which more or less legalized abortion nationally, and which some attributed in part to the pressure generated by the heightened political presence and mobilization of American women.

The 1970s saw a substantial increase in the number of women running for—and winning—local office as well, including positions as mayors. In 1974 San Jose's Janet Gray Hayes became the first woman to be elected mayor of a city with a population of more than 500,000. This event was followed in 1979 by the election of Jane Byrne as mayor of Chicago.

Another first in this period was the election of the Connecticut Democrat Ella Grasso as governor in 1974, the first woman who was neither the wife nor the widow of a previous governor to be elected chief executive of a state. Women were making steady gains in other state offices, too, with the proportion of female legislators elected throughout the nation rising from 4.5 percent in 1970 to 12.1 percent in 1980 and to 18.3 percent in 1990. In California, the level of female county supervisors went from 3 percent in 1972 to 28 percent in 1992. An increase in female officeholders at the local level expands the pool of women who are visible and qualified to run for state or national office.

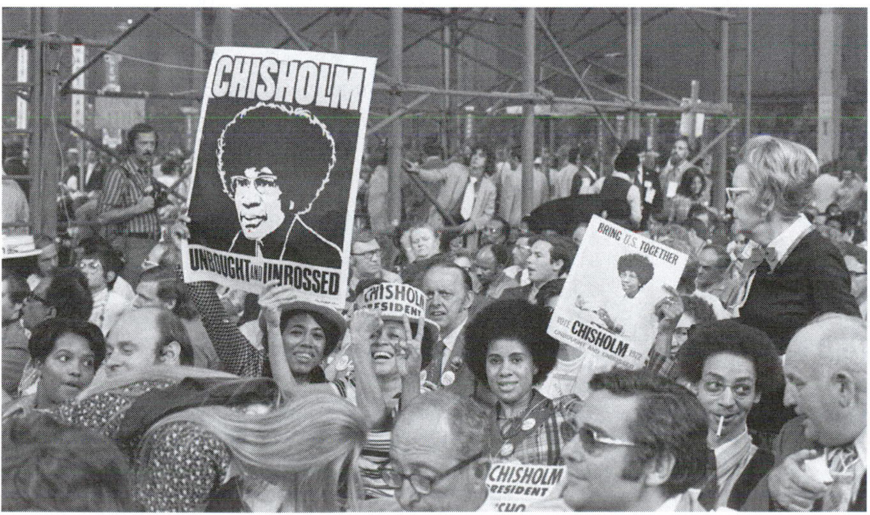

Shirley Chisholm addresses the Democratic National Convention in 1972 while her supporters cheer. (Jo Freeman)

During this period, the Democratic Party began to drive change for women in its strong advocacy of feminist legislation, a break with a past that had seen the Republican Party endorsing the ERA in the 1940s and nominating such well-respected moderate women as Maine's Senator Margaret Chase Smith, who served in the Senate from 1949 to 1973 and was the first high-profile woman in that body. The passage of the ERA in Congress mobilized right-wing women, led by Phyllis Schlafly, who helped defeat the measure. With the growth of the Religious Right, fueled in part by the social change unleashed by second wave feminism, the Republican Party continued the move to the right that had begun with Barry Goldwater in 1964. In 1980, for example, presidential candidate Ronald Reagan disavowed the ERA, and for the first time in American history, a gender gap was evident that November, as women voted significantly more Democratic than did men. Reading the poll numbers, the unsuccessful Democratic candidate for president in 1984, Walter Mondale, chose New York Congresswoman Geraldine Ferraro to be his running mate, the first woman on the national ticket of a major party. In 1981 Reagan nominated the first woman to serve on the U.S. Supreme Court, Sandra Day O'Connor.

Running as a Woman, 1990–2000

Though women were increasingly able to gain nominations and to win elections before 1990, and though legislation benefitting women was being enacted, the most outspoken advocates of such legislation were not necessarily female candidates or officeholders. Scholars used to refer to a "closet feminist" syndrome, because women candidates were often shy about "running as a woman" or about campaigning on an explicitly feminist platform. Margaret Chase Smith had once told an interviewer that she never ran as a "woman candidate" because that would have been a formula for losing. Women candidates were often fearful, too, about doing anything to call attention to their appearance or to their families, lest they reinforce invidious stereotypes.

This situation began to change around 1990, signaled by the successful campaign of Ann Richards for governor of Texas that year. A sharp-tongued woman with a lively personality, Richards was bold enough to mail a picture of herself having her hair done to every beauty salon in Texas as a way to reach out to women during the campaign, a break with the practices of the past and an indication of the extent to which Richards liberated herself from the usual constraints. Significantly, by this time, women had formed more professional fund-raising organizations for pro-choice women Democrats, most notably Emily's List ("Early Money Is Like Yeast"—It makes the dough rise), founded in time to help raise money for Maryland Democrat Barbara Mikulski's successful move from the House to the Senate in 1986. By 1990 Emily's List was able to give $1.5 million to 14 candidates, Richards among them. In 1992 the group raised $6 million—partly the result of a transformative event that took place in the intervening two years.

In 1991 President George H. W. Bush nominated Clarence Thomas to succeed the legendary civil rights lawyer Thurgood Marshall on the U.S. Supreme Court. Democrats were deeply unhappy about the choice of the conservative Thomas but were reluctant to go on the attack against an African American. After rather pro forma hearings, the Senate Judiciary Committee called a late witness against Thomas, African American attorney Anita Hill, then a law professor at the University of Oklahoma but formerly an employee of Thomas's at the Equal Employment Opportunity Commission. Hill testified that Thomas had sexually harassed her when he was her boss. Thomas counterattacked, charging that he was the victim of a "high-tech lynching." Thomas was confirmed, and polls showed that a majority of Americans believed his word rather than Hill's. What the polls did not fully reveal, however, was that millions of women were enraged by the spectacle of the then-all-male Senate Judiciary Committee sitting in judgment on the veracity of a woman who had testified about an experience shared by many other women. If women believed Hill, they were especially unhappy about the attacks and accusations she endured from a number of Republican politicians and writers.

The election cycle of 1992, which subsequently became known as "the year of the woman," saw more women candidates running at all levels of government, more money raised for them, and more electoral success than ever before. The 102nd Congress, elected in 1990, had included 4 women senators and 28 congresswomen. The 103rd Congress included 7 women senators and 47 congresswomen. Moreover, some of the newly elected made history. Carol Moseley Braun of Illinois, for example, became the first woman of color and the first African

American Democrat to serve in the Senate. Moreover, she defeated an incumbent to achieve this.

In 1992, for the first time in 16 years, a Democrat, Bill Clinton, was elected president. Nonetheless, the possibility that the increasing number of women in Congress could legislate in ways directly beneficial to women was greatly circumscribed in 1994 when control of Congress returned to Republicans for the first time since 1953. The charged rhetoric and political maneuverings of Republicans, moving even further right under the leadership of Speaker Newt Gingrich, increased the level of rancor in the nation's capital and made it difficult for any coalition of feminists of both sexes and varying political persuasions to advance their legislative agenda.

Yet even during this period, there were gains. Madeleine Albright became secretary of state during Clinton's second term, the first woman to hold the office and the highest-ranking woman to that date in the history of the U.S. government. Clinton appointed another woman to the U.S. Supreme Court, Ruth Bader Ginsburg, in 1993. He also made history by appointing an all-time high of 14 women to cabinet-level positions. The number of women in Congress continued to grow, though not as dramatically as in 1992: by the election of the 107th Congress in 2000, there were 13 women senators and 59 congresswomen. By that time the national proportion of women in state legislatures was 22.5 percent.

Going for Broke: Since 2001

By the early twenty-first century, women filled positions of authority in many realms of American society: acting as CEOs in the business world (though only a tiny percentage as CEOs of Fortune 500 companies), running organizations in the nonprofit sector, filling high-profile jobs in the media, serving as school principals and superintendents, and playing leadership roles in the academy. One symbol of dramatic change was the 2007 appointment of Drew Gilpin Faust as president of Harvard University—not only a woman (Harvard's first female president) but a historian of women. As of 2007 there were nine women serving as governors (six Democrats and three Republicans), a significant change because this position had historically been quite resistant to female leadership. And two women, Nancy Pelosi and Hillary Rodham Clinton, made even bigger history.

Nancy Pelosi, a San Francisco Democrat, became the minority leader of the House in 2002, poised to become speaker should the Democrats capture control of that body. In 2006 the Democrats gained control of both houses of Congress, and Pelosi became the first woman speaker in American history. On the occasion of her swearing in she surrounded herself with her grandchildren, thus calling attention to her status as the mother of five. Women politicians had come a long way from the days in which they had had to package themselves as honorary men in order to be taken seriously.

As for Clinton, she was the front-runner for the Democratic nomination for president in the waning days of 2007. A hard-working senator, married to a popular former president, she initially ran a highly professional campaign, with few missteps. Polling revealed that Clinton could count on an especially large gender gap among women voters in her favor. But then two things happened. First, Illinois Senator Barack Obama began to attract huge crowds, and his campaign caught fire. The Obama campaign, in fact, began to receive unprecedented sums of money in donations. Second, the Clinton campaign made some major miscalculations, most particularly in not putting enough resources into the caucus states (as opposed to those featuring a primary), and Obama swept those, giving him a lead in the delegate count, despite Clinton's wins in many populous states. In fact, Clinton and Obama both garnered about 18 million votes, though Obama led in delegates. Political observers also noted that her vote in favor of the war in Iraq had cost her among the Democratic base, and that she suffered from unusually high "negatives," a lingering effect of controversies from her days as First Lady to President Bill Clinton. Although she lost the nomination, she came closer to becoming the presidential nominee of a major party than any other woman in American history.

This was the good news. The bad news for such "women's issues" as child care, as well as for the politicians of either sex or party who advocated for them, lay in the spillover from the terrorist attacks on the United States on September 11, 2001. Following the attacks, President George W. Bush declared a "War on Terror"—a war that extended into a preemptive strike on Iraq in 2003. In response to the genuine and manufactured anxiety, the female vote splintered, with married women much less likely to vote for a Democrat than single women. Where Democratic-voting "soccer moms" had been the bellwether of change in the Clinton years, now the media invented the term *security moms* to characterize those (primarily married) women whose priorities had shifted

Nancy Pelosi, the first woman to serve as Speaker of the House, signs legislation in 2007. (http://speaker.house.gov)

from social issues to protection from terrorism and hence who tended to vote Republican. As of late 2007, Democratic pollster Celinda Lake was still finding very large differences between the political preferences of married and unmarried women, with the latter voting two to one Democratic—but not the former.

The 110th Congress, elected in 2006, contained more women than ever before: 16 in the Senate and 71 in the House (of whom slightly less than one-fourth were women of color). But those numbers still represented only 16.3 percent of the 535 members in the two houses. Trying to account for the slowness of change, scholars have concluded that being a woman does not make a candidate less viable or less able to raise money. But there is the power of incumbency—and most incumbents are still male—and the fact that even now fewer women run for office, especially at higher levels. Recent scholarship suggests that women still face the burden of disproportionate responsibility for child care and elder care, which impedes their political ambitions. Moreover, women still hold themselves to a high standard before they feel qualified to run for office, more so than do men. They've come a long way, but they still have a long way to go to enjoy full equality.

See also Democratic Party, 1968–2008; feminism; Republican Party, 1968–2008.

FURTHER READING

Burrell, Barbara. *A Woman's Place Is in the House: Campaigning for Congress in the Feminist Era*. Ann Arbor: University of Michigan Press, 1994.

Carroll, Susan J., and Richard L. Fox. *Gender and Elections: Shaping the Future of American Politics*. Cambridge: Cambridge University Press, 2006.

Center for American Women and Politics, Rutgers University. http://www.cawp.rutgers.edu.

Darcy, R., Susan Welch, and Janet Clark. *Women, Elections, and Representation*. 2nd ed. Lincoln: University of Nebraska Press, 1994.

Dolan, Kathleen A. *Voting for Women: How the Public Evaluates Women Candidates*. Boulder, CO: Westview Press, 2004.

Lawless, Jennifer L., and Richard L. Fox, *It Takes a Candidate: Why Women Don't Run for Office*. Cambridge, UK: Cambridge University Press, 2005.

Mikulski, Barbara, et al., with Catherine Whitman. *Nine and Counting: The Women of the Senate*. New York: William Morrow, 2000.

Reingold, Beth. *Representing Women: Sex, Gender, and Legislative Behavior in Arizona and California*. Chapel Hill: University of North Carolina Press, 2000.

Witt, Linda, Karen M. Paget, and Glenna Matthews. *Running as a Woman: Gender and Power in American Politics*. New York: Free Press, 1994.

GLENNA MATTHEWS

World War I

Few Americans could have predicted that conflict in Europe in the summer of 1914 would lead to four years of war, U.S. military intervention, and the transformation of American politics. Decades of rivalry among the European powers had prompted minor conflicts in the Balkans and North Africa between 1909 and 1914; war came after Gavrilo Princip, a Bosnian Serb nationalist, assassinated Archduke Franz Ferdinand, heir to the throne of the Austro-Hungarian Empire, on June 28, 1914. Ultimatums and secret treaties drew all Europe's major powers into war by the beginning of August, pitting the Central Powers of Germany, Austria-Hungary, and the Ottoman Empire against an alliance of France, Britain, and Russia. On the battlefield, an initial German drive met stiff resistance from the British and French; by September 1914, the two sides dug into a thousand-mile system of trenches that remained more or less unchanged until the war's end four years later.

Americans reacted with concern to the outbreak of war, but many thought the conflict would be a minor clash; most, even the normally bellicose former president Theodore Roosevelt, urged inaction. Isolationists eschewed entangling alliances; progressives who believed that a century of peace had advanced society beyond war urged the United States to stay out. So did President Woodrow Wilson. Elected in 1912 due to a divided Republican Party, Wilson wanted to continue his domestic agenda. Together with a heavily Democratic Congress, Wilson had spent the first year of his term shepherding through reforms in labor relations and political economy.

Both parties hailed President Wilson's call on August 19, 1914, that Americans be "impartial in thought as well as in action." But in practice, the United States was never entirely neutral. News coverage leaned toward support for Britain; the cutting of transatlantic cables connecting North America with Germany ensured that Americans received nearly all their war news from a British perspective. Awareness of German atrocities in Belgium and gruesome industrialized warfare in the trenches—including machine guns, tanks, mustard gas, and daily casualties in the tens of thousands—horrified the American public and tended to amplify support for the Allies. Nor was the United States ever fully neutral in its actions: Americans more or less ceased trading with the Central Powers (especially after a British blockade of continental Europe) and lent them little money; by contrast, loans to Allied governments expanded, and trade with the Allied Powers increased fourfold. U.S. dependence on transatlantic commerce meant that German submarine warfare would increasingly pose a threat to American lives and livelihood.

On May 7, 1915, a German submarine torpedoed the British passenger ship *Lusitania*, killing 1,198 people, including 128 Americans. Wilson continued to speak of neutrality, insisting that "there is such a thing as a nation being so right that it does not need to convince others by force that it is right," but his diplomatic communications with Germany were so stern that his antiwar secretary of state William Jennings Bryan resigned in protest on June 8, 1915. (Wilson replaced him with Robert Lansing, openly anti-German from the outset.) In Congress, supporters of neutrality—which included both southern Democrats and midwestern progressives—sought to keep the United States from being pulled into war by world events. Representative Jefferson McLemore (D-Texas) introduced a resolution blocking Americans from traveling on the ships of the warring powers. (Indeed, the *Lusitania* had been carrying munitions.) McLemore's resolution was narrowly defeated; war was delayed by a German announcement in the fall of 1916 that it would not attack passenger ships without warning.

The issue of war dominated the 1916 election. Democrats campaigned for Wilson as the man who "kept us out of war." The slogan referred not only to European events but to the Mexican Revolution as well. On March 9, 1916, revolutionary leader Pancho Villa led a raid on Columbus, New Mexico; Wilson responded with a massive deployment of U.S. troops under the leadership of Major General John J. Pershing. The border conflict raged as Congress debated the nation's wartime "preparedness." The National Defense Act of August 1916 increased the authorized strength of the U.S. Army and gave the president the power to federalize state militias for overseas service; the Naval Act of 1916 called for substantial construction of ships. At Chicago in June, Republicans nominated Supreme Court Justice Charles Evans Hughes, who ran a lackluster campaign. Nevertheless, the 1916 presidential election was one of the closest in American history. Wilson lost ten of the states he had won four years earlier, and had he not managed a 3,800-vote victory in California, Hughes would have entered the White House.

Soon after his reelection, Wilson proposed a negotiated end to the war. In a speech to the Senate on January 22, 1917, Wilson called for "peace without victory" and urged the formation of a postwar league of nations. Meanwhile, two weeks earlier, German war planners had adopted a new strategy in the hope of breaking the war's stalemate: submarine warfare to starve the British and a final push on Paris. Renewed submarine attacks were sure to bring the United States into the war, but the Germans gambled that they could win before Americans fully mobilized. The Germans announced their plan on January 31; three days later Wilson severed diplomatic relations.

On March 1, the American public learned of the Zimmermann telegram, a cable from a German diplomat inviting Mexico to join Germany's side of the war in exchange for the restoration of Mexican territory lost to the United States in 1848. Three attacks on American merchant ships in March 1917 brought renewed demands for U.S. entry into the war. Wilson called the newly elected 65th Congress into special session, and on April 6, 1917, Congress heeded his call to make the world "safe for democracy," declaring war on Germany by a vote of 373 to 50 in the House of Representatives and 82 to 6 in the Senate.

The United States began the war with a comparatively small military force. Despite defense legislation passed the previous year, in April 1917, the army numbered just 120,000 men, the navy had about 300 ships, and neither officers nor enlisted men in either service had substantial field experience. On May 18, 1917, Wilson signed the Selective Service Act, requiring the registration of eligible men for conscription. The bill sharply divided Democrats; Wilson relied on the leadership of Representative Julius Kahn (R-California) to see it through Congress. Overall, some 24 million men between the ages of 18 and 45 registered; about 2.7 million were drafted, and about 2 million more volunteered (particularly in the navy and the marines, which did not rely on the draft). The War Department constructed 32 training camps (carefully distributing 16 in the North and 16 in the South), and while initial mobilization was slow, the army eventually moved 2 million troops to Europe in the space of 18 months.

Mobilizing the Home Front

War mobilization required a substantial expansion of federal presence into areas of Americans' everyday lives. Lacking a large federal bureaucracy to manage the task—and drawing on the Progressive Era's political culture of voluntarism—the Wilson administration tapped existing organizations and social networks to carry out much of the work on the homefront. In Washington, D.C., those volunteers included "dollar-a-year men," corporate executives who took war leadership positions for a token salary. Among them was George Creel, an advertising executive who headed the Committee on Public Information (CPI). The CPI spread the Wilson administration's case for the war, spending its $100 million budget on a media blitz and mobilizing tens of thousands of volunteers, known as "four-minute men" for the brief speeches they made in movie theaters, urging Americans to enlist, to buy bonds, and save food. Voluntarist rhetoric also shaped the War Industries Board; Wilson tasked chairman Bernard M. Baruch with coordinating industrial production. In the winter of 1917–18, as fuel shortages hit consumers and tangled railroad schedules delayed needed war materials, the government took over control of both the coal and railroad industries. The National War Labor Board, established in April 1918, managed relations between business and labor. During the war, unions enrolled 1.5 million members and won such victories as the eight-hour workday, equal pay for women, and collective bargaining rights, but many of labor's gains were temporary and restricted to those in war industries.

The United States Food Administration (USFA), established in May 1917, was led by Herbert Hoover, a business leader who had already earned an international reputation for coordinating relief efforts for European civilians. Americans did not experience rationing, except for some regulations on wholesalers and restaurants and modest limits on sugar. USFA policies did far less to increase the food supply than did the incentives of market forces. But the 500,000 volunteers (most of them women) who led local campaigns made the USFA a public success and made Hoover the only American during the postwar era whose election to the presidency drew on his wartime record.

As the federal budget increased from $1 billion in 1916 to $19 billion in 1919, paying for the war became an ongoing political contest. Progressives supported increased taxation, and won modest victories in the application of income taxes and "excess profits" taxes on corporations; together these raised about one-third of the war's costs. Most, however, came from the $23 billion raised through the bond sales of the Liberty Loan program. As in other facets of war mobilization, bond sales depended on the arm-twisting of local volunteers, a mass media campaign, and substantial financial incentives for large-scale purchasers.

The Wilson administration mobilized its supporters and suppressed its opponents. In June 1917, the Espionage Act drastically restricted freedom of speech; in May 1918, amendments collectively known as the Sedition Act went even further. Thousands were arrested, most of them German Americans, pacifists, or radical leftists. Eugene V. Debs, leader of the Socialist Party and winner of over 900,000 votes in the 1912 election, was sentenced to ten years in prison for a speech he gave in Canton, Ohio, in June 1918; the radical Industrial Workers of the World was essentially crushed. German citizens in the United States lived under the Alien Enemies Act; about 6,000 were interned over the course of the war. States substantially amplified federal legislation; voluntary associations lent a hand as well. Various organizations challenged wartime restrictions, including several New York groups that coalesced into the American Civil Liberties Union after the war. They won few victories.

Wartime politics accelerated some political movements that had been on the national agenda for decades. Temporary measures meant to conserve grains and regulate soldiers' drinking prompted the adoption of Prohibition as national policy; in December 1917, Congress sent the Eighteenth Amendment, prohibiting the production or sale of alcohol, to the states; it was ratified in January 1919. Supporters of woman suffrage—who had been pressing the issue at the state level with little success—made a political breakthrough during the war. Millions of moderate suffragists in the National American Woman Suffrage Association called for the vote as a reward for wartime sacrifice; radicals in the smaller National Woman's Party marched before the White House to embarrass the Wilson administration. Bitter rivals, the two groups contributed separately to the passage of the Nineteenth Amendment, ratified in August 1920.

European immigrants found that war opened some avenues for inclusion and closed others. Jewish and Catholic groups participated prominently in war mobilization; elsewhere, concerns about ethnic diversity led to strictures against private schools and bilingual education and an early attempt to establish a federal Department of Education to regulate schools. Submarine warfare and European conscription all but closed off transatlantic migration after 1914, and the changing world situation heightened Americans' concerns with national identity. In February 1917, over Wilson's veto, Congress adopted legislation requiring a literacy test for migrants and effectively barring nearly all Asian migrants. Further restrictive acts in 1921 and 1924 shaped the demographic character of American society for two generations.

Despite the fact that African American organizations overwhelmingly supported the war effort, the black press and black political groups were subject to systematic surveillance. Individual black workers in the South—many of whom migrated to cities in the South or North—faced intimidation. Violence culminated in 1919, when some 70 African Americans were murdered in public lynchings and race riots rocked cities such as Washington, D.C.; Omaha, Nebraska; and Chicago, Illinois. Ideological shifts and the death of Booker T. Washington in 1915 opened the door for a new generation of leaders; the National Association for the Advancement of Colored People added thousands of names to its rolls in 1919, and Marcus Garvey began recruiting members to the Universal Negro Improvement Association, which established its first U.S. branches in 1917.

Postwar Politics

At the front, the American Expeditionary Force under General Pershing kept its distance; the United States insisted on being called an "associated" rather than an "allied" nation, lest its men be used as cannon fodder by the British and French generals whom Pershing disdained. American troops participated in large numbers in the Second Battle of the Marne in July 1918 and played a key role in the Battle of the Meuse-Argonne in September–October 1918, an extended assault that pushed back the Germans. Soon the armies of the Central Powers surrendered, and their governments collapsed; an armistice, signed on November 11, 1918, brought the fighting to an end. About 116,000 Americans had lost their lives, nearly half them from disease, especially the global influenza epidemic of 1918.

On May 27, 1918, President Wilson told congressional leaders that for the duration of the war, "politics is adjourned," but nothing was further from the truth. Wilson's wartime relations with Congress were never easy, and after the armistice, they worsened. Voters frustrated by Wilson's war policies and the increased cost of living targeted the Democrats in the 1918 midterm elections—all the more so because in October, Wilson had asked the American public to treat the election as a referendum on the war and vote for Democrats. The move backfired, and Republicans took decisive control of both houses.

The postwar Congress faced several pressing issues. Political and social unrest at home dominated the headlines in 1919. The Bolshevik Revolution of November 1917 had brought radical socialists to power in Russia; soon thereafter the Russians left the war, signing a treaty at Brest-Litovsk on March 3, 1918. Widespread belief in the United States that German agents had fomented the Bolshevik Revolution (Germany had given modest support to Vladimir Lenin) fanned fears of espionage and subversion in the United States. Conflict peaked during the Red Scare of 1919. A general strike in Seattle, Washington, in February and a shutdown of the steel industry in September galvanized popular support for drastic measures by states and the federal government aimed at radicals, unionists, and noncitizens. The Justice Department's Bureau of Investigation (later renamed the Federal Bureau of Investigation) expanded in size and power.

International issues also occupied Americans' minds, particularly the peace settlement. On January 8, 1918, Wilson had announced the famous Fourteen Points that he believed could guide postwar relations. Most of these 14 points were specific calls for territorial adjustment, reflecting Wilsonian principles of free trade, national self-determination, and freedom of the seas; the final point called for a "general association of nations." Wilson personally led the 1,300-person American delegation to the peace negotiations in Paris. The Treaty of Versailles finally signed on June 28, 1919, little resembled Wilson's proposals, but he hoped that a functioning League of Nations (as called for in Article Ten of the treaty) could hammer out any remaining details. Returning to Washington, Wilson urged the Senate on July 10, 1919, to adopt the treaty or "break the heart of the world."

In the Senate, supporters (mostly Democratic Wilson loyalists, now in the minority) had to sway the votes of senators who gathered in blocs of mild reservationists, strong reservationists, and "irreconcilables"—senators opposed to the treaty in any form. Wilson embarked on a national speaking tour to build support for the League of Nations but had to return to Washington after collapsing in Pueblo, Colorado, on September 25, 1919. Wilson suffered a stroke on October 2, 1919, and never fully recovered, and the nation entered a constitutional crisis that was carefully hidden from public view. First Lady Edith Wilson controlled access to the president and wielded extraordinary power together with Wilson's secretary Joseph Tumulty. (Vice President Thomas Marshall, widely regarded as a political nonentity, was excluded from decision making.) Wilson's illness meant that the League fight had lost its leader, and the treaty twice went down to defeat. On November 19, 1919, Senator Henry Cabot Lodge called for a vote on the treaty with some amendments, but Wilsonian Democrats and the irreconcilables joined together to block it. Then, on March 19, 1920, the Senate voted down Wilson's original version.

World War I substantially expanded the presence of the federal government in Americans' everyday lives, and brought the United States to leadership on the world stage. Wartime politics brought culminating victories for some progressive issues but an end to progressivism in general. The war divided the Democratic Party and united the Republicans, and set the course of American politics until the Great Depression a decade later.

See also foreign policy and domestic politics, 1865–1933; progressivism and the Progressive Era, 1890s–1920.

FURTHER READING

Capozzola, Christopher. *Uncle Sam Wants You: World War I and the Making of the Modern American Citizen*. New York: Oxford University Press, 2008.

Chambers, John Whiteclay. *To Raise an Army: The Draft Comes to Modern America*. New York: Free Press, 1987.

Cooper, John Milton. *Breaking the Heart of the World: Woodrow Wilson and the Fight for the League of Nations*. New York: Cambridge University Press, 2001.

Hawley, Ellis W. *The Great War and the Search for a Modern Order: A History of the American People and Their Institutions, 1917–1933*. New York: St. Martin's Press, 1979.

Kennedy, David M. *Over Here: The First World War and American Society*. New York: Oxford University Press, 1980.

Kornweibel, Theodore, Jr. *"Investigate Everything": Federal Efforts to Compel Black Loyalty during World War I*. Bloomington: Indiana University Press, 2002.

Link, Arthur S., et al., eds. *The Papers of Woodrow Wilson*. 69 vols. Princeton, NJ: Princeton University Press, 1966–94.

Livermore, Seward. *Politics Is Adjourned: Woodrow Wilson and the War Congress, 1916–1918*. Middletown, CT: Wesleyan University Press, 1966.

McCartin, Joseph A. *Labor's Great War: The Struggle for Industrial Democracy and the Origins of Modern American Labor Relations, 1912–1921*. Chapel Hill: University of North Carolina Press, 1997.

Murphy, Paul L. *World War I and the Origin of Civil Liberties in the United States*. New York: Norton, 1979.

CHRISTOPHER CAPOZZOLA

World War II

World War II had a powerful impact on American life. The most extensive conflict in human history changed political, diplomatic, economic, and social configurations and provided the framework for the postwar years. Forced to work closely with other members of the Grand Alliance—Great Britain and the Soviet Union—to defeat the Axis powers—Germany, Italy, and Japan—the United States became, in President Franklin D. Roosevelt's words, the "arsenal of democracy." In the process, the nation overcame the ravages of the Great Depression of the 1930s, became a dominant world power, and prepared for a new era of prosperity when the war was won.

Military victory was always the first priority. Roosevelt was willing to do whatever was necessary to defeat the nation's foes in Europe and Asia. He understood the need for American involvement in the struggle after Germany rolled into Poland in September 1939, even though formal entrance did not come until the surprise Japanese attack on the American fleet at Pearl Harbor, Hawai'i, on December 7, 1941. The United States had begun to prepare for war with a major increase in defense spending in 1940 but still found itself at a disadvantage with the destruction of ships and planes in Hawai'i. Japan's calculation that it could win the Pacific war before the United States could revive failed in the face of a huge mobilization effort. The tide turned at the Battle of Midway in mid-1942. American carrier-based planes defeated the enemy and dealt a major blow to Japanese military might. The United States continued its relentless campaign by attacking island after island in preparation for a final assault on the Japanese home islands.

Meanwhile, the United States was engaged in top-level diplomacy to craft a combined military strategy in Europe. Roosevelt met with British Prime Minister Winston Churchill even before American entrance into the war and settled on attacking the Axis first in North Africa through what Churchill called the "soft underbelly" rather than launching a frontal attack on Germany. Though Roosevelt initially favored direct engagement, and Joseph Stalin, autocratic leader of the Soviet Union, likewise sought action to reduce pressure on the Eastern front, Churchill, mindful of the huge losses in the trenches during World War I, refused to push ahead directly until he was assured of success. Roosevelt and Churchill met again at Casablanca, Morocco, in early 1943, after the successful North African campaign, and determined to move into Italy next. Other meetings—which now included Stalin, took place in Teheran, Iran, in late 1943; at Yalta, in the Crimea, in early 1945; and finally in Potsdam, Germany, in mid-1945. Those meetings called for the cross-channel invasion that began on D-Day, June 6, 1944, and culminated in the defeat of Germany a year later. They also confronted the larger political questions of the shape of the postwar world and determined on the future borders of Poland and Allied occupation zones for Germany.

Political considerations likewise played a part in bringing the war in the Pacific to an end. Atomic energy became an issue in this campaign. The Manhattan Project to create a new atomic bomb had its origins in a letter from the world-famous physicist Albert Einstein to Roosevelt in August 1939, suggesting that a rapid self-sustaining nuclear reaction splitting the atoms in the nucleus of uranium might unleash a tremendous amount of energy. Roosevelt was interested, and the committee he established grew into a huge operation, in time including 37 facilities in the United States and Canada. Significantly, the United States told Great Britain about the developmental effort but chose not to divulge that information to the Soviet Union, a decision that had important postwar implications. Meanwhile, Roosevelt assumed from the start that a bomb, if it could be created, was a weapon of war to be used when ready. But Roosevelt died in April 1945 before the bomb was available, and Harry S. Truman, his successor, had to make the decision about its use. As the end of the war approached, the U.S. Navy proposed a blockade of the Japanese islands, the U.S. Army prepared for a major invasion, and some American diplomats suggested that the Japanese might surrender if assured they could retain their emperor. Truman's decision was not to choose any of those actions but to let the process that was underway continue to its logical conclusion. So, two atomic bombs were dropped—on Hiroshima first, then Nagasaki—in August 1945. The war ended a week later.

A political commitment to focusing on military issues above all had significant consequences. Though some government officials understood the dimensions of Adolf Hitler's "Final Solution" to exterminate all Jews, a persistent anti-Semitism in the State Department prevented word from reaching those in authority who might have taken action to save some of the victims. Only toward the end of the war did the United States begin to deal effectively with refugees from Nazi Germany. Even so, Roosevelt was not ready to move aggressively in any way he deemed might compromise the military effort, and his single-minded concentration on what he felt were the major issues of the war made him less sensitive to the plight of people he might have helped.

Roosevelt also acquiesced in the internment of Japanese Americans on the West Coast of the United States. Tremendous hostility followed the Japanese attack on Pearl Harbor and led to demands that all Japanese—even those born in the United States and therefore American citizens—be evacuated, and eventually detained in ten camps in a number of Western states. In a debate at the top levels of government, FDR sided with Secretary of War Henry L. Stimson on the need to move out all West Coast Japanese to forestall sabotage and bolster national security. Executive Order 9066 gave military officials the power to "prescribe military areas . . . from which any or all persons may be excluded," and a new War Relocation Authority established the detention camps in which 110,000 Japanese Americans spent the war. It was a travesty based on the single-minded effort to win the war as quickly and expeditiously as possible.

Roosevelt used his political clout to embark on a major industrial mobilization effort. He understood that putting the nation on a war footing required enormous organizational adjustments. As Stimson observed, "If you are going to try to go to war, or to prepare for war, in a capitalist country, you have got to let business make money out of the process or business won't work." Business leaders who had incurred presidential wrath for resistance to New Deal programs now found themselves in demand to run the government agencies coordinating war production. Paid a dollar a year by the government, these businessmen remained on company payrolls and continued to be aware of the interests of their corporations. They helped devise different incentives to get business to cooperate, including the cost-plus-a-fixed-fee system, in which the government paid companies for all development and production costs for wartime goods, and then paid a percentage profit as well.

Political considerations surfaced as a huge network of wartime agencies developed to coordinate war pro-

U.S. sailors man boats at the side of the burning battleship USS *West Virginia* to fight the flames started by Japanese torpedoes and bombs at Pearl Harbor, Hawai'i, December 7, 1941. (Library of Congress)

duction. Military leaders assumed a dominant role and sometimes complicated the bureaucratic process. When mobilization failed to work effectively, Roosevelt, who never liked to dismantle administrative structures or fire people who worked for him, responded by creating one agency after another, with new ones often competing with old ones, to produce the weapons of war. That pattern let him play off assistants against one another and to retain final authority himself. "There is something to be said . . . for having a little conflict between agencies," he once said. "A little rivalry is stimulating, you know. It keeps everybody going to prove that he is a better fellow than the next man." And, of course, the final injunction was to "bring it to Poppa."

On the mobilization front, one agency also followed another. There was the National Defense Advisory Commission, then the Office of Production Management, then the War Production Board, and eventually the Office of War Mobilization. And there were comparable agencies dealing with employment, wage and price levels, and a host of other issues.

The system worked well. The economy, benefiting from a quadrupling of defense spending in 1940, quickly moved into high gear, and the corrosive unemployment, which had been the most prominent feature of the Great Depression, vanished. By the middle of 1945, the United States had produced 300,000 airplanes, 100,000 tanks and armored cars, and 80,000 landing craft, along with 15 million guns and 41 billion rounds of ammunition.

Always the astute politician, Roosevelt recognized that propaganda could help mobilize support for the war. Yet he was concerned with the excessive exuberance of the Committee on Public Information, which had been the propaganda agency during World War I, and he was intent on keeping control in his own hands. To that end, he established a new Office of War Information to help get the message about America's role in the war to people at home and abroad. Made up, in characteristic fashion, of a series of predecessor agencies, such as the Office of Facts and Figures and the Foreign Information Service, the Office of War Information sought to broadcast and illuminate the nation's aims in the war. It portrayed the liberal terms of Roosevelt's "four freedoms"—freedom of speech, freedom of worship, freedom from want, and freedom from fear—and the Atlantic Charter, endorsing the self-determination of nations, equal trading rights, and a system of general security agreed upon by Roosevelt and Churchill.

For groups suffering discrimination in the past, the war brought lasting social and economic gains that changed the political landscape. For women and African Americans, in particular, the war was beneficial and provided a model for future change.

Women were clearly second-class citizens at the start of the struggle. Many occupations were closed to them, and in the positions they did find, they usually earned less than men. The huge productive effort gave women the chance to do industrial work, especially as military service took men overseas. "Rosie the Riveter" posters encouraged women to work in the factories, and they did. At the peak of the industrial effort, women made up 36 percent of the civilian workforce. At the same time, demographic patterns changed. In the past, working women had usually been single and young. Now an increasing number of married women found their way into the workforce, and by the end of the war, half of all female workers were over 35.

African Americans likewise benefited from wartime needs. When the war began, their unemployment rate was double that of whites, and they found themselves concentrated in unskilled jobs. They faced constant slights. One black American soldier who was turned away from a lunchroom in Salina, Kansas, watched German prisoners of war served at the same counter. "This was really happening," he said. "It was no jive talk. The people of Salina would serve these enemy soldiers and turn away black American G.I.s."

Blacks pushed for equal opportunities. The *Pittsburgh Courier*, an influential African American newspaper, proclaimed a "Double V" campaign—V for victory in the war overseas and V for victory in the campaign for equality at home. In 1941, A. Philip Randolph, head of the Brotherhood of Sleeping Car Porters, pushed for a massive march on Washington, D.C., to dramatize the cause of equal rights, and only called it off when Roosevelt signed Executive Order 8802 creating the Fair Employment Practices Committee to investigate complaints about discrimination and take appropriate action. Meanwhile, black airmen finally got the chance to fly, and black students picketed segregated restaurants in Washington, D.C., thus foreshadowing the civil rights movement of the 1950s and 1960s.

The world of electoral politics reflected the transformations taking place at home. The political world has always mirrored major issues of the day, and electoral contests have long helped to articulate national values and views. The major wartime elections—presidential and congressional—clearly reflected wartime concerns.

The war brought a change of focus. Roosevelt recognized that New Deal reform had run its course by the time the war began. He summed up the transformation in a press conference at the end of 1943. The New Deal had come about when the patient—the United States—was suffering from a grave internal disorder. But then, at Pearl Harbor, the patient had been in a terrible external crash: "Old Dr. New Deal didn't know 'nothing' about legs and arms. He knew a great deal about internal medicine, but nothing about surgery. So he got his partner, who was an orthopedic surgeon, Dr. Win-the-War, to take care of this fellow who had been in this bad accident." At the end of the 1930s, Roosevelt began to encounter a coalition of Republicans and conservative Democrats who resisted further liberal initiatives. That congressional coalition remained intact for the duration of the war, dismantling remaining New Deal programs, but providing the president with full support for the military struggle. Democrats retained congressional majorities in both houses, but Roosevelt had to back away from programs not directly related to the war.

In 1940 Roosevelt sought an unprecedented third presidential term. Recognizing that American involvement in the European war was likely, he felt he had no choice but to run. He faced Republican Wendell Willkie, an Indiana business executive who argued that the New Deal had gone too far. When Willkie asserted that Roosevelt would lead the nation into war, the president declared, "I have said this before, but I shall say it again and again and again: Your boys are not going to be sent into any foreign wars." Reminded that an attack might leave him unable to keep his promise, he retorted that in case of an attack, it would no longer be a foreign war. Roosevelt won nearly 55 percent of the popular vote and a 449 to 82 victory in the Electoral College.

Four years later, Roosevelt chose to run again. The war was still underway, and while the president was politically strong, he was now ailing physically. He suffered from heart disease and appeared worn out. Because of the precarious state of his health, the choice of a running mate became increasingly important, and the Democratic Convention nominated Senator Harry Truman as the vice presidential candidate. This time, Roosevelt ran against Republican Thomas E. Dewey, governor of New York. Fighting back personal attacks, Roosevelt rose to the occasion and was victorious again. He won about 54 percent of the popular vote, with a 432-to-99 electoral vote margin.

World War II changed the course of U.S. history. It enlisted the support of the American people, on the battlefield and in factories back home. It forced the nation to work closely with its allies to defeat a monumental military threat. And in the process, it changed political configurations at home and abroad as the United States faced the postwar world.

See also foreign policy and domestic politics since 1933; New Deal Era, 1932–52.

FURTHER READING

Adams, Michael C. C. *The Best War Ever: America and World War II.* Baltimore, MD: Johns Hopkins University Press, 1994.

Blum, John Morton. *V Was for Victory: Politics and American Culture During World War II.* New York: Harcourt Brace Jovanovich, 1976.

Jeffries, John W. *Wartime America: The World War II Home Front.* Chicago: Ivan R. Dee, 1996.

O'Neill, William L. *A Democracy at War: America's Fight at Home and Abroad in World War II.* New York: Free Press, 1993.

Polenberg, Richard. *War and Society: The United States, 1941–1945.* New York: Lippincott, 1972.

Winkler, Allan M. *Franklin D. Roosevelt and the Making of Modern America.* New York: Pearson/Longman, 2006.

———. *Home Front U.S.A.: America during World War II.* 2nd ed. Wheeling, IL: Harlan Davidson, 2000.

———. *The Politics of Propaganda: The Office of War Information, 1942–1945.* New Haven, CT: Yale University Press, 1978.

ALLAN M. WINKLER

Appendix I: Documents

The Declaration of Independence

IN CONGRESS, July 4, 1776.

The unanimous Declaration of the thirteen united States of America, When in the Course of human events, it becomes necessary for one people to dissolve the political bands which have connected them with another, and to assume among the powers of the earth, the separate and equal station to which the Laws of Nature and of Nature's God entitle them, a decent respect to the opinions of mankind requires that they should declare the causes which impel them to the separation.

We hold these truths to be self-evident, that all men are created equal, that they are endowed by their Creator with certain unalienable Rights, that among these are Life, Liberty and the pursuit of Happiness.—That to secure these rights, Governments are instituted among Men, deriving their just powers from the consent of the governed,—That whenever any Form of Government becomes destructive of these ends, it is the Right of the People to alter or to abolish it, and to institute new Government, laying its foundation on such principles and organizing its powers in such form, as to them shall seem most likely to effect their Safety and Happiness. Prudence, indeed, will dictate that Governments long established should not be changed for light and transient causes; and accordingly all experience hath shewn, that mankind are more disposed to suffer, while evils are sufferable, than to right themselves by abolishing the forms to which they are accustomed. But when a long train of abuses and usurpations, pursuing invariably the same Object evinces a design to reduce them under absolute Despotism, it is their right, it is their duty, to throw off such Government, and to provide new Guards for their future security.—Such has been the patient sufferance of these Colonies; and such is now the necessity which constrains them to alter their former Systems of Government. The history of the present King of Great Britain is a history of repeated injuries and usurpations, all having in direct object the establishment of an absolute Tyranny over these States. To prove this, let Facts be submitted to a candid world.

He has refused his Assent to Laws, the most wholesome and necessary for the public good.

He has forbidden his Governors to pass Laws of immediate and pressing importance, unless suspended in their operation till his Assent should be obtained; and when so suspended, he has utterly neglected to attend to them.

He has refused to pass other Laws for the accommodation of large districts of people, unless those people would relinquish the right of Representation in the Legislature, a right inestimable to them and formidable to tyrants only.

He has called together legislative bodies at places unusual, uncomfortable, and distant from the depository of their public Records, for the sole purpose of fatiguing them into compliance with his measures.

He has dissolved Representative Houses repeatedly, for opposing with manly firmness his invasions on the rights of the people.

He has refused for a long time, after such dissolutions, to cause others to be elected; whereby the Legislative powers, incapable of Annihilation, have returned to the People at large for their exercise; the State remaining in the mean time exposed to all the dangers of invasion from without, and convulsions within.

He has endeavoured to prevent the population of these States; for that purpose obstructing the Laws for Naturalization of Foreigners; refusing to pass others to encourage their migrations hither, and raising the conditions of new Appropriations of Lands.

He has obstructed the Administration of Justice, by refusing his Assent to Laws for establishing Judiciary powers.

He has made Judges dependent on his Will alone, for the tenure of their offices, and the amount and payment of their salaries.

He has erected a multitude of New Offices, and sent hither swarms of Officers to harrass our people, and eat out their substance.

He has kept among us, in times of peace, Standing Armies without the Consent of our legislatures.

He has affected to render the Military independent of and superior to the Civil power.

He has combined with others to subject us to a jurisdiction foreign to our constitution, and unacknowledged by our laws; giving his Assent to their Acts of pretended Legislation:

For Quartering large bodies of armed troops among us:

For protecting them, by a mock Trial, from punishment for any Murders which they should commit on the Inhabitants of these States:

For cutting off our Trade with all parts of the world:

For imposing Taxes on us without our Consent:

For depriving us in many cases, of the benefits of Trial by Jury:

For transporting us beyond Seas to be tried for pretended offences

For abolishing the free System of English Laws in a neighbouring Province, establishing therein an Arbitrary government, and enlarging its Boundaries so as to render it at once an example and fit instrument for introducing the same absolute rule into these Colonies:

For taking away our Charters, abolishing our most valuable Laws, and altering fundamentally the Forms of our Governments:

For suspending our own Legislatures, and declaring themselves invested with power to legislate for us in all cases whatsoever.

He has abdicated Government here, by declaring us out of his Protection and waging War against us.

He has plundered our seas, ravaged our Coasts, burnt our towns, and destroyed the lives of our people.

He is at this time transporting large Armies of foreign Mercenaries to compleat the works of death, desolation and tyranny, already begun with circumstances of Cruelty & perfidy scarcely paralleled in the most barbarous ages, and totally unworthy the Head of a civilized nation.

He has constrained our fellow Citizens taken Captive on the high Seas to bear Arms against their Country, to become the executioners of their friends and Brethren, or to fall themselves by their Hands.

He has excited domestic insurrections amongst us, and has endeavoured to bring on the inhabitants of our frontiers, the merciless Indian Savages, whose known rule of warfare, is an undistinguished destruction of all ages, sexes and conditions.

In every stage of these Oppressions We have Petitioned for Redress in the most humble terms: Our repeated Petitions have been answered only by repeated injury. A Prince whose character is thus marked by every act which may define a Tyrant, is unfit to be the ruler of a free people.

Nor have We been wanting in attentions to our British brethren. We have warned them from time to time of attempts by their legislature to extend an unwarrantable jurisdiction over us. We have reminded them of the circumstances of our emigration and settlement here. We have appealed to their native justice and magnanimity, and we have conjured them by the ties of our common kindred to disavow these usurpations, which, would inevitably interrupt our connections and correspondence. They too have been deaf to the voice of justice and of consanguinity. We must, therefore, acquiesce in the necessity, which denounces our Separation, and hold them, as we hold the rest of mankind, Enemies in War, in Peace Friends.

We, therefore, the Representatives of the united States of America, in General Congress, Assembled, appealing to the Supreme Judge of the world for the rectitude of our intentions, do, in the Name, and by Authority of the good People of these Colonies, solemnly publish and declare, That these united Colonies are, and of Right ought to be Free and Independent States; that they are Absolved from all Allegiance to the British Crown, and that all political connection between them and the State of Great Britain, is and ought to be totally dissolved; and that as Free and Independent States, they have full Power to levy War, conclude Peace, contract Alliances, establish Commerce, and to do all other Acts and Things which Independent States may of right do.—And for the support of this Declaration, with a firm reliance on the protection of divine Providence, we mutually pledge to each other our Lives, our Fortunes and our sacred Honor.

The 56 signatures on the Declaration appear in the positions indicated:

COLUMN 1
Georgia:
Button Gwinnett
Lyman Hall
George Walton

COLUMN 2
North Carolina:
William Hooper
Joseph Hewes
John Penn
South Carolina:
Edward Rutledge
Thomas Heyward Jr.
Thomas Lynch Jr.
Arthur Middleton

COLUMN 3
Massachusetts:
John Hancock
Maryland:
Samuel Chase
William Paca
Thomas Stone
Charles Carroll of Carrollton
Virginia:
George Wythe
Richard Henry Lee
Thomas Jefferson
Benjamin Harrison
Thomas Nelson Jr.
Francis Lightfoot Lee
Carter Braxton

COLUMN 4
Pennsylvania:
Robert Morris
Benjamin Rush
Benjamin Franklin
John Morton
George Clymer
James Smith
George Taylor
James Wilson
George Ross
Delaware:
Caesar Rodney
George Read
Thomas McKean

COLUMN 5
New York:
William Floyd
Philip Livingston
Francis Lewis
Lewis Morris
New Jersey:
Richard Stockton
John Witherspoon
Francis Hopkinson
John Hart
Abraham Clark

COLUMN 6
New Hampshire:
Josiah Bartlett
William Whipple
Massachusetts:
Samuel Adams
John Adams
Robert Treat Paine
Elbridge Gerry
Rhode Island:
Stephen Hopkins
William Ellery
Connecticut:
Roger Sherman
Samuel Huntington
William Williams
Oliver Wolcott
New Hampshire:
Matthew Thornton

The Constitution of the United States

We the People of the United States, in Order to form a more perfect Union, establish Justice, insure domestic Tranquility, provide for the common defence, promote the general Welfare, and secure the Blessings of Liberty to ourselves and our Posterity, do ordain and establish this Constitution for the United States of America.

ARTICLE. I.

SECTION. 1.

All legislative Powers herein granted shall be vested in a Congress of the United States, which shall consist of a Senate and House of Representatives.

SECTION. 2.

The House of Representatives shall be composed of Members chosen every second Year by the People of the several States, and the Electors in each State shall have the Qualifications requisite for Electors of the most numerous Branch of the State Legislature.

No Person shall be a Representative who shall not have attained to the Age of twenty five Years, and been seven Years a Citizen of the United States, and who shall not, when elected, be an Inhabitant of that State in which he shall be chosen.

Representatives and direct Taxes shall be apportioned among the several States which may be included within this Union, according to their respective Numbers, which shall be determined by adding to the whole Number of free Persons, including those bound to Service for a Term of Years, and excluding Indians not taxed, three fifths of all other Persons. The actual Enumeration shall be made within three Years after the first Meeting of the Congress of the United States, and within every subsequent Term of ten Years, in such Manner as they shall by Law direct. The Number of Representatives shall not exceed one for every thirty Thousand, but each State shall have at Least one Representative; and until such enumeration shall be made, the State of New Hampshire shall be entitled to chuse three, Massachusetts eight, Rhode-Island and Providence Plantations one, Connecticut five, New-York six, New Jersey four, Pennsylvania eight, Delaware one, Maryland six, Virginia ten, North Carolina five, South Carolina five, and Georgia three.

When vacancies happen in the Representation from any State, the Executive Authority thereof shall issue Writs of Election to fill such Vacancies.

The House of Representatives shall chuse their Speaker and other Officers; and shall have the sole Power of Impeachment.

SECTION. 3.

The Senate of the United States shall be composed of two Senators from each State, chosen by the Legislature thereof for six Years; and each Senator shall have one Vote.

Immediately after they shall be assembled in Consequence of the first Election, they shall be divided as equally as may be into three Classes. The Seats of the Senators of the first Class shall be vacated at the Expiration of the second Year, of the second Class at the Expiration of the fourth Year, and of the third Class at the Expiration of the sixth Year, so that one third may be chosen every second Year; and if Vacancies happen by Resignation, or otherwise, during the Recess of the Legislature of any State, the Executive thereof may make temporary Appointments until the next Meeting of the Legislature, which shall then fill such Vacancies.

No Person shall be a Senator who shall not have attained to the Age of thirty Years, and been nine Years a Citizen of the United States, and who shall not, when elected, be an Inhabitant of that State for which he shall be chosen.

The Vice President of the United States shall be President of the Senate, but shall have no Vote, unless they be equally divided.

The Senate shall chuse their other Officers, and also a President pro tempore, in the Absence of the Vice President, or when he shall exercise the Office of President of the United States.

The Senate shall have the sole Power to try all Impeachments. When sitting for that Purpose, they shall be on Oath or Affirmation. When the President of the United States is tried, the Chief Justice shall preside: And no Person shall be convicted without the Concurrence of two thirds of the Members present.

Judgment in Cases of Impeachment shall not extend further than to removal from Office, and disqualification to hold and enjoy any Office of honor, Trust or Profit under the United States: but the Party convicted shall nevertheless be liable and subject to Indictment, Trial, Judgment and Punishment, according to Law.

SECTION. 4.

The Times, Places and Manner of holding Elections for Senators and Representatives, shall be prescribed in each State by the Legislature thereof; but the Congress may at any time by Law make or alter such Regulations, except as to the Places of chusing Senators.

The Congress shall assemble at least once in every Year, and such Meeting shall be on the first Monday in December, unless they shall by Law appoint a different Day.

SECTION. 5.

Each House shall be the Judge of the Elections, Returns and Qualifications of its own Members, and a Majority of each shall constitute a Quorum to do Business; but a smaller Number may adjourn from day to day, and may be authorized to compel the Attendance of absent Members, in such Manner, and under such Penalties as each House may provide.

Each House may determine the Rules of its Proceedings, punish its Members for disorderly Behaviour, and, with the Concurrence of two thirds, expel a Member.

Each House shall keep a Journal of its Proceedings, and from time to time publish the same, excepting such Parts as may in their Judgment require Secrecy; and the Yeas and Nays of the Members of either House on any question shall, at the Desire of one fifth of those Present, be entered on the Journal.

Neither House, during the Session of Congress, shall, without the Consent of the other, adjourn for more than three days, nor to any other Place than that in which the two Houses shall be sitting.

SECTION. 6.

The Senators and Representatives shall receive a Compensation for their Services, to be ascertained by Law, and paid out of the Treasury of the United States. They shall in all Cases, except Treason, Felony and Breach of the Peace, be privileged from Arrest during their Attendance at the Session of their respective Houses, and in going to and returning from the same; and for any Speech or Debate in either House, they shall not be questioned in any other Place.

No Senator or Representative shall, during the Time for which he was elected, be appointed to any civil Office under the Authority of the United States, which shall have been created, or the Emoluments whereof shall have been encreased during such time; and no Person holding any Office under the United States, shall be a Member of either House during his Continuance in Office.

SECTION. 7.

All Bills for raising Revenue shall originate in the House of Representatives; but the Senate may propose or concur with Amendments as on other Bills.

Every Bill which shall have passed the House of Representatives and the Senate, shall, before it become a Law, be presented to the President of the United States: If he approve he shall sign it, but if not he shall return it, with his Objections to that House in which it shall have originated, who shall enter the Objections at large on their Journal, and proceed to reconsider it. If after such Reconsideration two thirds of that House shall agree to pass the Bill, it shall be sent, together with the Objections, to the other House, by which it shall likewise be reconsidered, and if approved by two thirds of that House, it shall become a Law. But in all such Cases the Votes of both Houses shall be determined by Yeas and Nays, and the Names of the Persons voting for and against the Bill shall be entered on the Journal of each House respectively. If any Bill shall not be returned by the President within ten Days (Sundays excepted) after it shall have been presented to him, the Same shall be a Law, in like Manner as if he had signed it, unless the Congress by their Adjournment prevent its Return, in which Case it shall not be a Law.

Every Order, Resolution, or Vote to which the Concurrence of the Senate and House of Representatives may be necessary (except on a question of Adjournment) shall be presented to the President of the United States; and before the Same shall take Effect, shall be approved by him, or being disapproved by him, shall be repassed by two thirds of the Senate and House of Representatives, according to the Rules and Limitations prescribed in the Case of a Bill.

SECTION. 8.

The Congress shall have Power To lay and collect Taxes, Duties, Imposts and Excises, to pay the Debts and provide for the common Defence and general Welfare of the United States; but all Duties, Imposts and Excises shall be uniform throughout the United States;

To borrow Money on the credit of the United States;

To regulate Commerce with foreign Nations, and among the several States, and with the Indian Tribes;

To establish an uniform Rule of Naturalization, and uniform Laws on the subject of Bankruptcies throughout the United States;

To coin Money, regulate the Value thereof, and of foreign Coin, and fix the Standard of Weights and Measures;

To provide for the Punishment of counterfeiting the Securities and current Coin of the United States;

To establish Post Offices and post Roads;

To promote the Progress of Science and useful Arts, by securing for limited Times to Authors and Inventors the exclusive Right to their respective Writings and Discoveries;

To constitute Tribunals inferior to the supreme Court;

To define and punish Piracies and Felonies committed on the high Seas, and Offences against the Law of Nations;

To declare War, grant Letters of Marque and Reprisal, and make Rules concerning Captures on Land and Water;

To raise and support Armies, but no Appropriation of Money to that Use shall be for a longer Term than two Years;

To provide and maintain a Navy;

To make Rules for the Government and Regulation of the land and naval Forces;

To provide for calling forth the Militia to execute the Laws of the Union, suppress Insurrections and repel Invasions;

To provide for organizing, arming, and disciplining, the Militia, and for governing such Part of them as may be employed in the Service of the United States, reserving to the States respectively, the Appointment of the Officers, and the Authority of training the Militia according to the discipline prescribed by Congress;

To exercise exclusive Legislation in all Cases whatsoever, over such District (not exceeding ten Miles square) as may, by Cession of particular States, and the Acceptance of Congress, become the Seat of the Government of the United States, and to exercise like Authority over all Places purchased by the Consent of the Legislature of the State in which the Same shall be, for the Erection of Forts, Magazines, Arsenals, dock-Yards, and other needful Buildings;—And,

To make all Laws which shall be necessary and proper for carrying into Execution the foregoing Powers, and all other Powers vested by this Constitution in the Government of the United States, or in any Department or Officer thereof.

SECTION. 9.

The Migration or Importation of such Persons as any of the States now existing shall think proper to admit, shall not be prohibited by the Congress prior to the Year one thousand eight hundred and eight, but a Tax or duty may be imposed on such Importation, not exceeding ten dollars for each Person.

The Privilege of the Writ of Habeas Corpus shall not be suspended, unless when in Cases of Rebellion or Invasion the public Safety may require it.

No Bill of Attainder or ex post facto Law shall be passed.

No Capitation, or other direct, Tax shall be laid, unless in Proportion to the Census or enumeration herein before directed to be taken.

No Tax or Duty shall be laid on Articles exported from any State.

No Preference shall be given by any Regulation of Commerce or Revenue to the Ports of one State over those of another; nor shall Vessels bound to, or from, one State, be obliged to enter, clear, or pay Duties in another.

No Money shall be drawn from the Treasury, but in Consequence of Appropriations made by Law; and a regular Statement and Account of the Receipts and Expenditures of all public Money shall be published from time to time.

No Title of Nobility shall be granted by the United States: And no Person holding any Office of Profit or Trust under them, shall, without the Consent of the Congress, accept of any present, Emolument, Office, or Title, of any kind whatever, from any King, Prince, or foreign State.

SECTION. 10.

No State shall enter into any Treaty, Alliance, or Confederation; grant Letters of Marque and Reprisal; coin Money; emit Bills of Credit; make any Thing but gold and silver Coin a Tender in Payment of Debts; pass any Bill of Attainder, ex post facto Law, or Law impairing the Obligation of Contracts, or grant any Title of Nobility.

No State shall, without the Consent of the Congress, lay any Imposts or Duties on Imports or Exports, except what may be absolutely necessary for executing its inspection Laws; and the net Produce of all Duties and Imposts, laid by any State on Imports or Exports, shall be for the Use of the Treasury of the United States; and all such Laws shall be subject to the Revision and Controul of the Congress.

No State shall, without the Consent of Congress, lay any Duty of Tonnage, keep Troops, or Ships of War in time of Peace, enter into any Agreement or Compact with another State, or with a foreign Power, or engage in War, unless actually invaded, or in such imminent Danger as will not admit of delay.

ARTICLE. II.

SECTION. 1.

The executive Power shall be vested in a President of the United States of America. He shall hold his Office during the Term of four Years, and, together with the Vice President, chosen for the same Term, be elected, as follows:

Each State shall appoint, in such Manner as the Legislature thereof may direct, a Number of Electors, equal to the whole Number of Senators and Representatives to which the State may be entitled in the Congress: but no Senator or Representative, or Person holding an Office of Trust or Profit under the United States, shall be appointed an Elector.

The Electors shall meet in their respective States, and vote by Ballot for two Persons, of whom one at least shall not be an Inhabitant of the same State with themselves. And they shall make a List of all the Persons voted for, and of the Number of Votes for each; which List they shall sign and certify, and transmit sealed to the Seat of the Government of the United States, directed to the President of the Senate. The President of the Senate shall, in the Presence of the Senate and House of Representatives, open all the Certificates, and the Votes shall then be counted. The Person having the greatest Number of Votes shall be the President, if such Number be a Majority of the whole Number of Electors appointed; and if there be more than one who have such Majority, and have an equal Number of Votes, then the House of Representatives shall immediately chuse by Ballot one of them for President; and if no Person have a Majority, then from the five highest on the List the said House shall in like Manner chuse the President. But in chusing the President, the Votes shall be taken by States, the Representation from each State having one Vote; A quorum for this purpose shall consist of a Member or Members from two thirds of the States, and a Majority of all the States shall be necessary to a Choice. In every Case, after the Choice of the President, the Person having the greatest Number of Votes of the Electors shall be the Vice President. But if there should remain two or more who have equal Votes, the Senate shall chuse from them by Ballot the Vice President.

The Congress may determine the Time of chusing the Electors, and the Day on which they shall give their Votes; which Day shall be the same throughout the United States.

No Person except a natural born Citizen, or a Citizen of the United States, at the time of the Adoption of this Constitution, shall be eligible to the Office of President; neither shall any Person be eligible to that Office who shall not have attained to the Age of thirty five Years, and been fourteen Years a Resident within the United States.

In Case of the Removal of the President from Office, or of his Death, Resignation, or Inability to discharge the Powers and Duties of the said Office, the Same shall devolve on the Vice President, and the Congress may by Law provide for the Case of Removal, Death, Resignation or Inability, both of the President and Vice President, declaring what Officer shall then act as President, and such Officer shall act accordingly, until the Disability be removed, or a President shall be elected.

The President shall, at stated Times, receive for his Services, a Compensation, which shall neither be increased nor diminished during the Period for which he shall have been elected, and he shall not receive within that Period any other Emolument from the United States, or any of them.

Before he enter on the Execution of his Office, he shall take the following Oath or Affirmation:—"I do solemnly swear (or affirm) that I will faithfully execute the Office of President of the United States, and will to the best of my Ability, preserve, protect and defend the Constitution of the United States."

SECTION. 2.

The President shall be Commander in Chief of the Army and Navy of the United States, and of the Militia of the several States, when called into the actual Service of the United States; he may require the Opinion, in writing, of the principal Officer in each of the executive Departments, upon any Subject relating to the Duties of their respective Offices, and he shall have Power to grant Reprieves and Pardons for Offences against the United States, except in Cases of Impeachment.

He shall have Power, by and with the Advice and Consent of the Senate, to make Treaties, provided two thirds of the Senators present concur; and he shall nominate, and by and with the Advice and Consent of the Senate, shall appoint Ambassadors, other public Ministers and Consuls, Judges of the supreme Court, and all other Officers of the United States, whose Appointments are not herein otherwise provided for, and which shall be established by Law: but the Congress may by Law vest the Appointment of such inferior Officers, as they think proper, in the President alone, in the Courts of Law, or in the Heads of Departments.

The President shall have Power to fill up all Vacancies that may happen during the Recess of the Senate, by granting Commissions which shall expire at the End of their next Session.

SECTION. 3.
He shall from time to time give to the Congress Information of the State of the Union, and recommend to their Consideration such Measures as he shall judge necessary and expedient; he may, on extraordinary Occasions, convene both Houses, or either of them, and in Case of Disagreement between them, with Respect to the Time of Adjournment, he may adjourn them to such Time as he shall think proper; he shall receive Ambassadors and other public Ministers; he shall take Care that the Laws be faithfully executed, and shall Commission all the Officers of the United States.

SECTION. 4.
The President, Vice President and all civil Officers of the United States, shall be removed from Office on Impeachment for, and Conviction of, Treason, Bribery, or other high Crimes and Misdemeanors.

ARTICLE. III.

SECTION. 1.
The judicial Power of the United States shall be vested in one supreme Court, and in such inferior Courts as the Congress may from time to time ordain and establish. The Judges, both of the supreme and inferior Courts, shall hold their Offices during good Behaviour, and shall, at stated Times, receive for their Services a Compensation, which shall not be diminished during their Continuance in Office.

SECTION. 2.
The judicial Power shall extend to all Cases, in Law and Equity, arising under this Constitution, the Laws of the United States, and Treaties made, or which shall be made, under their Authority;—to all Cases affecting Ambassadors, other public Ministers and Consuls;—to all Cases of admiralty and maritime Jurisdiction;—to Controversies to which the United States shall be a Party;—to Controversies between two or more States;—between a State and Citizens of another State;—between Citizens of different States;—between Citizens of the same State claiming Lands under Grants of different States, and between a State, or the Citizens thereof, and foreign States, Citizens or Subjects.

In all Cases affecting Ambassadors, other public Ministers and Consuls, and those in which a State shall be Party, the supreme Court shall have original Jurisdiction. In all the other Cases before mentioned, the supreme Court shall have appellate Jurisdiction, both as to Law and Fact, with such Exceptions, and under such Regulations as the Congress shall make.

The Trial of all Crimes, except in Cases of Impeachment, shall be by Jury; and such Trial shall be held in the State where the said Crimes shall have been committed; but when not committed within any State, the Trial shall be at such Place or Places as the Congress may by Law have directed.

SECTION. 3.
Treason against the United States, shall consist only in levying War against them, or in adhering to their Enemies, giving them Aid and Comfort. No Person shall be convicted of Treason unless on the Testimony of two Witnesses to the same overt Act, or on Confession in open Court.

The Congress shall have Power to declare the Punishment of Treason, but no Attainder of Treason shall work Corruption of Blood, or Forfeiture except during the Life of the Person attainted.

ARTICLE. IV.

SECTION. 1.
Full Faith and Credit shall be given in each State to the public Acts, Records, and judicial Proceedings of every other State. And the Congress may by general Laws prescribe the Manner in which such Acts, Records and Proceedings shall be proved, and the Effect thereof.

SECTION. 2.
The Citizens of each State shall be entitled to all Privileges and Immunities of Citizens in the several States.

A Person charged in any State with Treason, Felony, or other Crime, who shall flee from Justice, and be found in another State, shall on Demand of the executive Authority of the State from which he fled, be delivered up, to be removed to the State having Jurisdiction of the Crime.

No Person held to Service or Labour in one State, under the Laws thereof, escaping into another, shall, in Consequence of any Law or Regulation therein, be discharged from such Service or Labour, but shall be delivered up on Claim of the Party to whom such Service or Labour may be due.

SECTION. 3.

New States may be admitted by the Congress into this Union; but no new State shall be formed or erected within the Jurisdiction of any other State; nor any State be formed by the Junction of two or more States, or Parts of States, without the Consent of the Legislatures of the States concerned as well as of the Congress.

The Congress shall have Power to dispose of and make all needful Rules and Regulations respecting the Territory or other Property belonging to the United States; and nothing in this Constitution shall be so construed as to Prejudice any Claims of the United States, or of any particular State.

SECTION. 4.

The United States shall guarantee to every State in this Union a Republican Form of Government, and shall protect each of them against Invasion; and on Application of the Legislature, or of the Executive (when the Legislature cannot be convened), against domestic Violence.

ARTICLE. V.

The Congress, whenever two thirds of both Houses shall deem it necessary, shall propose Amendments to this Constitution, or, on the Application of the Legislatures of two thirds of the several States, shall call a Convention for proposing Amendments, which, in either Case, shall be valid to all Intents and Purposes, as Part of this Constitution, when ratified by the Legislatures of three fourths of the several States, or by Conventions in three fourths thereof, as the one or the other Mode of Ratification may be proposed by the Congress; Provided that no Amendment which may be made prior to the Year One thousand eight hundred and eight shall in any Manner affect the first and fourth Clauses in the Ninth Section of the first Article; and that no State, without its Consent, shall be deprived of its equal Suffrage in the Senate.

ARTICLE. VI.

All Debts contracted and Engagements entered into, before the Adoption of this Constitution, shall be as valid against the United States under this Constitution, as under the Confederation.

This Constitution, and the Laws of the United States which shall be made in Pursuance thereof; and all Treaties made, or which shall be made, under the Authority of the United States, shall be the supreme Law of the Land; and the Judges in every State shall be bound thereby, any Thing in the Constitution or Laws of any State to the Contrary notwithstanding.

The Senators and Representatives before mentioned, and the Members of the several State Legislatures, and all executive and judicial Officers, both of the United States and of the several States, shall be bound by Oath or Affirmation, to support this Constitution; but no religious Test shall ever be required as a Qualification to any Office or public Trust under the United States.

ARTICLE. VII.

The Ratification of the Conventions of nine States, shall be sufficient for the Establishment of this Constitution between the States so ratifying the Same.

The Word, "the," being interlined between the seventh and eighth Lines of the first Page, the Word "Thirty" being partly written on an Erazure in the fifteenth Line of the first Page, The Words "is tried" being interlined between the thirty second and thirty third Lines of the first Page and the Word "the" being interlined between the forty third and forty fourth Lines of the second Page.

Attest William Jackson Secretary

Done in Convention by the Unanimous Consent of the States present the Seventeenth Day of September in the Year of our Lord one thousand seven hundred and Eighty seven and of the Independence of the United States of America the Twelfth In witness whereof We have hereunto subscribed our Names,

G°. Washington
Presidt and deputy from Virginia

Delaware
Geo: Read
Gunning Bedford jun
John Dickinson
Richard Bassett
Jaco: Broom
Maryland
James McHenry
Dan of St Thos. Jenifer
Danl. Carroll
Virginia
John Blair
James Madison Jr.

North Carolina
Wm. Blount
Richd. Dobbs Spaight
Hu Williamson
South Carolina
J. Rutledge
Charles Cotesworth Pinckney
Charles Pinckney
Pierce Butler
Georgia
William Few
Abr Baldwin
New Hampshire
John Langdon
Nicholas Gilman
Massachusetts
Nathaniel Gorham
Rufus King
Connecticut
Wm. Saml. Johnson
Roger Sherman
New York
Alexander Hamilton
New Jersey
Wil: Livingston
David Brearley
Wm. Paterson
Jona: Dayton
Pennsylvania
B Franklin
Thomas Mifflin
Robt. Morris
Geo. Clymer
Thos. FitzSimons
Jared Ingersoll
James Wilson
Gouv Morris

The Bill of Rights

Congress of the United States
begun and held at the City of New-York, on
Wednesday the fourth of March, one thousand seven hundred and eighty nine.

THE Conventions of a number of the States, having at the time of their adopting the Constitution, expressed a desire, in order to prevent misconstruction or abuse of its powers, that further declaratory and restrictive clauses should be added: And as extending the ground of public confidence in the Government, will best ensure the beneficent ends of its institution.

RESOLVED by the Senate and House of Representatives of the United States of America, in Congress assembled, two thirds of both Houses concurring, that the following Articles be proposed to the Legislatures of the several States, as amendments to the Constitution of the United States, all, or any of which Articles, when ratified by three fourths of the said Legislatures, to be valid to all intents and purposes, as part of the said Constitution; viz.

ARTICLES in addition to, and Amendment of the Constitution of the United States of America, proposed by Congress, and ratified by the Legislatures of the several States, pursuant to the fifth Article of the original Constitution.

Note: The following text is a transcription of the first ten amendments to the Constitution in their original form. These amendments were ratified December 15, 1791, and form what is known as the "Bill of Rights."

AMENDMENT I

Congress shall make no law respecting an establishment of religion, or prohibiting the free exercise thereof; or abridging the freedom of speech, or of the press; or the right of the people peaceably to assemble, and to petition the Government for a redress of grievances.

AMENDMENT II

A well regulated Militia, being necessary to the security of a free State, the right of the people to keep and bear Arms, shall not be infringed.

AMENDMENT III

No Soldier shall, in time of peace be quartered in any house, without the consent of the Owner, nor in time of war, but in a manner to be prescribed by law.

AMENDMENT IV

The right of the people to be secure in their persons, houses, papers, and effects, against unreasonable searches and seizures, shall not be violated, and no Warrants shall issue, but upon probable cause, supported by Oath or affirmation, and particularly describing the place to be searched, and the persons or things to be seized.

AMENDMENT V

No person shall be held to answer for a capital, or otherwise infamous crime, unless on a presentment or indictment of a Grand Jury, except in cases arising in the land or naval forces, or in the Militia, when in actual service in time of War or public danger; nor shall any person be subject for the same offence to be twice put in jeopardy of life or limb; nor shall be compelled in any criminal case to be a witness against himself, nor be deprived of life, liberty, or property, without due process of law; nor shall private property be taken for public use, without just compensation.

AMENDMENT VI

In all criminal prosecutions, the accused shall enjoy the right to a speedy and public trial, by an impartial jury of the State and district wherein the crime shall have been committed, which district shall have been previously ascertained by law, and to be informed of the nature and cause of the accusation; to be confronted with the witnesses against him; to have compulsory process for obtaining witnesses in his favor, and to have the Assistance of Counsel for his defence.

AMENDMENT VII

In Suits at common law, where the value in controversy shall exceed twenty dollars, the right of trial by jury shall be preserved, and no fact tried by a jury, shall be otherwise re-examined in any Court of the United States, than according to the rules of the common law.

AMENDMENT VIII

Excessive bail shall not be required, nor excessive fines imposed, nor cruel and unusual punishments inflicted.

AMENDMENT IX

The enumeration in the Constitution, of certain rights, shall not be construed to deny or disparage others retained by the people.

AMENDMENT X

The powers not delegated to the United States by the Constitution, nor prohibited by it to the States, are reserved to the States respectively, or to the people.

Constitutional Amendments XI–XXVII

AMENDMENT XI

Passed by Congress March 4, 1794. Ratified February 7, 1795. Note: Article III, Section 2, of the Constitution was modified by Eleventh Amendment.

The Judicial power of the United States shall not be construed to extend to any suit in law or equity, commenced or prosecuted against one of the United States by Citizens of another State, or by Citizens or Subjects of any Foreign State.

AMENDMENT XII

Passed by Congress December 9, 1803. Ratified June 15, 1804. Note: A portion of Article II, Section 2, of the Constitution was superseded by the Twelfth Amendment.

The Electors shall meet in their respective states and vote by ballot for President and Vice-President, one of whom, at least, shall not be an inhabitant of the same state with themselves; they shall name in their ballots the person voted for as President, and in distinct ballots the person voted for as Vice-President, and they shall make distinct lists of all persons voted for as President, and of all persons voted for as Vice-President, and of the number of votes for each, which lists they shall sign and certify, and transmit sealed to the seat of the government of the United States, directed to the President of the Senate;—the President of the Senate shall, in the presence of the Senate and House of Representatives, open all the certificates and the votes shall then be counted;—The person having the greatest number of votes for President, shall be the President, if such number be a majority of the whole number of Electors appointed; and if no person have such majority, then from the persons having the highest numbers not exceeding three on the list of those voted for as President, the House of Representatives shall choose immediately, by ballot, the President. But in choosing the President, the votes shall be taken by states, the representation from each state having one vote; a quorum for this purpose shall consist of a member or members from two-thirds of the states, and a majority of all the states shall be necessary to a choice. [And if the House of Representatives shall not choose a President whenever the right of choice shall devolve upon them, before the fourth day of March next following, then the Vice-President shall act as President, as in case of the death or other constitutional disability of the President.—* The person having the greatest number of votes as Vice-President, shall be the Vice-President, if such number be a majority of the whole number of Electors appointed, and if no person have a majority, then from the two highest numbers on the list, the Senate shall choose the Vice-President; a quorum for the purpose shall consist of two-thirds of the whole number of Senators, and a majority of the whole number shall be necessary to a choice. But no person constitutionally ineligible to the office of President shall be eligible to that of Vice-President of the United States.

**Superseded by Section 3 of the Twentieth Amendment.*

AMENDMENT XIII

Passed by Congress January 31, 1865. Ratified December 6, 1865. Note: A portion of Article IV, Section 2, of the Constitution was superseded by the Thirteenth Amendment.

SECTION. 1.
Neither slavery nor involuntary servitude, except as a punishment for crime whereof the party shall have been duly convicted, shall exist within the United States, or any place subject to their jurisdiction.

SECTION. 2.
Congress shall have power to enforce this article by appropriate legislation.

AMENDMENT XIV

Passed by Congress June 13, 1866. Ratified July 9, 1868. Note: Article I, Section 2, of the Constitution was modified by Section 2 of the Fourteenth Amendment.

SECTION. 1.
All persons born or naturalized in the United States, and subject to the jurisdiction thereof, are citizens of the United States and of the State wherein they reside. No State shall make or enforce any law which shall abridge the privileges or immunities of citizens of the United States; nor shall any State deprive any person of life, liberty, or property, without due process of law; nor deny to any person within its jurisdiction the equal protection of the laws.

SECTION. 2.
Representatives shall be apportioned among the several States according to their respective numbers, counting the whole number of persons in each State, excluding Indians not taxed. But when the right to vote at any election for the choice of electors for President and Vice-President of the United States, Representatives in Congress, the Executive and Judicial officers of a State, or the members of the Legislature thereof, is denied to any of the male inhabitants of such State, being twenty-one years of age,* and citizens of the United States, or in any way abridged, except for participation in rebellion, or other crime, the basis of representation therein shall be reduced in the proportion which the number of such male citizens shall bear to the whole number of male citizens twenty-one years of age in such State.

SECTION. 3.
No person shall be a Senator or Representative in Congress, or elector of President and Vice-President, or hold any office, civil or military, under the United States, or under any State, who, having previously taken an oath, as a member of Congress, or as an officer of the United States, or as a member of any State legislature, or as an executive or judicial officer of any State, to support the Constitution of the United States, shall have engaged in insurrection or rebellion against the same, or given aid or comfort to the enemies thereof. But Congress may by a vote of two-thirds of each House, remove such disability.

SECTION. 4.
The validity of the public debt of the United States, authorized by law, including debts incurred for payment of pensions and bounties for services in suppressing insurrection or rebellion, shall not be questioned. But neither the United States nor any State shall assume or pay any debt or obligation incurred in aid of insurrection or rebellion against the United States, or any claim for the loss or emancipation of any slave; but all such debts, obligations and claims shall be held illegal and void.

SECTION. 5.
The Congress shall have the power to enforce, by appropriate legislation, the provisions of this article.

**Changed by Section 1 of the Twenty-Sixth Amendment.*

AMENDMENT XV

Passed by Congress February 26, 1869. Ratified February 3, 1870.

SECTION. 1.
The right of citizens of the United States to vote shall not be denied or abridged by the United States or by any State on account of race, color, or previous condition of servitude—

SECTION. 2.
The Congress shall have the power to enforce this article by appropriate legislation.

AMENDMENT XVI

Passed by Congress July 2, 1909. Ratified February 3, 1913. Note: Article I, Section 9, of the Constitution was modified by the Sixteenth Amendment.

The Congress shall have power to lay and collect taxes on incomes, from whatever source derived, without apportionment among the several States, and without regard to any census or enumeration.

AMENDMENT XVII

Passed by Congress May 13, 1912. Ratified April 8, 1913. Note: Article I, Section 3, of the Constitution was modified by the Seventeenth Amendment.

The Senate of the United States shall be composed of two Senators from each State, elected by the people thereof, for six years; and each Senator shall have one vote. The electors in each State shall have the qualifications requisite for electors of the most numerous branch of the State legislatures.

When vacancies happen in the representation of any State in the Senate, the executive authority of such State shall issue writs of election to fill such vacancies: *Provided*, That the legislature of any State may empower the executive thereof to make temporary appointments until the people fill the vacancies by election as the legislature may direct.

This amendment shall not be so construed as to affect the election or term of any Senator chosen before it becomes valid as part of the Constitution.

AMENDMENT XVIII

Passed by Congress December 18, 1917. Ratified January 16, 1919. Note: The Eighteenth Amendment was repealed by the Twenty-First Amendment.

SECTION. 1.
After one year from the ratification of this article the manufacture, sale, or transportation of intoxicating liquors within, the importation thereof into, or the exportation thereof from the United States and all territory subject to the jurisdiction thereof for beverage purposes is hereby prohibited.

SECTION. 2.
The Congress and the several States shall have concurrent power to enforce this article by appropriate legislation.

SECTION. 3.
This article shall be inoperative unless it shall have been ratified as an amendment to the Constitution by the legislatures of the several States, as provided in the Constitution, within seven years from the date of the submission hereof to the States by the Congress.

AMENDMENT XIX

Passed by Congress June 4, 1919. Ratified August 18, 1920.

The right of citizens of the United States to vote shall not be denied or abridged by the United States or by any State on account of sex.

Congress shall have power to enforce this article by appropriate legislation.

AMENDMENT XX

Passed by Congress March 2, 1932. Ratified January 23, 1933. Note: Article I, Section 4, of the Constitution was modified by Section 2 of this amendment. In addition, a portion of the Twelfth Amendment was superseded by Section 3 of this amendment.

SECTION. 1.
The terms of the President and the Vice President shall end at noon on the 20th day of January, and the terms of Senators and Representatives at noon on the 3d day of January, of the years in which such terms would have

ended if this article had not been ratified; and the terms of their successors shall then begin.

SECTION. 2.
The Congress shall assemble at least once in every year, and such meeting shall begin at noon on the 3d day of January, unless they shall by law appoint a different day.

SECTION. 3.
If, at the time fixed for the beginning of the term of the President, the President elect shall have died, the Vice President elect shall become President. If a President shall not have been chosen before the time fixed for the beginning of his term, or if the President elect shall have failed to qualify, then the Vice President elect shall act as President until a President shall have qualified; and the Congress may by law provide for the case wherein neither a President elect nor a Vice President shall have qualified, declaring who shall then act as President, or the manner in which one who is to act shall be selected, and such person shall act accordingly until a President or Vice President shall have qualified.

SECTION. 4.
The Congress may by law provide for the case of the death of any of the persons from whom the House of Representatives may choose a President whenever the right of choice shall have devolved upon them, and for the case of the death of any of the persons from whom the Senate may choose a Vice President whenever the right of choice shall have devolved upon them.

SECTION. 5.
Sections 1 and 2 shall take effect on the 15th day of October following the ratification of this article.

SECTION. 6.
This article shall be inoperative unless it shall have been ratified as an amendment to the Constitution by the legislatures of three-fourths of the several States within seven years from the date of its submission.

AMENDMENT XXI

Passed by Congress February 20, 1933. Ratified December 5, 1933.

SECTION. 1.
The eighteenth article of amendment to the Constitution of the United States is hereby repealed.

SECTION. 2.
The transportation or importation into any State, Territory, or Possession of the United States for delivery or use therein of intoxicating liquors, in violation of the laws thereof, is hereby prohibited.

SECTION. 3.
This article shall be inoperative unless it shall have been ratified as an amendment to the Constitution by conventions in the several States, as provided in the Constitution, within seven years from the date of the submission hereof to the States by the Congress.

AMENDMENT XXII

Passed by Congress March 21, 1947. Ratified February 27, 1951.

SECTION. 1.
No person shall be elected to the office of the President more than twice, and no person who has held the office of President, or acted as President, for more than two years of a term to which some other person was elected President shall be elected to the office of President more than once. But this Article shall not apply to any person holding the office of President when this Article was proposed by Congress, and shall not prevent any person who may be holding the office of President, or acting as President, during the term within which this Article becomes operative from holding the office of President or acting as President during the remainder of such term.

SECTION. 2.
This article shall be inoperative unless it shall have been ratified as an amendment to the Constitution by the legislatures of three-fourths of the several States within seven years from the date of its submission to the States by the Congress.

AMENDMENT XXIII

Passed by Congress June 16, 1960. Ratified March 29, 1961.

SECTION. 1.
The District constituting the seat of Government of the United States shall appoint in such manner as Congress may direct:

A number of electors of President and Vice President equal to the whole number of Senators and Representatives in Congress to which the District would be entitled if it were a State, but in no event more than the least populous State; they shall be in addition to those appointed by the States, but they shall be considered, for the purposes of the election of President and Vice President, to be electors appointed by a State; and they shall meet in the District and perform such duties as provided by the twelfth article of amendment.

SECTION. 2.
The Congress shall have power to enforce this article by appropriate legislation.

AMENDMENT XXIV

Passed by Congress August 27, 1962. Ratified January 23, 1964.

SECTION. 1.
The right of citizens of the United States to vote in any primary or other election for President or Vice President, for electors for President or Vice President, or for Senator or Representative in Congress, shall not be denied or abridged by the United States or any State by reason of failure to pay poll tax or other tax.

SECTION. 2.
The Congress shall have power to enforce this article by appropriate legislation.

AMENDMENT XXV

Passed by Congress July 6, 1965. Ratified February 10, 1967. Note: Article II, Section 1, of the Constitution was affected by the Twenty-Fifth Amendment.

SECTION. 1.
In case of the removal of the President from office or of his death or resignation, the Vice President shall become President.

SECTION. 2.
Whenever there is a vacancy in the office of the Vice President, the President shall nominate a Vice President who shall take office upon confirmation by a majority vote of both Houses of Congress.

SECTION. 3.
Whenever the President transmits to the President pro tempore of the Senate and the Speaker of the House of Representatives his written declaration that he is unable to discharge the powers and duties of his office, and until he transmits to them a written declaration to the contrary, such powers and duties shall be discharged by the Vice President as Acting President.

SECTION. 4.
Whenever the Vice President and a majority of either the principal officers of the executive departments or of such other body as Congress may by law provide, transmit to the President pro tempore of the Senate and the Speaker of the House of Representatives their written declaration that the President is unable to discharge the powers and duties of his office, the Vice President shall immediately assume the powers and duties of the office as Acting President.

Thereafter, when the President transmits to the President pro tempore of the Senate and the Speaker of the House of Representatives his written declaration that no inability exists, he shall resume the powers and duties of his office unless the Vice President and a majority of either the principal officers of the executive department or of such other body as Congress may by law provide, transmit within four days to the President pro tempore of the Senate and the Speaker of the House of Representatives their written declaration that the President is unable to discharge the powers and duties of his office. Thereupon Congress shall decide the issue, assembling within forty-eight hours for that purpose if not in session. If the Congress, within twenty-one days after receipt of the latter written declaration, or, if Congress is not in session, within twenty-one days after Congress is required to assemble, determines by two-thirds vote of both Houses that the President is unable to discharge the powers and duties of his office, the Vice President shall continue to discharge the same as Acting President; otherwise, the President shall resume the powers and duties of his office.

AMENDMENT XXVI

Passed by Congress March 23, 1971. Ratified July 1, 1971. Note: Amendment 14, Section 2, of the Constitution was modified by Section 1 of the Twenty-Sixth Amendment.

SECTION. 1.
The right of citizens of the United States, who are eighteen years of age or older, to vote shall not be denied or

abridged by the United States or by any State on account of age.

SECTION. 2.
The Congress shall have power to enforce this article by appropriate legislation.

AMENDMENT XXVII

Originally proposed September 25, 1789. Ratified May 7, 1992.

No law, varying the compensation for the services of the Senators and Representatives, shall take effect, until an election of representatives shall have intervened.

Appendix II: Data

States, by Date of Entry into the Union

	State	Entered Union	Year Settled		State	Entered Union	Year Settled
1.	Delaware	Dec. 7, 1787	1638	26.	Michigan	Jan. 26, 1837	1668
2.	Pennsylvania	Dec. 12, 1787	1682	27.	Florida	Mar. 3, 1845	1565
3.	New Jersey	Dec. 18, 1787	1660	28.	Texas	Dec. 29, 1845	1682
4.	Georgia	Jan. 2, 1788	1733	29.	Iowa	Dec. 28, 1846	1788
5.	Connecticut	Jan. 9, 1788	1634	30.	Wisconsin	May 29, 1848	1766
6.	Massachusetts	Feb. 6, 1788	1620	31.	California	Sept. 9, 1850	1769
7.	Maryland	Apr. 28, 1788	1634	32.	Minnesota	May 11, 1858	1805
8.	South Carolina	May 23, 1788	1670	33.	Oregon	Feb. 14, 1859	1811
9.	New Hampshire	June 21, 1788	1623	34.	Kansas	Jan. 29, 1861	1727
10.	Virginia	June 25, 1788	1607	35.	West Virginia	June 20, 1863	1727
11.	New York	July 26, 1788	1614	36.	Nevada	Oct. 31, 1864	1849
12.	North Carolina	Nov. 21, 1789	1660	37.	Nebraska	Mar. 1, 1867	1823
13.	Rhode Island	May 29, 1790	1636	38.	Colorado	Aug. 1, 1876	1858
14.	Vermont	Mar. 4, 1791	1724	39.	North Dakota	Nov. 2, 1889	1812
15.	Kentucky	June 1, 1792	1774	40.	South Dakota	Nov. 2, 1889	1859
16.	Tennessee	June 1, 1796	1769	41.	Montana	Nov. 8, 1889	1809
17.	Ohio	Mar. 1, 1803	1788	42.	Washington	Nov. 11, 1889	1811
18.	Louisiana	Apr. 30, 1812	1699	43.	Idaho	July 3, 1890	1842
19.	Indiana	Dec. 11, 1816	1733	44.	Wyoming	July 10, 1890	1834
20.	Mississippi	Dec. 10, 1817	1699	45.	Utah	Jan. 4, 1896	1847
21.	Illinois	Dec. 3, 1818	1720	46.	Oklahoma	Nov. 16, 1907	1889
22.	Alabama	Dec. 14, 1819	1702	47.	New Mexico	Jan. 6, 1912	1610
23.	Maine	Mar. 15, 1820	1624	48.	Arizona	Feb. 14, 1912	1776
24.	Missouri	Aug. 10, 1821	1735	49.	Alaska	Jan. 3, 1959	1784
25.	Arkansas	June 15, 1836	1686	50.	Hawaii	Aug. 21, 1959	1820

Territorial Growth of the United States and Its Colonies from 1790 to 1960

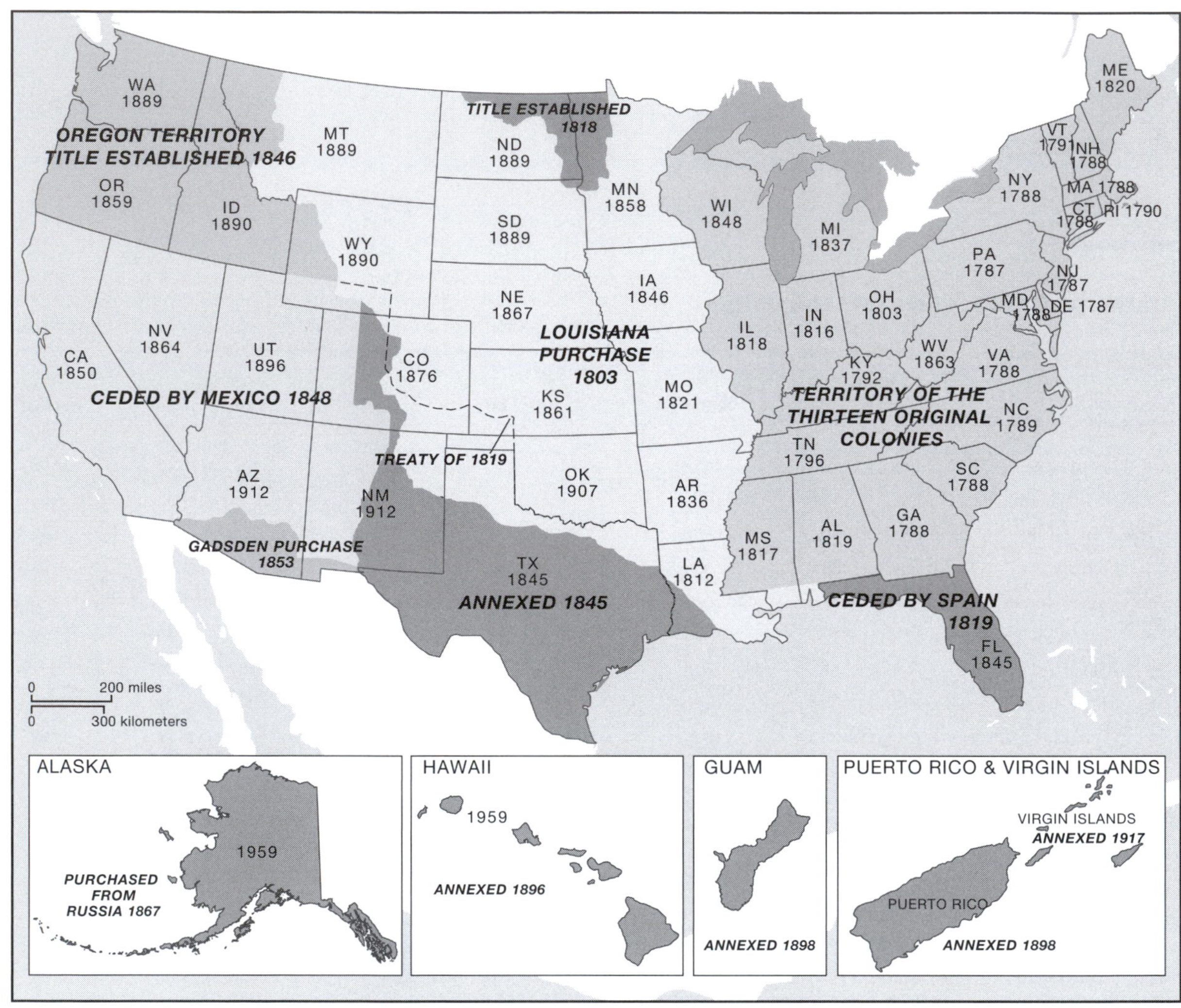

Population of the United States, 1790–2000

Year	U.S. Population	Year	U.S. Population	Year	U.S. Population
2000	281,421,906	1920	106,021,537	1850	23,191,876
1990	248,709,873	1910	92,228,496	1840	17,069,453
1980	226,542,199	1900	76,212,168	1830	12,866,020
1970	203,302,031	1890	62,979,766	1820	9,638,453
1960	179,323,175	1880	50,189,209	1810	7,239,881
1950	151,325,798	1870	38,558,371	1800	5,308,483
1940	132,164,569	1860	31,443,321	1790	3,929,214
1930	123,202,624				

Information compiled from the U.S. Census Bureau. As of May 2009, the U.S. Census Bureau projection for 2010 was 310,233,000.

Presidential Elections

Year	Number of States	Candidates	Parties	Popular Vote	% of Popular Vote	Electoral Vote	% Voter Participation
1789	11	**George Washington**	No party designations			69	
		John Adams				34	
		Other candidates				35	
1792	15	**George Washington**	No party designations			132	
		John Adams				77	
		George Clinton				50	
		Other candidates				5	
1796	16	**John Adams**	Federalist			71	
		Thomas Jefferson	Democratic-Republican			68	
		Thomas Pinckney	Federalist			59	
		Aaron Burr	Democratic-Republican			30	
		Other candidates				48	
1800	16	**Thomas Jefferson**	Democratic-Republican			73	
		Aaron Burr	Democratic-Republican			73	
		John Adams	Federalist			65	
		Charles C. Pinckney	Federalist			64	
		John Jay	Federalist			1	
1804	17	**Thomas Jefferson**	Democratic-Republican			162	
		Charles C. Pinckney	Federalist			14	
1808	17	**James Madison**	Democratic-Republican			122	
		Charles C. Pinckney	Federalist			47	
		George Clinton	Democratic-Republican			6	
1812	18	**James Madison**	Democratic-Republican			128	
		DeWitt Clinton	Federalist			89	

(continued)

Year	Number of States	Candidates	Parties	Popular Vote	% of Popular Vote	Electoral Vote	% Voter Participation
1816	19	**James Monroe**	Democratic-Republican			183	
		Rufus King	Federalist			34	
1820	24	**James Monroe**	Democratic-Republican			231	
		John Quincy Adams	Independent Republican			1	
1824	24	**John Quincy Adams**	Democratic-Republican	108,740	30.5	84	26.9
		Andrew Jackson	Democratic-Republican	153,544	43.1	99	
		Henry Clay	Democratic-Republican	47,136	13.2	37	
		William H. Crawford	Democratic-Republican	46,618	13.1	41	
1828	24	**Andrew Jackson**	Democratic	647,286	56.0	178	57.6
		John Quincy Adams	National Republican	508,064	44.0	83	
1832	24	**Andrew Jackson**	Democratic	688,242	54.5	219	55.4
		Henry Clay	National Republican	473,462	37.5	49	
		William Wirt	Anti-Masonic }	101,051	8.0	7	
		John Floyd	Democratic }			11	
1836	26	**Martin Van Buren**	Democratic	765,483	50.9	170	57.8
		William H. Harrison	Whig }	739,795	49.1	73	
		Hugh L. White	Whig }			26	
		Daniel Webster	Whig }			14	
		W. P. Mangum	Whig }			11	
1840	26	**William H. Harrison**	Whig	1,274,624	53.1	234	80.2
		Martin Van Buren	Democratic	1,127,781	46.9	60	
1844	26	**James K. Polk**	Democratic	1,338,464	49.6	170	78.9
		Henry Clay	Whig	1,300,097	48.1	105	
		James G. Birney	Liberty	62,300	2.3		
1848	30	**Zachary Taylor**	Whig	1,360,967	47.4	163	72.7
		Lewis Cass	Democratic	1,222,342	42.5	127	
		Martin Van Buren	Free Soil	291,263	10.1		
1852	31	**Franklin Pierce**	Democratic	1,601,117	50.9	254	69.6
		Winfield Scott	Whig	1,385,453	44.1	42	
		John P. Hale	Free Soil	155,825	5.0		
1856	31	**James Buchanan**	Democratic	1,832,955	45.3	174	78.9
		John C. Frémont	Republican	1,339,932	33.1	114	
		Millard Fillmore	American	871,731	21.6	8	
1860	33	**Abraham Lincoln**	Republican	1,865,593	39.8	180	81.2
		Stephen A. Douglas	Democratic	1,382,713	29.5	12	
		John C. Breckinridge	Democratic	848,356	18.1	72	
		John Bell	Constitutional Union	592,906	12.6	39	
1864	36	**Abraham Lincoln**	Republican	2,206,938	55.0	212	73.8
		George B. McClellan	Democratic	1,803,787	45.0	21	
1868	37	**Ulysses S. Grant**	Republican	3,013,421	52.7	214	78.1
		Horatio Seymour	Democratic	2,706,829	47.3	80	
1872	37	**Ulysses S. Grant**	Republican	3,596,745	55.6	286	71.3
		Horace Greeley	Democratic	2,843,446	43.9	*	

Year	Number of States	Candidates	Parties	Popular Vote	% of Popular Vote	Electoral Vote	% Voter Participation
1876	38	**Rutherford B. Hayes**	Republican	4,036,572	48.0	185	81.8
		Samuel J. Tilden	Democratic	4,284,020	51.0	184	
1880	38	**James A. Garfield**	Republican	4,453,295	48.5	214	79.4
		Winfield S. Hancock	Democratic	4,414,082	48.1	155	
		James B. Weaver	Greenback-Labor	308,578	3.4		
1884	38	**Grover Cleveland**	Democratic	4,879,507	48.5	219	77.5
		James G. Blaine	Republican	4,850,293	48.2	182	
		Benjamin F. Butler	Greenback-Labor	175,370	1.8		
		John P. St. John	Prohibition	150,369	1.5		
1888	38	**Benjamin Harrison**	Republican	5,477,129	47.9	233	79.3
		Grover Cleveland	Democratic	5,537,857	48.6	168	
		Clinton B. Fisk	Prohibition	249,506	2.2		
		Anson J. Streeter	Union Labor	146,935	1.3		
1892	44	**Grover Cleveland**	Democratic	5,555,426	46.1	277	74.7
		Benjamin Harrison	Republican	5,182,690	43.0	145	
		James B. Weaver	People's	1,029,846	8.5	22	
		John Bidwell	Prohibition	264,133	2.2		
1896	45	**William McKinley**	Republican	7,102,246	51.1	271	79.3
		William J. Bryan	Democratic	6,492,559	47.7	176	
1900	45	**William McKinley**	Republican	7,218,491	51.7	292	73.2
		William J. Bryan	Democratic; People's	6,356,734	45.5	155	
		John C. Wooley	Prohibition	208,914	1.5		
1904	45	**Theodore Roosevelt**	Republican	7,628,461	57.4	336	65.2
		Alton B. Parker	Democratic	5,084,223	37.6	140	
		Eugene V. Debs	Socialist	402,283	3.0		
		Silas C. Swallow	Prohibition	258,536	1.9		
1908	46	**William H. Taft**	Republican	7,675,320	51.6	321	65.4
		William J. Bryan	Democratic	6,412,294	43.1	162	
		Eugene V. Debs	Socialist	420,793	2.8		
		Eugene W. Chafin	Prohibition	253,840	1.7		
1912	48	**Woodrow Wilson**	Democratic	6,296,547	41.9	435	58.8
		Theodore Roosevelt	Progressive	4,118,571	27.4	88	
		William H. Taft	Republican	3,486,720	23.2	8	
		Eugene V. Debs	Socialist	900,672	6.0		
		Eugene W. Chafin	Prohibition	206,275	1.4		
1916	48	**Woodrow Wilson**	Democratic	9,127,695	49.4	277	61.6
		Charles E. Hughes	Republican	8,533,507	46.2	254	
		A. L. Benson	Socialist	585,113	3.2		
		J. Frank Hanly	Prohibition	220,506	1.2		
1920	48	**Warren G. Harding**	Republican	16,143,407	60.4	404	49.2
		James M. Cox	Democratic	9,130,328	34.2	127	
		Eugene V. Debs	Socialist	919,799	3.4		
		P. P. Christensen	Farmer-Labor	265,411	1.0		

(continued)

Year	Number of States	Candidates	Parties	Popular Vote	% of Popular Vote	Electoral Vote	% Voter Participation
1924	48	**Calvin Coolidge**	Republican	15,718,211	54.0	382	48.9
		John W. Davis	Democratic	8,385,283	28.8	136	
		Robert M. La Follette	Progressive	4,831,289	16.6	13	
1928	48	**Herbert C. Hoover**	Republican	21,391,993	58.2	444	56.9
		Alfred E. Smith	Democratic	15,016,169	40.9	87	
1932	48	**Franklin D. Roosevelt**	Democratic	22,809,638	57.4	472	56.9
		Herbert C. Hoover	Republican	15,758,901	39.7	59	
		Norman Thomas	Socialist	881,951	2.2		
1936	48	**Franklin D. Roosevelt**	Democratic	27,752,869	60.8	523	61.0
		Alfred M. Landon	Republican	16,674,665	36.5	8	
		William Lemke	Union	882,479	1.9		
1940	48	**Franklin D. Roosevelt**	Democratic	27,307,819	54.8	449	62.5
		Wendell L. Willkie	Republican	22,321,018	44.8	82	
1944	48	**Franklin D. Roosevelt**	Democratic	25,606,585	53.5	432	55.9
		Thomas E. Dewey	Republican	22,014,745	46.0	99	
1948	48	**Harry S Truman**	Democratic	24,179,345	49.6	303	53.0
		Thomas E. Dewey	Republican	21,991,291	45.1	189	
		J. Strom Thurmond	States' Rights	1,176,125	2.4	39	
		Henry A. Wallace	Progressive	1,157,326	2.4		
1952	48	**Dwight D. Eisenhower**	Republican	33,936,234	55.1	442	63.3
		Adlai E. Stevenson	Democratic	27,314,992	44.4	89	
1956	48	**Dwight D. Eisenhower**	Republican	35,590,472	57.6	457	60.6
		Adlai E. Stevenson	Democratic	26,022,752	42.1	73	
1960	50	**John F. Kennedy**	Democratic	34,226,731	49.7	303	62.77
		Richard M. Nixon	Republican	34,108,157	49.5	219	
1964	50	**Lyndon B. Johnson**	Democratic	43,129,566	61.1	486	61.92
		Barry M. Goldwater	Republican	27,178,188	38.5	52	
1968	50	**Richard M. Nixon**	Republican	31,785,480	43.4	301	60.84
		Hubert H. Humphrey	Democratic	31,275,166	42.7	191	
		George C. Wallace	American Independent	9,906,473	13.5	46	
1972	50	**Richard M. Nixon**	Republican	47,169,911	60.7	520	55.21
		George S. McGovern	Democratic	29,170,383	37.5	17	
		John G. Schmitz	American	1,099,482	1.4		
1976	50	**Jimmy Carter**	Democratic	40,830,763	50.1	297	53.55
		Gerald R. Ford	Republican	39,147,793	48.0	240	
1980	50	**Ronald Reagan**	Republican	43,901,812	50.7	489	52.56
		Jimmy Carter	Democratic	35,483,820	41.0	49	
		John B. Anderson	Independent	5,719,722	6.6	0	
		Ed Clark	Libertarian	921,188	1.1	0	
1984	50	**Ronald Reagan**	Republican	54,455,075	58.8	525	53.11
		Walter Mondale	Democratic	37,577,185	40.6	13	

Year	Number of States	Candidates	Parties	Popular Vote	% of Popular Vote	Electoral Vote	% Voter Participation
1988	50	**George H. W. Bush**	Republican	48,886,097	53.4	426	50.15
		Michael Dukakis	Democratic	41,809,074	45.6	111	
1992	50	**William J. Clinton**	Democratic	44,909,326	43	370	55.23
		George H. W. Bush	Republican	39,103,882	37.4	168	
		H. Ross Perot	Independent	19,741,657	18.9	0	
1996	50	**William J. Clinton**	Democratic	47,402,357	49.2	379	49.08
		Robert Dole	Republican	39,198,755	40.7	159	
		H. Ross Perot	Reform	8,085,402	8.4	0	
2000	50	**George W. Bush**	Republican	50,455,156	47.9	271	51.3
		Albert Gore Jr.	Democratic	50,992,335	48.4	266	
		Ralph Nader	Green	2,882,738	2.7	0	
2004	50	**George W. Bush**	Republican	62,040,610	50.7	286	55.27
		John F. Kerry	Democratic	59,028,444	48.3	251	
2008	50	**Barack Obama**	Democratic	69,456,897	52.9	365	56.8
		John McCain	Republican	59,934,814	45.7	173	

Candidates receiving less than 1 percent of the popular vote have been omitted. Thus the percentage of popular vote given for any election year may not total 100 percent.

Before the passage of the Twelfth Amendment in 1804, the Electoral College voted for two presidential candidates; the runner-up became vice president.

Before 1824, most presidential electors were chosen by state legislatures, not by popular vote.

*Greeley died shortly after the election; the electors supporting him then divided their votes among minor candidates.

Presidents, Vice Presidents, and Cabinet Members

The Washington Administration

President	George Washington	1789–1797
Vice President	John Adams	1789–1797
Secretary of State	Thomas Jefferson	1789–1793
	Edmund Randolph	1794–1795
	Timothy Pickering	1795–1797
Secretary of Treasury	Alexander Hamilton	1789–1795
	Oliver Wolcott	1795–1797
Secretary of War	Henry Knox	1789–1794
	Timothy Pickering	1795–1796
	James McHenry	1796–1797
Attorney General	Edmund Randolph	1789–1793
	William Bradford	1794–1795
	Charles Lee	1795–1797
Postmaster General	Samuel Osgood	1789–1791
	Timothy Pickering	1791–1794
	Joseph Habersham	1795–1797

The John Adams Administration

President	John Adams	1797–1801
Vice President	Thomas Jefferson	1797–1801
Secretary of State	Timothy Pickering	1797–1800
	John Marshall	1800–1801
Secretary of Treasury	Oliver Wolcott	1797–1800
	Samuel Dexter	1800–1801
Secretary of War	James McHenry	1797–1800
	Samuel Dexter	1800–1801

(continued)

The Washington Administration *(continued)*

Attorney General	Charles Lee	1797–1801
Postmaster General	Joseph Habersham	1797–1801
Secretary of Navy	Benjamin Stoddert	1798–1801

The Jefferson Administration

President	Thomas Jefferson	1801–1809
Vice President	Aaron Burr	1801–1805
	George Clinton	1805–1809
Secretary of State	James Madison	1801–1809
Secretary of Treasury	Samuel Dexter	1801
	Albert Gallatin	1801–1809
Secretary of War	Henry Dearborn	1801–1809
Attorney General	Levi Lincoln	1801–1805
	Robert Smith	1805
	John Breckinridge	1805–1806
	Caesar Rodney	1807–1809
Postmaster General	Joseph Habersham	1801
	Gideon Granger	1801–1809
Secretary of Navy	Robert Smith	1801–1809

The Madison Administration

President	James Madison	1809–1817
Vice President	George Clinton	1809–1813
	Elbridge Gerry	1813–1817
Secretary of State	Robert Smith	1809–1811
	James Monroe	1811–1817
Secretary of Treasury	Albert Gallatin	1809–1813
	George Campbell	1814
	Alexander Dallas	1814–1816
	William Crawford	1816–1817
Secretary of War	William Eustis	1809–1812
	John Armstrong	1813–1814
	James Monroe	1814–1815
	William Crawford	1815–1817
Attorney General	Caesar Rodney	1809–1811
	William Pinkney	1811–1814
	Richard Rush	1814–1817
Postmaster General	Gideon Granger	1809–1814
	Return Meigs	1814–1817
Secretary of Navy	Paul Hamilton	1809–1813
	William Jones	1813–1814
	Benjamin Crowninshield	1814–1817

The Monroe Administration

President	James Monroe	1817–1825
Vice President	Daniel Tompkins	1817–1825
Secretary of State	John Quincy Adams	1817–1825
Secretary of Treasury	William Crawford	1817–1825
Secretary of War	George Graham	1817
	John C. Calhoun	1817–1825
Attorney General	Richard Rush	1817
	William Wirt	1817–1825
Postmaster General	Return Meigs	1817–1823
	John McLean	1823–1825
Secretary of Navy	Benjamin Crowninshield	1817–1818
	Smith Thompson	1819–1823
	Samuel Southard	1823–1825

The John Quincy Adams Administration

President	John Quincy Adams	1825–1829
Vice President	John C. Calhoun	1825–1829
Secretary of State	Henry Clay	1825–1829
Secretary of Treasury	Richard Rush	1825–1829
Secretary of War	James Barbour	1825–1828
	Peter Porter	1828–1829
Attorney General	William Wirt	1825–1829
Postmaster General	John McLean	1825–1829
Secretary of Navy	Samuel Southard	1825–1829

The Jackson Administration

President	Andrew Jackson	1829–1837
Vice President	John C. Calhoun	1829–1833
	Martin Van Buren	1833–1837
Secretary of State	Martin Van Buren	1829–1831
	Edward Livingston	1831–1833
	Louis McLane	1833–1834
	John Forsyth	1834–1837
Secretary of Treasury	Samuel Ingham	1829–1831
	Louis McLane	1831–1833
	William Duane	1833
	Roger B. Taney	1833–1834
	Levi Woodbury	1834–1837
Secretary of War	John H. Eaton	1829–1831
	Lewis Cass	1831–1837
	Benjamin Butler	1837

Attorney General	John M. Berrien	1829–1831
	Roger B. Taney	1831–1833
	Benjamin Butler	1833–1837
Postmaster General	William Barry	1829–1835
	Amos Kendall	1835–1837
Secretary of Navy	John Branch	1829–1831
	Levi Woodbury	1831–1834
	Mahlon Dickerson	1834–1837

The Van Buren Administration

President	Martin Van Buren	1837–1841
Vice President	Richard M. Johnson	1837–1841
Secretary of State	John Forsyth	1837–1841
Secretary of Treasury	Levi Woodbury	1837–1841
Secretary of War	Joel Poinsett	1837–1841
Attorney General	Benjamin Butler	1837–1838
	Felix Grundy	1838–1840
	Henry D. Gilpin	1840–1841
Postmaster General	Amos Kendall	1837–1840
	John M. Niles	1840–1841
Secretary of Navy	Mahlon Dickerson	1837–1838
	James Paulding	1838–1841

The William Harrison Administration

President	William H. Harrison	1841
Vice President	John Tyler	1841
Secretary of State	Daniel Webster	1841
Secretary of Treasury	Thomas Ewing	1841
Secretary of War	John Bell	1841
Attorney General	John J. Crittenden	1841
Postmaster General	Francis Granger	1841
Secretary of Navy	George Badger	1841

The Tyler Administration

President	John Tyler	1841–1845
Vice President	None	
Secretary of State	Daniel Webster	1841–1843
	Hugh S. Legaré	1843
	Abel P. Upshur	1843–1844
	John C. Calhoun	1844–1845
Secretary of Treasury	Thomas Ewing	1841
	Walter Forward	1841–1843
	John C. Spencer	1843–1844
	George Bibb	1844–1845
Secretary of War	John Bell	1841
	John C. Spencer	1841–1843
	James M. Porter	1843–1844
	William Wilkins	1844–1845
Attorney General	John J. Crittenden	1841
	Hugh S. Legaré	1841–1843
	John Nelson	1843–1845
Postmaster General	Francis Granger	1841
	Charles Wickliffe	1841
Secretary of Navy	George Badger	1841
	Abel P. Upshur	1841
	David Henshaw	1843–1844
	Thomas Gilmer	1844
	John Y. Mason	1844–1845

The Polk Administration

President	James K. Polk	1845–1849
Vice President	George M. Dallas	1845–1849
Secretary of State	James Buchanan	1845–1849
Secretary of Treasury	Robert J. Walker	1845–1849
Secretary of War	William L. Marcy	1845–1849
Attorney General	John Y. Mason	1845–1846
	Nathan Clifford	1846–1848
	Isaac Toucey	1848–1849
Postmaster General	Cave Johnson	1845–1849
Secretary of Navy	George Bancroft	1845–1846
	John Y. Mason	1846–1849

The Taylor Administration

President	Zachary Taylor	1849–1850
Vice President	Millard Fillmore	1849–1850
Secretary of State	John M. Clayton	1849–1850
Secretary of Treasury	William Meredith	1849–1850
Secretary of War	George Crawford	1849–1850
Attorney General	Reverdy Johnson	1849–1850
Postmaster General	Jacob Collamer	1849–1850
Secretary of Navy	William Preston	1849–1850
Secretary of Interior	Thomas Ewing	1849–1850

(continued)

The Fillmore Administration

President	Millard Fillmore	1850–1853
Vice President	None	
Secretary of State	Daniel Webster Edward Everett	1850–1852 1852–1853
Secretary of Treasury	Thomas Corwin	1850–1853
Secretary of War	Charles Conrad	1850–1853
Attorney General	John J. Crittenden	1850–1853
Postmaster General	Nathan Hall Sam D. Hubbard	1850–1852 1852–1853
Secretary of Navy	William A. Graham John P. Kennedy	1850–1852 1852–1853
Secretary of Interior	Thomas McKennan Alexander Stuart	1850 1850–1853

The Pierce Administration

President	Franklin Pierce	1853–1857
Vice President	William R. King	1853–1857
Secretary of State	William L. Marcy	1853–1857
Secretary of Treasury	James Guthrie	1853–1857
Secretary of War	Jefferson Davis	1853–1857
Attorney General	Caleb Cushing	1853–1857
Postmaster General	James Campbell	1853–1857
Secretary of Navy	James C. Dobbin	1853–1857
Secretary of Interior	Robert McClelland	1853–1857

The Buchanan Administration

President	James Buchanan	1857–1861
Vice President	John C. Breckinridge	1857–1861
Secretary of State	Lewis Cass Jeremiah S. Black	1857–1860 1860–1861
Secretary of Treasury	Howell Cobb Philip Thomas John A. Dix	1857–1860 1860–1861 1861
Secretary of War	John B. Floyd Joseph Holt	1857–1861 1861
Attorney General	Jeremiah S. Black Edwin M. Stanton	1857–1860 1860–1861
Postmaster General	Aaron V. Brown Joseph Holt Horatio King	1857–1859 1859–1861 1861
Secretary of Navy	Isaac Toucey	1857–1861
Secretary of Interior	Jacob Thompson	1857–1861

The Lincoln Administration

President	Abraham Lincoln	1861–1865
Vice President	Hannibal Hamlin Andrew Johnson	1861–1865 1865
Secretary of State	William H. Seward	1861–1865
Secretary of Treasury	Samuel P. Chase William P. Fessenden Hugh McCulloch	1861–1864 1864–1865 1865
Secretary of War	Simon Cameron Edwin M. Stanton	1861–1862 1862–1865
Attorney General	Edward Bates James Speed	1861–1864 1864–1865
Postmaster General	Horatio King Montgomery Blair William Dennison	1861 1861–1864 1864–1865
Secretary of Navy	Gideon Welles	1861–1865
Secretary of Interior	Caleb B. Smith John P. Usher	1861–1863 1863–1865

The Andrew Johnson Administration

President	Andrew Johnson	1865–1869
Vice President	None	
Secretary of State	William H. Seward	1865–1869
Secretary of Treasury	Hugh McCulloch	1865–1869
Secretary of War	Edwin M. Stanton Ulysses S. Grant Lorenzo Thomas John M. Schofield	1865–1867 1867–1868 1868 1868–1869
Attorney General	James Speed Henry Stanbery William M. Evarts	1865–1866 1866–1868 1868–1869
Postmaster General	William Dennison Alexander Randall	1865–1866 1866–1869
Secretary of Navy	Gideon Welles	1865–1869
Secretary of Interior	John P. Usher James Harlan Orville H. Browning	1865 1865–1866 1866–1869

The Grant Administration

President	Ulysses S. Grant	1869–1877
Vice President	Schuyler Colfax	1869–1873
	Henry Wilson	1873–1877
Secretary of State	Elihu B. Washburne	1869
	Hamilton Fish	1869–1877
Secretary of Treasury	George S. Boutwell	1869–1873
	William Richardson	1873–1874
	Benjamin Bristow	1874–1876
	Lot M. Morrill	1876–1877
Secretary of War	John A. Rawlins	1869
	William T. Sherman	1869
	William W. Belknap	1869–1876
	Alphonso Taft	1876
	James D. Cameron	1876–1877
Attorney General	Ebenezer Hoar	1869–1870
	Amos T. Ackerman	1870–1871
	G. H. Williams	1871–1875
	Edwards Pierrepont	1875–1876
	Alphonso Taft	1876–1877
Postmaster General	John A. J. Creswell	1869–1874
	James W. Marshall	1874
	Marshall Jewell	1874–1876
	James N. Tyner	1876–1877
Secretary of Navy	Adolph E. Borie	1869
	George M. Robeson	1869–1877
Secretary of Interior	Jacob D. Cox	1869–1870
	Columbus Delano	1870–1875
	Zachariah Chandler	1875–1877

The Hayes Administration

President	Rutherford B. Hayes	1877–1881
Vice President	William A. Wheeler	1877–1881
Secretary of State	William B. Evarts	1877–1881
Secretary of Treasury	John Sherman	1877–1881
Secretary of War	George W. McCrary	1877–1879
	Alex Ramsey	1879–1881
Attorney General	Charles Devens	1877–1881
Postmaster General	David M. Key	1877–1880
	Horace Maynard	1880–1881
Secretary of Navy	Richard W. Thompson	1877–1880
	Nathan Goff Jr.	1881
Secretary of Interior	Carl Schurz	1877–1881

The Garfield Administration

President	James A. Garfield	1881
Vice President	Chester A. Arthur	1881
Secretary of State	James G. Blaine	1881
Secretary of Treasury	William Windom	1881
Secretary of War	Robert T. Lincoln	1881
Attorney General	Wayne MacVeagh	1881
Postmaster General	Thomas L. James	1881
Secretary of Navy	William H. Hunt	1881
Secretary of Interior	Samuel J. Kirkwood	1881

The Arthur Administration

President	Chester A. Arthur	1881–1885
Vice President	None	
Secretary of State	F. T. Frelinghuysen	1881–1885
Secretary of Treasury	Charles J. Folger	1881–1884
	Walter Q. Gresham	1884
	Hugh McCulloch	1884–1885
Secretary of War	Robert T. Lincoln	1881–1885
Attorney General	Benjamin H. Brewster	1881–1885
Postmaster General	Timothy O. Howe	1881–1883
	Walter Q. Gresham	1883–1884
	Frank Hatton	1884–1885
Secretary of Navy	William H. Hunt	1881–1882
	William E. Chandler	1882–1885
Secretary of Interior	Samuel J. Kirkwood	1881–1882
	Henry M. Teller	1882–1885

The Cleveland Administration

President	Grover Cleveland	1885–1889
Vice President	Thomas A. Hendricks	1885–1889
Secretary of State	Thomas F. Bayard	1885–1889
Secretary of Treasury	Daniel Manning	1885–1887
	Charles S. Fairchild	1887–1889
Secretary of War	William C. Endicott	1885–1889
Attorney General	Augustus H. Garland	1885–1889
Postmaster General	William F. Vilas	1885–1888
	Don M. Dickinson	1888–1889
Secretary of Navy	William C. Whitney	1885–1889

(continued)

The Cleveland Administration *(continued)*

Secretary of Interior	Lucius Q. C. Lamar William F. Vilas	1885–1888 1888–1889
Secretary of Agriculture	Norman J. Colman	1889

The Benjamin Harrison Administration

President	Benjamin Harrison	1889–1893
Vice President	Levi P. Morton	1889–1893
Secretary of State	James G. Blaine John W. Foster	1889–1892 1892–1893
Secretary of Treasury	William Windom Charles Foster	1889–1891 1891–1893
Secretary of War	Redfield Proctor Stephen B. Elkins	1889–1891 1891–1893
Attorney General	William H. H. Miller	1889–1891
Postmaster General	John Wanamaker	1889–1893
Secretary of Navy	Benjamin F. Tracy	1889–1893
Secretary of Interior	John W. Noble	1889–1893
Secretary of Agriculture	Jeremiah M. Rusk	1889–1893

The Cleveland Administration

President	Grover Cleveland	1893–1897
Vice President	Adlai E. Stevenson	1893–1897
Secretary of State	Walter Q. Gresham Richard Olney	1893–1895 1895–1897
Secretary of Treasury	John G. Carlisle	1893–1897
Secretary of War	Daniel S. Lamont	1893–1897
Attorney General	Richard Olney James Harmon	1893–1895 1895–1897
Postmaster General	Wilson S. Bissell William L. Wilson	1893–1895 1895–1897
Secretary of Navy	Hilary A. Herbert	1893–1897
Secretary of Interior	Hoke Smith David R. Francis	1893–1896 1896–1897
Secretary of Agriculture	Julius S. Morton	1893–1897

The McKinley Administration

President	William McKinley	1897–1901
Vice President	Garret A. Hobart Theodore Roosevelt	1897–1901 1901
Secretary of State	John Sherman William R. Day John Hay	1897–1898 1898 1898–1901
Secretary of Treasury	Lyman J. Gage	1897–1901
Secretary of War	Russell A. Alger Elihu Root	1897–1899 1899–1901
Attorney General	Joseph McKenna John W. Griggs Philander C. Knox	1897–1898 1898–1901 1901
Postmaster General	James A. Gary Charles E. Smith	1897–1898 1898–1901
Secretary of Navy	John D. Long	1897–1901
Secretary of Interior	Cornelius N. Bliss Ethan A. Hitchcock	1897–1899 1899–1901
Secretary of Agriculture	James Wilson	1897–1901

The Theodore Roosevelt Administration

President	Theodore Roosevelt	1901–1909
Vice President	Charles Fairbanks	1905–1909
Secretary of State	John Hay Elihu Root Robert Bacon	1901–1905 1905–1909 1909
Secretary of Treasury	Lyman J. Gage Leslie M. Shaw George B. Cortelyou	1901–1902 1902–1907 1907–1909
Secretary of War	Elihu Root William H. Taft Luke E. Wright	1901–1904 1904–1908 1908–1909
Attorney General	Philander C. Knox William H. Moody Charles J. Bonaparte	1901–1904 1904–1906 1906–1909
Postmaster General	Charles E. Smith Henry C. Payne Robert J. Wynne George B. Cortelyou George von L. Meyer	1901–1902 1902–1904 1904–1905 1905–1907 1907–1909

Secretary of Navy	John D. Long	1901–1902
	William H. Moody	1902–1904
	Paul Morton	1904–1905
	Charles J. Bonaparte	1905–1906
	Victor H. Metcalf	1906–1908
	Truman H. Newberry	1908–1909
Secretary of Interior	Ethan A. Hitchcock	1901–1907
	James R. Garfield	1907–1909
Secretary of Agriculture	James Wilson	1901–1909
Secretary of Labor and Commerce	George B. Cortelyou	1903–1904
	Victor H. Metcalf	1904–1906
	Oscar S. Straus	1906–1909
	Charles Nagel	1909

The Taft Administration

President	William H. Taft	1909–1913
Vice President	James S. Sherman	1909–1913
Secretary of State	Philander C. Knox	1909–1913
Secretary of Treasury	Franklin MacVeagh	1909–1913
Secretary of War	Jacob M. Dickinson	1909–1911
	Henry L. Stimson	1911–1913
Attorney General	George W. Wickersham	1909–1913
Postmaster General	Frank H. Hitchcock	1909–1913
Secretary of Navy	George von L. Meyer	1909–1913
Secretary of Interior	Richard A. Ballinger	1909–1911
	Walter L. Fisher	1911–1913
Secretary of Agriculture	James Wilson	1909–1913
Secretary of Labor and Commerce	Charles Nagel	1909–1913

The Wilson Administration

President	Woodrow Wilson	1913–1921
Vice President	Thomas R. Marshall	1913–1921
Secretary of State	William J. Bryan	1913–1915
	Robert Lansing	1915–1920
	Bainbridge Colby	1920–1921
Secretary of Treasury	William G. McAdoo	1913–1918
	Carter Glass	1918–1920
	David F. Houston	1920–1921
Secretary of War	Lindley M. Garrison	1913–1916
	Newton D. Baker	1916–1921
Attorney General	James C. McReynolds	1913–1914
	Thomas W. Gregory	1914–1919
	A. Mitchell Palmer	1919–1921
Postmaster General	Albert S. Burleson	1913–1921
Secretary of Navy	Josephus Daniels	1913–1921
Secretary of Interior	Franklin K. Lane	1913–1920
	John B. Payne	1920–1921
Secretary of Agriculture	David F. Houston	1913–1920
	Edwin T. Meredith	1920–1921
Secretary of Commerce	William C. Redfield	1913–1919
	Joshua W. Alexander	1919–1921
Secretary of Labor	William B. Wilson	1913–1921

The Harding Administration

President	Warren G. Harding	1921–1923
Vice President	Calvin Coolidge	1921–1923
Secretary of State	Charles E. Hughes	1921–1923
Secretary of Treasury	Andrew Mellon	1921–1923
Secretary of War	John W. Weeks	1921–1923
Attorney General	Harry M. Daugherty	1921–1923
Postmaster General	Will H. Hays	1921–1922
	Hubert Work	1922–1923
	Harry S. New	1923
Secretary of Navy	Edwin Denby	1921–1923
Secretary of Interior	Albert B. Fall	1921–1923
	Hubert Work	1923
Secretary of Agriculture	Henry C. Wallace	1921–1923
Secretary of Commerce	Herbert C. Hoover	1921–1923
Secretary of Labor	James J. Davis	1921–1923

The Coolidge Administration

President	Calvin Coolidge	1923–1929
Vice President	Charles G. Dawes	1925–1929
Secretary of State	Charles E. Hughes	1923–1925
	Frank B. Kellogg	1925–1929
Secretary of Treasury	Andrew Mellon	1923–1929
Secretary of War	John W. Weeks	1923–1925
	Dwight F. Davis	1925–1929

(continued)

The Coolidge Administration *(continued)*

Attorney General	Henry M. Daugherty	1923–1924
	Harlan F. Stone	1924–1925
	John G. Sargent	1925–1929
Postmaster General	Harry S. New	1923–1929
Secretary of Navy	Edwin Derby	1923–1924
	Curtis D. Wilbur	1924–1929
Secretary of Interior	Hubert Work	1923–1928
	Roy O. West	1928–1929
Secretary of Agriculture	Henry C. Wallace	1923–1924
	Howard M. Gore	1924–1925
	William M. Jardine	1925–1929
Secretary of Commerce	Herbert C. Hoover	1923–1928
	William F. Whiting	1928–1929
Secretary of Labor	James J. Davis	1923–1929

The Hoover Administration

President	Herbert C. Hoover	1929–1933
Vice President	Charles Curtis	1929–1933
Secretary of State	Henry L. Stimson	1929–1933
Secretary of Treasury	Andrew Mellon	1929–1932
	Ogden L. Mills	1932–1933
Secretary of War	James W. Good	1929
	Patrick J. Hurley	1929–1933
Attorney General	William D. Mitchell	1929–1933
Postmaster General	Walter F. Brown	1929–1933
Secretary of Navy	Charles F. Adams	1929–1933
Secretary of Interior	Ray L. Wilbur	1929–1933
Secretary of Agriculture	Arthur M. Hyde	1929–1933
Secretary of Commerce	Robert P. Lamont	1929–1932
	Roy D. Chapin	1932–1933
Secretary of Labor	James J. Davis	1929–1930
	William N. Doak	1930–1933

The Franklin D. Roosevelt Administration

President	Franklin D. Roosevelt	1933–1945
Vice President	John Nance Garner	1933–1941
	Henry A. Wallace	1941–1945
	Harry S. Truman	1945
Secretary of State	Cordell Hull	1933–1944
	E. R. Stettinius Jr.	1944–1945
Secretary of Treasury	William H. Woodin	1933–1934
	Henry Morgenthau Jr.	1934–1945
Secretary of War	George H. Dern	1933–1936
	Henry A. Woodring	1936–1940
	Henry L. Stimson	1940–1945
Attorney General	Homer S. Cummings	1933–1939
	Frank Murphy	1939–1940
	Robert H. Jackson	1940–1941
	Francis Biddle	1941–1945
Postmaster General	James A. Farley	1933–1940
	Frank C. Walker	1940–1945
Secretary of Navy	Claude A. Swanson	1933–1940
	Charles Edison	1940
	Frank Knox	1940–1944
	James V. Forrestal	1944–1945
Secretary of Interior	Harold L. Ickes	1933–1945
Secretary of Agriculture	Henry A. Wallace	1933–1940
	Claude R. Wickard	1940–1945
Secretary of Commerce	Daniel C. Roper	1933–1939
	Harry L. Hopkins	1939–1940
	Jesse Jones	1940–1945
	Henry A. Wallace	1945
Secretary of Labor	Frances Perkins	1933–1945

The Truman Administration

President	Harry S. Truman	1945–1953
Vice President	Alben W. Barkley	1949–1953
Secretary of State	James F. Byrnes	1945–1947
	George C. Marshall	1947–1949
	Dean G. Acheson	1949–1953
Secretary of Treasury	Fred M. Vinson	1945–1946
	John W. Snyder	1946–1953
Secretary of War	Robert P. Patterson	1945–1947
	Kenneth C. Royall	1947
Attorney General	Tom C. Clark	1945–1949
	J. Howard McGrath	1949–1952
	James P. McGranery	1952–1953
Postmaster General	Frank C. Walker	1945
	Robert E. Hannegan	1945–1947
	Jesse M. Donaldson	1947–1953
Secretary of Navy	James V. Forrestal	1945–1947
Secretary of Interior	Harold L. Ickes	1945–1946
	Julius A. Krug	1946–1949
	Oscar L. Chapman	1949–1953

Secretary of Agriculture	Clinton P. Anderson Charles F. Brannan	1945–1948 1948–1953
Secretary of Commerce	Henry A. Wallace W. Averell Harriman Charles W. Sawyer	1945–1946 1946–1948 1948–1953
Secretary of Labor	Lewis B. Schwellenbach Maurice J. Tobin	1945–1948 1948–1953
Secretary of Defense	James V. Forrestal Louis A. Johnson George C. Marshall Robert A. Lovett	1947–1949 1949–1950 1950–1951 1951–1953

The Eisenhower Administration

President	Dwight D. Eisenhower	1953–1961
Vice President	Richard M. Nixon	1953–1961
Secretary of State	John Foster Dulles Christian A. Herter	1953–1959 1959–1961
Secretary of Treasury	George M. Humphrey Robert B. Anderson	1953–1957 1957–1961
Attorney General	Herbert Brownell Jr. William P. Rogers	1953–1858 1958–1961
Postmaster General	Arthur E. Summerfield	1953–1961
Secretary of Interior	Douglas McKay Fred A. Seaton	1953–1956 1956–1961
Secretary of Agriculture	Ezra T. Benson	1953–1961
Secretary of Commerce	Sinclair Weeks Lewis L. Strauss Frederick H. Mueller	1953–1958 1958–1959 1959–1961
Secretary of Labor	Martin P. Durkin James P. Mitchell	1953 1953–1961
Secretary of Defense	Charles E. Wilson Neil H. McElroy Thomas S. Gates Jr.	1953–1957 1957–1959 1959–1961
Secretary of Health, Education, and Welfare	Oveta Culp Hobby Marion B. Folsom Arthur S. Flemming	1953–1955 1955–1958 1958–1961

The Kennedy Administration

President	John F. Kennedy	1961–1963
Vice President	Lyndon B. Johnson	1961–1963
Secretary of State	Dean Rusk	1961–1963
Secretary of Treasury	C. Douglas Dillon	1961–1963
Attorney General	Robert F. Kennedy	1961–1963
Postmaster General	J. Edward Day John A. Gronouski	1961–1963 1963
Secretary of Interior	Stewart L. Udall	1961–1963
Secretary of Agriculture	Orville L. Freeman	1961–1963
Secretary of Commerce	Luther H. Hodges	1961–1963
Secretary of Labor	Arthur J. Goldberg W. Willard Wirtz	1961–1962 1962–1963
Secretary of Defense	Robert S. McNamara	1961–1963
Secretary of Health, Education, and Welfare	Abraham A. Ribicoff Anthony J. Celebrezze	1961–1962 1962–1963

The Lyndon Johnson Administration

President	Lyndon B. Johnson	1963–1969
Vice President	Hubert H. Humphrey	1965–1969
Secretary of State	Dean Rusk	1963–1969
Secretary of Treasury	C. Douglas Dillon Henry H. Fowler	1963–1965 1965–1969
Attorney General	Robert F. Kennedy Nicholas Katzenbach Ramsey Clark	1963–1964 1965–1966 1967–1969
Postmaster General	John A. Gronouski Lawrence F. O'Brien Marvin Watson	1963–1965 1965–1968 1968–1969
Secretary of Interior	Stewart L. Udall	1963–1969
Secretary of Agriculture	Orville L. Freeman	1963–1969
Secretary of Commerce	Luther H. Hodges John T. Connor Alexander B. Trowbridge Cyrus R. Smith	1963–1964 1964–1967 1967–1968 1968–1969
Secretary of Labor	W. Willard Wirtz	1963–1969
Secretary of Defense	Robert F. McNamara Clark Clifford	1963–1968 1968–1969
Secretary of Health, Education, and Welfare	Anthony J. Celebrezze John W. Gardner Wilbur J. Cohen	1963–1965 1965–1968 1968–1969

(continued)

The Lyndon Johnson Administration *(continued)*

Secretary of Housing and Urban Development	Robert C. Weaver Robert C. Wood	1966–1969 1969
Secretary of Transportation	Alan S. Boyd	1967–1969

The Nixon Administration

President	Richard M. Nixon	1969–1974
Vice President	Spiro T. Agnew Gerald R. Ford	1969–1973 1973–1974
Secretary of State	William P. Rogers Henry A. Kissinger	1969–1973 1973–1974
Secretary of Treasury	David M. Kennedy John B. Connally George P. Shultz William E. Simon	1969–1970 1971–1972 1972–1974 1974
Attorney General	John N. Mitchell Richard G. Kleindienst Elliot L. Richardson William B. Saxbe	1969–1972 1972–1973 1973 1973–1974
Postmaster General	Winston M. Blount	1969–1971
Secretary of Interior	Walter J. Hickel Rogers Morton	1969–1970 1971–1974
Secretary of Agriculture	Clifford M. Hardin Earl L. Butz	1969–1971 1971–1974
Secretary of Commerce	Maurice H. Stans Peter G. Peterson Frederick B. Dent	1969–1972 1972–1973 1973–1974
Secretary of Labor	George P. Shultz James D. Hodgson Peter J. Brennan	1969–1970 1970–1973 1973–1974
Secretary of Defense	Melvin R. Laird Elliot L. Richardson James R. Schlesinger	1969–1973 1973 1973–1974
Secretary of Health, Education, and Welfare	Robert H. Finch Elliot L. Richardson Casper W. Weinberger	1969–1970 1970–1973 1973–1974
Secretary of Housing and Urban Development	George Romney James T. Lynn	1969–1973 1973–1974
Secretary of Transportation	John A. Volpe Claude S. Brinegar	1969–1973 1973–1974

The Ford Administration

President	Gerald R. Ford	1974–1977
Vice President	Nelson A. Rockefeller	1974–1977
Secretary of State	Henry A. Kissinger	1974–1977
Secretary of Treasury	William E. Simon	1974–1977
Attorney General	William Saxbe Edward Levi	1974–1975 1975–1977
Secretary of Interior	Rogers Morton Stanley K. Hathaway Thomas Kleppe	1974–1975 1975 1975–1977
Secretary of Agriculture	Earl L. Butz John A. Knebel	1974–1976 1976–1977
Secretary of Commerce	Frederick B. Dent Rogers Morton Elliot L. Richardson	1974–1975 1975–1976 1976–1977
Secretary of Labor	Peter J. Brennan John T. Dunlop W. J. Usery	1974–1975 1975–1976 1976–1977
Secretary of Defense	James R. Schlesinger Donald Rumsfeld	1974–1975 1975–1977
Secretary of Health, Education, and Welfare	Casper Weinberger Forrest D. Mathews	1974–1975 1975–1977
Secretary of Housing and Urban Development	James T. Lynn Carla A. Hills	1974–1975 1975–1977
Secretary of Transportation	Claude Brinegar William T. Coleman	1974–1975 1975–1977

The Carter Administration

President	Jimmy Carter	1977–1981
Vice President	Walter F. Mondale	1977–1981
Secretary of State	Cyrus R. Vance Edmund Muskie	1977–1980 1980–1981
Secretary of Treasury	W. Michael Blumenthal G. William Miller	1977–1979 1979–1981
Attorney General	Griffin Bell Benjamin R. Civiletti	1977–1979 1979–1981
Secretary of Interior	Cecil D. Andrus	1977–1981
Secretary of Agriculture	Robert Bergland	1977–1981

Secretary of Commerce	Juanita M. Kreps Philip M. Klutznick	1977–1979 1979–1981
Secretary of Labor	F. Ray Marshall	1977–1981
Secretary of Defense	Harold Brown	1977–1981
Secretary of Health, Education, and Welfare	Joseph A. Califano Patricia R. Harris	1977–1979 1979
Secretary of Health and Human Services	Patricia R. Harris	1979–1981
Secretary of Education	Shirley M. Hufstedler	1979–1981
Secretary of Housing and Urban Development	Patricia R. Harris Moon Landrieu	1977–1979 1979–1981
Secretary of Transportation	Brock Adams Neil E. Goldschmidt	1977–1979 1979–1981
Secretary of Energy	James R. Schlesinger Charles W. Duncan	1977–1979 1979–1981

The Reagan Administration

President	Ronald Regan	1981–1989
Vice President	George H. W. Bush	1981–1989
Secretary of State	Alexander M. Haig Jr. George P. Shultz	1981–1982 1982–1989
Secretary of the Treasury	Donald T. Regan James A. Baker III Nicholas F. Brady	1981–1985 1985–1988 1988–1989
Secretary of Defense	Caspar W. Weinberger Frank C. Carlucci	1981–1987 1987–1989
Attorney General	William French Smith Edwin Meese III Richard L. Thornburgh	1981–1985 1985–1988 1988–1989
Secretary of the Interior	James G. Watt William P. Clark Donald P. Hodel	1981–1983 1983–1985 1985–1989
Secretary of Agriculture	John R. Block Richard E. Lyng	1981–1986 1986–1989
Secretary of Commerce	Malcolm Baldrige C. William Verity Jr.	1981–1987 1987–1989
Secretary of Labor	Raymond J. Donovan William E. Brock Ann Dore McLaughlin	1981–1985 1985–1987 1987–1989
Secretary of Health and Human Services	Richard S. Schweiker Margaret M. Heckler Otis R. Bowen	1981–1983 1983–1985 1985–1989
Secretary of Housing and Urban Development	Samuel R. Pierce Jr.	1981–1989
Secretary of Transportation	Andrew L. Lewis Jr. Elizabeth H. Dole James H. Burnley IV	1981–1983 1983–1987 1987–1989
Secretary of Energy	James B. Edwards Donald P. Hodel John S. Herrington	1981–1983 1983–1985 1985–1989
Secretary of Education	T. H. Bell William J. Bennett Lauro F. Cavazos	1981–1985 1985–1988 1988–1989

The George H. W. Bush Administration

President	George H. W. Bush	1989–1993
Vice President	J. Danforth Quayle	1989–1983
Secretary of State	James A. Baker III Lawrence S. Eagleburger	1989–1992 1992–1993
Secretary of the Treasury	Nicholas F. Brady	1989–1993
Secretary of Defense	Richard Cheney	1989–1993
Attorney General	Richard L. Thornburgh William P. Barr	1989–1991 1991–1993
Secretary of the Interior	Manuel Lujan Jr.	1989–1993
Secretary of Agriculture	Clayton K. Yeutter Edward Madigan	1989–1991 1991–1993
Secretary of Commerce	Robert A. Mosbacher Sr. Barbara H. Franklin	1989–1992 1992–1993
Secretary of Labor	Elizabeth H. Dole Lynn Martin	1989–1990 1991–1993
Secretary of Health and Human Services	Louis W. Sullivan	1989–1993
Secretary of Housing and Urban Development	Jack F. Kemp	1989–1993
Secretary of Transportation	Samuel K. Skinner Andrew Card	1989–1992 1992–1993
Secretary of Energy	James D. Watkins	1989–1993

(continued)

The George H. W. Bush Administration *(continued)*

Secretary of Education	Lauro F. Cavazos Lamar Alexander	1989–1990 1991–1993
Secretary of Veterans Affairs	Edward J. Derwinski	1989–1992

The Clinton Administration

President	William J. Clinton	1993–2001
Vice President	Albert A. Gore Jr.	1993–2001
Secretary of State	Warren M. Christopher Madeleine Albright	1993–1997 1997–2001
Secretary of the Treasury	Lloyd Bentsen Robert E. Rubin Lawrence H. Summers	1993–1994 1995–1999 1999–2001
Secretary of Defense	Les Aspin William J. Perry William S. Cohen	1993–1994 1994–1997 1997–2001
Attorney General	Janet Reno	1993–2001
Secretary of the Interior	Bruce Babbitt	1993–2001
Secretary of Agriculture	Mike Espy Dan Glickman	1993–1994 1995–2001
Secretary of Commerce	Ronald H. Brown Mickey Kantor William M. Daley Norman Y. Mineta	1993–1996 1996–1997 1997–2000 2000–2001
Secretary of Labor	Robert B. Reich Alexis Herman	1993–1997 1997–2001
Secretary of Health and Human Services	Donna E. Shalala	1993–2001
Secretary of Housing and Urban Development	Henry G. Cisneros Andrew M. Cuomo	1993–1997 1997–2001
Secretary of Transportation	Federico F. Peña Rodney Slater	1993–1997 1997–2001
Secretary of Energy	Hazel R. O'Leary Frederico F. Peña Bill Richardson	1993–1997 1997–1998 1998–2001
Secretary of Education	Richard W. Riley	1993–2001
Secretary of Veterans Affairs	Jesse Brown Togo D. West Jr.	1993–1998 1998–2001

The George W. Bush Administration

President	George W. Bush	2001–2009
Vice President	Richard B. Cheney	2001–2009
Secretary of State	Gen. Colin L. Powell Condoleezza Rice	2001–2005 2005–2009
Secretary of the Treasury	Paul H. O'Neill John Snow Henry Paulson	2001–2002 2003–2006 2006–2009
Secretary of Defense	Donald H. Rumsfeld Robert Gates	2001–2006 2006–2009
Attorney General	Alberto Gonzales Michael Mukasey	2005–2007 2007–2009
Secretary of the Interior	Gale A. Norton Dirk Kempthorne	2001–2006 2006–2009
Secretary of Agriculture	Ann M. Veneman Mike Johanns Edward T. Schafer	2001–2005 2005–2007 2008–2009
Secretary of Commerce	Donald L. Evans Carlos Gutierrez	2001–2005 2005–2009
Secretary of Labor	Elaine L. Chao	2001–2009
Secretary of Health and Human Services	Tommy G. Thompson Mike Leavitt	2001–2005 2005–2009
Secretary of Homeland Security	Tom Ridge Michael Chertoff	2003–2005 2005–2009
Secretary of Housing and Urban Development	Melquiades R. Martinez Alphonso Jackson Steven C. Preston	2001 2003–2008 2008–2009
Secretary of Transportation	Norman Y. Mineta Mary E. Peters	2001–2006 2006–2009
Secretary of Energy	Spencer Abraham Samuel Bodman	2001–2005 2005–2009
Secretary of Education	Roderick R. Paige Margaret Spellings	2001–2005 2005–2009
Secretary of Veterans Affairs	Anthony Principi Jim Nicholson James Peake	2001–2005 2005–2007 2007–2009

The Obama Administration

President	Barack Obama	2009–
Vice President	Joseph R. Biden	2009–
Secretary of State	Hillary Rodham Clinton	2009–
Secretary of the Treasury	Timothy F. Geithner	2009–
Secretary of Defense	Robert M. Gates	2009–

The Obama Administration *(continued)*

Attorney General	Eric H. Holder Jr.	2009–
Secretary of the Interior	Kenneth L. Salazar	2009–
Secretary of Agriculture	Thomas J. Vilsack	2009–
Secretary of Commerce	Gary F. Locke	2009–
Secretary of Labor	Hilda L. Solis	2009–
Secretary of Health and Human Services	Kathleen Sebelius	2009–
Secretary of Housing and Urban Development	Shaun L. S. Donovan	2009–
Secretary of Transportation	Raymond L. LaHood	2009–
Secretary of Energy	Steven Chu	2009–
Secretary of Education	Arne Duncan	2009–
Secretary of Veterans Affairs	Eric K. Shinseki	2009–
Secretary of Homeland Security	Janet A. Napolitano	2009–

Members of the Supreme Court of the United States

Name	State Appointed From	Appointed by President	Judicial Oath Taken	Date Service Terminated
Chief Justices				
Jay, John	New York	Washington	(a) October 19, 1789	June 29, 1795
Rutledge, John	South Carolina	Washington	August 12, 1795	December 15, 1795
Ellsworth, Oliver	Connecticut	Washington	March 8, 1796	December 15, 1800
Marshall, John	Virginia	Adams, John	February 4, 1801	July 6, 1835
Taney, Roger Brooke	Maryland	Jackson	March 28, 1836	October 12, 1864
Chase, Salmon Portland	Ohio	Lincoln	December 15, 1864	May 7, 1873
Waite, Morrison Remick	Ohio	Grant	March 4, 1874	March 23, 1888
Fuller, Melville Weston	Illinois	Cleveland	October 8, 1888	July 4, 1910
White, Edward Douglass	Louisiana	Taft	December 19, 1910	May 19, 1921
Taft, William Howard	Connecticut	Harding	July 11, 1921	February 3, 1930
Hughes, Charles Evans	New York	Hoover	February 24, 1930	June 30, 1941
Stone, Harlan Fiske	New York	Roosevelt, F.	July 3, 1941	April 22, 1946
Vinson, Fred Moore	Kentucky	Truman	June 24, 1946	September 8, 1953
Warren, Earl	California	Eisenhower	October 5, 1953	June 23, 1969
Burger, Warren Earl	Virginia	Nixon	June 23, 1969	September 26, 1986
Rehnquist, William H.	Virginia	Reagan	September 26, 1986	September 3, 2005
Roberts, John G. Jr.	Maryland	Bush, G. W.	September 29, 2005	
Associate Justices				
Rutledge, John	South Carolina	Washington	(a) February 15, 1790	March 5, 1791
Cushing, William	Massachusetts	Washington	(c) February 2, 1790	September 13, 1810

(continued)

Name	State Appointed From	Appointed by President	Judicial Oath Taken	Date Service Terminated
Associate Justices *(continued)*				
Wilson, James	Pennsylvania	Washington	(b) October 5, 1789	August 21, 1798
Blair, John	Virginia	Washington	(c) February 2, 1790	October 25, 1795
Iredell, James	North Carolina	Washington	(b) May 12, 1790	October 20, 1799
Johnson, Thomas	Maryland	Washington	(a) August 6, 1792	January 16, 1793
Paterson, William	New Jersey	Washington	(a) March 11, 1793	September 9, 1806
Chase, Samuel	Maryland	Washington	February 4, 1796	June 19, 1811
Washington, Bushrod	Virginia	Adams, John	(c) February 4, 1799	November 26, 1829
Moore, Alfred	North Carolina	Adams, John	(a) April 21, 1800	January 26, 1804
Johnson, William	South Carolina	Jefferson	May 7, 1804	August 4, 1834
Livingston, Henry Brockholst	New York	Jefferson	January 20, 1807	March 18, 1823
Todd, Thomas	Kentucky	Jefferson	(a) May 4, 1807	February 7, 1826
Duvall, Gabriel	Maryland	Madison	(a) November 23, 1811	January 14, 1835
Story, Joseph	Massachusetts	Madison	(c) February 3, 1812	September 10, 1845
Thompson, Smith	New York	Monroe	(b) September 1, 1823	December 18, 1843
Trimble, Robert	Kentucky	Adams, J. Q.	(a) June 16, 1826	August 25, 1828
McLean, John	Ohio	Jackson	(c) January 11, 1830	April 4, 1861
Baldwin, Henry	Pennsylvania	Jackson	January 18, 1830	April 21, 1844
Wayne, James Moore	Georgia	Jackson	January 14, 1835	July 5, 1867
Barbour, Philip Pendleton	Virginia	Jackson	May 12, 1836	February 25, 1841
Catron, John	Tennessee	Jackson	May 1, 1837	May 30, 1865
McKinley, John	Alabama	Van Buren	(c) January 9, 1838	July 19, 1852
Daniel, Peter Vivian	Virginia	Van Buren	(c) January 10, 1842	May 31, 1860
Nelson, Samuel	New York	Tyler	February 27, 1845	November 28, 1872
Woodbury, Levi	New Hampshire	Polk	(b) September 23, 1845	September 4, 1851
Grier, Robert Cooper	Pennsylvania	Polk	August 10, 1846	January 31, 1870
Curtis, Benjamin Robbins	Massachusetts	Fillmore	(b) October 10, 1851	September 30, 1857
Campbell, John Archibald	Alabama	Pierce	(c) April 11, 1853	April 30, 1861
Clifford, Nathan	Maine	Buchanan	January 21, 1858	July 25, 1881
Swayne, Noah Haynes	Ohio	Lincoln	January 27, 1862	January 24, 1881
Miller, Samuel Freeman	Iowa	Lincoln	July 21, 1862	October 13, 1890
Davis, David	Illinois	Lincoln	December 10, 1862	March 4, 1877
Field, Stephen Johnson	California	Lincoln	May 20, 1863	December 1, 1897
Strong, William	Pennsylvania	Grant	March 14, 1870	December 14, 1880
Bradley, Joseph P.	New Jersey	Grant	March 23, 1870	January 22, 1892
Hunt, Ward	New York	Grant	January 9, 1873	January 27, 1882
Harlan, John Marshall	Kentucky	Hayes	December 10, 1877	October 14, 1911
Woods, William Burnham	Georgia	Hayes	January 5, 1881	May 14, 1887
Matthews, Stanley	Ohio	Garfield	May 17, 1881	March 22, 1889
Gray, Horace	Massachusetts	Arthur	January 9, 1882	September 15, 1902
Blatchford, Samuel	New York	Arthur	April 3, 1882	July 7, 1893
Lamar, Lucius Quintus C.	Mississippi	Cleveland	January 18, 1888	January 23, 1893

Name	State Appointed From	Appointed by President	Judicial Oath Taken	Date Service Terminated
Associate Justices *(continued)*				
Brewer, David Josiah	Kansas	Harrison	January 6, 1890	March 28, 1910
Brown, Henry Billings	Michigan	Harrison	January 5, 1891	May 28, 1906
Shiras, George Jr.	Pennsylvania	Harrison	October 10, 1892	February 23, 1903
Jackson, Howell Edmunds	Tennessee	Harrison	March 4, 1893	August 8, 1895
White, Edward Douglass	Louisiana	Cleveland	March 12, 1894	December 18, 1910*
Peckham, Rufus Wheeler	New York	Cleveland	January 6, 1896	October 24, 1909
McKenna, Joseph	California	McKinley	January 26, 1898	January 5, 1925
Holmes, Oliver Wendell	Massachusetts	Roosevelt, T.	December 8, 1902	January 12, 1932
Day, William Rufus	Ohio	Roosevelt, T.	March 2, 1903	November 13, 1922
Moody, William Henry	Massachusetts	Roosevelt, T.	December 17, 1906	November 20, 1910
Lurton, Horace Harmon	Tennessee	Taft	January 3, 1910	July 12, 1914
Hughes, Charles Evans	New York	Taft	October 10, 1910	June 10, 1916
Van Devanter, Willis	Wyoming	Taft	January 3, 1911	June 2, 1937
Lamar, Joseph Rucker	Georgia	Taft	January 3, 1911	January 2, 1916
Pitney, Mahlon	New Jersey	Taft	March 18, 1912	December 31, 1922
McReynolds, James Clark	Tennessee	Wilson	October 12, 1914	January 31, 1941
Brandeis, Louis Dembitz	Massachusetts	Wilson	June 5, 1916	February 13, 1939
Clarke, John Hessin	Ohio	Wilson	October 9, 1916	September 18, 1922
Sutherland, George	Utah	Harding	October 2, 1922	January 17, 1938
Butler, Pierce	Minnesota	Harding	January 2, 1923	November 16, 1939
Sanford, Edward Terry	Tennessee	Harding	February 19, 1923	March 8, 1930
Stone, Harlan Fiske	New York	Coolidge	March 2, 1925	July 2, 1941*
Roberts, Owen Josephus	Pennsylvania	Hoover	June 2, 1930	July 31, 1945
Cardozo, Benjamin Nathan	New York	Hoover	March 14, 1932	July 9, 1938
Black, Hugo Lafayette	Alabama	Roosevelt, F.	August 19, 1937	September 17, 1971
Reed, Stanley Forman	Kentucky	Roosevelt, F.	January 31, 1938	February 25, 1957
Frankfurter, Felix	Massachusetts	Roosevelt, F.	January 30, 1939	August 28, 1962
Douglas, William Orville	Connecticut	Roosevelt, F.	April 17, 1939	November 12, 1975
Murphy, Frank	Michigan	Roosevelt, F.	February 5, 1940	July 19, 1949
Byrnes, James Francis	South Carolina	Roosevelt, F.	July 8, 1941	October 3, 1942
Jackson, Robert Houghwout	New York	Roosevelt, F.	July 11, 1941	October 9, 1954
Rutledge, Wiley Blount	Iowa	Roosevelt, F.	February 15, 1943	September 10, 1949
Burton, Harold Hitz	Ohio	Truman	October 1, 1945	October 13, 1958
Clark, Tom Campbell	Texas	Truman	August 24, 1949	June 12, 1967
Minton, Sherman	Indiana	Truman	October 12, 1949	October 15, 1956
Harlan, John Marshall	New York	Eisenhower	March 28, 1955	September 23, 1971
Brennan, William J. Jr.	New Jersey	Eisenhower	October 16, 1956	July 20, 1990
Whittaker, Charles Evans	Missouri	Eisenhower	March 25, 1957	March 31, 1962
Stewart, Potter	Ohio	Eisenhower	October 14, 1958	July 3, 1981
White, Byron Raymond	Colorado	Kennedy	April 16, 1962	June 28, 1993
Goldberg, Arthur Joseph	Illinois	Kennedy	October 1, 1962	July 25, 1965

(continued)

Name	State Appointed From	Appointed by President	Judicial Oath Taken	Date Service Terminated
Associate Justices *(continued)*				
Fortas, Abe	Tennessee	Johnson, L.	October 4, 1965	May 14, 1969
Marshall, Thurgood	New York	Johnson, L.	October 2, 1967	October 1, 1991
Blackmun, Harry A.	Minnesota	Nixon	June 9, 1970	August 3, 1994
Powell, Lewis F. Jr.	Virginia	Nixon	January 7, 1972	June 26, 1987
Rehnquist, William H.	Arizona	Nixon	January 7, 1972	September 26, 1986*
Stevens, John Paul	Illinois	Ford	December 19, 1975	
O'Connor, Sandra Day	Arizona	Reagan	September 25, 1981	January 31, 2006
Scalia, Antonin	Virginia	Reagan	September 26, 1986	
Kennedy, Anthony M.	California	Reagan	February 18, 1988	
Souter, David H.	New Hampshire	Bush, G. H. W.	October 9, 1990	
Thomas, Clarence	Georgia	Bush, G. H. W.	October 23, 1991	
Ginsburg, Ruth Bader	New York	Clinton	August 10, 1993	
Breyer, Stephen G.	Massachusetts	Clinton	August 3, 1994	
Alito, Samuel A. Jr.	New Jersey	Bush, G. W.	January 31, 2006	
Sotomayor, Sonia	New York	Obama	August 8, 2009	

Notes: The acceptance of the appointment and commission by the appointee, as evidenced by the taking of the prescribed oaths, is here implied; otherwise the individual is not carried on this list of the Members of the Court. Examples: Robert Hanson Harrison is not carried, as a letter from President Washington of February 9, 1790, states Harrison declined to serve. Neither is Edwin M. Stanton who died before he could take the necessary steps toward becoming a Member of the Court. Chief Justice Rutledge is included because he took his oaths, presided over the August Term of 1795, and his name appears on two opinions of the Court for that Term.

The date a Member of the Court took his/her Judicial oath (the Judiciary Act provided "That the Justices of the Supreme Court, and the district judges, before they proceed to execute the duties of their respective offices, shall take the following oath . . .") is here used as the date of the beginning of his/her service, for until that oath is taken he/she is not vested with the prerogatives of the office. The dates given in this column are for the oaths taken following the receipt of the commissions. Dates without small-letter references are taken from the Minutes of the Court or from the original oath which are in the Curator's collection. The small letter (a) denotes the date is from the Minutes of some other court; (b) from some other unquestionable authority; (c) from authority that is questionable, and better authority would be appreciated.

[The foregoing was taken from a booklet prepared by the Supreme Court of the United States, and published with funding from the Supreme Court Historical Society.]

*Elevated.

Historical Party Strength in the U.S. Congress

Party Abbreviations

Ad: pro-administration (no parties)
C: coalition (no parties)
D: Democratic
DR: Democratic-Republican
F: Federalist
J: Jacksonian Democrat
NR: National Republican
Op: anti-administration (no parties)
R: Republican
U: Unionist
W: Whig

Period	Congress	Party of Majority		Party of Minority		Others	President
U.S. Senate							
1789–1791	1st	Ad	17	Op	9	—	Washington (F)
1791–1793	2nd	F	16	DR	13	—	Washington (F)
1793–1795	3rd	F	17	DR	13	—	Washington (F)
1795–1797	4th	F	19	DR	13	—	Washington (F)
1797–1799	5th	F	20	DR	12	—	J. Adams (F)
1799–1801	6th	F	19	DR	13	—	J. Adams (F)
1801–1803	7th	DR	18	F	13	—	Jefferson (DR)
1803–1805	8th	DR	25	F	9	—	Jefferson (DR)
1805–1807	9th	DR	27	F	7	—	Jefferson (DR)
1807–1809	10th	DR	28	F	6	—	Jefferson (DR)
1809–1811	11th	DR	28	F	6	—	Madison (DR)
1811–1813	12th	DR	30	F	6	—	Madison (DR)
1813–1815	13th	DR	27	F	9	—	Madison (DR)
1815–1817	14th	DR	25	F	11	—	Madison (DR)
1817–1819	15th	DR	34	F	10	—	Monroe (DR)
1819–1821	16th	DR	35	F	7	—	Monroe (DR)
1821–1823	17th	DR	44	F	4	—	Monroe (DR)
1823–1825	18th	DR	44	F	4	—	Monroe (DR)
1825–1827	19th	Ad	26	J	20	—	J. Q. Adams (C)
1827–1829	20th	J	28	Ad	20	—	J. Q. Adams (C)
1829–1831	21st	D	26	NR	22	—	Jackson (D)
1831–1833	22nd	D	25	NR	21	2	Jackson (D)
1833–1835	23rd	D	20	NR	20	8	Jackson (D)
1835–1837	24th	D	27	W	25	—	Jackson (D)
1837–1839	25th	D	30	W	18	4	Van Buren (D)
1839–1841	26th	D	28	W	22	—	Van Buren (D)
1841–1843	27th	W	28	D	22	2	W. H. Harrison (W)
1843–1845	28th	W	28	D	25	1	Tyler (W)
1845–1847	29th	D	31	W	25	—	Polk (D)
1847–1849	30th	D	36	W	21	1	Polk (D)
1849–1851	31st	D	35	W	25	2	Taylor (W)
1851–1853	32nd	D	35	W	24	3	Fillmore (W)
1853–1855	33rd	D	38	W	22	2	Pierce (D)
1855–1857	34th	D	40	R	15	4	Pierce (D)
1857–1859	35th	D	36	R	20	8	Buchanan (D)
1859–1861	36th	D	36	R	26	4	Buchanan (D)

(continued)

Period	Congress	Party of Majority		Party of Minority		Others	President
U.S. Senate *(continued)*							
1861–1863	37th	R	31	D	10	8	Lincoln (R)
1863–1865	38th	R	36	D	9	5	Lincoln (R)
1865–1867	39th	U	42	D	10	—	Lincoln (R)
1867–1869	40th	R	42	D	11	—	A. Johnson (R)
1869–1871	41st	R	56	D	11	—	Grant (R)
1871–1873	42nd	R	52	D	17	5	Grant (R)
1873–1875	43rd	R	49	D	19	5	Grant (R)
1875–1877	44th	R	45	D	29	2	Grant (R)
1877–1879	45th	R	39	D	36	1	Hayes (R)
1879–1881	46th	D	42	R	33	1	Hayes (R)
1881–1883	47th	R	37	D	37	1	Garfield (R)
1883–1885	48th	R	38	D	36	2	Arthur (R)
1885–1887	49th	R	43	D	34	—	Cleveland (D)
1887–1889	50th	R	39	D	37	—	Cleveland (D)
1889–1891	51st	R	39	D	37	—	B. Harrison (R)
1891–1893	52nd	R	47	D	39	2	B. Harrison (R)
1893–1895	53rd	D	44	R	38	3	Cleveland (D)
1895–1897	54th	R	43	D	39	6	Cleveland (D)
1897–1899	55th	R	47	D	34	7	McKinley (R)
1899–1901	56th	R	53	D	26	8	McKinley (R)
1901–1903	57th	R	55	D	31	4	McKinley (R)
1903–1905	58th	R	57	D	33	—	T. Roosevelt (R)
1905–1907	59th	R	57	D	33	—	T. Roosevelt (R)
1907–1909	60th	R	61	D	31	—	T. Roosevelt (R)
1909–1911	61st	R	61	D	32	—	Taft (R)
1911–1913	62nd	R	51	D	41	—	Taft (R)
1913–1915	63rd	D	51	R	44	1	Wilson (D)
1915–1917	64th	D	56	R	40	—	Wilson (D)
1917–1919	65th	D	53	R	42	—	Wilson (D)
1919–1921	66th	R	49	D	47	—	Wilson (D)
1921–1923	67th	R	59	D	37	—	Harding (R)
1923–1925	68th	R	51	D	43	2	Coolidge (R)
1925–1927	69th	R	56	D	39	1	Coolidge (R)
1927–1929	70th	R	49	D	46	1	Coolidge (R)
1929–1931	71st	R	56	D	39	1	Hoover (R)
1931–1933	72nd	R	48	D	47	1	Hoover (R)
1933–1935	73rd	D	60	R	35	1	F. D. Roosevelt (D)
1935–1937	74th	D	69	R	25	2	F. D. Roosevelt (D)
1937–1939	75th	D	76	R	16	4	F. D. Roosevelt (D)
1939–1941	76th	D	69	R	23	4	F. D. Roosevelt (D)
1941–1943	77th	D	66	R	28	2	F. D. Roosevelt (D)
1943–1945	78th	D	58	R	37	1	F. D. Roosevelt (D)
1945–1947	79th	D	56	R	38	1	F. D. Roosevelt (D)
1947–1949	80th	R	51	D	45	—	Truman (D)
1949–1951	81st	D	54	R	42	—	Truman (D)
1951–1953	82nd	D	49	R	47	—	Truman (D)
1953–1955	83rd	R	48	D	47	1	Eisenhower (R)
1955–1957	84th	D	48	R	47	1	Eisenhower (R)

Period	Congress	Party of Majority		Party of Minority		Others	President
1957–1959	85th	D	49	R	47	1	Eisenhower (R)
1959–1961	86th	D	65	R	35	1	Eisenhower (R)
1961–1963	87th	D	65	R	35	1	Kennedy (D)
1963–1965	88th	D	67	R	33	1	Kennedy (D)
1965–1967	89th	D	68	R	32	1	L. Johnson (D)
1967–1969	90th	D	64	R	36	1	L. Johnson (D)
1969–1971	91st	D	57	R	43	—	Nixon (R)
1971–1973	92nd	D	54	R	44	2	Nixon (R)
1973–1975	93rd	D	56	R	42	2	Nixon(R)
1975–1977	94th	D	60	R	37	3	Ford (R)
1977–1979	95th	D	61	R	38	1	Carter (D)
1979–1981	96th	D	58	R	41	1	Carter (D)
1981–1983	97th	R	53	D	46	1	Reagan (R)
1983–1985	98th	R	55	D	45	—	Reagan (R)
1985–1987	99th	R	53	D	47	—	Reagan (R)
1987–1989	100th	D	55	R	45	—	Reagan (R)
1989–1991	101st	D	54	R	46	—	G. H. W. Bush (R)
1991–1993	102nd	D	56	R	44	—	G. H. W. Bush (R)
1993–1995	103rd	D	57	R	43	—	Clinton (D)
1995–1997	104th	R	52	D	48	—	Clinton (D)
1997–1999	105th	R	55	D	45	—	Clinton (D)
1999–2001	106th	R	55	D	45	—	Clinton (D)
2001–2003	107th	D	50	R	49	1	G. W. Bush (R)
2003–2005	108th	R	51	D	48	1	G. W. Bush (R)
2005–2007	109th	R	55	D	44	1	G. W. Bush (R)
2007–2009	110th	R	49	D	49	2	G. W. Bush (R)
2009–2011	111th	D	58	R	40	2	Obama (D)
U.S. House of Representatives							
1789–1791	1st	Ad	37	Op	28	—	Washington (F)
1791–1793	2nd	Ad	39	Op	30	—	Washington (F)
1793–1795	3rd	Op	54	Ad	51	—	Washington (F)
1795–1797	4th	DR	59	F	47	—	Washington (F)
1797–1799	5th	F	57	DR	49	—	J. Adams (F)
1799–1801	6th	F	60	DR	46	—	J. Adams (F)
1801–1803	7th	DR	68	F	38	—	Jefferson (DR)
1803–1805	8th	DR	103	F	39	—	Jefferson (DR)
1805–1807	9th	DR	114	F	28	—	Jefferson (DR)
1807–1809	10th	DR	116	F	26	—	Jefferson (DR)
1809–1811	11th	DR	92	F	50	—	Madison (DR)
1811–1813	12th	DR	107	F	36	—	Madison (DR)
1813–1815	13th	DR	114	F	68	—	Madison (DR)
1815–1817	14th	DR	119	F	64	—	Madison (DR)
1817–1819	15th	DR	146	F	39	—	Monroe (DR)
1819–1821	16th	DR	160	F	26	—	Monroe (DR)
1821–1823	17th	DR	155	F	32	—	Monroe (DR)
1823–1825	18th	DR	189	F	24	—	Monroe (DR)

(continued)

Period	Congress	Party of Majority		Party of Minority		Others	President
U.S. House of Representatives *(continued)*							
1825–1827	19th	Ad	109	J	104	—	J. Q. Adams (C)
1827–1829	20th	J	113	Ad	100	—	J. Q. Adams (C)
1829–1831	21st	D	136	NR	72	5	Jackson (D)
1831–1833	22nd	D	126	NR	66	21	Jackson (D)
1833–1835	23rd	D	143	AM	63	34	Jackson (D)
1835–1837	24th	D	143	W	75	24	Jackson (D)
1837–1839	25th	D	128	W	100	14	Van Buren (D)
1839–1841	26th	D	125	W	109	8	Van Buren (D)
1841–1843	27th	W	142	D	98	2	W. H. Harrison (W)
1843–1845	28th	D	147	W	72	4	Tyler (W)
1845–1847	29th	D	142	W	79	6	Polk (D)
1847–1849	30th	W	116	D	110	4	Polk (D)
1849–1851	31st	D	113	W	108	9	Taylor (W)
1851–1853	32nd	D	127	W	85	5	Fillmore (W)
1853–1855	33rd	D	157	W	71	4	Pierce (D)
1855–1857	34th	R	100	D	83	51	Pierce (D)
1857–1859	35th	D	132	R	90	15	Buchanan (D)
1859–1861	36th	R	116	D	83	39	Buchanan (D)
1861–1863	37th	R	108	D	44	31	Lincoln (R)
1863–1865	38th	R	86	D	72	27	Lincoln (R)
1865–1867	39th	U	136	D	38	19	Lincoln (R)
1867–1869	40th	R	173	D	47	4	A. Johnson (R)
1869–1871	41st	R	171	D	67	5	Grant (R)
1871–1873	42nd	R	136	D	104	3	Grant (R)
1873–1875	43rd	R	199	D	88	5	Grant (R)
1875–1877	44th	D	182	R	103	8	Grant (R)
1877–1879	45th	D	155	R	136	2	Hayes (R)
1879–1881	46th	D	151	R	132	20	Hayes (R)
1881–1883	47th	R	147	D	128	14	Garfield (R)
1883–1885	48th	D	196	R	117	12	Arthur (R)
1885–1887	49th	D	182	R	141	2	Cleveland (D)
1887–1889	50th	D	167	R	152	6	Cleveland (D)
1889–1891	51st	R	179	D	152	1	B. Harrison (R)
1891–1893	52nd	D	238	R	86	8	B. Harrison (R)
1893–1895	53rd	D	218	R	124	14	Cleveland (D)
1895–1897	54th	R	254	D	93	10	Cleveland (D)
1897–1899	55th	R	206	D	124	27	McKinley (R)
1899–1901	56th	R	187	D	161	9	McKinley (R)
1901–1903	57th	R	200	D	151	6	McKinley (R)
1903–1905	58th	R	207	D	176	3	T. Roosevelt (R)
1905–1907	59th	R	251	D	135	0	T. Roosevelt (R)
1907–1909	60th	R	223	D	167	1	T. Roosevelt (R)
1909–1911	61st	R	219	D	172	—	Taft (R)
1911–1913	62nd	D	230	R	162	2	Taft (R)
1913–1915	63rd	D	291	R	134	10	Wilson (D)
1915–1917	64th	D	230	R	196	9	Wilson (D)
1917–1919	65th	D	214	R	215	6	Wilson (D)
1919–1921	66th	R	240	D	192	2	Wilson (D)

Period	Congress	Party of Majority		Party of Minority		Others	President
1921–1923	67th	R	302	D	131	2	Harding (R)
1923–1925	68th	R	225	D	207	3	Coolidge (R)
1925–1927	69th	R	247	D	183	5	Coolidge (R)
1927–1929	70th	R	238	D	194	3	Coolidge (R)
1929–1931	71st	R	270	D	164	1	Hoover (R)
1931–1933	72nd	D	216	R	218	1	Hoover (R)
1933–1935	73rd	D	313	R	117	5	F. D. Roosevelt (D)
1935–1937	74th	D	322	R	103	10	F. D. Roosevelt (D)
1937–1939	75th	D	334	R	88	13	F. D. Roosevelt (D)
1939–1941	76th	D	262	R	169	4	F. D. Roosevelt (D)
1941–1943	77th	D	267	R	162	5	F. D. Roosevelt (D)
1943–1945	78th	D	222	R	209	4	F. D. Roosevelt (D)
1945–1947	79th	D	242	R	191	2	F. D. Roosevelt (D)
1947–1949	80th	R	246	D	188	1	Truman (D)
1949–1951	81st	D	263	R	171	1	Truman (D)
1951–1953	82nd	D	235	R	199	1	Truman (D)
1953–1955	83rd	R	221	D	213	1	Eisenhower (R)
1955–1957	84th	D	232	R	203	—	Eisenhower (R)
1957-1959	85th	D	234	R	201	—	Eisenhower (R)
1959–1961	86th	D	283	R	153	1	Eisenhower (R)
1961–1963	87th	D	263	R	174	—	Kennedy (D)
1963–1965	88th	D	259	R	176	—	Kennedy (D)
1965–1967	89th	D	295	R	140	—	L. Johnson (D)
1967–1969	90th	D	247	R	187	—	L. Johnson (D)
1969–1971	91st	D	243	R	192	—	Nixon (R)
1971–1973	92nd	D	255	R	180	—	Nixon (R)
1973–1975	93rd	D	242	R	192	1	Nixon(R)
1975–1977	94th	D	291	R	144	—	Ford (R)
1977–1979	95th	D	292	R	143	—	Carter (D)
1979–1981	96th	D	277	R	158	—	Carter (D)
1981–1983	97th	D	242	R	192	1	Reagan (R)
1983–1985	98th	D	269	R	166	—	Reagan (R)
1985–1987	99th	D	253	R	182	—	Reagan (R)
1987–1989	100th	D	258	R	177	—	Reagan (R)
1989–1991	101st	D	260	R	175	—	G.H.W. Bush (R)
1991–1993	102nd	D	267	R	167	1	G.H.W. Bush (R)
1993–1995	103rd	D	258	R	176	1	Clinton (D)
1995–1997	104th	R	230	D	204	1	Clinton (D)
1997–1999	105th	R	228	D	206	1	Clinton (D)
1999–2001	106th	R	223	D	211	1	Clinton (D)
2001–2003	107th	R	221	D	212	2	G. W. Bush (R)
2003–2005	108th	R	229	D	204	1	G. W. Bush (R)
2005–2007	109th	R	232	D	202	1	G. W. Bush (R)
2007–2009	110th	R	202	D	233	1	G. W. Bush (R)
2009–2011	111th	R	178	D	256		Barack Obama (D)

Note: Before the first day of the 72nd Congress, 19 Representatives-elect died. In 14 cases, party control of the seat changed with the special election, and the Democrats ended up with a majority of House seats, enabling them to organize the House.

Source: Congressional Research Service, Office of the Clerk, U.S. House of Representatives. Biographical Directory of the U.S. Congress.

American Wars: Service Members and Casualties

American Revolution (1775–83)	
Total service members	217,000[1]
Battle deaths	4,435
War of 1812 (1812–15)	
Total service members	286,730
Battle deaths	2,260
Indian Wars (approx. 1817–98)	
Total service members	106,000
Battle deaths	1,000
Mexican-American War (1846–48)	
Total service members	78,718
Battle deaths	1,733
Other deaths in service	11,550
Civil War (1861–65)	
Total service members (Union)	2,213,363
Battle deaths (Union)	140,414
Other deaths in service (Union)	224,097
Total service members (Conf.)	1,050,000[2]
Battle deaths (Conf.)	74,524[3]
Other deaths in service (Conf.)	59,297[3]
Spanish-American War (1898–1902)	
Total service members (worldwide)	306,760
Battle deaths	385
Other deaths in service	2,061
World War I (1917–18)	
Total service members (worldwide)	4,734,991
Battle deaths	53,402
Other deaths in service	63,114

World War II (1941–45)	
Total service members (worldwide)	16,112,566
Battle deaths	291,557
Other deaths in service	113,842
Korean War (1950–53)	
Total service members (worldwide)	5,720,000
Battle deaths	33,741
Other deaths in service	20,505
Vietnam War (1964–75)	
Total service members (worldwide)	8,744,000[4]
Battle deaths	47,424[5]
Other deaths in service	42,785[5]
Gulf War (1990–91)	
Total service members (worldwide)	2,322,000
Battle deaths	147
Other deaths in service	1,825
War in Afghanistan (2001–)	
Service members	60,000[6]
Battle deaths	459*
Other deaths in service	227*
Iraq War (2003–)	
Service members	138,000[7]
Battle deaths	3,445*
Other deaths in service	856*

1. Exact number is unknown. Posted figure is the median of estimated range from 184,000 to 250,000.
2. Exact number is unknown. Posted figure is the median of estimated range from 600,000 to 1,500,000.
3. Battle death figures are based on incomplete returns. Other deaths in service figures do not include 26,000 to 31,000 who died in Union prisons.
4. Covers the period August 5, 1964–January 27, 1973 (date of cease-fire).
5. Covers period November 1, 1955 (commencement date for the Military Assistance Advisory Group)–May 15, 1975 (date last American service member left Southeast Asia, i.e., Vietnam).
6. Service members as of July 2009.
7. Service members as of January 2009.

*Casualties as of June 2009. Current casualty statistics are posted on the Department of Defense Web site http://www.defenselink.mil/news/casulty.pdf

Information compiled from the Department of Veterans Affairs.

Index

Main entries are indicated by bold type. Page numbers in italic type indicate an illustration, map, chart, or table on that page.